WileyPLUS

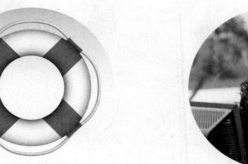

INTRODUCTION TO

CORPORATE FINANCE

MANAGING CANADIAN FIRMS IN A GLOBAL ENVIRONMENT

Third Edition

LAURENCE BOOTH
University of Toronto

SEAN CLEARY
Queen's University

WILEY

Library and Archives Canada Cataloguing in Publication

Booth, Laurence D.

Introduction to corporate finance / Laurence Booth, W. Sean Cleary.

Includes bibliographical references and index.
ISBN 978-1-118-30076-3

1. Corporations—Finance—Textbooks. 2. Business enterprises—Finance—Textbooks.
I. Cleary, W. Sean (William Sean)   II. Title.

HG4026.B65 2012   658.15   C2012-904216-1

Production Credits

Vice President and Publisher: Veronica Visentin
Acquisitions Editor: Darren Lalonde
Marketing Manager: Anita Osborne
Editorial Manager: Karen Staudinger
Production Manager: Tegan Wallace
Developmental Editor: Gail Brown
Media Editor: Channade Fenandoe

Editorial Assistant: Luisa Begani
Design: Joanna Vieira
Typesetting: Interrobang Graphic Design Inc.
Cover design: Interrobang Graphic Design Inc.
Cover photo: ©Getty Images/Photodisc
Printing & binding: QuadGraphics

Printed and bound in the United States of America.
2 3 4 5 QG 17 16 15 14 13

John Wiley & Sons Canada, Ltd.
6045 Freemont Blvd.
Mississauga, Ontario L5R 4J3
Visit our website at: www.wiley.com

PREFACE

In designing a textbook, we have tried to answer the basic question: What do we want students to learn? In this respect, we are very much aware that the target audience for this textbook is made up of bright students who seek careers in business management predominantly in Canada. This has dictated both what we have covered in the textbook and how we have tried to cover it.

A finance textbook designed for business students of necessity means that it should take a managerial focus. In this respect, it is important to note that finance is built on three "legs": accounting, law, and economics.

Accounting is the language of business, and financial analysts must be able to understand a firm's financial statements. This is a prerequisite to understanding anything in finance. In fact, for most non-financial companies, the terms "finance" and "accounting" are interchangeable. This is reflected in chapters 3 and 4 of the textbook, where we review the basic features of financial statements and financial analysis. We do this by studying a real Canadian company, Tim Hortons Inc., and using its financial statements throughout the textbook both to illustrate and develop basic financial concepts. We chose the financial statements of Tim Hortons because its statements are relatively uncomplicated and easy for beginning students to understand.

However, if you go back 50 years, you will discover that introductory finance textbooks were heavily based on *corporate* and *securities laws*. This is because financial securities are contracts and the terms of these contracts are partly determined by statute, while the ability to sell them to the general public and trade them in a market is determined by securities laws. Understanding the basics of the legal system is critical for understanding how finance works in practice. Here it is important to understand that there are differences between the United States and Canada that flow from differences in their legal systems. Coercive tender offers, for example, occur in the United States but not in Canada, while bought deal underwritings are common in Canada, but not in the United States.

Behind most corporate and securities law, there has been an action that has enriched one person at someone else's expense. While economists politely refer to these actions as "wealth transfers," more commonly they are referred to as "fraud." The legal system is simply the entrenchment of society's ethical or value system. For this reason, the text includes a series of ethical issues for analysis and discussion. If accounting provides the data, and the legal system provides the constraints on what can be done, *economics* provides most of the principles on how to get things done. Understanding the workings of the economy—where we are in the business cycle, industry market structure, and the response of competitors—is all critical to understanding how financial markets behave and how firms manage their finances. However, this is not a financial economics textbook. We are not proving the existence of equilibrium, but rather we are providing a framework to solve real problems. In this, we develop and use relevant accounting, legal, and economic skills that are used to solve financial problems faced by Canadians every day.

NEW TO THIS EDITION

The third edition of *Introduction to Corporate Finance* has been fully revised and updated in an effort to present the most current and relevant data and coverage of topics in the world of finance. We have continued our coverage of the financial market "crash" of 2008–9, as the effects and implications continue to influence the world of finance. This is reflected, for example, in the ongoing Eurozone debt crisis and in the general fragility and resilience demonstrated by financial markets around the globe and in Canada. These events have caused both academics and professionals to continue to re-evaluate many strongly held beliefs about the efficiency of financial markets, the functioning of the banking system, and the role of regulation. Canada was spared the enormous damage suffered in the United States, Europe, and the UK—a testament to the fundamental strength of the Canadian economy and financial system—but there are still lessons to be learned.

We have included an expanded discussion of International Financial Reporting Standard (IFRS), which have been adopted by Canadian public companies since January 2011. We have also included a general comparison with U.S. generally accepted accounting principles (GAAP), which are still used by many Canadian companies that list on U.S., as well as Canadian stock exchanges. We have also expanded our discussion of behavioural (neo-Keynesian) finance in our discussion of market efficiency, as academics and professionals continue to question the central ideas of market efficiency.

Also, we have selected new *Finance in the News* articles to reflect current thinking in the field of finance and to help students put the material and topics being discussed into context.

ORGANIZATION OF THE TEXTBOOK

There are underlying financial principles that every student of finance needs to know. This text develops these principles first, and then applies them to business finance. However, some instructors may prefer to cover the material in a different manner. To add flexibility, we have designed the material into "parts." Parts 1 and 2 are traditional. We start with an overview of the financial system and business finance, before reviewing basic financial statements and financial analysis. In parts 3 to 5, we deviate from the traditional structure by developing a general understanding of discounted cash flow models, modern portfolio theory, and options and futures. In our view, this is necessary to avoid undue duplication when discussing capital budgeting, corporate financing, and cost of capital. In particular, a general introduction to options and futures is useful for discussing real options in capital budgeting, as well as hybrid securities in corporate financing.

In Part 6, we then apply these ideas to the acquisition of long-lived assets (capital budgeting), in Part 7 to corporate financing, in Part 8 to financial policy, and in Part 9 to working capital management. Furthermore, topics relating to international issues and ethics are integrated throughout the text. In this way, none of the topics are "add ons," pushed to the end of the textbook, to be rarely covered.

For those instructors who prefer a more traditional structure, the textbook is flexible enough that Part 6 on capital budgeting may easily be moved forward to follow Part 3 and the discussion of discounted cash flow models. The discussion of modern portfolio theory and Part 4 may then be developed in conjunction with risk analysis in capital budgeting. However, the disadvantage of this structure would be that Part 5, on futures and options, would be relegated to a special topic when in reality it is too important to be left to the end of the course.

ORIENTATION

Many textbooks used in Canada are U.S. textbooks adapted for a Canadian market. In contrast, this text has been written from the ground up based on Canadian content and applications (such as the examples using Tim Hortons, our featured company). Issues such as the day count, how to quote interest rates, takeover rules, and securities law continue to be different between Canada and the United States. Canadians working for Canadian firms are expected to know what happens in Canada, as well as what happens in the United States.

However, Canadian content includes more than just describing different rules; it must also relate to current practice. We include news articles in the *Finance in the News* features to bring to life the finance issues and topics covered in the textbook. Relating basic issues to Canadian examples makes the material more relevant to students. For example, it is more relevant to understand the specific issues facing Canadian pension plans and investors, than those faced by U.S. or international investors, even though many of the general issues are the same.

On the other hand, in today's global business environment, what happens around the world impacts Canadians. Therefore, it is important to consider how global factors influence the Canadian environment, and hence the decisions made by Canadian managers and investors. In fact, global influences are so great in Canada that all Canadian financial managers have to be aware of these issues. We address this by integrating international issues on a topic-by-topic basis, as they arise, rather than in a separate chapter where they are just "lumped together." In this way, awareness of international issues develops naturally.

Finally, finance is a how-to subject. Students learn how to do things in a finance course; for example, how to evaluate securities, how to manage short-term cash, how to evaluate a plant expansion, and how to build a portfolio. In helping students develop these skills, this textbook has an extensive set of examples and problems worked out to show how to solve these problems in long hand or electronically using either a business calculator or spreadsheet. This approach is particularly important in the foundational Part 3, which deals with discounted cash flow valuation. This section develops the basics, and builds in a cumulative manner that allows the analysis of complex financial securities, while building students' confidence in their ability to solve real problems.

We believe that this textbook will stimulate students to understand finance, as well as to apply it. We believe that after working through this textbook, students will be able to solve basic financial problems, have the basic skills necessary to do more advanced work in finance, and go on to add value to the firms for whom they will eventually work. We hope this textbook will lead students to greater understanding of finance and that they will then share our enthusiasm for finance. These are our reasons for writing this textbook. We know that these are high standards for a finance textbook; if you feel we have not met these objectives, we welcome your feedback.

PEDAGOGICAL FEATURES

Learning Objectives: These are listed at the start of each chapter and then integrated throughout the chapter to reinforce key concepts and help guide students' learning.

Running Glossary: Key terms are highlighted throughout each chapter and defined in the text margin.

Concept Review Questions: At the end of each major section, questions are provided to help students check their understanding before moving on.

Examples: All examples in the text are numbered and labelled for easy reference, and include fully worked out solutions. Keystrokes for the TI BAII Plus financial calculator and Excel spreadsheet commands are included for each relevant example.

Chapter Summary: Each chapter concludes with a summary of the key concepts covered in that chapter, as well as a summary of the learning objectives.

Equations Summary: Equations are numbered, titled, and listed with page references at the end of each chapter.

Questions and Practice Problems: These are provided at the end of each chapter and allow students to practice and enhance their understanding and learning. Challenging problems are identified by this icon ⚙.

WileyPLUS

This online teaching and learning environment integrates the entire digital textbook with the most effective instructor and student resources to fit every learning style. With *WileyPLUS*:

- Students achieve concept mastery in a rich, structured environment that's available 24/7.
- Instructors personalize and manage their course more effectively with assessment, assignments, grade tracking, and more, and can access all resources, including all instructor supplements, from one easy-to-use website.

Wiley Custom Select

Wiley Custom Select offers your students a cost-efficient alternative to traditional texts. In a simple three-step process, create a solution containing the content you want, in the sequence you want, delivered in the way you want. Visit Wiley Custom Select at http://customselect.wiley.com.

INSTRUCTOR AND STUDENT RESOURCES

Instructors and student resources are available on the text's companion website, www.wiley.com/go/boothcanada.

For Instructors

Instructor's Manual: The instructor's manual includes complete solutions to all end-of-chapter questions and practice problems in the textbook and answers to the concept review questions.

Test Bank: The test bank includes a rich selection of multiple choice, short answer, and practice problems, with full solutions. These are coded by difficulty and knowledge level, with references to the relevant sections in the text. The test bank is available as Word files and as a computerized test bank, in an easy-to-use test-generating program.

PowerPoint© Presentations: A full series of PowerPoint© slides have been prepared for each chapter and includes key points from each chapter and worked-out demonstration problems where applicable.

For Students

Within *WileyPLUS*, students will find a variety of interactive and media-rich study and learning tools, including:

Practice Quizzes: Self-study practice questions, with immediate feedback, for every chapter of the textbook to help students gauge their understanding as they prepare for class or a test.

Laurence Booth and Sean Cleary Video Tutorials: A series of 10- to 15-minute videos by the textbook's authors that cover the key concepts and core material of a corporate finance course. The authors walk students through examples to help them master core concepts, and use current and relevant financial news to illustrate and apply key topics. This exciting new addition to the third edition package will enhance students' comprehension and facilitate students' learning in their corporate finance course.

Micro Cases with Excel©: Enhanced problems that test students' conceptual and applied knowledge using real-life scenarios, such as saving for retirement. These cases test students' understanding over multiple concepts in a chapter or across multiple chapters, and are solved using Excel©.

Prerequisite Course Reviews: Brief concept reviews with exercises and problems, which allow students to refresh their knowledge of basic topics in algebra, statistics, financial accounting, and microeconomics.

Spreadsheet Templates and Financial Calculator Keystrokes: These are included for all relevant worked-out examples.

HALLMARK FEATURES OF THIS TEXTBOOK

Because students are motivated to learn finance if they are shown how it is relevant to their world, each chapter of *Introduction to Corporate Finance* is written with engaging real-world examples and a wealth of detail. The following features are included to further enhance this presentation.

finance IN THE NEWS 22-3 Canadian Bank's Long History of Steady Dividends

SOME OF THE LARGEST banks in the world had collapsed and central bankers were still in the midst of a costly bail out of financial institutions.

The directors of the Bank of Montreal were carefully balancing the pressure to pay out a dividend to shareholders and the need to contain the effects of an international financial crisis.

The year was 1829, and as stock markets recovered from the failure of six English banks caught out by bad bets on Latin American credit markets, bank directors decided to proceed with a dividend payment to shareholders.

The move established a tradition that has endured for 180 years and was reaffirmed on Tuesday as Canada's oldest bank maintained its dividend at 70 cents.

There was no sign that BMO's management had given any serious consideration to cutting the dividend ahead of Tuesday's annual general meeting.

But Bill Downe, chief executive, took time out to reassure shareholders, saying dividends were of perennial importance to retail investors.

"Shareholders of Canadian banks place a high value on consistency,"

BMO Financial Group president and CEO William Downe addresses the audience at the bank's 2009 annual shareholder meeting. (Clement Allard/The Canadian Press)

Finance in the News: Each chapter includes at least one article or item from the financial press that is integrated into the main discussion of the chapter to help students draw the connection between theory and application, and to highlight the relevance of the topic being discussed.

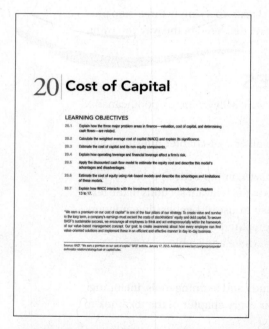

20 | Cost of Capital

LEARNING OBJECTIVES

20.1 Explain how the three major problem areas in finance—valuation, cost of capital, and determining cash flows—are related.

20.2 Calculate the weighted average cost of capital (WACC) and explain its significance.

20.3 Estimate the cost of capital and its non-equity components.

20.4 Explain how operating leverage and financial leverage affect a firm's risk.

20.5 Apply the discounted cash flow model to estimate the equity cost and describe this model's advantages and disadvantages.

20.6 Estimate the cost of equity using risk-based models and describe the advantages and limitations of these models.

20.7 Explain how WACC interacts with the investment decision framework introduced in chapters 13 to 17.

"We earn a premium on our cost of capital" is one of the four pillars of our strategy. To create value and survive in the long term, a company's earnings must exceed the costs of stockholders' equity and debt capital. To secure BASF's sustainable success, we encourage all employees to think and act entrepreneurially within the framework of our value-based management concept. Our goal: to create awareness about how every employee can find value-oriented solutions and implement these in an efficient and effective manner in day-to-day business.

Source: BASF. "We earn a premium on our cost of capital." BASF website. January 17, 2013. Available at www.basf.com/group/corporate/en/investor-relations/strategy/cost-of-capital/index.

Chapter Opener: These introduce students to the main focus of the chapter through an interesting and relevant discussion, showing its real-world application.

Lessons to Be Learned: These illustrate an important concept in the chapter, and how that basic tenet of finance was either ignored and thus fuelled the financial crisis, or was adhered to and helped to mitigate the effects of the crisis.

LESSONS TO BE LEARNED During the fall of 2008, stock markets around the world fell dramatically, and they fell in tandem. In other words, the correlation among equity returns was extremely high, with most global stock market returns displaying correlations greater than 0.95 with the returns on the S&P 500 Composite Index. For example, the S&P/TSX Composite Index displayed a 0.97 coefficient with the S&P. This led many market observers to question the value of diversification. Consider the following quote from Louis Gagnon: "Diversification works on the way up when we don't need it and it fails miserably when we do."[14] So what does this mean for investors? First of all, it suggests that diversification is no guarantee that you can never lose money, which is of course true—there are always risks associated with investing. We alluded to this point in the chapter opener.

So what does diversification do for us? Consider the following two points. First, even though diversification within and across stock markets would not have prevented investors from experiencing large losses on their common equity holdings, they would have been much better off than if they had not been diversified. For example, investors would have suffered if their investments had been concentrated in financial companies. Many of those stock prices declined by as much as 90 percent, before some rebounded somewhat in the spring of 2009. Of course, if investors were holding only those stocks that didn't recover, they would have been hit really hard.

Second, being diversified across asset categories would have helped cushion the blow. Recall from Figure 8-7B, for example, the low correlation between stock returns and T-bill returns, which was −0.077. Similarly, the correlation coefficient between stock returns and government bond returns over the 1938 to 2011 period was also close to zero (−0.01). So being invested in various asset categories would have softened the blow, due to the low correlations across the asset classes. For example, a portfolio of Canadian stocks would have lost 42.5 percent over the March 2008 to March 2009 period, while an equally weighted portfolio of Canadian stock and government bonds would have lost only 17.5 percent. On the other hand, the ending wealth for $1,000 invested in this equally weighted portfolio over the 1938 to 2011 period would have been $411,819, versus an ending

12-1 ETHICS AND CORPORATE GOVERNANCE
Audit Options Policies, CSA Urges

The Canadian Securities Administrators, or CSA, is recommending that all Canadian public companies assess their policies and controls for stock option grants to ensure they comply with legislation.

The notice comes as a scandal over backdated stock options continues to widen in the United States, where more than 40 companies have already said they will restate earnings or might do so once internal probes are completed. The restatements total at least $2.27 billion (U.S.).

Backdating occurs when a company sets the grant date for stock options retroactively, to a time when the company's stock price was lower, creating an instant paper gain for the executive or employee receiving the options.

Stock options allow recipients to buy shares at a future date, usually at the price on the day they were granted. They are given to managers as an incentive to find ways to boost the stock price.

A University of Michigan study released this week suggests shareholders bear the brunt of the practice, shouldering an average of $510 million per company in losses after the practice is made public. That far

Securities legislation also requires company insiders to file an insider-trading report within 10 days of receiving options.

Directors are responsible for ensuring that a company prices and discloses options appropriately, the CSA said.

It suggested boards set up a compensation committee that follows national corporate governance guidelines. It also suggested they adopt corporate disclosure and insider-trading policies and establish blackout periods around earnings announcements.

In October, the TSX Group sent a notice to listed companies reminding them of the rules around options.

"Staff has become aware that listed issuers may not be adhering to the requirements ... of the manual," the notice said.

In the United States, prosecutors and members of Congress have said backdating grants, or awarding them shortly before good news is announced, subverts their purpose and could involve criminal fraud.

Securities and Exchange Commission chairman Christopher Cox told Congress this week that more than 100 companies are being investigated.

Ethics and Corporate Governance: Found in various parts of the text, this feature discusses how issues of ethics and corporate governance affect corporations today. These features include questions to help launch in-class analysis and discussion.

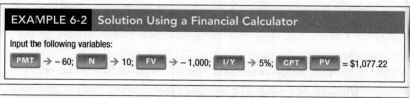

EXAMPLE 6-2 Solution Using a Financial Calculator

Input the following variables:

PMT → − 60;   N → 10;   FV → − 1,000;   I/Y → 5%;   CPT   PV = $1,077.22

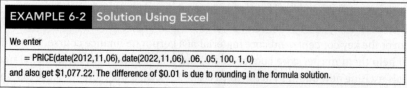

EXAMPLE 6-2 Solution Using Excel

We enter

= PRICE(date(2012,11,06), date(2022,11,06), .06, .05, 100, 1, 0)

and also get $1,077.22. The difference of $0.01 is due to rounding in the formula solution.

Financial Calculator Keystrokes: All relevant demonstration problems include actual keystrokes for the TI BAII calculator.

Excel Spreadsheet Commands: All relevant demonstration problems include Excel spreadsheet commands.

ABOUT THE AUTHORS

Sean Cleary (left) and Laurence Booth (right)

Laurence Booth, DBA, MBA, MA (Indiana University); BS (London School of Economics) is Professor of Finance and holds the CIT chair in structured finance at the Rotman School of Management, University of Toronto. His major research interests are in corporate finance and the behaviour of regulated industries. He has published over 50 articles in numerous academic journals including *Journal of Finance* and *Journal of Financial and Quantitative Analysis*, co-authored a textbook on international business, and is on the editorial board of four academic journals.

At the University of Toronto since 1978, Professor Booth has taught graduate courses in business finance, international financial management, corporate financing, mergers and acquisitions, financial management, financial markets, and financial theory, as well as short executive programs on money and foreign exchange markets, business valuation, mergers and acquisitions, and financial strategy. His advice is frequently sought by the media, and he has appeared as an expert financial witness before various regulatory tribunals in Canada.

Sean Cleary, CFA, is the BMO Professor of Finance and Director of the Master of Finance, Queen's School of Business, Queen's University. Dr. Cleary holds a PhD in finance from the University of Toronto, an MBA, is a Chartered Financial Analyst (CFA) charterholder, and is a former member of both the Atlantic Canada and Toronto CFA societies. He has also completed the Professional Financial Planning Course (PFPC), the Canadian Securities Course (CSC), and the Investment Funds Institute of Canada (IFIC) Mutual Fund Course.

Dr. Cleary has taught numerous university finance courses, as well as courses and seminars in many programs designed to prepare students to write exams for all three levels of the CFA program and the CSC. He is the Canadian author of the first three editions of *Investments: Analysis and Management*, and the co-author of the sixth edition of *Finance in a Canadian Setting*, both published by John Wiley & Sons Canada, Ltd. He is also the author of the first four editions of *The Canadian Securities Exam Fast Track Study Guide*, also published by Wiley.

Dr. Cleary has published numerous research articles in various journals, including *Journal of Finance*, *Journal of Financial and Quantitative Analysis*, *Journal of Financial Management*, *Journal of Banking and Finance*, and *Journal of Financial Research* among others. He has received several major research grants from the Social Sciences and Humanities Research Council of Canada (SSHRC). He currently serves as Associate Editor (Finance) at Canadian Journal of Administrative Sciences, and Associate Editor for European Journal of Finance.

Dr. Cleary frequently appears in the media on television, on the radio, and in newspapers.

ACKNOWLEDGEMENTS

A large scale textbook project such as this one is not the work of single authors; rather it is the combined effort of many people whom we wish to acknowledge. We thank the following reviewers who took the time to read and evaluate the draft manuscripts for this and previous editions:

Ashraf Al Zaman, St. Mary's University
Ben Amoako-Adu, Wilfrid Laurier University
Yunbi An, University of Windsor
Ata Assaf, University of Windsor
Reena Atanasiadis, Concordia University
Mohamed Ayadi, Brock University
Larry Bauer, Memorial University of Newfoundland
Ernest Biktimirov, Brock University
David Birkett, University of Guelph
Edward Blinder, Ryerson University
Trevor W. Chamberlain, McMaster University
Chris Duff, Royal Roads University
Alex Faseruk, Memorial University of Newfoundland
Bill Fletcher, Saint Mary's University
Louis Florence, University of Toronto
Merlyn Foo, Athabasca University
Cameron Gall, Mount Royal University
Myron Gordon, University of Lethbridge
Larbi Hammami, McGill University
Ken Hartviksen, Lakehead University
Margery Heuser, Okanagan College

Robert Ironside, University of Lethbridge
Raad Jassim, Concordia University
Lew Johnson, Queen's University
Kurt Loescher, University of Saskatchewan
András Marosi, University of Alberta
Mike McIntyre, Carleton University
Lukasz Pomorski, University of Toronto
Lynnette Purda, Queen's University
Ian Rakita, Concordia University
William Rentz, University of Ottawa
Michael W. Reynolds, Carleton University
Wilf Roesler, University of Lethbridge
Raina Rudko, MacEwan University
Shahbaz Sheikh, University of Western Ontario
David A. Stangeland, University of Manitoba
Vijay Vishwakarma, St. Francis Xavier University
Thomas Walker, Concordia University
Eric Wang, Athabasca University
Sherry Wang, Lakehead Univeristy
Jun Yang, Acadia University

We would also like to thank the team at John Wiley & Sons Canada, Ltd. who, as always, provided us with unparalleled support on so many levels. Special thanks to Veronica Visentin, Publisher; Darren Lalonde, Acquisitions Editor; Anita Osborne, Marketing Manager; Deanna Durnford, Supplements Coordinator, and especially Gail Brown, Developmental Editor, for her capable and tireless efforts. The editorial contributions of Ross Meacher, Audrey McClellan, Louise Oborne, and Yvonne Van Ruskenveld are also very much appreciated.

We are also particularly grateful to Bin Chang (University of Ontario Institute of Technology), Bill Fletcher (Saint Mary's University), Sorin Rizeanu (University of Victoria), Raina Rudko (MacEwan University), and Wilf Roesler (University of Lethbridge), for all their contributions to the end-of-chapter material and solutions and to the textbook's ancillaries. Thank you also to Karine Benzacar for her insightful contributions on IFRS in Chapter 3.

From Laurence Booth: My thanks to all my former students—you are the reason that faculty write books; your questions and challenges motivate us to do better. My thanks also to my family and those special people (you know who you are) who provided the emotional support when it was needed.

From Sean Cleary: Thanks to my colleagues and my students (past and present) for their inspiration. Special thanks to my wife, Grace, my children (Jason, Brennan, Brigid, and Siobhan) and to my parents (Bill and Beryl) for all of their support.

Laurence Booth
Toronto, Ontario

Sean Cleary
Kingston, Ontario

February 2013

BRIEF TABLE OF CONTENTS

TABLE OF CONTENTS

Part 1

THE FINANCIAL ENVIRONMENT

What is business finance? In these opening chapters, we examine the big picture in terms of the Canadian financial system, including the major actors in the system, the major securities issued, and the types of problems solved. We also discuss how Canadian markets are linked to international markets and how changes in one seemingly low-risk sector, the U.S. mortgage market, reverberated around the world to cause the biggest financial crisis in 75 years. After that crisis subsided, the knock-on effects for government finances created the sovereign debt (euro) crisis that still continues. As a result of the original crisis, Canadian businesses faced huge problems in financing and are currently quite cautious in both their spending and financing. The important lesson we point out is that corporate finance was affected by shocks elsewhere in the financial system. We then discuss the different ways a business can be organized and financed, and we introduce the income trust sector, in which billions of dollars in market value were wiped out overnight due to unexpected government policy changes. Finally, the role of management in diverse firms is explored, with a discussion of key careers available to finance majors.

1 | An Introduction to Finance

LEARNING OBJECTIVES

1.1   Define finance and explain what is involved in the study of finance.

1.2   List the major financial and real assets held by Canadians and the major sectors in the financial system.

1.3   Explain how money is transferred from lenders to borrowers and the role played by market and financial intermediaries.

1.4   Identify the basic types of financial instruments that are available and explain how they are traded.

1.5   Explain the importance of the global financial system and how Canada is impacted by events in the U.S. mortgage market.

We start this chapter with an introduction to Canada's balance sheet, which leads us to a discussion of the big-picture items that underlie much of finance. The debt on Canada's balance sheet is the accumulation of all budget deficits and surpluses since Confederation in 1867, when the debt was a mere $75 million. World War I pushed this number up to approximately $3 billion by 1920. In 1996–97, the debt had reached a high of $562.9 billion, with interest payments of around $45 billion. The debt was a whopping 68.4 percent of gross domestic product (GDP). Since then, efforts to eliminate budget deficits resulted in reduced debt and lower interest charges on the existing debt, so that by 2008, Canada's net debt-to-GDP ratio had dropped to only 28.6 percent. However, in September 2008, the world went into its first-ever global recession, and Canada has not been immune to its effects. With increased government spending to stimulate the economy and jump-start financial markets, government deficits and debt are increasing again. Canada's debt-to-GDP ratio is now at 36 percent, far off the long-run target of less than 20 percent.

Source: Data from Department of Finance, "Budget 2012." Available from the Department of Finance Canada website at www.budget.gc.ca.

CHAPTER 1 **PREVIEW**

Often, the first finance course business students take is a business finance course. Yet business finance cannot be taught in isolation. It is simply one part of finance, which includes personal or household finance, government finance, and international finance. The events of 2008–9 confirmed unequivocally that all parts of the financial system are interrelated. The crisis started in the U.S. residential mortgage market, but since then it has moved on to become the euro crisis, as the debt that some governments raised to stimulate their economies to offset the downturn in 2008–9 has, in turn, left them struggling to refinance their own debts. The result is that business finance in 2013 is heavily affected by household, government, and international finance.

So what is finance? In its broadest terms, **finance** is the study of how and under what terms savings (money) are allocated between lenders and borrowers. Here, the terms "lenders" and "borrowers" are also used in their broadest sense—as people and institutions that either have excess money to invest or need money for some reason. However, the key term in the definition is "allocated," and you may recognize the similarity between finance and economics, which studies how scarce resources are allocated in an economy. In many ways, finance is closely related to economics. However, finance is distinct from economics in that finance is not just about how resources are allocated; it also examines under what terms and through what channels the allocations are made.

Whenever funds are transferred, a financial contract comes into existence, and these contracts are called financial securities. As we will discuss in depth in later chapters, exchanging funds (money) for pieces of paper (securities) opens up an enormous number of opportunities for fraud. As a result, the study of finance requires a basic understanding of securities and corporate law and the institutions that facilitate and monitor this exchange of funds. This may seem dull, but it can be dramatic. For example, on December 11, 2008, Bernard Madoff was arrested for securities fraud in the United States, and on March 12, 2009, he pleaded guilty to defrauding his clients of an unbelievable $65 billion.

In this chapter, we will briefly review the structure of the Canadian financial system, considering how it links to the rest of the world and who the major agents are. Our objective is to help you understand the place of business finance in the financial system and how it is buffeted by events occurring elsewhere in "the markets."

1.1 REAL VERSUS FINANCIAL ASSETS

Canada's Balance Sheet

Let's start with the balance sheet, which is simply a snapshot of what is owned (assets) and what is owed (liabilities) at a particular time. The difference between the value of what is owned and what is owed is "net worth" or equity—as, for example, the equity someone has in a house. We can estimate balance sheets for individuals and for institutions (both businesses and governments). In Chapter 3, we will discuss the role of assets and liabilities in financial statements.

Table 1-1 aggregates the 2011 market value of the assets and liabilities of the three major domestic groups in our economy: (1) individuals, referred to as the household sector by Statistics Canada (StatsCan), (2) businesses, and (3) government. The Canadian assets and liabilities that are held by non-resident individuals, businesses, and governments compose the balance sheet of the non-resident sector, which we generally "net" out to determine what the country owes to or is owed by non-residents.

Table 1-1 shows that, at the end of 2011, Canadians had total real assets with a market value of $6,852 billion. At the same time, Canada had a net liability to non-residents of $236 billion, meaning a net worth of $6,616 billion or almost $200,000 for every Canadian. Canada had net foreign liabilities of $236 billion—that is, we owed more to non-residents than we owned as foreign assets. This has changed over the past few years due to the financial crisis, as non-residents have bought Canadian securities as a "safe haven" in response to serious concerns about the financial stability of southern European countries from Greece to Portugal. This is why Canada's balance sheet is very simple—as of the end of 2011, we had $6,852 billion in assets with a small net liability to non-residents. Within Canada, we had lots of debts, but these were simply to other Canadians. When we add everything up, these debts to ourselves net out to zero because one person's debt is another person's asset, as we will discuss shortly.

TABLE 1-1 Canada's Balance Sheet ($billion), 2011

Residential structures	1,908
Non-residential structures	1,687
Machinery and equipment	474
Consumer durables	441
Inventories	242
Land	2,100
Net foreign liabilities	236
Net worth or equity	6,616

Source: Statistics Canada, "Table 35." In *National Balance Sheet Accounts, 2011*. Ottawa: Minister of Industry, 2012 (Catalogue No. 13-022-X)

Real Assets

The balance sheet shows all real assets according to six major classifications. The assets included under these headings are **real assets**, representing the tangible things that compose personal and business assets. Personal assets are the value of houses (residential structures), the land the houses are on, the major appliances in the houses (televisions, washing machines, etc.), and cars. Major appliances and cars are referred to as consumer durables because they last many years. For businesses, the major assets are office buildings, factories, mines, and so on (non-residential structures); the machinery and equipment in those structures; the land they are on; and the stock or inventories of things waiting to be used or sold. [1]

real assets the tangible things that compose personal and business assets

We have introduced Canada's national balance sheet because finance is essentially the management of an entity's balance sheet. This management involves the real asset side and the liability side of the balance sheet. When we look at business finance, we will discuss how firms arrive at the decision to build a new factory, increase the level of their inventory holdings, and make strategic asset acquisition decisions, such as buying another firm (mergers and acquisitions). These are all examples of asset acquisitions, which we will generically refer to as capital expenditure (capex) decisions. On the liability side are ways to finance these expenditures, which we will refer to as corporate financing decisions. However, these same decisions are made by individuals when deciding to buy a house or a new car, and by the government, because all entities have a balance sheet.

However, there is a danger in looking simply at Canada's balance sheet in that it focusses attention on things that we can measure. In a recent United Nations report directed by Sir Partha Dasgupta at Cambridge University in England, researchers calculated a more inclusive definition of wealth by including both human capital—based on the skills and education of a country—and its natural capital, based on its land, forests, fossil fuels, and minerals. In contrast, StatsCan only estimates a part of this value. Table 1-2 and Figure 1-1 present the results

---

[1] These assets also include some owned by the different levels of government in Canada.

of this report, as summarized by *The Economist*. Canada comes out as the third-wealthiest country studied, after the United States and Japan, with total wealth of $331,919 per person in 2008. You are wealthier than you think.

TABLE 1-2 The Balance Sheet of Wealth

Country	Inclusive Wealth	
	2008, $trillion*	1990–2008 Growth, % †
United States	117.8	0.7
Japan	55.1	0.9
China	20.0	2.1
Germany	19.5	1.8
Britain	13.4	0.9
France	13.0	1.4
Canada	11.1	0.4
Brazil	7.4	0.9
India	6.2	0.9
Australia	6.1	0.1

* Constant 2000 $

† Average annual rate

Source: "The Real Wealth of Nations." *The Economist*, June 30, 2012, p. 78. Available at www.economist.com. Data from the United Nations. Copyright © The Economist Newspaper Limited, London 2012. Reprinted by permission.

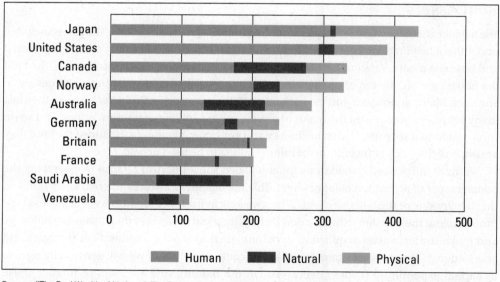

FIGURE 1-1 *Inclusive Wealth per Person, 2008, $'000 (Constant 2000 $)*

Source: "The Real Wealth of Nations." *The Economist*, June 30, 2012, p. 78. Available at www.economist.com. Copyright © The Economist Newspaper Limited, London 2012. Reprinted by permission.

Financial Assets

Although the national balance sheet presented in Table 1-1 is useful for understanding wealth and the different types of real assets, it removes most of the things that are of interest to students of finance. This is because it nets out all of the debts we Canadians owe to other Canadians, which is almost all of our debts! To understand these **financial assets** and how the financial system works, we need to disaggregate the data—that is, look at it in greater detail. This is what StatsCan does when it prepares the National Balance Sheet Accounts (NBSA).

financial assets a claim that one individual or institution has on another

The basic idea behind the NBSA is to collect financial data on the major agents in the financial system and then track the borrowing and lending between these agents. For example, StatsCan collects data on all persons and unincorporated businesses in Canada and groups them into the household sector.[2] This is because individuals as a group tend to lend to the other major agents in the system, thereby creating financial assets. However, within the household sector, what one person lends to another is offset by what that person owes. In this way, a positive financial asset is offset by a negative financial asset or a financial liability, so the numbers are the net real assets and the net financial assets of Canadian households. Figure 1-2 provides the overall breakdown of both the real and the net financial assets in Canada as of the end of 2011.

Figure 1-2 shows who owns and owes what in the Canadian economy. If we start with Canadian households and add up all the real (tangible) assets, such as homes and cars, in aggregate, Canadian households owned real assets with a market value of $3,612 billion at the end of 2011. In addition to these real assets, Canadian households owned net financial assets issued by the government, corporations, and non-residents with a market value of $2,697 billion. So, in aggregate, if we add the two together, Canadian households had total net assets with a 2011 market value of $6,308 billion, which is slightly smaller than the total net assets for Canada of $6,616 billion, as shown in Table 1-1.

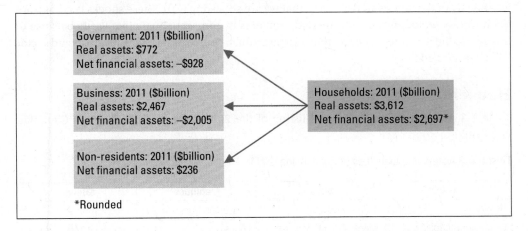

Source: Data from Statistics Canada, *National Balance Sheet Accounts, 2011.* Ottawa: Minister of Industry, 2012 (Catalogue No. 13-022-X).

FIGURE 1-2 *Borrowing and Lending: The Big Picture, 2011*

In 2011, all layers of Canadian government, in aggregate, had real assets worth $772 billion. The bulk of these assets are government office buildings and the machinery and equipment in them, but $166 billion represents the market value of government-owned land. That's the good news. The bad news is that all layers of government, in aggregate, had net financial assets of –$928 billion—that is, a net financial liability of $928 billion, which is the market value of all government debt outstanding. Similarly, Canadian corporations and government Crown corporations had real assets with a market value of $2,467 billion in 2011, representing the factories, mines, office buildings, and so on, needed to produce the goods and services that we buy. The market value of the net financial assets issued by the business sector to finance those real assets, or what we call corporate financing, was –$2,005 billion. Notice that if we add up the value of real assets owned by the three domestic sectors, we end up with a total market value of real assets of $6,851 billion. However, when we add up the total net financial assets of these three sectors, we end up with financial assets of –$236 billion, which equals exactly the net financial assets owed by Canadians to non-residents. Therefore, the value of the net assets owned by Canadian residents, or our net worth, is the sum of these two or

---

[2] We will discuss business organization in Chapter 2, but unincorporated businesses are basically individuals operating a business that, for tax purposes, is indistinguishable from themselves.

$6,615 billion, which but for rounding errors would equal the $6,616 billion in Table 1-1. Also, notice in Figure 1-2 that the net financial assets figure for the household sector equals *positive* $2,697 billion, while the total net financial assets of the combined government and business sectors equals *negative* $2,933 billion. Again, the difference reflects the net foreign liability of $236 billion. Overall, the NBSA data indicate that, as Canadians, we are in pretty good shape except for a relatively minor liability to non-residents, which in fact has fluctuated between positive and negative through the first three editions of this book and currently reflects Canada's "safe harbour" position as one of the few AAA-rated countries left in the world.

Although Figure 1-2 shows the flow of savings from households to governments and business, with some money flowing in from non-residents, it does not show the flows within each sector. However, it does highlight the importance of the four major areas of finance: personal finance, government finance, corporate finance, and international finance. Although the main focus of this text is on corporate finance, it is important to realize that all these sectors are part of the financial system and are affected by the same types of phenomena; a shock in the government or international sectors can quickly work through the system to affect personal and corporate finance and vice versa. Shortly, we will discuss exactly how a shock starting in the U.S. mortgage market in 2008 triggered the biggest financial crisis of the past 75 years and led directly to the sovereign debt crisis that we are still living with. These shocks from outside the business sector have caused myriad problems in corporate financing. Partly because of this shock, but also due to the fact that it is the primary source of savings, the household sector will be discussed first.

Households

Table 1-3 provides a comprehensive listing of the 2011 assets and liabilities of Canadian households.

TABLE 1-3 Assets and Liabilities of Households, 2011

Assets	$Billion	Liabilities	$Billion
Houses	1,693	Consumer credit	452
Consumer durables	476	Loans	140
Land	1,443	Mortgages	1,027
Real Assets	**3,612**	**Total Liabilities**	**1,619**
Deposits	1,045		
Debt	100		
Pensions and insurance	1,565		
Shares	1,450		
Foreign and other	156		
Financial Assets	**4,316**		
Total Assets	**7,928**		

Source: Data from Statistics Canada, *National Balance Sheet Accounts, 2011*. Ottawa: Minister of Industry, 2012 (Catalogue No. 13-022-X).

In aggregate, the household sector looks much as we would expect from our own experiences. The major real assets are houses, worth $1,693 billion; consumer durables, such as washing machines and cars (plus some other miscellaneous assets), worth $476 billion; and the land on which our houses are built, worth $1,443 billion.[3] Our major financial assets are money on deposit, mainly with the banks, worth $1,045 billion; debt securities, worth $100 billion; the value of pension and insurance assets, worth $1,565 billion; and the market value of the shares in corporations, worth $1,450 billion.

Offsetting these financial assets are $452 billion in consumer credit (mainly credit-card debt), $140 billion in loans (mainly bank loans), and $1,027 billion in mortgage debt taken out to buy our houses. So, in aggregate, Canadian households have $1,619 billion in financial liabilities to offset against the $4,316 billion in financial assets. This leaves net financial assets of $2,697 billion, which is the number reported in Figure 1-2. However, the household sector's liabilities are all different forms of debt, which can be netted out against the debt-like financial assets—namely, deposits at banks and loans. What is left constitutes the two major financial assets of the household sector: the market value of investments in shares and the market value of investments in insurance and pensions.

It's one thing to tell people that, on average, each Canadian has almost $200,000 in wealth, but many of them will respond, "I don't have that!" So who does have all that money? Understanding wealth distribution within a country is a complex issue. However, a good starting point is to consider how borrowing and lending changes throughout the life cycle of individuals as they get older. The key decisions most people make are saving to buy a house and saving for retirement. The basic problem in retirement planning is determining how to finance our non-working or retirement years, when we will be consuming but not earning. The basic problem when we want a house is figuring out how to save to buy it and then pay down the mortgage so we are mortgage free as we age and begin to think about retirement.

When considering these problems, think about the financial assets and liabilities in Table 1-3. We can expect, for example, to observe significant differences between people in the household sector, with younger individuals borrowing to buy houses and consumer durables and having a net *negative* financial asset position (i.e., they are in debt). Conversely, as they age, they pay down their mortgage and build up their financial assets, so older, higher-income individuals tend to save and be wealthier. Thus, within the household sector, we see older individuals lending and younger ones borrowing, but by aggregating across everyone within the household sector, this dynamic is lost.

Table 1-3 shows that a large part of household wealth consists of life insurance and pension claims, with the latter being promises made by a government or private company to pay money to individuals after they retire. But just how good are these promises? If the promises are made by a private company, its ability to fulfill them can be severely compromised if its own future is in doubt; as a result, pensions can be a major issue in salary and benefit negotiations, as illustrated by *Finance in the News 1-1*. We can also look at the mortgage market, for reasons that will become clear later in this chapter. In 2011, mortgage debt was $1,027 billion, and the value of the housing stock was $1,693 billion. So, on average, mortgages were worth 61 percent of the value of a house. However, some people were mortgage free, whereas many others had only recently taken out a mortgage and were heavily indebted. Therefore, a shock to the financial system, such as a recession and job loss or a collapse in house prices, can have a huge impact on the mortgage market and, through it, the whole financial system. So the key questions are: How does money flow from those who have it to those who want it? Who are the agents in the financial system? What are the types of securities issued?

---

[3] Some minor accounts from unincorporated businesses have been consolidated with household assets and liabilities.

finance IN THE NEWS 1-1   Strikes Highlight Canada's Pension Problems

ONE OF THE KEY STICKING POINTS in both the Air Canada and Canada Post strikes is pensions, an issue that experts say is going to take on more prominence for Canadians in the near future.

With more Canadians facing retirement age, many corporate pension plans are strained, and some have massive shortfalls because of the recession.

Air Canada says it has a $2.1-billion pension shortfall, and the company is now supporting more retired employees than it has current ones. Canada Post has a pension deficit of $3.22 billion.

Peter Merrick, author of *The Essential Individual Pension Plan Handbook*, says that with Canadians living much longer after retiring, pension plans are increasingly strained.

"These plans were never put into place to actually support people for 30 to 40 years. It's not maintainable or sustainable," he told CTV's *Power Play*.

"This is something many individuals as they approach retirement are going to be looking at: 'Are my pensions properly funded?' And right now they are not."

The average life expectancy of a Canadian is now about 81 years old.

Jim Stanford, an economist with the Canadian Auto Workers' union, says pension plans can recover from the hit they took from the recession.

"When the stock market is doing well, many pensions are in great shape...There's a bit of a boom and a bust factor," he said. "These things can be solved over time, what you don't want to do is throw the whole system out, which is what employers right now are trying to do."

Air Canada wants new employees to accept a defined contribution pension plan, rather than the defined benefit pension plan that is in place for current workers.

With a defined benefit plan, employees have a predictable income, but the airline is on the hook for additional costs if the pension fund's assets can't pay for the benefits.

But less than half of working Canadians have any sort of workplace pension plan. For those that do, the majority work for the government.

Merrick says Canadians need to put greater emphasis on personally planning for their retirement, either through RRSPs or other investments.

The issue of pensions is becoming more important, as is evident in labour negotiations and disputes. (top, Pat Hewitt/The Canadian Press; bottom, Graham Hughes/The Canadian Press)

"No longer can we rely on big government or big corporations to provide us for the rest of our lives," he said.

Stanford is calling on Ottawa to expand the Canada Pension Plan.

"Unfortunately, the Harper government, instead of expanding the CPP, is putting more emphasis on individual saving methods," he said.

Source: "Strikes Highlight Canada's Pension Problems." CTV News, June 15, 2011. Available at www.ctv.ca. Reprinted by permission.

CONCEPT REVIEW QUESTIONS

1. What is finance?
2. Distinguish between real and financial assets.
3. Which sector or sectors of the economy are net providers of financing and which are the net users of financing?

Learning Objective 1.3
Explain how money is transferred from lenders to borrowers and the role played by market and financial intermediaries.

1.2 THE FINANCIAL SYSTEM

Overview

Figure 1-3 provides an overview of the financial system of any economy, be it Canada, the United States, or the global economy. In Canada, as we have discussed, the household sector is the primary provider of funds to business and government. The basic financial flow is "intermediated" through the financial system, which comprises (1) **financial intermediaries** that transform the nature of the securities they issue and invest in, and (2) **market intermediaries** that simply make the markets work better. The whole package of institutions is the Canadian financial system. We discuss the various facets of this system in the following sections.

financial intermediaries entities that invest funds on behalf of others and change the nature of the transactions

market intermediaries entities that facilitate the working of markets and help provide direct intermediation but do not change the nature of the transaction; also called brokers

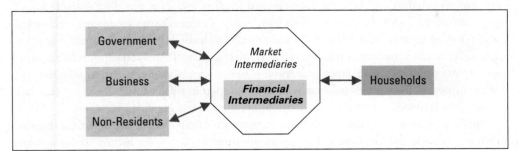

FIGURE 1-3 *The Financial System*

Channels of Intermediation

Figure 1-4 demonstrates that the financial system transfers money from those with a surplus (lenders) to those who need it (borrowers). This transfer occurs through **intermediation**, which is the process of bringing these parties together. If we think about how this intermediation can occur, one obvious way is for individuals to borrow directly from friends, relatives, and acquaintances. Another is to borrow from a specialized financial institution, such as the Royal Bank of Canada (RBC Financial Group). These are two extremes in terms of the transfer of money from lenders to borrowers. In the first case, borrowers obtain funds *directly* from individuals; in the second, they borrow *indirectly* from individuals who have first loaned their savings to (deposited them into) a financial institution, which in turn lends to the ultimate borrowers.

intermediation the transfer of funds from lenders to borrowers

These two patterns of intermediation are illustrated in Figure 1-4, with the three basic channels represented. In the first channel is *direct* intermediation, where the lender provides money directly to the ultimate borrower without any help from a specialist. This is a non-market transaction because the exchange is negotiated directly between the borrower and lender. An example would be a relative lending money to buy a car or helping to finance a degree program. The second channel also represents direct intermediation between the lender and borrower, but in this case, some help is needed because no one individual can lend the full amount needed or because the borrower is not aware of the available lenders. As a result, the borrower needs help to find suitable lenders, which is what market intermediaries do. A market intermediary is simply an entity that facilitates the working of markets and helps the direct intermediation process.

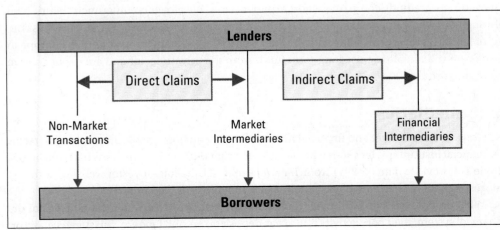

FIGURE 1-4 *Channels of Money Transfer*

Typically, market intermediaries are called "brokers." The real estate market has real estate and mortgage brokers, who help with the sale and financing of houses. The insurance market has insurance brokers, who facilitate the sale of insurance, and the stock market has stockbrokers, who facilitate the sale of financial securities, particularly shares. In each case, market intermediaries help to make the market work. Their responsibilities are to assist with the transaction and bring borrowers and lenders together, but they do not change the nature of the transaction itself. In this way, market intermediaries are agents, and we call these types of transactions "agency transactions." The most important financial market in Canada is the stock market, or the Toronto Stock Exchange (TSX), which supports a variety of market intermediaries, from stockbrokers who advise clients, through traders who buy and sell securities, to investment bankers who help companies raise capital. In each case, their raison d'être is to make markets work; in doing so, they effect agency transactions.

The third channel is completely different. It represents financial intermediation, a situation in which the financial institution or financial intermediary lends the money to the ultimate borrowers but raises the money itself by borrowing directly from other individuals. In this case, the ultimate lenders have only an *indirect* claim on the ultimate borrowers; their direct claim is on the financial institution. In Figure 1-4, the financial intermediary is in a rectangular box to indicate that it changes the nature of the transaction, whereas the market intermediary does not. We call these types of transactions "principal transactions" because the financial intermediary acts as a principal on its own behalf rather than as an agent on behalf of its clients. However, in the end, both individuals and financial intermediaries are involved in lending to the ultimate borrowers; it is just that the route to these ultimate borrowers differs. Additionally, market intermediaries help financial intermediaries, as well as individuals, in their dealings with the ultimate borrowers. Commonly, we refer to these two market segments as the "retail" and "institutional" markets. When market intermediaries help individuals, it is retail; when they help financial intermediaries, it is institutional.

Before we move on, it's important to note that financial intermediaries rely on the willingness of individuals to lend to them; otherwise, they cannot lend to the ultimate borrowers, who are the ones who really need the money. When people are not willing to lend to financial intermediaries, and those intermediaries, in turn, have to restrict whom they can lend to, we have a **credit crunch**. In 2008–9, as we will see shortly, Canada and the world experienced the worst credit crunch in over 75 years because major financial intermediaries in the United States and Europe purchased direct claims from issuers who could not repay them. Consequently, other lenders were unwilling to lend to major financial intermediaries, causing, in September 2008, both the biggest-ever bankruptcy in the United States (Lehman Brothers Holdings Inc.) and the biggest-ever bank failure in the United States (Washington Mutual, Inc.). The failures in the U.S. banking system generated a panic that quickly spread around the world, as the financial health of otherwise sound financial intermediaries was called into question. As credit dried up, the world experienced a full-blown credit crunch that rippled through the whole financial system and pushed the world into its first-ever global recession. As of July 2012, we are still living with the after-effects of this financial crisis as many European banks are still unable to raise long-term funds from the private sector and are dependent on state support.

credit crunch a situation in which financial intermediaries have to raise the cost of their loans by a significant amount due to their own inability to raise financing on reasonable terms

Intermediaries

So who are these market and financial intermediaries, and how important are they? In terms of financial institutions, let's start with the most familiar ones—the Canadian chartered banks. Table 1-4 provides data for 2011 from *The Globe and Mail's* Globe Investor website for the six biggest Canadian chartered banks in terms of revenue, assets, and profits.

What do the banks do? Although Canadian banks are involved in almost all areas of the financial system, their core activity is to act as deposit takers and lenders. This means that they take in deposits from individuals and institutions and then lend the money to others as loans. If we add up all the assets of the Big Six banks, we get $3,317 billion, which is much more than the net liabilities of the household sector, given in Table 1-3, of $452 billion in consumer credit, $140 billion in loans, and $1,027 billion in mortgage debt. The $3,317-billion figure reflects all of the lending within the household sector that StatsCan netted out, plus the corporate financing and foreign activities of the banks. You may not have a good benchmark for these numbers, but the Big Six banks are extremely large, whether they are judged by revenue, total assets, or profits.

TABLE 1-4 Chartered Banks—Financial Statistics, 2011

Bank	Revenue ($Million)	Assets ($Million)	Profits ($Million)
Royal Bank of Canada	36,651	815,016	4,843
Canadian Imperial Bank of Commerce (CIBC)	16,250	391,449	3,112
Bank of Nova Scotia	27,470	637,055	5,487
Toronto-Dominion Bank	28,808	773,186	6,161
Bank of Montreal	19,535	525,503	3,790
National Bank of Canada	6,203	175,247	1,233

Source: Data retrieved June 13, 2012, from the Globe Investor website at www.globeinvestor.com/.

The Canadian banks are among the soundest banks in the world and recently have become paragons of prudence. But with assets of $815 billion and profits of *only* $4.843 billion, all the Royal Bank has to lose on its assets is 0.594 percent after tax ($4,843/$815,016), and it will have no profits at all. In terms of a business model, banking is a low-margin, high-turnover business, which means a bank makes lots of "sales"—that is, loans—but each one is not very profitable. After a couple of years of losses, investors may start to worry about whether the bank can survive, and a full-scale credit crunch will erupt. This is exactly what happened throughout the U.S. banking system during 2008, when the largest bank in the world, Citigroup Inc., saw its overall market value drop from US$260 billion in 2006 to US$5 billion. Citigroup recorded a series of losses that peaked in 2010 at a pre-tax loss of US$140 billion, and global losses in banking rose to $1.24 trillion. The problems at the largest U.S. and UK banks in 2008, as customers defaulted on their loans, severely retarded the efforts of government agencies to stimulate the economy, since many of the banks were in a desperate "survival mode" and reluctant to make new loans. This led to some demands that the U.S. government nationalize its banks—that is, take them over or directly intervene in markets to get the U.S. banking system working again (see *Finance in the News 1-2*).

---

finance INTHENEWS 1-2 U.S., Europe Must Fix Bank Systems: Flaherty

FINANCE MINISTER Jim Flaherty says the U.S. and Europe need to move faster to fix their ailing banks or there will be no worldwide economic recovery.

"This is a must-do—the banks have to be fixed in the United States and in Europe for the economies to start to recover," he said at the G7 meeting of financial ministers and central bank governors in the U.S. capital.

"There has been concern with the delay in dealing with the problems with the banks in the United States and in Europe for that matter....The global lending has to take place, the credit markets have to function, the financial markets have to function."

Source: The Canadian Press, "Flaherty Urges U.S., Europe to Fix Their Banks, and Fast," April 24, 2009. Copyright © 2009 The Canadian Press. Reprinted by permission.

Although the banks are overwhelmingly the most important financial intermediaries, the major insurance companies are also very large. Table 1-5 provides financial data on the major insurance companies in Canada. The big three, Manulife Financial Corporation, Sun Life

Financial Inc., and Great-West Lifeco Inc., each had over $200 billion in assets at the end of 2011, although poor stock markets and low interest rates have taken their toll on the profitability of both Manulife and Sun Life.

TABLE 1-5 Insurance Companies: Financial Statistics, 2011

Insurer	Revenue ($Million)	Assets ($Million)	Profits ($Million)
Manulife Financial	51,072	462,102	129
Sun Life Financial	22,581	218,027	− 200
Great-West Lifeco	29,999	238,000	2,335

Source: Data retrieved June 14, 2012, from the Globe Investor website at www.globeinvestor.com/.

Technically, life insurance is not insurance—we are all going to die, so we can't insure against it—but it is often a form of savings.[4] Insurance companies are classified as contractual savers, because, in most cases, the premiums on a policy are paid on a monthly basis, so the insurers receive a steady flow of money: you buy life insurance and pay premiums; then you die and the policy pays off to your survivors. Before you die, the insurance company has all the premiums to invest, so many view selling insurance as simply a way of getting "free" money to invest.

As long as the insurance company can invest the proceeds from the premiums to earn a good return, things are fine. However, from 2006 to 2008, the world's biggest insurance company, American International Group (AIG), invested in exotic financial securities issued by major U.S. banks.[5] So far, these investments have forced the U.S. government to inject US$170 billion into AIG to "rescue" it; otherwise, its collapse would have dwarfed that of Washington Mutual and Lehman Brothers.

When we looked at the major financial assets of the household sector in Table 1-3, the two largest components were insurance and pension assets and direct investments in shares. The funds in pension plans are held directly for their pensioners, and they substitute for having individuals save for themselves for their retirement. Not surprisingly, the data provided in Table 1-6 on the major Canadian pension plans show that they are very large. Like the insurance companies, the pension plans are contractual savers and get a steady flow of money each month. The Caisse de dépôt et placement du Québec is the largest pension fund manager in Canada, with more than $159 billion in assets under management; however, it manages the assets of several Quebec-based pension funds.

TABLE 1-6 Pension Plan Assets, December 31, 2011

Pension Plan Managers	Net Assets ($Billion)
Caisse de dépôt et placement du Québec*	159
Canada Pension Plan (CPP)	148
Ontario Teachers (Teachers)	117
Ontario Municipal Employees (OMERS)	56

* The Caisse manages the investments of several pension plans.
Source: 2011 annual reports.

The three types of financial intermediaries discussed above are financial institutions that change the nature of the financial contract. Chartered banks take in deposits and make loans; insurance companies take in insurance premiums and pay off when an incident, such as a death or a fire, occurs; pension funds take in contributions and provide pension payments after plan members retire. These have traditionally been the three most important types of financial intermediaries.

---

[4] Term insurance is insurance in the sense that it pays off only if you die during the life of the policy.
[5] We discuss these credit default swaps in Chapter 11.

In contrast, mutual funds simply act as a "pass-through" for individuals, providing them with a convenient way to invest in the equity and debt markets. Like insurance and pension plans, many mutual funds receive their monies through monthly savings plans, but this is not always the case. Unlike other financial intermediaries, mutual funds do not transform the nature of the underlying financial security. Mutual funds perform two major functions: (1) they pool small sums of money so they can make investments that would not be possible for smaller investors, and (2) they offer professional expertise in the management of those funds. We will discuss the relative advantages of paying for professional money management through mutual funds versus simply investing directly in the stock and bond markets later. The mutual fund business has enormous amounts of money under management. The dollar amount of mutual fund assets under management has grown dramatically, particularly over the past 20 years, as demonstrated in Figure 1-5. As of December 2010, mutual fund assets totalled $636 billion, compared with $17.5 billion in 1986, and a mere $1 billion at the end of 1963. However, the total assets under management fell dramatically in 2008, by $197 billion, due to the severe financial and economic crisis that developed in the second half of the year and the associated stock market crash. The last time this happened was in 2002 when, again, the economy went into a slowdown and the stock market declined.

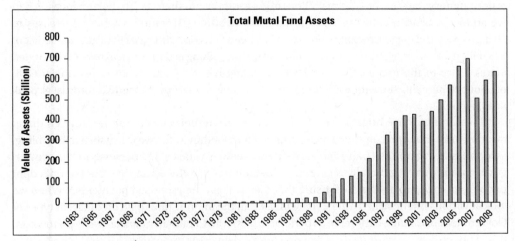

FIGURE 1-5 *Canadian Mutual Fund Assets, 1963–2010 ($Billion)*

Source: Data from the Investment Funds Institute of Canada website at www.ific.ca.

This brief look at the major players in the Canadian financial system should help you understand how the system works. At the core of the system are ordinary Canadians who want to buy houses and televisions, save for retirement, and protect themselves from the impact of accidents. They then channel their savings to the ultimate borrowers—that is, governments and business—either directly, as retail investors, or indirectly, through the major financial intermediaries, where the money is invested by institutional investors. So who are the major borrowers or issuers of financial securities?

The Major Borrowers

The previous sections introduced the central idea of intermediation—that is, money is transferred from lenders to borrowers either directly though market intermediaries or indirectly through financial intermediaries. Governments are important in this process. For example, the Canada Pension Plan (CPP) and the Quebec Pension Plan (QPP) play large roles in channelling funds from lenders to borrowers. In addition, governments provide many services to Canadians, some of which are paid for out of taxes and some of which are paid for by borrowing. Indeed, the Government of Canada (Canada) has 2011–12 total expenditures budgeted of $281 billion. After the federal government, the next biggest spenders were the Province of Ontario (Ontario) and the Province of Quebec (Quebec), with 2011–12 expenditures of $128.7 billion and $75.9 billion,

Crown corporations
government-owned companies that
provide goods and services needed
by Canadians

respectively.[6] Finally, government-owned **Crown corporations** provide goods and services needed by Canadians. Two of the largest, in terms of company assets, are Hydro-Québec and Ontario Power Generation Inc. (OPG), with assets in 2011 of $70 billion and $34.8 billion, respectively. Both of these Crown corporations issue debt to finance the development of electricity generation plants, but there is a difference: the debt of Hydro-Québec is provincially guaranteed, whereas that of OPG is not. We will discuss how this affects the pricing of their debt in Chapter 6.

We will talk about debt markets later, but note here that the government debt market plays a very important role in the financial system. Even though the federal government produced a surplus every year from 1997 to 2009, the financial crisis and recession of 2008–9 caused the federal government to return to a deficit, so the amount of Canadian debt outstanding increased to $642 billion by the end of May 2012. In other words, the federal government is a net debtor and a significant borrower at that. In terms of assessing how much debt this is, we normally divide the amount of debt by a country's gross domestic product (GDP). This standardizes the amount of debt by a country's income in the same way that we assess the burden of an individual's debt by dividing by their income. At the end of 2011, the Dominion Bond Rating Service estimated Canada's debt-to-GDP ratio to be 36 percent. However, Canada is not a unitary state, as the responsibilities of government are shared with the provinces. When we add in provincial debt, the total government debt-to-GDP ratio in Canada increases to 78.5 percent. The biggest recent contributor has been Ontario, with a 2011–12 annual deficit of $23 billion, as the province has been hit hard by the continuing economic weakness in the United States. Prior to the financial crisis of 2008–9, Ontario had a stable debt-to-provincial-GDP of about 26 percent. Since then it has inexorably increased to 39 percent and is forecast to peak at 45 percent in 2016.[7]

Governments have huge power to raise money from their citizens, either through direct taxation or by monopolizing and charging higher fees for things that we want, such as gambling, alcohol, and cigarettes (these fees are often called "sin taxes").[8] Because of this power, government debt is generally regarded as "default free," in the sense that it is the only debt people can invest in and know for sure that they will get the promised payments.[9] When we look at various financial securities, you will see that the interest rates paid on different types of Government of Canada debt serve as benchmarks for the Canadian financial system. However, this is not always the case, as the sovereign (euro) debt crisis indicates.

In *Finance in the News 1-3, The Globe and Mail* discusses some debt-to-GDP statistics for Europe as provided by Eurostat, including those countries that gave up their own currency in return for a common currency, the euro. Of all the monopolies that governments normally reserve for themselves, the most important is that of printing the national currency. However, among the countries of the European Community, 17 gave up this monopoly when they joined together to use a common currency. The problem is that some of these countries continued to borrow money to finance government expenditures and ignored the fact that there were limits to how much they could tax and also how much they could cut their expenditures without causing civil unrest. Without the ability to simply print money, these countries relied on others to lend to them, like any other borrower. However, for the past three years lenders have refused to lend to the most indebted countries. First Greece, then Ireland, then Portugal and Spain were all cut off from normal lenders and sought bailouts from the richer members of the European Community (mainly Germany). As a result, a new acronym was coined, PIIGS (for Portugal, Ireland, Italy, Greece and Spain), to refer to the indebted countries. For these

---

[6] Data from Dominion Bond Rating Service (DBRS), "2011 Canadian Federal and Provincial Governments Overview," December 2011.

[7] Quebec has the highest debt-to-GDP ratio at 61 percent.

[8] The most important government monopoly is the ability to print banknotes. Anyone who tries to make Bank of Canada banknotes in competition with the government goes to jail.

[9] Deposits in banks are also default free up to certain limits because they are, in turn, insured by the government.

countries, sovereign debt was regarded as anything but risk free as they became increasingly reliant on funding from fellow Eurozone members and the International Monetary Fund! In response to receiving "aid," they have had to implement austerity measures that have pushed Europe back into recession, as the article discusses.

---

finance INTHENEWS 1-3   Euro Crisis Deepens As Debt Hits 90% of GDP

THE EMBATTLED EURO ZONE is sinking ever deeper into crisis, as new reports highlight the debt and broader economic troubles plaguing the 17-member monetary union.

According to fresh data released today by Eurostat, government debt as a percentage of gross domestic product continues to climb, in some countries to extreme levels.

The key debt-to-GDP measure for the euro zone as a whole rose in the second quarter to 90 percent, from 88.2 percent in the first three months of the year, the statistics agency said.

For the full 27 countries of the European Union, it rose to 84.9 percent from 83.5 percent.

Compared to a year earlier, the ratio climbed from 87.1 percent in the euro zone and 81.4 percent in the EU.

But it is the currency union in particular where the troubles lie, and notably its most troubled members.

Greece, for example, posted the highest ratio, at 150.3 percent, followed by Italy at 126.1 percent, Portugal at 117.5 percent and Ireland at 111.5 percent.

Compared to the first quarter, Greece also had the dubious distinction of posting the highest increase despite its massive cutbacks as the measure climbed 13.4 percentage points.

The lowest levels, by the way, were in Estonia, at 7.3 percent, Bulgaria at 16.5 percent and Luxembourg at 20.9 percent.

Today's Eurostat report came amid new, disappointing economic readings, in the form of Markit's purchasing managers' index for the euro zone, which slipped in October.

"Advance readings on the European PMIs were weaker than expected with the euro zone's manufacturing PMI unexpectedly falling 0.8 points to 45.3 in October, while the services PMI ticked only a shade higher to a reading of 46.2, adding to concerns that the region's economic slump could be deepening with both measures remaining clearly in contraction territory to start the quarter," said Carl Campus of BMO Nesbitt Burns.

The 50 mark in a PMI separates contraction from expansion, so what today's reading shows is that in what is already an environment of contraction, it's getting worse.

It's also the worst showing in years. And it's not just in the troubled nations, but in Germany as well, for example, whose latest reading on business confidence also slumped. Germany is Europe's economic engine, and deeper troubles there are a particular concern.

"After Germany's PMI signalled rising optimism by climbing to the highest reading since March it fell back down again in the October print against expectations for an improvement," said Derek Holt and Dov Zigler of Bank of Nova Scotia.

"This shifts the picture away from perhaps signalling a more optimistic turning point back to renewed concerns over accelerated economic weakness," they said in a research note.

"This was reinforced by a deterioration in German business confidence. The reading weakened because of reduced confidence in near-term conditions while longer-run expectations remained unchanged at the weakest level since May 2009. If Europe is settling its affairs, then either Germans don't believe it or they are increasingly of the view that they'll take their lumps for the sake of bailing out more ineptly managed neighbours at the expense of their own competitiveness."

Although government debt is very important as a benchmark, and personal debt is important for financing houses and consumer credit, arguably the most important borrowing sector is business. The business sector makes the goods and services we consume, and it borrows to finance growth in this capacity. Indeed, when we looked at Figure 1-2, we noted that the business sector as a whole had net securities outstanding with a market value of $2,005 billion, approximately twice the market value of government securities outstanding.

We conclude this section with a look at the 10 largest non-financial companies in Canada, based on 2011 profits, as shown in Table 1-7. Although revenue is an indicator of size, in that it places a value on what we buy from a company, assets need to be financed and will be reflected in the firm's capital expenditure and corporate financing decisions, topics you will be studying in business finance. Typically, the profits of non-financial corporations are significantly less than those of the big five chartered banks, which reiterates the important role played by the banks in our financial system. Note, for example, that the profit rank in the first column does not start at 1; that's because the missing numbers all belong to the big financial institutions, which make up six of the 16 most profitable companies in Canada.

TABLE 1-7 Top 10 Non-Financial Companies Ranked by Profits, 2011 ($000s)

Rank	Companies	Profit	Revenues	Assets	Employees	Industry
4	Barrick Gold	4,484,000	14,662,000	48,884,000	46,169	Precious metals
5	Suncor Energy	4,304,000	39,790,000	74,777,000	46,156	Integrated oils
6	Imperial Oil	3,371,000	30,714,000	25,429,000	38,473	Integrated oils
9	Potash Corporation of Saskatchewan	3,081,000	9,127,000	16,257,000	36,160	Chemicals
10	Teck Resources	2,668,000	11,634,000	34,219,000	21,927	Integrated mines
11	Canadian Natural Resources	2,643,000	15,548,000	47,278,000	41,830	Oil and gas producers
12	Canadian National Railway Co.	2,457,000	9,429,000	26,026,000	36,821	Transportation
13	BCE Inc.	2,340,000	19,588,000	39,426,000	32,933	Telephone utilities
14	Husky Energy	2,224,000	24,774,000	32,426,000	23,508	Integrated oils
16	Brookfield Asset Management	1,957,000	19,273,000	91,030,000	17,365	Diversified

Source: "Ranking Canada's top 1,000 public companies by profit." *The Globe and Mail/Report on Business Magazine*, June 28, 2012. Retrieved from *The Globe and Mail* website, http://www.theglobeandmail.com/repor-on-business/rob-magazine/top-1000/2012-rankings-of-canadas-top-1000-public-companies-by-profit/article4371923/.

CONCEPT REVIEW QUESTIONS

1. Identify and briefly describe the three main channels of savings.
2. Distinguish between market and financial intermediaries.
3. Discuss how the three most important types of financial intermediaries operate.

1.3 FINANCIAL INSTRUMENTS AND MARKETS

Learning Objective 1.4
Identify the basic types of financial instruments that are available and explain how they are traded.

debt instruments legal obligations to repay borrowed funds at a specified maturity date and to provide interim interest payments

equity instruments ownership stakes in a company

common share an equity instrument that represents part ownership in a company and usually gives voting rights on major decisions affecting the company

preferred shares equity instruments that usually entitle the owner to fixed dividend payments that must be made before any dividends are paid to common shareholders

You now know who the biggest borrowers and lenders in Canada are, and you know that financial intermediaries coexist alongside market intermediaries to help the intermediation process. The next step is to look at the instruments and institutional arrangements that are used to transfer these funds.

Financial Instruments

Financial assets are formal legal documents that set out the rights and obligations of all the parties involved. Since we discuss the various types of securities in depth at several points later on, we will provide only a brief overview here.

There are two major categories of financial securities.

1. **Debt instruments**: These represent legal obligations to repay borrowed funds at a specified maturity date and provide interim interest payments as specified in the agreement. We will discuss these instruments in more detail in Chapter 6 but note here that some of the most common examples are bank loans, commercial paper, bankers' acceptances (BAs), treasury bills (T-bills), mortgage loans, bonds, and debentures.

2. **Equity instruments**: These represent an ownership stake in a company. The most common form of equity is the **common share**, which we will discuss at length in Chapter 7 and in later chapters. Companies may also issue **preferred shares**, which usually entitle the owner to fixed dividend payments that must be made before any dividends are paid to common shareholders.

Aside from the debt-versus-equity distinction, financial instruments can be categorized in several additional ways. One way is to distinguish between **non-marketable financial assets** and **marketable financial assets**. The most familiar forms of non-marketable assets are savings accounts or demand deposits with financial institutions, such as chartered banks. The funds invested here are available on demand, which guarantees the liquidity of these investments, but you can't sell them to someone else: you have to first withdraw the funds and then transfer the cash. Another widely used type of non-marketable financial asset in Canada is the Canada Savings Bond (CSB) and its provincial counterparts, which are issued by the federal or provincial governments. These bonds are non-marketable, unlike traditional bonds, because they are not tradable. However, CSBs can be cashed out by the owner at full par value plus eligible accrued interest at any bank in Canada at any time.

Marketable securities are those that can be traded among market participants. They are typically categorized not only according to whether they are debt or equity securities but also by their "term to maturity," or time until the obligation must be repaid. **Money market securities** include short-term (i.e., maturities less than one year) debt instruments, such as T-bills, commercial paper, and BAs. **Capital market securities** include debt securities with maturities greater than one year, such as bonds, debentures, and so on. They also include equity securities, which represent ownership in a company and generally have no maturity date.

Governments raise new financing via the debt markets. They issue T-bills as a source of short-term financing (i.e., less than one year), and they issue traditional bonds and CSBs for long-term financing. Businesses raise short-term financing in the form of debt through loans, or by issuing commercial paper, BAs, and so on (all of which will be discussed in greater detail in later chapters). They raise long-term financing in the form of debt (i.e., through loans, by issuing bonds, or by using other long-term debt instruments) or in the form of equity (i.e., by issuing common shares or preferred shares).

Financial Markets

We have provided a brief overview of the financial instruments that are available to transfer funds from lenders to borrowers. Now we provide a brief description of the financial markets that permit the issue and trading of these instruments. It is important to recognize that financial markets play a critical role in any open economy by facilitating the transfer of funds from lenders to borrowers. In addition, if markets are efficient (which is the topic of Chapter 10), these funds will be allocated to those who have the most productive use for them.

For discussion purposes, we will begin by distinguishing between primary and secondary markets. **Primary markets** involve the issue of new securities by the borrower in return for cash from investors (or lenders). For example, when the government sells new issues of T-bills or bonds or when a company sells new common shares to the public, these are primary market transactions; new securities are created, and the borrowing entity raises monies it can spend. Chapters 17 and 19 deal extensively with the primary markets.

Primary markets are the key to the wealth creation process, since they enable money to be transferred to those who can make best use of it in terms of developing new real assets, such as houses and factories. However, primary markets will not work properly without well-functioning **secondary markets**. Secondary markets provide trading (or market) environments that permit investors to buy and sell existing securities. This service is critical to the functioning of the primary markets because governments and companies would not be able to raise financing if investors were unable to sell their investments when necessary. Consider how reluctant investors would be to buy a 20-year corporate bond worth $1,000 or $1,000 worth of a company's common shares, if they knew they would be unable to sell these securities when they needed to raise money quickly or when they became nervous about the company's future prospects.

non-marketable financial assets invested funds that are available on demand in instruments that are not tradable

marketable financial assets those assets that can be traded among market participants

money market securities short-term debt instruments

capital market securities debt securities with maturities greater than one year and equity securities

primary markets markets that involve the issue of new securities by the borrower in return for cash from investors (or lenders)

secondary markets trading (or market) environments that permit investors to buy and sell existing securities

exchanges or auction markets secondary markets that involve a bidding process that takes place in a specific location

dealer or over-the-counter (OTC) markets secondary markets that do not have a physical location and consist of a network of dealers who trade directly with one another

brokers market intermediaries who facilitate the sale of financial securities and help to make the market work

There are two major types of secondary markets: (1) **exchanges or auction markets**; and (2) **dealer or over-the-counter (OTC) markets**. Exchanges have been referred to as auction markets because they involve a bidding process that takes place in a specific location (i.e., similar to an auction). Investors (both buyers and sellers) can be represented at these markets by **brokers**. In contrast, OTC or dealer markets do not have a physical location, but rather consist of a network of dealers who trade directly with one another. The distinction has become blurred in recent years because trading on most of the major exchanges in the world is now fully computerized, making the physical location of the exchanges of little consequence. At the same time, OTC markets have become increasingly automated, reducing the amount of direct haggling between dealers.

Money market instruments trade in dealer markets. They tend to be very large and are typically issued in sizes of $100,000 or more. As a result, money market trading is dominated by governments, financial institutions, and large corporations. Long-term debt instruments, such as bonds, are also traded primarily through dealer markets, although some are traded on exchanges.

Equity securities generally, and common shares in particular, are the major financial securities issued by corporations, and they represent a proportionate ownership (share) in a firm. Unlike debt securities, which are normally paid back and result in constant refinancing activity, common shares are generally issued once and then stay outstanding indefinitely.[10] As a result, secondary market trading in equity securities is many times the size of the primary market, whereas it is the opposite for debt securities. The overwhelming majority of equity market transactions take place through a stock exchange, although there is a small OTC equity market in Canada.

Toronto Stock Exchange (TSX) the major stock exchange in Canada, where most equity security transactions take place; it is the official exchange for trading Canadian senior securities

Dramatic changes have taken place in the major stock exchanges in recent years, both at home and abroad. At the start of 1999, Canada had five stock exchanges: the **Toronto Stock Exchange** or **TSX (formerly called the TSE)**, the Montréal Exchange (ME), the Vancouver Stock Exchange (VSE), the Winnipeg Stock Exchange (WSE), and the Alberta Stock Exchange (ASE). An overhaul of that structure occurred during 1999 and 2000, resulting in only two Canadian stock exchanges: the TSX and the newly created **TSX Venture Exchange**. Both of these exchanges are owned by the TSX Group Inc., which became the first North American exchange to be publicly listed in November 2002. Trading operations for both the TSX and the TSX Venture Exchange are conducted by **TSX Markets**, which is also a member of the TSX Group. On September 2007, the Winnipeg Commodity Exchange was acquired by the Intercontinental Exchange (ICE), as ICE expanded its trading to include agricultural contracts. On December 10, 2007, the Montreal Exchange and the TSX Group announced an agreement to combine both institutions to form the **TMX Group Inc.**, which was completed on May 1, 2008. In the space of 10 years, Canada has gone from five major exchanges to one, but there are still several distinct entities.

TSX Venture Exchange the stock exchange for trading the securities of emerging companies not listed on the TSX

TSX Markets the group that performs trading operations for the TSX and the TSX Venture Exchange

TMX Group Inc. the company that owns the TSX, the TSX Venture Exchange, and the ME

Since March 2000, the Montreal Exchange (**Bourse de Montréal**) has functioned as the Canadian national derivatives market, and it now carries on all trading in financial futures and options that previously occurred on the TSX, the ME, and the now-defunct Toronto Futures Exchange. Similarly, equity trading is now concentrated on the TSX, where oversight and regulation can be more uniformly implemented.

Bourse de Montréal the exchange that acts as the Canadian national derivatives market and carries on all trading in financial futures and options

Traditionally, stock exchanges were not-for-profit organizations. Membership in a stock exchange (in the form of a "seat") was sold to individuals to allow them to trade on the exchange. However, when the TSX converted into a regular corporation, these seats were exchanged for shares, so now the new TMX Group is a for-profit institution owned by its shareholders. This reflects a worldwide trend in the conversion of stock exchanges to competitive private companies, as global competition to list and trade securities has increased. The result is that market intermediaries, like stock brokerages, are now called "participating organizations" or "approved participants" and do not have to own seats in order to trade on the exchange.

---

[10] There are occasional share repurchases, but relative to the continuous retirement of debt, the amounts are generally insignificant.

On April 23, 1997, the TSX closed its trading floor, and trading is now mostly computerized. Brokers enter orders to either buy or sell securities based on their client orders, and the computer matches buyers with sellers. As of May 1, 2012, there were 3,755 firms listed in Canada (1,496 on the TSX and 2,259 on the TSX Venture Exchange), and many of the larger ones were also listed on U.S. markets. In mid-June 2011, the TSX had a market capitalization (that is, the total market value of all the listed firms) of $2.2 trillion and ranked eighth in the world in terms of market value. The barometer of the state of the Canadian equity market is the Standard & Poor's/Toronto Stock Exchange (S&P/TSX) Composite Index (formerly known as the TSE 300 Composite Index). The S&P/TSX Composite Index is the TSX's major stock market index and is maintained by Standard & Poor's (S&P), a major U.S. company that also maintains the S&P500 Index, which is one of the major indexes of the U.S. stock market. Figure 1-6 gives the value of the S&P/TSX Composite from 1984 to 2012.

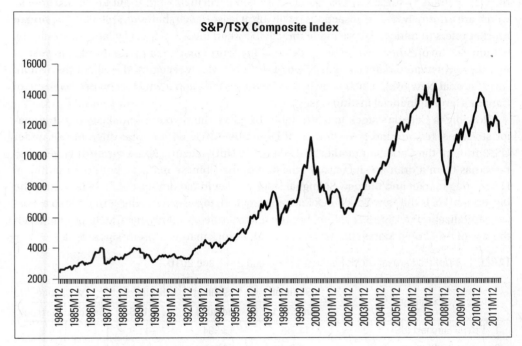

FIGURE 1-6 *TSX Composite Index, 1984–2012*

Source: Data from Statistics Canada, CANSIM V122620.

The S&P/TSX Composite Index reached a month-end high of 14,714.73 in May 2008. Then it was caught in the tailspin of the worldwide decline in equity markets as the U.S. banking system verged on collapse. For six months, from August 2008 to February 2009, the TSX dropped each month by some gut-wrenching, double-digit declines, with many daily price fluctuations exceeding 7 percent. By the end of February 2009, the TSX had dropped by 45 percent from its month-end high less than a year earlier. Globally, almost US$15 trillion in **market capitalization** had disappeared with the decline in stock markets around the world.

market capitalization the total market value of the securities of an entity

The extreme volatility in equity markets in the second half of 2008 triggered a very large increase in trading activity. In December 2008, volume on the TSX reached a record high of 10.2 billion shares, compared to 6.9 billion a year earlier. However, the decline in market values meant that the daily value of shares traded dropped from $6.5 billion to $5.6 billion. In such poor equity markets, it is hardly surprising that few firms came to the equity market for new financing. As discussed above, new equity financing is a primary market transaction. During 2008, $30.2 billion in new equity financing was raised in the public markets. Only $1.4 billion came from initial public offerings (IPOs), where companies raised money for the very first time; the balance was seasoned equity offerings (SEOs) by established firms. In contrast, the numbers for 2007 were $40 billion and $5.7 billion, respectively. By 2010, the markets had recovered to $37 billion and $7.8 billion, respectively.[11]

As mentioned above, in addition to listing on an organized stock exchange, common shares also trade in the OTC or unlisted markets. Trades in unlisted securities do not need to be reported, except in Ontario, where the **Ontario Securities Commission (OSC)** requires that they be reported on the Canadian Unlisted Board Inc. automated system. The first Canadian quotation and reporting system, the **Canadian Trading and Quotation System Inc. (CNQ)** was launched in July 2003. The CNQ provides an alternative market for very small emerging companies because the requirements to trade on this market are less stringent than those for the TSX Venture Exchange.

In addition to the primary and secondary markets, there are also the third and fourth markets. The **third market** refers to the trading of securities that are listed on organized exchanges in the OTC market. Historically, this market has been particularly important for "block trades," which are extremely large transactions involving at least 10,000 shares or $100,000. The **fourth market** refers to trades that are made directly between investors (usually large institutions), without the involvement of brokers or dealers. The fourth market operates through the use of privately owned automated systems. Two of the most widely recognized systems are Instinet (Institutional Network), which is owned by Reuters, and Alpha, which is owned by some of Canada's largest financial institutions.[12]

How big is Canada's stock market? Table 1-8 gives the market capitalization of the major stock markets around the world as of December 2011. With a total value of just under US$2 trillion, the Canadian market ranked eighth. Until recently it was the sixth largest, but there has been a dramatic increase in the size of the Chinese markets, both the traditional Hong Kong market and the new Shanghai stock market in "communist" China! Of course the biggest market is the New York Stock Exchange, which, together with the Nasdaq, had a market capitalization of US$15.6 trillion, but the normal rule of thumb that Canada is one-tenth the size of the United States suggests that Canada's stock market is pretty significant.

TABLE 1-8 World's Largest Stock Markets at Year End 2011 and 2010

	Exchange	US$Billion End 2011	US$Billion End 2010	% Change in US$	% Change in Local Currency
1	NYSE Euronext (US)	11,796	13,394	−11.9	−11.9
2	NASDAQ OMX (US)	3,845	3,889	−1.1	−1.1
3	Tokyo Stock Exchange Group	3,325	3,828	−13.1	−17.6
4	London Stock Exchange Group	3,266	3,613	−9.6	−6.6
5	NYSE Euronext (Europe)	2,447	2,930	−16.5	−13.7
6	Shanghai Stock Exchange	2,357	2,716	13.2	−17.1
7	Hong Kong Exchanges	2,258	2,711	−16.7	−16.8
8	TMX Group	1,912	2,170	−11.9	−9.7
9	BM&F BOVESPA	1,229	1,546	−20.5	−10.7
10	Australian Securities Exchange	1,198	1,454	−17.6	−17.6

Source: World Federation of Exchanges, "2011 WFE Market Highlights," January 19, 2012. Available at www.world-exchanges.org. Reprinted by permission.

---

[11] Data is from the Investment Industry Association of Canada website at www.iiac.ca.

[12] As of May 31, 2012, the owners of Alpha were part of the Maple Group and in the process of taking over the TMX Group to further consolidate stock trading in Canada.

CONCEPT REVIEW QUESTIONS

1. Distinguish among the various types of financial assets.
2. Identify the major sources of financing used by (a) governments and (b) businesses.
3. Distinguish between primary and secondary markets.

1.4 THE GLOBAL FINANCIAL COMMUNITY

In addition to the domestic financial markets discussed above, global financial markets represent important sources of funds for borrowers and provide investors with important alternatives. Indeed, Canadian debt and equity markets represent only a small proportion of the total global marketplace. Therefore, it makes sense for Canadians to borrow and invest abroad, which has become easier to do in today's global business environment as investment barriers are relaxed.

Learning Objective 1.5
Explain the importance of the global financial system and how Canada is impacted by events in the U.S. mortgage market.

Table 1-9 demonstrates the importance of global markets to Canadians, and vice versa. In particular, in 2011, Canadians had foreign investments totalling about $1.89 trillion (i.e., all the assets in the table). Approximately $691 billion of this figure represented investments in financial assets, such as foreign stocks, bonds, and so on (i.e., it excluded the $801.9 billion in direct investments). At the same time, foreign investment in Canadian assets exceeded $2.12 trillion (i.e., the liabilities), with over $1.1 trillion of this amount being in the form of financial securities and another $778.7 billion in foreign direct investment—that is, direct ownership of Canadian firms. Combining the two items, we had a net investment position of −$236 billion in 2011, which is also the figure reported in Table 1-1.

TABLE 1-9 Canada's International Investments, 2011

		$Billion
Total Assets		
Canadian direct investments		801.9
Canadian portfolio investments		691.5
Loans		89.6
Deposits		119.1
Official international reserves		63.9
Other assets		120.0
Total Liabilities		
Foreign direct investments		778.7
Foreign portfolio investments		1,108.0
Portfolio Canadian bonds	670.6	
Portfolio Canadian stocks	371.2	
Portfolio Canadian money	66.2	
Loans		53.6
Deposits		101.6
Other liabilities		79.9
Canada's Net International Investments		**−236**

Source: Data from Statistics Canada, "Table 64." In *National Balance Sheet Accounts.* Ottawa: Minister of Industry, 2012 (Catalogue No. 13-022-X).

The magnitude of Canadian investment abroad and foreign investment in Canada should come as no surprise. In today's financial markets, it is easier for Canadian companies and governments to issue securities in foreign markets. At the same time, it is easier for Canadian investors to invest in foreign markets and for foreign companies to raise funds in Canadian markets. The United States represents an important market for Canadians because of its size and proximity. In fact, as discussed, a large number of Canadian companies are listed on more than one stock market, primarily markets in the United States, such as National Association of Securities Dealers Automated Quotations (Nasdaq) or the New York Stock Exchange (NYSE), which are both discussed below.

Global Financial Markets

New York Stock Exchange (NYSE)
the world's largest stock market

The world's money markets and bond markets are very global in nature, with U.S. markets representing the largest and most active debt markets in the world. As in Canada, global debt markets are primarily dealer markets. The United States also possesses the largest equity markets in the world, which is convenient for Canadians who want to raise money or invest by using these markets. The **New York Stock Exchange (NYSE)** is the world's largest stock market. The market capitalization of the firms traded on NYSE Euronext was almost $12 trillion at the end of 2011.[13] However, the NYSE has steadily been losing ground in the trading of its listed securities to alternative trading mechanisms (ATMs).

The most important stock market in the United States is the Nasdaq Stock Market, or Nasdaq, which is the second-largest stock market in the world, based on its market capitalization of US$3.8 trillion in December 2011. In fact, Nasdaq has more listed companies than the NYSE, with approximately 3,200; the average number of shares traded per day (2 billion) is close to the figure for the NYSE.[14] However, larger firms tend to list on the NYSE, which is why its market capitalization far exceeds that of Nasdaq.

Like the Canadian exchanges, U.S. and global stock markets have been consolidating. In 2007, the NYSE and Euronext merged, creating the first truly global securities exchange, NYSE Euronext. On January 16, 2009, the American Stock Exchange was phased out after it was acquired by the NYSE and became the NYSE's trading platform for options, closed-end funds, and exchange-traded funds (ETFs). We will discuss these types of securities in more detail in later chapters, but as trading becomes computerized, the barriers between markets get smaller. The main constraint becomes the capacity and sophistication of the computer program that manages the trading. Consequently, even though there are almost 200 stock exchanges around the world, the industry is rapidly amalgamating, and many exchanges have various sorts of partnerships.

The globalization of the equity markets means that linkages between the markets are getting tighter. Never has this been better demonstrated than by the events of autumn 2008, when the crisis in the U.S. banking sector turned into the first global financial meltdown and recession. Such events reinforce the fact that there is only *one* finance; business finance is simply a subset of finance.

Recognizing that a mortgage is one of the simplest of financial products will help you understand how the crisis occurred. Normally, for homebuyers to qualify for a mortgage, the bank requires they have a 20 percent down payment before it will lend the balance with a loan secured on the value of the house. However, house prices in the United States started to increase quite dramatically as the country recovered from a serious recession in 2002. The increase was fuelled by better economic times, low mortgage rates, and a series of financial innovations that, in retrospect, reduced the checks in the mortgage-lending process. These factors, combined with loose regulation by the U.S. banking authorities, meant that credit was easily available. As Figure 1-7 shows, some hot markets in the United States, such as Miami, Los Angeles, and Las Vegas, experienced 150 percent increases over a short period of time.[15]

---

[13] World Federation of Exchanges, "2011 WFE Market Highlights," January 19, 2012.
[14] These statistics are from the Nasdaq website at www.nasdaq.com.
[15] House prices are all initialised to $100 in January 2000.

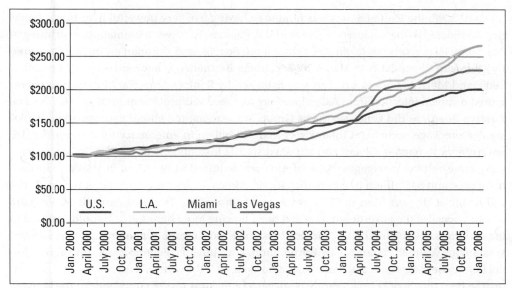

FIGURE 1-7 *Case-Shiller Index of U.S. House Prices, 2000–6*

Source: Booth, Laurence, "Collateral Damage." *Canadian Investment Review*, Winter 2008, Fig. 1, p. 13. Reprinted with the permission of *Canadian Investment Review*.

You might think that in an overheated housing market, lenders would reduce the amount of the mortgage they were willing to lend. However, in the United States, this did not happen, and banks often loaned more than 100 percent of the value of the house, with very little documentation. Such loans were known as "Ninja" loans: no income, no job, no assets. Any loan of more than 75 to 80 percent made to a weak borrower is called a sub-prime loan, and by 2006, the U.S. sub-prime market was exploding. Everything would have been fine if house prices had continued to increase, but gravity got in the way. Figure 1-8 shows the collapse in the U.S. housing market as lenders began to realize that credit was too generous and financing started to contract. By the summer of 2007, U.S. house prices had begun a downward spiral, which had only just begun to bottom out at the time of writing (July 2012).

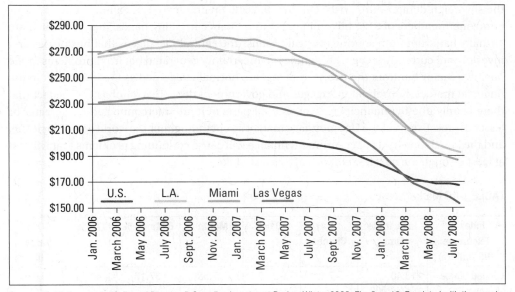

FIGURE 1-8 *Case-Shiller Index of U.S. House Prices, 2006–8*

Source: Booth, Laurence, "Collateral Damage." *Canadian Investment Review*, Winter 2008, Fig. 2, p. 13. Reprinted with the permission of *Canadian Investment Review*.

With U.S. house prices in hot markets off by an average 35 percent, even prime U.S. mortgage loans were often for more than the value of the houses they were secured against, so the owners had negative equity. The result was an increase in late payments, defaults, and huge losses for the banks that made the loans.

Until 2008, the United States was unique in having five very powerful investment banks that dominated as market intermediaries in U.S. markets. However, a dramatic restructuring of U.S. financial markets has taken place since then. Bear Stearns Companies, Inc. was acquired by JPMorgan Chase & Co. in March 2008; Lehman Brothers was allowed to fail in September 2008; and Merrill Lynch & Co., Inc. was acquired by Bank of America. Morgan Stanley required a capital injection from Asian investors and received protection from the U.S. Federal Reserve Board, as did Goldman Sachs Group, Inc. Among the elite U.S. commercial banks, similar wreckage occurred: Citibank received $65 billion in emergency funds from the U.S. government to remain solvent and obtained special insurance to cover $306 billion in toxic sub-prime-related mortgages. Bank of America acquired $109 billion in similar bad-loan insurance and $45 billion in emergency funds. Almost every major U.S. bank received special financial support from the U.S. government through its Troubled Asset Relief Program (TARP), because the government realized that allowing more banks to fail would have led to the complete collapse of the U.S. financial system. Even so, famous names such as Wachovia, Washington Mutual, National City Corporation, and IndyMac Federal Bank were allowed to fail before the magnitude of the crisis became clear.

The bankruptcy of Lehman Brothers triggered a massive loss of confidence in the banking sector and desperate efforts by the U.S. government to shore up its banks. Despite these efforts, by October 2008, stock markets worldwide crashed, as UK and European banks recognized losses incurred both on their U.S. investments and on their own souring mortgage loans. Table 1-10 provides data on stock market losses from the perspective of a U.S. investor on October 24, 2008, just after a severe crash in each of the major world markets.

The Canadian banking system was largely immune to the problems experienced in the United States and has not required any direct government support. However, Canada's trade is inextricably linked to that of the United States, and there was a similar sell-off of stocks on the TSX, as there was on all the major stock markets around the world.

After October 2008, the world moved into a serious recession, and a major depression was only averted by large-scale government intervention to stimulate spending. However, that level of spending has driven the finances of many countries into a perilous state and generated the sovereign debt or euro crisis. On June 9, 2012, Spain received a bailout from its fellow eurozone members of $125 billion in order to refinance its ailing banks, many of which are virtually bankrupt from souring mortgage loans. The central message is that businesses and investors are currently living with significant uncertainty generated not from problems in the business sector but from the two sectors that are normally regarded as the lowest risk in the financial market: household mortgages and government debt. This emphasizes the fact that there is only one big financial market, and all parts of it are interconnected to a greater or lesser degree. Events in the U.S. mortgage market swept throughout the world like a hurricane, and the knock-on effects in government finance will cause continuing problems that will last at least through the next few editions of this textbook.

TABLE 1-10 Market Losses

Index or Exchange (US Dollars)	Last Trade Date	1 Day Change	1 Day %	1 Month %	6 Month %	YTD %	2006 Value ($Billions)
United States Composite	213.40 10/24/2008	−7.52	−3.40	−27.53	−37.17	−40.46	18,039
Japan Composite	82.39 10/24/2008	−2.74	−3.21	−22.00	−32.07	−35.54	4,422
United Kingdom Composite	149.79 10/24/2008	−11.63	−7.21	−35.44	−48.66	−52.51	3,441

continued

TABLE 1-10 Market Losses *(Continued)*

Index or Exchange (US Dollars)	Last Trade Date	1 Day Change	1 Day %	1 Month %	6 Month %	YTD %	2006 Value ($Billions)
Canada Composite	278.25 10/24/2008	−4.74	−1.67	−40.46	−48.15	−49.61	1,636
Germany Composite	218.89 10/24/2008	−14.62	−6.26	−39.40	−51.88	−56.28	1,426
Hong Kong Composite	186.44 10/24/2008	−10.10	−5.14	−31.80	−51.39	−57.97	1,361
Spain Composite	388.93 10/24/2008	−26.01	−6.27	−34.22	−50.24	−51.93	1,146
Switzerland Composite	374.65 10/24/2008	−10.44	−2.71	−22.21	−32.06	−34.35	1,111

Source: Booth, Laurence, "Collateral Damage." *Canadian Investment Review*, Winter 2008, Table 1, p. 11. Reprinted with the permission of *Canadian Investment Review*.

LESSONS TO BE LEARNED

We will be discussing the impact of the credit crunch and financial meltdown of 2008–9 and the euro crisis throughout this text, because there are obvious lessons to be learned— or relearned. Figure 1-9 shows the market capitalizations of Canadian banks, as well as major banks worldwide. Market capitalization is simply the share price multiplied by the number of shares outstanding, and it measures the stock market valuation of the bank. We can see immediately the huge drop in market value of Citigroup, Bank of America, and the Royal Bank of Scotland, as well as other major international banks. The Canadian banks' market capitalization also declined, but nowhere near the same degree. The resulting stability of the Canadian banking system has been a source of pride for the Canadian government. Delegations of ministers and others from all over the world have travelled to Canada to discover our secret: how did we avoid the disasters that befell so many other banks? As President Barack Obama said, "I think Canada has shown itself to be a pretty good manager of the financial system in the economy in ways that we haven't always been here in the United States."

So why were Canadian banks so stable and the Canadian financial system relatively unaffected by the global meltdown? *Newsweek International* gave a simple answer: "common sense." Lending decisions by Canadian banks were still made the old-fashioned way. Banks required verification of income and the value of a house before arranging a mortgage and loaned only up to 80 percent of the value of the house, unless the loan could be guaranteed by an external government agency such as the Canada Mortgage and Housing Corporation (CMHC). Banks in other parts of the world forgot this basic lesson, and the financial system was severely damaged as a result. In recognition of this common-sense approach, the governor of the Bank of Canada, Mark Carney, was appointed to head the Financial Stability Board, which was tasked to alleviate the system-wide stress in financial markets and prevent a repeat of the 2008–9 crisis. In later chapters of this text, we will discuss how this failure to exercise "common sense" directly affected business finance.

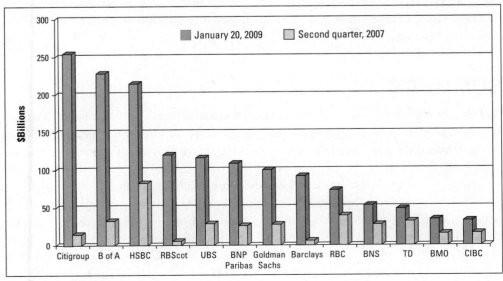

FIGURE 1-9 *Market Capitalization of Banks (January 20, 2009, versus Second Quarter, 2007)*

Source: Company annual reports

1.5 THE STRUCTURE OF THIS TEXT

corporate finance the financing and investment decisions made by corporations

investments the decisions made by the investors in financial securities

We have now introduced how financial systems work in general and have highlighted the importance of global influences and opportunities. In the rest of the text, we will focus on the study of business finance, which is introduced in Chapter 2. We will distinguish between **corporate finance**, which focuses on the financing and investment decisions made by corporations, and **investments**, which focus on the decisions made by the investors in financial securities. In fact, these two areas of finance are merely two sides of the same coin: investors purchase the financial securities that are issued by corporations. In Part 2, we will examine corporate accounting statements and present some essential tools for financial analysis.

Parts 3, 4, and 5 focus on the investment side of finance. In particular, we discuss the investment alternatives available to the suppliers of funds and some of the most important factors they need to consider during this investment process. Part 3 introduces the basic valuation process used in finance and applies it to the valuation of stocks and bonds. Part 4 discusses the importance to investors of modern portfolio theory and the notion of efficient markets. Finally, Part 5 discusses derivative securities, focusing on options and futures contracts in particular.

The second half of the text focuses on the corporate finance side of the coin. Part 6 examines corporate investment decisions and provides the framework on which such decisions should be made. We also show how this framework can be used to evaluate potential takeover decisions, as well as the decision of whether or not to enter into a leasing arrangement. In Part 7, we discuss the various long-term financing alternatives available to corporations. We follow this up in Part 8 by examining how firms decide on their long-term financing mix (or capital structure), and we also discuss the main considerations involved in corporate dividend decisions. Finally, Part 9 focuses on how firms manage their investment in short-term assets and how they determine their short-term financing mix, which is referred to as "working capital management."

SUMMARY

This chapter provides an overview of financial systems in general and the Canadian financial system in particular. We identify the major participants and discuss the different types of financial securities and financial markets. In doing so, we provide an overview of finance in general.

In the next chapter and for the balance of the text, we will focus on business (or corporate) finance, which is one very important part of the overall financial system. As you develop an understanding of the problems faced by corporations, it is important to realize that business finance is inextricably linked with government finance, personal finance, and international finance—the three other major agents in the financial system—because collectively they determine what happens in the financial system. The financial system is one huge market for borrowing and lending money—what happens in one part of the system affects all other parts.

SUMMARY OF LEARNING OBJECTIVES

1.1 Define finance and explain what is involved in the study of finance.

Finance is the study of how and under what terms savings (money) are allocated between lenders and borrowers.

Finance is not just about how resources are allocated but also under *what terms* and through *what channels* the allocations are made. Whenever funds are transferred, a financial contract comes into existence, and these contracts are called financial securities. As a result, the study of finance requires a basic understanding of securities and corporate law and the institutions that facilitate and monitor this exchange of funds.

1.2 List the major financial and real assets held by Canadians and the major sectors in the financial system.

The four sectors are government, business, households, and non-residents. On an aggregate level, the first three sectors own real assets. Households own positive net financial assets, while governments and businesses own negative net financial assets, which mean net debt. Non-residents own a small portion of positive net financial assets.

1.3 Explain how money is transferred from lenders to borrowers and the role played by market and financial intermediaries.

Money is transferred from lenders to borrowers through the following three channels: (1) financial intermediaries that transform the nature of the securities they issue and invest in, (2) market intermediaries that simply make the markets work better, and (3) non-market transactions in which the market is not involved.

1.4 Identify the basic types of financial instruments that are available and explain how they are traded.

The major types of financial instruments are debt and equity. Debt instruments are loans. Equity instruments involve ownership. Financial markets are divided into two divisions: primary and secondary (secondary markets come in two types: auction and dealer markets).

1.5 Explain the importance of the global financial system and how Canada is impacted by events in the U.S. mortgage market.

In addition to the domestic financial markets discussed above, global financial markets represent important sources of funds for borrowers and provide investors with important alternatives. Indeed, Canadian debt and equity markets represent only a small proportion of the total global marketplace. Therefore, it makes sense for Canadians to borrow and invest abroad, which has become easier to do in today's global business environment as investment barriers are relaxed.

Even though the Canadian banking system was largely immune to the problems in the United States and has not required any direct government support, Canada's trade is inextricably linked with that of the United States, and shares on the TSX were sold off as they were on all the major stock markets around the world.

KEY TERMS

Bourse de Montréal, p. 20
brokers, p. 20
Canadian Trading and Quotation System Inc. (CNQ), p. 22
capital market securities, p. 19
common share, p. 18
corporate finance, p. 28
credit crunch, p. 12
Crown corporations, p. 16
dealer or over-the-counter (OTC) markets, p. 20
debt instruments, p. 18
equity instruments, p. 18

exchanges or auction markets, p. 20
finance, p. 4
financial assets, p. 6
financial intermediaries, p. 11
fourth market, p. 22
intermediation, p. 11
investments, p. 28
market capitalization, p. 21
market intermediaries, p. 11
marketable financial assets, p. 19
money market securities, p. 19
New York Stock Exchange (NYSE), p. 24
non-marketable financial assets, p. 19

Ontario Securities Commission (OSC), p. 22
preferred shares, p. 18
primary markets, p. 19
real assets, p. 5
secondary markets, p. 19
third market, p. 22
TMX Group Inc., p. 20
Toronto Stock Exchange (TSX), p. 20
TSX Markets, p. 20
TSX Venture Exchange, p. 20

QUESTIONS AND PRACTICE PROBLEMS

Multiple Choice Questions

1. Which of the following is true about finance?
    a. Finance is the study of how and under what terms savings (money) are allocated between lenders and borrowers.
    b. Finance is different from economics because economics does not study how resources are allocated.
    c. All parts of finance are not integrated.
    d. Business finance is the only important part of finance.

2. According to Canada's national balance sheet, which of the following items is not a real asset?
    a. Land
    b. Machinery and equipment
    c. Stocks
    d. Residential structures

3. You have hired someone to purchase 100 shares of a technology firm for your portfolio. The person you have hired is acting as a
    a. financial intermediary.
    b. market intermediary.
    c. financial principal.
    d. market principal.

4. Which of the following is a correct combination of primary fund lenders and fund borrowers in the financial system?
    a. Households and government
    b. Households and non-residents
    c. Businesses and households
    d. Government and non-residents

5. Which of the following financial intermediaries does not transform the nature of the underlying financial securities?
    a. Banks
    b. Insurance firms
    c. Mutual funds
    d. Pension funds

6. A small investor from New Brunswick has just purchased 100 common shares of a telecommunications firm on the Toronto Stock Exchange. This is the first time the investor has purchased this stock. This transaction is an example of
    a. a primary market transaction because it is the first time the investor has bought the stock.
    b. a primary market transaction because the money the investor has invested will go directly to the firm.
    c. a secondary market transaction because the investor has bought the stock from other investors.
    d. none of the above; this is a large block trade and will be done using the OTC market (the "third market").

7. Which of the following "statements" is true about the global financial system?
    a. Canadian debt and equity markets represent the majority of the global financial market.
    b. Canada's net international investment position is always negative in any year.
    c. The globalization of the equity markets means that the linkages between the global markets are getting tighter.

    d. Canada's financial system is completely separated from the global financial market.

8. Which of the following "statements" is true about the financial crisis of 2008?
    a. The crisis in the Canadian banking sector turned into the global financial crisis.
    b. The Canadian stock market was not hit by the financial crisis.
    c. The Canadian government bailed out one major Canadian bank.
    d. The crisis in the U.S. banking sector turned into a global financial crisis.

Practice Problems

9. You are examining the economy of a very small, completely isolated island nation. There are only three people on this island: Fred, Robinson, and Friday. Fred owns a house valued at $1,000 and owes Friday $500. Robinson owns a house valued at $3,000 and owes Friday $2,000. Friday's house is valued at $1,500. Derive the balance sheet of this island economy.

10. List the four major financial sectors in the financial system and discuss how they relate to one another.

11. Explain how banks, pension funds, insurance firms, and mutual funds work in the financial system.

12. Describe why financial and market intermediaries exist in our financial system.

13. Describe the causes of a "credit crunch."

14. List the two main types of primary market transactions and describe them.

15. What are secondary market transactions? How do secondary markets facilitate the primary markets?

2 | Business (Corporate) Finance

LEARNING OBJECTIVES

2.1 List the four forms of business organizations and describe the advantages and disadvantages of each.

2.2 Describe the goals of the firm and the pressures exerted on corporations by various stakeholders.

2.3 Explain the importance of aligning the interests of management with the interests of shareholders in a corporation.

2.4 Explain what agency costs are and how they affect the interests of management and shareholders.

2.5 Identify the main corporate finance decisions involving the financial management of a firm's assets and its liabilities (corporate financing).

2.6 List some finance jobs available with financial and non-financial companies.

This chapter focuses on the different types of business organizations and what the role of one of these, the corporation, should be. These days, corporations are being called upon more than ever to act in a manner that is socially, economically, and environmentally responsible. However, being a good corporate citizen can put a firm at odds with its fundamental obligation, which is to maximize profits. Home Depot Canada has a solid track record of community involvement. The company uses its resources and expertise to build playgrounds and affordable housing, and it assists communities affected by natural disasters. It has also developed in-store programs that help customers identify environmentally preferred products and dispose of household materials safely.

Source: Home Depot website at www.homedepot.ca.

Natural Resources Canada, "Corporate Social Responsibility: Highlights of Company CSR Activities." Natural Resources Canada website at www.nrcan.gc.ca.

Natural Resources Canada, "Corporate Social Responsibility: Lessons Learned." Natural Resources Canada website at www.nrcan-rncan.gc.ca.

CHAPTER 2 **PREVIEW**

I n Chapter 1, we discussed the financial system and provided the context for the discussion of business finance. In this chapter, we discuss the role of the corporation and provide the background that is necessary to analyze how its investment and financing decisions are made. In the process, we discuss the goals of the corporation and how its internal affairs are organized. We conclude with a description of some available jobs in the field.

2.1 TYPES OF BUSINESS ORGANIZATIONS

Learning Objective 2.1
List the four forms of business organizations and describe the advantages and disadvantages of each.

In Chapter 1, we distinguished between real assets and financial assets, with real assets for the household being tangible things, such as houses, dishwashers, computers, and cars, while financial assets are loans, in the broadest sense, to other people and institutions. However, this discussion of Canadian households was limited by Statistics Canada's (StatsCan's) division of the economy into four main segments: households, business, government, and foreign (non-resident). The reason for this division is that the business sector makes the real investment decisions that increase our wealth over time. In contrast, the real investment decisions of households are to buy consumer durables—that is, consumption items that generate value over future periods. Ultimately, we can say that households consume—it's just that some of this consumption is of non-durables, like food, and some of it is of durables, like cars. The business sector, conversely, makes very different real investment decisions, which are intended to increase its ability to produce goods and services in the future—that is, to generate future growth in consumption and wealth.

As we noted in Chapter 1, StatsCan considers Canadian households to comprise "persons and unincorporated businesses," so some business is conducted within the household, rather than in the business sector. Businesses can be organized in different ways: the four major forms of business organizations are sole proprietorships, partnerships, trusts, and corporations. We discuss each of these below.

Sole Proprietorships

sole proprietorship a business owned and operated by one person

A **sole proprietorship** is a business owned and operated by one person. Starting one is as simple as drumming up business. Many important businesses have been started by someone trying to meet a market need, whether it's the neighbour's daughter who started a lemonade stand one hot summer day or the boy who cleans up yards in his spare time. These people have both started sole proprietorships, in which one person starts working on his or her own rather than for someone else.

The big advantage of a sole proprietorship is that setting one up is easy—no paperwork is involved, and the owner needs only to start doing business. Of course, if the business begins to grow, the owner might want to register a business name, or even patent a particular business process to keep imitators away or at least make them pay a royalty.[1] Purchasing some business cards is helpful too. However, the critical thing is that the business is almost inseparable from the owner; if that lemonade turns out to be bad, or if part of that yard isn't cleaned up, then the business owner is personally liable. This isn't a big factor for most very small businesses, but if that person's web page inadvertently damages a client by directing traffic elsewhere, then the owner is personally liable. More to the point, an owner can be sued for damages. If that person has other assets, he or she could lose them or, in extreme cases, be forced into bankruptcy and

---

[1] ServiceOntario charges to register a name and to search to make sure someone isn't already conducting similar business with a similar name. See www.ontario.ca/en/services_for_business/STEL02_039990. Most provinces have similar search and registration procedures.

lose everything because of a bad decision made in that sole proprietorship. This accountability is referred to as **unlimited liability**, because an owner is liable not only to the extent of what is invested in the business but also for any other assets owned. Lawyers generally advise wealthy people not to operate a sole proprietorship.

> **unlimited liability** the liability not only for what is invested in the business but also for any other assets owned

Sole proprietorships do have financial implications. The sources of finance available for sole proprietorships are the same ones that are available to individuals. No complicated finance options are available—owners borrow from relatives and friends, or from the bank, through either a loan or a credit card. If a business creates some revenue, its owner can use one of the many government programs designed to stimulate small businesses. If a business grows and the owner wants to sell it, it can be problematic, because all the contacts and relationships are personal and belong to the owner, since legally the owner and the business are identical. Selling a profitable window-cleaning business may mean visiting every contact and explaining that someone new is taking over the business and will be serving them in the future. The fact is, there is no continuity in a sole proprietorship, which makes it difficult to sell, and, of course, it dies with the owner.

Because legally a sole proprietorship is inseparable from the individual, the owner has to report the income to the Canada Revenue Agency (CRA) on an annual income tax return. Sole proprietors have to keep the same accounting records as big businesses do and report the income after deducting all reasonable expenses. However, the net income is simply added to any regular salary income and taxed at ordinary tax rates. For this reason, StatsCan cannot separate persons and unincorporated businesses from households, because most of the data come from individual income tax returns.

Partnerships

Suppose you are working on a new web page and need some help from a friend. The two of you start working together. After a while, it becomes a solid relationship and you always work together on jobs for clients. This relationship is a **partnership**, rather than a sole proprietorship. Some of the most prominent and successful businesses started out as partnerships—consider Bill Gates and Paul Allen (Microsoft Corporation), who started a partnership working on personal computers in their parents' garages. A partnership can be formalized by having a lawyer create a partnership agreement. The agreement sets out how decisions are made, such as how each partner can buy out the other in the event that one wants to dissolve the partnership. If the partnership grows, then the owners also need to document how new partners enter and their attendant obligations, as well as how others can cash out. The partnership agreement further stipulates how the partnership's income is allocated among the partners. Individuals have to be careful with partnerships, since a legal agreement is not required to be considered a partner. Sometimes a partnership can be implied by the actions of a group of people working together. This becomes a problem when a disaffected party sues everyone associated with a business, even people who are not formal partners.

> **partnership** a business owned and operated by two or more people

Some very big firms traditionally operated as partnerships, most of which were in the professional services area, such as accounting firms, investment banking firms, doctors' offices, and dentists' offices. Such firms needed more than one person to deliver a full range of services, yet "society" judged it important to hold each member individually responsible for both his or her own actions and those of his or her colleagues. However, over time, the increasing complexity of partnership operations—for example, in the accounting and investment banking areas—weakened this argument. With hundreds of partners, it is difficult to justify making all the partners responsible for the actions of one rogue partner. As a result, the importance of traditional partnerships has diminished.

Partnerships are still important, however, for smaller firms, because they maintain the integration of partnership income with other income for each partner. However, newer partnership models have emerged that maintain this tax treatment while removing the unlimited personal liability. The two main partnership forms are limited liability partnerships (LLPs) and limited and general partnerships.

LLPs are the latest form of organization for professional firms. Each partner has limited liability in the event of a lawsuit against the firm; however, each partner's income is still included as ordinary income and filed by using an individual tax return. Table 2-1 lists the leading accounting and law firms in Canada, according to the *Financial Post*'s FP500 tables for 2011. Notice that LLP is listed after each firm, indicating a limited liability partnership. Clearly, with the larger firms having hundreds of partners, it is unreasonable to impose unlimited liability on them all.

TABLE 2-1 Canadian Law and Accounting Firms, 2011

Law Firms	Employees	Lawyers	Partners
Borden Ladner Gervais LLP	1,309	762	412
Gowling Lafleur Henderson LLP	1,225	729	429
Fasken Martineau DuMoulin LLP	905	684	413
McCarthy Tétrault LLP	893	684	413
Accounting Firms	**Sales ($Million)**	**Partners**	**Professional Staff**
Deloitte & Touche LLP	1,505	538	6,051
PricewaterhouseCoopers LLP	1,180	420	4,339
KPMG LLP	1,138	428	3,887
Ernst & Young LLP	870	331	3,060
Grant Thornton LLP	515	416	2,974

Source: *Financial Post*, FP500 tables, 2011. Material printed with the express permission of National Post Company, a CanWest Partnership.

Limited and general partnerships are generally used for tax reasons. In this case, a general partner operates the business, and limited partners are passive investors. As long as the limited partners are not active in the business, they have the advantage of **limited liability**, in that all they can lose is their initial investment. The general partner, conversely, has unlimited liability as the operator of the business. However, in practice, most general partners are corporations (discussed below) and indirectly benefit from limited liability. Limited partnerships are often used in tax shelters, and, for this reason, Canada Revenue Agency looks very carefully at them to make sure they are not a vehicle for tax avoidance; however, there are also legitimate reasons to set up a limited partnership.

limited liability the liability for only the initial investment

Until 2010, Canada had some very large firms organized as partnerhsips. For example, the largest natural gas distribution company in Quebec is Gaz Métro, which had 2009 sales of $2.25 billion and profit of $158 million. Part of Gaz Métro was then publicly owned through Gaz Métro Limited Partnership (GMLP). However, the federal government changed the tax treatment of limited partnerships, along with that of income trusts (discussed next), and GMLP converted to a regular corporation, Valener, in October 2010.

Trusts

trust a legal organization in which assets are owned by one party and managed or controlled by a different party

The trust structure is not new by any means and is, in fact, a standard part of the lawyer's tool kit. **Trusts** are used to separate ownership from control. For example, a standard part of estate planning is transferring assets in trust to children to minimize any tax burden and yet control the use of those assets until death. In this way, ownership has been transferred to one party and yet control stays with the transferring party. Traditionally, open-end mutual funds have been organized as trusts. The mutual fund is owned by the unitholders, yet day-to-day control is exercised by the fund manager under the supervision of a board of directors, which appoints the manager. More important, because it is a trust, the income earned by the mutual fund passes through without any tax to the unitholders, who are then subject to taxes on the income received. The use of trusts expanded dramatically during the 2000s, from personal finance and mutual funds to **income trusts** and **royalty trusts**, which became very important in the Canadian financial system to the extent that they jeopardized the federal government's corporate income tax revenues.

Income and royalty trusts are set up to invest in the shares and debt obligations of a company. Because they are trusts, all the income passes through without any tax. Figure 2-1 is a simplified example of an income-trust structure.

income trusts and **royalty trusts**
trusts set up to invest in the shares and debt obligations of a company

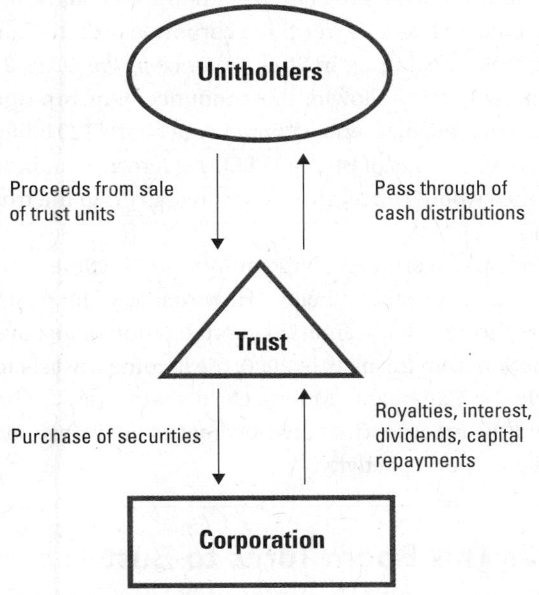

Unitholders of the trust provide financing to the trust. In return, they generally receive cash distributions of income and return of capital.

The income trust uses the funds to invest in assets. The assets provide a return to the trust based on the underlying active business in the form of interest, royalty, or lease payments, as well as dividends and return of capital from the corporation.

The corporation or the trust may borrow from third-party lenders, such as banks, or by issuing bonds.

FIGURE 2-1 *Simplified Example of an Income Trust Structure*

Source: Figure 1 from Tax and Other Issues Related to Publicly Listed Flow-Through Entities, http://www.fin.gc.ca/activty/pubs/toirplf_1-eng.asp, Department of Finance Canada, 2008. Reproduced with the permission of the Minister of Public Works and Government Services Canada, 2013.

Figure 2-1 shows that, because the trust owns both the debt and the equity of the company, the use of debt by the company can be maximized to reduce (or eliminate) any corporate income tax. The interest, dividends, and other payments then flow through to the trust, and provided the trust pays out most (or all) of its income to its unitholders, there is no tax paid. This is because interest payments on debt are a tax-deductible expense to the corporation, as we will discuss later, but it is unlikely that non-payment of interest will cause default since the trust is both the debt holder and the equity holder. In the jargon of finance professionals, trusts are "tax efficient." From 1998, and for almost 10 years, the use of trusts to structure business activity exploded. By March 31, 2006, there were 238 income trusts listed on the Toronto Stock Exchange (TSX), up from 73 in 2001 and only a handful in the mid-1990s. In fact, the total market capitalization of income trusts grew from $1.4 billion in 1994 to $192 billion by March 2006, representing approximately 10 percent of the quoted market value of the TSX.[2] As a result of this growth, the TSX fully incorporated income trusts into the Standard & Poor's/Toronto Stock Exchange (S&P/TSX) Composite Index as of March 2006, completing a gradual process that was initiated in November 2005.

---

[2] Statistics from the TSX website at www.tsx.com.

The tax-efficient structure of trusts, along with their popularity among investors, led many corporations to convert to the trust structure between 2000 and 2006. This fuelled concerns regarding the government's loss of corporate tax revenue, because the trust structure eliminates most of the income taxes paid by businesses. In addition, it generated a great deal of worry and speculation regarding the effect that this trend would have on the future growth of businesses in the Canadian economy, since trusts are inclined to pay out their earnings rather than reinvest in the business. All these worries came to a head in the fall of 2006 in response to announcements by Canadian telecommunications giants TELUS Corporation and BCE Inc. that they would be converting to the trust structure. Not only would these conversions add another $50 billion or so in market capitalization to the income trust market, but their conversion was also taken as a warning sign that many other large corporations could follow suit. As a result of these concerns, on October 31, 2006, Finance Minister Jim Flaherty announced that the distributions made by newly created trusts would be taxed at prevailing corporate tax rates, and that this new tax would apply to existing trusts beginning in 2011. *Finance in the News 2-1* describes the stock market fallout on November 1, 2006, following this announcement. In particular, income trust prices dropped about 12.4 percent on average, "wiping out nearly $20 billion in shareholder wealth." The market prices of the shares of BCE and TELUS were also hit hard, as the market anticipated, correctly, that they would cancel their plans to convert to the trust structure.

Since the change in tax policy by the federal government, large numbers of income trusts have converted back to regular corporate status, discussed below. However, as of June 2012 there were still 60 income trusts traded on the TSX, with a market capitalization of just over $60 billion. While this is a significant reduction from the peak in 2006, the income trust sector remains an important investment vehicle for Canadians. Moreover, in many ways, it has reverted to its original status, since most of the income trusts are now real estate investment trusts and royalty trusts, rather than regular corporate activity.

finance INTHENEWS 2-1   Billions in Value Disappear as This Boom Turns to Bust

CANADA'S GREAT INCOME trust boom turned into a bust yesterday as unit prices plunged, erasing billions in market value and sparking outrage from investors who said they were sideswiped by Ottawa's crackdown on the sector.

In a selloff that was as broad as it was deep, the S&P/TSX's capped income trust index sank 12.4 percent, wiping out nearly $20 billion in shareholder wealth. The rout hammered trusts large and small, from the giant Canadian Oil Sands Trust down to seafood canner Connors Bros. Income Fund.

It also helped slice nearly 300 points from Canada's benchmark stock index—the S&P/TSX Composite's biggest setback since June—and drove the dollar down eight-tenths of a cent (U.S.).

Foreign investors fled what had until yesterday been the market's fastest-growing sector.

"I don't think anybody expected it to be this dramatic and this quick," Kate Warne, Canadian market strategist with Edward Jones & Co. in St. Louis said of Ottawa's decision to close the loophole that allows trusts to largely avoid paying income taxes.

Seven of the 10 biggest contributors to the S&P/TSX composite's loss were trusts or would-be trusts, led by TELUS and BCE, whose plans to convert to the structure were widely seen to have forced the federal government to abandon its election promise to leave the sector untouched.

The decision angered investors who have flocked to trusts for their hefty payouts, which have made the $200-billion industry a favourite of seniors and others seeking steady income in an era of low interest rates.

"It makes me feel betrayed," said Cameron Avery, 54, a semi-retired filmmaker in Cobble Hill, B.C., whose income trust portfolio is valued in the "higher five figures."

But even as the trust market was collapsing yesterday, some money managers said they were finding bargains amid the carnage. Some trusts are now trading at valuations that make them attractive takeover targets, while the drop has pushed yields on others to tempting levels.

"I think this is a huge buying opportunity," said John Stephenson, who helps manage $1.1 billion at First Asset Investment Management Inc. in Toronto, including more than $500 million in income trusts.

His firm was nibbling at some trusts yesterday and may add to its positions, particularly in the pipeline and power sectors. Among the names he likes are Great Lakes Hydro Income Fund, Innergex Power Income Fund, Royal Utilities Income Fund and Inter Pipeline Fund. All suffered double-digit drops yesterday.

In effect, he said the stock market has already priced in the government's proposed tax on income trust distributions, even though the levy—assuming the legislation is approved—won't come into effect until 2011. That means investors have more than four years to enjoy

continued

Finance in the News 2-1: Billions in Value Disappear as This Boom Turns to Bust *(continued)*

the juicy distributions. In the meantime, now that the unit prices have tanked, "a lot of private buyers may come in and say these are attractive assets," he said.

Carl Hoyt, who manages the $120-million AGF Monthly High Income Fund, also believes some trusts are trading at attractive valuations. For example, Yellow Pages Income Fund, which tumbled 18.9 percent yesterday to levels not seen since 2004, is now trading at a multiple that's below that of some takeover deals for similar telephone directory assets in the United States.

"Regardless of the tax legislation, it's possible that a private equity player, of which there are a lot, would look at that and say, hmm, that's an attractive asset," he said of Yellow Pages, whose $6.3-billion market capitalization makes it one of Canada's largest trusts.

For those who lack the stomach for income trusts but still crave income, there's always dividend-paying stocks. Even as trusts were getting clobbered yesterday, shares of many banks, insurers and other dividend stocks were climbing.

Bank of Nova Scotia, Royal Bank of Canada, Canadian Imperial Bank of Commerce and Rogers Communications Inc.—which hoisted its dividend Tuesday—all rose. "The market is hungry for yield," said Marc Lalonde, portfolio manager with Louisbourg Investments Inc. in Moncton.

Corporations

Corporations are easy to recognize because they have "Inc." for incorporated, "Ltd." for limited, or, in Europe, "PLC" for private limited corporation, after their names. In each case, the abbreviations or initials indicate that the owners have the benefit of limited liability, so the maximum they can lose is their investment—that is, they cannot be forced to invest more in the firm to make up for any losses the firm incurs. Unlike a partnership or sole proprietorship, a business that operates as a corporation separates personal assets from any malfeasance or failure at the corporate level. Although the courts have occasionally "pierced the corporate veil" and extended that liability, it is very rare and happens only when significant public policy concerns are involved.

> **corporations** businesses organized as separate legal entities under corporate law, with ownership divided into transferable shares

How a corporation is formed depends on provincial corporate law; however, it is generally by either a certificate of incorporation or letters of patent. The articles of incorporation then indicate the most basic information about the firm, such as its mailing address, name, line of business, number of shares issued, names and addresses of the officers of the firm (that is, the people who can legally bind the firm by signing cheques), and so on. The critical feature is that the corporation is a *distinct* legal entity. For this reason, the corporation is entitled to sign contracts, file tax returns, borrow money, make investments, sue, and be sued—all in its own name.

As a distinct legal entity, the corporation has significant advantages over a partnership or a sole proprietorship. One advantage is that a corporation is "immortal." Early limited companies had to renew their charter or incorporation periodically, since politicians worried about the public policy implications of having a legal entity with an indefinite life; however, as the operations of corporations have become better understood, these concerns have waned. This indefinite life means that, unlike people, corporations can borrow by using debt that will be paid off in 40, and sometimes 50, years' time. Individuals, with finite lives, would have difficulty getting these terms from a bank. It also means that transferring and selling assets is relatively easy because all the contracts go with the company and the share ownership is simply transferred.

The most difficult aspects of corporations are their control and taxation (we will deal with taxes in Chapter 3). In partnerships and sole proprietorships, the owners run the business; in corporations, the owners are the shareholders. For smaller companies, this isn't a problem, but for larger companies, this becomes a serious concern: they usually have a very clear separation of ownership by the shareholders and control by management. This division is the fundamental problem of the governance structure of large companies. We will discuss governance later in the chapter and in Chapter 15 because it is integral to the role of mergers and acquisitions and to understanding valuation.

Every company has a set of bylaws that indicates how it is run. Some of the content of the bylaws is determined by corporate law, but most is discretionary and up to the company. What is not discretionary is the requirement that the company have a board of directors (BOD) whose responsibility is to "manage or supervise the management of the business and affairs of the corporation."[3] These directors are appointed at the annual general meeting of the company and serve at the discretion of the shareholders, which means that they can be removed without cause.[4]

In theory, the BOD is elected by the shareholders and acts in their best interests. The directors' statutory responsibilities are enshrined in the *Canada Business Corporations Act (CBCA)*, in Section 122 (1):

Every director and officer of a corporation in exercising their powers and discharging their duties shall

(a) act honestly and in good faith with a view to the best interests of the corporation;

and

(b) exercise the care, diligence, and skill that a reasonably prudent person would exercise in comparable circumstances.

Essentially, this legal requirement means that members of the BOD cannot fall asleep at a board meeting; they have to exercise the normal standards of professionalism expected of people in their position. This standard is known as the "due diligence" standard, and as long as it is met, members of the BOD cannot be sued for negligence. What should their goals be? The CBCA says only that they must act in the best interests (honestly and in good faith) of the corporation, but what are the best interests of the corporation? To answer this, we have to discuss corporate goals.

CONCEPT REVIEW QUESTIONS

1. Describe the main advantages and disadvantages of sole proprietorships and partnerships.
2. How are trusts distinct from corporations?
3. What are the main advantages and disadvantages of the corporation structure?

2.2 THE GOALS OF THE CORPORATION

Learning Objective 2.2
Describe the goals of the firm and the pressures exerted on corporations by various stakeholders.

You might remember from your economics course that the goal of the firm is to maximize its profits. However, many have challenged this objective, and the major reasons are illustrated in Figure 2-2.

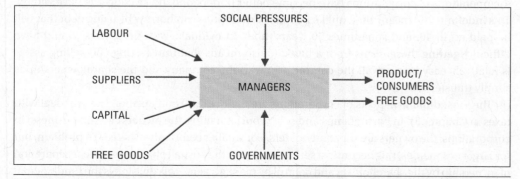

FIGURE 2-2 *The Firm as an Input-Output Function*

---

[3] Section 121 of the *Canada Business Corporations Act* allows the BOD to delegate this responsibility to officers of the corporation.
[4] In the United States, this is not the case; directors can only be removed for cause before the end of their term of appointment. This means that it is technically possible to own 51 percent of the company and yet not be able to immediately remove the board of directors and control the company.

What Figure 2-2 illustrates is that the firm is essentially an input-output mechanism. It takes inputs, such as raw materials, labour, and supplies, and transforms those inputs into something more useful to society when it produces goods or services. For all firms, this activity is regulated both by implicit societal pressures to be good and by laws passed by government to prevent firms from doing things it regards as bad. For example, minimum wage and employment laws prevent firms from paying wages that are too low or using underage labour. Similarly, laws on environmental protection, packaging of goods, and so on, ensure that the firm operates according to what is in consumers' interests. Apart from obeying the law, for sole proprietorships and partnerships, this is the end of the story; those firms are then run in the interests of their owners. Normally, this means that the firms enhance the owners' welfare and make profits.

In finance, we extend the idea of the firm's goal being to maximize its profits, because what the firm should really do is enhance the owner's wealth. Wealth is different from profits because it reflects the value of all profits—not just today's but also those expected in the future—where profits refer to genuine economic profits and not what the accountant creates (i.e., accounting profits). We will discuss wealth in more detail in Part 3 when we talk about valuation. When this definition of the firm's goal is applied to publicly traded firms, the goal of the firm is to maximize its market value or, alternatively, maximize shareholder value: the firm should take resources and create products that society values more highly than it values the inputs. Note that there are two very important things in Figure 2-2 that we have not discussed: the existence of externalities and the role of managers.

Externalities are things that the firm doesn't pay for or charge for, but which affect others. As a result, the firm creates value without taking into account its impact and may make decisions that are not in the public's best interests. A classic example on the input side is the use of water. Should firms be allowed to use water without paying a true market price for it? Water is something that Canada has in abundance, and it would be relatively easy to set up a plant to export water to, say, the U.S. southwest, which is largely desert. In fact, it is possible to reverse the flow of water down the Mackenzie Valley, moving it down the Colorado River to Arizona and California, instead of having it go to the Arctic. This was an issue in the Free Trade Agreement (FTA) between the United States and Canada: would the United States have the right to Canadian water, and would refusing a U.S. request for water be a violation of trade under the FTA? Clearly, large-scale diversion of water entails a cost that is not captured in the rates the public pays for water, and to charge this lower rate for large-scale water diversion is almost certainly not in the best interests of Canada, even though it may be in the best interests of people sponsoring the idea.

Another example involving externalities is the "too big to fail" argument, which has become extremely political in the aftermath of the 2008–9 financial crisis. During the financial crisis, the U.S. banking system was on the verge of collapse, and two of the Big Three U.S. car manufacturers became insolvent. During 2008, the price of oil skyrocketed to an all-time high of $122 a barrel, and *The Wall Street Journal* (*WSJ*), the major financial newspaper in the United States, openly questioned whether General Motors (GM), the largest car manufacturer in the world, could survive. GM's chief operating officer responded, and his letter was published in the *WSJ* on August 20, 2008 (see *Finance in the News 2-2*).

GM did survive the impact of high oil prices in the summer of 2008, but by fall 2008, the effect of the credit crunch and the onset of recession had forced GM and Chrysler to seek emergency funds from the U.S. and Canadian governments. True to form, the U.S. government bailed out GM and Chrysler, since the financial markets were so fragile at that time that the bankruptcy of the largest car company in the world was considered unthinkable. By April 2009, GM had received $19.2 billion in emergency bailout money from the U.S. government, was shutting plants all over the United States, and was cutting costs in order to meet a U.S. government deadline to produce a viable financial plan by June 1, 2009. On April 26, 2009,

finance INTHENEWS 2-2   GM's Letter to *The Wall Street Journal*

America's auto makers on the road for the long term

IN THE OP-ED "Can America's Auto Makers Survive?" (Aug. 7), Paul Ingrassia asks whether Detroit's auto makers can survive. In the case of General Motors, the answer is, emphatically, yes. And not only survive, but thrive.

There is no question the industry is facing significant pressure driven by the weak U.S. economy and rising fuel costs. At GM, we're taking the difficult and necessary steps to reduce our cost structure to be more competitive in the global marketplace and build a stronger foundation for our future.

Contrary to Mr. Ingrassia's notion that U.S. auto makers did not anticipate the risk of rising fuel prices, GM has been preparing for the shift for several years toward more fuel-efficient models and developing diverse alternative fuel solutions that will redefine the industry.

In fact, 11 of our last 13 U.S. launches have been cars or crossovers, as will 18 of the next 19. We have 17 models that get 30 mpg or better, and offer six hybrid models. Most significant is our commitment to produce the Chevy Volt, a plug-in electric vehicle that will deliver 40 miles of gasoline-free driving and a total range of about 400 miles using a small gasoline engine to recharge its electric battery. This truly revolutionary vehicle will be on the market in 2010.

It's also important to note that the auto industry has a significant impact on the U.S. economy—by directly employing a quarter of a million people and providing health care and pension benefits to millions. The auto industry has invested a quarter of a trillion dollars in the U.S. over the last 20 years, spends $12 billion a year in R&D and is the largest purchaser of raw materials and computer chips in the U.S. The future of the auto business is important to America, and we are dedicated to seeing that GM continues to be a significant part of the American landscape for decades to come.

Fritz Henderson
GM President and COO
Detroit

Source: Henderson, Fritz, "America's auto makers on the road for the long term." *The Wall Street Journal*, August 20, 2008. Available at http://online.wsj.com.

GM put a proposal to its lenders to swap their debt for equity, which would have left the old shareholders with only 1 percent of the company. However, the U.S. government decided that the plan was not viable, and the company went into bankruptcy protection. On June 1, 2009, it was reorganized, and a new GM emerged with the company's good assets, while all the bad assets were left for Motors Liquidation Corporation, the successor to the old GM. GM may indeed have been "too big to fail" as far as the company was concerned, but the shareholders lost almost every cent, and Fritz Henderson, temporary chief executive, was soon out of a job.

The main message from these examples is that very large firms are very visible, their actions often have a significant impact on other firms, and those actions are not necessarily in the best interests of Canada. After all, firms hold privileged status as corporations because they act in *the owners'* interests, so the government has the right to oversee their actions. Consequently, many argue that corporations should act in the "social interest," rather than in the interests of their owners.

The social welfare or social interest argument has validity for the largest firms in Canada because they are the ones that have these spinoff effects on others. Indeed, for the first time in a generation, policy-makers are considering reducing the size of major U.S. firms due to the significant problems their failure imposed on the U.S. economy in 2008. However, for most firms, what is good for the firm is also what is good for Canada; there are few spinoffs elsewhere. For this reason, the creation of shareholder value has been widely accepted as the proper goal for a corporation, not just by academic theorists but also by regulators. In 1994, the TSX issued a report entitled *Where Were the Directors?*—commonly called the Dey Report[5], after its chairman, Peter Dey. The report's mandate was to look at the governance of Canadian companies after the serious recession of the early 1990s. The Dey Report concluded, in Section 1.11:

---

[5] Toronto Stock Exchange, Committee on Corporate Governance in Canada, "Where Were the Directors? Guidelines for Improved Corporate Governance in Canada," (the Dey Report), TSE, Toronto: December, 1994.

> We recognize the principal objective of the direction and management of a business is to enhance shareholder value, which includes balancing gain with risk in order to enhance the financial viability of the business.

As you will see, this is exactly what finance takes as the objective of the firm. Further, the idea of balancing gain with risk is what we refer to as the risk-return trade-off, and you will become very familiar with it as it comes up in connection with virtually every topic we discuss in this textbook. The Dey Report went on to say, in Section 4.12:

> A board of directors is not a parliament where elected members represent the best interests of their constituency. Directors have only one constituency and that is the corporation and its shareholders generally.

Here, the Dey Report was explicitly pouring cold water on the social welfare theory that the firm should pay attention to special interests or other stakeholders. The BOD, in directing the strategy of the firm, should be guided only by what creates shareholder value. What of the other stakeholder interests? The Dey Report suggested the following:

> Their [stakeholders'] interests are generally protected in the terms of the contract establishing their relationship with the corporation and, in many instances, by "stakeholder statutes," such as environmental laws, which impose specific duties upon boards of directors in relation to the interests of the particular stakeholder.

In other words, the BOD can ignore stakeholders. The firm has a duty to do the right thing as enshrined in law and the contracts that it signs, for example, with employees. However, beyond these contractual responsibilities, the firm should not be forced to do more. Instead, the firm should operate legally and in compliance with its contractual responsibilities, in the interests of its owners, by creating value for them. In the process, this creates value for society at large by producing the things that we place the most value on. Ultimately, shareholder value creation simply puts the consumer, i.e., us, first.

CONCEPT REVIEW QUESTIONS

1. What is the primary goal of the corporation?
2. What role does the board of directors serve?
3. Explain the costs imposed on society if firms become too big to fail, and discuss whether the government should break up large firms when they pose such risks.
4. Should the government allow one of the Big Six Canadian banks to fail if it loses money on its loan portfolio?

2.3 THE ROLE OF MANAGEMENT AND AGENCY ISSUES

Most finance academics, as well as the governance guidelines of the TSX, assess the goal of the firm to be that of the creation or maximization of shareholder value. The problem is that neither group actually runs a firm; that is what managers do.

In smaller firms, managers and owners are often the same people, which solves the problem. Even some quite large Canadian companies have a controlling shareholder who ensures that managers act in the shareholders' best interests. However, for many companies, the shareholders are widely dispersed and the firm's chief executive officer (CEO) is able to pack the BOD with cronies who will not challenge his or her authority. In other words, the firm has poor governance and few checks on management, and it may be run in management's

Learning Objective 2.3
Explain the importance of aligning the interests of management with the interests of shareholders in a corporation.

Learning Objective 2.4
Explain what agency costs are and how they affect the interests of management and shareholders.

interest rather than in the interests of the shareholders. Further, the interests of managers and shareholders do not necessarily coincide.

As Gordon Donaldson has stated:

> To say that management and shareholders have much in common is only to state the obvious. So do management and the labour force, consumers, or any other group having a vested interest in the corporate entity. But to extend this by saying that management, in pursuing the corporate objectives as it sees them, necessarily serves the best interest of the stockholders, in either the short or long run, misstates the facts in certain important respects. It also leads to confusion in and misinterpretation of financial policy.[6]

Managers are employees, and we now think of them as agents working on behalf of the shareholders—this is referred to as an **agency relationship** in exactly the same way that we referred to agency transactions in Chapter 1 in the context of hiring a broker to act for and advise us. However, how hard managers work to serve the best interests of the shareholders depends on their personal interests and how they are compensated. This is the classic **agency problem** associated with the separation of ownership from management.

The costs associated with the agency problem are referred to as **agency costs**. There are two major types of agency costs: (1) *direct* costs, which arise because suboptimal decisions are made by managers when they act in a manner that is not in the best interests of their company's shareholders, and (2) *indirect* costs, which are incurred in an attempt to avoid direct agency costs. Indirect costs include those that arise from any restrictions placed on the actions of management, those associated with monitoring the actions of managers (which includes any compensation paid to the BOD), and those associated with management compensation schemes that will provide managers with incentives to act in the shareholders' best interests. We elaborate on this last topic below.

Suppose you hire the son of a friend to clean up your yard. You could sit on the back porch and watch him to make sure he does a good job. However, this monitoring of his work is expensive for you; after all, you probably hired him because your time is valuable and you have other things to do. Monitoring him defeats the purpose. Instead, you can compensate him to try to meet your objectives. Suppose you pay him $10 an hour and think the job will take four hours. What might happen when you come back after four hours? Unless he expects repeat business, which means his reputation is at stake, he'll probably be only partly done, because with a cost-plus contract, his incentive is to stretch out the job. Conversely, if you agree on a fixed fee, say $40, you'll probably come back after four hours and discover that he left two hours earlier. Then you'll have to check everything, because he's probably taken short cuts. In this case, his personal incentive is to finish early. What you want to do is align his interests with yours so you don't have to monitor and check his behaviour.

Like your interests and those of your friend's son, the interests of managers and shareholders are usually fundamentally different. For example, shareholders tend to have a short-term interest in the firm and hold the shares and other securities of many entities in a large investment portfolio. If they see the managers acting contrary to what they would like, they are likely to sell their shares and go elsewhere rather than try to remove management through a costly proxy fight at the annual general meeting. (We will discuss proxy fights later). It is simply too costly for most shareholders to fight to remove management in a large corporation; however, this is not to say it does not happen. U.S. hedge fund Pershing Square Capital Management waged an expensive, months-long war to change the CEO of Canadian Pacific Railway, discussed in *Finance in the News 2-3*. All too often, such proxy fights to change management fail because it is so expensive and time consuming for one party to bear the costs.

agency relationship the relationship between the shareholders who own the company and the managers hired to work on their behalf

agency problems problems that arise due to potential divergence of interests among managers, shareholders, and creditors

agency costs the costs associated with agency problems

---

[6] Donaldson, Gordon, "Financial Goals: Management vs. Stockholders." *Harvard Business Review*, May/June 1963.

finance INTHENEWS 2-3 | Canadian Pacific Railway Profits Fall in Second Quarter on Series of Expenses

A NINE-DAY STRIKE and costs related to a change in CEO dragged on Canadian Pacific Railway Ltd.'s second-quarter results, but the company's new boss has an upbeat view of what's next for the storied railroad.

"It's been fun. I've enjoyed the first three or four weeks of getting back in the saddle," Hunter Harrison, who used to lead CP's biggest rival, said in an interview. "It's been delightful."

Net income fell to $103 million, or 60 cents per share, in the three months ended June 30 from $128 million, or 75 cents per share, a year earlier.

Earnings per share would have been 30 cents higher if not for the $38-million costs related to Hunter Harrison's appointment as CEO following a bitter proxy fight, advisory costs and a change in Ontario's corporate income tax rate.

And a nine-day strike that started in May—and ultimately ended when Ottawa stepped in with back-to-work legislation—further reduced Canadian Pacific's (TSX:CP) earnings per share by 25 cents to 30 cents earnings per share.

"We've had a number of significant items that masked our true financial results. However with the noise aside, we have a solid performance to build on," said chief financial officer Kathryn McQuade.

"Our capital plan is on track and we are seeing real volume growth in strategic areas like energy and we continue to drive operating improvements into the network. This is a strong franchise with positive market opportunities and we are committed to providing quality service as we drive long-term value for our shareholders."

Activist hedge fund Pershing Square Capital Management bought a 14 percent stake in Canadian Pacific last fall and then agitated for months to oust then-CEO Fred Green.

Pershing Square CEO Bill Ackman argued the railway was languishing under Green's leadership and major changes at the top were necessary to get the company up to speed with its peers.

Ackman said Harrison, who retired as CEO of rival railway Canadian National Railway Co. (TSX:CNR) in 2009, was the right man for the job and last month he was appointed to the job.

Harrison had said the railway could cut expenses as a percentage of revenues to the mid-60 range in four years—an operating ratio target CP's former management and board deemed unrealistic.

During the second quarter, CP's operating ratio was 82.5, an increase of 80 basis points.

"I feel even stronger today than I did two or three months ago about the numbers that I was throwing around," Harrison told a conference call.

"I think they're in for some surprises," he said of the skeptics.

Revenue increased to $1.37 billion from $1.27 billion during the quarter.

(Jeff McIntosh/The Canadian Press))

Harrison said he's seen some pleasant surprises since taking the reins of Canadian Pacific.

"There's some strength the organization had that I didn't even appreciate, I think from a technology standpoint they're way ahead of the competition," said Harrison.

He also said he had been "too conservative" with respect to the railway's revenue growth prospects. If economic conditions remain steady, the railway shouldn't have trouble meeting its targets, he said.

"When I got here and looked, my confidence just became even stronger."

He said morale has been mixed at the railway following the rocky times it's experienced this year.

"I think there's some people out there that see me as the big bad wolf and think I'm gonna walk in here and not do things positive for the organization and they're not real pleased about that," he said.

"At the same time I've been pleasantly surprised as I've been out on the property shaking hands and meet railroaders that are very encouraged by the changes that the organization...is trying to make."

Harrison now has a condo in Calgary, where he's been spending most of his time since starting his new job. Once things settle down, he sees himself spending about a third of the time in Calgary and the rest on the road in Canada and the United States.

"And I'll work my family in somehow in those schedules," the Tennessee-born CEO told The Canadian Press.

Harrison doesn't expect to have any trouble honouring contractual obligations he signed with his former employer, CN, when he left. For its part, CN said it would closely monitor Harrison to make sure he doesn't spill confidential information to its competitor.

"I don't know what information I have that's confidential that hasn't been made public that I could divulge, even if I made a mistake," said Harrison.

Source: "Canadian Pacific Railway profits fall in second quarter on series of expenses." *The Canadian Press,* July 25, 2012. Reprinted by permission.

Finally, in terms of agency costs, there is a special cost that has become a veritable "hot potato": **moral hazard**. Suppose that, instead of hiring someone to clean up your yard, you accept your son's offer to volunteer to do the job. In this case, your son might think that he can do a quick job, knowing that you will finish it off—his behaviour changes because he knows

moral hazard the fact that individuals' behaviours may change if they are not exposed to the full consequences of their actions

that you will bail him out. So although your son might do a great job in someone else's yard, he does a poor job for you. If you think of your son as Lehman Brothers Holdings Inc. or Bear Stearns Companies, Inc., and the U.S. government as you, the parent, you can see how the concept of moral hazard became important in 2008.

In 1998, the U.S. government bailed out a hedge fund called Long-Term Capital Management (LTCM) because it was deemed to pose a systemic risk to the U.S. financial system—that is, it imposed an externality on others. This resulted in a common understanding that a financial institution could take risks because, in the event of failure, the U.S. government would bail out the institution. This is the moral hazard problem: knowing that the U.S. government had bailed out LTCM, the behaviour of other institutions changed. This problem is also why, on September 15, 2008, the U.S. government forced Lehman Brothers into bankruptcy, even though it was much larger than LTCM and its failure posed a much greater risk to the financial system. In retrospect, it is now acknowledged that forcing Lehman Brothers into bankruptcy was a huge mistake, since it triggered the credit crunch, financial market meltdown, and the worst recession since the Great Depression of the 1930s. In 2010, Mark Carney, Governor of the Bank of Canada, was still concerned about the issue of moral hazard, as discussed in *Finance in the News 2-4*. The U.S. government's bailout of its banks after the Lehman crisis illustrates that moral hazard is still with us and if left unchecked, could distort markets.

---

finance INTHENEWS 2-4   Carney Says Bailouts Created a 'Moral Hazard'

BANK OF CANADA governor Mark Carney says the bailout of the banks around the world created a moral hazard, that if left unchecked will distort behaviour and inflate costs.

Speaking to the International Centre for Monetary and Banking Studies in Geneva, the central bank governor called for steps to be taken to build the infrastructure needed to help restore market discipline to financial institutions.

He says the central bank was working with its partners to establish the mechanisms to help maintain liquidity in the financial markets in times of crisis.

Canada and its banks fared better than many of its G7 counterparts through a combination of a well-regulated mortgage market, less leverage, and a bit of good fortune.

But Carney says Canadians shouldn't be complacent.

He says the first line of defence will be investors, management and boards of directors.

(Cate Gillon/Getty Images)

Source: The Canadian Press, "Carney says bailouts created a 'moral hazard'," November 9, 2010. Copyright © 2010 The Canadian Press. Reprinted by permission.

Despite the moral hazard problem, the fact remains that institutions that are too big to fail cannot be allowed to fail. As a result, a new acronym has entered the financial lexicon: SIFI, a systemically important financial institution, which is just another way of saying a bank that is too important to be allowed to fail. Allowing a SIFI to fail, it is argued, would trigger a global financial meltdown similar to what happened in 2008–9. Assuming we cannot break up SIFIs, we have to regulate them more carefully. In 2011, the Basel Committee on Banking Supervision opted for this approach in its new regulations (Basel 3).[7] So far, about 30 large international financial institutions have been identified for this "extra careful" supervision and more extensive regulation, none of them in Canada. That may sound like a blow to Canada's prestige, but it means that the Canadian banks have more leeway to grow. They just have to be careful not to grow so large they become a SIFI and attract too much attention!

We have discussed a variety of agency problems that explain why managers don't necessarily pursue the best interests of the shareholders—mainly because their investment in the corporation goes much deeper than that of a typical shareholder. Donaldson argued that the main implication was that managers of regular corporations tend to be more conservative than would seem justified by the shareholder approach, since they don't face the moral hazard problem of being too big to fail. Donaldson further analyzed four key areas and found that in each area, managers would make different decisions than the ones shareholders would make. These are illustrated in Table 2-2.

TABLE 2-2 Areas of Disagreement

	Managers	Shareholders
Performance appraisal	Accounting ROI/cash	Market prices
Investment analysis	IRR of best division	WACC external
Financing	Retentions, debt, new equity	Debt, retentions, new equity
Risk	Preservation of firm	Portfolio

For example, when being appraised, managers want to be judged relative to accounting numbers, such as profits and return on investment (ROI), because they can control these numbers. In contrast, shareholders are interested in the stock market performance, because they want managers to create shareholder value. Similarly, in investment analysis (choosing projects), managers want to choose the internal rate of return (IRR) of their best project, relative to other divisions of the firm or past performance, because, again, this is what they control.[8] In contrast, shareholders are interested in what they can do with the money, which can be measured by comparing the return on a project with the firm's weighted average cost of capital (WACC). If the firm can't meet the shareholders' criterion, shareholders believe it should give the money to them so they can invest elsewhere. Obviously, managers don't like this idea!

Managers and shareholders also differ in their approach to risk and financing. Donaldson argued that shareholders take a portfolio approach because they hold many securities. This allows them to diversify risk and have the firm be more aggressive, whereas managers see their careers totally tied up with the firm and act conservatively. This approach is carried over to financing, where managers follow a "pecking order": they want to retain earnings first, rather than pay them out in dividends, then use bank debt, and finally issue new equity only as a last resort. In contrast, shareholders want the firm to use debt, which makes the firm riskier at first, then use only shareholders' money by retaining earnings, and lastly issue new equity.

There is no question that Donaldson correctly identified the key differences in the goals of managers and shareholders. But this situation is like hiring your friend's son to work in your yard: it is a question of providing the correct incentive to get managers to do what you want. At the time that Donaldson was writing, most managers were compensated through salary and bonuses, which has changed as BODs have become more aware of the need to make managers act like shareholders.

Table 2-3 lists the 12 highest-paid executives in Canada, with a breakdown of their compensation. The major components of income are straight salary, annual bonus, share receipts or options, and pension rights. Notice that, in all cases, straight salary compensation

---

[7] For details on Basel 3, see the Basel Committee on Banking Supervision website, http://www.bis.org/bcbs/basel3.htm.
[8] We will discuss IRR and WACC in later chapters.

is relatively low compared with the total package. Annual bonuses are generally somewhat larger, but the largest component by far is share compensation. This comes in two forms: grants of restricted stock awarded under incentive plans and stock options. With stock options, if the company's stock price goes above a certain level, the executive gets the right to buy the stock at a fixed lower price.

TABLE 2-3 Canadian Executive Compensation, 2011

Executive	Organization Name	Base Salary	Bonus	All Other Compensation	Share-Based Awards	Option-Based Awards	Pension Value	Total Reported Compensation
J. Michael Pearson	Valeant Pharmaceuticals International Inc.	$1,561,643	$2,964,894	$13,802,664	$12,038,730	$5,950,910	$0	$36,318,841
Bradley Shaw	Shaw Communications Inc.	$2,393,940	$4,675,000	$191,426	$825,000	$0	$7,765,970	$15,851,336
Donald J. Walker	Magna International Inc.	$307,192	$6,853,945	$378,444	$3,426,972	$3,874,532	$0	$14,841,085
Gerald W. Schwartz	Onex Corp.	$1,286,149	$12,851,496	$0	$0	$0	$0	$14,137,644
Robert Friedland	Ivanhoe Mines Ltd.	$890,411	$920,091	$0	$0	$10,767,310	$0	$12,577,811
Peter Marrone	Yamana Gold Inc.	$1,285,456	$4,311,838	$100,352	$5,631,299	$0	$1,091,517	$12,420,462
William A. Downe	Bank of Montreal	$1,026,250	$1,150,000	$12,069	$5,400,000	$2,300,000	$1,531,923	$11,420,242
Edmund Clark	Toronto-Dominion Bank	$1,500,000	$1,960,000	$105,696	$5,210,010	$2,605,024	$0	$11,380,730
Charles A. Jeannes	Goldcorp Inc.	$1,400,457	$4,862,555	$133,019	$2,697,884	$1,719,687	$510,167	$11,323,770
Gordon M. Nixon	Royal Bank of Canada	$1,476,712	$1,750,000	$44,417	$5,137,500	$1,712,500	$1,050,000	$11,171,129
Richard E. Waugh	Bank of Nova Scotia	$1,500,000	$1,400,000	$1,196	$3,858,000	$3,858,000	$0	$10,617,196
Gerald T. McCaughey	Canadian Imperial Bank of Commerce	$1,500,000	$3,404,000	$0	$4,146,000	$960,000	$591,000	$10,601,000

Source: Data retrieved from "Executive Compensation Report 2011." *The Globe and Mail*, Report on Business website at www.globeandmail.com. See the full table at http://www.theglobeandmail.com/report-on-business/careers/management/executive-compensation/executive-compensation-rankings-for-canadas-top-earners/article4243534/. ©The Globe and Mail, Inc. All rights reserved. Reprinted by permission.

The idea behind share incentive plans is to have the best interests of CEOs and senior managers coincide with those of shareholders. Often, shares are granted when the company reaches certain objectives, such as revenue targets or investment returns. In such cases, the manager has an incentive to get the share price up as high as possible. In the same way, if executives are given the right to buy shares at a price of $50 when they are selling for $40, then they have an incentive to get the share price over $50 to trigger the option. If the share price never reaches $50, the options are worthless. Both types of share programs have the basic objective of aligning the interests of shareholders and managers, and traditionally have been used to trump the comments made by management theorists like Gordon Donaldson.

It's doubtful that share compensation schemes have successfully met their objectives, however. The stock market peaked in October 2000, and prices subsequently dropped almost

50 percent by the spring of 2002. Technology shares dropped even more: some investors purchased Nortel at $122 and saw it go bankrupt in the 2000s. Many may have purchased Research In Motion (RIM) shares and watched an eerily similar performance.[9] It would be nice to think that the senior management groups at Nortel, RIM, and other tech companies suffered those losses along with their shareholders. However, what happened was that the option grants and share incentive schemes were retooled to continue to provide incentives to management. So if the stock fell 50 percent and made existing options worthless, new ones were granted to continue to provide incentives for managers; the argument was that otherwise management would leave and go elsewhere.

However, was such compensation necessary to keep these managers? Who would want to hire away the manager of a company whose stock price had fallen 50 percent? But then, the compensation committees of the BOD granting these options and share grants were not always completely independent of the CEO who received them.[10] However, the important point is that the interests of managers and shareholders are not aligned if, on the downside, managers do not suffer along with the shareholders. In fact, managers have an incentive to use short-sighted measures to pump up the share price so that they can exercise their options or share grants. For the managers, this is a "heads they win, tails they don't lose" strategy.

One final wrinkle in the use of executive stock options is that this practice has been linked to outright fraud by senior managers in the United States. The U.S. Securities and Exchange Commission investigated 74 firms for "backdating" executive stock options grants.[11] The fraud was that senior managers would get the compensation committee to award them stock options and then date them to an earlier period, when the company's stock price was low. Effectively, this meant that on the approval date, the stock was already worth a large amount of money, so there was little incentive value to the grant. Committing this type of fraud was slightly more difficult in Canada, because the rules on reporting executive stock options were tighter than those in the United States. However, in March 2007, RIM admitted to having backdated options, and Jim Balsillie resigned as chairman of the BOD (see *Ethics and Corporate Governance 2-1* at the end of this chapter). In February 2009, RIM's co-CEOs, Jim Balsillie and Mike Lazaridis, agreed, along with Chief Operating Officer Dennis Kavelman, to pay $77 million in penalties, costs, and compensation to end the Canadian investigation into their option backdating.[12]

If compensation schemes have largely been used to *reward* management,[13] rather than to provide them with *incentive* to act like shareholders, where does this leave the goal of the firm? Luckily, there is a more powerful argument: the threat of acquisition. Poor management translates into poor stock market performance and a share price that is less than its intrinsic value. If a firm owns assets with an intrinsic value of $50 a share, but is selling for $25 because management is incompetent and $25 reflects the value of the profits they are generating, then more efficient managers can afford to bid for the firm to turn it around for a profit. This is termed the "market for corporate control," because it is based on teams of managers competing for the right to manage corporate assets.

The most important thing Canada can do is make sure that the assets in the country are managed as efficiently as possible so that the country is as wealthy as possible. This requires that the best managers are given the chance to manage assets. In turn, this means that hostile takeovers should be encouraged and managers should be prevented from mounting defensive

---

[9] Research In Motion shares have dropped from over $130 to under $7 at the time of writing. James Balsillie and Mike Lazaridis, co-CEOs of RIM, both took in over $5 million in 2011 and ranked equal #51 on the Canadian executive compensation scale just as successive new RIM products bombed and the company's shares swooned. To their credit, Balsillie and Lazaridis moved aside to let new management take over RIM.

[10] The compensation committees of the BOD are supposed to be made up of outside directors to avoid this conflict of interest. However, "independent" is an elastic term.

[11] Henry, David, "How the Options Mess Got So Ugly and Expensive." *Business Week*, September 11, 2006.

[12] Middlemiss, Jim, "OSC and SEC: Different Views on Option Backdating." *Financial Post*, February 11, 2009. Retrieved from the *Financial Post* website at www.financialpost.com/news-sectors/legal/ story.html?id=1275417.

[13] Does $75 million really provide managers with that much more incentive than, say, $10 million? Or, alternatively, how many millions does it take to motivate management?

measures that simply entrench their ability to mismanage our corporate assets. Finance people believe the best defence against mergers and acquisitions (which we will discuss extensively in Chapter 15) is a high stock price. Ultimately, it is this market for corporate control, not managerial incentives, that will ensure shareholder value creation is the objective of every well-run firm in Canada.

LESSONS TO BE LEARNED

The old phrase "you get what you pay for" is relevant to corporate management. In terms of motivating managers, this means that firms get what they provide incentives for managers to do. If the incentive structure is poorly designed, you can expect managers to act on the basis of those incentives. We have already discussed RIM's stock option backdating scandal and the moral hazard problem following the bailout of LTCM, but in 2008, an even bigger scandal emerged in the United States. Following the bankruptcy of Lehman Brothers on September 15, 2008, the U.S. government bailed out American International Group, Inc. (AIG). AIG had provided default insurance on $441 billion of securities: this meant that if these securities were devalued, AIG had to pay up. Unfortunately for AIG, with the collapse in the U.S. housing market, it had to pay up and quickly ran into serious financial trouble, which is why the U.S. government had to inject about $170 billion into keeping AIG afloat.

The question of management compensation came up because other insurance companies started raiding AIG's managers, and AIG agreed to pay retention bonuses to keep key staff. When news that AIG had paid $165 *million* in bonuses, while the U.S. government was providing it with $170 *billion* in financial support, became public, it created a huge political uproar. On March 16, 2009, CBC News reported the following:

U.S. President Barack Obama declared Monday that he will do everything he can to stop insurance giant American International Group——a company kept alive by huge federal bailouts——from paying millions in bonuses to key employees.

AIG is in trouble because of "recklessness and greed," he said at the outset of an appearance to announce help for small businesses hurt by the deep recession.

"It's hard to understand how derivative traders at AIG warranted any bonuses, much less $165 million in extra pay," he said. "How do they justify this outrage to the taxpayers who are keeping the company afloat?"[14]

President Obama's statements are consistent with an earlier decision to impose a salary cap on all banks that have accepted U.S. government bailout funds. However, banks and insurance companies have many separate divisions; their problems originated in a small defined area. Without the ability to pay competitive salaries or retention bonuses to valued employees, it is difficult to see how these institutions can recover. The lesson to be learned is that the U.S. government may, in fact, bail out institutions deemed too big to fail, but once a firm gets into the political arena, politicians responding to populist rhetoric can cause all sorts of problems.

CONCEPT REVIEW QUESTIONS

1. Describe the nature of the basic owner-manager agency relationship.

2. Define agency costs and describe both types.

3. How have management compensation schemes been designed to better align owner-manager interests? How well have these schemes performed in this regard?

4. What is moral hazard and why did it become the buzz word of the 2008 financial crisis?

2.4 CORPORATE FINANCE

Learning Objective 2.5
Identify the main corporate finance decisions involving the financial management of a firm's assets and its liabilities (corporate financing).

So what do senior managers do? To answer this question and provide the focus for this textbook, let's refer back to Chapter 1 and remember where we discussed how the wealth of a country and its people depends on its stock of assets. The government has primary responsibility for developing the country's human capital through its education policy, and is also responsible for realizing the value of its resources through royalties charged for the use of property. This leaves the management of physical assets, such as buildings, machinery and equipment, inventory, and other private assets, which raises some basic management problems and questions to answer:

1. How does a firm decide to expand its existing buildings or construct or buy another building?

---

[14] "Obama, Voicing Outrage, Vows Battle to Block AIG Bonuses." CBC News website, www.cbc.ca/world/story/2009/03/16/aig-bonus-outrage.html, March 16, 2009.

2. How does a firm decide when to replace machinery and equipment? Just because a piece of equipment still works, does this mean that the firm should still use it?

3. How does a firm decide whether to buy or lease machinery and equipment?

4. How much stock or inventory should a firm carry? Should it keep stocks to meet every contingency or should it use just-in-time methods to reduce the investment?

These decisions are some of the most important that a firm can make, and the framework for analyzing these investment or asset decisions is called **capital budgeting** or **capital expenditure analysis**. Unlike most decisions, a decision to open a mine or build a nuclear reactor commits a firm to a particular course of action and to spend money that is almost irreversibly sunk in a particular application, since often the investment has no or very little alternative use. *Finance in the News 2-5* discusses a new $12-billion liquefied natural gas (LNG) facility that Shell and its partners plan for northwestern B.C. Even to a company the size of Shell and its partners, $12 billion is a lot of money to tie up in a facility that has very little alternative use.

In addition to decisions about physical or real assets, firms have to consider the management of their financial assets, which raises some more basic questions.

1. How do firms decide to extend credit to customers to purchase their product—that is, why do firms finance other firms?

2. How do firms manage their cash? Cash is a non-interest-bearing asset, so it seems that corporate holdings of cash should be minimized. However, in 2012, Canadian firms had very significant cash hoards, and U.S. cash holdings are at record levels.

3. How do firms manage any temporary surplus cash?

4. Why do firms take minority stakes in other firms, or, more generally, how do they decide to buy 100 percent or less of another firm? This question leads us into corporate acquisitions and valuation.

The combination of the real asset decisions and these financial asset acquisition decisions represent acquisition or investment decisions. Generally, we talk about investment decisions in terms of **financial management**. However, this is only one side of the balance sheet. In addition, we have to consider how these assets are financed and answer some more basic questions.

1. How does a firm decide between raising money through debt or equity?

2. In terms of equity, how does a firm raise the equity: by retaining earnings or by issuing new equity?

3. Why does a firm decide to go public and issue shares to the general public rather than remaining a non-traded private company?

4. If a firm decides to issue debt, what determines whether this is bank debt or bonds issued to the public debt market?

5. What determines whether firms access the short-term money market as opposed to borrowing from a bank?

These basic questions represent the core of liability management for corporations, which we refer to as their **corporate financing** decisions. Taken together, the financial management of assets and corporate financing decisions represent the area of **corporate finance**.

capital budgeting or **capital expenditure analysis** the framework for analyzing investment or asset decisions

financial management the process of managing the firm's investment decisions

corporate financing the sources of money for a company, which include using debt or equity, retaining earnings or issuing equity, going public, using bank debt or bonds, using the short-term money market, or borrowing from a bank

corporate finance the financial management of assets and corporate financing decisions

CONCEPT REVIEW QUESTIONS

1. Describe the two key decision areas with respect to the financial management of assets.

2. What are some of the key corporate financing decisions made by firms?

3. What are the two key topics covered in the study of corporate finance?

2.5 FINANCE CAREERS AND THE ORGANIZATION OF THE FINANCE FUNCTION

chief financial officer (CFO) the top financial manager in a company

senior vice-president of finance in some companies, functions as the CFO

treasurer one of the two main finance jobs in a non-financial firm; focuses on the finance side: forecasting, pension management, capital budgeting, cash management, credit management, financing, risk management

controller one of the two main finance jobs in a non-financial firm; focuses on the accounting side: compliance, tax management, systems/MIS, internal audit, accounting, and budgeting

FIGURE 2-3 *Finance in a Non-Financial Company*

Every manager should be a *financial* manager, in the sense that the ideas discussed in this textbook are important for all managers within a firm. However, when we think of finance jobs, we generally distinguish between jobs in corporate finance (i.e., within the finance function of a non-financial company, such as BCE) and "pure" finance jobs within a financial intermediary, such as the Royal Bank of Canada or Manulife Financial Corporation.

Figure 2-3 shows the basic breakdown of the finance function within a non-financial corporation. The top person is the **chief financial officer (CFO)** or, in more traditional companies, the **senior vice-president of finance**. Under the CFO are the two main finance jobs: the **treasurer** and the **controller**. Although the breakdown of responsibilities will vary from firm to firm, generally, the treasurer does the things that we discuss in this textbook and in the other finance courses normally taught at a university. The controller usually does the things normally discussed in accounting courses. As a result, anyone interested in working for a non-financial company, like Ford Motor Company of Canada, Ltd., or BCE, should study a lot of accounting, because what these firms regard as finance is heavily influenced by accounting.

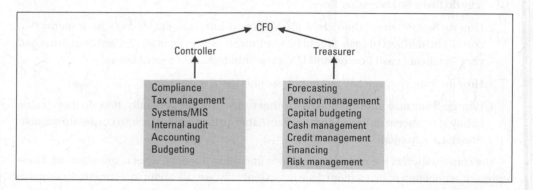

The controller, for example, is responsible for compliance. This entails making sure that the firm meets its statutory legal responsibilities with securities commissions and other regulatory bodies, makes its tax payments to the government, fulfills its responsibility to prepare and file financial statements, and ensures that its internal control systems eliminate fraud so that the financial statements fairly represent the company's financial position. As part of this financial system, the controller is normally responsible for the management information system (MIS), because its main purpose is to collect the data required for internal audits and the preparation of the firm's financial statements. Finally, the system that produces the financial statements is the same system that generates budgets and targets for the upcoming year.

From this brief description of the controller's functions, it follows that finance jobs in the controller's department require training in financial accounting, management accounting, taxes, MIS, and control systems. These are all regarded as "finance" in non-financial companies.

In contrast, the treasurer has the pure finance job in a company. The treasurer's basic function is to manage the treasury, which is the company's chequebook. To do this, the treasurer has to manage the company's cash and decide to whom the company will extend credit—in other words, cash and credit management. The treasurer must then pay the bills and make sure that cash is available when needed. This means forecasting the firm's future cash position, determining its capital expenditure plans, and arranging both debt and equity financing. If the firm has a pension plan, the treasurer is also responsible for managing these financial assets the same way a portfolio manager in a mutual fund would manage them. As we noted in Chapter 1, the largest private pension plans manage billions of dollars. Finally, the treasurer is responsible for risk management. Traditionally, this has meant arranging adequate insurance and making sure the firm was covered if a fire burned down the building. However, over the past 30 years, many new techniques have emerged to manage financial risks, such as the risk of serious exchange rate or interest rate movements. These new techniques of financial risk management are the responsibility of the treasurer.

The important thing about finance jobs within a non-financial firm is that the jobs are very broad and need a strong dose of accounting and knowledge developed in other courses in a business school as well as in finance. This is also true, though to a lesser extent, for the finance jobs within a financial intermediary.

Generally, in the major financial institutions, people start out as **analysts**, a position that requires an undergraduate degree, and then progress to **associates**. Analysts are usually responsible for gathering and analyzing data, and providing general assistance to associates. Normally, associates must have a masters of business administration (MBA) or a professional designation, such as chartered accountant (CA), certified general accountant (CGA), certified management accountant (CMA), or chartered financial analyst (CFA), before being promoted to **manager.** As we indicated earlier, the Canadian banks dominate the financial system, and Canadian banks offer different career paths, simply because they are such huge organizations. In traditional commercial banking, on the business lending side, the standard job is that of an **account manager** for small- and medium-sized businesses. The job entails managing the bank's relationships with companies by extending credit, helping to manage their receivables and cash, and directing them to the bank's more specialized services, such as foreign exchange services, mergers and acquisitions, and specialized credit. **Banking associates** generate reports on companies, prepare industry reports, and perform the background checks (due diligence) needed before extending credit.

In the major chartered banks, investment banking is structured as a separate division, referred to as an "investment dealer" or increasingly "capital markets" in Canada (such businesses are referred to as investment banks in the United States and in most other countries). People who work for investment dealers are either in sales/trading, or in "pure" investment banking. Pure investment banking, in turn, is divided into corporate financing and mergers and acquisitions (M&A), with jobs in both areas that mirror the corporate finance jobs in a non-financial company (i.e., analysts, associates, and managers).

Corporate financing workers, whether analysts, associates, or managers, advise their clients and help them access the capital markets to raise financing. Although a company may raise capital relatively infrequently, investment dealers constantly advise their clients on what is available in the capital market. On the M&A side, investment dealers, whether analysts, associates, or managers, advise their clients on suitable candidates for acquisition, or suggest how they can defend themselves against a hostile acquisition. This often involves restructuring operations, selling off divisions (divestitures), or changing the firm's financial structure.

Investment dealers, whether in corporate financing or M&A, derive part of their expertise from their knowledge of what is happening in the financial markets. Investment dealer **security analysts** monitor the valuations of the companies they follow and make recommendations to buy and sell a company's shares. They are generically referred to as sell-side analysts, because they generally recommend that their clients buy or sell securities. Their expertise in understanding a particular industry and their ability to value a company is vital to the dealer when it is considering how much a company would be worth if it were taken public and its shares sold in an initial public offering (IPO). **Sales and trading people** then execute trades on behalf of their clients and conduct proprietary trading for the dealer itself, using the bank's own capital. **Private bankers** and **retail brokers** help their clients manage their personal wealth. Retail brokers usually work with the general public and deal with small to medium-sized accounts, advising them on investment strategies to build their wealth. Private bankers deal with larger accounts and generally charge a flat fee of 1 percent of the value of the portfolio for their services; retail brokers generally charge per trade.

analysts first-level jobs in a financial institution, requiring an undergraduate degree; analysts are usually responsible for gathering and analyzing data, and providing general assistance to associates

associates second-level jobs in a financial institution; require an MBA or a professional designation, such as a CFA

managers third-level jobs in a financial institution

account managers people who manage a bank's relationships with companies, extending credit, helping to manage receivables and cash, and directing them to the bank's more specialized services

banking associates people who generate reports on companies, prepare industry reports, and perform background checks on credit applicants

security analysts people who monitor the valuations of companies and make recommendations to buy and sell a company's shares

sales and trading people those who execute trades on behalf of their clients and conduct proprietary trading for the dealer itself by using the bank's own capital

private bankers people who help clients, usually people who have large accounts, manage their personal wealth

retail brokers people who help clients, usually people who have small to medium-sized accounts, manage their personal wealth

financial and investment analysts people who do research, perform detailed analyses of individual investments, and make recommendations on overall financial strategy

portfolio managers professionals in charge of the overall management of a portfolio

fixed income traders or **equity traders** people who implement a company's investment strategies and either buy or sell the stakes in companies

corporate finance associates and consultants finance professionals who advise on restructuring, small scale M&A, and corporate financing

The larger insurance companies and pension funds, as we saw earlier, have significant long-term investments. As a result, they employ buy-side analysts to do research on which particular investments to buy or sell. In supporting these decisions, they have **financial and investment analysts** who do their own in-house research, performing detailed analyses of individual investments and making recommendations on overall financial strategy. **Portfolio managers** are the professionals in charge of the overall management of a portfolio. The analysts report to the portfolio managers, who make the ultimate decisions for their particular portfolio. Because these portfolios are very large, most of the larger companies employ **fixed income traders** or **equity traders** to implement their investment strategies and either buy or sell what are sometimes very large stakes in companies.

The final major sector with a significant number of finance jobs is management consulting and accounting firms. In their consulting practices, these firms need to analyze the financial health of a company, and often their advice contains a corporate finance element. Many of the smaller deals that do not involve significant capital market access are structured by accounting and consulting firms. The finance professionals are normally known as **corporate finance associates and consultants**, and they advise on restructuring, small-scale M&A, and corporate financing.[15]

2-1 ETHICS AND CORPORATE GOVERNANCE

Research In Motion to Restate Results by $250 Million

Research In Motion Ltd., maker of the BlackBerry e-mail phone, will restate results to cut earnings by about $250 million and said James Balsillie will give up his post as chairman after a review of its stock-options grants.

Research In Motion didn't find intentional misconduct by its executives, the Waterloo, Ontario-based company said today in a statement. The restatements, which aren't yet complete, cover more than three years of results dating back to 2004.

The adjustment exceeds an earlier prediction by Research In Motion, which forecast in January that restatements would cut past earnings by more than $45 million. In concluding its options probe, the company said Balsillie will remain co-chief executive officer as it separates the roles of chairman and CEO to increase corporate governance.

"The overall financial impact still looks pretty minor," said Tavis McCourt, an analyst at Morgan Keegan & Co. in Nashville, Tennessee. He rates the shares "market perform" and doesn't own any. "My biggest concern is what the impact of senior management involvement will be going forward."

Balsillie and co-CEO Michael Lazaridis will voluntarily contribute C$10 million ($8.5 million) to cover some costs of the review and the restatement, Research In Motion said. Directors and officers will return any benefit from mispriced options.

Shares of Research In Motion fell $1.45, or 1.1 percent, to $134.52 at 4 p.m. New York time in Nasdaq Stock Market trading. They had gained 90 percent this year before today.

Balsillie's Authority

Until the options review began, all grants except those to the company's co-CEOs were made "by or under the authority of" Balsillie, Research In

Motion said. All options granted prior to February 27, 2002 were accounted for incorrectly because the company didn't use variable accounting, the release said.

Balsillie said in an interview today that the company's options probe "hasn't affected our business one bit." The company also announced it won 1 million BlackBerry subscribers, a record number of additions, in the quarter ended March 3. "Our business is thriving," Balsillie said.

Research In Motion is one of at least 200 companies that have disclosed internal or federal investigations into options. Investigators are trying to determine whether companies inflated the value of employee options by backdating or timing the grants to coincide with days when the stock price was low.

A special committee of the board found the company had "failed to maintain adequate internal and accounting controls with respect to the issuance of options in compliance with the company's stock option plan," according to the statement.

Shareholders Lose

Of the grants the company made between Feb. 28, 2002, and August 2006, 321 awards had incorrect dates, Research In Motion said in its statement. That's about 63 percent of all grants made after Feb. 28, 2002, the company said.

"The shareholders here are the losers," said Richard Williams, director of research at ICAP in Jersey City, New Jersey. He rates the shares "sell" and doesn't own any. "Backdating creates greater dilution. More shares had to be created to pay for those greater profits."

As part of changes to management roles, Chief Financial Officer Dennis Kavelman will become chief operating officer and the position

continued

---

[15] A good guide to getting a job in finance is *The (Practical) Guide to Finding the (Right) Finance Job in Canada* (Redlader Publishing, 2005), written by David Price, MBA, a former student of one of the authors of this textbook.

> **ETHICS AND CORPORATE GOVERNANCE:** Research In Motion to Restate Results by $250 Million (continued)
>
> of CFO will be eliminated. Controller Brian Bidulka was named chief accounting officer to oversee all financial reporting and compliance activities.
>
> Research In Motion will also expand its board to nine members from seven, adding Royal Bank of Canada COO Barbara Stymiest and John Wetmore, former head of International Business Machines Corp.'s Canadian unit, as directors. The company has yet to appoint a new chairman. The company announced its internal review in September, and said in October that the U.S. Securities and Exchange Commission had begun an informal inquiry.
>
> **Source:** Fournier, Chris, and Ville Heiskanen, "Research In Motion Restates Results by $250 Mill on." Bloomberg, March 5, 2007. © 2007 Bloomberg LP. All rights reserved. Reprinted with permission.
>
> **DISCUSSION QUESTIONS**
>
> 1. What is "option backdating," and why would Richard Williams say "the shareholders are the losers here"?
>
> 2. Research In Motion (RIM)'s executive stock options were granted "by or under the authority of" Balsillie, and a special committee found that the BOD failed to maintain adequate internal accounting controls. How would the requirements of the *Sarbanes-Oxley Act (SOX)*, which is discussed in Chapter 3, affect these practices in the future?
>
> 3. The article does not mention that RIM is a Canadian company. Under what conditions, if any, should a Canadian company be subject to the requirements of U.S. legislation like SOX?
>
> 4. The article discusses governance changes and says that RIM will separate the functions of the chairman of the board from the CEO. Why should this improve RIM's governance structure?
>
> 5. In this chapter, we discussed the typical organization of the finance function. RIM has now abolished the CFO title, and the controller has become the chief accounting officer. Why do you think RIM did this, and what are the advantages and disadvantages of this action?

SUMMARY

In this chapter, we discuss the many different ways of organizing businesses, from sole proprietorships to corporations, and the recent innovations in the use of trusts that dramatically changed the Canadian business landscape. We also discuss some of the pressures exerted on corporations, and point out that although finance people take it for granted that firms should create shareholder value, this is not always the case. One important consideration that can detract from this goal is the agency relationship that exists between owners and managers, who act as agents on behalf of the company's shareholders (owners). Agency costs arise because managers may not act in the best interests of shareholders or because they must be induced to act optimally. We then discuss the main types of decisions made by corporations involving the financial management of their real and financial assets, as well as the associated corporate financing decisions. We conclude by discussing some of the major types of finance jobs that are available with both financial and non-financial companies. Many of these jobs require a solid background in accounting. This will lead us logically to the next section of this text, which reviews some of the most important concepts in financial accounting, at least from a finance point of view.

SUMMARY OF LEARNING OBJECTIVES

2.1 List the four forms of business organizations and describe the advantages and disadvantages of each.

- Sole proprietorship: a business owned and operated by one person

  Advantages: it is easy to set up

  Disadvantages: the business is inseparable from the owner; there is unlimited legal liability; net income is taxed at personal marginal tax rate; financing is limited to the resources of the single owner

- Partnership: a business owned and operated by two or more people.

  Advantages: it combines the financial resources and talents of its partners; liability is spread across the partners

Disadvantages: income is taxed at the individual's marginal tax rate; there is unlimited legal liability

- Trust: a legal organization in which assets are owned by one party and managed or controlled by a different party

  Advantages: there is no taxation of funds flowing through the trust; ownership and control are separated

  Disadvantage: there are no funds left for investment because all cash is passed to unitholders

- Corporation: a business organized as a separate legal entity under corporate law, with ownership divided into transferable shares

  Advantages: ownership and control are separated; it has the potential to attract great amounts of financing by expanding the base of shareholders; it has the potential to attract and use the expertise of its board of directors; it has the potential to hire professional managers to build value

  Disadvantages: formality and structure may slow the speed of response of the organization; there is double taxation of corporate income tax and personal dividend tax

2.2 Describe the goals of the firm and the pressures exerted on corporations by various stakeholders.

Corporations are owned by the shareholders but managed by the executives. The link between the groups is the board of directors (BOD). The BOD has a fiduciary responsibility to represent the best interests of shareholders when dealing with the executives. The BOD hires and fires the senior executives. Other stakeholder groups, such as employees and the general public, may have an interest in the company's activities but do not have any legal sway over corporate decisions.

2.3 Explain the importance of aligning the interests of management with the interests of shareholders in a corporation.

Management's personal interest and compensation may determine how hard it works to serve the best interests of the shareholders. This is the classic agency problem associated with the separation of ownership and management. Shareholders and management may disagree about performance appraisal, investment analysis, financing priorities, and risk consideration, which may result in management behaviour that reduces shareholders' value. Thus, it is important to align the interests of management with the interests of shareholders in order to maximize shareholders' value.

2.4 Explain what agency costs are and how they affect the interests of management and shareholders.

Agency costs are the costs associated with the agency problem. There are two major types of agency costs: (1) direct costs, which arise because suboptimal decisions are made by management when it acts in a manner that is not in the best interests of shareholders, and (2) indirect costs, which are incurred in an attempt to avoid direct agency costs. Indirect costs include those that arise from any restrictions placed on the actions of management, those associated with monitoring the actions of management, and those associated with management compensation schemes that provide managers with incentives to act in the shareholders' best interests.

2.5 Identify the main corporate finance decisions involving the financial management of a firm's assets and its liabilities (corporate financing).

Financial managers in corporations make both short-term working capital decisions and long-term capital budgeting decisions. Both short- and long-term decisions have implications for the capital needs of the company.

2.6 List some finance jobs available with financial and non-financial companies.

- Finance jobs in corporations include chief financial officer, treasurer, and controller.

- Jobs in the investment industry include portfolio managers, brokers, traders, and analysts.

- Jobs on the buy side of the investment industry include buyers of securities.

- Jobs on the sell side of the investment industry include sellers of securities, such as investment dealers.

- Investment banking (corporate finance) jobs involve advising firms on their interactions with the capital markets. Investment bankers are involved with such events as new issues of securities and mergers.

KEY TERMS

account managers, p. 53

agency costs, p. 44

agency problems, p. 44

agency relationship, p. 44

analysts, p. 53

associates, p. 53

banking associates, p. 53

capital budgeting or capital expenditure
analysis, p. 51

chief financial officer (CFO), p. 52

controller, p. 52

corporate finance, p. 51

corporate finance associates and
consultants, p. 54

corporate financing, p. 51

corporations, p. 39

financial and investment analysts, p. 54

financial management, p. 51

fixed income traders or equity traders, p. 54

income trusts and royalty trusts, p. 37

limited liability, p. 36

managers, p. 53

moral hazard, p. 45

partnership, p. 35

portfolio managers, p. 54

private bankers, p. 53

retail brokers, p. 53

sales and trading people, p. 53

security analysts, p. 53

senior vice-president of finance, p. 52

sole proprietorship, p. 34

treasurer, p. 52

trust, p. 36

unlimited liability, p. 35

QUESTIONS AND PRACTICE PROBLEMS

Multiple Choice Questions

1. Which of the following businesses is the *least likely* to be operated as a partnership?
   a. accounting firms
   b. doctors' offices
   c. lawyers' offices
   d. steel foundry

2. Which of the following statements is *false?*
   a. The limited liability partnership (LLP) is one of the two main partnership forms.
   b. Limited liability partnerships (LLP) have more tax advantages than income trusts.
   c. In the limited and general partnerships form, the limited partners are passive investors.
   d. In the limited and general partnerships form, the general partner has unlimited liability.

3. Which statement about sole proprietorships is *false?*
   a. The business has unlimited liability.
   b. The business is easy to set up.
   c. The business is hard to sell.
   d. The income is taxed at a corporate rate.

4. Which statement about trusts is *correct?*
   a. Compared with corporations, trusts provide greater tax advantages.
   b. Compared with corporations, trusts provide fewer tax advantages.
   c. Income usually passes through trusts, with corporate tax paid by the unitholders.
   d. Unitholders do not pay tax on the income received.

5. Which statement about corporations is *correct*?
   a. There is double taxation: corporations pay corporate tax and shareholders pay tax on dividends received.
   b. There is no separation of ownership and control.
   c. Corporations are taxed at the personal tax rate.
   d. Corporations are not as popular as sole proprietorships as a form of business organization.

6. Which of the following is the goal of a corporation?
   a. operate in the legal sense
   b. act in the "social interest"
   c. maximize the wealth of its shareholders
   d. all of the above

7. Which of the following is the main concern from the point of view of a company's shareholders?
   a. IRR of all divisions when investment is analyzed
   b. preservation of the firm where risk is concerned
   c. accounting return on investment when performance is appraised
   d. market prices when performance is appraised

8. What is the most important purpose of share incentive plans?
   a. compensate straight salary
   b. align the interests of managers and shareholders
   c. reward management
   d. boost the share price

9. Which statement about the areas of disagreement between managers and shareholders is *incorrect*?
   a. Performance appraisal: Managers use market prices while shareholders use accounting numbers like return on investment or cash.
   b. Investment analysis: Managers use the internal rate of return of the best division while shareholders use weighted average cost of capital.
   c. The order of financing: Managers prefer retentions to debt and prefer debt to new equity while shareholders prefer debt first.
   d. Risk concern: Managers' main concern is the preservation of the firm while shareholders' main concern is their portfolios.

10. Which of the following is *not* a concern related to capital budgeting?
    a. the percentage of debt financing in the capital structure
    b. whether or not to replace old equipment to boost output
    c. whether to purchase or lease machinery
    d. inventory level

11. Who is the person in charge of the pure finance job (cash and credit management, risk management, etc.) in a company?
    a. controller
    b. treasurer
    c. chief operating officer
    d. accountant

12. Which of the following responsibilities does *not* usually belong to the controller?
    a. compliance
    b. credit management
    c. tax management
    d. budgeting

Practice Problems

13. List and define the four major forms of business organization.

14. State the main differences and similarities between sole proprietorships and partnerships.

15. Summarize the main characteristics of corporations.

16. State the statutory responsibilities of directors that are described in the *Canada Business Corporations Act*.

17. Trustco Income Fund is an income trust whose units trade on the Toronto Stock Exchange. On October 31, 2006, just before the Government of Canada announced new taxes for businesses organized as trusts, the price of each Trustco unit was $15.12. The firm had been making regular payments to its unitholders at a rate of $1.03 per year; this means that unitholders were getting a yield (or return) of 6.8 percent per year. The day after the government's announcement, the unit price fell to $12.26, but there was no immediate change in the payments to unitholders. What was the yield on Trustco units on November 1, 2006?

18. Janice borrowed $100,000 from friends and family to start her company (a sole proprietorship). Business has been poor recently, and Janice has decided to cease operations and liquidate the firm. She expects to obtain $108,000 from selling the assets of the company. How much money will the debt holders receive, and how much will be left for Janice? Would these figures be different if the company had been a corporation?

19. Suppose Janice obtains only $93,000 when she sells all the assets of the firm described in Practice Problem 18. How much money would the debt holders receive if the business were a corporation? If it were a sole proprietorship? How much would Janice receive in each case?

20. List the four areas of conflict of interest between shareholders and managers.

21. When you hired Dan to manage your business, you agreed to pay him a bonus of 10 percent of profits at the end of each year. The company now has a choice between two projects (it can take on only one of them). Project A will generate profits of $50,000 per year, and detailed financial calculations show that it will increase the value of the firm by $123,100. Project B will generate profits of $40,000 per year but will increase the firm's value by $125,600. Which project is Dan likely to choose and why? Which project would you, the owner of the firm, prefer?

22. Describe the compensation structure of top Canadian executives.

23. What is the objective behind the stock option plan of executives? In reality, does it achieve this objective?

24. List the basic areas of capital budgeting.

25. List the basic areas of financial management.

26. List the basic questions related to corporate financing.

27. List the major jobs available in the financial industry.

28. Summarize the main responsibilities of the finance function (including CFO, treasurer, and controller) in a non-financial company.

29. As the CFO of your company, it falls to you to make the final decision on large expenditures. Recently, your controller has proposed purchasing a new computer system at a cost of $50,000. He believes the system will deliver savings of $60,000 in the accounting department and could be useful to other departments as well. Your treasurer takes a decidedly different view of the proposal. She claims that the company will have to borrow money to buy the computer system, and this will cost $11,000 in interest. As well, she is concerned that the amount of savings promised by the controller won't materialize. Should you purchase the computer system?

Part 2

FINANCIAL ANALYSIS TOOLS

If accounting is the language of finance, then what are we being told when accounting scandals involving billions of dollars lead to the downfall of mega companies, such as Sino Forest Corp., Lehman Brothers Holdings Inc., Washington Mutual, Inc., Enron Corporation, and WorldCom Corporation? Understanding how financial statements are prepared and what they mean to external investors is a key skill that is necessary for any student of finance. The tools of financial analysis are developed so that external investors can better understand and interpret financial statements. In Part 2, we discuss these skills in a detailed analysis of a real Canadian company.

3 | Financial Statements

LEARNING OBJECTIVES

3.1 Define international financial reporting standards (IFRS) and state their significance for Canadian firms.

3.2 Organize a firm's transactions, and explain what are the most important accounting principles related to this task.

3.3 Prepare a firm's financial statements.

3.4 Analyze a firm's financial statements.

3.5 Describe the Canadian tax system and explain the differences between how a corporation and an individual are taxed.

The following is an extract from Ford Motor Co.'s 2011 year-end financial release:

- Full year pre-tax operating profit was $8.8 billion, or $1.51 per share, an increase of $463 million from a year ago.

- Full year net income was $20.2 billion, or $4.94 per share, an increase of $13.7 billion, or $3.28 per share, from a year ago. Net income includes a favourable one-time, non-cash special item of $12.4 billion from release of almost all of the valuation allowance against net deferred tax assets in the fourth quarter.

- Fourth quarter net income was $13.6 billion, or $3.40 per share, a $13.4 billion increase from fourth quarter 2010. As noted, one-time special items positively affected net income.

- Revenue was $34.6 billion in the fourth quarter and $136.3 billion for the full year, an increase of $15.4 billion from full year 2010.

Source: Ford Motor Co. press release, January 27, 2012. Available at http://corporate.ford.com.

CHAPTER 3 **PREVIEW**

Accounting decisions can influence a company's stated performance, as well as perceptions regarding its future. Accounting is the language of business and one of the most important sources of corporate information. Gaining a good understanding of accounting is essential for any serious student of finance. As we discussed in Chapter 2, many "finance jobs" in non-financial companies require a significant knowledge of accounting. Even finance jobs with financial intermediaries require a good understanding of financial accounting. In this chapter, we will review the salient features of financial accounting. This chapter is no substitute for a course in financial accounting, but it does deal with the issues that are vital to understanding finance. It will also help explain how some accounting scandals occurred.

3.1 ACCOUNTING PRINCIPLES

Learning Objective 3.1
Define international financial reporting standards (IFRS) and state their significance for Canadian firms.

At its most basic level, accounting is simply an organized way of summarizing all of a firm's transactions and presenting them in such a way that external users can understand the firm's affairs. Clearly, problems arise when the firm tries to present its accounting statements in a way that does *not* fairly represent its affairs, either to creditors, like the bank, or to the common shareholders. Consequently, external users of the firm's financial statements have to become skilled in analyzing these statements and spotting signs that things may not be quite as management presents them. It is important to realize that management prepares the firm's financial statements, not the firm's auditors. Auditors, like Deloitte & Touche LLP, simply attest to whether or not the financial statements fairly represent the firm's financial position according to the appropriate accounting standards.[1]

International Financial Reporting Standards (IFRS) an internationally recognized set of accounting guidelines adopted by many countries around the world (including Canada as of 2011)

Over the past decade, a new set of accounting guidelines, **International Financial Reporting Standards (IFRS)**, has gained prominence throughout the financial world. Up until approximately 2005, each country throughout the world had its own accounting guidelines. However, with the increased globalization and prominence of international business, it became less suitable for each country to report financial results according to its own standards. For example, consider the situation of a Canadian investor wanting to invest in a Swiss company and desiring a full understanding of this company's financial health prior to investing. The investor would have to obtain an understanding of the Swiss accounting rules prior to reviewing the company's statements. Thus, it is only natural that the accounting practices in various countries came to be standardized. Since 2005, more than 100 countries throughout the world, including Canada, have either adopted IFRS or have converged their local accounting standards with IFRS.

generally accepted accounting principles (GAAP) the set of basic principles and conventions that are applied in the preparation of financial statements

IFRS have been the primary accounting standards for publicly accountable enterprises in Canada since January 2011, replacing our previous standard, which we refer to as our "former" Canadian **generally accepted accounting principles (GAAP)**. Publicly accountable enterprises include any company that has issued debt or equity that is or will be traded in a public market, or any organization, such as a bank or a mutual fund, that holds assets in a fiduciary capacity for a broad group of outsiders as one of its primary businesses. Private companies or not-for-profit organizations have the option to report their financial results under IFRS but are not required to do so. These organizations have special accounting standards, which were also introduced in Canada in January 2011, and which are designed to meet their unique needs as well as the needs of the users of their financial statements. Private companies may report under IFRS or they may choose to report under Accounting Standards for Private

---

[1]Much of this section was developed by Karine Benzancar, CMA, managing director of Knowledge Plus Corporation. We thank her very much for her assistance and her invaluable insights.

Enterprises (ASPE), which is simpler than IFRS and therefore is often less costly for private companies. Not-for-profit organizations have special accounting standards designed to meet the unique needs of the users of their financial statements—for example, users often wish to review the effectiveness of the entity's stewardship of resources. Most small and mid-sized private Canadian companies have chosen to report under ASPE as it is fairly similar to the former Canadian GAAP. Larger private companies, such as Irving Oil, have opted to adopt IFRS. In some cases, larger organizations chose IFRS to prepare for an eventual public offering of their stock, because of their more complex accounting needs, or because it makes it easier for them to benchmark their financial statements against those of their industry peers.

Given the multiple accounting platforms that exist in Canada, the terminology of Canadian GAAP is used to encompass the different reporting possibilities—IFRS, ASPE, or not-for-profit or pension accounting.[2] There is also a separate set of standards applicable to public entities or government. The various reporting options acceptable under current Canadian GAAP are depicted in Figure 3-1.

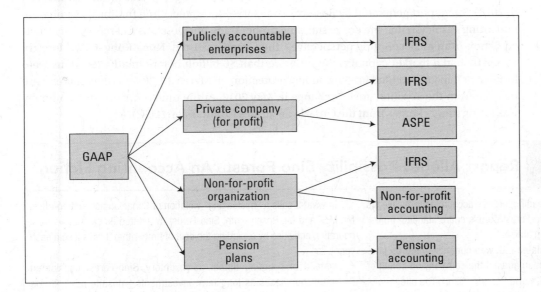

FIGURE 3-1 *Accounting Options Available to Various Forms of Organizations*

There is one final accounting option for Canadian companies. Since March 2005, Canadian securities laws permit a public company whose stock is listed on both Canadian and American stock exchanges to prepare its financial statements under U.S. GAAP.[3] There are approximately 75 Canadian companies that are interlisted in the United States, and rather than convert their financial statements to IFRS in 2011, some of these companies, such as Magna International and Canadian Pacific, chose to adopt U.S. GAAP instead. The differences between U.S. GAAP and the former Canadian GAAP were much smaller than those between Canadian GAAP and IFRS, so it was much easier and less expensive for these companies to convert to U.S. GAAP. Tim Hortons is another example of a company that reports its results using U.S. GAAP.

The United States is one of the few developed countries that had not adopted IFRS at the time this textbook was written. Instead, the Financial Accounting Standards Board (FASB) in the United States has been working with the regulators of IFRS, the International Accounting Standards Board (IASB), located in London, England, to converge U.S. GAAP with IFRS. Essentially, since 2002, the two regulators have been meeting regularly to revise the U.S. accounting rules and modify IFRS to achieve consistency between the two sets of accounting

---

[2] Regulators resisted eliminating use of the word "GAAP" because many legal documents, such as loan agreements, would have to be revised if the terminology changed.

[3] This option is included in Canada Business Corporations Regulations, section 71.

guidelines. The ultimate goal of the regulators is to have one set of high-quality accounting standards that can be used throughout the world. However, as FASB and the IASB work to develop consistent standards, IFRS continue to change. This fact has been a challenge for companies throughout the world who have adopted IFRS and then need to adjust their financial reporting to accommodate additional changes to the standards. We are expecting that the changes will continue happening for several more years.

The Impact of Accounting Scandals

The question of whether a firm's financial statements fairly represent its financial position has been a major concern throughout time. Unfortunately, we have two prominent Canadian examples—Nortel Networks Corp. (which will be discussed later in the chapter) and Sino-Forest Corp., which is discussed in *Finance in the News 3-1*—in which the statements did not accurately reflect the company's position. The Finance in the News article discusses the fraudulent nature of Sino-Forest's financial statements over a prolonged period of time (from 2006 to 2010). The report generated by Rosen & Associates Ltd. stated, "[the findings] corroborate our strong suspicion that the entire standing timber trade business was a carefully constructed fiction from an accounting perspective." The Canadian-listed, Hong Kong–based forestry company had a market capitalization of more than $6 billion before fraud allegations were levelled at it in 2011. It filed for bankruptcy protection on March 30, 2012, and its shares were delisted from the Toronto Stock Exchange in May 2012. At the time of writing, the company was facing fraud charges from the Ontario Securities Commission (OSC).

finance INTHENEWS 3-1 | Report Alleges Possibility Sino-Forest "An Accounting Fiction"

A REPORT BY one of the country's leading forensic accounting firms alleges there is a "serious possibility" Sino-Forest Corp.'s entire standing timber business in China is "an accounting fiction."

The report by Rosen & Associates Ltd. was commissioned by lawyers pursuing a potential class action against the company on behalf of investors. It was recently filed in Ontario Superior Court. The allegations have not been proven. A spokesman for Sino-Forest said the company had no comment.

The document is part of hundreds of pages of new court filings, the latest salvo from lawyers acting for investors who lost billions when the company was stung by fraud allegations that caused its stock to crash last year.

The accounting report, signed by accountants Alan Mak and Al Rosen, takes aim at Sino-Forest's auditors, Ernst & Young LLP and BDO McCabe Lo Ltd. Both firms are named as defendants along with the company in the potential class-action lawsuit.

The Rosen report says Sino-Forest's financial statements from 2006 to 2010 were "grossly overstated" and alleges the company had a "disconcerting business model" that included interrelationships among the company and its suppliers and a lack of independent verification of its forestry holdings. The report alleges the company engaged in a misleading "manipulation" of its cash flows.

The authors of the report say their findings "corroborate our strong suspicion that the entire standing timber trade business was a carefully constructed fiction from an accounting perspective."

In what it calls a "misleading" violation of Canadian accounting rules, Mr. Mak and Mr. Rosen write, Sino-Forest overstated its cash flows from operating activities by excluding the cost of timber that it says it sold each year.

Instead of counting timber as inventory, Sino-Forest considered its timber purchases as long-term investments—despite being in the business of frequently selling its holdings. Its auditors "accepted the inappropriate and misleading timber acquisition and sale reporting each year," the report states.

"Overall, it is our opinion that E&Y and BDO seriously failed to fulfill their basic obligations to test Sino-Forest's significant financial statement assertions," the report reads. Ernst & Young recently resigned as auditor.

For the year 2010, Ernst & Young's audit report said the company's "cash flows from operating activities" were $840 million (U.S.), but the report alleges they were just a fraction of that amount, or $94 million. Investors "were led to believe that Sino-Forest was far more successful in generating operating cash revenue than was actually the case," the report reads.

Peter Griffin, a lawyer for Ernst & Young, said in an e-mail that the firm "believes that the claims against it are without merit" and "will vigorously defend itself against all such claims and will deal with these allegations before the court at the appropriate time."

Peter Greene, a lawyer for BDO, slammed the report by Mr. Mak and Mr. Rosen, saying it contained inaccuracies. He said BDO Hong Kong

continued

Finance in the News 3-1: Report Alleges Possibility Sino-Forest "An Accounting Fiction" (continued)

was not involved in audits relevant to the case and should not have been named as a defendant.

"With respect to Mr. Rosen the opinions in his report are based upon wild factual speculation or alleged facts which are just wrong," Mr. Greene said in an e-mail. "I look forward to cross-examining him on his report."

In addition to the accounting report, the filings include an affidavit sworn by Stephen Gowan Chandler, a former chief inspector with the commercial crime bureau of the Royal Hong Kong Police, that alleges Sino-Forest engaged in undisclosed related-party transactions.

Among other deals, Sino-Forest engaged in an undisclosed related-party transaction with one of its executives named Chen Hua or Hua Chen, Mr. Chandler alleges. Citing Administration of Industry and Commerce (AIC) records, he says Ms. Chen was a major shareholder of a subsidiary of a company called Homix Limited when Sino-Forest bought Homix in 2010.

In September of 2011, *The Globe and Mail* reported similar filings after reviewing records from China. A report by an independent committee of Sino-Forest directors said it found evidence that Ms. Chen was not a shareholder of the Homix subsidiary at the time of the acquisition.

The possibility of related-party transactions with business partners has been a central part of the Sino-Forest saga. Despite more than seven months of work and spending $50 million, the independent committee was unable to unravel the relationships between Sino-Forest and many of the companies that supply and sell its trees in China.

Facing fraud allegations by the Ontario Securities Commission and an investigation by the RCMP, Sino-Forest's business has been effectively frozen, the company has said. It was granted protection from its creditors last month and has put itself up for sale.

Concerns over accounting fraud hit all-time highs in the United States after the failure of Enron Corporation in 2001. At the time, Enron was a respected and widely admired U.S. company that had been ranked as high as seventh on the Fortune 500 list of U.S. companies. Enron's collapse triggered dozens of lawsuits and criminal charges:

- Sixteen former Enron executives pleaded guilty to securities fraud, insider trading, and conspiracy.

- Four former Merrill Lynch & Co., Inc. executives and one mid-level Enron finance executive are in jail for misreporting loans.

- Merrill Lynch, JPMorgan Chase & Co., Citigroup Inc. and the Canadian Imperial Bank of Commerce (CIBC) have paid US$400 million to settle allegations that they helped Enron "cook its books," and they have also paid US$6.6 billion to settle a variety of shareholder lawsuits against them.

- The last two CEOs of Enron, Kenneth Lay and Jeffrey Skilling, were found guilty on 29 counts between them. They were on trial for "misleading investors, analysts, auditors and employees through false and sanitized financial statements, empty hype and shady accounting manoeuvres in finance broadband, trading and retail energy units."[4] Kenneth Lay died less than two months after being found guilty. Jeffrey Skilling is serving his sentence of 24 years and 4 months in a U.S. federal prison.

The fallout from Enron's bankruptcy has had enormous implications for accounting and finance. Quite simply, the financial collapse of Enron changed the accounting landscape and what is expected of a firm's financial statements. So many individuals were hurt by the collapse, and it happened so quickly, to such a widely admired firm, that the U.S. Congress had to

---

[4]This section is adapted from Hays, Kristen, "Trial of Enron Founder Ken Lay and Ex CEO Jeffrey Skilling Starts January 30." *Associated Press*, January 22, 2006.

act to restore public confidence in the U.S. financial system. As a direct consequence, the U.S. Congress in 2002 passed the *Sarbanes-Oxley Act (SOX)*. The following are the main provisions of this act:[5]

- the establishment of a Public Company Accounting Oversight Board to register and inspect public accounting firms and establish audit standards

- the separation of audit functions from other services, such as consulting, provided by the big accounting firms, with the auditors rotating every five years so that they do not get too close to the companies they are auditing

- the implementation of much stricter governance standards, including internal controls, with auditors reporting to the company's audit committee, which is to be composed of independent members of the board of directors (BOD) with the power to engage independent consultants

- the requirement that the company's annual report contain an internal control report that indicates the state of the firm's internal controls and assesses their effectiveness

- the requirement that both the chief executive officer (CEO) and the chief financial officer (CFO) "certify" that the firm's financial statements "fairly present, in all material respects, the operations and financial condition of the issuer"

As the key provisions of SOX indicate, the main targets are the company and its auditors. There was widespread belief that Enron's auditor, Arthur Andersen LLP, was too tight with Enron, as many former Andersen people worked with Enron, and the local auditors overruled head office in several key areas. Rotating the company's auditors every five years will promote their objectivity. Further, separating the non-audit functions of the major accounting firms from their audit functions will help prevent accounting firms from being in a conflict of interest. Previously, many felt the accounting firms were treating auditing as a "loss leader" to get consulting contracts. Consequently, they were not sufficiently objective in their audit responsibilities. This judgement is confirmed by the fact that the U.S. government set up an oversight body to regulate audit firms and take direct control of many accounting areas.

For U.S. companies, the major change is the requirement of stronger internal controls. One of the failures at Enron was apparently a weak audit committee that did not exercise proper oversight of the company's financial statements. Now, the audit committee has to be composed of independent and unrelated members of the BOD who have the power to engage external consultants and to have the external auditors report to them. Further, management has to report on, and the auditor has to comment on, the firm's internal controls, with the CEO and CFO certifying the statements are fair.

SOX has had a major impact in the United States, improving public confidence in the objectivity of the financial statements of U.S. companies. It also affects a significant number of Canadian companies (especially the large ones) that issue securities in the United States and have to comply with U.S. securities laws. Indeed, although Canada has had fewer accounting scandals, and those that have occurred are of a smaller scale than those in the United States, concerns over such misrepresentations and their impact on the business environment have dictated that Canadian regulatory authorities maintain strict controls over the auditing process, similar to those employed in the United States. On the other hand, increasing disclosure requirements does not solve many problems. It is still up to the users of these statements to identify the risks inherent in the disclosures, as discussed in the following *Lessons to Be Learned*.

---

[5]See the summary on the website of the American Institute of Certified Public Accountants (AICPA) at www.aicpa.org.

LESSONS TO BE LEARNED

Consider the following quotes from American International Group (AIG) Inc.'s 2007 annual report:

- "AIG is exposed to a number of significant risks, and AIG's risk management processes and controls may not be fully effective in mitigating AIG's risk exposures in all market conditions and for all types of risks."

- "AIG's liquidity could be impaired by an inability to access the capital markets or by unforeseen significant outflows of cash."

- "This situation may arise due to circumstances specific to AIG, such as a decline in its credit ratings."

- "Some of AIG's investments are relatively illiquid and would be difficult to sell, or sell at acceptable prices, if AIG required cash in amounts greater than its customary needs."

- "AIG's investments in certain securities, including certain structured securities, direct private equities, limited partnerships, hedge funds, mortgage loans, flight equipment, finance receivables and real estate are relatively illiquid. These asset classes represented approximately 23 percent of the carrying value of AIG's total cash and invested assets as of December 31, 2007."

- "AIG's liquidity may be adversely affected by requirements to post collateral."

- "Reporting the conclusion by AIG's independent auditors that AIG had a material weakness in internal control over financial reporting and oversight related to this valuation, the following credit rating actions were taken:..." [S&P, Moody's, and Fitch had given them a negative outlook.]

- "In the event of a downgrade of AIG, AIG would be required to post additional collateral."

Given that these statements were front and centre in the annual report and not "buried" in the footnotes, they were clear warning signals (in retrospect) that were to a large extent ignored by the so-called experts scrutinizing these reports. Consider what happened only a few months after the release of these statements—in fact, most of the risks identified above combined to lead to AIG's collapse and subsequent government bailout.

- On September 15, 2008, Lehman Brothers declared bankruptcy—the largest bankruptcy in U.S. history. Investors realized that AIG had valued its Alt-A and sub-prime MBS at 1.7 to 2 times the rates used by Lehman.

- On September 16, AIG's stock dropped 60 percent at the market's opening—down 97 percent to just US$1.25 from a 52-week high of US$70.13. AIG faced a liquidity crisis following the downgrade of its credit rating, forcing the company to post collateral with its trading counter-parties.

- The Federal Reserve announced the creation of a secured credit facility of up to US$85 billion, secured by the assets of AIG subsidiaries, in exchange for warrants for a 79.9-percent equity stake—the largest government bailout of a private company in U.S. history, though smaller than the bailout of Fannie Mae and Freddie Mac a week earlier.

- Total bailout funds as of March 18, 2009, reached US$173.3 billion.

In fact, the credit spreads began to widen several months before the recession and peaked in the fall of 2009. The spreads narrowed again during the recovery period in 2010, although they remained at high levels because of uncertainty over the economic recovery, the European debt crisis, and similar matters.

CONCEPT REVIEW QUESTIONS

1. What does IFRS stand for? What types of Canadian companies *must* prepare their financial statements in accordance with IFRS (or U.S. GAAP)?

2. Who prescribes GAAP for U.S. companies?

3. What are the major provisions of SOX?

3.2 ORGANIZING A FIRM'S TRANSACTIONS

Bookkeeping

Table 3-1 presents a series of transactions that someone, let's call him Jim, has made in setting up a company to make widgets.

Learning Objective 3.2
Organize a firm's transactions, and explain what are the most important accounting principles related to this task.

TABLE 3-1 Jim's Widget Business

1. December 1: Jim opens a business account with a $50,000 deposit.
2. December 5: Jim purchases a lathe for $30,000 using $20,000 cash and a $10,000 loan.
3. December 10: Jim buys $10,000 worth of inventory on credit.
4. December 11: Jim pays $5,000 to suppliers (creditors).
5. December 31: Jim sells $20,000 worth of widgets, $15,000 in cash and $5,000 on credit.
6. December 31: Jim recognizes cost of sales (inventory decline) of $8,000.
7. December 31: Jim pays hydro of $2,600 and rent of $2,400.
8. December 31: Jim withdraws $10,000 for himself.
9. January 5: Jim pays a further $5,000 to creditors.

The accountant must make sense of these transactions. Before we get into the accounting issues, we will first discuss bookkeeping, which is different from accounting. On December 1, Jim opened his business by putting in $50,000 of capital (i.e., he "capitalized" his business). The secret in bookkeeping and accounting is to recognize that every transaction is an exchange, so there must be two parallel transactions. This parallelism is called double-entry bookkeeping. For this transaction, the business received $50,000 in cash and gave Jim ownership rights, or capital, worth $50,000. Jim might decide that as far as his statements are concerned, this $50,000 represents 50,000 shares, each with a book value of $1.

By convention, increases in assets, like cash, are recorded as debits on the left side of a balance sheet. In contrast, increases in liabilities, like the capital owed to Jim, are recorded as credits on the right side of the balance sheet. So, after this transaction, the balance sheet for Jim's Widgets would look as follows:

Balance Sheet for Jim's Widgets (December 1)

Assets ($)		Liabilities and Equity ($)	
Cash	50,000	Owner's equity	50,000
Total assets	50,000	Total liabilities and equity	50,000

balance sheet a snapshot of the financial position of a firm, listing assets on the left and liabilities and owner's equity on the right

The **balance sheet** is a snapshot of the firm's financial position, listing assets on the left side, and liabilities and owner's equity on the right side. In practice, the firm's bookkeeper wouldn't make up a balance sheet after every transaction; he or she would record the transaction in a journal or ledger and then post all the transactions to the firm's total balance sheet after a certain period. So balance sheets are at a particular time, such as the end of a year or a quarter. Because he is just starting out, Jim will be doing his own bookkeeping. What would the balance sheet look like after Jim purchases a lathe to make his widgets? Well, he has a lathe with a cost of $30,000, so he debits (increases) equipment on the assets side for $30,000, credits (reduces) cash by $20,000, and credits (increases) loans for $10,000, because he paid $20,000 in cash and now owes $10,000.

Balance Sheet for Jim's Widgets (December 5)

Assets ($)		Liabilities and Equity ($)	
Cash	30,000	Loan	10,000
Equipment	30,000	Owner's equity	50,000
Total assets	60,000	Total liabilities and equity	60,000

The second transaction illustrates a couple of things. First, in accounting parlance, "debit" means to increase an asset or decrease a liability, while "credit" means to increase a liability or decrease an asset. Because Jim paid $20,000 in cash, he credited cash for this amount. Second, the balance sheet still balances, but it has now increased by the amount of the equipment ($10,000) that was not paid for in cash.

For the third transaction, Jim buys $10,000 worth of inventory (i.e., stock, wood, and other supplies) that he needs to produce his widgets. Because he has good credit, the suppliers simply ship him the goods with invoices for him to pay. So he debits (increases) inventory for $10,000 and credits (increases) accounts payable to indicate that he has to pay $10,000 to his suppliers. For the fourth transaction, Jim pays $5,000 to his suppliers (creditors), so he credits (reduces) cash for $5,000 and debits (reduces) payables for $5,000. After these transactions on December 11, the balance sheet will look like this:

Balance Sheet for Jim's Widgets (December 11)			
Assets ($)		**Liabilities and Equity ($)**	
Cash	25,000	Payables	5,000
Inventory	10,000	Loan	10,000
Machinery	30,000	Owner's equity	50,000
Total assets	65,000	Total liabilities and equity	65,000

By convention, items on balance sheets are listed in terms of their **liquidity**, which is how easily they are converted to cash. On the asset side, cash is the most liquid, then inventory, and finally machinery. On the liability side, payables are the most liquid, since they have to be paid in the normal course of business, then loans, and finally owner's equity.

Up to now, Jim has been buying things and getting ready to produce his widgets, so not much happens for the next few weeks. Then, at year end, he sells $20,000 worth of widgets, $15,000 for cash and $5,000 to someone who will pay in 30 days (Jim hopes). He debits (increases) cash for $15,000 and debits (increases) accounts receivable for $5,000, but what about sales (or revenues) of $20,000? For now, he will set up an account on the liability side for income from sales and called it the IS account. The balance sheet now looks as follows:

Balance Sheet for Jim's Widgets (December 31)			
Assets ($)		**Liabilities and Equity ($)**	
Cash	40,000	Payables	5,000
Receivables	5,000	Loan	10,000
Inventory	10,000	Owner's equity	50,000
Machinery	30,000	IS	20,000
Total assets	85,000	Total liabilities and equity	85,000

It is now year end. Jim has to prepare his balance sheet, but he faces some special problems. So far, all the transactions have been mechanical and verifiable in that he had the invoices and the receipts to document the transactions. Therefore, the process has been simple bookkeeping, with very little judgement needed. However, Jim recognizes in transaction 6 from Table 3-1 that he has used $8,000 of his inventory, because he does a quick check of what he has on hand and finds that he is short this amount. Jim also recognizes in transaction 7 that some of the $5,000 he has paid in hydro and rent is for the future, because he had to pay two months' rent on moving in and he also had to make a $2,300 deposit for hydro. Finally, he knows that the $10,000 he took out of his business (transaction 8) can't all be salary, because it is excessive compared with his sales of $20,000. Jim also notices that his lathe is a bit worn, and he realizes that he will have to pay some interest on his loan soon. In short, Jim recognizes that although he could do his own bookkeeping, he can't do the accounting, so he has to set up a meeting to talk to an accountant.

liquidity the ease with which assets and liabilities are converted to cash

Accounting Conventions: The Basic Principles

What is the difference between an accountant and a bookkeeper? In a crude sense, the book-keeper manages all the transactions in a firm, while the accountant uses them to create the firm's financial statements. Accountants do this by applying the accounting standards we described previously so that other accountants can understand and accept what was done. As noted earlier, IFRS are a set of basic principles and conventions applied in preparing financial statements. These principles are accepted by securities regulators, like the Ontario Securities Commission (OSC), for use in preparing statements for securities offered to the general public.

The following are the most basic accounting principles:

1. *The entity concept*: the accounting is for an economic entity, such as a corporation.

2. *The going concern principle*: the statements must reflect the accounts on the basis that the firm is not in imminent threat of bankruptcy; otherwise, they have to be qualified.

3. *A period of analysis*: the statements are for a particular period of time, such as a year-end balance sheet or quarterly statement.

4. *A monetary value*: in Canada, accountants use historical cost accounting, in which transactions are for the dollars actually involved, with no restatement for inflationary effects.

5. *The matching principle*: the revenues must be matched against the costs that generated those revenues.

6. *Revenue recognition*: Revenues are recognized only when there is a verifiable sale.

A particular entity's statements are prepared for a specific period, and the entity has to be a going concern (currently in business). The most powerful principle is the matching principle, which leads to accrual accounting: costs and revenues have to match the period, even if the cash components of the transactions occur in other periods. This is the point at which the accountant's judgement is needed to match up these revenues and costs.

General Themes of IFRS

According to IFRS, the primary objective of financial reporting standards is

> to provide financial information about the reporting entity that is useful to existing and potential investors, lenders, and other creditors in making decisions about providing resources to the entity.[6]

IFRS suggest that reported financial information should possess two fundamental qualitative characteristics:

1. *Relevance*: information is relevant if it could potentially affect users' decisions and has predictive and/or confirmatory power. This implies the information should be "material."

2. *Faithful representation*: the information provided should be complete, neutral (that is, bias-free), and free from error.[7]

IFRS suggest the following characteristics enhance the usefulness of relevant and faithfully represented information:

- *Comparability*: consistent comparisons can be made across entities and across time.
- *Verifiability*: information can be verified by an independent knowledgeable party.

---

[6] IFRS Foundation/International Accounting Standards Board (IASB), "Conceptual Framework for Financial Reporting 2010." London: IASB, paragraph OB2, p. 9.

[7] Paraphrased from ibid., paragraphs QC5–18, pp. 17–19.

- *Timeliness*: information is presented in a timely manner.

- *Understandibility*: information is presented in as clear and concise a manner as is possible (given the nature of material information provided).[8]

The preceding paragraphs demonstrate that IFRS have a very strong focus on the users of financial statements and consist of a number of guidelines to encourage companies to provide enough detail and transparency on a company's financial health that readers of financial statements can make informed decisions. Although there are substantial guidelines in IFRS, there is also room for managerial discretion in deciding how to present the results. In fact, many industry professionals find that IFRS are more subjective than the former Canadian GAAP or U.S. GAAP; as a result, they find it challenging to compare financial results of different companies.

On the surface, in terms of format, a set of statements prepared using IFRS will look very similar to the Tim Hortons' statements you will review in section 3.4, which were prepared using U.S. GAAP. There will still be an income statement, a balance sheet, and a statement of cash flows. The names of the first two statements will be slightly different though. Under IFRS, they are called "statement of comprehensive income" and "statement of financial position." However, the most significant difference between IFRS statements and U.S. GAAP statements lies in terms of how the numbers are determined.

Since companies have a substantial amount of management judgement when it comes to reporting financial results, they present their financial statements with accompanying notes, which provide further detail on how the numbers in the statements are calculated. When reviewing financial statements, it is important to review not only the statements themselves, but also all the information presented in the notes.

For example, under IFRS, each company will make an accounting policy choice to report on the value of a company's fixed assets, based either on its historical value less any accumulated amortization or on its fair market value. Reporting on fair value provides the user of the financial statements with an understanding of what the asset is worth as of the balance sheet date; however, the process of determining fair value can be onerous and expensive for the company, especially for assets where fair values are constantly changing, such as real estate. Fair value reporting requires independent valuations by external appraisers and will require a number of accounting adjustments to accurately reflect the market value, making it more complex and expensive for companies to report in this fashion. Many companies in the real estate sector have chosen this valuation method, however, as it permits them to show higher asset values and equity on their balance sheet. The method of reporting (i.e., historical cost or fair value) will be described in the notes to the financial statements.

Differences between IFRS and other acceptable forms of financial reporting can be fairly significant. For example, U.S. GAAP does not permit companies to value fixed assets using market values; only historical costs, adjusted for amortization, are allowed. The same holds true for the Canadian GAAP that existed prior to 2011. When Brookfield Asset Management switched its reporting from the former Canadian GAAP, where it reported its fixed assets at historical cost, and began reporting real estate values on the basis of fair value, its equity almost tripled on its balance sheet, increasing from $7.5 million under the former Canadian GAAP to $23 million under IFRS.[9]

The impairment, or loss in value, of assets is also treated differently under IFRS and other forms of reporting, such as U.S. GAAP. For example, when an asset loses value, this loss in value is reflected in the company's financial statements. If subsequent events cause the asset's value to increase, IFRS require that higher asset value be reflected on the company's financial statements. In contrast, U.S. GAAP does not allow a company to increase the value of its assets

---

[8] Paraphrased from ibid., paragraphs QC19–34, pp. 19–22.

[9] Brookfield Asset Management financial statements, Q1 2009.

once they have been reduced. An example of the impact of this policy can be seen in the 2003 financial statements of Lihir Gold, a company that reported $35 million of income under IFRS, $31 million of which resulted from reversing past impairments.[10]

In general, IFRS seek to present as much information as possible on the financial statements and to limit off-balance-sheet financing, a concept that can result in some of a company's financing costs not being reflected in the liabilities listed on their balance sheet. For example, if a company enters into an agreement to lease office space, typically the company's commitment is not seen on the balance sheet, even if it is a non-cancellable lease. This is an example of off-balance-sheet financing. Investors who are unaware of the extent of a company's off-balance-sheet financing can be unpleasantly surprised should the company be in a position where it fails to meet its obligations. At the time of writing, IFRS were being adjusted so that leases would be brought into the balance sheet.

Another difference between IFRS and other forms of reporting is the volatility of income. If a company incurs large losses in one period that are offset by corresponding gains in another period, the company will present large fluctuations in income under IFRS; other forms of financial reporting tend to have more options to smooth out financial results over the periods in question. Although this characteristic of IFRS reporting causes income to be more volatile, it is a more accurate depiction of the company's true economic situation.

As the FASB and the IASB continue their discussions to align their financial reporting guidelines, it is possible that we may see a new presentation format emerge for financial statements. Since 2002, the regulators have been seeking to redesign the format of financial statements so that they portray a more cohesive financial picture of an entity's activities and disaggregate information to provide more detail to the users of financial statements. Their efforts have met with a certain degree of resistance from the financial community, which may explain why their project is taking so long. The new format of financial statements is expected to segregate the firm's activities into operating, investing, and financing. For example, rather than having a balance sheet categorized as assets, liabilities, and equity, the balance sheet would be segregated into operating, investing, and financing sections. A substantially greater amount of detail would be displayed on the income statement and balance sheets, including information that companies currently consider to be proprietary. These new formats are still several years away; however, should this proposal go forward, we may see some of the techniques of financial analysis change dramatically. Some of these proposed future changes are discussed in *Finance in the News 3-2*.

---

finance INTHENEWS 3-2 — IFRS Brings a Radical Change to Financial Statement Presentation

A DISCUSSION PAPER released by international accounting regulators is proposing to change the look and feel of financial statements. The new financial statement presentation is a proposal by a joint committee of the key regulators involved in the international standards—the U.S. Financial Accounting Standards Board (FASB) and the International Accounting Standards Board (IASB).

Why Change the Look of Financial Statements?

The discussion paper explains that "how an entity presents information in its financial statements is vitally important because financial statements are a central feature of financial reporting—a principal means of communicating financial information to those outside an entity." The Boards contend that the existing presentation guidelines make it difficult to understand the relationship between financial statements and that information in different statements is inconsistently presented. These factors make it difficult to properly assess the financial health of an organization.

There are three objectives associated with the change. Information should be presented in the financial statements in a manner that:

a. Portrays a cohesive financial picture of an entity's activities. A cohesive financial picture means that the relationship between items across financial statements is clear and that an entity's financial statements complement each other as much as possible.

b. Disaggregates information so that it is useful in predicting an entity's future cash flows.

continued

---

[10] Lihir Gold, 2003 F-20 SEC filing, reconciliation between U.S. GAAP and IFRS.

Finance in the News 3-2: IFRS Brings a Radical Change to Financial Statement Presentation (continued)

c.   Helps users assess an entity's liquidity and financial flexibility.

How Are the Statements Changing?

The financial statements will have new names: an income statement will now be called a "Statement of Comprehensive Income" and a balance sheet will be called a "Statement of Financial Position." The required statement of retained earnings will be replaced by a "Statement of Changes in Shareholder's Equity." There is also a new statement reconciling net income to cash flow, which must be included in the financial statement notes.

The new names though, are just the beginning. In order to achieve the objective of cohesiveness between the statements, the format of the statements will change. All statements are to be subdivided into the same general categories—a business section (subdivided further into operating and investing components), a financing section, income taxes, discontinued operations, and equity. These classifications are similar to how today's cash flow statement is divided. Imagine having a balance sheet that doesn't look like it balances.[11] If there is one thing that accountants are used to doing it is quickly glancing at a balance sheet to see that the total assets equal the total of the liabilities plus equity. With the introduction of International Financial Reporting Standards (IFRS) in 2011 though, it may not be as easy to see that a balance sheet balances.

The following is a summary of the main items comprising these financial statements.

Statement of Financial Position	Statement of Comprehensive Income	Statement of Cash Flows
Business • Operating Assets and Liabilities • Investing Assets and Liabilities	Business • Operating Income • Investing Income	Business • Operating Cash Flows • Investing Cash Flows
Financing • Financing Assets • Financing Liabilities	Financing • Financing Income • Financing Expenses	Financing • Operating Cash Flows • Investing Cash Flows
Income Taxes	Income Taxes on Continuing Operations	Income Taxes
Discontinued Operations	Discontinued Operations (net of tax)	Discontinued Operations
Equity	Other Comprehensive Income (net of tax)	Equity

Source: Benzacar, Karine, CMA, "IFRS Brings a Radical Change to Financial Statement Presentation." *CMA Management*, February 28, 2009, pp.29-33. Reprinted by permission..

CONCEPT REVIEW QUESTIONS

1. Differentiate between debits and credits with respect to assets and liabilities.

2. What is the primary objective of financial reporting under IFRS?

3. Explain what is meant by the matching principle. How is this principle related to the use of accrual accounting?

3.3 PREPARING ACCOUNTING STATEMENTS

The Balance Sheet and the Income Statement

An accountant, armed with accrual accounting, looks at Jim's business and focuses on the matching and revenue recognition principles.

1. Inventory should be reduced by $8,000, and cost of sales of $8,000 should be expensed against revenues.

Learning Objective 3.3
Prepare a firm's financial statements.

---

[11] This is because of the new approach to formatting the statements, which entails grouping "like" assets and liabilities together (e.g., operating assets and liabilities).

2. Of the $5,000 in payments, the accountant expenses $300 for hydro for the month and $1,200 for rent, and records the balance of $3,500 as a prepaid expense.

3. Of the $10,000 that Jim withdrew, the accountant indicates that $4,000 is a reasonable salary for the month and the balance of $6,000 reflects a reduction or return of capital.

4. The lathe has suffered wear and tear, and its value should be reduced. After looking at similar pieces of equipment, the accountant reduces the lathe's value by $2,000. This cost is offset against revenues.

5. The accountant advises Jim to record an expense of $500 for the interest that he owes but hasn't paid for the period.

6. Finally, the accountant will prepare Jim's tax return and recognize that, for tax purposes, Jim is able to write off $5,000 for wear and tear on the lathe, rather than the actual $2,000, because the government is giving special incentives for firms to buy more modern equipment.

After making these judgement calls, the accountant records these transactions to the special IS account that Jim inserted on the balance sheet:

- Inventory is credited (reduced) by $8,000, and the IS account debited (reduced) with cost of sales of $8,000.

- Cash is credited (reduced) by $5,000, of which $1,500 is debited to rent and hydro in the IS account, and $3,500 is debited to a new asset account called "prepaid expenses."

- Cash is credited (reduced) by $10,000 for Jim's withdrawal. Capital is debited (reduced) by $6,000, and the IS account is debited (reduced) by $4,000 for Jim's salary.

- The equipment account is credited (reduced) by $2,000 for the wear and tear on the lathe, and the IS account debited (reduced) by $2,000 for equipment wear and tear.

- The IS account is debited (reduced) by $500 for interest expense, and a new account is credited (increased) by $500 for accrued interest payable.

- Finally, the IS account is debited with $2,000 for total tax expense at a 50 percent tax rate, and two new accounts are created and credited $500 for accrued taxes payable and $1,500 for deferred income taxes.

The accountant has made a lot of judgement calls and has used the matching concept to match up Jim's Widgets' revenues and costs over the period, which in this case is from the start of the business until year end. After all this debiting and crediting, the balance sheet looks like this:

Balance Sheet for Jim's Widgets (December 31)			
Assets ($)		Liabilities and Equity ($)	
Cash	25,000	Payables	5,000
Receivables	5,000	Accruals	1,000
Inventory	2,000	Loan	10,000
Prepaids	3,500	Deferred taxes	1,500
Machinery	28,000	Owner's equity	44,000
		IS	2,000
Total assets	63,500	Total liabilities and equity	63,500

income statement a firm's financial statement showing the sales, expenses, and net profit for a given period

Those of you familiar with accounting will recognize the IS account listed below the owner's equity as the **income statement**. While Jim was adding these transactions to the balance sheet account, he was actually making up the income statement. For convenience, let's write out the transactions and record the income statement for Jim's Widgets.

The balance of $2,000 is Jim's net income. Now that the accountant knows that Jim's Widgets made $2,000 in profit or net income, he or she could ask Jim if he wants some of the $10,000 withdrawal as a dividend payment, rather than as salary or a withdrawal of capital. To make these decisions, Jim has to understand the tax consequences, which we will defer explaining for the moment.

Income Statement for Jim's Widgets ($)	
Revenues	20,000
Cost of sales	8,000
Hydro	300
Rent	1,200
Salaries	4,000
Depreciation (lathe)	2,000
Interest	500
Before-tax income	4,000
Tax expense	500
Deferred income tax	1,500
Net income	2,000
Dividends	0
Retained earnings	2,000

The accountant reports one final number to Jim: because Jim capitalized his company with 50,000 shares, each with a $1 book value, his company earned $0.04 per share (i.e., $2,000/$50,000). This is the earnings per share (EPS) for Jim's Widgets and is a very important number, as you will see later. However, note that Jim could just as easily have capitalized his company using 10,000 shares with a book value of $5, in which case the $2,000 net income divided by the 10,000 shares would have given an EPS of $0.20. In isolation, the EPS is meaningless; it is only useful when we look at trends over time or compare it with other per-share figures, such as the stock price.

What is income? In economics, income is the amount that can be withdrawn from a business while keeping it whole, in the sense of not encroaching on the capital value. However, although this is the guiding principle behind the matching and revenue recognition principles, in practice the correlation between the two is loose. In accounting, income is the highest number consistent with GAAP that the auditor will accept. If this seems cynical, remember how loosely related Enron's net income was with any semblance of economic profit. For this reason, the external analyst must understand how the accountant creates the income statement and balance sheet.

Changing Accounting Assumptions

Suppose that Jim's accountant interpreted three things differently:

1. On reflection, the accountant feels that the lathe has not deteriorated that much and expenses only $1,000 for wear and tear.

2. The accountant talks to Jim and decides to recognize another $5,000 in sales to a customer who has promised to buy some of Jim's widgets. Another $5,000 is added to receivables, because no cash has been received.

3. On reflection, the accountant feels that $2,000 of Jim's salary reflects the development of a unique style and also suggests that Jim patent this style.

Obviously, these new interpretations will influence Jim's balance sheet, as well as his profits. For now, we will focus our discussion on the impact that these three decisions have on Jim's profits, which jump to $6,000, as follows:

Revised Income Statement for Jim's Widgets ($)	
Revenues	25,000
Cost of sales	8,000
Hydro	300
Rent	1,200
Salaries	2,000
Depreciation (lathe)	1,000
Interest	500
Before-tax income	12,000
Tax expense	4,000
Deferred income tax	2,000
Net income	6,000
Dividends	0
Retained earnings	6,000

The extra $4,000 in retained earnings comes from the recognition of the extra $5,000 in sales ($2,500 after tax),[12] the reduction (or understatement) of Jim's wear and tear on the lathe by $1,000 ($500 after tax), and the reduction (or understatement) of Jim's salary by $2,000 ($1,000 after tax). These changes certainly make Jim's business look more profitable, and the balance sheet will be stronger as well. There is now an extra $5,000 receivable, the equipment is worth $1,000 more, and there is a new $2,000 account for patents and brand names. All in all, Jim's business looks much better, all because of different judgement calls made by Jim's accountant.

The three areas in which the accountant changed the financial statements are all classic areas of financial statement manipulation. WorldCom Corporation's accounting fraud was a simple case of deciding that the rental payments for telephone lines were an asset, rather than an expense. So instead of deducting them as expenses and reducing income, they were added to the balance sheet as assets, exactly like the $2,000 of Jim's salary. Bristol-Myers Squibb had to restate its financial statements after it was revealed that a significant component of its sales were actually to controlled distributors, where there was an agreement to buy them back under certain circumstances, exactly like the $5,000 in additional sales to someone who had "promised" to buy some of Jim's widgets. The understatement of wear and tear on Jim's lathe is another classic case where conservatism in writing down the value of an asset makes the company's income statement and balance sheet look better.

What these three examples, along with the other adjustments, indicate is the significant scope for judgement in the preparation of a firm's annual statements and the ongoing need to seriously examine the assumptions underlying these judgements. The examples emphasize the old phrase "figures can lie and liars can figure."

Tax Statements

Let's assume that Jim decides against the aggressive adjustments discussed in the section above and keeps to his original statements. We now consider the two tax accounts: taxes payable and deferred taxes. To understand the tax accounts, you have to understand that corporations are allowed to say different things to different people. In particular, they are allowed to present one set of accounts to Canada Revenue Agency (the tax authorities) and another to the investing public. There are limits on how different they can be, but Canada is not like northern European countries, where only one set of statements is used and the accounts given to the tax authorities are the same as those presented to the general public. One of the biggest differences in the statements in Canada is wear and tear.

---

[12] With an assumed 50-percent tax rate, all the changes on an after-tax basis are half the amounts.

What we have been calling "wear and tear" has traditionally been referred to by accountants as **depreciation**, because the asset is depreciating or reducing in value through time. Depreciation is now referred to as **amortization expense** by accountants. For the financial statements, the accountant is allowed to use any reasonable (and GAAP-compliant) method for calculating depreciation (amortization). The most common method is to divide a depreciable asset's cost, less an estimated salvage value, by its estimated useful life and expense that amount per year. This is referred to as the "straight-line method." There are other, more sophisticated methods, such as by machine usage. However, for tax purposes, the government allows a special form of depreciation, which in Canada is called "capital cost allowance" (CCA). Essentially, every asset is allocated to a CCA asset class, and a fixed percentage of the undepreciated balance is allowed as an expense each year. So for tax purposes, Jim's income statement may look like this:

depreciation/amortization the reduction in value of an asset over time

Tax Return for Jim's Widgets ($)	
Revenues	20,000
Cost of sales	8,000
Hydro	300
Rent	1,200
Salaries	4,000
CCA	5,000
Interest	500
Taxable income	1,000
Tax expense	500

The only difference from Jim's original income statement is that the CCA expense of $5,000 replaces the depreciation expense of $2,000. As a result, the tax bill for Jim's Widgets is only $500, despite the fact that the financial statements report $4,000 in before-tax income. So what is the deferred tax bill of $1,500? It's actually a figment of the accountant's imagination; it is the amount Jim's Widgets would pay if the government didn't allow accelerated depreciation for tax purposes (i.e., CCA). One thing should be made very clear: this is not money that is presently owed to the government. Canada Revenue Agency, like tax authorities all around the world, tries to collect all the money owed it. The deferred income taxes are entirely a result of the accountant's judgement in using depreciation for the financial statements that differ from the CCA allowed for tax purposes.

Cash Flow Statements

By now, the element of judgement that permeates a firm's financial statements should be obvious. To outsiders, this is extremely annoying because external (non-accounting) observers tend to believe that there is one number that is waiting to be counted by the accountant, but this is not the case. A very good example to the contrary is provided by Nortel Networks Corporation. On March 11, 2006, Nortel announced that it was restating its financial results for at least the prior four years. This was Nortel's third attempt at preparing its financial statements for those years. Nortel's CFO, Peter Currie, blamed the misstatements on "misapplication of accounting theory."[13] However, an external telecommunications analyst expressed many people's frustration with Nortel by stating, "Really, how many accountants does it take to screw in a light bulb?"

How then can we assess the element of judgement in a firm's financial statements and determine how much money Jim has really made? One answer is to look at the third major financial statement, the **cash flow statement**, which essentially undoes the effects of judgement as much

cash flow statement a summary of a firm's cash receipts and disbursements over a specified period

---

[13] Hamilton, Tyler, "Nortel Accounting Woes Continue." *Toronto Star*, March 11, 2006.

as possible and tracks the actual flow of hard cash through a firm. There are two ways to calculate the cash flow statement: (1) by examining the changes in the balance sheet accounts, and (2) by adding back non-cash items to net income.

An increase of cash occurs when you decrease an asset. For example, if Jim sells some of his inventory, all else remaining constant, this sale generates cash. Alternatively, cash is generated when liabilities increase—for example, if loans go up. So for Jim's Widgets, he can estimate the sources of cash from increases in liabilities and decreases in assets, and he can estimate the uses of cash as the opposite. For this example, because Jim started out with nothing and he knows what his year-end balance sheet looks like, the changes are easy to determine because it is just a rearrangement of the balance sheet. This is demonstrated below, where the net change in cash (or net cash flow) is $25,000, which corresponds to the $25,000 in the cash account on the balance sheet for Jim's Widgets. This makes sense because the beginning cash balance was zero.

Sources and Uses of Funds for Jim's Widgets ($)	
Increase in payables	5,000
Increase in accruals	1,000
Increase in loans	10,000
Increase in deferred taxes	1,500
Increase in owner's equity	44,000
Increase in retained earnings	2,000
Total sources of cash	63,500
Increase in receivables	5,000
Increase in inventory	2,000
Increase in prepaid expenses	3,500
Increase in machinery	28,000
Total uses of cash	38,500
Increase in cash	25,000

Another way to arrive at the same result is to start with the net income figure of $2,000 and then add back the non-cash items in the income statement. This version of the cash flow statement is presented below:

Cash Flow Statement for Jim's Widgets ($)	
Net income	2,000
Depreciation	+2,000
Deferred income taxes	+1,500
Traditional cash flow	5,500
Increase in receivables	−5,000
Increase in prepaids	−3,500
Increase in inventory	−2,000
Increase in accruals	+1,000
Increase in payables	+5,000
Increase in net working capital	−4,500
Cash flow from operations	1,000
Capital expenditures	−30,000
Free cash flow	−29,000

In Jim's case, the major non-cash items in the income statement are depreciation and deferred income taxes. Remember that depreciation was a non-cash item because the accountant just "charged off" $2,000 to represent the wear and tear on the lathe, but no cash was involved in this. Similarly, the only taxes Jim owed were those that were calculated using

CCA, resulting in the $500 tax liability. The deferred or future income taxes were created from the accountant's judgement and do not reflect what is owed to the government. Adding these judgement calls back to net income indicates that Jim's Widgets had cash flow of $5,500. This figure is often referred to as the **traditional cash flow** figure.

traditional cash flow net income plus non-cash expenses, such as depreciation and deferred taxes

Historically, analysts have focused on traditional cash flow, since for many manufacturing firms depreciation is a major non-cash expense. Further, it adjusts for any aggressive choice of depreciation by adding back whatever was subtracted in the income statement. For example, if Jim had followed aggressive accounting practices and used depreciation of $1,000 instead of $2,000, this would have been added back in calculating traditional cash flow. Therefore, focusing on cash flow negates the effect of aggressive accounting for depreciation.

However, other subtle non-cash items are often even more important. For example, Jim's accounts receivable increased by $5,000 because $5,000 of his sales were credit sales and not cash sales. Instead of cash, all Jim got was someone's promise to pay him later. As a result, net income overstates cash flow by assuming that all sales are cash sales. Jim also paid $5,000 for rent and hydro, only $1,500 of which passed through the income statement; another $3,500 was classified as prepaid expenses but still involved cash payments. Similarly, Jim paid $10,000 for inventory but used only $8,000 of it, as $2,000 was still in inventory at the end of the year. Jim has to recognize that he paid $2,000 for this inventory. The sum of these three items is an increase in working capital and a decrease in cash of $10,500. We call this "working capital" simply because it represents short-term investments that turn over or are constantly "working."

Offsetting this increase in working capital is the fact that some of the expenses in the income statement similarly do not involve cash. For example, Jim recorded $500 in interest and $500 in taxes on the income statement as expenses, because the accountant wanted to match these expenses with Jim's revenues. However, neither the bank nor the government was actually paid, although the expenses have been accrued, and these obligations can be referred to as "accruals." Similarly, there are still accounts payable of $5,000 outstanding, which means that some of the inventory expenses on the income statement are not yet paid. When these two accounts of $6,000 are subtracted from the working capital of $10,500, net working capital increased by $4,500. The net working capital figure indicates that Jim made a cash investment of $4,500 in his widget business, reflecting the difference between what is recorded on the income statement and what went through his chequebook.

When we subtract the increase in net working capital of $4,500 from the traditional cash flow of $5,500, we get **cash flow from operations (CFO)** of $1,000. The value of looking at CFO is that it takes into account changes in net working capital. It brings to light any increases in receivables and inventory, so the analyst can ask why people aren't paying for their sales and why inventory is increasing. If sales are constant and yet the increase in net working capital is significant, it is one sign that the firm's net income numbers might be aggressive. For example, remember Jim's possible use of aggressive accounting in recording $5,000 of sales prematurely. If Jim had done this, then net working capital would have increased by this $5,000, since the sales would have shown up as credit sales and increased receivables. As a result, subtracting this larger increase in net working capital when calculating CFO would have corrected for this aggressive accounting assumption.[14]

cash flow from operations (CFO) the result of subtracting the increase in net working capital from traditional cash flow

The next step in the cash flow statement was to subtract capital expenditures (capex) of $30,000 from CFO. This gives a figure that is commonly called **free cash flow**, which is −$29,000 in Jim's case. Financial analysts focus on free cash flow to see whether a company is generating or using cash. In Jim's case, he is investing in his company and it is using cash. Free cash flow is important because it picks up the effect of all three of the aggressive accounting practices that Jim could have used. In the final case, where Jim could have claimed that $2,000 of his salary was to develop a brand or patent for his business, this would have been a capital expenditure. In that case, although Jim's income would have been higher, the

free cash flow the result of subtracting capital expenditures from cash flow from operations

---

[14] However, in this case, Jim's figures would be down because he would accrue more income tax.

increased capital expenditures would have been subtracted from CFO and reduced the free cash flow figure.

Financial analysts like to calculate free cash flow because it focuses on the financing of the firm: if the firm is using cash, it has to raise the money from somewhere. As a result, free cash flow indicates the firm's financing problems, or lack thereof. In practice, accountants prepare a variation of the free cash flow statement above that accounts for cash flow from financing (CFF) and is referred to as the cash flow statement. For Jim's Widgets, an abbreviated version of the cash flow statement would look like the following:[15]

Cash Flow Statement for Jim's Widgets ($)	
Cash flow from operations	1,000
Cash flow from investing	–30,000
Bank loan	10,000
Capital stock	44,000
Cash flow from financing	54,000
Change in cash	25,000

This presentation of the cash flow statement simply takes free cash flow of −$29,000 and adds CFF of $54,000 to it. Because Jim still owes the bank $10,000 and has invested $44,000 in owner's equity, CFF is $54,000. When this amount is added to the free cash flow deficit of $29,000, we arrive at the net cash flow (or change in cash) figure of $25,000, as calculated in the sources and uses of funds statement.

Most financial analysts focus on the cash flow statement. However, one problem with this statement is that the same information can be presented in many different ways. In fact, both the name and the presentation of the cash flow statement has changed several times over the past 20 years in response to user concerns.

We now leave our simple example, which was designed to show the basic accounting principles involved in determining financial statements, to look at the actual financial statements of Tim Hortons Inc.

CONCEPT REVIEW QUESTIONS

1. How is the balance sheet related to the income statement?

2. What happens to the net income figure when a firm's accountants make more aggressive accounting assumptions? Briefly explain.

3. How do cash flow statements alleviate the impact of most major accounting assumptions?

4. Why do income statements differ from tax statements? What is the major difference?

3.4 TIM HORTONS INC. ACCOUNTING STATEMENTS

Learning Objective 3.4
Analyze a firm's financial statements.

Tim Hortons Inc. is one of Canada's best known companies, a Canadian icon of sorts. In fact, Tim Hortons is the largest publicly traded quick service restaurant chain based in Canada. We present and discuss Tim Hortons' financial statements in this chapter, and in the next chapter, we provide some tools that can be used to analyze these statements.

---

[15] This statement is abbreviated because it leaves out the computation of CFO and cash flow from investing (or capex), which were calculated above.

Accompanying Statements

We begin by looking at the information the company files with its financial statements. Figure 3-2 shows two statements that include "Certifications of the CEO" (pursuant to two separate sections of SOX), which accompany Tim Hortons' 2011 annual report. The CFO provides similar certifications (although we have not included them here) in accordance with the provisions of SOX, as discussed at the beginning of this chapter. Although Tim Hortons is based in Toronto, it files its statements according to Securities and Exchange Commission (SEC) regulations (and according to the rules of SOX) in the form of a 10-K statement, since its common shares are listed on the New York Stock Exchange (NYSE), as well as on the Toronto Stock Exchange (TSX).[16]

Exhibit 31(a)

Certifications of the CEO
Pursuant to Section 302 of the Sarbanes-Oxley Act of 2002

I, Paul D. House, certify that:

1. I have reviewed this annual report on Form 10-K of Tim Hortons Inc.;

2. Based on my knowledge, this report does not contain any untrue statement of a material fact or omit to state a material fact necessary to make the statements made, in light of the circumstances under which such statements were made, not misleading with respect to the period covered by this report;

3. Based on my knowledge, the financial statements, and other financial information included in this report, fairly present in all material respects the financial condition, results of operations and cash flows of the registrant as of, and for, the periods presented in this report;

4. The registrant's other certifying officer and I are responsible for establishing and maintaining disclosure controls and procedures (as defined in Exchange Act Rules 13a-15(e) and 15d-15(e)) and internal control over financial reporting (as defined in Exchange Act Rules 13a-15(f) and 15d-15(f)) for the registrant and have:

   a) Designed such disclosure controls and procedures, or caused such disclosure controls and procedures to be designed under our supervision, to ensure that material information relating to the registrant, including its consolidated subsidiaries, is made known to us by others within those entities, particularly during the period in which this report is being prepared;

   b) Designed such internal control over financial reporting, or caused such internal control over financial reporting to be designed under our supervision, to provide reasonable assurance regarding the reliability of financial reporting and the preparation of financial statements for external purposes in accordance with generally accepted accounting principles;

   c) Evaluated the effectiveness of the registrant's disclosure controls and procedures and presented in this report our conclusions about the effectiveness of the disclosure controls and procedures, as of the end of the period covered by this report based on such evaluation; and

   d) Disclosed in this report any change in the registrant's internal control over financial reporting that occurred during the registrant's most recent fiscal quarter (the registrant's fourth fiscal quarter in the case of an annual report) that has materially affected, or is reasonably likely to materially affect, the registrant's internal control over financial reporting; and

5. The registrant's other certifying officer and I have disclosed, based on our most recent evaluation of internal control over financial reporting, to the registrant's auditors and the audit committee of the registrant's board of directors (or persons performing the equivalent functions):

   a) All significant deficiencies and material weaknesses in the design or operation of internal control over financial reporting which are reasonably likely to adversely affect the registrant's ability to record, process, summarize and report financial information; and

   b) Any fraud, whether or not material, that involves management or other employees who have a significant role in the registrant's internal control over financial reporting.

Date: February 27, 2012

/s/ PAUL D. HOUSE
Name: Paul D. House
Title: Chief Executive Officer

continued

FIGURE 3-2 *Tim Hortons Inc. Certifications of the CEO*

---

[16] Not all Canadian companies that list on U.S. exchanges prepare their annual reports using U.S. GAAP as Tim Hortons has chosen to do. Many Canadian companies, such as BCE Inc., prepare their annual reports using IFRS.

Exhibit 32(a)

**Certification of the CEO Pursuant to
18 U.S.C. Section 1350,
As Adopted Pursuant to
Section 906 of the Sarbanes-Oxley Act of 2002***

This certification is provided pursuant to 18 U.S.C. Section 1350, as adopted pursuant to Section 906 of the Sarbanes-Oxley Act of 2002, and accompanies the annual report on Form 10-K (the "Form 10-K") for the year ended January 1, 2012 of Tim Hortons Inc. (the "Issuer").

I, Paul D. House, the Chief Executive Officer of the Issuer certify that, to the best of my knowledge:

(i) the Form 10-K fully complies with the requirements of section 13(a) or section 15(d) of the Securities Exchange Act of 1934 (15 U.S.C. 78m(a) or 78o(d)); and

(ii) the information contained in the Form 10-K fairly presents, in all material respects, the financial condition and results of operations of the Issuer.

Dated: February 27, 2012

/s/ PAUL D. HOUSE
Name: Paul D. House

_____

*   This certification is being furnished as required by Rule 13a-14(b) under the Securities Exchange Act of 1934 (the "Exchange Act") and Section 1350 of Chapter 63 of Title 18 of the United States Code, and shall not be deemed "filed" for purposes of Section 18 of the Exchange Act or otherwise subject to the liability of that section. This certification shall not be deemed to be incorporated by reference into any filing under the Securities Act of 1933 or the Exchange Act, except to the extent that the Company specifically incorporates this certification therein by reference.

FIGURE 3-2 *Tim Hortons Inc. Certifications of the CEO (continued)*

Source: Tim Hortons Inc., *2011 Annual Report on Form 10-K*, Exhibit 31(a) and 32(a), pp. 173 and 175.

Notice in Figure 3-2 that the CEO acknowledges, among other things, that he has reviewed the annual report and, based on his knowledge, certifies that it contains no material misstatements of fact or omissions. He also acknowledges that the statements represent fairly the financial condition of Tim Hortons, and that he and the CFO are responsible for establishing and maintaining appropriate disclosure controls and procedures, and internal controls over financial reporting. In essence, the CEO and CFO assume responsibility for the integrity of the financial statements, as well as for the process under which they were prepared.

This is important to note, as it means the CEO and CFO are personally "liable" for the integrity of the financial statements. *Finance in the News 3-3* discusses the situation with Nortel Networks, in which the company officers were being held accountable for the fraudulent nature of Nortel's previous financial statements. Company officers were subsequently found "not guilty" in January of 2013.

finance 3-3
INTHENEWS   As Crown Wraps Up at Nortel Trial, Burden Shifts to Judge

IF A JUDGE has ever had a tough verdict to render, it would be Mr. Justice Frank Marrocco.

This week, the spotlight at the long-running trial of three former Nortel Networks Corp. executives will shift to Judge Marrocco, a seven-year veteran of the Ontario Superior Court, as the Crown wraps up five months of evidence in the marathon fraud case.

Defence lawyers have not said whether they intend to call any witnesses of their own, but are not expected to do so. If they do not, the legal battle will move to closing arguments, likely to be scheduled for September.

The volume of evidence alone makes Judge Marrocco's work daunting.

Former Nortel CEO Frank Dunn addresses reporters following the company's annual meeting in Ottawa on Thursday April 24, 2003. (Chris Wattie/The Canadian Press)

continued

Finance in the News 3-3: As Crown Wraps Up at Nortel Trial, Burden Shifts to Judge *(continued)*

Since it began in January, the Nortel trial has seen more than 2,500 documents tendered as part of almost 600 exhibits. Dozens of thick black binders of exhibits line bookshelves in a spacious courtroom on Toronto's University Avenue, representing a mere fraction of the 30 million pages of material disclosed to the RCMP in its investigation.

While the evidence is voluminous, the allegations in the case are relatively straightforward. The Crown alleges Nortel's executives manipulated the company's huge stockpile of accounting reserves on its books—amounts previously booked to cover anticipated future expenses—to push the company to profitability when most advantageous in the first and second quarters of 2003.

The alleged motive is that the executives wanted to trigger special "return to profitability" bonuses for themselves, ultimately earning payouts totalling a combined $12.8-million for former chief executive officer Frank Dunn, chief financial officer Douglas Beatty and controller Michael Gollogly.

The allegations may be the only straightforward thing about the case.

One of Judge Marrocco's biggest tasks will come as he weighs the often ambiguous evidence presented at the trial from 20 Crown witnesses, much of it coming from cautious accountants who at times sounded more like they were called by the defence than the Crown.

Judge Marrocco is left to piece through hundreds of hours of testimony to decide which evidence remains clear and uncontested, and which was shaken under examination.

The Crown's case, however, has several strengths.

Strength No. 1: The trial hinges on the clear fact that Nortel's accounting was wrong during 2002 and 2003, a fact supported by two successive restatements of the company's books.

The restatements have freed the Crown from having to demonstrate as a starting point that the accounting treatment was erroneous, which can be surprisingly difficult to do in the absence of a clear admission by the company. It means the starting point for the trial was whether the errors were intentional or not.

Strength No. 2: Internal reports dubbed "outlooks" and "road maps" for executives were introduced at Nortel in 2003—and, according to testimony, not shown to auditors or the board of directors—illustrating how the company could move from losses to profitability by using millions of dollars of accounting reserves to meet the targets.

Some of the outlooks included pages analyzing the profit levels needed to trigger payouts under Nortel's complex bonus and share unit plans.

The defence argues the documents were innocuous efforts at forecasting and planning, but the Crown alleges they are road maps to a fraud.

Strength No. 3: Testimony about closing the books for the fourth quarter of 2002 was possibly the best employee evidence at the trial. At least four non-head office employees testified about receiving unusual phone calls early in 2003 asking if their operating divisions had any more accounting reserves they could create for the fourth quarter of 2002.

All had submitted their year-end numbers by this time, and said they had never received such a phone call before asking them to look for more reserves they could book after the fact. While witnesses shifted their evidence under cross-examination to varying degrees, it will be hard for the defence to fully counter the sheer volume of people telling similar versions of events.

There are also weaknesses in the Crown's case that offer strength to the defence:

Weakness No. 1: There is no single smoking gun that clearly implicates the accused—no e-mail, memo or conversation where the accused openly discussed fraudulent manipulations. The Crown can only suggest the accused must logically have known about and directed the fraud, arguing no one else had the authority to make such key decisions.

Weakness No. 2: The three accused have stuck together and are presenting a combined defence with no one striking a deal to testify against the others. As a result Judge Marrocco is left with a challenge of separately weighing the guilt of each accused when there is little evidence which of the men made which key decisions at issue.

Weakness No. 3: There is plenty of evidence that many of the accounting decisions in question were reviewed and approved by Nortel's external auditors at Deloitte & Touche, helping the defence build its argument that the accused believed their decisions were appropriate at the time. Similarly, there are many reports, memos and e-mails showing that accounting treatment of reserves was being carefully studied internally by Nortel staff beginning in 2002.

It means the defence has grounds to suggest the executives were releasing reserves as part of a well-intentioned effort to get the accounting fixed. Lawyers for the accused have stressed Nortel was facing huge chaos in 2001 and 2002, allowing errors with accounting reserves to fester unnoticed. When problems with overstated accounting reserves finally came to light, the defence argues executives tried to fix them in the most expedient way possible by reversing the reserves—and booking the income—to try to get the mistaken entries off the books.

Figure 3-3 provides a sample of an independent auditor's report. Notice that the report is addressed to the shareholders of the company. The Auditor's Responsibility describes the scope of the auditor's examination, which includes various audits and tests to verify things were as management said they were. Previously, auditors checked everything, but that isn't feasible now, so auditors do spot checks. The auditor also checked on the judgement (e.g., the estimates and principles applied) that management used. Remember, a considerable amount of judgement is involved in the preparation of financial statements. The auditor also assessed the overall financial statement presentation. The audit Opinion states that "in our opinion" the statements "present fairly, in all material respects, the financial position of ..." The audit does not say that the statements fairly present in an absolute sense, simply that the company has chosen a set of allowable accounting principles and has prepared the statements fairly in accordance with those principles. This difference may seem picky, but sometimes financial statements that fairly present according to GAAP do not fairly present in an absolute sense.

To the Shareholders of [company]

We have audited the accompanying financial statements of [company], which comprise the balance sheet as at [date], and the consolidated statement of income, comprehensive income, and changes in shareholders' equity and cash flow for the year then ended, and a summary of significant accounting policies and other explanatory information.

Management's Responsibility for the Financial Statements
Management is responsible for the preparation and fair presentation of these financial statements in accordance with Canadian accounting standards and for such internal control as management determines is necessary to enable the preparation of financial statements that are free from material misstatement, whether due to fraud or error.

Auditor's Responsibility
Our responsibility is to express an opinion on these financial statements based on our audit. We conducted our audit in accordance with Canadian generally accepted auditing standards. Those standards require that we comply with ethical requirements and plan and perform the audit to obtain reasonable assurance about whether the financial statements are free from material misstatement.

An audit involves performing procedures to obtain audit evidence about the amounts and disclosures in the financial statements. The procedures selected depend on the auditor's judgment, including the assessment of the risks of material misstatement of the financial statements, whether due to fraud or error. In making those risk assessments, the auditor considers internal control relevant to the entity's preparation and fair presentation of the financial statements in order to design audit procedures that are appropriate in the circumstances, but not for the purpose of expressing an opinion on the effectiveness of the entity's internal control. An audit also includes evaluating the appropriateness of accounting policies used and the reasonableness of account-ing estimates made by management, as well as evaluating the overall presentation of the financial statements.

We believe that the audit evidence we have obtained is sufficient and appropriate to provide a basis for our audit opinion.

Opinion
In our opinion, the financial statements present fairly, in all material respects, the financial position of [company] as at [date], and the results of its operations and its cash flows for the year then ended in accordance with Canadian generally accepted accounting standards [or **International Financial Reporting Standards or U.S. GAAP**].

[Chartered accountant signature]
[Date]
[City, province]

FIGURE 3-3 *Sample Independent Auditor's Report*

Tim Hortons' Balance Sheet

Tim Hortons' financial statements are relatively straightforward for 2010 and 2011, which is one reason we chose them. Figure 3-4 shows Tim Hortons' balance sheets for 2010 and for 2011 as presented in its 2011 annual report.

TIM HORTONS INC. AND SUBSIDIARIES
Consolidated Balance Sheet
(in thousands of Canadian dollars)

	As at	
	January 1, 2012	January 2, 2011
Assets		
Current assets		
Cash and cash equivalents	$ 126,497	$ 574,354
Restricted cash and cash equivalents	130,613	67,110
Restricted investments	0	37,970
Accounts receivable, net (note 5)	173,667	182,005
Notes receivable, net (note 6)	10,144	12,543
Deferred income taxes (note 7)	5,281	7,025
Inventories and other, net (note 8)	136,999	100,712
Advertising fund restricted assets (note 21)	37,765	27,402
Total current assets	620,966	1,009,121
Property and equipment, net (note 9)	1,463,765	1,373,670
Intangible assets, net (note 10)	4,544	5,270
Notes receivable, net (note 6)	3,157	3,811
Deferred income taxes (note 7)	12,197	13,730
Equity investments (note 12)	43,014	44,767
Other assets (note 11)	56,307	31,147
Total assets	$2,203,950	$2,481,516
Liabilities and Equity		
Current liabilities		
Accounts payable (note 13)	$ 177,918	$ 142,444
Accrued liabilities:		
Salaries and wages	23,531	20,567
Taxes	26,465	65,654
Other (note 13)	179,315	209,663
Deferred income taxes (note 7)	0	2,205
Advertising fund restricted liabilities (note 21)	59,420	41,026
Current portion of long-term obligations	10,001	9,937
Total current liabilities	476,650	491,496
Long-term obligations		
Long-term debt (note 14)	352,426	344,726
Capital leases (note 16)	94,863	82,685
Deferred income taxes (note 7)	4,608	8,237
Other long-term liabilities (note 13)	120,970	111,930
Total long-term obligations	572,867	547,578
Commitments and contingencies (note 17)		
Equity		
Equity of Tim Hortons Inc.		
Common shares ($2.84 stated value per share). Authorized: unlimited shares. Issued 157,814,980 and		
170,664,295, respectively (note 18)	447,558	484,050
Common shares held in Trust, at cost: 277,189 and 278,082 shares, respectively (note 18)	(10,136)	(9,542)
Contributed surplus	6,375	0
Retained earnings	836,968	1,105,882
Accumulated other comprehensive loss	(128,217)	(143,589)
Total equity of Tim Hortons Inc.	1,152,548	1,436,801
Noncontrolling interests	1,885	5,641
Total equity	1,154,433	1,442,442
Total liabilities and equity	$2,203,950	$2,481,516

See Accompanying Notes to the Consolidated Financial Statements.

Approved on behalf of the Board:

By: /s/ PAUL D. HOUSE   By: /s/ MICHAEL J. ENDRES

    Paul D. House, Executive Chairman   Michael J. Endres, Director

FIGURE 3-4 *Tim Hortons Inc. Consolidated Balance Sheet*

Source: Tim Hortons Inc., *2011 Annual Report on Form 10-K*, Consolidated Balance Sheet, p. 104. (View the accompanying notes to the financial statements on the textbook's website.)

Figure 3-4 shows that in fiscal 2011, Tim Hortons had total assets of $2.204 billion. This figure included $621 million in current assets, including, among other items, $126.5 million in cash and equivalents, $130.6 million in restricted cash and equivalents (associated with customer cash cards), $173.7 million in accounts receivable, and $137 million in inventories. The items listed above are all called **current assets**, because they are expected to be

current assets assets (cash and equivalents, short-term investments, accounts receivable, inventories, prepaid expenses, and other items) that are expected to be converted into cash within a year or operating cycle

converted into cash within a year as receivables are collected, inventories sold, and so on. For longer-term assets, by far the largest item is property and equipment (net) at $1,463.8 million. Deferred income tax items arise due to timing differences between the tax and reporting values of certain assets and liabilities. Tim Hortons' tax status is complicated due to its previous relationship with Wendy's and as a result of maintaining both Canadian and U.S. operations. Consequently, Tim Hortons reports three deferred income tax figures on its balance sheet: $5.3 million under current assets (collectible within a year); $12.2 million under long-term assets (due to the company in the long term); and $4.6 million under long-term liabilities (due from the company in the long term). The equity investments figure of $43 million represents Tim Hortons' share in companies in which it has a substantial ownership position (typically between 20 and 50 percent ownership), but that do not qualify as subsidiaries, and thus would not be included in the consolidated statements.[17]

For **current liabilities**, Tim Hortons owed suppliers $177.9 million, owed salaries of $23.5 million, owed the government taxes of $26.5 million, and had accumulated advertising fund liabilities of $59.4 million (associated with advertising funds established to pay for advertising and promotional campaigns). The company also had $10 million representing the current portion of long-term obligations (i.e., the portion due to be repaid in the coming year). In total, Tim Hortons had current liabilities of $476.7 million. The main components of its long-term liabilities consisted of term debt of $352.4 million, capital leases of $94.9 million, and other long-term liabilities of $121 million, in addition to the $4.6 million in deferred income taxes mentioned previously. Tim Hortons' equity holders have contributed $1,154.4 million in shareholders' equity, either through original contributions or by having net income retained and reinvested within the business.

In looking at Tim Hortons' assets and liabilities, you should recognize the similarity to the simple statements prepared for Jim's Widgets. Of course, the preparation of the statements for a firm with $2,204 million in assets is more complex than it is for Jim's Widgets, but, in principle, the same GAAP have been followed. Just as Jim's Widgets does, Tim Hortons has cash, accruals, receivables, and plant and equipment. On the asset side, two notable differences are the $130.6 million in restricted cash and equivalents and the $43 million in equity investments. On the liability side, a notable difference is the advertising fund restricted liabilities.

Tim Hortons' Income Statement

How much money did Tim Hortons make in fiscal 2011? To see this, we look at the income statement (also known as statement of earnings or, as in the case of Tim Hortons, statement of operations), in Figure 3-5.

We can see from Figure 3-5 that in 2011, Tim Hortons had revenues of $2,853 million. Subtracting operating costs of $2,283.5 million from revenues gave it operating income or earnings before interest and taxes (EBIT) of $569.5 million, from which it paid $25.9 million in net interest expense (i.e., interest expense less interest income) and $157.9 million in income tax. Overall, in 2011, Tim Hortons produced $385.7 million in net income. So when Tim Hortons' net income is divided by the average (adjusted) number of shares outstanding, it produces a basic EPS figure of $2.36. Companies are also required to report "diluted" EPS, which is simply the adjusted net income divided by the total possible number of shares that

current liabilities liabilities (e.g., accounts payable, notes payable, bank loans, and so on) that are due within a year or operating cycle

---

[17] Technically, this is because such inter-company investments are accounted for using the "equity method." The equity method requires the company that owns the shares in other companies to report its "net equity" position in those other companies on its balance sheet, and also requires it to record a percentage of those companies' incomes (i.e., the percentage it owns) as "equity income." Generally, a company is denoted as a subsidiary when the "parent" company owns more than 50 percent of its common shares and is accounted for using the "consolidation method." The consolidation method requires the parent to include all of the subsidiary's assets, liabilities, and profits on its financial statements (less inter-company items). The percentage that the parent does not own of the subsidiary shows up as "minority interest" on the liability side of its balance sheet, and as a minority interest charge against income on the income statement. If a company owns less than 20 percent of another company, it accounts for this using the "cost method," which basically means it only accounts for any dividends received from the other company as dividend income.

TIM HORTONS INC. AND SUBSIDIARIES
Consolidated Statement of Operations
(in thousands of Canadian dollars, except per share data)

	Year ended		
	January 1, 2012	January 2, 2011	January 3, 2010
Revenues			
Sales	$2,012,170	$1,755,244	$1,704,065
Franchise revenues			
Rents and royalties	733,217	687,039	644,755
Franchise fees	107,579	94,212	90,033
	840,796	781,251	734,788
Total revenues	2,852,966	2,536,495	2,438,853
Costs and expenses			
Cost of sales	1,774,107	1,527,405	1,464,844
Operating expenses	259,098	246,335	236,784
Franchise fee costs	104,884	91,743	86,903
General and administrative expenses	161,444	147,300	141,739
Equity (income) (note 12)	(14,354)	(14,649)	(13,700)
Asset impairment and closure costs, net (note 3)	372	28,298	0
Other (income), net	(2,060)	(1,100)	(3,319)
Total costs and expenses, net	2,283,491	2,025,332	1,913,251
Gain on sale of interest in Maidstone Bakeries (note 4)	0	361,075	0
Operating income	569,475	872,238	525,602
Interest (expense)	(30,000)	(26,642)	(21,134)
Interest income	4,127	2,462	1,950
Income before income taxes	543,602	848,058	506,418
Income taxes (note 7)	157,854	200,940	186,606
Net income	385,748	647,118	319,812
Net income attributable to noncontrolling interests	2,936	23,159	23,445
Net income attributable to Tim Hortons Inc.	$ 382,812	$ 623,959	$ 296,367
Basic earnings per common share attributable to Tim Hortons Inc. (note 2)	$ 2.36	$ 3.59	$ 1.64
Diluted earnings per common share attributable to Tim Hortons Inc. (note 2)	$ 2.35	$ 3.58	$ 1.64
Weighted average number of common shares outstanding – Basic (in thousands) (note 2)	162,145	174,035	180,477
Weighted average number of common shares outstanding – Diluted (in thousands) (note 2)	162,597	174,215	180,609
Dividends per common share	$ 0.68	$ 0.52	$ 0.40

See Accompanying Notes to the Consolidated Financial Statements.

FIGURE 3-5 *Tim Hortons Inc. Income Statement*

Source: Tim Hortons Inc., *2011 Annual Report on Form 10-K*, Consolidated Statement of Operations, p. 102.

could be outstanding if all potentially "dilutive" securities outstanding were converted into common shares. For example, a company might have some "convertible" bonds outstanding, which, under certain circumstances, could be converted into common shares. The diluted EPS takes into account all the potential shares that could "dilute" the EPS by spreading the net income over a greater number of shares. Tim Hortons had negligible potential for equity dilution, so its diluted EPS figure is only $0.01 below its basic EPS figure at $2.35.

Tim Hortons' Cash Flow Statement

We examine Tim Hortons' statement of cash flows in Figure 3-6. In terms of non-cash items, the biggest item is depreciation and amortization, which represents an "expense," as fixed assets are written down; however, no cash is actually paid out. The net working capital adjustments are relatively minor, so CFO is very close to net income plus depreciation and amortization (net income plus depreciation and amortization is commonly referred to as "traditional cash flow"). This similarity in numbers essentially indicates that Tim Hortons is not prematurely recording sales, building up inventory, or avoiding paying its bills. Its net income figure is reliable.

TIM HORTONS INC. AND SUBSIDIARIES
Consolidated Statement of Cash Flows
(in thousands of Canadian dollars)

	Year ended		
	January 1, 2012	January 2, 2011	January 3, 2010
Cash flows provided from (used in) operating activities			
Net income	$ 385,748	$ 647,118	$ 319,812
Adjustments to reconcile net income to net cash provided by operating activities			
Depreciation and amortization	115,869	118,385	113,475
Asset impairment (note 3)	1,850	18,352	0
Stock-based compensation expense	17,323	14,263	8,869
Amortization of Maidstone Bakeries' supply contract (note 13)	(8,253)	(1,325)	0
Deferred income taxes	(5,433)	1,285	25,491
Changes in operating assets and liabilities			
Restricted cash and cash equivalents	(63,264)	(6,920)	789
Accounts receivable	2,099	(10,923)	(11,432)
Inventories and other	(32,057)	(29,275)	(329)
Accounts payable and accrued liabilities	349	104,829	(20,177)
Taxes	(39,197)	40,715	(317)
Gain on sale of interest in Maidstone Bakeries (note 4)	0	(361,075)	0
Other, net	16,433	(9,885)	6,441
Net cash provided from operating activities	391,467	525,544	442,622
Cash flows (used in) provided from investing activities			
Capital expenditures (including Advertising Fund (note 21))	(181,267)	(132,912)	(160,458)
Purchase of restricted investments	0	(37,832)	(20,136)
Proceeds from sale of restricted investments	38,000	20,240	0
Proceeds from sale of interest in Maidstone Bakeries (note 4)	0	475,000	0
Cash and cash equivalents of Maidstone Bakeries divested	0	(30,411)	0
Other investing activities	(9,460)	1,934	(19,719)
Net cash (used in) provided from investing activities	(152,727)	296,019	(200,313)
Cash flows (used in) provided from financing activities			
Purchase of treasury stock	0	0	(16,701)
Purchase of common shares (note 18)	(572,452)	(242,595)	(113,401)
Dividend payments to common shareholders	(110,187)	(90,304)	(72,506)
Distributions, net to noncontrolling interests	(6,692)	(22,524)	(29,179)
Proceeds from issuance of debt, net of issuance costs	3,699	300,823	3,507
Principal payments on long-term debt obligations	(8,586)	(307,023)	(6,582)
Other financing activities	6,398	(4,005)	1,420
Net cash used in financing activities	(687,820)	(365,628)	(236,052)
Effect of exchange rate changes on cash	1,223	(3,234)	(9,321)
(Decrease) Increase in cash and cash equivalents	(447,857)	452,701	(3,064)
Cash and cash equivalents at beginning of year	574,354	121,653	124,717
Cash and cash equivalents at end of year	$ 126,497	$ 574,354	$ 121,653

FIGURE 3-6 *Tim Hortons Inc. Consolidated Statement of Cash Flows*

Source: Tim Hortons Inc., *2011 Annual Report on Form 10-K*, Consolidated Statement of Cash Flows, p. 105.

In 2011, Tim Hortons' cash flow from investing activities (CFI) was –$152.7 million, mainly due to $181.3 million in capital expenditures on property and equipment. This figure is very different from the 2010 figure of +$296 million, which was primarily due to the sale of Maidstone Bakeries. Firms that are growing and constantly investing in (acquiring) new assets typically have negative CFI figures.

The CFF figure for 2011 of $687.8 million is due primarily to the purchase of $572.5 million of treasury stock (through its share repurchase program) and the payment of dividends ($110.2 million), with little impact made by debt and equity financing. This was much larger than the 2010 and 2009 figures, due to the large share repurchases in 2011. Finally, adding the CFO, the CFI, and the CFF shows that Tim Hortons had a net decrease in cash of $447.9 million.

The strength of Tim Hortons can be seen when we use the information from the cash flow statement to estimate the company's free cash flow, as shown in Table 3-2.[18]

TABLE 3-2 Tim Hortons Inc. Free Cash Flow Statement Estimated

Free Cash Flow (for the year ended Jan. 1, 2012 and Jan. 2, 2011)	2011 ($Million)	2010 ($Million)
Net income	385,748	647,118
Total cash flow from operations (CFO)	391,467	525,544
Capital expenditures (capex)	−181,267	−132,912
Free cash flow	210,200	392,632

Source: Data from Tim Hortons Inc. *2011 Annual Report on Form 10-K.*

The company had 2011 total earnings of $385.7 million and cash flow from operations of $391.5 million. After deducting capital expenditures of $181.3 million, the 2011 free cash flow was $210.2 million, well below the 2010 figure, which was inflated by the sale of Maidstone Bakeries. The free cash flow can be viewed as the funds available to the company and its subsidiary to pay dividends, which were actually $110.2 million in 2011. Overall, Tim Hortons' financial statements are "clean," in the sense that there are very few adjustments that make the statements difficult to understand.

CONCEPT REVIEW QUESTIONS

1. Who is responsible for the preparation of a company's financial statements?
2. What are the scope and purpose of the auditor's opinion?
3. Identify the main components of a firm's balance sheet and income statement.

3.5 THE CANADIAN TAX SYSTEM

Canadian taxes are levied on both personal and corporate income, but the government recognizes the potential for double taxation of income earned through a corporation and has designed a partially integrated system. We will explain what we mean by partially integrated as we develop our understanding of taxes. We begin by noting that the United States operates a classical system of double taxation, while Europe, by and large, operates a fully integrated system, which leaves Canada somewhere in the middle. How taxes are levied has important implications for corporate finance, so it is important to realize from the outset that the Canadian tax system differs in some fundamental ways from the U.S. system. As a result, corporate finance strategies that are based on the U.S. tax code are not directly applicable in Canada or Europe.

Corporate Taxes

As we saw in Chapter 2, corporations are distinct legal entities and are taxed as such. We saw in this chapter that corporations file income tax returns with Canada Revenue Agency that are determined in much the same way as they prepare their income statement for investors. However, we also noted that there are some differences. One main difference that we have

> **Learning Objective 3.5**
> Describe the Canadian tax system and explain the differences between how a corporation and an individual are taxed.

---

[18] This is a typical definition for free cash flow; however, several variations exist.

discussed previously is that different methods are used to calculate amortization expense. Another major difference is in the treatment of investment income and expenses. We will now elaborate on these two issues.

CCA is amortization for tax purposes, and the government has designed it to be as simple as possible. First, all assets are allocated to one of a number of CCA asset classes. Four of the major ones are listed in Table 3-3.[19]

TABLE 3-3 Major CCA Asset Classes

Asset Class	Type of Assets	CCA Rate
Class 1	Buildings	4%
Class 8	Office equipment	20%
Class 10	Computer hardware, system software	30%
Class 43	Manufacturing equipment	30%
Class 45	Computers	45%

Class 8 is, in fact, a general catch-all category, so when in doubt use a 20 percent CCA rate! The CCA rate is the rate that is applied to the **undepreciated capital cost (UCC)** of an asset class; the higher the rate, the faster the assets are depreciated. Notice that the general rates make sense in terms of the assets' economic lives. Computers may last a long time, but the rapid pace of technological progress means that you will generally replace them before they wear out. Their economic life is relatively short, and their CCA rate is high. In contrast, buildings last much longer, so their CCA rate of 4 percent is much lower. The asset classes or pools have been designed such that CCA is applied to the balance of the pool at the end of the fiscal year. So rather than calculating CCA for each item separately, it is calculated for the pool as a whole. For most firms, unless they make a special election, their fiscal year is the same as the calendar year.

One minor adjustment associated with CCA is that because it is taken on the year-end balance, Canada Revenue Agency allows only one-half of the CCA rate to be applied to net acquisitions to an asset class in the first year the assets are acquired. This is known as the **half-year rule**, which was implemented to reduce the incentive to purchase assets right at the end of the year and then claim a full year's CCA on them. Remember, CCA is a non-cash expense, but it reduces taxable income and therefore reduces current taxes payable. As a result, firms generally want to charge as much CCA as possible.

For example, suppose a company buys a new computer for $5,000. The CCA would be 45 percent of $5,000, or $2,250. Using the half-year rule, only $1,125 can be deducted in the first year. After deducting CCA of $1,125, the balance that remains to be depreciated (i.e., the associated UCC) is $3,875, which equals the asset class's UCC if it were the only asset in that class. For the following year, if no further class 45 assets were acquired, the CCA would be 45 percent of the UCC of $3,875, or $1,744. Notice that although 45 percent seems to be a high depreciation rate, it is applied to the UCC, which declines each year, so the firm will actually be taking CCA on this computer forever, even though its economic life may be only three years. Conversely, most of the asset's value will be depreciated within three years, and virtually all of it will be depreciated after six years, as illustrated in Figure 3-7. Notice that although CCA expenses technically go on forever, for practical purposes, they end after six years or so for this asset class. By year 10, the UCC is only $18 and CCA deductions are only $8.10, which is trivial when compared to the original investment of $5,000.

One advantage of using CCA asset classes or pools is that individual assets are not amortized separately, unless they are the only asset in the pool. This makes it easy to account for sales of assets: the proceeds are subtracted from, instead of added to, the pool, and the half-year rule comes into play only when the net acquisitions figure for an asset class is positive (i.e., when purchases exceed sales for that asset class). Example 3-1 illustrates how to apply the CCA system.

undepreciated capital cost (UCC) the undepreciated cost of assets, calculated by asset class and written off on a declining balance basis

half-year rule the rule by which Canada Revenue Agency allows only one-half of the CCA rate to be applied to net acquisitions to an asset class in the first year the assets are acquired

---

[19] There is no category for land, since it is a non-depreciable asset.

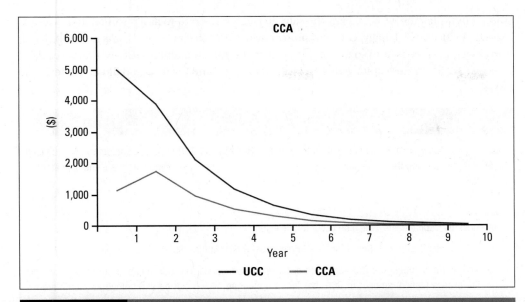

FIGURE 3-7 *CCA Expenses through Time*

EXAMPLE 3-1   Estimating CCA

A company purchases equipment for $650,000. The equipment is in asset class 38, which has a CCA rate of 30 percent (declining balance method). Assume this is the only asset in this class. Calculate the CCA associated with this asset class for the year of acquisition and for the subsequent two years.

Solution

For year one, apply the half-year rule, which states that only one-half of the CCA rate is applied in year 1. Therefore, we can calculate CCA in year 1 as

$$\text{CCA (year 1)} = (\$650{,}000) \times (0.3) \times (1/2) = \$97{,}500$$

Because the full CCA rate is applied to the UCC of the asset class in all years subsequent to the first year, we can calculate the CCA in years 2 and 3 as follows:

$$\text{UCC (beginning of year 2)} = \text{UCC (beginning of year 1)} - \text{CCA (year 1)} = \$650{,}000 - \$97{,}500 = \$552{,}500$$

$$\text{CCA (year 2)} = (\text{UCC}) \times (\text{CCA rate}) = (\$552{,}500) \times (0.3) = \$165{,}750$$

$$\text{UCC (beginning of year 3)} = \text{UCC (beginning of year 2)} - \text{CCA (year 2)} = \$552{,}500 - \$165{,}750 = \$386{,}750$$

$$\text{CCA (year 3)} = (\text{UCC}) \times (\text{CCA rate}) = (\$386{,}750) \times (0.3) = \$116{,}025$$

Other issues arise with respect to depreciable assets when they are sold. First, if the selling price is greater than the original capital cost, a **capital gain** arises, which is taxable. However, the converse is not true; when a depreciable capital asset is sold below its original purchase price, this does not generate a tax deductible **capital loss**, because this is expected (i.e., it is a depreciable asset and, as such, is expected to depreciate in value below its original cost). In fact, capital losses are generated only when a non-depreciable asset (such as land or financial assets) is sold at a price less than its original cost.

Aside from capital gains, additional tax consequences may arise in the form of **CCA recapture** or **terminal losses**. These may arise if the CCA asset class is terminated by selling the asset, which would occur only if there were no other assets included in that asset class for the firm. Under this scenario, the firm would have to pay additional taxes on "excess" CCA charged against the asset (or assets) if the salvage value is greater than the ending UCC for the asset (or asset class). The amount by which the salvage value exceeds the UCC is referred to as CCA recapture and is fully taxable.[20] However, if the salvage value is less than the ending UCC, the

capital gain a taxable gain realized when an asset is sold at a price greater than its original cost

capital loss a tax-deductible loss generated when a non-depreciable asset is sold at a price lower than its original cost

CCA recapture a tax on the amount by which the salvage value (sale price) of an asset exceeds the undepreciated capital cost; occurs only if the asset class is terminated or if an asset is sold for a price that exceeds the remaining UCC for that asset class

terminal loss a tax deduction equal to the amount by which the undepreciated capital cost exceeds the salvage value (sale price); occurs only if the asset class is terminated

---

[20] In other words, it is viewed as if the firm charged too much CCA (amortization), because the asset is sold for more than its depreciated book value for tax purposes (UCC). Therefore, the firm must pay back the amount of taxes it saved by charging too much CCA.

amount by which the UCC exceeds the salvage value is referred to as a terminal loss, which is fully tax deductible.[21] Finally, CCA recapture may occur even if an asset class is not terminated, if an asset (or assets) is (are) sold for a price that exceeds the remaining UCC for that asset class. Example 3-2 illustrates capital gains and CCA recapture, and Example 3-3 illustrates terminal losses.

EXAMPLE 3-2   Capital Gains and CCA Recapture

Assume that, during year 3, the company from Example 3-1 sells for $700,000 the equipment it purchased for $650,000. Estimate the tax consequences of this transaction, again assuming that this is the only asset in this class.

Solution

First, check for capital gains, which do occur in this example:

$$\text{Capital gains} = \text{Selling price} - \text{Original cost} = \$700,000 - \$650,000 = \$50,000$$

Next, determine whether a CCA recapture or terminal loss results. The CCA recapture (terminal loss) will equal the excess (deficit) amount of CCA that the firm charged, which can be determined as the difference between the lower of the selling price and the original cost, and the beginning UCC in year 3 (which was determined in Example 3-1):

$$\text{CCA recapture (terminal loss)} = \text{Lower of selling price and the original cost} - \text{UCC}$$

$$= \$650,000 - \$386,750 = \$263,250$$

This number is positive, so it represents a CCA recapture of $263,250. The firm must claim this taxable amount on its income tax return.

EXAMPLE 3-3   Terminal Loss

Ignore Example 3-2, and now assume that, during year 3, the company from Example 3-1 sells for $200,000 the equipment it purchased for $650,000. Estimate the tax consequences of this transaction, again assuming that this is the only asset in this class.

Solution

First, check for capital gains, which do not occur in this example, because the selling price of $200,000 is less than the original cost of $650,000.

Next, determine whether a CCA recapture or terminal loss results:

$$\text{CCA recapture (terminal loss)} = \text{Lower of selling price and the original cost} - \text{UCC}$$

$$= \$200,000 - \$386,750 = -\$186,750$$

The number is negative, so it represents a terminal loss of $186,750.

Firms often make temporary investments while waiting to pay bills. These assets generate investment income. Similarly, Tim Hortons has both debt and common shares outstanding, so it paid interest on its debt and dividends on its common shares. How investment income and expenses are treated for tax purposes is very important in finance. The basic rule is that interest is fully taxable when earned and fully deductible when paid. Usually, firms combine these two items into one "net interest" amount that is taxable.

Unlike interest, dividends are not tax deductible when paid; they are paid out of after-tax income. In return, when a Canadian corporation receives dividends from another Canadian corporation, they are not taxable, because they are paid out of the after-tax income of the

---

[21] In other words, the firm did not charge enough CCA, because the asset was sold below its book value for tax purposes (UCC). Therefore, the firm is permitted to amortize the asset to its selling price and deduct this charge for tax purposes.

issuing corporation. Otherwise, dividends flowing through multiple companies would attract tax at every stage, thereby increasing the effective tax rate. This represents another difference between accounting income and income for tax purposes. In particular, for accounting purposes, any dividends received are added to income. All else constant, the different tax treatment of interest and dividends means that companies prefer to pay interest (issue debt) and receive dividend income. We will return to this preference when we discuss corporate financing issues in Chapter 21. In terms of taxable income, it means that firms with significant dividend income and high CCA deductions will appear to pay lower rates of tax on their financial statements.

The basic tax rates for Canadian corporate income for 2012 consisted of a federal and a provincial rate, and are provided in Table 3-4. The basic rate of federal corporate income tax was 15 percent for active businesses—that is, for non-investment income—with a 4-percent reduction to 11 percent for small businesses earning less than $500,000.[22] Provincial taxes run from 0 percent for small businesses in Manitoba, for an overall rate of 11 percent, to 16 percent for larger businesses in Nova Scotia and Prince Edward Island, for an overall rate of 31 percent. **Operating losses** can also be important for corporations, since they can be used to reduce taxable income. If a company has a loss, it can carry it back three years to restate prior tax returns and get a refund on taxes that have been "overpaid." Alternatively, the operating loss can be stored and carried forward for 10 years to reduce future taxes payable.

operating loss loss generated when a firm's tax deductions are greater than its taxable income; losses can be carried back three years to get a refund on taxes paid or carried forward for 10 years to reduce future taxes payable

TABLE 3-4 Corporate Income Tax Rates (%)

		2012	2011	2010
Federal	General	15.00	16.50	18.00
	Small business CCPC	11.00	11.00	11.00
Alberta	General	10	10	10
	Small business CCPC	3	3	3
British Columbia	General	10	10	10.5
	Small business CCPC	2.5	2.5	2.5
Manitoba	General	12	12	12
	Small business CCPC	0	0	1/0
New Brunswick	General	10	10 (as of July 1, 2011)	11 (as of July 1, 2010)
	Small business CCPC	4.5	5	5
Newfoundland and Labrador	General	14	14	14
	Small business CCPC	4	4	4 (as of April 1, 2010)
Northwest Territories	General	11.5	11.5	11.5
	Small business CCPC	4	4	4
Nova Scotia	General	16	16	16
	Small business CCPC	4	4.5	5
Nunavut	General	12	12	12
	Small business CCPC	4	4	4
Ontario	General	11 (as of July 1, 2012)	11.5 (as of July 1, 2011)	12 (as of July 1, 2010)
	Small business CCPC	4.5	4.5	4.5 (after June 30, 2010)
Prince Edward Island	General	16	16	16
	Small business CCPC	1	1	1 (as of April 1, 2010)
Quebec	General	11.9	11.9	11.9
	Small business CCPC	8	8	8

continued

---

[22] Note that this is the federal limit. At the time of writing, provincial limits were $500,000 in every province or territory except Manitoba and Nova Scotia, where they were set at $400,000.

TABLE 3-4 Corporate Income Tax Rates (%) (*continued*)

		2012	2011	2010
Saskatchewan	General	12	12	12
	Small business CCPC	2	2 (as of July 1, 2011)	4.5
Yukon	General	15	15	15
	Small business CCPC	4	4	4

CCPC: Canadian-controlled private corporation

Source: Data from Canada Revenue Agency website, www.cra-arc.gc.ca, and provincial and territorial websites.

Personal Tax

Canada operates a progressive personal tax system in which the rates increase with income. For 2011, the basic federal income tax rates were the following:

- 15 percent on taxable income from $10,527 up to $41,544
- 22 percent on income between $41,544 and $83,088
- 26 percent on income between $83,088 and $128,800
- 29 percent on income above $128,800

In addition, each province operates a separate provincial tax system. It used to be that provincial taxes were a simple multiple of federal taxes, so that Ontario, for example, would add 52 percent (at its peak) of federal taxes. However, things have changed over the past 10 years, and most provinces have developed a parallel tax system.

Table 3-5 provides the 2011 federal and provincial marginal tax rates. In looking at the tax rates, remember that these rates are marginal rates, which means they are the rates on the next dollar of income. For example, the top federal rate of 29 percent is applied to every dollar of income above $128,800. Someone earning over $150,000 in Nova Scotia would pay this federal rate of 29 percent, plus a provincial rate of 21 percent—effectively, the governments are equal partners for these individuals. Remember too that interest income is taxed as ordinary income: the marginal tax rate for investment income differs depending on whether the individual earns interest from debt, dividends from common shares, or capital gains from increases in security prices.

Both cash and stock dividends received by individuals from Canadian corporations are taxable using the dividend tax credit system. The May 2006 budget revised the federal rules governing this system, increasing the amount of tax savings associated with dividend income. The system works in the following manner: first, the amount of the dividend is "grossed up" (by 45 percent as per the May 2006 budget versus 25 percent before that) to obtain the full taxable amount of dividend income included in taxable income. Then a federal dividend tax credit of 18.97 percent (previously 13.33 percent) and the appropriate provincial tax credit (which varies by province) are deducted from taxes paid. We will discuss how this interacts with corporate taxation later in the textbook (in chapters 21 and 22) when we consider how a firm should be financed. However, note for now that the tax rate on dividend income is always lower than that on interest income. This difference used to result in tax rates that were reduced by about 15 percent on average, but under the more recent rules the dividend tax rates will be 20 percent to 25 percent lower, depending on an investor's tax category and on the provincial rules.

TABLE 3-5 Provincial/Territorial Personal Income Tax Rates, 2011

Provincial / Territorial tax rates (combined chart)	
Provinces/Territories	**Rate(s)**
Federal	15% on the first $41,544 of taxable income, + 22% on the next $41,544 of taxable income, + 26% on the next $45,712 of taxable income, + 29% of taxable income over $128,800.
Alberta	10% of taxable income
British Columbia	5.06% on the first $36,146 of taxable income, + 7.7% on the next $36,147, + 10.5% on the next $10,708, + 12.29% on the next $17,786, + 14.7% on the amount over $100,787
Manitoba	10.8% on the first $31,000 of taxable income, + 12.75% on the next $36,000, + 17.4% on the amount over $67,000
Newfoundland and Labrador	7.7% on the first $31,904 of taxable income, + 12.5% on the next $31,903, + 13.3% on the amount over $63,807
New Brunswick	9.1% on the first $37,150 of taxable income, + 12.1% on the next $37,150, + 12.4% on the next $46,496, + 14.3% on the amount over $120,796
Northwest Territories	5.9% on the first $37,626 of taxable income, + 8.6% on the next $37,627, + 12.2% on the next $47,092, + 14.05% on the amount over $122,345
Nova Scotia	8.79% on the first $29,590 of taxable income, + 14.95% on the next $29,590, + 16.67% on the next $33,820 + 17.5% on the next $57,000 21% on the amount over $150,000
Nunavut	4% on the first $39,612 of taxable income, + 7% on the next $39,612, + 9% on the next $49,576, + 11.5% on the amount over $128,800
Ontario	5.05% on the first $37,774 of taxable income, + 9.15% on the next $37,776, + 11.16% on the amount over $75,550
Prince Edward Island	9.8% on the first $31,984 of taxable income, + 13.8% on the next $31,985, + 16.7% on the amount over $63,969

continued

TABLE 3-5 Provincial/Territorial Personal Income Tax Rates, 2011 (*continued*)

Provinces/Territories	Rate(s)
Quebec	16% on the first $41,100 of taxable income, + 20% on the next $41,100, + 24% on the amount over $80,200
Saskatchewan	11% on the first $40,919 of taxable income, + 13% on the next $75,992, + 15% on the amount over $116,911
Yukon	7.04% on the first $41,544 of taxable income, + 9.68% on the next $41,544, + 11.44% on the next $45,712, + 12.76% on the amount over $128,800

Source: Data from Canada Revenue Agency website www.cra-arc.gc.ca.

The final source of investment income is capital gains. These are currently taxed on the basis that 50 percent of the capital gain (i.e., the taxable capital gain) is included as ordinary income. As a result, the effective rate is simply half that of ordinary income. If an individual incurs a capital loss, it can only be used to offset capital gains income, but not ordinary income. That being said, if there is an excess of capital losses, it can be carried back three years, to reduce any taxes paid on previous capital gains, or carried forward indefinitely. Of course, tax rates and tax rules are constantly changing, and we suggest that you check the newest tax rules.

CONCEPT REVIEW QUESTIONS

1. Explain how to calculate the CCA expense for an asset class in a given year.
2. Explain why a firm cannot claim CCA recapture and a terminal loss for the same asset class in the same year.
3. Why would firms prefer to receive dividend income and make interest payments rather than make dividend payments and receive interest payments?
4. What form of investment income has the highest tax rate in Canada?

SUMMARY

This chapter provides a basic overview of accounting statements, beginning with a discussion of the principles on which they are constructed. We discuss the importance of using generally accepted accounting principles (GAAP) and the role of international financial reporting standards (IFRS) in creating financial statements that adhere to somewhat uniform standards. We then illustrate how to apply these principles by developing a simple set of financial statements from a series of transactions that an entrepreneur makes in setting up a business. We look at the financial statements of a large company (Tim Hortons Inc.) to show that these simple principles are the same basic ones needed to understand the financial statements of large corporations. Finally, because much accounting revolves around tax issues, we conclude the chapter with a brief discussion of the Canadian tax system.

SUMMARY OF LEARNING OBJECTIVES

3.1 Define international financial reporting standards (IFRS) and state their significance for Canadian firms.

International financial reporting standards (IFRS) set out the basic conventions for preparing financial statements in Canada and in many countries around the world. They are intended to ensure that a firm's financial position is fairly represented to those who use the firm's financial statements (e.g., shareholders and creditors) and that these users are able to understand the firm's transactions. The emergence of a common set of international standards is becoming more important in today's global environment as it allows easier comparability of financial statements across companies based in different countries.

3.2 Organize a firm's transactions, and explain what are the most important accounting principles related to this task.

The organization of a firm's transactions is presented in section 3.2. When organizing a firm's transactions, the most important accounting principles are:

The entity concept: The accounting is for an economic entity, such as a corporation.

The going concern principle: The statements must reflect the accounts on the basis that the firm is not in imminent threat of bankruptcy; otherwise, they have to be qualified.

A period of analysis: The statements are for a particular period of time, such as a year-end balance sheet or quarterly statement.

A monetary value: In Canada, accountants use historical cost accounting, in which transactions are for the dollars actually involved, with no restatement for inflationary effects.

The matching principle: The revenues must be matched against the costs that generated those revenues.

Revenue recognition: Revenues are only recognized when there is a verifiable sale.

3.3 Prepare a firm's financial statements.

The preparation of a firm's financial statements is presented in section 3.3.

3.4 Analyze a firm's financial statements.

A firm can be analyzed by comparing its historical statements with its current statements and by comparing its financial statements with those of other firms in the same industry. An analysis of the financial statements of Tim Hortons Inc. is presented in section 3.4.

3.5 Describe the Canadian tax system and explain the differences between how a corporation and an individual are taxed.

Canadian taxes are levied on both personal and corporate income, but the government recognizes the potential for double taxation of income earned through a corporation and has designed a partially integrated system. For a corporation, amortization and interest payments are deducted before tax is paid, but dividends are paid after tax; for an individual, there are different deductibles—interest payment is taxed as regular income, half of capital gains is taxed, and dividends are taxed but with a dividend tax credit.

KEY TERMS

balance sheet, p. 70
capital gain, p. 93
capital loss, p. 93
cash flow from operations (CFO), p. 81
cash flow statement, p. 79
CCA recapture, p. 93
current assets, p. 87
current liabilities, p. 88
depreciation/amortization, p. 79
free cash flow, p. 81
generally accepted accounting principles
   (GAAP), p. 64

half-year rule, p. 92
income statement, p. 76
International Financial Reporting Standards
   (IFRS), p. 64
liquidity, p. 71
operating loss, p. 95
terminal loss, p. 93
traditional cash flow, p. 81
undepreciated capital cost (UCC), p. 92

QUESTIONS AND PRACTICE PROBLEMS

Multiple Choice Questions

1. Which of the following is *correct*?
   a. In Canada, GAAP is contained in the Canadian Institute of Chartered Accountants Handbook.
   b. The differences between Canadian GAAP and American GAAP have become more important in the past two decades.
   c. Canadian GAAP is issued by the International Accounting Standards Board (IASB).
   d. Canada has adopted US GAAP.

2. What is the correct book entry when a firm increases its inventories by using its sound credit with the supplier?
   a. Credit inventories and debit cash.
   b. Credit inventories and debit accounts payable.
   c. Debit inventories and credit cash.
   d. Debit inventories and credit accounts payable.

3. The *CICA Handbook* contains the accounting principles of:
   a. Canada
   b. the United States
   c. all countries
   d. Canada and the United States

4. Which of the following is not a GAAP principle?
   a. the entity concept
   b. a period of analysis
   c. the idea that revenues must be matched against the costs that generated those revenues
   d. the idea that revenues are only recognized when cash is collected

5. Which of the following assets does *not* qualify for capital cost allowance (CCA)?
   a. land
   b. manufacturing equipment
   c. building
   d. computer

6. Which of the following is a source of cash inflows?
   a. decrease of property, plant, and equipment
   b. increase of accounts receivable
   c. payment of dividends
   d. decrease of accounts payable

7. Which of the following is a non-cash item?
   a. receipt of dividends
   b. payment of interest
   c. amortization
   d. purchase of inventory

8. Which of the following equations represents free cash flow?
   a. Net income + Depreciation + Deferred income taxes
   b. Net income + Depreciation + Deferred income taxes +/– Change in working capital
   c. Net income + Depreciation + Deferred income taxes +/– Change in working capital – Capital expenditures
   d. Net income + Depreciation + Deferred income taxes +/– Change in working capital – Capital expenditures +/– Financing cash flows

9. Which of the following is *not* classified as cash flow from financing?
   a. issuance of long-term debt
   b. repurchase of capital stock
   c. payment of dividends
   d. purchase of inventory

10. Which of the following is a cash outflow?
    a. decrease in inventories
    b. decrease in accounts receivable
    c. issue of common shares
    d. decrease in accounts payable

11. Which of the following is not classified as cash flow from operations?
    a. issuance of long-term bonds
    b. sale of goods
    c. purchase of inventories
    d. payment of employee salaries

12. Which of the following is most likely to report non-controlling interest in its balance sheet? (Non-controlling interest (NCI) is the portion of equity ownership in a subsidiary not attributable to the parent company, which has a controlling interest (greater than 50 percent but less than 100 percent) and consolidates the subsidiary's financial results with its own.)
    a. a subsidiary firm
    b. a firm that controls 20 percent of another firm
    c. a firm that controls 80 percent of another firm
    d. government

13. Which of the following is not a current asset?
    a. cash
    b. bonds
    c. inventories
    d. land

14. Capital gains occur in which of the following cases?
    a. Selling price of the asset < Initial cost of the asset
    b. Selling price of the asset > Initial cost of the asset
    c. Selling price of the asset < Ending UCC
    d. Selling price of the asset > Ending UCC

15. Which of the following statements is *false*?
    a. Canada operates a progressive personal tax system.
    b. When dividends are received, they are preferentially taxed.
    c. When interest is earned, it is fully taxable.
    d. Ontario residents and Quebec residents pay the same federal and provincial tax.

Practice Problems

16. State three of the most basic principles of GAAP in the *CICA Handbook*.

17. The balance sheet for a small firm shows total assets of $429,500 and total liabilities of $379,000. What is the shareholders' equity?

18. The firm in Practice Problem 17 had retained earnings of $5,000 at the beginning of the year. Its net income for the year was $7,500, and it paid out $4,000 in dividends. What are its retained earnings at the end of the year?

19. Randy's Rowboats Ltd. purchased and began to use its first six rowboats for a total cost of

$2,400. Randy believes the boats can be used for five years, providing the company with equal value each year. After five years, the boats will be worthless.

a. Use your best judgement to determine a reasonable amount to charge to amortization expense each year.

b. Find the book value (cost less amortization) of the boats for each of the five years they will be used.

c. If the company expects to sell the rowboats for $400 after five years, determine the reasonable amount to charge to amortization expense each year.

20. The rowboats Randy purchased (see Practice Problem 19) are a Class 7 asset, so they have a CCA rate of 15 percent. Determine the amount of the capital cost allowance for each of the five years the boats will be used (include the "half-year rule").

21. List the correct bookkeeping entries when a firm sells $40,000 worth of inventories for $70,000 using credit sales. (Ignore the tax effect.)

22. Based on the figures in practice problems 17 and 18, how much money did the shareholders actually invest in the firm (i.e., what is the value of the capital stock)?

Use the following information to answer practice problems 23 to 28.

Twin brothers David and Douglas Finn started a small business from their college dormitory room. Finns' Fridges purchased several small refrigerators to rent to other students for use in their rooms. At the end of their first year of operations, the brothers' records showed the information below.

Current assets (cash and accounts receivable)	$2,000
Interest payable	200
Other current liabilities	800
Property and equipment (net)	4,000
Long-term liabilities	3,200
Owners' equity	1,800
Revenues	2,000
Interest expense	200
Amortization expense	1,000

23. Construct a balance sheet and income statement for the business, assuming no income tax.

24. Based on the balance sheet you created, how much working capital does Finns' Fridges have?

25. Suppose Finns' Fridges is subject to corporate income tax at a rate of 30 percent. What will the company's net income be after tax?

26. David and Douglas invested $500 each to capitalize Finns' Fridges. To allow for future flexibility (such as selling shares to other investors), they placed a "par value" of $10 on each share; thus each brother owns 50 shares. Based on the net income figure from Practice Problem 23, assuming no tax, what were the earnings per share (EPS) of Finns' Fridges for its first year of operations?

✱ 27. David Finn notices that the local appliance store is now charging $210 for the same model of refrigerator his company bought for $200. Given that Finns' Fridges purchased 25 of these refrigerators, what should the company's balance sheet show as the value of property and equipment?

✱ 28. The Finn brothers are concerned that the financial statements for Finns' Fridges (see practice problems 23 to 27) don't reflect the true state of affairs. The company's 25 customers were charged $10 for rent at the end of each month. Now that the academic year is over, five of these customers (students) have vacated their dormitory rooms without paying the last month's rent on the refrigerators. Moreover, one student seems to have taken the refrigerator with him when he left! Douglas doubts the company will ever receive the late rental fees or retrieve the stolen fridge. Based on this, construct a new balance sheet and income statement for the company.

29. Corine's Candies Inc. paid dividends of $1.2 million during 2012. However, the company needed extra cash to open new stores, so it issued $1.3 million in new stock. What was Corine's cash flow from financing in 2012?

30. In 2012, a firm's revenue is $90,000, cost of sales is $40,000, rent is $10,000, depreciation is $2,000, and interest paid is $2,000. Its tax rate is 35 percent.
    a. Construct an income statement based on this information.
    b. If the company pays 30 percent of its net income as dividends, what is the increase in retained earnings for 2012?

31. Calculate cash flow from operations for Tina's Business Inc. using the following information.

Net income	$80,000
Depreciation	6,000
Deferred income taxes	2,000
Decrease in inventories	10,000
Decrease in accounts receivable	2,000
Decrease in accounts payable	1,500
Decrease in accruals	2,200
Decrease in prepaids	3,600

32. Estimate cash flow from operations for KER Inc. using the following information.

Net income	$90,000
Depreciation	10,000
Deferred income taxes	5,000
Increase in inventories	20,000
Decrease in accounts receivable	1,000
Increase in accounts payable	2,000
Decrease in accruals	2,500
Decrease in prepaids	5,000

33. The balance sheet for a small corporation shows total assets of $425,600, common equity of $125,000, and retained earnings of $85,000. Calculate the total liabilities.

34. A firm had retained earnings of $8,000 at the beginning of the year. Its net income for the year was $9,300, and its dividend payout ratio is 25 percent. What are its retained earnings at the end of the year?

35. A firm's net earnings are $105 million and it has 50 million shares outstanding. Determine its earnings per share.

36. A firm borrowed $2 million and paid 10 percent interest this year. It also paid a dividend of $1 per share on 500,000 shares outstanding. What is the firm's cash flow from financing?

37. In year 1, a firm had cash and cash equivalents of $100,000, accounts receivable of $25,000, and inventories of $13,000. In year 2, it had cash and cash equivalents of $80,000, accounts

receivable of $20,000, and inventories of $15,000. Calculate the change in total current assets in dollars and as a percentage.

Use the following information to answer practice problems 38 to 40.

Year 1 and Year 2 Balance Sheet ($ million)					
	Y1	**Y2**		**Y1**	**Y2**
Cash	100	112	Accounts payable	400	350
Accounts receivable	330	234	Notes payable	390	370
Inventory	410	435	Total	790	720
Total	840	781	Long-term debt	500	550
Net fixed assets	1,556	1,888	Owners' equity		
			Common stock	550	599
			Retained earnings	556	800
			Total	1,106	1,399
Total assets	2,396	2,669	Total liabilities and owners' equity	2,396	2,669

38. What is the firm's net working capital in year 2?

39. What are the firm's changes in net working capital in year 2?

✿ 40. The firm's dividend payout ratio is 40 percent. What was the firm's year 2 net income?

41. The firm has 150 million shares outstanding. What is the firm's year 2 earnings per share?

42. Using the net income and earnings per common share (EPS) figures from Tim Hortons' income statement (Figure 3-5), determine how many shares (approximately) the company had outstanding at the end of 2011.

43. Based on Tim Hortons' balance sheet (Figure 3-4), the firm's total current assets changed between the last two recent years. Which component of the current assets changed the most? By what dollar amount and percentage did it increase?

44. Tim Hortons paid $0.68 in dividends for each common share outstanding during 2011. Use the total "Dividend payments to common shareholders" figure from the firm's cash flow statement (Figure 3-6) to determine how many shares (approximately) the company had outstanding in 2011. Compare this number to your answer from Practice Problem 42.

45. The income statement for Tim Hortons (Figure 3-5) shows income before income taxes is $543.602 million in 2011 and income taxes are $157.854 million. What is the average tax rate (tax paid as a percentage of net income)?

46. What was the growth rate of sales at Tim Hortons Inc. in 2010 and 2011? Did the sales growth rate increase or decrease?

47. Mrs. Kwan lives in Ontario. Her annual salary is $195,000. What is the marginal tax on her salary?

48. Omar's business purchased several pieces of machinery some time ago for $25,000. At the beginning of the current year, this pool of assets had a UCC of $15,000. During the year, Omar decided to sell all the assets from this pool. For each of the three sale prices below, determine if the firm will report a capital gain and calculate the amount (if any) of CCA recapture and/or terminal loss.
   a. $30,000
   b. $20,000
   c. $10,000

49. Suppose firms A and B have identical revenues and operating expenses, so that each has earnings before amortization and taxes of exactly $1 million. Both firms will report amortization of $200,000 on their public financial statements. On its tax return, firm A claims $200,000 for CCA, whereas firm B is able to claim $400,000. Based on a tax rate of 30 percent of taxable income, how much tax will each firm pay?

50. What is the apparent tax rate (tax paid as a percentage of net income) for firms A and B in Practice Problem 49?

51. Given the following income statement for GG Inc. and the adjustments to be made, rebuild its income statement.
    a. GG Inc. should use the straight-line depreciation method, which incurred only $1,500 in depreciation.
    b. GG Inc. forgot to book $4,000 in salary paid during the year.
    c. GG Inc. should use the new corporate tax rate, which is 30 percent.

GG Inc. Income Statement for Y2012 (unadjusted)	
Revenue	$90,000
Cost of sales	10,000
Rent	10,000
Depreciation	2,500
Interest	2,000
Income before taxes	65,500
Taxes paid	26,200
Net income	39,300

52. Prince Rupert Fly 'n' Fish Inc. purchases one small plane in its first year of business for $70,000. In year 2, it purchases another plane for $90,000. Find the UCC at the end of year 3 if the CCA rate for aircraft is 25 percent.

53. Suppose Prince Rupert Fly 'n' Fish Inc. (see Practice Problem 52) decides to sell its first aircraft for $50,000 in year 2 (purchased for $70,000 in year 1). As before, the second plane costs $90,000 and is bought and put in service in year 2. Find the UCC at the end of year 3.

54. Tina's Business Inc. bought machines some time ago for $30,000. She decided to sell all the assets from this pool at the end of this year. The pool of assets had a UCC of $5,000 before the sale, and the whole asset class was sold for $40,000. Calculate the amount of any capital gain, and calculate the amount (if any) of CCA recapture and/or terminal loss.

55. Suppose firms A and B have identical revenues and operating expenses, so that each has earnings before amortization and taxes of $10 million. Both firms will report amortization of $1 million on their public financial statements. On its tax return, firm A claims $1 million for CCA, whereas firm B claims $2 million. The tax rate is 30 percent of taxable income.
    a. Is it legal to report different amortization for financial statement and for tax purposes?
    b. Which firm pays higher taxes?
    c. How much tax will each firm pay?
    d. What is the net income for each firm?

56. Tina's Business Inc. purchases one machine in its first year of business for $750,000. In year 2, it purchases another machine for $625,000. The CCA rate for these assets is 30 percent.
    a. Find the beginning UCC, CCA, and ending UCC in years 1 to 3 for the first machine.
    b. Find the beginning UCC, CCA, and ending UCC in years 2 and 3 for the second machine.
    c. Find the UCC at the end of year 3 for both machines in total.

57. Kash Kow Inc. pays out all its after-tax earnings to shareholders in the form of dividends. Suppose that in 2012 the company earned $1 per share before tax. Corporate income tax

was paid at a rate of 25 percent. For a high-income earner living in Ontario, the personal tax on dividend income was 31.34 percent. How much of the original $1 per share would such a shareholder have left after all the taxes were paid?

58. GG Inc. just bought a computer for $2,000. It belongs to asset class 45 and has a CCA rate of 45 percent. Calculate the first-year and second-year CCA expenses. (Assume this computer is the only asset in this asset class.)

4 | Financial Statement Analysis and Forecasting

LEARNING OBJECTIVES

4.1 Identify the issues that need to be considered in applying consistent financial analysis.

4.2 Explain why return on equity is one of the key financial ratios used to assess a firm's performance, and show how it can be used to provide information about three areas of a firm's operations.

4.3 Describe, calculate, and evaluate the key ratios relating to financial leverage.

4.4 Describe, calculate, and evaluate the key ratios relating to financial efficiency.

4.5 Describe, calculate, and evaluate the key ratios relating to financial productivity.

4.6 Describe, calculate, and evaluate the key ratios relating to financial liquidity.

4.7 Describe, calculate, and evaluate the key ratios relating to the valuation of a company.

4.8 Explain why financial forecasting is critical for both management and external parties, and explain how to prepare financial forecasts using the percentage of sales method.

4.9 Explain how external financing requirements are related to sales growth, profitability, dividend payouts, and sustainable growth rates.

4.10 Apply financial forecasting to a real company.

Canada's combined federal and provincial net debt will pass $1.1 trillion at 11 p.m. ET on October 3 [2011], according to a recent calculation. But while some observers are sounding the alarm bells about the country's balance sheet, others say Canada's fiscal situation is not nearly as bad as it may seem.

But according to Chris Ragan, an expert in monetary policy at McGill University, when it comes to government debt, "It is misleading to look at the total amount."

Much more relevant to Canada's fiscal well-being, says Ragan, is the debt-to-GDP ratio, which he describes as "fairly low."

"If you look at debt as a fraction of GDP, what you're doing is you're scaling it to the size of the economy," he says. "GDP is basically the tax base of governments. So if you look at debt as a fraction of GDP, you're getting an indication of the government's ability to service that debt."

Despite rising levels of government debt, Canada's combined federal and provincial debt-to-GDP ratio was 57.9 percent in 2010–2011—a far cry from the situation in Greece, where the debt-to-GDP ratio is expected to surpass 160 percent this year.

But Ragan says that an even more illustrative ratio is Canada's net government debt-to-GDP ratio, which accounts for existing financial assets. For 2010, he puts that figure at 44 percent.

Canada's current net debt-to-GDP ratio is less than half of what it was in the mid-1990s, when fear of hitting the so-called debt wall prompted drastic spending cuts.

Source: Mendleson, Rachel, "Canada's Public Debt Hits $1.1 Trillion, But That May Not Be as Bad as It Sounds." HuffPost Canada Business, October 3, 2011. Retrieved from www.huffingtonpost.ca/2011/10/03/canada-debt-cfib-road-to-greece_n_992480.html. By Rachel Mendleson, © 2011 TheHuffingtonPost. com, Inc.

CHAPTER 4 **PREVIEW**

If accounting is the language of business, what is it saying to us? This chapter answers this question and shows how external interested parties can use financial statements to evaluate a firm. Ratio analysis is part of this process, as ratios provide insight into the aggregate numbers, as alluded to in the chapter-opening vignette. Of course, no one uses financial statements in isolation; they look at additional information on the firm and the macroeconomic environment, and compare the firm's statements across time and with members of its peer group, such as other firms in the same industry or industry averages. The method of analyzing a firm's statements also depends on why it is being done. A bank making a short-term loan will look at different factors than would the same bank making a long-term loan. Further, in both cases, the bank will look at different factors than would an equity analyst trying to value the company's common shares.[1] In turn, both bank and equity analyst will look at different factors than would another firm interested in buying the first one or possibly lowering its prices to heighten competition. However, in all cases, a major source of information is the firm's financial statements, and financial analysis provides a standard framework of evaluation. Once the basics of financial analysis are understood, the same tools can be used to forecast whether the firm is likely to use or need cash over a forecast horizon.

Financial analysis is clearly important for the firm. Of course, financial analysis is also critical for a firm's creditors, like the bank, and for investment dealers, who need to advise the firm on its financing issues. In this chapter, we will introduce the basics of financial analysis and forecasting.

4.1 CONSISTENT FINANCIAL ANALYSIS

Learning Objective 4.1
Identify the issues that need to be considered in applying consistent financial analysis.

In Chapter 3, you learned about the significant role that judgement plays in the preparation of a firm's financial statements. With so much judgement involved, it is reasonable to ask whether financial analysis based on these statements is a bit like building a sand castle. To some extent it is, and this has led to significant efforts by third parties to reconcile and standardize the financial statements of firms, as discussed in Chapter 3. However, despite efforts to harmonize accounting standards, important differences still persist, as reflected in generally accepted accounting principles (GAAP). These differences have forced users of financial statements to attempt an external reconciliation of GAAP. This is important because users of financial statements need to be able to compare the financial statements of companies in the same industry that are based in different countries. For example, two of the world's largest oil and gas companies are Exxon Mobil Corporation (United States) and BP PLC (United Kingdom). How can their financial statements be compared if they are prepared using different forms of GAAP? On the other hand, as more countries adopt International Financial Reporting Standards (IFRS), the transition to these standards, should enhance comparability in the long term.

Aside from the use of different accounting standards (i.e., different forms of GAAP) in preparing financial statements, an additional complication arises because there are no generally accepted financial ratios. Thus, it is important, when looking at ratios generated by another

---

[1] It is possible for the same investment bank's credit and equity analysts to offer different advice for their debt and equity clients, since their perspectives differ.

party, to determine how they are calculated. Even some of the most basic ratios, such as return on equity, can vary when calculated by different institutions, even if the input data are the same.[2] Other ratios, such as the debt ratio, have multiple definitions and can vary quite widely in their calculation and, hence, their interpretation. Acting on the assumption that all ratios are prepared on the same basis can lead to misleading conclusions, and it is essential to always compare "apples with apples" and not "oranges."

CONCEPT REVIEW QUESTIONS

1. What difficulties do analysts face when trying to compare the financial statements of firms that are based in different countries?

2. Why should people be aware of the precise definition of a financial ratio employed by those who calculate the ratio?

4.2 A FRAMEWORK FOR FINANCIAL ANALYSIS

Return on Equity (ROE) and the DuPont System

Return on equity (ROE) is one of the most commonly referenced ratios, and for good reason: it measures the return earned by the equity holders on their investment in the company. It is calculated as the net income (NI) divided by shareholders' equity (SE), as shown in Equation 4-1.[3]

$$ROE = \frac{NI}{SE}$$

[4-1]

We will calculate the 2011 ROE for Tim Hortons Inc., using the figures reported in the company's financial statements, which were included in Chapter 3, and we will do the same for the other ratios introduced in this chapter. In 2011, NI was $385.748 million, while SE was $1,154.433 million, so Tim Hortons' ROE was as follows:

$$ROE = \frac{NI}{SE} = \frac{385.748}{1,154.433} = 33.41\%$$

This is a healthy ROE figure that would be rated above average, which suggests that Tim Hortons lies at the upper end of corporate profitability in Canada (or anywhere else for that matter).

> **Learning Objective 4.2**
> Explain why return on equity is one of the key financial ratios used to assess a firm's performance, and show how it can be used to provide information about three areas of a firm's operations.
>
> **return on equity (ROE)** the return earned by equity holders on their investment in the company; net income divided by shareholders' equity

---

[2] This is not because they make mistakes but because they employ different definitions of the same ratio.

[3] ROE can also be defined as NI available to the common shareholders (i.e., NI − preferred dividends) divided by common equity (CE). For Tim Hortons, there is no difference, because the company does not have any preferred equity. For some firms, it can make a difference.

ROE is not a "pure" financial ratio because it involves dividing an income statement (flow) item by a balance sheet (stock) item.[4] As a result, some people calculate the ROE as NI over the "average" SE—that is, the average of the starting and ending SE. This adjustment acknowledges that NI is earned throughout the year, so it makes sense to divide by an average of SE to recognize that not all of those funds were invested throughout the year. For example, the ending SE is partly the result of the retained earnings for the year, which, in turn, is dependent on the net income for the year; however, with three years of data, the use of the average SE causes the loss of an observation. This is why most analysts use the ending SE as the denominator simply to get more estimates of the ROE; that way, they can assess a trend over time. However, this tends to understate a firm's profitability on average, because the ending SE will usually exceed the average for the year if the firm is profitable.

The next step in financial analysis is to understand where Tim Hortons' ROE came from. The most popular approach to "decomposing" ROE is attributable to the DuPont Corporation, which pioneered a variation of the expansion of the ROE shown in Figure 4-1.

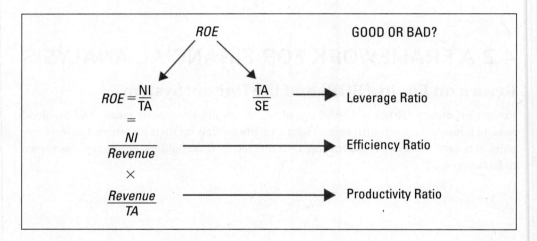

FIGURE 4-1 *DuPont System*

The DuPont system provides a good starting point for any financial analysis and is commonly included in research reports as a way of summarizing a firm's key financial ratios. As an example, Table 4-1 shows the DuPont information for Bombardier Inc. over the 2002 to 2011 period, as provided by Morningstar, Inc. We do not comment on the items in the table now, but you will see how all the reported figures and ratios are related as you proceed through this section, with particular emphasis on the 2011 numbers for Tim Hortons.

TABLE 4-1 Morningstar Ratios for Bombardier

Profitability	2002-01	2003-01	2004-01	2005-01	2006-01	2007-01	2008-01	2009-01	2010-01	2011-01
Tax Rate %	—	—	—	—	10	27.46	27.79	20.82	22.73	17.4
Net Margin %	1.81	−2.6	−0.56	−0.68	1.69	1.62	1.65	5.11	3.6	4.26
Asset Turnover (Average)	0.88	0.85	0.84	0.81	0.78	0.82	0.89	0.94	0.91	0.79
Return on Assets %	1.58	−2.21	−0.47	−0.55	1.33	1.33	1.48	4.82	3.28	3.38
Financial Leverage (Average)	7.32	13.15	9.42	10.29	8.41	7.79	7.42	9.7	6.34	5.97
Return on Equity %	10.41	−21.01	−5.14	−5.41	12.36	10.75	11.21	40.58	25.15	20.74
Return on Invested Capital %	2.84	−4.44	−1.04	−1.23	3.18	3.36	3.95	15.14	10.22	9.39

Source: Data from Morningstar website, www.morningstar.ca.

---

[4] "Pure" ratios involve dividing an income statement item by another income statement item, or dividing a balance sheet item by another balance sheet item.

The DuPont approach defines the firm's **return on assets (ROA)** as NI divided by total assets (TA), as shown in Equation 4-2.

$$ROA = \frac{NI}{TA}$$

[4-2]

return on assets (ROA) net income divided by total assets

For Tim Hortons in 2011,

$$ROA = \frac{NI}{TA} = \frac{385.748}{2,203.950} = 17.5\%$$

If the ROA is multiplied by TA and divided by SE, the TAs cancel out and produce the ROE. So what is TA divided by SE? This is called the **leverage ratio**, and it measures how many dollars of total assets are supported by each dollar of SE, or how many times the firm has "leveraged" the capital provided by the shareholders into total financing. It is shown in Equation 4-3.

$$Leverage = \frac{TA}{SE}$$

[4-3]

leverage ratio total assets divided by shareholders' equity; it measures how many dollars of total assets are supported by each dollar of shareholders' equity, or how many times the firm has leveraged the capital provided by the shareholders into total financing

The 2011 leverage ratio for Tim Hortons is as follows:

$$Leverage = \frac{TA}{SE} = \frac{2,203.950}{1,154.433} = 1.9091 \text{ or } 190.91\%$$

Thus, Tim Hortons has leveraged every dollar of shareholders' equity into $1.91 of total financing by using debt and other forms of liabilities to help finance its operations.

We interpret this ratio as saying that every dollar of total assets earned an ROA of 17.5 percent, but the shareholders didn't provide all this financing. They provided about 52.4 percent of the money to buy the firm's total assets (i.e., 1/1.9091)—that is, the firm leveraged each dollar of shareholders' equity by 1.9091. As a result, the ROE is the ROA of 17.5 percent multiplied by the leverage ratio of 1.9091, which gives an ROE of 33.41 percent. What this figure means is that part of the reason for Tim Hortons' high ROE is that it is extremely profitable and has a high ROA of 17.5 percent. The rest of the story is that Tim Hortons magnified this ROA using financial leverage. This is why, when we analyze corporate performance, we look at ROE, ROA, and a series of ratios that measure **financial leverage**, since how the firm finances its operations is very important.

financial leverage the use of capital provided by shareholders to increase total financing

We can now decompose ROA into two of its major components: the firm's **net profit margin** and its (asset) **turnover ratio**, which we show in Equation 4-4 and Equation 4-5.

$$Net\ profit\ margin = \frac{NI}{Revenues}$$

[4-4]

net profit margin part of return on assets; net income divided by revenues

$$Turnover\ ratio = \frac{Revenues}{TA}$$

[4-5]

turnover ratio part of return on assets; revenues divided by total assets

Multiplying the two ratios together cancels the revenues figure on the bottom of net profit margin with the revenues figure on the top of the turnover ratio, leaving NI/TA, or, simply, the ROA, as shown in Equation 4-6.

$$ROA = \frac{NI}{TA} = \frac{NI}{Revenues} \times \frac{Revenues}{TA}$$

[4-6]

For Tim Hortons, the 2011 net profit margin or (return on revenues) was as follows:

$$\text{Net profit margin} = \frac{NI}{Revenues} = \frac{385.748}{2,852.966} = 13.52\%$$

So Tim Hortons made profits of over 13 percent of revenues earned. We look at the net profit margin to determine how *efficiently* the firm converts revenues into profits. Later in the chapter, we will expand our analysis to include additional efficiency ratios.

So if every dollar of revenue earned Tim Hortons 13.5 percent in profits, how many dollars of revenues did it generate from each dollar invested in assets, or, alternatively, what was its turnover ratio?

$$\text{Turnover ratio} = \frac{Revenues}{TA} = \frac{2,852.966}{2,203.950} = 1.2945$$

For 2011, with total assets of $2,203.950 million, Tim Hortons generated revenues of $2,852.966 million. In other words, each dollar of assets generated about $1.2945 in revenues. The turnover ratio is a productivity ratio, as it measures how productive the firm is in generating revenues from its assets. As you will see, several productivity ratios can be calculated to determine the main drivers of this overall productivity.

Now we have the major ratios of the DuPont formula. Putting them all together produces Equation 4-7.[5]

[4-7]
$$ROE = \frac{NI}{SE} = \frac{NI}{Revenues} \times \frac{Revenues}{TA} \times \frac{TA}{SE}$$
$$= \text{Net profit margin} \times \text{Turnover ratio} \times \text{Leverage ratio}$$

For Tim Hortons in 2011,

$$ROE = \frac{NI}{SE} = \frac{NI}{Revenues} \times \frac{Revenues}{TA} \times \frac{TA}{SE}$$

$$= 0.1352 \times 1.2945 \times 1.909 = 33.41\% \text{ (as calculated at the start of this section)}$$

Each dollar of equity supported $1.909 of assets, which, in turn, generated $1.2945 in revenues, which, in turn, generated a net profit margin of 13.52 percent. In other words, overall, the ROE is determined by leverage, turnover, and profit margin. So what does this mean?

Interpreting Ratios

A single ratio on its own provides little information. To judge whether a given ratio is "good" or "bad" requires some basis for comparison. Two bases are commonly used for comparison:

1. the company's historical ratios, or the *trend* in its ratios

2. *comparable* companies—for this purpose, we can use a similar company or use industry average ratios

Table 4-2 includes Tim Hortons' DuPont analysis ratios for 2008–11.

---

[5]This is the simplest and most commonly used version of the DuPont system. There are other versions, which we do not discuss here, many of which break ROE into five or more components.

TABLE 4-2 Tim Hortons' DuPont Ratios

	2011	2010	2009	2008
ROE	0.3341	0.4486*	0.2547	0.2496
ROA	0.175	0.2608*	0.1527	0.1429
Net profit margin	0.1352	0.2551*	0.131	0.1393
Turnover	1.2945	1.0222	1.1645	1.0256
Leverage	1.9091	1.7204	1.6678	1.7473

* Excluding one-time gain: ROE = 0.2538; ROA = 0.1475; net profit margin = 0.1438

Often, unique factors drive a particular firm's ratios and make them difficult to compare with the ratios of other firms. For example, if a firm has made a recent large acquisition of another firm, key profitability and turnover ratios often drop. For this reason, it is important to look at a firm's ratios over time. What we can observe from Table 4-2 is that Tim Hortons was consistently profitable in all four years, with ROEs ranging from 24.96 percent to 44.86 percent. The 2010 figure of 44.86 percent was heavily influenced by a one-time gain on the sale of Maidstone Bakeries—if we adjust for the sale, we end up with a figure of 25.38 percent, which is in line with the other three years' figures. The net profit margin was in the 13 to 14 percent range in all four years (after adjusting the 2010 figure for the one-time gain), while both the turnover ratio and the leverage ratio increased slightly during 2011, resulting in an increase in the 2011 ROE.

So how does Tim Hortons compare with its competition? Ideally, we would compare Tim Hortons with another Canadian fast-service food and coffee franchise company of similar size and market presence, or even an industry average comprising several similar Canadian firms. Certainly, this would be a viable approach if we were comparing the Canadian banks, because they are so similar. However, no other Canadian companies compare to Tim Hortons very well along several dimensions such as size, product offerings, and nationwide market presence.[6] Therefore, we have chosen two well-known U.S. companies, McDonald's Corporation and Starbucks Corporation, which have market presence similar to Tim Hortons' in the markets in which Tim Hortons operates.[7] Both companies represent major competitors for Tim Hortons, even though they offer differentiated versions of Tim Hortons' product lines. McDonald's offers a wider variety of fast-food products, and Starbucks offers a "higher-end" version of Tim Hortons' product line but a narrower number of food offerings. Obviously, there are differences among the companies, but they represent reasonable benchmarks.

Table 4-3 provides the DuPont ROE data for McDonald's and Starbucks for 2008–11. These ratios are comparable to Tim Hortons' ratios, although it should be noted that Starbucks has a September year end, while McDonald's has a January 31 year end, and Tim Hortons has a December 31 year end.[8]

TABLE 4-3 McDonald's and Starbucks' DuPont Ratios

	McDonald's (January)				Starbucks (September)			
	2011	2010	2009	2008	2011	2010	2009	2008
ROE	0.3792	0.338	0.3243	0.3224	0.3091	0.2568	0.1285	0.1267
ROA	0.1691	0.1547	0.1506	0.1516	0.181	0.1481	0.0702	0.0556
Net profit margin	0.2038	0.2054	0.2001	0.1834	0.1065	0.0883	0.04	0.0304
Turnover	0.8297	0.7529	0.7525	0.8265	1.7	1.6767	1.7527	1.8304
Leverage	2.2425	2.185	2.1537	2.1267	1.71	1.7342	1.831	2.2773

---

[6] Also, recall that Tim Hortons' financial statements have been prepared in accordance with U.S. GAAP, and we want to compare "apples with apples" to the greatest extent possible.

[7] The ratios for these two companies have been calculated based on the financial statement information we found in their annual reports, as well as on information found at www.morningstar.ca.

[8] The choice of fiscal year end can have a significant impact on reported financial ratios, based on annual financial statements, especially for firms that face a seasonal sales cycle. As a result, several balance sheet items, such as loans outstanding, accounts receivable, inventory, and accounts payable, will vary considerably during the year. The analyst must be aware of these factors when evaluating the ratios and also when comparing to other "similar" firms that choose different fiscal year ends.

The 2011 ROE for McDonald's is 37.9 percent, and Starbucks' 2011 ROE is 30.9 percent, so Tim Hortons' 2011 ROE is near the middle at 33.4 percent. Notice that during 2008, which was a poor year for the economy (particularly in the second half of the year, when we officially entered a recessionary period), McDonald's (the lower-end competitor) maintained a high ROE, while Starbucks (the higher-end competitor) saw its ROE decline markedly. Tim Hortons' ROE remained near the middle. Over the period, Tim Hortons had stable profit margins of around 13 to 14 percent, which was below that for McDonald's, but above those for Starbucks. Tim Hortons' turnover ratio was consistently higher than McDonald's, but much lower than that for Starbucks. Tim Hortons' leverage ratios are consistently much lower than McDonald's, which indicates less financial risk; however, its leverage was higher than Starbucks' in 2011, as Timmies' leverage increased, while Starbucks' decreased.

On the surface, we could conclude that Tim Hortons has solid performance—providing stable results and generating similar ROEs to its main competitors. It does this with profit margins that are lower than McDonald's but higher than Starbucks'; with asset turnover that is higher than McDonald's but lower than Starbucks'; and using less financial leverage than McDonald's but slightly more than Starbucks, as of 2011. However, we should consider any possible contributing factors before reaching any conclusions. To get a better understanding of these results, we can extend the analysis of the leverage, efficiency, and productivity ratios.

CONCEPT REVIEW QUESTIONS

1. What three areas of a firm's operations does the DuPont system provide information about?

2. All else being equal, list three factors that will lead to higher ROE ratios.

3. What can we use as a basis for comparison when looking at financial ratios? What kind of information can we gain from this comparison?

4.3 LEVERAGE RATIOS

Learning Objective 4.3
Describe, calculate, and evaluate the key ratios relating to financial leverage.

Leverage is synonymous with magnification. It is good when a firm is low risk and earns a healthy ROA, since it magnifies these high ROAs into even higher ROEs. However, when the firm loses money, the use of leverage magnifies ROEs on the downside as well. This can get the firm into serious trouble, as discussed in the following Lessons to Be Learned.

LESSONS TO BE LEARNED

Figure 4-2 provides a graphical depiction of the five largest U.S. investment banks over the 2003–7 period. While the leverage ratios of financial institutions (FIs) are much higher than those for traditional companies due to the very nature of FIs, Figure 4-2 shows a steady increase in these ratios, all of which exceeded 25 by 2007, with three exceeding 30. More conservative figures for banks would be in the range of 12 to 20.

The leverage ratio is a measure of the risk taken by a firm; a higher ratio indicates more risk. It is calculated as total debt divided by shareholders' equity. Each firm's ratio increased between 2003 and 2007.

As mentioned above, the use of leverage works well during good times, as good results are magnified and transformed to even better results. Unfortunately, during tough times, leverage also magnifies poor results. Either way, dramatic increases in leverage, and high use of leverage in an absolute sense, represent a high-risk situation for any company. In this case, it suggested a high level of systemic risk in the U.S. investment banking industry. Thus, this heavy buildup of debt should have represented a warning signal to those following this industry.

So what happened to these banks? By the third quarter of 2008, these five investment banks (which do not have the stability afforded by depositors, which commercial banks enjoy) could no longer finance their operations and had either gone bankrupt (Lehman Brothers), merged with other institutions, or became depository banks to improve their ability to secure funds.

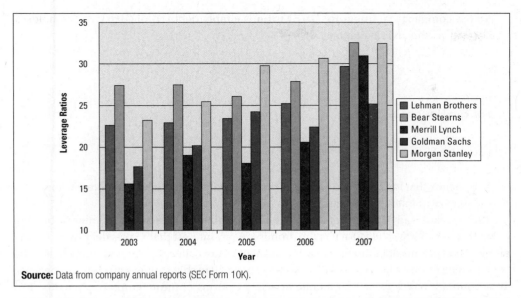

Source: Data from company annual reports (SEC Form 10K).

FIGURE 4-2 *Leverage Ratios for Major U.S. Investment Banks*

We will discuss the leverage decision in more detail when we discuss the firm's capital structure in chapters 20 and 21. But for now, we will introduce the major ratios to consider when discussing financial leverage. There are basically three types: stock ratios, flow ratios, and other ratios.

Stock ratios indicate the amounts of debt outstanding at a particular time. For leverage, there are three basic stock ratios: the leverage ratio (discussed above), the debt ratio, and the debt-equity ratio. The **debt ratio** is defined as total liabilities (TL) divided by total assets (TA), as shown in Equation 4-8.[9]

stock ratios the amounts of debt outstanding at a particular time

debt ratio total liabilities divided by total assets

$$Debt\ ratio = \frac{TL}{TA} \qquad\qquad [4\text{-}8]$$

For Tim Hortons in 2011,

$$Debt\ ratio = \frac{TL}{TA} = \frac{1{,}049.517}{2{,}203.950} = 0.4762$$

The debt ratio is just a rearrangement of the leverage ratio, which for Tim Hortons was 1.909.[10] The debt ratio as defined above includes all liabilities, including money that a company owes suppliers. But in a broad sense, these liabilities are not debt in the way that bank debt is debt. These liabilities arise as a result of normal operations, not from someone deciding to invest in, or lend money to, Tim Hortons.

To capture the use of "genuine" debt, we estimate the amount of interest-bearing debt the firm has outstanding relative to shareholders' equity. The sum of interest-bearing debt and shareholders' equity is referred to as **invested capital** to distinguish it from total assets, some of which are financed as a result of normal business operations. Tim Hortons' interest-bearing debt total of $516.71 million is calculated as follows:

invested capital the sum of interest-bearing debt and shareholders' equity

$10.001 million (Current portion of long-term debt) + $352.426 million (Term debt) + $59.42 million (Advertising fund restricted debt—which bears interest) + $94.863 million (Capital leases)

---

[9] There are many variations of this ratio that include the use of total debt or total long-term debt in the numerator and/or divide by total capital instead of total assets.

[10] In fact, the leverage ratio is simply one divided by one minus the debt ratio (i.e., 1/(1 − 0.4762) = 1.909).

debt-equity (D/E) ratio debt divided by shareholders' equity

So the company's **debt-equity (D/E) ratio** is simply debt (D) divided by shareholders' equity (SE), as shown in Equation 4-9.

[4-9]
$$D/E \ ratio = \frac{D}{SE}$$

For Tim Hortons in 2011,

$$D/E \ ratio = \frac{D}{SE} = \frac{516.710}{1,154.433} = 0.4476$$

This means that for every dollar of equity contributed by shareholders, Tim Hortons borrowed $0.4476 in interest-bearing debt.

The D/E ratio's advantage over the debt ratio is that it measures the use of interest-bearing debt. This is important because it is the promise to pay interest that makes debt risky. For example, Tim Hortons does not face risk as a result of its tax-collecting activities on behalf of the government, because its creditors think well enough of it to ship supplies on credit, or because an accountant has decided to generate accruals in terms of future employee benefits. Tim Hortons does face risk through its interest-bearing debt. In this respect, analysts often "net out" interest-bearing debt by subtracting cash and cash equivalents. In Tim Hortons' case, these two items total $126.497 million, approximately one-quarter of the amount of interest-bearing debt the company holds. However, the bulk of cash and cash equivalents is used in Tim Hortons' operations or held for tax payments to the government.

This discussion of the role of interest-bearing debt should remind you that not only is it important to determine the amount of debt, but it is also equally, if not more, important to evaluate how much the debt costs. More generally, we look at measures that indicate the flow of fixed commitments to income, which provides an estimate of a firm's ability to service its debt obligations. Of course, this concept also relates to individuals, as demonstrated in *Finance in the News 4-1*, which discusses the importance of the debt-to-income ratio for individuals. This ratio is closely related to the two ratios discussed below that are commonly used to evaluate companies' ability to service their debt.

finance INTHENEWS 4-1 Do You Know Your Debt-to-Income Ratio?

DO YOU KNOW your debt-to-income ratio? Is it 120 percent? 165? 200? And what does that number even mean?

Each quarter, Statistics Canada publishes the average Canadian's debt-to-personal-disposable-income ratio. It's a stat that gets cited often in stories about Canadians' onerous and rising debt loads.

The latest debt-to-income report from StatsCan shows that as of the third quarter of 2011, the average Canadian's debt-to-personal-disposable-income ratio was 153 percent. That's up from 150.6 percent in the previous quarter and higher than 148.3 percent a year ago. Seeing that makes me wonder how I compare.

Turns out, calculating your own ratio is not that difficult. To get your debt-to-personal-income percentage, add up your total debt (including mortgages, loans, credit lines, and credit cards) and find out what percent that is of your annual after-tax income. For example, if your total debt is $120,000 and your after-tax income is $85,000, your debt-to-income ratio is 141 percent.

Your next question might be: If my ratio is lower than the national average, does that mean I'm in better financial health than most? Or if I'm higher, am I in trouble?

Not necessarily. Though it's bandied about frequently in the press, the debt-to-income ratio is limited when it comes to measuring one's own financial health. For one thing, it doesn't take equity or assets into account. Also, as *The Globe and Mail* personal finance columnist Rob Carrick noted in this story, it measures things that are not directly comparable, namely your entire debt load vs. one year's net pay (one would hardly be expected to pay off all your debt in one year, right?).

"Another flaw in the debt-to-income ratio is that it lumps together people who have no debt with those who are heavily indebted," wrote Mr. Carrick. "So you get seniors who have paid off their mortgages combined with Vancouver and Toronto residents and their mega-mortgages."

Mr. Carrick pointed out that the debt-to-income ratio is used by economists for a "big picture" view on debt, and unless you are able to compare your ratio with others who are like you—say, young families with mortgage debt or boomers preparing for retirement—measuring yourself against the average number is largely meaningless.

continued

Finance in the News 4-1: Do You Know Your Debt-to-Income Ratio? (continued)

So are there better ways to calculate whether your debt load is financially sound?

Consolidated Credit Counseling Services of Canada has another way to determine your debt-to-income ratio and gauge whether you are in a good position to borrow money or if you are spending too much paying off debt.

Take your total monthly debt payments, including rent or mortgage, minimum credit card, car payments, etc., and divide by your total household monthly income. Multiply by 100. Because this way of calculating your debt-to-income ratio compares two numbers that are more directly comparable—what's coming in each month versus what's coming out each month—it might give you a better idea of whether your current situation is a healthy one.

According to Consolidated Credit, your debt-to-income ratio should be 36 percent or less. At 37 to 49 percent, you should be concerned about your level of debt, and at 50 percent or more, you should seek out professional assistance to severely reduce your debt.

The most important debt coverage measure, or at least the one most commonly referred to, is the **times interest earned (TIE)**, or coverage, ratio. This is defined as earnings before interest and taxes (EBIT) divided by interest expense (I), as shown in Equation 4-10:

$$TIE = \frac{EBIT}{I}$$ [4-10]

times interest earned (TIE) earnings before interest and taxes divided by interest expense; also called the "coverage ratio"

We estimate the TIE for Tim Hortons in 2011 using the operating income (or EBIT) figure of $569.475 million and the interest expense figure of $30 million, as shown below. (Both figures are found in Tim Hortons' income statement, which we presented in Chapter 3.)

$$TIE = \frac{EBIT}{I} = \frac{569.475}{30} = 18.98$$

So how do we evaluate the TIE? It means that for every dollar of interest expense, Tim Hortons had approximately $19 of income available to pay interest and taxes. In fact, this ratio would have been even higher had we "netted out" interest income against interest expenses and used this figure in the denominator of the ratio calculation above. In the interest of conservatism, we did not. Our approach demonstrates that Tim Hortons is in a stable position in the sense that the company is able to cover its interest payments from the profits it generates.[11]

A final ratio that is normally calculated is a mixture of the above ratios. The **cash flow to debt ratio** measures how long it would take to pay off a firm's debt (D) using its cash flow from operations (CFO). It is calculated as shown in Equation 4-11:

cash flow to debt ratio a measure of how long it would take to pay off a firm's debt using its cash flow from operations; cash flow from operations divided by debt

$$\text{Cash flow to debt ratio} = \frac{CFO}{D}$$ [4-11]

For Tim Hortons in 2011,

$$\text{Cash flow to debt ratio} = \frac{CFO}{D} = \frac{391.467}{516.710} = 0.7576$$

---

[11] There are other coverage ratios, which are variations of the TIE that are adjusted to include the impact of other fixed charges, such as preferred share dividends, lease obligations, and sinking fund payments, but these will be discussed later when we talk about other contractual commitments attached to different types of securities.

Given its CFO of $391.467 million and its total debt outstanding of $516.71 million, Tim Hortons could pay off 76 percent of its debt within a year if it devoted its operating cash flow to debt repayment. This indicates, once again, Tim Hortons' very strong credit position.

So what is the overall assessment of Tim Hortons' leverage position in 2011? The stock ratios (i.e., debt ratio, leverage ratio, and D/E ratio) indicate reasonably low to moderate levels of debt, while the interest coverage ratio and cash flow to debt ratios indicate that Tim Hortons' earnings or the related operating cash flows can very easily support the required debt payments.

To gain additional insight, look at the trend in Tim Hortons' leverage ratios, and compare them with those of McDonald's and Starbucks. These ratios are shown in Table 4-4.

TABLE 4-4 Tim Hortons', McDonald's, and Starbucks' Leverage Ratios

	Tim Hortons				McDonald's				Starbucks			
	2011	2010	2009	2008	2011	2010	2009	2008	2011	2010	2009	2008
Leverage	1.9091	1.7204	1.6678	1.7473	2.25	2.185	2.1573	2.1267	1.71	1.7342	1.831	2.2773
Debt ratio	0.4762	0.4187	0.4004	0.4277	0.5638	0.5423	0.5357	0.5298	0.4043	0.4234	0.4539	0.5609
D/E ratio	0.4476	0.3808	0.3875	0.3553	0.84	0.8946	0.8509	0.8562	0.13	0.1492	0.1804	0.7934
TIE	18.98	19.19*	24.86	18.06	11.58	11.62	9.62	12.78	51.91	43.41	14.37	9.6

*Adjusted for one-time gain of $361.075 million

Tim Hortons' leverage ratios show that the amount of debt as a percentage of total financing increased slightly during 2011, and the coverage ratio declined very slightly. Comparing Tim Hortons with McDonald's and Starbucks, we can see that Tim Hortons had a much lower percentage of debt financing than McDonald's, and its coverage ratios were much better, indicating Tim Hortons could cover its debt obligations much easier. However, as of 2011 it has more debt than Starbucks, with a lower coverage ratio. Based on the foregoing, we could conclude that Tim Hortons is in a relatively good position with respect to leverage.

CONCEPT REVIEW QUESTIONS

1. Why is it important to look at stock and flow leverage ratios to assess a firm's debt situation?

2. Briefly explain what type of information is provided about a firm's leverage position by the debt ratio, the D/E ratio, the TIE ratio, and the cash flow to debt ratio.

4.4 EFFICIENCY RATIOS

Efficiency ratios measure how efficiently a dollar of revenue is turned into profits, so we start with Tim Hortons' 2011 net profit margin of 13.52 percent, which is a very healthy figure. However, it is a measure of overall profitability and is frequently broken out into its major components. How this is done depends on the type of firm and the amount of data presented in its financial statements. Unfortunately, not all firms present a good breakdown of their cost structure on their income statements.

When looking at a firm's cost structure, economists like to think in terms of variable and fixed costs, where variable costs vary with the amount of production, and sales and fixed costs do not. Suppose a firm has revenues of $120 and variable costs of $72, or 60 percent of revenues. This means that the firm has a contribution margin of 40 percent, or $48 is available to contribute to the firm's fixed costs and profits. With fixed operating costs of $31 and fixed interest costs of $5, the firm has taxable income of $12. With a 50-percent income tax rate, its net income and taxes are both $6, and the firm has a net profit margin of 5 percent. This example is illustrated in Table 4-5, which also shows what happens with a 10-percent increase and decrease in revenues.

TABLE 4-5 Profit Margin and Revenue Variability

Revenues	$120	$132	$108
Contribution margin (40%)	48	53	43
Fixed operating cost	31	31	31
Fixed interest cost	5	5	5
Tax	6	8.5	3.5
Net income	6	8.5	3.5
Net profit margin	5%	6.4%	3.2%

If the firm sells more and revenues increase to $132, then only the variable costs increase. The gross profit, which is revenues minus variable costs, also increases by 10 percent to $53. However, because the fixed production and interest costs stay the same, the taxable income increases from $12 to $17 or 40 percent, and the net profit margin increases to 6.4 percent. Conversely, if revenues decrease by 10 percent to $108, the process works in reverse and the existence of the fixed costs causes net income to drop by 40 percent.[12]

The above example indicates that the more fixed costs the firm has, the greater its income variability. Note that although revenues varied by +/–10 percent, net income varied by +/–40 percent. We will discuss this more in chapters 20 and 21, when we discuss the financial and business risk of the firm. However, as shown in Equation 4-12, we can estimate the **degree of total leverage (DTL)** as the contribution margin (CM) divided by the earnings before taxes (EBT).[13]

degree of total leverage (DTL) contribution margin divided by earnings before taxes

$$DTL = \frac{CM}{EBT} \qquad [4\text{-}12]$$

For the previous example,

$$DTL = \frac{CM}{EBT} = \frac{48}{12} = 4.0$$

The DTL for our example firm shows a very significant exposure of profits to variability in revenues, because every 1 percent change in revenues causes a 4 percent change in earnings before taxes. This exposure depends on the firm's cost structure, which is crucial to the risk of the firm. It also allows the firm to estimate its **break-even point (BEP)**, which is the level of revenues at which the firm covers all its operating and fixed costs. In the above example, the firm needs revenues of $90 to cover these costs; if revenues fall below this level, it loses money.

break-even point (BEP) the level of revenues at which the firm covers all its operating costs and fixed costs; total fixed costs divided by the contribution margin ratio

This $90 break-even point is calculated as the total fixed costs (FC) divided by the contribution margin ratio, as shown in Equation 4-13:

$$BEP = \frac{FC}{CM} \qquad [4\text{-}13]$$

For our example firm,

$$BEP = \frac{FC}{CM} = \frac{31 + 5}{0.4} = \$90$$

---

[12] The actual numbers are rounded.

[13] We don't use net income to estimate the DTL. With a 50-percent tax rate, half the gain accrues to the government in income taxes because income taxes are not a fixed payment.

The contribution margin ratio is just the complement of the variable costs as a percentage of revenues, so with variable costs at 60 percent of revenues, the contribution margin is 40 percent or 0.4. Dividing the fixed operating and interest costs of $36 by 40 percent produces the break-even point of $90.

Clearly, it is important for the firm to know its break-even point and how its profits vary with revenues. As a result, internally it will have the information to estimate these important values. However, externally, the firm is not required to present this information in its financial statements. Further, the proxies that are available are often poor. From your managerial cost accounting course, you know that the cost of sales includes variable production costs, as well as the allocation of factory overhead—that is, it includes fixed costs. If the firm does only one thing, this factory overhead can include almost all of its operating fixed costs. Unfortunately, what is presented for most companies, including Tim Hortons, does not allow a breakout of variable and fixed costs, so we cannot estimate its break-even point or contribution margin, or the sensitivity of its profits to revenue increases or decreases.

However, consistent with the basic idea of calculating the contribution margin—that is, revenues minus variable costs—we can calculate a variation of it: the **gross profit margin**. Equation 4-14 shows that this ratio is defined as revenues (Rev) minus the cost of sales (COS) divided by revenues.

gross profit margin revenues minus the cost of sales divided by revenues

[4-14]
$$Gross\ profit\ margin = \frac{Rev - COS}{Rev}$$

For Tim Hortons in 2011,

$$Gross\ profit\ margin = \frac{Rev - COS}{Rev} = \frac{(2,852.966 - 1,774.107)}{2,852.966} = 37.82\%$$

A gross margin of 37.82 percent indicates that 37.82 percent of Tim Hortons' revenues is available to cover its other operating expenses

The other expenses, apart from cost of sales, that firms normally incur are period costs, which are often loosely called fixed costs, because, in the short run, they are unrelated to revenues. These costs consist of advertising, research and development, general sales and administrative expenses, and amortization expenses. For Tim Hortons, these expenses amounted to approximately $509.4 million in 2011.

operating margin operating income (OI) divided by revenues

operating income (OI) the earnings before interest and taxes (EBIT) figure

The final ratio is the **operating margin**, which is defined as **operating income (OI)** divided by revenues, as in Equation 4-15.

[4-15]
$$Operating\ margin = \frac{OI}{Rev}$$

For Tim Hortons, this ratio is relatively easy to calculate, since operating income (or earnings before interest and taxes—EBIT) is reported in the income statement, but this is not always the case.[14]

The operating income or EBIT figure for Tim Hortons in 2011 was $569.475 million. For Tim Hortons, the 2011 operating margin was as follows:

$$Operating\ margin = \frac{OI}{Rev} = \frac{569.475}{2,852.966} = 19.96\%$$

---

[14] Some analysts use EBITDA, or earnings before interest, tax, depreciation, and amortization, in their calculations since it is less susceptible to the effects of accounting judgement with respect to amortization.

For reference, 19.96 percent is a solid operating margin, which is consistent with Tim Hortons' solid gross profit margin, and it implies the company has good control over its other operating costs as well as its cost of sales.

Table 4-6 provides the efficiency ratios for Tim Hortons, McDonald's, and Starbucks for 2008–11, which allows us to further evaluate Tim Hortons' efficiency results. We can see that Tim Hortons maintained steady profitability, but lower gross profit margins than McDonald's and Starbucks. However, Tim Hortons maintained operating profit margins and net profit margins that were higher than Starbucks', but lower than McDonald's. Overall, we can say that Tim Hortons has displayed consistent, strong profitability over the 2008–11 period, above that of Starbucks, but below that of McDonald's.

TABLE 4-6 Tim Hortons', McDonald's, and Starbucks' Efficiency Ratios

	Tim Hortons				McDonald's				Starbucks			
	2011	**2010**	**2009**	**2008**	**2011**	**2010**	**2009**	**2008**	**2011**	**2010**	**2009**	**2008**
Net profit margin	0.1352	0.2551*	0.131	0.1393	0.2038	0.2054	0.2001	0.1834	0.1065	0.0883	0.04	0.0304
Operating profit margin	0.1996	0.3978*	0.2155	0.2146	0.316	0.3104	0.3008	0.5298	0.148	0.1326	0.0575	0.0633
Gross profit margin	0.3782	0.3978	0.3737	0.411	0.396	0.4	0.387	0.8562	0.577	0.584	0.58	0.1919

*Excluding one-time gain: net profit margin = 14.38%; operating profit margin = 20.15%

CONCEPT REVIEW QUESTIONS

1. What useful information is provided by the contribution margin, the degree of total leverage, and the break-even point?

2. Why is it uncommon to see the three ratios above reported by companies for external users of their financial statements?

3. What useful information is provided by the net profit margin, the gross profit margin, and the operating margin?

4.5 PRODUCTIVITY RATIOS

If the efficiency ratios measure how efficiently the firm turns revenues into profits, the next question is how productive the firm is in generating revenues from its assets. You saw that the turnover ratio is revenues divided by total assets, so the key to looking at different **productivity ratios** is to look at variations of the turnover ratio for each major asset class. For example, we can see how productive the firm is in using receivables, inventory, and plant and equipment, because these are the major categories of assets that all firms have.

We begin by defining the **receivables turnover ratio** as revenues (Rev) divided by accounts receivable (AR), as shown in Equation 4-16.

$$Receivables\ turnover = \frac{Rev}{AR}$$ [4-16]

For Tim Hortons in 2011,

$$Receivables\ turnover = \frac{Rev}{AR} = \frac{2,852.966}{173.667} = 16.4278$$

Learning Objective 4.5
Describe, calculate, and evaluate the key ratios relating to financial productivity.

productivity ratios measurements of how productive the firm is in generating revenues from its assets

receivables turnover ratio revenues divided by accounts receivables (AR)

For every dollar invested in receivables (i.e., credit extended to purchasers), Tim Hortons generated $16.4278 in revenues. Alternatively, we can say that Tim Hortons turned its AR account over 16.43 times during the year, on average.

The turnover ratio is useful, but it is common to calculate a variation of it called the **average collection period (ACP)**. To do this, divide the average daily credit sales into the accounts receivable, because only credit sales generate receivables; cash sales, obviously, generate cash! However, Tim Hortons, like most companies, does not break out sales into cash and credit sales, at least not in its external financial statements. Therefore, it is common to use average daily sales (ADS) or average daily revenue (ADR) in the denominator, which equals annual sales (or revenues) divided by 365 days. When we define ACP in this manner, ACP is 365 divided by the receivables turnover ratio, because if AR are "turned over" 10 times a year, it implies that the firm takes an average of 36.5 days to collect on its AR. Therefore, we can define the ACP as shown in Equation 4-17.

average collection period (ACP) accounts receivable divided by the average daily revenue

[4-17]
$$ACP = \frac{AR}{ADR} = \frac{365}{Receivables\ turnover}$$

For Tim Hortons in 2011,

$$ACP = \frac{AR}{ADR} = \frac{365}{Receivables\ turnover} = \frac{365}{16.4278} = 22.2184$$

This implies its receivables were paid on average within 22.22 days. For Tim Hortons, this is not a critical ratio, since it does not carry much in the way of receivables.

The second major current asset category for many companies is inventory. However, once again, this is not a significant investment amount for Tim Hortons ($136.999 million in 2011), which turns its inventory over very quickly. Conceptually, the **inventory turnover ratio** is calculated as the cost of sales divided by inventory, because when a widget is sold, its financial cost moves from inventory (INV) and is expensed through cost of sales. This ratio is shown in Equation 4-18.

inventory turnover ratio the cost of sales (or sales) divided by inventory

[4-18]
$$Inventory\ turnover = \frac{COS}{INV}$$

For Tim Hortons in 2011,

$$Inventory\ turnover = \frac{COS}{INV} = \frac{1,774.107}{136.999} = 12.9498$$

For some firms, the data on cost of sales (or cost of goods sold) is not reliable because of accounting differences in how such items as factory overhead are treated. In addition, publicly available ratios and industry ratios are often calculated using revenue due to the difficulty in determining cost of goods sold, which is often not separated out on corporate income statements. As a result, the cost of sales is often replaced by revenues in the inventory turnover ratio, as shown in Equation 4-19.

[4-19]
$$Inventory\ turnover = \frac{Rev}{INV}$$

When we calculate Tim Hortons' 2011 inventory turnover ratio using this equation, we get

$$Inventory\ turnover = \frac{Rev}{INV} = \frac{2,852.966}{136.999} = 20.8247$$

Notice the large difference in the inventory turnover ratio figures, depending on which version of the two equations is used. This difference makes it clear why we have stressed the importance of determining precisely how a ratio is calculated (i.e., so we can compare "apples with apples"). Similar to what we did with the receivables turnover ratio, it is common to invert the inventory turnover ratio and call it the **average days revenues in inventory (ADRI)**, as shown in Equation 4-20.

average days revenues in inventory (ADRI) inventory divided by average daily revenues

$$ADRI = \frac{INV}{ADR} = Inventory\ turnover \qquad [4\text{-}20]$$

For Tim Hortons in 2011,

$$ADRI = \frac{INV}{ADR} = \frac{136.999}{(2,852.966/365)} = 17.5272$$

Notice that this equals 365 divided by the inventory turnover ratio of 20.8247. So in 2011, Tim Hortons had 17.5 days of revenues tied up in inventory and 22.2 in receivables.

The final productivity ratio is the **fixed asset turnover ratio**, calculated as revenues divided by net fixed assets (NFA), which is simply the depreciated value of the fixed assets, as shown in Equation 4-21.

fixed asset turnover ratio revenues divided by net fixed assets

$$Fixed\ asset\ turnover = \frac{Rev}{NFA} \qquad [4\text{-}21]$$

For Tim Hortons in 2011,

$$Fixed\ asset\ turnover = \frac{Rev}{NFA} = \frac{2,852.966}{1,463.765} = 1.9491$$

As firms depreciate their assets, the fixed asset turnover ratio automatically increases, so many analysts also look at the fixed asset turnover ratio by using gross assets, which is the undepreciated cost of the fixed assets (i.e., without any depreciation deducted). Tim Hortons had fixed assets with an initial cost in 2011 of $2,291.327 million, but had accumulated depreciation of $827.562 million. So its fixed assets are 36 percent depreciated (i.e., 827.562/2,291.327 = 0.36).

In Table 4-7, we provide some context for Tim Hortons' 2011 ratios as calculated above by reporting its historical ratios, as well as those for McDonald's and Starbucks.

There are several things to note from Table 4-7. First, Tim Hortons' turnover, receivables turnover, and fixed asset turnover ratios increased during 2011, while the inventory turnover ratio decreased. The receivables and inventory turnover ratios are not particularly important

TABLE 4-7 Tim Hortons', McDonald's, and Starbucks' Productivity Ratios

	Tim Hortons				McDonald's				Starbucks			
	2011	2010	2009	2008	2011	2010	2009	2008	2011	2010	2009	2008
TA Turnover	1.2945	1.0222	1.1645	1.026	0.83	0.753	0.753	0.827	1.7	1.677	1.753	1.8304
Receivables Turnover	16.4278	13.9364	13.5536	12.813	21.49	20.418	21.449	25.26	33.95	35.373	36.069	31.511
ACP	22.22	26.19	26.93	28.49	16.98	17.88	14.93	14.45	10.75	10.32	10.12	11.58

continued

TABLE 4-7 Tim Hortons', McDonald's, and Starbucks' Productivity Ratios *continued*

	Tim Hortons				McDonald's				Starbucks			
	2011	**2010**	**2009**	**2008**	**2011**	**2010**	**2009**	**2008**	**2011**	**2010**	**2009**	**2008**
Inventory turnover (using sales)	20.82	25.19	30.3001	28.58	143.97	133.62	128.18	125.7	6.56	7.38	6.37	12.12
ADRI	17.53	14.49	12.05	12.77	2.54	2.73	2.859	2.9	55.64	49.46	57.3	30.12
FA turnover	1.9491	1.8465	1.6324	1.5333	1.2	1.0913	1.0563	1.1613	4.9	4.431	3.8537	3.512

for any of these companies, since they all maintain low levels of receivables and inventories, consistent with the nature of their businesses. Tim Hortons has higher fixed asset and total turnover ratios than McDonald's and lower ratios than Starbucks, which has a lower proportional investment in fixed assets.

CONCEPT REVIEW QUESTIONS

1. What information can be gained from examining a firm's receivables turnover, inventory turnover, and fixed asset turnover ratios?

2. Why is it common to estimate the ACP by using total revenues rather than credit sales, and to estimate inventory turnover by using revenues rather than cost of sales?

4.6 LIQUIDITY RATIOS

Learning Objective 4.6
Describe, calculate, and evaluate the key ratios relating to financial liquidity.

liquidity the ease with which something can be converted into cash

working capital ratio current assets divided by total assets

working capital current assets

As we discussed previously, DuPont analysis shows that, together, the leverage, efficiency, and productivity ratios help explain a firm's good or poor performance in terms of ROE. However, some financial statement users have a different interest when examining financial statements. Banks, for example, and suppliers shipping to Tim Hortons on credit, want to know whether a firm has the means to pay off its debts. This leads to a focus on the liquidity of the company. As mentioned in Chapter 3, **liquidity** refers to how easily something can be converted into cash.

The focus in analyzing the liquidity of the company is on the overall liquidity of a firm's assets and on the available assets to meet current liabilities. In terms of overall liquidity, we look at the ratio of current assets (CA) to total assets (TA). This is referred to as the **working capital ratio** because current assets are often called **working capital**. This is defined in Equation 4-22.

[4-22]
$$\text{Working capital ratio} = \frac{CA}{TA}$$

For Tim Hortons in 2011,

$$\text{Working capital ratio} = \frac{CA}{TA} = \frac{620.966}{2{,}203.950} = 0.2818$$

For Tim Hortons, this ratio indicates that its assets are not extremely liquid, with only 28 percent supposedly converting to cash within a year. Overall, Tim Hortons consists of larger amounts of net fixed assets and smaller amounts of current assets. So how liquid are these current assets?

One of the most important liquidity ratios is the **current ratio**, also called the bankers' ratio, which is estimated as current assets divided by current liabilities (CL), as shown in Equation 4-23.

current ratio also called the "bankers' ratio"; current assets divided by current liabilities

$$\text{Current ratio} = \frac{CA}{CL} \qquad\qquad [4\text{-}23]$$

For Tim Hortons in 2011,

$$\text{Current ratio} = \frac{CA}{CL} = \frac{620.966}{476.650} = 1.3028$$

Tim Hortons has \$1.30 in current assets for every dollar in current liabilities. This ratio is important for bankers because bank loans are normally short term and included in current liabilities. So a current ratio of 1.30 means that Tim Hortons has more than enough assets that will be soon converted to cash and may be available to help pay off a bank loan, although the coverage is by no means excessive at a factor of 1.30. However, if a bank has to seize assets or force a firm to liquidate assets, this is a sign that some of the firm's assets are probably not worth much. In particular, the inventory of a bankrupt or failing firm is normally not worth its book value, while it is unlikely a creditor could ever recover any funds from prepaid expenses. For this reason, banks also look at the **quick ratio** or **acid test ratio** which is cash (C) plus marketable securities (MS) plus accounts receivable (AR) divided by current liabilities, as shown in Equation 4-24.[15]

quick ratio or **acid test ratio** cash plus marketable securities plus accounts receivable divided by current liabilities

$$\text{Quick ratio} = \frac{C + MS + AR}{CL} \qquad\qquad [4\text{-}24]$$

For Tim Hortons in 2011,

$$\text{Quick ratio} = \frac{(C + MS + AR)}{CL} = \frac{(126.497 + 0 + 173.667)}{476.65} = 0.82$$

For Tim Hortons in 2011, the quick ratio is less than 1, which indicates the company could not pay off all its current liabilities from its "quick" (i.e., most liquid) assets. Table 4-8 contains the current and quick ratios for Tim Hortons, McDonald's, and Starbucks for 2008–11. Tim Hortons' current ratios were higher than McDonald's and Starbucks' over the entire period, except for 2008 when McDonalds had a higher ratio, and in 2011 when Starbucks' was higher. However, Tim Hortons' quick ratios were generally below those for McDonald's, but above those for Starbucks with the exception of 2011. Overall, Tim Hortons seems to display adequate liquidity, especially given its conservative leverage situation, which was noted previously. This reiterates one of the most important facets of ratio analysis that we have already touched on several times—ratios cannot be looked at in isolation!

TABLE 4-8 Tim Hortons', McDonald's, and Starbucks' Liquidity Ratios

	Tim Hortons				McDonald's				Starbucks			
	2011	2010	2009	2008	2011	2010	2009	2008	2011	2010	2009	2008
Current ratio	1.3028	2.0532	1.4697	1.2704	1.25	1.4937	1.1431	1.386	1.83	1.5493	1.2959	0.7983
Quick ratio	0.82	1.6161	0.9203	0.7134	1.05	1.22	0.969	1.18	1.175	0.99	0.59	0.3

Before we proceed to the next section, we will elaborate on the concept of adjusting book values to realizable values in the event of bankruptcy. We introduced this concept when we treated inventory as worthless in calculating the quick ratio, which is an extreme example of asset

---

[15]Sometimes the quick ratio is calculated as current assets minus inventory divided by current liabilities, which would include prepaid expenses.

adjustment. The objective is really to estimate a realizable value in the event of liquidation.

Finance in the News 4-2 discusses the importance of estimating the liquidation value of a company from an investing perspective, as advocated by legendary investing guru Benjamin Graham (Warren Buffett's mentor). The article discusses the rationale underlying the purchase of stocks in companies that are trading for less than their liquidation value.

While Graham suggests that the liquidation value of assets "will vary according to their character," he does provide some general guidelines, which can be adjusted according to the specific situation. He suggests valuing cash at 100 percent of its book value, because it is cash. Accounts receivable are valued at 75 to 90 percent, with an average of 80 percent; inventory between 50 and 75 percent, with an average of 66.6 percent; and fixed assets between 1 and 50 percent, with an approximate average of 15 percent. Liabilities should be valued at 100 percent, since this is the amount due.

Several things are important in this simple approach. First, the discounts from book value increase as the liquidity of the asset deteriorates; for example, receivables are worth 80 percent; inventories, 66.6 percent; and fixed assets, 15 percent. This occurs because a bank seizing the receivables has to wait only 30 or 60 days for customers to pay their bills. In contrast, the inventory of a failed firm is often not worth much, while plant and equipment often entail significant costs in physically removing them from one location and transporting them to another. The true liquidation value could deviate significantly from the figure calculated, and in order to value a company that is on the brink of liquidation, one would have to go through the assets in more detail. For example, 80 percent is slightly higher than the more commonly used percentages of 70 to 75 percent for collecting on receivables; however, any of these figures could be high depending on the quality and age of the receivables. Similarly, even using 50 percent of inventory (which is the commonly used rule of thumb) might be too high, especially if a lot of it is in the form of work in progress and/or obsolete inventory. On the other hand, it is possible that fixed assets might sell for their book value or more and not 15 percent,

---

finance INTHENEWS 4-2   About Liquidation Value Investing

LIQUIDATION VALUE INVESTING is the purchase of securities at a discount to the value of the securities in a liquidation.

The rationale for such an investment is straight forward. In the 1934 edition of *Security Analysis*, Benjamin Graham argued that the phenomenon of a stock selling persistently below its liquidation value was "fundamentally illogical." In Graham's opinion, it meant:

1. The stock was too cheap, and therefore offered an attractive opportunity for purchase and an attractive area for security analysis; and

2. Management was pursuing a mistaken policy and should take corrective action, "if not voluntarily, then under pressure from the stockholders."

Graham understood why these sort of stocks—also known as "net-net", "net-quick" or "net current asset value" stocks—traded at a discount to liquidation value:

"Common stocks in this category almost always have an unsatisfactory trend of earnings."

…

Graham then considered why investors should even contemplate liquidating values when companies were not going to liquidate, responding:

"The stockholders do not have it in their power to make a business profitable, but they do have it in their power to liquidate it. At bottom it is not a theoretical question at all; the issue is both very practical and very pressing.

…

In its simplest terms the question comes down to this: Are these managements wrong or is the market wrong? Are these low prices merely the product of unreasoning fear, or do they convey a stern warning to liquidate while there is yet time?"

continued

Finance in the News 4-2: About Liquidation Value Investing *(continued)*

How to determine a company's liquidation value

In *Security Analysis*, Graham wrote that, in determining the liquidation value, the current-asset value generally provides a rough indication:

"A company's balance sheet does not convey exact information as to its value in liquidation, but it does supply clues or hints which may prove useful. The first rule in calculating liquidating value is that the liabilities are real but the assets are of questionable value. This means that all true liabilities shown on the books must be deducted at their face amount. The value to be ascribed to the assets however, will vary according to their character."

Graham then provided the following guide for determining the value of various types of assets in a liquidation:

- Cash assets (including securities at market) – 100%

- Receivables (less usual reserves) – between 75% to 90% with an average of 80%   Graham noted that retail installment accounts should be valued for liquidation at a lower rate, between 30% to 60% with an average of about 50%

- Inventories (at lower or cost or market) – between 50% to 75% with an average of 66.6%

- Fixed and miscellaneous assets (real estate, buildings, machinery, equipment, nonmarketable investments, intangibles etc.) — between 1% to 50% with an approximate average of 15%.

Source: Excerpted from Carlisle, Tobias, "About liquidation value investing." Greenbackd.com, December 1, 2008. Available at http://greenbackd.com/2008/12/01/about-liquidation-value-investing. Reprinted by permission.

---

depending on the market value of real estate in the company's market—remember that fixed assets are carried at historical cost less depreciation.

While the liquidation value is a useful figure, as is the book value, the "market" value could be, and often is, much higher. The reason for this is that company market value is based on the company's value as a going concern; for profitable companies, the value of the assets in use is significantly more than their value to someone else. This leads to the final set of ratios that analysts often consider, which includes valuation ratios. These summarize how the market values the firm's operations.

CONCEPT REVIEW QUESTIONS

1. What type of financial statement user will be most interested in a firm's liquidity ratios?

2. What useful information do we obtain from a firm's working capital, current, and quick ratios?

3. Why might bankers focus more on the quick ratio than on the current ratio?

4.7 VALUATION RATIOS

We will discuss common share valuation in Chapter 7, but at this stage we introduce some of the standard ratios that people look at to understand the relative valuation of a company.

Some ratios that are useful in assessing a firm's relative value include earnings per share (EPS), which we discussed in Chapter 3, and the **equity book value per share (BVPS)**, which is the ending shareholders' equity (SE) divided by the ending number of shares outstanding, as shown in Equation 4-25.

$$BVPS = \frac{SE}{\text{Number of shares}}$$

[4-25]

Learning Objective 4.7
Describe, calculate, and evaluate the key ratios relating to the valuation of a company.

equity book value per share (BVPS) shareholders' equity divided by the number of shares outstanding

For Tim Hortons in 2011,

$$BVPS = \frac{SE}{Number\ of\ shares} = \frac{1,154.433}{157.815} = \$7.3151$$

Usually, reporters of financial information will adjust the previous per-share values to reflect any changes in the number of shares outstanding.

In terms of valuation, one of the most basic ratios an analyst can look at is a company's **dividend yield**, which is the current dividend per share (DPS) divided by the current share price (P), as shown in Equation 4-26.

dividend yield the dividend per share divided by the share price

[4-26]
$$Dividend\ yield = \frac{DPS}{P}$$

For Tim Hortons, the 2011 DPS was \$0.68, so at its year-end share price of \$49.36, we obtain the following:

$$Dividend\ yield = \frac{DPS}{P} = \frac{0.68}{49.36} = 0.0138$$

A dividend yield of 1.38 percent is quite low. Equation 4-26 tells us that a low dividend yield can be caused by low dividend payouts or high share prices or both. Because investors are concerned about the firm's ability to sustain its dividend payments, one ratio that is useful to assess this ability is the **dividend payout ratio**, which is the DPS divided by the EPS, as shown in Equation 4-27.

dividend payout ratio the dividend per share divided by the earnings per share

[4-27]
$$Dividend\ payout = \frac{DPS}{EPS}$$

We will use the basic EPS in this equation, which for Tim Hortons is the same as its diluted EPS figure. For Tim Hortons in 2011, we obtain the following:

$$Dividend\ payout = \frac{DPS}{EPS} = \frac{0.68}{2.36} = 0.2881$$

This ratio implies that, during 2011, Tim Hortons paid out 28.81 percent of its earnings as dividends.

We would expect this from a moderate-growth business, such as Tim Hortons. This dividend payout ratio allows the company to reinvest about three-quarters of each dollar earned back into the company.

One of the most important and widely followed value ratios is the **price-earnings (P/E) ratio**, which is estimated as the share price (P) divided by the EPS, as shown in Equation 4-28.

price-earnings (P/E) ratio the share price divided by the earnings per share

[4-28]
$$P/E = \frac{P}{EPS}$$

For Tim Hortons in 2011,

$$P/E = \frac{P}{EPS} = \frac{49.36}{2.36} = 20.92$$

This means that investors were willing to pay $20.92 for $1 of Tim Hortons' 2011 earnings. The higher the ratio, the more investors will pay and vice versa. We will discuss the determinants of P/E ratios at some length in Chapter 7 but will note here that P/E ratios increase when share prices increase or when EPS declines. Usually, analysts focus on prices, which are reflected in the numerator of the P/E, and some would argue that a company's shares become too expensive when its P/E ratio gets too high. Conversely, others might argue that a high P/E ratio is warranted because they expect substantial growth in the company's future earnings or because they feel that the company's shares represent a relatively low-risk investment. In either event, from the firm's point of view, higher P/E ratios are a good thing, because they suggest that the markets have confidence in the firm, all else being equal. Remember that, in Chapter 2, we suggested the goal of the firm is to maximize shareholder wealth, which is reflected in share price.

The P/E ratio estimated above is based on the "trailing," or last year's, EPS and is sometimes called the trailing P/E ratio. However, Tim Hortons' fiscal year runs until the end of December, so at the time of writing this EPS was about three months old. The analysts following Tim Hortons and making recommendations to investors estimated its 2012 fiscal EPS figure at $2.74. When we estimate the P/E ratio based on the current price and using a forecast or expected EPS (EEPS) figure, we refer to it as the **forward P/E ratio**, as shown in Equation 4-29.

forward P/E ratio share price divided by the expected earnings per share

$$\text{Forward } P/E = \frac{P}{EEPS}$$ [4-29]

If, as mentioned, the analyst "consensus" EPS estimate for Tim Hortons at the beginning of 2012 was $2.74, while its year-end share price was $49.36, that leaves us with the following forward P/E ratio:

$$\text{Forward } P/E = \frac{P}{EEPS} = \frac{49.36}{2.74} = 18.01$$

Security analysts recommending companies tend to use forward P/E ratios because they normally make shares look cheaper (i.e., as long as EPS continues to increase).

A forward P/E ratio of 18.01 means that if an investor held the stock for 18 years and the EPS stayed at the estimated 2012 value, the investor would get back in profits the $49.36 paid for the stock. In this sense, the P/E ratio is a simple example of a payback period, which will be discussed in Chapter 13. The higher the P/E ratio, the longer shareholders have to wait to recover the cost of their investment in future profits. Generally, low P/E shares are regarded as value stocks, since the payback period is shorter and there is less emphasis on any growth in the forecast EPS. In contrast, high P/E shares are generally regarded as *growth* stocks, because investors are relying more heavily on future growth in the EPS.

The P/E ratio and dividend yield are useful value indicators for many firms. However, P/E ratios are meaningless when EPS is negative or very low, while dividend yields will equal zero for firms that do not pay dividends. In such cases, analysts look for other ratios that provide an indication of a firm's relative value, and many relative value ratios exist. One commonly used ratio is the **market-to-book (M/B) ratio**, which is defined as the market price per share (P) divided by the book value per share (BVPS), as shown in Equation 4-30.

market to book (M/B) ratio the market price per share divided by the book value per share

$$[4\text{-}30] \qquad M/B = \frac{P}{BVPS}$$

Using the 2011 book value and year-end price for Tim Hortons,

$$M/B = \frac{P}{BVPS} = \frac{49.36}{7.3151} = 6.7477$$

EBITDA multiple the total enterprise value divided by earnings before interest, taxes, depreciation, and amortization

total enterprise value (TEV) equity market value plus the market value of the firm's debt

This ratio indicates that every dollar invested by the shareholders in Tim Hortons was worth $6.75 as of the end of December 2011. A dollar invested in Tim Hortons' operations is worth $6.75 in part because of the company's ROE of 33.41 percent. This ROE is attractive, and much better than what investors can get elsewhere, so they have bid up the share price to well above its book value.

Finally, another valuation ratio that is often considered is the **EBITDA multiple**, which is calculated as the **total enterprise value (TEV)** divided by earnings before interest, taxes, depreciation, and amortization (EBITDA), which is shown in Equation 4-31.

$$[4\text{-}31] \qquad EBITDA\ multiple = \frac{TEV}{EBITDA}$$

The total enterprise value is an estimate of the total market value of the firm, which equals the equity market value plus the market value of the firm's debt. This is the market value of what we called "invested capital" when we looked at the firm's financial statements. For Tim Hortons, its December 2011 equity market value, at a $49.36 share price with 157.815 million shares outstanding, was $7,789.748 million. Usually, it is reasonable to assume that the book value of debt provides a sufficient approximation of its market value, although this will not always be the case.[16] We will make this assumption for Tim Hortons' debt in 2011. Therefore, we add the amount of its total debt outstanding of $516.710 million (as calculated earlier) to the market value of its equity and estimate its total enterprise value at $8,306.458 million. Dividing this by Tim Hortons' 2011 EBITDA of $685.344 million (calculated as Tim Hortons' 2011 EBIT of $569.475 million + its depreciation and amortization of 115.869 million), we obtain the following:

$$EBITDA\ multiple = \frac{TEV}{EBITDA} = \frac{8,306.458}{685.344} = 12.1201$$

This ratio is of particular interest when a firm is considering the takeover or purchase of another firm, since it values the whole firm and not just the common equity. It also recognizes that the firm can always issue or buy back common equity and debt.

In Table 4-9, we can see that Tim Hortons' 2011 dividend yield of 1.38 percent is slightly higher than its 2010 value, but is still very low—well below McDonald's yield of 2.7 percent, but above Starbucks' ratio of 1.01 percent. The lower ratio for Tim Hortons relative to McDonald's is consistent with Tim Hortons' dividend payout ratio of 28.8 percent, which is much lower than McDonald's payout of 48 percent, but similar to Starbucks' payout ratio of 32 percent. Tim Hortons' 2011 P/E ratio is above its 2010 adjusted figure and is below Starbucks' ratio of 31.6, but above McDonald's of 18.5. Tim Hortons' M/B ratio increased during 2011 and is slightly below the figure for McDonald's and also below the figure for Starbucks, with the three companies valued similarly with respect to book values.

---

[16] We will elaborate in Chapter 6 on why this assumption may not be reasonable.

Overall, our analysis of the valuation ratios provided in Table 4-9 suggests that, based on the P/E ratio, it appears that Tim Hortons is valued slightly higher than McDonald's and lower than Starbucks. Overall, we can say that Tim Hortons' valuation seems in line with both companies.

TABLE 4-9 Tim Hortons', McDonald's, and Starbucks' Valuation Ratios

	Tim Hortons				McDonald's				Starbucks			
	2011	2010	2009	2008	2011	2010	2009	2008	2011	2010	2009	2008
Dividend yield	0.0138	0.0127	0.0124	0.0108	0.027	0.0294	0.0328	0.0262	0.01011	0.0139	0	0
Dividend payout	0.2881	0.1448*	0.2439	0.2322	0.4801	0.4871	0.4916	0.4335	0.321	0.2903	0	0
P/E	20.92	11.42*	19.59	21.41	18.5	16.54	14.97	16.55	31.6	20.92	38.13	34.58
M/B	6.75	4.86	4.62	5.28	6.9	5.59	4.86	5.18	8.3	5.38	4.89	4.36

*Adjusted for one-time gain: payout = 24.3% and P/E = 19.16

Summing up Valuation Ratios

Overall, what do we make of Tim Hortons as a potential investment? Our financial analysis indicates that it has a relatively low absolute level of debt, and the company can easily service its debt obligations from existing operating profits and cash flows. It also possesses high operating margins and good turnover, so it is quite profitable. These strengths are reflected in Tim Hortons' stock price, which is close to seven times its book value per share and is consistent with its high P/E ratio and EBITDA multiple.

CONCEPT REVIEW QUESTIONS

1. What useful information do we obtain from the dividend yield, P/E ratio, M/B ratio, and EBITDA multiple?

2. Why are P/E ratios and dividend yields often not useful indicators of value?

3. Why is it so difficult to assess whether a firm is properly valued?

4.8 FINANCIAL FORECASTING

To do a reasonable job of financial forecasting, we first must complete a comprehensive financial analysis in order to develop a good understanding of the relationships in the firm's financial statements. Financial forecasting is a critical job for the firm, its financial advisors, and its external analysts. The firm cannot decide how to finance itself until it first assesses the nature of the financing need to determine whether funds are required in the short or long run, whether the financing needs will grow through time, whether the financing need arises from a problem that is self-correcting, and so on. The firm's financial advisors also must consider the firm's needs when recommending a financial strategy, just as the bank must consider these when structuring a loan or credit facility. Finally, equity investors must consider the firm's financing needs when buying the company's shares, because the last thing they want is to invest in a company only to find that it has to raise more money.

Learning Objective 4.8
Explain why financial forecasting is critical for both management and external parties, and explain how to prepare financial forecasts using the percentage of sales method.

The Percentage of Sales Method

The most important input in financial forecasting is an accurate sales forecast, because sales growth drives a firm's financing requirements. As a result, financial forecasting requires input from most of the divisional managers of the firm but particularly the marketing

percentage of sales method a method of financial forecasting that uses a fixed percentage of sales from the previous period to determine amounts in a future period

managers. This will become evident when we consider the most basic forecasting technique: the **percentage of sales method**. We will first consider a stylized example and then return to our study of Tim Hortons.

The percentage of sales method involves the following steps:

1. Determine which financial policy variables you are interested in.

2. Set all the non-financial policy variables as a percentage of sales.

3. Extrapolate the balance sheet based on a percentage of sales.

4. Estimate future retained earnings.

5. Modify and iterate until the forecast makes sense.

external financing requirements (EFR) the money a firm has to raise by using equity or debt or both

Financial policy variables are the variables that the treasurer is concerned with. For example, the treasurer could be concerned with common equity (whether the firm has to issue equity or not), long-term funds (equity plus long-term debt), or the firm's total external financing requirement. To illustrate, we will assume that the treasurer is interested in total **external financing requirements (EFR)**. Let's look at a simple balance sheet for a hypothetical firm (Table 4-10) to see what this means.

TABLE 4-10 Balance Sheet ($)

Cash	5	Accruals	5
Securities	10	Payables	5
Receivables	10	Bank debt	20
Inventory	25	Current liabilities	30
Current assets	50	Long-term debt	40
Net fixed assets	100	Common equity	80
Total assets	150	Total liabilities and equity	150

This firm has total assets of $150 that have been financed with $80 of common equity, $40 of long-term debt, and $20 of short-term debt. Taken together, these are referred to as invested capital, because both the common shareholders and the bank and long-term debt investors have made a decision to invest in the firm. In contrast, the accruals and payables are referred

spontaneous liabilities accruals and payables that arise during the normal course of business

to as **spontaneous liabilities** because, as long as the firm is in business (i.e., a going concern), it will naturally generate payables and accruals: suppliers will ship goods on credit, and workers will work and collect their wages at the end of the month. In this sense, when we generate a five-year financial forecast, these accounts will be assumed to automatically increase with sales, and only the financial policy variables will initially be kept constant.[17]

The next step is to convert the non-policy variables to a percentage of sales. For the sake of our example, we will assume that sales are $120 and that the percentages that result from this sales level are reasonable for the future. In practice, we would look at the ratios over the previous five years or so, factor in current business conditions for the firm (e.g., new orders), and assess what values would be reasonable going forward.

The third step is to extrapolate the balance sheet based on the sales forecast by using these percentages of sales. For our purposes, we will assume that sales are forecast to increase by 10 percent a year. The result is the naive initial forecast shown in Table 4-11.

---

[17] This is not to say that these amounts are ignored: some financially constrained firms will decide to delay paying bills in order to meet their financial targets. This means that payables will increase more than proportionally with sales. We will discuss this in Chapter 24.

TABLE 4-11 Initial Forecast

Sales	$120	%	$132	$145	$160
Cash	5	4.2	5.5	6.1	6.7
Marketable securities	10	8.3	11	12.1	13.3
Accounts receivable	10	8.3	11	12.1	13.3
Inventory	25	20.8	27.5	30.3	33.3
Net fixed assets	100	83.3	110	121	133
Total assets	150	125	165	181.6	199.6
Accruals	5	4.2	5.5	6.1	6.7
Accounts payable	5	4.2	5.5	6.1	6.7
Short-term debt	20	16.7	20	20	20
Long-term debt	40	33.3	40	40	40
Equity	80	66.7	80	80	80
Total Liabilities and equity	150	125	151	152.2	153.4
Cumulative EFR			14	29.4	46.2

PERCENTAGES OF SALES

The top line is the sales forecast, with sales going from the current level of $120 to $132 one year out, and then to $145, and finally to $160. Then we express all the asset accounts and the spontaneous liabilities as a percentage of sales, because these are the non-policy variables and are extrapolated based on the sales forecast. Take cash, for example: it is $5 or 4.2 percent of the $120 sales level, so based on a 10 percent sales growth forecast, it increases by 10 percent to $5.5, $6.1, and $6.7. The values of the other assets are also increased by 10 percent per year, resulting in a forecast value of $199.60 for total assets.

On the liability side, as discussed, we assume that spontaneous liabilities increase at the rate of sales, so we get a forecasted value of $13.40. Subtracting this figure from the total assets forecast of $199.60, we get the required invested capital figure of $186.20. However, recall that we assumed no change in the amount of invested capital, leaving only $140 in invested capital, which suggests a shortfall of $46.20. This shortfall is the balance sheet plug, which we have labelled as the EFR.[18] Notice that this is a cumulative not an annual requirement—that is, the firm needs to raise $46.20 in total financing over the next three years.

However, this forecast is extremely naive or simple. For one thing, it ignores any new equity that the firm will generate simply by retaining some of its future earnings. For another, it assumes that the existing debt will still be there in three years. In practice, some of it may need to be refinanced, or the bank may refuse to renew the short-term loans. However, we'll assume that all the debt can be renewed and focus on the retained earnings. To do this, we need to look at the firm's income statement (Table 4-12).

TABLE 4-12 Income Statement ($)

Sales	120
Gross operating profit	48
Fixed costs	31
EBIT	17
Interest	5
Taxes (50%)	6
Net income	6
Dividends	3

If this looks familiar, it's because it is the example we used before when looking at efficiency ratios, where the firm has a cost structure of 60 percent variable costs and fixed costs of $31. So at the current sales level of $120, it has EBIT of $17, from which it subtracts $5 in interest on the $60 of debt and pays 50 percent income taxes or $6. As a result, it has net income of $6 and a net profit margin of 5 percent. However, it pays out 50 percent of its earnings as dividends, so only $3 is retained within the firm. What is important is that the firm's retained earnings as a percentage of sales are its net profit margin, multiplied by one minus the dividend payout, which equals 2.5 percent (i.e., 5% × 0.5) in this example.

If we use this information to revise our simple initial forecast, we add 2.5 percent of sales each year to retained earnings, which leaves us with our first revision to our naive forecast, depicted in Table 4-13.

[18] Remember, the balance sheet has to balance.

TABLE 4-13 First Revision of Forecast

Sales	$120	%	$132	$145	$160
Cash	5	4.2	5.5	6.1	6.7
Marketable securities	10	8.3	11	12.1	13.3
Accounts receivable	10	8.3	11	12.1	13.3
Inventory	25	20.8	27.5	30.3	33.3
Net fixed assets	100	83.3	110	121	133
Total assets	150	125	165	181.6	199.6
Accruals	5	4.2	5.5	6.1	6.7
Accounts payable	5	4.2	5.5	6.1	6.7
Short-term debt	20	16.7	20	20	20
Long-term debt	40	33.3	40	40	40
Equity	80	66.7	83.3	86.9	90.9
Total liabilities and equity	150	125	154.3	159.1	164.3
Cumulative EFR			10.7	22.5	35.3

The only difference between this revision and the initial forecast is that we have taken into account the future retained earnings of 2.5 percent per dollar of sales, which has reduced the EFR by $10.90. However, this forecast is still relatively naive and does not make use of skills in financial analysis. We can improve on this naive forecast. To do this, we will go through all the non-financial policy assumptions to see whether we can improve on them.

First, we have to recognize that the percentage of sales method automatically imposes a very strict relationship between the assets and sales. For example, when we assume that cash is 4.2 percent of sales, we assume that it will remain so whether sales are $10 or $1,000. Graphically, we are forcing the relationship between cash and sales to be a straight line going through the origin. A more reasonable assumption would be that there are economies of scale to managing cash and that the marginal impact of sales growth is less than the average percentage of sales of 4.2 percent. For example, the true relationship at a sales level of $120 might be $2 plus 2.5 percent of sales so that the marginal impact of sales growth is only 2.5 percent of sales. Figure 4-3 depicts the differences in the cash forecasts that arise by changing this assumption.

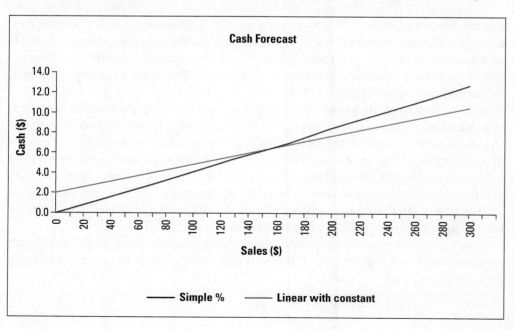

FIGURE 4-3 *Cash Forecast*

How cash varies with sales can be determined by statistically analyzing previous sales levels and cash balances. A linear relationship as graphed in Figure 4-3 can be estimated with or without a constant by using an ordinary least squares (OLS) linear regression. This regression can be done in Excel or by using various other statistical packages. For our forecast, we assume that the treasurer has done this analysis and is satisfied that, over the three-year horizon, operations can be managed from existing cash balances and no further investment is required. Cash will be held constant at $5.

We will temporarily skip marketable securities and consider accounts receivable, addressing the issue of whether assuming they are a strict percentage of sales is reasonable. In this case, it may be. Previously, when considering the investment in accounts receivable, we showed that the number of days of sales in receivables, or the ACP, gave essentially the same information as the receivables turnover ratio. As long as the firm maintains the same credit policy and the same mix between credit and cash sales, and the economy doesn't crash, then assuming a constant percentage of sales is reasonable. However, if the firm anticipates changing its credit policy and granting more lenient credit terms, then the percentage of sales tied up in receivables will increase, as it will if the proportion of credit to cash sales increases. Both of these events might happen in an economic downturn, where the firm might use more lenient credit as a way of maintaining its level of sales. Understanding the macroeconomic environment that generates the sales forecast will help the treasurer refine the percentage of sales tied up in receivables. For our purposes, we will assume that no slowdown is expected during the forecast period and that estimating receivables at 8.3 percent of sales is reasonable.

We treat inventory in a similar manner to receivables. As long as the inventory turnover ratio is expected to be constant, inventory will increase in line with sales. However, the same qualifications apply in terms of the macroeconomic environment. If a downturn is anticipated, then the firm might plan to increase the level of inventory in order to bolster sales by offering immediate delivery. In contrast, the firm might believe that it can reduce inventory, either because some of it is obsolete or because it plans to adopt new inventory management systems, such as "just-in-time" inventory planning. However, consistent with our treatment of receivables, we assume that using a constant percentage of sales is reasonable.

The last asset item is net fixed assets. Here, the reasonableness of assuming a constant percentage of sales largely depends on whether the firm is a single-plant or multi-plant firm. In a single-plant firm, assuming that a constant percentage of sales will be tied up in net fixed plant and equipment tends to be unreasonable; investment in plant and equipment usually lasts many years, and the firm does not replace a part of it each year. Instead, investment in plant and equipment is "lumpy." The firm will build its plant and equipment, and then each year the plant and equipment will reduce in value as the firm records depreciation. After a certain number of years, major refurbishment and replacement is needed, and the cycle begins again. For multi-plant firms, this effect gets smoothed out because the process is occurring over large numbers of plants.

This brings us back to the question of why firms hold marketable securities. Generally, firms do not create value by investing in marketable securities; they hold marketable securities as a temporary resting place for cash until it can be used. Suppose that the treasurer talks to the controller and realizes that the $10 in marketable securities is needed to fund a plant expansion next year, after which there will be no further capital expenditures over the forecast horizon. In this case, it makes no sense to extrapolate marketable securities into the future. Further, after the plant and equipment are expanded, plant and equipment will decline in the future as they are depreciated. So we'll assume that the firm depreciates the plant and equipment by $10 per year, but in the first year, it spends the $10 in marketable securities to maintain the plant and equipment at $100.

The final items to consider are the spontaneous liabilities. These act very much like accounts receivable, because the major item is accounts payable. As long as the firm does not anticipate changing its payment policy, then its payables will increase in line with sales, so assuming that payables will remain a constant percentage of sales is reasonable. Making the adjustments discussed above, we get the second revision to the forecast, which is shown in Table 4-14.

TABLE 4-14 Second Revision of Forecast

Sales	$120	%	$132	$145	$160
Cash	5	4.2	5	5	5
Marketable securities	10	8.3	0	0	0
Accounts receivable	10	8.3	11	12.1	13.3
Inventory	25	20.8	27.5	30.3	33.3
Net fixed assets	100	83.3	100	90	80
Total assets	150	125	143.5	137.4	131.6
Accruals	5	4.2	5.5	6.1	6.7
Accounts payable	5	4.2	5.5	6.1	6.7
Short-term debt	20	16.7	20	20	20
Long-term debt	40	33.3	40	40	40
Equity	80	66.7	83.3	86.9	90.9
Total liabilities and equity	150	125	154.3	159.1	164.3
Cumulative EFR			−11.2	−21.7	−32.7

This revision has profoundly different implications for the treasurer. Whereas, before, the firm had an external financing requirement, now it would be able to repay some financing obligations because the EFR is negative. The reasons for this are that the firm no longer needs the increase in cash or the marketable securities and, more important, the plant and equipment don't need new money spent on them during the forecast period.

The final step is to consider changes in the net profit margin. Previously, we assumed that the net profit margin remained the same even when sales changed. However, if the 10 percent sales growth forecast is due to a recovery from a recession, then the firm may be able to achieve this growth without adding to its fixed costs. In this case, the net profit margin may also increase, if the firm's fixed costs are indeed fixed. Table 4-15 reports the income statements that arise if we maintain gross profits at 40 percent of sales but maintain fixed costs at $31.

TABLE 4-15 Profit Margin and Sales

Sales	$120	$132	$145	$160
Gross margin (40%)	48	53	58	64
Fixed costs	31	31	31	31
Interest	5	5	5	5
Tax	6	8.5	11	14
Net income	6	8.5	11	14
Net profit margin	5%	6.4%	7.6%	8.8%

Notice that the profit margin increases dramatically from 5 percent to 8.8 percent over the four-year period. This is the typical "recovery from recession" pattern, in which the firm lowers fixed costs during a recession, through restructuring and cost-cutting, so that the immediate impact of a recovery causes greatly improved profit margins.

Finally, as we will discuss in Chapter 22, firms usually do not follow a constant dividend payout policy; they tend to cautiously increase dividends in line with sustainable earnings. We'll assume that the treasurer expects the dividend to stay at $3 for the next three years. This means that retained earnings will increase much more quickly than net income will. If this higher level of retained earnings is added to our forecast, we get the final forecast, as shown in Table 4-16.

TABLE 4-16 Final Revision of Forecast

Sales	$120	%	$132	$145	$160
Cash	5	4.2	5	5	5
Marketable securities	10	8.3	0	0	0
Accounts receivable	10	8.3	11	12.1	13.3
Inventory	25	20.8	27.5	30.3	33.3
Net fixed assets	100	83.3	100	90	80
Total assets	150	125	143.5	137.4	131.6
Accruals	5	4.2	5.5	6.1	6.7
Accounts payable	5	4.2	5.5	6.1	6.7
Short-term debt	20	16.7	20	20	20
Long-term debt	40	33.3	40	40	40
Equity	80	66.7	85.5	93.5	104.5
Total liabilities and equity	150	125	156.5	165.7	177.9
Cumulative EFR			−13	−28.3	−46.3

The upshot of this final revision is that the surplus is even greater, and the treasurer has to develop a plan for managing these funds, rather than arranging for the firm to raise money. This is quite a different scenario indeed! [19]

In considering how we changed the simple percentage of sales forecast, we have obviously exaggerated certain effects. For example, fixed costs are only fixed in the sense that they do not vary with sales. However, they still tend to increase over time as a result of wage increases and the general tendency to hire more staff as the firm's profits increase. Likewise, it would be difficult for the firm to maintain the dividend at $3 as profits and cash start to pile up. Alternative assumptions about the macroeconomic environment could soon cause the surplus to become a deficit. For example, if a slowdown is forecast, then a stable or declining sales forecast could cause the profit margin to contract while requiring more receivables and inventory as a percentage of sales. However, this is not the point of the exercise, because many different scenarios can be envisioned. What we wanted to demonstrate is how the simple percentage of sales forecasting method, when allied with basic skills in financial analysis, can produce an effective forecast. However, if it is employed "blindly," it may provide misleading results. Moreover, even though the percentage of sales forecasting method can be improved for short-term forecasts, it is very accurate for multi-plant firms over longer periods of time, which brings us to simple formula forecasting techniques. [20]

CONCEPT REVIEW QUESTIONS

1. Why is the sales forecast the most critical component of financial forecasting?

2. Describe the basic percentage of sales approach to financial forecasting. What is the main underlying premise to this forecasting approach?

3. What are some of the major limitations of the percentage of sales approach, and how may they be overcome?

---

[19] Note that some "sophisticated" financial planning models build in a further refinement so that, as debt changes, so too do the firm's interest charges and net profit margin. This can be done quite easily in Excel by simultaneously solving for all values. However, we find that this extension generally adds little to the usefulness of financial planning, particularly now that interest rates are so low.

[20] In fact, to get a detailed picture of cash flow needs throughout the year for a firm with seasonal sales, a cash flow forecast is needed, using a detailed cash budget. This is discussed in Chapter 23. The percentage of sales method allows you to forecast more permanent financing required to support projected sales growth, but throughout the year, actual financing requirements may be considerably greater. This effect may be further complicated by the firm's choice of fiscal year end.

4.9 FORMULA FORECASTING

Let's return to the simple percentage of sales forecasting method, as this works very well for longer periods and for multi-plant firms. From the initial forecast, total assets in our example were 125 percent of sales, and spontaneous liabilities were 8.4 percent, so invested capital was the balance of 116.6 percent. As we discussed previously, when we subtract spontaneous liabilities from total assets, we get the firm's invested capital, or net assets, as a percentage of sales. We will denote this as a, which represents the treasurer's financial policy variable, because it is the total invested capital requirement of the firm as a percentage of sales.

According to the assumptions of the percentage of sales method, if the firm doesn't grow, there is no need for additional net assets. This is because the firm will not need to provide additional credit to customers (accounts receivable) or inventory to meet demand, and the firm's fixed assets should be able to continue to produce enough to meet demand. Consequently, the current level of invested capital is sufficient for the firm. The corollary is that positive EFR mainly arises as a result of sales growth. We represent this sales growth as g, so if current sales are S, next period's sales growth is $S \times g$, and the incremental capital required is $a \times S \times g$. In our previous example, current sales were $120, and the forecast sales growth rate was 10 percent, so incremental sales were expected to be $12. With the net asset requirement of 116.6 percent of sales, the firm will acquire additional invested capital of $14.

From this additional invested capital, we need to subtract the forecast retained earnings. As we noted before, this is the net profit margin multiplied by one minus the dividend payout. We represent the net profit margin as PM, and we denote one minus the payout ratio as b, which is commonly referred to as the **retention (or plowback) ratio**. Therefore, we can express the forecast retained earnings as $b \times PM \times (1 + g) \times S$. In our example, with current sales of $120, the forecast sales $[(1 + g) \times S]$ are $132, using a sales growth rate of 10 percent. In this case, the forecast retained earnings are 2.5 percent of $132 or $3.30, since we are assuming a 5 percent net profit margin (PM) and a retention ratio (b) of 50 percent. The EFR of $10.70 is then exactly what we calculated in the first revision of our percentage of sales forecast in Table 4-13.

retention (or plowback) ratio one minus the payout ratio

Algebraically, we can represent this EFR as shown in Equation 4-32.

[4-32]
$$EFR = a \times S \times g - b \times PM \times (1+g) \times S$$

This is the invested capital requirement minus the forecast retained earnings. The advantage of the algebraic formulation is that it focuses on the key drivers of the EFR, which are the sales growth rate, the invested capital requirement, and the amount of earnings retained by the firm.

The EFR in our example can also be expressed as a linear function of the sales growth rate (g). We can see this more easily by dividing both sides of Equation 4-32 by the current sales level and rearranging, as shown in Equation 4-33.

[4-33]
$$\frac{EFR}{S} = -b \times PM + (a - b \times PM)g$$

This line can be graphed with EFR/S along the vertical (y) axis, and with g along the horizontal (x) axis, as shown in Figure 4-4.

This is an important graph. It tells us that, for negative and low forecast sales growth rates, EFR is zero or even negative (i.e., cash is freed up). The reason for this is twofold: first, the firm generates profits from its sales, some of which ($b \times PM$) are retained within the firm; second, it also liberates some of its investment in accounts receivable and inventory, which both decline as sales fall. At this point, it is important to remember that this is the forecast growth rate. If the firm plans for positive sales growth, and then sales decline, this often results in more receivables and inventory than planned and generates a positive EFR. In fact, many firms run

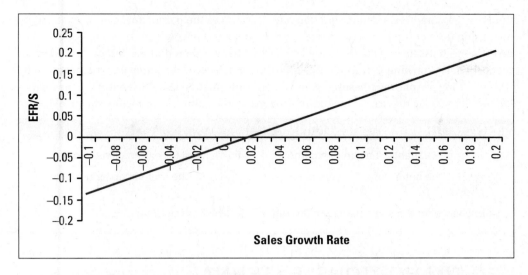

FIGURE 4-4 *External Financing Requirements*

into severe financing problems when sales decline dramatically and they are not able to cut production quickly enough, so they just produce for inventory.

The graph indicates a basic principle in finance, which is that declining- and low-growth firms tend to be cash cows, in that they generate cash. Notice from Equation 4-33 that at a zero growth rate, the firm does not need any new invested capital, so the EFR equals the forecast earnings retained within the business. Further, notice that the coefficient of growth is positive as long as $a > (b \times PM)$, which will almost always be the case. This means that the EFR increases as sales growth increases, all else being equal. In our example, $a > (b \times PM)$ because the sales growth causes the firm to increase its net assets by a, which in our example is 116.6 percent, and this is only partially offset by the retained earnings percentage of sales, which in our example is 2.5 percent. The result is that the sales growth generates an external financing need and problems for the treasurer. This is the norm—as sales grow, firms require external financing to support these sales, no matter how profitable they are.

Finance professors like linear relationships, such as those discussed above, because they generate a line that crosses the horizontal axis. This point is very important, because it measures a break-even point. We have already discussed the break-even point, which is the sales level at which the firm covers its fixed costs. However, there is also a sales growth rate at which the firm neither generates nor needs financing—that is, it breaks even in the financing sense. This is the point in Figure 4-4 at which the line crosses the horizontal axis, which we call the **sustainable growth rate (g*)**.[21] We can find this point by setting $EFR/S = 0$ in Equation 4-33 and solving for g, which leaves us with Equation 4-34.

sustainable growth rate (g*) the sales growth rate at which the firm neither generates nor needs financing—that is, it breaks even in terms of financing

$$g^* = \frac{b \times PM}{(a - b \times PM)} \qquad [4\text{-}34]$$

For our example, we have the following:

$$g^* = \frac{b \times PM}{(a - b \times PM)} = \frac{0.5 \times 0.05}{(1.166 - 0.5 \times 0.05)} = 0.0219$$

Sales for the firm in our example can grow at 2.19 percent per year before the firm needs external financing. The fact that sales are forecast to grow at 10 percent generates the EFR in the first revision of our percentage of sales forecast.

If sales for the firm in our example do in fact grow at 10 percent per year and exceed the sustainable growth rate, then one of two things has to happen. Either the firm has to raise external

---

[21] See Higgins, Robert, "Sustainable Growth under Inflation." *Financial Management* 10 (Autumn 1981), pp. 36–40.

funds or the parameters in our equation have to change. The parameters can be changed by increasing the net profit margin, decreasing the dividend payout rate, or decreasing the net investment in assets. In fact, these are the factors that we altered in our forecast revisions in section 4.8. By knowing the sustainable growth rate, as well as the target growth rate given by the marketing people, the treasurer gains valuable information about the nature of the financing problem facing the firm in the future—the rest of the effort is working out the details.

CONCEPT REVIEW QUESTIONS

1. What four variables have a direct impact on a firm's need for external financing?
2. What is the nature of the relationship between EFR and the four variables described above?
3. Explain what the sustainable growth rate is and why it is important.

4.10 TIM HORTONS' EXTERNAL FINANCING REQUIREMENTS

Learning Objective 4.10
Apply financial forecasting to a real company.

There are some useful lessons to be learned by repeating the forecasting exercise using Tim Hortons. We will keep the forecast as simple as possible, without making unrealistic assumptions. For this purpose, we begin by expressing Tim Hortons' 2008–11 balance sheet accounts as a percentage of sales, which is shown in Table 4-17.

TABLE 4-17 Tim Hortons Inc.'s Balance Sheet as a Percentage of Sales

Assets	% of Sales (2008)	% of Sales (2009)	% of Sales (2010)	% of Sales (2011)	Use
Current assets					
Cash and cash equivalents	**0.0497**	**0.0461**	**0.2264**	**0.0443**	2011 % sales
Accounts receivable	0.078	0.0762	0.0718	0.0609	2011 % sales
Other receivables	0.0111	0.0172	0.0049	0.0035	2011 % sales
Inventory	0.035	0.0305	0.0397	0.048	2011 % sales
Other current assets	0.0537	0.0495	0.055	0.0609	2011 % sales
Total Current Assets	**0.2275**	**0.2193**	**0.3978**	**0.2177**	**2011 % sales**
Gross fixed assets	0.9359	0.8907	0.8277	0.8031	2011 % sales
Accumulated depreciation	−0.2837	−0.2927	−0.2861	−0.29	2011 % sales
Net fixed assets	0.6522	0.598	0.5416	0.5131	2011 % sales
Notes receivable, net	0.0086	0.0044	0.0015	0.0011	2011 % sales
Intangibles	0.0013	0.0027	0.0021	0.0016	2011 % sales
Equity investments	0.0648	0.0539	0.0177	0.0151	2011 % sales
Other non-current assets	0.0206	0.0122	0.0177	0.024	2011 % sales
Total Assets	**0.9750**	**0.8905**	**0.9783**	**0.7725**	
Liabilities					
Accounts payable	0.0769	0.0578	0.0561	0.0624	2011 % sales
Salaries and wages payable	0.0091	0.0091	0.0081	0.0082	2011 % sales
Income taxes payable	0.0125	0.0112	0.0259	0.0093	2011 % sales

continued

TABLE 4-17 Tim Hortons Inc.'s Balance Sheet as a Percentage of Sales *continued*

Assets	% of Sales (2008)	% of Sales (2009)	% of Sales (2010)	% of Sales (2011)	Use
Other payables	0.0541	0.05	0.0827	0.0628	2011 % sales
Other current liabilities	0.0233	0.0198	0.017	0.0208	2011 % sales
Current portion of long-term debt	0.0033	0.0034	0.0039	0.0035	2011 % sales
Total current liabilities	**0.1791**	**0.1513**	**0.1938**	**0.1671**	**2011 % sales**
Long-term debt	0.1627	0.1499	0.1359	0.1235	2011 value
Other long-term debt	0.0034	0.0002	0.0002	0	2011 % sales
Capital leases	0.0289	0.03	0.0324	0.0333	2011 % sales
Deferred income taxes	0.0067	0.0021	0.0032	0.0016	2011 % sales
Other long-term liabilities	0.0363	0.0349	0.0441	0.0424	2011 % sales
Total long-term obligations	0.2379	0.217	0.2159	0.2008	2011 % sales
Total Liabilities	**0.417**	**0.3683**	**0.4097**	**0.3679**	
Shareholders' equity					
Preferred stock	0	0	0	0	
Common stock	0.2534	0.2243	0.1908	0.1569	2011 value
Retained earnings	0.3315	0.3551	0.436	0.2934	2011 value + RE
Other equity	−0.0269	−0.058	−0.0604	−0.0462	2011 % sales
Non-controlling interests	0	0	0.0022	0.0007	2011 value
Total shareholders' equity	**0.5580**	**0.5222**	**0.5687**	**0.4047**	
Total liabilities and shareholders' equity	**0.975**	**0.8905**	**0.9783**	**0.7725**	

For most of the items, the percentages are similar for 2008, 2009, and 2011, with the 2010 figures being skewed due to the one-time gain on the sale of Maidstone Bakeries. This implies that using the percentage of sales forecasting approach is reasonable. The only notable account that is an exception to the rule is common stock, which changed significantly over the period as a result of share repurchases.

Table 4-17 also includes an additional column entitled "Use," which shows the assumption we will use to construct our forecast. You will note that we have simply used the 2011 percentage of sales figures to forecast most of the balance sheet items, which simplifies our forecasting process considerably. We feel this is reasonable since this eliminates the influence of the 2010 percentages, which are atypical, and because it represents the company's most up-to-date figures. In addition, these numbers are reasonably close to the values in 2008 and 2009, which confirms their representativeness.

We note three exceptions where we do not apply the 2011 percentage of sales figures. These are non-controlling interests, long-term debt, and common stock, where we assume no change in the values. The non-controlling interest figure is so small as to be negligible, while the other two assumptions are equivalent to saying that the firm neither issues nor retires any long-term debt or common stock outstanding. If we go back through the actual balance sheets, we see there has been little change in the long-term debt item, so this seems to be a reasonable assumption. In addition, this is a useful assumption for forecasting purposes because these are two sources of external financing accounts that Tim Hortons might use.

The only other account that is not estimated as a direct percentage of sales is the retained earnings account, which we estimate using the procedures described in the preceding two sections.

In particular, we have derived an equation that helps us to determine how retained earnings will increase in the future, based on forecasted sales growth, profit margins, and retention rates. We will use 2011 averages for Tim Hortons to estimate future growth and profit margins, and use the 2011 dividend payout ratio to estimate the retention ratios. The 2011 dividend payout ratio was 28.81 percent, implying a 71.19 percent retention ratio. The net profit margin averaged 13.52 percent, and sales grew at an annual rate of 10.76 percent over the 2008–11 period, which is consistent with Tim Hortons' commonly employed revenue growth target of 10 percent per year. All of these estimates seem reasonable, for our purposes.

Based on these assumptions, we have chosen to use a sales growth rate of 10 percent. We start with this figure to construct our financial forecast for 2012–14, which is shown in Table 4-18.

TABLE 4-18 Tim Hortons Inc. Forecast ($ Millions)

	2012 ProForma	2013 ProForm	2014 ProForma
Assets			
Current assets			
Cash and cash equivalents	139.2	153.1	168.4
Accounts receivable	191.1	210.2	231.2
Other receivables	11.1	12.2	13.4
Inventory	150.7	165.8	182.3
Other current assets	191.1	210.2	231.2
Total Current Assets	**683.1**	**751.4**	**826.6**
Gross fixed assets	2,520.4	2,772.5	3,049.7
Accumulated depreciation	−910.3	−1,001.3	−1,101.4
Net fixed assets	1,610.2	1,771.2	1,948.3
Notes receivable, net	3.5	3.9	4.3
Intangibles	5	5.4	6
Equity investments	47.3	52	57.2
Other non-current assets	75.4	82.9	91.2
Total Assets	**2,424.4**	**2,666.8**	**2,933.5**
Liabilities			
Accounts payable	195.7	215.3	236.8
Salaries and wages payable	25.9	28.4	31.3
Income taxes payable	29.2	32.1	35.3
Other payables	197.2	217.0	238.6
Other current liabilities	65.3	71.9	79.1
Current portion of LT debt	11	12.1	13.3
Total current liabilities	**524.3**	**576.7**	**634.4**
Long-term debt	352.4	352.4	352.4
Other long-term debt	0	0	0
Capital leases	104.4	114.8	126.3
Deferred income taxes	5.1	5.6	6.1
Other long-term liabilities	133.1	146.4	161.1
Total long-term obligations	630.2	693.2	762.5
Total Liabilities	1,154.5	1,269.9	1,396.9

continued

TABLE 4-18 Tim Hortons Inc. Forecast ($ Millions) *continued*

	2012 ProForma	2013 ProForm	2014 ProForma
Shareholders' equity			
Preferred stock	0	0	0
Common stock	447.5	447.5	447.5
Retained earnings	1,138.3	1,469.7	1,834.2
Other equity	−160.2	−176.2	−193.8
Non-controlling interests	1.9	1.9	1.9
Total shareholders' equity	**1,425.6**	**1,741.0**	**2,087.9**
Total liabilities and shareholders' equity	**2,580.1**	**3,010.9**	**3,484.8**
Common shares outstanding (year end)	162,145	162,145	162,145
Cumulative EFR	**−155.6**	**−344.0**	**−551.2**

Notice from Table 4-18 that the bottom line is the cumulative EFR, which is negative $155.6 million for 2012, which means Tim Hortons could actually pay down some debt during that year. The projected cumulative EFR increases by an additional $188.4 million in 2013 and a further $207.2 million the following year, which implies Tim Hortons could continue to reduce its debt, increase its capital spending, increase its dividend payout, and/or continue to repurchase shares, as long as its sales continue to grow and its profit margins remain high.

The fact that Tim Hortons produced surplus EFR positions is hardly surprising if we look at its sustainable growth rate, which we can estimate by using the approach described in section 4.9. In 2011, total assets were 77.25 percent of sales, and spontaneous liabilities were 14.27 percent, so net assets (a) were 62.98 percent. To estimate the sustainable growth rate, we also need to estimate the retained earnings percentage of sales, which is the profit margin times the retention rate. We use the 2011 figures for Tim Hortons, which indicate a retention ratio (b) of 0.7119 and a net profit margin (PM) of 13.52 percent. By using Equation 4-34, we can estimate Tim Hortons' sustainable growth rate as the following:

$$g^* = \frac{b \times PM}{(a - b \times PM)} = \frac{(0.09625)}{(0.6298 - 0.09625)} = 0.1804$$

This is a relatively high sustainable growth rate, reflecting Tim Hortons' high profitability and relatively high retention rates. In fact, very few firms could grow at this rate without needing any external financing. Notice that Tim Hortons' revenues increased 12.5 percent during 2011, and 10.76 percent over the 2007–11 period, which are both well below the estimated sustainable growth rate. Thus, it is not surprising that, based on the 10 percent sales growth estimate we forecast, Tim Hortons would be in a surplus EFR position for the next three years. In fact, even if Tim Hortons grew at a rate of 12 percent per year, the company would still generate EFR surpluses of $135 million in 2012, an additional $169 million in 2013, and another $189 million in 2014, providing all else remained relatively constant.

CONCEPT REVIEW QUESTIONS

1. What is the relationship between the sustainable growth rate, the actual sales growth rate, external financing requirements, and dividend payments?

SUMMARY

Almost all corporate finance questions involve an analysis of macroeconomic conditions, followed by a financial analysis of the firm. It is critical to understand the sources of a firm's profitability or lack thereof. The basic analysis is to look at the ROE and then break this out into operating profitability, leverage, efficiency, and productivity ratios, with a look at liquidity ratios to see what the firm's financial reserves are. These same skills in financial analysis are then needed for financial forecasting, for which the external financing requirement is essentially the plug in a forecast balance sheet. All forecasts hinge on a sales forecast. For longer-term forecasts, the sustainable growth rate represents an easy shortcut to estimating the types of financing problems a firm is likely to have.

SUMMARY OF LEARNING OBJECTIVES

4.1 Identify the issues that need to be considered in applying consistent financial analysis.

Despite efforts to harmonize accounting standards, important differences in generally accepted accounting principles (GAAP) still persist. An additional complication arises because there are no generally accepted financial ratios. Thus, it is always important, when looking at ratios generated by another party, to examine how they are calculated. Even some of the most basic ratios, such as return on equity (ROE), can vary when calculated by different institutions, even if the input data are the same.

4.2 Explain why return on equity is one of the key financial ratios used to assess a firm's performance, and show how it can be used to provide information about three areas of a firm's operations.

The return on owner's equity (ROE) ratio is an accounting measure of the return on the owners' investment. It is a very important ratio for financial analysts as it measures overall profitability from the owners' (shareholders') perspective. The DuPont system is a system for analyzing ratios, and it explains changes in ROE. In the DuPont system, ROE is shown to be a function of leverage, margin, and turnover.

4.3 Describe, calculate, and evaluate the key ratios relating to financial leverage.

Leverage ratios measure the amount of borrowing that a company has done (debt), and the ability of the company to pay interest and repay principal on its debts. The calculation and evaluation of leverage ratios are presented in section 4.3.

4.4 Describe, calculate, and evaluate the key ratios relating to financial efficiency.

Efficiency ratios measure margins and profitability. The calculation and evaluation of efficiency ratios are presented in section 4.4.

4.5 Describe, calculate, and evaluate the key ratios relating to financial productivity.

Productivity ratios measure how efficiently a company uses its assets—that is, how much revenue it gets out of its assets. The calculation and evaluation of productivity ratios are presented in section 4.5.

4.6 Describe, calculate, and evaluate the key ratios relating to financial liquidity.

Liquidity ratios reflect net working capital—the amount of short-term assets relative to the amount of short-term liabilities. Liquidity ratios are of particular interest to short-term lenders who use the short-term assets as collateral. The calculation and evaluation of liquidity ratios are presented in section 4.6.

4.7 Describe, calculate, and evaluate the key ratios relating to the valuation of a company.

Valuation ratios provide insight into whether stock prices are overvalued or undervalued. The calculation and evaluation of valuation ratios are presented in section 4.7.

4.8 Explain why financial forecasting is critical for both management and external parties, and explain how to prepare financial forecasts using the percentage of sales method.

Financial forecasts help managers identify cash and capital shortages before they occur. Forecasting is also a critical part of discounted cash flow valuation—a primary tool of investment managers. Financial forecasting is usually performed using the percentage of sales method. Under this method, sales are forecast, and then most financial items are forecast using their historic ratio to sales, making adjustments to items when this assumption is not appropriate.

4.9 Explain how external financing requirements are related to sales growth, profitability, dividend payouts, and sustainable growth rates.

Financial forecasting yields a number called EFR—external financing requirements. EFR is the amount of capital necessary (from outside sources) to fund the forecasted increase in sales and the associated increased need for assets like inventory and fixed assets.

4.10 Apply financial forecasting to a real company.

See the example using Tim Hortons in section 4.10.

KEY TERMS

average collection period (ACP), p. 122
average days revenues in inventory (ADRI), p. 123
break-even point (BEP), p. 119
cash flow to debt ratio, p. 117
current ratio, p. 124
debt ratio, p. 115
debt-equity (D/E) ratio, p. 116
degree of total leverage (DTL), p. 119
dividend payout ratio, p. 128
dividend yield, p. 128
EBITDA multiple, p. 130
efficiency ratios, p. 118
equity book value per share (BVPS), p. 127

external financing requirements (EFR), p. 132
financial leverage, p. 111
fixed asset turnover ratio, p. 123
forward P/E ratio, p. 129
gross profit margin, p. 120
inventory turnover ratio, p. 122
invested capital, p. 115
leverage ratio, p. 111
liquidity, p. 124
market-to-book (M/B) ratio, p. 129
net profit margin, p. 111
operating income (OI), p. 120
operating margin, p. 120
percentage of sales method, p. 132

price-earnings (P/E) ratio, p. 128
productivity ratios, p. 121
quick ratio or acid test ratio, p. 125
receivables turnover ratio, p. 121
retention (or plowback) ratio, p. 138
return on assets (ROA), p. 111
return on equity (ROE), p. 109
spontaneous liabilities, p. 132
stock ratios, p. 115
sustainable growth rate (g^*), p. 139
times interest earned (TIE), p. 117
total enterprise value (TEV), p. 130
turnover ratio, p. 111
working capital, p. 124
working capital ratio, p. 124

EQUATIONS

Equation	Formula	Page
[4-1] Return on Equity	$ROE = \dfrac{NI}{SE}$	p. 109
[4-2] Return on Assets	$ROA = \dfrac{NI}{TA}$	p. 111
[4-3] Leverage Ratio (Equity Multiplier)	$Leverage = \dfrac{TA}{SE}$	p. 111
[4-4] Net Profit Margin	$Net\ profit\ margin = \dfrac{NI}{Revenues}$	p. 111
[4-5] Asset Turnover Ratio	$Turnover\ ratio = \dfrac{Revenues}{TA}$	p. 111
[4-6] Return on Assets (DuPont)	$ROA = \dfrac{NI}{TA} = \dfrac{NI}{Revenues} \times \dfrac{Revenues}{TA}$	p. 111
[4-7] Return on Equity (DuPont)	$ROE = \dfrac{NI}{SE} = \dfrac{NI}{Revenues} \times \dfrac{Revenues}{TA} \times \dfrac{TA}{SE}$ $= Net\ profit\ margin \times Turnover\ ratio \times Leverage\ ratio$	p. 112

continued

EQUATIONS *continued*

Equation	Formula	Page
[4-8] Debt Ratio	$Debt\ ratio = \dfrac{TL}{TA}$	p. 115
[4-9] Debt-to-Equity Ratio	$D/E\ ratio = \dfrac{D}{SE}$	p. 116
[4-10] Times Interest Earned (Coverage Ratio)	$TIE = \dfrac{EBIT}{I}$	p. 117
[4-11] Cash Flow to Debt Ratio	$Cash\ flow\ to\ debt\ ratio = \dfrac{CFO}{D}$	p. 117
[4-12] Degree of Total Leverage	$DTL = \dfrac{CM}{EBT}$	p. 119
[4-13] Break-Even Point	$BEP = \dfrac{FC}{CM}$	p. 119
[4-14] Gross Profit Margin	$Gross\ profit\ margin = \dfrac{Rev - COS}{Rev}$	p. 120
[4-15] Operating Profit Margin	$Operating\ margin = \dfrac{OI}{Rev}$	p. 120
[4-16] Receivables Turnover	$Receivables\ turnover = \dfrac{Rev}{AR}$	p. 121
[4-17] Average Collection Period	$ACP = \dfrac{AR}{ADR} = \dfrac{365}{Receivables\ turnover}$	p. 122
[4-18] Inventory Turnover Ratio (Using COS)	$Inventory\ turnover = \dfrac{COS}{INV}$	p. 122
[4-19] Inventory Turnover Ratio (Using Revenues)	$Inventory\ turnover = \dfrac{Rev}{INV}$	p. 122
[4-20] Average Days Revenues in Inventory	$ADRI = \dfrac{INV}{ADR} = Inventory\ turnover$	p. 123
[4-21] Fixed Asset Turnover	$Fixed\ asset\ turnover = \dfrac{Rev}{NFA}$	p. 123
[4-22] Working Capital Ratio	$Working\ capital\ ratio = \dfrac{CA}{TA}$	p. 124
[4-23] Current Ratio	$Current\ ratio = \dfrac{CA}{CL}$	p. 125
[4-24] Quick (Acid Test) Ratio	$Quick\ ratio = \dfrac{C + MS + AR}{CL}$	p. 125
[4-25] Equity Book Value per Share	$BVPS = \dfrac{SE}{Number\ of\ shares}$	p. 127
[4-26] Dividend Yield	$Dividend\ yield = \dfrac{DPS}{P}$	p. 128
[4-27] Dividend Payout Ratio	$Dividend\ payout = \dfrac{DPS}{EPS}$	p. 128
[4-28] Price-to-Earnings Ratio (Trailing)	$P/E = \dfrac{P}{EPS}$	p. 128

continued

EQUATIONS *continued*

Equation	Formula	Page
[4-29] Price-to-Earnings Ratio (Forward)	$Forward\ P/E = \dfrac{P}{EEPS}$	p. 129
[4-30] Market-to-Book ratio	$M/B = \dfrac{P}{BVPS}$	p. 130
[4-31] Earnings before Interest, Taxes, Depreciation, and Amortization (EBITDA) Multiple	$EBITDA\ multiple = \dfrac{TEV}{EBITDA}$	p. 130
[4-32] External Financing Required (EFR)	$EFR = a \times S \times g - b \times PM \times (1+g) \times S$	p. 138
[4-33] EFR/Sales	$\dfrac{EFR}{S} = -b \times PM + (a - b \times PM)g$	p. 138
[4-34] Sustainable Growth Rate	$g^* = \dfrac{b \times PM}{(a - b \times PM)}$	p. 139

QUESTIONS AND PRACTICE PROBLEMS

Multiple Choice Questions

1. Which of the following statements about consistent financial analysis is correct?
    a. Accounting standards are different across countries.
    b. If the input data are the same, the ratios for companies across countries are the same.
    c. We can directly compare ratios from annual reports of companies across countries.
    d. Debt ratio is calculated in the same way by companies across countries.

2. Which of the following ratios is not in the DuPont system?
    a. net profit margin
    b. leverage
    c. asset turnover
    d. current ratio

3. Which of the following components of the DuPont system for Hill Inc. is correct if sales are $5,600; earnings before tax (EBT) are $2,090; the tax rate is 40 percent; total liabilities are $30,900; and equity is $16,500?
    a. Net profit margin = 37.32 percent
    b. Asset turnover = 11.81 percent
    c. Leverage = 1.87
    d. Leverage = 0.53

4. To increase return on equity (ROE),
    a. increase equity, all else being unchanged.
    b. decrease debt outstanding, all else being unchanged.
    c. decrease corporate tax rate, all else being unchanged.
    d. decrease earnings after tax, all else being unchanged.

    Use the following information to answer practice problems 5 to 10.

Balance Sheet as of December 31, 2013

	$Million		$Million
Cash	400,000	Accounts payable	500,000
Marketable securities	500,000	Accrued liabilities	90,000

continued

Balance Sheet as of December 31, 2013 *continued*

	$Thousands		$Thousands
Inventory	250,000	Wages payable	150,000
Equipment	1,000,000	Long-term debt	2,000,000
Land	2,500,000	Common shares	2,800,000
Patent	980,000	Retained earnings	90,000
Total assets	5,630,000	Total liabilities and equity	5,630,000

Income Statement 2013

	$Thousands
Sales	1,090,000
COGS	380,000
Wages	200,000
Interest	150,000
EBT	360,000
Tax	108,000
NI	252,000

5. What is the company's debt ratio?
   a. 0.36
   b. 0.94
   c. 0.55
   d. 0.49

6. Calculate the debt-equity ratio and times interest earned ratio.
   a. 3.56; 0.32
   b. 0.95; 2.4
   c. 0.69; 3.4
   d. 2.4; 0.95

7. What is the company's gross profit and its operating margin? (Use EBIT as operating income.)
   a. 75 percent; 25 percent
   b. 65 percent; 47 percent
   c. 55 percent; 30 percent
   d. 70 percent; 49 percent

8. Which of the following is average days revenues in inventory?
   a. 84 days
   b. 70 days
   c. 66 days
   d. 82 days

9. Which of the following is the working capital ratio?
   a. 24.5 percent
   b. 18.5 percent
   c. 20.4 percent
   d. 15.5 percent

10. Which of the following is invested capital?
    a. $5,600,000
    b. $2,890,000

    c. $4,800,000

    d. $4,890,000

11. A financial ratio that measures the firm's ability to pay its interest obligations is
    a. debt ratio.
    b. debt-equity ratio.
    c. cash flow to debt ratio.
    d. times interest earned.

12. The current ratio is measured as
    a. current assets minus current liabilities.
    b. current assets divided by current liabilities.
    c. cash and cash equivalent divided by current liabilities.
    d. current liabilities divided by current assets.

13. The financial ratio measured as sales minus cost of goods sold, divided by sales, is the
    a. gross profit margin.
    b. break-even point.
    c. degree of total leverage.
    d. current ratio.

14. The average collection period is measured as
    a. accounts receivable divided by average daily sales.
    b. sales divided by accounts receivable.
    c. sales divided by inventory.
    d. 365 divided by inventory turnover.

15. The financial ratio measured as dividend per share divided by the current stock price is the
    a. dividend yield.
    b. book value per share.
    c. dividend payout.
    d. price-earnings ratio.

Practice Problems

Use the following information to answer practice problems 16 to 33 on Finns' Fridges.

    Finns' Fridges is a company created by twin brothers David and Douglas Finn, who rented small refrigerators to other students in their college dormitory. Use the following statements to answer the questions about Finns' Fridges.

Balance Sheet for Finns' Fridges (End of the year indicated)

	Year 1 ($)	Year 2 ($)
Assets		
Cash	1,150	493
Property and equipment (net)	3,840	3,888
Total assets	4,990	4,381
Liabilities and Owners' Equity		
Interest payable	200	160
Tax payable	177	182
Dividends payable	200	210
Long-term debt	3,200	2,400
Total liabilities	3,777	2,952

continued

Balance Sheet for Finns' Fridges (End of the year indicated) *continued*

	Year 1 ($)	Year 2 ($)
Common shares	1,000	1,000
Retained earnings	213	429
Total owners' equity	1,213	1,429
Total liabilities and owners' equity	4,990	4,381

Income Statement for Finns' Fridges (For the full year indicated)

	Year 1 ($)	Year 2 ($)
Revenues (net of bad debts)	1,950	2,200
Selling and administrative expenses	0	220
Loss (stolen equipment)	160	0
EBITDA	1,790	1,980
Amortization expense	1,000	1,212
EBIT	790	768
Interest expense	200	160
Earnings before tax	590	608
Tax (30%)	177	182
Net income	413	426
Earnings per share (100 shares)	4.13	4.26
Dividends per share	2.00	2.10

16. Find Finns' Fridges' return on equity (ROE) for years 1 and 2, using the owners' equity figure at the end of each year. Did this ratio improve or get worse between year 1 and year 2?

17. Use the definition of the leverage ratio in the DuPont system to determine if Finns' Fridges has become more or less leveraged between year 1 and year 2.

18. One key part of ROE in the DuPont system is the return on assets (ROA). Find the ROA for Finns' Fridges for both years and determine if it is increasing or decreasing.

19. The most recent financial statements for a large Canadian furniture and appliance rental chain show that its debt ratio was 0.256 and its debt-to-equity ratio (D/E) was 0.073. At the end of year 2, was Finns' Fridges more or less leveraged than this major competitor? (Remember to use only the interest-bearing liabilities—that is, long-term debt, when calculating the D/E ratio.)

20. The large competitor firm mentioned in Practice Problem 19 had net operating income of $4.426 million and sales of $30.16 million in its most recent accounting period. Find the operating margin for this competitor. Comment on Finns' Fridges level of operating efficiency compared to this real-world business.

21. In the DuPont system, there are two components of ROA. Determine whether efficiency or productivity (or both) is responsible for the increase in ROA for Finns' Fridges from year 1 to year 2.

22. We can calculate cash flow from operations (CFO) as net income + non-cash expenses + change in working capital. In year 2, the change in working capital for Finns' Fridges was −$25. Find the CFO and use this figure to calculate the cash flow to debt ratio. How many

years would it take the company to pay off its entire debt load if it devoted its cash flow to debt repayment?

23. Find the operating margin for Finns' Fridges for both years (you may assume that the net operating income is equal to the firm's EBIT). Was there an increase or a decrease in the operating margin, and is this a good trend or a bad one?

24. Calculate the fixed asset turnover for Finns' Fridges for years 1 and 2 (note that net fixed assets correspond to "property and equipment (net)" on the company's balance sheet). Has the company become more or less productive in terms of generating sales from assets?

25. At the end of its most recent fiscal period, the large appliance rental company mentioned in Practice Problem 19 had a working capital ratio of 4.3 percent and a current ratio of 18.2 percent. Calculate these ratios for Finns' Fridges at the end of year 1 and year 2. Is the company more or less liquid than its competitor?

26. The Finn brothers are planning their third year of operations. As a first step in the process, create a "percentage of sales" balance sheet for Finns' Fridges as of the end of year 2.

27. a. Suppose the Finns believe they can increase revenues to $2,600 in year 3. Use this figure and the percentage of sales balance sheet (Practice Problem 26) to forecast the company's balance sheet at the end of year 3. Remember that the "financing" components (long-term debt and total owners' equity) should be left unchanged from the year 2 figures.
    b. The forecast balance sheet does not balance! Determine the amount of external financing required by Finns' Fridges based on the initial forecast.

28. To achieve the target level of revenues in year 3 ($2,600), Finns' Fridges will have to buy some more equipment. This will increase the amortization expense to $1,422. Selling costs will be the same percentage of sales as in year 2, and the interest expense for the year will be $120. Use this information to determine the amount of net income the company should expect to earn in year 3.

29. Use the average dividend payout ratio from years 1 and 2, and the forecast net income figure from Practice Problem 28, to estimate the total amount of dividends that will be paid by the company in year 3.

30. Suppose that Finns' Fridges actually pays $270 in dividends in year 3. Determine the value of the retained earnings account at the end of year 3 based on the forecast net income calculated in Practice Problem 28.

31. The forecast for retained earnings (Practice Problem 30) changes the year 3 forecast for total liabilities and owners' equity to $4,770. With total assets forecast to be $5,177, determine how much external financing will be required in year 3.

✱ 32. Use the following information to create a revised forecast of the year 3 balance sheet for Finns' Fridges. Cash will increase by the forecast EBITDA amount (see Practice Problem 28); it will be reduced by $1,050 to purchase new equipment, $552 for year 2 payables, and $800 for debt repayment. The property and equipment (net) account will increase by $1,050 (new fridges purchased) but must be reduced by the $1,422 amortization expense. Interest and tax payable will reflect the respective expenses on the forecast income statement (again, see Practice Problem 28). Dividends payable will be $270. Long-term debt will be reduced by $800, and the retained earnings figure is $718. With this revised forecast, determine if any additional external financing is required.

⚙ 33. Use the year 2 financial statements for Finns' Fridges to determine the company's sustainable growth rate.

Use the following information to practice problems 34 to 38 on Corine's Candies.

34. At the end of 2011, Corine's Candies Inc. had total shareholders' equity of $13.8 million. In 2012, the company had net income of $5.2 million and paid out half this amount in dividends, resulting in shareholders' equity at the end of 2012 of $16.4 million. Use the average amount of shareholders' equity to determine Corine's ROE for 2012.

35. Corine's Candies Inc. registered a gross profit margin of 75 percent on sales of $16 million in 2012. What would the company's income statement show for the cost of goods sold?

⚙ 36. The shares of Corine's Candies Inc. are currently trading at $18.20. There are four million shares outstanding. The company's 2012 net income was $5.2 million. Find the market value of equity for the company and the P/E ratio of the shares.

⚙ 37. Other candy-making firms have an average forward P/E ratio of 12 at this time. With a share price of $18.20, what are the expected 2013 EPS for Corine's Candies if its forward P/E ratio is the same as the industry average?

⚙ 38. The managers of Corine's Candies like to use the EBITDA multiple to value the firm. EBITDA was approximately $10 million in 2012. Use the market value of equity from Practice Problem 36 and a debt value of $20 million to find the total enterprise value (TEV). Next, calculate the EBITDA multiple. Suppose the industry-average EBITDA multiple for candy producers is 8.65. Is the market valuing Corine's Candies Inc. more or less highly than its competitors?

Use the following information to answer practice problems 39 to 42 on GG Co.

39. For GG. Co., calculate the degree of total leverage (DTL) and break-even point of sales at which the firm covers all its operating and fixed costs, given the following information: sales are $5,050,000; variable cost is $1,850,000; net income is $685,750; tax rate (T) is 35 percent; and fixed cost is $2,100,000.

⚙ 40. GG Co. shows the following information on its financial statements: interest-bearing debt is $900,000; shareholders' equity (SE) is $2,500,000; sales are $5,050,000; net income is $685,750; dividends are $200,000; and sales growth (g) is 5 percent. Calculate EFR/S and discuss the relationship between dividend payout and EFR. Calculate the sustainable growth rate for GG Co. Discuss the relationship between profit margin and EFR.

41. Suppose that GG Co. would like to grow its sales by 30 percent, which is greater than its sustainable growth rate (see Practice Problem 40). If all the other financial information remains unchanged, how much external financing will the company require?

42. Calculate the degree of total leverage (DTL) and break-even point for a company, given the following information: sales are $400,088; variable cost is $120,000; net income is $180,000; tax rate (T) is 35 percent; fixed cost is $80,000.

43. Calculate the receivables turnover, inventory turnover, and average collection period for a firm, given the following accounting data: accounts receivable are $500,000; accounts payable are $305,000; inventory is $650,000; gross profit is $550,000; sales are $950,000. Interpret the receivables turnover, inventory turnover, and the average collection period.

44. Calculate book value per share, dividend yield, dividend payout, market-to-book ratio, earnings per share, and price-to-earnings ratio given the following information: shareholders' equity is $945,000; number of shares outstanding is 500,000; total dividends are $150,000; market price of each share is $9.50; net income is $433,000.

Use the following information to answer practice problems 45 to 58 on Excelsior Inc.

2012 Income Statement ($Million)

Net sales	1,850	Taxable income	985
Less: Cost of goods sold	605	Less: Taxes	156
Less: Depreciation	180	Net income	829
Earnings before interest and taxes	1,065	Addition to retained earnings	244
Less: Interest paid	80	Dividends paid	585

Year 1 and Year 2 December 31 Balance Sheet ($Million)

	Year 1	Year 2		Year 1	Year 2
Cash	100	112	Accounts payable	400	350
Accounts receivable	330	234	Notes payable	390	370
Inventory	410	435	Subtotal	790	720
Subtotal	840	781	Long-term debt	500	550
Net fixed assets	1,556	1,888	Owner's equity		
			Common shares	550	599
			Retained earnings	556	800
			Subtotal	1,106	1,399
Total assets	2,396	2,669	Total liabilities and equity	2,396	2,669

Number of shares = 100 million; share price = $15

45. Using the DuPont system, what are Excelsior Inc.'s net profit margin, asset turnover, and leverage ratio in year 2?

46. Use two approaches to determine ROE in year 2. (Hint: one approach is from definition and the other is to use the DuPont system.)

47. Determine leverage ratios, including debt ratio and debt-equity ratio, in both years. Has Excelsior Inc. improved on its leverage ratios in year 2?

48. Determine Excelsior Inc.'s efficiency ratio of times interest earned in year 2.

49. Determine the company's efficiency ratios including gross profit margin and operating margin in year 2. Explain the differences.

50. Determine productivity ratios including receivables turnover and average collection period in year 2.

51. Determine productivity ratios including inventory turnover and average days revenue in inventory in year 2.

52. Determine net fixed asset turnover in year 2.

53. Determine liquidity ratios including working capital ratio, current ratio, and quick ratio for year 2. Explain the differences among the ratios.

54. Determine valuation ratios including book value per share, dividend yield, and dividend payout for year 2.

55. If Excelsior Inc. keeps the same dividend payout ratio, what are the expected total dividends in year 3 if the sales growth rate is 5 percent?

56. Determine the price-earnings ratio, market-to-book ratio, and EBITDA ratio for year 2.

57. What sales growth rate must Excelsior Inc. achieve if it is to have a cash surplus?

58. If Excelsior Inc.'s expected sales growth rate is 5 percent, determine the external financing required. Will the corporation have a cash surplus or deficit?

Part 3

VALUATION BASICS

The three iron laws of finance are the time value, risk value, and tax value of money. In finance, the saying "time is money" is the building block for valuing securities. In this section, we develop the basic discounted cash flow model that is the workhorse of finance. We start with the time value of money and apply the basic discounting framework to valuing bonds and equities. In the process, we examine the widely used Gordon growth model for valuing low-risk equities and discuss fundamental approaches to equity valuation.

5 | Time Value of Money

LEARNING OBJECTIVES

5.1 Explain the importance of the time value of money and how it is related to an investor's opportunity costs.

5.2 Define simple interest and explain how it works.

5.3 Define compound interest and explain how it works.

5.4 Differentiate between an ordinary annuity and an annuity due, and explain how special constant payment problems can be valued as annuities and, in special cases, as perpetuities.

5.5 Differentiate between quoted rates and effective rates, and explain how quoted rates can be converted to effective rates.

5.6 Apply annuity formulas to value loans and mortgages, and set up an amortization schedule.

5.7 Solve a basic retirement problem.

5.8 Estimate the present value of growing perpetuities and annuities.

The discount rate used to determine the value of our money today is related to the opportunity cost of that money. What might be the opportunity cost of pursuing a master's degree in Canada? In a study by Statistics Canada (StatsCan), the opportunity cost was defined as tuition + additional fees + books + lost income − part-time income earned during the school year. StatsCan estimated the opportunity cost on average was $29,956. Its survey indicated that the returns from earning a post-graduate degree appear to outweigh the costs. Five years after graduation, master's graduates earned, on average, one-third more than those with bachelor's degrees. The employment rate for master's graduates was also higher than that of college, bachelor, or doctorate graduates, with 94 percent of men and 92 percent of women working fulltime in 2007.

Source: Bone, Alison, "Pursuing a Master's Degree: Opportunity Cost and Benefits." *Education Quarterly Review 8*, no. 4 (2002). Statistics Canada Catalogue no. 81-003-XIE. Ottawa.

Bayard, Justin and Greenlee, Edith, *Graduating in Canada: Profile, Labour Market Outcomes and Student Debt of the Class of 2005*. Statistics Canada, 2009, Catalogue no. 81-595-M, no. 074.

CHAPTER 5 **PREVIEW**

P art 1 was an introduction to the study of finance. In Part 2, we examined the importance of company financial statements. Now, in Part 3, we discuss the basic valuation process as it applies to financial securities. This valuation process relies heavily on discounting future expected cash flows, one of the tools discussed in this chapter. Mastery of the tools presented in this chapter is necessary for understanding finance.

This chapter will introduce you to everyday problems, such as taking out a loan, setting up a series of payments, and valuing them. The ideas in this chapter are important for all types of financial problems: determining the payments on a weekly versus a monthly mortgage, buying versus leasing a new car, appropriately valuing a bond or stock, determining whether a company should expand production or abandon a product line, and deciding how much a company should be willing to pay for another company. Although each situation involves unique circumstances that will be covered in subsequent chapters, the basic framework used to evaluate them is the same and relies on material covered in this chapter.

5.1 OPPORTUNITY COST

Learning Objective 5.1
Explain the importance of the time value of money and how it is related to an investor's opportunity costs.

time value of money the idea that a dollar today is worth more than a dollar in the future

medium of exchange something that can be used to facilitate transactions

required rate of return or **discount rate** the market interest rate (k) or the investor's opportunity cost

In this chapter, we are concerned with the **time value of money**. As we saw in Chapters 1 and 2, the financial system is designed to transfer savings from lenders to borrowers, so that savers have money to spend in the future. To illustrate this concept, we used the example of saving while working in order to have money when retired. Money, in this sense, represents our ability to buy goods and services—that is, it operates as a **medium of exchange** and has no value in and of itself. Of course, an investor could simply store the dollar bills (tuck them under the mattress!) and spend them later; a dollar is always worth at least a dollar in the future.[1] However, this option ignores the fact that the saver has other uses for that dollar, which in economics are called the "opportunity costs" or "alternative uses." Opportunity costs, such as investing the dollar to earn a return, are what produce the time value of money.

The opportunity cost of money is the interest rate that would be earned by investing it. For this reason, we also call the interest rate the "price of money." Knowing this rate helps us determine the value of money received at different times. Suppose, for example, a person has three choices: he or she could receive $20,000 today, $31,000 in five years, or $3,000 per year indefinitely. This choice could, for example, be the payoff from a lottery (though we are certainly not advocating gambling!). Making a choice from these different options requires that we know how to value the dollars received at different times—that is, the winner needs to adjust for the time value of money.

To make a decision, the person needs to know what the interest rate is. We will use k as a standard notation throughout the textbook for the market interest rate. We will refer to this market interest rate by several other names later in the textbook, such as the **required rate of return** or **discount rate**. The reason for these different names will become clear later, but in all cases, we are looking at the investor's opportunity cost—that is, what he or she can do with the money being invested. However, first we have to make some basic distinctions in terms of how this interest rate is earned and distinguish between simple interest and compound interest.

CONCEPT REVIEW QUESTIONS

1. Why does money have a "time value"?
2. What is an "opportunity cost"?

---

[1]This ignores the fact that what we are really concerned about is what that dollar will buy in terms of goods and services—that is, its purchasing power. We discuss this later in the chapter.

5.2 SIMPLE INTEREST

Simple interest is interest paid or received on only the initial investment (the principal). Although, in practice, simple interest is used for a limited number of applications, we introduce it first to contrast it with compound interest, which is the norm.

Learning Objective 5.2
Define simple interest and explain how it works.

simple interest interest paid or received on only the initial investment (the principal)

EXAMPLE 5-1 | **Simple Interest I**

Suppose someone invests $1,000 today for a five-year term and receives 10 percent annual simple interest on the investment. How much money would the investor have after five years?

Solution
Annual interest = $1,000 x 0.1 = $100 per year

Year	Beginning Amount	Ending Amount
1	$1,000	$1,100
2	1,100	1,200
3	1,200	1,300
4	1,300	1,400
5	1,400	1,500

In Example 5-1, the interest earned is $100 every year, regardless of the beginning amount each year, because interest is earned on only the original investment (principal). Interest is *not* earned on the accrued (or earned) interest.

Because the same amount of interest is earned each year—$100 in the example—we can use Equation 5-1 to find the value of the investment at any point in time.

$$\text{Value (time } n) = P + (n \times P \times k) \qquad [5\text{-}1]$$

where P = principal and n = number of periods.

Notice that $P \times k$ = interest. If we apply this equation to Example 5-1, P = 1,000, $n = 5$, and $k = 0.1$. The value in year 5 = 1,000 + (5 x 100) = $1,500. This is the amount shown in the table for Example 5-1 at year 5.

The basic point of simple interest is that in order to determine the future value of an investment, we calculate the annual interest—in our case, $100—multiply this by the number of years of the investment, and add it to the starting principal.

Understanding simple interest helps solve our earlier problem. For example, a person offered the choice between $20,000 today and $31,000 in five years can calculate the two annual interest payments. With the same 10 percent interest rate, the annual interest is $20,000 × 0.1 = $2,000 per year. In five years, it would generate $10,000 in interest, meaning that $20,000 today is worth $30,000 in five years. In this case, given the choice between $20,000 today and $31,000 in five years, with 10 percent simple interest, the correct choice is $31,000 in five years, because it is worth more. However, how do we solve the choice between these two options and $3,000 per year forever (indefinitely)?

EXAMPLE 5-2 | **Simple Interest II**

We'll repeat the example but assume that the investment is for 50 years.

Solution
Annual interest is still $100 per year ($1,000 x 0.1), so using Equation 5-1 we get
Value in year 50 = 1,000 + (50 x 100) = 1,000 + 5,000 = $6,000

One way to solve this problem is to assume a very long period, say 100 years. Receiving $3,000 each year for 100 years produces a future value of $3,000 × 100 = $300,000. We then compare this with investing $20,000 for 100 years, which has a future value of $20,000 + ($2,000 × 100) = $220,000. In this case, by assuming that "indefinitely" is 100 years, the solution would be to choose the $3,000 per year. However, apart from the fact that simple interest problems are relatively rare, it turns out that we are missing something very important, particularly when we invest for long periods. If we earn interest on the principal, then what about the interest earned on the subsequent interest payments since these can be regarded as (smaller) subsequent principal investments?

CONCEPT REVIEW QUESTIONS

1. Explain how simple interest payments are determined.
2. Why does simple interest take into account the time value of money?

Learning Objective 5.3
Define compound interest and explain how it works.

compound interest interest that is earned on the principal amount invested *and* on any accrued interest

5.3 COMPOUND INTEREST

Compounding (Computing Future Values)

Compound interest is interest that is earned on the principal amount invested *and* on the future interest payments. Compound interest can result in dramatic growth in the value of an investment over time. This growth is directly related to the length of the period, as well as to the level of return earned, which we will demonstrate shortly. Before we get to that, an example will show how compound interest arrangements work.

EXAMPLE 5-3   Compound Interest I

Suppose someone invests $1,000 today for a five-year term and receives 10 percent annual *compound* interest. How much would the investor have after five years?

Solution

Annual interest is earned on the original $1,000 (principal) *and* on accrued interest.

Year	Beginning Amount	Interest	Ending Amount
1	$1,000	1,000 × 0.1 = $100	$1,100
2	1,100	1,100 × 0.1 = $110	1,210
3	1,210	1,210 × 0.1 = $121	1,331
4	1,331	1,331 × 0.1 = $133.10	1,464.10
5	1,464.10	1,464.10 × 0.1 = $146.41	1,610.51

Unlike the annual interest for an investment earning simple interest, the amount of compound interest earned increases every year; the interest rate is applied to the *principal plus interest earned*, so the value of the investment increases. As a result, the interest received increases from $100 in year 1, to $146.41 in year 5; the ending amount of $1,610.51 is much higher than the $1,500 earned with simple interest.

To make the process clear, let's look at the first two years of interest using a little algebra. For the first year, everything is the same as the example with simple interest—that is, the ending amount is the starting principal plus the interest or

$$\$1,000 + (\$1,000 \times 0.1) = \$1,100 = \$1,000 \times (1 + 0.1) \text{ or } PV_0(1 + k)$$

where PV_0 = the present value today (i.e., at time 0). We have factored the $1,000 principal value, so to get the future value, we multiply the principal by 1 plus the market interest rate.

For year 2, the full $1,100 is **reinvested**—that is, we explicitly do not take the $100 of interest and spend it. As a result, we have the following equation:

$$\$1,100 + (\$1,100 \times 0.1) = \$1,210 = \$1,100 \times (1 + 0.1) \text{ or } PV_0(1 + k)^2$$

In this case, $1,100 is invested at the beginning of year 2 and earns the 10 percent interest. The interest earned increases to $110: the $100 interest on the starting principal plus $10 interest earned on the $100 of interest reinvested at the end of the first year. We can again factor the starting value of $1,100 and then factor the $1,000 principal value to get the formula for the future value at the end of year 2. This is the starting principal times one plus the interest rate squared. As we increase the period, we get the general formula

$$FV_n = PV_0 (1 + k)^n \qquad [5\text{-}2]$$

where FV_n = the future value at time n.

Equation 5-2 is the basic compounding equation, and the last term, $(1 + k)^n$, is the **compound value interest factor (CVIF)**.

Applying this equation to Example 5-3, we get $FV_5 = 1,000(1 + 0.1)^5 = 1,000(1.61051) = \$1,610.51$. This is $110.51 more than for the investment earning simple interest. Figure 5-1 illustrates what happens with the two types of interest over time. Note that for the first few years the difference is minimal, but over time it gets bigger and bigger.

reinvest to keep interest earned on an investment fully invested

compound value interest factor (CVIF) a term that represents the future value of an investment at a given rate of interest and for a stated number of periods: $(1 + k)^n$

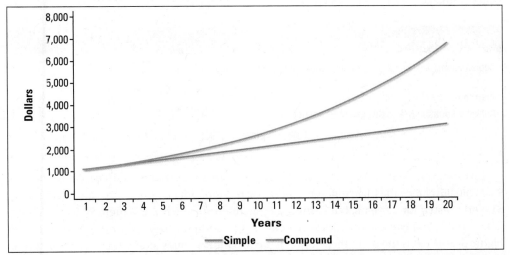

FIGURE 5-1 *Simple versus Compound Interest at 10%*

Example 5-3 can also be solved using a financial calculator. Although the keystrokes (and variable names) used will vary from one calculator to the next, the basic procedures do not. We will illustrate with one commonly used calculator: the Texas Instruments (TI) BA II Plus.[2]

(TI BA II PLUS)

EXAMPLE 5-3   Solution Using a Financial Calculator

Input the following variables:

`0` → `PMT` ; − `1,000` → `PV` ; `10` → `I/Y` ; and `5` → `N`

Press `CPT` (compute) and then `FV` . The answer will be 1,610.51.

PMT here refers to regular payments and will be discussed in a later section; FV is the future value; I/Y is the period interest rate; and N is the number of periods. The PV is entered with a negative sign on this calculator (this is not the case with all calculators) to reflect the fact that investors must pay money now to get money in the future. Alternatively, we could have left it positive. This would produce a negative sign in front of the FV, which we could simply ignore. We will do this in some of the ensuing applications.

---

[2]This is one of only two types of calculators permitted for the Chartered Financial Analyst (CFA) examinations, which are administered by the CFA Institute.

Time value of money problems can also be solved using Excel spreadsheets, which have time value of money functions. We illustrate this below by solving Example 5-3 using Excel.

EXAMPLE 5-3	Solution Using Excel
= FV	(rate, nper, pmt, pv, type)
where rate =	interest rate (expressed as a decimal)
nper =	number of periods
pmt =	the payment amount
pv =	present value
type =	0 if it is an ordinary annuity, 1 if it is annuity due. (We will explain what the difference is shortly; for now, our examples will involve ordinary annuities.)
For Example 5-3, we would enter the following in the appropriate cell:	
= FV	(0.10, 5, 0, −1000, 0), which yields → 1,610.51.

Let us now extend the time horizon for Example 5-3, as we did for the example relating to simple interest.

EXAMPLE 5-4   Compound Interest II

Repeat Example 5-3, but assume the investment is for 50 years.

Solution

Applying Equation 5-2 to this example, we get

$$FV_{50} = 1{,}000 \ (1 + 0.1)^{50} = 1{,}000 \ (117.39085) = \$117{,}390.85$$

Investing $1,000 for 50 years at an annual compound interest rate of 10 percent produces $117,390.85. Notice the huge difference between this amount and the future value of the same $1,000 invested for 50 years, but earning simple interest, which was a mere $6,000 ($1,000 + [50 × $100]). You can see the difference that compounding makes over this 50-year span in Figure 5-2. What is the difference between the two future values after 50 years? The answer is $111,390.85, which is the total interest-earned on interest.

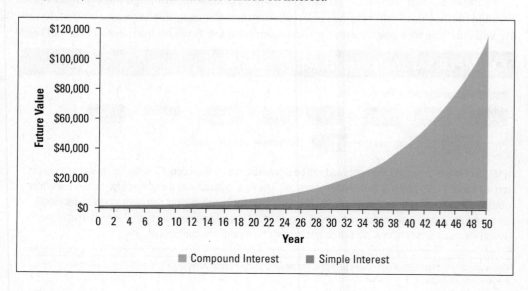

FIGURE 5-2 *Simple versus Compound Interest over 50 years*

You might be tempted to ask whether a 50-year term is realistic. It is for many investments. Consider someone who begins investing for retirement in his or her early 20s. Those early investments could earn compound returns for 40 years or so before the individual retires. Further, assuming the individual does not withdraw all the savings on the first day of retirement (which would have severe tax consequences), and assuming that this person lives another 20 to 25 years after retirement, some investment dollars may not be touched for more than 50 years. *Finance in the News 5-1* discusses the so-called miracle of compound interest, and shows why it is important to begin investing as early as possible.

finance INTHENEWS 5-1 | It Pays to Begin Saving for Retirement in Your 20s

ASK MY FINANCIAL ADVISER when young people should start saving for their retirement. The answer is always the same: they should start socking money away inside a registered retirement savings plan in the same year they begin earning income.

For those leaving high school and not going on to university or college, this can mean starting an RRSP as young as age 18. For others whose education years stretch longer, those first paycheques may not come until the late 20s.

No matter when they start working, however, many people sail clear through their 20s without giving a thought to retirement planning. A survey this year for Royal Trust found the average first-time RRSP contributor is 31 years old.

Yet to earn a healthy nest egg for retirement inside a tax-sheltered plan, it really pays to start early. Popular Canadian investment author Gordon Pape points this out in his 1999 Buyer's Guide to RRSPs.

"The greatest growth takes place in the later years," Pape writes. "So the longer you wait to begin, the less your RRSP will be worth when you retire.

"In fact, if you begin contributions in your early 20s and stop when you reach age 35, leaving the balance in your RRSP, you'll end up with more money at 65 than if you waited until you were 35 to begin and contributed every year thereafter."

Judy Willmer, a certified financial planner with Investors Group Inc. in St. Albert, Alta., has an 18-year-old client who just set up an RRSP. But younger people make up only a fraction of her client base; most are between ages 35 and 50.

"Let's say somebody comes in at age 25," Ms. Willmer says. "I'll show them a projection saying if you can save $200 a month up until age 65 you'll have over $1 million. But if you wait 10 years before you save and still want to have that $1-million at age 65, you now have to save $500 a month."

Geoff Anselmo, a 29-year old mutual fund investment specialist with Royal Trust, says it can be difficult to even reach young people to tell them they should start saving for retirement.

The young clients who do come his way are often referred to him by their parents. As a way of getting them to see the advantages of investing, he tells them that time is on their side.

Mr. Anselmo illustrates this point with an anecdote about Bill and Linda, who are twins.

At age 22, Bill starts investing $2,000 each year, earning a healthy 12 percent per year. He continues for six years, then stops and never invests another dime. Linda waits six years, starts investing $2,000 a year at age 28 and continues to do this until she reaches 65. Like her brother, she gets a 12 percent annual compound rate of return.

At 65, they each have about $1.4-million for their retirement. Yet Bill invested only $12,000 while his sister invested $76,000.

"I find that story in itself is very effective," Mr. Anselmo says. "It talks to people as to why to start early."

Mr. Anselmo encourages the new saver to start with something easy, such as putting $25 or $50 a month into a balanced mutual fund.

As their paycheques get larger, their deductions can increase. Mr. Anselmo finds that after saving up a base of $10,000 or $20,000 and doing some reading on investing, young people can comfortably start to tinker with their investment mixes.

Investors Group's Ms. Willmer takes a slightly different approach to her younger clients. She always works out cash flow statements, showing them where their money is going. Nights out for beer and pizza can eat up $200 a month if you're not careful, she warns them.

"You can show them that if they are earning $25,000 and they put $1,000 into an RRSP they will pay $250 less income tax that year," she says.

Happily, Ms. Willmer has discovered some of her younger clients do think ahead to retirement. "A lot of the kids are very knowledgeable," she says.

Source: Excerpted from Howell, David. "Get a Head Start on RRSP." *Financial Post*, May 20, 1999, p. D4. Material reprinted with the express permission of Edmonton Journal Group Inc., a CanWest Partnership.

Table 5-1 provides some evidence regarding the power of compound returns. It shows the future values that would have resulted from investing $1,000 at the beginning of 1938 and leaving that money invested for 74 years (until the end of 2011) in various investment assets.

TABLE 5-1 Ending Wealth of $1,000 Invested from 1938 to 2011 in Various Asset Classes

	Annual Compound Return (%)	Year-End Value, 2011 ($)
Government of Canada treasury bills	4.88	33,994
Government of Canada bonds	6.08	79,004
Canadian stocks	10.03	1,183,626
U.S. stocks	10.77	1,938,975

Source: Data to 2008 are from the Canadian Institute of Actuaries; data from 2009 to 2011 are from the Statistics Canada CANSIM database.

Compound return represents the average annual growth rate in the value of $1 invested at the start of the period. Compound return thus involves the same reinvestment rate assumption as compound interest rate— that is, all future returns are reinvested. Compound return is also often referred to as the geometric return and differs from the simple average or arithmetic average. We will discuss the difference between the two in detail in Chapter 8. Notice the impressive power of compounding over such a long period: $1,000 invested in Canadian equities would have made you a millionaire by 2011, and invested in U.S. equities, a millionaire times two (almost). However, remember that the cost of this investment is that the $1,000 invested in 1938 would have been locked away and not touched for 74 years, so in all likelihood whoever invested this money would have left it for their great-grand-children!

The dramatic difference in ending values results from differences in the rate of return. At a rate of return of 4.88 percent (i.e., the T-bill return), $1,000 would have grown to $33,994, while at 10.77 percent (i.e., the U.S. stock return), it would have grown to $1,938,975—more than 57 times as much! The difference in ending values is significant, even when the differences in returns are small. For example, consider the difference in ending values of approximately $750,000 when $1,000 is invested in Canadian stocks at 10.03 percent versus U.S. stocks at 10.77 percent. These data show why finance professionals struggle to increase the returns on their investments even by very small amounts. In fact, it is normal to look at returns down to 1/100 of 1 percent, which is called a **basis point**. Earning just a few basis points more on one investment causes the future value of the portfolio to compound that much faster. Unfortunately, this search for additional returns often leads investors to underestimate the associated risks, which can backfire. For example, during the period leading up to the 2007–2008 financial crisis, many investors purchased securitized structured debt products offered by investment banks in search of slightly higher returns over, for example, government bonds. However, instead of earning higher returns, they ended up generating huge losses.

basis point 1/100 of 1 percent

Let's return to our two choices of $20,000 today or $31,000 in five years' time, assuming the investor now earns *compound* interest of 10 percent. Using the CVIF formula, we get $CVIF = (1 + k)^5 = (1.1)^5 = 1.61051$. The $20,000 compounds to $32,210. So the choice is now $20,000 today, because it will grow to more than $31,000 in five years if invested at 10 percent with compound interest. However, we still have a problem comparing either of these single sums with the option of getting $3,000 a year forever. We could compound each of the $3,000 annual payments forward to, say, 100 years in the future, but there are easier ways of doing this, as we will discuss in section 5.4.

Discounting (Computing Present Values)

So far we have been concerned with finding future values, but there is a problem with comparing future values: there are many of them! We could choose an arbitrary common period to make the comparisons, which solves this problem. The obvious choice is to compare the values at the *current* time, so instead of calculating future values, we determine *present values*. This process is also called **discounting**. We will explain it with a simple example.

discounting finding the present value of a future value by accounting for the time value of money

EXAMPLE 5-5 Discounting

An investor estimates that she needs $1 million to live comfortably when she retires in 40 years. How much does she have to invest today, assuming a 10 percent interest rate on the investment?

Solution

To solve this example, first start with what is already known: the future value formula of Equation 5-2

$$FV_n = PV_0 (1 + k)^n$$

where $CVIF = (1 + k)^n$. With a starting present value, we multiply by the CVIF to get the future value. This means we can divide the future value by the CVIF to get the present value. Rearranging Equation 5-2 to solve for PV we get

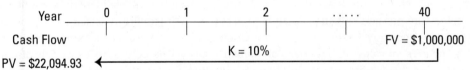

$$PV_0 = \frac{FV_n}{(1 + k)^n} = FV_n \times \frac{1}{(1 + k)^n} \qquad [5\text{-}3]$$

Equation 5-3 is the basic discounting equation, and the last term, $1/(1 + k)^n$, is called the discount factor or **present value interest factor (PVIF)**. Some older textbooks have tables of PVIF and CVIF for various periods and interest rates, although they are simply reciprocals of each other. The use of computers and calculators makes these tables obsolete.

Let's return to our example. If FV = 1,000,000; $k = 0.1$; and $n = 40$, we get

$$PV = 1,000,000 \times 1/(1.1)^{40} = 1,000,000 \times (1/45.259256)$$
$$= 1,000,000 \times 0.02209493 = \$22,094.93$$

We illustrate this in a timeline.

Year	0	1	2	.....	40
Cash Flow					FV = $1,000,000

K = 10%

PV = $22,094.93

An investment of $22,094.93 today, earning a 10 percent return per year, has a future value of $1 million in 40 years. With a 10 percent market interest rate, $22,094.93 today and $1 million in 40 years' time are worth the same amount, so the two figures are economically equivalent.

present value interest factor (PVIF) a formula that determines the present value of $1 to be received at some time in the future n based on a given interest rate k

We can also solve Example 5-5 using a financial calculator or Excel, as shown below.

EXAMPLE 5-5 Solution using a Financial Calculator

Input the following variables:

0 → **PMT** ; – **1,000,000** → **FV** ; **10** → **I/Y** ; and **40** → **N**

Press **CPT** and then **PV** . This will give an answer of 22,094.93.

(TI BA II PLUS)

EXAMPLE 5-5 Solution using Excel

The following function may be used in Excel:

= PV (rate, nper, pmt, fv, type)

For this example, we would enter the following in the appropriate cell:

= PV (0.1, 40, 0, –1000000, 0)

This would yield a PV of 22,094.93.

XLS

Now you know why we call this process "discounting." If people don't want to pay the full price for something, they ask for a discount or, in other words, they ask for something off the price. In the same way, $1 million in 40 years is not worth $1 million today, so you discount, or take something off, to get it to its true value. Discounting future values to find their present value is the same process, except that when we know the market interest rate, we can use Equation 5-3 to calculate the exact true value.

There are two important points from Example 5-5 and Equation 5-3: first, discount factors (the PVIF) are always less than one as long as discount rates are positive (i.e., $k > 0$). This means that future dollars are usually worth less than the same dollars today. However, this is not always the case. In Chapter 6, *Finance in the News 6-3* describes the impact of the euro crisis, whereby investors were willing to lend money to the German government at negative yields or interest rates. In other words, they were willing to pay the German government to lend them money. Why, you might ask, don't investors simply keep the money in cash? The answer is simply that the investors in question were major institutions, so going to the local bank to ask for €3.9 billion in ones and twos is not an option![3] Similar to the German government, major financial institutions are now considering imposing fees on deposits rather than paying interest, since the deposited money cannot be lent out to borrowers to earn positive rates of return to the bank.

The second important implication is that discount factors are the reciprocals of their corresponding compound factors and vice versa (PVIF = 1/CVIF). This means that **the greater the discount rate, the greater the CVIF (and future value), and the smaller the PVIF (and present value) and vice versa.**

This last point has been very important for the past several years when interest interest rates have been abnormally low. Consider the impact of these low interest rates on pension funds for example, which were discussed briefly in Chapter 1. Pension funds estimate the present value of their future pension payouts to plan members (i.e., their liabilities), based on discounting these future pension payments using current interest rates. As a result of these very low interest rates, the present value of these pension liabilities has increased dramatically. This discount rate effect on the liability side of their funding equation was largely offset by positive asset returns on the asset side of their equation (i.e., the value of their investment holdings) during 2010 and the first quarter of 2011. However, as discussed in *Finance in the News 5-2*, during the third quarter of 2011, volatile (and largely negative) capital market returns hit pension funds on both sides of their funding equation. This resulted in major funding issues, as indicated by the Mercer Pension Health Index falling to 60 percent by the end of December 2011, nearing its all-time low of 59 percent. The effect of these low interest rates, combined with poor investment returns has meant that many defined-benefit pension plans have significant deficits as their assets have not increased as fast as the present value of their liabilities.

finance INTHENEWS 5-2   Pension Plans' Funding Plummets

CANADIAN PENSION plans saw their funding plummet in the first nine months of 2011 but the bleeding was stanched in the final quarter of the year.

Surveys by two pension consulting firms—both tracking hypothetical pension plans with typical investments—show pension funding fell by almost 15 percentage points throughout 2011, leaving plans facing a severe financing shortfall.

Towers Watson said its pension index fell to 72 per cent by the end of December from 86 per cent at the beginning of 2011, while Mercer said its index dropped to 60 per cent from 73 per cent at the start of the year. The index measures the proportion of assets held by the pension plan compared with its estimated pension liability.

Paul Forestell, senior partner at Mercer, said the only good news is that pension health remained flat in the fourth quarter as stock markets posted modest gains.

"I think that's the best you can say this year—it's the only quarter that didn't do any damage," he said.

---

[3] In an attempt to reduce money laundering from illicit activity, most countries severely restrict the amount of money that can be withdrawn in cash. As a result, taking money out and "putting it under the bed" is only viable for very small investors.

Finance in the News 5-2: Pension Plan's Funding Plummets (continued)

Canada's benchmark S&P/TSX composite index fell 11 per cent in 2011, posting a decline of 13.5 per cent in the first nine months but recording a gain of 2.8 per cent in the final quarter.

Towers Watson said its model pension plan—with a typical asset mix of 60 per cent stocks and 40 per cent bonds—earned a meagre 0.5 per cent rate of return on its assets in 2011. But its financing was eroded by a 20-per-cent increase in the liability to pay pensions to members.

That's because pension liabilities are calculated based on long-term bond yields, which fell in 2011, driving funding costs far higher.

Both surveys look at the impact on pension plan health based solely on changes in interest rates and investment performance during the year. Real pension plans may have a different funded status because companies often add extra cash to their plans to make up shortfalls.

Nevertheless, the impact of the market turmoil means companies are facing sharply higher pension costs and growing obligations to put extra cash into their traditional defined-benefit (DB) pension plans, which pay a guaranteed level of income in retirement.

"DB plan sponsors will continue to feel the impact of the double whammy we experienced in 2011—a combination of declining long-term interest rates and poor equity-market performance," Towers Watson pension consultant Ian Markham said.

"For many organizations, these conditions have resulted in larger plan deficits at the end of 2011 and will lead to higher pension costs in 2012 and beyond."

Many large companies announced plans to add extra cash to their pension plans in 2011 or to reorganize their plans to lower liabilities. Royal Bank of Canada, for example, said it will no longer allow new hires to join its traditional DB pension plan as of Jan. 1, while Air Canada faced labour turmoil in June over its plans to close its DB plans to new hires.

Canadian Pacific Railway Ltd. said in November it will borrow $500 million to inject more cash into its pension plan—the third such lump sum payment in three years. Phone giant BCE Inc. said it would make an extra $750-million payment to its pension plan in December.

"There was a fair bit of press in December around companies making special contributions … and they were big amounts," Mr. Forestell said.

"I think what they were doing is anticipating the results that we're seeing here. So it will be a cash drain again this year."

Source: McFarland, Janet, "Funding for Canadian pension plans plummets." *The Globe and Mail*, January 4, 2012. Available at www.theglobeandmail.com. © The Globe and Mail Inc. All rights reserved. Reprinted by permission.

Determining Rates of Return or Holding Periods

When we looked at the discounting problem, we noted that we simply divided through by the CVIF but essentially used the same future value equation. Let's look at this again.

$$FV_n = PV_0 (1 + k)^n$$

We have used this equation to solve for future values (FV) and present values (PV), but notice that we can solve for two other values: the interest rate (k) and the period (n). If both the present and future values are known, and we know either the interest rate or the period, we can solve for the last unknown. We illustrate this in Examples 5-6 and 5-7.

EXAMPLE 5-6   Finding the Rate of Return

Suppose we modify the lottery example used earlier. The "prize" is now a $20,000 investment that has a payoff of $31,000 in five years. We have the present and future values and the period, so we can solve for the interest rate. This is an important interest rate, called the internal rate of return (IRR), because it is the rate of return that is *internal* to the values in the problem. Many problems in finance are IRR problems for which we need to compare the rates of return earned on different investments.

Solution

$$FV = 31,000; PV = 20,000; n = 5$$

Using Equation 5-2, we get $20,000 = 31,000/(1 + k)^5$.
We could solve for k in the following manner:

$$31,000/20,000 = 1.55 = (1 + k)^5$$

This is a simple problem, but it is still awkward to solve. One way to solve it is through trial and error, using a simple calculator. Put, say, 1.08 into memory and then enter 1 and press "multiply, memory recall, equals" five times. The result is 1.469. Doing the same thing with 10 percent (1.1) produces 1.6105, so we know that the internal rate of return is in between these two numbers and closer to 10 percent than to 8 percent. All we can then do is iterate to get closer and closer to 1.55. Eventually, we would end up with 9.161 percent. However, this is a laborious and inefficient process. Using a financial calculator or Excel makes these types of calculations much simpler, as we illustrate below.

(TI BA II PLUS)

EXAMPLE 5-6   Solution using a Financial Calculator

Input the following variables:

Press **CPT** and then **I/Y**. This will give an answer of 9.161 percent. Notice that either FV or PV needs to be input as a negative number, because to "receive" one cash flow (either today or in the future) you need to "pay" (or invest) either today or in the future.

EXAMPLE 5-6   Solution using Excel

The following function may be used:

= RATE (nper, pmt, pv, fv, type)

For this example, we would enter the following in the appropriate cell:

= RATE (5, 0, 20000, −31000, 0)

This also yields the correct answer of 9.161 percent.

EXAMPLE 5-7   Solving for Time or "Holding" Periods

In this example, we use the same data as before but change the problem to ask how long we have to invest $20,000 at 10 percent to get $31,000.

Solution

With our data, we now have to solve the following for *n*:

$$31{,}000/20{,}000 = 1.55 = (1.1)^n$$

Unfortunately, solving this equation with a simple calculator is even more complicated than the IRR problem was. We could put 1.1 into memory, enter 1, and again press "multiply, memory recall, equals" five times to find that the period is between four and five years but closer to five. However, we can't be more accurate than this. If you are familiar with logarithms, you can take logs of both sides and solve for *n* as follows:

$$n = \frac{Ln\,(FV/PV)}{Ln\,(1 + k)} = \frac{Ln\,(1.55)}{Ln\,(1.1)}$$

The natural log of 1.55 is 0.438255 and the natural log of 1.1 is 0.09531, so the answer is 4.6 years. However, logarithm tables are rarely used; we used the logarithm function in Excel and typed in = *Ln*(1.55). Using a financial calculator or Excel makes the calculations much easier.

(TI BA II PLUS)

EXAMPLE 5-7   Solution using a Financial Calculator

Input the following variables:

Press **CPT** and then **N**. This will give an answer of 4.5982 or 4.6 years.

EXAMPLE 5-7   Solution using Excel

The following function may be used:

= NPER (rate, pmt, pv, fv, type)

For this example, we would enter the following in the appropriate cell:

= NPER (0.1, 0, −20000, 31000, 0)

This would yield an answer of 4.5982 or 4.6 years.

We'll summarize what we have learned so far. We have Equation 5-2:

$$FV_n = PV_0 (1 + k)^n$$

This equation has four values. If we know any three of them, we can solve for the last one. Therefore, four different types of finance problems can be solved:

- *Future value problems*: How much will I have in n years at x percent if I invest $\$y$ today?

- *Present value problems*: What is the value today of receiving $\$z$ in n years if the interest rate is x percent?

- *IRR problems*: What rate of return will I earn if I invest $\$y$ today for n years and get $\$z$?

- *Period problems*: How long do I have to wait to get $\$z$ if I invest $\$y$ today at x percent?

All the problems that we have looked at are single-sum problems, looking at a single investment today and a single payoff in the future. In principle, we can solve almost any problem using the techniques we have discussed because, for example, valuing a series of receipts in the future can be done by valuing each one individually. However, special formulas exist for standard problems in finance for which the receipts or payments are the same each period. Think back to our first example about choosing between $\$20,000$ today, $\$31,000$ in five years, or $\$3,000$ each year forever. The last choice involves valuing a constant $\$3,000$ each year forever and is an example of an "annuity." In this case, it is a special class of annuity: a perpetual annuity, commonly referred to as a "perpetuity."

CONCEPT REVIEW QUESTIONS

1. Explain how to compute future values and present values when using compound interest.

2. What is the relationship between CVIFs and PVIFs? Why does this make sense?

3. Why does compound interest result in higher future values than simple interest?

5.4 ANNUITIES AND PERPETUITIES

The Importance of Investing Early

Similar to the example in *Finance in the News 5-1*, the example below illustrates the power of compound interest as time passes. Consider twins who follow two different investing approaches. Assume each earns a 12 percent annual return.

- Twin 1: At age 21, she decides to invest $\$2,000$ per year (at year end) for six years, and then she makes no further contributions (total amount invested is $\$12,000$). Note that she invests the same amount each year, so this is an example of an annuity. At age 65, she will have accumulated $\$1.2$ million for retirement.

- Twin 2: She postpones investing for six years, until she reaches age 28, and then invests $\$2,000$ per year for 38 years (total amount invested is $\$76,000$). At age 65, she will also have accumulated $\$1.2$ million for retirement.

Notice that both twins have the same ending amounts, but Twin 1 invested only $\$12,000$ in total, while Twin 2 invested $\$76,000$. This shows how the compounding effect is magnified as the time horizon increases.

We could solve these problems to find the ending value using "brute force," finding the future value of each payment the twins make individually. However, we will solve them after we develop more formally the concept of an annuity.

Learning Objective 5.4
Differentiate between an ordinary annuity and an annuity due, and explain how special constant payment problems can be valued as annuities and, in special cases, as perpetuities.

Ordinary Annuities

annuity regular payments on an investment that are for the same amount and are paid at the same interval

cash flows the actual cash generated from an investment

ordinary annuities equal payments that are made at the end of each period

So far, we have dealt with PV and FV concepts as they apply to only two cash flows—one today (i.e., the PV) and one in the future (i.e., the FV). In practice, we will often need to compare different series of receipts or payments that occur through time. An **annuity** is a series of payments or receipts, which we will simply call **cash flows**, that are for the same amount and paid at the same interval—that is, for example, they are paid annually, monthly, or weekly—over a given period. Annuities are common in finance; the one you may be familiar with is a loan or mortgage payment. This involves an identical payment made at regular intervals for a loan based on a single interest rate.

Ordinary annuities involve end-of-period payments. We have the same values as in our earlier discussion: FV, PV, n, and k. However, now we have another term, PMT, for the regular annuity payment or receipt. Example 5-8 demonstrates how to determine the FV and PV of an ordinary annuity.

EXAMPLE 5-8 FV and PV of an Ordinary Annuity

In 2011, the average NHL player earned $2.4 million per year, while the average career was approximately six years. Assuming a 41 percent tax rate, this would generate $1,416,000 in annual "disposable" (i.e., after-tax) income. Assume a player earning this average decides to invest 10 percent of his disposable income (i.e., $141,600) at the *end* of each year for the next six years (i.e., the average career span) and expects to earn 8 percent per year.

a.   How much will he have accumulated after six years?

b.   How much would he need to deposit today to have the same results?

Solution

a.   We can first depict the series of payments on a timeline diagram, which shows when the cash flows occur.

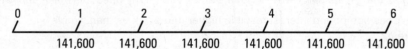

Timelines are very useful in finance. You should get into the habit of displaying the data in a problem in a timeline. For example, from this diagram we can see that by the end of year six, the first deposit of $141,600 will have earned a return for five years, because there are five years from the end of year 1 to the end of the period in year 6. In contrast, the second payment will earn a return for four years, the third for three years, the fourth for two years, the fifth for one year, and the final payment will not earn a return at all. Using this information, we could view this as a six-part problem in which we have to find the future value of each of the six payments.

$$FV_6 = 141,600\,(1.08)^5 + 141,600\,(1.08)^4 + 141,600\,(1.08)^3 + 141,600\,(1.08)^2 +$$
$$141,600\,(1.08)^1 + 141,600\,(1)$$

$$= 141,600\,(1.469328) + 141,600\,(1.360489) + 141,600\,(1.259712) +$$
$$141,600\,(1.166400) + 141,600\,(1.08) + 141,600\,(1)$$

$$= 141,600\,(7.335929) = \$1,038,768$$

We illustrate this in a timeline.

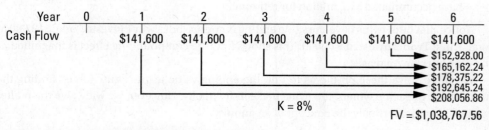

The player would have $1,038,768 after six years.

EXAMPLE 5-8   FV and PV of an Ordinary Annuity *continued*

This would be our brute-force calculation, in which we solve the problem with six separate calculations. This approach is fine for a six-period annuity problem, but it would be tedious for a 25-year monthly mortgage problem that has 300 payments. Fortunately, there is a much quicker way (even without the use of a financial calculator or a spreadsheet). If we look closely at our solution, we can see that we are multiplying $141,600 by the sum of six compound value interest factors (CVIF), based on an 8 percent return (i.e., the CVIF for $k = 8$ percent, with $n = 5, 4, 3, 2, 1,$ and 0, respectively).

The ordinary annuity equation, Equation 5-4, adds these CVIFs.

$$FV_n = PMT \left[\frac{(1 + k)^n - 1}{k} \right] \qquad [5\text{-}4]$$

PMT is the end-of-period annuity payment. This formula is usually called the compound value annuity formula or CVAF to distinguish it from the single-sum CVIF. The advantage of Equation 5-4 is that it involves only one formula and can be solved easily, even on a simple calculator.

Using this equation, we can solve Example 5-8a as follows:

$$FV_5 = PMT \left[\frac{(1 + 0.08)^6 - 1}{0.08} \right] = 141,600(7.335929) = \$1,038,768$$

We can get the CVAF for six years at 8 percent by using a simple calculator, putting 1.08 into memory, entering 1, and then pressing "times, memory recall, equals" six times, or by using Excel and entering = 1.08^6. Then we can take this number, subtract 1 from it, and divide by 0.08 to get 7.335929.

continued

EXAMPLE 5-8   Solution using a Financial Calculator

Input the following variables:

141,600 → PMT ; 6 → N ; 0 → PV (i.e., no deposit today); and 8 → I/Y

Press **CPT** and then **FV**. This will give you an answer of −1,038,768. Remember that you get a negative value because the calculator is programmed to consider cash outflows and cash inflows.

EXAMPLE 5-8   Solution using Excel

The following Excel function may be used:

= FV (rate, nper, pmt, pv, type)

For this example, we would enter the following in the appropriate cell:

= FV (0.08, 6, −141600, 0, 0)

This would yield an answer of $1,038,768.

EXAMPLE 5-8   FV and PV of an Ordinary Annuity *continued*

b.   To find the present value, we can again view this as a six-part problem for which we have to find the present value of each of the six annual payments:

$$PV_0 = 141,600 \, (1/1.08)^6 + 141,600 \, (1/1.08)^5 + 141,600 \, (1/1.08)^4 +$$

$$141,600 \, (1/1.08)^3 + 141,600 \, (1/1.08)^2 + 141,600 \, (1/1.08)^1$$

$$= 141,600 \, (0.630170) + 141,600 \, (0.680583) + 141,600 \, (0.735030) +$$

continued

EXAMPLE 5-8 FV and PV of an Ordinary Annuity *continued*

$$141,600 (0.793832) + 141,600 (0.857339) + 141,600 (0.925926)$$
$$= 141,600 (4.622880) = \$654,600$$

We illustrate this in a timeline.

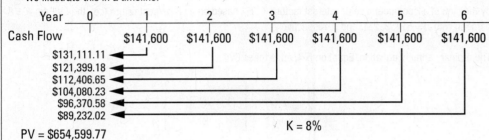

Year	0	1	2	3	4	5	6
Cash Flow		$141,600	$141,600	$141,600	$141,600	$141,600	$141,600

$131,111.11
$121,399.18
$112,406.65
$104,080.23
$96,370.58
$89,232.02

K = 8%

PV = $654,599.77

As before, notice that we are using brute force by multiplying $141,600 by the sum of the relevant six PVIF or discount factors, which add to 4.622880. Fortunately, the formula for determining the PV of ordinary annuities, Equation 5-5, will do this for us.

[5-5]

$$PV_0 = PMT \left[\frac{1 - \dfrac{1}{(1 + k)^n}}{k} \right]$$

This formula is usually called the present value annuity formula or PVAF to distinguish it from the PVIF used for valuing single-sum problems. By using this equation to solve Example 5-8b, we get

$$PV_0 = 141,600 \left[\frac{1 - \dfrac{1}{(1.08)^6}}{0.08} \right] = 141,600 (4.622880) = \$654,600$$

Again, we can get the PVAF for six years at 8 percent by using a simple calculator with memory. For longer-period problems, we can use a financial calculator or Excel.

(TI BA II PLUS)

EXAMPLE 5-8 **Solution using a Financial Calculator** *continued*

Input the following variables:

141,600 → PMT ; 6 → N ; 0 → FV ; and 13 → I/Y

Press CPT and then PV . This will give an answer of −654,600.

XLS

EXAMPLE 5-8 **Solution using Excel** *continued*

The following Excel function may be used:

= PV (rate, nper, pmt, fv, type)

For this example, we would enter the following in the appropriate cell:

= PV (0.08, 6, −141600, 0, 0)

This would yield an answer of $654,600.

We can ensure that our answer is correct by checking that $654,600 is the present value of the future value at year 6 (calculated earlier): $1,038,768 with an 8 percent interest rate. We leave this as an exercise for you.

In summary, the examples above illustrate the following relationships:

$654,600 today = $141,600 at the end of each of the next six years = $1,038,768 six years from today

Annuities Due

Sometimes annuities are structured so that the cash flows are paid at the *beginning* of a period, rather than at the end. For example, leasing arrangements are usually set up like this, with the **lessee** making an immediate payment on taking possession of the equipment, such as a car. Such an annuity is called an **annuity due**. Example 5-9 demonstrates how to evaluate these cash flows.

lessee a person who leases an item

annuity due an annuity (such as a lease) for which the payments are made at the beginning of each period

---

EXAMPLE 5-9   FV and PV of an Annuity Due

We will repeat Example 5-8, except we assume that the payments are made at the *beginning* rather than the end of each year.

a. How much will the investor have after six years?

b. How much would the investor have to deposit today to have the same results?

Solution

a. We begin as before by depicting the data on a timeline.

```
     0          1          2          3          4          5          6
     |          |          |          |          |          |          |
  141,600    141,600    141,600    141,600    141,600    141,600
```

Notice that, as in Example 5-8, we have six cash flows of $141,600 each. However, each cash flow appears one period earlier, and thus each receives an extra period of interest at the rate of 8 percent. Using the brute-force approach applied in Example 5-8a, we can find the future value of each of the six payments.

$$FV_6 = 141,600 \ (1.08)^6 + 141,600 \ (1.08)^5 + 141,600 \ (1.08)^4 + 141,600 \ (1.08)^3 +$$
$$141,600 \ (1.08)^2 + 141,600 \ (1.08)^1$$

$$= 141,600 \ (1.586874) + 141,600 \ (1.469328) + 141,600 \ (1.360489) +$$
$$141,600 \ (1.259712) + 141,600 \ (1.166400) + 141,600 \ (1.08)$$

$$= 141,600 \ (7.922803) = \$1,121,869$$

We illustrate this in a timeline.

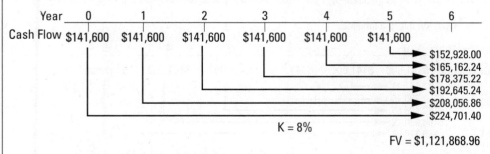

Notice that because each flow gets one extra period of compounding at 8 percent, the net result is that we multiply our answer to Example 5-8a by 1.08. In other words, the FV (annuity due) = [FV (ordinary annuity)](1 + *k*).

Therefore, we can alter Equation 5-4 to find the FV of an annuity due as follows:

$$FV_n = PMT \left[\frac{(1 + k)^n - 1}{k} \right] (1 + k) \qquad \text{[5-6]}$$

This is CVAF(1 + *k*), so in practice, we don't use a separate formula. However, we can now solve Example 5-9a as follows:

$$FV_6 = PMT \left[\frac{(1 + 0.08)^6 - 1}{0.08} \right] (1.08) = [141,600 \ (7.335929)] \ (1.08) = (1,038,768) \ (1.08) = \$1,121,869$$

Note that the value of the annuity due, $1,121,869, is 1.08 times higher than the value of the ordinary annuity that we calculated earlier, which was $1,038,768.

continued

EXAMPLE 5-9　Solution using a Financial Calculator

There is a "Begin" mode on the TI BA II Plus, as there is on most financial calculators. We need to activate "Begin" mode before solving this problem, which can be done as follows for the TI BA II Plus:

Press [2ND] [BGN] [2ND] [SET] . Then input the variables:

[141,600] → [PMT] ; [6] → [N] [0] → [PV] ; and [8] → [I/Y]

Press [CPT] and then [FV] . This gives an answer of −1,121,869. As before, recognize that the negative sign is due to the need for a series of cash inflows matched by a cash outflow.

EXAMPLE 5-9　Solution using Excel

The following Excel function may be used:

= FV (rate, nper, pmt, pv, type)

Now, we can see what the "type" stands for in the Excel formula. When type is set = 0, as in our previous examples, it refers to an ordinary annuity; when it is set = 1, it refers to an annuity due. So for this example, we would enter the following in the appropriate cell:

= FV (0.08, 6, −141600, 0, 1)

This yields an answer of $1,121,869.

EXAMPLE 5-9　FV and PV of an Annuity Due *continued*

b.　As before, to solve for the present value, we could view this as a six-part problem for which we have to find the present value of each of the six payments.

$$PV_0 = [141,600 (1/1.08)^6 + 141,600 (1/1.08)^5 + 141,600 (1/1.08)^4 +$$
$$141,600 (1/1.08)^3 + 141,600 (1/1.08)^2 + 141,600 (1/1.08)^1] \times (1.08)$$

$$= [141,600(4.622880)](1.08) = (654,600)(1.08) = \$706,968$$

We illustrate this in a timeline.

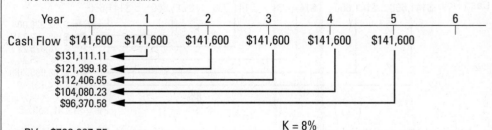

Year | 0 | 1 | 2 | 3 | 4 | 5 | 6
Cash Flow $141,600 $141,600 $141,600 $141,600 $141,600 $141,600

$131,111.11
$121,399.18
$112,406.65
$104,080.23
$96,370.58

K = 8%

PV = $706,967.75

　Note that, as in Example 5-9a, we are multiplying our answer to Example 5-8b by 1.08—that is, (1 + k). Accordingly, we can modify Equation 5-5 to arrive at the formula for determining the PV of an annuity due, which is given below:

[5-7]
$$PV_0 = PMT \left[\frac{1 - \dfrac{1}{(1 + k)^n}}{k} \right] (1 + k)$$

Equation 5-7 is PVAF (1 + k). Using this to solve Example 5-9b, we get

$$PV_0 = 141,600 \left[\frac{1 - \dfrac{1}{(1.08)^6}}{0.08} \right] (1.08) = [141,600(4.622880)](1.08) = (654,600)(1.08) = \$706,968$$

EXAMPLE 5-9   Solution using a Financial Calculator *continued*

First, activate the "Begin" function   BGN . Then input the following variables:

141,600 → PMT ; 6 → N ; 0 → FV ; and 8 → I/Y

Press   CPT   and then   PV . This gives an answer of −706,968.

EXAMPLE 5-9   Solution using Excel *continued*

The following Excel function may be used:

| = PV (rate, nper, pmt, fv, type) |

For this example, we would enter the following in the appropriate cell:

| = PV (0.08, 6, −141600, 0, 1) |

This would yield an answer of $706,968.

Perpetuities

Perpetuities are special annuities in that they go on forever, so n goes to infinity in the annuity equation. In this case, Equation 5-5 reduces to

perpetuity a special annuity that provides payments forever

$$PV_0 = \frac{PMT}{k} \qquad [5\text{-}8]$$

Perpetuities are easy to value because all we do is divide the cash payment or receipt by the interest rate.

EXAMPLE 5-10   Annuities and Perpetuities

a. An annuity pays $3,000 per year at year end and earns an annual return of 12 percent per year for 30 years. What is the present value?

b. What is the PV of a $3,000 per year annuity that goes on forever—that is, in perpetuity—if $k = 12$ percent?

Solution

a. $$PV_0 = 3,000 \left[\frac{1 - \dfrac{1}{(1.12)^{30}}}{0.12} \right] = 3,000 \,(8.05518) = \$24,165.55$$

b. $$PV_0 = \frac{3,000}{0.12} = \$25,000$$

Notice the small difference in the present value of these cash streams. This tells you that the PV of the cash flows of $3,000 per year from years 31 to infinity (∞) is only $834.45—that is, $25,000 − $24,165.55. This is a very important result and is behind many financial innovations. It means that cash flows far in the future are of little value because of the discounting involved in the time value of money.[4]

EXAMPLE 5-10   Solution using a Financial Calculator

Input the following variables:

3,000 → PMT ; PMT → N ; 0 → FV ; and 12 → I/Y

Press   CPT   and then   PV . This will give an answer of −24,165.55.

---

[4] This has also been behind many misleading advertisements for which something is 100 percent backed by a government bond. The small print indicates that the bond pays off in 25 years so is not worth much today!

EXAMPLE 5-10   Solution using Excel

The following Excel function may be used:
= PV (rate, nper, pmt, fv, type)
For this example, we would enter the following in the appropriate cell:
= PV (0.12, 30, −13000, 0, 0)
This yields an answer of $24,165.55.

Annuities and Perpetuities Summarized

So far, we have discussed constant annuities and perpetuities—that is, where the cash flows remain the same for every period. However, sometimes we want to evaluate growing (or shrinking) perpetuities or annuities—that is, where the cash flows grow (or shrink) at a certain rate every period. We will consider situations in which these assumptions may be appropriate in Chapter 7 (for valuing stocks) and in chapters 13 to 15 (for evaluating long-term investment and merger and acquisition decisions). Appendix 5A describes how to evaluate growing annuities and perpetuities.

We conclude by deriving the solution to the investing-early scenario described at the beginning of this section.

EXAMPLE 5-11   Investing Early

Solve for both twins from the scenario at the beginning of section 5.4.

Solution
This must be solved as a two-part problem, which can then be solved in several ways. We first estimate the future value of the six $2,000 payments at the end of six years.

$$FV_0 = PMT \left[\frac{(1 + k)^n - 1}{k} \right] = (2,000) \left[\frac{(1.12)^6 - 1}{0.12} \right] = (2,000)(8.11519) = \$16,230.38$$

Then we estimate the future value of the accumulated savings after 38 years (i.e., from age 27 to age 65).

$$FV_{38} = PV_0 (1+k)^n = (16,230.38)(1.12)^{38} = (16,230.38)(74.17966) = \$1,203,964.13$$

Solve for Twin 2 from the scenario above.

$$FV_{38} = PMT \left[\frac{(1 + k)^n - 1}{k} \right] = (2,000) \left[\frac{(1.12)^{38} - 1}{0.12} \right] = (2,000)(609.83053) = \$1,219,661.07$$

So they both end up with approximately $1.2 million.

CONCEPT REVIEW QUESTIONS

1. Explain how to calculate the present value and future value of an ordinary annuity and an annuity due.

2. Define "perpetuity."

3. Why is the present value of $1 million in 50 years' time worth very little today?

5.5 QUOTED VERSUS EFFECTIVE RATES

Determining Effective Annual Rates

So far, we have assumed that payments are made annually and that interest is compounded annually, so we have been able to use quoted rates to solve each problem. In practice, in many situations, payments are made (or received) at intervals other than annually (e.g., quarterly or monthly), and compounding often occurs more frequently than annually, so we need to be sure that we use the appropriate effective interest rate.

The **effective rate** for a period is the rate at which a dollar invested grows over that period. It is usually stated in percentage terms based on an annual period. To determine effective rates, we first recognize that the annual rates quoted by financial institutions will equal the annual effective rate only when compounding is done on an annual basis. We will use some examples to illustrate the process for determining effective rates.

Learning Objective 5.5
Differentiate between quoted rates and effective rates, and explain how quoted rates can be converted to effective rates.

effective rate the rate at which a dollar invested grows over a given period; usually stated in percentage terms based on an annual period

---

EXAMPLE 5-12 | Effective versus Quoted Rates

a. Suppose someone invests $1,000 today for one year at a quoted annual rate of 16 percent compounded annually. What is the FV at the end of the year?

b. What if someone invests $1,000 at a quoted rate of 16 percent compounded quarterly?

Solution

a. FV $= 1,000(1.16)^1 = \$1,160$.
   This means that each dollar grows to $1.16 by the end of the period, so we can say that the "effective" annual interest rate is 16 percent.

b. When the rate is "quoted" at 16 percent, and compounding is done quarterly, the appropriate adjustment (by convention) is to charge 16 percent/4 = 4 percent per quarter, so we have FV $= 1,000(1.04)^4 = \$1,170$ (rounded).

   Notice that even though the quoted rate is 16 percent, each dollar invested grows to $1.17—that is, by 17 percent—by the end of the period. In this case, we say that the "effective" annual interest rate is 17 percent.

We can use the following equation to determine the effective *annual* rate for any quoted annual rate, if given the compounding interval:

$$k = \left(1 + \frac{QR}{m}\right)^m - 1 \qquad [5\text{-}9]$$

where k = effective annual rate, QR = quoted rate, and m = the number of compounding intervals per year.

Applying this equation to Example 5-12, we see the following:

For 5-12a, $m = 1$, QR = 0.16, and we get

$$k = \left(1 + \frac{0.16}{1}\right)^1 - 1 = 0.16 = 16\%$$

so the quoted and effective rates are the same.

For 5-12b, $m = 4$, QR = 0.16, so we get

$$k = \left(1 + \frac{0.16}{4}\right)^4 - 1 = 0.1699 = 17\%$$

The effective rate is higher than the quoted rate. This is why it is important to examine the compounding frequency of investments and loans; looking at the rate alone is often not enough.

When compounding is conducted on a continuous basis, we use Equation 5-10 to determine the effective annual rate for a given quoted rate.

[5-10]
$$k = e^{QR} - 1$$

where e is the unique Euler number (approximately 2.718) and is found on your calculator and in Excel. It is used frequently in finance. If we use the Excel function "enter = exp (.16)," and subtract 1, we get 17.351 percent.

Example 5-13 shows that as the frequency of compounding increases, the effective annual rate also increases.

Example 5-13 shows that as the compounding frequency increases, the quoted rate of 12 percent increases to a maximum effective rate of 12.75 percent, achieved with instantaneous or continuous compounding. However, the daily rate is almost the same, at 12.747 percent.

EXAMPLE 5-13   Effective Annual Rates for Various Compounding Intervals

What are the effective annual rates for the following quoted rates?

a.   12 percent, compounded annually

b.   12 percent, compounded semi-annually

c.   12 percent, compounded quarterly

d.   12 percent, compounded monthly

e.   12 percent, compounded daily

f.   12 percent, compounded continuously

Solution

a.   Annual compounding, $m = 1$: $k = \left(1 + \dfrac{0.12}{1}\right)^{1} - 1 = 12\%$

b.   Semi-annual compounding, $m = 2$: $k = \left(1 + \dfrac{0.12}{2}\right)^{2} - 1 = 12.36\%$

c.   Quarterly compounding, $m = 4$: $k = \left(1 + \dfrac{0.12}{4}\right)^{4} - 1 = 12.55\%$

d.   Monthly compounding, $m = 12$: $k = \left(1 + \dfrac{0.12}{12}\right)^{12} - 1 = 12.68\%$

e.   Daily compounding, $m = 365$: $k = \left(1 + \dfrac{0.12}{365}\right)^{365} - 1 = 12.747\%$

f.   Continuous compounding: $k = e^{0.12} - 1 = 12.75\%$

You can, of course, solve effective interest rate problems by using a calculator or Excel.

EXAMPLE 5-13   Solution using a Financial Calculator *continued*

Perform the following keystrokes:

`2ND` `ICONV`

`2ND` `CLRWORK`

The screen will show NOM = some value.

Make NOM = 12 (this is the nominal rate).

Then `ENTER` `↓` `↓` .

This should show C/Y = some value.

For daily compounding, for example, input:

C/Y = 365 (this is the number of compounding periods per year)

Then `ENTER` `↓` `↓` , which should show EFF = some value.

Then `CPT` , which gives an answer of 12.747 percent.

EXAMPLE 5-13   Solution using Excel

Excel has a special function for solving for effective rates: the Effect(nominal, npery) function, for which "nominal" is the nominal interest rate and "npery" is the compounding frequency.[6] For any of the previous periods, we would enter

  = effect(0.12, *n*)

with *n* = 1, 2, 4, 12, 365, and a very large number to approximate *n* = ∞, and we would get the answers above.

Effective Rates for "Any" Period

In Example 5-12b, the effective quarterly rate is 4 percent, because each dollar grows to $1.04 by the end of one quarter. Similarly, in Example 5-13 (which uses a quoted rate of 12 percent), the effective semi-annual rate for 5-13b is 6 percent (i.e., 12 percent/2), the effective quarterly rate for 5-13c is 3 percent (i.e., 12 percent/4), and the effective monthly rate for 5-13d is 1 percent (i.e., 12 percent/12).

However, suppose we need to know the effective monthly rate associated with the annual effective rate of 12.36 percent from Example 5-13b, perhaps to make monthly payments on a loan. It is not appropriate to divide 12.36 percent by 12, because it is an effective rate, not a quoted rate. Remember, we are looking for the effective monthly rate (i.e., how much $1 would grow over a given month), based on an annual effective rate of 12.36 percent. In this case, we know that after 12 compounding intervals at a monthly effective rate of $k_{monthly}$, each $1 would have grown to $1.1236. In other words, we have

$$\left(1 + k_{monthly}\right)^{12} = 1.1236$$

We could solve this equation by taking the 12th root of each side:

$$\left(1 + k_{monthly}\right) = \left(1.1236\right)^{1/12}$$

So $k_{monthly} = (1.1236)^{1/12} - 1 = 0.0097588$ or 0.97588 percent.

We can verify this by compounding $1 at the rate of 0.97588 percent per month for 12 months as follows: $(1.0097588)^{12} = 1.1236$. In other words, investing $1 at 0.97588 percent per

---

[5] You may need to add the Analysis ToolPak in Excel, which can be done by clicking on Tools, then Add-Ins, then Analysis ToolPak, and then OK.

month produces the same amount at the end of one year (1.1236) as does investing $1 for one year with semi-annual compounding at 6 percent per six-month period.

The following equation, which is a variation of Equation 5-9, can be used to determine the effective rate for any period, given any quoted rates:

[5-11]

$$k = \left(1 + \frac{QR}{m}\right)^{\frac{m}{f}} - 1$$

where f = frequency of payments per year (i.e., f = 1 when we are looking for an annual effective rate; f = 12 when looking for a monthly effective rate, etc.). Notice that when f = 1, we have Equation 5-9.

There is no specific function to solve for "other than annual" effective rates by using the TI BA II Plus calculator. We could find the effective annual rate for a 12 percent nominal rate with quarterly compounding (as demonstrated in the previous example), and then do the following:

$$\left(1 + k_{monthly}\right)^{12} = 1.1236$$

$$\text{So } \left(1 + k_{monthly}\right) = \left(1.1236\right)^{1/12}, \text{ and}$$

$$k_{monthly} = \left(1.1236\right)^{1/12} - 1 = 0.0097588 \text{ or } 0.97588\%$$

In Excel, we can go back to the rate function that we used previously. For example, if the annual rate is 12.36 percent and we want to know the effective monthly rate, we can use the following function,

$$= \text{Rate}\left(nper, pmt, pv, fv, type\right),$$

entering the following in the appropriate cell,

$$= \text{Rate}\left(12, 0, -1, 1.1236, 0\right),$$

where there are 12 periods and no intervening payments, and we are interested in a $1 outflow growing to 1.1236. Because we are not interested in annuities, we put in 0 for type. This produces the same answer: 0.975879 percent.

CONCEPT REVIEW QUESTIONS

1. Why can effective rates often be very different from quoted rates?

2. Explain how to calculate the effective rate for any period.

5.6 LOAN OR MORTGAGE ARRANGEMENTS

Learning Objective 5.6
Apply annuity formulas to value loans and mortgages, and set up an amortization schedule.

mortgage a loan, usually secured by real property, that involves "blended" equal payments (both interest and a principal repayment) over a specified payment period

amortize to retire a loan over a given period by making regular payments

One common and important application of annuity concepts is in the form of loan or **mortgage** arrangements. Typically, these arrangements involve "blended" payments for equal amounts that include both an interest and a principal repayment component. The loan payments are designed to **amortize** the loan, which means that, at the end of the loan term, the balance due (or principal outstanding) will equal zero—in other words, the loan and all associated interest obligations will have been paid off in their entirety. Note that both "amortize" and "mortgage" contain the French word *mort*, which means "death." So a mortgage is "killed off" over the mortgage period, and no money is owed at the end. Similarly, amortize means to "kill off" financially.

Because these loans involve equal payments at regular intervals, based on one fixed interest rate specified when the loan is taken out, the payments can be viewed as annuities. Therefore, we can determine the amount of the payment, the effective period interest rate, and so on, by using Equation 5-5 and recognizing that the PV equals the amount of the loan.

An amortization schedule divides the blended payments into the interest portion and the principal repayment portion. This is of importance to businesses, where the interest portion is a deductible expense for tax purposes. The interest portion is determined by applying the effective period interest rate to the principal outstanding at the beginning of each period. The remaining portion of the payment is then used to reduce the amount of principal outstanding. The example below shows the development of an amortization schedule.

It is important to understand how this amortization table is created. The loan is a simple annual payment loan, so the cost of the loan is the annual interest rate times the outstanding balance; in this case, 10 percent times $5,000, or $500. This is the first charge on the loan payments; the residual, which is $1,510.57 in the first year, goes to reduce the amount of the loan.

EXAMPLE 5-14 Loan Payments and Amortization Schedule

Determine the required year-end payments for a three-year $5,000 loan with a 10 percent annual interest rate. Complete an amortization schedule.

Solution

First, determine the required payments by solving Equation 5-5 for PMT.

$$PMT = \frac{PV_0}{\left[\dfrac{1 - \dfrac{1}{(1+k)^n}}{k}\right]} = \frac{5{,}000}{\left[\dfrac{1 - \dfrac{1}{(1.10)^3}}{0.10}\right]} = \frac{5{,}000}{2.48685} = \$2{,}010.57$$

Second, determine the loan amortization schedule

Period	(1) Beginning Principal Outstanding	(2) PMT	(3) Interest [(1)*k]	(4) Principal Repayment [(2) − (3)]	End Principal Outstanding [(1) − (4)]
1	5,000.00	2,010.57	500.00	1,510.57	3,489.43
2	3,489.43	2,010.57	348.94	1,661.63	1,827.80
3	1,827.80	2,010.57	182.77	1,827.80	0.00

EXAMPLE 5-14 Solution using a Financial Calculator

(TI BA II PLUS)

Input the following variables:

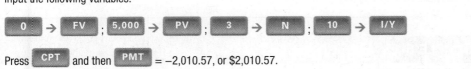

Press CPT and then PMT = −2,010.57, or $2,010.57.

EXAMPLE 5-14 Solution using Excel

XLS

Use the Excel payment function (PMT):

= PMT (rate, nper, pv, fv, type),

which for our example gives = PMT (0.1, 3, 5000, 0, 0), and the same answer of $2,010.57.

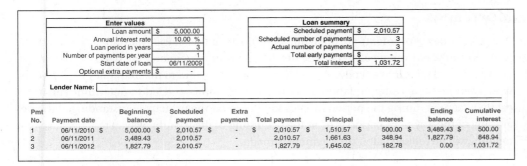

Enter values			Loan summary		
Loan amount	$ 5,000.00		Scheduled payment	$ 2,010.57	
Annual interest rate	10.00 %		Scheduled number of payments	3	
Loan period in years	3		Actual number of payments	3	
Number of payments per year	1		Total early payments	$ -	
Start date of loan	06/11/2009		Total interest	$ 1,031.72	
Optional extra payments	$ -				

Lender Name: _____

Pmt No.	Payment date	Beginning balance	Scheduled payment	Extra payment	Total payment	Principal	Interest	Ending balance	Cumulative interest
1	06/11/2010	$ 5,000.00	$ 2,010.57	$ -	$ 2,010.57	1,510.57	$ 500.00	$ 3,489.43	$ 500.00
2	06/11/2011	3,489.43	2,010.57	-	2,010.57	1,661.63	348.94	1,827.79	848.94
3	06/11/2012	1,827.79	2,010.57	-	1,827.79	1,645.02	182.78	0.00	1,031.72

FIGURE 5-3 *Excel Amortization Table for Example 5-14, Showing Mortgage Loan Payments*

For the next year, the outstanding balance on the loan is now $3,489.43 and the cost of the loan goes down to $348.94, even though the payment is the same at $2,010.57. As a result, the amount going toward the repayment of the loan increases to $1,661.63.

Note that Excel users can automate the whole process of generating an amortization table by typing amortization into the online help and downloading the amortization template. For our example, Excel produced the information presented in Figure 5-3 on the previous page.

However, even though you can use Excel, you should practise generating your own schedule by using the PMT function and writing out each line separately, since Excel sometimes presents the data in a way that your instructor might not accept. Note the heading of the loan amortization schedule and the last line of the schedule compared with the one we developed.

EXAMPLE 5-15   Determining the Principal Outstanding

Determine the principal outstanding on the loan in Example 5-14 after one year, without referring to the amortization schedule found in the solution.

Solution

This problem can be solved by recognizing that the principal outstanding at any time on a loan equals the PV of all future payments at that time. For this example, we find the PV for the given payments and interest rate when $n = 2$ (i.e., the number of payments remaining on the loan after one year).

$$PV_0 = PMT \left[\frac{1 - \dfrac{1}{(1 + k)^n}}{k} \right] = 2{,}010.57 \left[\frac{1 - \dfrac{1}{(1.08)^6}}{0.08} \right]$$

$$= (2{,}010.57)(1.735537) = \$3{,}489.42$$

EXAMPLE 5-15   Solution using a Financial Calculator

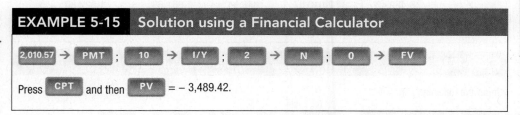

$2{,}010.57 \rightarrow$ PMT ; $10 \rightarrow$ I/Y ; $2 \rightarrow$ N ; $0 \rightarrow$ FV

Press CPT and then PV $= -3{,}489.42$.

EXAMPLE 5-15   Solution using Excel

Use the Excel PV function

= PV (rate, nper, pmt, fv, type),

which for our example gives = PV (0.1, 2, 2010.57, 0, 0) and the same answer of $3,489.42.

Notice again that the answers are the same except for $0.01 because of rounding. Remember that the answer will come out as a negative because we are investing money and then receiving a payoff.

Mortgages

In practice, loan repayments are often not made on an annual basis. Many loans call for quarterly, monthly, or even weekly repayments. For these arrangements, we need to convert the quoted annual rates into effective period rates that correspond to the frequency of payments, which can be done using Equation 5-11. This conversion is needed to determine the interest that accrued during the period in question based on the principal outstanding at the beginning of the payment period (i.e., at the beginning of the month, week, etc.), because that amount will be reduced after the payment is made.

Mortgages represent an example of a loan that requires that payments be made more frequently than annually. In fact, mortgage payments must be made at least monthly, and many offer the opportunity to make biweekly or weekly payments. In Canada, mortgages are further complicated by the fact that compounding is done on a semi-annual basis, similar to bonds, which we will discuss in Chapter 6. When we deal with mortgages in Canada, $m = 2$ in Equation 5-11, while $f > 2$ (in fact, f must be greater than or equal to 12, since payments must be made at least monthly).

Finally, there is one other thing to be familiar with: the distinction between the "term" and the "amortization period" associated with long-term loans, such as mortgages. In particular, the term of a loan refers to the period for which investors can "lock in" at a fixed rate. This is usually shorter than the period over which the loan is to be repaid, or amortized, which is called the amortization period. The payments are based on the amortization period. For example, a loan with a 25-year amortization period may be structured so that the investor locks in a fixed rate of 6 percent for five years (which is the term of the loan). The payments for this loan would be determined based on the 6 percent quoted rate, assuming equal payments for 25 years even though after five years the payments will change if the interest rate on the mortgage changes.

The choice of amortization period can have a large impact on the amount of each mortgage payment (and hence on the maximum amount mortgagees can borrow), and also on the total amount of interest paid during the duration of the loan. *Finance in the News 5-3* demonstrates this point very clearly by showing that a $600,000 mortgage loan that is amortized over 25 years, would require monthly payments of $3,201.83, resulting in total interest payments of $360,545. In contrast, a 40-year amortization period would require monthly payments of only $2,546.86 and much higher total interest payments of $622,488. *Finance in the News 5-3* also refers to recent regulatory changes designed to reduce the length of amortization periods, in an effort to reduce household debt loads In 2012, the federal government further reduced the maximum amortization period allowable to 25 years.

finance INTHENEWS 5-3   Factoring New Mortgage Rules into the Market

THROWING A bucket of cold water on an already-cooling housing sector is not a step any government takes lightly.

This week, Finance Minister Jim Flaherty did just that. As of March 18, the government will no longer insure mortgages with amortization periods of more than 30 years. That will keep some potential home buyers out of the market, and in theory, help stop already debt-burdened households from going even deeper. Ottawa will also make home refinancing rules tighter, among other moves.

The consumer debt habit is widely viewed as a risk to the economy, and the move to curb its growth seen as necessary. But when it comes to the housing market, Ottawa has waded into muddy waters.

While the effective elimination of the 35-year mortgage could diminish housing prices, economists say it's not possible to calculate the degree of dampening with any certainty.

That's in part because some homeowners take long mortgages initially and then change the terms later, paying more than required in order to retire the debt sooner.

And there are a host of other factors that determine housing prices such as interest rates, employment growth, and housing supply.

"Given the structure of the mortgage market, this is like a surgical strike," said Benjamin Tal, deputy chief economist at CIBC World Markets.

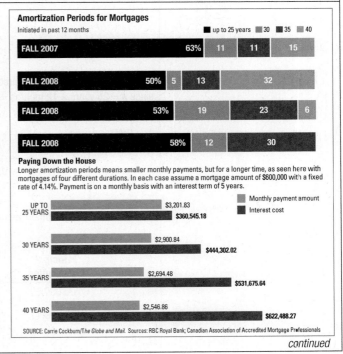

Amortization Periods for Mortgages
Initiated in past 12 months

■ up to 25 years ■ 30 ■ 35 ■ 40

FALL 2007	63%	11	11	15
FALL 2008	50%	5	13	32
FALL 2008	53%	19	23	6
FALL 2008	58%	12	30

Paying Down the House
Longer amortization periods means smaller monthly payments, but for a longer time, as seen here with mortgages of four different durations. In each case assume a mortgage amount of $600,000 with a fixed rate of 4.14%. Payment is on a monthly basis with an interest term of 5 years.

■ Monthly payment amount
■ Interest cost

UP TO 25 YEARS — $3,201.83 / $360,545.18
30 YEARS — $2,900.84 / $444,302.02
35 YEARS — $2,694.48 / $531,675.64
40 YEARS — $2,546.86 / $622,488.27

SOURCE: Carrie Cockburn/*The Globe and Mail*. Sources: RBC Royal Bank; Canadian Association of Accredited Mortgage Professionals

continued

Finance in the News 5-3: Factoring New Mortgage Rules into the Market (continued)

"They are able to aim without too many side effects because of the way the mortgage market is structured in Canada. The impact is insignificant."

There's little data examining the issue.

The new rules can be expected to dampen both home sales and prices as potential home buyers face new limits on how much they can borrow, encouraging them to opt for cheaper homes, economists said.

Douglas Porter, deputy chief economist with BMO Nesbitt Burns Inc., said the changes would reduce the amount that people can borrow by up to 7 per cent.

Corresponding price declines, though, are hard to predict. Canada's housing market has been cooling for months and interest rates are widely predicted to begin rising again during the latter half of this year.

"I suspect that what we'll end up seeing is home prices about flat this year," Mr. Porter said.

Bank of Nova Scotia economists Adrienne Warren and Derek Holt suggest the new limits on amortization will add about $100 to the monthly principal and interest payment on an average priced house, compared with a 35-year mortgage.

"Looking further ahead, as interest rates begin to move higher in 2012 and beyond, the cumulative impact from shorter amortization options on housing affordability could be substantial," their report said.

The Bank of Canada hinted at a link between prices and amortization rates last year, when deputy governor Sheryl Kennedy said "financial innovations" such as longer amortization rates can "encourage speculation in quick flip financial investment."

That surge in home buying helped drive up prices, particularly in large urban centres. As a result, since 2007, increasing numbers of Canadians have opted for mortgages with amortization periods stretching well past 25 years.

Initially, 40-year mortgages saw the most explosive growth until Mr. Flaherty took action in 2008 to do away with those unconventional loans.

The following year, however, marginal consumers increasingly turned to 35-year mortgages to fill the void, a trend that continued well into 2010.

EXAMPLE 5-16   Determining Mortgage Payments and Amortization Schedule

Determine the monthly payments and the amortization schedule for the first three months of a $200,000 mortgage loan with an amortization period of 25 years, based on a quoted rate of 6 percent and a 10-year term.

Solution

First, determine the effective period rate. Because it is a Canadian mortgage, we know that $m = 2$. Since payments are made monthly, we need to find the effective monthly rate, so $f = 12$. Using Equation 5-11,

$$k_{monthly} = \left(1 + \frac{0.06}{2}\right)^{\frac{2}{12}} - 1 = 0.4938622\%$$

Second, determine the required monthly payments by using Equation 5-5. There are 300 payments in total, since $n = 25$ years $\times$ 12 months $= 300$. PV $= 200,000$ (i.e., the loan amount).

$$\text{PMT} = \frac{PV_0}{\left[\dfrac{1 - \dfrac{1}{(1 + k)^n}}{k}\right]} = \frac{200,000}{\left[\dfrac{1 - \dfrac{1}{(1.004938622)^{300}}}{0.004938622}\right]} = \frac{200,000}{156.2972258} = \$1,279.61$$

Third, construct an amortization schedule similar to the one in Example 5-14 above.

Period	(1) Beginning Principal Outstanding	(2) PMT	(3) Interest [$k \times$ (1)]	(4) Principal Repayment [(2) − (3)]	End Principal Outstanding [(1) − (4)]
1	200,000.00	1,279.61	987.72	291.89	199,708.11
2	199,708.11	1,279.61	986.28	293.33	199,414.78
3	199,414.78	1,279.61	984.83	294.78	199,120.00

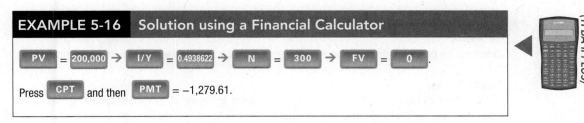

EXAMPLE 5-16   Solution using a Financial Calculator

PV = 200,000 → I/Y = 0.4938622 → N = 300 → FV = 0 .

Press CPT and then PMT = −1,279.61.

Note that unlike the simple annual payment loan, for which the cost of the loan was the annual interest cost, now the cost is the monthly interest rate of 0.4938622 percent, because we have a monthly amortization schedule. It is this monthly rate applied to the outstanding balance that determines how much of the mortgage's monthly payments represent the cost of the loan. As is clear from the amortization schedule, very little of the early payments go toward reducing the principal. The greater portion of the early payments are for interest. This is true for all long-term loans because, by definition, the repayment of the loan is being done over a longer period. As time passes, the interest cost of the fixed payments continues to decrease, and the payment of principal correspondingly increases. The reason for this is simply that the interest rate is the cost of borrowing money, and this cost has to be subtracted first from the monthly payment.

As before, Excel simplifies the whole process. However, note that Excel reports mortgage costs according to U.S., not Canadian, practice. In Canada, mortgage rates are quoted equivalent to bonds, so a 6 percent quoted mortgage rate is actually 3 percent every six months, and the monthly rate is then determined as a monthly rate that compounds to 3 percent over six months or 0.49386 percent. In the United States, the same 6 percent quote means 0.5 percent per month. In other words, the annual rate is simply divided by 12. As a result, the same quoted mortgage rate in the United States and Canada will produce different results. The first three months of the Excel amortization table for Example 5-16 are shown in Figure 5-4.

Enter values	
Loan amount	$ 200,000.00
Annual interest rate	0.06
Loan period in years	25
Number of payments per year	12
Start date of loan	06/11/2010
Optional extra payments	$ -

Loan summary	
Scheduled payment	$ 1,288.60
Scheduled number of payments	300
Actual number of payments	300
Total early payments	$ -
Total interest	$ 186,580.84

Lender Name:

Pmt No.	Payment date	Beginning balance	Scheduled payment	Extra payment	Total payment	Principal	Interest	Ending balance	Cumulative interest
1	06/12/2010	$ 200,000.00	$ 1,288.60	$ -	$ 1,288.60	$ 288.60	$ 1,000.00	$ 199,711.40	$ 1,000.00
2	06/01/2011	199,711.40	1,288.60	-	1,288.60	290.05	998.56	199,421.35	1,998.56
3	06/02/2011	199,421.35	1,288.60	-	1,288.60	291.50	997.11	199,129.86	2,995.66

FIGURE 5-5 *Mortgage Loan Payments*

Note that for the first month, the interest payment is simply 0.5 percent times the principal of $200,000, or $1,000, versus $987.72 for the true (Canadian) cost. Also note that the monthly payment is $9 higher, at $1,288.60.

Excel is a wonderful software program, but before using the sophisticated functions, always check the answers by using the basic functions first to make sure that the macros written by the programmers are consistent with what you want to estimate. For Canadian mortgages, you can check with a variety of mortgage calculators, available free on the Internet, that also produce amortization schedules.[6]

One item of interest to a mortgagee would be how much of the loan has been retired after a certain time. We can solve this problem in the same manner that we did in Example 5-15.

Notice in Example 5-17 that slightly less than 25 percent of the loan has been repaid after 10 years, even though 40 percent of the amortization period (i.e., 10 out of 25 years) has elapsed. This is consistent with our earlier observation with respect to the high proportion of each of the early payments that goes toward interest versus principal reduction.

---

[6] A well-presented calculator is available on the website of Bankrate.com: www.bankrate.com/calculators/mortgages/mortgage-calculator.aspx.

EXAMPLE 5-17 Determining the Principal Outstanding on a Mortgage

Determine the principal outstanding on the mortgage in Example 5-16 at the end of the 10-year term.

Solution

Trying to solve this by constructing an amortization schedule to the end of 10 years would be cumbersome. However, it is easily solved by recognizing that the principal outstanding is the PV of all future payments after 10 years. We find the PV for the payments when n = 15 years × 12 months = 180 months—that is, for the balance of the payments after 10 years.

$$PV_0 = \$1,279.61 \left[\frac{1 - \dfrac{1}{(1.004938622)^{180}}}{0.004938622} \right] = (\$1,279.61)(119.0642325) = \$152,355.78$$

EXAMPLE 5-17 Solution using a Financial Calculator

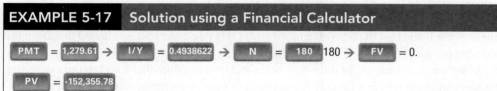

PMT = 1,279.61 → I/Y = 0.4938622 → N = 180 180 → FV = 0.

PV = -152,355.78

EXAMPLE 5-17 Solution using Excel

= PV (0.004938622, 180, 1279.61, 0, 0) gives the same answer of − $152,355.78. Note as before that the interest rate is inserted in decimals.

CONCEPT REVIEW QUESTIONS

1. Explain how loan and mortgage payments can be determined using annuity concepts.

2. What complications arise when dealing with mortgage loans in Canada?

3. Why is a 6 percent U.S. mortgage not the same as a 6 percent Canadian mortgage?

5.7 COMPREHENSIVE EXAMPLES

Learning Objective 5.7
Solve a basic retirement problem.

We conclude this chapter by providing a few comprehensive examples that involve applying the concepts you have learned to more challenging situations. The second of these examples is a common problem facing investors with respect to planning for retirement.

Notice that the two problems in this section appear complicated at first but are quite manageable if you break them down into their components. Timelines are very useful for this purpose because they help you visualize what information you have and what is needed to solve the problem. If you are able to solve these problems, then you have a good understanding of the basic concepts involving the time value of money.

EXAMPLE 5-18 Multiple Annuities

a. What is the PV of $1,000 received at year end for the next four years, followed by $2,000 per year end for years 5 to 7, assuming a 10 percent rate of interest, compounded annually?

b. Suppose an investor needed $15,000 at the end of seven years and can only invest $1,000 per year for years 1 to 4 (as above). How much would the investor need to deposit in each of years 5 to 7 to achieve this objective, assuming a 10 percent interest rate as above?

EXAMPLE 5-18 Multiple Annuities *continued*

Solution

a.   This problem is best solved by first constructing a timeline:

0	1	2	3	4	5	6	7
	1.000	1.000	1.000	1.000	2.000	2.000	2.000

Notice that we can view this problem in several ways. It can be viewed as a four-year annuity of $1,000 followed by a three-year annuity of $2,000, or as a seven-year annuity of $1,000, with a three-year annuity of an "extra" $1,000 beginning at the end of year 5, and so on. Also, we could solve it by finding the future value of both annuities at $t = 7$ and then discounting them, or by finding the PV of the second annuity at $t = 4$ and discounting it back to $t = 0$, which is the approach we have chosen.

Viewing this problem as a four-year ordinary annuity (A1) that pays $1,000 per year, followed by a three-year ordinary annuity (A2) that pays $2,000 per year, we can determine the PV as follows:

$$PV(A1) = 1,000 \left[\frac{1 - \frac{1}{(1.10)^4}}{0.10} \right] = 1,000\,(3.16987) = \$3,169.87$$

$$PV(A2) = 2,000 \left[\frac{1 - \frac{1}{(1.10)^3}}{0.10} \right] \left[\frac{1}{(1.10)^4} \right] = 2,000(2.48685)(0.683013) = \$3,397.10$$

We illustrate this in a timeline.

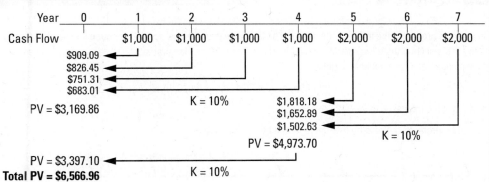

Notice that for PV(A2), we first determine the PV of the three-year annuity starting at time $t = 4$ (i.e., 4,973.70), and then we discount this amount back to today.   *continued*

EXAMPLE 5-18   Solution using a Financial Calculator

Enter the following:

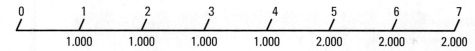

Then CPT → PV = −3,169.87

Then enter the following:

Then CPT → PV = 4,973.70

continued

EXAMPLE 5-18   Solution using a Financial Calculator *continued*

This is the PV of the three-year annuity at time $t = 4$, which must be discounted back to time $t = 0$.

Next, enter the following:

4,973.70 → **FV** ; **0** → **PMT** ; **10** → **I/Y** ; **4** → **N**

Then **CPT** → **PV** = −3,397.10

EXAMPLE 5-18   Solution using Excel

Using Excel, calculate PV (A1) = PV (0.1, 4, − 1000, 0, 0)
We can calculate PV (A2) by first calculating the PV of the three-year annuity as
= PV (0.1, 3, −2000, 0, 0),
which gives $4,973.70. Then use
= PV (0.1, 4, 0, −49737.70, 0),
which gives $3,397.10.
However, we can calculate PV (A2) in one step with Excel, because we can nest Excel functions within each other. In this case, we can write it in one step as
= PV (0.1, 4, 0, PV (0.1, 3, −2000, 0, 0), 0)
and we would get the same answer.

EXAMPLE 5-18   Multiple Annuities *continued*

So the PV(Total) = PV(A1) + PV(A2) = 3,169.87 + 3,397.10 = $6,566.97.

In all these problems, the interest rate need not be the same over the two periods. For our example, the interest rate for the second three-year period could be 10 percent, while for the first four periods it could be 5 percent. In this case, the Excel solution would be

$$= PV (0.05, 4, 0, PV (0.1, 3, −2000, 0, 0), 0)$$

and the value increases to $6,943.05.

b.   This problem can also be best represented by using a timeline:

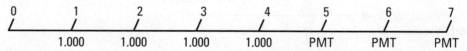

We can solve this problem in several ways. We have chosen to solve it by finding the future value of the first annuity (A1) at $t = 7$, and then determining the FV of the second annuity (A2) at $t = 7$, required to achieve the $15,000 target. Then, knowing the required FV of the three-year annuity, we can determine the payments for years 5 to 7.

Determine the FV of A1 at time $t = 4$:

$$FV_4 (A1) = 1,000 \times \left[\frac{(1 + 0.10)^4 - 1}{0.10} \right] = (1,000)(4.641) = \$4,641$$

Second, determine the FV of A1 at time $t = 7$:

$$FV_7(A1) = 4,641 \times (1.10)^3 = (4,641)(1.331) = \$6,177.17$$

Third, determine the required FV of A2 at time $t = 7$:

$$\text{Required } FV_7(A2) = \text{Required amount} - FV_7(A1) = 15,000 - 6,177.17 = \$8,822.83$$

continued

EXAMPLE 5-18   Multiple Annuities *continued*

We illustrate this in a timeline.

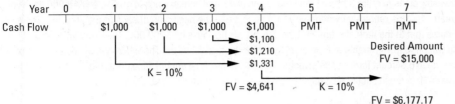

Fourth, determine the required payments for A2:

$$PMT = \frac{8,822.83}{\left[\dfrac{(1.10)^3 - 1}{0.10}\right]} = \frac{8,822.83}{3.31} = \$2,665.51$$

EXAMPLE 5-18   Solution using a Financial Calculator *continued*

Enter the following:

then CPT → FV = 4,641

Second, enter the following:

Then CPT → FV = −6,177.17

Third, enter the following:

Then press CPT → PMT = −2,665.51

EXAMPLE 5-18   Solution using Excel *continued*

= FV (0.1, 4, −1000, 0, 0) gives an answer of $4,641.
= FV (0.1, 3, 0, 4641, 0) gives an answer of $6,177.17.
Then we can use the payment function,
= PMT (rate, nper, pv, fv, type), so that inserting our values
= PMT (0.1, 3, 0, 8822.83, 0) gives the same answer of $2,665.51.
If we are really ambitious, we can collapse all three Excel functions into a single one and input
= PMT (0.1, 3, 0, 15000 + FV(0.1, 3, 0, FV(0.1, 4, − 1000, 0, 0), 0), 0)

and get the right answer. However, although this shows the power of Excel, it is not recommended. Much can be learned by breaking the problem into its three constituent parts because you need to develop an understanding of what is approximately the right answer. This opportunity is lost when you collapse it all into one function. Furthermore, you have to be careful: Excel provides a negative present value if the payoff is positive because it treats the values as those from an investment. In our case, we have to add the future value from the annuity since Excel provides a negative value for this.

EXAMPLE 5-19   Retirement Problem

An investor plans to retire 35 years from today and have sufficient savings to guarantee $48,000 each year for 20 years. Assume retirement withdrawals will be made at the beginning of each of the 20 years. The investor estimates that at the time of retirement, he can sell his business for $200,000. The expectation is that interest rates will be relatively stable at 8 percent a year for the next 35 years. Thereafter, the interest rate is expected to decline to 6 percent forever. The investor wants to make equal annual deposits at the end of each of the next 35 years. How much should be deposited each year in order to meet the stated objective?

Solution

A timeline helps visualize the problem:

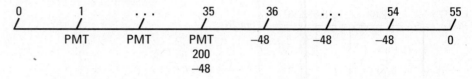

0	1	. . .	35	36	. . .	54	55
	PMT	PMT	PMT	−48	−48	−48	0
			200				
			−48				

$k = 8$ percent for years 1 to 35 $k = 6$ percent for years 35 to 55

First, determine how much is needed after 35 years. At this time, the investor wants a 20-year annuity due of $48,000, because he is drawing down funds immediately on retirement, at a 6 percent interest rate. In other words, find the PV of a 20-year annuity due, when $k = 6$ percent:

$$PV_{35} = 48,000 \left[\frac{1 - \dfrac{1}{(1.06)^{20}}}{0.06} \right] (1.06) = (48,000)(11.46992122)(1.06) = \$583,589.59$$

(TI BA II PLUS)

EXAMPLE 5-19   Solution using a Financial Calculator

First, set your calculator to "Begin" mode and then enter

FV = 0 ; PMT = 48,000 ; I/Y = 6 ; N = 20 .

Press CPT and then PV = −583,589.59 or $583,589.59.

EXAMPLE 5-19   Retirement Problem *continued*

Second, subtract the $200,000 expected from the sale of the business, leaving the amount needed to be raised through investments:

$$\text{Need } FV_{35} = 583,589.59 - 200,000 = \$383,589.59$$

Third, determine the required year-end payments over the next 35 years:

$$PMT = \left[\frac{383,589.59}{\dfrac{(1.08)^{35} - 1}{0.08}} \right] = \frac{383,589.59}{172,3168037} = \$2,226.07$$

EXAMPLE 5-19   Solution using a Financial Calculator *continued*

Finally, take your calculator out of "Begin" mode.

Enter PV = 0 ; FV = 383,589.59 ; I/Y = 8 ; N = 35

Then press CPT and then PMT = − 2,226.07 or $2,226.07

EXAMPLE 5-19   Solution using Excel

Or, using Excel,

= PV (0.06, 20, 48000, 0, 1)

gives the same answer of $583,589.59. However, now that we need an annuity due, we have to put a 0 in for the future value to let Excel know that the 1 in the last column refers to an annuity due and is not a future value. If we then use the payment function to calculate the annuity, we get

= PMT (0.08, 35, 0, 383589.59, 0)

The answer is $2,226.07. As before, we can collapse this into one function as PMT (0.08, 35, 0, PV(0.06, 20, −48000, 0, 1) −200000, 0)

But this is not advisable until you have more experience with Excel.

LESSONS TO BE LEARNED

Example 5-19 demonstrates a relatively simple version of the basic retirement "problem" that is central to finance, as it faces all individual investors, as well as pension funds. Notice that this problem is based on "assumed" returns of 8 percent per year during the investor's "earnings" phase. So what options do investors have when the invested funds do *not* earn this rate of return, and they find themselves in a shortfall position?

Basically, they have four options: (1) increase their contributions; (2) try to earn a higher rate of return (although they do not have control over capital market returns, so this might involve taking on more risk, which could backfire and result in even lower returns); (3) reduce the amount withdrawn upon retirement; and/or, (4) postpone retirement (i.e., work longer).

Unfortunately, many individuals, as well as many pension plans, have been forced to deal with this situation over the past few years, as their investment funds were hit by volatile and weak market returns. In fact, a recent survey by the Conference Board of Canada indicates that by 2011, one in five individuals had been forced to delay retirement by at least one year. In addition, many pension plans have been dealing with severe underfunding problems (as alluded to in *Finance in the News 5-2*), and have been forced to consider (or implement) some combination of reducing benefits paid to retirees and/or increasing required contributions. All of this comes at a time when the returns offered by "safe" investments (i.e., government debt securities) are very low, and stock returns have been volatile, thus requiring some very tough decisions by investors at all levels.

CONCEPT REVIEW QUESTIONS

1. Explain how timelines can be used to break a complicated time value of money problem into manageable components.

2. Demonstrate how to solve a typical retirement problem.

APPENDIX 5A

GROWING PERPETUITIES AND ANNUITIES

Growing Perpetuities

Sometimes we may want to evaluate a stream of cash flows that will grow (or shrink) at a constant rate per period (g) indefinitely.[7] In this case, our payments (PMT) will change from one period to the next, as shown below:

$$PMT_1 = PMT_0 (1 + g)$$

$$PMT_2 = PMT_1 (1 + g) = PMT_0 (1 + g)^2$$

$$PMT_3 = PMT_2 (1 + g) = PMT_0 (1 + g)^3$$

and so on.[8]

The present value of this stream of payments can be calculated as follows:

[5A-1]
$$PV_0 = \frac{PMT_0 (1 + g)}{(1 + k)^1} + \frac{PMT_0 (1 + g)^2}{(1 + k)^2} + \frac{PMT_0 (1 + g)^3}{(1 + k)^3} + \ldots + \frac{PMT_0 (1 + g)^\infty}{(1 + k)^\infty}$$

Notice that what we are doing here is multiplying PMT_0 by a factor of $(1 + g)/(1 + k)$ every period. This is easily solved because it represents the sum of a geometric series, so we can reduce this to the following expression:

[5A-2]
$$PV_0 = \frac{PMT_0 (1 + g)}{k - g} = \frac{PMT_1}{k - g}$$

Equation 5A-2 has several important points:

1. This relationship holds only when $k > g$. Otherwise, the answer is negative, which is uninformative.

2. Only *future* estimated cash flows and estimated growth in these cash flows are relevant.

3. The relationship holds only when growth in payments is expected to occur at the same rate indefinitely.

EXAMPLE 5A-1 | Valuing a Growing Perpetuity

You are attempting to determine the present value of cash flows to be generated from a rental property you are considering purchasing. You have estimated that the after-tax cash flows from this property will grow at 4 percent per year indefinitely due to rental increases. The cash flow this past year was $100,000, and the appropriate discount rate is 15 percent. Find the present value of these cash flows.

Solution

$$PMT_0 = 100,000; \; g = 4\%; \; k = 15\%$$

Using the equation above, we get

$$PV_0 = \frac{PMT_0 (1 + g)}{k - g} = \frac{(100,000)(1.04)}{.15 - .04} = \frac{104,000}{.11} = \$945,454.55$$

---

[7] For example, in Chapter 7, we will make this assumption about dividends paid on common shares.
[8] Notice that if the cash flows are shrinking, it merely means that g is a negative rate.

Growing Annuities

Sometimes we may want to evaluate a stream of cash flows that will grow (or shrink) at a constant rate per period (g) over a given period of time, ending at some terminal point (n). Such a stream represents a growing annuity.

The present value of this stream of payments can be calculated as follows:

$$PV_0 = \frac{PMT_0\,(1 + g)}{(1 + k)^1} + \frac{PMT_0\,(1 + g)^2}{(1 + k)^2} + \frac{PMT_0\,(1 + g)^3}{(1 + k)^3} + \cdots + \frac{PMT_0\,(1 + g)^n}{(1 + k)^n} \quad \text{[5A-3]}$$

Notice that this equation is identical to Equation 5A-1, except that the last payment occurs at time n—that is, the payments do not go on to infinity. Equation 5A-3 reduces to the following expression:

$$PV_0 = \frac{PMT_1}{k - g} \times \left[1 - \left(\frac{1 + g}{1 + k}\right)^n \right] \quad \text{[5A-4]}$$

Notice that this equation estimates the present value of a growing perpetuity and then subtracts the present value of the payments from period $n + 1$ to infinity from this value.

EXAMPLE 5A-2 | Valuing a Growing (Shrinking) Annuity

A mining company is attempting to determine the present value of cash flows to be generated from a new mining operation. They have estimated that the after-tax cash flows from this mine will shrink at a rate of 10 percent per year as the reserves are depleted, and that after 10 years, the mine will be abandoned. Next year's cash flow is estimated to be $200,000, and the appropriate discount rate is 20 percent. Find the present value of these cash flows.

Solution

$$PMT_1 = 200,000;\ g = -10\%;\ k = 20\%;\ n = 10$$

Using Equation 5A-4, we get

$$PV_0 = \frac{PMT_1}{k - g} \times \left[1 - \left(\frac{1 + g}{1 + k}\right)^n \right] = \frac{200,000}{.20 - (-.10)} \times \left[1 - \left(\frac{1 + (-.10)}{1 + .20}\right)^{10} \right] = \$629,124.32$$

CONCEPT REVIEW QUESTIONS

1. Explain how to evaluate a growing perpetuity.
2. Explain how to calculate the present value of a growing annuity.

SUMMARY

In this chapter, we demonstrate how to compare cash flows that occur at different points in time, after accounting for the time value of money. This process is applied to virtually every topic that is studied in finance, so it is extremely important. We show how to determine economically equivalent future values from values that occur in previous periods by applying the process of compounding at an appropriate rate of return. Similarly, we show how to determine economically equivalent present values (in today's dollars) for cash flows that occur in the future by discounting them, which is the reciprocal of compounding. These processes can be applied to several cash flows simultaneously.

Annuities represent a special type of cash flow stream involving equal payments at the same interval, with the same interest rate being applied throughout the period. We see that these kinds of cash flow streams are commonplace in finance applications (e.g., loan payments), and that there are relatively simple formulas that enable us to determine the present or future value of these cash flows. We also illustrate how to adjust quoted interest rates to find effective rates, which is important because compounding often takes place at other than annual intervals. Finally, we conclude with some more involved applications of the concepts discussed in the chapter.

SUMMARY OF LEARNING OBJECTIVES

5.1 Explain the importance of the time value of money and how it is related to an investor's opportunity costs.

Time value of money is the idea that money invested today has more value than the same amount invested later. This concept helps us to understand how interest is earned and why investors are indifferent to investment today and future value later.

The opportunity cost of money is the interest rate that would be earned by investing it. For this reason, we also call the interest rate the "price of money."

5.2 Define simple interest and explain how it works.

Simple interest is interest earned on the original principal. The growth in the value of an investment is simply the sum of annual interest earned.

5.3 Define compound interest and explain how it works.

Compound interest is interest earned on the principal amount invested and on any accrued interest. Compound interest can result in dramatic growth in the value of an investment over time.

5.4 Differentiate between an ordinary annuity and an annuity due, and explain how special constant payment problems can be valued as annuities and, in special cases, as perpetuities.

Annuities are streams of level payments at regular time intervals. An ordinary annuity has payments at the end of each period. An annuity due has the same number of payments as an ordinary annuity, but the payments occur at the beginning of each period. The present value of an ordinary annuity can be found with a formula that is equal to the sum of the present value factors. The future value of an ordinary annuity can be found with a formula that is equal to the sum of the future value factors. To get the present

and future value factors for an annuity due, just multiply the ordinary annuity factors by $(1 + k)$.

5.5 Differentiate between quoted rates and effective rates, and explain how quoted rates can be converted to effective rates.

Quoted rates are also called stated rates or annual percentage rates, which are measured annually and used for quoting purposes. The effective rate for a period is the rate at which a dollar invested grows over that period. It is usually stated in percentage terms based on an annual period. The relation can be found in the formula $k = \left(1 + \frac{QR}{m}\right)^m - 1$, where QR is the quoted rate, m is the compounding frequency, and k is the annual effective rate.

5.6 Apply annuity formulas to value loans and mortgages, and set up an amortization schedule.

Loans can be valued as an annuity since they meet the three characteristics of an annuity in that they have equal payments, are for a fixed period of time, and are based on the same discount rate.

To set up an amortization schedule, five variables are calculated for each period: beginning principal outstanding, payment, interest, principal repayment, and ending principal outstanding.

5.7 Solve a basic retirement problem.

A simple retirement problem can be solved by equating the present value of the retirement annuity and the future value of the savings annuity. Comprehensive examples are presented in section 5.7.

5.8 Estimate the present value of growing perpetuities and annuities.

Growing perpetuities can be solved using Equation 5A-2, while growing annuities can be solved using Equation 5A-4.

KEY TERMS

amortize, p. 180
annuity, p. 170
annuity due, p. 173
basis point, p. 164
cash flows, p. 170
compound interest, p. 160
compound value interest factor
   (CVIF), p. 161

discounting, p. 164
effective rate, p. 177
lessee, p. 173
medium of exchange, p. 158
mortgage, p. 180
ordinary annuities, p. 170
perpetuity, p. 175

present value interest factor
   (PVIF), p. 165
reinvest, p. 161
required rate of return or discount rate,
   p. 158
simple interest, p. 159
time value of money, p. 158

EQUATIONS

Equation	Formula	Page
[5-1] Future Value (Simple Interest)	$\text{Value (time } n) = P + (n \times P \times k)$	p. 159
[5-2] Future Value (Compound Interest)	$FV_n = PV_0 (1 + k)^n$	p. 161
[5-3] Present Value	$PV_0 = \dfrac{FV_n}{(1 + k)^n} = FV_n \times \dfrac{1}{(1 + k)^n}$	p. 165
[5-4] Future Value (Ordinary Annuity)	$FV_n = PMT \left[\dfrac{(1 + k)^n - 1}{k} \right]$	p. 171
[5-5] Present Value (Ordinary Annuity)	$PV_0 = PMT \left[\dfrac{1 - \dfrac{1}{(1 + k)^n}}{k} \right]$	p. 172
[5-6] Future Value (Annuity Due)	$FV_n = PMT \left[\dfrac{(1 + k)^n - 1}{k} \right] (1 + k)$	p. 173
[5-7] Present Value (Annuity Due)	$PV_0 = PMT \left[\dfrac{1 - \dfrac{1}{(1 + k)^n}}{k} \right] (1 + k)$	p. 174
[5-8] Present Value (Perpetuity)	$PV_0 = \dfrac{PMT}{k}$	p. 175
[5-9] Effective Annual Rate	$k = \left(1 + \dfrac{QR}{m}\right)^m - 1$	p. 177
[5-10] Effective Annual Rate (with continuous compounding)	$k = e^{QR} - 1$	p. 178

EQUATIONS *continued*

Equation	Formula	Page
[5-11] Effective Period Rate (for any period f)	$k = \left(1 + \dfrac{QR}{m}\right)^{\frac{m}{f}} - 1$	p. 180
[5A-1] Growing Perpetuity (long version)	$PV_0 = \dfrac{PMT_0\,(1+g)}{(1+k)^1} + \dfrac{PMT_0\,(1+g)^2}{(1+k)^2} + \dfrac{PMT_0\,(1+g)^3}{(1+k)^3} + \ldots + \dfrac{PMT_0\,(1+g)^\infty}{(1+k)^\infty}$	p. 192
[5A-2] Growing Perpetuity (reduced version)	$PV_0 = \dfrac{PMT_0\,(1+g)}{k-g} = \dfrac{PMT_1}{k-g}$	p. 192
[5A-3] Growing Annuity (long version)	$PV_0 = \dfrac{PMT_0\,(1+g)}{(1+k)^1} + \dfrac{PMT_0\,(1+g)^2}{(1+k)^2} + \dfrac{PMT_0\,(1+g)^3}{(1+k)^3} + \ldots + \dfrac{PMT_0\,(1+g)^n}{(1+k)^n}$	p. 193
[5A-4] Growing Perpetuity (reduced version)	$PV_0 = \dfrac{PMT_1}{k-g} \times \left[1 - \left(\dfrac{1+g}{1+k}\right)^n\right]$	p. 193

QUESTIONS AND PRACTICE PROBLEMS

Multiple Choice Questions

1. What is the total amount accumulated after five years if someone invests $1,000 today with a simple annual interest rate of 8 percent? How about with a compound annual interest rate of 8 percent?
    a. $600, $680
    b. $1,400, $1,469
    c. $1,469, $1,400
    d. $5,400, $1,016

2. An investment of $5,000 invested for three years has an expected future value of $6,100. The simple annual interest rate is closest to _____ and the compound annual interest rate is closest to _____.
    a. 6.01%; 6.41%
    b. 7.33%; 6.85%
    c. 6.85%; 7.33%
    d. 6.41%; 6.01%

3. At the end of 2009, Malcolm invested $10,000 in two bank accounts. The expected value of each bank account for the years 2009 to 2020 are represented in the following graph. In the graph, "Series 1" represents an account paying _____ interest, while "Series 2" represents an account paying _____ interest.

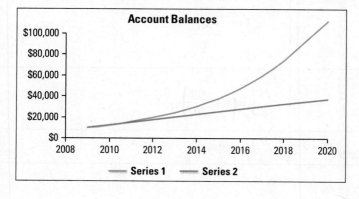

    a. simple; compound

    b. compound; simple

    c. simple; simple

    d. compound; compound

4. Which of the following has the largest future value if $1,000 is invested today?

    a. Five years with a simple annual interest rate of 10%

    b. 10 years with a simple annual interest rate of 8%

    c. Eight years with a compound annual interest rate of 8%

    d. Eight years with a compound annual interest rate of 7%

Interest rates in the following questions are compound rates unless otherwise stated.

5. Suppose an investor wants to have $15 million to retire 25 years from now. How much would she have to invest today if her annual rate of return is equal to 5 percent?

    a. $6,666,666.67

    b. $4,429,541.58

    c. $600,000

    d. $21,345

6. Which of the following is false?

    a. The longer the time period, the smaller the present value, given a $100 future value and holding the interest rate constant.

    b. The greater the interest rate, the greater the present value, given a $100 future value and holding the time period constant.

    c. A future dollar is always less valuable than a dollar today if interest rates are positive.

    d. The discount factor is the reciprocal of the compound factor.

7. Maggie deposits $10,000 today and is promised a return of $17,000 in eight years. What is the implied annual rate of return?

    a. 6.86%

    b. 7.06%

    c. 5.99%

    d. 6.07%

8. How long will it take Mike to triple his investment if he can earn an annual rate of return of 9%?

    a. 15.5 years

    b. 13.9 years

    c. 12.7 years

    d. 10 years

9. Which of the following statements is incorrect?

    a. An ordinary annuity has payments at the end of each year.

    b. An annuity due has payments at the beginning of each year.

    c. A perpetuity is considered a perpetual annuity.

    d. An ordinary annuity has a greater PV than an annuity due, if they both have the same periodic payments, discount rate, and time period.

10. Jan plans to invest $2,000 in an equity fund every year end beginning this year. The expected annual return on the fund is 15 percent. How much would she expect to have at the end of 20 years?

    a. $237,620

    b. $176,424

    c. $204,887

    d. $178,424

11. Jan plans to invest $2,000 in an equity fund every year end beginning this year. The expected annual return on the fund is 15 percent. She plans to invest for 20 years. What is the present value of Jan's investments?
    a. $12,625
    b. $12,519
    c. $14,396
    d. $12,396

12. What is the present value of a perpetuity with an annual year-end payment of $1,500 and expected annual rate of return equal to 12 percent?
    a. $14,000
    b. $13,500
    c. $11,400
    d. $12,500

13. What is the present value of a perpetuity with an annual payment of $1,500 if the first payment is due immediately? The expected annual rate of return is equal to 12 percent.
    a. $14,000
    b. $13,500
    c. $11,400
    d. $12,500

14. Ten years ago you borrowed $250,000. The term of the loan was 20 years and required monthly payments of $2,752.72. The interest rate on the loan was 12 percent compounded monthly. You have just made the 120th payment. What is the principal outstanding?
    a. $200,000
    b. $196,697
    c. $191,866
    d. $125,000

15. Which of the following statements is correct?
    a. The future value of a perpetuity cannot be computed.
    b. The future value of a perpetuity can be computed.
    c. The present value of a perpetuity cannot be computed.
    d. The present value of an annuity cannot be computed.

Practice Problems

16. 16. Franklin is trying to decide whether or not to take a philosophy course next semester. He finds the topic interesting, but being a business student, he wants to measure the cost of taking the course. After detailed thought and analysis, he has identified the following items that he feels may be relevant to his decision:

    Tuition fees for the course: $500
    Textbook for the course: $200
    Rent for his apartment: $5,000
    Food for next semester: $3,200
    Currently Franklin earns $2,000 per semester as a teaching assistant.

    Franklin estimates that the philosophy course will require considerable study so he will have to reduce his teaching assistant hours by 25 percent. Determine the cost of taking the philosophy course.

17. Dmitri Chekov has made an investment of $25,000, and it promises to pay him 8 percent simple interest per year for 10 years. Determine how much interest he will earn in the:
    a. first year
    b. ninth year

18. After a summer of travelling (and not working), a student finds himself $1,500 short for this year's tuition fees. His parents have agreed to lend him the money for three years at a simple interest rate of 6 percent, with interest due at the end of each year.
    a. How much interest will he owe his parents after one year?
    b. How much money will he have paid, in total, at the end of three years?

19. Your sister has been forced to borrow money to pay her tuition this year. If she makes annual interest payments on the loan at year end for the next three years, and the loan is for $2,500 at a simple interest rate of 6 percent, how much will she pay each year?

20. Khalil's summer job has given him $1,200 more than he needs for his tuition this year. The local bank pays simple interest at a rate of 0.5 percent per month. How much interest will he earn in one year?

21. A new Internet bank pays compound interest of 0.5 percent per month on deposits. How much interest will Khalil's summer savings of $1,200 earn in one year with this online bank account?

22. History tells us that a group of Dutch colonists purchased the island of Manhattan from the Native American residents in 1626. Payment was made with wampum (likely glass beads and trinkets), which had an estimated value of $24. Suppose the Dutch had invested this money back home in Europe and earned an average return of 5 percent per year. Determine how much this investment would be worth 387 years later (rounding to the nearest dollar), using:
    a. simple interest
    b. compound interest

23. David has been awarded a scholarship that will pay $2,500 one year from now. However, he really needs the money today and has decided to take out a loan. If the interest rate is 8 percent, how much can he borrow so that the scholarship will just pay off the loan?

24. On the advice of a friend, Gilda invests $20,000 in a mutual fund that has earned 10 percent per year, on average, in recent years. If this rate of return continues, determine how much her investment will be worth in:
    a. one year
    b. five years
    c. 10 years

25. When Jon graduates in three years, he wants to throw a big party, which will cost $800. To have this amount available, how much does he have to invest today if he can earn a compound return of 5 percent per year?

26. Veda has to choose between two investments that have the same cost today. Both investments will ultimately pay $1,300 but at different times, as shown in the table below. If Veda does not choose one of these investments, she could leave the funds in a bank account paying 5 percent per year. Which investment should Veda choose?

Year	Investment A	Investment B
1	$0	$200
2	$500	$400
3	$800	$700

27. A firm has just declared that its dividend next year will be $3 per share. That rate of payment will continue for an additional four years, after which the dividends will fall back to their usual $2 per share. The discount rate is 12%. What is the present value of all the future dividends?

⚙ 28. After living in a university residence for one year, Mary-Beth decides to rent an apartment for the remaining three years of her degree. She has found a nice location that will cost $450 per month. Rent for the first and last month must be paid up front. How much money would Mary-Beth need to have in her bank account right now to be sure she will always have enough for rent? The bank account pays 3.75 percent interest, compounded monthly.

⚙ 29. A 65-year-old man intends to use his retirement funds to purchase an annuity from a life insurance company. Given the amount of money the man has available to invest, the insurance company is able to offer two alternatives. The first option is to receive $2,785 each month for as long as he lives; the second option is to receive $3,500 each month, but for only 20 years (payments will be made to his estate if he should die before that time). The relevant interest rate is 6 percent per year monthly compounding. How long must the man live so that the first option is a better deal?

30. Grace, a retired librarian, would like to donate some money to her alma mater to endow a $5,000 annual scholarship. The university will manage the funds and expects to earn 3 percent per year. How much will Grace have to donate so that the endowment fund never runs out?

31. Grace, a retired librarian, would like to donate some money to her alma mater to endow a $5,000 annual scholarship. The first scholarship will be awarded in 5 years. The university will manage the funds and expects to earn 3 percent per year. How much will Grace have to donate so that the endowment fund never runs out?

32. Muriel would like to support the education of her favourite grand-nephew, Stephen, who plans to begin university in three years. How much will Muriel have to invest today, at 7 percent, to be able to give Stephen $4,000 at the end of each year for four years?

33. You have just won $50 million in a lottery and are offered two options: receive $40 million today or receive $5 million per year for the next 10 years. At what interest rate are you indifferent to the choice between the two options? If the interest rate is greater than the indifference rate, which do you prefer and why? If the interest rate is less than the indifference rate, which do you prefer and why?

⚙ 34. Two friends, Abe and Betty, are planning for their retirement. Both are 20 years old and plan on retiring in 30 years with $1 million each. Betty plans on making annual deposits beginning in one year (total of 30 deposits) while Abe plans on waiting and then depositing twice Betty's deposits. If both can earn 5 percent per year, how long can Abe wait before he has to start making his deposits?

⚙ 35. You are planning on buying your first home and need to borrow $250,000 from the bank. The manager offers you two mortgages: the long option will take 25 years to be paid off, and your annual payments will be $17,738. The short option will take only 10 years to be paid off, and your annual payment will be $35,200. The manager offers you the following advice: if you take the long option, you will pay $193,450 in interest ($17,738 × 25 – $250,000), while if you take the short option, you will pay only $102,000 in interest ($35,200 × 10 – $250,000)—a savings of over $91,000. Do you agree or disagree with the manager's advice? Briefly explain your reasoning. Hint: consider opportunity cost.

36. Bank A pays 7.25 percent interest compounded semi-annually, Bank B pays 7.20 percent compounded quarterly, and Bank C pays 7.15 percent compounded monthly. Which bank pays the highest effective annual rate?

37. Jimmie is buying a new car. His bank quotes a rate of 9.5 percent per year for a car loan. Calculate the effective annual rate if the compounding occurs:

   a. annually

   b. quarterly

   c. monthly

38. If Alysha puts $50,000 in a savings account paying 6 percent per year, determine how much money she will have in total at the end of the first year if interest is compounded:

   a. annually

   b. monthly

   c. daily

39. A bank is currently offering a savings account paying an interest rate of 8 percent compounded quarterly. It would like to offer another account, with the same effective annual rate, but compounded monthly. What is the equivalent rate compounded monthly?

40. Public corporations have no fixed lifespan; as such, they are often viewed as entities that will pay dividends to their shareholders in perpetuity. Suppose a firm pays a dividend of $2 per share every year. If the discount rate is 12 percent, what is the present value of all the future dividends?

41. Mary-Beth is planning to live in a university residence for four years while completing her degree. The annual cost for food and lodging is $5,800 and must be paid at the start of each school year. What is the total present value of Mary-Beth's residence fees if the discount rate (interest rate) is 6 percent per year?

42. Calculate the effective annual rates for the following:

   a. 24%, compounded daily

   b. 24%, compounded quarterly

   c. 24%, compounded every four months

   d. 24%, compounded semi-annually

   e. 24%, compounded continuously

   f. Calculate the effective monthly rate for parts (a) to (d).

43. Amanda would like to borrow $50,000 to pay one year's tuition at a private U.S. university. She would like to make quarterly payments and finish repaying the loan in five years. If the bank is quoting her a rate of 6 percent compounded monthly, determine her quarterly payment.

44. Wilma would like to borrow $150,000 to start her own business. She would like to make monthly payments to repay the loan in five years. If the bank is quoting her a rate of 6 percent compounded quarterly, determine her monthly payment.

45. At the age of 10, Felix decided that he wanted to attend a very prestigious (and expensive) university. How much will his parents have to save each year to accumulate $40,000 by the time Felix needs the funds in eight years? Assume Felix's parents can earn 7 percent (compounded annually) on their savings, and that each year's savings are deposited at the end of the year.

46. Jane's parents save $1,000 per year for 17 years to pay for her university tuition costs. They deposit the money into a Registered Education Savings Plan (RESP) account so that no tax is payable on the interest income. This RESP account provides a return of 6 percent per year.

   a. How much will Jane's account be worth when she begins her university studies?

   b. As an incentive to save for higher education, the government will add 20 percent to any money contributed to an RESP each year. Including these grants, how much will Jane have in her account?

47. Stephen has learned that his great-aunt intends to give him $4,000 each year he is studying at university. Tuition must be paid in advance, so Stephen would like to receive his payments at the beginning of each school year. How much will his great-aunt have to invest today at 7 percent, to make the four annual (start-of-year) payments? Assume that Stephen will be starting school in four years.

48. Felix will need $10,000 per year for four years to pay for tuition. How much will Felix's parents have to invest at the end of each year for the eight years before he begins his studies if their savings earn compound interest at 7 percent per year? Assume the tuition payments occur at the end of each year.

49. Roger has his eye on a new car that will cost $20,000. He has $15,000 in his savings account, earning interest at a rate of 0.5 percent per month.
    a. How long (to the nearest month) will it be before he can buy the car?
    b. How long will it be before Roger can buy the car if, in addition to his existing savings, he can save $250 per month?

50. How many years will it take for an investment to double in value if the rate of return is 9 percent, and compounding occurs:
    a. annually?
    b. quarterly?

51. Céline has just won a lottery. She will receive a payment of $6,000 at the end of each year for nine years. As an alternative, she can choose an immediate payment of $50,000.
    a. Which alternative should she pick if the interest rate is 5 percent?
    b. What would the interest rate have to be for Céline to be indifferent about the two alternatives?

52. Jimmie wishes to buy a new car that will cost $29,000.
    a. How much will his monthly car payments be if he obtains a loan that is amortized over 60 months, and the nominal interest rate is 8.5 percent per year with monthly compounding?
    b. Create an amortization schedule for Jimmie's car loan. What portion of the first monthly payment goes toward repaying the principal amount of the loan? What portion of the last monthly payment goes toward the principal?
    c. Using the amortization schedule, determine how much Jimmie still owes on the car loan after three years of payments on the five-year loan. What is the present value of this amount?

53. Michelle is offered a loan of $29,000 that requires 60 monthly payments of $588.02. What is the effective annual interest rate on this loan? What would the quoted rate be?

54. To start a new business, Su Mei intends to borrow $25,000 from a local bank. If the bank asks her to repay the loan in five equal annual instalments of $6,935.24, determine the bank's effective annual interest rate on the loan transaction. With annual compounding, what nominal rate would the bank quote for this loan?

55. The Business Development Bank is willing to loan Su Mei the $25,000 she needs to start her new business. The loan will require monthly payments of $556.11 over five years.
    a. What is the effective monthly rate on this loan?
    b. With monthly compounding, what is the nominal (annual) interest rate on this loan?

56. After losing money playing online poker, Scott visits a loan shark for a $750 loan. To avoid a visit from the "collection agency," he will have to repay $800 in just one week.
    a. What is the nominal interest rate per week? Per year?
    b. What is the effective annual interest rate?

57. Josephine needs to borrow $180,000 to purchase her new house in Yarmouth, Nova Scotia. She would like to pay off the mortgage in 20 years, making monthly payments. For the initial three-year term, Providence Bank has offered her a quoted annual rate of 6.40 percent.
    a. What is the effective annual interest rate?
    b. What is the effective monthly interest rate?
    c. How much will Josephine's monthly mortgage payments be?
    d. Yarmouth Credit Union will provide Josephine with a mortgage at a rate of 6.36 percent, but unlike most Canadian mortgages, the compounding will occur monthly. Should Josephine take out the mortgage loan from Yarmouth Credit Union or from Providence Bank?

58. A lakefront house in Kingston, Ontario, is for sale with an asking price of $499,000. The real estate market has been quite active, so the house will almost certainly attract several offers, and may sell for more than the asking price. Charlie is very eager to purchase this house, but is concerned that he may not be able to afford it. He has $130,000 available for a down payment, and can pay up to $1,950 per month on a mortgage loan. As Charlie is a long-time customer, his bank has offered him a great mortgage rate of 3.90 percent on a one-year term. If the loan will be amortized over 25 years, what is the most that Charlie can afford to pay for the house?

59. Five years ago, Franklin borrowed $300,000 to purchase a house in Sandy Lake. At the time, the quoted rate on the mortgage was 6 percent, the amortization period was 25 years, the term was 5 years, and the payments were made monthly. Now that the term of the mortgage is complete, Franklin must renegotiate his mortgage. If the current market rate for mortgages is 8 percent, what is Franklin's new monthly payment?

60. Timmy sets himself a goal of amassing $1 million in his retirement fund by the time he turns 61. He begins saving $3,000 each year, starting on his 21st birthday (40 years of saving).
    a. If his savings earn 10 percent per year, will Timmy achieve his goal?
    b. At what age will the value of Timmy's savings plan be worth $1 million?

61. Tommy has a goal of amassing $1 million by the time he retires. However, there always seemed to be a reason not to save money, so he put it off for many years. Finally, with just 15 years before his retirement, he began to save. Fortunately, Tommy's executive-level job allowed him to save $30,000 per year. If these savings earn 10 percent per year, will Tommy achieve his $1-million goal at the desired time?

62. Jack is 28 years old now and plans to retire in 35 years. He works in a local bank and has an annual after-tax income of $45,000. His expected annual expenditure is $36,000, and the rest of his income will be invested at the beginning of each of the next 35 years at an expected annual rate of return of 12.6 percent. Calculate the amount Jack will have accumulated when he retires.

63. a. Determine the month-end payment for a $200,000, 10-year loan with an interest rate of 12 percent, compounded monthly, assuming there is no down payment.
    b. Calculate the outstanding loan amount after 18 months.
    c. Redo part (a), assuming it is a mortgage loan with 12% annual interest rate and monthly payments.

64. Investor A just turned 20 years old and currently has no investments. She plans to invest $5,500 at the end of each year for eight years, beginning in five years. The rate of return on her investment is 15 percent, continuously compounded. Investor B is 40 years old and he has just started to invest an equal amount of money at the beginning of every year. He will invest for 10 years. The rate of return on his investment is 16 percent, compounded quarterly. Determine the yearly payment Investor B has to make in order to have the same present value as Investor A.

65. Paul and Maria want to have enough money to travel around the world when they retire. They both just turned 30 and will retire when they turn 60. They earn a total of $9,000 after taxes each month. Their monthly expenditures include $3,000 in mortgage payments, $850 in car payments, and $1,450 in other expenses. They approached a fund manager and decided to invest the rest of their income at the end of each year. They expect to earn a 10 percent annual rate of return for each of the next 30 years. When they retire, they will sell their cottage for an expected price of $50,000.
    a. Determine how much they will have when they retire.
    b. How much can Paul and Maria withdraw annually at the beginning of each year after they retire if they expect to live until they are 90?

66. Alysha has decided to use her $50,000 in savings to make a down payment on a house. She will live in the house for the next two years while still at university and then sell it when she graduates. The bank has offered her a mortgage rate of 5.1 percent compounded semi-annually on a two-year term, with an amortization period of 25 years. The house she is interested in purchasing costs $280,000.
    a. If two friends rent rooms from Alysha and pay her $475 each for rent at the end of each month, how much additional money does she need to meet her monthly mortgage payment?
    b. In two years, Alysha wants to sell the house for a high enough price to cover the remaining principal amount on the mortgage, as well as recoup her down payment. What is the minimum sale price she should accept?

67. An investment promises to pay you $100 per year starting in one year. The cash flow from the investment is expected to increase by 3 percent per year forever. If alternative investments of similar risk earn a return of 9 percent per year, determine the maximum you would be willing to pay for the investment.

68. An investment promises to pay you $100 per year starting immediately. The cash flow from the investment is expected to increase by 3 percent per year forever. If alternative investments of similar risk earn a return of 9 percent per year, determine the maximum you would be willing to pay for the investment.

69. An investment promises to pay you $100 per year starting in five years. The cash flow from the investment is expected to increase by 3 percent per year forever. If alternative investments of similar risk earn a return of 9 percent per year, determine the maximum you would be willing to pay for the investment.

70. Shirley has been offered two perpetuities: Grow and Shrink. Grow promises her $100 in one year and an annual cash flow that will increase by 4 percent per year forever. Shrink, in contrast, promises her $1,000 in one year but the annual cash flow will decline by 2 percent forever. If her opportunity cost is 5 percent per year and both annuities cost $1,000, which annuity offers her the greater value?

71. Xiang wishes to have $1 million in 30 years. He cannot afford to make large deposits at the moment; however, he believes that he will be able to increase his deposits by 3 percent per year for the next 30 years. He will make his first deposit in one year. If his opportunity cost is 5 percent, how large an initial deposit is needed? If instead of increasing his deposit each year, Xiang invested the same amount each year, how large a deposit would he need to make each year?

6 | Bond Valuation and Interest Rates

LEARNING OBJECTIVES

6.1   Describe the basic structure and the various features of different types of bonds.

6.2   Explain how to value a bond given an appropriate discount rate.

6.3   Determine the discount rate or yield for a given market value of a bond.

6.4   List and describe the factors, both domestic and global, that affect interest rates.

6.5   List and describe the characteristics and pricing of other debt instruments.

6.6   Explain how interest rate parity works.

The Toronto stock market was set for a positive start to the session Thursday as successful bond auctions in Italy and Spain raised the appetite for risk and sent commodity prices higher.

There was relief on financial markets as Italy saw its borrowing costs drop sharply while easily selling €12 billion in bonds in its first test of market sentiment of the new year.

Among other issues, investors bought €8.5 billion in 12-month bonds at a yield of 2.735 percent, sharply down from last month's rate of 5.95 percent.

And Spain successfully raised nearly €10 billion in debt auctions Thursday in a sign of investor confidence in the new conservative government's attempts to get a grip on the country's debt.

The treasury said demand for the three bonds, which mature in 2015 and 2016, was strong and the amount sold was double the maximum sought.

Borrowing costs shot up late last year as markets grew increasingly frustrated with the lack of a comprehensive plan to deal with the eurozone's debt crisis.

At one point, Italy was forced to offer yields of over 7 percent for 10-year bonds, a level considered unsustainable in the long run.

Source: Excerpted from The Canadian Press, "TSX poised to open higher," January 12, 2012.

CHAPTER 6 PREVIEW

Chapter 5 introduced the basic concept of the time value of money. In this chapter, we discuss bonds, which provide investors with predetermined future payments. As such, the analysis of bonds provides an important application of compounding and discounting. Understanding the topics covered in this chapter will increase your ability to apply the tools of valuation and improve your knowledge of financial securities.

The importance of bond and money markets to the global financial system and the overall global economy has gained more attention than usual over the past few years. Bond markets represent a major source of financing for companies, financial institutions, and governments. Thus, the fallout from collapses in corporate bond and commercial paper markets contributed greatly to the financial crisis of 2007 and 2008 and forced central banks to take action to support these markets. More recently, the European debt crisis has been one of the most important stories since 2009, while other issues such as the downgrading of the United States' credit rating have also been prevalent. The article excerpt in the chapter opener demonstrates well the influence that bond market activity can have on stock markets as well as on global economies.

We will refer to bonds generically as long-term debt instruments that promise fixed payments to their owners. However, specific terms are used depending on the maturity of the bond. Short-term bonds, with a maturity of less than one year, are called **bills** or **paper**; those with maturities between one and seven years are called **notes**; and those with terms of longer than seven years are called **bonds**. Because all of these instruments are valued in the same manner, we will refer to them all as bonds in this textbook.

The main bond issuers include federal, provincial, and municipal governments; government agencies (e.g., Canada Mortgage and Housing Corporation, Hydro-Québec); corporations; and non-resident issuers (e.g., the Maple bond market, discussed in Chapter 11). The main purchasers are institutional investors; in particular, insurance companies, pension funds, and bond mutual funds.

6.1 THE BASIC STRUCTURE OF BONDS

The key feature of a bond is that the issuer agrees to pay the bondholder (investor) a regular series of cash payments and to repay the full principal amount by the maturity date. These promises are stipulated in the bond contract and are a fixed contractual commitment. (You will hear this phrase again as it is important in corporate financing.) Although many payment structures are possible, the traditional "coupon-paying" bond provides for identical payments at regular intervals (usually semi-annually or annually), with the full principal to be repaid at the stated maturity date. We call the interest payment a "coupon" because at one time bonds literally had coupons, and the investor had to cut the coupon from the bond certificate and send it in for payment.[1] Today, almost all bonds in Canada are registered, and the payments are made directly into individual bank accounts, providing a record of who has paid and who has received the interest. When the principal payment is made in one lump sum at maturity, it is called a **bullet payment** or **balloon payment**.

Bonds are often referred to as fixed income securities because the interest payments and the principal repayment are specified, or fixed, at the time the bond is issued. In other words, the bond purchaser knows the amount and timing of the future cash payments to be received, barring default by the issuer. However, if the buyer decides to sell the bond before maturity, the price received will depend on the level of interest rates at that time, which we will illustrate shortly.

To understand how bonds are valued, we can use timelines, as developed in Chapter 5. A typical pattern of cash payments is depicted in Figure 6-1. Two things are obvious. First, the

---

bills or **paper** short-term bonds with a maturity of less than one year

notes bonds with maturities between one and seven years

bonds long-term debt instruments that promise fixed payments and have maturities of longer than seven years

Learning Objective 6.1
Describe the basic structure and the various features of different types of bonds.

bullet payment or **balloon payment** a principal payment made in one lump sum at maturity

---

[1]The coupons were attached to the bond and could be mailed in by whoever had the bond. Such bonds were called "bearer bonds" and are still widely used in parts of the world where personal tax rates are high.

structure of the payments differs from that of the loan or mortgage discussed in Chapter 5, because those involved "blended" payments that included both interest and principal components. In contrast, a typical bond has interest payments throughout its life and a balloon payment of principal at maturity. Second, a bond can be viewed as two separate components: an annuity consisting of the identical and regular interest payments, plus a lump-sum principal payment at maturity. In this way, valuing a traditional bond becomes a straightforward application of the time-value-of-money concept developed in Chapter 5.

Note: I = interest payments; F = principal repayment (face value)

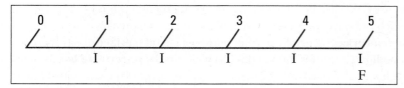

FIGURE 6-1 *Cash Flow Pattern for a Traditional Coupon-Paying Bond*

Basic Bond Terminology

Before discussing how to value bonds, we will introduce some terminology and institutional features attached to different types of bonds. Most bonds are sold to a variety of investors, and someone must make sure that the payments are made on time. This problem is solved by including all relevant details for a particular bond issue in a **bond indenture** that is held and administered by a trust company. This is a legal document that specifies the payment requirements, all other salient matters relating to the issue (such as any assets that might serve as security or **collateral** for the bond), any protective provisions, and other additional features. The trust company then makes sure that these **covenant provisions** within the indenture are observed by the issuer. In this way, the bond is a legal contract between the issuer and the holder, and the trust company has the job of ensuring that the terms of the contract are upheld. Any change to the contract normally requires the approval of either one-half or two-thirds of the value of the outstanding bonds.

All bond indentures include the basic features attached to the cash payments. The **par value**, also known as **face value** or **maturity value**, represents the amount that is paid at maturity for traditional bonds. The par value of most bonds is $1,000, although bond prices are typically quoted based on a par value of 100. In other words, if the price of a bond is quoted at $99.583, a $1,000 par value bond would be selling for $995.83. The **term to maturity** of the bond is the time remaining until the maturity date. The regular **interest payments**, or **coupons**, for any bond are determined by multiplying the coupon rate (which is stated on an annual basis) by the par value of the bond. For example, a bond with a coupon rate of 6 percent and a par value of $1,000 would pay coupons of $60 if they are paid annually, or $30 every six months if they are paid semi-annually.

Security and Protective Provisions

Technically, bonds are debt instruments that are secured by real assets. They are often called **mortgage bonds**. However, not all bonds are secured by real property. For example, **debentures** are similar to bonds but are generally unsecured, or are secured by a general floating charge over the company's unencumbered assets (i.e., those assets that have not been pledged as security for other debt obligations). Government bonds are debentures because no specific security is pledged as collateral. However, they are referred to as bonds as a matter of convention.

Collateral trust bonds are secured by a pledge of other financial assets, such as common shares, bonds, or treasury bills. **Equipment trust certificates** are secured by equipment, such as the rolling stock of a railway. The assets pledged as security are owned by investors through a lease agreement with, in this case, a railway until the loan has been retired. The certificates have serial numbers that dictate their maturity date, with a certain amount maturing every year.

Protective covenants are clauses in the trust indenture that restrict the actions of the issuer. Negative covenants prohibit certain actions. For example, a company may be restricted

---

bond indenture a legal document that specifies the payment requirements and all other salient matters relating to a particular bond issue, held and administered by a trust company

collateral assets that can serve as security for the bond in case of default

covenant provisions clauses within the indenture that lay out the legal rights of the bondholder and the obligations of the issuer

par value, face value, maturity value the amount paid at maturity for traditional bonds

term to maturity time remaining to maturity date

interest payments or **coupons** amounts paid on a bond at regular intervals

mortgage bonds debt instruments that are secured by real assets

debentures debt instruments that are similar to bonds but are generally unsecured or are secured by a general floating charge over the company's unencumbered assets

collateral trust bonds bonds secured by a pledge of other financial assets, such as common shares, bonds, or treasury bills

equipment trust certificates a type of debt instrument secured by equipment, such as railway rolling stock

protective covenants clauses in a trust indenture that restrict the actions of the issuer; covenants can be positive or negative

from making a dividend payment larger than a certain amount or prevented from pledging its assets to another lender. Positive covenants specify actions that the firm agrees to undertake. For example, a company may promise to provide quarterly financial statements or maintain certain working capital levels.

Additional Bond Features

So far, we have focused our discussion on traditional or regular coupon-paying bonds that provide for full principal repayment at the maturity date. However, some bonds have additional features (or options) that may provide for some, or all, of the principal to be repaid before maturity. We discuss a few of the more common provisions here.

callable bonds bonds that give the issuer the option to "call," or repurchase, outstanding bonds at predetermined prices at specified times

Callable bonds give the issuer the option to "call," or repurchase, outstanding bonds at predetermined **call prices** (generally at a premium over par) at specified times. These types of bonds create an additional risk for the bondholder. Conversely, **retractable bonds** allow the bondholder to sell the bonds back to the issuer at predetermined prices at specified times earlier than the maturity date. In this way, the maturity of the bond is retracted, or shortened. In contrast, **extendible bonds** allow the bondholder to extend the maturity date of the bond. "Extendibles" and "retractables" give bondholders the flexibility to change the maturity of the bonds to their advantage. We will discuss why they might want to do this after we show how bonds are valued.

call prices prices, generally at a premium over par, at which issuers can repurchase bonds

retractable bonds bonds that the bondholder can sell back to the issuer at predetermined prices at specified times earlier than the maturity date

Sinking fund provisions require the issuer to set money aside each year so that funds are available at maturity to pay off the debt. Provisions are made in two ways. In the first, the firm repurchases a certain amount of debt each year so that the amount of debt goes down. In the second, the firm pays money into the sinking fund to buy other bonds, usually government bonds, so that money is available at maturity to pay off the debt, although the amount due at maturity is unchanged. Sinking fund provisions benefit the issuers, because the issuers avoid paying the entire face value of the issue at the maturity date. However, if the bonds are actually repurchased, sinking fund provisions are not always beneficial to investors, because the bonds may be randomly called and repaid. Furthermore, the bonds are normally repaid at par value and the investors may suffer a loss if the bonds are worth more. Finally, as the amount of the issue declines, there may be a loss in liquidity as the bonds become less attractive. These disadvantages are offset by the operation of a sinking fund in which funds are used to buy government bonds.

extendible bonds bonds that allow the bondholder to extend the maturity dates of the bonds

sinking fund provisions the requirement that an issuer set aside funds each year to be used to pay off the debt at maturity

purchase fund provisions the requirement that a certain amount of debt be repurchased only if it can be repurchased at or below a given price

Purchase fund provisions are similar to sinking fund provisions, but require the repurchase of a certain amount of debt only if it can be repurchased at or below a given price. These provisions are generally advantageous to the debt holder, since they provide some liquidity and downward price support for the market price of the debt instruments.

convertible bonds bonds that can be converted into common shares at predetermined conversion prices

Convertible bonds can be converted into common shares at predetermined conversion prices. Convertible bonds may be offered to make debt issues more attractive to investors. These are discussed in greater depth in Chapter 19.

From this brief review of the institutional features attached to bonds, two things should be very clear: a bond is a contract, and what is in that contract varies from one bond to another. Unlike common shares, which we discuss later, each bond contract has to be reviewed separately, because one differs from another. If investors don't recognize this, the differences can come back to haunt them years after the bond has been issued.[2]

CONCEPT REVIEW QUESTIONS

1. In what ways are bonds different from mortgages?
2. How is a traditional bond structured?
3. What is a bond indenture?
4. What is the difference between a positive and a negative covenant provision?
5. How do sinking funds work?

---

[2]In particular, issuers have to do only what they have contracted to do in the indenture. A famous case involved bonds issued by CP Railway that were redeemable "after 1953." Investors expected the bonds to be redeemed in 1953 and sued the company when it refused. The company won the suit.

6.2 BOND VALUATION

We are now ready to examine how bonds are valued. Once investors know the par value, the term to maturity, and the coupon rate, they know both the amount and the timing of all the future promised payments on a bond. The price of a bond is determined by discounting these future payments using an appropriate discount rate, often referred to as the "market rate of interest." We will discuss the factors that affect this discount rate in greater detail later in the chapter. For now, you should be aware that it is a function of market conditions (i.e., other market interest rates) as well as factors specific to the issue and issuer.

The price of a bond equals the present value of the future payments on the bond, which is the present value of the interest payments and the par value repaid at maturity. By using the concepts developed in Chapter 5, we can use Equation 6-1 to price the bond:

$$B = I \times \left[\frac{1 - \frac{1}{(1+k_b)^n}}{k_b} \right] + F \times \frac{1}{(1+k_b)^n}$$

[6-1]

Learning Objective 6.2
Explain how to value a bond given an appropriate discount rate.

where B = the bond price
I = interest (or coupon) payments
k_b = the bond discount rate (or market rate)
n = the term to maturity
F = the face (par) value of the bond

In Equation 6-1, note that the interest or coupon payments are multiplied by the standard present value annuity factor (PVAF) developed in Chapter 5, while the par value is multiplied by the present value interest factor (PVIF). Valuing a traditional bond is an example of applying the time-value-of-money concept.

EXAMPLE 6-1 | Bond Valuation with Annual Coupons I

Find the price of a $1,000 par value bond that matures in 10 years if it pays interest annually, if it is based on a 6-percent coupon rate, and if the market rate of interest is 7 percent.

Solution

$F = \$1,000$; I = coupon rate $\times F = 0.06 \times \$1,000 = \$60$; $n = 10$; $k_b = 0.07$

With this information, we can use Equation 6-1 to find the price, or we can solve it by using a financial calculator or Excel.

$$B = 60 \times \left[\frac{1 - \frac{1}{(1.07)^{10}}}{0.07} \right] + 1,000 \times \frac{1}{(1+0.07)^{10}}$$

$$= (60 \times 7.02358) + (1,000 \times 0.50835) = 421.41 + 508.35 = \$929.76$$

We illustrate this with a timeline.

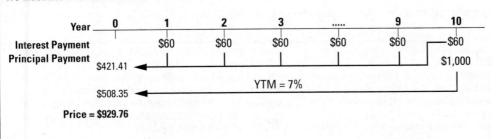

(TI BA II PLUS)

EXAMPLE 6-1   Solution Using a Financial Calculator

Input the following variables:

PMT → – 60;   **N** → 10;   **FV** → – 1,000;   **I/Y** → 7%;   **CPT**   **PV** → $929.76

As in Chapter 5, with the calculator solution we have to be careful with the signs. The calculator program assumes that there is an outflow (negative value) for an investment and then a payoff (positive value).

XLS

EXAMPLE 6-1   Solution Using Excel

Excel contains a range of special functions for valuing bonds. The basic function is the following "price" function.[3]

| = PRICE(settlement, maturity, rate, yld, redemption, frequency, basis) |

The terms refer to the following pieces of information:

- Settlement is the day on which the bond is paid for or "settled."
- Maturity is the date when the terminal principal is paid.
- Rate is the coupon rate on the bond.
- Yld is the discount rate or yield required on the bond.
- Redemption is the principal amount paid at maturity.
- Frequency indicates how often the coupon is paid—for example, annually.
- Basis we will ignore for now, so we will enter 0.

To solve this problem in Excel, we would enter

| = PRICE(date(2012,11,06), date(2022,11,06), .06, .07, 100, 1, 0) |

and get the correct answer of $929.76.

The Excel function has several special features. Be careful in entering the dates. In this example, we used "date(2012,11,06)" to indicate November 6, 2012. The date must be entered in this way for Excel to convert it into a number that can be used for calculations. Then we specified the maturity date as exactly 10 years in the future. Excel is sophisticated enough that if we had entered a different maturity date—for example, "date(2022,8,06)"—it would have automatically taken into account that it was nine months to the next interest payment, and all of the payments would then be brought forward by three months. With this maturity date, the bond is now worth $930.62, reflecting the fact that the investor is getting all the payments a little earlier.[4] Excel also requires that you enter the par value of the bond in the same way it is quoted—for example, as $100—and not the actual value of $1,000.

As with all problems, you should first solve them using the basic formula. Then you can determine whether the Excel answer is correct and whether you are inputting the values in the correct way. Errors in inputting the data will produce incorrect answers, and these will be easier to catch if you have used the basic formula first.

discount the difference between a bond's par value and the price it trades at when it trades below the par value

In Example 6-1, the bond trades at a **discount** from its par value. This happens because the coupon rate is less than the market interest (discount) rate, which means that investors require a return greater than 6 percent on equivalent bonds under current market conditions. Because the future payments are fixed, the only way to get a return higher than the coupon rate on this bond is to pay less than the par value for it. If an investor bought the bond at its par value of $1,000 and held it to maturity, he or she would earn a return equal to the coupon rate of 6 percent. In other words, the person would invest $1,000, get a 6 percent return on

---

[3] You may need to add the Analysis ToolPak in Excel, which can be done by clicking on Tools, then Add-Ins, then Analysis ToolPak, and then OK.

[4] In valuing the bond, we need to know how many days there are in a year and the length of time until the interest payment, given that every month does not have 30 days. In Canada, we use the actual number of days in a month and 365 days in a year or "actual/365 basis." The U.S. convention is to use 30 days in a month and 360 days in a year, the so-called 30/360 basis. These conventions are called the "basis," and Excel requires that you enter 0 for the United States and 3 for Canada. There are other conventions used elsewhere in the world; generically, these are called "the day count convention."

that investment per year—that is, $60 in interest each year—and then receive $1,000 back at maturity. Thus, when market rates equal the coupon rate, bonds trade at par.[5] Similarly, if market interest rates are below the coupon rate of 6 percent, the bond will trade at a **premium** to par, which we illustrate in Example 6-2.

premium the difference between a bond's par value and the price it trades at when it trades above the par value

---

EXAMPLE 6-2 Bond Valuation with Annual Coupons II

Find the price of a $1,000 par value bond that matures in 10 years. It pays interest annually, is based on a 6-percent coupon rate, and the market rate of interest is 5 percent.

Solution

$F = \$1,000$; $I = $ coupon rate $\times F = 0.06 \times \$1,000 = \$60$; $n = 10$; $k_b = 0.05$

We can use Equation 6-1 to find the price. We can also find the price by using a financial calculator or Excel.

$$B = 60 \times \left[\frac{1 - \dfrac{1}{(1.05)^{10}}}{0.05} \right] + 1{,}000 \times \frac{1}{(1+0.05)^{10}}$$

$$= (60 \times 7.72173) + (1{,}000 \times 0.61391) = 463.30 + 613.91 = \$1{,}077.21$$

EXAMPLE 6-2 Solution Using a Financial Calculator

Input the following variables:

PMT → − 60;   N → 10;   FV → − 1,000;   I/Y → 5%;   CPT   PV = $1,077.22

(TI BA II PLUS)

EXAMPLE 6-2 Solution Using Excel

We enter

= PRICE(date(2012,11,06), date(2022,11,06), .06, .05, 100, 1, 0)

and also get $1,077.22. The difference of $0.01 is due to rounding in the formula solution.

XLS

So, the bond in Example 6-2 trades at a premium over par, because the coupon rate of 6 percent is greater than the market rate of 5 percent.

The two examples assume that interest payments (or coupons) are made annually. However, in reality, most bonds pay coupons semi-annually. Fortunately, this does not change the valuation process, but we must make the appropriate adjustments to reflect the fact we are dealing with semi-annual periods rather than annual ones. Specifically, we must divide the annual coupon payments by two to determine the amount of semi-annual coupons and multiply the number of years to maturity by two to obtain the number of semi-annual periods to maturity. Finally, we need a semi-annual discount rate because that coincides with the frequency of payments. For bonds, as a matter of convention, the appropriate adjustment is to divide the market bond yield by two to obtain the six-month market yield (notice that this implies that the bond yields are not effective rates). Example 6-3 shows how to apply this process.

EXAMPLE 6-3 Bond Valuation with Semi-Annual Coupons

Determine the price of a 15-year bond that pays interest semi-annually and has a par value of $1,000 and a coupon rate of 5 percent, when the appropriate market rate is 6 percent.

continued

---

[5]Bonds are often issued at (or very close to) par by setting the coupon rate equal to the market rate at the time of issue.

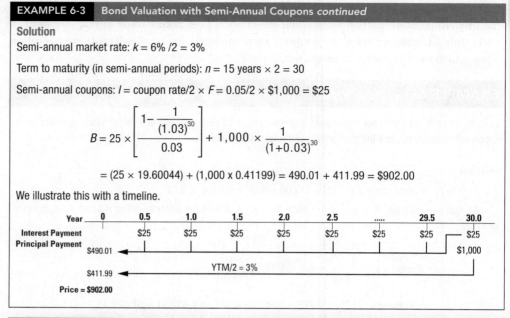

EXAMPLE 6-3   Bond Valuation with Semi-Annual Coupons *continued*

Solution

Semi-annual market rate: $k = 6\% / 2 = 3\%$

Term to maturity (in semi-annual periods): $n = 15$ years $\times 2 = 30$

Semi-annual coupons: $I = $ coupon rate$/2 \times F = 0.05/2 \times \$1,000 = \$25$

$$B = 25 \times \left[\frac{1 - \dfrac{1}{(1.03)^{30}}}{0.03} \right] + 1,000 \times \frac{1}{(1+0.03)^{30}}$$

$$= (25 \times 19.60044) + (1,000 \times 0.41199) = 490.01 + 411.99 = \$902.00$$

We illustrate this with a timeline.

Year	0	0.5	1.0	1.5	2.0	2.5	.....	29.5	30.0
Interest Payment		$25	$25	$25	$25	$25	$25	$25	$25

Principal Payment

$490.01 ◄──────────────

$411.99 ◄────────── YTM/2 = 3%

Price = $902.00

$1,000

(TI BA II PLUS)

EXAMPLE 6-3   Solution Using a Financial Calculator

Input the following variables:

PMT → –25;   N →30;   FV → –1,000;   I/Y → 3%;   CPT   PV = $902.00

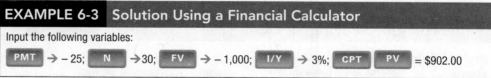

XLS

EXAMPLE 6-3   Solution Using Excel

We enter

= PRICE(date(2012,11,06), date(2027,11,06), .05, .06, 100, 2, 0)

and we get $901.997 or $902.

Factors Affecting Bond Prices

The examples above illustrate the most important property of fixed income investments, such as bonds: *if interest rates decrease, the market prices of bonds increase and vice versa.* This is clear from *Finance in the News 6-1*, which discusses the good year enjoyed by Canadian bonds during 2011 due to declining bond yields throughout that year, which caused Canadian bond prices to increase and resulted in a 9.6 percent return. Similarly, declining rates on U.S. government treasury bonds during 2011, as a result of heavy demand, led to price increases and resulted in annual returns that year of over 17 percent.

finance INTHENEWS 6-1   Canadian Bonds Continue to Shine

SINCE JANUARY, Canadian government and corporate bonds have returned 9.6 percent, almost doubling the global average of 5.5 percent. Much like last year, the thirst for these bonds, from both domestic and foreign buyers, stems from a relatively healthy Canadian economy.

Gross domestic product is growing, slowly but surely, and Canada has proven to be a relative haven with its triple-A federal debt rating. Contrarily, Standard & Poor's (S&P) threw markets into a tailspin in August by downgrading the United States' debt.

On Wednesday, during a typically quiet trading period, investor concern about the U.S. and European economies in the early part of 2012 pushed U.S. stocks down over 1 percent and sent the euro to a 10-year low against the yen. This year, those same worries drove central banks around the world to diversify their holdings beyond the greenback and the euro, weakening those currencies and creating strong support for the loonie.

The more Canadian dollars that central banks pick up as a result of worries elsewhere, the more will be reinvested in Canadian bonds.

"The hype around Canada is still intact," said Jean-François Godin, senior fixed-income market analyst at Desjardins Securities. "Maybe not as high as before, because it's becoming old news, but the fiscal situation remains very favourable."

Finance in the News 6-1: Canadian Bonds Continue to Shine (continued)

Canada ranked behind only Germany in a new economic report card from Bank of Montreal, which compared inflation, jobless rates, budget deficits, and credit ratings among the world's biggest industrialized economies. But Canada's picture isn't entirely rosy, according to the bank. BMO warned that demand for the country's bonds could evaporate if fiscal prudence isn't maintained, and that the country's second-place ranking speaks more to its peers' poor performance than anything else.

Canada's holes begin to appear when compared with Germany, the top-ranked country. Germany's debt load is much more manageable, and the country exports more than it imports. "The major weak spot for Canada—and this is a relatively new development—is our 3 percent of GDP current account deficit, compared with a surplus for Germany," BMO economists Doug Porter and Benjamin Reitzes wrote.

"As well, on the budget deficit front, Germany made big strides to rein in its shortfall, while Canada's deficit remains relatively large at 5 percent of GDP (in part due to a still-wide gap at the provincial level)."

After Canada's bond market beat the Global Broad Market Index in 2010, fixed-income analysts weren't sure demand would die down. "We thought it was going to wane," Mr. Godin said. "But it didn't.

This strength is largely owed to provincial bonds, which domestic buyers and foreigners continue to scoop up.

A jaw-dropping $57-billion of provincial debt was raised from April 2010, the start of the provinces' fiscal year, to December, and 2011 churned out the exact same figure as provinces continue to borrow to fund their deficits. Demand for these bonds has been so strong that in several instances, buyers have approached the provinces directly and promised to purchase a certain amount, typically $200 to $500 million of a new public offering, giving the provinces confidence to come to market.

Still, much like the feds, provinces have reason to be cautious. Earlier in December, ratings agency Moody's Investors Service lowered Ontario's outlook from "stable" to "negative," following similar moves by S&P and DBRS 9 (Dominion Bond Rating Service) Ltd.

Plus, the Canadian story may eventually grow old as investors find solace in another developed country.

"The danger obviously is that some investors reallocate their cash eventually," Mr. Godin said. "We're not saying that yet … but some people may start thinking about it."

Consider a bond that has a 5 percent coupon paid semi-annually and matures in 10 years. If the yield is less than 5 percent, the bond trades at a premium. If the yield is greater than 5 percent, the bond trades at a discount, as you can see when we look at yields to maturity ranging from 0 percent to 10 percent (Table 6-1).

TABLE 6-1 Bond Yields

Yield to Maturity	Discount Rate per Period	Number of Periods	Coupon Payment	Face Value	Price
0%	0.0%	20	$25	$1,000	$1,500.00
1%	0.5%	20	$25	$1,000	$1,379.75
2%	1.0%	20	$25	$1,000	$1,270.68
3%	1.5%	20	$25	$1,000	$1,171.69
4%	2.0%	20	$25	$1,000	$1,081.76
5%	2.5%	20	$25	$1,000	$1,000.00
6%	3.0%	20	$25	$1,000	$925.61
7%	3.5%	20	$25	$1,000	$857.88
8%	4.0%	20	$25	$1,000	$796.15
9%	4.5%	20	$25	$1,000	$739.84
10%	5.0%	20	$25	$1,000	$688.44

You can also see this inverse relationship between yields and bond values in Figure 6-2, in which we depict the bond price-yield curve for this bond for yields from 0 percent to 20 percent.

Figure 6-3 provides a general depiction of the bond price-yield curve for any regular coupon-paying bond. We can also see clearly from this graph that the relationship between market rates and bond price is *not* linear; the curve representing this relationship is convex. This fact is evident if we look at the bond pricing equation, in which the discount rate is raised to powers other than one.

FIGURE 6-2 *Value of a $1,000 Face Value Bond, with a 5% Coupon Maturing in 15 Years, for Different Yields to Maturity*

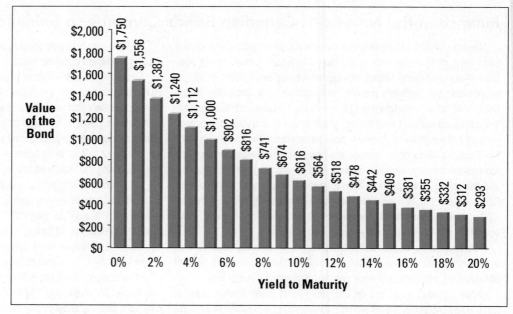

FIGURE 6-3 *Bond Price-Yield Curve*

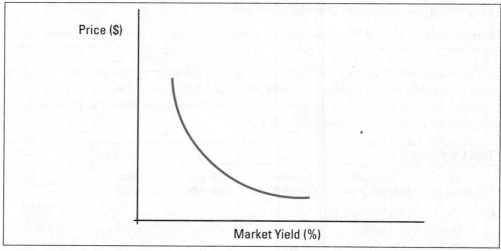

The shape of this curve shows two additional factors in the relationship between bond prices and market rates. First, for a given change in interest rates, bond prices will increase more when rates decrease than they will decrease when rates increase. Note, for example, that the curve is steeper to the left of any point than it is to the right, which indicates that the impact of decreasing interest rates is different from the impact of increasing ones. Second, the curve is steeper for lower interest rates, which means that a given change in interest rates will have a much greater impact on bond prices when rates are lower than it will if they are higher.

The second most important property of bonds is that *the longer the time to maturity, the more sensitive the bond price is to changes in market rates.* Intuitively, this makes sense, because the longer the term to maturity, the longer the investor has "locked-in" fixed payments based on the bond's coupon rate. When market rates rise above this rate, the bond price will fall more because the coupon rate is unattractive relative to prevailing rates for a longer period. The longer an investor is locked in, the greater the disadvantage and the more the bond price will fall to adjust. Similarly, when rates fall below the coupon rate, the longer an investor is locked in, the greater the attractiveness of the higher coupon. Example 6-4 illustrates this property.

EXAMPLE 6-4 Estimating Prices for Bonds with Different Terms to Maturity

Consider the bond from Example 6-3 with a $1,000 par value and a coupon rate of 5 percent, paying interest semi-annually, with market rates at 6 percent. Recalculate the price on this bond, assuming that the term to maturity is not 15 years, but is either

a.   5 years or

b.   30 years

Solution

$k = 3\%;\ I = \$25;\ F = \$1,000$

a. $n = 5 \text{ years} \times 2 = 10$

$$B = 25 \times \left[\frac{1 - \dfrac{1}{(1.03)^{10}}}{0.03}\right] + 1,000 \times \frac{1}{(1+0.03)^{10}}$$

$$= (25 \times 8.53020) + (1,000 \times 0.74409) = 213.26 + 744.09 = \$957.35$$

continued

EXAMPLE 6-4 Solution Using a Financial Calculator

Input the following variables:

 PMT → − 25; N → 10; FV → − 1,000; I/Y → 3%; CPT PV = $957.35

(TI BA II PLUS)

EXAMPLE 6-4 Solution Using Excel

We enter

   = PRICE(date(2012,11,06), date(2017,11,06), .05, .06, 100, 2, 0)

which again gives $957.35.

Notice that this 5-year bond sells at a lower "discount" (higher price) to its par value than does the 15-year bond, reflecting the fact that investors are not locked in to the unattractive 5-percent rate for as long.

EXAMPLE 6-4 Estimating Prices for Bonds with Different Terms to Maturity
continued

b. $n = 30 \text{ years} \times 2 = 60$

$$B = 25 \times \left[\frac{1 - \dfrac{1}{(1.03)^{60}}}{0.03}\right] + 1,000 \times \frac{1}{(1+0.03)^{60}}$$

$$= (25 \times 27.67556) + (1,000 \times 0.16973) = 691.89 + 169.73 = \$861.62$$

EXAMPLE 6-4 Solution Using a Financial Calculator

Input the following variables:

 PMT → − 25; N → 60; FV → − 1,000; I/Y → 3%; CPT PV = $861.62

(TI BA II PLUS)

EXAMPLE 6-4 Solution Using Excel

We enter

   = PRICE(date(2012,11,06), date(2042,11,06), .05, .06, 100, 2, 0)

which again gives $861.62.

With the longer maturity, the 30-year bond sells at a much bigger "discount" (lower price) to its par value than does the 15-year bond (and the 5-year bond), reflecting the fact that investors are locked in to the unattractive 5-percent rate for a longer time.

Bond prices' sensitivity to interest rates is directly related to interest rate levels and to the term to maturity. It is also related to the level of the coupon rate associated with the bond, although this factor is much less important than either interest rate levels or the term to maturity. In particular, the price of bonds with lower coupon rates will be more sensitive to interest rates than the price of higher-coupon-paying bonds will be. This is intuitive, if we recall from Chapter 5 that the compounding (or discounting) effect is accentuated with time, which suggests that a change in the discount rate will have the greatest impact on the most distant cash flows, including the par value to be received at maturity in the case of bonds. For bonds that pay lower coupons, the principal repayment, which occurs at the maturity date, represents a higher proportion of the total payments to be received by the bondholder. As a result, the prices of such bonds will fluctuate more for a given change in interest rates than will otherwise identical higher-coupon-paying bonds. Example 6-5 illustrates this property.

EXAMPLE 6-5 Estimating Prices for Bonds with Different Coupon Rates

Consider the semi-annual, $1,000 par value, 5-percent bond examined in Example 6-3 (call it Bond 1) along with another 15-year bond that pays semi-annual coupons based on a 6-percent coupon rate (Bond 2). Calculate the price of each bond when market rates are

a. 5 percent

b. 6 percent

Solution

For both bonds: $F = \$1,000$; $n = 30$

For Bond 1: $I = \$25$

For Bond 2: $I = \$30$

a. $k = 5\%/2 = 2.5\%$

Bond 1: $B = \$1,000$ (i.e., it trades at par, since market yield = coupon rate)

Bond 2:

$$B = 30 \times \left[\frac{1 - \dfrac{1}{(1.025)^{30}}}{0.025} \right] + 1,000 \times \frac{1}{(1+0.025)^{30}}$$

$$= (30 \times 20.93029) + (1,000 \times 0.47674) = 627.91 + 476.74 = \$1,104.65$$

b. $k = 6\%/2 = 3\%$

Bond 1:

$$B = 25 \times \left[\frac{1 - \dfrac{1}{(1.03)^{30}}}{0.03} \right] + 1,000 \times \frac{1}{(1+0.03)^{30}}$$

$$= (25 \times 19.60044) + (1,000 \times 0.41199) = 490.01 + 411.99 = \$902.00$$

Bond 2: $B = \$1,000$ (i.e., it trades at par, since market yield = coupon rate)

(TI BA II PLUS)

EXAMPLE 6-5 Solution Using a Financial Calculator

a. Bond 2:

PMT → – $30; N → 30; FV → – 1,000; I/Y → 2.5%; CPT PV = $1,104.65

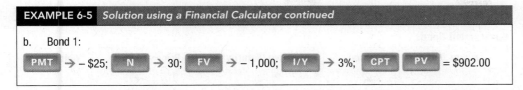

EXAMPLE 6-5   *Solution using a Financial Calculator continued*

b.   Bond 1:

PMT → − $25;   N → 30;   FV → − 1,000;   I/Y → 3%;   CPT   PV = $902.00

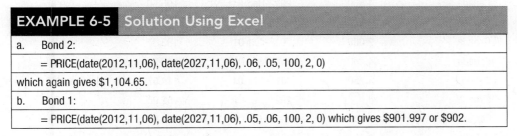

EXAMPLE 6-5   **Solution Using Excel**

a.   Bond 2:

= PRICE(date(2012,11,06), date(2027,11,06), .06, .05, 100, 2, 0)

which again gives $1,104.65.

b.   Bond 1:

= PRICE(date(2012,11,06), date(2027,11,06), .05, .06, 100, 2, 0) which gives $901.997 or $902.

As we would expect, based on our discussion, if we look at the change in the price of each bond in Example 6-5 for a 1 percent change in interest rates, we can see that Bond 1 (with the lower coupon rate) experienced a higher percentage change (decline) in price than Bond 2 (the higher-coupon-rate bond) did, although the difference is not dramatic.

Percentage change in price of Bond 1
= (902 − 1,000)/1,000 = −0.0980 = −9.8%

Percentage change in price of Bond 2
= (1,000 − 1,104.65)/1,104.65 = −0.0947 = −9.47%

The sensitivity of bond prices to changes in interest rates is generally referred to as **interest rate risk**. All else constant, longer-term bonds with lower coupon rates and lower market yields will possess greater interest rate risk than will shorter-term, higher-coupon bonds with higher market yields. An important measure of interest rate risk, **duration**, incorporates all these factors into a single measure. Technically, duration measures the approximate percentage change in the price of a bond for a given change in the appropriate market interest rate. For example, the price of a bond with a duration of 10 would be expected to increase approximately 10 percent if interest rates fell 1 percent. This approximation tends to work quite well for small changes in interest rates, but is less accurate for larger changes in rates.

While a detailed discussion of duration is beyond the scope of this textbook, we note the following important points:

1. The prices of bonds with higher durations are more sensitive to interest rate changes than are those with lower durations.

2. All else being equal, durations will be higher when (1) market yields are lower, (2) bonds have longer maturities, and (3) bonds have lower coupons.[6]

interest rate risk the sensitivity of bond prices to changes in interest rates

duration an important measure of interest rate risk that incorporates several factors

Bond Quotes

Table 6-2 shows some typical bond quotes that appear in the financial media.

---

[6]Excel has a duration function—DURATION(settlement, maturity, coupon, yld, frequency, basis)—where all of the same values needed to value a bond are the inputs and the duration function measures the sensitivity of the bond to interest rate changes.

TABLE 6-2 Selected Bond Quotes, January 9, 2012

Government Bonds

Issuer	Coupon	Effective Maturity	Price	Yield
Canada	5.250	2012-Jun-01	101.72	0.83
Canada	1.500	2012-Dec-01	100.50	0.93
Canada	3.000	2015-Dec-01	107.07	1.14
Canada	2.000	2016-Jun-01	103.37	1.21
Canada	4.250	2018-Jun-01	116.91	1.47
Canada	**3.750**	**2019-Jun-01**	**114.57**	**1.65**
Canada	8.000	2023-Jun-01	159.96	2.06
Canada	9.000	2025-Jun-01	178.85	2.18
Canada	8.000	2027-Jun-01	173.70	2.29
Canada	5.750	2029-Jun-01	147.22	2.41
Canada	5.750	2033-Jun-01	153.29	2.51
Canada	4.000	2041-Jun-01	130.65	2.52
Canada	3.500	2045-Dec-01	121.99	2.53
Alberta	4.000	2019-Dec-01	111.98	2.33
Alberta	4.500	2040-Dec-01	124.06	3.21
BC	4.100	2019-Dec-18	111.87	2.44
BC	4.300	2042-Jun-18	118.08	3.35
New Brunswick	4.400	2019-Jun-03	113.28	2.43
Nova Scotia	4.150	2019-Nov-25	111.54	2.52
Ontario	4.400	2019-Jun-02	113.56	2.39
Quebec	4.500	2019-Dec-01	113.79	2.56
Saskatchewan	6.400	2031-Sep-05	145.92	3.23

Corporate Bonds

Issuer	Coupon	Effective Maturity	Price	Yield
407 Intl	4.990	2020-Jun-16	114.54	3.02
BC Gas Inc	5.560	2014-Sep-15	109.39	1.94
BMO	4.609	2025-Sep-10	111.93	3.50
BNS	4.100	2017-Jun-08	107.88	2.53
Bell CDA	7.650	2031-Dec-30	120.80	5.87
CIBC	6.000	2018-Jun-06	116.36	3.16
CdnTire Corp	6.250	2028-Apr-13	109.57	5.36
Emera Inc.	4.830	2019-Dec-02	108.31	3.61
EnCana Corp	4.300	2012-Mar-12	100.50	1.35
Fairfax FinH	7.250	2020-Jun-22	109.00	5.88
Hydro One	5.360	2036-May-20	121.08	4.00
JohnDeere Cr	5.450	2015-Sep-16	111.91	2.07
LaurentianBk	3.700	2015-Nov-02	102.11	3.11
Loblaw CoLtd	5.220	2020-Jun-18	109.61	3.87
Manitoba Tel	5.625	2019-Dec-16	109.19	4.25

TABLE 6-2 Selected Bond Quotes, January 9, 2012 *continued*

Corporate Bonds *continued*

Issuer	Coupon	Effective Maturity	Price	Yield
National Bk	4.700	2015-Nov-02	107.16	2.71
RogersComm	5.340	2021-Mar-22	110.08	4.02
Royal Bank	3.770	2018-Mar-30	106.80	2.58
Royal Bank	0.000	2017-Apr-30	99.39	2.04
Shaw Commun	5.650	2019-Oct-01	110.24	4.09
Suncor	5.800	2018-May-22	116.16	2.99
Sunlife Fin	5.700	2019-Jul-02	109.47	4.21
TD Bank	9.150	2025-May-26	155.36	3.82
Telus Corp	5.050	2019-Dec-04	110.48	3.52
TransAlta Co	6.400	2019-Nov-18	113.81	4.31
TransCdaPipe	8.050	2039-Feb-17	161.75	4.21
Wcoast Enrgy	4.570	2020-Jul-02	109.27	3.31

Source: Data from Canadian Fixed Income.ca website: http://www.pfin.ca/canadianfixedincome/Default.aspx

Let's consider the following quote from the table:

Issuer	Coupon	Effective Maturity	Price	Yield
Canada	3.75	2019-Jun-01	114.57	1.65

This quote shows the issuer (Canada—that is, the Government of Canada), the associated coupon rate (3.75 percent), the date the bond matures (June 1, 2019), the previous trading day's closing bid price (114.57), and the associated yield to maturity (1.65 percent). The price is based on $100 of face value. For example, if the face value of the bond was $1,000, you would have to pay $1,145.70 ($1,000 × 1.1457) plus accrued interest (discussed below) to purchase the bond. The yields refer to the market (discount) rates that we have been using to value bonds. These are discussed in the next section.

Notice that the Government of Canada bond is trading at a relatively large premium, because market yields are well below the coupon rate of 3.75 percent. This is true of almost all of the bonds listed in Table 6-2, since interest rates were extremely low relative to historical levels in January 2012. However, several bonds were also trading below par at that time, including the Royal Bank bond shown in Table 6-2. This is because bonds are issued at various points in time, and the coupon rates are set approximately equal to prevailing market rates at that time. Therefore, with different levels of prevailing interest rates, at any given point we will observe some bonds trading at discounts and others trading at premiums.

Cash Prices versus Quoted Prices

The prices discussed in this section, as well as those reported in the media, such as in Table 6-2, are typically referred to as "quoted" prices. These differ from the actual prices investors pay for bonds whenever bonds are sold at a date other than the date of a coupon payment. The reason is that interest will accrue to bondholders between such payment dates. For example, investors who held bonds for 45 days since the last coupon was paid have "earned" 45 days of interest, even though they will not receive those 45 days of interest if they sell the bonds now because coupons are paid semi-annually—in fact, the bond purchasers will receive those 45 days of interest when they receive the next scheduled coupon payment. As a result, a bond purchaser must pay the bond seller the quoted price plus the accrued interest on the bond. This amount is referred to as the "cash price" of the bond. Example 6-6 demonstrates how the cash price is calculated.

EXAMPLE 6-6   The Cash Price of a Bond

Consider the bond in Example 6-3, which pays interest semi-annually, has a $1,000 maturity value and a 5-percent coupon rate, and is sold on July 14 at a quoted price of $902. Assume this bond matures on June 30, which implies the semi-annual interest payments on this bond are made on June 30 and on December 31. Calculate the cash price of this bond.

Solution

The cash price for this bond would equal $902 plus 14 days of accrued interest at the coupon rate of 5 percent. In other words,

Cash price = Quoted price + Accrued interest

Cash price = $902 + ($1,000 × 0.05 × [14/365]) = $902 + $1.92 = $903.92

Note that we have to choose a convention in terms of how much interest has been earned. Because this is a Canadian bond, we use the Canadian day count, which uses the actual number of days that have elapsed and assumes that there are 365 days in a year.

CONCEPT REVIEW QUESTIONS

1. What two time-value-of-money formulas do we need to value a bond?
2. When market interest rates are above the coupon rate on a bond, is it a premium or discount bond?
3. If market interest rates go up, what happens to bond prices?
4. Which types of bonds have more interest rate risk: short-term or long-term bonds?
5. What is the day count convention in Canada and in the United States?

6.3 BOND YIELDS

Yield to Maturity

The discount rate used to evaluate bonds is referred to as the **yield to maturity (YTM)**. It is the yield that an investor would realize if he or she bought the bond at the current price, held it to maturity, received all the promised payments on their scheduled dates, and reinvested all the cash flows received at the YTM. Given the price of a bond and all the details regarding the amount and timing of interest and principal repayments, we can always estimate the bond's YTM using Equation 6-1, which is reproduced below.

Learning Objective 6.3
Determine the discount rate or yield for a given market value of a bond.

yield to maturity (YTM) the discount rate used to evaluate bonds

$$B = I \times \left[\frac{1 - \frac{1}{(1+k_b)^n}}{k_b} \right] + F \times \frac{1}{(1+k_b)^n}$$

The difference is that now we will solve for k_b, given B, instead of solving for B, given k_b. k_b represents the discount rate that equates the known market price (B) with the present value of the future interest payments and face value repayment. It should be obvious that this rate is simply a special form of internal rate of return (IRR), which was discussed in Chapter 5. For bonds that pay annually, n is the number of years to maturity, and YTM is k_b. For semi-annual bonds, n is the number of years to maturity multiplied by two, and YTM is k_b multiplied by two.

Unfortunately, as we found out in Chapter 5, solving for IRRs is difficult because of the various powers involved in Equation 6-1: solutions require logarithms, a business calculator, Excel, or a lot of time-consuming trial and error. The same problems occur in calculating the

YTM on a bond. In fact, an exact algebraic solution for the YTM is not available. Fortunately, financial calculators and Excel are good at repetitive calculations and can solve the problem easily. However, if you don't have access to a financial calculator or Excel,[7] you have to use a trial-and-error approach to estimate the approximate yield that satisfies Equation 6-1.[8] In Example 6-7, we will use the formula with trial and error, and then find the solution using a financial calculator and Excel.

We follow the same process to estimate the YTM on a bond that pays semi-annual

---

EXAMPLE 6-7 Estimating the YTM on an Annual-Pay Bond

Estimate the YTM on a 10-year, 5-percent bond that pays annual coupons and is selling for $980.

Solution

$B = \$980$; $F = \$1{,}000$; $I = 0.05 \times 1{,}000 = \$50$; $n = 10$

$$980 = 50 \times \left[\frac{1 - \dfrac{1}{(1+k_b)^{10}}}{k_b} \right] + 1{,}000 \times \frac{1}{(1+k_b)^{10}}$$

Essentially, we begin by estimating the discount rate, k_b. We try the coupon rate first, even though we know the yield must be greater than 5 percent, as the bond is selling at a discount. Substituting this rate into the equation for k_b gives us a price of $1,000. Therefore, k_b must be higher than this rate because $1,000 is more than the price we want ($980). Substituting 6 percent for k_b gives us a price of $926.40, so 6 percent is too high a discount rate. Therefore, we know that the rate we are looking for is between 5 and 6 percent.

We can obtain a close approximation by using linear interpolation, which involves setting up two equivalent ratios:

Rate	Price
5%	1,000
k_b	980
6%	926.40

We find k_b by forming one ratio of the rates and putting the corresponding prices in the same position in a ratio of the prices:

$$\frac{k_b - 5}{6 - 5} = \frac{980 - 1{,}000}{926.40 - 1{,}000}$$

$$\frac{k_b - 5}{1} = \frac{-20}{-73.60} = 0.2717$$

So, $k_b = 5.27$ percent.

Since this is an annual-pay bond, the YTM $= k_b = 5.27\%$. Notice that this is close to the exact solution of 5.26 percent obtained using a financial calculator.

We illustrate this also with a timeline.

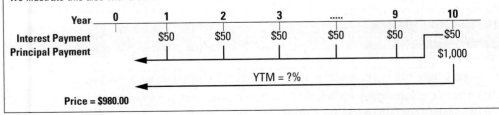

---

[7] Old-fashioned bond tables, which show yields corresponding to various prices, coupon rates, and maturity dates, are also available.
[8] An approximation formula does exist, but it can be off by a significant amount sometimes, especially for longer-term bonds that are trading at prices quite different from their par value.

(TI BA II PLUS)

EXAMPLE 6-7   Solution Using a Financial Calculator

Input the following variables:

PMT = 50;   **PV** = − 980;   **FV** = 1,000;   **N** = 10

Then, **CPT** **PV** will give 5.26 percent, which is an annual rate, so YTM (annual) = 5.26 percent.

XLS

EXAMPLE 6-7   Solution Using Excel

Excel has a special function for calculating YTM.

= YIELD(settlement, maturity, rate, pr, redemption, frequency, basis)

This is the same as the bond pricing formula, except that the yield (yld) has been replaced by the market price (pr). If we input our values, we get

= YIELD(date(2012,11,06), date(2022,11,06), .05, 98.0, 100, 2, 0), so we get 5.26 percent, the same as with the calculator. Note that Excel automatically converts the yield to an annual rate.

This answer appears reasonable because the bond is trading at a slight discount from par, which implies that the discount rate (YTM) is greater than the coupon rate of 5 percent. Compare the simplicity of this solution to the long trial-and-error solution, at the beginning of this example.

coupons, except that we first solve Equation 6-1 for a semi-annual rate (k_b), which we then convert to an annual rate by multiplying it by two.[9] Example 6-8 demonstrates this process.

EXAMPLE 6-8   Estimating the YTM on a Semi-Annual Bond

Estimate the YTM on a 20-year, 6-percent bond that pays semi-annual coupons and is selling for $1,030.

Solution
$B = \$1,030; F = \$1,000; I = 0.06/2 \times 1,000 = \$30; n = 20 \times 2 = 40$

$$1,030 = 30 \times \left[\frac{1 - \frac{1}{(1+k_b)^{40}}}{k_b} \right] + 1,000 \times \frac{1}{(1+k_b)^{40}}$$

(TI BA II PLUS)

EXAMPLE 6-8   Solution Using a Financial Calculator

Input the following variables:

PMT → 30;   **PV** → − 1,030;   **FV** → 1,000;   **N** = 40

Then, **CPT** **PV** will give 2.87 percent, which is a semi-annual rate (k_b), so we multiply by two to find the annual YTM: 2.87% × 2 = 5.74%.

XLS

EXAMPLE 6-8   Solution Using Excel

We enter

= YIELD(date(2012,11,06), date(2032,11,06), .06, 103, 100, 2, 0) and we get 5.746 percent.

Notice that the answers appear reasonable because the bond is trading at a premium over par, which implies that the discount rate (YTM) is less than the 6-percent coupon rate.

[9]We multiply the semi-annual rate by two in order to reflect the manner in which bond yields are quoted. As discussed previously, bond yields are not effective annual rates when semi-annual coupons are paid.

Yield to Call

We mentioned earlier that bonds often have flexible maturity dates because some bonds are callable by the issuer; for others, the maturity can be retracted or extended by the investor. This means that we can calculate the yield to maturity for these different dates. Suppose, for example, that the bond in the previous example was callable after five years at par.[10] This means that it is possible the bond will not be outstanding for 20 years, because it may be called after five years. The yield that is associated with a bond's first call date is known as its yield to call (YTC). It can be estimated in the same way as we estimated the YTM, using Equation 6-1, except that we replace the time to maturity (n) with the time to first call (c); we replace the face value (F) with the call price (CP); and we denote the appropriate discount rate as k_c instead of k_b. This gives us Equation 6-2.

$$B = I \times \left[\frac{1 - \dfrac{1}{(1+k_c)^c}}{k_c} \right] + CP \times \frac{1}{(1+k_c)^c} \qquad \text{[6-2]}$$

EXAMPLE 6-9 Estimating the Yield to Call (YTC)

Estimate the YTC on a 20-year, 6-percent bond that is callable in five years at a call price of $1,050, if the bond pays semi-annual coupons and is selling for $1,030.

Solution

$B = \$1,030$; $CP = \$1,050$; $I = 0.06/2 \times 1,000 = \$30$; $n = 5 \times 2 = 10$

$$1,030 = 30 \times \left[\frac{1 - \dfrac{1}{(1+k_c)^{10}}}{k_c} \right] + 1,050 \times \frac{1}{(1+k_c)^{10}}$$

We illustrate this also with a timeline.

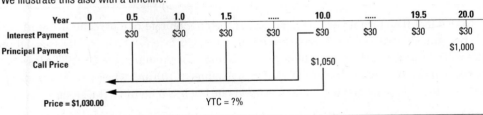

EXAMPLE 6-9 Solution Using a Financial Calculator

(TI BA II PLUS)

Input the following variables:

PMT → 30; **PV** → −1,030; **FV** → 1,050; **N** = 10

Then, **CPT** **I/Y** will give 3.081 percent. This is a semi-annual rate (k_c), so we multiply by two to find the annual YTC: 3.081% × 2 = 6.16%.

EXAMPLE 6-9 Solution Using Excel

We enter

= YIELD(date(2012,11,06), date(2017,11,06), .06, 103, 105, 2, 0)

and we get 6.16 percent.

Notice that in Example 6-9, the YTC is greater than the coupon rate, because the call price of $1,050 is greater than the bond's current price of $1,030. So what can we say about the 5.74 percent YTM on this bond, calculated in Example 6-8, compared with the 6.16 percent

YTC? Because the call price is above its current market price, it is unlikely that the bond would be called back by the issuer, so it is selling based on its YTM rather than its YTC. It would trade on its YTC if it were likely the bond would be called, which would occur if the bond were trading above its call price and, correspondingly, if the YTC were lower than the YTM. Generally, the bond trades off whichever of the two is lower. We can confirm this by looking at five-year and 20-year yields on equivalent non-callable bonds, which takes us into the determination of market interest rates. However, before doing this, we should touch on another simple interest rate measure.

Current Yield

current yield (CY) the ratio of the annual coupon interest divided by the current market price

The **current yield (CY)** is defined as the ratio of the annual coupon interest divided by the current market price. As such, it is not a true measure of the return to a bondholder because it disregards the bond's purchase price relative to all the future cash flows and uses just the next year's interest payment. The current yield is also sometimes referred to as the flat or cash yield. It can be calculated using Equation 6-3.

[6-3]

$$CY = \frac{Annual\ interest}{B}$$

EXAMPLE 6-10   Current Yield

Determine the current yield for the bond used in Example 6-8, which was trading for $1,030.

Solution

$B = \$1,030$; Annual interest $= \$30 \times 2 = \$60$ (or simply $\$1,000 \times 0.06$)

$CY = \dfrac{60}{1,030} = 0.0583$ *or* 5.83%

Notice that the current yield does not equal the coupon rate of 6 percent or the YTM of 5.74 percent. This will hold unless the bond is trading at its face value, in which case all three rates will be equal. It is clear that whenever bonds trade at a premium, the CY will be less than the coupon rate but greater than the YTM (as in Example 6-10); and whenever they trade at a discount, the CY will be greater than the coupon rate but less than the YTM, as shown here:

Price-Yield Relationships

Bond Price	Relationship
Par	Coupon rate = CY = YTM
Discount	Coupon rate < CY < YTM
Premium	Coupon rate > CY > YTM

CONCEPT REVIEW QUESTIONS

1. Why is there no simple analytical formula for the yield to maturity?
2. When bonds sell above their par value, is the yield to maturity greater or less than the coupon rate?
3. Is the yield to call always greater than the yield to maturity?

6.4 INTEREST RATE DETERMINANTS

Base Interest Rates

Learning Objective 6.4
List and describe the factors, both domestic and global, that affect interest rates.

Interest rates are usually quoted on an annual percentage basis. However, it is common to refer to changes in interest rates in terms of "basis points," each of which represents 1/100th of 1 percent. For example, a decrease of 10 basis points indicates that interest rates declined by 0.1 percent.

As we discussed in Chapter 5, the interest rate is the price of money and, just like the price of any other commodity, it is determined by the laws of supply and demand. In the case of interest rates, it is the supply of and demand for "loanable funds." All else being constant, as the demand for loanable funds increases so does their price and, as a result, interest rates increase. Conversely, interest rates decrease as the supply of loanable funds increases. The interest rates that we have been discussing so far are called **nominal interest rates**, because they are the rates charged for lending today's dollars in return for getting dollars back in the future, without taking into account the purchasing power of those future dollars. One of the most important factors in determining these nominal interest rates is the expected rate of inflation, because this determines the purchasing power of those future dollars.

In structuring our discussion of actual interest rates, we refer to the base rate as the **risk-free rate (RF)**. We will discuss risk at length shortly, but the term "risk-free," although conventional, is a bit of a misnomer. What it actually refers to is **default free**, in that the investors know exactly how many dollars they will get back on their investment. It is common to use the yield on short-term government treasury bills (T-bills), which are discussed in greater detail later in this chapter, as a proxy for this risk-free rate. Federal government T-bill yields are considered risk free because they possess no risk of default: the government essentially controls the Bank of Canada and can always have it buy any bonds that are issued, using Bank of Canada banknotes. Furthermore, government T-bills have little interest rate risk because their term to maturity is short.

As a result, we have the approximate relationship as shown in Equation 6-4:

$$RF = Real\ rate + Expected\ inflation \qquad [6\text{-}4]$$

This relationship is an approximation of the direct relationship between inflation and interest rates that is often referred to as the "Fisher effect," after Irving Fisher, who described how investors attempt to protect themselves from the loss in purchasing power caused by inflation by increasing their required nominal yield.[11] As a result, interest rates will be low when expected inflation is low and high when expected inflation is high.

The "precise" Fisher relationship is shown in Equation 6-5:

$$RF = [\ (1 + Real\ rate)(1 + Expected\ inflation)\ ] - 1 \qquad [6\text{-}5]$$

Applying a bit of algebra, we see that the risk-free rate is not only the sum of the real rate and the expected inflation rate, but also the cross-product term, real rate × expected inflation:

$$RF = 1 + Real\ rate + Expected\ inflation + (Real\ rate \times Expected\ inflation)$$

We often see the approximation simply because the cross-product term (the right-most term) is generally so small when inflation rates are low.

The average return on Government of Canada T-bills over the 1938 to 2011 period was 5.14 percent. Over the same period, inflation averaged 3.839 percent, which indicates that the average real return over this period was 130 percent, or 130 basis points.[12]

nominal interest rates the rates charged for lending today's dollars in return for getting dollars back in the future, without taking into account the purchasing power of those future dollars

risk-free rate (RF) the rate of return on risk-free investments, which is often used as the base interest rate

default free having no risk of non-payment

EXAMPLE 6-11	Estimating the Real Rate of Return

If T-bill rates are currently 4.5 percent and the expected level of inflation is 2 percent, estimate the approximate real rate of return.

continued

---

[11] See Fisher, Irving, "Appreciation and Interest." *Publications of the American Economic Association* (August 1896), pp. 1–1001.
[12] Notice that we are looking at returns "after the fact" in this example. In practice, the return is based on expected inflation, which will usually not be the same as actual inflation.

EXAMPLE 6-11   Estimating the Real Rate of Return *continued*

Solution
Real rate = 4.5 − 2 = 2.5%

The graph in Figure 6-4 provides the history of the annual inflation rate as measured by the consumer price index (CPI) and the yield to maturity on long-term Government of Canada bonds over the 1957 to 2011 period. Notice that the level of nominal interest rates generally tracked the increase in inflation throughout the 1960s and early 1970s, until inflation unexpectedly peaked at more than 12 percent in 1973, at which point the actual inflation rate exceeded government bond yields. Since then, interest rates have generally declined with the rate of inflation.

As we just discussed, one measure of the real rate is the difference between the ongoing inflation rate and the level of nominal interest rates, which averaged 3.36 percent over the 1957 to 2011 period. This difference was considerably larger throughout the 1980s and 1990s, before narrowing considerably since 2002. This difference actually became negative in 2011, as interest rates remained abnormally low relative to inflation rates for several reasons (which are discussed in the remainder of this chapter).

FIGURE 6-4 *Interest Rates and Inflation*

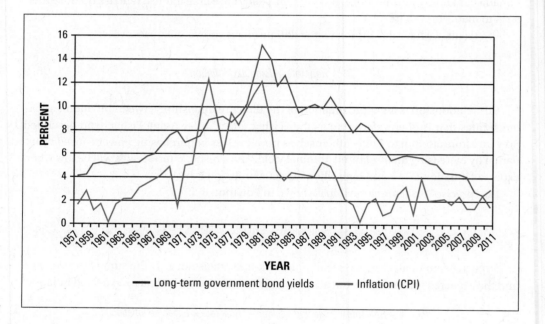

YEAR
── Long-term government bond yields   ── Inflation (CPI)

Global Influences on Interest Rates

We have already discussed the effect that global factors have played in influencing domestic interest rates, which has been painfully obvious over the past few years. For example, the excellent returns experienced by Canadian and U.S. bond markets during 2011 are a direct result of the influence of the European debt crisis, which led bond investors to seek safer places for their funds. While global influences can dominate in times of such crises, even under normal circumstances these effects are present, as discussed below.

Although interest rate levels vary from one country to the next, global interest rates interact with one another. This occurs because most countries have now removed foreign exchange restrictions, allowing capital to flow from one country to another in search of higher rates of return. As a result, interest rates in Canada are heavily influenced by prevailing rates in other countries, especially those in the United States. This influence is inevitable in today's capital markets because money is the most generic of all commodities. If there are no restrictions, one price will prevail in the capital market.

Exactly how do foreign interest rates affect domestic interest rates? For example, why do investors not invest in the bonds of countries that are offering higher interest rates, and why do companies not issue bonds in countries with lower rates? The answer to these questions lies in the functioning of foreign exchange markets. For example, although it may be tempting to buy bonds in countries offering higher interest rates, the additional gains could easily be cancelled out (and even large losses incurred) as a result of adverse movements in the foreign exchange rates prevailing when funds are converted back into the domestic currency. In other words, investing or issuing debt abroad creates foreign exchange risk, which offsets the potential advantages that may arise from inter-country interest rate differentials.

The **interest rate parity (IRP) theory** demonstrates how differences in interest rates between countries are offset by expected changes in exchange rates. If this were not the case, capital would flow from countries with low interest rates to those with high interest rates, increasing the supply of capital in the country with higher rates, which would ultimately drive down borrowing costs. Similarly, the capital outflows from countries with low rates would cause their rates to rise in order to have the supply of funds equal the demand for these funds.

interest rate parity (IRP) theory a theory that demonstrates how differences in interest rates between countries are offset by expected changes in exchange rates

The IRP theory, which is discussed in greater detail in Appendix 6A, uses forward currency exchange rates to describe the precise relationship between interest rates and currency levels, because forward currency contracts can be used to eliminate foreign exchange risk. Essentially, the IRP theory states that forward exchange rates, which can be locked in today in order to eliminate foreign exchange risk, will be established at levels that ensure investors will end up with the same amount whether they invest at home or in another country (with no foreign exchange risk). Important factors that affect both interest rates and currency exchange rates are inflation and inflation differentials between countries. For example, if Canadian inflation exceeded that in the United States, we would expect that interest rates would be higher in Canada than in the United States. However, the inflation would cause the value of our currency to depreciate in relation to the U.S. dollar so that we could remain competitive in international trade. Thus, a U.S. investor who bought Canadian bonds in an attempt to benefit from our higher rates would lose these gains when he or she converted the Canadian-dollar payments back into U.S. dollars.

In short, although interest rates are heavily influenced by inflation and other domestic macroeconomic variables, global factors, such as foreign exchange rates and inflation differentials, also play an important role in the level of interest rates at any given time.

The Term Structure of Interest Rates

So far, we have discussed the major factors affecting the base level of interest rates, or RF, which we use as a proxy for the yield on short-term government T-bills. The yields on other debt instruments will differ from RF for several reasons. One important factor affecting debt yields is the term to maturity. This is obvious if we look at the Canadian bond quotes from Table 6-2, where we can see various yield levels for bonds with different maturity dates, even though they were issued by the same entity. For example, at the top of the chart, the Government of Canada benchmarks are yields ranging from 0.83 percent for bonds maturing in five months to 2.53 percent for 34-year bonds.

The relationship between interest rates and the term to maturity on underlying debt instruments is referred to as the **term structure of interest rates**. The graphic representation of this relationship (as displayed in Figure 6-5) is often referred to as the **yield curve**. Yield curves must be constructed based on interest rates on debt instruments that are from the same issuer. Otherwise, default risk (discussed below) and other risk factors, in addition to maturity differentials, will affect the difference in yields. Therefore, the yield curve is almost

term structure of interest rates the relationship between interest rates and the term to maturity on underlying debt instruments

yield curve the graphic representation of the term structure of interest rates, based on debt instruments from the same issuer

always constructed using federal government issues because they possess the same default risk, as well as similar issue characteristics. In addition, the government tends to have a large number of issues outstanding at any given time, so we can construct a yield curve with rate estimates for a wide variety of maturities.

Figure 6-5 shows five historical Government of Canada yield curves at the end of June in 1990, 1994, 1998, and 2004, and as at January 2012. Although yield curves are usually upward sloping, they can assume a wide variety of shapes, which is evident in this figure. The 2012 yield curve slopes upward, with one-month rates sitting at 0.72 percent and longer-term rates at just over 2.5 percent. This illustrates that although long-term government bonds are virtually free from default risk—just as short-term government T-bills are—long-term bonds typically yield more than medium-term bonds, which in turn typically yield more than T-bills.

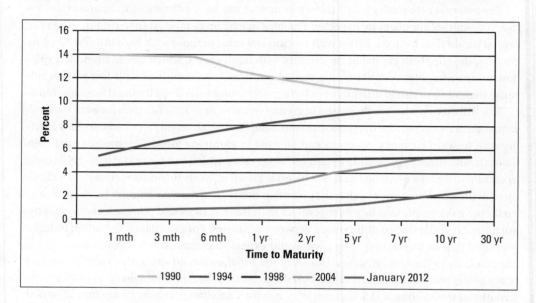

FIGURE 6-5 *Historical Yield Curves 1990, 1994, 1998, 2004, and 2012*

Similar to the curve for 2012, the curves for 1994 and 2004 are upward sloping. However, these three curves vary significantly in terms of their shapes and their starting points, with long-term rates exceeding the short-term rates by about 4 percent in 1994 and 2004, but by less than 2 percent in 2012. In addition, the short-term rates vary from under 1 percent in 2012 to just more than 2 percent in 2004 and almost 6 percent in 1994. The downward-sloping (or inverted) yield curve from 1990, when short-term rates exceeded long-term rates, is less common. Some market participants believe these inverted curves indicate that short-term rates will fall. In fact, short-term interest rates did decline in the subsequent 1991–1993 period. Another less common shape is the relatively flat yield curve in 1998, which indicates that long- and short-term rates are similar.

Several theories attempt to account for the various shapes and movements of the yield curve. We describe three of the most popular theories here.

liquidity preference theory a theory that suggests that investors prefer short-term debt instruments because they exhibit less interest rate risk, while debt issuers prefer to lock in borrowing rates for longer periods to avoid the risk of having to refinance at higher rates

1. The **liquidity preference theory** suggests that investors prefer short-term debt instruments (i.e., more liquid instruments) because they exhibit less interest rate risk, while debt issuers prefer to lock in borrowing rates for longer periods to avoid the risk of having to refinance at higher rates. Therefore, issuers must provide investors with higher yields to induce them to invest in longer-term bonds. As a result, yield curves will generally be upward sloping because long-term rates will be higher than short-term rates. Although this theory is intuitive and does a good job of explaining why yield curves are usually upward sloping, it does not properly account for downward-sloping or flat term structures.

2. The **expectations theory** argues that the yield curve reflects investor expectations about future interest rates. Therefore, an upward-sloping yield curve reflects expectations of interest rate increases in the future, and a downward-sloping curve reflects expectations of interest rate decreases in the future. Unlike the liquidity preference theory, this theory provides a reasonable explanation for downward-sloping and flat term structures, as well as for upward-sloping curves. However, it does not account for the predominance of upward-sloping curves, because it is unreasonable to believe that people expect rates to increase most of the time.

3. The **market segmentations theory** suggests that distinct markets (or market segments) exist for interest rate securities of various maturities and that rates are determined within these independent market segments by the forces of supply and demand within that market. The resulting term structure merely depicts the consequences of the forces of supply and demand within these markets.

> **expectations theory** a theory that argues that the yield curve reflects investor expectations about future interest rates

> **market segmentations theory** a theory that suggests that distinct markets (or market segments) exist for interest rate securities of various maturities and that rates are determined within these independent market segments by the forces of supply and demand within that market

Each of these theories provides useful insights into the factors that affect the shape of term structures. However, each theory has its limitations and therefore does not provide a comprehensive explanation. It is best to realize that liquidity preferences by investors, investor expectations about interest rates, and the demand and supply forces within various maturity segments all affect the shape of the yield curve at any given time, and that the relative importance of each of these factors will vary through time.

Risk Premiums

In addition to differences in terms to maturity, the yield on bonds will differ from the risk-free rate because of additional risks or features associated with these instruments. In other words, investors expect extra compensation for assuming additional risks, and therefore they require higher returns. We can express this relationship using Equation 6-6.

$$k_b = RF + / - \text{Maturity yield differential} + \text{Spread} \qquad [6\text{-}6]$$

The maturity yield differential refers to the term structure impact, which we discussed in the section above, so we now turn our attention to the last term in Equation 6-6. The **spread** is a difference in yield that compensates the investor for the assumption of additional risks, which may include some or all of (1) default or credit risk, (2) liquidity, and (3) issue-specific features. We will discuss each of these in turn.

The most obvious difference in yield arises because of the different levels of **default risk** associated with the bond issuer. In other words, bondholders require higher yields to compensate them for the possibility that the borrower may default on the promised debt payments. This factor is an obvious influence on the yields shown in Table 6-2. For example, if we consider three bond issues that have similar coupon rates and mature on or about the same date, we can observe that their yields differ when they are from separate issuers, which reflects different levels of default risk. For example, the 3.75 percent Government of Canada bonds with a June 1, 2019, maturity date are priced to yield 1.65 percent, while the 4.4 percent Government of New Brunswick bonds maturing two days later yield 2.43 percent, and the 5.70 percent Sunlife Financial bonds maturing approximately one month later yield 4.21 percent.

Debt ratings are assigned by professional debt-rating services, which perform detailed analyses of bond issuers to determine their ability to sustain their required payments of interest and principal repayments. The ratings may be modified by "high" or "low" to indicate the relative ranking within a category. Figure 6-6 lists the debt-rating categories for S&P and DBRS, and Moody's.

> **spread** a difference in yield that compensates the investor for the assumption of additional risks

> **default risk** the risk associated with the bond issuer and its ability to pay

> **debt ratings** ratings assigned by professional debt-rating services after detailed analyses of bond issuers to determine their ability to sustain the required interest and principal payments

S&P and DBRS	Moody's	Description		
AAA	Aaa	highest credit quality	} High quality	Investment grade
AA	Aa	very good quality		
A	A	good quality	} Medium grade	
BBB	Baa	medium quality		
BB	Ba	lower medium quality		Non-investment grade
B	B	poor quality		
CCC	Caa	speculative quality		
CC	Ca	very speculative quality		
D	C	default		In default
Suspended		rating suspended		

Source: Standard & Poor's, www.standardandpoors.com; DBRS, www.dbrs.com; Moody's: www.moodys.com

FIGURE 6-6 *Debt-Rating Categories for Standard & Poor's, Dominion Bond Rating Service, and Moody's*

investment-grade debt debt obligation with a credit rating of AAA, AA, A, or BBB (or Aaa, Aa, A, or Baa)

speculative debt debt that is not investment grade, being rated below BBB or Baa; also commonly referred to as "high-yield debt," "junk bonds," or "low-grade debt"

Investment-grade debt is debt with a rating at or above BBB (DBRS, S&P, and Fitch Ratings), Baa (Moody's), or higher. In other words, investment-grade debt includes the top four major classes. **Speculative debt** has a credit rating below investment grade. If a rated bond is not investment grade, then it is speculative. Some other names for speculative debt are "high-yield debt," "junk bond," or "low-grade debt."

Why have an issue evaluated by a credit-rating firm? The answer is that many investors want to have, or are required to have, a third-party assessment of the credit worthiness of the debt. For example, many pension funds and insurance companies (the two largest holders of bonds) are restricted to investing in investment-grade debt.

Is all debt rated? No, it isn't. Some issuers will place an issue directly with an investor and will not have the issue rated if the investor does not require it.

National governments issue debt obligations (referred to as sovereign debt). In theory, this debt is considered to be risk free because the government can print money or raise revenues through taxes to meet the cash flow obligations of this sovereign debt. We say "in theory" because there have been situations in which this debt has been viewed as not risk free. This is the case for many European countries today facing possible debt default, such as Greece, Ireland, Italy, Portugal, and Spain. Other nations in the past have defaulted, including Venezuela, Russia, Argentina, the Ukraine, and Belize. In some cases, the debt has been restructured, allowing the nation to repay the debt under more favourable terms.[13]

Sovereign debt ratings are similar to those of corporate debt ratings in terms of a ratings scheme, but the factors are different. Sovereign debt ratings take into account:

- fiscal performance
- debt burden
- external liquidity and international investment position
- institutional effectiveness
- political risks
- monetary flexibility
- economic structure
- growth prospects

[13]An exception is the case of Ecuador in 2008. That country's government decided simply not to pay its debts on the basis of moral grounds, though the country likely could have paid its debts.

Consider the case of Greece (Hellenic Republic), which is part of the European Union. As the country's economic conditions have worsened, its debt credit rating has deteriorated over time (Table 6-3).[14]

TABLE 6-3 Greece Debt Credit Rating

Date	Debt Rating
March 26, 1997	A–
March 13, 2001	A
June 10, 2003	A+
November 17, 2004	A
January 14, 2009	A–
December 16, 2009	BBB+
April 27, 2010	BB+
March 29, 2011	BB–
May 9, 2011	B
June 13, 2011	CCC
July 27, 2011	CC

These credit ratings reflect the burgeoning debt relative to the country's gross domestic product (GDP). For example, the ratio of debt to GDP climbed from 94 percent in 1999 to 142.8 percent in 2010. Additionally, GDP growth went from positive 1 percent in 2008 to negative 2 and negative 4.5 percent in 2009 and 2010, respectively. Greece is part of the European Union and, as such, cannot print more money and must seek assistance from the European Central Bank. It therefore has limited flexibility in dealing with its economic woes.

As the example of Greece illustrates, the credit ratings of countries reflect varying economic conditions. The ratings for 13 major nations in the world as at June 30, 2011, are listed in Table 6-4.

TABLE 6-4 Credit Ratings for Various Countries

Country	Credit Rating as at June 30, 2011
Canada	AAA
Germany	AAA
Iceland	BBB–
India	BBB–
Israel	AA–
Italy	A+
Japan	AA–
Mexico	A
People's Republic of China	AA–
Russian Federation	BBB+
Sweden	AAA
United Kingdom	AAA
United States	AAA

On August 5, 2011, Standard & Poor's lowered the rating on the debt of the United States from AAA to AA+. The United States had had an AAA rating since 1917. This downgrade followed a rancorous debate over the debt ceiling, the budget, and deficit spending.[15] Canada has been able to retain its AAA credit rating from Moody's, as discussed in *Finance in the News 6-2*. Moody's cites "comfortable" government finances and Canada's ability to survive the recession better than most countries as factors affecting its outlook for Canada.

---

[14]Standard & Poor's *Sovereign Rating and Country T&C Assessment Histories*, July 5, 2011; Standard & Poor's *Sovereign Government Rating Methodology and Assumptions*, June 30, 2011.

finance INTHENEWS 6-2   Moody's Confirms Canada's AAA Credit Rating

MOODY'S INVESTOR SERVICE gave Canada a vote of confidence on Friday, reaffirming the country's pristine AAA credit rating while calling the federal government's finances "comfortable."

"Canada's ratings appear unlikely to move downward in the near future," the credit agency said.

The credit and debt crises that started in 2008 did some damage to the country's finances. But Moody's repeated a theme heard from many sources already—that Canada wasn't hurt quite as badly by the recession, and has done comparatively better than other countries in the aftermath.

"The country was affected less than most other advanced economies by the global credit crisis and recession, and its government financial position remains comfortable," Moody's said.

Moody's cites the risk of Quebec separation and the possibility of waning commitment to debt reduction as major long-term threats to Canada's sovereign debt rating, but the agency says the risk of both those things is quite low.

The company noted Canada posted a strong current account surplus in the decade up to 2008, but a combination of the global recession and lower commodity prices have brought it back to deficit since then.

Pressure on the public purse because of pension liabilities is lower in Canada than it is in many other developed economies, Moody's noted.

Source: CBC News, December 23, 2011. Retrieved April 18, 2012 from http://www.cbc.ca/news/business/story/2011/12/23/moodys-canada.html.

liquidity premium an additional yield offered on bonds that are less liquid

Most of the differences in yields for bonds of the same term to maturity that we observe as we move from Government of Canada bonds to provincial government bonds to corporate bonds are due to differences in the default risk associated with the issuers. However, a portion of the difference is also due to the fact that Government of Canada bonds trade more actively than provincial bonds, which trade more actively than most investment-grade corporate bonds, which trade more actively than junk bonds. In other words, some bonds are more liquid than others, meaning they are easier to buy and sell and that the required price concessions are lower. Bonds that are less liquid generally have to offer investors a higher yield to compensate for this illiquidity. This additional yield is referred to as the **liquidity premium**. Researchers at the Bank of Canada have estimated that 63 percent of the change in spreads for investment grade issuers results from liquidity rather than risk differences.[16] For non-investment grade issuers this is reversed, with changes in default risk dominating.

The importance of liquidity has been more critical than ever throughout the current global financial concerns, especially in the wake of the European debt crisis. *Finance in the News 6-3* alludes to this, referring to a recent auction of German T-bills that resulted in a negative yield. As discussed in Chapter 5, this implies that investors were willing to pay the German government to lend them money. While the article cites the importance of "security" (i.e., getting paid back), it also discusses the importance of "liquidity." Indeed, liquidity is a big reason there was steady and growing demand for U.S. treasury bonds throughout 2011 (resulting in higher prices and returns—exceeding 17 percent—for T-bond holders) despite the well-documented U.S. financial woes that prompted the S&P downgrade.

---

[15]Congress passed the *Budget Control Act of 2011* [Public Law 112-25, S. 365], and the bill was signed into law on August 2, 2011, to increase the debt limit, attempting to avert a credit downgrade or default on the debt. Standard & Poor's downgraded the U.S. debt within one week of this bill being signed into law. This debt crisis brought to the forefront the issue of how much debt the federal government should or could bear. At the time of this writing, both Moody's and Fitch Ratings rated the United States as AAA. However, both agencies had put the U.S. on a "negative watch," which means that conditions are present that may result in a downgrade.

[16]A. Garcia and J. Yang, "Understanding Corporate Bond Spreads Using Credit Default Swaps," *Bank of Canada Review*, Autumn 2009.

finance INTHENEWS 6-3   Germany Sells Treasury Bills at a Negative Yield for First Time

AN AUCTION of German government short-term bonds produced a negative yield for the first time ever, providing stark evidence that an increasingly nervous European financial community is opting for security and liquidity over any semblance of returns.

Germany's issue of €3.9 billion ($5.1 billion) of six-month treasury bills on Monday resulted in an average yield of minus 0.0122 percent. German officials confirmed it was the first time the country had ever sold government debt securities at a negative yield—a rare circumstance in which buyers actually pay for the privilege of lending money to the debt issuer.

"It just underpins how nervous the overall market is," David Schnautz, fixed-income strategist with Commerzbank AG in London, told Bloomberg News. "[Investors] are okay donating some of their money to Germany, just to make sure they get it back."

The auction took place in the shadow of a key meeting between German Chancellor Angela Merkel and French President Nicolas Sarkozy, after which the two leaders stressed the need for faster progress on the proposed restructuring of Greece's troubled debts.

Negative yields have begun to pop up with growing frequency as Europe's sovereign debt woes linger. High-quality government issuers such as Switzerland, Denmark, and the Netherlands have all sold bonds at negative yields recently, and German short-term bills have traded in negative territory on the open market for the past several weeks.

"It's a sign that risk avoidance is the main name of the game," said Marlene Puffer, managing editor of Global Fixed Income Strategy at BCA

Research Inc., an independent investment research firm based in Montreal. "Investors are looking to hide their money somewhere where at least they'll still get most of it back."

Market watchers said the main participants in the auction—commercial and investment banks, primarily in Europe—use short-term government debt more as a means to manage their cash and maintain liquidity than as an income-generating investment. As a result, they said, the yield plays a minor role, next to the predominant concern of having their funds secure and readily available.

Ms. Puffer added that for European banks, the German T-bills can be used as collateral for borrowing from the European Central Bank, thus allowing them to put their cash holdings to work to generate additional liquidity. This makes the T-bills particularly attractive—even at negative yields—for banks trying to keep money flowing amid an ever-tightening European credit environment.

Experts also point out that negative yields aren't new territory for the bond market. In "real" terms, once inflation is taken into account, many safe-haven government issues have long been in negative territory.

"Nominal returns are a fiction. The return that matters is the real return—that is, the purchasing power of your money," said Eric Lascelles, chief economist at RBC Global Asset Management. "By this standard, even a German 10-year bond offers a negative return.

"The Rubicon was crossed long ago."

Source: Excerpted from Parkinson, David. "Germany Sells Treasury Bills at a Negative Yield for First Time," *The Globe and Mail*, January 10, 2012. ©The Globe and Mail, Inc. All rights reserved. Reprinted by permission.

Issue-specific premiums arise when bonds have features that cause them to be more or less attractive to investors, relative to straight (option-free) bonds. For example, as discussed earlier in the chapter, the call feature is detrimental to bondholders because these bonds are likely to be called by the issuer when interest rates are low (so that they can be refinanced at lower rates), which is exactly when the market prices of these bonds are increasing. As a result, investors will not pay as much for a callable bond as they would for an otherwise identical non-callable bond (i.e., they will demand a higher return). Conversely, retractable bonds permit investors to sell the bonds back to the issuer at predetermined prices when interest rates rise (and bond prices fall), which provides protection against rising rates. Similarly, extendible bonds will only be extended by investors if the coupon rates on such bonds are competitive. If rates increase, the investors will choose not to extend and could invest in other bonds that offer higher coupon rates. Because extendible and retractable bonds, as well as convertible bonds, offer the investor an additional privilege, they will trade at higher prices than otherwise identical straight bonds (i.e., they will provide a lower return).

All three of these factors are embedded in what is commonly called the corporate spread over equivalent-maturity Canada bonds. In practice, it is difficult to separate these three components of the corporate spread. The *Lessons to Be Learned* feature here discusses the corporate yield spread, as measured by the difference between AAA-rated bonds and BBB-rated bonds. These spreads vary over time with the business cycle and often provide clues as to future economic activity. Notice that despite the variation, the AAA-rated bonds always provide lower yields than their riskier BBB-rated counterparts.

issue-specific premiums premiums that arise when bonds have features that cause them to be more or less attractive to investors, relative to straight (option-free) bonds

LESSONS TO BE LEARNED

Corporate bond yields change along with the changing economy. Not only do credit spreads—the difference between corporate bond yields and government yields—increase in a recession, but the spread between yields on corporate bonds that have different credit risk increases, as indicated by the spread between yields on AAA-rated bonds and BBB-rated bonds. We can see these characteristics when examining the credit spreads leading up to and beyond the financial crisis of 2008 and 2009, illustrated in Figure 6-7

In fact, the credit spreads began to widen several months before the recession and peaked in the fall of 2009. The spreads narrowed again during the recovery period in 2010, although they remained at high levels because of uncertainty over the economic recovery, the European debt crisis, and similar matters.

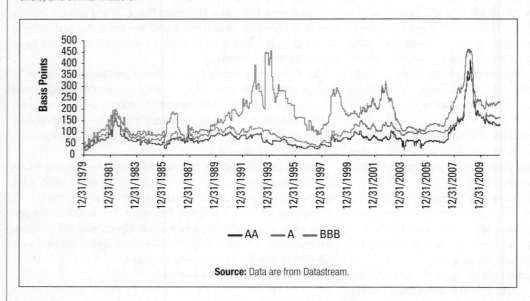

— AA — A — BBB

Source: Data are from Datastream.

FIGURE 6-7 *Default Credit Spreads, December 1979 to December 2009*

CONCEPT REVIEW QUESTIONS

1. How does the expected rate of inflation affect nominal interest rates?
2. Why do interest rates differ between Canada and the United States?
3. Why do interest rates on different-maturity Canada bonds differ?
4. What is a corporate spread?

6.5 OTHER TYPES OF BONDS/ DEBT INSTRUMENTS

Treasury Bills

Learning Objective 6.5
List and describe the characteristics and pricing of other debt instruments.

Treasury bills (T-bills) are short-term government debt obligations that mature in one year or less. Partly because of this short term to maturity, they do not make regular interest payments but are sold at a discount from their par (or face) value, which is paid on the maturity date. The interest earned is the difference between the purchase price and the face value. In Canada, T-bills are issued by the federal government and, in recent years, have also been issued by many provincial governments.

Similar to bonds, T-bills can be priced by estimating the present value of the expected future payment (i.e., the par value that is to be repaid at maturity). Equation 6-7 is used to value T-bills in Canada, with k_{BEY} being the bond equivalent yield and n the term to maturity expressed as number of days.

$$P = \frac{F}{\left(1 + k_{BEY} \times \dfrac{n}{365}\right)} \qquad [6\text{-}7]$$

EXAMPLE 6-12   Determining the Price of T-bills

Find the price of a 91-day T-bill with a face value of $10,000 that has a quoted yield of 4.2 percent.

Solution

$F = \$10,000;\ k_{BEY} = 0.042;\ n = 91$

$$P = \frac{F}{\left(1 + k_{BEY} \times \dfrac{n}{365}\right)} = \frac{10,000}{1.010471233} = \$9,896.37$$

Similar to bonds, T-bill prices are usually quoted on the basis of $100 of par value, so the price quote for the T-bill in Example 6-12 would be $98.9637.

Rearranging Equation 6-7, we can determine the yield on T-bills using Equation 6-8.

$$k_{BEY} = \frac{F - P}{P} \times \frac{365}{n} \qquad [6\text{-}8]$$

EXAMPLE 6-13   Estimating the Yield on a T-bill

Estimate the yield on a 182-day T-bill that is currently selling at a price of $98.20.

Solution

$F = \$100;\ P = 98.20;\ n = 182$

$$k_{BEY} = \frac{100 - 98.20}{98.20} \times \frac{365}{182} = 0.018329939 \times 2.005494505 = 0.03676 = 3.676\%$$

In the United States, yields on T-bills are usually quoted based on the "bank discount yield," which is determined by using a different procedure from that used to calculate the bond equivalent yield in Canada. The differences arise because of the use of face value instead of price in the denominator of the first term, and because 360 days is used instead of 365 days to annualize the rate. The resulting equation, in which k_{BDY} is the bank discount yield, is:

$$k_{BDY} = \frac{F - P}{F} \times \frac{360}{n} \times 100$$

Zero Coupon Bonds

A **zero coupon bond** (or, simply, "zero") is structured similarly to a long-term T-bill, in the sense that it does not make regular interest payments but is issued at a discount and repays the par value at the maturity date. The return earned represents the difference between the purchase price and the redemption price. Obviously, the lower the price paid for the bond, the higher the return. "Zeroes" were initially created by financial intermediaries who purchased traditional bonds, stripped the cash flows (both the interest and the principal repayment components) from them, and sold these cash flows separately. Today, most zeroes are created this way, but some are also initially issued as zero coupon bonds. These instruments are very popular with financial institutions, which often use them for hedging purposes to cover

zero coupon bond a bond that is issued at a discount, pays no coupons, and repays the par value at the maturity date; also commonly referred to simply as a "zero"

their outstanding liabilities. Zeroes are ideally suited for this purpose because, unlike with traditional bonds, there are no issues tied to reinvesting interest payments that are received before maturity.

Zero coupon bonds are easy to evaluate using a variation of Equation 6-1 in which we drop the first term (because there are no interest payments to discount). This leaves us with Equation 6-9.

[6-9]
$$B = F \times \frac{1}{(1 + k_b)^n}$$

Remember that, by convention, we value these bonds by assuming semi-annual discounting periods and convert our quoted yield to a semi-annual yield. Therefore, the number of periods should also be expressed in terms of semi-annual periods.

EXAMPLE 6-14 Estimating the YTM on a Semi-Annual Bond

Determine the price of a 15-year zero coupon bond with a face value of $1,000 and a market yield of 5 percent.

Solution
$F = \$1,000$; $n = 15$ years $\times 2 = 30$; $k_b = 0.05/2 = 0.025$

$B = 1,000 \times \dfrac{1}{(1 + 0.25)^{30}} = 1,000 \times 0.47674 = \$476.74$

EXAMPLE 6-14 Solution Using a Financial Calculator

(TI BA II PLUS)

Input the following variables:

PMT → 0; N → 30; FV → 1,000; I/Y → 2.5%; CPT PV → −$476.74

EXAMPLE 6-14 Solution Using Excel

We enter

= PRICE(date(2012,11,06), date(2027,11,06), 0, .05, 100, 2, 0)

and get the same answer of $476.74. Note that with Excel, the only difference for a regular bond is to enter 0 for the coupon rate.

From Equation 6-9, notice that if market rates fell, the price of the zero would increase and vice versa, just as is the case for a regular coupon-paying bond. In fact, the market prices of zeroes are even more sensitive to interest rate changes, because they make no coupon payments at all.

Finally, it is relatively straightforward to solve for the YTM on a zero if we are given the price. In particular, we can rearrange Equation 6-9 to determine an exact solution for the semi-annual rate (k_b), as shown in Equation 6-10. This value is then doubled to find the annual YTM. Notice that this differs from the coupon-paying bonds, for which there was no finite solution for YTM.

[6-10]
$$k_b = \left[\frac{F}{B} \right]^{\frac{1}{n}} - 1$$

EXAMPLE 6-15   Estimating the YTM on a Zero Coupon Bond

Determine the YTM on a 10-year zero coupon bond with a face value of $1,000 that is selling for $560.

Solution

$F = \$1,000$; $n = 10$ years $\times 2 = 20$; $PV = \$560$

$$k_b = \left[\frac{1,000}{560} \right]^{\frac{1}{20}} - 1 = (1.785714286)^{\frac{1}{20}} - 1 = 1.0294 - 1 = .0294 = 2.94\%$$

EXAMPLE 6-15   Solution Using a Financial Calculator

(TI BA II PLUS)

Input the following variables:

$\boxed{\text{PMT}} \rightarrow 0$; $\boxed{\text{N}} \rightarrow 20$; $\boxed{\text{FV}} \rightarrow 1,000$; $\boxed{\text{PV}} \rightarrow -560$; $\boxed{\text{CPT}}\ \boxed{\text{PV}} = 2.94\%$

Doubling this gives a YTM of 5.88 percent.

EXAMPLE 6-15   Solution Using Excel

XLS

We enter

= YIELD(date(2012,11,06), date(2022,11,06), 0, 56, 100, 2, 0)

which gives 5.883 percent.

Floating Rate and Real Return Bonds

Floating rate bonds (floaters) have adjustable coupons that are usually tied to some variable short-term rate, such as the T-bill rate, although many variations exist. They differ significantly from traditional fixed-income bonds because the coupon rates increase as interest rates increase and vice versa. Therefore, floaters provide protection against rising interest rates and tend to trade near their par value.

Government of Canada **Real Return Bonds** provide investors with protection against inflation by providing a real yield, which was 4.25 percent at the time they were introduced and is currently sitting at 0.40 percent. This is achieved by pegging the face value to the rate of inflation (as measured by the CPI) and having the coupon rate apply to the inflation-adjusted face value.

floating rate bonds (floaters) bonds that have adjustable coupons that are usually tied to some variable short-term rate

Real Return Bonds bonds issued by the Government of Canada that provide investors with protection against inflation

Canada Savings Bonds

Canada Savings Bonds (CSBs) differ significantly from the bonds discussed above. Because they cannot be traded, CSBs have no secondary market and therefore their prices do not change over time. They are registered in the name of the investor at the time of purchase and can be cashed out by the owner, at their full par value plus eligible accrued interest, at any bank in Canada at any time. Currently, CSBs may be purchased only by individuals, estates, and certain trusts. This restriction differs significantly from the restrictions on traditional bonds, which tend to be held mainly by institutional investors.

The rates of return on CSBs may vary through time. At present, CSBs are available in two forms: (1) regular interest bonds, which pay out the annual interest amounts; and (2) compound interest bonds, which reinvest the interest, meaning interest is also earned on accumulated interest (producing the power of compounding, as discussed in Chapter 5).

Canada Savings Bonds (CSBs) bonds issued by the Government of Canada that cannot be traded and therefore have no secondary market, which means their prices do not change over time

CONCEPT REVIEW QUESTIONS

1. How does the formula for determining the price of a T-bill resemble the formula for determining the price of a zero coupon bond? Why is this so?
2. How do U.S. bank discount yields differ from bond equivalent yields?
3. How do floaters and Real Return Bonds provide protection against inflation?

APPENDIX **6A**

INTEREST RATE PARITY

Learning Objective 6.6
Explain how interest rate parity works.

Interest rates vary from one country to the next, yet wise investors do not invest merely in the bonds of countries that are offering the highest interest rates. Any attempt to exploit such opportunities would expose investors to foreign exchange risk, which offsets the potential advantages that may arise from inter-country interest rate differentials. The interest rate parity (IRP) theory demonstrates why the differences in interest rates between countries should be offset by forward exchange rates. In particular, the IRP states that the relationship shown in Equation 6A-1 should hold or else "arbitrage opportunities" (i.e., the opportunity to earn riskless profits) will exist.

[6A-1]
$$\frac{F}{S} = \frac{(1 + k_{domestic})}{(1 + k_{foreign})}$$

where F = the current forward exchange rate, expressed in number of units of domestic currency required to purchase one unit of the foreign currency

S = the current spot exchange rate

$k_{domestic}$ = the domestic interest rate

$k_{foreign}$ = the foreign interest rate

Example 6A-1 uses this equation to determine the predicted forward exchange rate.

EXAMPLE 6A-1   Using Interest Rate Parity (IRP)

Assume British interest rates are currently 10 percent on one-year British T-bills. Assume that sterling is quoted at £1 = C$1.75 and the interest rate on one-year T-bills in Canada is 6 percent. Find the one-year forward exchange rate.

Solution
Notice that the interest rate differential for the specified one-year term is 4 percent, which implies that the forward exchange rate should be approximately 4 percent lower (in Canadian dollar terms) than the spot rate to ensure that IRP holds.

To be more precise, we can rearrange the IRP equation to solve for the forward rate:

$$F = S \times \frac{(1 + k_{domestic})}{(1 + k_{foreign})} = \$1.75 \times \frac{1.06}{1.10} = \$1.6864$$

The IRP implies that an investor cannot benefit from higher foreign interest rates without assuming risk, which is demonstrated in Example 6A-2.

EXAMPLE 6A-2   An Arbitrage Opportunity When IRP Does Not Hold

Determine the ending wealth of two Canadian investors with C$1,000 to invest, assuming the conditions identified in Example 6A-1 exist. Investor 1 invests domestically, while Investor 2 invests in Britain and eliminates foreign exchange risk using the forward contract.

Solution

Investor 1: Ending wealth = C$1,000 × 1.06 = C$1,060

Investor 2: First, convert C$ into £: C$1,000/1.75 = £571.43

Second, £571.43 invested at 10% grows to £628.57

Third, convert £ into C$ through forward contract = £628.57 × 1.6864 = C$1,060.02

Notice that if this is the prevailing forward rate, neither investor is better off by investing in either country (the $0.02 difference is due to rounding error).

Why does this relationship hold? If it didn't, investors could earn arbitrage (riskless) profits without putting up any initial investment. Example 6A-3 demonstrates how.

EXAMPLE 6A-3   An Arbitrage Opportunity When IRP Does Not Hold

In Example 6A-2, if the forward exchange rate was set at C$1.70 instead of C$1.6864, demonstrate how an investor (arbitrageur) could earn arbitrage (riskless) profit. Assume that anyone can borrow and lend (invest) at the quoted rates.

Solution

When the arbitrageur observes the forward price of C$1.70, she would first note that it violates IRP, because $F \neq 1.75 (1.06)/(1.1) = $ C$1.6864.

This means that the forward rate is pricing sterling too dearly and Canadian dollars too cheaply. The arbitrageur will therefore want to sell sterling for Canadian dollars through the forward contract. She borrows Canadian dollars to buy sterling now in the spot market, and invests it in Britain until the maturity date of the forward contract.

Assuming the arbitrageur borrows C$2 million, we obtain the following:

1. Borrow C$2 million (at 6 percent) to buy sterling today. Convert C$2 million at spot of (1/C$1.75) = £1,142,857.

2. Invest in sterling for one year at 10 percent.

3. The total investment at maturity = £1,142,857(1.1) = £1,257,143.

   Convert back to Canadian dollars at the C$1.70 forward rate: £1,257,143 × C$1.70 = C$2,137,143.

   Pay back loan: (C$2 million)(1.06) = C$2.12 million.

   Arbitrage profit = C$2,137,143 − C$2,120,000 = C$17,143

The arbitrageur would make a riskless (arbitrage) profit (of C$17,143) without assuming any risk and without making any initial investment of her own funds

---

The condition in Example 6A-3 could not persist, however. As investors rushed to exploit such an opportunity, the forward price would quickly fall to C$1.6864.[17]

---

[17]Although the example illustrates the existence of an arbitrage possibility, it disregards transaction costs and the fact that borrowing and lending rates are not usually equal. Both of these factors affect the potential for arbitrage and explain why IRP need not hold precisely, but rather should hold within reasonable boundaries.

In similar fashion, if the forward exchange rate were $1.66, arbitrageurs would note that this violates IRP because the rate is £1 = C$1.6864. However, this time the forward rate prices sterling too cheaply and Canadian dollars too dearly. Investors will want to sell Canadian dollars for sterling through the forward contract, which means they will borrow sterling (at 10 percent), convert it to Canadian dollars in the spot market, and invest the amount in Canada (at 6 percent) until the maturity date of the forward contract.

SUMMARY

In this chapter, we discuss the nature of bonds as an investment. We examine the standard format of a traditional coupon-paying bond and consider additional features or variations of this structure. We then examine how these instruments can be valued, using the discounting concepts developed in Chapter 5, after we determine an appropriate discount rate. One of the most important factors affecting bond prices is the level of interest rates. The most important property of bond prices is that they increase when interest rates decrease and vice versa. Finally, we consider the various factors, both domestic and global, that affect the basic levels of market interest rates.

SUMMARY OF LEARNING OBJECTIVES

6.1 Describe the basic structure and the various features of different types of bonds.

A bond is a security that represents a loan from the buyer (investor) to the issuer. The issuer of the bond promises a series of cash payments to the buyer—the cash payments represent interest and repayment of principal. Bonds are often referred to as "fixed income securities" because the interest payments and the principal repayment are specified, or fixed, at the time the bond is issued. A coupon bond pays the bondholder semi-annual or annual interest payments (coupons) and the face value at the maturity date.

6.2 Explain how to value a bond given an appropriate discount rate.

The cash price of a bond is equal to the present value of the promised cash payments. The cash price of a bond is the sum of the quoted price and accrued interest. The bond prices shown in newspapers or on websites are the quoted price and not the cash price. The quoted price is the sum of the discounted future cash flow. Thus, discount rate plays an important role in bond pricing: the higher the discount rate, the lower the bond prices.

6.3 Determine the discount rate or yield for a given market value of a bond.

The yield to maturity (YTM) is the discount rate that equates future payments with the current selling price. It represents the return investors would get if they purchased the bond at the given price, held it to maturity, and re-invested all interest payments at this rate of return.

6.4 List and describe the factors, both domestic and global, that affect interest rates.

Interest rates are affected by domestic factors, including inflation, default risk, and liquidity risk. They are also affected by global factors, including foreign interest rates and foreign exchange risk.

6.5 List and describe the characteristics and pricing of other debt instruments.

Other debt instruments include treasury bills, zero coupon bonds, floating rate bonds, and Real Return Bonds. The price equals the sum of the discounted future cash flow.

6.6 Explain how interest rate parity works.

Interest rates vary from one country to another, yet wise investors do not invest merely in the bonds of countries that are offering the highest interest rates. Any attempt to exploit such opportunities would expose investors to foreign exchange risk, which offsets the potential advantages that may arise from inter-country interest rate differentials. The interest rate parity (IRP) theory demonstrates why the differences in interest rates between countries should be offset by forward exchange rates. In particular, the IRP states that the relationship shown in Equation 6A-1 should hold or else "arbitrage opportunities" (i.e., the opportunity to earn riskless profits) will exist.

KEY TERMS

EQUATIONS

Equation	Formula	Page
[6-1] Bond Valuation and Yield to Maturity	$B = I \times \left[\dfrac{1 - \dfrac{1}{(1+k_b)^n}}{k_b} \right] + F \times \dfrac{1}{(1+k_b)^n}$	p. 209
[6-2] Yield to Call	$B = I \times \left[\dfrac{1 - \dfrac{1}{(1+k_c)^c}}{k_c} \right] + CP \times \dfrac{1}{(1+k_c)^c}$	p. 223
[6-3] Current Yield	$CY = \dfrac{Annual\ interest}{B}$	p. 224
[6-4] Fisher Relationship (approximation)	$RF = Real\ rate + Expected\ inflation$	p. 225
[6-5] Fisher Relationship (precise)	$RF = [\,(1 + Real\ rate)(1 + Expected\ inflation)\,] - 1$	p. 225
[6-6] Bond Yield Components	$k_b = RF + / - Maturity\ yield\ differential + Spread$	p. 229
[6-7] T-Bill Price	$P = \dfrac{F}{\left(1 + k_{BEY} \times \dfrac{n}{365}\right)}$	p. 235
[6-8] T-Bill Yield	$k_{BEY} = \dfrac{F - P}{P} \times \dfrac{365}{n}$	p. 235
[6-9] Price – Zero Coupon Bond	$B = F \times \dfrac{1}{(1 + k_b)^n}$	p. 236
[6-10] YTM – Zero Coupon Bond	$k_b = \left[\dfrac{F}{B} \right]^{\frac{1}{n}} - 1$	p. 236
[6A-1] Interest Rate Parity	$\dfrac{F}{S} = \dfrac{(1 + k_{domestic})}{(1 + k_{foreign})}$	p. 238

QUESTIONS AND PRACTICE PROBLEMS

Multiple Choice Questions

1. Which of the following statements concerning bonds is incorrect?
    a. They involve blended payments of principal and interest.
    b. They have a fixed maturity date, at which time the issuer repays the full principal amount.
    c. Bondholders are paid a series of fixed periodic amounts before the maturity date.
    d. The bond indenture is a legal document, specifying payment requirements and so on.

2. Which of the following statements is incorrect?
    a. Callable bonds give the bond issuer an option to call the bond at a predetermined price.
    b. All debentures are secured bonds.
    c. Extendible bonds allow bondholders to extend the maturity date.
    d. Convertible bonds give the bondholders an option to convert into common shares at a predetermined conversion ratio.

3. What is the price of a 10-year, 8-percent, annual coupon bond when the market rate is 10 percent? The face value is $100.
    a. $100
    b. $100.57
    c. $87.71
    d. $113.42

4. Which of the following bond prices is most sensitive to market rate changes? The par value is $100 for all.
    a. 5-year, 5-percent coupon rate, yield 5.5 percent
    b. 3-year, 8-percent coupon rate, yield 5.6 percent
    c. 7.5-year, 4.5-percent coupon rate, yield 5.5 percent
    d. 10-year, 4.5-percent coupon rate, yield 5.5 percent

5. What is the yield to maturity on an eight-year, 9-percent bond that pays interest semi-annually, which is now priced at $980? Use a financial calculator.
    a. 9.05 percent
    b. 9 percent
    c. 4.68 percent
    d. 9.36 percent

6. Which of the following statements is correct?
    a. Current yield is the ratio of annual coupon payment divided by the par value.
    b. When the coupon rate is higher than the market rate, the bond is priced at a discount.
    c. When the market rate is higher than the coupon rate, the bond is priced at a premium.
    d. If a bond is at a discount, the coupon rate is less than the current yield, which is less than YTM.

7. Which statement is incorrect?
    a. The liquidity preference theory states that investors prefer short-term debt.
    b. According to the expectations theory, a downward-sloping yield curve implies that interest rates are expected to decline in the future.
    c. The risk premium in the bond yield reflects default risk, liquidity risk, and issue-specific features.
    d. A debt rating of AAA is a worse rating than BB for S&P.

8. What is the *quoted* price of a 182-day Canadian T-bill that has a face value of $10,000 and a quoted yield of 4 percent?
   a. $9,804.45
   b. $9,478.67
   c. $98.0445
   d. $94.7867

9. Which of the following statements is false?
   a. Zero coupon bonds are deep-discount bonds.
   b. Zero coupon bonds are often created when cash flows are stripped from traditional bonds.
   c. Floating rate bonds provide protection against decreasing interest rates.
   d. There are two forms of return available for Canada Savings Bond buyers: regular interest and compound interest

10. Which statement is correct according to interest rate parity (IRP) theory?
    a. IRP states that differences in interest rates between countries cannot be totally offset by expected changes in exchange rates.
    b. Forward exchange rates may be locked in today to eliminate foreign exchange risk and ensure investors can profit from moving capital to countries with higher interest rates.
    c. Inflation differentials between countries affect both interest rates and currency exchange rates.
    d. The country with a higher inflation rate will see its currency appreciate against another country with a lower inflation rate.

Practice Problems

11. Describe the difference between positive and negative bond covenants.

12. State the relationship between market rates and bond prices.

13. Calculate the price of a bond with FV of $1,000, a coupon rate of 8 percent (paid semi-annually), and five years to maturity when:
    a. k_b = 10 percent
    b. k_b = 8 percent
    c. k_b = 6 percent

14. Calculate the price of the following bond: FV = $1,000; coupon rate = 6 percent, paid semi-annually; market rate = 4 percent; term to maturity = 10 years.

15. Describe the relationship between bond interest rate risk and the coupon rate, the market yield, and the term to maturity.

16. Suppose that, several years ago, the Canadian government issued three very similar bonds; each has a $1,000 face value and a 10-percent coupon rate and will mature in five years. The only difference between the bonds is the frequency of the coupon payments. If the market yield is now 6.5 percent, determine the price of the bond that pays coupons:
    a. annually
    b. semi-annually
    c. monthly

17. The following is data for two bonds at a time when the market yield is 7 percent.

Bond	Coupon Rate	Price
A	6%	$958.42
B	8%	$1,041.58

These bonds are otherwise identical (FV = $1,000, five years to maturity, semi-annual coupon payments). Which bond's price will change more, and by how much, if the market yield increases by 100 basis points?

18. The following two bonds are identical (FV = $1,000, 8-percent coupon rate paid semi-annually), except that they mature at different times.

Bond	Time to maturity	Price
C	3 years	$1,026.64
D	8 years	$1,060.47

If the market yield, currently 7 percent, increases by 100 basis points, which bond's price will change more and by how much?

19. A 10-year bond has just been issued with its coupon rate set at the current market yield of 6 percent. How much would the price of the bond change (in percentage terms) if the market yield suddenly fell by 50 basis points? How much would the price change if the yield rose by 50 basis points?

20. Consider a bond with five years to maturity, FV of $1,000, and a coupon rate of 6.5 percent (semi-annual payments).
    a. Calculate the price of this bond if the market yield is: i) 7.75 percent   ii) 5.25 percent
    b. In each case, calculate the percentage change in the price of the bond if the market yield rises by 1 percent.

21. A zero coupon bond has a par value of $1,000 and will mature in eight years.
    a. Calculate the current price of this bond if the market yield is: i) 7.75 percent   ii) 5.25 percent
    b. In each case, calculate the percentage change in the price of the bond if the market yield rises by 1 percent.

22. It is now March 1, 2013, and Peter has just purchased a five-year U.S. government bond (FV = $1,000) with a quoted price of 93.863. This bond has a 5-percent coupon rate, and the last semi-annual coupon payment was made on January 1, 2013.
    a. How much will Peter actually pay for this bond?
    b. Had this been a Canadian government bond, what would be the cash price?

23. Calculate the price change for a 1-percent decrease in market yield for the following bond: par = $1,000; coupon rate = 6 percent, paid semi-annually; market yield = 6 percent; term to maturity = 10 years.

24. Calculate the cash price of the following bond, sold on September 21: par = $1,000; coupon rate = 4 percent, paid on January 1 and July 1; quoted price = $956. Explain why the cash price is different from the quoted price.

25. You bought a bond last year for $102.50 and just sold it for $98.50. What has happened to the interest rate over that period?

26. A bond is currently trading at $825. It has 12 years to maturity. If you require a rate of return of 12 percent, what should be the bond's coupon rate if the bond pays semi-annual coupons?

27. A bond with semi-annual coupons at a rate of 10 percent will mature in one year. If the bond's price is $1,010, use the trial-and-error method to find the YTM. Check your answer by using a financial calculator or Excel spreadsheet. What would the YTM be if the bond made annual coupon payments?

28. For each of the following YTM figures, calculate the price and current yield for a two-year, 7-percent, annual-pay bond with a face value of $1,000.

   a.   YTM = 6 percent
   b.   YTM = 7 percent
   c.   YTM = 8 percent

29. At maturity, each of the following zero coupon bonds (pure discount bonds) will be worth
     $1,000. For each bond, fill in the missing quantity in the following table. Assume semi-annual
     compounding.

	Price	Maturity (Years)	Yield to Maturity
A	$450	10	
B	$400		6%
C		15	12%

30. Suppose that a 6-percent, annual-pay, Government of Canada bond that matures in two
     years has a yield to maturity of 6.75 percent. If inflation is expected to be 2.5 percent per year
     over the next two years, what coupon rate would you expect to find on a Real Return Bond
     that is otherwise identical?

31. Suppose the inflation rate in Canada, as measured by the CPI, has been averaging 3.5 percent
     in recent years. The most recent Bank of Canada announcement indicates that it expects
     3-percent inflation over the next year. If the real rate of return on Canadian T-bills is 1.5 percent,
     what is the nominal risk-free rate?

32. The following values are the spread for corporate bond yields.

Bond Rating	Spread over AAA
AA	30 basis points
A	45 basis points
BBB	70 basis points
BB	110 basis points

   a.   One-year T-bills are trading with a YTM of 6 percent. What yield would you expect to find
        on A-rated corporate bonds maturing in one year?
   b.   Five-year government bonds have a maturity yield differential of 50 basis points. What
        yield would you expect to observe on non-investment grade (BB-rated) corporate bonds
        with a five-year maturity?

33. Using the Fisher relationship, calculate the exact real interest rate and the approximate real
     rate, given a T-bill rate of 9 percent and an expected inflation rate of 4.5 percent.

34. Calculate the bank discount yield on a 92-day U.S. T-bill that is currently quoted at $97.75.

35. a.   What is the value of a 10-year zero coupon bond with a face value of $1,000 when the
          market rate is 8 percent.
     b.   Calculate the YTM of the above zero coupon bond if the current price is $760.

36. Sapna would like to receive a real return of 5 percent per year on a bond investment at a time
     when the expected inflation rate is 2.5 percent. How much would she be willing to pay for a
     bond maturing in two years if it pays annual coupons at a (nominal) rate of 7 percent? If a
     Real Return Bond were available with a 4.5-percent coupon (annual payments) and the same
     two-year maturity, how much would Sapna be willing to pay for it to achieve her desired rate
     of return?

37. A 90-day U.S. T-bill has a bank discount yield (k_{BDY}) of 4.673 percent. Find the quoted price.
     Find the bond equivalent yield (k_{BEY}) on a 90-day Canadian T-bill with the same quoted price.

38. The Slice & Dice Investment Co. needs some help understanding the intricacies of bond pricing. It has observed the following prices for zero coupon bonds that have no risk of default:

Maturity	Price per $1 face value
1 year	0.97
2 years	0.9
3 years	0.81

   a. How much should Slice & Dice be willing to pay for a three-year bond that pays a 6-percent coupon, assuming annual coupon payments start one year from now?

   b. What is the yield to maturity of the three-year coupon bond?

   c. Suppose Slice & Dice purchases this coupon bond and then "un-bundles" it into its four component cash flows: three coupon payments and the par value amount. At what price(s) can Slice & Dice resell each of the first three cash flows (the coupon payments) today?

   d. The remaining cash flow (the face value amount) is a "synthetic" three-year zero coupon bond. How much must this "strip bond" be sold for if Slice & Dice is to break even on the investment?

   e. What is the yield to maturity on the synthetic three-year zero coupon bond?

   f. Why are the answers for (b) and (e) different?

39. A bond that matures in 10 years is callable in three years at a call price of $1,025. The bond has a semi-annual coupon rate of 8 percent. If the YTM is 7.3 percent and the YTC is 6.92 percent, what is the bond's current price? Is this bond likely to be called?

40. If you have a retractable bond, under what conditions will you exercise your right to sell the bond back to the bond issuer?

41. Altech Inc. has a convertible bond with a face value of $1,000 and coupon rate of 6 percent. The bond will mature in 10 years, and its current price is $950. The bond can be converted at any time into 25 shares of Altech Inc., whose current share price is $40. If the holder decides to convert the bond into shares, what is the percentage premium/discount of the conversion relative to the current share price?

42. If a bond-rating agency downgrades the rating of a bond, how will it affect the price of that bond?

43. A bond has a yield to maturity of 8 percent and a current yield of 6 percent. Is the bond trading at par, at a premium, or at a discount? What can you say about the coupon rate?

44. Explain yield to maturity in terms of the spot rate.

45. The present value of a dollar to be received one year from today is 0.91743. The present value of a dollar to be received two years from today is 0.82645. What is the price of a bond that pays an annual coupon of 8 percent and matures in two years? Find its yield to maturity.

46. You are a financial advisor and one of your clients comes to you with a convertible bond that has a coupon rate of 8 percent. The market interest rate is 6 percent. The share price of the company that issued the bond is going down, and you don't expect the company to recover in the near future. Your client is thinking of converting the bond into shares and wants your advice. What will you recommend to your client?

47. Adam has saved C$1,000 and plans to go surfing in Australia next summer. He won't need the money for a year, so he decides to invest it. Adam could invest the money in Canada, where a T-bill will earn 4.5 percent, and then convert it to Australian dollars (AU$) just before he leaves. Alternatively, Adam could convert the funds today and invest in an Australian T-bill earning 5.2 percent. Which approach should he take if the currency spot rate is C$0.90431/AU$ and the one-year forward rate is C$0.89829/AU$?

48. Bower is a Canadian investor. He noticed that the euro spot rate is currently quoted at C$1.4161/euro. The European interest rate is 7 percent on one-year T-bills, and the one-year interest rate in Canada is 5 percent. The one-year forward rate is C$1.409/euro. Determine whether there is an arbitrage opportunity. State the transactions Bower should apply to profit from the arbitrage opportunity if one exists. Explain what would happen if many other investors also seized such an arbitrage opportunity, if one existed.

7 | Equity Valuation

LEARNING OBJECTIVES

7.1   Identify the basic characteristics of equity securities (i.e., preferred shares and common shares).

7.2   Explain how to value preferred shares.

7.3   Explain how to value common shares using the dividend discount model.

7.4   Explain how to value common shares using the price-earnings (P/E) ratio.

7.5   Explain how to value common shares using additional relative value ratios.

7.6   Apply the principles of fundamental valuation and relative valuation.

7.7   Explain how speculative price bubbles occur.

We have long recognized that the value of the stock of a corporation is not likely the same as the value of the stock on the company's books. For example, for a company without any debt, it was recognized over 100 years ago, in "Ryan v. Board of County Commissioners of Leavenworth Coal Co., and Others," that

> if a company has special privileges or monopoly of any kind of business, its franchises may have a separate and independent value, and the value of the stock of the company may exceed largely the value of all the tangible property of the corporation. (p. 159)

The valuation of stock based on the future dividends of a company has also long been recognized. For example, Benjamin Graham and David Dodd, back in 1934, remarked that

> the investor may look to future dividends or even to future enhancement of market value, instead of to the current dividend. (p. 320)

The many forces that influence the value of stock were first recognized in the early 20th century and continue to be today. For example, Charles A. Conant wrote in 1905:

> Among the influences which affect prospective earning power, are all the facts and rumors which indicate the economic future—not only whether crops are to be large or small, but whether consumption is to be greater or less; whether given properties are managed well or ill; whether the rate of growth of population and wealth promises increased earning power in the future, or whether competitive establishments threaten to reduce the margin or profit; whether legislatures are disposed to grant new franchises and continue old ones, or to impose direct burdens to be paid out of dividends, and indirect burdens, which gradually cripple the producing power and the initiative of the community. (p. 351)

In other words, it's complicated. But that is what makes the value of stock interesting and rewarding.

Source: "Ryan v. Board of County Commissioners of Leavenworth Coal Co., and Others," filed July 5, 1883, *The Pacific Reporter* 2, pp. 156–61; Graham, Benjamin, and David Dodd, *Security Analysis*. McGraw-Hill Companies, Inc., 1934; Conant, Charles A, "How the stock-market reflects values." *The North American Review* 180, no. 580 (March 1905), pp. 347–59.

CHAPTER 7 **PREVIEW**

The chapter-opening vignette alludes to various factors that have affected the value of common shares for over a century: (1) "intangibles" that can generate future cash flows; (2) dividends; and (3) earnings power. We discuss each of these factors in this chapter. Recall that in Chapter 6, we discussed how to estimate the value of bonds based on the present value of their expected future cash flows and how to estimate the implied yield based on given prices. In this chapter, we apply the same concepts to equity valuation. We begin by examining how to evaluate both preferred and common shares based on the present value of their expected future dividend stream. We proceed to show how this approach is related to the fundamentals that affect stock prices (i.e., future profitability and dividends, interest rates, and risk). We conclude with a discussion of relative valuation approaches and show how they too can be related to company fundamentals.

7.1 EQUITY SECURITIES

Learning Objective 7.1
Identify the basic characteristics of equity securities (i.e., preferred shares and common shares).

equity securities ownership interests in an underlying entity, usually a corporation

common share a certificate of ownership in a corporation; the most common type of equity security

preferred share the other major type of equity security, which gives the owner a claim to a fixed amount of equity that is established when the shares are first issued

Equity securities are ownership interests in an underlying entity, usually a corporation. Generally, equity securities have no fixed maturity date. Equities pay dividends from after-tax earnings, so, unlike interest payments, they do not provide the issuer with a tax-deductible expense. However, shareholders pay lower taxes on dividends received from Canadian corporations than they would on interest payments, as discussed in Chapter 3.

By far the most common type of equity security is the **common share**, which represents a certificate of ownership in a corporation. A purchaser of 200 common shares owns $(200/n \times 100)$ percent of the corporation (where n is the total number of common shares outstanding). Common shareholders represent the true "owners" of the corporation. They are the residual claimants of the corporation, which means that they are entitled to income remaining only after all creditors and preferred shareholders (discussed below) have been paid. Similarly, in the case of liquidation of the corporation, common shareholders are entitled to the remaining assets only after all other claims have been satisfied. As owners, they can exert control over the corporation through their power to vote, which allows them to elect the board of directors and to vote on major issues, such as takeovers, corporate restructuring, and so on. In Chapter 19, we discuss the characteristics of common shares in more detail.

The other major category of equities is **preferred shares**. These provide the owner with a claim to a fixed amount of equity that is established when the shares are first issued. Most preferred shares have preference over common shares with respect to income and assets (in the event of liquidation), but they rarely have any voting rights. Traditionally, preferred shares had no maturity date, but over the past 30 years preferred shares have been increasingly issued with a fixed maturity date, similar to a bond. The main difference between preferred shares and bonds is that the board of directors declares any dividends. Unlike interest payments, dividends are not a legal obligation of the firm until that declaration is made. Usually no payments can be made to common shareholders until preferred shareholders have been paid the entire amount of the dividends they are due. We discuss the characteristics of preferred shares in more detail in Chapter 19.

Valuation of Equity Securities

A commonly used method for valuing equity securities follows the discounted cash flow approach used to estimate the value of bonds. Specifically, we estimate the expected future cash flows associated with the security and then determine the discounted present value of those future cash flows, based on an appropriate discount rate (k). The discount rate for equities will equal the risk-free rate of return plus a risk premium (as was the case for bonds). This is shown in Equation 7-1 below.

$$k = RF + \text{Risk Premium}$$ [7-1]

where k = the required return on an equity security and RF = the risk-free rate of return.

Recall from Chapter 6 that the risk-free rate comprises the real rate of return plus expected inflation and is often proxied by the return on short-term government T-bills. However, for long-lived investments like common shares, the use of a short-term interest rate often introduces problems, since it is directly affected by the Bank of Canada's monetary policy. To offset this, many analysts use long-term Canada bond yields as the risk-free rate.[1] The risk premium will be based on an estimate of the risk associated with the security; the higher the risk, the higher the risk premium, because investors will require a higher return as compensation. We will discuss the factors affecting the risk premium and methods for estimating a discount rate for equities in chapters 8 and 9.

In addition to determining the discount rate, investors must estimate the size and timing of the expected cash flows associated with an equity security. Making this estimate is straightforward for a bond, because the amount and timing of the coupons and principal repayments are specified in the bond indenture. For equities, this issue is more complex, especially for common shares, as will be discussed shortly. We will first deal with preferred shares because they are easier to value.

CONCEPT REVIEW QUESTIONS

1. How do equity shareholders exert their influence over a company?
2. What are the two main components of the required rate of return on equity securities?

7.2 PREFERRED SHARE VALUATION

As mentioned above, traditional preferred shares have no maturity date and pay dividends of a fixed amount at regular intervals indefinitely, as depicted in Figure 7-1:

Learning Objective 7.2
Explain how to value preferred shares.

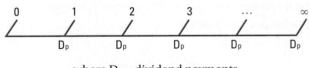

where D_p = dividend payments.

FIGURE 7-1 *The Cash-Flow Pattern for a Straight Preferred Share*

Because the payments are essentially fixed when the preferred shares are issued, such shares are often referred to as fixed income investments, just as bonds are. The payment of a fixed dividend amount at regular intervals indefinitely means we can view these investments as "perpetuities," which were discussed in Chapter 5. The value of preferred shares can be estimated using Equation 7-2, which determines the present value of a perpetuity. P_{ps} is the market price (or present value), D_p is the dividend amount (or payment), and k_p is the required rate of return on the preferred shares (or discount rate).

$$P_{ps} = \frac{D_p}{k_p}$$

[7-2]

---

[1] For example, 91-day treasury bills are only risk free over a 91-day horizon.

The amount of the dividend payments is usually based on a stated par (or face) value and a stated dividend rate, which is similar to the coupon rate on a bond. For example, a preferred share with a par value of $100 and an 8 percent dividend rate would pay an annual dividend of $8 per year. In practice, dividends are paid quarterly; however, for valuation purposes, we will assume they are paid annually.[2] This will not have a big influence on the valuation process because of the long time period involved (i.e., assuming the dividends are paid to infinity).

EXAMPLE 7-1   Determining the Market Price of Preferred Shares

Determine the market price of a $50 par value preferred share that pays annual dividends based on a 7 percent dividend rate when market rates are

a.   7 percent.

b.   8 percent.

c.   6 percent.

Solution

$$D_p = \$50 \times 0.07 = \$3.50$$

$$\text{a.} \quad P_{ps} = \frac{D_p}{k_p} = \frac{\$3.50}{0.07} = \$50$$

$$\text{b.} \quad P_{ps} = \frac{\$3.50}{0.08} = \$43.75$$

$$\text{c.} \quad P_{ps} = \frac{\$3.50}{0.06} = \$58.33$$

Notice that, like bonds, preferred shares will trade at par when the dividend rate equals the market rate, at a discount from par when market rates exceed the dividend rate, and at a premium when market rates are less than the dividend rate. Also note that the market prices of preferred shares increase when market rates decline, and vice versa.

Equation 7-2 can be rearranged to determine the required rate of return on the preferred shares for a given market price, as follows:

[7-3]
$$k_p = \frac{D_p}{P_{ps}}$$

EXAMPLE 7-2   Estimating the Required Rate of Return on Preferred Shares

Determine the required rate of return on preferred shares that provide a $6 annual dividend if they are selling for $70.

Solution

$$k_p = \frac{D_p}{P_{ps}} = \frac{\$6}{\$70} = 8.57\%$$

---

[2] We will also assume annual dividends when valuing common shares, even though they also usually pay quarterly dividends.

7.3 COMMON SHARE VALUATION: THE DIVIDEND DISCOUNT MODEL (DDM)

The Basic Dividend Discount Model

Valuing common shares involves several complications that arise with respect to the appropriate future cash flows that should be discounted. Which cash flows should be discounted? The most popular model for valuing discounted cash flows, which is discussed below, uses dividends. However, unlike bonds or even preferred shares, there is no requirement that common shares pay dividends at all. In addition, the level of dividend payments is also discretionary, which means we must make estimates regarding the amount and timing of any dividend payments.

The **dividend discount model (DDM)** assumes that common shares are valued according to the present value of their expected future cash flows. Based on this premise, today's price can be estimated using Equation 7-4, if we have an *n*-year holding period.

> **Learning Objective 7.3**
> Explain how to value common shares using the dividend discount model.

> **dividend discount model (DDM)**
> a model for valuing common shares that assumes they are valued according to the present value of their expected future dividends

$$P_0 = \frac{D_1}{(1 + k_c)^1} + \frac{D_2}{(1 + k_c)^2} + ... + \frac{D_n + P_n}{(1 + k_c)^n}$$

[7-4]

where P_0 = the estimated share price today

D_1 = the expected dividend at the end of year 1

P_n = the expected share price after *n* years

k_c = the required return on the common shares

Consider Example 7-3, in which the investor plans to hold the stock for one year.

EXAMPLE 7-3   Estimating the Price of a Common Share for a One-Year Holding Period

An investor buys a common share and estimates she will receive an annual dividend of $0.50 per share in one year. She estimates she will be able to sell the share for $10.50. Estimate its value, assuming the investor requires a 10 percent return on this investment.

Solution

$$P_0 = \frac{0.50 + 10.50}{(1 + 0.10)^1} = \$10.00$$

According to the DDM, the selling price at any point (say, time *n*) will equal the present value of all the expected future dividends from period *n* + 1 to infinity. So the price next year, for example, is the present value of the expected dividend and share price for year 2. By repeatedly substituting for the future share price, we replace it with the present value of the dividend and share price expected the following year. As a result, we remove P_n in Equation 7-4 and eventually get the following:

$$[7\text{-}5] \qquad P_0 = \frac{D_1}{(1 + k_e)^1} + \frac{D_2}{(1 + k_e)^2} + \dots + \frac{D_\infty}{(1 + k_e)^\infty} = \sum_{t=1}^{\infty} \frac{D_t}{(1 + k_e)^t}$$

In other words, the price today is the present value of all future dividends to be received (i.e., from now to infinity).

Why use dividends? Well, if investors buy a particular stock, the only cash flows they will receive until they sell the stock will be the dividends. Although a firm's residual earnings technically belong to the common shareholders, corporations generally do not pay out all their earnings as dividends. Another reason is that dividends can only be paid out of earnings (otherwise they are a return of capital), so dividends are a good signal of the long-run earnings of the firm. Of course, it is really the earnings that are important, since without them the corporation could not sustain dividend payments for long. In fact, earnings receive more attention from investors than any other single variable. However, corporations typically re-invest a portion of their earnings to enhance future earnings and, ultimately, future dividends. *Finance in the News 7-1* discusses the importance of dividends to investors, both as a source of income and as a positive signal regarding the company's future prospects. The importance of this positive signal can be seen in the following quotation from this article: "The paying of a dividend reflects tangible evidence of the underlying financial strength of a company."

finance INTHENEWS 7-1 | An Apple Dividend Could Be Sweet Indeed

HOW WILL Apple Inc.'s stock react if the company initiates a dividend? For a clue, look at Starbucks Corp., Cisco Systems Inc., Dollarama Inc., and Lexmark International Inc.

All of these companies initiated a dividend within the past two years, and in each case the stock is higher now than it was when the payment was declared. The gains range from about 13 percent for Lexmark, which announced its first dividend in October, to 91 percent for Starbucks, which initiated a dividend in March 2010.

Not every company that initiates a dividend goes on to post double-digit gains, of course. And there are no guarantees that Apple's high-flying stock will keep rising if—as a growing number of analysts expect—it shells out some of the nearly $100-billion (U.S.) in cash on its balance sheet. But a dividend initiation is often a bullish signal, partly because of what it says about management's outlook and also because it brings new investors into a stock.

"The paying of a dividend reflects tangible evidence of the underlying financial strength of a company," said Charles Carlson, chief executive officer of Horizon Investment Services in Hammond, Ind., and author of *The Little Book of Big Dividends*. "Once a company initiates a dividend, it doesn't want to cut it two quarters later. So there's a confidence factor that the company is going to be able to continue to generate the cash flow needed to support that dividend."

In most cases, investors expect that the company won't just maintain the dividend, but will raise it.

Starbucks, for example, initially paid a quarterly dividend of 10 cents a share. Less than four months later it hiked its dividend by 30 percent, and in November it announced another increase of 31 percent. Starbucks' stock price has followed the dividend higher, richly rewarding investors who jumped in after the first dividend was declared.

The dividend, per se, doesn't necessarily drive the stock up. Rather, it's what the dividend signals about the health of the company and management's growth expectations. Sometimes, it takes a while for the stock to react to the improving fundamentals that a dividend declaration reflects.

"Do the shares react immediately? The answer is, not necessarily," said George Vasic, chief economist and equity strategist at UBS Securities Canada in Toronto. For some companies, such as gold and silver producers, investors don't buy the stock for the dividend, which is typically puny. So a dividend hike usually doesn't have much impact on the share price.

With industrial or consumer-oriented stocks, on the other hand, a dividend initiation could attract income-oriented funds and other investors that otherwise wouldn't be interested in the company. That extra demand pushes up the price.

"Income and dividend funds are seeing all the inflows [of investor cash] for the last several years, and that could be positive in terms of attracting new investors" to a company, Mr. Vasic said.

Shares of Canadian discount retailer Dollarama, for instance, have surged about 35 percent since it initiated a small dividend last June.

Finance in the News 7-1: An Apple Dividend Could Be Sweet Indeed *(continued)*

Fellow Canadian chain Tim Hortons has soared 73 percent since initiating a dividend in 2006, and the company has raised its dividend four times, with a fifth increase expected in February.

Apart from Apple, cash-rich U.S. companies that could initiate a dividend include Google Inc., Berkshire Hathaway Inc., and Amazon.com. Other companies with modest dividend yields, such as Wal-Mart Stores Inc. and Microsoft Corp., are in a position to hike their payments substantially, analysts say.

Consumer advocate Ralph Nader, a Cisco shareholder, has gone public with demands that Cisco reduce share buybacks and instead more than double its quarterly dividend and pay a $1 special dividend.

"Most studies show that company buybacks have not increased shareholder value …" he wrote. "Other data [have] convincingly shown over the last 40 years that dividend-paying stocks are better for share-holder appreciation than non-dividend-paying companies."

With corporate cash at record levels and more investors agitating for companies to share the wealth, dividends are bound to rise in the next few years.

"The payout ratio [dividends as a percentage of profits] in this country is around 30 percent. It historically was between 40 and 50 percent,"

said Daniel Peris, a dividend fund manager at Federated Investors in Pittsburgh and author of *The Strategic Dividend Investor*. "It's been abnormally low and … it really has to go further up."

Some companies are getting the message. On Tuesday, toy giant Mattel Inc. boosted its quarterly dividend by 35 percent after reporting fourth-quarter profit that beat Wall Street estimates.

Still, not everyone is convinced Apple will initiate a regular quarterly dividend. Mr. Carlson thinks the company might start with a special one-time dividend of about 1 percent, or $4 to $5 a share. That would placate investors who want the company to give back some of its cash, but would give Apple greater flexibility than if it started a regular quarterly payment.

It's more likely that Google, which is coming off a disappointing quarter, will initiate a regular dividend in an attempt to boost its sagging stock price, he said.

Google "may be at a point where they may be looking to broaden the buyer market for their stock, more so than Apple," Mr. Carlson said. "Apple stock certainly hasn't been penalized at all by not offering a dividend."

Equation 7-5 is the workhorse of share valuation because it says that the value of a share is the present value of expected future dividends. However, by repeatedly substituting for the share price, we are implicitly making a very important assumption: that investors are rational. We assume that, at each point, investors react rationally and value the share based on what they rationally expect to receive the next year. This assumption specifically rules out "speculative bubbles," which illustrate what is colloquially known as the "bigger fool theorem."

Suppose, for example, a broker tells a client to buy XYZ at $30. The investor refuses because the stock is only worth $25. The broker replies, "I know, but there is momentum behind it and I am seeing a lot of interest. I think it will go to $40 by next year." The investor is a fool to pay $30 for something she thinks is worth $25, but it is not the fool theorem but the bigger fool theorem. If the investor does buy it, she is a fool, but she is also assuming that an even bigger fool will buy it in a year's time for $40.

This type of speculative bubble, in which prices keep increasing and become detached from reality, is specifically ruled out by the assumption of rational investors coolly calculating the present value of the expected cash flows each year, so that prices never get detached from these fundamentals. Of course, there have been speculative bubbles when it has been very difficult to estimate these fundamental values. In Appendix 7A, we review the famous bubble involving the South Sea Company in 1720, when Sir Isaac Newton almost bankrupted himself and then proclaimed, "I can calculate the motions of the heavenly bodies, but not the madness of people." The madness of people was what caused the share price of the South Sea Company to become completely detached from its fundamentals. The Internet bubble of the late 1990s, in which the price of shares in Nortel Networks Corporation rose from $20 to $122 and then fell back to less than $2, indicates that the madness of people may not have changed much in almost 300 years. However, it is difficult to build pricing models based on irrationality, so we will continue with the development of models based on fundamental cash flows.

The Constant Growth DDM

Obviously, it is impractical to estimate and discount *all* future dividends one by one, as required by Equation 7-5. Fortunately, this equation can be simplified into a usable formula by assuming that dividends grow at a constant rate (g) indefinitely. We can then estimate all future dividends, assuming we know the most recent dividend paid (D_0).

$$D_1 = D_0(1+g)$$

$$D_2 = D_1(1+g) = D_0(1+g)^2$$

$$D_3 = D_2(1+g) = D_0(1+g)^3$$

and so on.

Therefore, assuming constant growth in dividends to infinity, Equation 7-5 reduces to the following expression:

[7-6]
$$P_0 = \frac{D_0(1+g)^1}{(1+k_c)^1} + \frac{D_0(1+g)^2}{(1+k_c)^2} + \dots + \frac{D_0(1+g)^\infty}{(1+k_c)^\infty}$$

constant growth DDM a version of the dividend discount model for valuing common shares, which assumes that dividends grow at a constant rate indefinitely

In Equation 7-6 we are multiplying D_0 by a factor of $(1+g)/(1+k_c)$ every period. This represents a "growing perpetuity," which is easily solved because it represents the sum of a geometric series. In fact, Equation 7-6 reduces to the following expression, which is the constant growth version of the DDM, or simply the **constant growth DDM:**

[7-7]
$$P_0 = \frac{D_0(1+g)}{k_c - g} = \frac{D_1}{k_c - g}$$

There are several important points to note about Equation 7-7.

1. This relationship holds only when k_c is greater than g. Otherwise, the value is negative, which is uninformative.[3]

2. Only *future* estimated cash flows and estimated growth in these cash flows are relevant.

3. The relationship holds only when growth in dividends is expected to occur at the same rate indefinitely.

EXAMPLE 7-4 Using the Constant Growth DDM

Assume a company is currently paying $1.10 per share in dividends. Investors expect dividends to grow at an annual rate of 4 percent indefinitely, and they require a 10 percent return on the shares. Determine the price of these shares.

Solution

$$D_1 = (\$1.10)(1 + 0.04) = \$1.144$$

$$P_0 = \frac{D_1}{k_c - g} = \frac{\$1.144}{0.10 - 0.04} = \$19.07$$

---

[3] The negative answer occurs because if g is greater than k_c in Equation 7-6, each future dividend is worth more in today's terms than the previous one. The value never converges but increases to infinity.

Estimating the Required Rate of Return

The constant growth DDM can be rearranged as Equation 7-8 to obtain an estimate of the rate of return required by investors on a particular share.

$$k_c = \frac{D_1}{P_0} + g \qquad [7\text{-}8]$$

The first term (D_1/P_0) in Equation 7-8 represents the expected dividend yield on the share, which we discussed in Chapter 4. Therefore, we may view the second term, g, as the expected capital gains yield, because the total return must equal the dividend yield plus the capital gains yield. It is important to recognize that this equation provides an appropriate estimate for required return *only* if the conditions of the constant growth DDM are met (i.e., in particular, the assumption regarding constant growth in dividends to infinity must be satisfied).

EXAMPLE 7-5   **Estimating the Required Rate of Return Using the DDM**

The market price of a company's shares is $12 each; the estimated dividend at the end of this year (D_1) is $0.60; and the estimated long-term growth rate in dividends (g) is 4 percent. Estimate the implied required rate of return on these shares.

Solution

$$k_c = \frac{D_1}{P_0} + g = \frac{0.60}{12} + 0.04 = 0.05 + 0.04 = 0.09 = 9\%$$

The result in Example 7-5 suggests that the expected return on these shares comprises an expected dividend yield of 5 percent and an expected capital gains yield of 4 percent.

Estimating the Value of Growth Opportunities

The constant growth DDM can also provide a useful assessment of the market's perception of growth opportunities available to a company, as reflected in its market price. Let's begin by assuming that a firm with no profitable growth opportunities should not reinvest residual profits in the company, but rather should pay out all its earnings as dividends. Under these conditions, we have $g = 0$ and $D_1 = EPS_1$, where EPS_1 represents the expected earnings per common share in the upcoming year. Given these assumptions, the constant growth DDM reduces to the following expression:

$$P_0 = \frac{EPS_1}{k_c} \qquad [7\text{-}9]$$

We are not likely to find a company that has exactly "zero" growth opportunities, but the point is that we can assume the share price of any common stock that satisfies the assumptions of the constant growth DDM will be made up of two components: its no-growth component and the remainder, which is attributable to the market's perception of the growth opportunities available to that company. We denote this as the present value of growth opportunities (*PVGO*). These growth opportunities will generally represent a company's ability to generate substantial growth in future profits and cash flows. This growth may be attributable to several factors, including the prospects for its industry, its competitive position within that industry, the value of its "brand" name, and its long-term investment and research and development programs. We will discuss these issues in greater detail throughout the text, and in chapters 13, 14, and 20 in particular.

Taking into account *PVGO*, we get Equation 7-10.

[7-10]
$$P_0 = \frac{EPS_1}{k_c} + PVGO$$

EXAMPLE 7-6   Estimating PVGO

A company's shares are selling for $20 each in the market. The company's EPS is expected to be $1.50 next year, and the required return on the shares is estimated to be 10 percent. Estimate the *PVGO* per share.

Solution

This can be solved by rearranging Equation 7-10 to solve for *PVGO*:

$$PVGO = P_0 - \frac{EPS_1}{k_c} = \$20 - \frac{1.50}{0.10} = \$20 - \$15 = \$5$$

Examining the Inputs of the Constant Growth DDM

From Equation 7-7, we can see that the constant growth DDM predicts that, all else remaining equal, the price of common shares (P_0) will *increase* as a result of

1. an increase in D_1

2. an increase in g

3. a decrease in k_c

This list illustrates the intuitive appeal of the DDM. It links common share prices to three important fundamentals: corporate profitability, the general level of interest rates, and risk. In particular, expected dividends are closely related to profitability, as is the growth rate of these dividends, while the required rate of return is affected by the base level of interest rates (RF) and by risk (as reflected in the risk premium required by investors). In particular, *all else being equal*, the DDM predicts that common share prices will be higher when profits are high (and expected to grow), when interest rates are lower, and when risk premiums are lower.

Finance in the News 7-2 alludes to two of these fundamentals as they pertain to Tim Hortons. The excerpt discusses the favourable responses of analysts to Tim Hortons' announcement of earnings that exceeded expectations (which increases growth expectations). It also discusses the favourable light shed on Tim Hortons' decision to share its good fortune with investors in the form of increased dividends and share repurchases. *Finance in the News 7-3* examines the critical impact of central banks on stock markets through their influence on interest rates, which in turn affects the risk premium. Indeed, the role that governments played in capital markets after 2008 is in many ways unprecedented.

---

finance INTHENEWS 7-2   Tim Hortons Inc.— Growth and Income

TIM HORTONS Inc. announced a lot of good news for investors on February 23. It (1) reported better than expected fourth quarter results, (2) announced a $200 million stock buyback, and (3) increased its dividend by 24%.

This prompted analysts to revise their estimates higher for both 2012 and 2013. It is a Zacks #2 Rank (Buy) stock.

Finance in the News 7-2: Tim Hortons Inc.—Growth and Income *(continued)*

Fourth Quarter Results

Tim Hortons delivered strong fourth quarter results on February 23. Earnings per share came in at 65 cents, beating the Zacks Consensus Estimate of 61 cents. It was a stellar 25% increase over the same quarter in 2010.

Total revenues surged 21% to $779.8 million, well ahead of the Zacks Consensus Estimate of $726.0 million. This was driven by a solid 5.5% increase in same-store sales in Canada and a 7.2% increase in the U.S.

Adjusted operating income was up 15% year-over-year as the company was able to somewhat offset higher commodity costs with operating leverage.

Estimates Rising

Analysts have revised their earnings estimates significantly higher following Tim Hortons' solid Q4 results. It is a Zacks #2 Rank (Buy) stock.

The Zacks Consensus Estimate for 2012 is now $2.74, representing 14% EPS growth over 2011. The 2013 consensus estimate is currently $3.08, corresponding with 13% growth.

Analysts expect the company's solid same-store sales momentum to continue in the near future. This, along with the company's plans to eventually expand to 4,000 stores in Canada, should drive double-digit earnings growth over the foreseeable future.

Returning Value to Shareholders

Management has also made a couple of shareholder-friendly moves lately. It announced on February 23 that it will repurchase up to $200 million worth of shares (representing about 10% of the company's float).

It also announced on that day that it was raising its quarterly dividend by 24% to 21 cents per share. It yields a solid 1.6%.

The company has a target payout ratio of 30-35% of net income, so as long as EPS continues to grow, expect more dividend increases down the road.

Valuation

Although shares of THI don't look cheap, the valuation picture still looks reasonable. The stock trades at 18.9 x 12-month forward earnings, in-line with its historical median. And it sports a PEG ratio of 1.4 based on a consensus 5-year EPS growth ratio of 13.5%.

The Bottom Line

With rising earnings estimates, strong growth projections and shareholder-friendly management, Tim Hortons offers investors a lot to like.

Source: Bunton, Todd, "Growth and income: Tim Hortons Inc." Zacks.com, March 8, 2012. Avaliable at www.zacks.com.

---

finance INTHENEWS 7-3 Markets Overly Dependent on Central Banks

FOR MUCH of the past three years, the world's stock markets have relied on central bankers the way junkies rely on drug dealers. The question now is whether the next fix will come—and what will happen if the markets are forced to go cold turkey.

More than any other single factor, the recovery in equities has been fuelled by the largesse of the world's leading central banks, especially the U.S. Federal Reserve Board, as those key financial institutions have expanded their balance sheets to prime the struggling global financial system and keep money flowing.

From the Fed's initial ramp-up of quantitative easing (now known as QE1) that revived stocks from the depths of the bear market in March, 2009, to the launch of the European Central Bank's long-term refinancing operation (LTRO) last December, equities climbed higher each time central banks poured new cash into the financial system.

Last week, rumblings that the Fed is looking into another round of quantitative easing (which would be QE3, for those keeping score) underpinned another strong gain for stocks—despite the fact that the Fed is highly unlikely to announce any such moves at Tuesday's policy-setting meeting.

"The key catalyst for the equity rally, in our view, was global central bank easing," said Barry Knapp, head of U.S. portfolio strategy at Barclays Capital in New York, in a recent research note. "It served to mitigate (for now) the two most significant external risks to U.S. equities: European bank deleveraging and slowing emerging markets' growth.

Any sign the spigot might be closing could prove disruptive."

Balance-sheet expansions by central banks affect stock prices by shifting the equity risk premium (ERP)—the difference between the earnings yield on stocks (annual earnings per share as a percentage of stock price) and the yield on government bonds. This reflects the higher returns that investors demand from equities to compensate them for the perceived risk in these investments relative to the near-zero risk of a stable government bond (the 10-year U.S. Treasury is a typical benchmark). When the ERP falls, that pushes stock valuations higher and vice-versa.

Mr. Knapp found that since the financial crisis began, ERFs have consistently declined during each new Fed program of balance-sheet expansion (QE1, QE2 and the so-called Operation Twist). The resulting rise in price-to-earnings multiples fuelled stock-market rallies each time.

Similarly, research by Montreal-based BCA Research Inc. found that lower interest rates—the typical result of central-bank monetary easing, whether it be balance-sheet expansions or more traditional cuts in policy rates—have long been closely linked to lower ERPs. In the past decade, global equities have twice staged rallies that more than doubled their prices after global central banks reached extreme levels of easing; those same conditions are in place again this year.

"Expansive monetary policy almost always eases equity multiple compression, allowing stock prices to rise," BCA said in a report last week. "With virtually all central banks in easing mode, and in the

continued

Finance in the News 7-3: Markets Overly Dependent on Central Banks *(continued)*

absence of negative exogenous shocks, the tendency will be for stocks to rise."

Indeed, the stock market actually seemed disappointed in late February when Fed chairman Ben Bernanke, in his semi-annual report to Congress, sounded more positive about the economy—because, presumably, that implies no more QE is coming down the pipe.

"The fact that this reaction was mostly negative points to a surprising fragility in the prices of risk assets," said Capital Economics chief international economist Julian Jessop in a note to clients. "If equity investors are banking both on stronger economic growth and further monetary easing to support current valuations, they are almost certain to be disappointed."

We can usually assume that current dividends (D_0) are given, so it is the movements in k_c and g that determine the price of a share (i.e., because $k_c - g$ is the denominator, and because $D_0[1 + g]$ is the numerator). In fact, given the long period involved in the discount process (i.e., to infinity), price estimates are very sensitive to these inputs, as illustrated in Example 7-7 and Example 7-8.

EXAMPLE 7-7 More Pessimistic Inputs of the Constant Growth DDM

Revisit the company in Example 7-4 that is currently paying $1.10 per share in dividends. This time, revise the expectations for annual growth in dividends to 3 percent (from 4 percent) and revise the estimated required rate of return to 11 percent (from 10 percent). Re-estimate the price of these shares.

Solution

$$D_1 = (\$1.10)(1 + 0.03) = \$1.133$$

$$P_0 = \frac{D_1}{k_c - g} = \frac{\$1.133}{0.11 - 0.03} = \$14.16$$

Notice the substantial drop in price (i.e., 25.7 percent, from $19.07 to $14.16) that results when we increase the discount rate from 10 percent to 11 percent and lower the growth rate from 4 percent to 3 percent (which are both bad things for stock prices). Similarly, Example 7-8 illustrates the large price increase that results from the use of improved estimates for these inputs.

EXAMPLE 7-8 More Optimistic Inputs of the Constant Growth DDM

Redo Example 7-7 by assuming annual growth in dividends is 5 percent and the required rate of return is 9 percent.

Solution

$$D_1 = (\$1.10)(1 + 0.05) = \$1.155$$

$$P_0 = \frac{D_1}{k_c - g} = \frac{\$1.155}{0.09 - 0.05} = \$28.88$$

In this case, the price estimate is 51.4 percent higher than the original estimate of $19.07, yet we only changed each of our inputs by 1 percentage point. Obviously, we need to be careful when determining these inputs, which are in fact merely estimates.

Estimating DDM Inputs

Estimating the inputs into the constant growth DDM generally requires a great deal of analysis and judgement. Assuming we know the most recent year's dividend payment (D_0), we need to estimate g because $D_1 = D_0(1 + g)$. As discussed earlier, the discount rate for equities will equal the risk-free rate of return plus a risk premium, as depicted in Equation 7-1. We defer further discussion of estimating the discount rate for equities to chapters 8 and 9.

Several methods can be used to estimate the expected annual growth rate in dividends (g). One of the most common approaches is to determine the company's **sustainable growth rate,** which can be estimated by multiplying the earnings retention ratio by the return on equity, as shown in Equation 7-11:

sustainable growth rate the earnings retention ratio multiplied by return on equity

$$g = b \times \text{ROE}$$
[7-11]

where b = the firm's earnings retention ratio = 1 – firm's dividend payout ratio; and ROE = the firm's return on common equity = net profit/common equity (as defined in Chapter 4).

Growth in earnings (and dividends) will be positively related to the proportion of each dollar of earnings reinvested in the company (b) multiplied by the return earned on those reinvested funds, which we measure using ROE. For example, a firm that retains all its earnings and earns 10 percent on its equity would see its equity base grow by 10 percent per year. If the same firm paid out all of its earnings, it would not grow. Similarly, a firm that retained a portion (b) of its earnings would earn 10 percent on that portion, resulting in $g = b \times \text{ROE}$.[4]

EXAMPLE 7-9   Estimating a Firm's Sustainable Growth Rate

A firm has an ROE of 12 percent, and its dividend payout ratio is 30 percent. Use this information to determine the firm's sustainable growth rate.

Solution

$$g = b \times \text{ROE} = (1 - 0.3) \times (0.12) = (0.7) \times (0.12) = 0.084 = 8.4\%$$

Recall from Chapter 4 that we can use the DuPont system to decompose ROE into three factors, as shown in Equation 7-12.

$$
\begin{aligned}
\text{ROE} &= \text{(Net income/Sales)} \times \text{(Sales/Total assets)} \times \text{(Total assets/equity)} \\
&= \text{Net profit margin} \times \text{Turnover ratio} \times \text{Leverage ratio}
\end{aligned}
$$
[7-12]

The ROE, and hence g, increases with higher profit margins, higher asset turnover, and higher debt (although higher debt implies higher risk and, therefore, higher k_c).

EXAMPLE 7-10   Estimating a Firm's Sustainable Growth Rate Using the DuPont System

A company just paid an annual dividend of $1.00 per share and had an EPS of $4.00 per share. Its projected values for net profit margin, turnover ratio, and leverage ratio are 4 percent, 1.25, and 1.40, respectively. Determine the firm's sustainable growth rate.

continued

---

[4] A major weakness of this approach is its reliance on accounting figures to determine ROE, because it is based on book values and the accrual method of accounting. As a result, it may not represent the "true" return earned on reinvested funds.

EXAMPLE 7-10	Estimating a Firm's Sustainable Growth Rate Using the DuPont System *(continued)*

Solution

$$ROE = (0.04)(1.25)(1.4) = 0.07 = 7\%$$

$$\text{Payout ratio} = DPS/EPS = \$1/\$4 = 0.25, \text{ so } b = 1 - 0.25 = 0.75$$

$$g = b \times ROE = (0.75)(7\%) = 5.25\%$$

Another method of estimating g is to examine historical rates of growth in dividends and earnings levels, including long-term trends in these growth rates for the company, the industry, and the economy as a whole. Predictions regarding future growth rates can be determined based on these past trends by using arithmetic or geometric averages, or by using more involved statistical techniques, such as regression analysis. Finally, an important source of information regarding company growth, particularly for the near term, can be found in analyst estimates. Investors are often especially interested in "consensus" estimates, because market values are often based to a large extent on these estimates. However, a word of caution is in order: analysts have been shown to be biased—that is, they tend to be overly optimistic—in part because their major source of information is frequently the company itself. Research by Easton and Sommers has put the "optimism" bias in analysts' growth forecasts at an average of 2.84 percent.[5] As a result, analyst forecasts tend to be used with the two-stage growth model (discussed in the next section) to mitigate this optimism.

It is important to remember, when applying any of these approaches, that "future" growth is being estimated, and the inputs require judgement on the part of the analyst. If researchers believe past growth will be repeated in the future, or if they want to eliminate period-to-period fluctuations in b and ROE, they may choose to use three- to five-year averages for these variables. Conversely, if the company has changed substantially, or if analysts have good reason to believe the ratios for the most recent year are the best indicators of future sustainable growth, they will use these figures. In addition, an analysis of macroeconomic, industry-specific, and company-specific factors may lead researchers to develop predicted values for these variables independent of their historical levels.

The Multiple-Stage Growth Version of the DDM

The constant growth DDM relationship holds only when we are able to assume constant growth in dividends from now to infinity. In many situations, it may be more appropriate to estimate dividends for the most immediate periods up to some point (t), after which it is assumed there will be constant growth in dividends to infinity. Several situations lend themselves to this structure. For example, it is reasonable to assume that competitive pressures and business-cycle influences will prevent firms from maintaining extremely high growth in earnings for long periods. In addition, short-term earnings and dividend estimates should be much more reliable than those covering a longer period, which are often calculated using very general estimates of future economic, industry, and company conditions. To use the best information available at any point, it may make the most sense to estimate growth as precisely as possible in the short term before assuming some long-term rate of growth.

Equation 7-13 can be applied when steady growth in dividends to infinity does not begin until period t:

[7-13]
$$P_0 = \frac{D_1}{(1 + k_e)^1} + \frac{D_2}{(1 + k_e)^2} + \ldots + \frac{D_t + P_t}{(1 + k_e)^t}$$

---

[5] Easton, Peter D., and Gregory A. Sommers, "Effect of analysts' optimism on estimates of the expected rate of return implied by earnings forecasts," *Journal of Accounting Research* 45, no. 5 (December 2007), pp. 983–1016.

where $P_t = \dfrac{D_{t+1}}{k_c - g}$

Notice that this is Equation 7-4, with n replaced by t and with an estimate for P_t. Figure 7-2 depicts the cash flows associated with this type of valuation framework.

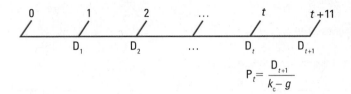

FIGURE 7-2 *The Cash Flow Pattern for Multiple-Stage Growth in Dividends*

Essentially, whenever we use multiple-period growth rates, we estimate dividends up to the beginning of the period in which it is reasonable to assume constant growth to infinity. Then we can use the constant growth DDM to estimate the market price of the share at that time (P_t). Finally, we discount all the estimated dividends up to the beginning of the constant growth period, as well as the estimated market price at that time.[6] This provides us with today's estimate of the share's market price.

EXAMPLE 7-11 Using the Multi-Stage DDM

A company is expected to pay a dividend of $1.00 at the end of this year, a $1.50 dividend at the end of year 2, and a $2.00 dividend at the end of year 3. It is estimated dividends will grow at a constant rate of 4 percent per year thereafter. Determine the market price of this company's common shares if the required rate of return is 11 percent.

Solution

First, estimate dividends up to the start of constant growth to infinity. In this example, they are all given, so no calculations are required:

$D_1 = \$1.00$

$D_2 = \$1.50$

$D_3 = \$2.00$

Second, estimate the price at the beginning of the constant growth to infinity period:

$$D_4 = (\$2.00)(1 + 0.04) = \$2.08$$

$$P_3 = \frac{D_4}{k_c - g} = \frac{\$2.08}{0.11 - 0.04} = \$29.71$$

Third, discount back the relevant cash flows to time 0:

$$P_0 = \frac{1.00}{(1 + 0.11)} + \frac{1.50}{(1 + 0.11)^2} + \frac{2.00 + 29.71}{(1 + 0.11)^3} = 0.90 + 1.22 + 23.19 = \$25.31$$

---

[6] Recall that P_t represents the present value of all the expected dividends from time $t + 1$ to infinity, so we are essentially discounting *all* the expected future dividends associated with the stock.

(TI BA II PLUS)

EXAMPLE 7-11   Solution Using a Financial Calculator

Input the following variables:

(D_1) **PV** : **N** → 1; **I/Y** → 11%; **PMT** → 0; **FV** → −1.00; **CPT** **PV** gives 0.90

(D_2) **PV** : **N** → 2; **I/Y** → 11%; **PMT** → 0; **FV** → −1.50; **CPT** **PV** gives 1.22

$(D_3 + P_3)$ **PV** : **N** → 3; **I/Y** → 11%; **PMT** → 0; **FV** → −31.71; (i.e., 2 + 29.71);

CPT **PV** gives 23.19

Then we add these figures to get $25.31, as above.

A well-known version of the multiple-growth DDM is the two-stage growth rate model, which assumes growth at one rate for a certain period, followed by a steady growth rate to infinity. This is illustrated in Example 7-12.

EXAMPLE 7-12   Two-Stage Dividend Growth

A company just paid a dividend of $2.00 per share. An investor estimates that dividends will grow at 10 percent per year for the next two years and then grow at an annual rate of 5 percent to infinity. Determine the market price of this company's common shares if the required rate of return is 12 percent.

Solution

First, estimate dividends up to the start of constant growth to infinity. In this example, we use the first-period growth rate of 10 percent:

$D_1 = (\$2.00)(1.1) = \$2.20$

$D_2 = (\$2.20)(1.1) = \$2.42$

Second, estimate the price at the beginning of the constant growth to infinity period:

$D_3 = (\$2.42)(1 + 0.05) = \$2.541$

$$P_2 = \frac{D_3}{k_c - g} = \frac{\$2.541}{0.12 - 0.05} = \$36.30$$

Third, discount the relevant cash flows back to time 0:

$$P_0 = \frac{2.20}{(1.12)^1} + \frac{2.42 + 36.30}{(1.12)^2} = 1.96 + 30.87 = \$32.83$$

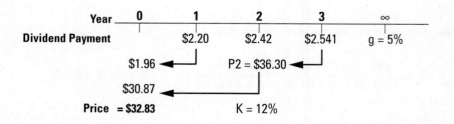

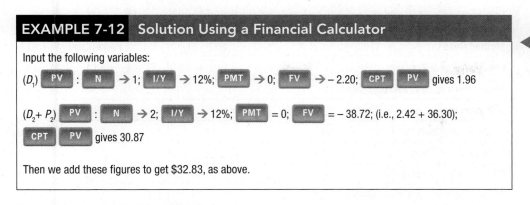

EXAMPLE 7-12 Solution Using a Financial Calculator

Input the following variables:

(D_1) **PV** : **N** → 1; **I/Y** → 12%; **PMT** → 0; **FV** → − 2.20; **CPT** **PV** gives 1.96

$(D_2 + P_2)$ **PV** : **N** → 2; **I/Y** → 12%; **PMT** = 0; **FV** = − 38.72; (i.e., 2.42 + 36.30);
CPT **PV** gives 30.87

Then we add these figures to get $32.83, as above.

(TI BA II PLUS)

Limitations of the DDM

Although the DDM provides significant insight into the factors that affect the valuation of common shares, it is based on several assumptions that are not met by a large number of firms, especially in Canada. In particular, it is best suited for companies that (1) pay dividends based on a stable dividend-payout history that they want to maintain in the future, and (2) are growing at a steady and sustainable rate. As such, the DDM works reasonably well for large corporations in mature industries with stable profits and an established dividend policy. In Canada, the banks and utility companies fit this profile, while in the United States, there are numerous NYSE-listed companies of this nature. Not surprisingly, the DDM does not work well and/or is difficult to apply for many resource-based companies, which are cyclical in nature and often display erratic growth in earnings and dividends. Many of these companies (especially the smaller ones) do not distribute much in the way of profits to shareholders as dividends. The model will also not work well for firms in distress, firms that are in the process of restructuring, firms involved in acquisitions, and private firms. Finally, if a company enters into substantial share-repurchase arrangements, the model will require adjustments, because share repurchases also represent a method of distributing wealth to shareholders.

Due to the limitations of the DDM discussed above, and because common share valuation is a challenging process, involving, as it does, predictions for the future, analysts often use several approaches to value common shares. This is evident from the survey results reported in Table 7-1. The study surveyed the percentage of analysts who use a particular share valuation method, and the fact that the percentages far exceed 100 percent suggests that most analysts use several methods.

In addition to the DDM and the relative valuation approaches discussed in the next section, another discounted cash flow approach—the free cash flow approach—is used frequently, which is obvious from Table 7-1. The free cash flow approach is implemented almost identically to the DDM, except that instead of discounting estimated future dividends, you discount expected future free cash flows. The underlying rationale is that dividends are discretionary, and many firms may choose not to pay out the amount of dividends they could. Therefore, instead of using dividends, you use free cash flow, which is in some sense a measure of what a firm could pay out if it chose, after taking account of expenses, changes in net working capital, and capital expenditures. We will not discuss this model in detail but would note that there are two variations of this approach: (1) using free cash flows to equity holders and discounting them using the required return to equity holders (as in the DDM), and (2) using free cash flows to the firm and discounting them using the firm's weighted average cost of capital (which will be discussed in Chapter 20).[7] This approach is often more appropriate when firms do not pay out a significant portion of their earnings as dividends or pay out well below their capacity.

---

[7] Free cash flow available to equity holders can be estimated as Net income + Depreciation and Amortization + Deferred taxes − Capital spending +/− Change in net working capital − Principal repayments + New external debt financing. Free cash flow to the firm can be estimated as Net income + Depreciation and Amortization + Deferred taxes − Capital spending +/− Change in net working capital + Interest expense × (1 − Tax rate).

TABLE 7-1 Common Share Valuation Approaches

Method Used	Percentage
Price-earnings (P/E) approach	88.1
Discounted free cash flow approach	86.8
Enterprise value multiple approach	76.7
Price-to-book-value approach	59.0
Price-to-cash-flow approach	57.2
Price-to-sales approach	40.3
Dividend-to-price or price-to-dividend approaches	35.5
Dividend discount model approach	35.1

Source: Model Selection from "Valuation Methods" presentation, October 2007, produced by Tom Robinson, Ph.D., CFA, CPA, CFP®, Head, Educational Content, CFA Institute. Copyright 2007, CFA Institute. Reproduced and republished with permission from CFA Institute. All rights reserved.[8]

CONCEPT REVIEW QUESTIONS

1. Why is share value based on the present value of expected future dividends?
2. What is the "bigger fool theorem" of valuation?
3. Why does an increase in the expected dividend growth rate increase share prices?
4. Why can't the expected growth rate exceed the investor's required return in the constant growth model?
5. How can we estimate future growth rates?

7.4 USING MULTIPLES TO VALUE SHARES

The Basic Approach

Learning Objective 7.4
Explain how to value common shares using the price-earnings (P/E) ratio.

Relative valuation approaches determine the value of common shares by comparing the market prices of similar companies relative to some common variable, such as earnings, cash flow, book value, or sales. Conceptually, these approaches are relatively simple to apply: all we need to do is find a group of comparable firms and then use their financial data and market values to infer the value of the firm in question. However, finding comparable firms is difficult: what firm is similar to Microsoft, for example? Even after we find a group of comparable firms, we have to estimate the appropriate multiple because values will differ even for comparable firms, so the exercise involves substantial analysis and judgement. We will illustrate the approach by using the most commonly used relative valuation multiple: the **price-earnings (P/E) ratio**. In the first edition of *Security Analysis* (1934), Benjamin Graham and David L. Dodd described common stock valuation based on price-earnings ratios as the standard method of that era. Table 7-1 suggests that, over 70 years later, the P/E ratio is still the most familiar valuation measure. Recall that the P/E ratio, which was introduced in Chapter 4, represents the number of times investors are willing to pay for a company's earnings, as expressed in the share price, or the share price divided by the earnings per share. The P/E approach is implemented by estimating the firm's earnings per share (EPS) and multiplying that figure by an appropriate (or justifiable) P/E multiple. The typical P/E formulation uses

price-earnings (P/E) ratio the share price divided by the earnings per share; the most commonly used relative valuation multiple

---

[8] The results are based on a survey of about 13,500 CFA Institute members, 2,369 of whom accepted the invitation. Of those surveyed, 2,063 evaluate individual securities in order to make an investment recommendation or portfolio decision. They are primarily buy-side investment analysts and portfolio managers. For those managing portfolios, the sample was split fairly equally between members managing institutional and individual (private wealth) portfolios.

estimated earnings per share (EPS$_1$) for the next 12 months. The basic valuation equation can then be expressed as shown in Equation 7-14.

$$P_0 = \text{Estimated EPS}_1 \times \text{Justified P/E ratio} = \text{EPS}_1 \times P_0/E_1 \qquad [7\text{-}14]$$

Notice that the P/E ratio used in Equation 7-14 differs from the one we discussed in Chapter 4. This one is based on expected future earnings (EPS$_1$) and is called the "leading P/E ratio." By comparison, when we analyze financial ratios, the reported P/E ratios are based on earnings over the previous 12 months (EPS$_0$), which are called "lagging P/E ratios." For valuation purposes, we typically focus on the leading P/E ratio because market values are based on expectations about the future.

Using the P/E ratio is easy: if the firm's forecast earnings per share are $2 and the P/E ratio for comparable firms is 20X, then the P/E approach would say that a fair share price is $40. We can see from this example why this approach is also called "using multiples." In this case, the multiple of earnings is 20X. What this means is that if this level of earnings stays constant, it will take 20 years to earn back the price of the shares. In this sense, the multiple is an example of a payback period. The higher the multiple, the longer the payback period and the more the investor is expecting earnings to increase. Alternatively, it could be that the shares are simply more expensive shares.

We can also see why the approach is commonly called **relative valuation**: we are valuing the firm relative to other comparable firms. This means that if the comparable firms are all overvalued, then using the P/E approach will overvalue the firm in question. If the market is in a speculative bubble, the P/E approach will not detect it directly. In that case, what we need is some yardstick or benchmark P/E. We can approximate this by looking at the P/E ratio for the S&P/TSX Composite Index, which is shown in Figure 7-3.

relative valuation valuing a firm relative to other comparable firms

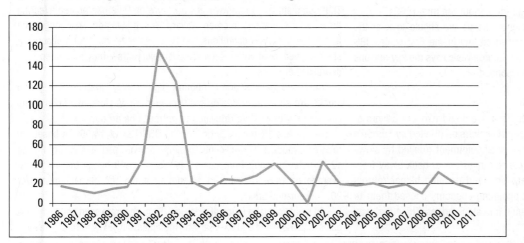

FIGURE 7-3 *S&P/TSX Composite P/E*

The P/E in Figure 7-3 is based on trailing or lagging earnings for the firms in the S&P/TSX Composite Index. It vividly demonstrates the problems with the P/E ratio: very low earnings cause the value of the P/E to skyrocket. Despite the fact that the P/E is based on up to 300 companies, these problems are not minimal. In the early 1990s, Canada experienced a severe recession as a result of high interest rates as well as the costs of adjusting to free trade with the United States, and many Canadian companies incurred large losses. Earnings for corporate Canada almost disappeared, causing the P/E to increase dramatically. For this reason, the P/E is often set at a maximum of 100. In fact, during the slowdown in 2002, after the Internet bubble was punctured, two Canadian companies, Nortel and JDS Uniphase Canada Ltd., lost so much money that the overall earnings of the firms in the TSX Index were not just low but were actually negative.[9]

---

[9] Most of the losses were due to writing off the value of investments in other firms that no longer had any value.

When we take these problems into account, we can see that, typically, the P/E is 15X to 20X. In fact, the median value over the 1986 to 2011 period was 19.72.[10] When P/E ratios fall below 15X, we tend to think the stock market is undervalued; when the P/E creeps above 20X, we take it as a warning signal that equities are overvalued. At the time of writing, in March 2012, the P/E ratio for the S&P/TSX Index was slightly below this lower threshold, sitting at 14.92.

The P/E ratio is an attractive (and commonly reported) statistic for investors and analysts for several reasons. First, it relates the price to the earnings owned by the shareholders. Second, it is easy to compute and, as a result, is commonly available. This makes comparisons relatively straightforward. Third, it is intuitive, as it indicates the payback period and can be related to a number of other firm characteristics, such as growth opportunities and risk. The common usage of these ratios, and their relationship to growth opportunities and risk, is illustrated in *Finance in the News 7-4*. For example, the article suggest two factors driving low P/E ratios are increased "risk aversion," and "slowing global growth."

finance INTHENEWS 7-4   Maybe It's Time for a Dash of Rational Exuberance

AS STOCK VALUATIONS slumped in the past year, market pundits debated whether we had any more room to beat them down further. Perhaps a better question is whether we have any more excuses.

The S&P/TSX composite index is priced at a little more than 12 times its estimated earnings per share for the next 12 months (its "forward price-to-earnings" ratio)—a valuation that, while low compared with the market's historical average, is not wildly outside the range of normal. P/Es fell below eight in the depths of the 2008 financial crisis. Even in less unusual circumstances, the current P/E levels aren't unheard of—P/Es were in the 11 to 13 range throughout the mid-1990s.

But rather than look at precedents, maybe we should look at the reasons P/E multiples have been driven so low in the first place. UBS Securities Canada Inc. equity strategist George Vasic says the key reasons have eased—but P/Es haven't yet responded.

The Pressures Subside

In a research report this week, Mr. Vasic identified two key drivers of the decline in P/Es over the past year: risk aversion (fuelled by Europe's sovereign debt crisis) and economic disappointment (fuelled by slowing global growth). Risk aversion caused investors to back away from so-called "risk assets" such as equities, and demand higher returns in exchange for volatility; the disappointing economy caused them to question the growth assumptions built into stock prices. The effect was to drive valuations lower.

But now, Mr. Vasic said, both the risk pressures and the economic disappointments have abated. UBS's global equity risk indicator has returned to historically normal levels, while the VIX index—a measure of volatility in U.S. stocks, usually equated with investors' fear levels—has retreated to an 18-month low, and below its long-term average. Meanwhile, UBS's global growth surprise index has turned decidedly upward, indicating that economic data are again exceeding expectations.

Who Needs P/Es, Anyway?

That suggests that the downward pressure on P/Es has abated, clearing the way for valuations to creep upward. Still, if investors lack confidence that these improved conditions can be sustained—not an unreasonable stance, given what we've seen the past few years—they may keep P/Es depressed anyway.

But even if P/Es don't rebound significantly, that doesn't mean stocks are stuck in the doldrums this year, Mr. Vasic said. "Solid gains can occur without P/Es returning to normal," he argued.

Mr. Vasic's 12-month target for the S&P/TSX of 14,000 is based on relatively modest 10-per-cent earnings growth and a forward P/E of 12.7—little changed from current levels and well below the long-term average of 14.5. That would amount to a tidy 17 percent gain over 2011's year-end price.

"It would not take much of a rise in P/Es to generate solid equity market gains in 2012—and end the year with multiples still below normal," he said.

LESSONS TO BE LEARNED

It is common to hear that stock prices are "undervalued" when their P/E ratio is low, or overvalued when it is high. This belief is alluded to in Finance in the News 7-4 in relation to stock prices in general. However, it is important to recognize, as is also acknowledged in the article, that there are often good reasons why P/E ratios are low. In particular, P/E ratios will be low when future earnings are expected to decline or to grow more slowly than they did in the past, or when there is a great deal of risk associated with the expected future earnings. Many investors learned this lesson the hard way as they poured money into the shares of banks and other companies in the financial sector during the summer and fall of 2008, based on the belief that they were undervalued. Unfortunately, many of these stocks continued to decline, and some of the financial institutions went bankrupt, rendering their shares worthless. On the other hand, the share prices of many financial institutions that weathered the storm recovered nicely during the spring of 2009. The lesson to be learned is that sometimes low P/E ratios represent a buying opportunity, but in other cases they may be a sign of bad things to come. Only detailed analysis (and a little luck) can tell the difference.

---

[10] The average, which is 34.5, is less meaningful, since it is impacted by the outliers exceeding 100.

Applying the P/E Ratio Approach

Equation 7-14 suggests that we need two estimates in order to implement the P/E ratio approach. Unfortunately, obtaining reasonable estimates requires a substantial amount of analysis and also an element of judgement. EPS_1 can be determined using several approaches, which are similar to those described above for estimating future dividends. In particular, we can analyze historical earnings data, project trends, and the company's present situation, and forecast future earnings (see our discussion of forecasting financial statements in Chapter 4). In addition, the use of analyst estimates (and consensus estimates) may provide reasonable forecasts of EPS_1.

Estimating justifiable P/E ratios is even more involved, and several approaches are typically used. One commonly used approach is to find *comparable* companies and estimate an appropriate P/E ratio for the company being analyzed based on a comparison of this company with the others in terms of risk and growth opportunities. This method often involves using an industry-average P/E ratio, which is then scaled up or down, based on an assessment of whether the company is above or below average. Unfortunately, this approach involves a great deal of subjectivity regarding several company-specific characteristics, including risk, potential for growth, and the overall financial health of the company. In addition, it may build market errors into the value estimation process. For example, even though a firm may be average within its industry, the industry-average P/E ratio may be too high if the market has overvalued this particular industry at a particular time.

Another commonly used approach is to examine historical averages for the company or the company's industry. However, using historical averages may be inappropriate if the company has changed substantially or if market and industry conditions have changed or are changing.

Given these potential problems associated with the use of industry or historical averages to estimate the appropriate P/E ratio, it is beneficial to obtain corroborating estimates based on economic, industry, and company fundamentals, if possible. Fortunately, the P/E ratio can be estimated by relating it to the fundamentals in the DDM.[11] We will illustrate this by using the simplest DDM model, the constant growth model:

$$P_0 = \frac{D_1}{k_c - g}$$

Dividing both sides of this equation by expected earnings (EPS_1), we get Equation 7-15.

$$\frac{P_0}{EPS_1} = \frac{P}{E} = \frac{D_1/EPS_1}{k_c - g} \qquad [7\text{-}15]$$

We are left with the P/E ratio on the left side of the equation. Notice that D_1/EPS_1 is the expected dividend payout ratio at time 1.

Equation 7-15 indicates that the following fundamental factors affect the justified P/E ratio, and hence share prices:

1. the expected dividend payout ratio (D_1/EPS_1)

2. the required rate of return (k_c)

3. the expected growth rate of dividends (g)

Notice that it is *expected earnings*, not historical earnings, that is the relevant input. Also note that k and g are typically the most important factors in the determination of the P/E ratio because a small change in either can have a large effect on its value.

---

[11] Like the DDM, this method for estimating P/E ratios will work best for companies with relatively stable dividend and growth patterns.

The following relationships should hold, *all else being equal*:

1. The higher the expected payout ratio, the higher the P/E.

2. The higher the expected growth rate, *g*, the higher the P/E.

3. The higher the required rate of return, k_c, the lower the P/E.

However, "all else being equal" is a brave assumption, because many of these variables are interrelated. For example, raising the payout ratio and thus increasing the dividend seems to increase the P/E, but raising the payout may also reduce growth, because one estimate of the growth rate is the sustainable growth rate, where $g = (1 - \text{Payout}) \times \text{ROE}$. We might also try to increase the growth rate by taking on risky investment projects that could increase future earnings and dividends, but this could also cause the discount rate, *k*, to increase (i.e., recall $k = RF + \text{Risk premium}$). However, we can say that P/E ratios tend to be higher when future growth in earnings and dividends is also expected to be high, and when interest rates or risk premiums are low (because they both affect k_c).

EXAMPLE 7-13   Using the P/E Ratio Approach

Assume that a firm has just reported an EPS of $2.00 and expects to maintain a 40 percent payout ratio. Estimate the firm's P/E ratio and its market price, assuming its ROE is 10 percent and investors require a 9 percent return on their shares.

Solution

First, estimate growth:

$$g = (1 - \text{Payout})(\text{ROE}) = (1 - 0.4)(10\%) = 6\%$$

Second, estimate earnings per share for the next 12 months:

$$\text{EPS}_1 = (\text{EPS}_0)(1 + g) = (2.00)(1.06) = \$2.12$$

Third, estimate the price-earnings ratio:

$$\frac{P}{E} = \frac{D_1/\text{EPS}_1}{k_c - g} = \frac{0.40}{0.09 - 0.06} = 13.33$$

Fourth, estimate the current share price:

$$P_0 = \text{EPS}_1 \times P_0/E_1 = (\$2.12)(13.33) = \$28.26$$

In Example 7-14, we assume the payout ratio remains constant at 40 percent, but we vary the main subjective inputs, k_c and *g*, to assess the effect on the P/E ratio and on price.

Notice the wide range of P/E and price estimates that arise for relatively small changes in our estimates of k_c and *g*.

EXAMPLE 7-14   Varying the Inputs for the P/E Ratio Approach

Revisit the firm in Example 7-13, assuming the same reported EPS of $2.00 and the same payout ratio of 40 percent. However, now assume that the growth rate and required return on the shares are, respectively,

a.   5 percent and 10 percent

b.   7 percent and 8 percent

Solution

$$\text{a.} \quad \textit{EPS}_1 = (2.00)(1.05) = \$2.10$$

$$\frac{P}{E} = \frac{0.40}{0.10 - 0.05} = 8$$

$$\text{So } P_0 = (\$2.10)(8) = \$16.80$$

EXAMPLE 7-14	Varying the Inputs for the P/E Ratio Approach *continued*

b. $EPS_1 = (2.00)(1.07) = \$2.14$

$$\frac{P}{E} = \frac{0.40}{0.08 - 0.07} = 40$$

So $P_0 = (\$2.14)(40) = \$85.60$

Limitations of P/E Ratios

Aside from the difficulties in estimating an appropriate P/E ratio and in estimating future EPS, there are several other practical concerns regarding the use of P/E ratios. First, P/E ratios are uninformative when companies have negative, or very small, earnings. As we saw for the S&P/TSX Composite in Figure 7-3, we sometimes get large or meaningless numbers for the P/E ratio, even when we aggregate across all companies. For a particular firm, the potential for these problems is much higher. Second, the volatile nature of earnings implies a great deal of volatility in P/E multiples. For example, the earnings of cyclical companies fluctuate dramatically throughout a typical business cycle. For these reasons, P/E ratios are normally based on smoothed or normalized estimates of earnings for the forecast year. It is also the reason analysts use other, similar relative-value approaches. Some of these alternative measures, including variations of the P/E ratio, are discussed in *Finance in the News 7-5*.

finance INTHENEWS 7-5   There's More Than One Way to Measure the Market

I BELIEVE STRONGLY in using cold, hard data when investing. The problem is that any single piece of data can lie. That's why it's so important to consider a variety of information. You might say that, when it comes to the numbers, there is safety in numbers.

My Guru Strategies, each of which is based on the approach of a different investing great, examine dozens of different data points when analyzing individual stocks.

You can apply a similar approach to assessing the broad market. Rather than focusing on a single measure of whether the S&P 500 is expensive, you can consider several. Here are some of my favourites:

The price/earnings ratio: The trailing 12-month P/E takes the market's current price and divides it by the amount of per-share earnings companies have reported over the past four quarters. Using Standard & Poor's earnings data and the Dec. 12 close, the S&P 500's P/E was about 14.2. The figure is lower than the 1872 to 2000 historical average for U.S. stocks of 14.5.

The 10-year P/E ratio: Yale economist Robert Shiller believes a better way to measure the market is to look back on current prices in relation to the average of the previous 10 years' earnings, adjusted for inflation. The benefit of this approach is that it compensates for short-term anomalies in earnings. The downside is that the period it examines is arbitrary. Typically, business cycles run about six years. So the 10-year P/E ratio can be skewed if the past decade has happened to include an unusual combination of recessionary and expansionary periods.

The 10-year P/E has hovered around 20 for the past couple of months. That's significantly above its 140-year historical average of about 16, though far from the peaks hit in 1999 (44.2) and 2007 (about 27.5).

The stock market/GDP ratio: This compares the total market value of the stock market to the value of all the goods and services produced in the U.S. for the year—the gross domestic product.

Warren Buffett has said the stock market/GNP (gross national product) is one of his favourite valuation metrics, and GDP and GNP tend to run quite close to each other. The website GuruFocus.com tracks the daily stock market/GDP ratio, and as of Dec. 13, the ratio was 86.1 percent. That sits in the "fair value" range (75 percent to 90 percent), which was derived by an analysis of historical data, the site says.

The price/sales ratio: The money manager Ken Fisher pioneered the price/sales ratio (PSR) in the 1980s as a way to value individual stocks. His logic: While earnings can fluctuate wildly from year to year, sales are far more stable, and provide a better gauge of a company's position.

Two of my Guru Strategies use the PSR. My Fisher-based model finds PSRs below 0.75 to be tremendous values, and those between 0.75 and 1.5 to be good values. My James O'Shaughnessy-based model looks for PSRs below 1.5. According to data from Morningstar, the S&P 500 currently has a PSR of 1.2.

The market yield: Just as bonds have yields, so too do stocks. One key indicator is the earnings yield, which is generally calculated as the inverse of the P/E ratio. Using the trailing 12 months' reported earnings, the earnings yield of the S&P 500 is 7.0 percent.

That's a pretty healthy figure. According to data from New York University finance professor Aswath Damodaran, the average earnings yield for the S&P 500 from 1960 to 2010 was 6.86 percent. In what has been a rarity in recent decades, the other main type of stock yield—dividend yield—is actually significantly higher than the 10-year Treasury yield. The

continued

Finance in the News 7-5: There's More Than One Way to Measure the Market *(con't)*

S&P's dividend yield is 2.54 percent, while the 10-year Treasury yields about 2.03 percent. That's a bullish sign.

Projected P/E: Rather than using past earnings, analysts will often look at the market P/E using projected earnings for the next year. Using this approach, the S&P 500 is trading for 11.9 times operating earnings, and 12.8 times as-reported earnings.

Over all, these indicators paint an attractive picture. P/E ratios and earnings yields that use one year's worth of earnings are now cheaper than historical averages. The market's price/sales ratio seems reasonable, and the stock market/GDP ratio is in "fair value" territory. Only the 10-year P/E looks high.

All of that suggests that the market is trading pretty close to its fair value. Throw in the fact that the market's dividend yield is more than 25 percent higher than the yield on the 10-year Treasury, and stocks seem priced to perform much better over the long term than the Treasury bonds that everyone has been piling into.

Source: Reese, John, "There's more than one way to measure the market." *The Globe and Mail*, December 21, 2011, p. B10. John Reese is founder and CEO of Validea.com, Validea.ca, and portfolio manager for the Omega American & International Consensus funds. Reprinted by permission.

CONCEPT REVIEW QUESTIONS

1. Why can the P/E ratio be viewed as a type of payback period?

2. What drives P/E ratios?

3. Why do P/E ratios differ even between comparable firms?

4. How are multiples linked to a discounted cash flow valuation?

7.5 ADDITIONAL MULTIPLES OR RELATIVE VALUE RATIOS

Learning Objective 7.5
Explain how to value common shares using additional relative value ratios.

market-to-book (M/B) ratio the market price per share divided by the book value per share

The **market-to-book (M/B) ratio**, which was defined in Chapter 4 as the market price per share divided by the book value per share, can also be used to value stocks. This is achieved by multiplying a justifiable M/B ratio by a company's book value per share (which was also defined in Chapter 4). Recall that the book value per share equals the book value of equity (i.e., assets minus liabilities) divided by the number of common shares outstanding. As such, valuing stocks relative to their M/B is an attractive approach for several reasons. Book value provides a relatively stable, intuitive measure of value relative to market values, which can be easily compared to those of other companies, provided accounting standards do not vary greatly across the comparison group. Using book value eliminates the problems arising from the use of P/E multiples, because book values are rarely negative and do not exhibit the volatility associated with earnings levels. However, book values may be sensitive to accounting standards and may be uninformative for companies that do not have a large proportion of fixed assets, such as service firms.

The use of the M/B ratio fell out of favour in the 1980s and 1990s when high rates of inflation distorted the book value of equity for many firms because of their use of historical cost accounting in an inflationary period. However, the low rate of inflation of the past 10 to 15 years has removed most of these problems, while changes in accounting standards have made the book value of equity more useful.[12]

price-to-sales (P/S) ratio market price per share divided by sales per share

The **price-to-sales (P/S) ratio** possesses several properties that make it attractive for valuation purposes. It is similar to the P/E and M/B approaches in that it is implemented by multiplying a justifiable P/S ratio by the sales per share figure. Unlike earnings and book value, sales are relatively insensitive to accounting decisions and are never negative. Sales are not as volatile as earnings levels, hence P/S ratios are generally less volatile than P/E multiples.

---

[12] At one point, firms were required to write off goodwill, which seriously affected both earnings and the book value of equity. Now the goodwill arising from an acquisition is only written off when it is impaired by a drop in value. This is what caused the huge losses to Nortel and JDS Uniphase in 2002.

In addition, sales figures provide useful information about corporate decisions, such as pricing. However, sales do not provide information about expenses and profit margins, which are important determinants of company performance.

Another commonly used relative valuation ratio is the **price-to-cash-flow (P/CF) ratio**, for which cash flow (CF) is often estimated as Net income + Depreciation and amortization + Deferred taxes. (Some analysts focus on "free" cash flow available to equity holders, as defined previously.) By focusing on cash flow rather than accounting income, this ratio alleviates some of the accounting concerns regarding measures of earnings. The **market (enterprise) value to EBIT** or the **market (enterprise) value to EBITDA ratio** can also be used. Using earnings before interest and taxes (EBIT) or earnings before interest, taxes, depreciation, and amortization (EBITDA) instead of net income eliminates a significant proportion of the volatility in EPS figures caused by the use of debt and amortization (which is a non-cash expense). We use the market value of the firm's capital (both debt and equity) to reflect the fact that EBIT and EBITDA represent income available to both debt and equity holders. However, although there are many different valuation ratios or "multiples," they are all related to the fundamental valuation drivers, as we now show.

Suppose an investor requires a 15 percent return on his or her shares, expects the firm to pay a $1 dividend, and expects dividends and earnings to grow at 10 percent. In this case, we can use the constant growth model to value the shares at $20.

$$P = \frac{\$1}{0.15 - 0.10} = \$20$$

If 0.5 million shares are outstanding, this firm would have a total market value for the equity or equity market capitalization (cap) of $10 million.

If the firm has the forecast income statement and financial data shown in Table 7-2, we can link all these valuation multiples.

price-to-cash-flow (P/CF) ratio market price per share divided by per share cash flow

market (enterprise) value to EBIT ratio total firm market value divided by earnings before interest and taxes

market (enterprise) value to EBITDA ratio total firm market value divided by earnings before interest, taxes, depreciation, and amortization

TABLE 7-2 Forecast Income Statement

Sales volume	1 million units
Unit price $10	$10 million
Variable costs	5.0
Fixed cash costs	1.7
EBITDA	3.3
Depreciation	0.8
EBIT	2.5
Interest	0.5
EBT	2.0
Income tax (@50 percent)	1.0
Net income	1.0
Dividends	0.5
Book value of equity	5.0
Book value of debt	5.0

For example, the share price is $20 and the dividend is $1, so the dividend yield is 5 percent (i.e., 1/20). In valuing this company, one valuation metric is to simply compare its dividend yields to those of other comparable companies. A high dividend yield relative to other companies might indicate an undervalued stock. Another way to use the dividend yield is to take its reciprocal and look at the dividend multiple—that is, the market price divided by the dividend. In this case, it is selling at 20X its dividend.

In practice, we don't often talk about the dividend multiple because the dividend yield provides the same information, and yields on stocks are often compared directly with yields on income trusts, bonds, and other interest-earning securities. However, there is a fundamental problem with using dividend multiples: many firms do not pay dividends. To get around this problem, we can work up the income statement and use the next item, which is earnings. In this case, with an equity market value of $10 million and $1 million in net income, the P/E ratio is 10X. Immediately we can see that although many firms don't have dividends, they should all expect to have some earnings. The problem here is that earnings are cyclical and industry specific, so let's move up the income statement a bit farther.

The next item is earnings before interest and tax (EBIT), which in our example is $2.5 million. The difference between EBIT and net income is that EBIT does not belong to the shareholders; some of it flows through to the firm's creditors and some to the government. This is why we usually calculate the total firm (enterprise) value (EV)—that is, the value of the debt plus the value of the equity—for all the ratios "above" net income. For our example, this comes to $15 million (the debt market value is assumed to be the book value of $5 million). The EV/EBIT multiple is then 6X (EBIT of $2.5 million divided into the total market value of $15 million).

However, as we know from our accounting discussion, depreciation is a non-cash charge, so we go farther up the income statement and add depreciation to get EBITDA. This adds back all the accounting items that do not involve cash. Depreciation of fixed assets is by far the largest component, but there are also some other amortizations, such as issue costs attached to debt, and so on. Again, with a total value of $15 million, the EV/EBITDA multiple is 4.5X. The EV/EBITDA multiple is the most commonly used multiple when firms look at acquiring other firms; it is a good proxy for the cash flow the firm generates, which can be used by the acquiring firm. Another good valuation is to look at the contribution generated by the firm, which is EBITDA with all the fixed costs added back. In our example, this is $5 million, giving a 3X multiple. This is useful for firms valuing other firms when they can consolidate operations and remove the fixed costs.

The final valuation multiple comes from going right to the top line, instead of the bottom line, and looking at sales. In our case, the sales multiple is a $10-million common equity value for buying $10 million in revenues or 1.0X. This would be useful if the entire sales of the firm could be switched to another firm and the existing plant and facilities closed down. Another variant is to look at the equity value per unit of sales. In our case, $10 million for 1 million unit sales means that the firm's shares are selling for $10 per unit of sales.

If we add to these valuation multiples the market-to-book ratio, which in our case is 2X (i.e., $10 million/$5 million), and the firm's return on equity (ROE) of 20 percent, we have a comprehensive list of key valuation ratios for the firm, all flowing from the fundamental valuation model.

Not all of these ratios are equally useful for every firm. Cable companies, for example, usually sell on a value per unit of output—in their case, a price per subscriber, because the more subscribers a cable company has, the more revenue it can generate. "Old-line" manufacturing firms generally sell on a market-to-book or P/E ratio basis because they tend to have stable earnings. Growth companies with large amounts of amortization because of their increasing asset base tend to sell on EBITDA or sales multiples. However, in all cases, these valuation multiples are simply shortcuts for the fundamental discounted cash flow valuation.

CONCEPT REVIEW QUESTION

1. What other relative valuation multiples are useful in valuation?

7.6 A SIMPLE APPLICATION: TIM HORTONS INC.

We now revisit Tim Hortons Inc. to illustrate fundamental valuation and relative valuation in practice, using Tim Hortons' 2011 accounting figures and market data as at March 2012.

Learning Objective 7.6
Apply the principles of fundamental valuation and relative valuation.

We begin by applying the DDM to Tim Hortons Inc. This requires the use of a discount rate. We will use 6.84 percent for this purpose (we will discuss how this figure was derived in Chapter 9). As of March 2012, the analyst consensus for EPS is $2.74. Rather than applying the 2011 dividend payout ratio of 28.94 percent to this expected EPS figure (which would give us an expected 2012 annual dividend of $0.79), we use $0.84, which reflects Tim Horton's announcement that it would increase its quarterly dividend to $0.21 per quarter. This implies a dividend payout ratio of 30.66 percent, which is close to the 2011 figure and is in line with the company's stated target range of 30 to 35 percent.

We begin by using the relatively simple constant growth version of the DDM, employing the commonly used long-term growth rate in dividends and earnings to infinity of 5 percent, which corresponds to the approximate nominal growth rate in the economy. Using Equation 7-7, we get:

$$P = 0.84 / (0.0684 - 0.05) = \$45.65$$

This is well below the price of Tim Horton's common stock at the time of analysis, which was $52.56. It is also well below the mean (median) analyst target price of $55.65 ($57.00). We assume for now that the discount rate used is appropriate and that the estimate of D_1 is reasonable, which they both appear to be. Let's consider our growth rate assumptions again. Consider that, at the time of analysis, the analyst consensus five-year growth rate in earnings for Tim Hortons was 12 percent (including the 2011 to 2012 period), which suggests the 5 percent constant growth rate we used could be too low a growth rate, at least for the next five years. While 12 percent might seem a bit on the optimistic side, Tim Hortons' operating income has increased over the past five years at an average annual rate of 14.5 percent. In addition, Tim Hortons has typically maintained a 10 percent growth target, which is in line with the 2011 increase in operating income of 9.9 percent. It is also consistent with its 2012 targets of a 4 to 6 percent increase in same-store sales, along with opening 250 to 290 new stores in 2012 (an increase in the number of stores of 6.1 to 7.1 percent). We could also calculate the sustainable growth rate as 23.56 percent, using Equation 7-11 and the 2011 ROE figure and payout ratio:

$$g = (1 - \text{Payout}) \times \text{ROE} = (1 - 0.2894) \times 33.16\% = 23.56\%$$

While this number is extremely high and therefore not sustainable over an extended period of time, it nonetheless suggests that Tim Hortons could be expected to grow faster than 5 percent per year, at least in the short term.

Let's now consider the possibility that 5 percent growth to infinity is too conservative. This suggests we could use a multi-stage version of the DDM to account for higher growth in the short-term. We do this below, using the discount rate and D_1 figures from above, but now assuming 12 percent growth over the four years after 2012 (i.e., we still assume $D_1 = \$0.84$), and then assuming 5 percent growth to infinity. Using Equation 7-13, and the process described in Example 7-12, we obtain an estimate of $54.18. If we were to be slightly more conservative in terms of the short-term growth rate and assumed a 10 percent growth rate, rather than 12 percent, for the next five years, our estimate would be $50.41. These analyses suggest that Tim Hortons' shares are reasonably valued at $52.56.

Now let's consider what the relative valuation approaches suggest about Tim Hortons' share price. Let's focus first on the P/E ratio. There are several ways to estimate a justifiable P/E ratio. First, we could use Equation 7-15 and Tim Hortons' implied 2012 payout ratio of 30.66 percent, along with $k = 6.84$ percent and $g = 5$ percent. This gives us a justifiable forward P/E ratio of 16.66 (i.e., P/E = 0.3066/(0.0684 − 0.05)). Using the 2012 analyst consensus EPS figure of $2.74 gives us a price estimate of $45.65 (i.e., $2.74 × 16.66). This estimate is identical to the figure we obtained using these inputs into the constant growth DDM. This should not be surprising, since Equation 7-15 is merely a rearrangement of the DDM, and we are using the same inputs.

We can obtain alternative estimates of a justifiable P/E ratio by looking at Tim Hortons' historical averages, industry averages, or averages of comparable companies. The five-year average P/E ratio for Tim Hortons was 20.04, while the industry average P/E was 22.2. The average P/E for McDonald's and Starbucks (the two comparable companies we chose in Chapter 4) was 25.05 (i.e., 18.5 for McDonald's and 31.6 for Starbucks). Since these averages all relate to trailing P/E ratios, we will multiply them by Tim Hortons' 2011 EPS figure of $2.36.

Using Tim Hortons' average: $P = 20.04 \times \$2.36 = \$47.29$

Using the 2012 industry average: $P = 22.2 \times \$2.36 = \$52.39$

Using McDonald's and Starbucks' average: $P = 25.05 \times \$2.36 = \$59.12$

So, based on these comparables, which range from $47.29 to $59.12, with an average of $52.93, Tim Hortons appears to be priced reasonably at $52.56, which is similar to our conclusion based on the two-stage DDM. When we use three alternative relative valuation methods (the market-to-book ratio, the price-to-sales ratio, and the price-to-cash flow ratio), the results suggest Tim Hortons is overvalued at $52.56 (although we have not reported the details here). Using Tim Hortons' five-year averages, as well as the 2012 industry averages, and averages for McDonald's and Starbucks for these ratios, and applying them to the appropriate Tim Hortons' figures (i.e., book value, sales, and cash flow), we get estimates ranging from $35.28 (using price-to-cash flow and the industry average) to $62.12 (using price-to-sales and the average for McDonald's and Starbucks). The overall average for the three methods is $46.71.

So where does this leave us? Figure 7-4 depicts the results of all these estimates graphically. The first thing to note is that the current price of $52.56 lies within the boundaries of all the estimates, with the exception of price-to-cash flow, where it lies just slightly above the upper boundary. The overall average of all five methods (and all 15 estimates) is $48.63, which suggests that the shares could be overvalued; however, such a conclusion suggests all approaches and all inputs are equally valid. If we rely primarily on the two-stage DDM estimates (since the single-stage DDM growth input seemed too low) and on the P/E ratio estimates, the estimates are consistent with the current price and also with the current analyst price target of $55.65. These approaches and estimates seem most reasonable, since they account for Tim Hortons' healthy profit margins and reasonably high short-term growth prospects.[13] However, some of the other estimates caution us that this target may be on the high side and that, in fact, the shares may be overvalued at their current price.

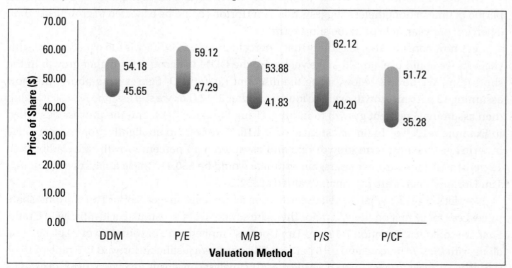

FIGURE 7-4 *Summary of Various Valuation Technique Estimates for Tim Hortons Inc.*

---

[13] It is also noteworthy that at the time of writing, Tim Hortons had just announced a new share repurchase program of up to $200 million, which will reduce the number of shares outstanding. We discuss how this will influence share price, as well as earnings and dividends per share, when we discuss dividend policy in Chapter 22. For now, we can recognize that many investors view this as a positive signal regarding the company, since it can be viewed as a form of "special" dividend, and it may have a positive impact on the share price.

It is worth noting that the market price of Tim Hortons stock reflects the combined opinions of thousands of investors. This estimate of the underlying true value of Tim Hortons' equity should not be easily disregarded in favour of a price determined by a formula using values based on assumptions about future growth, discount rates, etc. This point will be further addressed in Chapter 10 on market efficiency. However, in this example, our estimated values seem to be fairly close to the market price.

CONCEPT REVIEW QUESTION

1. What are some of the key assumptions that must be made when applying the valuation concepts discussed in this chapter to a real-life valuation situation?

7-1 ETHICS AND CORPORATE GOVERNANCE
IDA Must Tighten Its Rules for Analysts

There's a situation playing out in the oil patch that raises serious concerns about how research analysts employed by investment dealers are governed by the Investment Dealers Association of Canada [now the Investment Industry Regulatory Organization of Canada (IIROC)].

The plot is simple: A research analyst covering a company for his firm offered to buy a property being sold by that company for his own private company. This particular case involves Roger Serin, who covers the oil patch for TD Newcrest, and Peyto Energy Trust.

Peyto's CEO, Don Gray, recently sent a letter to the IDA calling its attention to Mr. Serin's offer to buy the property from Peyto while publishing opinions on the trust. (The offer itself was made in 2002, when Mr. Serin was covering Peyto for another brokerage, Raymond James. A deal was never done.)

What's interesting—or frightening—is that the IDA, which oversees the activities of brokerage firms, doesn't seem to have a problem with research analysts straddling both sides of the fence. As long as the analyst discloses what's going on, the IDA says the activity is not prohibited. The assumption here is that investors will read the disclosure statements and be able to make up their own minds as to whether the research should or shouldn't be relied on. In fact, the IDA's position is that it's the responsibility of the firm to ensure its analysts are not engaged in deals that could affect their objectivity.

Nonsense. There is no way research analysts should be allowed to both cover a firm and do business with it, too. Period. Full stop.

(I should note here that my husband is an analyst for an investment dealer, and he follows the energy sector.)

Research analysts are not allowed to publish reports on companies if their firms are involved in corporate transactions of any sort. How is it different if the analyst, rather than the firm, is involved in a transaction? In fact, the notion that an analyst may act for their own self interest from time to time is more than a tad frightening because one never knows in whose interest they are acting—theirs or the client's.

By turning a blind eye to this issue, the IDA isn't ensuring a level playing field for investors. It's not reasonable to expect investors to rely on the opinions of individuals who appear just as concerned with looking after their own interests by trying to do business with the companies they are following.

Some might say: "But what about analysts who own shares in the companies they follow?" Well, that is different because they are required to disclose their holdings and once those shares are held in personal accounts, that's where they sit until the analyst puts out a "sell" recommendation; they can't be selling for themselves while having a "buy" recommendation out to clients. Some firms aren't even comfortable with this and don't allow their analysts to hold shares in companies that they cover.

Even so, the most glaring difference is that the buying and selling of shares is done in the public markets and, in the case of analysts, is governed by a bevy of rules and regulations. Property deals, by contrast, are private transactions on which information is not as readily available to the public and which are not governed in the same way as stock transactions.

In this regard, it makes sense to look south of the border, to the Series 87 exams that anyone involved in research for an investment dealer must write—including Canadian analysts with U.S. institutional clients. These exams are run by the National Association of Securities Dealers to test the knowledge of securities rules and regulations of people in the industry.

The regulations specify that any activities that have the potential to compromise the perspective of an analyst—and put the client in second place—are forbidden.

The oil patch has worked hard over the past several years to dispel a widely held notion among investors, primarily in eastern Canada, that it was an insider's game and the only way anyone made money was if they were in Calgary and plugged in. One of the ways investment dealers opted to handle this perceived disadvantage was to move their research operations westward; back in the early 1990s, many energy analysts followed the sector from Toronto or Montreal. Today, the opposite is true, with only a handful of veterans clinging to their Bay Street perches. And there isn't an investment dealer that regrets the decision to do this because they are, in fact, better plugged in to what is going on.

In a sector as tight as the oil patch, which has been criticized for a bit of "nudge, nudge, wink, wink" behaviour over the years, it's even more important that there be specific rules governing what analysts can and cannot do beyond disclosing share ownership positions and not publishing opinions when their firm is involved in a transaction.

And an analyst approaching a company he or she follows to do a property deal for private benefit must be on that list. Simply disclosing it doesn't go far enough. Moreover, this is the kind of change in regulations that would be applicable in every sector of the economy that involves investment dealers, investors, opinions, and publicly traded companies; this isn't just an oil patch hot button. *continued*

7-1 ETHICS AND CORPORATE GOVERNANCE: IDA Must Tighten Its Rules for Analysts *continued*

What it really comes down to is an issue of transparency and maintaining the integrity of Canada's capital markets. The IDA is a crucial part of making this happen.

Source: Yedlin, Deborah, "IDA must tighten its rules for analysts." *The Globe and Mail*, April 11, 2006, p. B2. ©The Globe and Mail, Inc. All rights reserved. Reprinted by permission.

DISCUSSION QUESTIONS

1. What is the conflict of interest that the article is referring to and how might this damage investors?

2. Louis Brandeis, a former chief justice of the U.S. Supreme Court, once stated, "Sunlight is said to be the best of disinfectants; electric light the most efficient policeman." Do you think the IDA's position that transparency is sufficient is adequate?

3. What would be the implications of following U.S. practice and prohibiting "any activities that have the potential to compromise the perspective of an analyst"?

APPENDIX **7A**

A SHORT PRIMER ON BUBBLES[14]

Learning Objective 7.7
Explain how speculative price bubbles occur.

In 1711, the South Sea Company (SSC) was given a monopoly on all English trade to the South Seas—that is, South America.[15] Unfortunately, South America was largely under the control of Spain, and England was at war with Spain. Nevertheless, the hope was that in the ensuing peace, England would be able to dictate a freeing-up of trade to the company's benefit. As it turned out, the peace was to England's benefit but not very much to the company's. Meanwhile, John Law, a Scottish promoter in France, set up the Mississippi Company, which was draining investment from England to France. In response, the South Sea Company offered to have investors convert England's national debt into shares of the company. The company would pay a one-time fee to the government for this conversion and receive the fixed annual payments on the national debt. The certainty of receiving the interest payments would allow the company to borrow to fund its South Seas trade.

It was an audacious plan in an age of optimism and jubilation at England's defeat of both Spain and France. In April 1720, the government accepted the offer, and the stock price took off. It was clear that the plan could only be accepted if the stock price went up enough to encourage investors to convert their national debt into SSC equity. Consequently, the company issued shares on an instalment basis. As the cash came in, the company lent it back so that investors could buy more shares. The stock obviously took off, and in doing so sucked in a whole group of neophyte investors.

It also spawned imitators. One of the most interesting of these declared that it was "a company for carrying on an undertaking of great advantage, but nobody was to know what it is." Prices soared, and small investors got in for fear of missing out. Sir Isaac Newton sold his stock in the SSC in April 1720 for a 100 percent gain. However, the company's stock price rocketed up from £300 to its peak of more than £1,000 and Newton bought back in. In August, the bubble burst, and by September prices were back to £300. The *London Gazette* was full of bankruptcy announcements, and Newton lost £20,000. Philosophically, he made his famous statement, "I can calculate the motions of the heavenly bodies, but not the madness of people."

We have learned from this, haven't we? Leaving aside the Great Crash of 1929, there is the little matter of the Crash of 2000, and our recent experience with technology and Internet

---

[14] This appendix is based on Laurence Booth, "Investments, 'alternative' investments, and bubbles." In *Advisor's Guide to New Investment Opportunities* (2001), pp. 12–19.
[15] See Jim Harrison, "The Damn'd South Sea." *Harvard Magazine*, May–June 1999.

stocks. The most recent crashes stemmed from the high valuation of the equity market as a result of the long bull markets of the late 1990s.

Long bull markets pull in inexperienced investors who have unrealistic expectations. As we saw in Chapter 5, over long periods, average returns of the equity market have exceeded 10 percent a year, which is not enough to get investors really excited. However, a couple of 25-percent-plus years bring in the people who then come to expect 25-percent-plus returns. Moreover, plenty of people are willing to tell them that they can get 25 percent returns and that this time it is different: it is a new world of investing with new metrics.

In the September 1999 issue of *Atlantic Monthly*, James Glassman and Kevin Hassett discussed their prediction that the Dow would go to 30,000. They stated, "Stocks were undervalued in the 1980s and 1990s and they are undervalued now. Stock prices could double, triple or even quadruple tomorrow and still not be too high." They went on to suggest that "a profound change has occurred in the attractiveness of stocks since the early 1980s, as investors have become more rational. The old limits of yields and P/Es do not apply anymore, if they ever did." And finally they insisted: "In truth there is no extra risk in stocks."[16]

A familiar refrain during times of speculative bubbles is "This time it is different." After all, the little investors get in only after a run-up in prices, so it has to be different this time; otherwise, they have missed the boat. On May 15, 1929, the publications *Outlook* and *Independent* remarked, "But apparently there has been a fundamental change in the criteria for judging security values. Widespread education of the public in the worth of equity securities has created a new demand." Similarly, before the correction in 1969, *Barron's* stated, "The failure of the general market to decline during the last three years despite its obvious vulnerability, as well as the emergence of new investment characteristics, has caused investors to believe that the U.S. has entered a new investment era to which old guidelines no longer apply."[17]

The fact is that "old guidelines" are perennial; the only thing that changes is that the old investors die off and a new generation has to learn the same old lessons. Does that 1720 English company that promised "carrying on of an undertaking of great advantage, but nobody to know what it is," sound familiar? It should. On January 25, 2000, Michael Lewis, the author of *Liar's Poker*, pointed out that there was an Internet company, NetJ.com, that had filed statements with the U.S. Securities and Exchange Commission with the confession that "the company is not currently engaged in any substantial activity and has no plans to engage in any such activity in the foreseeable future." The company had $127,631 in accumulated losses and so little money on hand that the directors would have had to chip in to pay any filing costs to raise capital. The only snag was that NetJ.com had a market capitalization of $22.9 million.

SUMMARY

This chapter reviews the basic approaches to valuing preferred and common shares. It begins by introducing the preferred share valuation process, which is based on estimating the present value of expected future dividends. This approach is then extended to common stock valuation in the form of the dividend discount model (DDM). We show how the constant growth version of the DDM is related to the fundamentals that affect stock prices (i.e., future profitability and dividends, interest rates, and risk). We then show how the multiple-growth version of the DDM could be used to estimate common share prices. We conclude by examining relative valuation models, the P/E ratio approach in particular, and how they interact with the discounted cash flow model. Throughout our discussion, we highlight the importance of

---

[16] They also went through an interesting valuation of Cisco, in which they stated, "Using the standard formula for calculating a stock's present value according to the flow of cash it generates over time, we find that Cisco's PRP should be $399 a share. In other words, Cisco's price last June would need to sextuple. Its P/E would rise to 539 (no that's not a misprint)." At the time of writing, Cisco's price was $19. Glassman, James, and Hassett, Kevin, "Dow 36,000." *Atlantic Monthly* 284, no. 3 (September 1999).

[17] Quoted in Jim Stack, *The New Paradigm Era or Bubble* (Whitefish, MT: InvesTech Research, 1997).

recognizing the sensitivity of the valuation process to assumptions regarding input variables, such as growth rates, discount rates, and general market conditions, and the fact that valuation is as much an art as it is a science.

SUMMARY OF LEARNING OBJECTIVES

7.1 Identify the basic characteristics of equity securities (i.e., preferred shares and common shares).

Equity securities are ownership interests in a company. Common shares have voting rights and pay a dividend (at the discretion of the board of directors). Preferred shares have no voting rights and pay a fixed, regular dividend. Preferred shares have a par value. In the event of bankruptcy or liquidation, preferred shareholders are entitled to their par value before common shareholders are paid (if there is enough money to pay the par value after creditors are paid).

7.2 Explain how to value preferred shares.

Preferred shares are valued as perpetuities, with annual dividends divided by the discount rate.

7.3 Explain how to value common shares using the dividend discount model.

The general framework is that price equals the sum of the discounted future cash flow. So we need to estimate the amount and timing of future cash flow and the appropriate discount rate. In the dividend discount model, we make simplifying assumptions that the dividend grows at a constant rate.

7.4 Explain how to value common shares using the price-earnings (P/E) ratio.

The common share price is the benchmark P/E ratio multiplied by the firm's earnings.

7.5 Explain how to value common shares using additional relative value ratios.

The common share price is the benchmark relative value ratio multiplied by some measure of the firm's performance, such as earnings, book assets, and so on, which is the other side of the ratio.

7.6 Apply the principles of fundamental valuation and relative valuation.

The application of the principles of fundamental valuation and relative valuation are presented using Tim Hortons as an example in section 7.6.

7.7 Explain how speculative price bubbles occur.

Speculative bubbles illustrate what is colloquially known as the "bigger fool theorem." Suppose, for example, a broker tells a client to buy XYZ at $30. The investor refuses because the stock is only worth $25. The broker replies, "I know, but there is momentum behind it and I am seeing a lot of interest. I think it will go to $40 by next year." The investor is a fool to pay $30 for something he thinks is worth $25, but this is not the fool theorem but the bigger fool theorem. If the investor does buy it, he is a fool, but he is also assuming that an even bigger fool will buy it in a year's time for $40.

KEY TERMS

common share, p. 248
constant growth DDM, p. 254
dividend discount model (DDM), p. 251
equity securities, p. 248
market (enterprise) value to EBIT ratio, p. 271
market (enterprise) value to EBITDA ratio,
    p. 271

market-to-book (M/B) ratio, p. 270
preferred share, p. 248
price-earnings (P/E) ratio, p. 264
price-to-cash-flow (P/CF) ratio, p. 271
price-to-sales (P/S) ratio, p. 270
relative valuation, p. 265
sustainable growth rate, p. 259

EQUATIONS

Equation	Formula	Page
[7-1] Required Rate of Return on a Risky Security	$k = RF + \text{Risk Premium}$	p. 249
[7-2] Market Price of Preferred Share	$P_{ps} = \dfrac{D_p}{k_p}$	p. 249
[7-3] Required Return on Preferred Shares	$k_p = \dfrac{D_p}{P_{ps}}$	p. 250
[7-4] Dividend Discount Model (DDM) (Over n Periods)	$P_0 = \dfrac{D_1}{(1 + k_c)^1} + \dfrac{D_2}{(1 + k_c)^2} + \ldots + \dfrac{D_n + P_n}{(1 + k_c)^n}$	p. 251
[7-5] Dividend Discount Model (DDM)	$P_0 = \dfrac{D_1}{(1 + k_c)^1} + \dfrac{D_2}{(1 + k_c)^2} + \ldots + \dfrac{D_\infty}{(1 + k_c)^\infty} = \sum\limits_{t=1}^{\infty} \dfrac{D_t}{(1 + k_c)^t}$	p. 252
[7-6] Dividend Discount Model (DDM) with Constant Growth	$P_0 = \dfrac{D_0(1 + g)^1}{(1 + k_c)^1} + \dfrac{D_0(1 + g)^2}{(1 + k_c)^2} + \ldots + \dfrac{D_0(1 + g)^\infty}{(1 + k_c)^\infty}$	p. 254
[7-7] Constant Growth Dividend Discount Model (DDM)	$P_0 = \dfrac{D_0(1 + g)}{k_c - g} = \dfrac{D_1}{k_c - g}$	p. 254
[7-8] Implied Rate of Return (Using Constant Growth DDM)	$k_c = \dfrac{D_1}{P_0} + g$	p. 255
[7-9] No-Growth Value	$P_0 = \dfrac{EPS_1}{k_c}$	p. 255
[7-10] Price in Terms of Assets in Place and Present Value of Growth Opportunities	$P_0 = \dfrac{EPS_1}{k_c} + PVGO$	p. 256
[7-11] Sustainable Growth Rate	$g = b \times \text{ROE}$	p. 259
[7-12] DuPont Equation (Three-Point)	ROE = (Net income/Sales) × (Sales/Total assets) × (Total assets/equity) = Net profit margin × Turnover ratio × Leverage ratio	p. 259
[7-13] Dividend Discount Model (DDM)	$P_0 = \dfrac{D_1}{(1 + k_c)^1} + \dfrac{D_2}{(1 + k_c)^2} + \ldots + \dfrac{D_t + P_t}{(1 + k_c)^t}$	p. 261
[7-14] P/E Ratio Approach	$P_0 = \text{Estimated } EPS_1 \times \text{Justified P/E ratio} = EPS_1 \times P_0/E_1$	p. 265
[7-15] P/E Ratio (Using Constant Growth DDM)	$\dfrac{P_0}{EPS_1} = \dfrac{P}{E} = \dfrac{D_1/EPS_1}{k_c - g}$	p. 267

QUESTIONS AND PRACTICE PROBLEMS

Multiple Choice Questions

1. Jason bought 30,000 shares of CTB Inc. on January 12, 2013. At that time, CTB Inc. had 2 million common shares outstanding. Calculate the portion of CTB Inc. that Jason owns.
   a. 2.3 percent
   b. 1.4 percent
   c. 6.0 percent
   d. 1.5 percent

2. You bought 100 shares at $20 each. At the end of the year, you received a total of $400 in dividends, and your stock was worth $2,500 total. What was your total return?
   a. 45 percent
   b. 50 percent
   c. 90 percent
   d. 25 percent

3. Which of the following is not a difference between equity securities and debt securities?
   a. Incur a tax-deductible expense
   b. Have a fixed maturity date
   c. Always involve fixed periodic payments
   d. Represent ownership of the security

4. Given that the government short-term T-bill yield is 4 percent, and the risk premium of Takashi Group is 6.5 percent, calculate Takashi Group's required rate of return.
   a. 8.5 percent
   b. 10.5 percent
   c. 7.25 percent
   d. 11.5 percent

5. Which of the following statements about equities is correct?
   a. Every firm pays dividends to common shareholders each year.
   b. Preferred dividends are usually paid annually in practice.
   c. Common shareholders are entitled to a firm's earnings before preferred shareholders.
   d. Common shareholders can vote on issues, such as mergers, election of board members, and so on.

6. Westlake Ltd. just paid a dividend of $2.00 per share, which is expected to grow at a constant rate of 4.5 percent indefinitely. The T-bill rate is 3 percent and the risk premium of Westlake Ltd. is 6.5 percent. Calculate Westlake's current share price.
   a. $42.60
   b. $41.80
   c. $46.05
   d. $40.00

7. Grace Holdings recently paid an annual dividend of $1.50 per share, and its estimated long-term growth rate in dividends is 4 percent. The current market price of each share is $26. The implied rate of return on the share is
   a. 9.77 percent.
   b. 10 percent.
   c. 12.5 percent.
   d. 13.33 percent.

8. Park Recreational Vehicles Ltd. shares are currently selling for $37.50 each. You bought 200 shares one year ago at $34 and received dividend payments of $1.50 per share. What was your total dollar capital gain this year?
    a. $400
    b. $300
    c. $700
    d. none of the above

9. Park Recreational Vehicles Ltd. shares are currently selling for $37.50 each. You bought 200 shares one year ago at $34 and received dividend payments of $1.50 per share. What was your total dollar return?
    a. S700
    b. S1,000
    c. $300
    d. none of the above

10. Limestone Co. just paid a dividend of $1.50 per share and its EPS is $9.00. Its book value per share (BVPS) is $36. Calculate Limestone's sustainable growth rate.
    a. 20.83 percent
    b. 25 percent
    c. 4.17 percent
    d. 5.25 percent

11. The sustainable growth is negatively related to
    a. net profit margin.
    b. leverage ratio or equity multiplier.
    c. payout ratio.
    d. retention ratio.

12. Which of the following is not a limitation of the DDM?
    a. It cannot be applied to firms without dividend payments.
    b. It can only be applied to constant growing firms.
    c. It cannot be used to value private firms.
    d. It cannot be applied to firms with negative earnings.

13. Which of the following is false regarding the relative valuation approach?
    a. The most commonly used one is the P/E ratio approach.
    b. The M/B ratio may be used instead of the P/E ratio if the firm has negative earnings.
    c. We can use the average P/E ratio of the firm's industry when appropriate.
    d. The leading P/E ratio can be estimated as: (Payout ratio)$(1 + g)/(k − g)$.

14. High P/E ratios tend to indicate that a firm will _____, all things being equal.
    a. grow quickly
    b. grow at the same speed as the average firm
    c. grow slowly
    d. not grow

Practice Problems

15. Describe the characteristics of preferred shares.

16. List the elements needed for the calculation of a share price using the constant growth DDM.

17. Describe the constant growth DDM valuation method.

18. Describe how to estimate the present value of growth opportunities (PVGO) and what it represents.

19. Fill in the missing information in the following table:

			Preferred Shares in Canada		
Company	Price	Par Value	Required return	Dividend rate	Dividends paid per share
A		$100	8%	5%	$5.00
B	$60	$50	3%		
C	$70	$75			$8.00
D	$50	$50		14%	
E	$150	$30	7%		
F		$100	4%		$9.50
G			7%	9%	$18.00
H	$18		5%	6%	

20. The preferred shares of Chinook Electrical Co. have a par value of $100 and a dividend rate of 8 percent. The current price is $110. If the risk-free rate is 2 percent, what is the risk premium associated with these preferred shares?

21. FinCorp Inc. purchased a stock for $50. It expects to receive a dividend of $5 in one year and to sell the stock immediately afterwards.
    a. If the sale price is $75, what is the expected one-year holding period return?
    b. If the sale price is $35, what is the expected one-year holding period return?
    c. If the actual return was –4 percent, what was the sale price?
    d. If the actual return was 15 percent, what was the sale price?

22. FinCorp Inc. purchased a stock for $50. It expects to hold the stock for two years, receive a dividend of $1.50 at the end of each year, and sell the stock immediately after receiving the second dividend. Assume dividends are held in a zero interest savings account.
    a. If the sale price is $75, what is the expected annual return?
    b. If the sale price is $35, what is the expected annual return?
    c. If the actual return was –4 percent, what was the sale price?
    d. If the actual return was 15 percent, what was the sale price?
       (Excel or financial calculator recommended.)

23. Fill in the missing information in the following table:

		Common Shares in Canada			
Company	Price	Required return	Dividend growth	Current dividend	Dividend expected in 1 year
A		15%		$4.50	$5.00
B	$600	3%	1%		
C	$70		5%		$8.00
D	$55			$10.00	$11.00
E		14%	6%	$9.50	
F		15%	0%		$18.00
G	$40	5%	–2%		

24. ToolWerks Company is expected to earn $10 million next year. There are 2 million shares outstanding and the company uses a dividend payout ratio of 40 percent. The required rate of return for companies like ToolWerks is 8 percent. The current share price of ToolWerks is $75.
    a. What are the expected earnings per share for ToolWerks?
    b. What are the expected dividends per share for ToolWerks?
    c. What is the dividend growth rate expected for ToolWerks?
    d. What is the present value of growth opportunities for this firm?

25. Determine the present value of growth opportunities for a company with a leading EPS of $1.85, a required rate of return of 8 percent, and a current stock price of $50.

26. Oak Furniture Company's most recent earnings were $300,000. From these earnings, it paid dividends on common equity totalling $175,000. There are 50,000 common shares outstanding. The ROE for Widget is 12 percent. Determine the following:
    a. i) Earnings per share.   ii) Which can you calculate: leading or lagging EPS?
    b. Dividends per share
    c. Earnings retention ratio
    d. Sustainable growth rate

27. State the relationship that the required rate of return, the expected growth rate, and expected dividends have with the market share price, according to the constant growth DDM.

28. Star Corporation has issued $1 million in preferred shares to investors with a 7.25 percent annual dividend rate on a par value of $100. Assuming the firm pays dividends indefinitely and the required rate is 10.5 percent, calculate the price of the preferred shares.

29. Calculate the leading P/E ratio, given the following information: retention ratio = 0.6, required rate of return = 10 percent, expected growth rate = 5 percent.

✿ 30. Global Systems Inc. has just paid $2 in dividends ($D_0 = \$2$). The firm is expected to continue paying dividends in perpetuity.
    a. Suppose that the dividends are constant ($D_i = \$2$ for all i). What will be the stock price of a share of Global Systems Inc. in 17 years if the required rate of return is 10 percent?
    b. Suppose that the dividends are expected to grow by 5 percent each year in perpetuity. What will be the price of a share of Global Systems Inc. in 17 years if the required rate of return is 10 percent? What will be the price in 15 years and in 25 years?

31. You have just been to see your broker at Acclaim Capital Inc. for advice about investing in the Empire Bank. The broker indicates that the Empire Bank has three different types of securities: debt, preferred shares, and common shares. She states: "Debt is safe because it is a bank and Canadian banks are safe. Empire Bank preferred shares entitle you to vote at the annual general meeting. The Empire Bank has paid a common share dividend of $2.50 per year for the past 18 years so you are guaranteed to receive $2.50 next year; if you don't, the bank will go bankrupt." Comment on your broker's statement. Is she correct?

32. Ibis Company is expected to pay a $1.50 dividend next year. Dividends are expected to grow at 3 percent forever and the required rate of return is 7 percent.
    a. What is the price of Ibis today?
    b. What is the expected dividend yield?
    c. What is the expected capital gains yield?
    d. In one year, immediately after the dividend is paid,

    i. what is the price of the stock?

    ii. what was the one-year holding period return?

    iii. Looking forward one year, what are the expected dividend and capital gains yields?

    e. In year 10, immediately after the dividend is paid,

    i. what is the price of the stock?

    ii. what was the one-year holding period return (year 9 to 10)?

    iii. Looking forward one year, what are the expected dividend and capital gains yields?

33. Parker Imports Ltd. is expected to pay a $2.00 dividend in one year. The required rate of return is 9 percent. The firm uses a dividend payout ratio of 25 percent. Calculate the leading P/E ratio in the following cases:

a. Expected growth rate = 4 percent
   i. Today

   ii. In one year (immediately after dividend paid)
b. Expected growth rate = 8 percent
   i. Today

   ii. In one year (immediately after dividend paid)
c. If a firm is expected to have a constant dividend growth rate, do you expect the P/E ratio to change over time? Explain.

34. Spinnaker Supplies Ltd. currently doesn't pay any dividends but is expected to start paying dividends in five years. The first dividend is expected to be $1.00 and to grow at 6 percent thereafter. The required rate of return for the firm is 10 percent. What is Spinnaker's current stock price?

35. Latta Incorporated has announced an annual dividend of $5.00. The firm has zero growth and the required rate of return for this type of firm is 10 percent. Assuming that the ex-dividend date is January 20, calculate the expected stock price for Latta on January 19 and January 21.

36. OK Natural Foods' current dividend is $5.00. You expect the growth rate to be 0 percent for years 1 to 5, and 2 percent for years 6 to infinity. The required rate of return on this firm's equity is 10 percent. Determine the following:
   a. The expected dividend at the end of year 5
   b. The expected dividend at the end of year 6
   c. The expected price of the stock at the end of year 5 (immediately after the year 5 dividend)
   d. The price of the stock today

37. Peak's Organic Foods' current dividend is $5.00. You expect the growth rate to be 8 percent for years 1 to 5, and 2 percent from years 6 to infinity. The required rate of return on this firm's equity is 10 percent. Determine the following:
   a. The expected dividend at the end of year 5
   b. The expected dividend at the end of year 6
   c. The expected price of the stock at the end of year 5 (immediately after the year 5 dividend)
   d. The price of the stock today

38. Peele Clothiers Ltd.'s current dividend is $3.60. Dividends are expected to grow by 9 percent for years 1 to 3, 6 percent for years 4 to 7, and 2 percent thereafter. The required rate of return on the stock is 12 percent. What is the current stock price for Company C?

39. Prime Tire's current dividend is $4.00. Dividends are expected to grow by 25 percent for years 1 to 3 and 10 percent thereafter. The required rate of return on the stock is 15 percent. What is Prime's current stock price?

40. Investors demand a rate of return of 15 percent on Sweet Life Food Inc.'s common shares. These shares are currently trading at $20 per share. Dividend payout for the current year is expected to be $1 per share.
   a. What is the implied long-term growth rate that shareholders expect?
   b. If, because of a recession, the dividend growth rate is projected to be 0, what will be the new share value?
   c. Conversely, if, because of a booming economy, investors reassess their growth expectations to 15 percent per year, what will happen to the market price of Sweet Life Food's common shares?

41. Dillon Mechanical Inc.'s first dividend of $2 per share is expected to be paid six years from today. From then on, dividends will grow by 10 percent per year for five years. After five years, the growth rate will then slow to 5 percent per year in perpetuity. Assume that Dillon's required rate of return is 15 percent. What is the price of a share of Dillon Mechanical today?

42. TelTec Inc. stock is expected to sell for $10 per share four years from now. TelTec has just paid a dividend of 50 cents per share. Dividends are expected to grow at a rate of 5 percent per year for the next four years. Assume that the required rate of return for TelTec stock is 15 percent.
    a. What is the expected constant growth rate beginning in year 5?
    b. What will the price of TelTec stock be five years from now?
    c. What is TelTec's current stock price?

43. JINX Ltd. had earnings per share of $5 as at December 31, 2012, but paid no dividends. Earnings were expected to grow at 15 percent per year for the following five years. JINX Ltd. will start paying dividends for the first time on December 31, 2017, distributing 50 percent of its earnings to shareholders. Earnings growth will be 6 percent per year for the next six years (that is, from January 1, 2018 through to December 31, 2023). Starting on December 31, 2023, JINX Ltd. will begin to pay out 80 percent of its earnings in dividends and earnings growth will stabilize at 2 percent per year in perpetuity. The required rate of return on TJINX stock is 10 percent. What should be the current share price of JINX?

44. Karlyle Inc. has just paid a dividend of $4. An analyst forecasts annual dividend growth of 9 percent for the next five years; then dividends will decrease by 1 percent per year in perpetuity. The required return is 8 percent (effective annual return, EAR). What is the current value per share according to the analyst?

45. Next year Dillon Mechanical Inc.'s EPS is expected to be $2. The firm is not expected to pay any dividends for the next four years. In year 5, a dividend of $1 is expected and subsequent dividends are expected to grow at 5 percent per year. Another firm's (Sterling Inc.'s) next-year EPS is expected to be $5. Sterling has just paid a dividend of $5 (cheques were mailed out today). Its dividends are expected to grow at 1 percent per year. Assume that the cost of capital for both firms is 15 percent.
    a. What should be the current share price of Dillon Mechanical Inc.?
    b. What should be the current share price of Sterling Inc.?
    c. What is the PVGO of Dillon Mechanical?
    d. What is the PVGO of Sterling?

46. Apex Financial Ltd. is concerned about the impact of errors in its estimates of the future dividend payout ratio for Barnett Steel Corporation. Assume that the current dividend is $1, ROE is fixed at 10 percent, and the required rate of return is 15 percent. Using Excel, calculate the current stock price for dividend payout ratios ranging between 5 percent and 75 percent in 5 percentage point increments. Is the percentage change in the stock price for a 5 percentage point change in dividend payout ratio constant?

47. List three reasons why one firm may have a higher leading P/E ratio than a comparable firm.

48. TelTec Inc. has a patent that will expire in two years. The firm is expected to grow at 10 percent for the next two years and dividends will be paid at year end. It just paid a dividend of $1.00. After two years, the growth rate will decline to 4 percent immediately, and the firm will grow at this rate forever. If the required rate of return is 11 percent, value the firm's current share price.

49. INV Design Ltd. just paid a dividend of $4.00 and its current earnings per share is $5. The current T-bill rate is 3 percent and DE's risk premium is 12 percent. The net profit margin, asset turnover, and debt-to-equity (D/E) ratio are 20 percent, 1.5, and 0.67, respectively. Calculate the current share price by using the P/E ratio approach.

50. Dillon Mechanical Ltd.'s preferred shares have a par value of $50, a dividend rate of 7 percent, and trade at a price of $70. Sherwood Inc.'s preferred shares have a par value of $60, a dividend rate of 4 percent, and trade at a price of $45. Which company's preferred stock is riskier?

⚙ 51. Barchuk Mining Inc.'s share is currently selling for $150. The current dividend is $10 and the required rate of return is 10 percent. What is the expected dividend growth rate?

⚙ 52. Apex Financial Ltd. is interested in investing in Scion Systems Inc. Scion's current dividend is $5.50 and its shares are selling for $40. The required rate of return for firms like Scion is 8 percent. Apex has conducted an extensive analysis of the company and believes that the dividend growth rate should be 5 percent.
   a. Should Apex buy the stock at $40? Why or why not?
   b. Do you expect the stock price to stay at $40? Explain.

53. As part of your duties at Apex Financial Ltd. you have been asked to review the analysis carried out by a rival company—Prime Group—of the WX Media Company. WX has had a constant P/E ratio for the past five years. Prime's analyst has made the following statement: "WX's constant P/E ratio is due to zero growth in its earnings, and therefore, WX is not a good investment." Comment on Prime's statement.

⚙ 54. Selkirk Inc. has an expected profit margin of 10 percent, turnover ratio of 1.8, and a leverage ratio of 0.30. The leading EPS is $2.50 and the firm uses a dividend payout ratio of 35 percent. The required return on firms with Selkirk's risk characteristics is 5 percent. Calculate the expected current stock price of Selkirk.

⚙ 55. Larch Foods Inc.'s current dividend is $4.00. Dividends are expected to decline by 4 percent per year for the next three years, and then remain constant thereafter. The required rate of return for this type of company is 15 percent. What is the current stock price for Larch Foods?

56. Apex Financial Ltd. has completed a fundamental analysis of Spark Energy Inc. Spark Energy is a young company and expects to invest heavily in facilities and research and development during the next five years. It expects to reap the benefits of its research and development during years 6 to 10. However, it expects rivals to enter the market and margins and profitability to stabilize at a lower level after year 10. The details of the analysis are presented below:

Period	Net profit margin	Turnover	Leverage	Dividend payout ratio
Years 1–5	1%	0.75	3.0	0.05
Years 6–10	15%	3.00	2.0	0.10
Years 11–?	5%	1.40	1.0	0.50

The current dividend for Spark Energy is $3.00 and the required rate of return for this type of firm is 15 percent. Determine the current stock price for Spark Energy.

Part 4

PORTFOLIO AND CAPITAL MARKET THEORY

This section of the text discusses the key topics of risk, return, and portfolio theory. We discuss various measures of risk and methods for estimating the required rate of return for securities and portfolios. In Chapter 10, we discuss market efficiency and the importance of this issue for both investors and corporations.

8 | Risk, Return, and Portfolio Theory

LEARNING OBJECTIVES

8.1   Distinguish between ex post and ex ante returns and explain how they are estimated.

8.2   Distinguish between arithmetic and geometric means.

8.3   Explain how common risk measures are calculated and what they mean.

8.4   Describe what happens to risk and return when securities are combined in a portfolio.

8.5   Explain what is meant by the "efficient frontier."

8.6   Define diversification and explain why it is important to investors.

8.7   Construct two-security portfolio risk-return frontiers.

The average annual return on Canadian stocks for the decade ending December 31, 2010, was a mere 6.6 percent, while the average return on U.S. and global stocks over the same period was −2.6 and −1.3 percent, respectively. This decade (which has been referred to as the "lost decade" in the United States) was extremely volatile, including negative stock returns in Canada of approximately −12.5 percent in 2001 and 2002, as the high tech market crashed, and −33 percent in 2008 as the financial crisis hit its peak. So what can investors do to deal with this volatility? Tom Bradley, president of Steadyhand Investment Funds, suggests that you view your investments as a "portfolio" and that you be aware of the following three points:

1. Losing money in a year is part of life as an investor, even if you have a diversified portfolio: "Good returns over the long term will come with some periods of negative returns."
2. Healthy portfolios may have holdings that are money losers over a year or longer: "If you feel comfortable about everything that you own, you're not diversified."
3. Weak returns do not necessarily mean changes are needed: "Just because bonds, for example, didn't do much for my portfolio this year doesn't mean they're not playing a useful role."

Source: Carrick, Rob, "Measure your portfolio with the right yardstick." *The Globe and Mail,* January 21, 2011 p. B13. ©The Globe and Mail, Inc. All rights reserved. Reprinted by permission.

CHAPTER 8 PREVIEW

This chapter defines risk and return, which is the basic relationship in finance. Unfortunately, at any point in time, people tend to focus on only one of the "R's." When times are good, nobody thinks about risk; when times are bad, people only see risks—the truth lies somewhere between. This chapter establishes the relationship between risk and return, with particular emphasis on equity securities. As such, it lays the foundation for Chapter 9, which discusses some of the most important concepts in finance.

8.1 MEASURING RETURNS

Learning Objective 8.1
Distinguish between ex post and ex ante returns and explain how they are estimated.

In Chapter 7, we discussed the basics of the discounted cash flow (DCF) valuation of equities and finished with an analysis of Tim Hortons' common shares that placed Tim Hortons' stock price in the $50 to $55 range at a time when it was trading at $52.56.

Risk is typically defined as "the possibility of incurring harm." Purchasing shares in Tim Hortons at $52.56 and then holding them could prove wise, but no one can say for sure—there is an element of uncertainty, or risk, involved. This chapter is concerned with ways to analyze and manage this risk. First, we develop some basic definitions.

Ex Post versus Ex Ante Returns

ex post returns past or historical returns

ex ante returns future or expected returns

We must distinguish between **ex post returns** and **ex ante returns**. "Ex post" means "after the fact," so ex post returns are past or historical returns. "Ex ante" means "before the fact," so ex ante returns are expected returns. Advertisements for mutual funds and other investments show historical, or ex post, returns. Then, in smaller print, they have a disclaimer that says past returns do not necessarily reflect future, or ex ante, returns. Of course, what investors are interested in are these future or expected returns, but their judgement in terms of what they can reasonably expect is informed by what has happened in the past. The 33-percent negative return on Toronto Stock Exchange (TSX) stocks during 2008 shows that sometimes what happens is outside of what anyone expects. Even the experts never anticipated such a collapse in stock markets. Similarly, at the end of 2008, few would have predicted a banner year in 2009, when stocks returned 35 percent.

income yield the return earned by investors as a periodic cash flow

So how can investors measure these ex post or historical returns? As we saw in chapters 6 and 7, the return on an investment consists of two components: the income yield and the capital gain (or loss) yield. The **income yield** is the return earned in the form of a periodic cash flow received by the investors. These cash flows are interest payments from bonds and dividends from equities. The income yield measures these cash receipts by dividing them by the purchase price or the beginning-of-period market price. This is shown in Equation 8-1.

[8-1]

$$\text{Income yield} = \frac{CF_1}{P_0}$$

where CF_1 = the expected cash flows to be received
P_0 = the purchase price (or beginning market price)

The graph in Figure 8-1 shows the earnings yield (E/P) on the S&P/TSX Composite Index and the yield to maturity on the long Canada bond since 1986.[1] Notice that since 2005, earnings yields have been higher than bond yields (especially in 2008 and 2011) due to declines in stock prices, and also because bond yields remained extremely low over this period.

---

[1] The earnings yield depicted here is measured as EPS_0/P_0—that is, it is based on earnings per share over the previous 12 months, not the expected EPS.

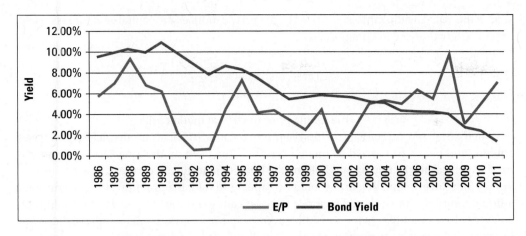

FIGURE 8-1 *Market Yields, 1986 to 2011*

Remember that the yield to maturity on the long Canada bond is the return earned by buying the bond and holding it to maturity. In this sense, it is also an expected return over that very long investment horizon. Investors often compare bond yields to the aggregate market dividend yield, such as that on the S&P/TSX Composite Index in Canada. The dividend yield, on the other hand, is the cash that investors can expect to earn if the dividend payments over the next year are the same as they were over the previous period. The dividend yield is a measure of the current dividend payments divided by the current value of the index; it is not a forecast of future dividends. The dividend yield on the TSX was very similar to that on long Canada bonds during the 1950s. During that decade, Canada bonds yielded, on average, only 0.82 percent more than the S&P/TSX dividend yield. In fact, during December 1957, the dividend yield on the TSX was 4.41 percent, exceeding the 3.83 percent yield on the long Canada bond. Obviously, 4.41 percent dominates 3.83 percent, so a piece of the puzzle is missing; otherwise, everyone would buy common shares and no one would buy long Canada bonds. The missing piece is the risk attached to investing in common shares.

After the late 1950s, the yield gap between common shares and the long Canada bond became significant, as Table 8-1 indicates. The spread increased to 2.35 percent in the 1960s, 4.54 percent in the 1970s, and 8.14 percent in the 1980s. The average yield gap decreased to 5.51 percent in the 1990s and to 2.02 percent so far in the 2000s. In fact, the spread was slightly negative in 2008, and hit −1.33 percent by the end of 2011, as bond yields fell to 1.52 percent and dividend yields were 2.85 percent due to the relatively low level of stock prices.

TABLE 8-1 Average Yield Gap between Common Shares and the Long Canada Bond (%)

1950s	0.82
1960s	2.35
1970s	4.54
1980s	8.14
1990s	5.51
2000s (to 2011)	2.02
Overall	3.90

capital gain the appreciation in the price of an asset from some starting price, usually the purchase price or the price at the start of the year

capital loss the depreciation in the price of an asset from some starting price, usually the purchase price or the price at the start of the year

The main reason this yield gap has varied so much over time is that the return to investors is not just the income yield but also the capital gain (or loss) yield.

The **capital gain** (or **capital loss**) component measures the appreciation (or depreciation) in the price of the asset from some starting price, usually the purchase price or the price at the start of the year. Dividing this gain or loss by the price produces the capital gain (or loss) yield or return, as expressed in Equation 8-2.

[8-2]

$$\text{Capital gain (loss) return} = \frac{P_1 - P_0}{P_0}$$

where P_1 = the selling price or current market price

When we take the capital gain (or loss) yield into account, it is clear why the yield gap between equities and bonds has varied so much over time. The yield on the long Canada bond is a fixed return earned by buying and holding the bond to maturity. In contrast, as a firm retains money for reinvestment, that firm should become more valuable over time; investing in such a firm's common shares should give rise to significant long-term capital gains. In addition, common shares should gain from inflation over the long run as their prices and cash flows are not fixed; in aggregate, they should increase with inflation. As a result, we would expect the yield gap to increase with the rate of inflation, which it generally does. Remember, for example, from Figure 6-4, that the high level of long Canada bond yields coincided with the very high rates of inflation in the 1970s into the 1980s, when the yield gap was the highest.

To get the complete picture of the return from investing in bonds versus common shares, we have to add the income yield and the capital gain (or loss) yield together. The **total return** is then calculated using Equation 8-3.

total return income yield plus the capital gain (or loss) yield

[8-3]

$$\text{Total return} = \text{Income yield} + \text{Capital gain (or loss) yield}$$
$$= \frac{CF_1 + P_1 - P_0}{P_0}$$

EXAMPLE 8-1   Calculating Returns

Estimate the income yield, capital gain (or loss) yield, and total return for the following securities over the past year:

a.   A $1,000 par value, 6-percent bond that was purchased one year ago for $990 and is currently selling for $995.

b.   A stock that was purchased for $20, provided four quarterly dividends of $0.25 each, and is currently worth $19.50.

Solution

a. $CF_1 = 0.06 \times \$1,000 = \$60$; $P_0 = \$990$; $P_1 = \$995$
Income yield = 60/990 = 0.0606 = 6.06%
Capital gain (loss) return = (995 − 990)/990 = 0.0051 = 0.51%
Total return = 6.06% + 0.51% = 6.57%
Or total return = (60 + 995 − 990)/990 = 0.0657 = 6.57%

b. $CF_1 = \$0.25 \times 4 = \$1.00$; $P_0 = \$20$; $P_1 = \$19.50$
Income yield = 1/20 = 0.05 = 5%
Capital gain (loss) return = (19.50 − 20)/20 = −0.025 = −2.5%
Total return = 5% − 2.5% = 2.5%
Or total return = (1 + 19.50 − 20)/20 = 0.025 = 2.5%

In Example 8-1, notice that the bond has not been held to maturity, so the return over one year may be different from the yield to maturity. In this case, the bond has increased in value from $990 to $995, so there is a capital gain of 0.51 percent from holding the bond, in addition to the income yield of 6.06 percent, so the total return is 6.57 percent. This raises an important question: in calculating the rate of return, does it matter whether or not the bond is sold? Take part (b) in Example 8-1, where there is a capital loss of 2.5 percent. This reduces the return from holding the common share from 5 percent to 2.5 percent, so it is less than the return from the bond. Should we add this capital loss to the overall return if we do not actually sell the shares?

The answer may seem obvious to most people, but psychologists have observed that people make different decisions if they own something than if they do not own it. For example, people will keep something for years because it cost $100 and is "valuable," even after they see the identical object selling for $1 in a flea market and yet wouldn't buy it for $1. Owning assets includes an attachment effect, and with such an attitude, many people refuse to accept capital losses in the total return calculation until they actually sell the asset and realize them. Until then, people refer to them as **paper losses**, with the implication that they are not real. This attitude is reinforced by the tax rules: capital gains and losses are only taxable on realization.

A second important point is that our decision to acknowledge paper gains and losses depends, in part, on our "investment horizon." For example, we can look at rates of return over daily, weekly, monthly, annual, or even longer periods. A **day trader** is someone who buys and sells based on intraday price movements. In that case, the total return for a day's trading will include the effect of capital gains and losses daily and sometimes over even shorter periods. In contrast, most people review their investments less frequently, perhaps quarterly or sometimes annually. For them, the intraday price variability and total return are not a concern. What is of concern is the total return over, say, a quarter or a year. They are not concerned about rates of return over shorter periods or the paper losses that are involved.[2]

The contrary view is that investors have to **mark to market** the prices of all financial securities over the relevant investment horizon. This means that investors always carry securities at the current market value regardless of whether they sell them. As a result, the total return includes the effect of paper gains and losses on securities not yet sold. This view is based on the basic opportunity cost argument, which asks what the alternative use is for the funds tied up in the investment. Clearly, an investor cannot sell the security at its historical cost; he or she can sell at the current market value, and this is the value that can be reinvested elsewhere. In this textbook, we will always mark to market and consider the total return as including paper gains and paper losses over the relevant investment horizon, because this reflects the economic value of past investment decisions.

paper losses capital losses that people do not accept as losses until they actually sell and realize them

day trader someone who buys and sells based on intraday price movements

mark to market carrying securities at the current market value regardless of whether they are sold

Measuring Average Returns

How can we measure these ex post or historical returns? Recall Table 5-1 from Chapter 5, which reported the arithmetic and geometric average annual rates of return for various types of investments from 1938 to 2011. These returns assume that the investor buys and holds the security for each year. Part of that table is reproduced in Table 8-2. It is important that you understand how these returns are calculated.

Learning Objective 8.2
Distinguish between arithmetic and geometric means.

---

[2] This brings to mind the philosophical question, "Does a tree falling in a forest make a noise if there is no one there to hear it?" Similarly, does a daily total return matter to an investor who only reviews his or her investments once a month? Perhaps it depends on the month—during September 2008, when global stock markets plummeted, it could have mattered a lot!

TABLE 8-2 Average Investment Returns and Standard Deviations, 1938 to 2011

	Annual Arithmetic Mean (%)	Annual Geometric Mean (%)[3]	Standard Deviation of Annual Returns (%)
Government of Canada treasury bills	4.96	4.88	4.24
Government of Canada bonds	6.44	6.08	8.99
Canadian stocks	11.35	10.03	16.82
U.S. stocks	12.16	10.77	17.53

Source: Annual geometric mean data from Table 5-1 are from the Canadian Institute of Actuaries (data to 2008) and from Statistics Canada CANSIM database (data from 2009 to 2011). Other data are from the Canadian Institute of Actuaries and from Datastream.

arithmetic mean or **arithmetic average** the most commonly used value in statistics; the sum of all returns divided by the total number of observations

The **arithmetic mean** or **arithmetic average** is the most commonly used value in statistics. It is calculated as the sum of all of the returns divided by the total number of observations, as expressed in Equation 8-4.

[8-4]
$$\text{Arithmetic mean (AM)} = \frac{\sum_{i=1}^{n} r_i}{n}$$

where r_i = the individual returns
n = the total number of observations

geometric mean the average or compound growth rate over multiple time periods

The **geometric mean**, in contrast, measures the compound growth rate over multiple periods, which was discussed in Chapter 5. For investments, this is the growth rate in the value invested or, equivalently, the compound rate of return. Recall that in Chapter 5, Table 5-1 showed that the future value of $1,000 invested in Canadian stocks at the start of 1938 would have grown to $1,183,626 by the end of 2011 (i.e., after 74 years) if all the income was reinvested each period. In fact, the precise geometric mean return was 10.03476580 percent, which means that $1,000 invested in 1938 and compounded at 10.03 percent grew to $1,183,626 after 74 years, or $FV = (\$1,000)(1.100347658090)^{74} = \$1,183,625.56$ (the difference is due to rounding the compound rate). In fact, the geometric mean is the rate of return used to find the future value, as discussed in Chapter 5. It is calculated using Equation 8-5.

[8-5]
$$\text{Geometric mean (GM)} = [(1+r_1)(1+r_2)(1+r_3)...(1+r_n)]^{1/n} - 1$$

EXAMPLE 8-2   Calculating Arithmetic Mean and Geometric Mean

Estimate the arithmetic mean (AM) and geometric mean (GM) for the following returns: 4.3 percent, 3.2 percent, 5.6 percent, 10.5 percent, and −7.6 percent.

Solution

AM = (4.3 + 3.2 + 5.6 + 10.5 − 7.6)/5 = 16/5 = 3.2%

GM = [(1.043)(1.032)(1.056)(1.105)(0.924)]^{1/5} − 1 = (1.1605455)1/5 − 1 = 1.0302 − 1 = 0.0302 or 3.02%

In Example 8-2, notice that the geometric mean is less than the arithmetic mean. This will always be the case unless the values are all identical. The more the returns vary, the bigger the difference between the AM and GM will be.

[3] This was referred to as the annual compound return in Table 5-1. This is because the geometric mean is the mean used in compounding.

We will formally discuss statistical measurement of how much returns vary in section 8.2, but note that the last column in Table 8-2 gives the **standard deviation** of the annual returns. The standard deviation measures the "typical" variation of the return: the larger the standard deviation, the more variable the return. When the standard deviation is squared, we get a measure called the variance. The difference between the AM and GM returns is approximately half this variance.

For example, the standard deviation of the annual treasury bill (T-bill) returns was 4.24 percent or 0.0424. Squaring this to get the variance gives us 0.00179776, and half this is 0.00089888 or 0.089888 percent. Note that the difference between the AM and GM T-bill returns is 4.96 percent minus 4.88 percent or 0.08 percent! So the approximation is very close. For Canadian equities, the standard deviation and variance were 16.82 percent (or 0.1682) and 0.02829124 respectively, so half the variance is 1.4146 percent. In this case, the difference between the AM and GM equity returns is 11.35 percent minus 10.03 percent or 1.32 percent, so the approximation is less precise.

As we indicated before, the more variable the annual returns, the bigger the difference between the AM and GM measures of return. Looking again at Table 8-2, the biggest difference is for the common stock returns and then the long bond returns. The smallest is for the T-bill returns. So when should we use the AM and when the GM to describe the average return from an investment? The answer depends on what we are trying to do.

The AM is appropriate when we are trying to estimate the typical return for a given period, such as a year. If we wanted to know the best estimate for the rate of return over the next year, we would use the AM of the annual rates of return because, by definition, this measures the average annual rate of return. We use the GM when we are interested in determining the "true" average rate of return over multiple periods—for instance, if we wanted to know how our investment (and wealth) will grow over time. We use the GM because it measures the compound rate of growth in our investment value over multiple periods. In this sense, the difference between the AM and GM is dependent on the relevant investment horizon.

If the investment horizon is one year, the AM is the best estimate. If the investment horizon is multiple years, the GM is better. Example 8-3 demonstrates why the geometric mean is superior for estimating returns over multiple periods.

standard deviation a measure of risk over all the observations; the square root of the variance, denoted as σ

EXAMPLE 8-3 | Geometric Mean versus Arithmetic Mean

Estimate the annual arithmetic mean return and the geometric mean return on an investment that is purchased for $100, rises to $110 after one year, and falls to $100 by the end of the second year. Assume the investment provided no income during the two-year period.

Solution

Total return (Year 1) = (110 − 100)/100 = 0.1 = 10%

Total return (Year 2) = (100 − 110)/110 = −9.09%

AM = (10 − 9.09)/2 = 0.455%

GM = $[(1.1)(0.9091)]^{1/2} - 1 = 0.0000 = 0.00\%$

The annual arithmetic mean return is 0.455 percent because this is simply the average of the two annual rates of return. However, to tell an investor that he or she has made on average 0.455 percent, when the investment is worth exactly what it started with, is misleading. In contrast, the geometric mean or compound rate of return provides the correct annual return of 0 percent.

Why the AM and GM differ in Example 8-3 can be seen by looking at the two rates of return. As we mentioned before, the annual rates of return have to vary to make a difference between the AM and GM, which they did in Example 8-3. Now notice that the gain of 10 percent is made when the investment is worth $100, whereas the loss of 9.09 percent is made when the investment is worth $110. Clearly, a gain of 10 percent on $100 is $10 and a loss of 9.09 percent on $110 is also $10, which is why the investor ends up with the same $100 that he or she started with. However, the AM simply averages the annual rates of return without taking into account that the amount invested varies across time. For this reason, the GM is a better way to estimate the average return when we are interested in the performance of an investment over time.

Estimating Expected Returns

expected returns estimated future returns

Although it is important to be able to estimate the ex post returns realized from past investments, investors are generally interested in the returns they *expect* to realize from an investment made today. In practice, **expected returns** are often estimated based on historical averages, but the problem is that there is no guarantee the past will repeat itself. For example, the years 1938 to 2011 included World War II (1939–45), a period of significant inflation (the 1970s and into the 1980s), a recession caused, in part, by the passing of the North American Free Trade Agreement between Canada, the United States, and Mexico (early 1990s), a bubble in technology stock prices, and a catastrophic 2008 for investors at the height of the recent financial crisis. For investors interested in expected returns, such events as these can have unexpected effects.

An alternative approach is to use all available information to assess the most likely returns under various future scenarios and then attach probabilities to the likelihood of each occurring. Using this approach, the expected return is estimated as the weighted average of the expected returns under each scenario; the weights correspond to the probability of each scenario actually occurring. This is expressed by Equation 8-6.

[8-6]
$$ER = \sum_{i=1}^{n} (r_1 \times Prob_i)$$

where ER = the expected return on an investment
r_i = the estimated return in scenario i
$Prob_i$ = the probability of state i occurring

EXAMPLE 8-4   Estimating Expected Returns

Suppose you are given the following information for two stocks, A and B, where the return on each varies with the state of the economy.

State of the Economy	Probability of Occurrence†	Expected Return on Stock A in This State	Expected Return on Stock B in This State
High growth	0.1	60%	5%
Moderate growth	0.2	20%	25%
No growth	0.5	10%	5%
Recession	0.2	−25%	0%

Estimate the expected return for each stock.

Solution

$ER_A = 0.1(60) + 0.2(20) + 0.5(10) + 0.2(-25) = 10\%$

$ER_B = 0.1(5) + 0.2(25) + 0.5(5) + 0.2(0) = 8\%$

Conceptually, the expected return in Example 8-4 is calculated the same way we calculate AM from historical data; the only difference is how we calculate the probabilities. In Example 8-4, we estimate the probabilities of each event directly. For example, economists might estimate the likelihood of different economic growth scenarios for the upcoming year, and security analysts will estimate the prospects for each firm. This sort of scenario data can then be packaged into data similar to what we have in the table in Example 8-4. In contrast, the AM simply assumes that each observation is equally likely, so the probability of each event is reflected in the number of times we observe it in the data. For example, the data from 1938 to 2011 will reflect the historical probabilities of the four different economic scenarios in the table without paying any attention to where we are today.

There are pros and cons to each method of determining expected rates of return. For short-term forecasts, the scenario-based approach makes more sense, because where we are today has a huge bearing on what is likely to happen over a short period. However, for longer-run forecasts, the historical approach tends to be better because it reflects what actually happens, even if it was not expected. In the next sections, we will use the scenario-based approach.

CONCEPT REVIEW QUESTIONS

1. What is the difference between ex ante and ex post returns?

2. Why do the income and capital gains components of the total return differ between common shares and bonds?

3. Why is the GM return a better estimate of long-run investment performance than the AM return?

4. Why might a scenario-based estimate be more accurate for a short-run expected return than a historical AM estimate?

8.2 MEASURING RISK

We have already touched on the idea of risk several times. Risk is the probability of incurring harm, and for investors, harm generally means losing money or earning an inadequate rate of return. In the rest of this chapter, we will use the term "risk" to mean the probability that the actual return from an investment is less than the expected return.[4] This means that the more variable the possible returns, the greater the risk. We can see this in Figure 8-2, which graphs the actual returns for various investments from 1938 to 2011 whose averages were reported in Table 8-2. One thing that is obvious from the graph is the wide variation in returns for Canadian stocks and U.S. stocks relative to the returns for bonds and T-bills. For example, Canadian stock returns varied from a maximum of 48.43 percent to a minimum of −33 percent, while T-bill returns varied much less, with a maximum of 20.37 percent and a minimum of 0.37 percent.

Learning Objective 8.3
Explain how common risk measures are calculated and what they mean.

---

[4] Often, risk is defined as the probability that the actual return is less than the risk-free rate, because this reflects the alternative investment. However, for our purposes this distinction is not material.

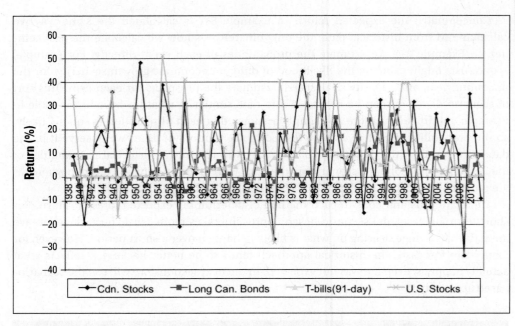

FIGURE 8-2 *Annual Returns, 1938 to 2011*

range the difference between the maximum and minimum values

The difference between the maximum and minimum values is called the **range**, so Canadian common stocks had a range of annual returns of 81.43 percent, which is greater than that for T-bills at 20 percent. The range summarizes the visual evidence that the returns on common stocks are more variable than those for bonds or T-bills. However, a more accurate measure of risk is the *standard deviation*, because the range only uses two observations, the maximum and minimum, whereas the standard deviation uses all the observations.

We reported the standard deviation of the 1938 to 2011 annual returns in Table 8-2 and discussed it when we pointed out the difference between the AM and GM returns. The standard deviation, like the range, clearly shows that common stock returns had a higher standard deviation in their annual returns than did bonds and T-bills over this period. This ranking of investments according to risk mirrors the ranking in terms of AM and GM returns, and it hints at a basic result in finance: risk and return go hand in hand. In other words, we normally see a trade-off between risk and return: securities offering higher expected rates of return tend to be riskier. So let's measure this risk using the standard deviation.

The definition of the standard deviation for a series of historical or ex post returns is shown in Equation 8-7.

[8-7]
$$\text{Ex post } \sigma = \sqrt{\frac{\sum_{i=1}^{n} (r_i - \bar{r})^2}{n-1}}$$

where

σ = the standard deviation
$\bar{r}$ = the average return
r_i = the return in year i
n = the number of obervations

variance the standard deviation squared; denoted as σ^2 and expressed in units of %²

The term inside the square root sign in Equation 8-7 is called the **variance**, which is denoted as σ^2. Therefore, the standard deviation is the square root of the variance, and, conversely, the variance is the square of the standard deviation. We focus on the standard deviation because it is easier to interpret: the standard deviation for a series of returns is expressed in the same unit as the returns—that is, as a percentage. In contrast, the variance is expressed as %², which makes its interpretation less obvious.

EXAMPLE 8-5   Calculating the Ex Post Standard Deviation

Estimate the standard deviation of the returns provided in Example 8-2 (i.e., 4.3 percent, 3.2 percent, 5.6 percent, 10.5 percent, and −7.6 percent).

Solution

Recall from Example 8-2 that the arithmetic mean for this series of returns was 3.2 percent Therefore, we can estimate the standard deviation as follows:.

$$\sigma = \sqrt{\frac{(4.3-3.2)^2 + (3.2-3.2)^2 + (5.6-3.2)^2 + (10.5-3.2)^2 + (-7.6-3.2)^2}{5-1}}$$

$$= \sqrt{\frac{1.21 + 0 + 5.76 + 53.29 + 116.64}{4}} = \sqrt{\frac{176.9}{4}} = \sqrt{44.225} = 6.65\%$$

Notice that the variance of this return series is 44.225%².

The standard deviation, as we have measured it, estimates the variability of the returns over the sample period. In the case of Example 8-5, this is 6.65 percent. For the investment returns from 1938 to 2011, the standard deviation of the annual returns for common shares was 16.82 percent; that for bonds was 8.99 percent. This raises the question of whether this relative risk was constant over the entire period. The graph in Figure 8-3 shows the ratio of the standard deviation of the returns on common shares to that on long Canada bonds over the 1947 to 2011 period. To see how this has changed over time, the estimates are based on rolling 10-year periods going back to 1938, so the first estimate is the ratio for 1938 to 1947, the second for 1939 to 1948, and so on.

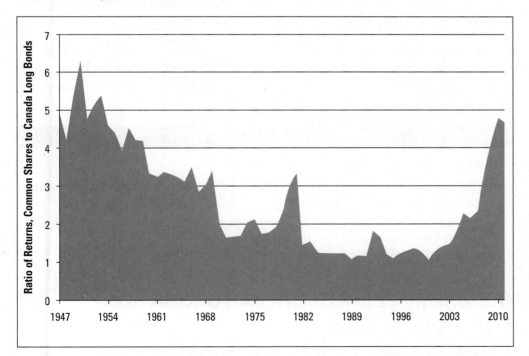

FIGURE 8-3 *Relative Uncertainty: Equities versus Bonds*

What is clear is that the relative risk of equities versus bonds has not been constant over this long period. Until the 1960s, the annual rates of return on common shares were about four to six times more variable than those on bonds. During the 1960s, they were approximately three times as volatile. Since then, they have been only approximately twice as variable, until the 2009 to 2011 period, when the ratio increased markedly into the 4 to 5 range. Just as the AM estimate of the annual return reflects the economic circumstances of the period over which it is estimated, so too does the standard deviation. For this reason, we also calculate the scenario-based standard deviation as a measure of risk.

The scenario-based standard deviation can be estimated using Equation 8-8 (where all variables are as defined in Equation 8-6). We will refer to this as the "ex ante measure" because we are explicitly taking into account updated probabilities of future events happening.

[8-8]
$$\text{Ex ante } \sigma = \sqrt{\sum_{i=1}^{n} (Prob_i)\,(r_i - ER)^2}$$

EXAMPLE 8-6   Estimating Ex Ante Standard Deviations

Estimate the standard deviations for stocks A and B from Example 8-4, using the information provided in that example.

Solution

$$\sigma_A = \sqrt{0.10(60 - 10)^2 + 0.20(20 - 10)^2 + 0.50(10 - 10)^2 + 0.20(-25 - 10)^2}$$
$$= \sqrt{250 + 20 + 0 + 245} = \sqrt{515} = 22.69\%$$
$$\sigma_B = \sqrt{(0.10(5 - 8)^2 + 0.20(25 - 8)^2 + 0.50(5 - 8)^2 + 0.20(0 - 8)^2}$$
$$= \sqrt{0.9 + 57.8 + 4.5 + 12.8} = \sqrt{76.00} = 8.72\%$$

Notice that A has the higher standard deviation; therefore, it appears to have the most risk, based on the variability of the forecast for its expected return.

Another commonly used measure of risk is "value at risk" (VaR). VaR is a probability-based measure of loss potential to a firm. Technically, it represents the estimated loss (in money terms) that could be exceeded (minimum loss) at a given level of probability. A lower probability translates into a higher potential loss, all else being equal. For example, a $1-million daily VaR at the 5-percent probability level means that there is a 5-percent chance of losing at least $1 million in one day (or a 95-percent chance that one day's losses will be lower than $1 million). Appendix 8B discusses VaR in greater detail.

CONCEPT REVIEW QUESTIONS

1. Why is the range sometimes a poor measure of risk?
2. What is the difference between a scenario-based (probability) estimate of risk versus a historical data-based estimate of risk?
3. Why would we sometimes want to use scenario-based risk measures rather than the standard deviation of actual returns over a long period?

Learning Objective 8.4
Describe what happens to risk and return when securities are combined in a portfolio.

portfolio a collection of securities, such as stocks and bonds, that are combined and considered a single asset

8.3 EXPECTED RETURN AND RISK FOR PORTFOLIOS

A **portfolio** is a collection of securities, such as stocks and bonds, that are combined and considered a single asset. A portfolio may refer to the holdings of a single investor or to holdings that are managed as a unit by one or more portfolio managers on behalf of their clients. It is a basic proposition in finance that securities should be managed within a portfolio, rather than individually, because it is possible to realize risk-reduction gains by combining securities into a portfolio. The study of portfolios and the potential gains related to them is called **modern portfolio theory (MPT)**, and we will be using the statistical ideas that we have just discussed to explore it. The basic idea is as simple as the old adage "don't put all your eggs in one basket": investors should diversify their investments so that they are not unnecessarily exposed to a single negative event. MPT takes this basic idea and operationalizes it to show how to form portfolios with the highest possible expected rate of return for any given level of risk. First, we will examine how to calculate the expected return and risk of a portfolio.

The expected return on a portfolio is simply the weighted average of the expected returns on the individual securities in the portfolio, as expressed in Equation 8-9. The "portfolio weight" of a particular security is the percentage of the portfolio's total value that is invested in that security. These weights sum to one, because 100 percent of the portfolio must be invested in something, even if it is simply cash.

$$ER_p = \sum_{i=1}^{n} (w_i \times ER_i)$$
[8-9]

where ER_p = the expected return on the portfolio
ER_i = the expected return on security i
w_i = the portfolio weight of security i

EXAMPLE 8-7   Estimating Expected Portfolio Return

Using the data from Example 8-4, estimate the expected return for a portfolio that has $600 invested in stock A and $1,400 invested in stock B.

Solution

Portfolio value = 600 + 1,400 = $2,000

$w_A = 600/2,000 = 0.3$

$w_B = 1,400/2,000 = 0.7$

So, $ER_p = w_A ER_A + w_B ER_B = (0.3)(10\%) + (0.7)(8\%) = 8.6\%$

The result of Example 8-7 means that if an investor puts 70 percent of his or her investment in security B, the remaining 30 percent has to be in A. We can simplify the expected return formula in the two-security case to make it more informative. Let us define w as simply the weight placed on security A, so that $(1 - w)$ is the weight placed on security B. In this case, we can rearrange the expected return for a two-security portfolio formula to get Equation 8-10.

$$ER_p = ER_B + w(ER_A - ER_B)$$
[8-10]

For example, if we place a weight of 0 on A, then, by definition, 100 percent is invested in B, and we expect to earn 8 percent, the expected return on B. Conversely, if we invest 100 percent in A and nothing in B, then we expect to earn 10 percent. Incrementally, as we increase w and put more money (weight) in A, we pick up the difference in the expected returns between A and B, which, with the numbers from Example 8-7, is 2 percent. In financial terms, the cost of investing in A is the lost 8-percent expected return from not investing in B, whereas the benefit is its expected return of 10 percent. There is a net advantage in terms of expected return of 2 percent.

modern portfolio theory (MPT)
the theory that securities should be managed within a portfolio, rather than individually, to create risk-reduction gains; also stipulates that investors should diversify their investments so as not to be unnecessarily exposed to a single negative event

We graph this relationship in Figure 8-4. Note that the graph sets the base return at 8 percent, where everything is invested in B, and then increases to 10 percent as we invest more and more in A.[5]

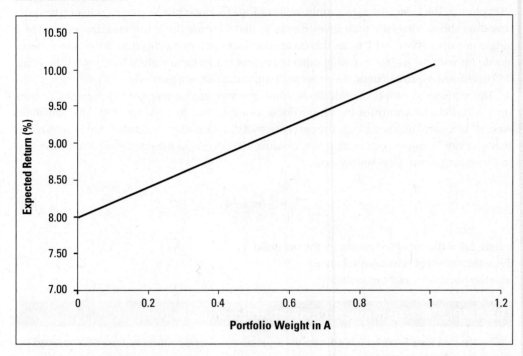

FIGURE 8-4 *Expected Portfolio Return*

Regardless of the number of assets held in a portfolio or the portfolio weights, the expected return on the portfolio is *always* a weighted average of the expected return on each individual asset. However, this is *not* the case for the portfolio standard deviation, because we must account for correlations, or co-movements, among the individual security returns included in the portfolio, which in turn affect the variability in total portfolio returns. Therefore, the standard deviation for a portfolio will reflect the weighted impact of the individual securities' standard deviations and the relationship among the co-movements of the returns on those individual securities.

The standard deviation of a two-security portfolio can be estimated using Equation 8-11. Notice that the first two terms inside the square root sign account for the weighted standard deviations (or variances) of individual securities, while the third term accounts for the weighted co-movement of the returns on the two securities. This is denoted by the **covariance** of the returns on A and B (COV_{AB}), which we define below.

covariance a statistical measure of the correlation of the fluctuations of the annual rates of return of different investments

[8-11]
$$\sigma_p = \sqrt{(w_A)^2(\sigma_A)^2 + (w_B)^2(\sigma_B)^2 + 2(w_A)(w_B)(COV_{AB})}$$

where σ_p = the portfolio standard deviation
COV_{AB} = the covariance of the returns on security A and security B

[5] For the purposes of this discussion, we have limited the investment weights to a range from 0 percent to 100 percent. However, if we are allowed to "short sell" either security, then the weights can be less than 0 (i.e., negative) and more than 100 percent. Short selling means investors sell shares in a stock that they do not own. This can be done through a broker, who "lends" investors shares that they can sell on the condition that the investors agree to "replace" these borrowed shares in the future (i.e., by buying them in the market). Thus, it provides investors with a way to profit from the belief that share prices will decrease. There are several technicalities associated with short selling that we will not discuss here. The main implication of short selling for our present discussion is that investors can maintain a negative position in one of the two stocks, so they can short sell A and use the proceeds to invest in B and vice versa.

The covariance is calculated using Equation 8-12.[6]

$$COV_{AB} = \sum_{i=1}^{n} Prob_i(r_{A,i} - \bar{r}_A)(r_{B,i} - \bar{r}_B)$$ [8-12]

where $r_{A,i}$ = the ith return on security A

EXAMPLE 8-8 Estimating Covariance

Using the data from Example 8-4, estimate the covariance of the returns on securities A and B.

Solution

$COV_{AB} = 0.1(60{-}10)(5{-}8) + 0.2(20{-}10)(25{-}8) + 0.5(10{-}10)(5{-}8) + 0.2(-25{-}10)(0{-}8)$

$= -15 + 34 + 0 + 56 = 75\%^2$

EXAMPLE 8-9 Estimating Portfolio Standard Deviation Using Covariance

Use the covariance estimate in Example 8-8 to estimate the standard deviation of the portfolio described in Example 8-7, which has 30 percent invested in stock A and 70 percent invested in stock B.

Solution
Using Equation 8-11, we get:

$$\sigma_p = \sqrt{(0.30)^2(22.69)^2 + (0.70)^2(8.72)^2 + 2(0.30)(0.70)(75)}$$

$$= \sqrt{46.335 + 37.259 + 31.500} = \sqrt{115.094} = 10.73\%$$

Notice that the portfolio standard deviation of 10.73 percent is less than the weighted average of the standard deviations of each individual security, which is 12.91 percent—that is, (0.30)(22.69) + (0.70)(8.72). This is always the case, except for one special situation, which we will discuss momentarily. However, before this discussion, we will demonstrate, in Figure 8-5, the implication of the difference between the portfolio standard deviation and the weighted average of the standard deviations of each security by graphing the standard deviation of the return on the portfolio as we put a greater share of our investment in the riskier security.

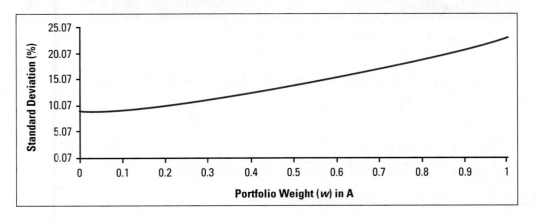

FIGURE 8-5 *Portfolio Risk*

---

[6] The ex post covariance can be calculated as $COV_{AB} = \dfrac{\sum_{i=1}^{n} (r_{A,i} - \bar{r}_A)(r_{B,i} - \bar{r}_B)}{n-1}$

We start out with the standard deviation of the portfolio at 8.72 percent because all funds are in B, and we finish up at 22.69 percent because all funds are in A, but the line between these points is not a straight one. In fact, the standard deviation of the portfolio's return barely moves as we increase investment in the riskier security to 20 percent, even though we expect to earn a higher rate of return. This is a clear win for the investor: more expected return and virtually the same amount of risk.

The curve that shows the standard deviation of the portfolio's return as we increase the investment in the risky security is distinctly "bowed." To see this, think of rotating the graph counterclockwise 180 degrees and then pulling on the bottom of the bow: you get the shape of the standard deviation of the portfolio return. We will return to this bow shape again as it is one of the most important ideas in MPT. For now, we turn to a discussion of another measure of return co-movements.

Although covariance provides a useful measure of the relationship of the co-movements of returns on individual securities, it is difficult to interpret intuitively because, as was the case with the variance, the unit is percent squared ($\%^2$). Fortunately, covariance is related to another statistical measure, the **correlation coefficient** (ρ_{AB}), which can be interpreted more intuitively. The correlation coefficient is related to covariance and individual standard deviations according to the relationship shown in Equation 8-13.

correlation coefficient a statistical measure that identifies how security returns move in relation to one another; denoted by ρ_{AB}

[8-13]
$$\rho_{AB} = \frac{COV_{AB}}{\sigma_A \sigma_B}$$

This equation can be solved for covariance to provide Equation 8-14.

[8-14]
$$COV_{AB} = \rho_{AB}\sigma_A \sigma_B$$

Finally, we can replace the covariance term in Equation 8-11 to produce Equation 8-15, which is commonly used to estimate portfolio standard deviation.

[8-15]
$$\sigma_p = \sqrt{(w_A)^2(\sigma_A)^2 + (w_B)^2(\sigma_B)^2 + 2(w_A)(w_B)(\rho_{AB})(\sigma_A)(\sigma_B)}$$

EXAMPLE 8-10   Estimating Portfolio Standard Deviation Using the Correlation Coefficient

Redo Example 8-9 using Equation 8-15 instead of Equation 8-11.

Solution
First, we need to estimate the correlation coefficient between the returns on stocks A and B.

$$\rho_{AB} = \frac{COV_{AB}}{\sigma_A \sigma_B} = \frac{75}{(22.69)(8.72)} = 0.379$$

By using Equation 8-15, we get

$$\sigma_p = \sqrt{(0.30)^2(22.69)^2 + (0.70)^2(8.72)^2 + 2(0.30)(0.70)(0.379)(22.69)(8.72)}$$

$$= \sqrt{46.335 + 37.259 + 31.495} = \sqrt{115.089} = 10.73\%$$

Example 8-10 yields the same answer as in Example 8-9. We can now separate the standard deviation component from the correlation component. This is useful because we already have the standard deviation of both securities in the first two terms, so the correlation coefficient is the only new information.

Correlation Coefficient

The correlation coefficient measures how security returns move in relation to one another. It is a relative measure that has a maximum value of +1.0, which denotes perfect positive correlation, and a minimum value of –1.0, which denotes perfect negative correlation. Positive correlation coefficients imply that the returns on security A tend to move in the same direction as those on security B. In other words, when the return on security B increases, the return on security A also tends to increase, and vice versa. It doesn't mean to say that they always increase together; if they did, they would be perfectly positively correlated. Negative correlation coefficients imply the opposite: the returns on security A tend to move in the opposite direction to those on security B. In other words, on average, when the return on security B increases, the return on security A tends to decrease, and vice versa.

The closer the absolute value of the correlation coefficient is to one, the stronger the relationship between the returns on the two securities. In fact, when $\rho_{AB} = +1$—that is, perfect positive correlation—and we know the return on one security, we can predict the return on the other security with certainty.[7] The same applies when we have $\rho_{AB} = -1$, perfect negative correlation, which implies the returns have a perfect negative relationship with each other. When $\rho_{AB} = 0$ (i.e., zero correlation), there is no relationship between the returns on the two securities. Therefore, knowing the return on one security provides no useful information for predicting the return on the second security. We illustrate various correlations in Figure 8-6, including perfect positive and perfect negative correlation, positive correlation, negative correlation, and no correlation. You can recognize perfect positive and perfect negative correlation right away, because the pairwise observations of returns lie on a perfectly straight line.

FIGURE 8-6 *Correlation between the Returns on Stocks*

Figure 8-6 is continued on next page.

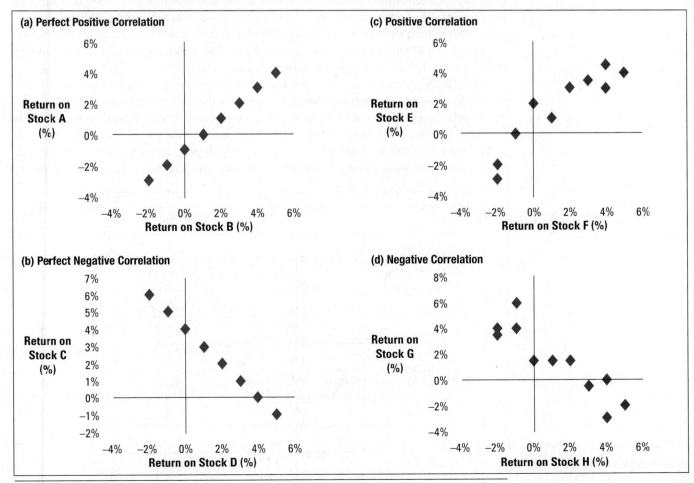

7 Technically, when $\rho = +1$ or -1 and we plot the returns of one asset on the x-axis and the returns of the other security on the y-axis, a line drawn through all the points would be straight. Such a line would be upward sloping when $\rho = +1$, and it would be downward sloping when $\rho = -1$.

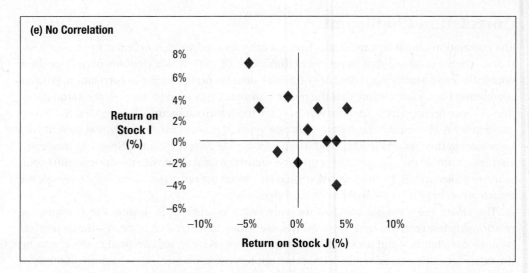

FIGURE 8-6 *Correlation between the Returns on Stocks (continued)*

The extreme correlation coefficient values described above do not occur for traditional common shares in practice, because so many different factors influence security returns. Generally, returns display positive correlations with one another, but they are less than one. This is logical because all securities tend to follow the movements of the overall market. As expected, the correlations tend to be higher among securities whose companies are similar in nature, for example, if they are in the same industry, are about the same size, and so on. For example, the correlation coefficient on the common share returns for the Big Six Canadian banks tends to be high, in the 0.7 to 0.8 range, while the correlation coefficient between bank stocks and mining stocks tends to be much lower, in the 0.2 to 0.4 range. So the correlation coefficient of 0.379 in Example 8-10 indicates the two securities are not in the same industry or are not affected similarly by common economic forces.

Figure 8-7A provides a scatter plot diagram of the returns on Canadian common shares relative to those on U.S. common shares. As expected, these returns possess a high and positive correlation coefficient of 0.686. Indeed, the graph shows that the returns tend to move in the same direction—that is, they both tend to be high or low at similar times. If we attempted to fit a line to these observations, it would be upward sloping, and the points would be relatively close to this line. Figure 8-7B depicts the returns on Canadian common shares relative

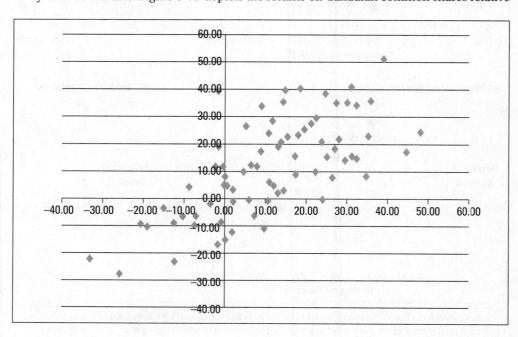

FIGURE 8-7A *Canadian versus U.S. Stock Returns, 1938 to 2011 (Correlation coefficient = 0.686)*

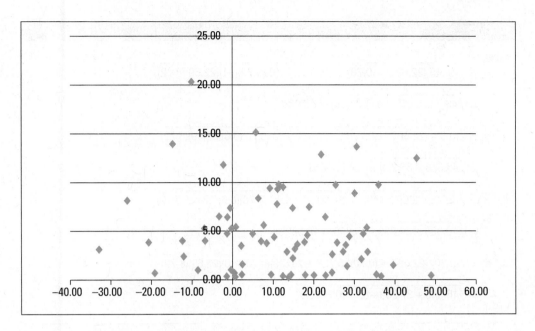

FIGURE 8-7B *T-Bill Returns versus Canadian Stock Returns, 1938 to 2011 (correlation coefficient = –0.077)*

to those on 91-day T-bills, which display a correlation coefficient that is close to zero, but is slightly negative (–0.077). The graph shows that knowing the return on one security provides little information about the return on the other. In other words, it would be hard to draw a line through these returns that depicts any kind of relationship.[8]

Finally, we can compare the correlation coefficient with the covariance. As noted in Equation 8-14, the covariance is the correlation coefficient multiplied by the two standard deviations. As a result, the covariance measures the strength, or magnitude, of the relationship between two variables. For example, two variables might be perfectly correlated, so that they always move together, but one of them might barely move at all: it might always go up when the other goes up, and vice versa, but not by very much. As a result, the covariance between these two variables might be lower than that between two other variables that are not so highly correlated.

Correlation Coefficients and Portfolio Standard Deviation

Recall that Equation 8-15 showed that the correlation between the returns on the two securities included in a portfolio affected the portfolio standard deviation. Holding the weights and the individual standard deviations constant, it is clear that the lower the correlation coefficient, the lower the standard deviation, a conclusion illustrated by Example 8-11.

EXAMPLE 8-11	Estimating Portfolio Standard Deviation as the Correlation Coefficient Changes

Redo Example 8-10 using Equation 8-15, but now assume that the correlation coefficient between the returns on A and B is

a.   –1

b.   0

c.   0.6

d.   1

continued

---

[8] If we d d draw a line, it would be downward sloping, as indicated by the slight negative correlation coefficient. However, the small absolute value of the coefficient indicates that it would not fit the data very well.

EXAMPLE 8-11   Estimating Portfolio Standard Deviation as the Correlation Changes *continued*

Solution

a. $\sigma_p = \sqrt{(0.30)^2(22.69)^2 + (0.70)^2(8.72)^2 + 2(0.30)(0.70)(-1)(22.69)(8.72)}$

$= \sqrt{46.335 + 37.259 - 83.100} = 0.703\%$

b. $\sigma_p = \sqrt{(0.30)^2(22.69)^2 + (0.70)^2(8.72)^2 + 2(0.30)(0.70)(0.0)(22.69)(8.72)}$

$= \sqrt{46.335 + 37.259 + 0} = 9.143\%$

c. $\sigma_p = \sqrt{(0.30)^2(22.69)^2 + (0.70)^2(8.72)^2 + 2(0.30)(0.70)(0.6)(22.69)(8.72)}$

$= \sqrt{46.335 + 37.259 + 49.860} = 11.552\%$

d. $\sigma_p = \sqrt{(0.30)^2(22.69)^2 + (0.70)^2(8.72)^2 + 2(0.30)(0.70)(1.0)(22.69)(8.72)}$

$= \sqrt{46.335 + 37.259 + 83.100} = 12.911\%$

There are several things to note from Example 8-11. First, the lower the correlation coefficient, the lower the portfolio standard deviation. In fact, the portfolio standard deviation for Example 8-11a is much lower than either individual standard deviation and is actually very close to zero. Obviously, the benefits will be greater as the correlation coefficient approaches −1. This highlights the importance of security return correlations in determining portfolio risk.

Second, the portfolio standard deviation is less than the weighted average of the individual security standard deviations (of 12.911 percent) in parts (a) to (c), as it was in Example 8-10, for which the correlation coefficient was +0.379. Only in Example 8-11d, for which the correlation coefficient equals +1, which is its highest possible value, was it a weighted average. Because +1 is the maximum value for the correlation coefficient, it must be the case that for all other possible correlation coefficients, we have $\sigma_p < w_A\sigma_A + w_B\sigma_B$. This implies there will be benefits from diversification as long as ρ_{AB} is less than +1, which is virtually always the case.

This result is very important because we have just shown the secret of MPT: by combining securities in a portfolio, we can reduce risk. This risk reduction increases as we combine securities that are less than perfectly correlated. It supports the basic finance argument that investors should hold diversified portfolios; otherwise, they are throwing away the magic of diversification, which is that they can lower risk without cost. We will return to this concept shortly, but first we graph the standard deviation of the portfolio return as the correlation coefficient changes in Figure 8-8.

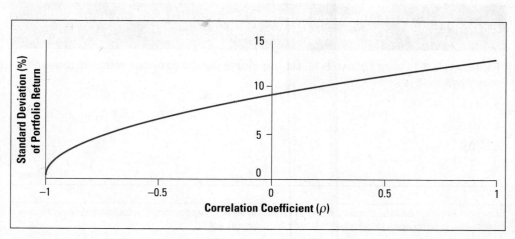

FIGURE 8-8 *The Impact of the Correlation Coefficient*

This graph shows several interesting things. First, the slope is not linear, as discussed before. This means that to demonstrate the effect of the correlation coefficient, we can use a zero correlation as an example, because this simplifies the arithmetic. Second, with perfectly negative correlation, the variability of the portfolio is reduced to almost zero, which means there is almost no risk. In fact, whenever the correlation coefficient equals −1, there exists one set of portfolio weights for the two securities such that we can eliminate risk completely. This suggests that to discuss how the standard deviation and expected return of a portfolio varies as we change its composition, we can look at three special cases: when the correlation coefficient between the two securities is zero, +1, or −1.

Let's go back to Equation 8-15, which, for ease of reference, we repeat below.

$$\sigma_p = \sqrt{(w_A)^2(\sigma_A)^2 + (w_B)^2(\sigma_B)^2 + 2(w_A)(w_B)(\rho_{AB})(\sigma_A)(\sigma_B)}$$

The three special cases produce simplified versions of the standard deviation of the portfolio's return, shown below.[9]

If $\rho = 0$ $\sigma_p = \sqrt{(w_A)^2(\sigma_A)^2 + (w_B)^2(\sigma_B)^2}$

If $\rho = +1$ $\sigma_p = \sqrt{(w_A)^2(\sigma_A)^2 + (w_B)^2(\sigma_B)^2 + 2(w_A)(w_B)(\sigma_A)(\sigma_B)}$

If $\rho = -1$ $\sigma_p = \sqrt{(w_A)^2(\sigma_A)^2 + (w_B)^2(\sigma_B)^2 - 2(w_A)(w_B)(\sigma_A)(\sigma_B)}$

The zero correlation coefficient case is obvious, as the covariance term disappears. However, in the other two cases, the correlation coefficient also disappears because it is either +1 or −1. We now get a perfect square: for a perfect positive correlation, think $(a + b)^2$, and for a perfect negative correlation, $(a - b)^2$, where a is the standard deviation of security A times its portfolio weight (i.e., $w_A\sigma_A$) and b is the same for security B (i.e., $w_B\sigma_B$). This allows us to simplify the equation for the standard deviation of the portfolio return.

Figure 8-5 showed how the portfolio risk (standard deviation) varied with the composition of the portfolio (i.e., based on the weights invested in A and B) for our example case, in which the correlation coefficient was 0.379. Now we can consider how the variability changes with the portfolio composition for these three special cases, because they contain everything of interest. The results are shown in Figure 8-9.

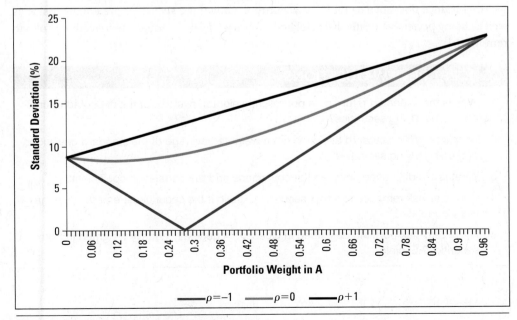

FIGURE 8-9 *Portfolio Risk and Composition*

---

[9] Remember these, as they often appear on tests and exams.

Note that with perfect positive correlation, the variability changes in a linear (straight line) fashion with the portfolio weights. As we discussed before, in this case, the standard deviation of the portfolio is a weighted average of each security's standard deviation, which is similar to the expected return. However, when the correlation is less than perfectly positive, the relationship is "bowed." It becomes more bowed as the correlation decreases until, with a perfect negative correlation, we can remove all risk. In this case, the bow becomes two straight lines that touch the horizontal axis. At this point in the $\rho = -1$ case, we can create a portfolio with a standard deviation of zero and no variability at all.

To calculate the portfolio that removes all risk (i.e., creates a portfolio with no variability), consider the special case of Equation 8-15, which reduces to Equation 8-16 when $\rho = -1$.

[8-16]
$$\sigma_p = w\sigma_A - (1 - w)\sigma_B$$

Here we have set the portfolio weights as w and $(1 - w)$ rather than w_A and w_B because they have to add to 100 percent. If we set the standard deviation of the portfolio equal to zero, we can solve for this weight using Equation 8-17.

[8-17]
$$w = \frac{\sigma_B}{\sigma_A + \sigma_B}$$

In our case, the weight is 27.76 percent, so if we put 27.76 percent of our investment in security A and 72.24 percent in the lower-risk security B, we get a portfolio that is risk free—that is, it has no variability at all. We can see this point in Figure 8-9, in which the two lines for the perfect negative correlation case touch the horizontal axis at just below 0.3.

The perfect negative correlation case is of great importance in finance, because it is the basis of hedging (taking an offsetting position so as to minimize risk; we will discuss hedging in more detail in chapters 11 and 12, when we deal with futures and options). Note that although the two securities in our example are perfectly negatively correlated, we do not create an equally weighted portfolio in which we invest the same amount in each security. Instead, we put 27.76 percent in the security with the greater standard deviation and 72.24 percent in the one with the smaller standard deviation. This is because when A goes up, B goes down, but they go up and down by different amounts, as indicated by their different standard deviations. As a result, we have to put more in the lower-variability security B to compensate for the fact that it does not move as much as security A. Only if the securities are equally risky, as well as being perfectly negatively correlated, would we form an equally balanced portfolio to remove risk.

CONCEPT REVIEW QUESTIONS

1. Why is the expected return on a portfolio a weighted average of the expected returns of the underlying securities?

2. Why is portfolio standard deviation not a weighted average of the standard deviations of the underlying securities?

3. What is the difference between the covariance and the correlation coefficient?

4. Why is all risk removed in a two-security portfolio if the securities are perfectly negatively correlated?

5. Is the zero-risk portfolio described in Question 4 generally equally weighted in both securities? Explain.

8.4 THE EFFICIENT FRONTIER

Two-Security Portfolio Combinations

Figure 8-4 showed how the expected return of a two-security portfolio (with a correlation coefficient of 0.379) changed as we changed the composition by shifting more of our investment toward security A (the riskier security), while Figure 8-5 showed how the portfolio standard deviation changed. If we plot these expected return–standard deviation combinations, with expected return on the vertical axis and standard deviation on the horizontal axis, we get Figure 8-10, which represents all possible portfolio combinations that can be constructed by varying the weights in our two securities, A and B.[10]

Learning Objective 8.5
Explain what is meant by the "efficient frontier."

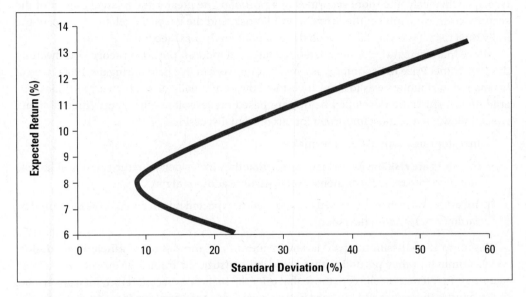

FIGURE 8-10 *Two-Security Portfolios*

The hyperbola-shaped frontier depicted in Figure 8-10 was created using only securities B and A, which had expected returns of 8 percent and 10 percent, standard deviations of 8.72 percent and 22.69 percent, and a correlation coefficient of 0.379. If we had combined two other securities, we would obtain a slightly different shape. However, as long as the correlation coefficient is not close to either extreme value (i.e., –1 or +1), this general hyperbola shape will prevail. Further, because risky securities in general tend to have positive correlation coefficients that are less than one, the shape depicted in Figure 8-10 can be generalized for portfolios formed by using most actual securities.

The Efficient Frontier

We can generalize from the two-security to the *n*-security case, for which the expected return will continue to be a weighted average of the expected returns on the individual securities, regardless of the number of securities in the portfolio. As a result, Equation 8-9 for estimating portfolio expected returns still applies, and the portfolio weights still have to sum to 100 percent. However, calculating the standard deviation on a portfolio of more than two securities becomes cumbersome quickly as the number of securities increases. For example, a three-

---

[10] Note that in order to construct this entire diagram, we have allowed the weights invested in either security to assume values above 1 and below 0 (i.e., we have permitted short selling—refer to footnote 5 for an explanation).

security portfolio can be calculated using Equation 8-18, which has three weighted variance terms and three weighted co-movement terms.

[8-18]
$$\sigma_p = \sqrt{\begin{array}{l} (w_A)^2(\sigma_A)^2 + (w_B)^2(\sigma_B)^2 + (w_C)^2(\sigma_C)^2 + 2(w_A)(w_B)(\rho_{AB})(\sigma_A)(\sigma_B) \\ + 2(w_A)(w_C)(\rho_{AC})(\sigma_A)(\sigma_C) + 2(w_B)(w_C)(\rho_{BC})(\sigma_B)(\sigma_C) \end{array}}$$

The four-security portfolio would similarly have four variance terms and six co-movement terms: the five-security portfolio would have five variance terms and 10 co-movement terms; and so on. A 100-security portfolio would have 100 variance terms and 4,950 co-movement terms.[11] Obviously, the more securities in a portfolio, the greater the relative impact of the security co-movements on the overall portfolio risk, and the lower the relative impact of the individual risks. (We will elaborate on this last point in the next section.)

Harry Markowitz, who is considered the father of modern portfolio theory, was awarded the 1990 Nobel Prize in Economics as a result of his work in this field during the 1950s. One of his main contributions was to show investors how to optimally diversify their portfolios. His arguments, which are developed below, are based on several assumptions. Three of them, which follow, are the most important for our present discussion.

1. Investors are rational decision-makers.

2. Investors are **risk averse**, which means that they like expected returns and dislike risk, and therefore require compensation to assume additional risk.

3. Investor preferences are based on a portfolio's expected return and risk (as measured by variance or standard deviation).

Based on these assumptions, Markowitz introduced the notion of **efficient portfolios**, which dominate other portfolios that could be constructed from a given set of available securities. Efficient portfolios are those that offer the highest expected return for a given level of risk or offer the lowest risk for a given expected return. Investors can identify efficient portfolios by specifying an expected portfolio return and minimizing the portfolio risk at this level of return, or by specifying a portfolio risk level they are willing to assume and maximizing the expected return given that level of risk.

The first step in the Markowitz analysis is to determine the expected return-risk combinations available to investors from a given set of securities by allowing the portfolio weights to vary, just as we did in Figure 8-10 when we considered only two securities. The entire curve, which is referred to as the **minimum variance frontier**, is illustrated in Figure 8-11.[12] Although our discussion has focused on plotting expected return against standard deviation, remember that the variance is just the standard deviation squared.

Notice that the shape is virtually identical to the frontier we constructed using only two securities in Figure 8-10. However, although the shape is similar, by using all available securities, we can generate a set of more efficient portfolios, in the sense that the portfolios will offer higher expected return for a given risk level or lower risk for a given expected return level.

The other difference between figures 8-10 and 8-11 is that we have included five portfolios marked A through E in Figure 8-11. All the portfolios that lie along the efficient frontier, including B, D, and E, can be attained by combining the underlying securities. They are referred to as the **attainable portfolios**. Portfolios A and C, conversely, which lie above and below the

risk averse to dislike risk and require compensation to assume additional risk

efficient portfolios those portfolios that offer the highest expected return for a given level of risk or offer the lowest risk for a given expected return

minimum variance frontier the curve produced when determining the expected return-risk combinations available to investors from a given set of securities by allowing the portfolio weights to vary

attainable portfolios portfolios that may be constructed by combining the underlying securities

---

[11] We can represent all these terms in a compact way using matrix algebra.

[12] Appendix 8A shows how to solve for all available portfolio weights in the two-security case, but this is impractical when a large number of securities are available. However, the problem can easily be solved using a quadratic programming model that chooses optimal "portfolio weights" in the available securities in order to minimize the risk of the portfolio for a given level of expected return. This optimization problem is subject to a wealth constraint (i.e., the sum of the weights in the individual securities must equal total wealth or 1) and is also constrained by the return-risk characteristics of the available set of securities.

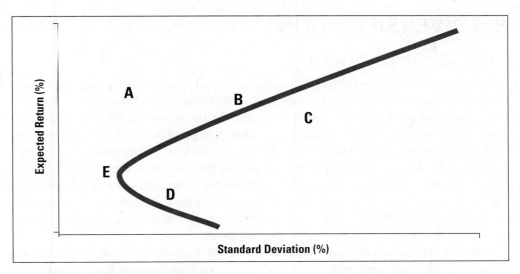

FIGURE 8-11 *The Minimum Variance Frontier*

efficient frontier, are not attainable. Portfolio A is not attainable in the sense that there is no way the underlying securities can be combined in such a way as to achieve this combination of expected return and risk. It is simply impossible. Portfolio C is unattainable in a different sense: it can be attained only by deliberately wasting money—that is, by simply not investing some portion of wealth and leaving money to earn zero return. It means that the portfolio is not formed by efficient combinations of the underlying securities.

This leaves us with portfolios B, D, and E, which do lie on the minimum variance frontier. We can ignore portfolio D, because it is a dominated portfolio, even though it lies on the minimum variance frontier. Like portfolio C, which is inefficient (as well as dominated), portfolio D offers a lower expected rate of return for the same risk as another portfolio on the upper half of the minimum variance frontier. We can see this by drawing a vertical line though D. The point where that line intersects the top part of the minimum variance frontier indicates a portfolio with the same standard deviation of return but a higher expected rate of return. Portfolio E is a special portfolio: it lies on the efficient frontier and also has the minimum amount of portfolio risk available from any possible combination of available securities. It is referred to as the **minimum variance portfolio (MVP)**.

The importance of the MVP is that portfolios lying below it, on the bottom segment of the minimum variance frontier, are dominated by portfolios on the upper segment. The segment of the minimum variance frontier above the global minimum variance portfolio, therefore, offers the best risk-expected return combinations available to investors from this particular set of securities. This segment includes the set of efficient portfolios that is commonly referred to as the **efficient frontier**. Rational, risk-averse investors will be interested in holding only those portfolios, like B, that offer the highest expected return for their given level of risk. (We will discuss risk aversion further in Chapter 9.) In this sense, these portfolios are not dominated by other attainable portfolios. In fact, the efficient frontier is the cornerstone of MPT.

Finally, the particular portfolio chosen by an investor will depend on his or her risk preferences. A more aggressive (i.e., less risk averse) investor might choose portfolio B, while a more conservative (i.e., more risk averse) investor might prefer portfolio E (i.e., the MVP).

minimum variance portfolio (MVP) a portfolio that lies on the efficient frontier and has the minimum amount of portfolio risk available from any possible combination of available securities

efficient frontier the set of portfolios that offer the highest expected return for their given level of risk; the only portfolios that rational, risk-averse investors will want to hold

CONCEPT REVIEW QUESTIONS

1. How do you form the minimum variance frontier in the two-security case?
2. What assumptions about investors underlie Markowitz's theories regarding efficient portfolios?
3. Why is the efficient frontier bowed?
4. What is an unattainable portfolio, and what is a dominated portfolio?

8.5 DIVERSIFICATION

Domestic Diversification

diversification the process of investing funds across several securities, which results in reduced risk

random diversification or **naïve diversification** the act of randomly buying securities without regard to relevant investment characteristics, such as company size, industry classification, and so on

We previously demonstrated that the expected portfolio return is always a weighted average of individual security returns, and as long as P_{AB} is less than +1, portfolio risk is always less than a weighted average (i.e., $\sigma_p < w_A\sigma_A + w_B\sigma_B$) of the risk of the two (or more) securities. Therefore, there is a benefit to combining securities into portfolios. In other words, we can eliminate risk by investing our funds across several securities, or by "not putting all of our eggs in one basket." This principle is called **diversification**. We have already seen how Markowitz showed that efficient diversification leads investors to hold a portfolio along the efficient frontier, which is one of the cornerstones of MPT. However, we have also seen that calculating all those correlation coefficients and generating the efficient frontier is not easy. So an important question is: how good is random or naïve diversification?

Random diversification or **naïve diversification** refers to the act of randomly diversifying without regard to relevant investment characteristics, such as company size, industry classification, and so on. An investor practising naïve diversification randomly selects a relatively large number of securities. Figure 8-12 plots the actual monthly data for Canadian stocks over the 1985–97 period, based on the data reported in Table 8-3, to illustrate naïve diversification in practice. Portfolio risk for a randomly selected portfolio was reduced to approximately 4.5 percent per month over this period. As securities are added to the portfolio, the total risk associated with the portfolio declines rapidly. The first few stocks cause a large decrease in portfolio risk. Based on these data, 46 percent of portfolio standard deviation is eliminated as we go from 1 to 10 securities.

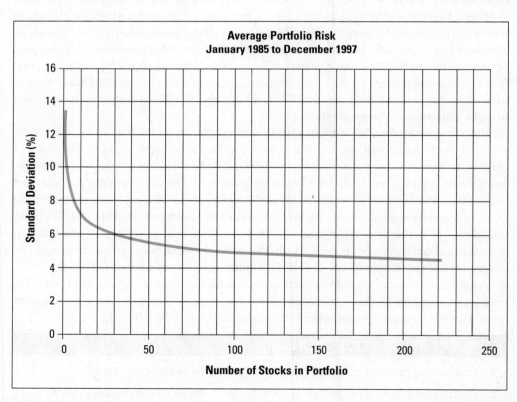

FIGURE 8-12 *Diversification with Canadian Stocks*

Source: Adapted from Cleary, S., and Copp, D. "Diversification with Canadian Stocks: How much is enough?" *Canadian Investment Review* (Fall 1999), Figure 1.

TABLE 8-3 Monthly Canadian Stock Portfolio Returns, January 1985 to December 1997

Number of Stocks in Portfolio	Average Monthly Portfolio Return (%)	Standard Deviation of Average Monthly Portfolio Return (%)	Ratio of Portfolio Standard Deviation to Standard Deviation of a Single Stock	Percentage of Total Achievable Risk Reduction (%)
1	1.51	13.47	1.00	0.00
2	1.51	10.99	0.82	27.50
3	1.52	9.91	0.74	39.56
4	1.53	9.30	0.69	46.37
5	1.52	8.67	0.64	53.31
6	1.52	8.30	0.62	57.50
7	1.51	7.95	0.59	61.35
8	1.52	7.71	0.57	64.02
9	1.52	7.52	0.56	66.17
10	1.51	7.33	0.54	68.30
12	1.51	7.03	0.52	71.58
14	1.51	6.80	0.50	74.19
16	1.52	6.63	0.49	76.04
18	1.52	6.51	0.48	77.41
20	1.52	6.39	0.47	78.65
22	1.52	6.25	0.46	80.30
24	1.52	6.15	0.46	81.32
26	1.52	6.07	0.45	82.25
28	1.52	5.99	0.44	83.18
30	1.52	5.91	0.44	84.06
35	1.52	5.76	0.43	85.68
40	1.52	5.62	0.42	87.24
45	1.52	5.50	0.41	88.56
50	1.52	5.41	0.40	89.64
60	1.52	5.25	0.39	90.40
70	1.51	5.12	0.38	92.86
80	1.51	5.02	0.37	94.00
90	1.51	4.93	0.37	94.94
100	1.51	4.86	0.36	95.70
150	1.51	4.64	0.34	98.18
200	1.51	4.51	0.34	99.58
222	1.51	4.48	0.33	100.00

Source: Cleary, S., and Copp, D. "Diversification with Canadian Stocks: How much is enough?" *Canadian Investment Review* (Fall 1999), Table 1.

Figure 8-12 also demonstrates that the benefits of random diversification do not continue indefinitely. As more and more securities are added, the marginal risk reduction per security becomes extremely small, eventually producing an almost negligible effect on total portfolio risk. For example, going from 10 to 20 securities eliminates an additional 7 percent of the monthly portfolio standard deviation, but going from 20 to 30 securities eliminates only 3 percent of the monthly standard deviation. Thus, although a large number of securities are not required to achieve substantial diversification benefits, the monthly portfolio risk levels out as additional securities are added to the portfolio.

unique (non-systematic) risk or **diversifiable risk** the company-specific part of total risk that is eliminated by diversification

market (systematic) risk or **non-diversifiable risk** the systematic part of total risk, directly influenced by overall movements in the general market or economy, that cannot be eliminated by diversification

The part of the total risk that is eliminated by diversification is the company-specific **unique (non-systematic) risk** or **diversifiable risk**. The part that is not eliminated by diversification is the **market (systematic) risk** or **non-diversifiable risk**. This portion of the risk cannot be eliminated because all the securities in the portfolio will be directly influenced by overall movements in the general market or economy. Total risk is often divided into these two components, which are additive, as reflected in Equation 8-19.

[8-19]   Total risk = Market (systematic) risk + Unique (non-systematic) risk

We show the total and market risk components in Figure 8-13.

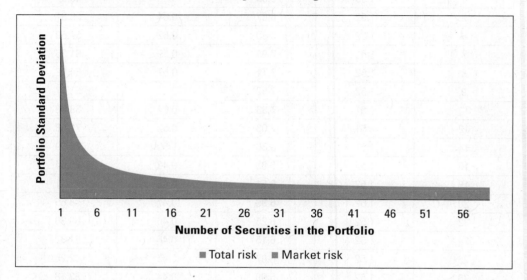

FIGURE 8-13 *Total and Market Risk for Different-Size Portfolios, Assuming Naïve Diversification*

The declining relationship between portfolio risk and the number of securities in a portfolio, illustrated in Figure 8-12 for Canadian stocks, is a well-known result that holds for diversification among stocks in all developed domestic stock markets around the world. Figure 8-12 highlights the benefits, in terms of risk reduction, of holding a well-diversified portfolio, when diversification is achieved by random security selection. Not surprisingly, diversification can be achieved more efficiently when we take a structured approach to forming portfolios, consciously selecting securities that can be expected to have lower correlations among their returns (i.e., to choose them from different industries).

A common and logical question to ask is: "how many stocks should I hold to be well diversified?" While the number of stocks for adequate diversification is much debated, 20 to 30 stocks seem to be the most accepted range, representing a compromise between higher transaction and monitoring costs and additional benefits from more diversified holdings. However, many would disagree and suggest that the actual number of stocks required is much higher. *Finance in the News 8-1* discusses this topic, with proponents from both sides of the diversification issue: those supporting a higher number of stocks and those supporting a lower number.

finance INTHENEWS 8-1   Diversification Dilemma

How many stocks do you need for a properly diversified portfolio?

THIS IS A SUBJECT of much debate among academics and investors. Before we delve into the controversy, let's review why diversification is important.

You've heard the expression "don't put all your eggs in one basket." The investing equivalent is: "don't put all your cash in one stock or even one industry." By investing in a mixed bag of stocks and sectors, you spread your bets around, reducing the impact that any one stock or sector will have on your portfolio.

continued

Finance in the News 8-1: Diversification Dilemma *(continued)*

What's more, if you choose stocks that have a low or inverse correlation with one another—that is, they don't move up or down together—you further reduce the volatility in your portfolio. For example, banks and resource stocks plunged in response to worries about China and the debt crisis in Europe, but utilities, pipelines, and telecoms—which are less economically sensitive—were largely unscathed.

Pick a number

In his influential 1949 book, *The Intelligent Investor*, legendary value investor Benjamin Graham argued that a portfolio of just 10 to 30 stocks provides adequate diversification. Increasing the number beyond that may reduce volatility marginally, but at the expense of higher transaction costs and more time required to monitor the portfolio.

In a similar vein, a classic 1968 paper entitled "Diversification and the Reduction of Dispersion," by professors John Evans and Stephen Archer at the University of Washington, argued that a portfolio of 15 randomly chosen stocks would have similar risk, as measured by standard deviation, to the market as a whole. More recent studies, however, have concluded that the ideal number of stocks could be 50, 100, or even more.

"The academics disagree over how many separate stocks are required to secure the benefits of diversification, but most professionally managed equity portfolios have at least 30 or so individual securities in them," U.S. fund manager Daniel Peris wrote in his 2011 book, *The Strategic Dividend Investor*.

Chasing the superstocks

Some investors pooh-pooh the notion that a few dozen stocks provides adequate diversification.

"To be blunt, if you think that you can do an adequate job of minimizing portfolio risk with 15 or 30 stocks, then you are imperilling your financial future and the future of those who depend on you," investment adviser and author William Bernstein said in a paper called "The 15-Stock Diversification Myth."

While a 15- or 30-stock portfolio would significantly reduce volatility, it would also have a high probability of missing out on the small number of "superstocks" that drive most of the market's gains, he said. He cited a study by researcher Ron Surz, who constructed 1,000 portfolios of 15 randomly chosen stocks, and tracked their returns over 30 years.

The top-performing random portfolios beat the market handily, but the worst portfolios missed out on most of the big gainers and trailed the market badly.

"Yes, picking a small number of stocks increases your chances of getting rich, but ... it also increases your chances of getting poor," Mr. Bernstein wrote in his 2010 book, *The Investor's Manifesto*.

What to do?

To reduce the risk of ending up in the poorhouse, Mr. Bernstein recommends investing in broadly diversified, low-cost index funds that provide exposure to hundreds, if not thousands, of stocks.

What about investors who want to manage their own portfolios? While there is no magic number, it's safe to say that the more stocks you own, and the more sectors you cover, the more diversified you'll be.

Of course, you could always take a hybrid approach—invest in diversified funds for the core of your portfolio, and allocate a portion of your funds to individual stocks.

Source: Heinzl, John, "The diversification dilemma: How many eggs? And how many baskets?" *The Globe and Mail*, October 14, 2011, p. B13. ©The Globe and Mail, Inc. All rights reserved. Reprinted by permission.

International Diversification

Our discussion above assumed random diversification in domestic securities only. However, it is reasonable to assume that if domestic diversification is good for reducing risk, international diversification must be better. This is logical, because we would expect the returns among stocks in different global markets to have lower correlation coefficients than those in the same market. Figure 8-14 demonstrates the benefits of international diversification in reducing portfolio risk, based on evidence provided in a classic research article by Bruno Solnik. Throughout the entire range of portfolio sizes, the risk is reduced when international investing is compared with investing in only domestic stocks (U.S. stocks in this example), and the difference is dramatic—about one-third less. Several studies confirm similar risk-reduction benefits are available to Canadian investors who diversify internationally.

Although almost all experts agree that diversification in general, and international diversification in particular, is one of the most critical components of good portfolio management, evidence suggests the benefits of international diversification have been declining as global equity markets become more integrated, to the point where many have suggested it is not a worthwhile exercise. This especially has been the case in Canada where our heavy exposure to resource stocks has served us well over the past decade.[13] However, there are still many valid reasons to diversify globally to some extent. *Finance in the News 8-2* discusses a few of

FIGURE 8-14 *International Diversification*

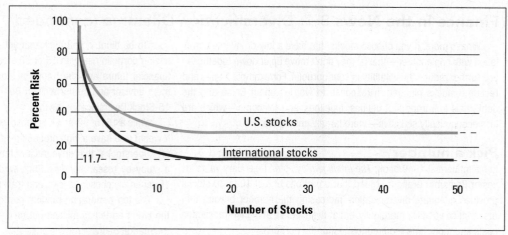

these reasons, from a Canadian perspective. The first two reasons allude to the inadequate diversification provided by Canadian markets, which are dominated by resource stocks and financials, and are underweight in many other industries, such as health care and technology. The remaining reasons refer to the influence of currency value, and the fact that recent returns do not necessarily imply future returns.

---

finance INTHENEWS 8-2   The Case for Embracing Global Markets

WITH THE MONSTER weighting our stock market has in oil and mining stocks, that's been the investing story of the past decade. Global investing? Strictly for suckers who bought into the theoretical benefits of diversification and ignored what was actually happening in the world.

It's time for a rethink now, and not just because one of the most basic investing rules is that no trend lasts forever. In fact, there are five good reasons to build up your exposure to global markets:

1. The Canadian market is dangerously lopsided.

Of the top 10 largest stocks in Canada, nine are banks or resource companies. That's our stock market: Rocks and Bucks R Us.

In fact, financials, energy, and materials (basically mining companies) account for almost 80 percent of the S&P/TSX Composite Index. Once thought of as volatile and speculative, energy and materials have grown in influence to the point where they alone account for 50 percent of the index. That defies common sense diversification.

There are plenty of great Canadian companies in other sectors, but investors aren't much interested. They keep pouring money into banks and resource companies, which in turn reinforces their stock market dominance and susceptibility to a fall.

2. The Canadian market is sadly deficient in some sectors.

Here are two notable examples: health care, which accounts for 1.25 percent of the S&P/TSX Composite, and technology, which accounts for 2.3 percent. We're a technology-obsessed society, and an aging population that will spend increasing amounts on health care. Yet our stock market barely acknowledges this.

Globally, it's a much different story. The most heavily weighted sector on the S&P 500, the most-watched U.S. index, is technology at almost 18 percent, while health care comes in fourth at 11 percent.

Investing globally gives you the chance to own the likes of Apple, whose shares are up a cumulative 400 percent in the past five years. It can also give you exposure to the hefty dividends and bear market sturdiness of health care companies.

3. The dollar is your friend.

Ten years ago, the Canadian dollar was worth about US$0.65 cents. The currency's long climb to levels above par with the U.S. dollar is one of the big reasons why investors have either made nothing or lost money in U.S. equity funds and global equity funds, most of which have large U.S. weightings.

continued

---

[13] Recall that in the chapter opener we mentioned the 2000 to 2010 average annual return of 6.6 percent on Canadian stocks versus −1.3 percent on global stocks and −2.6 percent on U.S. stocks.

Finance in the News 8-2: The Case for Embracing Global Markets *(continued)*

A rising dollar erodes returns in other currencies, but you don't have to worry about that right now because the long-term outlook for our currency is lower, not higher. It may take a while—years, even. But when our dollar slides, it will turbo-charge your returns from U.S. and global equity funds.

In the meantime, so high is our dollar right now that you can convert it into American funds and still get more than US$1.00, even after those egregious foreign exchange fees are applied. You might say U.S. dollars are on sale right now, limited time only.

4. History is your friend.

No one talks much about it now, but there was a time when Canada regularly had its butt kicked by the rest of the world. The year 1998 is a classic example. While the average Canadian equity fund lost 3 percent, the average global equity fund delivered a gain of 15.4 percent.

In fact, the decade of the 1990s saw global funds outperform Canadian equity funds in six of 10 years. Long-term numbers offer a further argument for global investing. The average annual return for the S&P/TSX Composite over the 30 years to March 31 was 9.1 percent,

while the S&P 500 made 10.1 percent in Canadian dollars and the MSCI Europe Australasia Far East Index averaged 9.1 percent, again in Canadian dollars.

5. Global funds have busted out of their slump.

The 10-year numbers from global equity funds are pure financial poison. We're talking about a compound average annual loss of 0.02 percent, which would have turned a $1,000 investment into $998. An investment in the average near zero-risk money market fund would have left you with $1,207 over the same time frame.

Today, global equity funds are on the move. Year to date, many of the biggest names are up about 4 percent. For the 24 months ended March 31, the average annual gain for the category was 18 percent.

The S&P/TSX Composite Index made 23.3 percent annually over that same two-year period, and its 10-year average annual return was 8.9 percent. Investors who like to buy low, where will you put your money? Canada or the world?

LESSONS TO BE LEARNED

During the fall of 2008, stock markets around the world fell dramatically, and they fell in tandem. In other words, the correlation among equity returns was extremely high, with most global stock market returns displaying correlations greater than 0.95 with the returns on the S&P 500 Composite Index. For example, the S&P/TSX Composite Index displayed a 0.97 coefficient with the S&P. This led many market observers to question the value of diversification. Consider the following quote from Louis Gagnon: "Diversification works on the way up when we don't need it and it fails miserably when we do."[14] So what does this mean for investors? First of all, it suggests that diversification is no guarantee that you can never lose money, which is of course true—there are always risks associated with investing. We alluded to this point in the chapter opener.

So what does diversification do for us? Consider the following two points. First, even though diversification within and across stock markets would not have prevented investors from experiencing large losses on their common equity holdings, they would have been much better off than if they had not been diversified. For example, investors would have suffered if their investments had been concentrated in financial companies. Many of those stock prices declined by as much as 90 percent, before some rebounded somewhat in the spring of 2009. Of course, if investors were holding only those stocks that didn't recover, they would have been hit really hard.

Second, being diversified across asset categories would have helped cushion the blow. Recall from Figure 8-7B, for example, the low correlation between stock returns and T-bill returns, which was –0.077. Similarly, the correlation coefficient between stock returns and government bond returns over the 1938 to 2011 period was also close to zero (–0.01). So being invested in various asset categories would have softened the blow, due to the low correlations across the asset classes. For example, a portfolio of Canadian stocks would have lost 42.5 percent over the March 2008 to March 2009 period, while an equally weighted portfolio of Canadian stock and government bonds would have lost only 17.5 percent. On the other hand, the ending wealth for $1,000 invested in this equally weighted portfolio over the 1938 to 2011 period would have been $411,819, versus an ending wealth of $1,183,626 if invested entirely in stocks. That is obviously a big sacrifice in returns if investors were in it for the long term and could live with the additional risk (i.e., the standard deviation of the equally weighted portfolio was 9.50 percent versus 16.82 percent for the stock portfolio). On the other hand, if investors had a short-term investment horizon and/or a low risk tolerance for other reasons, the reduction in risk might have been well worth it—recall that, at the beginning of this chapter, we said there is a trade-off between risk and return!

---

[14] Ladurantaye, Steve. "World markets start trading on their own merits." *The Globe and Mail*, April 14, 2009.

CONCEPT REVIEW QUESTIONS

1. What is naïve diversification?
2. What is the difference between diversifiable and non-diversifiable risk?
3. Why is it logical to believe that international diversification will provide benefits to investors?

APPENDIX 8A

TWO-SECURITY PORTFOLIO FRONTIERS

Learning Objective 8.7
Construct two-security portfolio risk-return frontiers.

Figures 8-4 and 8-9 show how the expected return and the standard deviation of a portfolio change as we change the portfolio's composition by shifting more of our investment toward security A, which is the riskier security. Rather than creating two graphs, we can combine them into one that implicitly shows all the portfolios. We do this by noting, from Equation 8-10, that rather than writing the expected return as the portfolio weight is varied, we instead write the portfolio weight as we change our expected return, as shown in Equation 8A-1.

[8A-1]
$$w = \frac{ER_p - ER_B}{(ER_A - ER_B)}$$

Or, using the numbers in our example,

$$w = \frac{ER_p - 8\%}{2\%}$$

Think about this by supposing that an investor wants a portfolio with an expected rate of return of 8 percent. In this case, look at the equation above, substitute 8 percent for ER_p, and learn that a zero weight has to be placed in security A—that is, the 8-percent expected return can be met with 100 percent in B. If the expected return on the portfolio is set at 10 percent, then we get 2 percent in the numerator and denominator of Equation 8A-1, and the portfolio weight has to be 100 percent—that is, all the investment has to be placed in security A. Between these two expected returns, we get different portfolio weights as we vary how much is invested in each security.[15]

We can now use Equation 8A-1 to remove the portfolio weights in Equation 8-15 and express the standard deviation of the portfolio solely in terms of the expected returns, standard deviations, and the correlation coefficient, as is done in Equation 8A-2.

[8A-2]
$$\sigma_p = \sqrt{\left(\frac{ER_p - ER_B}{ER_A - ER_B}\right)^2 (\sigma_A)^2 + \left(1 - \frac{ER_p - ER_B}{ER_A - ER_B}\right)^2 (\sigma_B)^2 + 2\left(\frac{ER_p - ER_B}{ER_A - ER_B}\right)\left(1 - \frac{ER_p - ER_B}{ER_A - ER_B}\right)(\rho_{AB})(\sigma_A)(\sigma_B)}$$

Although this is cumbersome, it indicates all the combinations of expected return and risk (standard deviation) created from these two securities.

With our example, we can substitute in and get the following:

$$\sigma_p = \sqrt{\left(\frac{ER_p - 8\%}{2\%}\right)^2 (22.69\%)^2 + \left(\frac{10\% - ER_p}{2\%}\right)^2 (8.72)^2 + 2\left(\frac{ER_p - 8\%}{2\%}\right)\left(\frac{10\% - ER_p}{2\%}\right)(\rho_{AB})(22.69\%)(8.72\%)}$$

This is a bit simpler, but you need to enter the numbers into Excel to work everything out. If you do this, you will get Figure 8A-1 for our three special cases and anything in between.

---

[15] As we mentioned before, there is no conceptual reason why the weights can't be more than 100 percent, and we will relax this constraint later.

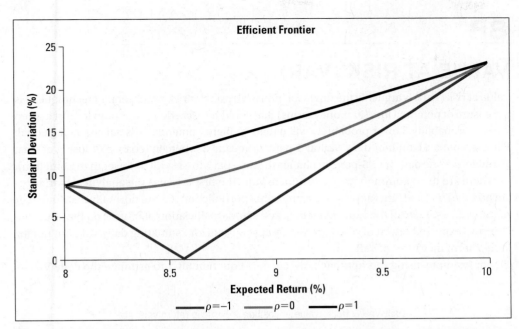

FIGURE 8A-1 *Two-Security Portfolios*

As we saw before, if we start out with all investment in security B ($w = 0$), we get an 8-percent expected return and a standard deviation of 8.72 percent. If we move to a portfolio with 100 per-cent invested in A, we get a 10-percent expected return and a 22.69-percent standard deviation. In between, interesting things happen! Notice that the risk of the portfolio falls as we add the risky security A, unless the securities are perfectly correlated; this decline is much more dramatic if the securities are negatively correlated. Regardless, adding A to the portfolio increases the expected return and lowers the risk, which means the investor is better off. It also means that no one should hold security B in isolation. (Think about why an investor might want to hold A in isolation.) Even-tually, the risk-reduction opportunity from holding A falls and the risk is minimized, after which the standard deviation of the portfolio's return starts to increase.

These diagrams show all the combinations of expected return and standard deviation that re-sult from creating portfolios of the two securities. Now we can return to our example, in which the correlation coefficient was 0.379, and graph the efficient frontier with a non-special correlation coefficient. We can also flip the axes, because normally, in finance, we have the expected return on the vertical axis and the standard deviation or risk on the horizontal axis, as shown in Figure 8A-2.[16]

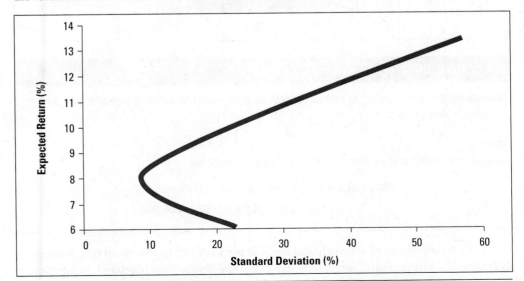

FIGURE 8A-2 *Two-Security Portfolios*

[16] Notice that we have also allowed the security weights to go below zero or above one in order to construct Figure 8A-2.

APPENDIX 8B

VALUE AT RISK (VAR)

Value at risk (VaR) is arguably the financial industry's premier risk-management technique. It is a measure of potential loss (in money terms) that could be exceeded (minimum loss) at a given level of probability. Lower probability will equate to higher potential loss, all else being equal. For example a $1-million daily VaR at 5 percent means a 5-percent chance of losing at least $1 million in one day (or a 95-percent chance that one day's losses will be lower than $1 million).

There are three common ways to estimate VaR. The first is to use the analytical (variance-covariance) method. This approach assumes that portfolio returns are normally distributed. It requires an estimate of the expected return and standard deviation of returns on the portfolio. Using an expected return of zero is generally appropriate for estimating daily VaR, but not for longer-term measures of VaR.

For example, using this approach, we can use Equation 8B-1 to estimate the daily VaR as follows:

[8-B1]   Daily VaR = Dollar value of position × Portfolio return volatility

where portfolio return volatility is defined as the portfolio period standard deviation multiplied by the appropriate Z-score (from the normal distribution normalized Z-scores).

For a 5-percent VaR estimate, we would use a Z-score of 1.65 (rounded from 1.645), since 95 percent of the observations would lie above a Z-score of −1.645. This can be seen in Figure 8B-1. For a 99-percent VaR, we would use a Z-score of 2.33, since 99 percent of the observations would lie above a Z-score of −2.33.

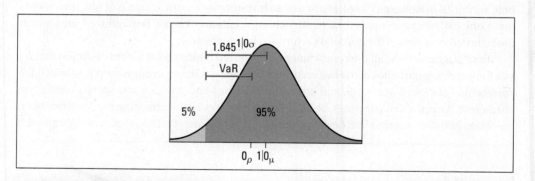

FIGURE 8B-1 *Standardized Normal Distribution*

EXAMPLE 8B-1	Estimating Daily VaR

Estimate the 5-percent daily VaR of a $2-million position in the market, which has a 2-percent daily standard deviation in price changes.

Solution

Since we are looking for the 5-percent VaR, we use the Z-score of 1.65.

$$\text{Daily VaR} = \text{Market value of position} \times \text{Price volatility}$$
$$= \$2,000,000 \times (1.65 \times 0.02) = \$66,000$$

The main advantage of the analytical method is its simplicity. The main disadvantage is its reliance on assumptions, particularly that of normal distribution of returns. In addition, it requires estimates of standard deviation of returns.

VaR can also be estimated using the historical method, which uses actual daily returns from some user-specified past period. If you have 1,000 observations, the 1-percent and 5-percent probabilities would be of a loss greater than the 10th- or 50th-worst out of the observations, respectively. As the name suggests, this approach reflects historical results, not the future, which is of course what concerns us. The main advantage is that it is nonparametric (i.e., we don't need to assume a certain probability distribution, such as the normal one). The main disadvantages are that the future could differ significantly from the past, and there is a some-what limited number of past observations.

In order to overcome the problem of a limited number of observations associated with the historical method, the Monte Carlo simulation method synthesizes additional observations. For example, we might generate 10,000 real and synthetic observations. These observations are generated by using historical variance and covariance estimates and then employing a random number generator to synthesize observations. The objective is to replicate the distri-bution of observed outcomes with synthetic data.

The Monte Carlo method produces random outcomes to examine the effects of particular sets of risks, using a probability distribution for each variable of interest. We can use normal or non-normal distributions for modelling purposes. As a result, this method is often useful for determining important risk-management information about various sources of risk. For large portfolios, this approach may require extensive commitments of computer resources.

The advantages of VaR are that it quantifies potential loss in simple terms, is widely accepted by regulators, and is versatile. The limitations are that it can be difficult to estimate, and various estimation methods can lead to significant estimate differences. It can create a false sense of security for risk managers, and it may underestimate the severity of worst-case returns.

Based on the strengths and limitations of VaR, there is substantial debate about its useful-ness. Consider the following comments from an article in the *GARP Risk Review*.[17] One of the co-authors, Aaron Brown, espouses the benefits of VaR, stating that "a risk manager has two jobs: make people take more risk the 99 percent of the time it is safe to do so, and survive the other 1 percent of the time. VaR is the border." The second co-author, David Einhorn, com-pares VaR to "an airbag that works all the time, except when you have a car accident." He further charges that VaR:

- led to excessive risk-taking and leverage at financial institutions

- focused on the manageable risks near the centre of the distribution and ignored the tails

- created an incentive to take "excessive but remote risks"

- was "potentially catastrophic when its use creates a false sense of security among senior executives and watchdogs"

SUMMARY

In this chapter, we discuss the expected return and risk characteristics of risky securities. We show how the standard deviation is calculated, and how it is commonly used as a measure of risk because it represents the variability in a security's rate of return. We also discuss different defini-tions of rates of return, including the arithmetic and geometric rates of return, and explain why they differ. We then discuss how portfolios are formed by varying the weight invested in different securities and what happens to the portfolio's expected rate of return and risk. In particular, we emphasize the importance of the correlation coefficient in determining portfolio risk and show how diversification can be used to reduce risk, as well as how to create the efficient frontier.

---

[17] Einhcrn, David, and Brown, Aaron. "Private Profits and Socialized Risk." *GARP Risk Review* (June/July 2008).

In Chapter 9, we will further develop these ideas. At the moment, they are mechanical in the sense that we show how a given set of securities can be combined into efficient portfolios. This won Harry Markowitz the Nobel Prize, but it was left to one of his students, William Sharpe, to take these ideas and think through what it means for a capital market dominated by Markowitz-type investors, rationally forming efficient portfolios using the ideas in this chapter. This led to another seminal idea in finance and another Nobel Prize.

SUMMARY OF LEARNING OBJECTIVES

8.1 Distinguish between ex post and ex ante returns and explain how they are estimated.

"Ex post" means "after the fact," so ex post returns are past or historical returns. "Ex ante" means "before the fact," so ex ante returns are expected returns. They are defined as the sum of dividends and capital gain (loss) divided by the beginning-of-the-period price.

8.2 Distinguish between arithmetic and geometric means.

The arithmetic mean is the most commonly used value in statistics. It is the sum of all returns divided by the total number of observations. The geometric mean is the average or compound growth rate over multiple time periods.

8.3 Explain how common risk measures are calculated and what they mean.

A common ex post risk measure is the ex post standard deviation, which is the standard deviation of the historical return. Ex ante standard deviation is scenario based, which is given by Equation 8-8.

8.4 Describe what happens to risk and return when securities are combined in a portfolio.

Expected return will be the value weighted return of securities. Risk measure is the standard deviation, which decreases with the number of securities in the portfolio unless all securities are perfectly correlated.

8.5 Explain what is meant by the "efficient frontier."

Efficient frontier is the set of portfolios that offer the highest expected return for their given level of risk—the only portfolios that rational, risk-averse investors will want to hold.

8.6 Define diversification and explain why it is important to investors.

Diversification is the process of investing funds across several securities, which results in reduced risk. It is important to investors because it reduces risk.

8.7 Construct two-security portfolio risk-return frontiers.

With two securities with known expected returns, standard deviation, and correlation coefficient, we can construct the risk-return frontier by changing the weight of the securities and calculating and plotting the expected return and standard deviation of the portfolio of these two securities.

KEY TERMS

arithmetic average, p. 294
arithmetic mean, p. 294
attainable portfolio, p. 312
capital gain, p. 291
capital loss, p. 291
correlation coefficient, p. 304
covariance, p. 302
day trader, p. 293
diversifiable risk, p. 316
diversification, p. 314
efficient frontier, p. 313
efficient portfolio, p. 312

ex ante returns, p. 290
ex post returns, p. 290
expected returns, p. 296
geometric mean, p. 294
income yield, p. 290
mark to market, p. 293
market (systematic) risk, p. 316
minimum variance frontier, p. 312
minimum variance portfolio (MVP), p. 313
modern portfolio theory (MPT), p. 301
naïve diversification, p.314
non-diversifiable risk, p.316

paper losses, p. 293
portfolio, p. 300
random diversification, p. 314
range, p. 298
risk averse, p. 312
standard deviation, p. 295
total return, p. 292
unique (non-systematic) risk, p. 316
variance, p. 298

EQUATIONS

Equation	Formula	Page
[8-1] Income Yield	$\text{Income yield} = \dfrac{CF_1}{P_0}$	p. 290
[8-2] Capital Gains (Loss) Yield	$\text{Capital gain (loss) return} = \dfrac{P_1 - P_0}{P_0}$	p. 292
[8-3] Total Return	$\text{Total return} = \text{Income yield} + \text{Capital gain (or loss) yield}$ $= \dfrac{CF_1 + P_1 - P_0}{P_0}$	p. 292
[8-4] Arithmetic Mean (AM)	$\text{Arithmetic mean (AM)} = \dfrac{\sum\limits_{i=1}^{n} r_i}{n}$	p. 294
[8-5] Geometric Mean (GM)	$\text{Geometric mean (GM)} = [(1+r_1)(1+r_2)(1+r_3)...(1+r_n)]^{1/n} - 1$	p. 294
[8-6] Expected Return (Individual)	$ER = \sum\limits_{i=1}^{n} (r_1 \times Prob_i)$	p. 296
[8-7] Standard Deviation for Individual Returns Ex-Post	$\text{Ex post } \sigma = \sqrt{\dfrac{\sum\limits_{i=1}^{n}(r_i - \bar{r})^2}{n-1}}$	p. 298
[8-8] Standard Deviation for Individual Returns Ex Ante	$\text{Ex ante } \sigma = \sqrt{\sum\limits_{i=1}^{n}(Prob_i)\,(r_i - ER)^2}$	p. 300
[8-9] Expected Portfolio Return	$ER_p = \sum\limits_{i=1}^{n}(w_i \times ER_i)$	p. 301
[8-10] Expected Return on a Two-Security Portfolio	$ER_P = ER_B + w(ER_A - ER_B)$	p. 301
[8-11] Standard Deviation of a Two-Security Portfolio (Using Covariance)	$\sigma_p = \sqrt{(w_A)^2(\sigma_A)^2 + (w_B)^2(\sigma_B)^2 + 2(w_A)(w_B)(COV_{AB})}$	p. 302
[8-12] Covariance of Returns	$COV_{AB} = \sum\limits_{i=1}^{n} Prob_i(r_{A,i} - \bar{r}_A)(r_{B,i} - \bar{r}_B)$	p. 303
[8-13] Correlation Coefficient of Returns	$\rho_{AB} = \dfrac{COV_{AB}}{\sigma_A \sigma_B}$	p. 304
[8-14] Covariance of Returns (Using Correlation Coefficient)	$COV_{AB} = \rho_{AB}\sigma_A\sigma_B$	p. 304
[8-15] Standard Deviation of a Two-Security Portfolio (Using Correlation Coefficient)	$\sigma_p = \sqrt{(w_A)^2(\sigma_A)^2 + (w_B)^2(\sigma_B)^2 + 2(w_A)(w_B)(\rho_{AB})(\sigma_A)(\sigma_B)}$	p. 304
[8-16] Standard Deviation of a Two-Security Portfolio (where Correlation Coefficient = –1)	$\sigma_p = w\sigma_A - (1-w)\,\sigma_B$	p. 310
[8-17] Portfolio Weights to Obtain Portfolio Standard Deviation = 0 (where Correlation Coefficient = –1)	$w = \dfrac{\sigma_B}{\sigma_A + \sigma_B}$	p. 310
[8-18] Standard Deviation of a Three-Security Portfolio	$\sigma_p = \sqrt{\begin{array}{l}(w_A)^2(\sigma_A)^2 + (w_B)^2(\sigma_B)^2 + (w_C)^2(\sigma_C)^2 + 2(w_A)(w_B)(\rho_{AB})(\sigma_A)(\sigma_B) \\ + 2(w_A)(w_C)(\rho_{AC})(\sigma_A)(\sigma_C) + 2(w_B)(w_C)(\rho_{BC})(\sigma_B)(\sigma_C)\end{array}}$	p. 312

EQUATIONS *continued*

Equation	Formula	Page
[8-19] Total Risk Decomposition	Total risk = Market (systematic) risk + Unique (non-systematic) risk	p. 316
[8A-1] Portfolio Weight (in Terms of ERs)	$w = \dfrac{ER_p - ER_B}{(ER_A - ER_B)}$	p. 320
[8A-2] Standard Deviation of a Two-Security Portfolio (in Terms of ERs)	$\sigma_p = \sqrt{\left(\dfrac{ER_p - ER_B}{ER_A - ER_B}\right)^2 (\sigma_A)^2 + \left(1 - \dfrac{ER_p - ER_B}{ER_A - ER_B}\right)^2 (\sigma_B)^2 + 2\left(\dfrac{ER_p - ER_B}{ER_A - ER_B}\right)\left(1 - \dfrac{ER_p - ER_B}{ER_A - ER_B}\right)(\rho_{AB})(\sigma_A)(\sigma_B)}$	p. 320
[8B-1] Value at Risk (Daily)	Daily VaR = Dollar value of position × Portfolio return volatility	p. 322

QUESTIONS AND PRACTICE PROBLEMS

Multiple Choice Questions

1. Calculate the capital gain return for a stock that was purchased at $25 one year ago and is now worth $26. It paid four quarterly dividends of $1 per share each throughout the year.
   a. 4 percent
   b. 16 percent
   c. 20 percent
   d. 12 percent

2. In Question 1, what is the total return of the security?
   a. 4 percent
   b. 8 percent
   c. 16 percent
   d. 20 percent

3. Which of the following is *false*?
   a. The income yield of a security that has a $3 cash flow during a period, with a beginning price of $15, is 20 percent.
   b. The arithmetic mean is always less than the geometric mean of a series of returns.
   c. The geometric mean of 50 percent and –50 percent is –13.4 percent.
   d. The greater the dispersion of a distribution, the greater the spread between the geometric mean and the arithmetic mean.

4. Calculate the expected return on a stock that has a 35-percent probability of a 30-percent return, a 40-percent probability of a 40-percent return, and a 25-percent probability of a 15-percent return.
   a. 28.33 percent
   b. 33.33 percent
   c. 30.25 percent
   d. 20 percent

5. In Question 4, what is the standard deviation?
   a. 11.12 percent
   b. 9.99 percent
   c. 9.81 percent
   d. 12 percent

6. Which of the following is *false*?
    a. The expected return of a portfolio is always the weighted average of the expected return of each asset in the portfolio.
    b. Covariance measures the co-movement between the returns of individual securities.
    c. The standard deviation of a portfolio is always the weighted average of the standard deviations of individual assets in the portfolio.
    d. Standard deviation is easier to interpret than variance as a measure of risk.

7. The correlation coefficient
    a. equals covariance times the individual standard deviations.
    b. measures how security returns move in relation to one another.
    c. may be greater than +1.
    d. shows a stronger relationship between the returns of two securities when its absolute value is closer to 0.

8. Which of the following is *false*?
    a. The standard deviation of a portfolio that contains two individual securities is the weighted average of individual standard deviations only when the correlation coefficient is equal to +1.
    b. It is impossible to eliminate all the risk for a two-security portfolio.
    c. There are $n(n-1)/2$ co-movement terms and n variance terms for an n-security portfolio.
    d. The more securities added, the lower the marginal risk reduction per security added.

9. According to the diagram below, which statement is *false*?

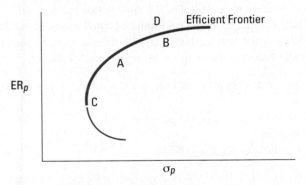

    a. Portfolio C is the minimum variance portfolio (MVP).
    b. Portfolios on the upper segment above C dominate those on the bottom segment below C.
    c. Portfolios A, B, and D are attainable, but C is not.
    d. A more risk-averse investor will prefer portfolios on the left side of the efficient frontier.

10. Which of the following correlation coefficients will provide the greatest diversification benefits for a given portfolio?
    a. 0
    b. 0.5
    c. 1
    d. −0.9

Practice Problems

11. At the beginning of the year you bought 250 shares of Lycel Ltd. at $82 each. During the year you received dividends of $750. At the end of the year the stock is trading for $87 and you decide to sell all your shares. Calculate your capital gain, total dollar return, and percentage return.

12. At the beginning of last year you invested $30,000 in 1,500 shares of Goran Products Inc. During the year you received $4,500 as a dividend. At the end of the year you sold the shares for $18 each. Calculate your total dollar return, capital gain, percentage return, and dividend yield.

13. Explain when to use the arithmetic mean and when to use the geometric mean to describe a return series.

14. State three of the most important assumptions underlying Markowitz's notion of efficient portfolios.

15. Data on the daily performance of Carraway Corporation have been partially completed in the following table. Fill in the missing data.

Carraway Corporation Performance

	Opening price	Dividend	Closing† price	Income yield	Capital gain	Total daily return
Monday	$100	$7	$115			
Tuesday	$115	$2			7%	
Wednesday		$8				10%
Thursday				4%	3%	
Friday		$0				15%

†The closing price on one day is assumed to be the opening price for the next day.

16. FinCorp Inc. conducted an extensive analysis of the economy and concluded that the probability of a recession next year is 35 percent, the probability of a boom is 45 percent, and the probability of a stable economy is 20 percent. Your boss has estimated that the price of PakCom Ltd. will be $60 if there is a recession, $110 if there is a boom, and $85 if the economy is stable. Currently, PakCom is trading for $80. Calculate the ex ante expected return on PakCom.

17. You have observed the following returns: 18 percent, –15 percent, 8 percent, 6 percent, and –12 percent.
    a. Calculate the geometric mean return.
    b. Calculate the arithmetic mean return.
    c. Calculate the variance and standard deviation of returns.

18. On Monday you invested $190 in Dettall Ltd. Dettall has earned daily returns of –8 percent, 18 percent, –30 percent, 6 percent, and 5 percent. What is the value of your investment at the end of the five days?

19. You observed the following daily returns for two companies, ABC and DEF.

	Daily returns	
	ABC	DEF
Monday	5%	4%
Tuesday	4%	16%
Wednesday	– 18%	14%
Thursday	2%	10%
Friday	5%	4%

a. Calculate the following for each stock:

i. five-day cumulative return

ii. geometric mean daily return

iii. arithmetic mean daily return

     iv. standard deviation of daily returns
- b. Calculate the covariance and correlation between the two stocks.

20. FinCorp Inc. is exploring different portfolio allocations between two stocks. Complete the following table.

	Case 1	Case 2	Case 3	Case 4	Case 5
$ invested in stock 1	$500			$200	
$ invested in stock 2	$500		$5,000		
Total $ invested		$2,000	$5,000		$1,000
Weight in stock 1		20%		40%	15%
Weight in stock 2					
Expected return of stock 1	8%	3%		5%	2%
Expected return of stock 2	3%				10%
Expected return of portfolio		8%	6%	7%	

21. Your portfolio consists of two securities: Transcomm and MidCap. The expected return for Transcomm is 15 percent, while for MidCap it is 5 percent. The standard deviation is 6 percent for Transcomm and 20 percent for MidCap. If 35 percent of the portfolio is invested in Transcomm, calculate the portfolio standard deviation if
- a. the correlation between the stocks is 0.75
- b. the correlation between the stocks is −0.75

22. FinCorp Inc. is exploring the risk of different portfolio allocations between two stocks. Complete the following table.

	Case 1	Case 2
Weight in stock 1		15%
Weight in stock 2	25%	
Standard deviation of stock 1	15%	2%
Standard deviation of stock 2	3%	10%
Covariance between stocks 1 and 2		
Correlation between stocks 1 and 2	−0.2	0.4
Portfolio variance		
Portfolio standard deviation		

23. You have the following return data on six stocks:

Day	XYZ	ABC	DEF	GHI	JKL	MNO
Monday	1%	−18%	3%	6%	7%	3%
Tuesday	2%	−15%	8%	3%	5%	−4%
Wednesday	3%	−12%	13%	1%	3%	8%
Thursday	4%	−9%	18%	3%	2%	−2%
Friday	5%	−6%	22%	−5%	0%	0%

- a. Graph the returns of each stock (ABC, DEF, GHI, JKL, and MNO) against the returns of XYZ.
- b. Based on the five graphs, which stocks are positively correlated with XYZ?
- c. Based on the five graphs, which stocks are negatively correlated with XYZ?
- d. Based on the five graphs, which stocks are uncorrelated with XYZ?
- e. Calculate the correlation between the five stocks and XYZ to check your results from parts (b) to (d).

24. Calculate the annual arithmetic mean and geometric mean return on the following security, and state which method is more appropriate for the situation: purchase price = $30; first-year dividend = $5; price after one year = $35; second-year dividend = $5; selling price after two years = $28.

25. Calculate the ex post standard deviation of returns for the following: 50 percent, 30 percent, 20 percent, 35 percent, 55 percent.

26. An investor owns a portfolio of $45,000 that contains $15,000 in stock A, with an expected return of 12 percent; $10,000 in bonds, with an expected return of 8 percent; and the rest in stock B, with an expected return of 20 percent. Calculate the expected return of the portfolio.

27. On January 1, FinCorp Inc. published the following forecasts for the economy:

State of the economy	Probability	Forecasted quarterly returns
Poor	20%	–3%
Average	50%	5%
Boom	30%	8%

During the year you observed quarterly returns of 2 percent, –5 percent, 3 percent, and 8 percent.

a. Calculate the ex ante expected quarterly return.
b. Calculate the ex ante standard deviation of quarterly returns.
c. Calculate the ex post average quarterly return.
d. Calculate the ex post standard deviation of quarterly returns.
e. Explain the difference between the ex ante and ex post returns.

28. On January 1, FinCorp Inc. completed its analysis of the prospects for the Geriatric Toy Store and concluded that there was a 15-percent chance the stock price would be $150 in one year and an 85-percent chance the stock price would be $200. Six months later, FinCorp Inc. revised its estimated probabilities to a 35-percent chance of a stock price of $150 and a 65 percent chance of $200. If the market agrees with FinCorp Inc.'s revised probabilities, what is the expected change in stock price from January 1 to July 1? Assume the discount rate is zero.

29. As an analyst for FinCorp Inc., you are responsible for many firms, including ADFC. Currently you have a "hold" recommendation on ADFC.[18] The current price of ADFC is $140. You have conducted an extensive analysis of the industry and you feel that the probability the firm will capture a substantial share of the new market is 35 percent. If the firm is able to capture the new market, you are expecting earnings to grow at a rate of 45 percent per year for the next five years. In that case, the stock price would rise to $220 due to the unusually high growth rate of future earnings. However, you feel there is a 40-percent probability that the firm will face serious difficulties in the near future, in which case the stock price will fall to $100, and the earnings growth rate will drop to 3 percent. There is a 25-percent chance that nothing will change for the firm and its earnings growth rate will remain at 12 percent. Should you change your recommendation?

30. FinCorp Inc. has been using the services of San Bernadino Brokerage Company (SBBC) for the past six months. SBBC has informed FinCorp Inc. that the geometric mean monthly return was 7 percent and that over the past six months FinCorp Inc. earned 16 percent, 19 percent, –23 percent, 14 percent, –8 percent, and an unknown amount in the last month. Determine the missing return.

⚙ 31. FinCorp Inc. is interested in the tradeoff between investing in two stocks, ABC and DEF. The expected return on ABC is 6 percent and on DEF is 18 percent.

---

[18] Basically, you are indicating that you believe the stock is fairly priced--it isn't a bargain, so people who don't currently own it shouldn't buy, and it isn't overpriced, so people who own it shouldn't sell.

a. Graph the relationship between the expected return on the portfolio and the weight in DEF.

Weight in DEF	Portfolio return
0%	6%
1%	6.12%
2%	6.24%
3%	6.36%
—	—
—	—
—	—
99%	17.88%
100%	18%

b. What is the tradeoff between investing in ABC and DEF (i.e., if we increase the weight in DEF by 1 percent, what is the change in the expected return on the portfolio)?

c. Your boss has just looked at your results and disagrees. He says the tradeoff between DEF and ABC is negative and, therefore, your results are wrong. Explain to your boss how you are both correct.

32. You wish to combine two stocks, Encor and Maestro, into a portfolio with an expected return of 16 percent. The expected return of Encor is 2 percent with a standard deviation of 1 percent. The expected return of Maestro is 25 percent with a standard deviation of 10 percent. The correlation between the two stocks is 0.4.
    a. What is the composition (weights) of the portfolio?
    b. What is the portfolio standard deviation?

33. You wish to combine two stocks, Peledon and Mexcor, into a portfolio with a standard deviation of 6 percent. The expected return of Peledon is 2 percent with a standard deviation of 1 percent. The expected return of Mexcor is 25 percent with a standard deviation of 10 percent. The correlation between the two stocks is 0.4.
    a. What is the composition (weights) of the portfolio?
    b. What is the expected return on the portfolio?

34. Calculate the covariance and correlation coefficient between the two securities of a portfolio that has 40 percent in stock X (with an expected return of 40 percent and a standard deviation of 12 percent) and 60 percent in stock Y (with an expected return of 30 percent and a standard deviation of 15 percent). The portfolio standard deviation is 6 percent.

35. Calculate the correlation coefficient (ρ_{AB}) for the following situation:

State of the economy	Probability of occurrence	Expected return on stock A in this state	Expected return on stock B in this state
High growth	25%	40%	55%
Moderate growth	20%	20%	25%
Recession	55%	−10%	−20%

36. To achieve a zero standard deviation for a portfolio, calculate the weights of stock A and stock B in Practice Problem 35, assuming the correlation coefficient is −1.

37. An investor purchased 500 shares of stock A at $22 per share and 1,000 shares of stock B at $30 per share one year ago. Stock A and stock B paid quarterly dividends of $2 per share and $1.50 per share, respectively, during the year. One year later, the investor sold both stocks at $30 per share. Calculate the total return of stock A and stock B and the total return of the portfolio.

38. In Practice Problem 37, the correlation coefficient P_{AB} is 0.3 and the standard deviations of stock A and stock B are 20 percent and 15 percent, respectively. Calculate the standard deviation of the portfolio.

39. FinCorp Inc. is exploring the risk of different portfolio allocations between two stocks. Complete the following table.

	Case 1	Case 2
Weight in stock 1	35%	40%
Weight in stock 2		
Standard deviation of stock 1	3%	
Standard deviation of stock 2	25%	20%
Covariance between stocks 1 and 2		0.022
Correlation between stocks 1 and 2		
Portfolio variance	0.027	
Portfolio standard deviation		26%

40. You are interested in using short selling to increase the possible returns from your portfolio.[19] You have short sold $200 of ABC and invested $1,200 in DEF. The following data are available on ABC and DEF:

	ABC	DEF
Expected return	3%	15%
Standard deviation	7%	35%

The correlation between ABC and DEF is 0.4. Calculate the expected return and standard deviation of the portfolio. (Hint: The total invested is $1,000, and while individual weights can be greater than one or less than zero, the sum of the weights must still be one.)

41. Using the following information, calculate the expected return and the standard deviation of ABC.

State of the economy	Probability	ABC stock return (%)
Depression	0.15	−5
Recession	0.2	1
Normal	0.4	6
Boom	0.25	18

42. Five years ago, your dad bought 250 shares of ABC for $6 each and 300 shares of DEF for $7.50 each. He has now given you all his shares, when both stocks are trading at $8. What are the weights of the two stocks in your portfolio?

43. The expected return of ABC is 18 percent, and the expected return of DEF is 23 percent. Their standard deviations are 12 percent and 20 percent, respectively. If a portfolio is composed of 35 percent ABC and the remainder DEF, calculate the expected return and the standard deviation of the portfolio, given a correlation coefficient between ABC and DEF of 0.35. Calculate the standard deviation if the correlation coefficient is −0.35.

44. The expected return of ABC is 15 percent, and the expected return of DEF is 23 percent. Their standard deviations are 10 percent and 23 percent, respectively, and the correlation coefficient between them is zero.

---

[19] When you short sell, you borrow stock from a broker and sell it. At a later date, you will have to buy the same number of shares back and return them to the broker.

a. What is the expected return and standard deviation of a portfolio composed of 25 percent ABC and 75 percent DEF?

b. What is the expected return and standard deviation of a portfolio composed of 75 percent ABC and 25 percent DEF?

c. Would a risk-averse investor hold a portfolio made up of 100 percent of ABC?

45. Using the following information, calculate the expected return and standard deviation of a portfolio with 50 percent in ABC and 50 percent in DEF. Then calculate the expected return and standard deviation of a portfolio where you invest 30 percent in ABC, 30 percent in DEF, and the rest in T-bills with a return of 2.5 percent.

State of the economy	Probability	ABC stock return (%)	DEF stock return (%)
Depression	0.15	−5	−7
Recession	0.2	−3	0
Normal	0.4	5	6
Boom	0.25	8	10

46. You are interested in two stocks: Alcon and Beldon. Both stocks have an expected return of 8 percent. The standard deviation of Alcon is 3 percent, and the standard deviation of Beldon is 5 percent. You want the weights to be greater than or equal to zero. You want to minimize the standard deviation of the portfolio. What should the portfolio composition be if

a. the correlation between the two stocks is −0.8?

b. the correlation between the two stocks is 0.8?

47. You are interested in two stocks: Alcon and Beldon. Both stocks have a standard deviation of 8 percent. The expected return of Alcon is 10 percent, and the expected return of Beldon is 20 percent. You want the weights to be greater than or equal to zero. You want to maximize the expected return of the portfolio. What should the portfolio composition be if

a. the correlation is 0.0?

b. the correlation is 1?

48. FinCorp Inc. wishes to examine the effect of correlation on the efficient frontier that can be created by investing in ABC and FGI. The expected return of ABC is 6 percent, with a standard deviation of 10 percent. The expected return of FGI is 10 percent, with a standard deviation of 25 percent. Graph the efficient frontier for

a. a correlation of 0.0

b. a correlation of −0.5

c. a correlation of 0.5

49. You have observed the following monthly returns for ABC and DEF.

Monthly returns

	ABC	DEF
January	6%	1%
February	−3%	3%
March	−2%	5%
April	−1%	7%
May	0%	2%
June	3%	1%
July	4%	−3%
August	8%	−2%
September	5%	−4%
October	3%	−2%
November	4%	1%
December	5%	2%

a. Graph the relationship between the weight in ABC and the portfolio returns (restrict all weights to be greater than or equal to zero).

b. Graph the relationship between the weight in ABC and the portfolio standard deviation (use the same weights as in (a)).

c. Using the data you have created in (a) and (b), graph the relationship between the risk and return for the portfolio (put return on the y-axis).

d. Which portfolio weights do you prefer and why?

50. FinCorp Inc. wants to examine a "real" efficient frontier involving Research in Motion (RIM.TO) and the Royal Bank (RY.TO).

a. Using monthly data for these two companies from January 2011 to December 2011, graph the relationship between risk and return.

b. Explain the difference between the frontier you developed in (a) and the efficient frontier.

c. Where do you expect the S&P/TSX Composite Index to plot relative to the frontier? Explain.

d. Download the S&P/TSX Composite Index data for the same period (ticker: ^GSPTSE) and plot the S&P/TSX on your graph.

e. Based on your graph, is the S&P/TSX an efficient portfolio? Explain.

f. What do you expect will happen to the frontier if you increase the number of stocks? Explain your reasoning.

51. Richards & Co. Analysts has recently published a study claiming that the benefits to diversification are constant. In other words, adding one more stock to a three-stock portfolio will have the same impact as adding one more stock to a 500-stock portfolio. You are not convinced and you decide to evaluate the claim.

a. Assume that all the stocks have the same standard deviation, 10 percent, and all are independent (correlation equals 0.0). Create equally weighted portfolios of 1 to 10 stocks and calculate the standard deviation for each portfolio. Graph the portfolio standard deviation as a function of the number of stocks. Based on the results of your analysis, evaluate the Richard & Co. Analysts' claim.

b. As the number of firms increases, what do you expect will happen to the risk of the portfolio? Can the risk of the portfolio come close to zero?

9 The Capital Asset Pricing Model (CAPM)

LEARNING OBJECTIVES

9.1 Describe how the efficient frontier is affected once the possibility of risk-free borrowing and investing is introduced.

9.2 Explain how modern portfolio theory is extended to develop the capital market line (CML), which determines how expected returns on efficient portfolios are determined.

9.3 Explain how the capital asset pricing model's (CAPM) security market line (SML) is developed from the capital market line (CML), and how the SML can be used to estimate the required return on individual securities and portfolios.

9.4 List alternative risk-based pricing models and describe how they differ from the CAPM.

Some innovations spread quickly. The web browser is a case in point. Others are adopted more slowly. Between 1952, when Harry Markowitz showed how to factor both the risks and the expected returns of securities into a portfolio construction decision, and 1964, when William Sharpe published the best-known rendition of the capital asset pricing model, the idea that the returns on an asset (any asset) consist of a market part and a nonmarket part came to fruition. The market part, now called "beta," is the part of the return that is explained by correlation with one or more broad-based market indices. The part of the return not explained by beta is the "alpha," usually interpreted as the return from active management skill. This idea was solidified in a 1967 article by Michael Jensen, and the meanings of alpha and beta have changed little since then. Thus, alpha and beta have been clearly separate—as concepts—for about 40 years.

Source: Siegel, Laurence, foreword to *Investing Separately in Alpha and Beta*, by Roger G. Clarke, Harindra de Silva, CFA, and Steven Thorley, CFA. CFA Institute, 2009. Page vi of Foreword.

CHAPTER 9 **PREVIEW**

T his chapter continues the discussion of the relationship between risk and return initiated in Chapter 8. We expand upon this discussion and use it to develop asset pricing models, including the capital asset pricing model, which formalize the risk-return relationship.

9.1 THE NEW EFFICIENT FRONTIER

Learning Objective 9.1
Describe how the efficient frontier is affected once the possibility of risk-free borrowing and investing is introduced.

The Efficient Frontier with Risk-Free Borrowing and Lending

In Chapter 8, we introduced the efficient frontier, which is depicted in Figure 9-1. Recall that the portfolios of risky securities that lie along the efficient frontier—that is, on the curve above the minimum variance portfolio (MVP)—are efficient and dominate all other possible portfolios of risky securities. This means that for a given level of risk, as defined by the standard deviation of their return, these portfolios offer the highest expected rate of return. As we showed in Chapter 8, the derivation of the efficient frontier is a mechanical exercise.

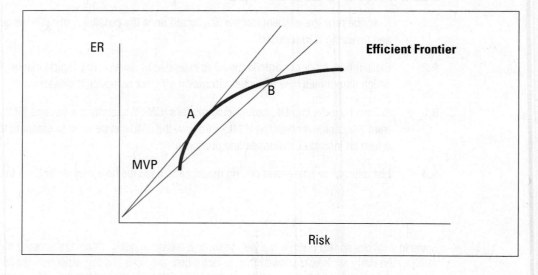

FIGURE 9-1 *Efficient Portfolios*

In the two-security case in Appendix 8A, we showed how to generate the efficient frontier from the expected return and standard deviation for each security and the correlation coefficient between their returns. The procedure is slightly cumbersome, but we can calculate the expected return on the portfolio, estimate its standard deviation, and graph the efficient frontier, which is what we did for Figure 8A-2. As the number of securities increases, the complexity of this mechanical exercise increases as well, but the general principle doesn't, because it is still mechanical. What we didn't fully explain in Chapter 8 are the reasons for graphing the efficient frontier.

In considering how investors make decisions between different securities, we assume that the investors are "risk averse": they will not willingly undertake fair gambles. Consider a game in which a coin is tossed. If it comes up heads, someone pays the player $100, but if it comes up tails, the player pays $100. The player will likely wait and see the coin tossed many times to make sure that the game is fair and that the odds really are 50-50. In this case, it is called a "fair gamble" because the expected payoff is 0—that is, the expected payoff = 0 = 0.50 × (+$100) + 0.50 × (−$100). If someone turns down a fair gamble, he or she is defined as risk averse. A risk-averse person prefers the risk-free situation to gambling on a risky situation where there is an equal probability of winning or losing the same amount of money.

The corollary to turning down a fair gamble is that the risk-averse person needs a **risk premium** to be induced to enter into a risky situation. For example, someone might be willing to take part in the game if the heads payoff were $150 instead of $100. In this case, the expected payoff increases to $25, and it is no longer a fair gamble because there is a risk premium of $25. Another person might require that the heads payoff increase to $200 before undertaking the gamble, so the risk premium increases to $50. The second individual is more risk averse and requires a larger expected payoff or risk premium to get into the risky situation. Generally, investor behaviour is consistent with risk aversion and the existence of risk premiums to induce individuals to bear risk. We can represent this risk aversion in terms of the required risk premium per unit of risk, with higher risk premiums indicating greater risk aversion.

risk premium the expected payoff that induces a risk-averse person to enter into a risky situation

We can also reverse the situation by putting the individual in a risky situation and asking how much he or she is willing to pay to get out of the risky situation. Suppose, for example, someone is faced with a fair gamble; how much would he or she pay to get out of it? A very risk-averse individual would pay a large amount, say $25, to get out of a fair gamble with equally likely payoffs of +/−$100. In this case, the payment to get out of a risky situation is called an **insurance premium**.

insurance premium the payment to get out of a risky situation

Recall that in Chapter 1 we discussed the basic institutions in the financial market and listed the major Canadian companies. One set of companies was the insurance companies, including Manulife Financial Corporation, Sun Life Financial Inc., and Great-West Lifeco Inc., which all had more than $100 billion in assets and $20 billion in revenues. These companies buy risky situations from individuals and institutions that do not want to bear them themselves. The risk of a house burning down, a car being stolen, or a spouse dying prematurely are all risks that individuals are willing to pay an insurance company to bear so that the individuals reduce the probability they will suffer financial harm. In this case, the gross profit margin on most insurance products is about 50 percent, so only 50 cents of every insurance premium dollar actually goes to pay claims; the remainder ends up in administrative expenses, profits, and taxes. The fact that individuals are willing to pay insurance premiums that generate 50-percent gross margins indicates how risk averse they are.[1]

The existence of insurance markets indicates how risk aversion creates a demand to remove risk, whereas the existence of capital markets indicates how risk aversion generates the risk premiums required to induce people to bear risk. In the following discussion, we will assume that investors are risk averse—that is, they require a risk premium to bear risk—and that the more risk averse they are, the higher the risk premium they require. Further, we will continue to assume that we can represent risk in terms of the standard deviation of the return on the portfolio. These assumptions lead to the result that investors will choose only portfolios on the efficient frontier above the MVP.

We can't say where on the efficient frontier a particular person will be, because individuals differ in terms of their risk aversion. However, a very risk-averse individual might choose portfolio A, shown in Figure 9-1, and a less risk-averse individual might choose portfolio B. Why do we know that the investor choosing A is more risk averse than the investor choosing B? The line going through A to the origin is steeper than the line through B and the origin. The slope of the line is the height, which is the expected return on the portfolio, divided by the length, which is the standard deviation of the portfolio. Because the line through A is steeper than the line through B, the individual who invests in A requires a higher expected rate of return per unit of risk—that is, he or she is more risk averse.

Many lines go through the origin and touch different points on the efficient frontier. Portfolios on the flatter lines are chosen by less risk-averse investors. These investors choose a portfolio with a lower expected rate of return per unit of risk and gradually move out along the

---

[1] It could also indicate that people do not understand the probabilities or the payoffs. People seem to be willing to pay very high premiums to remove low-probability risks that offer relatively low payoffs.

efficient frontier. Apart from knowing that investors differ in terms of their risk aversion, we know only that their preferred portfolio will lie somewhere along the efficient frontier.[2]

The origin is the point with a zero expected rate of return and zero risk. Zero risk is another way of describing a risk-free asset, such as a treasury bill (T-bill), where the return on the asset is guaranteed with no possibility of earning more or less. We usually use T-bills as the example of a risk-free asset simply because they are obligations of the Government of Canada, which also has a monopoly on issuing Government of Canada bank notes; T-bills are default free because investors know that they will always be paid off in full.[3] While this is a reasonable assumption for Canada, the United States, and most countries, the concept of risk-free government debt has come under many challenges in recent years, with the European debt crisis and the restructuring of the Greek government's debt obligations, for example. This is nothing new, since other nations have defaulted on their debt obligations in the past, such as Venezuela, Russia, Argentina, the Ukraine, and Belize, among others.

Risk-Free Investing

Consider any point on the efficient frontier in Figure 9-1, such as portfolio A. Now assume an investor places a portion of his or her wealth (w) in risky portfolio A, and the remainder ($1 - w$) in the risk-free asset, the T-bill. Remember that the expected return on a portfolio is always a weighted average of the expected returns on the individual assets, so we can estimate the expected return on this portfolio according to Equation 8-10, reproduced here as Equation 9-1, with RF in place of ER_B.

[9-1]
$$ER_p = RF + w(ER_A - RF)$$

ER_p is the expected return on the portfolio that starts out with $w = 0$, because 100 percent is invested in the T-bill. As w increases, more is placed in the risky portfolio, so the investor picks up ER_p at the cost of taking money out of the T-bill. As a result, the expected return on the portfolio increases by the difference: $ER_A - RF$.

We can estimate the standard deviation on this portfolio using Equation 8-15 from Chapter 8, which is reproduced below.

$$\sigma_p = \sqrt{(w_A)^2(\sigma_A)^2 + (w_B)^2(\sigma_B)^2 + 2(w_A)(w_B)(\rho_{AB})(\sigma_A)(\sigma_B)}$$

If we replace RF for risky portfolio B, w for w_A, and ($1 - w$) for w_B, we get the following:

$$\sigma_p = \sqrt{(w)^2(\sigma_A)^2 + (1-w)^2(\sigma_{RF})^2 + 2(w)(1-w)(\rho_{A,RF})(\sigma_A)(\sigma_{RF})}$$

With the risk-free asset, we know exactly what we are going to get, so the standard deviation of its return is zero. Because the return does not vary, the correlation between the return on the risk-free asset and that on risky portfolio A is also zero. So the standard deviation reduces to

$$\sigma_p = \sqrt{(w)^2(\sigma_A)^2 + (1-w)^2(0)^2 + 2(w)(1-w)(\rho_{A,RF}=0)(\sigma_A)(0)} = \sqrt{w^2\sigma_A^2}$$

---

[2] The previous discussion may seem a bit loose for those with extensive economics training. We could represent each individual by his or her indifference curve, symbolizing his or her risk aversion and personal trade-off between risk and return. However, this adds little to our discussion.

[3] Treasury bills have not always been default free. John Ilkiw points out that sovereign debt used to be very risky because monarchs were above the law, as it was their law, and could repudiate debt without recourse. Only with the establishment of the Bank of England and parliamentary assumption of the British national debt in 1688 did the notion of a risk-free asset come into being. Interest rates on British debt dropped noticeably, by 4 percent, after this assumption as the default risk of lending to the government disappeared. In some parts of the world, government debt still remains risky. See Ilkiw, John, "The 100% Guarantee—The Reign of the Risk-Free Rate: Past Times, Present Value." *Canadian Investment Review* 19, no. 3 (Fall 2006), p. 7.

Taking the square root of the final term leaves us with Equation 9-2.[4]

$$\sigma_p = w\sigma_A \qquad\qquad [9\text{-}2]$$

Equation 9-2 is very important as it shows that portfolio risk increases in direct proportion to the amount invested in the risky asset. Therefore, the higher the portfolio allocation (weight) directed to the risky asset, the higher the portfolio risk. Because both the expected return and the standard deviation of a portfolio comprising any risky portfolio and a risk-free asset (RF) can be represented by a line that is based on the weights invested in RF and in the risky asset, all of the expected returns and risks for various portfolio combinations can be expressed as a straight line. We can show this by rearranging Equation 9-2 in terms of the portfolio weight:

$$w = \frac{\sigma_P}{\sigma_A}$$

Substituting for w in Equation 9-1, we get Equation 9-3.

$$ER_p = RF + \left(\frac{ER_A - RF}{\sigma_A}\right)\sigma_p \qquad\qquad [9\text{-}3]$$

Equation 9-3 is the equation of a straight line. It indicates that the line touches the vertical axis at the risk-free rate and then has a constant slope. The slope is the rise over the run, or the increased expected return divided by the increased risk. The increased expected return, as discussed, is the incremental return on the risky portfolio minus the lost return by taking money out of the risk-free asset. We represent this portfolio in Figure 9-2.

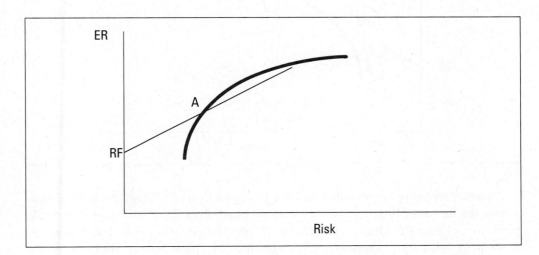

FIGURE 9-2 *Efficient Portfolios and a Risk-Free Asset*

The interpretation of this figure is the same as before: if $w = 0$, all the investment is in the risk-free asset (T-bill), and the portfolio has no risk and earns RF. As w increases, the expected return on the portfolio increases by $(ER_A - RF)$, and its risk by σ_p, until $w = 100$ percent, the expected return is ER_A, and the risk is σ_A. Portfolios formed from A and the risk-free asset are formed using RF and other portfolios on the efficient frontier. In each case, the equation will be the same as in Equation 9-3. In particular, think about portfolio T in Figure 9-3.

All portfolios composed of risky portfolio T and the risk-free rate lie along the line RF to T and offer a higher expected rate of return for the same risk as do portfolios composed of the

---

[4]Technically, this equation holds when short selling is not permitted, so that w is positive. If short selling were permitted, this would need to be replaced by the absolute value of w.

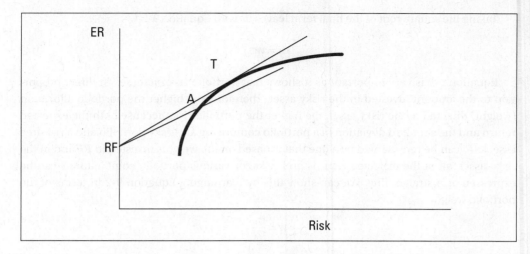

FIGURE 9-3 *Tangent Portfolios*

tangent portfolio the risky portfolio on the efficient frontier whose tangent line cuts the vertical axis at the risk-free rate

new (or super) efficient frontier portfolios composed of the risk-free rate and the tangent portfolio that offer the highest expected rate of return for any given level of risk

risk-free rate and risky portfolio A. Portfolio T is called the **tangent portfolio**, because it is the risky portfolio on the efficient frontier whose tangent line cuts the vertical axis at the risk-free rate. Portfolios composed of the risk-free rate and portfolio T offer the highest expected rate of return for any given level of risk and represent the **new (or super) efficient frontier**, which is depicted in Figure 9-4.

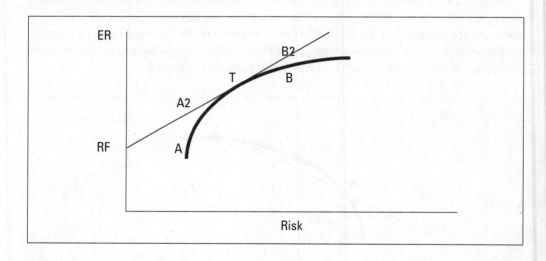

FIGURE 9-4 *The New Efficient Frontier*

Consider, for example, portfolio A, which was optimal for a very risk-averse investor without the risk-free asset. Now this investor could hold a portfolio of the risk-free asset and risky portfolio T, which offers a higher expected rate of return for the same risk as A. This is the new portfolio A2. What this demonstrates is that a portfolio partially invested in the risk-free asset reduces the portfolio risk but can achieve a higher expected rate of return than any portfolio on the efficient frontier of risky assets.

EXAMPLE 9-1	Expected Return and Standard Deviation for a Two-Asset Portfolio That Includes Investment in a Risk-Free Asset

Assume that portfolio T has an expected return of 10 percent, with a standard deviation of 25 percent, and the risk-free rate is 4.5 percent. Estimate the expected return and standard deviation for a portfolio that has 30 percent invested in the risk-free asset and 70 percent in T.

continued

| EXAMPLE 9-1 | Expected Return and Standard Deviation for a Two-Asset Portfolio That Includes Investment in a Risk-Free Asset *continued* |

Solution

$w = 0.7; (1 - w) = 0.3$

Therefore,

$ER_p = (0.3)(4.5\%) + (0.7)(10\%) = 1.35\% + 7\% = 8.35\%$

and

$\sigma_p = (0.7)(25\%) = 17.5\%$

Risk-Free Borrowing

Now consider a less risk-averse investor who held portfolio B in Figure 9-4. He or she could now hold portfolio B2 and get a higher expected rate of return for the same level of risk as B. However, creating portfolio B2 involves having more than 100 percent invested in the risky portfolio T ($w > 100$ percent), and thus having a negative or **short position** in the risk-free asset. We create a short position in the risk-free asset by borrowing. One way to do this is to buy stocks on "margin," which means the investor borrows part of the purchase price from the stockbroker. For example, some stocks have margin requirements as low as 30 percent, indicating an investor could buy $1,000 worth of stocks by investing only $300 and borrowing the remaining $700 from the broker. In this case, the portfolio weights are $w = 1,000/300$ or 333 percent in the risky asset and −233 percent in the risk-free asset. Of course, investors must pay interest on the borrowed money. In addition, short sellers face other risks including: experiencing unlimited losses (i.e., there is "theoretically" no maximum price the share prices could hit); risking being asked to "cover" their short position (by purchasing the amount of shares sold short); and having to cover dividends paid on the underlying stock while they are in the short position. *Finance in the News 9-1* discusses some of these risks.

short position a negative position in an asset; the investor achieves a short position by borrowing part of the asset's purchase price from the stockbroker

finance INTHENEWS 9-1 | Short Sellers Target Canadian Life Insurers

HERE IS A $2-BILLION QUESTION. Why do some investors hate Canada's big three life insurance companies so much they're selling them short?

A short sale is a high-risk strategy because it exposes investors to unlimited losses if they're wrong. Even worse, anyone shorting has to pay dividends to the owners of the shares, so it's not a step to be taken on a whim.

Yet Manulife Financial (MFC-T12.640.050.40%) is the most heavily shorted stock on the TSX, with more than 62 million shares sold in this way. Sun Life (SLF-T20.75-0.13-0.62%) and Great-West Lifeco (GWO-T23.330.090.39%) also rank high on the most-shorted list. As a group, the three life insurers, the best known companies in their industry in Canada, have a total short position on the TSX amounting to a tidy $2-billion worth of stock, a multibillion-dollar bet on their share prices sagging. There are also additional shares in the companies sold short in the U.S., but the amounts are not as large as in Canada.

Short-selling is the sale of a stock an investor doesn't own, in the hopes of profiting by buying it back later at a lower price to close out the transaction. The shares that are sold are borrowed through a friendly broker from another investor. Although it sounds complicated, short-selling is merely the reverse of the normal transaction of being "long"—or buying a stock in the expectation of making a profit when the share price goes up.

Given that short selling is a bet on a company slipping on a banana peel, the technique suffers from an image problem of not being a decent thing to do. It's the reason short sellers are typically a publicity-shy bunch. No investors have publicly claimed credit for the gargantuan anti-life insurance company bet, even though it has been a brilliant strategy in recent months.

Insurers' share prices were clobbered by last year's decline in interest rates, which made it harder for life insurance companies to earn high returns on their investments, the source of their profits.

"This short interest, this pessimism, is a reflection of the concern that interest rates, that bond yields, could go lower," observes Michael Goldberg, an analyst at Desjardins Capital Markets in Toronto.

One explanation for the trade is that some hedge funds are trying to goose their returns on the Canadian financial sector by simultaneously buying shares in banks, the strongest part of the financial system, and selling short the insurers, speculates Martin Braun, president of Adaly Investment Management Corp., a money management firm.

This approach—a kind of giant paired trade—was a definite money spinner in 2011, when the TSX bank index dropped a modest 2.9 percent, while life insurance companies plunged 30.4 percent.

Mr. Braun says the shorting may be targeting insurance as a sector, rather than making a judgement on the merits of individual companies.

continued

Finance in the News 9-1: Short Sellers Target Canadian Life Insurers *(continued)*

The bet against the insurers is sizable, by international standards. Data Explorers published a screen last month of 66 global life insurers, and found two of the Canadian companies were among the most shorted in the world, based on how much of the stock was sold this way compared to the total amount outstanding.

Sun Life was tied for being the most heavily shorted, while Manulife was no. 5. In the case of Sun Life, 9 percent of its stock has been sold short, while for Manulife it was 5 percent. Data Explorers says the average in the sector is 2 percent.

Shorting is an expensive proposition. Sun Life sports a 7-percent dividend, Great-West 5.5 percent, and Manulife 4.1 percent, money that the shorts have to fork over to the owners of the shares they've borrowed. To be sure, those shorting can offset some of the cost of these dividends by using the proceeds of the sale to buy other high-yielding stocks, such as the major banks, which pay out around 4 percent.

Mr. Goldberg, for one, says interest rates will be the determining factor for the performance of insurance companies. If interest rates rise this year, which is his most likely scenario, "then those shorts are going to get their clock cleaned," he predicts.

Given the huge short position, there could also be an explosive rally in insurers' share prices if things turn out better for the industry, aided by short sellers themselves. That's because any sharp rally would pressure the shorts, and could force them to exit their positions by bidding for the stock, further fuelling any rally.

Selling Them Short

Company	Ticker (TSX)	Recent Price $	12-Month % Chg.	Short Position (no. of shares)*
Manulife Financial	MFC	$12.76	−27.2%	62,322,404
Sun Life Financial	SLF	$21.18	−32.1%	29,738,248
Great-West Lifeco	GWO	$22.79	−13.8%	25,671,592

*As of January 15, 2012. Source: Bloomberg, TSX Datalinx.

For simplicity, we assume that short sellers borrow at the same risk-free rate as investors can lend at.[5] This situation is illustrated in Example 9-2.

EXAMPLE 9-2	Expected Return and Standard Deviation for a Two-Asset Portfolio That Includes Borrowing at the Risk-Free Rate

Assume that an investor invests all of her wealth ($1,000) in portfolio T from Example 9-1, with an expected return of 10 percent and a standard deviation of 25 percent. She borrows an additional $700 at the risk-free rate of 4.5 percent, which she also invests in T. Estimate the expected return and standard deviation for this portfolio.

Solution

$w = 1,700/1,000 = 1.7$; $(1 - w) = 1 - 1.7 = -0.7$

Therefore,

$ER_p = (-0.7)(4.5\%) + (1.7)(10\%) = -3.15\% + 17\% = 13.85\%$

and

$\sigma_p = (1.7)(25\%) = 42.5\%$

The portfolio described in Example 9-2 is similar to B2 and lies on the straight line depicted in Figure 9-4 beyond portfolio T, as would any portfolio formed by borrowing funds at RF and investing them in portfolio T.

The New Efficient Set and the Separation Theorem

We showed above that any point along the tangent line from the risk-free rate is attainable by either investing or borrowing at *RF*, and then investing all remaining proceeds in risky

[5]Although borrowing rates are generally higher than the risk-free rate in practice, this assumption can be relaxed without greatly affecting our key results. For more details, refer to any investments text, such as Cleary, W. S., and Jones, C.P., *Investments: Analysis and Management*, 3rd Canadian ed. (Toronto, Ontario: John Wiley & Sons Canada Ltd., 2009), p. 236.

portfolio T. From Figure 9-4, we see that all the points along this line dominate all the points on the efficient frontier, except for point T. As we showed, A2 is better than A and B2 is better than B. Therefore, allowing for the possibility of risk-free investing and borrowing has expanded the efficient set and provided investors with a *more efficient* set of portfolios from which to choose. This line is often called the new (or super) efficient frontier, or the previous efficient frontier is specifically referred to as the "efficient frontier of risky portfolios" to distinguish it from the efficient frontier of the risk-free asset and the tangent portfolio.

Investors can achieve any point on this new efficient frontier by borrowing or investing desired amounts at RF and investing the remainder in one portfolio of risky assets, which is the tangent portfolio T. Therefore, each investor can choose the point on this line that suits his or her personal risk preferences: more risk-averse investors can choose portfolios like A2, which are heavily invested in the risk-free asset (T-bills); whereas more aggressive investors can choose portfolios like B2, which involve borrowing.

A very important concept arises from this discussion. Suppose investors all agree on the expected rates of return and the risk attached to each security. In that case, the efficient frontier of risky assets is the same for all investors. This would occur, for example, if the investors were clients of an investment company that estimated all these values and then discussed the best portfolio for a particular client. It would no longer be necessary to match each investor's risk preferences with a specific risky portfolio. Instead, the investment company would recommend the same tangent portfolio to all its clients. It might then refer to this portfolio as its model portfolio, and some investors would invest in this and the risk-free asset (T-bills), whereas others would borrow to invest in the model portfolio.

Suppose, further, that all investment companies agreed on the set of expected returns and the risk attached to the securities. In that case, the tangent or model portfolio would also be the same. This result provides the basis for the **separation theorem**, which states that the *investment decision*—that is, the decision on how to construct the portfolio of risky assets—is separate from the *financing decision*—that is, the decision about how much should be invested or borrowed at the risk-free rate. In other words, the tangent portfolio T is optimal for every investor regardless of his or her degree of risk aversion. Further, if everyone holds the same portfolio, it must be the **market portfolio** of all risky securities, because every security has to be held by someone.

Theoretically, the market portfolio should contain all risky assets worldwide, including stocks, bonds, options, futures, gold, real estate, and so on, in their proper proportions. Such a portfolio, if it could be constructed, would be completely diversified. However, in practice, the market portfolio is unobservable, so we use proxies to measure its behaviour. Common stock market indexes, such as the S&P/TSX Composite Index in Canada and the S&P 500 Composite Index in the United States, are often used as proxies.

The fact that every investor would hold the same portfolio (the market portfolio) is referred to as an "equilibrium condition," because supply equals demand for all the risky securities, and we replace T with M, which is not just the tangent portfolio but also the market portfolio. This hypothesis is the basis for the most common model we use in finance to price securities, the capital asset pricing model, which is discussed in the next section.

separation theorem the theory that the investment decision (how to construct the portfolio of risky assets) is separate from the financing decision (how much should be invested or borrowed at the risk-free rate)

market portfolio a portfolio that contains all risky securities in the market

CONCEPT REVIEW QUESTIONS

1. What is risk aversion and how do we know investors are risk averse?
2. What is the risk of a portfolio consisting of a risk-free asset and a risky security?
3. Why is the tangent portfolio so important?
4. How do we generate a portfolio with a higher expected rate of return than that of the tangent portfolio?

9.2 THE CAPITAL ASSET PRICING MODEL (CAPM)

Learning Objective 9.2
Explain how modern portfolio theory is extended to develop the capital market line (CML), which determines how expected returns on efficient portfolios are determined.

capital asset pricing model (CAPM) a pricing model that uses one factor, market risk, to relate expected returns to risk

Professor William Sharpe of Stanford University won the Nobel Prize for developing the best-known equilibrium asset pricing model, the **capital asset pricing model (CAPM)**, which relates expected returns to risk. The initial development of the CAPM was based on a number of assumptions that we have already briefly discussed:

1. All investors have identical expectations about expected returns, standard deviations, and correlation coefficients for all securities.

2. All investors have the same one-period time horizon.

3. All investors can borrow or lend money at the risk-free rate of return (RF).

4. There are no transaction costs.

5. There are no personal income taxes, so investors are indifferent whether they receive capital gains or dividends.

6. There are many investors, and no single investor can affect the price of a stock through his or her buying and selling decisions. Therefore, investors are price-takers.

7. Capital markets are in equilibrium.

These assumptions may appear unrealistic at first. For example, the assumption of identical expectations is needed so that the efficient frontier of risky portfolios is the same for all investors. However, not all investors matter; the most important are the big institutions that invest most of the money. They all have access to the same information, and they all have expert security analysts analyzing the data. Similarly, borrowing rates differ from lending rates for small investors, but for large institutional investors the difference is not material. The same applies to transaction costs. The result is that most of the assumptions can be relaxed without significantly affecting the CAPM or its main implications. However, before discussing the CAPM, we will discuss what happens to the overall capital market.

The Market Portfolio and the Capital Market Line (CML)

The assumptions for the CAPM listed above give rise to the following important implications, which have been discussed previously:

1. The "optimal" risky portfolio is the one that is tangent to the efficient frontier on a line that is drawn from RF, as shown in Figure 9-4. This portfolio will be the same for all investors.

2. This optimal risky portfolio will be the "market portfolio" (M), which contains all risky securities. The value of this portfolio will equal the aggregate of the market values of all the individual assets composing it. Therefore, the weights of these assets in the market portfolio will be represented by their proportionate weight in its total value.

capital market line (CML) a line depicting the highest attainable expected return for any given risk level that includes only efficient portfolios; all rational, risk-averse investors want to be on this line

Figure 9-5 is similar to Figure 9-4, but it does not include the efficient frontier portion, and the only portfolio is M, the tangent portfolio, because the market portfolio (M) is the optimal portfolio of risky securities that is combined with RF. Recall that this line produces the highest attainable expected return for any given risk level; therefore, it includes only efficient portfolios. Further, all rational, risk-averse investors will seek to be on this line. In Figure 9-5, it is called the **capital market line (CML)**.

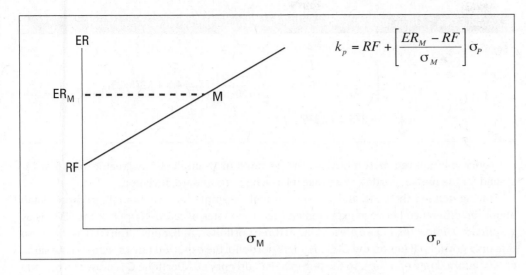

$$k_p = RF + \left[\frac{ER_M - RF}{\sigma_M} \right] \sigma_P$$

FIGURE 9-5 *The Capital Market Line (CML)*

We can see from Figure 9-5 that the CML has an intercept of RF, just like any portfolio consisting of the risk-free asset and a risky portfolio. But the risky portfolio is not arbitrary: now it is the market portfolio. So we have a special version of Equation 9-3:

$$\text{Slope of the CML} = \frac{ER_M - RF}{\sigma_M} \qquad [9\text{-}4]$$

As in Equation 9-3, the slope of the capital market line is the incremental expected return divided by the incremental risk. However, this is a special trade-off of risk and return called the **market price of risk** for efficient portfolios or the equilibrium price of risk in the capital market. It indicates the additional expected return that the market demands for an increase in a portfolio's risk. Adding the risk-free rate (*RF*) gives the CML as:

market price of risk the incremental expected return divided by the incremental risk; indicates the additional expected return that the market demands for an increase in risk

$$ER_p = RF + \left[\frac{ER_M - RF}{\sigma_M} \right] \sigma_p \qquad [9\text{-}5]$$

where
ER_M = the expected return on the market portfolio M
σ_M = the standard deviation of returns on the market portfolio
σ_p = the standard deviation of returns on the efficient portfolio being considered

The CML is a special version of Equation 9-3 in another important way. As always, the CML indicates an expected rate of return, just as Equation 9-3 gave the expected return on a portfolio of A and the risk-free rate. However, now we have made enough assumptions to identify the portfolio as the market portfolio and as an equilibrium condition in the capital market, where supply equals demand. As a result, the CML determines not just an expected rate of return but also a **required rate of return**, which we denote as k_p.

required rate of return the rate of return investors need to tempt them to invest in a security

---

EXAMPLE 9-3 **Using the CML to Determine the Required Rate of Return**

Assume the risk-free rate is 4.5 percent. The expected return on the market is 10 percent, and it has a standard deviation of 20 percent. Determine the required rate of return necessary for investors to hold an efficient portfolio with a standard deviation of 25 percent.

continued

EXAMPLE 9-3	Using the CML to Determine the Required Rate of Return *continued*

Solution

$$k_p = RF + \left[\frac{ER_M - RF}{\sigma_M}\right]\sigma_p = 4.5 + \left[\frac{10 - 4.5}{20}\right](25) = 4.5 + (.275)(25)$$

$$= 4.5 + 6.875 = 11.375\%$$

Notice that the required return on the portfolio in Example 9-3 is greater than that expected for the market portfolio, because it has a higher standard deviation.

Having defined the CML and worked through Example 9-3, we can talk in more detail about the difference between expected and required rates of return. Suppose the CML is as graphed in Figure 9-6, and we are looking at three portfolios: A, B, and C. The CML is drawn so that only portfolio B lies on the CML. For this portfolio, the expected rate of return is the same as the required rate of return, so the portfolio is "fairly priced." Portfolio C is drawn so that the expected portfolio return is higher than that of B. However, this portfolio is below the CML, which indicates that the required rate of return is higher than this expected rate of return. If we look at just the expected rate of return, C would seem to be a good buy, but this is wrong because it is a very risky portfolio. Given its risk, it is a bad buy and its price would drop, forcing up its expected rate of return until it was fairly priced and the expected and required rates of return were the same. Portfolio A presents the opposite situation: it has a high expected rate of return and relatively low risk. In this case, the expected rate of return exceeds the required rate of return, and investors would bid up its price and cause its expected rate of return to fall until it lies on the CML.

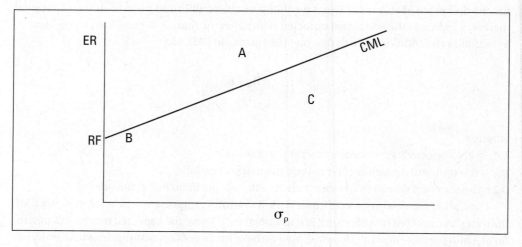

FIGURE 9-6 *Expected and Required Rates of Return*

It is also important to recognize that the CML must always slope *upward,* because with risk-averse investors the risk premium must always be positive, and the CML predicts r*equired* returns. As a result, risk-averse investors will not invest unless they expect to be compensated for bearing risk. The greater the risk, the greater the required rate of return. However, as we discussed in Chapter 8, there is a big difference between ex post and ex ante returns. After the fact (ex post) returns can be (and often have been) less than the T-bill yield. If this were never the case, investing in the equity market would have no risk and no one would hold T-bills. The observation of ex post poor returns on risky securities does not negate the validity of the CML; however, it merely indicates that returns actually realized differ from those that were expected. In other words, investors sometimes get it wrong and their expectations are not realized. If investors were never wrong, there would be no risk in the equity market!

The ideas that we have just described have become a critical part of the evaluation of investment performance in a financial system. Consider the slope of the CML in Equation 9-4 again. In equilibrium, all portfolios should lie along the CML, as those offering expected rates of return that are higher than required will have their prices bid up and vice versa. The CML is based on expected rates of return, so it is ex ante. However, if expectations are realized—if, on average, the actual return is what was expected—we can use the CML to judge the performance of different portfolios ex post—that is, the actual portfolio performance.

Risk-Adjusted Performance and Sharpe Ratios

When the ideas underlying the CML are used in this way, it leads to a discussion of the **Sharpe ratio**, named after William Sharpe of Stanford University, who developed the ratio and first applied it to assessing portfolio performance. The Sharpe ratio generally uses realized (or ex-post) returns, and is formally defined as

Sharpe ratio a measure of portfolio performance that describes how well an asset's return compensates investors for the risk taken

$$\text{Sharpe ratio} = \frac{ER_p - RF}{\sigma_p}$$

[9-6]

When the portfolio is the market portfolio, the Sharpe ratio is the ex-post version of Equation 9-4, which is the ex post slope of the CML. So what would be typical values for the Sharpe ratio? Table 8-2 showed that from 1938 to 2011, the arithmetic mean return for Canadian equities was 11.35 percent and for T-bills was 4.96 percent, so the ex post excess return of equities over T-bills was 6.39 percent. If the T-bill return is taken to be the risk-free rate, and if the standard deviation for equities is 16.82 percent (also taken from Table 8-2), the ex post Sharpe ratio for Canadian equities in this period was 0.380 (i.e., 6.39/16.82). What this means is that for every 1-percent increase in risk (standard deviation of the portfolio's return), the Canadian equity market rewarded the investor with an extra 0.380 percent of return.

Sharpe ratios are commonly used to assess the performance of portfolios, including professionally managed funds, as discussed in *Finance in the News 9-2*. The reason is that it measures excess returns (i.e., returns in excess of a risk-free rate) and scales them by the volatility of the returns. In other words, its value is increasing in returns but is decreasing in risk, all else being equal. As *Finance in the News 9-2* suggests, the "trick" to effective fund management is "to capture high returns without taking on too much risk."

finance INTHENEWS 9-2   CAPM and the Sharpe Ratio

WILLIAM SHARPE, AN American academic and consultant, is one of the founders of what is known universally as the capital asset pricing model (CAPM) and also of a ratio that bears his name that is used to measure the riskiness of an investment relative to the returns it generates.

We can deal with the CAPM first by noting that Sharpe's main contribution to portfolio theory was the insight that an individual investment contained two types of risk: specific risk, unique to that investment; and market risk, sometimes called systemic risk. Specific risk can be removed through diversification.

Coping with systemic risk is what really plagues investors, according to Sharpe.

The CAPM evolved as a way of quantifying this risk. Sharpe found that the return on an individual investment or portfolio of investments should equate to the risk-free rate of return plus the excess return that the market

provided over that risk-free rate multiplied by a factor, which Sharpe called beta. Beta is the measure of an individual investment's (or portfolio's) sensitivity to the movement in the market.

Each individual investment has a beta, which varies over time and for the time period chosen over which to measure it. A beta for a stock with measurements taken hourly over the course of a week, for example, might be different to one calculated daily over a period of three months. In both cases, though, beta means the same thing. A stock with a beta of 1.5 could, for example, be expected to rise 15 percent if the market rose 10 percent and fall 15 percent if the market fell 10 percent.

Beta is found by statistical analysis of share price returns compared with the market's returns over precisely the same period. Betas of individual stocks can be combined together to give a portfolio beta. The importance of Sharpe's model is that it allows one to predict the expected re-

continued

Finance in the News 9-2: CAPM and the Sharpe Ratio *(continued)*

turn from a portfolio given its beta, the market rate of return and the risk-free rate.

Say the portfolio beta was 2.0, the risk-free rate 3 percent, and the market rate of return 7 percent. Then the market's excess return is 4 percent (7 − 3), the portfolio's excess return is 8 percent (2 × 4, multiplying market excess return by beta), and the portfolio's total expected return is 11 percent (8 + 3, the portfolio's excess return plus the risk-free rate). What this means is that it is possible, by knowing these individual components of the CAPM, to establish whether the current price of an investment is consistent with it or not, in other words whether or not the investment is cheap or dear.

One other offshoot of Sharpe's work is a ratio for standardizing the measuring of the performance of funds, notably hedge funds. Known as the Sharpe ratio, this compares the excess return that a fund earns, over and above the risk-free rate, with the volatility of those returns. The argument underlying this is that any investment manager can earn higher returns by assuming more risk.

Risk is equated with volatility of returns. The trick is to capture high returns without taking on too much risk.

By comparing excess return with volatility, investments can be ranked on the basis of degree of return provided per unit of risk. The higher is the Sharpe ratio, the more favourable are the risk-return characteristics of the individual investment or fund. Just as funds can have Sharpe ratios, so too can markets.

This might all sound rather dry and academic, but the work of Sharpe and others led directly to the creation of index-tracking investments.

Sharpe, for example, by devising the concept of beta, demonstrated that it would not be necessary for an index-tracking portfolio to hold all of the constituents of an index in the exact proportions they represented of it to produce a performance that matched the index. All one needed to do was construct a portfolio that had, over time, a consistent beta of 1 and it would mimic the performance of the index.

It is perhaps significant that among the firms that used Sharpe's services as a consultant was Wells Fargo. Back in the mists of time, Wells Fargo Nikko Investment Advisors was a predecessor firm of Barclays Global Investors, creator of the iShares concept and now the biggest providers of exchange traded index funds for investors. If you hold an index-tracking investment, you have Sharpe to thank for the fact that the product is available for you to invest in.

Source: Temple, Peter, "CAPM and the Sharpe Ratio." *Interactive Investor,* March 24, 2011. First published on Interactive Investor www.iii.co.uk.

CONCEPT REVIEW QUESTIONS

1. What is the slope of the CML, and why can it be viewed as the market price of risk for efficient portfolios according to the CML?

2. Assuming the CAPM holds, if the expected return on a diversified portfolio lies above the CML, should an investor buy or sell that portfolio?

3. When is the expected return equal to the required return?

4. Why is the Sharpe ratio frequently referred to as a "risk-adjusted" measure of performance?

9.3 THE CAPM AND MARKET RISK

Learning Objective 9.3
Explain how the capital asset pricing model's (CAPM) security market line (SML) is developed from the capital market line (CML), and how the SML can be used to estimate the required return on individual securities and portfolios.

The CML provides a method of estimating the required return on equity securities relative to their risk, but it applies only to efficient portfolios and not to individual securities. In addition, the risk premium is based on portfolio risk, as measured by the standard deviation of the return on the portfolio. In corporate finance, we are usually concerned with the risk attached to individual firms and the required return for investing in them. Recall from our discussion in Chapter 8 that as the number of securities included in a portfolio increases, unique (nonsystematic or diversifiable) risk is eliminated, and only market (systematic or non-diversifiable) risk remains. This relationship is depicted in Figure 9-7.

Figure 9-7 shows that the average risk of an individual security—that is, a one-stock portfolio—is at the point where the curve gets very close to the vertical axis. Therefore, with randomly built diversified portfolios, the risk of a portfolio falls until it reaches a baseline and cannot be reduced below this market level. What this means is that part of a security's risk is diversifiable. Further, if it can be diversified away by holding a portfolio of more than, say, 20 securities, it is not important to rational investors. This is the key insight of the CAPM.

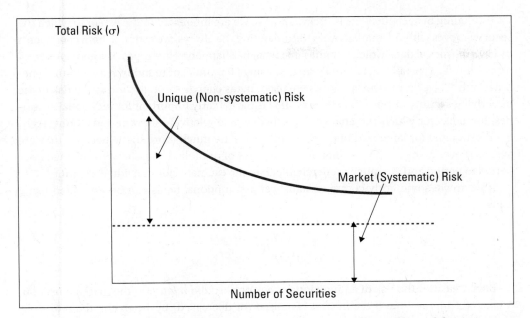

FIGURE 9-7 *Portfolio Risk and Diversification*

The CAPM points out that rational investors should not be compensated for unique or diversifiable risk, because it can be eliminated through diversification. This implies that market risk is the appropriate measure of risk to determine the risk premium required by investors for holding a risky security. We now introduce a new term, **beta (β_i)**, which is a commonly used measure of market risk that relates the extent to which the return on a security moves with that on the overall market. It is typically estimated by first plotting the returns on an individual security on the vertical axis relative to the returns for the market, which are plotted along the horizontal axis, and then fitting a line through the observations, as shown in Figure 9-8. The line is called the **characteristic line** and is determined by using a statistical technique called regression analysis. The slope of the line is the security's beta coefficient. For example, in Figure 9-8, the slope coefficient is 0.85, which indicates that if the market return goes up or down by 1 percent, the return on this security is expected to go up or down by 0.85 percent—that is, it changes by 0.85 of the return on the market.[6]

beta (β_i) a measure of market risk, or performance volatility, that relates the extent to which the return on a security moves with that on the overall market; the covariance between an investment and the market divided by variance of the market

characteristic line a line of best fit through the returns on an individual security, plotted on the vertical axis, relative to the returns for the market, plotted along the horizontal axis

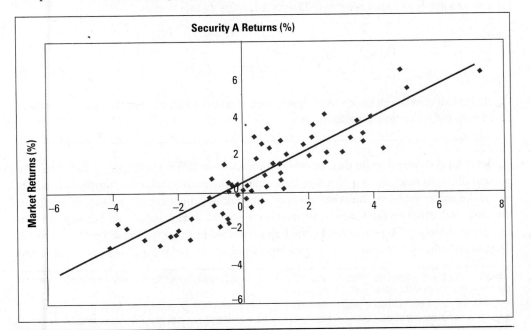

FIGURE 9-8 *The Characteristic Line for Security A*

[6]The characteristic line is also often estimated by using excess returns. The excess return is calculated by subtracting the risk-free rate from both the return on the stock and the return on the market. In excess return form, the same analysis applies.

Estimating beta coefficients is tricky, because we are interested in the extent to which the security moves with the market over a future period. As always, we estimate beta coefficients by using historical data, which assumes that what has happened in the past is a good predictor for the future. Typically, betas are estimated using 60 months of monthly returns, but sometimes only 52 weeks of weekly returns are used. Betas change through time as the risk of the underlying security or portfolio changes. This is particularly important for individual securities, the betas for which can change dramatically over relatively short periods. Conversely, betas estimated for large portfolios or for industries are much more stable because they are averaged over many securities. Therefore, estimates of portfolio betas show less change from period to period and are much more reliable than the estimates for individual securities.

If we make some fairly common statistical assumptions, betas can be estimated using Equation 9-7.[7]

[9-7]
$$\beta_i = \frac{COV_{i,M}}{\sigma_M^2} = \frac{\rho_{i,M}\sigma_i}{\sigma_M}$$

Beta measures the risk of an individual stock or portfolio *relative* to the market portfolio. A beta of 1 implies that if the market increased (or decreased) by 1 percent, the return on the security (or portfolio) would increase (decrease) by 1 percent *on average*. Therefore, the market has a beta of 1. A security with a beta of 1.2 has returns that are 1.2 times as volatile as market returns, either up and down. In other words, if the market increased 10 percent, that security's returns would increase by 12 percent, and so on. Securities with betas greater than 1 are generally considered to be more volatile (or risky) than average. Similarly, securities with betas less than 1 are less volatile (risky). The risk-free asset has a beta of zero, because it has a covariance of zero with the market and has no risk. Finally, negative betas are possible, although they are rare. Equation 9-7 shows that negative betas can only occur if a security has a negative correlation coefficient with market returns, which is uncommon.[8]

EXAMPLE 9-4   Estimating Beta

The returns on stock X have a standard deviation of 25 percent and a correlation coefficient of 0.7 with market returns, which have a standard deviation of 20 percent. Estimate the beta for stock X.

Solution

$$\beta_x = \frac{\rho_{x,M}\sigma_x}{\sigma_M} = \frac{(0.70)(25)}{20} = 0.875$$

Notice that even though stock X has a higher standard deviation than the market, its beta is less than one because of the correlation coefficient of 0.7.

Betas tend to vary a great deal between companies in different industries, because they possess different risk profiles. Although betas tend to be more similar for companies operating in the same industry, they can still vary substantially, because even companies within the same industry can differ across various dimensions, such as financial risk, size, and so on. These comments are validated by the betas reported in Table 9-1 for several well-known Canadian companies that operate in a variety of industries. Betas for 2011 range from a low

---

[7] The technical assumptions required ensure that ordinary least squares (OLS) is the appropriate regression estimation approach to determine the equation of the characteristic line discussed above.

[8] This is the only way a negative beta is possible, because the standard deviation terms in Equation 9-7 are always positive. Gold stocks have sometimes had negative betas because, in the past, the price of gold tended to go in the opposite direction to the market; investors would invest in gold when they were nervous about future market movements. However, this relationship is not as strong as it used to be, and negative betas rarely occur, even for gold stocks.

of 0.35 for BCE Inc. (a telecommunications company) to a high of 1.73 for AGF Management Ltd. (a mutual fund company).

TABLE 9-1 Canadian Betas

Company	Industry Classification	2009	2011
AGF Management Ltd.	Financials	1.36	1.73
Alamos Gold Inc.	Materials–Precious Metals & Minerals	0.87	0.41
Bank of Montreal	Financials–Banks	0.50	0.87
Bank of Nova Scotia	Financials–Banks	0.63	0.91
Barrick Gold Corp.	Materials–Precious Metals & Minerals	0.62	0.46
BCE Inc.	Communications–Telecommunications	0.32	0.35
Canadian Imperial Bank of Commerce	Financials–Banks	0.58	0.76
Cogeco Cable Inc.	Consumer Discretionary–Cable	0.99	0.37
Imperial Oil Ltd.	Energy–Oil & Gas: Integrated Oils	1.13	0.58
Magna International	Consumer Discretionary–Auto Parts	0.80	1.49
Royal Bank	Financials–Banks	0.60	0.72
Suncor Energy Inc.	Energy–Oil & Gas	1.80	1.62
Toronto-Dominion Bank	Financials–Banks	0.64	0.97
TSX Group Inc.	Financials–Diversified Financials	0.79	0.62
WestJet Airlines Ltd.	Industrials–Transportation: Airlines	0.49	0.41

Table 9-1 also shows how betas change through time (as discussed previously). Notice that the betas for all of the banks increased markedly to their more traditional 0.72 to 0.97 range in 2011 compared to the 0.50 to 0.64 range in 2009. Over this two-year period, the betas of AGF Management and Magna also increased markedly, while those for Alamos Gold, Cogeco Cable, and Imperial Oil decreased substantially.

Unlike portfolio standard deviations, portfolio betas are weighted averages of the betas for the individual securities in the portfolio. Therefore, we can estimate the beta for an n-security portfolio by using Equation 9-8.

$$\beta_p = w_1\beta_1 + w_2\beta_2 + \ldots + w_n\beta_n \qquad [9\text{-}8]$$

Consider a security with a beta of zero. This means that its return is unrelated to the return on the market as a whole. As a result, all of the variability in this security's return is diversifiable by any investor holding a well-diversified portfolio. If this security is added to a diversified portfolio with a beta of 1, it will reduce the portfolio's beta. In contrast, if we add a security with a beta of 2 to the same portfolio, its beta will increase, thus increasing the risk of the portfolio and making it more sensitive to market movements.

EXAMPLE 9-5 Estimating a Portfolio Beta

An investor has a portfolio that consists of $10,000 invested in stock B, which has a beta of 1.2; $20,000 in stock C, which has a beta of 0.8; and $20,000 in stock D, which has a beta of 1.3. Estimate the beta of this portfolio.

Solution

$$w_B = \frac{10,000}{(10,000 + 20,000 + 20,000)} = 0.20; \; w_C = \frac{20,000}{50,000} = 0.40; \; w_D = \frac{20,000}{50,000} = 0.40$$

$$\beta_p = w_B\beta_B + w_C\beta_C + w_D\beta_D = (0.20)(1.2) + (0.40)(0.8) + (0.40)(1.3)$$

$$= 0.24 + 0.32 + 0.52 = 1.08$$

We can see from the result of Example 9-5 why diversified portfolios end up with only market risk. First, the beta on the market portfolio, by definition, is 1. We can see this from Equation 9-7 by substituting M for the standard deviation of the security and noting that a security is perfectly correlated with itself. So if the average beta is 1, as we randomly add securities to a portfolio, we eventually end up with an average risk portfolio with a beta of 1, composed of all market risk. This is also why most large portfolios made up of a large number of securities are essentially the same as the market portfolio and earn the same rate of return.[9]

The Security Market Line (SML)

Based on the argument made earlier that investors should be compensated for market risk, as measured by beta, it is easy to use the CML to derive the **security market line (SML)**, which is given in Equation 9-9.[10]

[9-9]
$$k_i = RF + (ER_M - RF)\beta_i$$

where k_i = the required return on security (or portfolio) i
$(ER_M - RF)\beta_i$ = the risk premium

The SML is the most important and widely used contribution of the CAPM, and it is depicted graphically in Figure 9-9. It represents the trade-off between market risk and the required rate of return for any risky investment, whether it is an individual security or a portfolio.

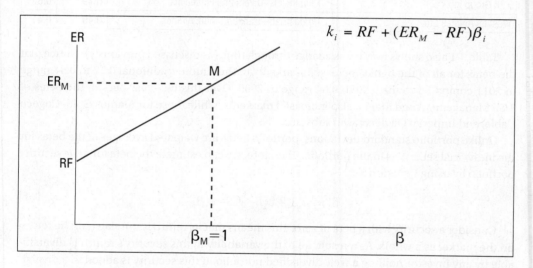

$$k_i = RF + (ER_M - RF)\beta_i$$

FIGURE 9-9 *The Security Market Line (SML)*

The SML slopes upward, which indicates that investors require a higher expected return on riskier—that is, higher-beta—securities. In essence, the SML formalizes the notion discussed previously at several junctures since Chapter 6: the required rate of return on an asset equals the risk-free rate plus a risk premium. According to the SML, the size of the risk premium varies directly with a security's market risk, as measured by beta.

The risk premium is also a function of market conditions, as reflected in the $ER_M - RF$ term, which is often referred to as the **market risk premium**. The historical averages provided in Table 8-2 of Chapter 8 suggest that the ex post risk premium from 1938 to 2011 in Canada was 6.39 percent (i.e., the average return on the market portfolio of Canadian common stocks was 11.35 percent, while the average T-bill return was 4.96 percent). (Whether this is a reasonable ex ante market risk premium is doubtful given market developments since then.)

---

[9] This is what is commonly referred to as "closet indexing," because although they charge large fees, most mutual funds have similar performance.

[10] For a formal derivation of the SML from the CML, refer to any investments textbook. For example, see Cleary, W.S., and Jones, C.P., *Investments: Analysis and Management*, 3rd Canadian edition (Toronto: John Wiley & Sons Canada Ltd., 2009), pp. 258–59.

According to the SML, securities or portfolios with betas greater than the market beta of 1 will have larger risk premiums than the "average" stock and will therefore have larger required rates of return. Conversely, securities with betas less than that of the market are less risky and will have lower required rates of return.

EXAMPLE 9-6   Using the SML

Given that the expected return on the market is 10 percent and the risk-free rate is 4.5 percent, estimate

a. the market risk premium

b. the required return for security X in Example 9-4, which had a beta of 0.875

c. the required return for the portfolio in Example 9-5, which had a beta of 1.08

Solution

a. $ER_M - RF = 10 - 4.5 = 5.5\%$

b. $k_X = RF + (ER_M - RF)\beta_X = 4.5 + 5.5(0.875) = 4.5 + 4.813 = 9.313\%$

Notice that the required return for X is *less* than the expected market return because its beta is less than 1.

c. $k_p = RF + (ER_M - RF)\beta_p = 4.5 + 5.5(1.08) = 4.5 + 5.94 = 10.44\%$

Notice that the required return for this portfolio is *greater* than the expected market return because its beta is greater than 1.

LESSONS TO BE LEARNED

Estimating required returns using the CAPM is fraught with difficulties. We need estimates of beta as well as the expected return on the market. Generally, betas are estimated using past data, with two years of weekly data or five years of monthly data being the most commonly employed approaches. Of course, what we really want is an estimate of beta for future periods, so beta estimates can and do vary through time as illustrated in Table 9-1. In many cases, they might not be good measures of a stock's future market sensitivity over a given period for a variety of reasons—we discuss one such instance in detail in Chapter 20.

Similarly, we often use historical averages to estimate the expected market return. Obviously, such estimates can often be way off the mark for any given period. Consider, for example, that the average Canadian stock market return over the 1938 to 2011 period was 11.35 percent, which is quite different from the −33 percent return experienced by the market in 2008, or the +35 percent return in 2009.

One has to keep in mind that beta represents the "average" market sensitivity and that this sensitivity may vary from one period to the next. The same applies to expected market returns. The realistic approach is to recognize that CAPM does a reasonable job of predicting returns on average, over the long run.

The SML and Market Equilibrium

In equilibrium, the expected return on all properly priced securities will lie *on* the SML, just as the expected return on all portfolios will lie on the CML. As with the CML, when investors expect a return equal to the required return, the security is correctly priced. However, at any given time, some securities may be temporarily mispriced according to CAPM. Whenever analysis suggests that the expected return on a security differs from its required rate of return according to CAPM, then that security is either undervalued or overvalued. Securities or portfolios that have expected returns *greater* than their required rate of return are *undervalued*, because they provide investors with an expected return that is higher than the return required given their risk. As with the CML, undervalued securities will lie *above* the SML, reflecting the fact that the expected return exceeds the required return, which is the return along the SML that corresponds to the beta coefficient. Security A in Figure 9-10 represents an example of an undervalued security. Similarly, securities or portfolios whose expected returns are *less* than their required rate of return, such as B in Figure 9-10, are *overvalued* and will lie below the SML.

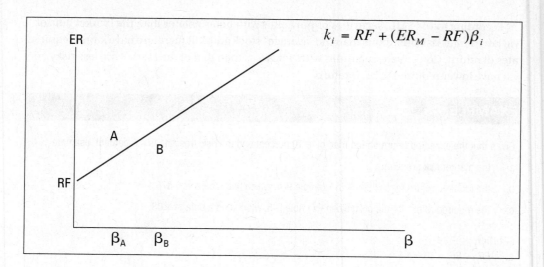

FIGURE 9-10 *The SML and Security Valuation*

$$k_i = RF + (ER_M - RF)\beta_i$$

If markets are efficient, we would expect prices to be correct (we will discuss the notion of market efficiency in Chapter 10). Therefore, whenever rational investors observe an under-valued security, such as A, they will rush to purchase it because it offers a higher expected return than its required return. As a result of this increase in demand for security A, its price will increase until it eventually equals the price level at which its expected return equals the required return according to the SML. In other words, security A's price will adjust until it lies along the SML. In similar fashion, selling pressure for security B (which is overvalued) would increase, causing B's price to decline until it too lies along the SML.

Of course, markets will not always be in equilibrium, and over a given period of time a security or portfolio might over- or under-perform the market and earn a return above or below that predicted by the SML. Let's consider the possibility that point A in Figure 9-10 depicts the actual returns and beta for portfolio A over some prior period in time, while *RF* and *RM* represent the risk-free returns and market returns, respectively, over that same period. The risk-adjusted excess returns earned by portfolio A (i.e., the return above that predicted by this "ex post" SML) over this period would be referred to as the portfolio's "alpha." Alpha (α) measures the risk-adjusted excess return (above or below that predicted by its beta) earned by a security or portfolio over a given period. It is a commonly used measure of portfolio manager performance. Of course, alpha need not always be positive; if point B in Figure 9-10 was also based on historical observations, it would indicate risk-adjusted "under-performance."

Alpha can be estimated by substituting ex post average returns (i.e., no more "expected" returns) into the SML and then rearranging as shown to create Equation 9-10.[11]

[9-10]
$$\alpha_i = (R_i - RF) - [\beta_i(R_M - RF)]$$

Equation 9-10 indicates that α_i is the difference between the actual excess return on a security or portfolio during some period and the return that should have been earned according to its level of systematic risk (beta) and the use of the CAPM. This difference can be positive, negative, or zero. It is important to recognize the role of statistical significance in the interpretation of alpha. Although the estimated alpha may be positive or negative, it may not be significantly different (statistically) from zero. If it is not, we would conclude that the manager of the portfolio being evaluated performed as expected. That is, the manager earned an average risk-adjusted return, neither more nor less than would be expected given the risk assumed.

This discussion of the security market line is similar to the discussion of the capital market line. The two main differences are: (1) the measure of risk (CML uses standard deviation,

---

[11] Technically, alpha is the intercept coefficient estimate obtained when we regress past excess returns ($R_i - RF$) on excess market returns ($R_M - RF$), while the slope coefficient estimate is the beta.

while SML uses beta); and (2) the CML applies only to efficient portfolios, while the SML applies to individual stocks and portfolios.

Using the SML to Estimate Long-Term Discount Rates

Technically, the CAPM is a one-period model, and the government T-bill rate should be used as the appropriate risk-free rate, since it is virtually guaranteed and does not fluctuate. However, analysts often use the CAPM to estimate the required return on common shares over many periods, such as when they are trying to estimate the share price using the dividend discount model or free cash flow models. As discussed in Chapter 7, these models require the discounting of expected cash flows that occur over many periods in the future. It is also normal to use the CAPM to estimate the cost of a firm's common equity financing component when estimating the firm's overall cost of capital. The cost of capital is then used to discount the expected future cash flows associated with capital expenditure decisions, which will be discussed in chapters 13, 14, and 20.

When using the CAPM to estimate a long-term required return on common equity, such as in the situations described above, analysts often use the yield on long-term government bonds instead of T-bills. Like T-bills, bond yields have virtually no default risk, but they do fluctuate widely in response to changes in interest rates (i.e., due to interest rate risk), as discussed in Chapter 6. So while T-bills represent a better one-period risk-free rate (because they don't fluctuate over one period), their rates often fluctuate from one period to the next. Long-term bond rates are more representative of the rate that could be obtained over longer investment horizons.

The market risk premium, as measured by the return on the market less the long-term government bond yield over the 1900-to-2010 period, averaged about 5 percent in developed stock markets around the world, which is lower than the U.S. and Canadian averages, over that period, of 6.4 percent and 5.3 percent, respectively.[12] Figure 9-11 shows the expected market risk premiums according to a 2010 survey of analysts, companies, and finance professors. Notice that the estimates were in the 5 to 6 percent range for all regions, which corresponds to their long-term averages.

We will discuss the process of estimating the required rate of return on a firm's common equity in greater detail when we examine the cost of capital in Chapter 20. At this point, we will briefly review how we obtained the discount rate of 6.84 percent for Tim Hortons, which we used to estimate that company's price in Chapter 7, using the dividend discount model (and also in the price-earnings ratio model).

When we estimated Tim Hortons' share price in March of 2012, we obtained a beta estimate for Tim Hortons of 0.68, using five years of monthly return data and the S&P/TSX Composite Index. However, as mentioned, beta estimates for individual stocks are always subject to some degree of estimation error. Therefore, it is common practice to also refer to industry beta estimates. This estimate for Tim Hortons is in line with the historical beta for this sector, which is typically close to 0.5. So we have decided to use our estimate of 0.68 as the beta estimate going forward; remember, we are interested in what the future beta is, and we use historical data for this purpose only.

In March 2012, the yield on long-term Government of Canada bonds was 2.70 percent, which we used as our risk-free rate. The long-term average market risk premium (over bond yields) in Canada is 5.3 percent, while the range of expected market risk premiums reported in Figure 9-11 ranges between 5 and 6 percent. If we choose the mid-point of this range (i.e., 5.5%) as our risk premium and use the bond yield of 2.70 percent as RF, we get:

$$k_e = 2.70 + (5.5\%)(0.68) = 6.44\%$$

---

[12] Dimson, E., Marsh, P., and Staunton, M., "Equity Premiums Around the World," in *Rethinking the Equity Risk Premium*. Research Foundation of the CFA Institute, December 2011.

This is not totally unreasonable. However, government bond yields were extremely low in early 2012, while bond yield spreads were very high as a result of nervousness at the slow pace of recovery in the United States, and due to recessionary and sovereign debt fears in Europe, as discussed in chapters 1 and 2 and throughout the textbook. Normally A-rated corporate bonds sell at spreads of 100 basis points (bps) above equivalent-maturity long Canada bonds, but currently these spreads are at 180 bps. While this spread is not anywhere near the record highs experienced during the financial crisis, it is still indicative of heightened risk aversion. Researchers at the Bank of Canada indicate that much of this increased spread is due to liquidity problems, but some still reflect increased risk premiums for even low-risk companies like Tim Hortons.[13] Consistent with the research at the Bank of Canada, we add half of the "above average" credit spread or 0.40 percent to our CAPM estimate to account for this time-varying risk premium. We would therefore place the equity cost for Tim Hortons at:

$$k_e = 6.44 + 0.40 = 6.84\%$$

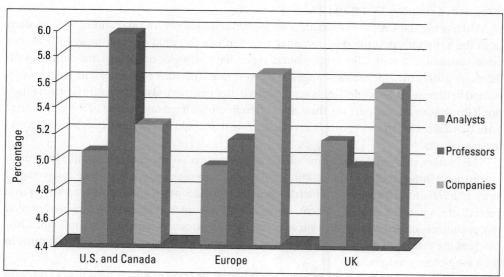

FIGURE 9-11 *Estimated Market Risk Premiums (2010)*

Source: Data from Fernandez, Pablo, and del Campo, Javier, *Market Risk Premium used in 2010 by Analysts and Companies: A Survey with 2,400 Answers*, May 21, 2010. Retrieved from http://www.iese.edu/research/pdfs/DI-0912-E.pdf.

CONCEPT REVIEW QUESTIONS

1. Why is beta a measure of market risk for a security?
2. If a security's correlation with the market return increases, will its beta get larger or smaller?
3. What is a characteristic line, and why is it useful?
4. If the market risk premium increases, will securities become overvalued or undervalued?

9.4 ALTERNATIVE ASSET PRICING MODELS

Learning Objective 9.4
List alternative risk-based pricing models and describe how they differ from the CAPM.

The CAPM is a "single-factor" model because it suggests that the required return on equities is determined by only one risk factor: market risk. The CAPM is often criticized because it is based on several assumptions, many of which are called into question in the real world. In addition, a substantial amount of empirical evidence finds that the CAPM does not hold well in practice. In particular, although empirical estimates of the ex post SML suggest that it is indeed an upward-

---

[13] Refer to A. Garcia and J. Yang, "Understanding Corporate Bond Spreads Using Credit Default Swaps," *Bank of Canada Review*, Autumn 2009.

sloping straight line, the ex ante *y*-intercept has been found to be higher than *RF*, and the slope of the SML is less than that predicted by theory—that is, it is "flatter" than it should be. Although this research remains very controversial, a 1992 study of U.S. stock returns by Fama and French concluded that beta, the sole risk factor in the CAPM, possessed no explanatory power for predicting stock returns.[14] In addition, they found that two other factors (discussed in the next subsection) do a much better job of explaining common stock returns. Indeed, there is a great deal of controversy and debate about the validity of the CAPM, as discussed in *Finance in the News 9-3*.

---

finance INTHENEWS 9-3 | The CFA Institute Centre for Financial Market Integrity Proposed Risk Management Requirement

Benjamin Graham and Risk

Beta is a more or less useful measure of past price fluctuations of common stocks. What bothers me is that authorities now equate the beta idea with the concept of risk. Price variability yes; risk no. Real investment risk is measured not by the percent that a stock may decline in price in relation to the general market in a given period, but by the danger of a loss of quality and earnings power through economic changes or deterioration in management.

—Benjamin Graham

Introduction

This paper draws on diverse sources, including

1. MPT: "Capital Ideas" by Peter Bernstein, recent articles by Harry Markowitz, William Sharpe, and Eugene Fama and Kenneth French,

2. Benjamin Graham: "The Intelligent Investor" by Ben Graham, and "Value Investing from Graham to Buffett and Beyond" by Bruce Greenwald et al.,

3. Behavioural: "Behavioural Investing" by James Montier.

This paper is not intended as another challenge to MPT—that significant body of theory consisting of mean-variance analysis (MVA) (Harry Markowitz-1952), the capital asset pricing model (CAPM) (William Sharpe-1964), and the efficient markets hypothesis (EMH) (Eugene Fama-1965).

There is already ample ongoing debate among very sophisticated commentators, including the above-noted original authors themselves, who acknowledge MPT's limitations and advocate broader perspectives. The paper is intended to discuss the MPT concept of risk, including the advice of the three original authors, discuss the value investors' concept of risk, and in conclusion, advocate the CFAI take a broader investor perspective with respect to its proposed risk management requirement. [. . .] Markowitz, Sharpe, Fama and French all suggest that alternatives to CAPM should be taught in finance courses.

The Evidence

The above sets out the theory of beta as a measure of risk. As noted, a fairly large body of research challenges the theory. Value stocks (those with low price/earnings ratios (P/Es) and low price/book ratios (P/Bs)) have lower betas, but have higher returns than growth stocks. This is contrary to the notion that returns go hand in hand with risk—which is at the heart of MPT. Such research emerged not long after Sharpe's paper in 1964—with the first studies appearing in 1970 . . . and they are still coming. The . . .

exhaustive study by Fama and French (2004) examined all NYSE, ASE, and NASDQ listed stocks between 1929 and 2003. It found there was almost no relationship between returns and beta.

As behaviouralist author James Montier says: "There is an overwhelming amount of evidence that CAPM simply does not work . . . CAPM woefully underpredicts the returns to low beta stocks and massively overestimates the returns to high beta stocks."

Benjamin Graham and Value Investors' Concept of Risk

In addition to Benjamin Graham's quote at the very beginning, most value investors have different views on beta.

Warren Buffet says in Berkshire Hathaway's "1993 Annual Report":

We define risk, using the dictionary terms, as "the possibility of loss or injury." Academics . . . like to define investment "risk" differently, averring that it is the relative volatility of a stock or portfolio of stocks . . . compared to a large universe of stocks. Employing data bases and statistical skills, these academics compute with precision the "beta" of a stock . . . and then build . . . investment and capital allocation theories around this calculation . . . for a single statistic to measure risk. . . . For the owners of a business— and that's the way we think of shareholders, the academics' definition of risk is far off the mark.

Charles Brandes says in "Value Investing Today":

Volatility is measurable, uncertainty is not . . . defining volatility as risk (as MPT does) obscures the true definition of investment risk as the possibility of losing money . . . Beta is used primarily by those who are looking at the whole market (or large numbers of stocks within it) and who don't look in detail at the fundamentals of specific companies. As I have shown for value investors, this concept is irrelevant and downright dangerous at worst.

An interesting thing about the value investor's definition of risk is that it is not a theory, nor an equation, but a common sense expression of how to avoid losing money. As Bernstein says in "Capital Ideas":

Ben Graham had devised a method for determining whether a stock is cheap or expensive. That method has stood many if not all the tests of time, but it is still not a theory. Graham told the investor what to do but said little about why his prescriptions would work.

Quite often Warren Buffett uses his investment in the Washington Post Company to explain risk. Buffett says:

continued

Finance in the News 9-3: The CFA Institute Centre for Financial Market Integrity Proposed Risk Management Requirement *(continued)*

Sometimes risk and reward are correlated in a positive fashion . . . the exact opposite is true in value investing. If you buy a dollar for 60 cents, it is riskier than if you buy a dollar for 40 cents, but the expectation for reward is greater in the latter case.

The Washington Post Company in 1973 was selling for $80 million in the market. At that time . . . the assets were worth $400 million, probably more. Now if the stock had declined even further to a price that made the valuation $40 million instead of $80 million, its beta would have been greater. And to people who think beta measures risk, the cheaper price would have made it look riskier. This is truly Alice in Wonderland.

Conclusions and Recommendations

It is clear that MPT has some limitations. As noted, the theory on beta simply does not hold up well empirically. Fama and French's exhaustive study found that value stocks have lower risk but higher returns than growth stocks—a direct contradiction of MPT, and ironically, exactly what the value investors say. Helping to explain why this is so, Fama and French went on to show that the low betas of value stocks and high betas of growth stocks converge as value stocks surprise on the upside and growth stocks surprise on the downside.

On the other hand, as all three original authors say, MPT should still be taught. An example of the usefulness of the CAPM concept is: how would one explain the concept of "portable alpha" without using the CAPM concepts of alpha and beta.

The recent comments of Harry Markowitz, William Sharpe, and Eugene Fama and Kenneth French make eminent sense though. MPT is a useful, though not the only, theory that should be taught in finance courses.

I would suggest that Benjamin Graham's definition of risk is the correct one and that of MPT is not.

Source: Grantier, Bruce, *The CFA Institute Centre for Financial Market Integrity Proposed Risk Management Requirement, Asset Manager Code of Professional Conduct—Benjamin Graham and Risk.* Originally published by the Brandes Institute: www.brandes.com/institute. Bruce Grantier is an Advisory Board member of the Brandes Institute.

An important theoretical problem associated with tests of the CAPM was identified by Richard Roll in 1976 and is commonly referred to as Roll's critique.[15] Roll argued that the CAPM cannot be tested empirically because the market portfolio, which consists of all risky assets, is unobservable. Therefore, researchers are forced to use market proxies, which may or may not be the optimal mean-variance efficient portfolio. In effect, Roll argued that tests of the CAPM are actually tests of the mean-variance efficiency of the chosen market portfolio. He showed that the basic CAPM results will hold whenever the chosen proxy is mean-variance efficient and will not hold if the converse is true. As a result the empirical tests have no power.

Despite the criticisms of the CAPM, it remains, for both academics and practitioners, the most commonly used method of estimating the required rate of return on individual securities (see Table 9-2). Two of the other models listed (Fama-French and APT) are discussed below, while the remainder will be discussed in Chapter 20. One of the main reasons for the CAPM's staying power is its intuitive appeal for assessing the trade-off between risk and expected return and the observation that individuals hold diversified portfolios. Further, the

TABLE 9-2 Percentage of Analysts Using Various Methods to Estimate the Required Return on Common Shares

CAPM	68.2%
APT	4.8%
Fama-French	4.0%
Bond yield plus risk premium	42.7%
Judgementally determined hurdle rate	47.5%
Other (Build up or market derived)	6.3%

Table Source: Model Selection from "Valuation Methods" presentation, October 2007, produced by Tom Robinson, Ph.D., CFA, CPA, CFP®, Head, Educational Content, CFA Institute. Copyright 2007, CFA Institute. Reproduced and republished from Valuation Methods with permission from CFA Institute. All rights reserved. The results are based on a survey of about 13,500 CFA Institute members, 2,369 of whom accepted the invitation. Of those surveyed, 2,063 evaluate individual securities for the purpose of making an investment recommendation or portfolio decision. They were primarily buy-side investment analysts and portfolio managers. For those managing portfolios, the sample was fairly equally split between members managing institutional and individual (private wealth) portfolios.

---

[15] See Roll, R. "A Critique of the Asset Pricing Theory's Tests; Part I: On Past and Potential Testability of the Theory," *Journal of Financial Economics* 4 (1976), pp. 129–76.

contenders have had at least as much difficulty as the CAPM in generating statistical support. However, in response to some of the problems associated with the CAPM, alternative asset pricing models have been developed, and two of the better-known alternatives are discussed in the next section. In contrast to the CAPM, both of these models are multi-factor models: they assume that more than one factor affects stock returns.

The Fama-French Model

As mentioned in the previous section, Fama and French found that two additional factors, beyond market returns, affected stock returns. These factors are the market value of a firm's common equity (MVE) and the ratio of a firm's book equity value to its market value of equity (BVE/MVE). Based on this discovery, they developed a three-factor pricing model. Like the CAPM, their model includes an overall market factor; however, it also includes MVE (which is related to firm size) and the BVE/MVE.[16]

The **Fama-French (FF) model** has become popular over the past decade because some believe it does a better job than the CAPM of explaining ex ante stock returns. For example, Ibbotson Associates, Inc., a major provider of financial information, now gives estimates of companies' required return on equity based on this model, in addition to estimates determined by the more widely recognized CAPM. However, the FF model has been criticized because it is not based on sound economic fundamentals, while the CAPM is. Further, many believe that the FF model is simply an example of "data mining," in which the data have been examined so many times that eventually some variables are bound to be discovered that explain returns better than the CAPM.

Fama-French (FF) model a pricing model that uses three factors (a market factor, the market value of a firm's common equity, and the ratio of a firm's book equity value to its market value of equity) to relate expected returns to risk

The Arbitrage Pricing Theory (APT)

Another well-known multi-factor asset pricing model is the **arbitrage pricing theory (APT)**. The APT holds under very few assumptions, unlike the CAPM. In particular, the APT does not depend on the existence of an underlying market portfolio, and it allows for the possibility that several types of risk may affect security returns. In fact, APT is based on the **no-arbitrage principle**, which states that two otherwise identical assets cannot sell at different prices.

Development of the formal APT assumes that asset returns are linearly related to a set of indexes, which proxy risk factors that influence security returns. The underlying risk factors in the APT represent broad economic forces, which are unpredictable. The APT can be expressed as in Equation 9-11.

arbitrage pricing theory (APT) a pricing model that uses multiple factors to relate expected returns to risk by assuming that asset returns are linearly related to a set of indexes, which proxy risk factors that influence security returns

no-arbitrage principle a rule stating that two otherwise identical assets cannot sell at different prices

$$ER_i = a_0 + b_{i1}F_1 + b_{i2}F_2 + \ldots + b_{in}F_n \qquad [9\text{-}11]$$

where ER_i = the expected return on security i

a_0 = the expected return on a security with zero systematic risk

b_{ij} = the sensitivity of security i to a given risk factor j

F_i = the risk premium for a given risk factor j

Equation 9-11 demonstrates that a security's risk is based on its sensitivity to basic economic factors, while expected return increases proportionately to this risk. The sensitivity measures (b_i) play a role similar to beta in the CAPM, because they measure the relative sensitivity of a security's return to a particular risk premium. In fact, the APT would "collapse" into the CAPM if there were only one risk factor (market returns) influencing security returns.

The main problem with the APT is that the factors are not specified ahead of time. In fact, APT does not even specify the number of risk factors that exist, or state which factors will be the most important. As a result, these factors, as well as their relative importance, must be identified empirically. Most empirical evidence suggests that three to five factors influence

---

[16] See Fama, E., and French, K., "Size and Book-to-Market Factors in Earnings and Returns," *Journal of Finance 50* (1995), pp. 131–55.

security returns and are priced in the market. For example, Roll and Ross identify the following five systematic factors:[17]

1. changes in expected inflation

2. unanticipated changes in inflation

3. unanticipated changes in industrial production

4. unanticipated changes in the default-risk premium[18]

5. unanticipated changes in the term structure of interest rates

---

CONCEPT REVIEW QUESTIONS

1. Why is the CAPM called a single-factor model?

2. Describe some of the criticisms of the CAPM, including Roll's critique.

3. Briefly describe the strengths and weaknesses of the Fama-French model and the APT.

SUMMARY

In this chapter, we show how the efficient frontier can be expanded by introducing the possibility of risk-free borrowing and lending. Based on certain assumptions that underlie the capital asset pricing model (CAPM), we show that this new (or super) efficient frontier can be depicted as a straight line that begins at RF and is tangent to the old efficient frontier at point M, the market portfolio. This line is called the capital market line (CML) and depicts the required return for efficient portfolios based on their standard deviations.

The security market line (SML), which represents the most important contribution of the CAPM, can be derived from the CML. The SML provides a way to estimate the required return for any security or portfolio, based on its market risk, as measured by beta. Criticisms of the CAPM have led to the development of alternative asset pricing models. We conclude the chapter with a brief description of two of these models: the Fama-French model and the arbitrage pricing theory (APT).

SUMMARY OF LEARNING OBJECTIVES

9.1 Describe how the efficient frontier is affected once the possibility of risk-free borrowing and investing is introduced.

Once the possibility of risk-free borrowing and investing is introduced, the efficient frontier becomes a straight line. The new (or super) efficient frontier portfolios are composed of the risk-free rate and the tangent portfolio that offer the highest expected rate of return for any given level of risk.

9.2 Explain how modern portfolio theory is extended to develop the capital market line (CML), which determines how expected returns on efficient portfolios are determined.

The "optimal" risky portfolio is the one that is tangent to the efficient frontier on a line that is drawn from RF, as shown in Figure 9-4. This portfolio will be the same for all investors. This optimal risky portfolio will be the market portfolio (M), which contains all risky securities. The value of this portfolio will equal the aggregate of the market

---

[17] Roll, R., and Ross, S., "An Empirical Investigation of the Arbitrage Pricing Theory," *Journal of Finance* 35, no. 5 (December 1980), pp. 1073–1103.

[18] This variable is commonly defined as the yield on long-term corporate bonds minus the yield on long-term government bonds.

values of all the individual assets composing it. Therefore, the weights of these assets in the market portfolio will be represented by their proportionate weight in its total value.

9.3 Explain how the capital asset pricing model's (CAPM) security market line (SML) is developed from the capital market line (CML), and how the SML can be used to estimate the required return on individual securities and portfolios.

Because of diversification, the individual risk can be diversified away, but the market risk remains. So the security price will finally depend on its co-movement with the market, which is measured by beta. Then CML is developed into SML. SML can be applied easily into asset pricing; see Equation 9-9.

9.4 List alternative risk-based pricing models and describe how they differ from the CAPM.

Alternative asset pricing models include the Fama-French model and the arbitrage pricing theory. The Fama-French model includes the market factor, value factor, and size factor, and is empirically successful. The arbitrage pricing theory introduces more factors, while CAPM has only one factor: the market portfolio.

KEY TERMS

arbitrage pricing theory (APT), p. 359
beta (β_i), p. 349
capital asset pricing model (CAPM), p. 344
capital market line (CML), p. 344
characteristic line, p. 349
Fama-French (FF) model, p. 359

insurance premium, p. 337
market portfolio, p. 343
market price of risk, p. 345
market risk premium, p. 352
new (or super) efficient frontier, p. 340
no-arbitrage principle, p. 359
required rate of return, p. 345

risk premium, p. 337
security market line (SML), p. 352
separation theorem, p. 343
Sharpe ratio, p. 347
short position, p. 341
tangent portfolio, p. 340

EQUATIONS

Equation	Formula	Page
[9-1] Expected Portfolio Return	$ER_p = RF + w(ER_A - RF)$	p. 338
[9-2] Portfolio Standard Deviation (Risky Asset and Risk-Free Asset)	$\sigma_p = w\sigma_A$	p. 339
[9-3] Expected Portfolio Return (Risky Asset and Risk-Free Asset) in Terms of Standard Deviations	$ER_p = RF + \left(\dfrac{ER_A - RF}{\sigma_A}\right)\sigma_p$	p. 339
[9-4] Slope of CML	$\text{Slope of the CML} = \dfrac{ER_M - RF}{\sigma_M}$	p. 345
[9-5] Capital Market Line (CML)	$ER_p = RF + \left[\dfrac{ER_M - RF}{\sigma_M}\right]\sigma_p$	p. 345
[9-6] Sharpe Ratio	$\text{Sharpe ratio} = \dfrac{ER_p - RF}{\sigma_p}$	p. 347
[9-7] Beta	$\beta_i = \dfrac{COV_{i,M}}{\sigma_M^2} = \dfrac{\rho_{i,M}\sigma_i}{\sigma_M}$	p. 350
[9-8] Portfolio Beta	$\beta_p = w_1\beta_1 + w_2\beta_2 + \ldots + w_n\beta_n$	p. 351
[9-9] Security Market Line (SML)	$k_i = RF + (ER_M - RF)\beta_i$	p. 352
[9-10] Jensen's Alpha	$\alpha_i = (R_i - RF) - [\beta_i(R_M - RF)]$	p. 354
[9-11] Arbitrage Pricing Theory (APT)	$ER_i = a_0 + b_{i1}F_1 + b_{i2}F_2 + \ldots + b_{in}F_n$	p. 359

QUESTIONS AND PRACTICE PROBLEMS

Multiple Choice Questions

1. What is the expected return and standard deviation of a portfolio consisting of $2,500 invested in a risk-free asset with an 8-percent rate of return, and $7,500 invested in a risky security with a 20-percent rate of return and a 25-percent standard deviation?
   a. 11 percent, 6.25 percent
   b. 17 percent, 18.75 percent
   c. 6.25 percent, 11 percent
   d. 18.75 percent, 17 percent

2. Which of the following statements is correct?
   a. The new efficient frontier is a curved line similar to the original efficient frontier.
   b. All the portfolios along the new efficient frontier dominate those along the original efficient frontier including the tangency portfolio.
   c. The weight of the risk-free asset is positive in calculating expected return when investors buy stocks on margin.
   d. Investors who are more risk averse invest to the left of the tangent portfolio.

3. What is the standard deviation of an efficient portfolio with a 20-percent expected rate of return, given that RF is 5 percent, ER_M is 8 percent, and σ_M is 24 percent?
   a. 50 percent
   b. 20 percent
   c. 60 percent
   d. 120 percent

4. Which of the following statements is false?
   a. The standard deviation of a risk-free asset is zero.
   b. Portfolios on the efficient frontier dominate all other attainable portfolios for a given risk or return.
   c. The covariance of any combination of a risky security and a risk-free asset is zero.
   d. The risk measurement associated with the security market line (SML) is the standard deviation of the portfolio.

5. If portfolio A lies above the SML, portfolio A is
   a. overvalued
   b. undervalued
   c. properly valued
   d. undetermined

6. All of the following are differences between the CML and SML, except
   a. the slope
   b. the risk measurement
   c. the y-intercept
   d. the application to the required return on individual securities

7. A portfolio with a beta greater than 1 is
   a. more volatile than the market
   b. less volatile than the market
   c. as volatile as the market
   d. not volatile

8. Which of the following statements is false?
   a. Systematic risk cannot be diversified away.
   b. The market portfolio includes all risky assets including stocks, bonds, real estate,

derivatives, and so on.
c. The market portfolio is observable.
d. The y-intercept of both the SML and the CML is *RF*.

9. Systematic risk (beta)
    a. is also called unique risk
    b. equals total risk divided by non-systematic risk
    c. estimates do not change through time
    d. measures of portfolios are more stable than those of individual assets

Practice Problems

10. TrenStar Inc. is planning to offer several investments to investors and is in the process of designing its marketing materials. Each investment's value in the future will be related to the return on the S&P/TSX Composite Index over the year. The cost and value of the investments are outlined as follows:

| Investment | Cost today | Value of investment if: | |
		S&P/TSX return < 0%	S&P/TSX return ≥ 0%
A	$7	0	$15
B	$12	$15	$15
C	$9	$20	$0
D	$0	–$10	$10
E	$0	$10	–$10

Assume that the probability of the S&P/TSX falling (i.e., having a return less than 0 percent) is 40 percent and that the risk-free rate is zero. Risk-averse investors are only willing to invest in a risky undertaking if the expected value is sufficiently greater than the cost. Which investments will be preferred by a risk-averse investor? Explain your reasoning.

11. For the following decisions, indicate if they are consistent with risk aversion or risk loving.
    a. Buying a lottery ticket
    b. Buying fire insurance on your house
    c. Jaywalking on St. Catherine Street in Montreal
    d. Backing up your computer

12. TrenStar Inc. has five clients with different risk and return preferences. The market portfolio has an expected return of 10 percent, with a standard deviation of 7 percent. The risk-free rate is 6 percent. Each client has $1,200 to invest. Fill in the missing information in the following table.

Investor	Weight in risk-free asset	$ amount invested in risk-free asset	Expected portfolio return	Portfolio standard deviation
Charles	20%			
Sonja		Borrowed $300		
Fritz			9%	
Eddy			16%	
Nellie				3%

13. Jackie borrowed $500 at the risk-free rate of 8 percent. She invested the borrowed money and her own money of $1,500 in a portfolio with a 15-percent rate of return and a 30-percent standard deviation. What is the expected return and standard deviation of her portfolio?

✿ 14. A lawyer prosecuting a lawsuit against The Brokerage Company has hired you to conduct an investigation into the advice the company has been giving its clients. You observe that clients have invested in the following portfolios:

Investor name	Portfolio	Expected return	Standard deviation
Charles	A	2%	0.4%
Rina	B	4%	0.6%
Xiang	C	5%	0.3%
Amanda	D	7%	0.5%
Amir	E	9%	0.45%
Geeta	F	10%	0.7%

Evaluate the advice the Brokerage Company has been giving its clients. (Assume that investors can only invest in one of the six portfolios.)

a. Evaluate the investors who are holding inefficient portfolios.
   i. Which investors are holding inefficient portfolios? Examine it by a graph with standard deviation on the x-axis and expected return on the y-axis.
   ii. The broker under investigation argues that these portfolios are appropriate because the investors are risk loving. Are inefficient portfolios appropriate for risk-loving investors?
b. Use return/risk to evaluate the investors who are holding efficient portfolios. Who is
   i. the most risk averse?   ii. the least risk averse?

✿ 15. Three of your friends (Jean, Evan, and Lee) are having an argument about investments and, because you have taken this course, have come to you for advice. The possible investments are set out in the following table. (Assume you cannot mix risky investments.)

Risky portfolio	Expected returns	Standard deviation
A	8%	5%
B	13%	7%
C	17%	11%

Jean says they should all invest in portfolio A because it has the lowest risk. Evan says they should all invest in portfolio C because it has the highest return. Lee is just confused.

a. If there is no risk-free asset, can you recommend the same portfolio for each of the friends? Why or why not?
b. If the expected risk-free rate is 2 percent, can you recommend the same set of risky assets for each of the friends? Why or why not?
c. Use Equation 9-3 to complete the table below and plot it.

	Portfolio of $RF + A$	Portfolio of $RF + B$	Portfolio of $RF + C$
Standard deviation	Expected return	Expected return	Expected return
0			
0.01			
0.02			
0.03			
0.04			
0.05			

continued

	Portfolio of RF + A	Portfolio of RF + B	Portfolio of RF + C
Standard deviation	Expected return	Expected return	Expected return
0.06			
0.07			
0.08			
0.09			
0.1			
0.11			
0.12			

    d. Does the existence of a risk-free asset make the friends better off? Explain your reasoning.

16. Today, you observe the market portfolio has an expected return of 13 percent, with a standard deviation of 7 percent. The risk-free rate is 2 percent. If only the risk-free rate increases (i.e., there are no changes to the expected risk and returns of the risky securities), will the composition of the market portfolio change? Will the expected risk and return on the market portfolio change? Explain your reasoning.

17. State three of the assumptions underlying the capital asset pricing model (CAPM).

18. Calculate the missing values for the following five efficient portfolios. The expected return on the market is 8 percent, with a standard deviation of 5 percent, and the risk-free rate is 2 percent.

Portfolio	Expected return	Standard deviation	Sharpe ratio	Required rate of return
Portfolio 1	14%	9%		
Portfolio 2	9%	3%		
Portfolio 3	3%	10%		
Portfolio 4	8%	4%		
Portfolio 5	4%	6%		

19. Which of the portfolios identified in Practice Problem 18 are undervalued, correctly valued, and overvalued?

✿ 20. Obtain monthly returns for RIM, the Royal Bank of Canada, and the S&P/TSX Composite Index for January to December 2011. (Note: Monthly historical prices, adjusted for dividends, are available from http://ca.finance.yahoo.com. To obtain the data, go to the website and search using the ticker symbol, RIM.TO.)
    a. Which firm do you expect to have a larger beta? Explain your reasoning.
    b. Calculate the beta for each company.
    c. Create a portfolio consisting of 50 percent in RIM and 50 percent in Royal Bank.
       i. Calculate the monthly returns for the portfolio and calculate the beta of the portfolio using those monthly returns.
      ii. Using Equation 9-8, calculate the beta of the portfolio.
     iii. Compare the two betas.

21. TrenStar Inc. obtained the following incomplete information from ABC Company and has given you the task of completing the table.

	Security 1 Beta	Security 2 Beta	Weight in Security 1	Portfolio Beta
Case 1	0.5	1.5	0.6	
Case 2		0.45	0.5	1.3

continued

	Security 1 beta	Security 2 beta	Weight in Security 1	Portfolio Beta
Case 3	1.1	1.9		2.1
Case 4	1.25	0.6	0.75	
Case 5	1.3		0.15	3

22. What is the beta of the following?
    a. Risk-free asset   b. Market portfolio

23. Stock FM has a standard deviation of 25 percent and a correlation coefficient of 0.6 with market returns. The standard deviation of market return is 20 percent, and the expected return is 16 percent. The risk-free rate is 6.5 percent.
    a. What is the beta of stock FM?
    b. What is the required rate of return of stock FM by the CAPM model?
    c. Compare FM's required return to the expected market return. What causes the difference?

24. Estimate the beta of the following stock: market risk premium = 25 percent, RF = 6 percent, P_0 = $10, expected dividend at the end of the year = $2.50, P_1 = $12.50. Assume the market is in equilibrium.

25. You are following five different stocks and need to issue a recommendation (buy, hold, or sell) to your customers. The market return is 7 percent, with a standard deviation of 4 percent. The risk-free rate is 3 percent. The CAPM is assumed to hold.

Security	Expected return	Standard deviation	Beta	Recommendation
ABC	5%	9%	1.5	
RTS	10%	3%	1.1	
DKF	6%	10%	0.95	
OPL	9%	4%	0.75	
WEQ	14%	6%	1.25	

To determine the recommendations, begin by calculating the required returns for each security using the CAPM. Comparing the expected and required returns will indicate which securities are underpriced, overpriced, or correctly priced.

26. If a security's total risk (variance) increases, does that mean the beta must have increased? Explain.

27. You are valuing the Vancouver Rain-Making Company (VRM) and need to calculate the following:
    a. required rate of return (assume the market risk premium is 8 percent, the risk-free rate is 2 percent, and the beta is 1.2)
    b. price of VRM based on the current dividend of $1.25 and a dividend growth rate of 3 percent

28. Which of the following are examples of systematic (market) risks? Which are examples of unsystematic (unique) risks?
    a. inflation risk
    b. CFO's fraudulent activities
    c. changes in interest rates
    d. product tampering

e. political risk

f. CEO's aversion to working on Fridays

29. Which security, A, B, or C, will provide the greatest return per unit of risk when combined with the risk-free asset with a 5 percent rate of return?

ER_A = 20 percent, σ_A= 5 percent

ER_B= 25 percent, σ_B= 10 percent

ER_C= 30 percent, σ_C= 15 percent

30. The current price of a stock is $20. It is expected to rise to $22 in one year and pay an annual dividend of $0.50 during the year. The RF is 5 percent, the ER_M is 9 percent, and the stock's beta is 2.6. Determine whether the stock is overvalued, undervalued, or properly valued. Is the stock above, below, or on the SML?

31. Suppose you have a portfolio that has $100 in stock A with a beta of 0.9, $400 in stock B with a beta of 1.2, and $300 in the risk-free asset. You have another $200 to invest. You wish to achieve a beta for your whole portfolio to be the same as the market beta. What is the beta of the added security? Give an example of a firm that may have such a beta.

32. Portfolio A has a beta of 1.2. Portfolio B has a beta of 0.9. RF is 5 percent and the market risk premium is 3 percent. Calculate the required rate of return of A and B. If the expected rate of return for both portfolio A and B is 8 percent, what investment strategy should apply?

⚙ 33. Your client is confused. He owns shares in the Whistler Snow-Making Company (WSMC) and wants you to explain your recommendation. Both of you agree on the following: WSMC has an expected return of 12 percent, a standard deviation of 9 percent, and a beta of 1.25; the expected return on the market is 8 percent, with standard deviation of 3 percent; and the risk-free rate is 4 percent.

   Your client has a basic understanding of the CAPM and, based on the capital market line, feels he should sell the stock. However, you are recommending that he buy more of the stock (or at least hold what he has). Explain your recommendation to your client.

34. Determine the beta of QTax based on the following information:
   - market expected return is 8 percent; standard deviation is 3 percent
   - risk-free rate is 3 percent
   - current dividend is $4.50
   - dividend growth rate is 5 percent
   - current stock price is $25

⚙ 35. You are forecasting the returns for PVC Company, a plumbing supply company, which pays a current dividend of $10. The dividend is expected to grow at a rate of 3 percent. You have identified two public companies, ABC and VJK, that appear to be comparable to PVC. ABC has the same total risk as PVC and a beta of 1.2. VJK, in contrast, has a very different total risk but the same market risk as PVC. VJK's beta is 0.75. The market risk premium is 5 percent and the risk-free rate is 1 percent.
   a. Determine the required return for PVC using the appropriate beta.
   b. Determine the price of PVC.

36. The idea behind CAPM is that investors should not be compensated for diversifiable risk. Why not?

37. Assuming CAPM is valid, can we have a situation where stock A has a required rate of return of 15 percent and a beta of 1.4, and stock B has a required rate of return of 20 percent and beta of 1.2?

38. The risk-free rate is 6 percent, the risk premium is 5 percent, and stock A has an expected return of 15 percent. What is the beta of stock A?

39. Stock A has a beta of 1.8 and an expected return of 20 percent. Stock B has a beta of 1.2 and an expected return of 14 percent. If CAPM holds, what should the return on the market and the risk-free rate be?

40. The expected return on stock A is 12 percent. The expected return on stock B is 8 percent. Assuming CAPM holds, if the beta of stock A is higher than the beta of stock B by 0.2, what should the risk premium be?

41. The variance of the market returns is 0.0625, and the covariance of the returns on ABC stock and the market is 0.09375. If the risk-free rate is 6 percent and the market risk premium is 8 percent, what is the required rate of return of ABC?

42. You invested $100,000 in the following stocks:

Stock	Amount	Beta
ABC	$20,000	0.8
DEF	$30,000	1.2
GHI	$15,000	1.35
JKL	$35,000	1.15

If the risk-free rate is 5 percent and the market risk premium is 8 percent, what is the expected return on your portfolio?

43. State Roll's critique concerning the CAPM.

44. Four risk factors, F_1, F_2, F_3, and F_4, have been identified to determine the required rate of return, as follows: $ER_i = a_0 + b_{i1}F_1 + b_{i2}F_2 + b_{i3}F_3 + b_{i4}F_4$, where a_0 is the expected return on a security with zero systematic risk. Calculate the required rate of return of a portfolio where b_{i1}, b_{i2}, b_{i3}, and b_{i4} are 0.4, 0.5, 1, and 1.5, respectively; $RF = 8$ percent; $F_1 = 10$ percent; $F_2 = 5$ percent;

$F_3 = 9$ percent; and $F_4 = 12$ percent.

10 | Market Efficiency

LEARNING OBJECTIVES

10.1   Explain the importance of the concept of market efficiency.

10.2   Explain what is meant by "market efficiency."

10.3   Differentiate among the different levels of efficiency.

10.4   Discuss the general consensus based on empirical evidence of market efficiency, as well as the existence of some well-known anomalies.

10.5   Differentiate between behavioural finance and the traditional view of finance.

10.6   Explain the implications of market efficiency.

James (Jimmy) Cayne, the former head of Bear Stearns, says there was nothing he or anyone else could have done to save the venerable Wall Street bank from collapse.

Telling his side of the story for the first time, Mr. Cayne emerged from months of seclusion, blaming a cast of others, including suspicious trading in its shares by hedge funds, panicky investors and shoddy work by credit rating agencies.

"The market's loss of confidence, even though it was unjustified and irrational, became a self-fulfilling prophecy," Mr. Cayne told the commission.

He also pointed to "some very unnatural trades" in the bank's shares before its demise, which he urged the commission to investigate.

Alan Schwartz, who succeeded Mr. Cayne as chief executive in January 2008, offered a similar explanation for Bear Stearns' sudden demise.

"In my heart, I think there was stuff going on," Mr. Schwartz testified of the sudden panic by investors and clients to flee the bank. "When everyone is running from a crowded theatre, it's hard to figure out who yelled 'fire,'" he added.

Those answers didn't sit well with commission chairman Phil Angelides, a real estate developer and former California state treasurer.

"There's a form of financial Russian roulette that Bear Stearns was playing along with other investment banks," Mr. Angelides said.

He pointed out that by the end of 2007—just three months before its collapse—Bear Stearns was leveraged 38-to-one, measured strictly by tangible assets and common equity.

Just prior to its failure, the bank had about $12.5-billion (U.S.) in loans that were poorly documented—more than the value of its equity, Mr. Angelides remarked.

"It seems like there were a lot of warning signs, a lot of red and yellow lights going off," he said.

Source: McKenna, Barrie, "Bear Stearns CEO blames market for firm's fall." *The Globe and Mail*, May 6, 2010, p. B12. ©The Globe and Mail, Inc. All rights reserved. Reprinted by permission.

CHAPTER 10 **PREVIEW**

The chapter-opening vignette presents two perspectives on market efficiency. On one hand, we have the former CEO of Bear Stearns blaming the company's fall on market irrationality, and there is no doubt investor panic contributed to the collapse. On the other hand, the head of the Financial Crisis Commission points to several valid risks and warning signs that led to the investment bank's decline, so one could argue that market participants had several good reasons to dump Bear Stearns' stock. Indeed, never has the concept of market efficiency been more severely criticized by its detractors than it has been over the early part of this century, as stock markets, corporate bond markets, structured debt product markets, etc., have experienced unprecedented declines and associated levels of volatility. A number of high-profile finance professionals (legendary investors, Nobel laureates, etc.) have lined up on different sides of this issue, which attests to its importance. In addition, this debate has been fuelled by the rapid rise to prominence of the theory of behavioural finance, which challenges many of the key assumptions underlying market efficiency, and many other theories of finance.

An understanding of these topics is critical for students of finance and financial professionals. In fact, market efficiency is central to most of the topics in finance. For example, the capital asset pricing model, which was discussed in Chapter 9, is based on the notion that markets are efficient, as are most of the theories and processes discussed throughout the textbook. In this chapter, we will examine some of the evidence on the issue and discuss the implications that arise for investors and businesses.

10.1 THE IMPORTANCE OF MARKET EFFICIENCY

Learning Objective 10.1
Explain the importance of the concept of market efficiency.

In Chapters 5 to 9, we talked about valuing different types of securities and estimating discount rates or required rates of return. We did this because, in corporate finance, firms have to know what investors want when they invest in a firm's securities, which is why discount rates are also called required rates of return. Once a firm knows what investors want, it can then make decisions that increase the value of those securities and enhance shareholder value. Never forget that firms have owners, and it is a legal requirement, as well as managerial responsibility, that managers act in the owners' best interests. Correctly estimating discount rates is only part of the process. A second important element is whether or not market prices reflect the actions of managers. This introduces the question of market efficiency.

operational efficiency a market condition in which transaction costs are low

allocational efficiency a market condition in which there are enough securities to efficiently allocate risk

There are three components to market efficiency. The first is **operational efficiency**. When a market is operationally efficient, it means that transaction costs are low. If it is too expensive to trade securities, it will be difficult for firms to raise capital, and investment will be lower than it should be. The second component is **allocational efficiency**. This means that there are enough securities to efficiently allocate risk. For example, a capital market in which firms can issue only short-term notes would not be very efficient, even if transaction costs were low. These two types of efficiency are important for Canadian capital markets but are not the main concern in this chapter. For now, take it as a given that the Canadian markets have a broad array of financial securities, from short-term treasury bills to common shares and what we will later call hybrids, and these are issued at relatively low cost. So on most criteria, the Canadian capital markets are both operationally and allocationally efficient. What is important in this chapter is whether the markets have **informational efficiency**.

informational efficiency a market condition in which important information is reflected in share prices

If managers make decisions that they think should increase market values—for example, if they decide to introduce a new product—they will call a press conference and announce the details. Investors will then analyze the information in the announcement, and market prices will likely increase. The managers will have the satisfaction of knowing that their owners (the shareholders) reacted positively to their decision. However, if share prices are chaotic (this is actually a technical term which means, loosely, that share prices reflect past actions in a predictable way that is magnified many times), they will not reflect the information in the press announcement; they will reflect these other past actions. If this occurs, managers will have no idea whether their owners agree or disagree with their decisions.

For shareholder value maximization to mean anything, there has to be a connection between the decisions made by managers and the level of share prices. In this way, share prices are like a score sheet used to evaluate management. The closer the link between the actions of managers and this score sheet, the more informationally efficient the capital market. It is therefore critical, in corporate finance, to understand how informationally efficient the capital market, and particularly the stock market, is. In this chapter, we will drop the adjective "informational" before references to "efficiency," because our focus is entirely on how to assess whether or not important information is reflected in share prices.

In Chapter 17, we will discuss the basics of securities regulation in Canada. However, the key element is that all **material facts** should be disclosed to the capital market. Material facts are anything that can be expected to affect the share price. In the previous example, we mentioned a press conference. In Ontario, it is a legal requirement for a firm to divulge material facts through a press release that is then filed with the securities commission.[1] If all material facts are disclosed to the stock market, managers should be able to see how good the score sheet is or, in other words, how efficient the capital markets are.

material facts anything that can be expected to affect the share price

CONCEPT REVIEW QUESTIONS

1. Distinguish from among operational efficiency, informational efficiency, and allocational efficiency.

10.2 DEFINING MARKET EFFICIENCY

An **efficient market** is one in which the prices of all securities accurately reflect all relevant and available information about the securities. This definition implies that security prices, as determined in the capital markets, are "correct." In other words, the current price of a common share reflects all known information, both past and present, about the firm, including information about a company's earnings, financial strength, management strengths and weaknesses, and future plans as announced through press releases and the management discussion and analysis (MD&A) in its financial statements. As discussed in Chapter 7, prices will reflect rational expectations about what will happen in the future and will therefore mirror today's beliefs about future interest rate changes, future profits, potential mergers, and so on. Events that cause these beliefs about the future to change will have a corresponding impact on today's prices.

Several conditions must exist before markets can operate efficiently. One critical condition is integrity of the market, such that all market participants are treated fairly. This requirement is the reason that such a heavy emphasis is placed on **disclosure**: the revelation of all material facts so that everyone in the market is buying and selling based on the same disclosed material facts about the firm.

Learning Objective 10.2
Explain what is meant by "market efficiency."

efficient market a market that reacts quickly and relatively accurately to new public information, which results in prices that are correct on average

disclosure the revelation of all material facts so that everyone in the market is buying and selling based on the same material facts about the firm

---

[1] In other provinces, such as British Columbia, for example, the firm has to disclose material facts in a different way, such as by filing a material change form with the provincial securities commission.

securities law the body of law that ensures, through capital market regulations, that all investors have equal access to, and an equal opportunity to react to, new and relevant information; the body of law that governs the buying and selling of securities

A lack of disclosure is one reason that "black markets," or smaller and more loosely regulated markets, tend to be less efficient and that the prices in these markets do not accurately reflect available information. In this case, information is either not disclosed, is disclosed late, or is disclosed in such a way that not all market participants are aware of what is going on. Information disclosure is an important part of **securities law**, and significant attention is devoted to maintaining and enforcing capital market regulations designed to ensure that all investors have equal access to, and an equal opportunity to react to, new and relevant information.[2] For example, insider trading laws prevent "insiders" from acting on private information before that information is made public.[3]

The technical definition of market efficiency suggests that market prices are *always* correct, which requires *instantaneous* and *perfect* price adjustments in response to the arrival of new information in the marketplace. This type of efficiency is not a practical reality; however, efficient markets do react quickly and relatively accurately to new information, and therefore prices are correct *on average*. This is a reasonable definition of an efficient market. We can expand on this logic and note that market efficiency is a matter of degree. In other words, more efficient markets process information faster and more accurately than do inefficient ones; therefore, the prices in these efficient markets are closer to the true values.

The following assumptions underlie the existence of efficient markets:

1. There are a large number of rational, profit-maximizing investors who actively participate in the market by analyzing, valuing, and trading securities. The markets are assumed to be competitive, which means that no one investor can significantly affect the price of a security.

2. Information is costless and widely available to market participants at the same time.

3. Information arrives randomly; therefore, announcements are not related to one another.

4. Investors react quickly and fully to the new information, which is reflected in stock prices.

sell-side analysts securities analysts whose job is to monitor companies and regularly report on their value through earnings forecasts and buy/sell/hold recommendations; they work for the investment banks that underwrite and sell securities to the public

buy-side analysts securities analysts whose job is to evaluate the research and recommendations produced by the sell-side analysts; they work for institutions in the capital market that invest in securities

Although these conditions are stringent, and are not met in the strictest sense in the real world, they are not unreasonable today. A large number of market participants actively follow the prices of securities trading in the market and devour information that may affect these prices. For example, all the major investment banks have securities analysts whose job is to monitor companies and regularly report on their value through earnings forecasts and buy/sell/hold recommendations. These analysts are called **sell-side analysts**, because they work for the investment banks that underwrite and sell securities to the public. In chapters 1 and 2, we saw that there are many institutions in the Canadian capital market that invest in securities, such as insurance companies, mutual funds, and pension funds. These institutions also employ securities analysts to evaluate the research and recommendations produced by the sell-side analysts. Because these institutions buy securities, their analysts are commonly referred to as **buy-side analysts**.

With all these analysts following firms, we might expect prices to be rationally based on available information and economic fundamentals. In addition, there is an abundance of free or inexpensive information available about most actively traded securities; some would even argue that an overabundance of such information makes it difficult to separate the wheat from the chaff. This information generally arrives randomly and is not predictable. If it were predictable, the prices would already reflect the information. Therefore, it is reasonable to assume that markets could be efficient. However, whether they are efficient is another matter, as the assumptions above may hold to various degrees.

---

[2] Securities law in Canada is a provincial responsibility. There has been considerable discussion as to whether or not Canada needs a national regulator, but at the moment, critical provinces are unwilling to give up their responsibilities. As a result, information must be disclosed and securities registered in most provinces separately. However, there is a forum for coordination across the provinces, and increasingly *national* policies are being developed.

[3] Several definitions exist for "insiders." We suggest the use of a broad definition that includes any party that has access to private information about a security as a result of a special relationship with the underlying entity. For example, this would include anyone who sat on the board of directors for a corporation, as well as that company's officers, lawyers, bankers, and so on.

The assumption most commonly under attack is the belief that investors are rational. The argument, espoused by former Bear Stearns CEO James Cayne in the chapter-opening vignette, is that analysts and market participants are human and may not process information rationally or efficiently. For example, "group think" may take over and, to paraphrase John Maynard Keynes, one of the greatest economists of the 20th century, it may be better to fail conventionally than succeed unconventionally.[4] It is indicative that Keynes's seminal work was published in 1936, after the great stock market crash and during the worst of the Great Depression, when financial economists were questioning the efficient functioning of markets, just as they do today. For example, Keynes noted:

> It might have been supposed that competition between expert professionals, possessing judgment and knowledge beyond that of the average private investor, would correct the vagaries of the ignorant individual left to himself. It happens, however, that the energies and skill of the professional investor and speculator are mainly occupied otherwise. For most of these persons are, in fact, largely concerned, not with making superior long-term forecasts of the probable yield of an investment over its whole life, but with foreseeing changes in the conventional basis of valuation a short time ahead of the general public. They are concerned, not with what an investment is really worth to a man who buys it "for keeps," but with what the market will value it at, under the influence of mass psychology, three months or a year hence.[5]

Apart from the fact that Keynes was a great investor and substantially increased the endowment of his college at Cambridge University in England, he raised the basic question of whether or not the actions of many specialist investors and analysts made the stock market more or less efficient. Keynes was under no illusions: he believed that their actions destabilized markets. Further, he believed that the stock market should have high transaction costs—that is, it should be *operationally inefficient*—in order to keep out small investors who didn't know what they were doing and contributed to stock market instability.[6]

Keynes's view, in part, reflected the fact that he was writing in the 1930s, just after the stock market crash of 1929.[7] However, it was a common belief: Bernard Baruch, a prominent U.S. investor in the 1920s, reportedly exited the U.S. stock market just before the crash after hearing elevator boys talking about which stocks to invest in. However, as the memories of 1929 and its aftermath receded, the notion that speculation or the actions of specialist investors were stabilizing took hold again, essentially producing a return to the pre-Keynesian belief that markets were inherently stable.

In this view, if prices are pushed up too high, then other experts will sell the stocks, driving prices down to an equilibrium level. This is the basic idea we discussed in Chapter 9 in the context of the market portfolio, and it is the dominant view in finance. However, the Internet bubble of the 1990s, the stock market crash of 2000, and the global collapse of stock and credit markets during 2008 again had people questioning investor rationality, the stabilizing role of professional investors, and market efficiency in general. As they did in the 1930s, politicians have brought up the idea of a transactions tax, discussed in *Finance in the News 10-1*, which describes how France and Germany have been pushing for such a tax to reduce "speculative excesses," while the United Kingdom, home to Europe's largest financial sector, is steadfastly resisting. Similarly, finance academics have rediscovered the idea that there are limits to

---

[4] A common axiom used to be "No one ever got fired for buying IBM," either the computers or the stock. In fact, the argument that "everyone else is doing it," backed by extensive reports from respected security analysts, is very powerful.

[5] One of the best discussions of the role of information in the stock market remains Chapter 12, "The State of Long-Term Expectations," of Keynes's *The General Theory of Employment, Interest and Money* (London: Macmillan, 1936), pp. 147–64. Keynes invented what is now called macroeconomics.

[6] This idea was resurrected in the 1990s in the form of the "Tobin tax," which was a transaction tax suggested by James Tobin of Yale University to reduce short-term speculation.

[7] It took investors 30 years to get back to the price level of 1929, and a generation of investors largely ignored the stock market.

arbitrage and that speculation can be destabilizing. In fact, a whole new field of financial thought has evolved in recent years. Known as *behavioural finance*, it suggests that investors make systematic mistakes in both their processing of information and their investing activities. We will discuss this topic in more detail later in the chapter.

Before we discuss the different levels of market efficiency, and the related empirical evidence, we should note a theoretical impediment to market efficiency known as the Grossman-Stiglitz paradox. Grossman and Stiglitz argued that markets can never be fully efficient. If they were, then all prices would be correct and would reflect all available information. Under this scenario, investors could realize no added value by conducting any type of information gathering or analysis, since prices would already reflect such information. Of course, the paradox is that if nobody has any incentive to gather and process information about security values, how can the prices reflect this information? However, not even the most ardent supporter of market efficiency would expect the market to be completely efficient. Hence, the key insight of the Grossman-Stiglitz argument lies in its message regarding the costs of information gathering and processing. It suggests that market participants will exert efforts to obtain and analyze information up to the point where the marginal benefits obtained from this process equal the associated marginal costs. Presumably, the more inefficient the market, the larger the potential benefits will be, since it is less likely that all information will be fully and properly reflected in market prices.

We conclude this section by noting that it remains an open question as to how informationally efficient the capital markets are.[8] We will elaborate on this debate in the sections that follow and discuss some of the empirical evidence.

finance IN THE NEWS 10-1   Euro Zone Split over Financial Transaction

EUROPEAN FINANCE MINISTERS are discussing a proposed EU financial transaction tax on Tuesday, but the bloc is hopelessly divided on the issue. Not even Germany and France's plan B, to only introduce the tax in the euro zone, has much chance of success. Key euro-zone members such as Ireland and the Netherlands are afraid of losing out.

It's being greeted as a breakthrough—but it remains open whether it really is. When the 27 European Union finance ministers meet in Brussels on Tuesday, they plan to discuss the introduction of a financial transaction tax in Europe. It's the first time that the issue has been on the agenda at such a meeting, and supporters of the tax argue that is a sign that the tax is making progress in its long journey through the EU's institutions.

Indeed, a certain amount of progress can be seen in the ongoing battle over a tax on financial transactions—at least on paper. French President Nicolas Sarkozy and German Chancellor Angela Merkel, the EU's two most powerful leaders, have made the issue a priority. And in September 2011, the European Commission presented a draft directive which foresees a financial transaction tax on all stock, bond and derivative transactions within the EU. The tax could come into force in 2014—provided all 27 EU members agree to it.

Therein lies the rub. There is little chance of such an agreement. Officially, supporters of the tax are still hoping for the "comprehensive solution," as the Commission's proposal is dubbed by the German government. But an agreement is already regarded as a pipedream. A whole row of naysayers, led by Britain and Sweden, are opposed to the tax unless it is introduced globally. They consider it to be detrimental to growth and fear that they will become less competitive on the international playing field if they introduce

European Union finance ministers meet in Brussels, May 2, 2012. (Virginia Mayo/AP/The Canadian Press)

a tax. The unanimity principle applies to tax matters within the EU, so even a single veto would be sufficient to derail the plan.

Considerable Resistance

Internally, the governments in Paris and Berlin seem to have already accepted the fact that some EU partners cannot be convinced. As a result, talk in recent months has focused on the idea of only introducing the tax in the euro zone. But even this contingency plan seems doomed to failure. The euro zone is divided on the issue, as can be seen from a letter that was

continued

---

[8] The equivalent of Bernard Baruch's elevator boys was the proliferation of day traders in the 1990s. These people gave up their full-time jobs to trade in and out of securities within the day.

Finance in the News 10-1: Euro Zone Split over Financial Transaction Tax *(continued)*

recently sent to the Danish finance minister. In it, nine euro-zone members called for Denmark, which currently holds the EU's rotating presidency, to "accelerate" efforts to introduce the financial transaction tax. It was signed by the finance ministers of Germany, Austria, Finland, France, Belgium, Spain, Portugal and Greece, as well as Italian Prime Minister Mario Monti, who is also the country's finance minister.

The most significant thing, however, is the fact that eight euro-zone countries did not sign the letter, namely Ireland, Netherlands, Luxembourg, Slovakia, Slovenia, Estonia, Malta and Cyprus. Admittedly, they are not the largest and most influential countries in the currency union, and not all of them are explicitly opposed to the tax—but some of them are putting up considerable resistance.

For example, the Irish government, with an eye to neighbouring Britain, only wants to introduce the financial tax if the rest of the EU plays along. Sources in Dublin say that, as long as the tax does not apply in London, the Irish will not support it. The coalition government of the conservative Fine Gael and the centre-left Labour Party are worried about the prospects for its young international funds sector, which the republic has wooed and supported over the past three decades. Should a levy be introduced only in the euro zone, Dublin fears that many companies would simply move from Ireland to London. Unlike financial firms' routine threats to move to Asia, which are usually empty, this risk has to be taken seriously.

There are similar reservations in the Netherlands. Two recent studies by the Dutch central bank and the country's independent statistical agency have advised against the financial transaction tax. The minority conservative coalition government, which is dependent on support from the opposition centre-left Labour Party on European issues, has so far not taken a position on the issue, and is said to be examining the proposals. They are in fact playing for time: The government is hoping that the issue will resolve itself.

In Slovakia, which previously opposed the tax, the political situation has taken a decisive turn. After the victory of Robert Fico and his centre-left Direction–Social Democracy party in this weekend's election, Slovakia has suddenly joined the ranks of the tax's supporters. It is not hard for the country to support the levy, as it has no significant financial sector and therefore does not need to fear any side effects.

The Stamp Solution

Nevertheless, there are still plenty of governments that are opposed to the euro zone going it alone in introducing the tax. The government in Luxembourg is divided. Even in Germany, where Merkel's conservatives are pushing for the tax, their junior coalition partner, the business-friendly Free Democratic Party (FDP), opposes it.

There is, however, a possible way out of the impasse. A number of parties, including Germany's FDP, have proposed, as an alternative to a comprehensive financial transaction tax, a so-called stamp duty based on the British model. In London, stamp duty already applies to trades in stocks, but not to bonds and derivatives. Such a stamp duty already exists in Ireland, and France will also introduce one in August, if Sarkozy gets his way.

The advantage of opting for a stamp duty would be that it would probably be possible to get all 27 EU members on board. There is, however, one serious flaw in the plan. The Europeans would have failed in their goal to curtail speculation in complex financial products.

Source: Volkery, Carsten, "Euro Zone split over financial transaction tax." *Der Spiegel*, March 13, 2012. Available at www.spiegel.de. Reprinted by permission.

CONCEPT REVIEW QUESTIONS

1. Define market efficiency in terms of information.
2. Discuss the reasonableness of the assumptions underlying market efficiency.

10.3 THE EFFICIENT MARKET HYPOTHESIS (EMH)

The **efficient market hypothesis (EMH)** states that markets are efficient. Therefore, in its strictest sense, it implies that prices accurately reflect *all* available information at any point in time. This statement goes well beyond our "weaker" definition of efficient markets, proposed in the previous section, where we said that prices in efficient markets are correct *on average*. Because the strictest form of the EMH represents such a high hurdle, it is common to break the EMH down into the following three different, and cumulative, levels, based on the extent to which prices reflect different types of available information:

1. The **weak form EMH** states that security prices fully reflect *all market data*, which refers to all past price and volume trading information. If markets are weak form efficient, historical trading data will already be reflected in current prices and should be of no value in predicting future price changes. In particular, weak form EMH implies that looking at

Learning Objective 10.3
Differentiate among the different levels of efficiency.

efficient market hypothesis (EMH) the theory that markets are efficient and, therefore, that prices accurately reflect all available information at any given time

weak form EMH the theory that security prices fully reflect all market data, which refers to all past price and volume trading information

graphs of previous stock prices is of no value. Consequently technical trading rules based on "patterns" observed in previous prices should be of no value.

semi-strong form EMH the theory that all publicly known and available information, including market data, is reflected in security prices

2. The **semi-strong form EMH** states that *all publicly known and available information* is reflected in security prices. This includes information about earnings, dividends, corporate investments, management changes, and so on. It would also include market data, which are publicly available. Therefore, this version of the EMH encompasses the weak form. In other words, if a market is semi-strong form efficient, then it must also be weak form efficient. A market that quickly incorporates all publicly available information into its prices is semi-strong form efficient. Semi-strong form EMH implies that it is futile to analyze publicly available information, such as financial statements, in an attempt to identify underpriced or overpriced securities; similarly, buying "undervalued" stocks based on P/E ratios or dividend yields is of no value.

strong form EMH the theory that stock prices fully reflect all information, which includes both public and private information

3. The **strong form EMH** asserts that stock prices fully reflect *all information*, which includes both public and private information. It is obviously the most stringent form of market efficiency, and it encompasses both the weak and semi-strong versions, because market data and all other publicly available information must be reflected in prices, as well as any private information that is possessed by some market participants but not by all. Strong form EMH implies that no investor can take advantage even of "inside" information that has not yet been released to the stock market. In this case, the possession of superior information or the superior processing of information to identify mispriced securities is not possible, since the prices already properly reflect all information. Obviously, this is a very strong assertion. *Ethics & Corporate Governance 10-1* discusses the role of inside information and market efficiency later in the chapter.

CONCEPT REVIEW QUESTIONS

1. Explain the efficient market hypothesis (EMH).
2. Describe the various forms of the EMH.

10.4 EMPIRICAL EVIDENCE REGARDING MARKET EFFICIENCY

Learning Objective 10.4
Discuss the general consensus based on empirical evidence of market efficiency, as well as the existence of some well-known anomalies.

A perfectly efficient market is one in which all information is reflected in stock prices quickly and fully. Therefore, all security prices equal their true economic (or intrinsic) value. In practice, not even the strongest supporters of the EMH would claim that markets are perfectly efficient, so it becomes a matter of degree—in other words, exactly how efficient are the markets? Empirical tests of market efficiency tend to be organized around how market prices react to certain kinds of information, and it is common to organize the evidence with respect to the implications about the three different forms of the EMH discussed above.

Countless studies have been conducted to test market efficiency, and we can't discuss them all. However, we will present the general consensus reached on many of the issues involved. Before we begin this discussion, note that, in order to be valid, any evidence supporting the existence of market inefficiencies must be *consistent* over reasonably long periods, because random or short-lived inefficiencies may appear from time to time, even in efficient markets. Similarly, many researchers have produced evidence that is *statistically* significant, but it would be difficult to translate these findings into *economically* significant gains, after accounting for risk, trading costs, and so on. Therefore, it makes sense to talk about an economically efficient market, in which securities are priced correctly enough that investors cannot exploit any discrepancies and earn unusual returns after consideration of all risks and trading costs. In fact, it is common for people involved in finance to suggest "There is no such thing as a free lunch." In such a market, some securities could be priced slightly above their intrinsic values and some slightly below, and time lags could exist in the processing of information, but the discrepancies would be too small to be exploited economically.

Weak Form Evidence

If markets are weak form efficient, current market prices will reflect all historical trading data. Therefore, past price changes (and total returns) should be unrelated to future price changes. This idea is related to the **random walk hypothesis**, which states that prices follow a random walk, with price changes over time occurring independently of one another. This hypothesis is logical if information arrives randomly, as it should, and if investors react to it immediately.

> **random walk hypothesis** the theory that prices follow a random walk, with price changes over time occurring independently of one another

Several tests of weak form efficiency are possible. One approach is to test whether price changes are, in fact, independent of one another. This assertion can be statistically tested in many different ways, so we will mention only two of the more commonly cited tests here. Serial correlation tests measure the correlation between successive price changes for various lags, such as one day, two days, one month, and so on. There have been numerous variations of these tests performed on Canadian, U.S., and global stock price data throughout the years. The general consensus of these studies has been that the correlations between successive price changes are not related in an economically significant manner, even though some, but not all, studies found statistically significant relationships. In other words, the pattern is too weak to be exploited by investors.

Another statistical test of price-change independence is the runs (or signs) test, which involves classifying each price change by its sign (i.e., whether the price change was +, 0, or –), and then examining whether there are any "runs" in the series of signs. The evidence provided by numerous studies that used the signs test also supports return independence. In particular, although "runs" have been documented, they could be consistent with random price changes, because even a truly random series will display some runs. Consider the following quote from *Graham and Dodd's Security Analysis*: "Elaborate tests of the correlation of successive prices, runs, and filter rules find some weak relationships, but they are not sufficient to generate trading profits after taking account of transactions costs."[9]

Although the evidence reported above is far from exhaustive, we can say that for the most part it supports the notion that price changes in the capital markets are independent of one another.

An alternative method of testing weak form efficiency is to examine specific trading rules that attempt to exploit historical trading data. If any such trading rule could be implemented in a manner that consistently generated abnormal risk-adjusted returns after trading costs, this evidence would contradict weak form efficiency.

Technical analysis involves the analysis of historical trading information in order to identify patterns in trading data that can be used to invest successfully. Technical analysts argue that simple statistical tests, such as the ones discussed above, are inconclusive because they are not applied to more sophisticated trading strategies. It is difficult to definitively refute this assertion because there are a virtually unlimited number of technical trading rules. However, most of the evidence suggests that technical trading rules, on average, have not been able to outperform a simple buy-and-hold strategy, after accounting for risk and trading costs.

> **technical analysis** the analysis of historical trading information to identify patterns in trading data that can be used to invest successfully

In summary, most of the evidence supports the notion that markets are weak form efficient. However, a few important exceptions, or **anomalies**, have been documented. (We will discuss some anomalies with respect to the other forms of market efficiency in the next subsections.) Anomalies are exceptions to a rule or theory—in this case, exceptions to market efficiency. We will discuss a few well-known anomalies; however, there is no guarantee that any trading strategy based on exploiting these anomalies would prove fruitful. Recall that any evidence

> **anomalies** exceptions to a rule or theory

---

[9] Cottle, Sidney, Murray, Roger F., and Block, Frank E., *Graham and Dodd's Security Analysis: Principles and Technique*, 5th ed. (New York: McGraw Hill, 1988).

supporting the existence of such market inefficiencies must be consistent over reasonably long periods of time to be valid; otherwise, sample selection could be a major contributing factor to the apparent validity of the evidence. In addition, given the widespread attention devoted to uncovering profitable anomalies, many findings are attributed to a process called *data mining*. This is the process of examining data in various manners and forms, and using various empirical approaches, until you find an interesting observation and/or the result you were looking for before you began the analysis. Consider the following quote from the late Fischer Black (co-developer of the Black-Scholes option pricing model and the CAPM): "Most so-called anomalies don't seem anomalous to me at all. They seem like nuggets from a gold mine, found by one of the thousands of miners all over the world." Documented anomalies are also often disputed based on the fact that while they may be statistically significant, it would be difficult to translate these findings into economically significant gains after accounting for risk, trading costs, and so on.

DeBondt and Thaler examined U.S. stock returns and found evidence that people overreact to information, and these overreactions lead to stock price "reversals."[10] They found that stocks that had performed poorly over the most recent three- to five-year periods ("losers") tended to outperform in the subsequent three- to five-year periods, while stocks that displayed superior performance in the past ("winners") tended to underperform in the future. Trading strategies that are designed to exploit this pattern are commonly referred to as "contrarian strategies," because the idea is based on the notion of investing *contrary* to the past performance record of stocks. Several subsequent studies have confirmed these results for U.S. stock returns; however, international evidence has been mixed. Interestingly, Kryzanowski and Zhang found no such pattern for Canadian stocks over a period (1950–88) similar to that studied by DeBondt and Thaler.[11] This tendency for stock prices to reverse contradicts weak form efficiency, because it implies that future stock returns can be predicted merely by examining past trading data.

momentum the tendency for stocks that have experienced high returns in the previous 3- to 12-month period to outperform in the subsequent 3- to 12-month period

An even more important contradiction of weak form efficiency is the existence of **momentum** in stock returns: stocks that have experienced high returns in previous 3- to 12-month periods tend to outperform in the subsequent 3- to 12-month periods. Notice that this pattern is in sharp contrast to the longer-term reversal pattern. There is strong empirical support for the existence of momentum in stock returns in most stock markets around the world. Probably the most famous of these studies dealing with U.S. stock returns was conducted by Jegadeesh and Titman in 1993.[12] They formed portfolios by ranking stocks based on their past 3- to 12-month returns and found that buying the top-performing stocks ("winners") and selling the worst-performing stocks ("losers") produced significant positive abnormal returns.

Several studies have confirmed the existence of this pattern in Canadian stock returns, as demonstrated in Figure 10-1. This figure shows that from 1980 to 1999, the returns for a "winner" portfolio (based on the most recent six-month performance) averaged 20.76 percent in the subsequent six-month period, well above the returns for the "loser" portfolio (5.99 percent) and the S&P/TSX Composite Index (6.10 percent).[13] *Finance in the News 10-2* further suggests that such a strategy has generated higher returns than the market in 24 of the 26 years ending in 2011. Strong international evidence supports the existence of momentum.[14]

---

[10] See DeBondt, W., and Thaler, R., "Does the stock market overreact?" *Journal of Finance* 40, no. 3 (1985), pp. 793–805.

[11] See Kryzanowski, L., and Zhang, H., "The contrarian strategy does not work in Canadian markets." *Journal of Financial and Quantitative Analysis* 27 (1992), pp. 389–95.

[12] See Jegadeesh, N., and Titman, S., "Returns to buying winners and selling losers: Implications for stock market efficiency." *Journal of Finance* 48 (1993), pp. 65–91.

[13] See Cleary, S., Schmitz, J., and Doucette, D., "Industry affects do not explain momentum in Canadian stock returns." *Investment Management and Financial Innovations* 2 (2005), pp. 49–60.

[14] For example, see Rouwenhorst, K.G., "International momentum strategies." *Journal of Finance* 53, no. 1 (February 1998), pp. 267–84.

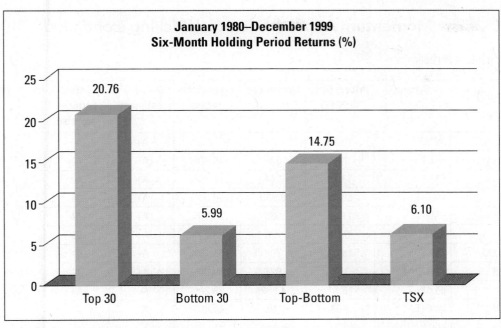

FIGURE 10-1 *Momentum in Canadian Stock Returns, 1980–99*

Source: Cleary, S., Schmitz, J., and Doucette, D., "Industry affects do not explain momentum in Canadian stock returns." *Investment Management and Financial Innovations* 2 (2005), pp. 49–60. Reprinted by permission.

---

finance INTHENEWS 10-2   The Momentum Approach to Stock Picking

What Are We Looking For?

Momentum. Stocks that are going up have a tendency to keep going up— at least for the short term.

More on Today's Screen

Craig McGee, senior consultant at CPMS, a division of Morningstar Canada, constructed the screen. He looked for rising stocks that are accompanied by improving expectations.

To make the list, a stock had to be:

- among the 350 largest stocks in the Canadian market, based upon market capitalization;

- among the 25 stocks in that group with the best combination of one-year total return, upward revisions in earnings estimates over the past 90 days, and positive earnings surprises, as calculated by CPMS.

More about CPMS

CPMS provides quantitative North American equity research and portfolio analysis to primarily institutional clients. It covers more than 700 Canadian and 2,200 U.S. stocks, and spends a lot of time adjusting for unusual accounting items in each company's quarterly results to make sure screens can perform correctly.

What We Learned

A momentum approach can work—if you can shoulder the hefty transaction costs involved in constantly shuffling your portfolio.

Mr. McGee tested how the particular momentum strategy outlined above would have performed over the past 25 years. He assumed an equally weighted 25-stock portfolio that was refreshed every three months.

He found that the approach would have generated an annualized return of 24.6 percent since the end of 1985, nearly tripling the 8.3-percent return for the S&P/TSX Total Return Index over the same period. The portfolio outperformed the index in 24 of 26 years, and lagged behind only in 2008 and 2009.

Mr. McGee says the success of the strategy highlights the importance of focusing on stocks with improving expectations. He cautions, however, that the approach would have required a tremendous amount of discipline to follow in real life.

Someone taking this momentum approach would, on average, have turned over every stock in the portfolio more than twice a year. Transaction costs weren't factored into the return calculations, so the cost of buying and selling shares would have eaten into profits.

An investor would also have had to endure losing 46 per cent of his or her portfolio's value from the end of June 2008 to the end of February 2009. Momentum can work, it seems—but you have to be prepared for volatility along the way.

continued

Finance in the News 10-2: The Momentum Approach to Stock Picking (continued)

TABLE 10-1 CPMS High Momentum Portfolio

Rank	Company	Symbol	Price $ (Feb. 3, 2012)	Market cap ($ mil.)	1-year total return	90-day EPS estimate	Latest earnings surprise
1	Poseidon Concepts Corp.	PSN-T	15.26	1,237	573.50%	A+	A−
2	EnerCare Inc.	ECI-T	9.67	544	40.00%	A+	A+
3	Parkland Fuel Corp.	PKI-T	13.11	844	17.70%	A+	A+
4	MEG Energy Corp.	MEG-T	46.18	8,935	0.50%	A+	A+
5	Killam Properties Inc.	KMP-T	11.86	585	20.10%	A+	A+
6	Argonaut Gold Inc.	AR-T	8.69	796	83.30%	A+	B+
7	Black Diamond Group Ltd.	BDI-T	18.99	708	65.10%	A−	A−
8	Northern REIT Stp Unit	NPR.UN-T	31.5	927	19.00%	A+	A−
9	Inter Pipeline Fund	IPL.UN-T	18.31	4,832	28.20%	A−	A+
10	Whitecap Resources Inc.	WCP-T	9.63	695	41.80%	A+	C−
11	lululemon athletica	LLL-T	64.15	6,936	79.70%	A−	C−
12	Cdn. Utilities Ltd., A	CU-T	61.56	7,856	18.80%	B−	A+
13	Constellation Software	CSU-T	84.98	1,487	72.20%	B−	B+
14	Kirkland Lake Gold Inc.	KGI-T	18.6	1,300	24.80%	A+	C−
15	Major Drilling Grp Intl	MDI-T	17.4	1,374	17.30%	B+	A+
16	Lumina Copper Corp.	LCC-X	14.59	572	184.40%	B+	B−
17	Endeavour Silver Corp.	EDR-T	10.98	959	64.60%	A−	C−
18	Surge Energy Inc.	SGY-T	9.77	693	15.60%	A+	B−
19	TransForce Inc.	TFI-T	17.03	1,627	32.00%	A−	B+
20	Total Energy Serv. Inc.	TOT-T	17.35	544	20.80%	B+	A−
21	NGEx Resources Inc.	NGQ-T	2.95	466	94.10%	C+	C−
22	Algonquin Power Corp.	AQN-T	6.02	820	27.10%	A−	B+
23	Precision Drilling Corp	PD-T	10.81	2,984	3.70%	B+	A−
24	Open Text Corp.	OTC-T	60.37	3,494	8.00%	B+	A−
25	Wajax Corp.	WJX-T	42.3	703	19.40%	C+	A−

Grades are relative to 738 securities in the CPMS Canadian database. Source: Morningstar Canada.

Source: McGugan, Ian, "The momentum approach to stock picking." *The Globe and Mail*, February 8, 2012, p. B18. Available at www.theglobeandmail.com. ©The Globe and Mail, Inc. All rights reserved. Reprinted by permission.

There is also evidence of seasonal patterns in stock returns. The best-known pattern is the "January effect," sometimes called the Santa Claus rally, since it occurs in the trading period following Christmas. Particularly for smaller firms, the returns are statistically higher in January than they are over the other 11 months of the year, with most of these returns arriving in the first five trading days. This pattern has been documented in the Canadian, U.S., and global markets. Recent evidence suggests the January effect is not as prevalent as it used to be, implying that market participants have "traded away" or exploited most of the pattern, as you would expect in a reasonably efficient market.

A wide array of reasons has been put forward to explain the January effect. One of the most commonly cited arguments is known as the "tax-loss selling hypothesis." This argument asserts that investors sell their "losers" of the previous year in late December to create capital losses, which can be used to offset their capital gains in order to reduce their taxes payable. By nature, many of these losers have lower prices and hence may be dominated by small cap stocks. This increased supply of stocks depresses the prices, so these stocks are bought in early January at relatively attractive prices. This demand then drives their prices up again. While this is a plausible argument, the evidence has only weakly supported the claim that this behaviour accounts for the January effect—i.e., while tax-loss selling may account for a portion of January returns, it does not explain all of it.

Another argument advanced is that professional portfolio managers engage in "window dressing" and attempt to get rid of their riskier holdings (i.e., small cap stocks, high-yield bonds, etc.) prior to December 31. According to the argument, this is a significant date because professional managers prepare their annual reports as of December 31, and these reports typically includes portfolio holdings. As such, they want their portfolios to look as attractive as possible for these widely distributed documents. After this critical date, managers may purchase riskier securities in an attempt to earn the associated higher expected returns. Similar to the tax-loss selling hypothesis, the evidence supporting this argument suggests it may explain some, but not all, of the January pattern.

Other seasonal patterns have been noted, such as the day-of-the-month effect, which reflects the fact that returns tend to be higher on the last trading day of the month and the first three trading days of the next month. The day-of-the-week effect refers to the fact that the average Monday return has historically tended to be negative and significantly different from the average returns for the other four weekdays, which are all positive. Although these patterns are interesting to note, it would be difficult and very risky to attempt to exploit them, because the evidence refers to "averages," which means the effects do not occur all the time, and because of the trading costs involved. Consider, for example, the following comment from Laszlo Birinya, Jr.: "Fact is that most seasonal tendencies are only 'statistically significant'— meaning you can write a dissertation on the subject, but don't try to make money on it."[15]

Semi-Strong Form Evidence

Most tests of the EMH focus on the semi-strong version. This is logical, because most analysis of security prices, as well as most corporate finance decisions, involve the use of publicly available information. Most studies support the semi-strong EMH; however, some do not. We discuss two broad categories of testing the semi-strong form below.

One way of testing for semi-strong market efficiency is to examine the speed of adjustment of stock prices to announcements of significant new information. In a semi-strong form efficient market, prices would adjust quickly and accurately to this new information so that investors could not act on it and earn abnormally high risk-adjusted returns. In contrast, if the market overreacts or underreacts or if there are time lags before stock prices adjust, and investors can exploit these flaws, then the market is not semi-strong form efficient.

Figure 10-2 illustrates the price-adjustment process for an efficient market (A), for an inefficient market that overreacts to new information (B), and for an inefficient market that reacts too slowly to new information (C). In this example, the stock is trading at $20 on the announcement date of the significant event (*t*). Market A is efficient, and the price adjusts immediately and accurately to the new information, which is obviously good news, because the price increases to $23. Market B overreacts to the new information, which provides investors with a window of opportunity to earn abnormal profits as a result of the information, if this overreaction occurs consistently and is of sufficient magnitude. In this case, investors could sell or short sell the stock shortly after the information becomes public and profit when the price subsequently declines. Market C, conversely, reacts too slowly to the new information, which again provides an opportunity for investors to exploit the information (i.e., by purchasing the stock after the information becomes public). Of course, many other possible patterns are displayed by inefficient markets.

---

[15] Birinya, Laszlo, Jr., "The window dressing anomaly." *Forbes*, December 20, 1993.

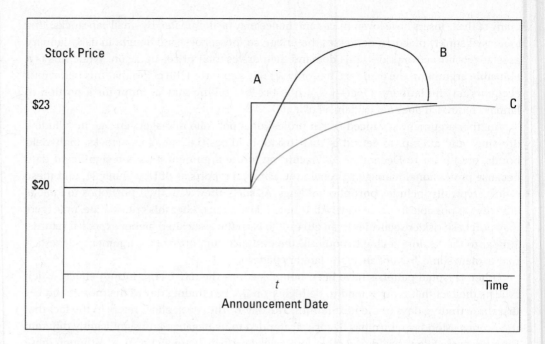

FIGURE 10-2 *Efficient and Inefficient Markets*

event study an examination of stock returns to determine the impact of a particular event on stock prices

abnormal returns returns that exceed the expected return on a stock according to a model of stock returns, such as the CAPM

There are numerous examples of these types of studies. Most of them take the form of an **event study**: stock returns are examined to determine the impact of a particular event on stock prices. Most of these studies support the notion that the market adjusts to new public information rapidly and accurately, and that investors could not earn **abnormal returns** based on inefficient market reactions to significant information announcements.

Many event studies have examined the impact of a variety of significant types of information events. For example, researchers have examined the price behaviour surrounding company-specific announcements regarding such events as stock splits, takeover announcements, dividend changes, accounting changes, and so on. Researchers have also examined significant economy-wide announcements, such as unexpected interest rate changes, that could be expected to influence aggregate price levels. The results of most of these studies are similar: prices begin to react to the event before the announcement is made public, and the final price adjustment occurs rapidly when the actual announcement is made. This is depicted in Figure 10-3, which obviously alludes to the announcement of some positive news. Notice that this evidence supports the presence of the semi-strong form of market efficiency, because investors could not have earned abnormal returns after the information was made public. This evidence does not provide support for strong form efficiency, because the price increase that occurs before the announcement suggests that some investors are profiting from private information about upcoming price changes by buying the securities before the information is made public.

One exception to the efficient processing of new information has been documented with respect to earnings "surprises." These refer to earnings announcements that either exceed or fall short of consensus earnings estimates. Several studies have confirmed that a lag exists in the adjustment of stock prices to earnings surprises. In particular, companies displaying the largest positive earnings surprises displayed superior *subsequent* performance, while *poor* subsequent performance was displayed by companies with low or negative earnings

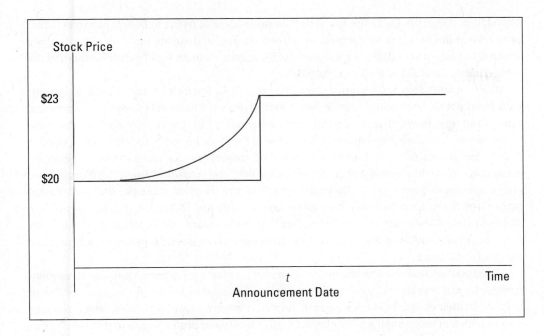

FIGURE 10-3 *The "Typical" Event Study Result for Good News Events*

surprises. Although substantial price adjustments occurred before, and on the date of, the actual announcement, similar to those noted in the studies discussed above, the substantial adjustments occurring *after* the announcement date contradict semi-strong form efficiency. In addition, stocks that have experienced positive earnings forecast revisions have been found to produce positive abnormal returns subsequent to the revision, on average. The larger the revisions, the greater the excess returns. This also contradicts the semi-strong form of the EMH.

This anomaly may be related, to a certain extent, to the momentum anomaly discussed in the previous subsection. In particular, it has been argued that the slow reaction of markets to earnings announcements, as well as to other news items, contributes to the price momentum effect. In other words, prices react positively to good news (and negatively to bad news), but the full extent of the reaction is insufficient; therefore, prices will continue to appreciate (depreciate).

A second general method of testing for semi-strong market efficiency is to examine the performance of investors to see if they are able to use publicly available information to consistently generate abnormal risk-adjusted returns over sustained periods. A variety of active strategies have been tested, with most results suggesting that such strategies do not outperform a simple buy-and-hold strategy. Perhaps the strongest evidence of semi-strong market efficiency is the fact that professional fund managers, with all of their training, expertise, technological capability, and access to data, do not outperform the market on a risk-adjusted basis, on average. In fact, most studies indicate the performance of the average active portfolio manager, after expenses, is substantially worse than the performance of their passive benchmarks. Some studies suggest they may underperform their benchmarks by as much as 50 to 200 basis points. Empirical evidence also suggests that pension fund managers consistently underperform their benchmarks.

These results reflect how difficult it is to "beat the market" and are not meant as a commentary on the abilities of active managers. For example, consider the following comment from Charles Ellis, a well-known investment consultant and author, who has studied the results of professional managers over many years: "The problem is not that professional managers lack skill or diligence. Quite the opposite. The problem with trying to beat the market is that professional investors are so talented, so numerous, and so dedicated to their work that as a group they make it very difficult for any one of their number to do significantly better than the others, particularly in the long run."[16]

While an abundance of evidence supports semi-strong form efficiency, several exceptions have been noted. For example, some investment styles have been able to produce abnormal returns (an investment style is a method of forming portfolios that consist of stocks that have some common underlying characteristics). One of the most important of these exceptions is that "value" stocks have consistently outperformed "growth" stocks. Value stocks are generally those that have below-average price-to-earnings (P/E) and market-to-book (M/B) ratios and above-average dividend yields. They are thought to provide good value per dollar of market price. Growth stocks, conversely, have above-average P/E and M/B ratios, but below-average dividend yields. Their name refers to the fact that investors are willing to pay a premium for these companies because they expect them to display above-average future growth in earnings and share price.

Based on the value phenomena noted above, value investing has been a popular investment strategy for many years. In fact, this approach was advocated by Benjamin Graham and David L. Dodd in their classic 1934 book *Security Analysis Principles and Techniques*, which remains a cornerstone of investment philosophy for many investment professionals to this day.[17] They argued that future growth was difficult to predict; therefore, investors should concern themselves with demonstrated performance. Graham and Dodd went on to show how analysts could identify bargain stocks by analyzing company financial statements.

Numerous studies of U.S., Canadian, and global market returns through the years have supported the superior returns generated by value stocks—in fact, there are too many studies supporting this assertion to even begin to list them. Of course, the higher returns could exist in perfectly efficient markets if value stocks are riskier than growth stocks. However, the evidence suggests this is not the case, at least not according to traditional risk measures, such as standard deviation and beta. In fact, most of the evidence suggests the opposite result with respect to risk—that is, value stocks appear to be less risky than growth stocks. This anomaly involving value stocks contradicts semi-strong market efficiency, because all the ratios used to categorize stocks in this manner are publicly available. The fact that this pattern has not disappeared in response to its widespread recognition by the investment community is troublesome to advocates of efficient markets. In efficient markets, when investors recognize this pattern, they should increase their demand for value stocks, driving up their prices and causing the excess returns to disappear. Similarly, the prices of growth stocks should decline in response to a decrease in demand for these types of stocks. However, these patterns have persisted. In any event, it is not a foolproof strategy because, in any given year, growth stocks could outperform value stocks, even though value stocks have continued to outperform over the long run.

Finance in the News 10-3 points out that just buying stocks that appear "cheap" will not generally lead to a successful value investing strategy. It alludes to the importance of buying reasonably priced stocks that also provide some "offense" (i.e., growth). The article also provides some commentary from Benjamin Graham's most famous student, Warren Buffett. For example, Mr. Buffett suggests that determining "value" isn't as simple as comparing a stock's price to one variable, and he reveals that he analyzes several different factors to determine estimated future values.

Another commonly used investing style involves forming portfolios based on the "size" of the underlying common stocks. Size is commonly measured using the stock's market

---

[16] See Ellis, Charles, *Winning the Loser's Game* (New York: McGraw Hill, 2002).
[17] Graham, Benjamin, and Dodd, David L., *Security Analysis: Principles and Technique* (New York: McGraw Hill, 1934).

finance INTHENEWS 10-3 Good Stocks Are a Lot Like Bobby Orr

WITH THE NATIONAL HOCKEY LEAGUE playoffs coming to a climax, it's the time of year that brings to mind history's greatest Stanley Cup moments. To be sure, it's debatable which of those great moments is, in fact, the greatest. But one that has to be in the running is Bobby Orr's 1970 Cup-clinching goal—a moment the Boston Bruins recently immortalized with the unveiling of a bronze statue of the Hall of Famer, mid-flight in the famous celebratory leap he made after scoring his historic goal.

Of course, as hockey fans are well aware, Mr. Orr's special place in hockey history goes far beyond that famed goal. A defenceman blessed with tremendous offensive abilities, Mr. Orr was the first—and only—defender to lead the National Hockey League in scoring, redefining his position and paving the way for the likes of Paul Coffey, Brian Leetch, and other great "offensive defencemen" who followed.

So, what does all of this have to do with investing? While on the surface it might seem an odd comparison, Mr. Orr's exceptional combination of offensive firepower and stalwart defence has something of a counterpart in the stock market. To understand how, you have to consider the two main categories into which most investors, commentators and investment companies put stocks: growth and value.

Because they are increasing earnings at a fairly rapid pace (and are expected to continue to do so) growth plays are usually the stocks that catch most investors' eyes—they're the goal scorers of the stock market, if you will. And, as with a great goal scorer, you often (though not always) have to pay a premium to get them.

Value stocks, meanwhile, tend to be large, established companies that, because of real problems, perceived problems or investor apathy, are trading at low levels compared with their earnings, cash flow, or book values. Like a solid defenceman, they often don't come with the attention—or price tag—of a growth stock/goal scorer.

While most of the investment world splits stocks into one of those two categories, however, "growth" and "value" are not mutually exclusive.

In fact, in a 2000 letter to Berkshire Hathaway shareholders, the great investor Warren Buffett wrote that "market commentators and investment managers who glibly refer to 'growth' and 'value' styles as contrasting approaches to investment are displaying their ignorance, not their sophistication. Growth is simply a component—usually a plus, sometimes a minus—in the value equation."

Mr. Buffett knows that determining "value" isn't as simple as comparing a stock's price to one variable, be it earnings, book value, dividend yield, or some other barometer. He instead analyzes several different factors to determine what he thinks an investment will be worth at some future point—and what he is willing to pay for it now, given the risk that his estimate will prove too high. A high earnings growth rate in and of itself thus doesn't mean a company is a good bet to fare well in the future. "Indeed, growth can destroy value if it requires cash inputs in the early years of a project or enterprise that exceed the discounted value of the cash that those assets will generate in later years," Mr. Buffett explained.

What that also means is that companies can have characteristics typically associated with strong "growth" stocks (that is, rapidly expanding earnings), and usually associated with top "value" plays (cheap shares, high yields, etc.). In fact, while most of my Guru Strategies (each of which is based on the approach of a different investing great, including Mr. Buffett) lean one way or the other in terms of growth/value orientation, most look for both qualities. That is, almost all of the growth-oriented models have at least one value test, and many of the value-oriented models include some type of earnings-growth assessment.

With all of that in mind, I thought it would be interesting to take a look at a couple of stocks that possess the market's equivalent of Mr. Orr's "offensive defenceman" skill set. These stocks have some of the defensive qualities one would typically expect from value plays, as well as the offensive qualities typically associated with growth plays.

Source: Reese, John, "Good stocks are a lot like Bobby Orr." *The Globe and Mail*, June 6, 2010. John Reese is founder and CEO of Validea.com, Validea.ca, and portfolio manager for the Omega American & International Consensus funds. Reprinted by permission.

---

capitalization (or market cap), which equals the number of shares outstanding times the market price per share. This investing style has emerged in response to the **size effect** anomaly, which has been well documented in the finance literature since the early 1980s. The size effect refers to the fact that small cap stocks tend to outperform large cap stocks, even after adjusting for risk. Interestingly, a large portion (as much as 50 percent) of the size effect has occurred in January. In fact, the January effect noted in the previous section is driven to a large extent by the performance of small stocks in January and is sometimes referred to as the "small firm in January effect." However, small cap returns are generally more volatile, and while they have outperformed over a reasonably long period, in some years, such as 2008, they underperformed, so they are by no means a "free lunch." In addition, small caps generally have substantially higher trading costs than larger cap stocks because they tend to trade less actively.

Another long-standing, semi-strong EMH anomaly is related to the information provided by Value Line Inc., one of the largest and best-known investment advisory services in the world, in its Value Line Investment Survey. Value Line ranks a large universe of stocks from

size effect an anomaly in which small market cap stocks tend to outperform large cap stocks even after adjusting for risk

1 (best) to 5 (worst), based on its expectations regarding the stocks' performance over the next 12 months. Substantial evidence suggests that the performance of stocks in the first two categories has been clearly superior in the subsequent period, while the lower-ranked stocks have performed poorly. Of course, this evidence contradicts semi-strong form efficiency, because investors could profit by using these ratings after they have been made public. However, evidence also suggests that it would be hard to exploit this anomaly after trading costs, because the market adjusts relatively quickly to this information.

Strong Form Evidence

The strong form version of the EMH asserts that prices reflect all public and private information, which is a very stringent requirement. For example, this suggests that insiders could not profit from inside information that is not known to the public, because prices would already reflect this information. However, it is impossible that prices could reflect all the information that is not publicly available. In fact, as discussed in *Finance in the News 10-4*, in the United States the CEO of the Galleon hedge fund was sentenced to 11 years in jail for setting up a network of informants at different companies who would provide him with inside information the hedge fund could trade on. It is not surprising that, on balance, the evidence does not support this version of the EMH.

finance INTHENEWS 10-4 CEO Jailed for 11 Years for Insider Trading

FALLEN HEDGE FUND tycoon Raj Rajaratnam has been sentenced to a record 11 years in prison after his conviction in the biggest Wall Street insider trading case in decades.

Prosecutors had pushed for a 25-year sentence after convicting Rajaratnam, 54, in the biggest insider trading investigation ever conducted by US authorities.

Legal experts said that while prosecutors may have been disappointed with the decision, the sentence was still the highest ever given for insider dealing.

"His crimes and the scope of his crimes reflect a virus in our business culture that needs to be eradicated," US district judge Richard Holwell told the Manhattan court. The judge also ordered Rajaratnam to pay a $10m fine.

"He is arguably the most egregious insider trader to face sentencing in a courthouse in the US," assistant US attorney Reed Brodsky said. He called Rajaratnam the "modern face of insider trading."

Prosecutors found that Rajaratnam had used a network of insiders to gain illegal tips on some of the world's biggest companies including Goldman Sachs, Google, Hilton and Intel. The scandal also dragged in Rajat Gupta, a former Goldman Sachs director and ex-boss of the McKinsey management consultant group, who is now facing a criminal investigation over tips he allegedly gave to Rajaratnam.

The secretly tapped conversations that the Galleon founder held with Gupta and other associates were instrumental in securing his conviction. Such extensive wire tapping in a white-collar criminal case is unusual. The practice is more usually associated with Mafia investigations and Rajaratnam's lawyer fought unsuccessfully to have the tapes banned from court.

Raj Rajaratnam, billionaire co-founder of Galleon Group, leaves Manhattan federal court. In October 2011, Rajaratnam was sentenced to 11 years for insider trading. (Mary Altaffer/AP/The Canadian Press)

The recordings proved extremely damaging for Rajaratnam and his associates. Out of 26 charged in Galleon-related cases, Rajaratnam and three others were convicted at trial; 21 pleaded guilty and one defendant is at large.

Rajaratnam's sentencing follows a 10-year sentence for Zvi Goffer, a former trader at Galleon. The average sentence of the 13 other defendants connected to the Galleon case has been about three years.

Eli Richardson, a partner in Bass, Berry & Sims, said Rajaratnam should "consider himself lucky." He said the sentencing guidelines would have justified a significantly longer sentence and that the prosecutors must have been disappointed.

continued

Finance in the News 10-4: CEO Jailed for 11 Years for Insider Trading (continued)

"The judge gets the best of both worlds here. He has handed out the stiffest sentence in an insider dealing case but at the same time displayed mercy," said Richardson.

The crackdown on insider dealing comes as US and UK authorities are trying to cooperate on cross-border regulation and enforcement.

Mary Schapiro, the chairwoman of the top US financial watchdog the Securities and Exchange Commission, met Hector Sants, the UK's Financial Services Authority chief executive officer, in London on Thursday to discuss topics including high-frequency trading and cross-border enforcement cases.

But legal experts said the Rajaratnam case would be difficult to replicate in the UK. Simon Hart, partner at law firm Reed Smith, said: "Rajaratnam's conviction was in large part secured through the use of phone-tap evidence. That is simply not an avenue available to the FSA when investigating and prosecuting insider dealing.

"Furthermore, even if there was a successful prosecution of this nature, the sentencing precedents in the UK don't come anywhere near the magnitude of those we have seen in the US."

Source: Rushe, Dominic, "Raj Rajaratnam jailed for 11 years for insider trading." *The Guardian* (UK), October 13, 2011. Copyright Guardian News and Media Limited 2011. Reprinted by permission.

Strong form efficiency tests examine whether any group of investors has information, public or private, that allows it to earn abnormal profits consistently. Therefore, it is common to examine the performance of groups that are thought to have access to "private" information, such as insiders. Given insiders' access to privileged information, it is not surprising that several studies have found they have consistently earned abnormal returns on their stock transactions, which refutes strong form efficiency. However, some studies have found that their returns are only slightly better than average. It should be noted that the trading activity of insiders is restricted in order to protect the general investing public. Therefore, their potential to exploit this insider knowledge is limited.

Summary of Empirical Evidence

Overall, based on the available empirical evidence, we can draw the following conclusions regarding the capital markets of Canada, the United States, and most developed countries:

1. Weak form efficiency is very well supported, and it is reasonable to conclude that markets are weak form efficient, although a few anomalies do exist.

2. Semi-strong form efficiency is well supported; however, more contradictory evidence exists for this version of the EMH than for the weak form.

3. Strong form efficiency is not very well supported by the evidence, and it is reasonable to conclude that markets are not strong form efficient in the strictest sense.

One final observation: in Chapter 9, we introduced the Fama-French three-factor model and noted that two of the factors are the size of the firm (measured by the market value of its common equity) and the ratio of the firm's book equity value to its market value of equity. As remarked in this chapter, small firms tend to outperform large ones, and value stocks outperform growth stocks. The market value of equity used by Fama-French identifies small and large firms, while the market-to-book ratio identifies value and growth stocks and is the reciprocal of the Fama-French risk factor. However, it is an ongoing debate as to whether the Fama-French "risk" factors identify riskier firms or simply identify these stock market anomalies or departures from efficiency. Eugene Fama, as the "temple guardian" of market efficiency, views these as risk factors and the market as efficient. Others are more sceptical; nevertheless, many investment professionals acknowledge the importance of many of these factors. This is obvious in *Finance in the News 10-5*, where MSCI Barra announces several "factor indices" related to volatility, momentum, value, earnings yield, and leverage.

---

finance INTHENEWS 10-5   MSCI Barra Expands Range of Factor Indices

MSCI INC., a leading provider of investment decision support tools worldwide, announced today the launch of a unique range of long/short factor indices based on MSCI indices and Barra risk models. The new indices are designed to reflect the returns of a single Barra risk factor and a designated market in a replicable manner. They target the Barra Momentum, Value, Volatility, Earnings Yield and Leverage risk factors.

"By combining MSCI's considerable index construction and risk modeling expertise, we have been able to develop unique indices that aim to reflect high factor returns within the European and US equity markets," said David Brierwood, Chief Operating Officer at MSCI Inc. "Factors such as Volatility and Leverage can play a significant role in determining portfolio risk and performance, and the availability of these long/short factor indices provides institutional investors with a valuable analytical tool for factor-based hedging and investment strategies."

Designed for use by institutional investors in US and European equities, the eight new factor indices are:

1. MSCI Europe Barra Momentum Index

2. MSCI Europe Barra Low Leverage Index

3. MSCI Europe Barra Low Volatility Index

4. MSCI Europe Barra Value Index

5. MSCI USA Barra Momentum Index

6. MSCI USA Barra Low Leverage Index

7. MSCI USA Barra Low Volatility Index

8. MSCI USA Barra Earnings Yield Index

The new indices use an optimization process that, based on specified constraints, aims to achieve a specified high level of exposure to a single Barra factor, very low exposure to other factors and low tracking error to the corresponding MSCI index.

"We have already seen considerable interest from our clients in using the MSCI Factor Indices to support innovative portfolio analysis and portfolio configuration, as well as to enable the creation and monitoring of more tradable products in this area," said Theodore Niggli, Managing Director and Head of MSCI Indices.

The indices are available on request from MSCI, with real time index levels expected to be available on Bloomberg and Reuters shortly after index launch.

Source: From MSCI Barra news release, June 16, 2009. Available at www.mscibarra.com.

CONCEPT REVIEW QUESTIONS

1. Is the weak form EMH well supported by empirical evidence? Discuss any exceptions.

2. Is the semi-strong form EMH well supported by empirical evidence? Discuss any exceptions.

3. Is the strong form EMH well supported by empirical evidence? Discuss any exceptions.

10.5 BEHAVIOURAL FINANCE

Learning Objective 10.5
Differentiate between behavioural finance and the traditional view of finance.

behavioural finance a field of financial thought that suggests that investor behaviour is not always rational but is influenced by psychological biases that cause investors to make systematic errors in judgement

According to a developing field of finance—**behavioural finance**—many of the anomalies described above have been attributed to human behaviour. Consider the following comment from David Dreman, a well-known financial commentator and huge supporter of value investing:

> Graham's observations that investors pay too much for trendy, fashionable stocks and too little for companies that are out-of-favour, was on the money...Why does this profitability discrepancy persist? Because emotion favours the premium-priced stocks. They are fashionable. They are hot. They make great cocktail party chatter. There is an impressive and growing body of evidence demonstrating that investors and speculators don't necessarily learn from experience. Emotion overrides logic time after time.[18]

Dreman's comments about stocks being "fashionable" and investors letting "emotion" outweigh logic are references to some of the underlying tenets of behavioural finance.

Many of the theories and activities in finance are based on what is sometimes called "the traditional view of finance." This view suggests that investors:

1. consider all available information;

---

[18] Dreman, David, "Ben Graham was right—again." *Forbes*, May 6, 1996. Reprinted by Permission of Forbes Media LLC © 2010.

2. act rationally and do not make systematic errors, either in processing information or in implementing investment decisions; and

3. adhere to the basic tenets of modern portfolio theory (MPT), which implies they are risk averse, they diversify, and they consider risk in the context of a well-diversified portfolio.

Conceptually, there seems to be little to dispute in the assertions above. However, in practice, human behaviour gets in the way. For example, a legendary investor, the late Peter Bernstein, suggested that, contrary to the traditional view of finance, the evidence "reveals repeated patterns of irrationality, inconsistency, and incompetence in the ways human beings arrive at decisions and choices when faced with uncertainty."[19] Behavioural finance examines human psychology in an attempt to explain how and why investor behaviour can deviate significantly from the predictions associated with the traditional view, which may lead to persistent market inefficiencies—that is, bubbles, crashes, etc.

Much of the rationale underlying behavioural finance is consistent with the thoughts expressed by Keynes, who was mentioned earlier in the chapter. Consider one of his famous quotations regarding the stock market: "Professional investment may be likened to those newspaper competitions in which the competitors have to pick out the 6 prettiest faces from 100 photographs, the prize being awarded to the competitor whose choice most nearly corresponds to the average preferences of the competitors as a whole."[20] That is, investors don't pick the stock they like; they pick the ones they think other investors are going to like and which as a result will increase in price.

While Keynes's ideals no doubt influenced the development of behavioural finance, its roots as a formal field of finance can be attributed to the 1979 work of Tversky and Kahneman, who provided the first significant alternative to the expected utility theory underlying traditional rational financial decision-making. Contrary to what the standard theory predicts, they found evidence that people place different weights on gains and losses, being affected more adversely by a loss than they were affected positively by a gain of the same amount. Based on these results, Tversky and Kahneman developed "prospect theory" as a way to reconcile the observed behaviour that people exhibited when making decisions under uncertainty.

Indeed, the number of believers in the importance of behavioural finance continues to grow dramatically as people try to account for recent market bubbles and subsequent collapses. Robert Shiller, in the first edition of *Irrational Exuberance*, which examines the reasons underlying market bubbles and subsequent crashes, went so far as to say: "Much of the evidence is drawn from the emerging field of behavioural finance, which as the years go by, is looking less and less like a minor subfield of finance and more and more like a central pillar of finance theory."[21] Clear recognition of the impact of behavioural finance came in 2002, when the Nobel Prize in Economics was awarded to Daniel Kahneman, a Princeton psychologist, and Vernon Smith, of George Mason University, whose economic experiments were at odds with the efficient market hypothesis. Furthermore, two recent John Bates Clark medals in economics (awarded every two years) have gone to behaviourists.

Behavioural finance suggests that investors are motivated by numerous "irrational" forces, such as overconfidence and extreme loss aversion. Recognizing these consistent errors in judgement provides us with the opportunity to avoid making such common errors ourselves, and/or to exploit market inefficiencies that present themselves due to the mistakes made by other market participants. Warren Buffet echoed these sentiments when he noted that, in order to be a successful investor, "what you need is the temperament to control the urges that get other people into trouble in investing." This means that examining past trends and observed behaviours can be beneficial.

---

[19] Bernstein, Peter, L., *Against the Gods: The Remarkable Story of Risk* (Hoboken, NJ: Wiley, 1998); Bernstein, Peter, L., *Capital Ideas: The Improbable Origins of Modern Wall Street* (Hoboken, NJ: Wiley, 2005).

[20] Keynes, John Maynard, "The state of long-term expectations." Chapter 12 in *The General Theory of Employment, Interest and Money* (London: Macmillan, 1936), pp. 147–64.

[21] Shiller, Robert, *Irrational Exuberance* (Princeton, NJ: Princeton University Press, 2000).

When the market is extremely volatile, it is often taken as an indicator that market prices may not reflect underlying fundamentals. One commonly used indicator of market volatility is the VIX Index, which measures investors' expectations of future volatility based on the implied volatilities derived from options-trading data on the Chicago Board Options Exchange. (Implied volatilities will be discussed in detail in chapters 11 and 12.) The Canadian version of the VIX Index is the Montreal Exchange Implied Volatility Index (VIXC). Figure 10-4 depicts the value of the VIXC Index for the period from December 2002 to March 2012—a period during which stock prices plummeted in the fall of 2008, bounced up and down during the winter of 2009, and then showed signs of more permanent recovery in 2009 and 2010 as investors became more confident in the future of the economy and, hence, in future stock returns. Figure 10-4 shows that during the fall of 2008, the VIXC Index increased dramatically, mimicking the dramatic rise in investor uncertainty. It declined significantly during 2009 and 2010, returning to the upper end of previous values, before increasing again in 2011 above historical levels, reflecting concerns over the European debt crisis and its impact on stock markets.

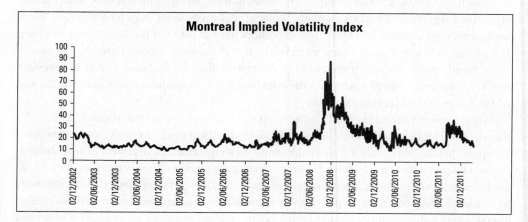

FIGURE 10-4 *Montreal Exchange (MX) Implied Volatility Index (VIXC) (December 2002– March 2012)*

loss aversion the tendency to place a heavier emphasis on losses than on comparable gains

risk aversion the tendency for investors to dislike risk while still being willing to assume it if they are adequately compensated

One important behavioural bias is extreme **loss aversion**, as identified above by Tversky and Kahneman, which refers to investors' unwillingness to place "fair bets." This is not the same thing as risk aversion, which is an underlying assumption of traditional finance. **Risk aversion** implies that investors dislike risk but are willing to assume risk if they are adequately compensated in the form of higher expected returns. Loss aversion, on the other hand, implies that investors may engage in suboptimal investing decisions to avoid losses, which they dislike more than they like comparable gains.

Loss aversion is related to several behavioural biases. For example, traditional finance suggests that investors will hold well-diversified portfolios that are consistent with their investing objectives in terms of return requirements and risk tolerance. Risk-averse investors will evaluate potential investments on this basis. In contrast, behavioural finance suggests that investors may invest too conservatively, especially if they have experienced losses recently. This could cause them to hold investments that are inappropriate for their investing objectives; as a result, their portfolios may not be adequately diversified. Loss aversion can also lead investors to hold on to "losers" too long (so they can avoid recognizing the loss) and sell "winners" too early (so they will realize the gains and avoid potentially losing these gains). This pattern of investing behaviour has been well documented.

Throughout history there have been numerous asset price "bubbles." For example, Sir Isaac Newton once said, "I can calculate the motions of heavenly bodies, but not the madness of people." He was referring to losses he experienced in 1720 while "following the herd" and investing in the South Sea Company, a London-based shipping company. Apparently Newton had sold all of his shares in the company in April 1720, after experiencing a gain of 100 percent on an original investment of £7,000. However, as the stock continued to soar, he was unable to stay on the sidelines and ended up buying an even larger number of shares near the peak of the market, eventually losing £20,000—a sizable amount at the time (see Chapter 7 for a fuller discussion of this bubble).

Certainly, there have been numerous examples of this herd-like mentality over the past decade, as reluctant investors could no longer stand on the sidelines, but put their money into Internet stocks and U.S. real estate just as those bubbles were about to burst. It is indeed difficult to sit and watch as others make fantastic gains on their investments, without feeling you are missing out on a "sure thing." In contrast, traditional finance suggests that investors should make their decisions based on their perceived investing needs and their beliefs regarding the appropriateness of market prices.

Once these bubbles burst, loss-averse investors are reluctant to invest in anything but the safest investments and are slow to re-enter stock markets. This behaviour is sometimes referred to as the "snake bite" effect. It also reflects the fact that investors tend to give recent information more weight than more distant information. Of course, when recent news has been positive, this same trait fuels the bubbles. As Warren Buffett has said, "People tend to underestimate low probability events when they haven't happened recently, and overestimate them when they have." Traditional finance, on the other hand, suggests investors consider all available information and place the appropriate rational weight on each item, regardless of when it was received.

Consider, for example, one of the most prolific investors of all time, Peter Lynch. He regretted that many of his fund holders did not realize the full gains that his fund made over the 1977–90 period, when his fund beat the market in 11 of 13 years, earning a 29 percent average annual return. How could this happen? Well, they did not stay fully invested in his Fidelity Magellan Fund, selling after periods of poor performance (i.e., selling low), then buying back after times of strong performance (i.e., buying high). Of course, this behaviour is the opposite of what you want to do as an investor, which is to buy low and sell high. Unfortunately, these tendencies to follow the herd and focus on the immediate past seem to be common behavioural flaws that doom many investors to experience subpar investment performance. Successful investing suggests, among other things, that you focus on your short-term and long-term investing objectives and risk tolerance and design a portfolio that is consistent with these objectives.

Another important behavioural flaw is investor overconfidence. This manifests itself in several ways. First, investors tend to focus on information that they consider important and downplay other pertinent information. They also tend to attribute their investing successes to their ability rather than to market factors. On the other hand, they tend to attribute investing failure to factors beyond their control. Overconfidence can lead investors to hold overly risky securities that might produce huge payoffs, which they take credit for, or huge losses, which they can blame on external factors they can't control. It might also lead them to hold poorly diversified portfolios, either because they hold too many risky securities or because they don't hold a sufficient number of securities. Clearly, this does not represent rational behaviour.

Anchoring refers to the tendency to become emotionally tied to some initial price or perception. For example, investors are often reluctant to sell investments below their original purchase price, or below some historically higher price (i.e., the price they could have sold it for a month ago). This may also cause them to not invest, because they could have done so at a lower price in the past. Investors can become anchored to some initial impression about the quality of an investment and either over- or undervalue it accordingly. This causes investors to adapt too slowly to new information as it is released. For example, they may assess the quality and value of a company's shares based on their embedded (historic) beliefs about the strength (or weakness) of the company, rather than in light of the actual health and future growth prospects of the company today. As a result, they may pay too much for companies whose fortunes have declined, or miss out on attractive "buy" opportunities for companies whose fortunes have improved.

anchoring the tendency to become emotionally tied to some initial price or perception

mental accounting the process of accounting for individual investments separately

Price anchoring tends to go hand in hand with **mental accounting**, which refers to the process of accounting for individual investments separately. This can cause investors to be poorly diversified, among other things. A good example of mental accounting is when investors employ different investing approaches to manage their investments, depending on the source of the money. In particular, investors often invest their "winnings" more aggressively than monies earned (this is known as the "house money effect"). This causes them to maintain separate mental accounts—i.e., "speculative" accounts, conservative accounts, and so on. Obviously, this can lead to poorly diversified portfolios that may not be consistent with investor objectives.

This discussion of behavioural investing flaws is far from exhaustive, but it does provide an overview of how psychological elements can affect the implementation of the investment decision. It is important to remember that these behaviours can be displayed by institutional investors as well as individual ones. After all, professional investors are also human and are subject to the same biases and emotional reactions as the rest of us. No matter what guidelines professional investors put in place in the form of clear, unambiguous investing restrictions and policies, the role of human behaviour usually comes into play at some point during the process. The important role of emotion in making financial decisions is alluded to in *Finance in the News 10-6*, in which behavioural economist Dan Ariely describes how he deliberately locked himself out of his trading account because he "wanted to separate... emotion from...decisions."

finance INTHENEWS 10-6   The Role of Emotion

WHEN THE FINANCIAL world came crashing down in 2008, Dan Ariely realized he would be tempted to do something drastic to his investment portfolio that he might later regret. So he deliberately punched in the wrong password enough times to lock himself out of his online brokerage account.

"I did it after I made a mistake," says the professor of behavioural economics at Duke University in Durham, N.C., who often uses his personal experiences as a springboard for his research into why people do the seemingly irrational things they do.

"What happened was that when the recession started, I kept on checking where I was [financially]. Every time I lost money, it kind of ruined the next few hours of my day. A year of savings was gone in one day of randomness. But I also didn't feel my allocation was off. There was nothing specific I wanted to change. And I wanted to separate my emotion from my decisions."

That's not something most of us are capable of doing, because of very human tendencies that run counter to rational investing, says Prof. Ariely, 42, an Israeli native who has emerged as a prominent voice in the hot field of behavioural economics.

"We are all far less rational in our decision making than standard economic theory assumes," he declared in his 2008 book on the subject, *Predictably Irrational: The Hidden Forces That Shape Our Decisions*. But as the title indicates, the irrational in us is neither random nor senseless.

Two of the key roadblocks that keep most of us from becoming the next Warren Buffett are known in psych-speak as anchoring and loss aversion.

Put simply, we can't help focusing on how much we paid for something (the reference point or anchor that affects how we value it), and we really hate losing money. When translated to the marketplace, the upshot is that we tend to stay with losers too long and sell winners too soon.

"The fact that you remember the starting point creates the loss aversion," Prof. Ariely says affably between sips of tea. "Losses loom larger than gains. It's more painful to lose, so this tendency grows even stronger by keeping losers for too long. And even when you're making money, you worry about losing it."

He illustrates this with a time-tested student experiment, offering a bet on a flipped coin. If the coin comes up heads, you win $100. If it's tails, you lose $80. If your instinct is to reject what is actually a good gamble out of a fear of losing, you shouldn't be investing in the stock market.

We also seek to avoid any regrets, which typically causes us to run with the herd, another obstacle to market success. "We have an instinctive initial reaction to assume other people are doing the right thing."

The stock market and commodity gains of recent months are a case in point.

"You're seeing all your friends investing in X, which could be gold, oil, indexes, whatever. It seems like everybody around you is doing the right thing, aside from you. So every day that you are not in this market and your friends are, you feel like an idiot."

Yet more investors are talking a bullish game than playing one, because money is still pouring into fixed income. And if you asked most people their view of economic fundamentals, few would say things are going particularly well.

"In some sense, everybody has learned a little bit too much economics," he says, by which he means "the Chicago school of rationality" has permeated popular thinking.

"It's somehow in the air, it's in the politics. I don't know where people are getting this deep belief in the rationality of institutions and markets," says Prof. Ariely, who describes himself as a conservative investor who didn't see the bust coming.

continued

Finance in the News 10-6: The Role of Emotion *(continued)*

The all too human traits he describes "make for very bad behaviour in markets. If you think that markets are supposed to be [made up of] these independent, cold, calculating actors who work against each other in the hope of getting a joint outcome to be better, human nature doesn't create a good recipe for that," says Prof. Ariely, who signs off his notes: "Irrationally yours."

Bank directors should make a point of getting their hands on his next book, *Perfectly Irrational*, due out in June. He will reveal the findings of his research into the impact of fat bonuses on the performance of those who receive them. As many of us have long suspected, the huge incentives—and the stress that comes with trying to achieve them—make for less productive people.

"In the experiments we show that they're counterproductive," Prof. Ariely says.

Now that's one irrational behaviour worth stamping out.

One of the most damaging observations related to the notion of market efficiency is the number of speculative bubbles in asset prices that have occurred so regularly throughout history, as discussed in Appendix 7A of Chapter 7. Bubbles refer to significant and generally unwarranted increases in asset prices that lead to unsustainably high price levels. Consider the following comment from *Manias, Panics, and Crashes* by Charles Kindleberger and Robert Aliber: "Bubbles always implode; by definition a bubble involves a non-sustainable pattern of price changes or cash flows."[22]

Some of the more notable bubbles through history include the Dutch Tulip Bulb bubble (1636), the South Sea bubble and the Mississippi bubble (1720), the late 1920s stock price bubble (1927–29), the Japanese bubble in real estate and stock prices (1985–89), the Internet bubble (1995–2000), and of course the recent U.S. real estate bubble, which precipitated the sub-prime crisis and subsequent global financial crisis. An important behavioural trait contributing to these bubbles is the herd-like behaviour that investors have exhibited for centuries, which was discussed above. Of course, with almost all of these bubbles, there have been other important contributing factors, such as fraudulent representations, excessive availability of credit, and so on.

Consider for example, the bubble in high-technology stock prices from 1995 to 2000, which translated into an average annual return of more than 40 percent for Nasdaq stocks over this period, prior to the market collapse in 2000. The Dow Jones Industrial Average (DJIA) also experienced dramatic increases over this period (tripling in value), as did high-tech stocks around the world. Indeed, as the DJIA surpassed 10,000 for the first time in 1999, it led many so-called experts to make bold predictions of the DJIA hitting 36,000, 40,000, and even 100,000 going forward. This kind of dramatic increase in prices inspired Robert Shiller to title his 2000 book *Irrational Exuberance*, reflecting an earlier comment made by Alan Greenspan, chairman of the U.S. Federal Reserve from 1987 to 2006, in reference to his concerns about market prices being overblown. At the time he wrote the first edition, which was just before the "bursting of the tech bubble" during the summer of 2000, Shiller suggested that this term was "a good description of the mood behind the market."

In the first edition, Shiller devoted considerable effort to describing some common behavioural biases that contributed to this bubble and to bubbles in general. In the preface to the second edition of his book, which was published in 2005, he elaborated on several of the behavioural traits he observed in investors while promoting his first text: herd behaviour, heavy emphasis on the importance of recent events, overconfidence, fear of regret, and so on. He then went on to note the existence of similar beliefs about the U.S. housing market, which subsequently collapsed in 2007, as illustrated in Figure 10-5.

---

[22] Kindleberger, Charles P., and Aliber, Robert, *Manias, Panics, and Crashes: A History of Financial Crises*, 5th edition (Toronto: Wiley, 2005).

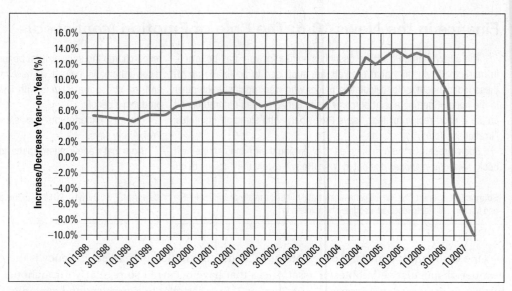

FIGURE 10-5 *U.S. House Prices (1998–2007)*

Source: Center for Responsible Lending/FHFA

LESSONS TO BE LEARNED   **One of the lessons** of the recent financial crisis is that we don't always take these lessons to heart. Consider a few of the bubbles in our financial history. Alan Greenspan, former chairman of the Federal Reserve Bank of the United States noted in a speech in 1996:

> Clearly, sustained low inflation implies less uncertainty about the future, and lower risk premiums imply higher prices of stocks and other earning assets. We can see that in the inverse relationship exhibited by price/earnings ratios and the rate of inflation in the past. But how do we know when irrational exuberance has unduly escalated asset values, which then become subject to unexpected and prolonged contractions as they have in Japan over the past decade? [23]

His comments were followed by declines in the stock markets around the world.

Robert Shiller used the phrase "irrational exuberance" to describe the dot.com frenzy in markets around the world, when stocks with little or no earnings prospects displayed values that made little sense using almost any valuation model. In his book *Irrational Exuberance*, published in 2000, Shiller discussed speculative bubbles in general, but also the speculative bubble that is often referred to as the "dot.com" or "Internet bubble."[24] The publication of this book preceded the bursting of the Internet bubble in 2001.

In the second edition of his book, published in 2005, Shiller added an analysis of the real estate bubble.[25] He discussed the problems associated with personal bankruptcies leading to financial difficulties for financial institutions. The publication of this book preceded the sub-prime mortgage-fuelled boom that went bust in 2007.

The challenge, as you can see, is that participants in markets do not always learn, and there is a psychological dimension to how market participants value stocks.

One of the reasons the field of behavioural finance has grown so dramatically in importance is that it provides practical and useful insights for investors, corporate managers, and the ordinary person. This is because it is important to recognize why behavioural characteristics may lead others (whether professionals or not) toward certain decisions. However, it is probably even more important to recognize that we too are human, and many of our decisions can be influenced by these same emotions. Consider the following quote from Arnold S. Wood, partner, president, and CEO of Martingale Asset Management:

> Aristotle Onassis is famous for saying "The secret of business is to know something that nobody else knows." One must ask oneself, "What is it that I know that nobody else knows as well as I do?" The answer is yourself. This is not just a matter of casual introspection, nor is it a useless existential thought. It is a practical answer.[26]

---

[23] Greenspan, Alan, "The challenge of central banking in a democratic society." Speech to the American Enterprise Institute, December 5, 1996.

[24] Shiller, Robert, *Irrational Exuberance* (Princeton, NJ: Princeton University Press, 2000).

[25] Shiller, Robert, *Irrational Exuberance*, 2nd ed. (Princeton, NJ: Princeton University Press, 2005).

[26] Wood, Arnold S., "Editor's Preface." In *Behavioral Finance and Investment Management*, pp. v–viii (Charlottesville, VA: Research Foundation of CFA Institute, December 2010).

CONCEPT REVIEW QUESTIONS

1. Contrast behavioural finance with the traditional view.

2. Explain why behavioural flaws could result in investors holding portfolios that are not as predicted by modern portfolio theory.

3. Explain why behavioural traits can cause asset price bubbles.

10.6 IMPLICATIONS OF MARKET EFFICIENCY

The EMH states that security prices will fully and accurately reflect all available information at any given time. The evidence suggests this strict interpretation of market efficiency does not hold; however, we can conclude that markets react quickly and relatively accurately to new public information. As a result, market prices are correct on *average*, and we can say that although markets may not be perfectly efficient, they are relatively efficient. This statement has several important implications for investors and for corporate officers.

Learning Objective 10.6
Explain the implications of market efficiency.

Some of the implications for investors include the following:

1. Technical analysis, which involves examining trading data for patterns, is not likely to be rewarded by substantial abnormal returns, because markets appear to be weak form efficient.

2. Fundamental analysis based on various forms of publicly available information is also likely to be unsuccessful at generating abnormal profits, although some opportunities appear to be available. The implication is that to benefit from such data, the analysis must be of superior and consistent quality. Average, or below-average, analysis will likely be unfruitful. This notion is consistent with the subpar performance reported by the "average" professional portfolio manager.

3. In light of items 1 and 2 above, "active" trading strategies are unlikely to outperform "passive" portfolio management strategies on a consistent basis. Passive strategies involve buy-and-hold tactics and the purchase of such products as index mutual funds or exchange-traded funds (ETFs) that replicate the performance of a market index. The lack of success for active strategies is partially attributable to the extra costs associated with collecting and processing information, as well as to the additional trading costs associated with active strategies. Obviously, these extra costs can be justified only if the approach generates sufficient additional returns to compensate for them. Passive strategies minimize these costs and therefore provide "average" results.

A notable champion of efficient markets has been Burton Malkiel, renowned for his book *A Random Walk down Wall Street*, the first edition of which was published in the early 1970s. In it, he proclaimed that "the market prices stocks so efficiently that a blind-folded chimpanzee throwing darts at the Wall Street Journal can select a portfolio as [good as] those managed by the experts." Based on such beliefs, Malkiel was a staunch advocate of the benefits to investors of buying index funds, which hold the stocks comprising an underlying market index. Malkiel argued that these funds would outperform actively managed funds, especially on an after-tax basis, due to their reduced trading costs and greatly reduced management fees. In the eighth edition of his text, published in 2002, he stated: "Now, over thirty years later, I believe even more strongly in that original thesis, and there's more than a six figure gain to prove it." Malkiel was referencing the fact that a $10,000-investment in an S&P 500 Index Fund, made at the beginning of 1969, would have grown to $327,000 by June 2002 (after management expenses of 0.2 percent), versus $213,000 for the average actively managed equity fund. Malkiel was not alone in his beliefs, and index funds experienced dramatic growth during the 1970s, 1980s, and 1990s.

At the time Malkiel wrote his first edition, there were no such things as ETFs, which are similar to index funds in that they hold the securities comprising an underlying stock or bond index. However, ETFs are not mutual funds; their units trade on stock exchanges just like common shares, and the associated management expenses tend to be much lower. ETFs have experienced dramatic growth in the past 10 years. First launched in the early 1990s, ETFs grew steadily to reach about three dozen in number and $40 billion in assets before the end of the decade. As of the end of February 2012, propelled by their low cost, tax efficiency, and intraday liquidity advantages, ETFs numbered 3,145 worldwide, with total assets under management (AUM) of US$1.52 trillion, as can be seen in Figure 10-6. In Canada, as of the end of January 2012, there were 222 funds, with C$45.3 billion under management.

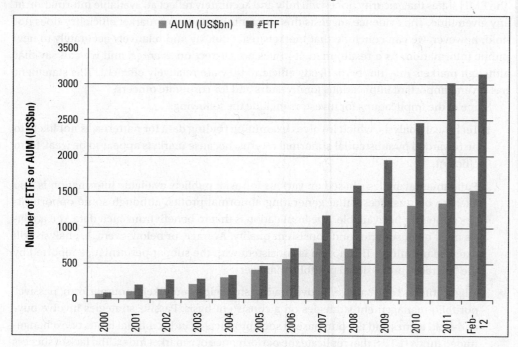

FIGURE 10-6 *Global ETFs (2000–February 2012)*

4. Whether investors decide to pursue a passive or active strategy, it is critical that they focus on the basics of good investing by defining their objectives in terms of expected return and acceptable risk levels, and by maintaining an adequately diversified portfolio. When markets are relatively efficient, as they appear to be, paying attention to these factors will do more to promote success than will the analysis of individual security prices.

Two of the most important implications of the preceding statement for corporate officers are the following:

1. The timing of security issues or repurchases is unimportant in an efficient market because prices will be correct, on average. In other words, prices will not become inflated, so there is no optimal time to sell new securities, and securities will not be undervalued, so there is no optimal time to repurchase outstanding securities.

2. If short-run momentum and overreaction continue, we would expect the opposite: that firms should sell equity after a price run-up and repurchase shares after a price decline. Therefore, management should monitor the price of the company's securities and determine whether price changes reflect new information or short-run momentum and/or overreaction.

CONCEPT REVIEW QUESTION

1. What are the main implications of the EMH for investors? For corporate officers?

10-1 ETHICS AND CORPORATE GOVERNANCE
Capitol Gains

Earlier this year, Senate Majority Leader Bill Frist told the trustee in charge of managing his stock portfolio to sell all of his shares in Hospital Corporation of America, the giant company founded by the Senator's father and brother. Just two weeks after the shares were sold, H.C.A. announced that its earnings would not meet Wall Street expectations, and the company's stock price tumbled almost nine percent. Frist, it happened, had got out pretty much at the top, and his continued connections to H.C.A.—his brother, for instance, is on the company's board of directors—raised the possibility that he'd been tipped off.

Frist is now the target of a probe by the Securities and Exchange Commission, although he insists that he did nothing wrong, and that he sold the shares to defuse concerns about potential conflicts of interest. Frist's colleagues in the Senate, meanwhile, have remained noticeably quiet about the affair. Perhaps that's because he's far from the only senator to demonstrate uncanny investing smarts. Last year, Alan Ziobrowski, a professor at Georgia State, headed the first-ever systematic study of politicians as investors. Ziobrowski and his colleagues looked at six thousand stock transactions made by senators between 1993 and 1998. Over that time, senators beat the market, on average, by twelve percent annually. Since a mutual-fund manager who beats the market by two or three percent a year is considered a genius, the politicians' ability to foresee the future seems practically divine. They did an especially good job of picking up stocks at just the right time; their buys were typically flat before they bought them, but beat the market by thirty percent, on average, in the year after. By those standards, Frist actually looks like a bit of a piker.

Are senators really that smart? The authors of the study suggest a more likely explanation: at least some senators must have been trading "based on information that is unavailable to the public"—in other words, they were engaged in some form of insider trading. It's impossible to pin down exactly how it happened, but it's easy to imagine senators getting occasional stock tips from corporate supplicants, and their own work in Congress often deals with confidential matters that have a direct impact on particular companies.

That the senators have done this without a hint of censure shouldn't come as a surprise. Corporate insider trading is illegal, in theory, but prosecutions are rare. Economists have known for a long time that corporate insiders outperform the market by something like six or seven percent a year. The only way they could pull that off is by trading on privileged information. And some people think that's as it should be. Beginning in the nineteen-sixties, when Henry Manne published "Insider Trading and the Stock Market," many theorists have argued that insider trading is a victimless offense, or even a positive good. After all, some investors always have better information than others, and if a well-informed trader didn't have the incentive of trading on what he knew, the stock market would dry up. Furthermore, since insider trading is, by definition, based on accurate information, it moves stock prices in the right direction. Isn't this just market efficiency in action?

Not really. Ultimately, insider trading is an inefficient way of achieving market efficiency, because insiders earn all their profits on the lag between when they start selling and when the market figures out what's going on. This gives them every reason to hoard information, with the result that stock prices are out of whack for longer than they otherwise would have been. Markets thrive on transparency, but insider trading thrives on opacity.

Insider trading therefore encourages executives to put their own interests before those of their shareholders. In fact, the real scandal of insider trading is not what's illegal but what's legal. For instance, although many companies have a rule that their employees can buy or sell company stock only during preordained periods, known as "trading windows," they don't need to announce in advance if they're going to buy or sell during a window. So executives who get bad news can still dump shares relatively freely (or, if they get wind of good news, buy freely).

Source: Surowiecki, James, "Capitol Gains." *The New Yorker,* October 31, 2005. Copyright © 2012 Condé Nast. All rights reserved. Article by James Surowiecki. Reprinted by permission.

DISCUSSION QUESTIONS

1. According to Henry Manne, insider trading is a victimless crime—even a positive good. Why do some argue that it is a good thing?

2. How do you think insider trading makes capital markets more efficient? If it were legal, what measures should be in place to make the markets even more efficient?

3. Why is insider trading illegal despite the claims of Manne? Would you participate in a market where insiders trade using information that is not available to you?

4. In this case, it is claimed that politicians have inside information as a result of their dealings with firms and lobbyists. What special policies would you recommend to manage the stock portfolios of politicians while they are in office?

SUMMARY

In this chapter, we define an efficient market as one that reacts quickly and relatively accurately to new information; as a result, its prices are correct *on average.* The efficient market hypothesis (EMH) suggests that market prices fully and accurately reflect all available information. The EMH is commonly broken down into three cumulative levels that are based on the extent to which prices reflect different types of available information. The weak form EMH states that security prices reflect all market data; the semi-strong form states that prices reflect all publicly known and available information; and the strong form states that prices reflect all public and private information.

Most of the assumptions required for markets to be efficient are reasonable; however, behavioural finance theory posits that some of the key assumptions related to human behaviour do not hold in the real world—namely investor rationality and risk aversion. Empirical evidence suggests that markets are reasonably efficient, but not perfectly so. In particular, the evidence suggests that markets are weak form efficient, are reasonably semi-strong form efficient, but are not strong form efficient. We discuss several important implications that arise from these conclusions, both for investors and for corporate decision-makers.

SUMMARY OF LEARNING OBJECTIVES

10.1 Explain the importance of the concept of market efficiency.

For shareholder value maximization to mean anything, there has to be a connection between the decisions made by managers and the level of share prices. In this way, share prices are like a score sheet used to evaluate management. The closer the link between the actions of managers and this score sheet, the more informationally efficient the capital market.

10.2 Explain what is meant by "market efficiency."

There are three components to market efficiency. The first is operational efficiency—whether transaction costs are low. The second is allocation efficiency—whether there are enough securities to efficiently allocate risk. The third is information efficiency, a market condition in which important information is reflected in share prices.

10.3 Differentiate among the different levels of efficiency.

(1) Weak form efficient market hypothesis (EMH) is the theory that security prices fully reflect all market data, which refers to all past price and volume trading information. (2) Semi-strong form EMH is the theory that all publicly known and available information, including market data, is reflected in security prices. (3) Strong form EMH is the theory that stock prices fully reflect all information, which includes both public and private information.

10.4 Discuss the general consensus based on empirical evidence of market efficiency, as well as the existence of some well-known anomalies.

Weak form efficiency is very well supported, and it is reasonable to conclude that markets are weak form efficient, although a few anomalies do exist. Semi-strong form efficiency is well supported; however, more contradictory evidence exists for this version of the EMH than for the weak form. Strong form efficiency is not very well supported

by the evidence, and it is reasonable to conclude that markets are not strong form efficient in the strictest sense.

10.5 Differentiate between behavioural finance and the traditional view of finance.

Behavioural finance is a field of financial thought which suggests that investor behaviour is not always rational but is influenced by psychological biases that cause investors to make systematic errors in judgement. The traditional view of finance suggests that investors consider all available information; act rationally and do not make systematic errors, either in processing information or in implementing investment decisions; and adhere to the basic tenets of modern portfolio theory, which implies they are risk averse, they diversify, and they consider risk in the context of a well-diversified portfolio.

10.6 Explain the implications of market efficiency.

(1) Technical analysis, which involves examining trading data for patterns, is not likely to be rewarded by substantial abnormal returns, because markets appear to be weak form efficient. (2) Fundamental analysis based on various forms of publicly available information is also likely to be unsuccessful at generating abnormal profits, although some opportunities appear to be available. To benefit from such data, the analysis must be of superior and consistent quality. (3) "Active" trading strategies are unlikely to outperform "passive" portfolio management strategies on a consistent basis. Passive strategies involve buy-and-hold tactics and the purchase of products such as index mutual funds or exchange-traded funds (ETFs) that replicate the performance of a market index. (4) Whether investors adopt a passive or active strategy, it is critical that they focus on the basics of good investing by defining their objectives in terms of expected return and acceptable risk levels, and by maintaining an adequately diversified portfolio. When markets are relatively efficient, these factors may do more to promote success than the analysis of individual security prices.

KEY TERMS

QUESTIONS AND PRACTICE PROBLEMS

Multiple Choice Questions

1. Which of the following statements about an efficient market is *false*?
   a. It reflects all relevant and available information.
   b. Prices will reflect such information as firm financial strength and earnings.
   c. It reacts to new information quickly and correctly.
   d. Price changes follow predictable patterns through time.

2. Which of the following is *not* a form of the efficient market hypothesis (EMH)?
   a. semi-strong
   b. strong
   c. semi-weak
   d. weak

3. The main difference between the three forms of market efficiency is that:
   a. the definition of excess return differs
   b. the definition of prices differs
   c. the definition of information differs
   d. There is no difference between the three forms

4. Which of the following is useful in attempting to identify mispriced securities if the semi-strong form of EMH is assumed?
   a. past stock price changes
   b. earnings expectations
   c. past and current published trading volumes
   d. relevant insider information

5. Which of the following statements is *true*?
   a. The weak form of the EMH encompasses the semi-strong form.
   b. The strong form of the EMH encompasses the semi-strong form.
   c. The semi-strong form of the EMH encompasses the strong form.
   d. The strong form of the EMH does not encompass the weak form.

6. If a test is statistically significant,
   a. it must be economically significant as well

   b. it cannot be economically significant at all
   c. it could be economically significant if the test is still significant after accounting for risk, trading costs, and so on
   d. None of the above

7. Which of the following conclusions is *false*?
    a. Evidence strongly supports the weak form of EMH.
    b. Evidence strongly supports the semi-strong form of EMH, with more contradictory evidence than for the weak form.
    c. Evidence strongly supports the strong form of EMH.
    d. Evidence does not support the strong form of EMH.

8. In an efficient market:
    a. security prices react quickly to new information
    b. security analysts will not enable investors to realize superior returns consistently
    c. one cannot make money
    d. a and b

9. Proponents of the efficient market hypothesis think technical analysts:
    a. should focus on relative strength
    b. should focus on resistance levels
    c. should focus on support levels
    d. are wasting their time

10. According to proponents of the efficient market hypothesis, the best strategy for a small investor with a portfolio worth $25,000 is probably to:
    a. perform fundamental analysis
    b. invest in individual stocks
    c. invest in derivative securities
    d. invest in mutual funds

11. Although markets may not be perfectly efficient, they are relatively efficient. An implication of this statement is:
    a. Fundamental analysis based on publicly available information is likely to successfully generate abnormal profits.
    b. Technical analysis is not likely to be rewarded by substantial abnormal returns.
    c. As it relates to fundamental analysis, average or below average analysis of publicly available information will likely be fruitful.
    d. As it relates to technical analysis and fundamental analysis, active trading strategies are likely to outperform passive portfolio management strategies.

12. Which of the following statements is *false*?
    a. Stock returns tend to produce statistically higher returns in January than in the other 11 months of the year.
    b. Average Monday returns tend to be negative, while average returns for the other four trading days tend to be positive.
    c. Growth stocks have consistently outperformed value stocks.
    d. Small cap stocks tend to outperform large cap stocks.

13. Which of the following characteristics is *not* typical of a value stock?
    a. below average P/E ratio
    b. below average M/B ratio
    c. above average dividend yield
    d. None of the above

14. If an investor observes a stock that experienced a price increase before an announcement of new information, as shown in the figure below, what can he or she conclude?
    a. The market is semi-strong form efficient.
    b. The market is strong form efficient.
    c. The market is not weak form efficient.
    d. The market is not efficient in any form.

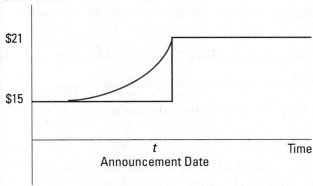

15. When investors dislike risk but are willing to undertake risk if they are compensated in the form of higher returns, this is an example of:
    a. loss aversion
    b. anchoring
    c. mental accounting
    d. risk aversion

16. Researchers have found that most of the small firm effect occurs:
    a. during the spring months
    b. during the summer months
    c. in January
    d. randomly

Practice Problems

17. Identify the types of inefficiency (allocational, operational, or informational) described below:
    a. The Lower Red River stock market is characterized by very high transaction costs and, due to frequent flooding, transaction orders are often lost.
    b. In the markets of the country of Upper Lachine, firms can only issue very long-term debt (35-year maturity or more) and stock.
    c. The Middle Bow River Market is a small stock market where trading can only occur on Thursdays. Newspapers are published every day.

18. Explain whether each of the following is an example of informational efficiency.
    a. Every time my broker tells me to buy, the stock price subsequently goes down. Every time my broker tells me to sell, the stock price subsequently goes up.
    b. Three months after receiving the financial statements of the Canada Bank, I finally look at them and decide to trade. I rarely make money.
    c. I use a simple trading rule: if the stock has risen for the past three days—sell; if the stock has fallen for the past three days—buy. I usually make money.
    d. You have been studying the trading behaviour of the CEO of the Parchyk Company and find that for the past 10 years, 90 percent of the time the stock rises after the CEO buys and 98 percent of the time the stock falls after the CEO sells stock.

e. I carefully examine the financial statements of the firm, the industry prospects, and general economic conditions. Because of my skill, I am able to complete this analysis within five minutes of the financial statement disclosure. I usually make money.

19. Parker Investments Inc. has just completed an investigation of strong form efficiency in the Canadian stock market and has concluded that its evidence is statistically significant but not economically significant. Explain to your client how this is possible.

20. Which type of analyst, buy side or sell side, is more likely to "sell" their recommendation to the public?

21. Describe two common tests for the weak form and for the semi-strong form of the EMH.

22. State the main assumptions required for the existence of efficient markets.

23. What is the momentum effect? What form of the EMH does it contradict?

24. Summarize the empirical conclusions regarding the three forms of the EMH.

25. Elvira, the CEO of AT Pharmaceutical Ltd., has hired Dome Financial Inc. to advise her on issuing new stock. Her company will need to issue more stock soon to finance the development of a new product— a Hair Growth formula. Elvira has noticed that, on average, the stock price of pharmaceutical companies is higher in the spring than the rest of the year. She would like to issue the Hair Growth stock in the spring to obtain the highest price possible. Given your understanding of the efficiency of the Canadian market, what advice do you have for Elvira regarding the timing of the new stock issue?

26. You are on the board of directors of Marlin Company. The stock price of Marlin has suddenly increased by 20 percent and the CEO has come to the board asking for a substantial pay increase. The CEO argues that the company's prospects have dramatically improved—after all, why else would the stock price increase? Do you feel that the CEO should receive a large pay increase? Explain.

27. On Monday, the stock of the Wicker Company was trading at $25. The CEO was satisfied with this price as it reflected the prospects of the firm (future dividend growth and required rate of return). The firm's scientists worked all Monday night to complete a top secret project, which will dramatically improve the quality of Wicker's products and result in a huge increase in sales for the next 10 years. On Tuesday evening, you have dinner with the CEO (he is a client of yours) who is complaining that the "markets cannot be efficient" because the stock price of WC has not changed despite this dramatic change in the firm's prospects. Provide the CEO with two different explanations about why there was no reaction on Tuesday.

28. State four important implications of the EMH for investors and two implications for corporate officers.

29. The manager of Quest Adventures Ltd. is puzzled. Analysts are saying that the future prospects for his company are poor because the stock price has dropped 5 percent.
    a. Explain to the manager the relationship between stock prices and market expectations.
    b. Would you be as concerned about the company's future prospects if the company had a beta of 1.5 and the market has fallen 4 percent?

30. On the morning of March 15, Decker Marketing Inc. announced that it will pay its first dividend of $5 this year. The ex-dividend date will be July 3.
    a. If the announcement is a complete surprise to the market, what do you expect will happen to the stock price on March 15?
    b. If the announcement has been forecasted by the financial analysts, what do you expect to happen to the stock price on March 15?

c. What do you expect to happen to the price of Decker Marketing Inc. on July 3?

31. On Monday evening, Codina Model Steam Engine Company announced that it would be restating its financial statements for the past five years, and its CFO was arrested for fraud. Interpret the following Tuesday stock reactions:
   a. stock price drops
   b. stock price does not change
   c. stock price increases

32. Assume that the information system is so advanced that the market, as confirmed by numerous unbiased studies, is efficient. Investment firms therefore decide to retire all portfolio managers and financial analysts and let random choice govern the security selection process. What impact will this action have on market efficiency?

33. A news story about United Airline's decision to seek protection from creditors was originally published December 10, 2002 by the *Chicago Tribune*. The story was recirculated by a Florida news service in 2008. Following the recirculated story there was a steep sell-off in United's shares. When the story hit Bloomberg News, United's stock fell from about $12 per share to $3 per share. Once the truth was out, the stock got back to a slightly lower $10.
   a. Use your knowledge of behavioural biases among investors to explain the market reaction to the incorrect news.
   b. Why didn't the share price immediately return to $12 after the truth was known?
   c. Does this market behaviour contradict the efficient market hypothesis?

34. Would you expect investors to be more overconfident during a boom or a recession? Why?

35. How would you expect increasing access to the Internet to affect investor behaviour?

Part 5

DERIVATIVE SECURITIES

In Part 4, we discussed how to value stocks and bonds and build portfolios. These are all basic securities issued by corporations. In this section, we consider derivative securities—that is, securities that are derived from these basic underlying securities. This has been one of the most dynamic areas of finance over the past 20 years, with a mushrooming derivatives market and the Nobel Prize–winning option pricing model developed by Fischer Black and Myron Scholes.

11 | Forwards, Futures, and Swaps

LEARNING OBJECTIVES

11.1 Describe forward contracts and identify the associated payoffs with long and short positions in forward contracts.

11.2 Explain how simple forward contracts are priced.

11.3 Describe futures contracts and explain why futures contracts can be viewed as the public market version of forward contracts.

11.4 Describe the mechanics of simple swap structures, including interest rate swaps and currency swaps.

11.5 Explain how the credit default swap market contributed to the financial crisis.

11.6 Explain how the general principles of forward contracts can be applied to fixed income securities.

Many corporations rely on derivative instruments, including forwards, futures, and swaps, to manage risk. The use of these instruments is popular with governments as well. The Canadian federal government has been using interest rate and currency swaps since 1985 to manage its liabilities; past and future savings are estimated to be approximately $500 million. The government has a swap management policy, which governs the "use, procurement, and execution of swaps." Interest rate swaps, for example, are used to exchange fixed rates for floating rates, and currency swaps are used to manage foreign exchange risk. Cross-currency swaps, in which principal and interest payments in a foreign currency are exchanged for the term of the swap, are the third type of swap permitted for use by the government.

Source: Bank of Canada website at www.bankofcanada.ca and Department of Finance Canada website at www.fin.gc.ca.

CHAPTER 11 **PREVIEW**

underlying assets the securities on which derivative contracts are based

Suppose your teacher returned an English essay you had written, with the comment, "This is derivative." You wouldn't be happy. Derivative means "not original," and the teacher's comment means your essay contained nothing new; it was derived from other things. So it is with derivative securities: they are not original because their behaviour is derived from other **underlying assets**, the securities on which derivative contracts are based. There are two basic types of derivative securities: (1) forwards, futures, and swaps, which are discussed in this chapter, and (2) options, which are discussed in Chapter 12.

11.1 FORWARD CONTRACTS

Basic Characteristics of Forward Contracts

Learning Objective 11.1
Describe forward contracts and identify the associated payoffs with long and short positions in forward contracts.

forward contract a price that is established today for future delivery

spot contract a price that is established today for immediate delivery

Appendix 6A introduced forward contracts in the discussion on interest rate parity (IRP). At that time, the forward rate was introduced as a forward foreign exchange rate. In fact, a **forward contract** is a price that is established today for future delivery, in contrast to a **spot contract**, which is a price that is established today for immediate delivery. The definition of immediate delivery depends on the nature of the underlying contract. For foreign exchange contracts, it is generally defined as the next day when exchanging the Canadian dollar for the U.S. dollar, and two days for many other less actively traded currencies. In contrast, forward delivery can be specified for almost any future date. Table 11-1 shows the foreign exchange rates provided by Thomson Reuters to the *Financial Post* for March 15, 2012.

TABLE 11-1 Foreign Exchange Rates (Foreign currency per Canadian dollar)

	US($)	GB(£)	JAP(¥)	Euro(€)
Spot	1.0067	0.6427	84.29	0.773
1 month	1.0063	0.6424	84.21	0.772
3 month	1.0058	0.6419	84.05	0.771
6 month	1.0028	0.6410	83.77	0.769
1 year	0.9984	0.6392	83.89	0.764
3 year	0.9816	0.6327	79.27	0.748
5 year	0.9746	0.6282	74.73	0.738

Source: Data from Thomson Reuters, *Financial Post*, March 15, 2012.

In each case, these prices reflect the amount of the foreign currency that one Canadian dollar would buy. The U.S. dollar rate of 1.0067, for example, means that if you exchanged one Canadian dollar on March 14, 2012, you could get 1.0067 U.S. dollars. The rates are mid-day rates for very large "wholesale" transactions between major banks, so these are not the rates that ordinary investors or retail clients of the bank would pay. At this point, the Canadian dollar (referred to as CDN by traders) was at a slight premium to the U.S. dollar. We can take the reciprocal of this rate, known as the "inverse" rate, to get the value of the Canadian dollar in terms of the U.S. dollar, which was 0.9933. Also note from the table that there is an extensive set of quotes for forward rates for the four major currencies out to five years. U.S.-dollar transactions out this long are routine since so much of Canada's trade is with U.S. customers or denominated in U.S. dollars. However, such long transactions are not as routine for the other currencies, so while it is possible to "do a forward" in five-year Japanese yen, this would require a call to one of the major banks to get an exact quote.

What do these quotes mean? In Chapter 5, we discussed the time value of money and emphasized that, because of the opportunity cost of money, a dollar in the future is not worth a dollar today; we can always invest a dollar today to get *more* than a dollar in the future. The time value of money is the reason we calculated present values. So it is with foreign currency; because forward rates are the price today for future delivery, they reflect the fact that foreign currency is not worth the same amount when it is received at different points in time.[1] For example, according to Table 11-1, if you bought US$1 million on March 15, 2012 (spot), the cost to a large wholesale investor would have been about C$993,200. However, if the investor wanted to fix a price on March 15 for US$1 million to be bought in five years' time, the investor would have had to pay about C$1.02606 million (using the reciprocal of 0.9746), indicating that U.S. dollars are worth more in the future than they are now relative to CDN.

This brings up an important feature associated with forward foreign exchange contracts: they are bank instruments. Buying or selling a forward contract requires that a customer have a banking relationship. It is not possible for ordinary individuals to access the forward foreign exchange market, as forward contracts are not traded in any open market. Instead, forwards are over-the-counter (OTC) markets. This means that they are traded OTC with a principal— in this case, the bank—in exactly the same way that we buy most things. We will return to this topic later, because it has important implications for the futures markets. Also note that although the quotes in the newspaper are for discrete units of time—such as one month, two months, and so on—in practice, forwards can be tailored to any specific date in the future and for any amount of money. This makes them incredibly flexible.

Using Forward Contracts

What can investors do with forwards? To make the arithmetic simple, suppose the Canadian dollar is trading at par with the U.S. dollar as it has been for much of 2012—that is, the exchange rate is C$1 for US$1. To make it even simpler, suppose that both the spot and the one-year forward rates are both at 1.0. In this case, an investor decides to **speculate** on the value of the U.S. dollar in the future and is able to buy US$1 million forward. This obligates the investor to pay C$1 million and receive US$1 million in one year. Because the investor is speculating, he or she does not have any underlying U.S. dollars. This is called a **naked position**—that is, the investor is exposed to changes in the value of the underlying asset, which in this case is the U.S. dollar. Because the investor has agreed to buy U.S. dollars and sell Canadian dollars forward, he or she is **long** U.S. dollars and **short** Canadian dollars. In this case, "long" just means that an investor *owns* something and "short" means that an investor *owes* something, so by selling Canadian dollars forward for U.S. dollars, the investor is long U.S. dollars and short Canadian dollars. The payoff possibilities that arise from this position based on various exchange rates are depicted in Figure 11-1, where the horizontal axis is the value of the C$ in terms of the US$—that is, the inverse quote.

speculate make an educated guess about the future value of something in hopes of profiting from it

naked position a position that leaves the investor exposed to changes in the value of the underlying asset

long the investor owns something

short the investor owes something

---

[1] They are not present values because the Canadian dollars are received in the future.

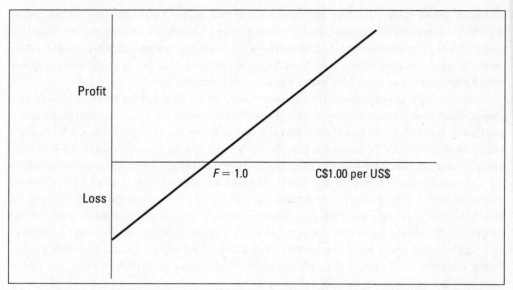

FIGURE 11-1 *Long Position in U.S. Dollars*

Suppose that, in one year, the spot exchange rate for the U.S. dollar is either C$1.20 (i.e., the Canadian dollar depreciates or loses value) or C$0.80 (i.e., the Canadian dollar appreciates or increases in value). Of course, if the Canadian dollar appreciates in value, then the U.S. dollar depreciates (at least on a relative basis), and vice versa, because the exchange rate is just the ratio of Canadian dollars to U.S. dollars. If the Canadian dollar goes to 1.2, then each U.S. dollar is now worth C$1.20, so the U.S. dollar has appreciated in value and the Canadian dollar has depreciated. In this case, the investor fulfills the forward foreign exchange contract and exchanges C$1 million for US$1 million, and then immediately sells the U.S. dollars in the spot market to get C$1.2 million. In this case, the investor earns a profit of $200,000. If the opposite happens and the Canadian dollar appreciates to 0.8, the investor still has to fulfill the forward contract and sell C$1 million to get US$1 million. However, now when the investor sells the U.S. dollars in the spot market, they can be exchanged for only C$0.8 million and he or she incurs a $200,000 loss.

If we denote the future spot price of Canadian for U.S. dollars as S_T, the forward price of Canadian for U.S. dollars as F, and the number of contracts entered into as n, the profit (loss) from a long position in a forward contract can be determined by using Equation 11-1:

[11-1]   Profit (loss) from long position $= (S_T - F) \times n$

The important point about a forward contract is that the investor *has* to fulfill the contract regardless of what happens to the value of the underlying asset. As a result, a forward contract has the possibility of either gains *or* losses, and the payoff is "linear" in the value of the underlying asset (that is, the payoff goes up "one for one" with increases in S_T and goes down "one for one" with decreases in S_T).[2] Figure 11-1 shows the possible payoff from the forward contract as a 45-degree line going through the forward rate. If the spot exchange rate in the future exceeds the forward rate by $0.01, then the speculator earns $0.01 profit for every Canadian dollar sold forward for U.S. dollars, and vice versa. The reason for this payoff is that the forward contract is a legal contract between the speculator and the bank to exchange funds in the future at a price fixed today. However, think about the cost of the contract. The forward rate is the price for future delivery, but whereas the bank makes money by buying and selling forward contracts at slightly different prices,[3] there is no immediate cash outlay for the contract. It is a contract stipulating the terms for future delivery.

---

[2] This is the distinction between the derivatives discussed in this chapter, which are linear, and those discussed in Chapter 12 (i.e., options), which are non-linear.

[3] The bank sells at the "ask" rate and buys at the "bid" rate. Its profit is the spread between these two rates, which differs according to the maturity of the contract and the size—that is, who the bank is dealing with.

This raises an interesting problem as far as the bank is concerned. If the Canadian dollar depreciates to 1.2, the investor will obviously execute the forward contract, buy the more valuable U.S. dollar, and make a profit of $200,000. However, if the Canadian dollar appreciates to 0.8, there is **credit risk** involved for the bank, as the investor suffers a loss of $200,000 and may decide to renege on the contract. This credit risk is also called **counterparty risk**, as it is the risk that the bank's counterparty to the transaction will not fulfill the contract. The bank can reduce this risk by dealing only with companies with which it already has a banking relationship and a line of credit. In this way, banks can control the risk that the counterparty imposes on them. This is an important issue that we will return to later in the chapter because it figures prominently in the financial crisis of 2008–9.

credit (counterparty) risk the risk that a borrower will not fulfill a contract or make a required payment

Finally, banks will only sell forward contracts for legitimate business purposes, and then only up to a company's approved credit limit. Banks do not want to be seen selling forward contracts for speculative purposes because this often runs counter to the objectives of the central bank, which may involve targeting a specific exchange rate. This is particularly true in countries where the bank regulator is that same central bank.

Most corporations and financial institutions become involved in forward markets for **hedging** purposes, rather than for speculation. In fact, most businesses and financial institutions are prohibited from engaging in speculation. Hedgers enter into derivative contracts to protect a short or long position in the underlying asset, as described below.

hedging reducing the risk of adverse price movement by taking an offsetting position in a derivative to eliminate exposure to an underlying price

Suppose, in the previous example, that a Canadian corporation is owed US$1 million by a U.S. company and expects to receive this in one year. In this case, the Canadian corporation has a naked position in U.S. dollars or, more formally, it has a U.S. dollar foreign exchange **exposure**, because it is long in the underlying asset (i.e., U.S. dollars). However, even though this position arises because of a commercial contract, the payoff is identical to the speculative purchase of the U.S. dollar forward that we just discussed. If the Canadian dollar depreciates to C$1.20, then the Canadian company will receive C$1.2 million when it exchanges the proceeds at the future spot rate. Alternatively, if the Canadian dollar appreciates to C$0.80, the Canadian company will receive only C$0.80 million. The only difference between the two payoffs is that one arises as the result of normal business operations and the other as the result of a speculative transaction.

exposure the extent to which value is affected by an external event, such as a change in exchange rate

This scenario of long U.S. dollar exposure is a standard problem facing Canadian companies that compete in the United States and invoice in U.S. dollars. In this case, if a Canadian company exports to the United States and waits for its U.S. customer to pay, it has long U.S. dollar exposure. Similarly, short U.S. dollar exposure arises when a Canadian company imports goods from the United States and then has to pay the U.S. dollar invoice at some future time, such as in 90 days. Because almost 90 percent of Canada's foreign trade is either with U.S. companies or denominated in U.S. dollars, these long and short U.S. dollar exposures are very common. A Canadian exporting company could avoid this problem by insisting that the U.S. company remit Canadian rather than U.S. dollars, but this normally isn't possible. Even if it were possible, it simply transfers the problem to the U.S. company. If a company cannot avoid this long U.S. dollar exposure, what can it do?

Most companies in this situation are not willing to speculate, because they are in business to manufacture and sell things, not to speculate on future exchange rates. In this regard, however, note that doing nothing and exchanging the U.S. dollars when they are received is equivalent to engaging in currency speculation. Some large Canadian companies with extensive U.S. dollar business do find that it makes sense to hold U.S. dollar bank accounts and actively manage their U.S. dollar exposure, but most simply want to remove this exposure. Removing a naked position is called **covering** (or hedging). In fact, the dictionary definition of hedging describes it as betting on both sides in order to remove risk. From our previous discussion of forward markets, we know that the opposite of a firm's long position in U.S. dollars is a short position in U.S. dollar forward contracts, so the company needs to sell

covering removing a naked position

U.S. dollars forward for Canadian dollars. Before we discuss the "hedged" position, we should first consider the payoff diagram for a naked sale of U.S. dollars forward, which is depicted in Figure 11-2.

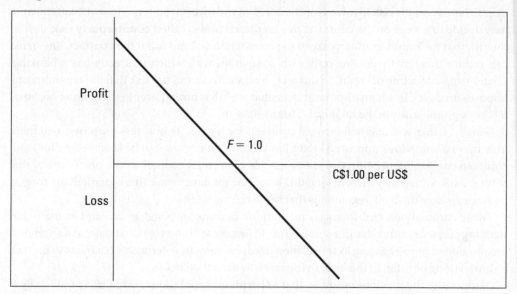

FIGURE 11-2 *Short Position in U.S. Dollars*

Notice that the payoff for the naked short position is the mirror image (or complete opposite) of the naked long position. If US$1 million is sold forward for C$1 million, and the Canadian dollar depreciates to C$1.20, then the forward contract loses money. In this case, the forward contract requires that US$1 million be exchanged for C$1 million. However, to get the US$1 million now requires C$1.2 million in the spot market, causing a C$200,000 loss. Alternatively, if the Canadian dollar appreciates to C$0.80, then buying US$1 million to fulfill the forward contract requires only C$800,000, meaning a C$200,000 profit. So the gains and losses from the naked short position are the exact opposite of a naked long position and can be determined by using Equation 11-2:

[11-2] $$\text{Profit (loss) from short position} = (F - S_T) \times n$$

Now consider the company with a long U.S. dollar exposure of US$1 million that buys a forward contract to sell U.S. dollars forward for Canadian dollars, thereby creating a US$1-million short position. Their combined position is simply the sum of the two previous diagrams, shown in Figure 11-3.

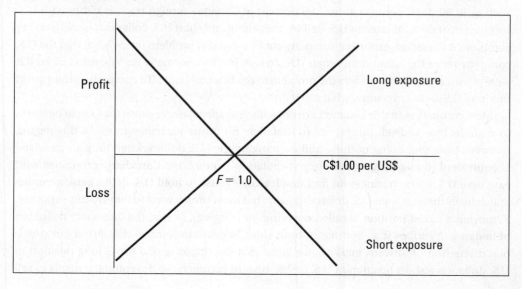

FIGURE 11-3 *Long and Short Forward Positions*

If the Canadian dollar depreciates to C$1.20, the company earns a profit of $200,000 on its underlying U.S. dollar exposure but then loses $200,000 on the forward sale of U.S. dollars. Similarly, if the Canadian dollar appreciates to C$0.80, it loses $200,000 on its underlying U.S. dollar exposure but gains $200,000 on its forward sale of US dollars. Regardless of what happens to the value of the exchange rate, it is locked in (or covered or hedged) against any future fluctuations in the exchange rate, so the company is no longer exposed to exchange rate changes.

We conclude this section with some examples illustrating the profits that materialize from assuming various positions in forward contracts.

EXAMPLE 11-1 Profits from a Long Position

Suppose the spot exchange rate is C$1.50 per €1, while the six-month forward rate is C$1.52 per euro. What will be the profit for an investor who assumes a €100,000 long position in the forward contract if the spot rate in six months equals the following amounts?

a. C$1.50 per euro

b. C$1.55 per euro

Solution

a. Profit (loss) long position = $(S_T - F) \times n = (1.50 - 1.52) \times$ C$100,000 = −$2,000 (loss)

b. Profit (loss) long position = $(S_T - F) \times n = (1.55 - 1.52) \times$ C$100,000 = $3,000 profit

EXAMPLE 11-2 Profits from a Short Position

Assume another investor takes a €100,000 short position in the six-month euro forward contract discussed in Example 11-1. Determine the investor's profit (loss) if the spot rate in six months equals the following amounts:

a. C$1.50 per euro

b. C$1.55 per euro

Solution

a. Profit (loss) short position = $(F - S_T) \times n = (1.52 - 1.50) \times$ C$100,000 = $2,000 profit

b. Profit (loss) long position = $(F - S_T) \times n = (1.52 - 1.55) \times$ C$100,000 = −$3,000 (loss)

EXAMPLE 11-3 How to Hedge a Short Position in the Underlying Asset

Assume the spot rates and forward rates from Example 11-1. Suppose a firm has to pay a foreign supplier €100,000 in six months and decides to eliminate its foreign exchange exposure by entering into a six-month forward contract.

a. Should it enter into a short or a long forward position? For how much?

b. Assuming it enters into the appropriate forward position, determine the cost in Canadian dollars for the following future spot rates:
    i. C$1.50 per euro
    ii. C$1.55 per euro

Solution

a. Because the firm has a short position in the underlying asset (i.e., euros), it should take a long position in the forward contract. To hedge itself for the full amount of its obligation, it needs to enter into a €100,000 forward contract.

continued

EXAMPLE 11-3   How to Hedge a Short Position in the Underlying Asset *continued*

a.   i. The cost in Canadian dollars = €100,000 × C$1.52 per euro = C$152,000
      ii. The cost in Canadian dollars = €100,000 × C$1.52 per euro = C$152,000

Notice that the cost is the same regardless of what the six-month spot rate is— thus, the position is hedged.

EXAMPLE 11-4   How to Hedge a Long Position in the Underlying Asset

Assume the spot rates and forward rates from Example 11-1. Suppose a firm expects to receive €100,000 in six months from a foreign customer and decides to eliminate its foreign exchange exposure by entering into a six-month forward contract.

a.   Should it enter into a short or a long forward position? For how much?

b.   Assuming it enters into the appropriate forward position, determine the proceeds in Canadian dollars for the following future spot rates:
      i. C$1.50 per euro
      ii. C$1.55 per euro

Solution

a.   Because the firm has a long position in the underlying asset (i.e., euros), it should take a short position in the forward contract. To hedge itself for the full amount, it needs to enter into a €100,000 forward contract.

b.   i. The proceeds in Canadian dollars = €100,000 × C$1.52 per euro = C$152,000
      ii. The proceeds in Canadian dollars = €100,000 × C$1.52 per euro = C$152,000

Notice that the proceeds are the same regardless of what the six-month spot rate is—thus, the position is hedged.

Interest Rate Parity (IRP) Revisited

The simple examples above illustrate why the forward foreign exchange market is a bank market. The bank is selling forward contracts to its customers for commercial purposes to allow them to manage their foreign exchange exposure. The banks are not buying and selling foreign exchange for speculative purposes.[4] If a bank finds that it has sold too many U.S. dollar forward contracts to its customers, so that the bank itself is now exposed, it can either enter the inter-bank market to offset its exposure by trading with other banks or synthetically create forward foreign exchange contracts. A bank can synthetically create a forward contract through the interest rate parity (IRP) condition that was discussed in Appendix 6A.

[11-3]
$$\frac{F}{S} = \frac{(1 + k_{domestic})}{(1 + k_{foreign})}$$

Recall that the IRP condition is where the exchange rates are expressed as Canadian dollars per foreign currency. Equation 11-3 means that the ratio of the forward to the spot rate must equal the ratio of one plus the interest rate in both markets. If we rearrange this condition, it tells us what determines the forward rate:

[11-4]
$$F = S \times \frac{(1 + k_{domestic})}{(1 + k_{foreign})}$$

---

[4] Many banks have suffered huge losses when rogue traders incur losses on forward foreign exchange contracts and then hide these trades and take bigger positions in the hope of covering their losses, only to end up with even bigger losses. Allied Irish Bank lost US$691 million as a result of John Rusnak's rogue trading in the Japanese yen at its Baltimore (U.S.) office in 2003. Rusnak ended up with a 7½-year prison sentence for bank fraud.

In other words, the forward rate is the ratio of one plus the interest rate in both markets times the spot rate. The important point is that all the Canadian banks deal in the spot market and can also borrow and lend in the major currencies. Thus, they can create a forward contract.

EXAMPLE 11-5   Estimating Forward Rates

Assume the one-year euro interest rate is presently 3.5 percent, and the one-year Canadian interest rate is 5 percent. Assume today's spot rate is C$1.50 for €1. Find the one-year forward exchange rate.

Solution

Notice that the interest rate differential for the specified one-year term is 1.5 percent, which implies that the forward exchange rate should be approximately 1.5 percent higher (in Canadian dollar terms) than the spot rate to ensure IRP holds.

To be more precise, we can use Equation 11-4 to solve for the forward rate:

$$F = S \times \frac{(1 + k_{domestic})}{(1 + k_{foreign})} = \$1.50 \times \frac{(1.05)}{(1.035)} = \$1.522$$

Suppose that a bank has sold too many U.S. dollar forward contracts and wants to create forward foreign exchange contracts to offset its own exposure. It can do so by first borrowing Canadian dollars for one year and then exchanging Canadian dollars for U.S. dollars at the spot rate. Finally, the bank would invest the U.S. dollar proceeds for one year at the U.S. interest rate. The result is that it knows exactly how many U.S. dollars it will own at the end of the year, because this is the amount invested times one plus the U.S. interest rate. It also knows exactly how many Canadian dollars it will owe, because this is the amount borrowed times one plus its borrowing cost. In effect, by borrowing Canadian dollars, converting them to U.S. dollars, and investing in the United States, the bank has synthetically sold Canadian dollars forward for U.S. dollars. This process generates a payoff identical to a straightforward sale of Canadian dollars for U.S. dollars, which is why interest rate parity tells us that the rates have to be the same. Otherwise, limitless profits could be made without assuming any risk—and the Canadian banks are not known for passing up the opportunity to make limitless profits!

For a bank with large-scale international operations, like all the major Canadian banks, these operations are routine. To synthetically create this forward contract, a Canadian bank would borrow in the Canadian money market by issuing what are termed "bankers' acceptances" (BAs). These are short-term notes that are fully guaranteed or "accepted" by the bank. The U.S. dollars would then be lent at what is referred to as the **London inter-bank offered rate (LIBOR)**. This is the key interest rate for Canadian banks when they are borrowing and lending U.S. dollars because it is a "free market" rate and not under direct government control. Further, it can be accessed by the banks to effect very large transactions.

London inter-bank offered rate (LIBOR) the key interest rate for Canadian banks when borrowing and lending U.S. dollars; a "free market" rate that is not under direct government control

Pricing Forward Contracts

The interest rate parity condition is a special case for pricing forward contracts. The general condition is that investors can always create a forward position in a storable **commodity** by buying it spot and holding it for future delivery. It has to be storable because if its condition deteriorates, it will not be acceptable in fulfilling the contract. Similarly, a commodity is something like a precious metal, whose value is immediately recognizable and not subject to dispute. This is essentially what the bank did above to create a forward contract; it simply purchased U.S. dollars and then "stored" them in a one-year investment. The only difference was that it first borrowed the Canadian dollars and then exchanged them for U.S. dollars However, suppose the storable commodity is a base metal that the investor has sold forward for $100. How is the forward synthetically created?

Learning Objective 11.2
Explain how simple forward contracts are priced.

commodity something traded based solely on price, because it is undifferentiated and can be traded without requiring physical examination

contango when the forward price exceeds the spot price

If the metal is currently selling for $80, the metal is regarded as having a forward **contango** of $20 or 25 percent. In this case, the investor borrows $80 and buys the metal spot. The investor then has to store it for a year, but because it is a storable commodity, at the end of the year the investor has the metal needed to meet the forward sale. The only question is the cost involved. First are the **storage costs**, which we assume are $5 for one year. Second are the financing costs, and we will assume the interest cost is 10 percent. With these assumptions, the investor can generate the metal for the forward sale at a future cost of $93. This is the principal and interest payment of $88 ($80 in principal and $8 interest) plus the storage cost of $5. If these were the actual prices and costs, an arbitrageur could generate gains of $7 simply by selling the metal forward for $100 and then buying it spot and storing it for a total cost of $93.

storage costs the price charged for holding a commodity for future delivery

The above example is a simplified version of actual commodity arbitrage, because it assumes that there is no income or **convenience yield** associated with holding the asset.[5] However, this sort of commodity arbitrage is common with storable commodities.

convenience yield the benefit or premium derived from holding the asset rather than holding a derivative

The London Metal Exchange (LME) is the premier metal exchange in the world and traces its origins back to the Royal Exchange in 1751. The LME trades eight non-ferrous metals, including aluminium, copper, lead, nickel, zinc, and tin, as well as steel, molybdenum, and cobalt. To encourage the efficiency of the metal market, the LME lists major warehouses in 37 locations that accept and store metals. These warehouses are located around the world in the major markets, so that consumers can, if need be, take delivery. For example, the following is the first entry in its warehouse list:

> C. Steinweg NV,
> Albert Dock,
> 131 Vrieskaai,
> 2030 Antwerp
> AH, CA, PB, ZS

This indicates the company, C. Steinweg NV, in Antwerp, Belgium, accepts metals at this warehouse in the Albert Dock. The metals accepted at this location are primary aluminium (AH), copper (CA), lead (PB), and zinc (ZS). This particular warehouse does not accept some of the other metals, but C. Steinweg has other warehouses in the Albert Dock that do. The LME has strict guidelines that companies must follow to have their warehouses accepted for the list, so that people taking delivery know the quality of the metal they are buying. However, in actual practice, less than 1 percent of contracts are actually closed out with physical delivery.

The existence of these warehouses and an organized exchange means that it is very easy to buy spot, store, and then sell forward these commodities. A profit of $7 on a $100 forward sale is more than enough to increase the spot demand for the metal and generate a forward sale. In the process, the spot price rises and the forward price falls until there are no risk-free profits. If, for example, the forward price drops to $95 and the spot price rises to $81.82, then the arbitrage opportunity disappears. The difference between the spot and forward rate is $13.18 or 16.11 percent, made up of the interest cost of 10 percent plus the storage cost of 6.11 percent (i.e., $5/$81.82). Together, the storage and financing costs are referred to as the **cost of carry**, because they represent the total cost of buying the commodity spot and then carrying it or effecting physical delivery when the forward contract expires—in a year, for our example.

cost of carry the total cost of buying a commodity spot and then carrying it or effecting physical delivery when the forward contract expires

---

[5] Note that when we were dealing with foreign currencies, the interest earned in the currency held could be viewed as the convenience yield.

The cost of carry links spot and forward rates so that, unless it changes, spot and forward rates will move in unison. For example, if the price of the metal increases in the spot market from $81.82 to $90, then the forward rate will also increase. This also means that a future disruption in supply that changes the forward rate will also change spot rates, even if there is no change in spot market conditions. All that is required is that the items are storable commodities. If they are not storable, they can't be bought and held to meet future delivery, and the forward and spot markets would be disconnected. The items also have to be commodities, which essentially means that they are undifferentiated and can be traded without requiring physical examination. It would be difficult to buy spot and hold to meet future delivery if there was uncertainty about what was being delivered against the forward contract.

Equation 11-5 expresses the relationship between cost of carry, and spot and forward prices:

$$F = (1 + c) \times S \qquad \text{[11-5]}$$

where c = the cost of carry, as a percentage of S, over the period in question.[6]

There was an enormous amount of arbitrage activity in the crude oil market toward the end of 2008. Huge tankers were being chartered simply so that arbitrageurs could buy oil spot and store it in the tankers to meet the delivery requirements on forward crude oil contracts. If that sounds strange, imagine it: tankers sitting idly offshore or moving aimlessly around for six months or even a year simply to deliver crude oil against a forward contract.

EXAMPLE 11-6   Estimating Prices for Commodity Forward Contracts

Find the forward price for a one-year forward contract for a metal that is selling for $90 spot, if storage costs are $5 for the year and financing costs are 10 percent per year.

Solution

$S = \$90$; $c = [(0.10 \times \$90) + \$5]/\$90 = 0.1556$

$F = (1 + 0.1556) \times \$90 = \$104$

In comparison with our discussion above, notice that when the spot price increases by $8.18 (i.e., from $81.82 to $90), the forward price increases $9 (i.e., from $95 to $104).

CONCEPT REVIEW QUESTIONS

1. Why do forward contracts involve a credit risk for banks?

2. When would a speculator assume a long position in a forward contract on an underlying asset? When would a speculator assume a short position?

3. When would a hedger assume a long position in a forward contract on an underlying asset? When would a hedger assume a short position?

4. What is the relationship among spot rates, forward rates, and the cost of carry?

---

[6] Notice that interest rate parity is a special example of forward pricing in which the cost of carry is the ratio of one plus the interest rates in both countries. In other words, for IRP $(1 + c) = \dfrac{(1 + k_{domestic})}{(1 + k_{foreign})}$ Appendix 11A expands on this discussion, showing the relationship between *forward interest rates* and *forward rate agreements (FRAs)*, which are interest-rate derivative products offered by banks.

11.2 FUTURES CONTRACTS

The Mechanics of Futures Contracts

Learning Objective 11.3
Describe futures contracts and explain why futures contracts can be viewed as the public market version of forward contracts.

futures contract a standardized exchange-traded contract in which the seller agrees to deliver a commodity to the buyer at some point in the future

clearing corporation a company that is responsible for reducing the credit risk of futures contracts and option contracts and for making sure that delivery takes place

margin a good faith deposit with a clearinghouse that is made by both the buyer and the seller to ensure they complete the transaction

initial margin a relatively small deposit made with the clearinghouse, usually between 2 and 10 percent of the value of the contract

maintenance or **variation margin** a minimum amount that must be maintained in a margin account

margin call a requirement to add money and increase an equity position to a minimum level

daily resettlement marking to market and adjusting investors' equity positions

settlement price the price used to settle futures contracts; usually the daily closing price

notional amount the dollar amount upon which a contract is valued

We started our discussion of derivatives with forward contracts for two reasons. First, they are primarily a bank instrument and represent one of the basic instruments used by corporations to manage their interest rate and foreign exchange rate exposures. The second reason is that they are centuries old. There are reports of forward-like contracts going back at least to the time of the Romans. Like the modern bank instruments of today, forwards have always been contracts between two parties and have largely been non-traded. However, over the past 30 years a new traded instrument that does much the same thing has rapidly developed. This is the **futures contract**. Remember that forward contracts involve credit risk, which is the reason investors need a line of credit with a bank before it will sell them. Once this requirement has been met, forwards are incredibly flexible in both the term and the amount of money involved. However, what makes them flexible for corporations also makes them difficult to trade. For something to be tradable, it has to be standardized so that people buying or selling it over the telephone or Internet know exactly what they are getting. The dramatic growth in the development of futures markets occurred because these problems have been solved. Let's look at how this happened.

First let's consider credit risk, which arises with the forward contract because the bank worries a borrower will renege on the forward contract if he or she suffers a loss. To solve this problem, all futures contracts are made with a futures exchange, not with an individual. Investor A might buy a futures contract and investor B might sell one, but instead of one contract between A and B, there are two contracts involving each individual and the exchange. The exchange then assigns responsibility for reducing the credit risk and making sure that delivery takes place to a **clearing corporation**. In Canada, the Canadian Derivatives Clearing Corporation (CDCC) of the Montreal Exchange handles these responsibilities for futures contracts, as well as option contracts, which we discuss in Chapter 12.

To ensure that people fulfill their contractual obligations, the CDCC enforces two types of **margins**: an **initial margin** and a **maintenance** or **variation margin**. The margin is essentially a good faith deposit made by both the buyer and the seller to ensure they complete the transaction. In effect, it is a performance bond. The margin is set by each clearinghouse based on the risk involved in the underlying asset: the riskier the asset, the higher the margin. The initial margin is relatively small and varies between 2 percent and 10 percent of the value of the contract, but it is required of both the buyer and the seller. Usually, the brokerage house managing the transaction for the customer imposes a higher margin, particularly for new or smaller clients, but it is not permitted to impose smaller margins. (Members of CDCC are allowed to post margin by depositing securities; CDCC has an extensive list of securities issued by the U.S. and Canadian governments, as well as Ontario and Quebec provincial bonds, that it accepts.)

All futures contracts are then marked to market each day, as the value of the contract changes. This means that all profits and losses on a futures contract are credited to investors' accounts every day to calculate their equity position in the underlying contract. If the equity position increases, these profits can be withdrawn; losses reduce investors' equity positions. Whenever an investor's equity position drops below the maintenance margin requirement (normally 75 percent of the initial margin), he or she will receive a **margin call** and will be forced to contribute more money to increase the equity position. If he or she fails to make this margin call, the position will automatically be closed out. This process of marking to market is called **daily resettlement** and is based on the contract's **settlement price**, which is normally, but not always, the daily closing price.

For example, suppose a futures contract is for 1,000 units of some underlying asset, and the starting unit price is $50; the contract value is $50,000. This is referred to as the **notional amount** of the contract, even though the investor does not have to come up with $50,000 to enter into it. The buyer and seller of this contract both need to deposit the initial margin requirement, which we assume is $2,000 (i.e., 4 percent of $50,000). Assume the maintenance margin is 75 percent of the initial margin (or $1,500). The buyer's commitment is to buy 1,000 units at $50, and the seller's commitment is to sell 1,000 units at $50. If the price closes up $0.25 on the first day, at $50.25, then the futures contract is now worth $250 to the buyer. This is because the buyer has contracted to buy the asset for $50,000, and it is now worth $50,250, so the equity increases from $2,000 to $2,250. Conversely, the seller's equity has declined from $2,000 to $1,750. Like all futures contracts, the gains and losses offset each other. In this case, the buyer has gained $250 at the expense of the seller, and the clearinghouse will transfer this $250 from the seller's account to the buyer's. The next day, the process starts all over again. If the buyer feels that, now that the price has gone up, he or she wants to cancel the contract, the buyer makes an **offsetting** sale, and the purchase is cancelled. The buyer can then withdraw the $2,250.[7] In this case, the buyer has a $250 profit on the margin deposit of $2,000.

offsetting cancelling a futures position by making an equivalent but opposite transaction

Suppose instead that both parties leave their contract outstanding, and the next day the price increases again, only this time it jumps to $51. Now the buyer's equity position has increased by $1,000 from its starting position, and the seller's equity position has correspondingly decreased by $1,000. The clearing corporation will transfer this amount from the seller's margin account, which means the seller's equity is now $1,000, which is below the maintenance margin. This drop in margin would result in the seller getting a call from the broker, telling him or her to post more money or the position will be closed. It is this daily resettling, combined with the enforcement of margin requirements, that ensures that both the buyer and the seller meet their commitments. This is the reason the margin is viewed as a performance bond: both the buyer and the seller have to post margin to make sure they deliver on their promise. The result is the elimination of credit risk, which means individuals can trade futures contracts without worrying about the identity of their counterparty—that is, the party they are trading with.

Examples 11-7 and 11-8 illustrate the concepts associated with marking to market.

EXAMPLE 11-7 Daily Marking to Market: Long Position

An investor enters into a long position in a futures contracts that requires a $50,000 initial margin and has a maintenance margin that is 75 percent of this amount. The futures price associated with this contract is $20. Assume the spot price of the underlying asset closes at the following prices for the next five days: $20.50, $20.75, $21.00, $19.75, and $19.25. Estimate the daily profit (loss) for this investor, as well as the equity position, assuming no cash deposits or withdrawals are made from the account.

Solution

Day	Spot Price	Daily Profit	Equity Position (Margin Balance)
0	$20	–	$50,000
1	$20.50	$0.50 × 50,000 = $25,000	$50,000 + $25,000 = $75,000
2	$20.75	$0.25 × 50,000 = $12,500	$75,000 + $12,500 = $87,500
3	$21.00	$0.25 × 50,000 = $12,500	$87,500 + $12,500 = $100,000
4	$19.75	−$1.25 × 50,000 = − $62,500	$100,000 − $62,500 = $37,500
5	$19.25	−$0.50 × 50,000 = −$25,000	$37,500 − $25,000 = $12,500

Notice that the investor would have received a margin call on day 5, when the equity position fell below the maintenance margin requirement of $37,500.

---

[7] Similarly, investors with the short position in the futures contract could enter into an offsetting purchase to close their position. Entering into offsetting transactions is the most common way to close futures positions. Actual delivery of the underlying asset occurs very rarely, in less than 5 percent of all futures transactions.

EXAMPLE 11-8   Daily Marking to Market: Short Position

An investor enters into a short position in a futures contract that requires a $50,000 initial margin and has a maintenance margin that is 75 percent of this amount. The futures price associated with this contract is $20. Assume the spot price of the underlying asset closes at the following prices for the next five days: $20.50, $20.75, $21.00, $19.75, and $19.25. Estimate the daily profit (loss) for this investor, as well as the equity position, assuming no cash deposits or withdrawals are made from the account.

Solution

Day	Spot Price	Daily Profit	Equity Position (Margin Balance)
0	$20	–	$50,000
1	$20.50	$-0.50 \times \$50,000 = -\$25,000$	$50,000 - 25,000 = \$25,000$
2	$20.75	$-0.25 \times \$50,000 = 12,500$	$25,000 - 12,500 = \$12,500$
3	$21.00	$-0.25 \times \$50,000 = 12,500$	$12,500 - 12,500 = \$0$
4	$19.75	$1.25 \times \$50,000 = \$62,500$	$0 + 62,500 = \$62,500$
5	$19.25	$0.50 \times \$50,000 = \$25,000$	$62,500 + 25,000 = \$87,500$

Notice that the investor would have received a margin call on day 1, when the equity position fell below the maintenance margin requirement of $37,500. Because the price continued to go up and additional losses were incurred, the investor might also have had to contribute on days 2 and 3 as well, depending on how much he or she contributed each day. Therefore, in practice, the margin account numbers after day 1 would reflect these contributions.

Futures Contracts Markets

Producing a standardized contract requires that both the underlying asset and the term of the contract be standardized. The term of the contract is set by the individual exchange, but most exchanges follow the lead of the Chicago Mercantile Exchange (CME), which has been consolidating the derivatives exchange business by buying up exchanges around the world, including the Chicago Board of Trade (CBOT) and the New York Mercantile Exchange (NYMEX), which are all now part of the CME Group. The most common delivery months are March, June, September, and December. In practice, physical delivery rarely takes place, as most positions are closed out with an offsetting transaction before the final day of trading, which is generally a couple of days before delivery. In this way, futures contracts are designed to share the price risk and not actually transfer the underlying asset. Most futures generally have a rolling 18-month term. This means that, at any point, investors can normally buy and sell futures on the same commodity with six different maturity dates.

To standardize the underlying asset, the exchange specifies precisely what is being traded, so that even though delivery rarely takes place, people know exactly what they are buying or selling. For the rare occasions when delivery does take place, the exchange will specify both the location and how delivery will occur. This is why, for example, the London Metal Exchange keeps a list of recognized warehouses.

Finally, the exchange determines how much of the asset is traded in each contract. In the example above, we used $50,000 as a notional contract amount. In reality, the actual amount varies with the needs of the individuals who are trading. So what does all this mean in practice?

Understanding the futures market means understanding the basic distinction between futures on physical commodities and financial futures. Some of the major assets traded and the locations of the trading are shown in Table 11-2. However, these contracts are constantly changing as there have been enormous changes in futures markets over the past few years, with the CME Group consolidating several previously distinct exchanges. New market entrants have also appeared as the International Commodity Exchange (ICE) and the New York Stock Exchange (NYSE) have both bought smaller exchanges and expanded the range of contracts to compete with the CME Group.

TABLE 11-2 Major Futures Contracts and Markets

Underlying Asset	Exchange
Commodities	
Wheat/oats/soybeans/rice	Chicago Board of Trade (CBOT)
Cattle/pigs/lumber/corn/milk	Chicago Mercantile Exchange (CME)
Crude oil/heating oil/natural gas/cocoa	New York Mercantile Exchange (NYMEX)
Cotton/orange juice/coffee/sugar	NY Cotton Exchange
Gold/silver/copper	The Commodity Exchange (Comex)
Lead/nickel/tin/aluminium/zinc	London Metal Exchange (LME)
Canola/western barley/wheat	International Commodity Exchange (ICE)
Financial Futures	
Treasury notes and bonds/DJIA	CBOT
S&P Index/Nikkei225/C$/£/€	CME
BAs/Canada bonds/TSX/S&P 60 Index	Montreal Exchange (MX)
German bonds/European equities	Euronext/NYSE Liffe
Other	
Weather derivatives	CME

Note the variety of commodities traded, ranging from traditional agricultural products to newer energy and base metal contracts. Recently the CME even introduced both futures and options contracts on the regional Case/Shiller U.S. housing indexes. Essentially, we see that futures contracts exist on almost any asset that will generate sufficient interest from companies wanting to hedge risk against changes in its price or that will generate sufficient speculative trading activity. Also note the intense competition. Competition appears when new contracts are introduced, such as weather derivatives and futures contracts on real estate and the consumer price index; some of these survive, while others disappear due to lack of interest. *Finance in the News 11-1* discusses the introduction of a new futures contract for heavy oil coming out of Alberta's oil sands and the competition between the CME and Montreal Exchange to generate trading volumes. The discussion also alludes to the benefits, in terms of liquidity, of having futures contracts trade on exchanges, as opposed to OTC forward contract trading.

It is interesting to note that relatively little trading takes place on Canadian exchanges. Commodity futures trading in Canada is concentrated in Winnipeg on ICE Canada, the former Winnipeg Commodity Exchange (WCE). ICE Canada trades western barley, durum wheat, and canola futures and has in the past also had contracts on rapeseed and other agricultural commodities. However, the wheat contract is in direct competition with the wheat contract on the CBOT, even though the CBOT contract is priced in U.S. dollars with a contract size of 5,000 bushels, while the Canadian contract is priced in Canadian dollars for 20 metric tonnes. The larger volume of trading in Chicago has meant that many Canadian farmers use the U.S. contract. As a result, the ICE contract has had an uneven history with minimal contracts traded in Canada relative to the United States. In June 2006, just before trading in Canada was suspended, there was open interest of fewer than 5,000 contracts in Winnipeg versus open interest of more than 500,000 contracts on the CBOT. **Open interest** represents the number of contracts that are outstanding, so when someone buys and another person sells a futures contract, although two transactions are recorded with the exchange, the open interest is just one contract. Open interest, therefore, represents the true amount of futures market activity.

open interest the number of contracts that are outstanding; the true amount of futures market activity

Trading in financial futures was concentrated in Montreal when the Canadian exchanges were reorganized in 2000. In this reorganization, the Montreal Stock Exchange gave up trading in common stocks to the Toronto Stock Exchange, and the Toronto Futures Exchange closed down so that all derivatives trading would be concentrated in Montreal. Today, the major futures contracts traded on the Montreal Exchange (MX) are the bankers' acceptances futures contracts (BAX), those on two-year (CGZ) and 10-year (CGB) Government of Canada bonds, and one on the S&P/TSX 60 Index (SXF). In total, there is open interest of typically just fewer than 1 million contracts, with the BAX accounting for slightly more than half the total.

finance INTHENEWS 11-1   A New Way to Play Alberta Crude

THE WORLD'S TOP FUTURES EXCHANGE will add its first Canadian oil contract later this month as Alberta's fast-growing oil sands command an increasingly important role in energy markets.

The CME group, which owns the New York Mercantile Exchange, will launch a cash-settled futures contract for Western Canadian Select heavy crude on July 28, an important step for Alberta's oil sands on to the global stage.

"There's no secret in the U.S. energy markets how important [the oil sands] are, both to refiners and to end users," said Joseph Raia, CME's New York-based managing director of energy and metals, who came to Calgary this week to market the product to the city's oil patch.

The major question is, will anyone want it? The CME contract is not the first of its kind; the Montreal Exchange launched a similar Western Canadian Select (WCS) product on June 18, but it hasn't been a runaway hit.

"The contract has not yet traded," said Carolyn Quick, director of corporate communications with Montreal Exchange owner TMX Group. "We are now focusing our efforts on training and educational efforts and we expect a progressive buildup of this new market."

Western Canadian Select producers have been cool to the new CME product. Talisman Energy Inc., for example, said that it has no intention of helping boost the contract's liquidity.

Elsewhere, smaller contracts have become important innovations: the Dubai Mercantile Exchange's Oman crude oil futures contract, for example, has delivered more than 235 million barrels of crude since its inception in June 2007.

But CME has no committed volumes for the WCS contract, and has warned it could take time to develop. And traders are far from bullish on the CME contract, saying that while it is sensible, success is not certain,

given that markets have historically preferred established contracts such as West Texas Intermediate (WTI) and Brent crude.

Both the new Montreal and New York Western Canadian Select futures products have a similar aim: to capitalize on a perceived need for a better financial instrument to trade Canadian crude, at a time when Alberta alone has surpassed all other countries as the largest source of U.S. oil imports.

"We truly believe that we're at the cusp of an explosion in trading volumes in Alberta," said Tim Gunn, chief executive officer of Net Energy Inc., a broker whose platform trades nearly one million barrels of oil a day, and whose index will form the basis of the new CME product.

One reason is the financial exposure Canadian oil producers must currently endure. Companies regularly hedge their production, meaning they contract to sell future production at a certain price. Today, they can do that by buying futures of WTI, the U.S.-based benchmark for intermediate oil.

Because WCS is a heavy oil that contains sulfur, it takes more effort to refine into end products such as gasoline or jet fuel, and therefore trades at a discount to WTI. Companies currently have no way to shield against those moves, which can be problematic because the discount can change quickly.

The CME contract, which is based on the heavy product coming out of Alberta's oil sands will give them that ability.

"It is a massive change," Mr. Gunn said.

"If this thing starts trading actively it can lead to all types of other vehicles. We could start an options market here. We could get an ETF on Canadian oil sands," he said. "This puts us on the map. We're in the big leagues now."

Trading/Hedging with Futures Contracts

For illustrative purposes, let's look at the futures contract on the 10-year Government of Canada bond to see how it works. The notional contract is for a $100,000 10-year Government of Canada bond at 6 percent. Prices for the CGB contract are quoted in the same way as for a regular bond—that is, they are quoted as a price per $100, such as $92.50, and then move in increments of $10 or 0.01 per $100.

In setting the initial margin requirement, the MX divides purchasers into speculators and hedgers, with the former posting a $2,350 margin and the latter $2,250. The MX classifies everyone as a speculator except for a small list of "institutions, counterparties, regulated entities, and bona fide hedgers as defined in its rules and procedures." As of February 8, 2012, the maximum position limit for the 10-year Canada bond future is set at 37,575 contracts, and individuals have to report to the MX when they have 250 or more contracts. This is to make sure that no single institution dominates trading.

With most futures contracts, the underlying asset is clearly specified, and the party responsible for delivering the asset has no choice. However, bond futures generally provide a choice. For example, if someone does choose to take delivery of the underlying asset in the CGB contract, the MX specifies a list of bonds with their "conversion factor" to make their values equivalent to the notional bond. The MX lists Government of Canada bonds that:

- have a remaining time to maturity of between 8 years and 10½ years as of the first day of the delivery month, calculated by rounding down to the nearest whole three-month period;

- have an outstanding amount of at least C$3.5-billion nominal value;

- are originally issued at 10-year auctions;

- are issued and delivered on or before the 15th day preceding the first delivery notice day of the contract.

So what can an investor do with this bond future? Well, imagine that a portfolio manager on December 1, 2012, who owns $1 million in market value of long Canada bonds, plans to sell the bonds in four months, and wants to protect their value in case interest rates increase. Because the fund is long the Canada bond, the investor needs to sell (i.e., go short) long Canada bond futures to protect the value of the underlying bond portfolio. In this case, the manager sells ten April 2013 10-year Government of Canada bond futures, because each contract has a notional value of $100,000.

If interest rates increase by April 1, 2013, then the market value of the fund's long Canada bonds will fall, causing a loss in their value. At the same time, the price of the futures contract falls, and because the futures have been sold, this generates a capital gain. This type of hedge, which we illustrated previously using forward contracts, is called a short hedge, because a futures sale or a short position in the futures contract is hedging a long position in the underlying asset.

Whether the gain on the futures contract exactly equals the loss on the long Canada bond portfolio depends on how sensitive both are to interest rate changes. If the bond portfolio's value changes exactly mimic those of the asset underlying the CGB contract, the portfolio will be completely hedged. However, when this is not the case, the investor will be exposed to **basis risk**. Basis risk is the risk associated with a hedged position that is attributable to the fact that the asset to be hedged is not identical to the asset used as the hedge. As a result, it may be impossible to create a perfectly hedged position because changes in the price of the underlying asset in the contract will not move in a totally predictable manner with respect to changes in the price of the asset position to be hedged. One of the advantages of forward contracts is that they can be structured to minimize (or even eliminate) basis risk. This is because, unlike futures contracts, forwards are not standardized and can therefore be tailor-made with respect to underlying assets and maturity dates.

In our example, if the bond portfolio is not exactly the same as the 6 percent notional 10-year Government of Canada bonds used in the futures contract, there is basis risk because their prices will not move identically. For bonds, this risk can be reduced by adjusting the number of bond futures sold to create a weighted hedge. In our example, perhaps selling 9.5 contracts would be more accurate than selling 10.[8] However, the principle remains the same—the portfolio manager can sell bond futures to hedge the portfolio's underlying exposure to long Canada bonds.

We conclude this section with an example of hedging foreign exchange risk. The CME trades a futures contract on the Canadian dollar to allow Americans to hedge their Canadian dollar exposure, but where is the U.S. dollar futures contract that Canadians can use

basis risk the risk associated with a hedged position that is attributable to the fact that the asset to be hedged is not identical to the asset used as the hedge

---

[8] In fact, the appropriate hedge ratio can be determined by calculating the bond's duration, but this is beyond the scope of our discussion.

to hedge their U.S. dollar exposure? The fact is, it doesn't exist, because the CME futures contract that involves a minimum 100 contracts, each with a notional value of C$100,000, works fine for Canadians as well. Foreign exchange rates are just reciprocals, so sellinCanadian dollar futures on the CME is exactly the same as buying U.S. dollar futures—that is, the futures contract involves selling Canadian dollars and buying U.S. dollars. In February 2012 the CME reported volume of 1,790,318 contracts on the US$/C$ futures contract, a 19 percent increase from the previous year. A significant amount of this involved Canadian parties hedging their U.S. dollar exposure, as well as Americans hedging their Canadian dollar exposure.

Summary of Forward and Futures Contracts

Table 11-3 lists the major differences between forward and futures contracts. The bottom line is that forward contracts offer more flexibility because they are customized OTC contracts; however, they possess additional risks because the contracts are not actively traded and because they possess credit risk. In other words, while forwards and futures serve the same basic purposes, one may be preferred over the other in some situations.

TABLE 11-3 Forwards versus Futures

	Forwards	**Exchange Futures**
Contracts	Customized	Standardized
Trading	Dealer or OTC markets	Exchanges
Default (credit) risk	Important	Unimportant—guaranteed by clearinghouse
Initial deposit	Not required	Initial margin and maintenance margin required
Settlement	On maturity date	Marked to market daily

CONCEPT REVIEW QUESTIONS

1. Define initial margin, maintenance margin, margin call, open interest, and notional amount.
2. Explain what is meant by "marked to market."
3. What is basis risk? Why is it important for hedgers?
4. Compare and contrast forwards and futures.

Learning Objective 11.4
Describe the mechanics of simple swap structures, including interest rate swaps and currency swaps.

swap an agreement between two parties to exchange cash flows in the future

counterparties two parties in a swap agreement

interest rate swap an exchange of interest payments on a principal amount in which borrowers switch loan rates

11.3 SWAPS

The final type of linear hedging contract we will discuss is the **swap**. A swap is an agreement between two parties, called **counterparties**, to exchange cash flows in the future. Note at the outset that this is a direct agreement between two parties; there is no formal exchange to guarantee performance, so the situation involves a dealer or OTC market, and there is credit risk. As a result, like forward contracts, swaps have evolved into a bank instrument, with the banks or swap dealers serving as intermediaries between the two counterparties to the swap. As with most things, the initial contracts were the simplest and the easiest to understand, so let's start with a simple **interest rate swap** example from the mid-1980s.[9]

---

[9] The example comes from the Bankers Trust sponsor's supplement to *Euromoney* (January 1986).

Interest Rate Swaps

We illustrate how an interest rate swap can be initiated by considering two hypothetical companies, A and B. Company A is a top-rated AAA company, whereas company B is a lower-rated BBB company. Credit (bond) ratings are discussed briefly in Chapter 6, and again in greater detail in Chapter 17, but for now, all you need to know is that AAA is the highest rating a company can have, and although BBB is a good bond rating, it is the lowest "investment grade" bond rating. Assume that company A wants to raise debt and pay a floating interest rate, which is usually done to finance short-term receivables and credit that earn a short-term interest rate. Company B, conversely, wants long-term fixed rate financing, perhaps to finance the purchase of machinery and equipment. Both companies approach the capital market, and company A is quoted a rate of 10.8 percent for fixed rate financing or a floating rate of 0.25 percent over LIBOR. In contrast, company B is quoted fixed rate financing at 12 percent and floating rate financing at a 0.75 percent spread over LIBOR.

As mentioned earlier, corporate borrowing rates are not generally priced with reference to the Government of Canada Treasury bill (T-bill) yield. Floating rate financing in Canadian dollars is generally priced relative to the bankers' acceptances (BA) rate, which is why the Montreal Exchange's most popular hedging contract is the BAX. In contrast, floating rate notes in U.S. dollars are normally priced off LIBOR. Why U.S. dollar financing would be based off a rate established in London, rather than New York, is partly a historical accident, but it is a rate that reflects true market activity. In contrast, rates in New York have historically reflected the intervention and credit controls established by U.S. monetary authorities and have not been true market rates.

Regardless of how the rates are determined and quoted, let's consider what these two companies would do. The quotes look reasonable; the BBB-rated borrower is quoted a higher yield in both the fixed rate and the floating rate markets and would have borrowed at 12 percent. The AAA company would have borrowed at LIBOR + 0.25 percent. However, 25 years ago, someone asked the basic question: why is the BBB credit quoted a spread of 1.2 percent more than the AAA in the fixed rate market and only 0.5 percent more in the floating rate market? This person recognized that although firm A had an absolute financing advantage in both the fixed and the floating rate markets, it also had a **comparative advantage** in the fixed rate market, where its costs were 1.2 percent lower than those of firm B. In contrast, firm B had a comparative advantage in borrowing in the floating rate market, where it paid only 0.5 percent more than A.

comparative advantage a benefit that one firm has relative to another

To take advantage of this difference in spreads, the companies should both borrow where they have a comparative advantage and then swap payments to get what they really want. From this, the swap market was born. So firm A should borrow what it does not need, which is fixed rate financing, say $50 million, at 10.8 percent, and B should borrow what it doesn't need through a floating rate note at LIBOR + 0.75 percent, say $50 million.

Company A then signs a five-year swap contract agreeing to make payments to B at LIBOR; in return, A will receive from B a fixed 10.9 percent rate. Thus, the overall cost to A is LIBOR–0.1 percent, because it pays LIBOR to B and pays 10.8 percent on its direct financing, but it receives 10.9 percent from B through the swap. Therefore, A saves 0.35 percent over its direct quote, which was LIBOR + 0.25 percent. Firm B borrows at LIBOR + 0.75 percent and makes payments to A based on a 10.9 percent fixed rate, while receiving payments based on LIBOR from A. The net effect is that it ends up paying an 11.65 percent fixed rate (i.e., 10.9 percent + 0.75 percent) for financing and also saves 0.35 percent over its direct quote.[10] Table 11-4 depicts the swap scenario, where borrowings are represented by minus signs.

---

[10] Note that this assumes that the 0.75 percent credit spread over LIBOR is fixed; otherwise its "fixed" rate financing will vary with the credit spread.

TABLE 11-4 An Interest Rate Swap

	A	B
Quotes	**(AAA)**	**(BBB)**
Floating	LIBOR + 0.25	LIBOR + 0.75
Fixed	10.8	12.0
Initial		
Floating		− (LIBOR + 0.75)
Fixed	−10.8	
Swap	B pays A fixed and A pays B floating	
	+10.9	−10.9
	−LIBOR	+LIBOR
Net	− (LIBOR − 0.1)	−11.65
Saving	0.35%	0.35%

plain vanilla interest rate swap the "fixed for floating" interest rate swap; the simplest and most commonly used type of swap

A "fixed for floating" interest rate swap denominated in one currency, such as the one described in Table 11-4, is commonly referred to as a **plain vanilla interest rate swap**, reflecting the fact that it is the simplest and most commonly used type of swap. Although the example was developed to show that both parties gain 0.35 percent, in reality the amount they gain depends on negotiation between the two. However, in principle there is the spread in the spreads, which total 0.7 percent and which can be shared in a variety of ways between the two parties.[11]

The comparative advantage argument is a basic one in finance: anyone offered a good deal in floating rate funds should borrow them, whether they are needed or not, and use a swap to exchange them for what is needed, locking in the financing advantage. In addition, although the swap market may have developed in response to such comparative advantages, today's swap markets have evolved beyond that. Today, many firms enter into swap arrangements to convert an existing fixed rate liability into a floating rate liability and vice versa. We discuss this in more detail later in this chapter.

The swap arrangement above is not without its problems. One main concern is that company A, which is a highly rated AAA company, is relying on the payments from B, a BBB-rated company, to make its fixed rate payments. In this example, firm A is assuming additional credit risk. If B defaults, then A is stuck with its own 10.8 percent fixed rate financing and, depending on legal interpretation, may also have to continue to pay LIBOR to B even after B stops making the 10.9 percent fixed rate payment to A. For this reason, early swap contracts were directly negotiated between the two counterparties based on documentation used for parallel loan transactions and included "set-off" rights. These rights meant that if either party defaulted, the other party stopped making payments. This was soon changed, and the required payments for interest rate swaps became **net payments**. This meant that instead of exchanging the total amount of interest, parties involved in interest rate swaps exchanged payments representing the difference between the fixed and floating rates.

net payments payments representing the difference between the fixed and floating rates

Table 11-5 shows how this would work for our interest rate swap example based on various values for LIBOR during the first five periods of the swap. The payments are assumed to be made every six months, which is the norm in practice, so the interest payments are half the quoted rates.

---

[11] In practice, swap dealers will also "pocket" some of the spread as payment for their services.

TABLE 11-5 Interest Rate Swap Net Payments

Period	LIBOR (%)	Floating Pay (%)	Fixed Pay (%)	Net Pay (%)
1	8.0	−4.0	+5.45	+1.45
2	9.0	−4.5	+5.45	+0.95
3	9.8	−4.9	+5.45	+0.55
4	11.0	−5.5	+5.45	−0.05
5	12.0	−6.0	+5.45	−0.55

The cash flows depicted in Table 11-5 are from company A's point of view. A receives half the fixed rate of 10.9 percent from B each period, or 5.45 percent of the notional value of the swap; in return, A pays LIBOR. For the first six-month period, LIBOR is 8 percent, so A pays half this, or 4 percent, and receives 5.45 percent. The net cash payment is that B pays A 1.45 percent of the notional value of the swap, which is why the sign is positive. From B's perspective, all the signs would be reversed, as it pays the difference of 1.45 percent.

Notice from Table 11-5 that the net payments depend on how LIBOR changes, because the fixed rate does not vary. In the above example, LIBOR increases consistently, and by period 5 (two-and-a-half years away), when it has increased to 12 percent, A finds that it is making a net payment to B of 0.55 percent of the notional amount.

This example illustrates two important points. First, the net payment is expressed as a percentage of the notional amount. The actual cash flows would depend on the notional value of the swap—for a $10-million swap, the percentage would be multiplied by $10 million, so the period 1 payment would be $145,000 (i.e., 0.0145 × $10,000,000); payment 2 would be $95,000; and so on. Equation 11-6 depicts the semi-annual payments from the fixed rate payee's perspective.[12]

$$\text{Payment (fixed rate payee)} = \text{NP} \times (\text{Fixed} - \text{FR}) \times \tfrac{1}{2} \qquad [11\text{-}6]$$

where NP = notional principal, Fixed = fixed rate, and FR = floating rate (usually LIBOR).

Second, when only net payments are required, the credit risk from A's perspective decreases significantly because it no longer relies on B to make the entire fixed rate payment. All that A gets from B is the much smaller difference between the LIBOR and fixed rate, which may be positive or negative. If B does default, A is still at risk, but only for this future stream of differences, rather than for the full interest payments.

EXAMPLE 11-9 Estimating Payments from an Interest Rate Swap

Company C enters into a two-year, $1-million, plain vanilla interest rate swap and agrees to pay a fixed rate of 5 percent and receive LIBOR. Payments are exchanged every six months, based on LIBOR at the beginning of the six-month period. Determine the amount of the required semi-annual payments that C must make, assuming that LIBOR has the following values for each six-month period, beginning now: 5%, 5.5%, 5.25%, and 4.75%.

Solution

After 6 months: Payment = $1 million × (0.05 − 0.05) × 1/2 = $0

After 12 months: Payment = $1 million × (0.05 − 0.055) × 1/2 = − $2,500 (i.e., they receive $2,500)

After 18 months: Payment = $1 million × (0.05 − 0.0525) × 1/2 = − $1,250 (i.e., they receive $1,250)

After 24 months: Payment = $1 million × (0.05 − 0.0475) × 1/2 = $1,250 (i.e., they pay $1,250)

---

[12] Notice that, to determine what the floating rate payee pays (receives), all we need to do is change the sign of the cash flow.

The Evolution of Swap Markets

currency swap the exchange of principal and interest in one currency for the same in another currency

As it turns out, the first swap was not an interest rate swap but a **currency swap** that involved IBM and the World Bank. At the time, the World Bank was required to borrow where it was cheapest in absolute dollars, which turned out to be either Swiss francs or German marks. In fact, it borrowed so much in those currencies that it made up the largest holding in most Swiss franc bond portfolios, and it ended up facing higher interest rates as a result. In contrast, it could issue U.S. dollar bonds quite easily because it was not a large U.S. dollar issuer. IBM, in contrast, was a well-known name but had never issued Swiss franc financing and was offered a good borrowing rate. Given our discussion of comparative advantage above, you might guess what happened next. IBM issued Swiss franc bonds, the World Bank issued U.S. dollar bonds, and each got its preferential rates. They then agreed to swap both the principal and the interest payments. In fact, the World Bank continued to make heavy use of currency swaps, and by the early 1980s it was routinely lowering its borrowing cost by a colossal 1.28 percent a year.[13]

The original swap transactions were extremely profitable for both counterparties, as indicated by the fact that the World Bank was able to lower its borrowing cost by 1.28 percent. This was because the credit spreads between risky borrowers and governments in different types of debt markets were largely unconnected. Theoretically, spreads in the floating rate and fixed rate markets should be the same, just as they should be between U.S. dollar and Canadian dollar financing. This is because most bonds have cross-default clauses in their debt contracts, so that default on any debt instrument anywhere in the world means a default on all debt obligations. As a result, the credit risk is the same. However, although the swap market has caused these spreads to narrow considerably, spread differences continue to exist. Swapping still makes sense, but it doesn't make as much sense as it used to.

Knowing what a swap is allows us to understand the reasons behind some strange actions. For example, we may see "tombstone" advertisements in the newspaper, in which a Canadian company announces that it has issued debt in New Zealand or Australian currencies. Taken on its own, this may not make much sense, especially if the company has no operations in New Zealand or Australia. However, when we realize that the company can swap those New Zealand or Australian dollars into Canadian dollars, we know that it has issued bonds in the foreign currencies because it got a "good" deal, and it then swapped the bonds for what it really needed—Canadian dollars. In fact, it has been estimated that as much as 75 percent of the bond issues in the international Eurobond market have ended up being swapped into something else.

The flip side to Canadian companies issuing foreign bonds in obscure locations is the recent development of the Maple bond market. Until January 2005, Canadian tax-preferred investors, such as pension funds, were restricted from holding more than 30 percent of the value of their portfolio in foreign-issued securities. To maximize the value of the 30 percent foreign content, investors tended to hold foreign equities rather than bonds. However, after the foreign content rule was removed, Canadian pension funds started buying Canadian dollar–denominated bonds issued by foreign companies—a market that was quickly termed the Maple bond market. Similar to Canadian firms' issuing Kiwi or Aussie bonds in order to swap back into Canadian dollars, the proceeds of these Maple bonds were almost always swapped back into the currency needed by the issuer.

As swap markets have matured, another major change has taken place. Initially, the major investment banks would bring two parties together and arrange the swap for a fee. However, as the market's liquidity grew, the major banks increasingly acted as principals, directly signing a swap with one party, and then "warehousing" the swap until they could do an offsetting transaction with another party. This development was helped by the increasing standardization in the market. The International Swap Dealers Association (ISDA) has developed standard legal

---

[13] Wallich, Christine, "The World Bank's Currency Swaps." *Finance and Development*, June 1984.

documentation so that everyone knows his or her rights and duties under a standard swap agreement. This standardization means that plain vanilla interest rate swaps and currency swaps have become commodities that can be bought and sold through a telephone call to a bank's swaps desk. As such, swaps have become traded commodities and major instruments for managing interest rate and currency exposures, with enormous ramifications that we will discuss shortly.

Consider, for example, the original IBM–World Bank currency swap. This was a primary market transaction, because both IBM and the World Bank used it to raise capital as cheaply as possible. In both cases, their intention was to raise the capital and then forget about it. However, once swaps became standardized, it was possible to constantly change the nature of an institution's liability stream.

Recall, for example, the foreign exchange exposure problem discussed earlier. At that time, we considered a firm that had a US$1-million receivable due in a year. Let's change this and say that a Canadian company has a five-year U.S. dollar bond outstanding, with fixed semi-annual interest payments of $1 million and a principal of US$30 million due in five years. In this case, the Canadian company has a U.S. dollar liability stream, so it is short the U.S. dollars. Now suppose the company looks at the current exchange rate and feels that it is at an all-time high and will depreciate in the future. As the Canadian dollar depreciates, it will cost the company more Canadian dollars to make those U.S. dollar interest and principal payments.

What can the company do? The most obvious thing is to repay the loan, but if this is a bond held by several U.S. institutions, that may not be possible. An alternative is to enter into a currency swap. The structure of currency swaps permits firms to adjust their foreign exchange exposure. In particular, one distinguishing feature of currency swaps is that, unlike interest rate swaps, they require the exchange of *all* cash flows. This is logical because exchange rates change as well as interest rates. Although this feature increases the credit risk associated with currency swaps, it also provides firms with the opportunity to manipulate the underlying currency associated with a series of future cash flows that it expects to pay (or receive).

In this case, the company can talk to the swaps desk at its bank and swap the U.S. dollar liability stream into a Canadian dollar liability stream. Unlike the original IBM–World Bank currency swap, which was arranged by an investment bank between the two counterparties, the bank is now capable of executing a secondary market transaction with itself as a principal— that is, it doesn't need a counterparty. The reason is that a currency swap can be viewed as a series of forward transactions. Think of the firm's five-year bond not as one transaction but as 10 individual transactions. The first nine transactions involve a US$1-million outflow every six months for interest, while the last one is a US$31-million outflow for both the final interest payment and the principal payment. So rather than going through a search for a counterparty, the bank could always execute 10 forward sales of Canadian dollars for U.S. dollars and directly change the U.S. dollar liability stream into a Canadian dollar liability stream. Once it has been converted into a fixed Canadian dollar stream, an interest rate swap can convert it into any other Canadian dollar liability, such as a floating rate liability.

If currency swaps have become a bank market through their links to the forward foreign exchange market, what of interest rate swaps? To understand the link with other instruments, let's go back to our circa 1985 example of an interest rate swap. At that time, all the rates were unique to the issuers, and the interest rates in the swap were negotiated. However, the core of the swap was simply a LIBOR-based rate and a fixed rate. To make a standardized product, suppose we fix both the floating and the fixed rates so that everyone knows what they are. Let's fix the floating rate at LIBOR and the fixed rate with reference to the government bond rate, with the choice of rate depending on whether it is a five-year, 10-year, or other maturity contract. Suppose the BBB bond issue was a five-year bond, so that we have a five-year interest rate swap. Let's say the five-year government bond rate was 10.65 percent at the time. In this way, the swap could be quoted simply as 10.65 percent. In fact, this is the way that swaps are now quoted, and this rate is called the **swap rate**.

swap rate the rate or the fixed portion of a swap used for quoting swap prices

We revisit our previous example and assume the swap rate was 10.65 percent at the time. This transaction is depicted in Table 11-6.

TABLE 11-6 Percent Interest Rate Swap

	A	B
Quotes	**(AAA)**	**(BBB)**
Floating	LIBOR + 0.25	LIBOR + 0.75
Fixed	10.8	12.0
Initial		
Floating		− (LIBOR + 0.75)
Fixed	−10.8	
Swap	B pays A fixed and A pays B floating	
	+10.65	− 10.65
	− LIBOR	+LIBOR
Net	− (LIBOR + 0.15)	− 11.4
Saving	0.10%	0.60%

In this case, unlike our original example, the 0.7 percent difference in spreads has been allocated as 0.1 percent to company A and 0.6 percent to company B. This generally has been the trend over time, as the gains to the higher-rated AAA are relatively small, given that it has good access to most markets. In contrast, it is the lower-rated issuers that sometimes face very large spread differences across different markets. Further, the AAA-rated firm is often a bank, and banks now make money trading swaps rather than acting as counterparties. In the above example, the swap rate of 10.65 percent would actually be the mid-point of an "ask" or "bid" rate of 10.63 percent and an "offer" rate of 10.67 percent. If a company wants to swap floating for fixed, it would pay the 10.67 percent fixed (offer) rate, but if it wanted to swap fixed for floating, it would receive the 10.63 percent fixed (ask) rate from the bank. The spread of 0.04 percent between these two rates rewards the bank for trading swaps.

Interest rate swaps are now standard around the world. Table 11-7 provides the "ask or offer" swap rates for the euro, U.S. dollar, and pound sterling as of March 16, 2012.

TABLE 11-7 Interest Rate Swap Quotes

Fixed Rate	Euro(€) Current	US($) Current	UK(£) Current
1 year	1.13	0.51	0.98
2 year	1.19	0.63	1.31
3 year	1.35	0.82	1.43
5 year	1.75	1.36	1.78
7 year	2.11	1.87	2.16
10 year	2.48	2.37	2.66
12 year	2.64	2.60	2.89
15 year	2.80	2.81	3.11
20 year	2.85	2.98	3.30
25 year	2.81	3.06	3.39
30 year	2.75	3.11	3.43

Source: Data retrieved from http://markets.ft.com on March 17, 2012. Swap rates are also available from the U.S. Federal Reserve website, www.federalreserve.gov.

Notice that the swap rates follow the full spectrum of the yield curve out to 30 years, so interest rate swaps are very useful for managing interest rate exposure. This also provides the link to other interest rate products. The link in this case is to the forward rate agreements (FRAs) that are discussed in Appendix 11A. Appendix 11A notes that by selling a one-year bond and investing in a two-year bond, a bank can create forward contracts on the one-year interest rate for the next year. In the same way, it can sell a six-month bond and invest in a one-year bond to create a six-month interest rate forward for hedging LIBOR. Doing the same thing at six-month intervals creates an FRA. The FRA can be seen as a series of forward interest rates equivalent to an interest rate swap. What this means is that the two core products in the swap market, the interest rate and currency swaps, are simply combinations of forward contracts—either on interest rates or on exchange rates. Creating swaps is therefore a key component of the skill set of all the major banks.

The integration of the swap markets with the forward market has allowed the enormous expansion of the market. If a company has a banking relationship with an outstanding line of credit, we have already seen that a company can call and buy and sell forward foreign exchange contracts. The same thing now happens in the swap market. If a company wants to change a floating rate liability into a fixed rate liability, it calls the bank and executes an interest rate swap. More than 80 percent of swap transactions are now worth around $10 million as secondary market transactions executed against a bank line of credit.

CONCEPT REVIEW QUESTIONS

1. Explain how plain vanilla interest rate swaps are structured and what purposes they serve.

2. Explain how currency swaps are structured and how they can be used for hedging purposes.

3. Why does it make sense that interest rate swaps involve an exchange of net payments, while currency swaps exchange all cash flows?

11.4 THE FINANCIAL CRISIS AND THE CREDIT DEFAULT SWAP MARKET

Interest rate and currency swaps have been the main focus of this section because they are the major vehicles for managing interest rate and currency exposure. However, there are more applications for swaps. If an investor doesn't like what's happening in the bond market and wants to increase exposure to the equity market, that investor could sell bonds and buy equities. The downside is that the bond market is not very liquid and the transaction costs are high. The investor could instead turn to the swap market and enter into a **total return swap**. This can be accomplished by first entering into an interest rate swap to convert the fixed rate bond payments into payments that vary with a floating rate, such as LIBOR, because almost all swaps go through LIBOR. The investor would then enter into a total return swap, paying LIBOR and receiving the total return from an equity index, such as the S&P 500 Index or the S&P/TSX 60 Index, plus or minus some spread. The existence of futures contracts on stock market indexes—on the S&P/TSX 60 Index on the Montreal Exchange, for example, or the S&P 500 Index on the CME—allows the equity market exposure to be hedged. These types of swaps are not for the small investor, as the notional principal amount involved is usually $100 million.

What the total return swap does indicate is how swaps have emerged as a major vehicle for managing exposure to any traded commodity that can be hedged. The result is a huge proliferation of specialized swap contracts and a huge transfer of risk, since, for example, if someone is to receive the return on the S&P 500 index, then someone else has to pay it. This dramatically increases counterparty or credit risk because some of the newer swaps are for highly volatile underlying securities. It is for this reason that Warren Buffett, one of the world's

Learning Objective 11.5
Explain how the credit default swap market contributed to the financial crisis.

total return swap an exchange of an interest rate return for the total return on an equity index, plus or minus a spread

greatest investors, termed derivatives in general "financial weapons of mass destruction." His warning was ignored, but in the summer of 2007 his words came back to haunt policy-makers around the world as credit default swaps began to self-destruct and threw the world into its first genuine global economic crisis.

A **credit default swap (CDS)** is just like any other swap. In this case, the agreement is essentially to swap the payments on a risk-free government bond in return for the proceeds of a default risky bond. Consider, for example, a default risky corporate bond paying 10 percent interest. The investor does not like the risk but for some reason is unable to sell the bond. She can enter into a CDS in which she pays the difference between the bond's 10 percent interest and, say, the 4 percent interest on the government bond; in this way, the investor's interest receipts are reduced to the level of a risk-free bond. In return for these payments, the counterparty gives the investor the right to receive the par value of the bond should it default. In this way, a CDS is essentially the same as buying default insurance on the risky corporate bond, where the buyer pays for the default protection and the seller sells the protection.

However, there are two big differences between a CDS and insurance. First, the risk attached to regular insurance, such as house or car insurance, is essentially random since the risk depends on factors unique to an individual. As a result, by pooling a lot of these unique risks, the insurer's exposure becomes predictable. In contrast, for a CDS, the underlying risk depends on the economy, as defaults tend to be clustered during a slowdown or recession, when individuals and companies are more likely to reorganize or go bankrupt. As a result, CDS contracts have market risk.

The second problem is that the CDS market is simply part of the swap market, and, as an OTC market, everything depends on the two counterparties fulfilling their promise. A heavily regulated insurance company is required to keep reserves to ensure it can fulfill its promises. In the swap market, in contrast, this risk is mitigated by restricting counterparty risk to large stable financial companies, such as American International Group (AIG), and requiring them to put up "margin" or other collateral should their financial health decline. However, in 2007–8 these measures proved inadequate simply because of the size of the market and the limited number of major participants. Table 11-8 displays data compiled by the Bank for International Settlements that includes aggregate global data for OTC and exchange-listed derivatives.

credit default swap (CDS) an agreement in which one party makes a series of interest payments and then is compensated by the counterparty in the event of default on the bond; it is essentially default insurance on the bond

TABLE 11-8 Notional Amounts of Derivative Contracts Outstanding Globally, June 2011

Organized Exchanges	US$ Billions	
	Futures	**Options**
Interest rate	24,999	49,081
Currency	204	119
Equity	1,109	5,008
Over the Counter (OTC)		
Foreign exchange	53,341	11,358
Interest rate	497,457	56,423
Commodity	1,846	883
Credit default swaps	32,409	

Source: Data from Bank for International Settlements website at www.bis.org/publ/otc_hy1111.htm. Futures data includes swap contracts.

As long as these markets were small and the underlying products were clearly understood, they could flourish. However, by 2007 the CDS market was worth US$45 trillion or about three times the value of the U.S. stock market. Even worse than the increased size of the CDS market was the fact that many of the newer CDS contracts were on securities tied to the U.S. sub-prime mortgage market (which is discussed in Chapter 1). As the sub-prime market grew, many of the banks generating the risky mortgages bought CDS contracts to swap out of the risk. Essentially, they bought insurance against the possibility of the risky mortgages defaulting. The protection sellers of these CDS contracts varied, but by 2007, AIG alone had written "protection" on US$440 billion worth of mortgage-backed securities or about a third of the entire U.S. sub-prime market. From AIG's point of view, it was receiving the insurance premiums on underlying securities with a very low risk of default, since most of these mortgage-backed securities were rated AAA. However, as the sub-prime market in the United States collapsed in 2007 and into 2008, AIG was increasingly called on to make good on these CDS contracts until the very solvency of AIG became questioned. As AIG faced the prospect of posting collateral or margin to make sure it fulfilled its CDS contracts, it simply ran out of cash and was forced to turn to the U.S. government for help.

The U.S. government eventually pumped $180 billion into AIG to save it from bankruptcy as part of the Troubled Asset Relief Program (TARP), which was designed to save the U.S. banking system from collapse. To avoid similar problems in the future the U.S. government passed the *Dodd-Frank Wall Street Reform and Consumer Protection Act* on July 21, 2010. This act represents the most extensive overhaul of the regulation of the U.S. financial services industry in history, most of it aimed at the banking system. However, one key component is an attempt to move derivatives trading away from OTC markets onto exchanges, where trades would attract margin. Similar regulatory changes are in the works in Canada and have been pushed by the International Monetary Fund.

As the data in Table 11-8 shows the OTC market is many times bigger than the exchange traded market; by June 2011, the notional amounts covered by all OTC derivatives was US$707 trillion versus "only" US$80 trillion for exchange-traded derivatives. By moving more of the OTC market onto organized exchanges, the hope is that a company like AIG will never again be able to place such large bets as to imperil the stability of the financial system. Instead, by posting margin, as on any futures exchange, all market participants will be aware of each participant's position and their ability to fulfill their commitments. However, *Finance in the News 11-2* warns that the derivatives industry is still growing, while a backlash is developing to delay the implementation of these rules in the United States as trade groups warn that the requirement to post margin will divert cash that would otherwise be spent on capital expenditures, resulting in the loss of 130,000 jobs.[14]

finance INTHENEWS 11-2   Another Financial Crisis Is on the Way, Mobius Says

WARREN BUFFETT CALLED them weapons of mass destruction. Now those same products, known as derivatives, are pushing the world closer to another financial crisis.

That's according to Mark Mobius, executive chairman of Templeton Asset Management's emerging markets group. Mobius, who oversees more than $50 billion in assets, says another financial crisis is "around the corner" because little has changed since recent collapse of the markets.

"There is definitely going to be another financial crisis around the corner because we haven't solved any of the things that caused the previous crisis. Are the derivatives regulated? No. Are you still getting growth in derivatives? Yes."

That was his response to a question about price swings at the Foreign Correspondents' Club of Japan in Tokyo today, according to Bloomberg.

Derivatives are financial instruments whose value is based on some underlying asset, like a mortgage for instance, and can be used to either hedge risk or for completely speculative positions. There are all kinds of derivatives investors can invest in or against including something called the death derivative where, you guessed it, investors bet on people's deaths.

The most infamous derivatives are the ones tied to residential mortgages and which led to the demise of the financial system back in 2008. When homeowners began defaulting on their mortgages, the effect was nearly detrimental to all the financial institutions that shared the risk through these exotic derivatives.

An IMF report from 2010 puts it this way:

Over-the-counter (OTC) derivatives markets have grown considerably in recent years, with total notional outstanding amounts exceeding $600 trillion at the end of June 2009...

continued

Finance in the News 11-2: Another Financial Crisis Is on the Way, Mobius Says
(continued)

During the financial crisis, the credit default swap (CDS) market, a part of the OTC derivatives market, took center stage as difficulties in financial markets began to intensify and the counterparty risk involved in a largely bilaterally cleared market became apparent. Authorities had to make expensive decisions regarding Lehman Brothers and AIG based on only partially informed views.

In fact, the derivatives battle at Lehman Brothers is still waging on with the counterparties in Lehman Brothers derivatives trades still looking to get paid for their bets. Bankrupt Lehman has been in talks for over a year with about a dozen big-bank counterparties about the value of the claims.

Meanwhile, Mobius says the derivatives market today is still so rife with bets made in different directions that major volatility is inevitable and the equity markets will suffer. He said the total value of derivatives in the world exceeds total global gross domestic product by a factor of 10, according to the Bloomberg report.

The derivatives market is one that regulators are attempting to reform right now with new rules scheduled to be implemented this year. The new rules would require more disclosure and transparency.

But like in other attempts at regulating lucrative lines of business, regulators are facing resistance from Wall Street–friendly lawmakers looking to extend the deadline.

Last week, U.S. Rep. Spencer Bachus co-sponsored a bill that would approve a measure to delay the implementation to September 2012. The legislation to delay the implementation of rules was passed last week with Bachus saying the move was necessary to "restore order to the Dodd-Frank Act derivatives rulemaking process."

The pushback in the United States is not unusual. On November 25, 2011, the Canadian Securities Administrators issued a consultation paper (91-403) and concluded: "It is the view of the Committee that effective surveillance and monitoring, harmonized market conduct rules and consistent enforcement will bring about greater transparency in the OTC derivatives markets, combat improper market conduct, and help support Canada's G20 commitments." However, its first recommendation was for "further study," its second to obtain data, and a final recommendation was to obtain legislative authority for new rules if "such rules are determined to be appropriate." The problem, as the committee noted, is that the majority of transactions entered into by Canadian participants involve foreign counterparties. As a result, Canada has to wait until major markets like those in New York and London have implemented specific policies on trading derivatives.

LESSONS TO BE LEARNED

There is an old adage "If it sounds too good to be true, it probably is." Nowhere is this more relevant than in the derivatives market. Derivatives are not inherently bad, but then neither are guns. In both cases, it is a question of how they are used. The collapse of AIG has shown that many derivative products pose systemic risk—that is, they pose risks to the entire financial system—even when their use is restricted to highly trained professionals and large, sophisticated companies. The essence of derivatives is that they enable risk to be transferred in the same way that insurance contracts transfer risk from the insured to the insurer. The financial system has functioned very efficiently with heavily regulated insurance companies for many decades, but the swap market allowed these functions to be carried out in an unregulated market. The resulting meltdown has ensured that we will now see more heavily regulated derivatives markets as we relearn the lessons our grandparents learned decades ago: *plus ça change, plus c'est la même chose …*

CONCEPT REVIEW QUESTIONS

1. Explain the difference between an insurance contract and a credit default swap.

2. How and why did AIG fail?

3. Why would making CDSs an exchange-traded product have avoided the collapse of AIG and averted the 2008–9 financial crisis?

APPENDIX 11A

FORWARD INTEREST RATES AND FORWARD RATE AGREEMENTS (FRAS)

Forward Interest Rates

Interest rate parity is a special example of forward pricing simply because the cost of carry is the ratio of one plus the interest rates in both countries. In other words, for IRP,

$$(1 + c) = \frac{(1 + k_{domestic})}{(1 + k_{foreign})}$$

Learning Objective 11.6
Explain how the general principles of forward contracts can be applied to fixed income securities.

For our synthetic forward example in the chapter, the cost of carry is the cost of borrowing in Canadian dollars relative to the investment income earned in U.S. dollars. If the Canadian one-year interest rate is 10 percent and the U.S. interest rate is 5 percent, then the cost of synthetically creating the forward rate is 1.1/1.05 − 1, or 4.76 percent. The income lost as a result of the Canadian dollar borrowing cost is higher than the income earned on the U.S. investment. As a result, the cost of carry is positive, and the forward rate of Canadian dollars for U.S. dollars has to show a 4.76 percent depreciation in the Canadian dollar. That is, if the spot rate is 1.0, the forward rate has to be 1.0476. In this way, the income loss of 4.76 percent is offset by a 4.76 percent capital gain on the exchange rate. Alternatively, if the Canadian borrowing rate is 5 percent and the U.S. rate is 10 percent, then the cost of carry is negative at − 4.55 percent. The forward rate has to show a 4.55 percent appreciation of the Canadian dollar to 0.95. In this way, the income gain from borrowing at 5 percent in Canada and investing at 10 percent in the United States— that is, a negative cost of carry—is offset by a capital loss from being in U.S. dollars.

Note that in the IRP condition, it is the ratio of one plus the interest rate in both countries that determines whether the forward rate exceeds or is less than the spot rate. However, in Table 11-1 there were forward foreign exchange rates for the Canadian dollar against the U.S. dollar extending five years into the future. This brings up another very important forward rate: the **forward interest rate**. In Chapter 6, we discussed the term structure of interest rates and the yield curve, and noted that the yield curve constantly shifts, based on the state of the economy and expectations about where interest rates are going. Figure 11A-1 shows the yield on 91-day T-bills issued by the Government of Canada and the yield on a portfolio of long Canada bonds with an average maturity exceeding 10 years. The two yields represent the very short and very long end of the yield curve, respectively.

forward interest rate an interest rate that is specified now for some time in the future

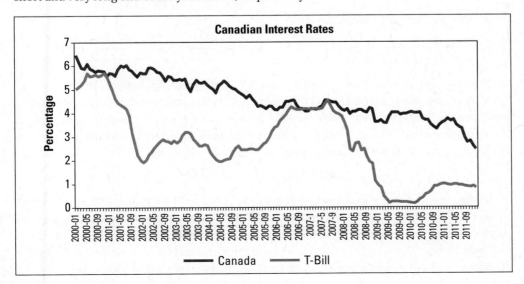

FIGURE 11A-1 *Canadian Interest Rates*

We can see that near the start of the period, in the summer of 2000, the yields on T-bills and on long Canada bonds were very similar; in fact, at the end of 2000, both yielded 5.6 percent. This was an example of a flat yield curve, in which interest rates were essentially the same across all maturities. Short-term interest rates then declined to the 2 percent level, where they remained until the end of 2004, when the Bank of Canada started increasing interest rates again, and they consistently increased to reach the same 4.2 percent level as the yields on long Canada bonds by mid-2006. T-bill yields actually exceeded those on long Canada bonds for the first few months of 2007, a situation referred to as an inverted yield curve, which usually implies a slowdown or recession. Sure enough, shortly afterward, T-bill yields started to fall, and by spring 2009 they were barely positive. Since then, T-bill yields have marginally increased, while long Canada bond yields have fallen. T-bill yields were actually negative for a short time in the United States as central banks around the world tried to stimulate rapidly worsening economies. With the spread between T-bill yields and those on long Canada bonds at 1.80 percent in 2012, the yield curve was upward or normally sloping.

However, for illustrative purposes, let's go back to mid-2004, when T-bill yields were at 2 percent, and see what the yield curve indicated.

Suppose at that time that the yields on zero coupon bonds, which were discussed in Chapter 6, were as follows:

One year	2.00%	Four year	3.65%
Two year	2.75%	Five year	4.00%
Three year	3.25%	Ten year	5.00%

Remember that zero coupon bonds are discount bonds; they do not pay interest explicitly, so the return is earned by buying them at a discount and then selling them at maturity for their par value. Now, suppose an investor wanted to invest for two years. There are several ways to invest for two years, but let's look at two alternatives: an investor can either buy a two-year bond or buy a one-year bond and then invest in another one-year bond at whatever interest rate is available in one year. Figure 11A-2 represents these choices schematically.

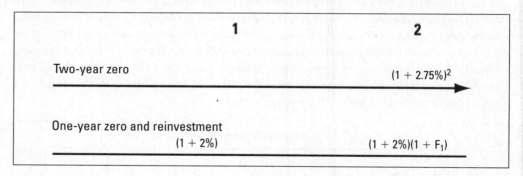

FIGURE 11A-2 *Zero Coupon Bonds*

The two-year bond will earn the investor 2.75 percent compounded for two years or 5.576 percent in total (i.e., $(1.0275)^2 - 1$). Conversely, if the investor invests for one year only and gets 2 percent for the first year, he or she will have to reinvest the next year at an unknown rate for a one-year bond. We can work out a break-even rate, denoted F1, which sets these two strategies equal, using the following equation:

$$(1 + 2.75\%)^2 = (1 + 2\%)(1 + F_1)$$

Solving, we find that $F_1 = 3.51$ percent, because $(1.0275)^2 = 1.05576 = (1.02)(1.0351)$. We have called this rate F_1 because this interest rate is also a forward rate. It is actually the forward rate for a one-year bond, one year in the future. In fact, embedded in the yield curve are a host of forward rates. For example, we could use the three-year and two-year zero coupon yields to calculate a forward rate for a one-year bond starting in two years, which would be:

$$(1 + 3.25\%)^3 = (1 + 2.75\%)^2(1 + F_2)$$

which is 4.26 percent. Equivalently, we could calculate the forward rate for a one-year bond for time period 3 by using the yields on three- and four-year bonds, for time period 4 by using four- and five-year bonds, and so on. In the same way, we could also calculate the forward rate on a two-year bond by using the current yield on the one-year and three-year bonds.

These break-even interest rates are also forward rates because a bank can lock in the rate on a one-year bond for one year in the future. It does this by borrowing using the current one-year rate and then using the proceeds to simultaneously invest for two years at the two-year rate. In one year's time, the bank will owe $102 when it has to repay the one-year 2 percent loan. However, the proceeds from that loan will have been invested in the two-year bond, and the bank is still owed the $105.576 payoff from this bond in the next year. As far as the bank is concerned, this is the same as investing $102 next year in a one-year bond that pays $105.576 at the end of that year, or pays 3.51 percent. As a result, the 3.51 percent break-even rate is also the forward rate for a one-year bond, one year in the future.

Equation 11A-1 is the general formula for calculating forward interest rates (F_t) for the one-year bond:

$$F_t = \frac{(1 + R_t)^t}{(1 + R_{t-1})^{t-1}} - 1 \qquad \text{[11A-1]}$$

Equation 11A-1 says (1) find the future value of investing for t periods by investing in the t period discount bond, then (2) divide by the future value generated by investing for $t - 1$ periods by using the $t - 1$ bond, and (3) subtract 1. This gives the break-even rate as the forward rate for the one-period bond available at the start of time period $t - 1$.

EXAMPLE 11A-1 Estimating Forward Rates

Estimate the one-year forward rate for years 4 and 5, given that zero coupon bonds were yielding the following: three-year, 3.25 percent; four-year, 3.65 percent; and five-year, 4 percent.

Solution

Year 4 forward rate $F_4 = \dfrac{(1 + .0365)^4}{(1 + .0325)^3} - 1 = 0.0486 = 4.86\%$

Year 5 forward rate $F_5 = \dfrac{(1 + .0400)^5}{(1 + .0365)^4} - 1 = 0.0541 = 5.41\%$

Forward Rate Agreements (FRAs)

Banks actually use these forward rates to offer a product called a **forward rate agreement (FRA)** to manage a firm's exposure to interest rate risk. Suppose, for example, that a firm has issued a floating rate bond for which it is required to pay the one-year T-bill yield plus a 0.5 percent credit spread, and the rate adjusts annually with the one-year T-bill yield. The firm may have issued this note in 2000, when it thought short-term interest rates would fall and it wanted to avoid locking in at a higher fixed-term interest rate. But in 2004, suppose that it thinks interest rates are going to increase and it wants protection against rising interest rates. This is the same as saying that it wants to hedge the interest rate exposure from its floating rate note.

If the firm's floating rate note has two years left before it matures, the first year's interest cost is fixed, so what it wants to do is fix next year's interest cost. Because this cost is based on the one-year T-bill rate, the bank would offer an FRA based on the one-year forward rate of 3.5 percent. If the T-bill yield is higher than 3.5 percent—say 4 percent—then the bank would

forward rate agreement (FRA) an agreement that uses forward rates to manage a firm's exposure to interest rate risk; an agreement to borrow or lend at a specified future date at an interest rate that is fixed today

pay the firm the difference of 0.5 percent. If the T-bill yield is less than 3.5 percent—say 3 percent—the firm would pay the bank the difference of 0.5 percent. The cash flows as far as the firm is concerned are shown in Table 11A-1.

Regardless of the T-bill yield, the firm has locked in an overall cost of 4 percent, which is the forward rate for the one-year T-bill of 3.5 percent, plus the 0.5 percent credit spread.

In comparing this interest rate example with our foreign exchange example, we can see that the FRA is a forward contract on the one-year T-bill yield. In this case, the firm starts out with a series of short positions in the one-year T-bill because it is obligated to pay the one-year T-bill yield plus 0.5 percent as long as its floating rate note is outstanding. To cover or hedge this short exposure, it goes long by buying an interest rate forward contract or FRA, which obligates it to pay the difference between the T-bill yield and the forward rate of 3.5 percent.

TABLE 11A-1 Forward Rate Agreements

T-Bill Yield	Spread 0.50%	FRA	Total
3.0	0.5	+0.5	4.0
3.5	0.5	0.0	4.0
4.0	0.5	−0.5	4.0

The example illustrates how banks offer FRAs to help firms manage their interest rate exposure in the same way that they offer forward foreign exchange contracts to help them manage their foreign exchange exposure. In practice, FRAs are more complex than the one in our simple example. This is because most floating rate notes have interest rates that fluctuate with LIBOR every three or six months, rather than with the T-bill yield every year. The second major difference is that forward foreign exchange contracts are generally one-shot deals to cover a single exposure. However, floating rate notes cover a series of future interest payments extending to the note's maturity. As a result, FRAs are tailored to the maturity of the note and are equivalent to a series of interest rate forward contracts. However, there is a basic similarity between FRAs and forward contracts—they are both bank instruments designed to help manage a firm's exposure to interest rates and foreign exchange.

On March 15, 2012, the *Financial Post* gave the quotes for FRAs in U.S. and Canadian dollars, as shown in Table 11A-2.

TABLE 11A-2 Forward Rate Agreements in U.S. and Canadian Dollars

	C$	US$
Three month	1.27	0.45
Six month	1.34	0.51
Nine month	1.41	0.56

Source: Data from *Financial Post*, March 15, 2012.

In each case, the FRAs are for three months. As the upward sloping yield curve in Figure 11A-1 also indicated, the FRAs are for increasing short-term interest rates, implying a recovery in the Canadian and U.S. economies that will cause borrowing costs to rise. The reader will know by now whether or not this market interest rate forecast was correct.

CONCEPT REVIEW QUESTIONS

1. Discuss three different strategies you can follow to invest in Canadian securities to obtain a return over a three-year period.

2. If the yield curve is upward (downward/inverted) where is the market expecting short-term interest rates to go?

SUMMARY

In this chapter, we learn how to diagnose long and short positions in foreign currency and how these positions can be hedged by using forward foreign currency contracts. Interest rate parity is discussed again and used to derive forward interest rates and to show how banks could derive synthetic securities. Futures contracts are then discussed, and we see that they can be viewed as the public market version of forward contracts. We then discuss swap markets and show how basic interest rate and currency swaps can be used to lower borrowing costs or to hedge interest rate or foreign currency exposures.

The forward, futures, and swap markets are all derived from the underlying asset, whether it is foreign exchange rates or interest rates. It is in this sense that these contracts are all derivatives. Market participants regularly use the futures market to offset positions in the swap market, the swap market to offset positions in the forward market, and the forward market to offset positions in the futures market. Moreover, they do this by making contracts with a variety of other market participants, creating a web of linkages, which means that defaults by one party can quickly affect other parties in the financial system, as the failure of AIG has reminded us.

SUMMARY OF LEARNING OBJECTIVES

11.1 Describe forward contracts and identify the associated payoffs with long and short positions in forward contracts.

Spot contracts are agreements for immediate exchange—the price is agreed now, and money and goods (or securities) are exchanged now. Forward contracts are agreements for exchange in the future—the price is agreed now, but money and goods (or securities) are exchanged at a future date. A long position with a spot contract means that you own something, whereas a long position with a forward contract means that you agree to buy the underlying asset in the future. A short position with a spot contract means that you have sold something, and a short position with a forward contract means that you agree to sell the underlying asset in the future. Investors in a long forward position make money when the underlying asset's price rises. Investors in a short forward position make money when the underlying asset's price falls. Forwards (and futures) are instruments that can be used to hedge risk or to speculate on price movements. Hedgers with a short position in the underlying asset use long positions in forwards or futures to eliminate their price risk, and hedgers with a long position in the underlying asset use short positions in forwards or futures to eliminate their price risk.

11.2 Explain how simple forward contracts are priced.

Forward prices are tied to spot prices through the cost-of-carry relationship. Forward prices are equal to the spot price plus the cost of carry.

11.3 Describe futures contracts and explain why futures contracts can be viewed as the public market version of forward contracts.

Futures contracts are standardized forward contracts that are traded on exchanges. Everything in a futures contract is fixed (by the exchange) except the price. Futures contracts feature a clearinghouse that guarantees counterparty performance—that is, it protects against counterparty default. An integral part of the clearinghouse system is the margin account and daily marking to market. These institutions help assure counterparty performance. With daily marking to market, daily profits and losses are added to (subtracted from) each counterparty's account.

11.4 Describe the mechanics of simple swap structures, including interest rate swaps and currency swaps.

A plain vanilla interest rate swap involves one party borrowing at a fixed rate and another borrowing at a floating rate. The two parties then swap interest payments. In addition to interest rates, swaps can also involve different currencies. The mechanics are the same.

11.5 Explain how the credit default swap market contributed to the financial crisis.

By 2007, the CDS market was worth US$45 trillion, or about three times the value of the U.S. stock market. Even more critical than the increased size of the market was the fact that many of the newer CDS contracts were on securities tied to the U.S. sub-prime mortgage market. As the sub-prime market grew, many of the banks generating the risky mortgages bought CDS contracts to hedge their risk. Essentially, they bought insurance against the risky mortgages defaulting. The protection sellers of these CDS contracts varied, but by 2007, AIG alone had written "protection" on US$440 billion worth of mortgage-backed securities or about a third of the entire U.S. sub-prime market. As the sub-prime market in the United States collapsed in 2007 and into 2008, AIG was increasingly called on to make good on these CDS contracts until the very solvency of AIG was at risk. Eventually, AIG was forced to turn to the U.S. government for help. The failure of AIG precipitated fears that other financial institutions would also fail, so banks began conserving cash to ride out the storm. Also, since CDS contracts were with so many different parties, it was difficult for regulators to estimate the extent of the problem and to address it.

11.6 Explain how the general principles of forward contracts can be applied to fixed income securities.

The Canadian government bond market contains a rich array of securities in terms of differing maturities. One can invest for three years, for example, by buying a three-year bond, or a two-year bond and then reinvesting in a one-year bond in two years' time. We can then define the forward for time period 2 on a one-year bond as the interest rate that sets these two strategies equal. Assuming the market is indifferent to any risk differences between these strategies provides a free market interest rate forecast. It also provides the banks with a way to provide simple hedging instruments (FRAs) to allow companies to manage their interest rate risk.

KEY TERMS

basis risk, p. 423
clearing corporation, p. 418
commodity, p. 415
comparative advantage, p. 425
contango, p. 416
convenience yield, p. 416
cost of carry, p. 416
counterparties, p. 424
covering, p. 411
credit (counterparty) risk, p. 411
credit default swap (CDS), p. 431
currency swap, p. 428
daily resettlement, p. 418
exposure, p. 411

forward contract, p. 408
forward interest rate, p. 435
forward rate agreement (FRA), p. 437
futures contract, p. 418
hedging, p. 411
initial margin, p. 418
interest rate swap, p. 424
London inter-bank offered rate (LIBOR), p. 415
long, p. 409
maintenance or variation margin, p. 418
margin, p . 418
margin call, p. 418
naked position, p. 409

net payments, p. 426
notional amount, p. 418
offsetting, p. 419
open interest, p.421
plain vanilla interest rate swap, p. 426
settlement price, p. 418
short, p. 409
speculate, p. 409
spot contract, p. 408
storage costs, p. 416
swap, p. 424
swap rate, p. 429
total return swap, p. 431
underlying assets, p. 408

EQUATIONS

Equation	Formula	Page
[11-1] Profit (loss) from long position	Profit (loss) from long position $= (S_T - F) \times n$	p. 410
[11-2] Profit (loss) from short position	Profit (loss) from short position $= (F - S_T) \times n$	p. 412
[11-3] Forward Premium or Discount	$\dfrac{F}{S} = \dfrac{(1 + k_{domestic})}{(1 + k_{foreign})}$	p. 414
[11-4] Forward Exchange Rate	$F = S \times \dfrac{(1 + k_{domestic})}{(1 + k_{foreign})}$	p. 414

Equation	Formula	Page
[11-5] Forward Rate for Storable Commodities	$F = (1 + c) \times S$	p. 417
[11-6] Payment on an Interest Rate Swap	Payment (fixed rate payee) = NP × (Fixed − FR) × ½	p. 427
[11A-1] Forward Interest Rate	$F_t = \dfrac{(1 + R_t)^t}{(1 + R_{t-1})^{t-1}} - 1$	p. 437

QUESTIONS AND PRACTICE PROBLEMS

Multiple Choice Questions

1. Which of the following statements is false?
    a. A spot price is a price today for immediate delivery.
    b. If a Canadian firm has to pay U.S. dollars in the future, it worries about the potential depreciation of the U.S. dollar.
    c. The forward price is a price today for future delivery.
    d. We say long Canadian dollar and short U.S. dollar when you buy Canadian dollars and sell U.S. dollars.

2. What is the one-year forward rate if the spot rate is C$1.25/US$ and interest rates in Canada and the United States are 5 percent and 4 percent, respectively?
    a. C$1.26/US$
    b. C$1.27/US$
    c. C$1.24/US$
    d. C$1.05/US$

3. Which of the following statements is false?
    a. Removing a naked position is called hedging.
    b. To hedge, you take a long position in a U.S. dollar forward contract if you have a long position in U.S. dollars.
    c. There is no initial cash outlay for a forward contract.
    d. Forward contracts could be used to hedge against exchange rate changes.

4. Using the interest rates in Question 2, what is the cost of carry of synthetically creating a forward rate by borrowing in Canadian dollars and investing in U.S. dollars?
    a. 1.24%
    b. 0.86%
    c. 0.96%
    d. 1.05%

5. Which of the following statements is false?
    a. Cost of carry could be either positive or negative.
    b. The forward rate will change if the spot rate changes.
    c. An income loss is offset by a capital gain on the exchange rate if IRP holds.
    d. The spot rate is the forward rate multiplied by (1 + cost of carry percentage).

6. Which of the following statements about forward contracts is false?
    a. In a naked position, the investor is exposed to changes in the value of the underlying asset.
    b. When an investor has agreed to buy U.S. dollars and sell Canadian dollars forwards, she is long U.S. dollars and short Canadian dollars.
    c. Long means investors own something.
    d. Short means investors own something.

7. Which of the following statements about the profit (loss) from a forward contract is false?
    a. Profit from a long position is negatively affected by the spot price.
    b. Profit from a long position is the difference between the spot price and strike price, multiplied by the number of contracts.
    c. Profit from a short position is negatively affected by the spot price.
    d. Profit from a short position is the difference between the strike price and spot price, multiplied by the number of contracts.

8. Which of the following is false concerning forward contracts and futures contracts?
    a. Futures contracts involve more credit risk than forward contracts do.
    b. The Canadian Derivatives Clearing Corporation (CDCC) takes responsibility for reducing credit risk.
    c. The higher the credit risk, the higher the margin.
    d. Futures contracts are marked to market every day.

9. Suppose a futures contract is for 1,000 units of a certain asset and the starting price is $30. The initial margin is 5 percent and the price closed on the first day at $45. Which of the following statements is *true*?
    a. Only the buyer puts down a $1,500 deposit when entering into the contract; the seller does not put down an initial deposit.
    b. The futures contract is worth $15,000 to the seller at the end of the first day.
    c. The buyer's commitment is to buy 1,000 units of the asset at $30 on a certain date.
    d. At the end of the first day, the seller's equity increased by $45,000.

10. Which of the following statements concerning futures contracts is *false*?
    a. The initial value of the futures contract is zero.
    b. The values of the buyer and the seller of the futures contract offset each other.
    c. If the seller gains, the clearinghouse will transfer the gained value from the seller's account to the buyer's account.
    d. If an investor's account falls below the maintenance margin, she receives a margin call.

11. In practice, most futures contracts are closed out
    a. with an offsetting transaction before the final day of trading.
    b. by actual deliveries of the underlying assets.
    c. by leaving the contracts to expire.
    d. by cash settlement.

12. Which of the following statements concerning Government of Canada bond futures is *false*?
    a. The contract price is quoted per $100.
    b. A maximum position limit is set to prevent a single dominant holding.
    c. Basis risk exists when the underlying asset to be hedged is not identical to the asset used as the hedge.
    d. To hedge, an investor should short a Government of Canada bond futures contract when he needs to buy the same bonds in the future.

13. Which of the following statements about the mechanics of futures contracts is *false*?
    a. All futures contracts are made with a futures exchange, not with an individual.
    b. Investor A might buy a futures contract and investor B might sell one, but instead of one contract between A and B, there are two contracts involving each individual and the exchange.
    c. The riskier the asset, the higher the margin.
    d. All futures contracts are marked to market each month, as the value of the contract changes.

14. Which of the following statements about hedging with futures contracts is *false*?
    a. Futures have less basis risk than forwards.
    b. Basis risk is the risk associated with a hedged position that is attributable to the fact that the asset to be hedged is not identical to the asset used as the hedge.
    c. One of the advantages of forward contracts is that they can be structured to minimize (or even eliminate) basis risk.
    d. Unlike futures contracts, forwards are not standardized and can therefore be tailor-made with respect to underlying assets and maturity dates.

15. What are NOT traded on the Montreal Exchange?
    a. Futures on the bankers' acceptances futures contracts (BAX)
    b. Futures on two-year and 10-year Government of Canada bonds
    c. Futures on S&P/TSX 60 Index (SXF)
    d. Futures on S&P 500 Index

16. Which of the following statements about forwards and futures is *true*?
    a. Forwards are customized and futures are standardized.
    b. Forwards are traded on exchanges while futures are traded on the dealer or OTC markets.
    c. Credit risk is less important for forwards because they are guaranteed by the clearing-house.
    d. Forwards are marked to market daily.

17. Suppose ABC Inc. pays a fixed rate of 9.5 percent and DEF Inc. pays a floating rate of LIBOR + 1.5 percent. They enter into a swap in which ABC Inc. agrees to pay LIBOR to DEF Inc. and DEF Inc. agrees to pay 9.5 percent to ABC Inc. What is the net paying interest rate for ABC Inc.?
    a. LIBOR + 1%
    b. LIBOR
    c. 12%
    d. LIBOR + 0.5%

18. Suppose ABC Inc. borrows at a fixed rate of 9.5 percent or a floating rate of LIBOR + 1 percent. DEF Inc. borrows at a fixed rate of 12 percent or a floating rate of LIBOR + 1.5 percent. Currently, ABC Inc. borrows at its fixed rate and DEF Inc. borrows at its floating rate. They enter into a swap in which ABC Inc. agrees to pay LIBOR to DEF Inc. and DEF Inc. agrees to pay 9.5 percent to ABC Inc. How much, in percentage, could ABC Inc. and DEF Inc. save through the swap, respectively?
    a. 1% and 1%
    b. 0.5% and 1.5%
    c. 1.5% and 0.5%
    d. 2% and 0%

19. Which of the following statements about interest rate swaps is false?
    a. Credit risk exists in interest rate swaps.
    b. The actual cash flows depend on the notional value of the swap.
    c. Net cash settlement increases the credit risk of the interest rate swap.
    d. Interest rate swaps are settled by paying a net amount between the two parties.

20. Which of the following statements about currency swaps is false?
    a. The swap rate for currency swaps is the exchange rate.
    b. The swap rate for currency swaps is the interest rate.
    c. The notional amounts of the currency swap are exchanged at the beginning and end of the swap only.
    d. Usually, one party pays a fixed rate, while a counterparty pays a floating rate.

21. Which of the following statements about plain vanilla interest swaps is false?
    a. It is a "fixed for floating" interest rate swap denominated in one currency.
    b. Counterparties exchange payments representing the difference between the fixed and floating rates.
    c. The semi-annual payment from the fixed rate payee is the notional amount multiplied by the difference between the fixed rate and the floating rate, and divided by two.
    d. The semi-annual payment from the floating rate payee is exactly the same as that from the fixed rate payee.

22. Which of the following are traded over the counter?
    a. equities
    b. bonds
    c. futures
    d. credit default swaps

23. Which of the following statements is *false*?
    a. FRAs are normally based on six-month LIBOR.
    b. FRAs are designed to hedge against exchange rates only.
    c. FRAs are tailored to match the maturities of floating rate notes.
    d. FRAs could be viewed as a series of interest rate forward contracts.

Practice Problems

24. Simon manages a large bond portfolio and wishes to hedge against interest rate risk. His portfolio includes Government of Canada bonds and high-grade Canadian corporate bonds. The correlation between the returns on his fund and the Government of Canada 6-percent 10-year bond is 1.00.
    a. Describe how Simon can hedge against changes in interest rates.
    b. Your analysis has just shown that the actual correlation between the returns on Simon's portfolio and the 6-percent 10-year Government of Canada bond is only .65. What are the implications for the hedge described in part (a)?
    c. Simon strongly believes that interest rates will fall in the near future. Describe how he can speculate on that belief. What risks are inherent in that position (i.e., what happens if interest rates rise?)

25. You have received the following incomplete information about a set of currency forwards. All the forwards are for C$1,000 in one year. Complete the following table.

	Position	Number of contracts	Spot (C$/US$)	Cost today (C$)	Forward (C$/US$)	Spot (C$/US$)	Payoff (C$)	Profit (Loss) C$
			Today			**In one year**		
A	Long	1	1.15	$0	1.20	1.40		
B	Short	1	1.15		1.20	1.40		
C	Long	2	.80	$0		.65	$100	
D		3	1.05		1.30	1.20		$(300)
E	Long	5	1.10	$0	1.25			$800
F			1.00		1.05	1.30		$(2,500)

26. Complete the following table. The underlying asset is ounces of gold. Assume no arbitrage.

	Spot	Cost of carry	1-year forward price	1-year interest rate	Annual storage cost
A	$200			8%	4% of spot
B	$235		$285		2% of spot
C			$300	7%	3% of spot
D	$350		$400	4%	
E	$200			9%	$20 per ounce
F			$300	3%	$5 per ounce
G	$250		$285		$15 per ounce

27. The Health Bracelet Company will need 1,000 kg of copper in one year and is trying to decide between buying the copper on the spot market and using a forward contract. The spot price of copper is $15 per kilogram. The forward price is $19 per kilogram. Health Bracelet will need to rent a warehouse space to store the copper at a cost of $100 per month. Health Bracelet is able to borrow and lend at 4 percent per year. Should Health Bracelet buy its copper using the spot market or the forward market? Explain.

28. Suppose the spot exchange rate is C$1.4665 per €1, while the six-month forward rate is C$1.50 per euro. What will be the profit for an investor who assumes a €100,000 long position in the forward contract if the spot rate in six months equals the following amounts?
    a. C$1.40 per euro   b. C$1.60 per euro

29. Assume another investor takes a €100,000 short position in the six-month euro forward contract with forward rate of C$1.50 per euro. Determine the investor's profit (loss) if the spot rate in six months equals the following amounts.
    a. C$1.40 per euro   b. C$1.60 per euro

30. Suppose the spot exchange rate is C$1.4665 per €1, while the six-month forward rate is C$1.50 per euro. Suppose a firm has to pay a foreign supplier €100,000 in six months and decides to eliminate its foreign exchange exposure by entering into a six-month forward contract.
    a. Should it enter into a short or a long forward position, and if so, for how much?
    b. Assuming it enters into the appropriate forward position, determine the cost in Canadian dollars for the following future spot rates:
        i. C$1.40 per euro   ii. C$1.60 per euro

31. Suppose the spot exchange rate is C$1.4665 per €1, while the six-month forward rate is C$1.50 per euro. Suppose a firm expects to receive €100,000 in six months from a foreign customer and decides to eliminate its foreign exchange exposure by entering into a six-month forward contract.
    a. Should it enter into a short or a long forward position, and if so, for how much?
    b. Assuming it enters into the appropriate forward position, determine the proceeds in Canadian dollars for the following future spot rates:
        i. C$1.40 per euro   ii. C$1.60 per euro

32. CanComp, a Canadian computer manufacturer, will be delivering a large computer system to a German firm in six months. CanComp expects to receive payment of US$1.5 million at that time. Currently the spot rate is C$1.15 per US$ and the six-month forward rate is C $1.25 per US$.
    a. What risks does CanComp face with the sale of the computer system?
    b. Describe how CanComp can hedge the currency risk.
    c. Determine CanComp's profit or loss on the hedge if the actual spot rate in six months is:
       i.   C $0.75 per $US   ii.   C $1.50 per $US
    d. Given your answers to (a) and (b), should CanComp hedge? *Hint*: Remember ex ante versus ex post.

33. CanComp has a contract to deliver a large computer system to a South African company in one year and would like to hedge the currency risk. CanComp will receive payment of R3.5 million (the currency of South Africa is the rand) in one year for the computer system. CanComp can borrow and lend in Canada at 3 percent per annum and can borrow and lend in South Africa at 7 percent per annum. Assume the borrowing and lending is risk free. The current spot exchange rate is C$/Rand .35 and there is no one-year forward exchange rate. Describe how CanComp can hedge the currency risk by creating a synthetic forward contract. Demonstrate that your synthetic forward contract hedges the currency risk. Assume all investments are risk free.

⚙ 34. Bert, the business reporter for the *Sidney Driftwood*, a small newspaper, has contacted you for information about the oil market. Provide responses to his questions below with arbitrage opportunities.
    a. "I understand supply and demand and the difference between the spot and the forward market. I understand that there will be an effect on the forward price of oil if an oil field in Iraq, which is expected to go into production in one year, does not go into production. There will be a decrease in the expected supply so it makes sense that the price expected in the future (the forward price) will increase. What I don't understand is why this causes a change in the spot price—after all the supply of oil today hasn't changed, so why would today's price change?"
    b. "The second thing that puzzled me was the effect of hurricane Katrina on the forward price of oil. The area around New Orleans is a major storage depot for oil in the United States and there was extensive damage to the storage facilities in the hurricane. Consequently, there would have been a decrease in the amount of oil available today and, logically, the spot price would have gone up. What I don't understand is why the forward price also rose— future oil production doesn't depend on the availability of storage facilities today."

35. Describe the process of marking to market for futures contracts.

36. Describe open interest with respect to futures contracts.

37. Explain the difference between forwards and futures.

38. Explain basis risk and the advantage of forward contracts over future contracts in minimizing basis risk.

39. Explain why two counterparties would enter into an interest rate swap even when one has an absolute financing advantage in both the fixed and the floating rate markets.

40. Ethel and Egbert have decided to invest in the futures market. Both entered into 1,000 futures contracts, which required a $30,000 initial margin. The maintenance margin for each investor is $22,500. Ethel and Egbert disagree about the future so Ethel went long while Egbert went short. Estimate each investor's daily profit (loss) and equity position (assuming no cash deposits or withdrawals).

		Ethel		Egbert	
Day	Spot price	Daily profit (loss)	Equity position (margin balance)	Daily profit (loss)	Equity position (margin balance)
0	$100		$30,000		$30,000
1	$75				
2	$50				
3	$80				
4	$130				
5	$100				

41. An investor enters into a long position in 50,000 futures contracts that requires a $50,000 initial margin and has a maintenance margin that is 75 percent of this amount. The futures price associated with this contract is $20. Assume the spot price of the underlying asset closes at the following prices for the next five days: $20.50, $20.75, $21.00, $19.75, and $19.25. Estimate the daily profit (loss) for this investor, as well as the equity position, assuming no cash deposits or withdrawals are made from the account.

42. An investor enters into a short position in 50,000 futures contracts that requires a $50,000 initial margin and has a maintenance margin that is 75 percent of this amount. The futures price associated with this contract is $20. Assume the spot price of the underlying asset closes at the following prices for the next five days: $20.50, $20.75, $21.00, $19.75, and $19.25. Estimate the daily profit (loss) for this investor, as well as the equity position, assuming no cash deposits or withdrawals are made from the account.

43. Ethel decided to invest in the futures market. She entered a long position in 1,000 futures contracts that require a $30,000 initial margin. The maintenance margin is $22,500. Assume that Ethel deposits the minimum amount of cash required to satisfy any margin calls and makes no cash withdrawals. Assume also that the cash earns no interest. At the end of day 5, Ethel closed her position.

Complete the following table.

Day	Spot price	Daily profit (loss)	Equity position before cash deposit	Margin call?	Cash deposit	Equity position (margin balance)
0	$100		$0		$30,000	$30,000
1	$92	−$8,000	$22,000	Yes	$500	$22,500
2	$95					
3	$103					
4	$90					
5	$100					

44. Aqua Boat Company recently issued floating rate debt. The rate is LIBOR + 3 percent, reset semi-annually. Compost Earth Company has recently issued fixed rate debt. The rate is 5 percent per year. Aqua and Compost have entered into a two-year interest rate swap with a notional value of $1.0 million. Aqua agrees to pay 6 percent fixed; Compost agrees to pay LIBOR + 2 percent. Payments are exchanged every six months based on LIBOR at the beginning of the six-month period. Determine the interest rate swap net payments for Aqua.

Start of period	LIBOR %	Floating pay %	Fixed pay %	Net pay %	Net pay $
1	4%				
2	5%				
3	3%				
4	1%				

45. Joyce and Anthony are in the process of renewing their mortgages. Each mortgage is an interest-only mortgage (i.e., the borrower pays only interest and has a balloon payment at the end) for $100,000. Anthony, having an excellent credit history, is offered the choice between a fixed rate mortgage at + 3 percent and a floating rate mortgage at prime + 1 percent ("prime" rate is the domestic version of LIBOR). Joyce is offered the choice between a fixed rate mortgage at 7 percent and a floating rate mortgage at prime + 3 percent. The current prime rate is 3 percent. Floating rate mortgages are reset at the start of each year.

    Anthony and Joyce have both recently retired—Anthony's future income is closely tied to market interest rates (he has his retirement funds invested in bonds) while Joyce has a fixed retirement income (the Canada Pension Plan).

    a. Ignoring interest costs, which mortgage would Anthony prefer—fixed or floating? Why? Which mortgage would Joyce prefer—fixed or floating? Why?

    b. Assume that Anthony chose a fixed rate mortgage and Joyce chose a floating rate mortgage.

       i. Design a swap agreement between Anthony and Joyce that will make them both better off.

       ii. What is this type of swap called and what are the risks associated with it?

       iii. If the prime rate for the next four years is: 3%, 5%, 4%, and 2%, respectively:

           1. Show the cash flows between Anthony and Joyce.

           2. Demonstrate that the swap will make Anthony and Joyce better off.

46. For Question 18, explain how the spreads are shared between the two parties, and describe the absolute advantage and comparative advantage in the swap.

47. CanGold Mining Company borrowed €100 million in France at an annual interest rate of 3.5 percent. The principal plus interest is due in one year. CanGold used the funds to purchase machine parts in Germany for use in its Indonesian gold mine. In one year, the mine is expected to produce 1 million ounces of gold. Gold is sold on the world market in U.S. dollars. CanGold would like to hedge its currency and commodity risk. The CFO of CanGold has been quoted the following forward contracts:

    i. One year C$/euro forward exchange rate: 1.60

    ii. One year C$/US$ forward exchange rate: 1.05

    iii. One year US$/euro forward exchange rate: 1.10

    iv. One year gold forward contract: US$250 per ounce

    Design two hedging strategies for CanGold so that CanGold has profit in C$. Which strategy is better? *Hint:* Are there any arbitrage opportunities?

48. Angela, a new investor, has contacted you with a question about the swap market. Provide a response to her question: "A swap agreement allows two companies to swap payments. Presumably, both parties believe that this agreement will make them better off. If the markets are efficient, how can a swap make both participants better off?" Answer this with respect to both interest rate and currency swaps.

49. Describe how total return swaps work.

50. David says that "CDS is essentially the same as buying default insurance on the risky corporate bond, where the buyer pays for the default protection and the seller sells the protection." Thus he concludes that CDS is the same as other insurance. Comment on David's conclusion.

51. You are in the process of developing forecasts of short-term interest rates. In order to determine a bond trading strategy, you want to determine the market's short-term (one-year) interest forecasts for different future periods. You have obtained the following data on traded Government of Canada zero coupon bonds of different maturities. Determine the implied one-year forward rates.

Maturity	Observed YTM%
1 year	3%
2 years	5%
3 years	7%
4 years	6%
5 years	5%

1-year forward rate expected in	Implied 1-year forward rate %
1 year	
2 years	
3 years	
4 years	
5 years	

52. Calculate the F_1, F_2, F_3, given the following interest rates on zero coupon bonds:

One year	2.10%	Four year	3.75%
Two year	2.65%	Five year	4.05%
Three year	3.25%		

53. At the end of the current year, you observe the following data about Government of Canada pure discount bonds (zero coupon bonds):

Bond issue: A	Years to maturity: 1	YTM%: 5
Bond issue: B	Years to maturity: 2	YTM%: 7
Bond issue: C	Years to maturity: 3	YTM%: 10

a. What price do you expect bond C to sell for at the end of year 2?

b. The Government of Canada is considering issuing a coupon bond. The bond will pay a 7-percent coupon, paid annually. The face value of the bond will be $1,000. What price would you expect the bond to sell for today?

12 | Options

LEARNING OBJECTIVES

12.1 Describe the basic nature of call options and the factors that influence their value.

12.2 Describe the basic nature of put options and the payoffs associated with long and short positions in put options.

12.3 Explain how to use put-call parity to estimate call and put prices, and explain how it can be used to synthetically create call, put, and underlying positions.

12.4 Explain how to use the Black-Scholes option pricing model to price call options.

12.5 Explain how options are traded and what is meant by implied volatility.

12.6 Understand by means of the simplest option pricing model what factors affect the value of a call option and provide a guide to their order of magnitude.

Companies often grant stock options to employees in an attempt to attract and retain talented workers. In fact, for some of the highest-paid CEOs in Canada, stock options are a larger component of total compensation than their salaries. However, the manner in which these options are awarded has left the door open for manipulation. In the United States, regulators have focused on the illegal practice of backdating options. Canadian stock exchanges and regulators are keeping an eye out for options abuses as well, and penalties can be severe. One TSX rule stipulates that companies may not issue options based on market prices that do not fully reflect non-public material information.

Source: Torys LLP website at www.torys.com and TMX Group website at www.tmx.com.

CHAPTER 12 **PREVIEW**

In Chapter 11, we discussed linear derivative contracts, in which the payoffs directly reflect the behaviour of the underlying asset, so both gains and losses are generated. In this chapter, we discuss contracts that produce non-linear payoffs, which may be limited in some way through a maximum gain, loss, or both. The most basic contract is a call option, for which the payoff is limited on the downside, so losses are restricted. Working out the value of an asset that in some cases can generate only positive payoffs led to a Nobel Prize for the development of the celebrated Black-Scholes option pricing model (OPM). We show why the OPM is such a powerful model and how it can be derived by creating a risk-free asset. You will learn what determines the value of options, how to use the OPM on the Montreal Exchange's website, and what all those Greek letters mean. This chapter introduces ideas that are often used in business finance, as you will see in Chapter 19, for example, when you learn how options have been used to design innovative new financing instruments.

12.1 CALL OPTIONS

Call Option Basics

Learning Objective 12.1
Describe the basic nature of call options and the factors that influence their value.

call option the right, but not the obligation, to buy an underlying asset at a fixed price for a specified time

exercise price or **strike price** the price at which an investor can buy the underlying asset

exercise to implement the rights of options by buying (in the case of call options) or selling (in the case of put options)

expiration date the last date on which options can be converted or exercised

payoff the proceeds that would be generated from the option if today was the expiration date

We begin by considering the characteristics of the basic **call option**, which is defined as the *right, but not the obligation*, to *buy* an underlying asset at a fixed price for a specified time. The price at which an investor can buy the underlying asset is called the **exercise price** or **strike price**, and the last date at which the option can be converted or **exercised** is called the **expiration date**.

We begin our discussion with a simple example in which the forward price on an underlying asset is $50. We assume a call option is available on that asset with an exercise price (X) of $50. We set the exercise price equal to the forward price to simplify some of the discussion; however, it is not a necessary assumption. For now, we will not specify the expiration date of the option. The **payoff** for the buyer (holder) of this call (i.e., a long call position) for various underlying asset prices is depicted in Figure 12-1. The payoff refers to the proceeds that would be generated from the call option if today was the expiration date and the option holder had to decide whether to exercise the option or not. It does not exactly reflect the investor's profits, because it does not account for the purchase price of the option, which we will discuss later. We have also included the payoff from a long position in the underlying asset (i.e., from holding it) in Figure 12-1.

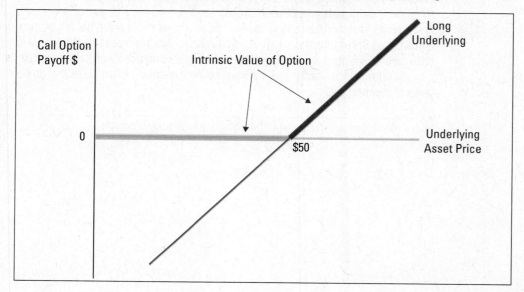

FIGURE 12-1 *Call Holder's Payoff*

First, think about a long position in the underlying asset. In this case, the payoff is a 45-degree line going through the origin, because the value varies one to one with the price of the underlying asset. In other words, the underlying asset is worth (or pays off) $1 if the price goes to $1, $2 if it goes to $2, $50 if the price goes to $50, and so on. Now let's shift the 45-degree line over so it cuts the horizontal axis at the strike price, which in this case is the forward price of $50. The result is the payoff from a forward contract, as discussed in Chapter 11. If an investor buys the asset forward, then he or she has a long position; if the asset price exceeds the forward price, the investor has a profit, and if the asset price is less than the forward price, the investor has a loss. The fact that the payoff on the forward contract is a straight line (which happens to be 45 degrees) is the reason that we previously referred to it as a linear payoff.

Now think about the call with the strike price equal to the forward price of $50. If at expiration the underlying asset's price is above $50, say $55, the investor exercises the call. This means that he or she pays $50 and "calls" the asset away from the counterparty—that is, the person who has sold the call. The investor could then obtain a payoff of $5 by selling the asset for $55 in the open market, exactly as we discussed with respect to the forward contract. In this case, we say the call is **in the money**. Conversely, if the underlying asset's price is below $50, the call is worthless and would not be exercised. No one would pay the strike price to call the asset away from its owner for $50 when it can be bought for less in the open market. This is the crucial fact about options: they give the owner the *right*, but not the *obligation*, to do something. In contrast to the long position in the forward contract, the investor doesn't incur losses in a long call position when the price of the underlying asset is below the strike price, which we refer to as being **out of the money**.[1] As a result, the investor gets the payoff from the forward contract above the strike price and gets zero below. For this reason, options are examples of securities with non-linear payoffs.[2]

in the money the option would generate a positive payoff if exercised today

out of the money the option would generate a negative payoff if exercised today

---

EXAMPLE 12-1   Call Holder's Payoffs

Complete the following table, giving the payoffs for various underlying asset prices for a call option buyer who buys a call option with a strike price of $50.

Asset price ($)	30	40	50	55	60	70
Call holder's payoff ($)						

Solution

Asset price ($)	30	40	50	55	60	70
Call holder's payoff ($)	0	0	0	5 $(55-50)$	10 $(60-50)$	20 $(70-50)$

Notice that the payoff is zero for all prices at or below the strike price of $50. Beyond $50, the payoff increases by $1 for every $1 increase in the underlying asset price.

The previous discussion leaves out one important detail—namely, the seller from whom investors are buying the option. The contracts we are examining in this chapter are secondary market options, which means that the supply and trading of these options has no impact on the underlying asset. When investors buy a call option, they buy it from some other market participant unrelated to the underlying asset. Until 30 years ago, investment bankers arranged option contracts directly between two parties, so there was significant credit risk attached to the counterparty. In other words, when investors exercised the call, they could not be certain that the counterparty would deliver it. In this way, option markets were similar to the original swap and forward markets. Today, as with the swap markets, option markets consist of unique

---

[1] An option is said to be "at the money" when the market price of the underlying asset equals the strike price.

[2] Strictly speaking, the payoffs are piecewise linear.

over-the-counter (OTC) options that are still arranged between two parties with credit risk. However, there are a significant number of exchange-traded options, similar to futures, which have been designed to remove credit risk. In fact, traded options markets are tightly integrated with futures markets. For now, we will ignore credit risk and consider the payoff for the person who sells a call option; such a person is called an **option writer**, because he or she has written the call option that is purchased by someone else. It is common to say that option writers have assumed a **short position** in the option.

option writer the person who sells an option

short position the position taken by the option writer

If someone sells a call option, the payoff is the mirror image of that received by the person who buys it, just as the payoff to a short forward position is the mirror image of that of a long forward position. For example, we have already looked at the payoff to the $50 call holder and noted that, as the asset price increases—say to $55—the payoff on the call also increases—in this case to $5. This $5 payoff occurs as the asset is called away from the option writer for $50 and sold for $55. The payoff to the call option writer is the opposite, as he or she has to go into the market and buy this asset for $55, then surrender it for only $50, losing $5. Conversely, when a call expires out of the money and is not exercised, the option writer doesn't lose anything. The payoff of this $50 call for the option writer is depicted in Figure 12-2.

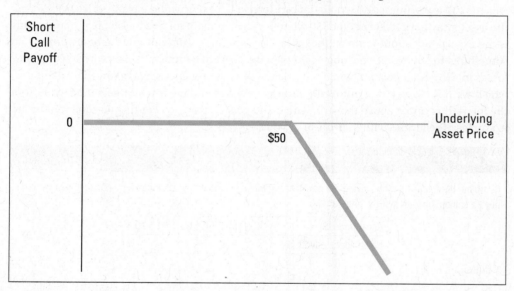

FIGURE 12-2 *Call Option Writer's Payoff*

Notice that the payoff from writing the call is the mirror image of that from buying the call. It is the payoff from buying the call "folded" downward at the exercise price.

EXAMPLE 12-2   Option Writer's Payoffs

Complete the following table depicting the payoffs for various underlying asset prices for an option writer who sells a call option with a strike price of $50.

Asset price ($)	30	40	50	55	60	70
Option writer's payoff ($)						

Solution

Asset price ($)	30	40	50	55	60	70
Option writer's payoff ($)	0	0	0	−5 (50 − 55)	−10 (50 − 60)	−20 (50 − 70)

Notice that the payoff is zero for all prices at or below the strike price of $50. Beyond $50, the payoff decreases by $1 for every $1 increase in the underlying asset price, because the option writer has agreed to sell the asset for $50.

Call Option Values

So what is the value of a call option? At expiration, when the call is in the money, the value of the option is the asset price (S) minus the exercise price (X). When it is out of the money, the value is zero. This is called the **intrinsic value (IV)** and is depicted by the bold line in Figure 12-1. Equation 12-1 shows how we can estimate the intrinsic value of a call option.

$$\text{IV (Call)} = \text{Max} (S - X, 0) \qquad [12\text{-}1]$$

Equation 12-1 states that the IV of a call equals $S - X$ when the call is in the money and equals 0 otherwise.

The IV is the value of an option on the expiration date. However, before expiration, the value of a call will exceed its intrinsic value because of the option's **time value (TV)**. The market value of the option, commonly known as the **option premium**, is the sum of its IV and its TV. This relationship is given in Equation 12-2.

$$\text{IV(Put)} = \text{Max}(X - S, 0) \qquad [12\text{-}2]$$

We can rearrange this equation to solve for the time value, as shown in Equation 12-3.

$$\text{TV} = \text{Option premium} - \text{IV} \qquad [12\text{-}3]$$

> **intrinsic value (IV)** the value of an option at expiration; it is positive when the option is in the money and zero when it is out of the money

> **time value (TV)** the difference between the option premium and the intrinsic value

> **option premium** the market value of the option; the sum of an option's IV and TV

EXAMPLE 12-3 | **Estimating Call Option Intrinsic and Time Values**

Assume the $50 call option referred to above is selling for $3 in the market. Determine the intrinsic value and time value of this call option, assuming the following prices for the underlying asset:

a. $48

b. $50

c. $52

Solution

a. IV = Max(48 − 50, 0) = 0; TV = 3 − 0 = $3

b. IV = Max(50 − 50, 0) = 0; TV = 3 − 0 = $3

c. IV = Max(52 − 50, 2) = 2; TV = 3 − 2 = $1

It has long been known that the option value depends on the price of the underlying asset, as indicated in Figure 12-1. However, it was not until Fischer Black and Myron Scholes, two finance professors from the University of Chicago, came up with the Black-Scholes option pricing model that the relationship was clearly understood.[3] We discuss this option pricing model later in the chapter; for now, let's step back and think intuitively about what drives option values.

The option value is influenced by the ratio of the price of the underlying asset to the strike price. Because X is fixed for each call, this essentially means that as S falls far below X, not only is the IV of the option zero, but so is the TV because there is less chance of the price of the underlying asset recovering to exceed the strike price. At the other extreme, when the price of the underlying asset is far above the strike price, the time value gets smaller, as discussed below. This means that **deep** in the money and deep out of the money calls are easier to value, because their values get closer to their intrinsic values as their time values get smaller.

> **deep** describes options that are so far in (out of) the money that they are almost certain (not) to be exercised

---

[3] Robert Merton was also a pioneer in option pricing. Both he and Myron Scholes (from Timmins, Ontario) won Nobel prizes for their work. Unfortunately, Fischer Black died before he could be similarly honoured.

For example, suppose over the next period it is equally likely that the price of the underlying asset will increase or decrease by $5. If the asset price is currently $10 and the strike price $50, the call is deep out of the money. With a decrease in the asset price to $5, the call remains deep out of the money. Even with an increase in the asset price to $15, it is still deep out of the money. With deep out of the money calls, the investor needs a sequence of very positive returns on the underlying asset to generate any value. This makes the time value very small.

Now take the opposite situation, in which the asset price is $100. This means the intrinsic value of the call is $50, so it is deep in the money. When the price changes by $5, the intrinsic value of the call also changes by close to $5. If the time value is zero, then the change in the value of the call is exactly the same as the underlying asset. In the extreme case of a call on an asset with a strike price of $0, then the call is deep in the money and exactly the same as the underlying asset.[4]

The impact of the underlying asset's price on the call's value means that a curve connects the intrinsic value of the option when it is deep in and deep out of the money. This relationship is illustrated in Figure 12-3, and it means that the call value is related in a non-linear way to the underlying asset price.

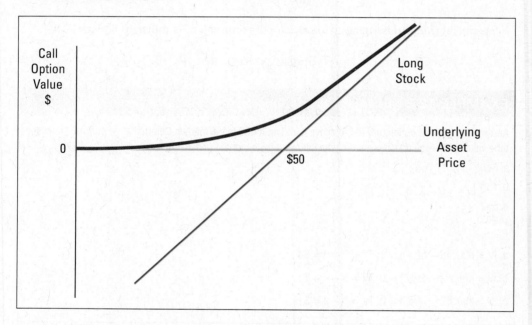

FIGURE 12-3 *The Value of a Call Option*

The fact that deep in and out of the money call options are relatively easy to value means that the most difficult options to value are those for which the price of the asset is close to the strike price. For options that are at the money (i.e., where $S = X$), the TV is at its largest and, by definition, the IV is zero. Unfortunately, most options start out with the strike price set close to the price of the underlying asset, so they have lots of time value and little intrinsic value. This factor is what makes option valuation complicated.

The discussion above directs our attention to the most important component of the option value, which is the *risk* of the underlying asset. In most areas of finance, risk is estimated as the variability or standard deviation of an asset's return. However, this is closely related to the range of possible outcomes, and it was the *range* that we used when we said the outcomes could be plus or minus $5, or a range of $10. Now suppose we are valuing two at the money calls on different assets that both have the same $50 strike price. The first call is on an asset with two equally likely outcomes of plus or minus $5 for a price range of $10, while the second is on a riskier asset with two equally likely outcomes of plus or minus $10 or a range of $20. Which call is more valuable?

---

[4] This assumes that the value of the asset, like that of a common share, cannot become negative.

First, consider what happens when the price of the underlying asset falls below X. We know that we are not going to exercise the call and will let it expire worthless, so whether the asset price is $5 or $10 below the strike price does not matter. Conversely, the amount by which the asset price exceeds X does matter. The call on the low-risk asset will now have an intrinsic value of $5, whereas that on the riskier asset will have an intrinsic value of $10. An important aspect of option pricing is the fact that call options on riskier assets are worth more than those on low-risk assets. This is because the call protects you from "downside" risk, so how far down you go doesn't matter since the payoff is still zero. All that matters is the upside or how far above the strike price the asset price can get. Anything that expands the range of outcomes or risk of the underlying asset makes a call on the asset more valuable.

Now consider *time*. Risk itself is important, but option values also depend critically on how much time is left until expiration. No matter how risky an underlying asset, if a deep out of the money call is close to expiration—say a day away—it will not be worth much. A deep out of the money call on a risky asset with a long time to expiration may be very valuable. Take our previous example of a plus or minus $5 change in the price of an underlying asset currently worth $10. If this is the possible weekly change, then a one-week call at $50 is worthless, because it is not possible for the price of the underlying asset to exceed $50. However, if the same call has nine weeks left, it is possible that the price of the underlying asset can increase by $5 each week and go from $10 to $55, thereby giving the call value.

Over long periods, all sorts of things can happen to give value to the underlying asset and, therefore, to a call on that asset. For example, in 2001, the value of the Canadian dollar was barely US$0.65, the price of a barrel of oil was $20, and the price of one share of Nortel Networks Corporation, a major Canadian telecom company, was $122. Eleven years later, the Canadian exchange rate was at parity with the US dollar; oil was consistently over US$100 a barrel; and Nortel had gone into bankruptcy protection, rendering its shares almost worthless. Such dramatic price movements illustrate why call options on risky assets with a long time to expiration are very valuable.

We will discuss the impact of risk and time more formally when we discuss a model of option pricing, but for now it's important to remember that risk compounds through time, causing the range of outcomes to increase. This compounding or magnification is greater for high-risk stocks than it is for low-risk stocks, which makes long-dated call options on risky assets more valuable than options on short-dated low-risk assets. For any given call option, if everything else is constant, its value will *decrease* over time. For example, an at the money call starts out with maximum time value and no intrinsic value. If nothing else changes, and it is still at the money at expiration, then it is worthless. Generally, the time value decreases at an increasing rate as the call gets closer to expiration.

We should also consider the factors driving the underlying asset's price. For example, from Chapter 7, we know that the value of a common share is the present value of a stream of dividends, so call options on equities depend on these dividend payments. We will discuss dividend policy in Chapter 22, but suppose a resource company has very large profits because natural resource prices are at an all-time high, which is not expected to continue. As a result, a company's stock price is $38, consisting of a $26 value for its continuing operations and $12 for its cash. If the firm decides to pay out this cash as a dividend, the stock price will drop by $12, reducing the value of a call on the stock.

Generally, options are not protected from any dividend payments made by the underlying asset, so options on high-dividend-paying stocks or assets with large cash distributions are worth less than those on non-dividend-paying stocks. In 1989, Inco Ltd., one of the largest nickel producers in the world, was in the situation described in the preceding paragraph and unexpectedly paid out a US$10 dividend, which was worth about C$12 at the time, causing a dramatic drop in its stock price. This illustrates how important it is to pay attention to the dividend payments of the underlying asset, because they can affect the price of both the underlying asset and the option.

The final factor that affects option prices is the *risk-free interest rate*. Normally, when interest rates go up, the values of securities go down. For example, bond prices always go down when interest rates rise, as discussed in Chapter 6, but equity prices also tend to go down, because the equity discount rate may go up. However, option prices behave differently, because the main effect of increasing interest rates is to decrease the present value of the strike price. An increase in the interest rate has a similar effect on a call price as decreasing the strike price. As a result, call options tend to increase with increases in interest rates.

To summarize our discussion, call option prices display the following characteristics:

- They approach their intrinsic value for deep in and deep out of the money calls.
- They increase with the price of the underlying asset.
- They decrease with a higher strike price.
- They increase if the underlying asset is riskier.
- They increase as the time to expiration increases.
- They decrease as the dividend payments of the underlying asset increase.
- They increase as interest rates increase.

That's a lot of factors to consider in a pricing model, and it is important to remember that we considered each of them in isolation, looking at the impact of a change in only one factor at a time. In reality, of course, many of these factors are changing all the time, and they affect one another. For example, an increase in interest rates or a change in risk may have a negative effect on option prices if the indirect effect on the asset price is greater than the *direct* effects discussed above. However, before we consider how to incorporate these factors into a pricing model, we can bracket the value of the call option by considering the characteristics of put options.

CONCEPT REVIEW QUESTIONS

1. Explain why the payoff from a call option is non-linear.
2. Explain how to estimate the intrinsic value and time value for a call option.
3. Briefly describe the main factors that affect a call option's value and how they affect the value.

12.2 PUT OPTIONS

Put Option Payoffs

A **put option** is the opposite of a call option: it gives the owner the *right, but not the obligation,* to *sell* an underlying asset at a fixed price for a specified time. Consider the value of a put on an underlying asset with a strike price equal to the forward price of $50. The payoff for the holder of a put is depicted in Figure 12-4.

In considering the behaviour of a call option, we first examined a long position in the asset. Because a put is the opposite of a call, we start with the opposite of a long position in the underlying asset, which is a short position. When the underlying asset is sold forward and its price exceeds the forward price at $55, the investor loses $5. This occurs because he or she has to go into the market and pay $55 to buy the asset to deliver against the forward contract, for which he or she gets only $50. Conversely, if the asset price falls to $45, the investor generates a $5 profit. He or she buys the asset for $45 and then delivers it to meet the forward commitment and receives the $50 forward price. Graphically, the short position is a 45-degree line going through the forward price of $50, as depicted in Figure 12-4. Notice that this is the mirror image of the long position.

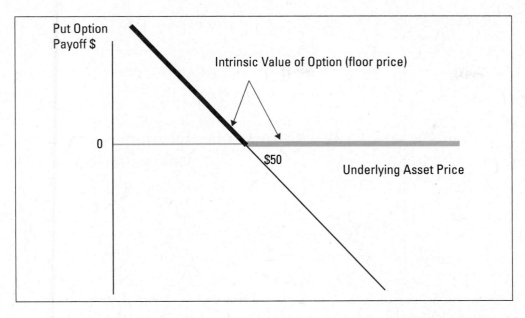

Put Option Payoff $

Intrinsic Value of Option (floor price)

0

$50

Underlying Asset Price

FIGURE 12-4 *Put Holder's Payoff*

Now consider the payoff on the put option. If the asset price increases, the investor does not exercise the put option, because there is no reason to sell the asset for $50 when the investor can sell it in the open market for, say, $55. Conversely, if the asset price drops to $45, the investor exercises the put. It is better to use the put contract and sell it to the counterparty for $50 than to sell it in the open market for $45. The result is the opposite of the call option; put options pay off when the asset price drops below the strike price, and they are worthless when the asset price is above the strike price. The put allows an investor to take advantage of the downside risk attached to an asset, just as the call allows an investor to take advantage of the upside.

EXAMPLE 12-4   Put Holder's Payoffs

Complete the following table depicting the payoffs for various underlying asset prices for an investor who buys a put option with a strike price of $50.

Asset price ($)	30	40	50	55	60	70
Put holder's payoff ($)						

Solution

Asset price ($)	30	40	50	55	60	70
Put holder's payoff ($)	20 (50 − 30)	10 (50 − 40)	0	0	0	0

Notice that the payoff is zero for all prices at or above the strike price of $50. Below $50, the payoff increases by $1 for every $1 decrease in the underlying asset price.

Now we consider the payoff for the put writer, who has assumed what is commonly called a short position in the put. We know that when the asset price increases above the strike price, the put expires worthless, so the payoff to both the put owner and writer is zero. When the asset price drops below the strike price, say, to $45, then the owner of the put buys the asset for $45 in the open market and sells it to the put writer for $50, making a $5 profit. The put writer's payoff is the opposite of the put holder's, because he or she has to pay $50 for an asset that can be sold for only $45, thereby incurring a $5 loss. The payoff for the put writer is given in Figure 12-5.

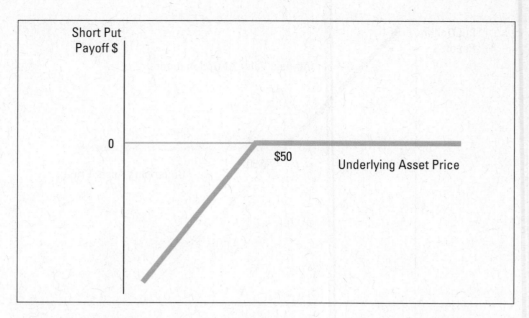

FIGURE 12-5 *Put Writer's Payoff*

Notice that it is the mirror image of the put holder's payoff, or the put holder's payoff folded downward.

EXAMPLE 12-5   Put Writer's Payoffs

Complete the following table depicting the payoffs for various underlying asset prices for a put option writer who sells a put option with a strike price of $50.

Asset price ($)	30	40	50	55	60	70
Put writer's payoff ($)						

Solution

Asset price ($)	30	40	50	55	60	70
Put writer's payoff ($)	−20 (30 − 50)	−10 (40 − 50)	0	0	0	0

Notice that the payoff is zero for all prices at or above the strike price of $50. Below $50, the payoff decreases by $1 for every $1 decrease in the underlying asset price, because the put writer has agreed to buy the asset for $50.

Put Option Values

Equation 12-4 shows how we can estimate the intrinsic value of a put option.

[12-4]
$$IV(Put) = Max(X - S, 0)$$

Equation 12-4 states that the IV of a put equals $X - S$ when the put is in the money, and equals 0 otherwise. Equations 12-2 and 12-3, regarding the time value and option premium of an option, apply to puts in the same way as they did for calls.

EXAMPLE 12-6   Estimating Put Option Intrinsic and Time Values

Assume the $50 put option referred to above is selling for $2.25 in the market. Determine the intrinsic value and time value of this put option, assuming the following prices for the underlying asset:

continued

EXAMPLE 12-6   Estimating Put Option Intrinsic and Time Values *continued*

a. $48

b. $50

c. $52

Solution

a. IV = Max(50 − 48, 0) = 2; TV = 2.25 − 2 = $0.25

b. IV = Max(50 − 50, 0) = 0; TV = 2.25 − 0 = $2.25

c. IV = Max(50 − 52, 0) = 0; TV = 2.25 − 0 = $2.25

The factors that drive put prices are the same factors that affect call prices. However, the effects are usually in the opposite direction. When the asset price is significantly above the strike price, the put is deep out of the money, so the price approaches its intrinsic value of zero. Conversely, when the asset price drops and is well below the strike price, the put is deep in the money, and again the put's price approaches its intrinsic value. This is opposite to the call but, like the call, the put's maximum time value occurs at the strike price, when its intrinsic value is zero. In contrast to the call, an increase in the asset price will decrease the put price, while a higher strike price will increase its value. However, an increase in either the expiration date or the risk (uncertainty) in the underlying asset will increase the put price in the same manner as it would a call price. A decrease in interest rates or an increase in cash dividend payments will increase the put price.

All of the effects discussed above are predictable, given the intuitive understanding of these factors' impact on call prices. However, there is a major difference between puts and calls when it comes to whether or not an investor can exercise the option before the expiration date. Note that **European options** can be exercised only at maturity, whereas **American options** can be exercised at any time up to and including the expiration date. This distinction is no longer geographic, as the names imply, because European options are traded in North America and vice versa. For call options on non-dividend-paying assets, the distinction is not important; as long as the option can be sold, it should never be exercised before maturity, because there is always some time value.[5] However, the distinction is important for put options. Consider what happens if the underlying asset price goes to zero, perhaps because it is a common share and the firm goes bankrupt. Because the underlying asset can never go below zero, the put reaches its maximum value. In this case, all American options would be exercised, because the put holder gets the maximum payoff immediately, and that cash can then be reinvested elsewhere.

We summarize the impact of these basic factors on option prices in Table 12-1.

European options options that can be exercised only at maturity

American options options that can be exercised at any time up to and including the expiration date

TABLE 12-1 Factors Affecting Option Prices

	Call Prices	Put Prices
Higher asset price (S)	↑	↓
Higher exercise price (X)	↓	↑
Longer expiration	↑	↑
Increased volatility	↑	↑
Higher interest rates	↑	↓
Higher dividends	↓	↑

[5] For interest- or dividend-paying assets, premature exercise may occur in the case of a very large payment that significantly reduces the value of the underlying asset.

1. Contrast the payoff from a put option with that from a call option.

2. Explain how to estimate the intrinsic value and time value for a put option.

3. Briefly describe the main factors that affect a put or a call option's value, and explain how they affect the value of each.

12.3 PUT-CALL PARITY

The Four Basic Option Positions

Learning Objective 12.3
Explain how to use put-call parity to estimate call and put prices, and explain how it can be used to synthetically create call, put, and underlying positions.

The four basic option positions are (1) long call, (2) short call, (3) long put, and (4) short put. These positions were diagrammed in Figures 12-1, 12-2, 12-4, and 12-5. We will consider these four positions again, only this time we will put them all in one figure. Note that if we combine a long call and a short put, we have a 45-degree line going through the strike price, which in our example is also the forward price of $50. This is a long forward contract with gains and losses around the strike price. Similarly, if we combine a long put and a short call, we have a 45-degree line going through the forward price. This is a short forward contract with losses and gains around the strike price. The payoffs on these contracts are depicted in Figure 12-6.

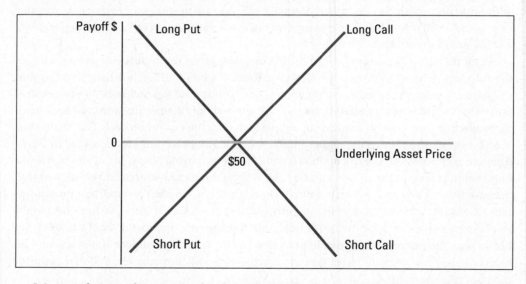

FIGURE 12-6 *Combining Option Positions*

It is now obvious why we started with puts and calls with a strike price equal to the forward price. In this special case, the long call and short put are the equivalent of a forward contract, and the long put and short call are the equivalent of a short forward contract. Examples 12-7 and 12-8 demonstrate.

EXAMPLE 12-7	Long Call Plus Short Put Payoffs

Complete the following table depicting the payoffs for various underlying asset prices for an investor who simultaneously buys a call and sells a put, each with a strike price of $50.

Asset price ($)	30	40	50	55	60	70
Long call payoff ($)						
Short put payoff ($)						
Net payoff ($)						

continued

EXAMPLE 12-7   Long Call Plus Short Put Payoffs *continued*

Solution

Asset price ($)	30	40	50	55	60	70
Long call payoff ($)	0	0	0	5	10	20
Short put payoff ($)	−20	−10	0	0	0	0
Net payoff ($)	−20	−10	0	5	10	20

Notice that the payoff for the net position is exactly the same as that from a long forward position at a forward price of $50.

EXAMPLE 12-8   **Short Call Plus Long Put Payoffs**

Complete the following table depicting the payoffs for various underlying asset prices for an investor who simultaneously sells a call and buys a put, each with a strike price of $50.

Asset price ($)	30	40	50	55	60	70
Short call payoff ($)						
Long putl payoff ($)						
Net payoff ($)						

Solution

Asset price ($)	30	40	50	55	60	70
Short call payoff ($)	0	0	0	−5	−10	−20
Long put payoff ($)	20	10	0	0	0	0
Net payoff ($)	20	10	0	−5	−10	−20

Notice that the payoff for the net position is exactly the same as that from a short forward position at a forward price of $50.

If an investor simultaneously established all four basic option positions, the net position would be zero, because in aggregate the four contracts are a "zero sum game": wealth is neither created nor destroyed. This is shown in examples 12-7 and 12-8, because the investor would be combining the two net payoff positions, which add to zero for any underlying asset price. With secondary market options, wealth is simply rearranged among market participants.[6]

Deriving the Put-Call Parity Relationship

Understanding how these four contracts end up looking like long and short forward contracts is the key to understanding **put-call parity**. Consider two portfolios. The first, portfolio A, consists of buying a put (P) with X = $50 and simultaneously purchasing the underlying asset (S). The second, portfolio B, consists of buying a call (C) with X = $50 and investing the present value of the exercise price, PV(X), in a risk-free asset paying interest at the risk-free rate (RF), so that the investor has $50 available to exercise the call option. We assume the options are European so that they can be exercised only at maturity. We also assume the underlying asset provides no dividends or other income. Table 12-2 shows the payoffs from these two portfolios, assuming the underlying asset price can be either $45 or $55.

Notice that the payoff from either strategy is the same, whether the ending share price is $45 or $55. In fact, it is easy to demonstrate that the payoffs for these two portfolios will always be the same, as depicted in Table 12-3.

put-call parity the relationship between the price of a call option and a put option that have the same strike price and expiry dates; assumes that the options are not exercised before their expiration

---

[6] This ignores the option prices, the fees charged by brokers, and the exchange to make the market. This is why many experts argue that, in aggregate, options waste scarce resources in the economy.

TABLE 12-2 Payoff from Combining Calls, Puts, and Underlying Asset Positions

Underlying Price	$55	$45
Portfolio A		
Long put payoff	0	+$5
Long asset payoff	+$55	+$45
Total payoff for A	$55	$50
Portfolio B		
Long call payoff	+$5	0
Invest present value of $50 at RF	+$50	+$50
Total payoff for B	$55	$50

TABLE 12-3 Payoff from Combining Calls, Puts, and Underlying Asset Positions: The General Case

Underlying Price at Expiration Date (S_T)	$S_T > X$	$S_T < X$
Portfolio A		
Long put payoff	0	$X - S_T$
Long asset payoff	S_T	S_T
Total payoff for A	S_T	X
Portfolio B		
Long call payoff	$S_T - X$	0
Invest PV of X	$+X$	$+X$
Total payoff for B	S_T	X

The payoff from either strategy is the same no matter what the ending share price is. Because early exercise is not possible, and the payoffs at the expiration date (T) will always be the same, the *cost* of constructing each portfolio must be the same. Denoting the cost of the put as P, the cost of the call as C, and the price of the underlying asset as S, we get Equation 12-5, which states that

[12-5]
$$P + S = C + PV(X)$$

Rearranging Equation 12-5, we get the basic put-call relationship:

[12-6]
$$C - P = S - PV(X)$$

It is important to recognize that this relationship holds for European options on non-dividend-paying assets. It is also important to recognize that we can solve this equation to determine the call option price, given P, S, X, and RF, and we can also determine the put option price given C, S, X, and RF. Both of these equations are shown below.

[12-7]
$$C = P + S - PV(X)$$

[12-8]
$$P = C - S + PV(X)$$

Although put-call parity doesn't help us to price the call, unless we know the price of the put and vice versa, it does demonstrate again that these contracts are all derivative—that is, not original. There is evidence that the basic properties of put-call parity have been known for centuries. We demonstrate how to apply put-call parity in examples 12-9 and 12-10.

EXAMPLE 12-9   Finding a Call Price by Using Put-Call Parity

A company's common shares are selling for $20, and a one-year European put option on those shares, with a $20 strike price, is selling for $0.50. If the risk-free rate is 5 percent, find the value of a one-year European call on the same stock with a $20 exercise price.

Solution

$C = P + S - \text{PV}(X) = 0.50 + 20.00 - 20/(1.05) = 20.50 - 19.05 = \$1.45$

EXAMPLE 12-10   Finding a Put Price by Using Put-Call Parity

A company's common shares are selling for $20, and a six-month European call option on those shares, with a $20 strike price, is selling for $0.90. If the risk-free rate is 5 percent, find the value of a six-month European put on the same stock with a $20 exercise price.

Solution

Six-month discount rate = 5%/2 = 2.50%

$P = C - S + \text{PV}(X) = 0.90 - 20.00 + 20/(1.025) = -19.10 + 19.51 = \$0.41$

The put-call parity equation can also be solved for S, as shown in Equation 12-9.

$$S = C - P + \text{PV}(X) \qquad\qquad \text{[12-9]}$$

Equation 12-9 shows that a long position in the underlying asset is equivalent to a long position in a call, a short position in a put with the same strike price, and an investment of $\text{PV}(X)$ in a risk-free asset. If we multiply this equation –1, we can see that a short position in the underlying asset is equivalent to a short position in a call, a long position in a put with the same strike price, and borrowing $\text{PV}(X)$ at the risk-free rate.

Creating Synthetic Positions by Using Put-Call Parity

The put-call parity relationships are particularly important for hedging purposes. Applying our discussion of how to create synthetic positions by using forward contracts from Chapter 11, we can see how we could use equations 12-7 through 12-9 to synthetically create long or short positions in puts, calls, or the underlying asset. For our present purposes, we ignore the $\text{PV}(X)$ term, which involves borrowing or lending at RF, because it does not affect the shape of the net payoff diagram.

We begin by considering a long position in the underlying asset; for example, assume that the asset is U.S. dollars receivable, as we discussed in Chapter 11. We already showed that an investor can sell U.S. dollars at the forward rate (F) to remove the exposure completely, but perhaps the investor thinks the Canadian dollar is going to weaken and wants the possibility of getting more Canadian dollars for those U.S. dollars. In other words, the investor wants downside-risk protection if the Canadian dollar strengthens and wants to maintain upside potential if it weakens. Suppose the contract is priced so that if the Canadian dollar appreciates to $0.90 per U.S. dollar, the investor will break even, but below this, he or she loses money. In this case, the investor might not want to risk a depreciation of the U.S. dollar below C$0.90, so he or she buys a put option to sell U.S. dollars at C$0.90 to fix the minimum Canadian dollars the investor will get out of the contract.

Buying a put option to protect a long position in an underlying asset is generally referred to as entering into a **protective put**. In this case, the purchase of the put option gives the right to sell the U.S. dollar at a fixed price for Canadian dollars, which insures the long position

protective put the purchase of a put option to protect a long position in an underlying asset against losing money. The net payoff from this overall position resembles that of a long call position, as predicted by put-call parity in Equation 12-7 and as depicted by the solid bolded line in Figure 12-7.

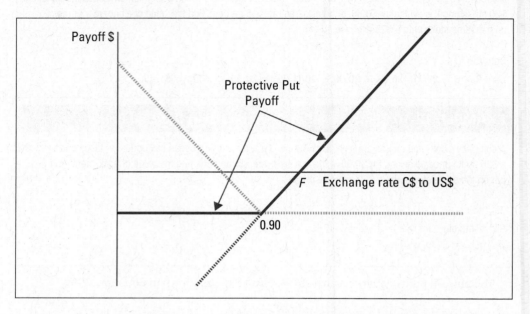

FIGURE 12-7 *A Protective Put*

The 45-degree line indicates the long position in U.S. dollars from the contract; the green dotted line indicates the long put position we discussed earlier. If the value of the U.S. dollar is above C$0.90, the investor does not exercise the put and exchanges U.S. dollars at the spot rate. However, as the U.S. dollar depreciates below C$0.90, say to C$0.80, the investor exercises the put and exchanges the depreciating U.S. dollar for C$0.90 instead of taking the spot rate. The combination is depicted by the bold line in Figure 12-7, which looks like a long call, as predicted by put-call parity. This example indicates a very important result: although buying puts and calls "naked" is regarded as risky, it is not risky when the investor already has the asset. In that case, the combination of being long in puts and in the underlying asset is equivalent to being long in a call option, so the put acts like insurance.

The insurance argument has been used extensively to sell put options. Consider basic house insurance. If homeowners don't have insurance, either nothing happens or they suffer a loss when, for example, their house burns down. Buying insurance removes the loss at the cost of the insurance premium. If nothing happens, homeowners are out the insurance premium, but if the house burns down, they sell the ashes to the insurance company in return for a new house. Car insurance works the same way: if drivers don't have an accident, nothing happens, but if drivers do have an accident, they transfer the loss—that is, vehicle damage and other personal liability—to the insurance company. In both cases, insurance is just a put option, where the buyer has the right to transfer the loss to the insurance company.

EXAMPLE 12-11   A Protective Put

Complete the following table depicting the payoffs for an investor who buys an underlying asset for $50 and simultaneously buys a put with a strike price of $50.

Asset price ($)	30	40	50	55	60	70
Long asset payoff ($)						
Long put payoff ($)						
Net payoff ($)						

continued

EXAMPLE 12-11 A Protective Put *continued*

Solution

Asset price ($)	30	40	50	55	60	70
Long asset payoff ($)	−20	−10	0	5	10	20
Long put payoff ($)	20	10	0	0	0	0
Net payoff ($)	0	0	0	5	10	20

Notice that the payoff for the net position is exactly the same as that for buying a call at a strike price of $50.

Let's consider another situation where the investor is long the asset but doesn't think the asset is going to increase in value. Normally, he or she would sell the asset. However, suppose the investor is a large pension fund and the asset is a stock market portfolio of $20 billion. In practice, it is difficult to sell that much without causing the price to drop. The investor can sell call options, because he or she doesn't think the price is going to increase to make the calls valuable. (The payoff from this strategy is explained below.) This is called a **covered call writing** strategy, because the investor has sold a call but owns the underlying asset. As Figure 12-8 indicates, the net payoff position resembles a short put position, which is what put-call parity (i.e., Equation 12-8) predicts.

covered call writing selling call options while owning the underlying asset

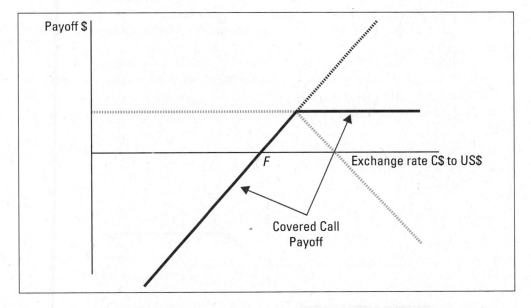

FIGURE 12-8 *Covered Call Writing*

The long position in Figure 12-8 is the 45-degree line; the short call position is the dotted green line; and the combined position is the bold blue line. If the asset value increases above the call price, it is called away from the investor, so all he or she gets is the strike price, which is set above the forward price. However, below the strike price, the call expires worthless and the investor gets the full value of the long position. Essentially, by selling a call, the investor has sold away some of the upside in the value of the underlying asset. This makes sense if he or she doesn't think there is much upside.

EXAMPLE 12-12 A Covered Call

Complete the following table depicting the payoffs for an investor who buys an underlying asset for $50 and simultaneously writes a call with a strike price of $50.

continued

EXAMPLE 12-12   A Covered Call (continued)

Asset price ($)	30	40	50	55	60	70
Long asset payoff ($)						
Short call payoff ($)						
Net payoff ($)						

Solution

Asset price ($)	30	40	50	55	60	70
Long asset payoff ($)	−20	−10	0	5	10	20
Short call payoff ($)	0	10	0	−5	−10	−20
Net payoff ($)	−20	−10	0	0	0	0

Notice that the payoff for the net position is exactly the same as that for writing a put at a strike price of $50.

If an investor is long the asset, then buying a put places a floor under how much he or she can lose, whereas selling a call places a ceiling on how much he or she can earn. So far, we have talked about how much these options are worth, but clearly they are very valuable, as anyone pricing car insurance (i.e., puts) knows! So buying a put and insuring your asset is costly; one way of financing this is to sell a call, as in Figure 12-9.

Notice that if the asset price goes above S_2, the strike price in the call, the asset is called away, so this is a ceiling price. Below S_1, the strike price in the put, the put is exercised, so it is a floor price. In between S_1 and S_2 is the payoff from a long position in the underlying asset. The net position is the bold line, and is generically called a **collar**, because the put and call options provide a collar for the price range. In foreign exchange, such contracts have been called flexible forwards or range forwards, while in financing cases they are referred to as floor-ceiling loans.

collar a position between the floor and ceiling price

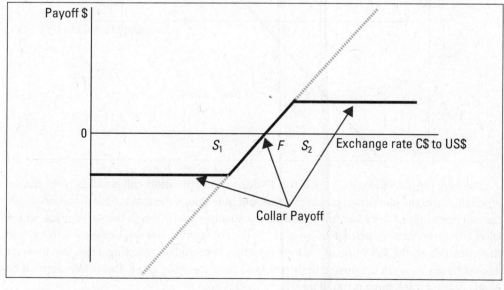

FIGURE 12-9 *A Collar*

Finance in the News 12-1 discusses a May 17, 2009, suggestion to use put options when the S&P 500 closed at 892.76, up from its March 10, 2009, low of 679.28 or up 31 percent. It turns out that this was not very good advice, as apart from a minor drop to 887 a week later, the S&P 500 index has not been below 892.76 since. However, as the article states, you would have been out only $11.20, the cost of a put option on the index at 600. On the other hand, you might have slept a lot better knowing you were protected from another calamitous fall in the stock market!

---

finance INTHENEWS 12-1   Betting against the Rally to Protect Your Portfolio

THIS RALLY MAY have further to run. But investors might want to think about taking out some portfolio insurance—just in case.

Luckily, the insurance, in the form of put options, is getting cheaper as optimism about the market grows. There are plenty of reasons for caution. Here are nine things the bulls should chew over.

1. Almost everyone on Wall Street is now bullish. Many sentiment indices are alarmingly complacent. The State Street Investor Confidence index is back to levels seen a year ago.

2. Meanwhile, according to companies that track this data, like Vickers and Form 4 Oracle, company insiders have actually been taking some profits. They were heavy buyers over the winter.

3. The market has already priced in a V-shaped economic recovery. That's possible, but hardly that likely. Total household debt is about twice the levels of just 10 years ago. How are people going to borrow to spend more?

4. Yes, the economy steadied during the winter. Great news. But it's worth remembering consumers got a huge one-off financial adrenaline boost from the collapse in fuel prices. That's now over. Oil has jumped back up.

5. Consumers also got another big adrenaline shot from the collapse in mortgage rates, to about 4.5% at the lows. That, too, appears to have ended.

6. Ominously, a lot of residential real estate simply hasn't corrected that much from the bubble. While prices in distressed sales—like foreclosures and short sales—have collapsed, other real estate prices haven't fallen that hard. They may have further to fall in due course. That's bad for the economy.

7. Business inventories haven't dropped as far as some bulls seem to think. They're only down about 8% from the peak. Inventories in March were actually about the same as they were two years earlier. Fat inventories are a bearish sign because they mean manufacturers don't have to ramp up production any time soon.

8. The unemployment situation is worse than the headline rates would suggest. According to the Bureau of Labor Statistics, when you factor in all those who have given up working, and those working part-time because they can't get a full-time job, the total "under-employment" rate is 15.8%. That's about one worker in six. Yes, it's a lagging indicator. But it's hardly bullish. The worst this got in the last downturn, in 2003, was 10.4%.

9. And, of course, the higher shares go the worse an investment they are. The average share now sells for 85% of company revenues, up from about 60% in early March. That's still OK by long term measures. But it's not as cheap as it was.

Those interested in insuring against another possible downturn might take a look at so-called index put options. The options are a bet that shares will take another tumble. They can be purchased through any broker, though you may need to add an options feature to your investment account. Put options that bet on an index can work like a lottery ticket or insurance: A small stake can get you a lot of action.

These puts are getting cheaper as shares rise. As an illustration: "December 600" puts on the Standard & Poor's 500 have slumped from $63 in early March to just $11.20 now. If the S&P closes below 600 when the contract expires in mid-December, you'll get a dollar for each point below. If it closes at 500, you'd get $100. If it closes at 450, you'd get $150. And so on. (The options are effectively sold in batches of 100).

If the S&P closes above 600, all you'll lose is the $11.20 stake.

If another crash or slide occurs, puts can at least counterbalance some of those losses. And you don't have to wait till expiry to exercise them. If Wall Street slumps next month, you could expect the price of these options to rise sharply, and investors could cash in their insurance.

No one knows what's going to happen next. Which is why insurance may be a wise idea.

We have discussed the most basic option strategies, which in practice are limited only by an investor's imagination. For example, an investor could have a long position and sell two options instead of one, or could buy both puts and calls at different exercise prices or expiration dates. However, in order to make sense of such strategies, we need to discuss how much these options are worth.

EXAMPLE 12-13 A Collar

Complete the following table depicting the payoffs for an investor who buys an underlying asset for $50 and simultaneously buys a put with a strike price of $45 and sells a call with a strike price of $55.

Asset price ($)	30	40	50	55	60	70
Long asset payoff ($)						
Long $45 put payoff ($)						
Short $55 call payoff ($)						
Net payoff ($)						

Solution

Asset price ($)	30	40	50	55	60	70
Long asset payoff ($)	−20	−10	0	5	10	20
Long $45 put payoff ($)	15	5	0	0	0	0
Short $55 call payoff ($)	0	0	0	0	−5	−15
Net payoff ($)	−5	−5	0	5	5	5

The payoff for the net position equals −$5 for all prices below $45 (the put's strike price), equals +$5 for all prices above $55 (the call's strike price), and increases by $1 for each $1 increase in the underlying asset price between $45 and $55.

CONCEPT REVIEW QUESTIONS

1. Illustrate how to combine the four basic option positions to create a variety of net payoff positions.

2. Explain why the put-call parity relationship should hold if markets are efficient.

3. Explain how to synthetically create long and short positions in calls, puts, and the underlying assets by using put-call parity.

12.4 OPTION PRICING

Learning Objective 12.4
Explain how to use the Black-Scholes option pricing model to price call options.

Appendix 12A discusses the binomial option pricing model, which can be used to value complicated securities. That model is based on the assumption that the underlying asset price can go either up or down to some value over a given period. Although this assumption may seem simplistic, so far we haven't specified the period involved. We can shorten the period from a month to a week, a day, a minute, or a second, and the model still holds. We can then think of a whole sequence of up and down movements representing the possible movement in the asset price, and use numerical procedures,[7] similar to those above, to calculate the option price. Although this is possible, it ignores one of the advantages of the Black-Scholes formula, which reduces to a simple "plug-in" formula, shown in Equation 12-9.

[12-10]

$$C = SN(d_1) - Xe^{-rt}N(d_2)$$

where

$$d_1 = \frac{\text{Ln}(S/X) + (r + \sigma^2/2)t}{\sigma\sqrt{t}}$$

$$d_2 = d_1 - \sigma\sqrt{t}$$

---

[7] See Hull, John, *Options, Futures and Other Derivatives*, 6th ed. (New York: Prentice-Hall, 2006).

Technically, Equation 12-10 applies to European call options on non-dividend-paying stocks; however, variations of this equation exist for calls on dividend-paying stocks and for puts.

It might be difficult to think of this as a plug-in formula, but it is. First, some of the numbers are straightforward, such as S, which is the current asset price, and X, which is the strike price. Recall from Chapter 5 that the term e^{-rt} is the present value formula when we are discounting in continuous time, so just think of Xe^{-rt} as the present value of the strike price, where r is the risk-free rate and t is the time to the expiration of the option. If we set $N(d_1)$ and $N(d_2)$ equal to one for now, the Black-Scholes formula says the value of a call is the value of the asset minus the present value of the exercise price. If the asset increases in value at the risk-free rate, then it is in or out of the money at expiration.

The key to option pricing is understanding the $N(d_1)$ and $N(d_2)$ terms—the cumulative standard normal density functions for the values d_1 and d_2—because we need to know the cumulative probability that the asset price will exceed the strike price at expiration. To estimate this probability, Black and Scholes assumed that the underlying asset followed a lognormal distribution. This means that the natural logarithm (Ln) of the asset price S is normally distributed, which explains why the term $Ln(S/X)$ is in the equation. To simplify, assume that the call is issued at the strike price, so this is the natural logarithm of 1.0, which is zero. We can also simplify by assuming that this is a single-period call option and the risk-free rate is zero, so $r = 0$ and $t = 1$. This leaves a formula for $d_1 = \sigma/2$. Because we are looking for the value of $N(\sigma/2)$, we need the cumulative probability of being half a standard deviation above the mean of the normal distribution. We can look at a table for the standard normal distribution or use Excel and find this value as 0.68. Similarly, $d_2 = -\sigma/2$, which is the cumulative probability of being half a standard deviation below the mean of the distribution, which is 0.32.

To understand d_1, think of it as the number of standard deviations that the call is expected to be in the money, so we will call this the expected "moneyness" of the call. The value for $N(d_1)$ is then the cumulative probability of being in the money. The larger the risk of the underlying asset, the larger $N(d_1)$ and the moneyness of the call will be. This reiterates that the more volatile the underlying asset, the more valuable the call. All we are doing is shifting this estimate of the call's expected moneyness. For example, if the asset price is currently above the strike price, $Ln(S/X)$ is no longer zero; instead, it is positive, and moneyness increases. Similarly, a higher risk-free rate simply increases the expected moneyness of the call. Finally, the time to expiration of the call increases both the risk-free rate and the standard deviation, so it compounds both, thereby increasing the call's moneyness. We illustrate all this in Example 12-14.

EXAMPLE 12-14   Using Black-Scholes I

Assume that an asset is selling for $50 and an investor wants to price a call with an exercise price of $55. The expiration date is 182 days or 182/365 of a year, the risk-free rate is 6 percent, and the standard deviation of the return on the underlying asset is 30 percent. What's the value of the call?

Solution

First, we calculate the present value of the strike price:

$$PV(S) = Se^{-rt} \text{ or } \frac{S}{(1+r)^t}$$

We can use either continuous compounding or approximate with discrete compounding. Let's approximate and discount back at 3 percent to get $53.398. With continuous compounding, we would get $53.375.

continued

EXAMPLE 12-14   Using Black-Scholes I *(continued)*

Next, we calculate d_1 as

$$d_1 = \frac{\text{Ln}(50/55) + (0.06 + .30^2/2) \times 182/365}{.30 \times \sqrt{182/365}} = -0.2028$$

and $d_2 = -0.4146$. Inserting these results into the cumulative normal density function, we get $N(d_1) = 0.4197$ and $N(d_2) = 0.3392$. The call is worth \$2.876.

$N(d_1)$ and $N(d_2)$ can be calculated from standard statistical tables. Table 12-4 includes a portion of such a table. The extended version can be found in Table A-1 at the end of the textbook.

We can also determine $N(d_1)$ by using a spreadsheet, such as Excel. In Excel, the "Normdist" function calculates the normal distribution function. Entering the following:

$$N(d_1) = Normdist(\text{a1},0,1,true)$$

returns the value for $N(d_1)$. The values to enter in order are a1, which is the spreadsheet cell entry for the value d_1; 0, which indicates a zero mean; and 1, which is the standard deviation for a unit normal density function. The final value, "true," indicates the cumulative normal distribution; "false" would indicate the individual point estimate of the probability. Calculating the Black-Scholes value for a call option is then straightforward in Excel, since the only part of Equation 12-10 that is difficult is the $N(d)$ function.

TABLE 12-4 The Cumulative Probabilities for a Standard Normal Distribution

d	N(d)	d	N(d)	d	N(d)	d	N(d)	d	N(d)
−0.50	.3085	−0.48	.3156	−0.46	.3228	−0.44	.3300	−0.42	.3373
−0.40	.3446	−0.38	.3520	−0.36	.3594	−0.34	.3669	−0.32	.3745
−0.30	.3821	−0.28	.3897	−0.26	.3974	−0.24	.4052	−0.22	.4129
−0.20	.4207	−0.18	.4286	−0.16	.4365	−0.14	.4443	−0.12	.4523
−0.10	.4602	−0.08	.4681	−0.06	.4761	−0.04	.4841	−0.02	.4920
0.00	.5000	0.02	.5080	0.04	.5160	0.06	.5239	0.08	.5319
0.10	.5398	0.12	.5478	0.14	.5557	0.16	.5636	0.18	.5714
0.20	.5793	0.22	.5871	0.24	.5948	0.26	.6026	0.28	.6103
0.30	.6179	0.32	.6255	0.34	.6331	0.36	.6406	0.38	.6480
0.40	.6556	0.42	.6628	0.44	.6700	0.46	.6773	0.48	.6844
...	...	...	...	...	...	...	...	...	...
2.00	.9772	2.10	.9821	2.20	.9861	2.30	.9893	2.40	.9918
2.50	.9938	2.60	.9953	2.70	.9965	2.80	.9974	2.90	.9981
3.00	.9986	–	–	–	–	–	–	–	–

Rather than using a spreadsheet, we can use one of several calculators that are available on the Internet. The Montreal Exchange (MX) has an online option pricing calculator at www.m-x.ca/accueil_en.php. By using the MX option pricing model and entering the values for our example, the model produces the output shown in Figure 12-10.

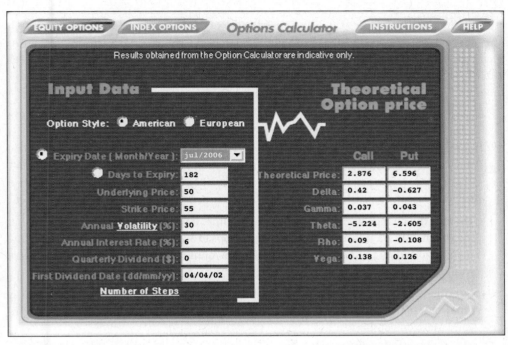

FIGURE 12-10 *Using Black-Scholes*

MX's value for the option is also $2.876. The calculator gives the price of a $55 put on the same asset as $6.596.[8] It also provides some other values, which we will discuss in the next section.

EXAMPLE 12-15   Using Black-Scholes II

Find the value of a three-month call option with a $20 strike price if the price of the non-dividend-paying underlying asset is $20.50 and its standard deviation is 25 percent. Assume the risk-free rate is 5 percent.

Solution
$S = \$20.50$; $X = \$20$; $r = 5\%$; $t = 3/12 = 0.25$; $\sigma = 25\%$.

$$d_1 = \frac{Ln(S/X) + (r + \sigma^2/2)t}{\sigma\sqrt{t}} = \frac{Ln(20.50/20) + (.05 + (.25)^2/2)(0.25)}{(0.25)\sqrt{0.25}}$$

$$= \frac{0.02469 + 0.0203}{0.125} = \frac{0.0450}{0.125} = 0.3600$$

$$d_2 = d_1 - \sigma\sqrt{t} = .3600 - .25\sqrt{0.25} = 0.2350$$

Using the MX's online option pricing calculator or Excel, we can find

$N(d_1) = 0.6406$ and $N(d_2) = 0.5929$

So, $C = SN(d_1) - Xe^{-rt}N(d_2) = (20.50)(0.6406) - (20)e^{-(0.05)(0.25)}(0.5929) = 13.13 - 11.71 = \$1.42$

---

[8] The numbers provided in the output are for American options, based on more complicated variations of Black-Scholes equations, which technically apply only to European options. In any event, because the underlying asset in this example does not pay any dividends, the value of a European call option will equal that of an American call option. Conversely, the corresponding European put option would be worth $6.255, approximately $0.34 less than the American put.

the Greeks the values—delta (δ), gamma (γ), theta (θ), rho (ρ), and vega—that indicate the sensitivity of the option price to changes in the underlying parameters

The "Greeks"

The other values provided by the MX in Figure 12-10—delta, gamma, theta, rho, and vega—indicate the sensitivity of the option price to changes in the underlying parameters. These Greek letters are commonly referred to as **the Greeks** in option pricing (though vega is not a Greek letter).

delta the change in the price of the option for a given change in the price of the underlying asset

- As the stock price increases, so does the call value. The change in the price of the option for a given change in the price of the underlying asset is referred to as **delta**. In our example, if the stock price increases to $50.10, when we use the MX website to recalculate the value of the call it shows an increase to $2.918 (from $2.876), for a change of $0.042. This change is consistent with the 0.42 delta provided by the MX, which means the call will increase in value by $0.42 for every $1 increase in the price of the underlying asset.

theta the change in the option value with time

- **Theta** is the change in the option value with time. If we move forward one day so that the call has 181 days to expiration, its value drops to $2.862, a loss of $0.014 per day. The theta reported by the MX is approximately this number multiplied by 365 days, so we would get –5.224.

gamma the change in delta with respect to a change in the underlying asset

- **Gamma** is the change in delta with respect to a change in the underlying asset. This is important for hedging, but we don't include a full discussion of gamma here as it is beyond the scope of this text.

rho the change in the option value with respect to a change in the interest rate

- **Rho** is the change in the option value with respect to a change in the interest rate. For example, if the interest rate in our example increases from 6 percent to 7 percent, the option value increases to $2.967, a rise of $0.091, so a 1 percent change in the interest rate causes a $0.091 change in the option value, consistent with the rho reported by the MX.

vega the change in the option value with respect to a change in the volatility of the underlying asset

- **Vega** is the change in the option value with respect to a change in the volatility of the underlying asset. If the standard deviation in our example increases by 1 percent to 31 percent, the option value increases to $3.014. Thus, a 1 percent increase in volatility increases the option value by $0.138, consistent with the vega reported by the MX.

Running the numbers through our Black-Scholes calculator indicates that the call option price behaves the way that it should: it goes up with increases in volatility, the risk-free rate, and the price of the underlying asset, and it falls as time passes.

Finally, what about the extremes? If the current asset price is deep out of the money at $30, the value of the call is $0.008; at $25, it is $0.0003. This shows why deep out of the money calls are essentially worthless. Similarly, if the asset price is $100, so that it is deep in the money, the call option is worth $46.628, where $45 is the intrinsic value. So the value of a call mainly reflects its intrinsic value.

CONCEPT REVIEW QUESTIONS

1. How can the Black-Scholes equation be used to price options?
2. What is measured by each of the five Greeks discussed in this section?

12.5 OPTIONS MARKETS

Learning Objective 12.5
Explain how options are traded and what is meant by implied volatility.

Like swaps, options are either traded over the counter, mainly with the major banks, or on organized exchanges. In Canada, options trading is focused on the MX, which has a standard practice of listing options on all the constituents of the S&P/TSX 60 Index, as well as on the S&P/TSX MidCap Index. Each option class has to have the interest of two market makers who stand ready to buy and sell the options to create an orderly market. These options follow a short expiration cycle based on the next two months, and there is a minimum daily volume of 40 contracts. If the volume exceeds 80, then longer-dated options are introduced based on months in the next quarterly cycle, and if there is enough interest, long-dated options are introduced with a January expiration date.

Apart from the S&P/TSX 60 Index (XIU), during March 2012 the two most active equity options were on the Bank of Nova Scotia (BNS) and Canadian Oil Sands (COS), with 15,109 and 11,898 contracts traded, respectively. Each contract is for 100 common shares, so for BNS there were effectively options traded to buy or sell 1,510,900 common shares—at the same time, 7,950,808 common shares in BNS were traded. The volume of trading for BNS was about three times greater than normal,[9] so let's look at some of the information for these options from the MX web page as of March 16, 2012, in Table 12-5.

At the time, BNS's last stock price of the day was $55.86, and four options were chosen from the dozens that were listed. Two are calls (c) and two are puts (p), with two different expiration dates for a very short-dated option expiring in March 2012 and a longer-dated option expiring in January 2014. Both these had a $54 exercise price. At the last BNS stock price of the day, the March call was in the money by $1.86, so the time value was only $0.06 if investors sold it back to the market maker at the price the maker was willing to buy it for (i.e., the bid price). The time value was $0.13 if investors bought it from the market maker at the price the maker was willing to sell it for (i.e., the ask price). The difference between the bid and ask of $0.07 was the profit the market maker or trader would make by standing ready to buy and sell options to "make" the market. Note that on Friday, March 16, 2012, there were 156 of these $54 calls traded.

For the January 2014 call option, the ask price increases from $1.99 to $5.90, even though the exercise price is the same, $54; the additional $3.91 is the time value, since the option has 21 months to run. However, note that there were none of these long-dated options traded on March 16. This is not unusual, since, unlike common shares, there are a large number of options listed with different expiration dates and strike prices. Also note that the MX provides the last trade price, which for the January 2014 $54 call was $7.00. However, since trades for many of these options are so infrequent, this price could have been established days earlier and is not as useful a reference point as the last price is for common shares.

In contrast to the call option, the March 2012 $54 put is out of the money, since the exercise price of $54 is below the current market price. Further, it is so close to expiration that the bid price quoted by the market maker for this option is zero, and the maker is willing to sell the put for only $0.03. In contrast, although the January 2014 puts are also out of the money, they have significant time value. If you already held the BNS common shares, then buying the January 2014 put for $6.90 would ensure that you could sell it for $54, even if the stock price crashed. Also note that, like the $54 calls, there were no January 2014 $54 puts traded on March 16, 2012.

TABLE 12-5 Bank of Nova Scotia Options Quotes, March 16, 2012

Date	Strike	Bid	Ask	Last	Volume
March 2012	54c	1.92	1.99	1.83	156
	54p	0.00	0.03	0.04	N/A
January 2014	54c	5.10	5.90	7.00	0
	54p	6.10	6.90	8.65	0

For option prices, most of the data are objective and verifiable, such as the strike price, the current price of the underlying asset, the risk-free rate, and the expiration date. The only "soft" number is the volatility of the underlying asset's price. However, once we know the price of the option, we can work back and find the volatility that matches this price. For BNS's $54 January 2014 call option, we can use the average of the bid-ask price and BNS's current dividend per

---

[9] The U.S. government released the results of its "stress tests" of banks on this day, and there was increased trading in bank stocks worldwide.

implied volatility an estimate of the price volatility of the underlying asset based on observed option prices

share with the Black-Scholes option pricing model to estimate this volatility by trial and error. It turns out to be about 21 percent. This number is the **implied volatility** of the option. In actual practice, the MX calculates this number for options when there are enough trades, and it also reports the 30-day historic volatility, which in the case of BNS was given as 10.82 percent.

Implied volatilities provide useful information. Remember from our discussion of the capital asset pricing model in Chapter 9 that the volatility of the market portfolio is a key number in deriving expected rates of return. The MX trades options on the S&P/TSX 60 Index, which reflects the biggest and most valuable companies in Canada. Every minute of every trading day, the MX calculates the implied volatility of the S&P/TSX 60 Index from a cross section of option prices. These are then used to estimate the 30-day implied volatility for the Canadian market. Calculations used to create the MX volatility index (VIXC) are analogous to those used to create the Chicago Board of Exchange (CBOE) Volatility Index (VIX) for the U.S. market.

The graph in Figure 12-11 shows the implied volatilities for the MX index from December 2, 2002, until March 2012.[10] Note that volatility changes over time. In early 2003, it was just less than 25 percent before falling to around 15 percent, where it remained until late 2005, after which it began increasing and reached the 25 percent level again. By June 2006, the options markets were indicating increased volatility, but this was just the beginning as the implied volatility increased until it peaked at 88 percent on November 11, 2008, during the worst of the financial crisis. Since then the VIXC has gradually receded to more normal levels.

Remember that the volatility of the S&P/TSX 60 is the volatility of a market portfolio of securities. This is always much lower than the volatility of an individual security due to the fact that the returns on individual companies are not perfectly correlated. This puts the volatility of BNS in perspective. We generally regard the Canadian banks as being low risk, but with an implied volatility of over 20 percent, holding shares in a Canadian bank in isolation is still riskier than holding the S&P/TSX 60. This simply reinforces the central message of modern portfolio theory, which is that there is a "free lunch" called diversification and risk reduction.

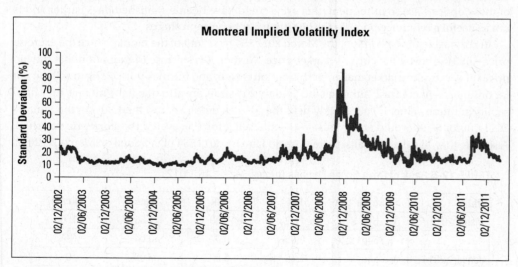

FIGURE 12-11 *Implied Volatilities for the S&P/TSX 60 Index*

LESSONS TO BE LEARNED   **The key insight from option** pricing theory is that "flexibility" is valuable. Remember, a call option is the right to be able to do something but is not an obligation, which means there is flexibility. Think about all the call options you experience in everyday life. For example, consider course grading, where some instructors give students the option of having their mid-term exam count as their final grade if it is higher than their final exam grade. Is this a valuable option, and if so, is it more valuable in the winter, where the chance of being "under the weather" is higher than in the summer? This is an example of a real option rather than a financial option. We will discuss real options at various points in the text, but the absence of options or flexibility can dramatically increase risk and be very dangerous.

continued

---

[10] Data prior to October 2009 is from an earlier, slightly different, MX volatility index.

Finance in the News 12-2 presents a *Calgary Herald* article about Oilexco, a small oil and gas exploration company headquartered in Calgary. In the summer of 2008, when oil hit $147 a barrel, Oilexco's stock price rose to $19.50, and Oilexco looked to a syndicate of banks, led by the Royal Bank of Scotland (RBS), for financing of its exploration program rather than locking in equity financing. As the credit crunch hit in the fall, RBS lost $42 billion and was rescued by the British government. However, in the process it reined in all its "risky" financing and pulled Oilexco's loan, forcing Oilexco into bankruptcy protection. By relying on bank financing, Oilexco had no alternative sources of financing, and on May 21, 2009, substantially all of its assets were sold to a British oil and gas exploration company that had financing.

As the article mentions, good firms can normally either raise financing or sell assets, but in the middle of the worst credit crunch in 70 years, these options were not available, and Oilexco went bankrupt when more prudent financing would have allowed it to survive. In subsequent chapters, we will see how difficult it is to value these real options. However, just because they are more difficult to value does not mean that they are free. In fact, option pricing has become a critical part of strategy and management precisely because these options are so valuable.

finance INTHENEWS 12-2 Oilexco Credit Denied

OILEXCO INC. WILL ring in the new year filing for bankruptcy protection for its North Sea subsidiary, foreshadowing a bleak future for other oil and gas exploration companies, analysts said.

The year came to a crashing end for the troubled corporation Wednesday after key creditors advised they would not advance any more funding to Oilexco North Sea Ltd.

The refusal by the Royal Bank of Scotland and a syndicate of lenders prompted Calgary-based Oilexco to announce it would file for creditor protection as soon as possible.

"Oilexco does not have any other source of funding at this time and has therefore concluded that an administration must be pursued," the company said in a statement.

Once the darling of the oil patch for its promising finds and extensive prospects in the North Sea, Oilexco shares dropped 98 percent in value during 2008 to hit 21 cents on the last day of the year after the announcement.

While industry had speculated the troubled company faced insolvency if not sold, the news came as a surprise as Oilexco had secured bridge financing of $47.5 million in early December, enough to last until the end of January.

"Obviously creditors have gotten more aggressive and pushed Oilexco to the point where they've got to file for administration," said Martin Molyneaux with First Energy Capital Corp.

The scenario likely will be played out more often as oil prices remain low, financial institutions tighten credit requisites and public equity slams the door on risky ventures such as exploration and development, he said.

"The biggest single ingredient is credit markets," Molyneaux said. "We don't see it as much in Canada, but the rest of the world has seen credit markets seize up."

Junior oil and gas companies without cash flow from producing assets and/or with heavy debt from developing prospects are faring the worst in such environments, analysts said.

For example, oil sands producer Opti Canada Inc. recently sold 15 percent of its interest in the Long Lake project to partner Nexen Inc. for $735 million to meet debt payments, just weeks from first production and revenues. Opti said it needed the cash from the sale to meet a debt covenant in the new year and to pay debt and interest due in June.

The company lost 89 percent of its share value in 2008, closing Wednesday at $1.80 per share.

Nexen had been tagged as a prospective suitor for Oilexco assets after the company announced in November it was seeking strategic options—industry speak for going on the auction block. But the Opti buy drained much of Nexen's ready cash, Molyneaux noted.

Oilexco was caught in the vise as low oil prices collided with disappearing funds at the same time the Royal Bank of Scotland grappled with a $14-billion potential loss in the U.S. subprime mortgage fiasco.

Arthur Millholland thanked the bank and trade creditors "for their continued support in these difficult times" when the bridge deal was announced in December.

"The board remains focused on achieving a satisfactory outcome to our strategic and financing initiatives in the near future," Millholland said in a statement.

However, as the noose tightened on the Scottish bank and the syndicate of lenders, the risk of Oilexco defaulting likely proved too strong.

It used to be companies with good assets and an experienced management team with proven track record could sell a company, said John Stephenson, senior vice-president and portfolio manager with First Asset Fund Inc. in Toronto.

But the combination of a global recession pulling down commodity prices and increasingly wary debt and equity markets spell "no go" to risky ventures, he said.

"The ones who aren't producing cash flow right now and are dependent on the banks to get financing are the ones getting hit hard because they have nothing to negotiate with," Stephenson said. "Unless you see a dramatic snap back in the economy it's going to continue to get worse."

Companies that have oil and gas production can scale back and ride the storm of low prices and little financing, but companies stuck between exploring and developing likely will run out of funds.

"You're going to see more bankruptcies," he warned.

Source: O'Meara, Dina, "Oilexco credit denied." *Calgary Herald*, January 1, 2009. Reprinted by permission.

CONCEPT REVIEW QUESTIONS

1. Where are options traded?

2. How are implied volatilities calculated? What information do they provide?

3. What real options have you been given over the past year and how valuable were they? What factors do you think influenced your valuation of them?

12-1 | ETHICS AND CORPORATE GOVERNANCE
Audit Options Policies, CSA Urges

The Canadian Securities Administrators, or CSA, is recommending that all Canadian public companies assess their policies and controls for stock option grants to ensure they comply with legislation.

The notice comes as a scandal over backdated stock options continues to widen in the United States, where more than 40 companies have already said they will restate earnings or might do so once internal probes are completed. The restatements total at least $2.27 billion (U.S.).

Backdating occurs when a company sets the grant date for stock options retroactively, to a time when the company's stock price was lower, creating an instant paper gain for the executive or employee receiving the options.

Stock options allow recipients to buy shares at a future date, usually at the price on the day they were granted. They are given to managers as an incentive to find ways to boost the stock price.

A University of Michigan study released this week suggests shareholders bear the brunt of the practice, shouldering an average of $510 million per company in losses after the practice is made public. That far outweighs the average $600,000 annual gain for a company's executives.

"If CSA staff become aware, through disclosure reviews, tips, or otherwise, of abuses by reporting issuers, they may take enforcement action against the issuers or their directors and officers," the administrators said yesterday.

Regulations in Canada may reduce the opportunity for companies to backdate options here, the CSA said.

Under Toronto Stock Exchange rules, the exercise price for options cannot be less than the market price of the stock when the options are granted, and the exercise price cannot be based on market prices that don't reflect undisclosed material information.

There are similar rules on the TSX Venture Exchange, except issuers are allowed to set the exercise price at a certain discount to the market price.

Securities legislation also requires company insiders to file an insider-trading report within 10 days of receiving options.

Directors are responsible for ensuring that a company prices and discloses options appropriately, the CSA said.

It suggested boards set up a compensation committee that follows national corporate governance guidelines. It also suggested they adopt corporate disclosure and insider-trading policies and establish blackout periods around earnings announcements.

In October, the TSX Group sent a notice to listed companies reminding them of the rules around options.

"Staff has become aware that listed issuers may not be adhering to the requirements ... of the manual," the notice said.

In the United States, prosecutors and members of Congress have said backdating grants, or awarding them shortly before good news is announced, subverts their purpose and could involve criminal fraud.

Securities and Exchange Commission chairman Christopher Cox told Congress this week that more than 100 companies are being investigated.

Source: Perkins, Tara, "Audit options policies, CSA urges." *Toronto Star*, September 9, 2006, p. D01. Reprinted with permission of Torstar Syndication Services.

DISCUSSION QUESTIONS

1. Explain what option backdating is and how it hurts shareholders.

2. How do you think the University of Michigan researchers came up with an estimated shareholder loss of $510 million?

3. The CSA indicates that staff may take action if they become aware of option backdating. Do you think they should have the option of not taking action?

APPENDIX 12A

BINOMIAL OPTION PRICING AND RISK-NEUTRAL PROBABILITIES

Binomial Option Pricing

Learning Objective 12.6
Understand by means of the simplest option pricing model what factors affect the value of a call option and provide a guide to their order of magnitude.

In the chapter, we discussed the Black-Scholes option pricing model, but here we consider a simpler model. Previously, we used an example of an asset selling for $50 with an equal probability of the price going up or down by $5. Now let's give the price a 60 percent chance of going up to $55, and a 40 percent chance of going down to $45. We do this to set the expected value on the asset at $51 (i.e., [0.6 × $55] + [0.4 × $45]), for a 2 percent expected rate of return. For simplicity, let's assume that this refers to a one-month period and that the monthly risk-free rate is 1 percent. This is an example of what is termed the **binomial model** (i.e., two numbers), because the asset price can only go up or down.

binomial model an option pricing model that uses two numbers, assuming the asset price can only go up or down

Now let's consider a one-period call option on this asset with a strike price of $50. In this case, when the asset price is $55, the investor exercises the option and realizes a $5 payoff, but when the asset price is $45, the option expires worthless. The payoffs on the asset and the call are provided in Figure 12A-1.

In the figure, S_0 and S_1 represent the asset prices at times 0 and 1, respectively; C is the payoff on the call, and P is the probability of a given price occurring. To understand how to price the call, we take advantage of the fact that it is a derivative and its payoff depends on the underlying asset value. This is the motivation for the central insight of Black and Scholes, which is that although we may not know how to value the call directly, we do know how to value a risk-free asset. Thus, we can derive the value of the call indirectly if we create a portfolio of the asset and the call, which generates the same payoff regardless of the price of the underlying asset. If the payoff of the portfolio is the same, regardless of whether the price of the asset goes up or down, then by definition it is risk-free, and we can value it by discounting at the risk-free rate.

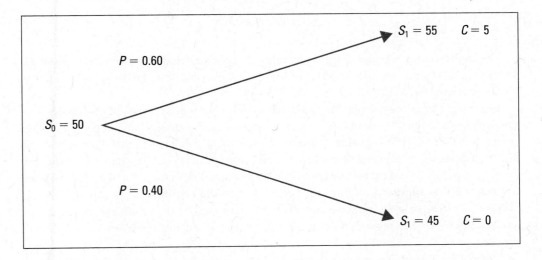

FIGURE 12A-1 *Binomial Prices*

When the price of the asset goes down to $45, the value of the call is zero. So if an investor builds a portfolio of the asset and the call, it doesn't matter how many calls he or she has, the value of the portfolio is still $45. To create a risk-free payoff, we have to think about a portfolio of the asset and the call that generates a payoff of $45 when the price of the asset is $55. For example, suppose the investor has a portfolio of the asset and sells one call—that is, the investor is long the asset and short the call. When the asset is worth $55, the call is exercised against the investor and he or she gets $50 for the asset, which is the payoff from the portfolio. Clearly, this is too high. Suppose the investor sells two calls against the asset. Now when the asset price goes to $55, two calls are exercised against the investor, but he or she has one underlying asset to deliver against two calls, so the investor has to go and buy another one. The payoff to the portfolio is $45, the same as if the asset value dropped to $45.

What we have discovered is that a portfolio that is long the asset and short two calls gives a payoff of $45 regardless of the price of the underlying asset. This means we have the following:

$$S - 2C = \frac{\$45}{1 + r} = 44.55$$

A portfolio long the asset and short two calls has a payoff of $45, which, given the 1 percent risk-free rate, is worth $44.55 today. However, we know that the asset is worth $50 today, so rearranging we get

$$C = \frac{1}{2}\ (\$50 - \$44.55) = \$2.725$$

The call is worth $2.725.

To provide the solution for the general case, we denote the increased price for the asset as PU (price up) and the decreased price as PD. The number of calls that an investor needs to sell to establish the same payoff whether the asset price goes up or down is called the **hedge ratio (h)**, which we can estimate as $PU - h(PU - X) = PD$.

This can be solved to give the following:

hedge ratio (h) the number of calls the investor needs to sell to hedge a long position in the underlying asset

[12A-1]

$$h = \frac{PU - PD}{PU - X}$$

In our example, the price can go to either $45 or $55, which means the hedge ratio is $(55 - 45)/(55 - 50)$, or 2, so two calls have to be sold for every long position in the asset. The value of the call is then estimated by solving the following equation:

[12A-2]

$$C = \frac{1}{h}\left(S - \frac{PD}{(1 + r)}\right)$$

The asset value is $50 and the present value of the asset when the price drops to $45 is $44.55, so the amount in brackets is $5.45—that is, 50 − 45/1.01. With the hedge ratio of 2, that means the call is worth $2.725—that is, 1/2 × $5.45.

The simplicity of the calculation is deceiving: some of the best minds in economics and finance spent decades trying to find the correct formula for valuing a call and could not. The reason was that they tried to value it *directly* by estimating the expected cash flow on the call and then using a risk-adjusted discount rate to value that cash flow. Although this is what we do in most areas of finance, no one could derive the correct discount rate. Black and Scholes did not use this approach,[11] and they came up with the central idea of valuing the call *indirectly* by valuing something we knew how to value: a risk-free payoff. Essentially, Black and Scholes took advantage of the central insight of option pricing, which is that the option is a derivative.

The use of a hedge to generate a risk-free payoff is the central idea of option pricing. With our example, a financial institution selling two calls has to go long the underlying asset to remove or hedge its risk. This is the central reason that the use of derivatives has exploded: rather than selling calls and creating risk for themselves, financial institutions now know how to hedge that exposure. They simply need to calculate the hedge ratio required to create a risk-free payoff. In our example, this hedge ratio is two: two calls have to be sold to hedge a long position in the asset.

Note also the factors that determine the value of the call in the general formula. The critical three factors are the hedge ratio, the asset value, and the present value of the down payoff on the asset. We will consider the second two first, as the hedge ratio is more complex. So, with our numbers, we have

$$C = \frac{1}{h}\left(50 - \frac{45}{1.01}\right)$$

---

[11] See Cox, J., S. Ross, and M. Rubinstein, "Option Pricing: A Simplified Approach." *Journal of Financial Economics* 7, no. 3 (1979), pp. 229–63. The arbitrage argument has also been credited to Robert Merton.

We make the following observations:

- First, the call is clearly worth more as the asset price goes up. If the current price is $50.25, the call price increases to $2.85.

- Second, the call is worth more as the risk-free rate goes up. Because the present value gets smaller when the price of the asset goes down, less is subtracted from the current asset value. With a 1.5 percent risk-free rate, the call is worth $2.83.

- Third, the call price goes up as the risk of the asset increases. As the range of possible outcomes increases, the asset value falls when the price goes down, making the call worth more. If the range increases to $20, lowering the payoff when the asset goes down to $40, the value of the call increases to $5.20.

- Fourth, as the strike price increases, the denominator in the hedge ratio (Equation 12A-1) gets smaller, so the investor has to sell more calls, which reduces the value of the call. At a strike price of $54, the hedge ratio increases to 10 and the call price drops to $0.545.

- Fifth, the call price increases if the up price increases, and the call price decreases if the up price decreases. For example, at $54 the hedge ratio increases to 2.25 and the call price drops to $2.42. We can think of a decrease in the up price as the impact of a dividend payment. Consider two firms. One pays a dividend and the other does not. In good economic conditions, the dividend-paying firm increases its dividend by $1, so its stock price drops to only $54, whereas the stock price of the non-dividend-paying firm goes to $55.[12]

These five observations are consistent with the intuitive results that we discussed in the chapter. The time to expiration can't be applied to this example, however, because this is a single-period binomial model. We also have not discussed the expected return on the asset as a factor in the option price. Nor have we discussed any of the factors that directly affect the market price of risk discussed in the CAPM earlier. In fact, the problem that bedevilled the pricing of options for many decades—determining the correct discount rate to value the option's payoff—is absent completely. In this case, we have an amazing result: we can behave as if the investor is risk neutral and value the option accordingly.

Risk-Neutral Probabilities

Let's go back to our simple example in which the payoff is either $55, with a probability of 60 percent, or $45, with a probability of 40 percent, so the expected rate of return is 2 percent— that is, $0.60 \times (55 - 50) + 0.40 \times (45 - 50) = 0.60 \times 10\% + 0.40 \times (-10\%)$. This 2 percent expected rate of return exceeds the risk-free rate of 1 percent because investors are risk averse. However, because the option price does not depend on risk aversion, we will keep things simple and assume the investor is **risk neutral**. In this case, we can calculate the probabilities that will earn a risk-neutral investor the same 1 percent rate of return as the risk-free rate does. We can do this because this is what risk neutrality means: investors ignore the risk involved in determining expected rates of return.

We can calculate the probabilities that will generate a 1 percent return on the asset given the two possible payoffs of $55 and $45. Because a 1 percent return means that the price of the asset has to be $50.50 in the next period, we use the formula of an expected value to get

$$50(1.01) = 55P + 45(1 - P)$$

$$P = \frac{50.5 - 45}{10} = 0.55$$

risk neutral the state of ignoring the risk involved in determining expected rates of return

---

If instead of a 60 percent chance of going up to $55, there is only a 55 percent chance, then the expected rate of return is 1 percent, the same as the risk-free rate. We can value the option directly as the payoff is still $5 when the asset price is $55. The only difference is that now we use the probability of 55 percent, so the expected payoff is $2.75, while there is a 45 percent chance of getting zero. If this expected cash flow of $2.75 is discounted back one period at the risk-free rate, the result is the option price of $2.72.

As we indicated before, this is an amazing result, but to get it we have derived new probabilities that ensure the asset price goes up with the risk-free rate, instead of dealing with the actual probabilities of the asset going up and down. These probabilities are called the **risk-neutral probabilities**. They are the probabilities that would exist if the investor were risk neutral; of course, they are not the true probabilities, because investors are not risk neutral. However, because the call option can be valued as if the investor were risk neutral, we can use these risk-neutral probabilities to determine the expected payoff on the call and value it directly. This insight has generated a huge industry in option pricing, where complicated securities are valued in a risk-neutral world, as if the underlying asset always earned the risk-free rate. It has proven to be an incredibly useful construct in solving complex problems and comes directly from the Black-Scholes and binomial option pricing models.

risk-neutral probabilities derived probabilities that ensure the asset price goes up with the risk-free rate; the probabilities that would exist if the investor were risk neutral

---

CONCEPT REVIEW QUESTIONS

1. Explain how to create a risk-free portfolio from the stock and the option's payoff.
2. What is a hedge ratio?
3. Why don't the probabilities of going up and down affect the option's value?
4. What are risk-neutral probabilities?

SUMMARY

This chapter discusses the Nobel Prize–winning ideas of Fischer Black, Myron Scholes, and Robert Merton. Continuing our discussion from Chapter 11, in which we looked at derivatives with linear payoffs, in this chapter we look at non-linear payoffs, where either the gains or the losses are truncated or changed at some points. We discuss the payoffs from call and put options and look at how the value of these options are determined by the underlying asset's price and volatility, the strike price and time to expiration of the option, and the conditions in the economy in terms of the risk-free rate. We go on to discuss put-call parity and how options can be used for hedging. We also show how options can be valued using the Black-Scholes option pricing model and then discuss how options are traded. Finally, we discuss the very important topic of real options and why the central ideas of option pricing have dramatically changed the way we look at a variety of finance and management topics.

SUMMARY OF LEARNING OBJECTIVES

12.1 Describe the basic nature of call options and the factors that influence their value.

A call option is the right, but not the obligation, to buy an underlying asset at a fixed price for a specified time. A call option value

- increases with the price of the underlying asset
- decreases with a higher strike price

- increases if the underlying asset is riskier
- increases as the time to expiration increases
- decreases as the dividend payments of the underlying asset increase
- increases as interest rates increase
- approaches its intrinsic value for deep in and deep out of the money calls

12.2 Describe the basic nature of put options and the payoffs associated with long and short positions in put options.

A put option is the opposite of a call option: it gives the owner the right, but not the obligation, to *sell* an underlying asset at a fixed price for a specified time. A put option value:

- decreases with the price of the underlying asset
- increases with a higher strike price
- increases if the underlying asset is riskier
- increases as the time to expiration increases
- increases as the dividend payments of the underlying asset increase
- decreases as interest rates increase

12.3 Explain how to use put-call parity to estimate call and put prices, and explain how it can be used to synthetically create call, put, and underlying positions.

Put-call parity is the relationship between the price of a call option and the price of a put option that has the same strike price and expiry date; it assumes that the options are not exercised before their expiration. See $P + S = C + PV(X)$.

- You can create a synthetic call option by longing a put and the underlying stock and shorting cash. See $C = P + S - PV(X)$.
- You can create a synthetic put option by longing a call and cash and shorting the underlying stock. See $P = C - S + PV(X)$.
- You can create the underlying positions by longing a call and cash and shorting a put. See $S = C - P + PV(X)$.

12.4 Explain how to use the Black-Scholes option pricing model to price call options.

The Black-Scholes option pricing model provides a formula to calculate the premium for European call options. (Put prices can be solved using the put-call parity condition.) The Black-Scholes model shows that the option premium is a function of the underlying asset's price, the option strike price, the volatility of the underlying asset's price, the risk-free interest rate, and the time remaining to maturity. The Black-Scholes option pricing model can be used to calculate the "Greeks": delta, gamma, theta, rho, and vega. The "Greeks" measure the sensitivity of the option premium to changes in the model parameters, except for gamma, which measures the sensitivity of delta to changes in the underlying asset's price.

12.5 Explain how options are traded and what is meant by implied volatility.

Options are traded over the counter and on exchanges. In Canada, options are traded on the Montreal Exchange (in the United States, options are traded on the CBOT [Chicago Board of Trade], the Chicago Mercantile Exchange, and the Philadelphia Exchange, to name three). Implied volatility is solved from the Black-Scholes option pricing model using the market price of the option and solving for the level of volatility, which yields the market price.

12.6 Understand by means of the simplest option pricing model what factors affect the value of a call option and provide a guide to their order of magnitude.

The binomial option pricing model shows how the intuitive factors that affect option prices, as discussed in section 12.2, affect option prices.

KEY TERMS

American options, p. 461
binomial model, p. 479
call option, p. 452
collar, p. 468
covered call writing, p. 467
deep, p. 455
delta, p. 474
European options, p. 461
exercise, p. 452
exercise price, p. 452
expiration date, p. 452

gamma, p. 474
Greeks, the, p. 474
hedge ratio (h), p. 480
implied volatility, p. 476
in the money, p. 453
intrinsic value (IV), p. 455
option premium, p. 455
option writer, p. 454
out of the money, p. 453
payoff, p. 452
protective put, p. 465

put option, p. 458
put-call parity, p. 463
rho, p. 474
risk neutral, p. 481
risk-neutral probabilities, p. 482
short position, p. 454
strike price, p. 452
theta, p. 474
time value (TV), p. 455
vega, p. 474

EQUATIONS

Equation	Formula	Page
[12-1] Intrinsic Value (IV) of a Call	IV (Call) = Max $(S - X, 0)$	p. 455
[12-2] Option Premium	IV(Put) = Max$(X - S, 0)$	p. 455
[12-3] Time Value (TV)	TV = Option premium − IV	p. 455
[12-4] Intrinsic Value (IV) of a put	IV (Put) = Max $(X - S, 0)$	p. 460
[12-5] Put-Call Parity	$P + S = C + PV(X)$	p. 464
[12-6] Put-Call Relationship.	$C - P = S - PV(X)$	p. 464
[12-7] Call Option Price	$C = P + S - PV(X)$	p. 464
[12-8] Put Option Price.	$P = C - S + PV(X)$	p. 464
[12-9] Underlying Asset Price	$S = C - P + PV(X)$	p. 465
[12-10] Black-Scholes' Option Pricing Model	$C = SN(d_1) - Xe^{-rt}N(d_2)$	p. 470
[12A-1] Hedge Ratio	$h = \dfrac{PU - PD}{PU - X}$	p. 480
[12A-2] Binomial Call Price	$C = \dfrac{1}{h}\left(S - \dfrac{PD}{(1 + r)}\right)$	p. 480

QUESTIONS AND PRACTICE PROBLEMS

Multiple Choice Questions

1. Which of the following statements about a call option is false?
   a. A call option is the right, not the obligation, to buy the underlying asset.
   b. A call option is in the money if the asset price is less than the strike price.
   c. A call option is at the money if the asset price is the same as the strike price.
   d. On the expiration date, a call option has no time value.

2. Before the expiration of a call option, if its intrinsic value is $13 and the market value of the option is $19, what is the time value of the option? What do we call the market value of the option?
   a. $32; option premium
   b. $6; option premium
   c. $32; option price
   d. $6; option price

3. Which of the following increases the value of a call option?
   a. The price of the underlying asset decreases.
   b. The volatility of the price of the underlying asset decreases.
   c. The remaining time to expiration of the call option increases.
   d. The underlying stock increases its dividend payment.

4. Which of the following *decreases* the value of a put option?
   a. The price of the underlying asset decreases.
   b. The underlying asset becomes riskier.

    c. The interest rate decreases.

    d. The strike price decreases.

5.   Which of the following may create a synthetic loan?

    a. Long a put, short the stock, and long a call.

    b. Long a put, long the stock, and long a call.

    c. Short a put, long the stock, and long a call.

    d. Long a put, long the stock, and short a call.

6.   What is the intrinsic value (IV) of a put if the underlying asset price (S) is $40 and the strike price (X) is $45? What is the IV if it is a call?

    a. $0, $5

    b. $5, $0

    c. $5, $5

    d. $0, $0

7.   Which of the following positions is the most risky?

    a. long a call

    b. short a call

    c. long a put

    d. short a put

8.   Which of the following statements about the Black-Scholes model is *false*?

    a. It uses a continuously compounded risk-free rate.

    b. d_1 can be thought of as the expected moneyness of the call.

    c. $N(d_1)$ is the cumulative probability of being out of the money.

    d. The model assumes that the underlying asset price follows a lognormal distribution.

9.   Which of the following statements is *correct*, given the following information?

January 2014	Strike	Bid	Ask	Last
Call A	25	1.85	2.05	1.85
Put B	36	1.10	1.35	1.15
Call C	30.75	1.50	1.75	1.60

    a. The market maker's profit of call A is 0.25.

    b. If the market price of the underlying asset is 35, then the time value of put B is 0.1.

    c. The time value for a put is usually higher than that for a call.

    d. By using the market price of an option, we can calculate the implied volatility of the option.

10. What is the hedge ratio (h) for a call if PU is $52, PD is $45, and the strike price (S) is $48?

    a. 1.33

    b. 2.05

    c. 1.75

    d. 2.33

11. Which of the following is the correct meaning of a hedge ratio of 1/3?

    a. Short one call to hedge a long position of three units of the underlying asset

    b. Short three calls to hedge a long position of the underlying asset

    c. Long one call to hedge a long position of three units of the underlying asset

    d. Long three calls to hedge a long position of the underlying asset

12. Which of the following statements about risk-neutral probabilities is false?

    a. Risk-neutral probabilities are probabilities that exist if investors are risk neutral.

    b. Risk-neutral probabilities are the actual probabilities of the asset price going up and down.

    c. Risk-neutral probabilities are the probabilities that ensure the asset price goes up with the risk-free rate.

    d. Risk-neutral probabilities assume the underlying asset earns the risk-free rate.

Practice Problems

13. You are in the process of interviewing for a promotion at FinCorp Inc. and have to identify the type of security based on the payoff diagrams below. All options expire on January 15, 201x, and the underlying asset is the index. Match the series from the diagrams to the appropriate security and position.

	Position	Series
A	Long index	
B	Short index	
C	Long call	
D	Short call	
E	Long put	
F	Short put	
G	Long bond	
H	Short bond	

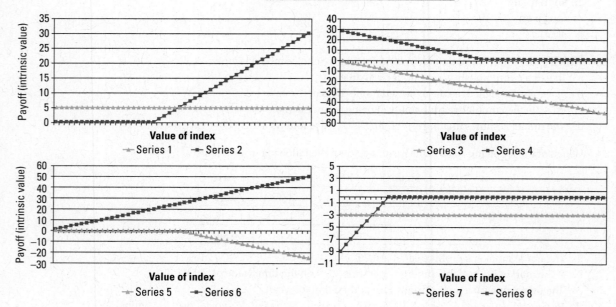

14. Richards & Co. Analysts has provided FinCorp Inc. with incomplete information, and it is your job to fill in the missing information in the table below.

				At expiration		
Long or short	Call or put	Strike price	Value of option today	Value of underlying asset	Payoff (intrinsic value)	Profit (loss)
Long	Call	150	5	175		
Short	Call	150	5	175		
Long	Put	150	5	110		
Short	Put	150	5	110		
Long	Call	175	5	150		
Short	Call	175	5	150		
Long	Put	175	5	200		
Short	Put	175	5	200		

15. Mr. Cabinet, your boss at FinCorp Inc., prefers to have his information presented visually. At his request, graph the payoffs (intrinsic values) and profits at expiration for the following option investments.
    a. long call, strike = $55, cost today = $10
    b. short call, strike = $55, cost today = $10
    c. long put, strike = $55, cost today = $10
    d. short put, strike = $55, cost today = $10

16. Briefly state all the factors that affect the value of a call option and a put option.

17. Your boss has observed that the call options on XCT and BRG are trading at different prices. Both options have the same strike price and the same time to expiration. Provide two possible explanations for this observation.

18. Mr. Cabinet is interested in the payoffs to combinations of options. Graph the intrinsic values of the following portfolios (all options expire on the same day and are written on the same non-dividend-paying asset).
    a. long one call, strike = $25; long one put, strike = $20
    b. short one call, strike = $25; long one put, strike = $15
    c. long one call, strike = $25; short one put, strike = $25
    d. long one call, strike = $25; short one share of underlying asset
    e. long one call, strike = $25; short one share; $25 in cash
    f. long one put, strike = $25; long one share; short $25 in cash (i.e., repay loan)

19. You have observed that a very smart and successful investor has bought a call and a put on the S&P/TSX Index. The options have the same strike prices and expire on the same day. What does the smart investor think is going to happen to the S&P/TSX Index? (Hint: When will she make money on this investment?)

✿ 20. Complete the following table.

| | | | | | | At expiration | | |
	Long or short	Call or put	Strike price	Value of option today	Value of under-lying asset	In/Out of the money	Payoff (intrinsic value) of option	Profit (loss)
A	Long	Put	80	0.05				−0.05
B	Long	Call	80	2				−1
C	Short	Put	80	0.05				−0.95
D	Short	Call	80	0.05				−0.95
E	Long	Call		1	125			25
F	Short	Put	124		125		0	−2
G			25	2	95		0	−2
H			25	2	95		70	68
I		Call	75		90			2
J		Put	75		90			2
K		Call	75	5	90			−10
L		Put	75		90			−2
M	Short	Call	110				0	2
N		Put	80	3			−25	−22

21. Mr. Kent, one of your clients, has been reading his daughter's finance textbook and has a question about options. He says: "If I buy a call option, I have the right to buy the asset at the strike price. If I buy a put option, I have the right to sell the asset at the strike price. And if I

sell a put, I have to buy the asset at the strike price. Therefore, buying a call option is the same as selling a put. So if I observe that puts and calls have different prices, I can make money because they should have the same price!" Comment on Mr. Kent's statement. Is he correct?

22. The current price of a stock is $97. You expect the price of the stock to be in the range of $95 to $105 in the next period. The call option with an exercise price of $105 is $1.30; the put option with an exercise price of $95 is $1.00. Both options expire in the next period. Using options only, explain how you can earn a profit.

23. You observe the following data on different options (all are European options with the same exercise date, and all are written on the same underlying security). What are the profits you would earn for every possible price of the underlying stock at the exercise date for each of the following strategies?

Security	Current price	Strike price
IBL Stock	50	
Call	C1	60
Call	C2	70
Call	C3	40
Call	C4	30

a. Using arbitrage arguments, rank the prices of the calls.
b. Buy one call with an exercise price of $40 and buy one share.
c. Buy two calls with a strike price of $70 and short sell one share.
d. Write two calls with a strike price of $30 and buy one share.

24. Compare the payoff of a call option and the underlying security. Show that the price of a call option must always be less than the value of the underlying security.

25. Richards & Co. Analysts have provided the following partially completed table of information about different securities. All options are written on XCT, a non-dividend-paying stock, and expire on the same day in one year. Fill in the missing information.

	XCT stock price	Price of call	Price of put	Strike price	Risk-free rate
A	90		6	75	5%
B	120	30		100	5%
C		3	2	15	6%
D		5	5	25	10%
E	85	25	30	90	
F	130	25	20		5%

26. Fill in the missing information in the following table for a non-dividend-paying stock and European call options.

	S	X	r	σ	T	d_1	d_2	$N(d_1)$	$N(d_2)$	Xe^{-rt}	Call value
A	100	98	2%	0.03	1						
B	100	98	2%	0.04	1						
C	100	98	3%	0.03	1						
D	100	99	2%	0.03	1						
E	100	98	2%	0.03	0.3						
F	99	98	2%	0.03	1						

27. Does put-call parity hold for the following? Risk-free rate = 5%, P_0 = $13, C_0 = $ 10, stock price (S) = $30, t = 4 years, strike price (X) = $33. If not, what is the put price according to put-call parity, assuming the other figures are correct?

28. Briefly explain "the Greeks" (delta, theta, vega, and rho) in option pricing.

29. Determine the call price (C), given the following information: stock price (S) = $36, strike price ($X$) = $32, risk-free rate ($r$) = 5% , t = 2 years, σ = 20%.

30. In Practice Problem 29, if the time value is $5, calculate the intrinsic value.

31. Calculate the put price (P), according to put-call parity, given the information in Practice Problem 29.

32. What is the price of a put option with a strike price of $50 and six months to maturity when the stock price is currently trading at $45? Assume the stock-price variance is 0.5 and the risk-free rate is 5 percent.

33. QBV, a non-dividend-paying stock, is currently trading for $100 a share. There is a 25-percent chance that the stock will trade for $85 in one year, and a 75-percent chance that the price will increase to $135. The risk-free rate is 5 percent per year. All options expire in one year. You would like to purchase a call with a strike price of $125. Unfortunately, it is not available on the market, so you will have to create it synthetically. Design a portfolio to create a call with a strike price of $125 and demonstrate that it will give the same payoff as the desired call.

⚙ 34. You have just been appointed manager of the equity portfolio of a large pension plan. The portfolio has a current value of $100 billion and is well diversified; consequently, it has a beta close to one. The trustees of the pension plan are very risk averse, and in order to prevent you from taking on too much risk, they have structured your compensation as follows: if the value of the fund drops below $90 billion in one year, you will be fired with no severance pay. If the fund is between $90 billion and $120 billion, you will be paid $2 million + 0.01 percent of the difference between the fund value and $90 billion (i.e., if the fund is worth $95 billion in one year, you will be paid $2 million + $500,000 = $2.5 million). If the fund is worth more than $120 billion, your salary will be capped at $5 million. You are allowed to invest in options on the S&P/TSX. The current value of the S&P/TSX is 1,000, and there are puts and calls traded that expire in one year. The puts and calls both have multipliers of $100. The standard deviation of returns on the S&P/TSX is 10 percent per year, and the risk-free rate is 3 percent per year. Assume that there are no dividends for either the portfolio or the S&P/TSX and that the options are European.
    a. Describe how you can best protect your personal interests.
    b. How much will these actions cost the portfolio?

35. FinCorp Inc. has both a call option and a put option with exercise prices of $50. Both expire in one year. The call is currently selling for $10 per share, while the put is currently selling for $2 per share. If the risk-free rate is 5 percent per year, what should the stock price be so that there is no arbitrage opportunity?

⚙ 36. In the next period, the economy can be in either state 1 or state 2, with a probability of 50 percent. You may trade any combination, including fractions of shares, of the following three securities:

Security	Value today	Value in future	
		State 1	State 2
MCD	15	25	20
SB	5	10	25
BK	3	75	17.50

   a. Are these securities correctly priced? If not, why not? (Hint: set up a portfolio with proper weight in MCD and SB so that the portfolio has the same payoff as security BK.)

   b. If there is an arbitrage opportunity, explain how you would exploit it.

   c. What is the maximum you would be willing to pay for SB? (Hint: The maximum I would be willing to pay for a share of SB is the cost of the portfolio that replicates one share of SB.)

37. The current price of TSY Inc. is $75. In one year, the price could be either $50 or $100. The risk-free rate is 5 percent per year. Construct a portfolio with the same payoff as a call option. What is the most you would pay for a call on TSY Inc. with a strike price of $90?

38. In most markets, you are not permitted to short sell if the stock price has fallen. That is, you can only short sell on an "uptick." Using put-call parity, show that you can replicate the cash flows of a short sale.

39. QBV, a non-dividend-paying stock, is currently trading for $80 a share. There is a 25-percent chance that the stock will trade for $65 in one year, and a 75-percent chance that the price will increase to $105. The risk-free rate is 5 percent per year. All options expire in one year.

   a. A call option has a strike price of 100. Determine the hedge ratio.

   b. Use the binomial option pricing formula to determine the value of a call with a strike price of $100.

   c. Use the put-call parity to determine the value of a put with a strike price of $100.

40. QBV, a non-dividend-paying stock, is currently trading for $100 a share. There is a 25-percent chance that the stock will trade for $85 in one year, and a 75-percent chance that the price will increase to $135. The risk-free rate is 5 percent per year. All options expire in one year.

   a. If the call option on QBV with a strike price of $115 is actually trading for $10, show that there is an arbitrage opportunity.

   b. If the put option on QBV with a strike price of $98 is actually trading for $0.50, show that there is an arbitrage opportunity.

41. DPG, a non-dividend-paying stock, is currently trading for $150 a share. There is a 30-percent chance that the stock will trade for $125 in one year, and a 70-percent chance that the price will increase to $175. The risk-free rate is 5 percent per year. There is a one-year call with a strike price of $165.

   a. What is the price of the call?

   b. b. What is the delta of the call? Define and calculate.

⚙ 42. Xiang Zhu, a client of FinCorp Inc., has phoned you with a question. She has been reading a finance textbook and cannot understand how to use the binomial option pricing model to value a call option. The underlying stock is currently trading for $100. There is a 30-percent chance it will increase to $190 in one year, and a 70-percent chance it will fall to $85 in the same period. The risk-free rate is 10 percent. There is a call option with a strike price of $170, which according to the binomial model should have a value of $4.329. Xiang is confused because she calculates that if there is a 30-percent chance the call will be worth $20 and a 70-percent chance it will be worth zero, the expected value should be $6. Why is it only worth $4.329?

   a. Demonstrate that if the call was trading for $6, there would be an arbitrage opportunity.

   b. Calculate the risk-neutral probabilities.

   c. Calculate the expected present value of the call option using the risk-neutral probabilities.

   d. Why can we value options as if the investors are risk neutral?

43. What is the strike price (X) if PU is $50, PD is $42, and the hedge ratio (h) is 2?

44. Assume stock XYZ does not pay dividends and has a market value of $98 per share. There is a 60-percent chance that the stock will trade for $130 in one year, and a 40-percent chance that it will trade for $55 in one year. What is the value of a put option with an exercise price of $90 if the risk-free rate is 5 percent per year?

Part 6

LONG-TERM INVESTMENT DECISIONS

Assets are on the left of the balance sheet and liabilities are on the right. In Part 6, we consider the left-hand side: assets. In chapters 13 and 14, we look at the internal acquisition of assets through capital budgeting and apply the workhorse of finance—discounting future cash flows—to evaluate capital expenditures. In chapters 15 and 16, we consider special cases: buying another firm's assets (commonly referred to as mergers and acquisitions) and leasing, which combines the asset-acquisition and financing decision into one.

13 Capital Budgeting, Risk Considerations, and Other Special Issues

LEARNING OBJECTIVES

13.1 Describe the capital budgeting process and explain its importance to corporate strategy.

13.2 Identify and apply the main tools used to evaluate investments.

13.3 Analyze independent projects and explain how they differ from interdependent projects.

13.4 Explain what capital rationing is and how it affects firms' investment criteria.

13.5 Explain the importance of international foreign direct investment both inside and outside Canada.

13.6 Understand how the modified internal rate of return (MIRR) is calculated and why this represents a conceptual improvement over the way the IRR is calculated.

Canada's productivity, defined as output per unit hour worked, outpaced the U.S. for the first time in five years in 2011, advancing 1.1 per cent in the fourth quarter above the corresponding period in 2010.

Jack Mintz, chair of the School of Public Policy at the University of Calgary pointed out that Canadian firms have dramatically hiked spending on new machinery and equipment over the past two years and some of those investments may be paying off.

The Bank of Canada has had productivity on its radar screen for years, and has often chided business on their lack of investments in machinery and equipment. Finance Minister Jim Flaherty is expected to take another run at the productivity issue in his March 29 federal budget, although it will be called "innovation."

Source: Beltrame, Julian, "Canada's productivity on the rise." The Canadian Press, March 13, 2012. Copyright © 2012 The Canadian Press. Reprinted by permission.

CHAPTER 13 **PREVIEW**

The chapter-opening vignette alludes to the critical role of business investment in productivity. In this chapter, we discuss long-term investment decisions made by firms, particularly decisions about investments in real assets, such as property, plant, and equipment. In previous chapters, we have seen that a firm's investment decisions are critical to firm value, because market values are based on the expected future growth in company earnings, dividends, and distributable cash flows.

In this chapter, we will also revisit several concepts we discussed when describing how to value bonds and shares, and we will emphasize that the basic techniques are identical: we have to estimate future cash flows, determine appropriate discount rates, convert those expected future cash flows back into their corresponding present values, and compare them with their cost. The essential difference between valuing shares and valuing projects or companies is not in the approach but in the judgement necessary because of the differing "quality" of the inputs.

13.1 CAPITAL EXPENDITURES

The Importance of the Capital Expenditure Decision

Learning Objective 13.1
Describe the capital budgeting process and explain its importance to corporate strategy.

capital expenditures a firm's investments in long-lived assets, which may be tangible or intangible

Capital expenditures are a firm's investments in long-lived assets, which may be tangible assets, such as property, plant, and equipment, or intangible assets, such as research and development (R&D), copyrights, brand names, and franchise agreements. Tangible assets are hard, physical assets, while intangible ones are more abstract; it is easier for a firm to borrow against tangible assets than against intangible ones.[1]

These long-term investment decisions determine a company's future direction and could be viewed as the most important decisions a firm can make, because a firm's capital expenditures (capex) usually involve large amounts of money, and the decisions are frequently irrevocable. For example, TransCanada PipeLines Ltd. transmits natural gas from western Canada to central Canada and Chicago. Once its pipeline assets are in place, they are largely unique to that application and have very little alternative use. It is therefore important that any decision related to these capex investments is made on sound financial and economic grounds.[2] The irrevocable and unique nature of real investments has its parallel in investments in intangible assets, where a decision to bring out a new soft drink, for example, with the attendant new product development costs and marketing campaign, is also irrevocable. In this case, it is almost impossible to get back the investment costs of a failed new product launch.

The importance of capex decisions lies in their ability to affect the risk of the firm. In some cases, the very survival of the firm depends on the success of a new product produced from prior capex decisions. Ford, for example, was saved from extinction in the 1980s when it brought out the then revolutionary Ford Taurus, which went on to become the most popular family car in North America.

---

[1] Under Canadian GAAP, spending to generate certain intangible assets, such as R&D and advertising, is expensed rather than capitalized. Such items do not appear on the balance sheet as assets. As a result, most intangible assets that do appear on the balance sheet result from a firm taking over another one at a premium to its book value. This premium, called "goodwill," is then allocated to different assets and often results in patent or copyright values or "other" assets appearing on the balance sheet.

[2] These types of decisions are so important that the National Energy Board (NEB) requires that TransCanada gets NEB approval before it can significantly expand its system. New pipelines have to undergo a thorough public examination, as was conducted for the Mackenzie Valley Pipeline (MVP), which is to bring natural gas down from the Arctic. The NEB gave "conditional approval" for the project in December 2010, subject to meeting 264 environmental, financial, and cultural commitments that were outlined in the NEB report. The tab for the MVP was estimated at approximately $7 billion in 2007, but 2011 estimates were over $16 billion.

Capital budgeting refers to the process through which a firm makes capital expenditure decisions, as shown below.

Identify investment alternatives → Evaluate these alternatives → Implement the chosen investment decisions → Monitor and evaluate the implemented decisions

We will focus most of our discussion on the general framework that should be used to evaluate various investment alternatives, because the remaining decisions are firm-specific and covered in managerial accounting (which develops the firm's control and audit systems). First, we will briefly discuss some important factors in the investment process.

The chapter-opening vignette suggests that one of the factors contributing to improved productivity is increased investment in machinery and equipment. Conversely, one could surmise that if a firm does not invest effectively, it will find itself at a competitive disadvantage, which in the extreme will affect its long-term survival. In the short run, poor investment decisions will make a firm less attractive than those that have better prepared themselves for the future. This will show up in the market price of the firm's debt and equity securities, which will decline, and will hence increase its cost of capital.

Finance in the News 13-1 discusses the critical role of capital expenditures and R&D outlays for Canada's long-term productivity. The author suggests that "contributors to our growing productivity gap" include "chronic underinvestment in machinery and equipment [and] insufficient levels of R&D," among other things. Of course, the opening vignette, which was written four months later, noted that Canadian businesses have made some recent improvements on these items.

> **capital budgeting** the process through which a firm makes capital expenditure decisions by (1) identifying investment alternatives, (2) evaluating these alternatives, (3) implementing the chosen investment decisions, and (4) monitoring and evaluating the implemented decisions

---

finance INTHENEWS 13-1   Canada Needs to Stimulate Productivity

CANADA'S PERFORMANCE DURING the financial crisis and subsequent recession is rightly a point of pride. Canadians, and the world, have developed a new-found appreciation for the institutional prudence of our banking system and regulatory regime. However, the risk-averse attitudes that helped us avoid taking dangerous financial bets also hold us back from taking the risks necessary to build more competitive companies and a more productive economy.

Neither our relative stability through the financial crisis nor our high standard of living should distract us from the reality that we lag many other countries in terms of productivity, one of the most important long-term drivers of prosperity. The average Australian now generates $2 more per hour than the average Canadian; the average American generates $13 more; the average Norwegian generates $29 more.

Productivity can be significantly influenced by risk appetite. Canada has long been regarded as a risk-averse country, but there has been little evidence to support this—until now. Deloitte conducted interviews about risk tolerance with 450 Canadian and 452 American executives from small, medium, and large companies across a broad array of industries and the results have provided valuable insight into the Canadian risk profile.

Canadian and American executives self-reported similar levels of risk tolerance, with Canadian business leaders more optimistic than their U.S. counterparts about the state of the economy. One would expect that this optimism, combined with similar risk tolerance levels, would translate into a greater—or at least equal—propensity for investment among Canadian business leaders.

Surprisingly, this is not the case. In the survey, Canadian executives indicated that they are not planning to invest in the types of activities required to improve productivity. When we look at the actual decisions Canadian business leaders make about activities that bolster productivity, such as investing in R&D and commercializing innovation, Americans are 13 percent more tolerant of risk than Canadians, according to the Deloitte Executive Risk Behaviour Index.

Canadians may label themselves as equally risk-tolerant to Americans, but when it comes to putting their money where their attitude is, they hesitate. This "action gap" is a key cause of the Canadian productivity conundrum.

It should be noted that this gap does not have an impact on all Canadian business leaders equally. Through their actions, our leading risk takers accept as much risk as their U.S. counterparts. However, with self-identified risk avoiders, we see a significant difference. Canadian risk avoiders accept far less risk than their American peers.

Canadian business leaders' aversion to risk is especially important because it underlies other critical contributors to our growing productivity gap, including a lack of risk capital for startups, chronic underinvestment in machinery and equipment, insufficient levels of private sector R&D, and an unwillingness to engage international markets.

continued

Finance in the News 13-1: Canada Needs To Stimulate Productivity *(continued)*

We need business leaders to be more willing to undertake intelligent risk by making investments in R&D, launching innovative products, developing improved production techniques, implementing international best practices, integrating state-of-the-art machinery, and expanding into new markets. Combined, these activities would contribute significantly to Canada's productivity and international competitiveness.

Continued economic growth will only be sustained through ongoing, persistent improvements in the productivity of our work force. The courage to lead this transformation must come from within the highest levels of business, government, and academia. In particular, business leaders must fundamentally re-examine their attitudes about taking intelligent risks. Canada's strength through the recession has created a finite window during which our productivity trajectory can be reset. To overlook this opportunity is to threaten our country's long-term prosperity.

Michael Porter has written extensively on the notion that successful companies will create a "competitive strategy" for themselves. He identifies five critical factors that determine the attractiveness of an industry:

- entry barriers
- the threat of substitutes
- the bargaining power of buyers
- the bargaining power of suppliers
- rivalry among existing competitors

five forces the five critical factors that determine the attractiveness of an industry: entry barriers, the threat of substitutes, the bargaining power of buyers, the bargaining power of suppliers, and rivalry among existing competitors

These are often called the **five forces**.[3] Porter argues that, after inception, firms have little immediate control over the attractiveness of the industry they are in. This implies that industry structure will have a significant input into every firm's investment decisions. However, Porter points out, firms *do* exert control over the manner in which they strive to create a competitive advantage within their industry. Obviously, these decisions will also be closely related to a firm's long-term investment decisions, as discussed below.

Porter argues that firms can create competitive advantages for themselves by adopting one of the following strategies:

1. *Cost leadership: strive to be a low-cost producer*. This strategy is viable for firms that are able to take advantage of economies of scale, proprietary technology, or privileged or superior access to raw materials. Obviously, investment outlays should be made in accordance with a firm's potential advantage. For example, if economies of scale or technological advantages are possible, firms should invest in a manner that will enable them to exploit these opportunities.

2. *Differentiation: offer "differentiated" products*. Firms can provide products that are differentiated from others in several ways. The most obvious is to have a product that is itself unique by virtue of its physical or technological characteristics. However, firms can also differentiate their products by providing customers with unique delivery alternatives, or by establishing a marketing approach that distinguishes their products from those of their potential competitors.

Either of these strategies can be applied with a broad (industry-wide) focus or with a narrow (industry-segment) focus, and both have their corollary in capex decisions. As we will discuss, cost leadership usually follows from *replacement* decisions, when firms are constantly striving to use the latest technology to lower the costs of production. Product

---

[3]Porter, M. "How Competitive Forces Shape Strategy." *Harvard Business Review*, March-April 1979.

differentiation usually follows from *new product development decisions*, such as the launch of a new flavoured soft drink or a new model of car.

Porter suggests that it is difficult to sustain a competitive advantage once one has been created. This is particularly true in industries where competition is heated or where barriers to entry are low or nonexistent. Therefore, companies must continually plan (and invest) strategically. This brings up the question: what is the relationship between corporate strategy and the capex decision?

A basic premise of finance suggests that when a senior executive justifies a project on non-financial grounds, either the analysis is not rigorous enough, with the advantages not fully developed, or it is a pet project and should not be pursued. Every project is amenable to the analytical techniques that we discuss below—the only difference is that the more qualitative the inputs, the more strategic the analysis. However, this does bring up a basic distinction—the difference between bottom-up and top-down analysis.

Bottom-up analysis is based on the idea that a firm is simply a set of capex decisions. Equipment replacement is a typical bottom-up analysis, in which an engineer estimates the savings that will be realized—in terms of labour hours, power, material costs, and so on—by replacing one piece of equipment with another. A financial analyst then translates these savings into financial parameters to determine whether the replacement savings are worth the cost of the equipment. However, at no point does the engineer or the financial analyst consider whether the firm should continue in this business. An analogy might be the engineer on the Titanic deciding to replace some equipment just after the ship struck the iceberg. In isolation, it might be a good decision but obviously it is irrelevant on a larger scale.

In contrast, **top-down analysis** focuses on strategic decisions about which industries or products the firm should be involved in. For example, Ford's F150 trucks were the best-selling vehicles in North America for several years, while its car division was losing money. Consequently, there was serious discussion about whether Ford should "do a Volvo" and sell its car business to someone or shut some plants and become a truck manufacturer. The strategic decision was whether Ford should produce passenger cars or focus solely on trucks, rather than the decision of which passenger cars should be developed. Of course, Ford didn't shut down its car division, and the car lines have been doing much better recently. *Finance in the News 13-2* discusses a top-down approach to investment decisions from an entire economy's perspective, referring to soaring "investment in China's medical and healthcare industry" in response to the increased number of participants who are in (and are projected to join) this system.

bottom-up analysis an investment strategy in which capex decisions are made in isolation, without considering general industry and economic trends or whether the firm should continue in this particular business

top-down analysis an investment strategy that focuses on strategic decisions, such as which industries or products the firm should be involved in, looking at the overall economic picture

finance INTHENEWS 13-2   Medical and Healthcare Investment Soars

INVESTMENT IN CHINA'S medical and healthcare industry reached a record $3.5 billion in the first nine months of the year, 2.7 times more than the total amount over the whole of 2010, according to a leading consultancy in the venture capital (VC) and private equity (PE) industry.

The 132 investments in 2010, more than double the 60 registered in 2009, totaled $1.3 billion, the Beijing-based Zero2IPO Group said in a report on Friday to the China Bio & Healthcare Industry Investment Forum 2011, held in Beijing.

This year, investors, both at home and abroad, have shown a stronger interest in promising medical and healthcare projects. Ni Zhengdong, founder and chief executive officer of Zero2IPO Group, described the period as having "an explosive increase."

According to the report, the major incentive for the increase in investment was that more people are now included in China's medical insurance system.

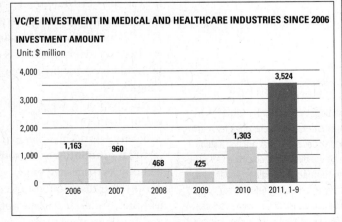

VC/PE INVESTMENT IN MEDICAL AND HEALTHCARE INDUSTRIES SINCE 2006

INVESTMENT AMOUNT
Unit: $ million

continued

Finance in the News 13-2: Medical and Healthcare Investment Soars *(continued)*

The government announced guidelines for healthcare reform in 2009, aiming to establish a medical care system for all Chinese residents by 2011. More than 96 percent of residents, or 1.29 billion people, have joined the system so far, the report said.

An aging population and rising individual incomes have increased demand for medical and healthcare products and services, said Xiao Jun, an analyst with Zero2IPO.

Those aged 60 or over accounted for about 13.3 percent of the country's total population in 2010, a rise from the figure of 10.3 percent seen 10 years ago, according to the Ministry of Health. Meanwhile, the disposable income of urban Chinese residents climbed threefold to 19,109 yuan ($3,000) between 2000 and 2010.

Zhang Zhenzhong, director of the development research centre at the Ministry of Health, said that areas such as drug development and production, medical equipment manufacture and healthcare insurance could be profitable and promising market segments for investors.

"We are particularly interested in research into traditional Chinese medicines and their production, which we see is enjoying a rapid growth in revenue," said Xu Xiaolin, general manager of the wealth management department at CCB International (Holdings) Ltd.

CCB launched a medical industry fund in 2009 and has invested in 12 projects so far.

Foreign investors have also been keen to invest in China's medical and healthcare industries. Antony Leung, chairman of Greater China at Blackstone Group, the world's largest private equity firm, said Blackstone is very interested in investing in China's consumer industry, especially in such sectors as healthcare and medical services.

The US-based VC company IDG Capital Partners has already invested in 12 Chinese medical enterprises.

INVESTMENT CASES

Source: www.zdbchina.com

ZHANG YE/CHINA DAILY

Source: Jingting, Shen, "Medical and healthcare investment soars." *China Daily*, November 5, 2011, p. 9.

In looking at bottom-up versus top-down analysis, the capital budgeting framework is identical. What is different is the quality of the estimates. In replacement decisions, the analysis is one of risk, in which the analyst estimates the cost savings with clearly defined probabilities. It may be possible, for example, to estimate that that there is a 30-percent chance of saving $50,000 and a 70-percent chance of saving $100,000 per year. In this way, replacement decisions are similar to the evaluation of equity investments for which there is a long price history, and for which means, variances, and so on can be estimated to say there is a 50-percent chance of a share going up 15 percent in price and a 50-percent chance of its going down 5 percent. In contrast, top-down or strategic decisions often involve a situation of *uncertainty*, in which it is almost impossible to estimate probabilities for the possible outcomes. In these situations, as we will discuss later, it is important for the analysis to involve different scenarios, so the firm can respond to different situations. This flexibility in top-down decision-making is an application of the theory of option pricing to capex decisions and is called real option valuation (ROV). ROV is difficult to implement but is one of the hottest areas in financial management. We will discuss it in detail in Chapter 14.

In Chapter 2, we pointed out that the firm's goal should be to maximize shareholder wealth. In this chapter, we develop techniques for making capex decisions that are consistent with this overriding objective. These techniques are generally called **discounted cash flow (DCF) methodologies**. As their name suggests, they are the capex analogues to the valuation techniques discussed earlier. DCF valuation involves estimating future cash flows and comparing their discounted values with investment outlays required today. In this way, they are technically identical to the approaches used to evaluate bonds (see Chapter 6) and preferred and common shares (see Chapter 7).

discounted cash flow (DCF) methodologies techniques for making capex decisions that are consistent with the overriding objective of maximizing shareholder wealth; they involve estimating future cash flows and comparing their discounted values with investment outlays required today

The only practical difference is that whereas the cash flows are fixed when valuing bonds and shares (in the sense that the analyst cannot change them) when making capex decisions the analyst can affect the underlying cash flows by changing the structure of the project. For example, after the analysis, the firm can decide to defer a project for a year or change the form of a product. If the firm is developing a new car, it may decide some parts will become optional extras in order to hit a target price point, or a substitute sweetener may be used in a new soft drink. As a result, the application of DCF valuation techniques in capex decisions is, by its nature, more of an *iterative* process than a one-time decision.

In discussing DCF techniques, we defer our discussion of how to estimate cash flows until Chapter 14. In this chapter, we will focus on the application of the approaches themselves and discuss their relative advantages, assuming that we already know the expected cash flows. In this way, we first focus on the capital budgeting framework.

CONCEPT REVIEW QUESTIONS

1. What is the difference between a tangible asset and an intangible asset?

2. What are irrevocable investment decisions? Why are they important for capital budgeting?

3. Contrast top-down and bottom-up analysis.

4. In what ways is DCF capex analysis similar to valuing common shares, and in what ways is it different?

13.2 EVALUATING INVESTMENT ALTERNATIVES

Learning Objective 13.2
Identify and apply the main tools used to evaluate investments.

Net Present Value (NPV) Analysis

The **net present value (NPV)** of a project is defined as the sum of the present value (PV) of all future after-tax incremental cash flows generated by an initial cash outlay, minus the present value of the investment outlays. The NPV is the present value of the expected cash flows net of the costs needed to generate them. This process is depicted graphically in Figure 13-1, where, for simplicity, there is a single outlay at time zero.

net present value (NPV) the sum of the present value of all future after-tax incremental cash flows generated by an initial cash outlay, minus the present value of the investment outlays; the present value of the expected cash flows net of the costs needed to generate them

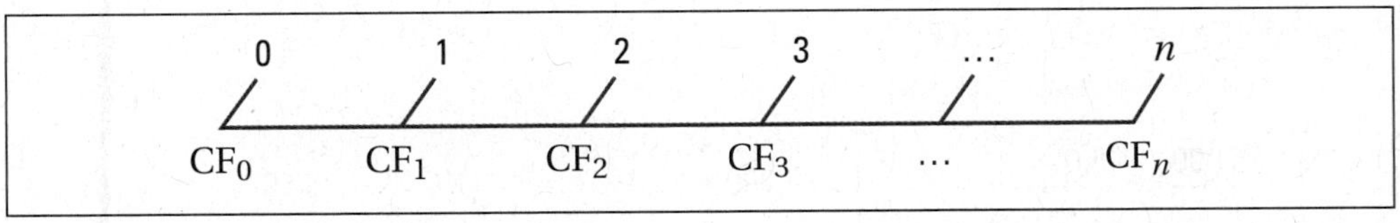

FIGURE 13-1 *The Cash Flow Pattern for a Traditional Capital Expenditure*

Usually we use the firm's after-tax marginal cost of capital as the appropriate discount rate for projects that are similar to the normal operations of the firm, because it should reflect the firm's normal financing costs. (We will revisit the reasonableness of using this discount rate later in this chapter.) The NPV of an n-year project can therefore be determined using Equation 13-1.

$$NPV = \frac{CF_1}{(1+k)^1} + \frac{CF_2}{(1+k)^2} + \frac{CF_3}{(1+k)^3} + \dots - CF_0 = \sum_{t=1}^{n} \frac{CF_t}{(1+k)^t} - CF_0 \qquad [13\text{-}1]$$

where CF_t = the estimated future after-tax incremental cash flow at time t

CF_0 = the initial after-tax incremental cash outlay

k = the appropriate risk-adjusted after-tax discount rate (which is usually the firm's after-tax marginal cost of capital)

incremental in capital budgeting, the change in revenues or costs resulting from the investment decision

Note that we described the cash flows as **incremental**, which means they change as a result of the decision. Cash flows that have already been incurred are referred to as "sunk" costs and are ignored, since they do not change as a result of the firm's investment decision. For example, in 2008, Petro-Canada decided to halt a $25-billion oil sands project in response to declining oil prices, despite having already spent $1.7 billion on the project. What mattered were the future cash flows generated from the firm's future expenditures. In this way, finance is always forward looking.

risk-adjusted discount rate (RADR) a discount rate that is set based on the overall riskiness of a project

We have discussed previously that the market value of any firm in an efficient market should equal the present value of its expected after-tax cash flows, discounted at an appropriate **risk-adjusted discount rate (RADR)**, which is set based on the overall riskiness of the project. Therefore, we can say that projects that have a *positive* NPV add value to the firm and should be accepted because, by definition, a positive NPV implies that the PV of the expected future cash flows will exceed the cash outlay today—that is, it increases the value of the firm. Because the firm's creditors have a fixed claim on the firm's income, regardless of the value of the project, this NPV drops down to the shareholders and increases the market value of the firm's common shares. In this way, accepting positive-NPV projects maximizes the firm's market value and creates shareholder value. In contrast, accepting *negative*-NPV projects destroys firm value, and such projects should be rejected because, by definition, the destruction of shareholder value is not in the best interests of the shareholders.

We would expect positive NPVs to arise only in situations in which a company has a competitive advantage. Because of the competitive nature of today's business environment, we would not expect to see an abundance of such opportunities, nor would we expect them to persist for very long. Therefore, projects that produce an NPV of zero will be the norm where firms operate in competitive markets. These projects should be accepted, because they provide the appropriate return required to compensate for the financing costs (and risks) associated with the investment.

EXAMPLE 13-1 Calculating NPV

Suppose a company has an investment that requires an after-tax incremental cash outlay of $12,000 today. It estimates that the expected future after-tax cash flows associated with this investment will be $5,000 in years 1 and 2, and $8,000 in year 3. Using a 15-percent discount rate, determine the project's NPV.

Solution

$$NPV = \frac{CF_1}{(1+k)^1} + \frac{CF_2}{(1+k)^2} + \frac{CF_3}{(1+k)^3} + \ldots - CF_0$$

$$= \left[\frac{5,000}{(1.15)^1} + \frac{5,000}{(1.15)^2} + \frac{8,000}{(1.15)^3} \right] - 12,000 = 13,388.67 - 12,000 = +1,388.67$$

The project would be accepted, because it has a positive NPV and would increase firm value by $1,388.67.

(TI BA II PLUS)

EXAMPLE 13-1 Solution Using a Financial Calculator

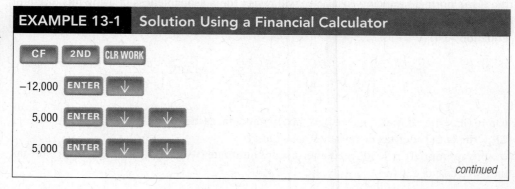

continued

EXAMPLE 13-1   Solution Using a Financial Calculator *(continued)*

8,000 ENTER ↓

NPV 15 ENTER ↓

CPT gives $1,388.67

EXAMPLE 13-1   Solution Using Excel

The following function can be used to determine the PV of the future CFs (not including CF_0):

= NPV (rate, value 1, value 2, ..., value n)

where rate = discount rate, value 1 = CF_1, value 2 = CF_2, and so on

For this example, we would enter the following in the appropriate cell:

= NPV (0.15, 5000, 5000, 8000)

This would yield an answer of $13,388.67 for the PV of the future CFs.

When we subtract the initial cash outlay of $12,000 from this amount, this translates into NPV = 13,388.67 − 12,000 = + $1,388.67.[4]

EXAMPLE 13-2   Calculating NPV When Future CFs Represent an Annuity

A project that requires an initial investment of $30,000 is expected to generate after-tax cash flows of $5,000 per year for the next nine years, and then $6,000 in year 10. Estimate the NPV using a 12-percent discount rate.

Solution

The "long version" of the solution, which involves discounting each of the nine future cash flows separately, is time-consuming and unnecessary. This is because the future CFs are all equal, at $5,000 (i.e., they form an annuity), except for the ending cash flow of $6,000, which we can view as another $5,000 payment, plus an additional one-time cash flow of $1,000. Therefore, we can solve the PV of the future cash flows by finding the sum of the PV of a 10-year annuity of $5,000 and the PV of a $1,000 cash flow, arriving at t equals 10, as follows:

$$PV_0 = 5,000 \left[\frac{1 - \frac{1}{(1.12)^{10}}}{0.12} \right] + \frac{1,000}{(1.12)^{10}} = 5,000 (5.650223) + (1,000)(0.32197)$$

$$= 28,251.12 + 321.97 = \$28,573.09$$

So, NPV = 28,573.09 − 30,000 = − $1,426.91

The project should be rejected, because it has a negative NPV and would destroy firm value.

Example 13-2 is solved more easily using a calculator and using only the time value of money functions, as shown below.

EXAMPLE 13-2   Solution Using a Financial Calculator

Input the following variables:

FV → 1,000 ; PMT → 5,000 ; N → 10 ; I/Y = 12

Press CPT and then PV = −28,573.09 or, 28,573.09 (which is the PV of future CFs).

So NPV = 28,573.09 — 30,000 = −$1,426.91

---

[4]If we had the discount rate in our Excel spreadsheet cell B2 and had the year 1, 2, and 3 cash flows in cells B3, B4, and B5, respectively, we could express the Excel function above as follows: = NPV (B2, B3:B5).

Of course, Example 13-2 can also be solved using the NPV function, as shown below.

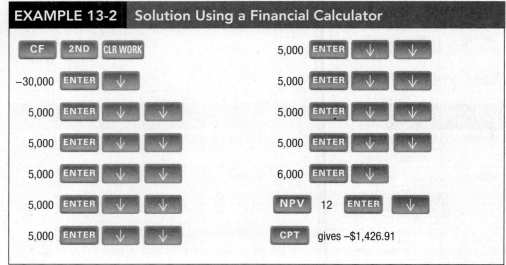

EXAMPLE 13-2   Solution Using a Financial Calculator

| CF | 2ND | CLR WORK | | 5,000 | ENTER | ↓ | ↓ |

−30,000 ENTER ↓

5,000 ENTER ↓ ↓

5,000 ENTER ↓ ↓

5,000 ENTER ↓ ↓

5,000 ENTER ↓ ↓

5,000 ENTER ↓ ↓

5,000 ENTER ↓ ↓

5,000 ENTER ↓ ↓

5,000 ENTER ↓ ↓

5,000 ENTER ↓ ↓

5,000 ENTER ↓

6,000 ENTER ↓

NPV 12 ENTER ↓

CPT gives −$1,426.91

In fact, we can use a shortcut when using the NPV function available on the TI BA II Plus calculator.

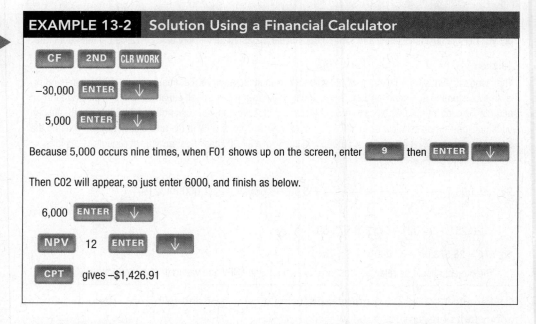

EXAMPLE 13-2   Solution Using a Financial Calculator

CF 2ND CLR WORK

−30,000 ENTER ↓

5,000 ENTER ↓

Because 5,000 occurs nine times, when F01 shows up on the screen, enter 9 then ENTER ↓

Then C02 will appear, so just enter 6000, and finish as below.

6,000 ENTER ↓

NPV 12 ENTER ↓

CPT gives −$1,426.91

EXAMPLE 13-2   Solution Using Excel

For this example, assuming we have the discount rate in cell B1 and the future cash flows for year 1 through 10 in cells B2 to B11, we would enter the following in the appropriate cell:

= NPV (B1, B2:B11)

This would yield an answer of $28,573.09 for the PV of the future CFs.

When we subtract the initial cash outlay of $30,000 from this amount, this translates into
NPV = 28,573.09 − 30,000 = − $1,426.91.

The Internal Rate of Return (*IRR*)

The **internal rate of return (IRR)** is the same as the yield to maturity (YTM) for a bond, which we estimated earlier. In fact, the YTM is the IRR of a bond for a given purchase price. As we showed then, the IRR is the discount rate that makes the NPV equal to zero for a given set of cash flows. This implies that it is the discount rate that sets the PV of future CFs equal to the initial cash outlay. Thus, it is a rate of return that is internal to this particular set of cash flows; for this reason, it is often called the "economic rate of return" of a given project. We can rearrange Equation 13-1 to obtain Equation 13-2, which can be used to estimate the IRR.

internal rate of return (IRR) the discount rate that makes the present value of future cash flows equal to the initial cash outlay

$$\frac{CF_1}{(1 + IRR)^1} + \frac{CF_2}{(1 + IRR)^2} + \frac{CF_3}{(1 + IRR)^3} + \ldots = CF_0 \text{ or } \sum_{t=1}^{n} \frac{CF_t}{(1 + IRR)^t} = CF_0 \qquad [13\text{-}2]$$

The general rule for IRR evaluation criteria is that a firm should accept a project whenever the IRR is greater than the appropriate risk-adjusted discount rate (k), which is usually the firm's cost of capital. Just like NPV, the IRR represents a discounted cash flow approach; in general, it will lead to the same accept/reject decisions as NPV does. However, note that in Equation 13-2 we could multiply through by $(1 + IRR)^n$, and it then becomes clear that in finding the IRR, we are solving for the roots of an nth-order polynomial. Unfortunately, every time the sign of the polynomial changes—that is, every time the cash flows change from positive to negative—there is a root, so for complex cash flow streams, we often find that there is more than one IRR or more than one root. (This is a common problem in evaluating leases, which we discuss in Chapter 16.)

Also note that in solving Equation 13-2, just as for the bond YTM case, there is no finite solution for the IRR. What this means is that solving for the IRR requires a trial-and-error process similar to the one used to estimate the YTM for a bond. Fortunately, financial calculators or computer spreadsheets make this process manageable, but be warned that in the case of multiple roots, these procedures give the IRR closest to your starting guess. We didn't worry about this for the bond's YTM because there is only ever one change in cash flow sign: when we buy the bond and there is a cash outflow followed by a series of cash inflows. We illustrate the calculation process in Example 13-3.

EXAMPLE 13-3 | Calculating the IRR

Revisit Example 13-1 and estimate the IRR of the project under consideration.

Solution

The IRR solves the following expression:

$$\left[\frac{5{,}000}{(1 + IRR)^1} + \frac{5{,}000}{(1 + IRR)^2} + \frac{8{,}000}{(1 + IRR)^3} \right] = 12{,}000$$

Solving by trial and error is very complicated, even for this simple three-period problem. We start by estimating the IRR and try IRR = 20 percent. Substituting this rate into the equation above gives us a value on the left side of $12,268.52. Therefore, the IRR must be higher than this, because the PV amount is greater than the $12,000 initial outlay. So now we try IRR = 25 percent, which produces a corresponding value on the left side of $11,296. We can conclude that 25 percent is too high. Therefore, we know that the rate we are looking for is between 20 percent and 25 percent.

continued

EXAMPLE 13-3 *continued*

We can obtain a reasonable approximation by using linear interpolation, which was discussed in Chapter 6:

Discount rate	V(LHS)
20%	12,268.52
IRR	12,000
25%	11,296

We find the IRR as follows:

$$\frac{IRR - 20}{25 - 20} = \frac{12,000 - 12,268.52}{11,296 - 12,268.52}$$

$$\frac{IRR - 20}{5} = \frac{-268.52}{-972.52}$$

$$IRR - 20 = 5 \times \frac{-268.52}{-972.52} = 1.3805$$

So, IRR ≈ 21.38%.

This is one case for which it is worthwhile to use a financial calculator or Excel—and this is only a three-period project. Imagine if it were a 20-year project!

(TI BA II PLUS)

EXAMPLE 13-3   **Solution Using a Financial Calculator**

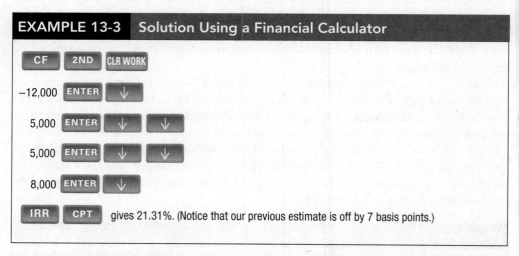

CF   2ND   CLR WORK

−12,000   ENTER   ↓

5,000   ENTER   ↓   ↓

5,000   ENTER   ↓   ↓

8,000   ENTER   ↓

IRR   CPT   gives 21.31%. (Notice that our previous estimate is off by 7 basis points.)

XLS

EXAMPLE 13-3   **Solution Using Excel**

The following function can be used to solve for the IRR:

= IRR (value 0, value 1, value 2, ..., guess)

where value 0 = CF_0 (expressed as a negative number), value 1 = CF_1, value 2 = CF_2, and so on, and guess = a guess as to what the IRR is (if nothing is entered, Excel enters 0.1 or 10 percent as the default). For this example, if we had the year 0, 1, 2, and 3 cash flows in cells B2, B3, B4, and B5, respectively, we could express the Excel function above as follows:

= IRR (B2:B5, 0.20)

Notice in Example 13-3 that the IRR of 21.31 percent exceeds the firm's cost of capital of 15 percent, which implies that the project increases shareholder value and should be accepted. This will always be the case when the NPV is positive, as it was in this case (recall from Example 13-1 that the NPV for this project was +$1,388.67). In fact, this should be obvious when we look at equations 13-1 and 13-2, because the NPV will equal zero when the IRR equals *k*.

Therefore, when IRR is greater than *k*, the NPV will be positive because the PV will be higher when we use a *lower* discount rate (i.e., *k*) than it will be when we use the *higher* discount rate (i.e., IRR). This is intuitive: a positive NPV implies that a project earns a return (IRR) that is higher than the cost of funds (which is reflected in *k*). Similarly, we can say that a negative NPV implies that IRR is less than *k*, and vice versa.

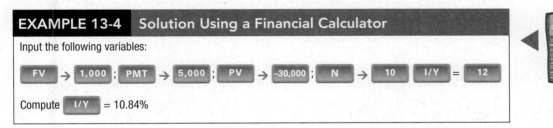

EXAMPLE 13-4   **Calculating the IRR When Future CFs Represent an Annuity**

Estimate the IRR for the project in Example 13-2.

Solution

We will skip the long trial-and-error version of the solution, because it is unnecessary here: the future CFs are equal at $5,000 (i.e., they form an annuity), except for the ending cash flow of $6,000, which we can view as another $5,000 payment plus an extra $1,000 that can be discounted separately. Therefore, we can solve the IRR by using a financial calculator.

EXAMPLE 13-4   **Solution Using a Financial Calculator**

Input the following variables:

FV → 1,000 ; PMT → 5,000 ; PV → −30,000 ; N → 10   I/Y = 12

Compute I/Y = 10.84%

The problem can also be solved using the IRR function, as shown below.

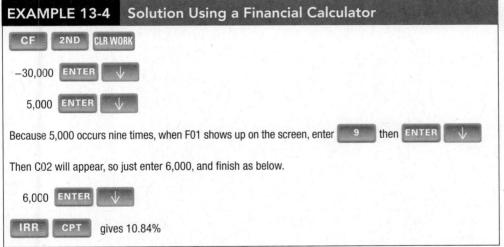

EXAMPLE 13-4   **Solution Using a Financial Calculator**

CF   2ND   CLR WORK

−30,000 ENTER ↓

5,000 ENTER ↓

Because 5,000 occurs nine times, when F01 shows up on the screen, enter 9 then ENTER ↓

Then C02 will appear, so just enter 6,000, and finish as below.

6,000 ENTER ↓

IRR   CPT   gives 10.84%

EXAMPLE 13-4   **Solution Using Excel**

For this example, assuming a guess of 10 percent (0.1) for the discount rate and that the cash flows for years 0 through 10 are located in cells B1 to B11, we would enter the following in the appropriate cell:

= IRR (B1:B11, 0.1)

This would yield an answer of 10.84 percent.

Notice that the IRR of 10.84 percent is less than the firm's cost of capital of 12 percent, which implies the project should be rejected. This is consistent with the negative NPV that we calculated in Example 13-2 using the 12-percent discount rate.

A Comparison of NPV and IRR

The relationship between the NPV and the IRR can be seen from an NPV profile diagram, such as the one shown in Figure 13-2 for two separate projects. NPV profiles depict the NPV of a project for various discount rates.

Figure 13-2 graphs the NPV against the discount rate. It shows how the NPV depends critically on the appropriate discount rate—of course, this is obvious from the NPV equation (i.e., Equation 13-1). As the discount rate increases, the NPV decreases and eventually becomes negative for higher discount rates. By definition, we know that the IRR occurs at the discount rate that makes the NPV equal zero. This corresponds to the point at which the NPV curve crosses the x-axis in Figure 13-2. For project A, the IRR is 12 percent, while for project B, the IRR is 15 percent. The diagram shows that whenever the discount rate exceeds the IRR, we have a negative NPV, and whenever the discount rate is less than the IRR, we have a positive NPV. We have previously noted these relationships between NPV and IRR.

We can make several useful observations from Figure 13-2. We begin by noting that the decision to accept the project depends on the discount rate used (k). According to either the NPV or the IRR evaluation criteria, project A should be accepted if k is less than 12 percent, because the NPV will be positive for these discount rates and because IRR will be greater than k. Conversely, if k is greater than 12 percent, project A should be rejected, because the NPV will be negative and because IRR is less than k. Similarly, project B should be accepted if k is less than 15 percent, and it should be rejected if k is greater than 15 percent. So if we are independently evaluating a project using either the NPV or the IRR evaluation criteria, we should arrive at the same conclusion.[5]

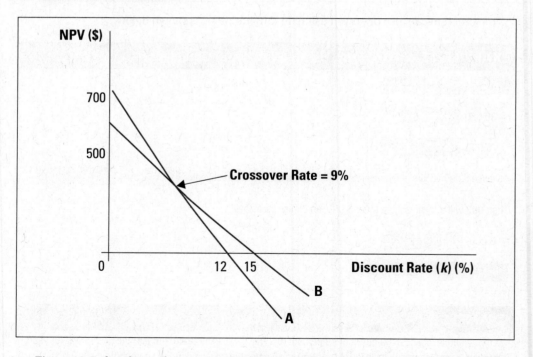

FIGURE 13-2 *Two NPV Profiles*

mutually exclusive projects a situation in which the acceptance of one project precludes the acceptance of one or more alternative projects

Figure 13-2 also shows that we can rank projects differently when we use NPV than when we use IRR. Suppose, for example, these two were **mutually exclusive projects**, which means that a firm has to decide between them and can accept only one. Because the IRR of project B is 15 percent, while the IRR of project A is only 12 percent, project B appears to be superior, according to the IRR approach. However, when we use the NPV approach, we arrive at different rankings depending on the firm's cost of capital (k). In this example, the NPV profiles cross

---

[5]As previously mentioned, this will not be true if we pick the wrong IRR when there are multiple reversals in the signs of the cash flows. This does not happen often in normal projects, but it does happen sometimes, to the surprise of analysts who forget this fact.

over and have the same NPV at one special discount rate, which is the **crossover rate**. If k is greater than the crossover rate of 9 percent, then project B is preferable to project A, because it generates a higher NPV. If k is less than 9 percent, project A is preferred.

The two approaches rank projects differently, so which one is better? To answer this question, we have to understand why the slopes of the two NPV profiles differ. The slope reflects the change in the NPV as the discount rate changes. If a project has cash flows that are far in the future, then changes in the discount rate have a big impact on the NPV of the project. In this case, project A has cash flows that are farther away, so at a high discount rate, these cash flows are valued less and the NPV falls by more than the NPV of project B. As a result, beyond the crossover point, B is preferred to A, because A's far-off cash flows are worth less, whereas at lower discount rates, the reverse happens and A is preferred to B.

The fact that the NPV decision depends on the discount rate, whereas the IRR decision does not, is important and relates to the different reinvestment rate assumptions of the two techniques. The NPV assumes that all cash flows are reinvested at one consistent discount rate (i.e., the cost of capital). The IRR assumes instead that all cash flows are reinvested at the IRR. If we remember that most projects will have low or zero NPV in a competitive market and that the discount rate reflects the opportunity cost or the all-in required return of the firm's investors, it is clear that the NPV assumption is more realistic. To put it another way, if an executive estimates an IRR of, say, 30 percent because he or she finds a wonderful project, the executive is then implicitly assuming that the cash flows generated by this wonderful project can be reinvested in another similarly wonderful project. This means that the executive is assuming that he or she has many wonderful projects, which is not normally a very realistic assumption. In Appendix 13A, we discuss an adjustment to the traditional calculation of IRR, called the modified internal rate of return (MIRR), which adjusts for this limitation of the traditional IRR.

We summarize this discussion by comparing the NPV and IRR criteria in Table 13-1. Figure 13-3 summarizes the results of a survey of Canadian chief financial officers (CFOs) that inquired about their capital budgeting decisions (as well as financing issues).[6] Their responses regarding the capital budgeting criteria they used are reported in Figure 13-3. What is clear is that the NPV and IRR methods are the most widely used. NPV is the most widely used (74.6 percent said they use it "Often" or "Always"). Despite the limitations of the IRR method, discussed above, it is also widely used in practice (sitting at 68.4 percent), falling just short of NPV. This is because, in most cases, the IRR gives the "correct" accept/reject decision, and the criticisms of the IRR do not often appear in practical applications. More important, it holds intuitive appeal because it provides a rate of return on particular investment projects that can be compared with the firm's financing costs. However, as we pointed out earlier, using this approach can cause problems later for the analyst who is unaware of its shortcomings.[7]

crossover rate a special discount rate at which the net present value profiles of two projects cross

TABLE 13-1 NPV versus IRR

Issue	NPV	IRR
1. Future cash flows change sign	NPV works the same way for both accept/reject and ranking decisions.	Multiple IRRs may result—in this case, the IRR cannot be used for either accept/reject or ranking decisions.

continued

---

[6]Source: Baker, Kent H., Shantanu Dutta, and Samir Saadi, "Corporate finance practices in Canada: Where do we stand?" *Multinational Finance Journal* 15, no. 3/4 (September/December 2011), pp. 157–92. In a similar survey of the CFOs of major U.S. companies, Graham and Harvey produced results that were similar qualitatively and very close in terms of the actual percentages as those found by Baker, Dutta, and Saadi in Canada. See Graham, John R., and Campbell R. Harvey, "The Theory and Practice of Corporate Finance: Evidence from the Field." *Journal of Financial Economics* 60 (2001), pp. 187–243.

[7]We have sometimes been approached by former students when they have problems with their analysis. Often, these problems occur because they have forgotten the problems with the use of the IRR.

TABLE 13-1 NPV versus IRR *continued*

Issue	NPV	IRR
2. Ranking projects	Higher NPV implies greater contribution to firm wealth—it is an absolute measure of wealth.	The higher IRR project may have a lower NPV and vice versa, depending on the appropriate discount rate and the size of the project. For example, would analysts prefer an IRR of 100 percent on $1,000 or 20 percent on $1 million?
3. Reinvestment rate assumed for future cash flows received	Assumes all future cash flows are reinvested at the discount rate. This is appropriate because it treats the reinvestment of all future cash flows consistently, and *k* is the investor's opportunity cost.	Assumes cash flows from each project are reinvested at that project's IRR. This is inappropriate, particularly when the IRR is high.

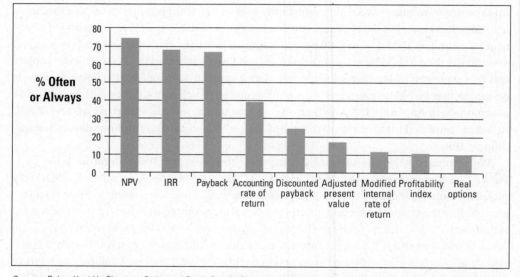

FIGURE 13-3 Survey Results of *Capital Budgeting Techniques Used by Canadian Firms When Deciding Which Projects or Acquisitions to Pursue*

Source: Baker, Kent H., Shantanu Dutta, and Samir Saadi, "Corporate Finance Practices in Canada: Where Do We Stand?" *Multinational Finance Journal* 15, no. 3/4 (September/December 2011), Table 3, p. 173.

Payback Period and Discounted Payback Period

The next most popular evaluation technique mentioned by CFOs, after NPV and IRR, was the use of payback period, with 67.2 percent of those surveyed saying they used it "often" or "always." The **payback period** is defined as the number of years required to fully recover the initial cash outlay associated with a capital expenditure. Shorter payback periods are better, and usually this decision criterion is implemented by choosing a cutoff date and rejecting projects whose payback period goes past the cutoff date. Example 13-5 illustrates how it is calculated.

payback period the number of years required to fully recover the initial cash outlay associated with a capital expenditure

---

EXAMPLE 13-5 | **Calculating Payback Period**

Revisit Example 13-1 and estimate the payback period of the project under consideration.

Solution

Year	Cumulative CFs recovered
1	5,000
2	10,000
3	18,000

continued

EXAMPLE 13-5 *continued*

Payback = 2 + (2,000/8,000) = 2.25 years

With a $12,000 cash outlay, $10,000 is recovered in two years, and the additional $2,000 is recovered a quarter of the way through the third year, assuming that the cash flows are evenly spaced throughout the year.

The payback period provides a useful intuitive measure of how long it takes to recover an investment and is sometimes used as an informal measure of project risk. This is because, in some sense, the quicker a firm recovers its investment outlay, the less risky the project is. However, the payback period has some important drawbacks. In particular, it disregards the time and risk value of money, because it treats a dollar of cash flow received in year 3 the same as those received in year 1, and so on. In addition, the payback period does not account for the cash flows received after the cutoff date, which could be substantial for some long-lived projects. Finally, the choice of the cutoff date is somewhat arbitrary and may vary from one firm to the next. *Finance in the News 13-3* gives an example of a situation where the limitations of the payback period measure surface. In particular, while the payback period for the investment associated with pursuing an MBA degree isn't attractive (8 to 10 years), the NPV ranged from $360,000 to $700,000, representing a substantial increase in terms of "today's" wealth for business professionals considering pursuing their MBA.

finance 13-3 ROI on the MBA
INTHENEWS

MANY WORKING BUSINESS professionals consider returning to school to earn an MBA. But is it worth it? It depends.

Antony Davies and Thomas Cline considered the cost and potential earning power from individuals who pursued an MBA in the years 1993 to 2001 and found:

- The return on investment in an MBA was better than Treasury bills, the return on triple-A rated bonds, and the Dow Jones Industrial Average.

- The payback period ... to recover tuition and fees is 8–10 years.

- The NPV—the present value of the benefits from increased salary and benefits, less the present value of the costs of tuition and fees—ranges from $360,000 (in 1993) to around $700,000 in 1998, with the NPV in 2001 of $550,000.

They also observed that there is variation in the benefits from an MBA. In other words, your experience may differ from that of the "average."

Source: Excerpted from Davies, Antony, and Thomas Cline, "The ROI on the MBA." *BizEd*, January/February 2005, pp. 42–45.

The **discounted payback period** alleviates the first shortcoming of the payback period by accounting for the time value of money. It is defined as the number of years required to fully recover the initial cash outlay in terms of discounted cash flows. Shorter periods are better, and projects with discounted payback periods before the cutoff date will be accepted. Unfortunately, as was the case for the payback period criterion, the discounted payback period ignores cash flows beyond the cutoff date, and the cutoff date is somewhat arbitrary. Example 13-6 shows how the discounted payback period is calculated.

> **discounted payback period** the number of years required to fully recover the initial cash outlay associated with a capital expenditure in terms of discounted cash flows

EXAMPLE 13-6 Calculating Discounted Payback Period

Revisit Example 13-1 and estimate the discounted payback period of the project under consideration.

Solution

Year	Cumulative CFs recovered	PV of cumulative *CFs* recovered
1	5,000	$5,000/(1.15) = 4,348$
2	10,000	$4,348 + 5,000/(1.15)^2 = 8,129$
3	18,000	$8,129 + 8,000/(1.15)^3 = 13,389$

continued

EXAMPLE 13-6   *continued*

Discounted Payback = 2 + [(12,000 − 8,129)/(8,000/(1.15)^3)]

$\qquad\qquad\qquad\quad$ = 2 + [3,871/5,260] = 2.74 years

In Example 13-6, the discounted payback period is longer than the simple payback period; the future cash flows are worth less because they have been discounted for time and risk. If a firm is going to use discounting, it might as well discount all the future cash flows and calculate the NPV. For this reason, the discounted payback period is a compromise between the payback period and the NPV, which is probably why it is not rated highly by CFOs.

Of the other techniques mentioned in the survey, we will, as noted, discuss modified internal rate of return in Appendix 13A. We will also discuss real options in Chapter 14; however, this is not really an independent technique but, rather, a more sophisticated implementation of the above techniques. While accounting rate of return is important to determine how a project will affect the firm's financial statements and is valuable for very large projects, it is not commonly used for small projects. Similarly, adjusted present value can be ignored for our purposes. It is a sophisticated technique that is very difficult to implement and rarely used. This leaves the last technique mentioned, the profitability index.

Profitability Index (PI)

profitability index (PI) another discounted cash flow approach used to evaluate capital expenditure decisions; defined as the ratio of a project's discounted net incremental after-tax cash inflows over the discounted cash outflows, which are usually the initial after-tax cash outlays

The **profitability index (PI)** is another DCF approach used to evaluate capital expenditure decisions. Like the IRR, the PI is a *relative* measure of project attractiveness. It is defined as the ratio of a project's discounted net incremental after-tax cash inflows divided by the discounted cash outflows, which are usually the initial after-tax cash outlays. Equation 13-3 shows how the PI is calculated.

[13-3]
$$PI = \frac{PV\ (cash\ inflows)}{PV\ (cash\ outflows)}$$

It should be obvious from Equation 13-3 that projects with ratios greater than one should be accepted because, by definition, they have positive NPVs; projects with ratios less than one should be rejected. It is also obvious that larger ratios are favoured because their NPVs are higher. The discount rate to be used is the same as the one used for calculating the NPV, usually the firm's cost of capital. Therefore, we observe the following relationship between NPV and PI: when the PI is greater than one, the NPV is greater than zero (and vice versa); when the PI is less than one, the NPV is less than zero and vice versa.

EXAMPLE 13-7   Calculating the PI

Revisit Example 13-2 and estimate the PI of the project under consideration.

Solution

$$PI = \frac{PV\ (cash\ inflows)}{PV\ (cash\ outflows)} = \frac{\dfrac{5,000}{(1.15)^1} + \dfrac{5,000}{(1.15)^2} + \dfrac{8,000}{(1.15)^3}}{12,000} = \frac{13,388.67}{12,000} = 1.116$$

Therefore, the project should be accepted because the PI is greater than 1. Of course, we knew this already, because we found that its NPV was greater than 0 in Example 13-1, and that its IRR was greater than *k* in Example 13-3.

We could also have answered Example 13-7 by solving for the NPV (by long hand, by using a financial calculator, or by using Excel) and adding the NPV to the initial outlay of $12,000 to find the numerator of the equation above (i.e., 1,388.67 + 12,000 = $13,388.67), and then proceeding as above.

EXAMPLE 13-8	Calculating the PI When Future CFs Represent an Annuity

Revisit Example 13-2 and estimate the PI of the project under consideration.

Solution

$$PI = \frac{\$5,000 \left[\dfrac{1 - \dfrac{1}{(1.12)^{10}}}{0.12} \right] + \dfrac{1,000}{(1.12)^{10}}}{30,000} = \frac{28,573.09}{30,000} = 0.952$$

Therefore, this project should be rejected because its PI is less than 1.

As discussed above, the PI produces the same accept/reject decisions as do the NPV and, normally, the IRR. In addition, the PI does not suffer from two of the weaknesses of the IRR, because it uses one consistent and reasonable discount rate and because it works even when future cash flows change signs. Like the IRR, the PI is attractive because it can be expressed as a percentage, so rather than 1.116 in Example 13-7, we could have said the PI was 111.6 percent.

One weakness that the PI shares with IRR is that it is a relative measure and not an absolute measure of wealth, like NPV. Although it is useful as a starting point for ranking projects when some projects must be rejected, final decisions should be based on which projects maximize the total NPV for the firm. (We will elaborate on this point later in this chapter, when we discuss mutually exclusive projects and capital rationing.) In this case, the PI is often used when firms are constrained by their capital budget, as we will discuss later.

CONCEPT REVIEW QUESTIONS

1. What discount rate do we use to determine the NPV of a project and why?
2. Why do we sometimes get multiple IRRs for a project?
3. What are the reinvestment rate assumptions underlying NPV and IRR?
4. What is the crossover rate?
5. Why is the payback period a poor evaluation technique?
6. Is the PI rule consistent with the NPV rule?

Learning Objective 13.3
Analyze independent projects and explain how they differ from interdependent projects.

13.3 INDEPENDENT AND INTERDEPENDENT PROJECTS

Independent projects have no relationship with one another. For example, a firm's decision to accept one project (e.g., purchase a new computerized accounting system) has no impact on the firm's decision to accept another project that is independent of the first one (e.g., replace an aging piece of machinery that is used in the production process). As long as there

independent projects projects that have no relationship with one another; accepting one project has no impact on the decision to accept another project

interdependent projects projects that are related such that accepting or rejecting one has an impact on the value of other projects under consideration

contingent projects projects for which the acceptance of one requires the acceptance of another either beforehand or simultaneously

are no capital spending restrictions,[8] the decision rule is to accept projects that generate a positive NPV (or an IRR greater than *k*, or a PI greater than one), and reject those that don't. However, many projects do have relationships with one another. These types of projects are referred to as **interdependent projects**. We must take these relationships into account in our decision process, as discussed below.

Capital expenditures can represent **contingent projects**. A firm can implement investment A (e.g., purchase the newest accounting software package) only if it also undertakes investment B (e.g., change the operating system to Microsoft Windows). In other words, one project is feasible only if another project is undertaken either beforehand or simultaneously. For these types of investment projects, the rule is to estimate the total NPV of *all* contingent projects and accept them if this total NPV is positive. In such a situation, even if the initial project (e.g., the updating of an operating system) does not generate a positive NPV on its own, it can be accepted if the benefits provided by the contingent projects more than offset the losses it generates. In fact, this is often the case with operating systems.

Mutually exclusive projects, as defined earlier, require that a firm choose among two or more alternatives. In other words, if a firm is considering replacing an old computer system with either system A or system B, it would never buy both, even if the analysis suggested that they both generated positive NPVs.[9] In such a case, the firm must decide which project is best. Recall from our previous discussion on IRR versus NPV that whenever a firm has to rank projects, NPV is superior. The decision will be straightforward if the projects have identical time horizons, because the firm will choose the one that produces the highest NPV, assuming the NPV is positive. However, when the projects under consideration have different time horizons, the firm must take this into consideration in its analysis.

chain replication approach a way to compare projects with unequal lives by finding a time horizon into which all the project lives under consideration divide equally and then assuming each project repeats until it reaches this horizon

Projects with unequal lives can be compared by using two approaches, both of which assume that the project can be replicated at the end of its useful time horizon. The **chain replication approach** involves finding a time horizon into which all the project lives under consideration divide equally and then assuming each project is repeated until they all reach this horizon. For example, if a firm is comparing a three-year project with a four-year project, it would assume the three-year project could be replicated four times and that the four-year project could be replicated three times (for a total of 12 years each). It then finds the PV of all the replicated projects for each individual project and chooses the one that generates the highest NPV over the entire period, assuming the NPV is positive. This approach is demonstrated in Example 13-9.

EXAMPLE 13-9   The Chain Replication Approach

A company is considering three separate, mutually exclusive projects, A, B, and C. Project A requires a $10,000 cash outlay today and is expected to generate after-tax cash flows of $7,000 in year 1 and $6,000 in year 2. Project B requires an $8,500 cash outlay today and is expected to generate after-tax cash flows of $4,000 in year 1 and $7,000 in year 2. Project C requires a $10,600 cash outlay today and is expected to generate after-tax cash flows of $5,000 for each of the next three years. Assume that 15 percent is the appropriate discount rate, and use the chain replication approach to determine which project the firm should choose.

Solution

Notice that projects A and B both have two-year time horizons, so we can calculate their respective NPVs and choose the one that generates the higher NPV, provided it is positive.

continued

---

[8]We will elaborate on this point later in the chapter, when we discuss mutually exclusive projects and capital rationing.

[9]If A and B were independent projects that generated positive NPVs, a firm would accept both projects.

EXAMPLE 13-9 *continued*

$$NPV_A = \left[\frac{7,000}{(1.15)^1} + \frac{6,000}{(1.15)^2}\right] - 10,000 = 10,623.82 - 10,000 = +623.82$$

$$NPV_B = \left[\frac{4,000}{(1.15)^1} + \frac{7,000}{(1.15)^2}\right] - 8,500 = 8,771.27 - 8,500 = +271.27$$

Therefore, the firm would choose project A over project B.
Now the firm would compare project A with project C, which has a three-year life.
First, it would calculate the NPV for project C.

$$NPV_C = \left[\frac{5,000}{(1.15)^1} + \frac{5,000}{(1.15)^2} + \frac{5,000}{(1.15)^3}\right] - 10,600 = 11,416.13 - 10,600 = +816.13$$

Project C is also attractive. Notice that it generates an NPV ($816.13) that is higher than the one A generates ($623.82) over a two-year period. If C produced an NPV that was lower than (or equal to) project A's NPV, which was generated over a shorter period, the firm would accept A over C. However, because this is not the case, the firm needs to determine the project that is best over a six-year period (i.e., because the projects have two- and three-year horizons).

The firm would now estimate the total NPV generated by projects A and C over a six-year time horizon, assuming A is replicated twice and C is replicated once.

Assuming A generates an NPV at time 0 of $623.82 (over years 1 and 2), the same NPV at time 2 (over years 3 and 4), and the same NPV at time 4 (over years 5 and 6), the total NPV at time 0 is as follows:

$$NPV_A = \left[623.82 + \frac{623.82}{(1.15)^2} + \frac{623.82}{(1.15)^4}\right] = 623.82 + 471.70 + 356.67 = \$1,452.19$$

Similarly, for project C, the total NPV is as follows:

$$NPV_C = \left[816.13 + \frac{816.13}{(1.15)^3}\right] = 816.13 + 536.62 = \$1,352.75$$

Therefore, project A should be accepted instead of project C, because it would generate a higher total NPV over a six-year period than project C would, assuming both projects can be replicated.

The chain replication approach is a reasonable method for solving Example 13-9, which had to extend to only six years to find a common time horizon for projects A and C. But what if we had to compare a five-year project with a seven-year project? This would force us to go out to 35 years, which would be cumbersome indeed! Fortunately, another approach leads to the same conclusions as the chain replication approach, but is much more computationally efficient. The **equivalent annual NPV (EANPV) approach** finds the NPVs of individual projects and then determines the amount of an annual annuity that is economically equivalent to the NPV generated by each project over its respective time horizon.[10] We then choose the project that generates the highest EANPV, which is defined in Equation 13-4.[11] Examples 13-10 and 13-11 demonstrate how the EANPV approach could be used.

equivalent annual NPV (EANPV) approach a way to compare projects by finding the net present value of the individual projects and then determining the amount of an annual annuity that is economically equivalent to the NPV generated by each project over its respective time horizon

[10] This approach is sometimes referred to as the equivalent annual annuity (EAA) approach, since essentially what it involves is estimating an annual NPV annuity.

[11] It would be incorrect to take the NPV and divide by the number of years required to generate the NPV, because this would disregard the time value of money.

[13-4]
$$EANPV = \frac{Project\ NPV}{\left[\dfrac{1-\dfrac{1}{(1+k)^{n}}}{k}\right]}$$

where n is the project's time horizon, and the term inside the parentheses in the denominator is the PV annuity factor for an n-year annuity, as discussed in Chapter 5.

EXAMPLE 13-10   The EANPV Approach

Redo Example 13-9 using the EANPV approach instead of the chain replication approach.

Solution

We already solved for the NPVs of all three projects in the solution to Example 13-9, so we will not replicate those calculations here. The NPVs for A, B, and C were $623.82, $271.27, and $816.13, respectively, and that would rule out project B, because it has the same lifespan as A but has a lower NPV. Therefore, all we need to do is compare the EANPV of A with the one for C.

$$EANPV_A = \frac{Project\ NPV_A}{\left[\dfrac{1-\dfrac{1}{(1+k)^{2}}}{k}\right]} = \frac{623.82}{\left[\dfrac{1-\dfrac{1}{(1.15)^{2}}}{0.15}\right]} = \frac{623.82}{1.625709} = \$383.72$$

$$EANPV_C = \frac{Project\ NPV_C}{\left[\dfrac{1-\dfrac{1}{(1+k)^{3}}}{k}\right]} = \frac{816.13}{\left[\dfrac{1-\dfrac{1}{(1.15)^{3}}}{0.15}\right]} = \frac{816.13}{2.283225} = \$357.45$$

(TI BA II PLUS)

EXAMPLE 13-10   Solution Using a Financial Calculator

Project A: [FV] → [0] ; [PV] → [623.82] ; [N] → [2] ; [I/Y] → [15]

Compute: [PMT] = −383.72 or $383.72

Project C: [FV] → [0] ; [PV] → [816.13] ; [N] → [3] ; [I/Y] → [15]

Compute: [PMT] = −357.45 or $357.45

XLS

EXAMPLE 13-10   Solution Using Excel

The following function can be used: PMT (rate, nper, pv, fv, type)
For Project A, we would enter the following in the appropriate cell:
= PMT (0.15, 2, − 623.82, 0, 0)
This would yield an answer of $383.72.
For Project C, we would enter the following in the appropriate cell:
= PMT (0.15, 3, − 816.13, 0, 0)
This would yield an answer of $357.45.

Therefore, the firm would choose project A over project C, just as we determined by using the chain replication approach. The EANPV approach shows that project A generates a higher NPV per year than does project C.

EXAMPLE 13-11 Applying the EANPV Approach

In May 2012, you decided to compare the long-term contract for Brad Richards of the NHL's New York Rangers to the one that was previously "rejected" by the NHL for the New Jersey Devil's Ilya Kovalchuk. Kovalchuk's contract was rejected (and New Jersey was fined $3 million and otherwise penalized) because it was deemed to be structured in a manner to circumvent the "salary cap" that the NHL imposes on its teams (by, for example, calculating small—well, relatively small—continuing payments far into the future). Ironically, the two players happened to be playing against each other in the 2012 Eastern Conference Finals at that time. The details are provided below.

Year	Richards ($millions)	Kovalchuk ($millions)
1	12	6
2	12	6
3	9	11.5
4	8.5	11.5
5	8.5	11.5
6	7	11.5
7	1	11.5
8	1	10.5
9	1	8.5
10	0	6.5
11	0	3.5
12	0	0.75
13	0	0.55
14	0	0.55
15	0	0.55
16	0	0.55
17	0	0.55

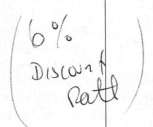

(6%
Discount
Rate)

Solution

At first glance, you might be tempted to say that Kovalchuk's contract is superior—clearly the total payments are much higher ($102 million versus $60 million). Therefore, it is not surprising that the NPV is also much higher ($72.73 million versus $49.46 million). However, this ignores the fact that Richards' contract is only over 9 years, while Kovalchuk's spans 17 years, with some very small payments in the future. While Richards would be older after 9 years and perhaps not able to command as high a salary as he could in 2011, barring injuries he could probably sign another contract and earn much more than $0.55 million per year.

So how do you determine which contract is better given the "unequal lives"? One approach would be to determine the EANPV. It turns out that the EANPV is higher for Richards' contract ($7.27 million per year) than for Kovalchuk's ($6.94 million). For this situation, however, this might not be the "precise" answer because it assumes their contracts would be "replicated." This is unlikely since both players will age and market salary conditions will change. Nonetheless, it does provide a useful comparison of the two contracts.

CONCEPT REVIEW QUESTIONS

1. What is the difference between independent and mutually exclusive projects?

2. How can we compare two choices, one involving a wooden bridge lasting 10 years and another involving a steel bridge lasting 25 years that costs more?

13.4 CAPITAL RATIONING

Learning Objective 13.4
Explain what capital rationing is and how it affects firms' investment criteria.

capital rationing when the total amount of investment capital available is restricted and must be allocated among available investment projects

investment opportunity schedule (IOS) the internal rate of return expected on each potential investment opportunity, ranked in descending order

Theoretically, firms should accept all independent projects that generate positive NPVs, which will enhance firm value. However, in practice, firms often face capital budget constraints, which may force them to turn down attractive projects. Theoretically, this constraint should not exist in an efficient market because firms should always be able to source new financing to take advantage of investment opportunities that generate returns (i.e., IRRs) that exceed the cost of raising the required investment funds. However, these constraints may arise because of market inefficiencies, which restrict the firm's ability to raise funds in the capital markets or because they are imposed internally (i.e., management may set certain budget limits that cannot be exceeded). When firms face capital budget constraints, it is common to say that **capital rationing** prevails—that is, investment capital must be rationed among available investment projects.

Figure 13-4 depicts the cash flow situation for Tim Hortons Inc. in fiscal 2011. With $391 million in cash flow from operations, and cash flows for investing of only $152.7 million, Tim Hortons had positive free cash flow and was the antithesis of a capital-constrained company. It could accept all the projects listed on its **investment opportunity schedule (IOS)** until the IRR equalled its weighted average cost of capital (WACC)[12] —or until the last project accepted had an NPV of zero—and still have money left over to pay a dividend or pay down debt. However, suppose Tim Hortons had only $100 million of internal funds; in that case, it could not accept all its projects and would be capital rationed unless it raised new financing, which many firms are reluctant to do.

The important point about capital rationing is that the cost of capital is no longer the appropriate opportunity cost, since the firm no longer has sufficient funds to accept all the projects that it should. This means that now the cash flows generated by a project can be reinvested at a higher rate than assumed by the cost of capital, because the firm is leaving some positive-NPV projects on the table because of lack of financing. The reinvestment rate assumption underlying the IRR has more validity, because the firm can reinvest the cash flows from a project at the IRR of the marginal project, rather than at its cost of capital. The problem is that the IOS schedule is rarely the nice smooth downward-sloping function shown in Figure 13-4.

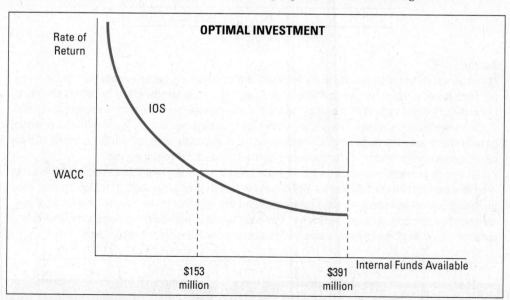

FIGURE 13-4 *Tim Hortons' Investment and Internal Cash Flow, 2011*

When firms with limited funds have to choose among discrete, lumpy projects, they must consider the cost of the investment, because this is constrained by the capital budget. In this case, we can first estimate the NPVs and the IRRs, but we can't fully rely on either of them as a

---

[12]We will discuss the WACC in detail in Chapter 20 and explain why we have defined it the way we have. At this stage, simply treat the WACC as the company's hurdle rate for evaluating investments.

criterion, because they ignore the cost of the investment and the capital constraint. The PI is often a useful starting point because it gives the highest present value relative to the initial cash outlay, which is constrained. However, the final decision should be based on which combination of projects generates the highest total NPV while satisfying the capital budget constraint. This is because the PI, like the IRR, may lead to incorrect decisions because it is a relative measure. Example 13-12 shows the correct procedure for dealing with capital rationing.[13]

EXAMPLE 13-12 Applying the EANPV Approach

A firm is considering the following independent investments:

Project	CF$_0$ (Initial Cash Outlay)	NPV	Project Life	PI
A	$100,000	$13,646	4	1.136
B	$50,000	−$3,342	6	0.933
C	$80,000	$10,558	3	1.132
D	$60,000	$4,320	7	1.072
E	$75,000	$10,825	5	1.144
F	$90,000	$7,225	6	1.080

a. In the absence of capital rationing, which projects should be selected? Determine the size, in total dollars, of the firm's capital budget under this scenario. What is the total NPV of all the projects selected?

b. Now suppose a capital budget constraint of $250,000 is placed on new investments. Determine which projects should be selected. What is the total NPV under this scenario? What is the loss to the company from the capital rationing constraint?

Solution

a. In the absence of capital rationing, the firm should select projects A, C, D, E, and F because they all have positive NPVs and are assumed to be independent.

Capital budget $=100,000 + 80,000 + 60,000 + 75,000 + 90,000 = \$405,000$

Total NPV $= 13,646 + 10,558 + 4,320 + 10,825 + 7,225 = \$46,574$

b. The firm should take on the combination of positive-NPV projects that maximizes total NPV, within the given budget constraints.

Combination	Total NPV	Capital Budget	Within Budget
A, C, D	$28,524	$240,000	Yes
A, D, E	$28,791	$235,000	Yes
C, E, F	$28,608	$245,000	Yes
A, C, E	$35,029	$255,000	No

If the capital budget constraint is fixed, the firm should select projects A, D, and E.[14] The total NPV is now only $28,791 under capital rationing, and the "loss" to the company is $46,574 − $28,791 = $17,783. Notice that the loss of $17,783 equals the sum of the NPVs of the two forgone positive-NPV projects (i.e., C and F). This is detrimental to firm value as it is forced to turn down two "good" positive-NPV investments because the firm lacks the capital to proceed with them. The PI criterion indicates A, C, and E have the highest PIs, but unfortunately they cost more than the budget allows. Although the PIs are a good starting point, they rarely give the optimal solution.

Although we have come up with the maximum NPV given the budget constraint, in reality the firm would conduct further analysis. For example, the company would forecast its budget for the following year and look at the deferral possibilities. It may turn out, for example, that C can be deferred and it is better to go with A and E this year and roll over the excess in the budget to take on C and other projects next year.

---

[13] This problem can be solved using integer programming techniques, but rarely is the problem difficult enough to justify the analysis.

[14] If there was $5,000 "slack" in the constraint, the combination of A, C, and E would generate the highest NPV; however, it requires a $255,000 outlay, which exceeds the $250,000 constraint.

How relevant is a situation of capital rationing? Theoretically, financing should always be available for good (i.e., positive-NPV) projects, which by their nature should increase firm value. This belief underlies the justification for using the WACC as the discount rate and basing decisions on the NPV criterion. However, this does not always hold true in practice, as financing is often limited or is sometimes simply not available, as happened to many firms during the financial crisis of 2008–9. Consider, for example, Maple Leaf Foods Inc.'s decision in October 2011 to shut down six meat plants, upgrade others, and shed 1,500 jobs. Maple Leaf CEO Michael McCain suggested that part of the impetus for such a drastic decision was that Canadian factories are "starved for capital."[15]

The Appropriate Discount Rate

As mentioned in the previous section, it is usually appropriate to use a firm's weighted average cost of capital (WACC) as the discount rate to evaluate long-term investment projects. Figure 13-5 shows that this is, in fact, the case in practice. Baker, Dutta, and Saadi's survey of Canadian CFOs suggests that 63.6 percent of CFOs use the WACC often or always. The WACC represents the after-tax cost of the average dollar of long-term financing to the firm, and we assume that firms will finance long-term investments by using long-term financing. This is appropriate if the project under consideration is an "average" risk investment for the company—in other words, if it is a typical investment and will not substantially change the asset mix of the company.

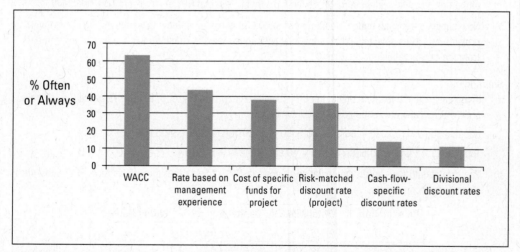

FIGURE 13-5 Survey Results of *Discount Rates Used by Canadian Firms When Evaluating a New Project*

Source: Baker, Kent H., Shantanu Dutta, and Samir Saadi, "Corporate finance practices in Canada: Where do we stand?" *Multinational Finance Journal* 15, no. 3/4 (September/December 2011), Table 5, p. 176.

However, if a company is considering a project that is "atypical" in the sense that it is either more or less risky than the average investment for that company, this fact should be reflected in the discount rate used to evaluate that project. For example, a company could be considering introducing a new product line that entails greater (or lower) risks than its traditional offerings. Under these circumstances, a higher discount rate should be used for projects that possess above-average risk, and a lower discount rate should be used for projects that possess below-average risk. If a firm does not adjust the discount rate under these circumstances and merely uses a constant WACC to select investment projects, it will make inappropriate decisions. In particular, this could lead the firm to reject positive-NPV low-risk projects that appear unattractive if evaluated using a discount rate that is too high. It could also lead the firm to accept negative-NPV high-risk projects that appear attractive if evaluated using a discount rate that is too low.

[15]Source: McNish, Jacquie. "Maple Leaf's big move." *The Globe and Mail*, October 20, 2011, p. B1/5.

A good example of this problem is provided by Marathon Oil Corporation in the United States. For a time, the company was made up of two divisions: the original oil company and US Steel. Suppose that the oil company's WACC was 8 percent and the steel company's was 12 percent. If each division made up 50 percent of the overall company, the company WACC would be 10 percent. Applying the company WACC of 10 percent to capital projects would cause some of the steel division's bad projects, with IRRs of 11 percent, to be accepted, even if stand-alone steel companies were rejecting similar projects. Likewise, good oil projects earning 9 percent would be rejected, even if they were being accepted by equivalent oil companies. If Marathon Oil did this over time, it would gradually become a bad steel company, because it would be doing things that good steel companies weren't. Similarly, it would be rejecting many good opportunities that good oil companies would have accepted.

The common response to the Marathon Oil problem is to estimate risk-adjusted discount rates (RADRs) by adjusting the cost of capital up or down based on the risk level and financing of a specific project under consideration. For example, Marathon Oil would use a discount rate of 8 percent in its oil division and 12 percent in its steel division. Estimating these different discount rates involves estimating betas and the risk associated with the investment and the optimal financing. One method of doing this is the **pure play approach**, which involves estimating the WACC of firms in an industry associated with the project. Another approach is to estimate beta for the project by regressing the return on assets (ROA) of the project against the ROA of the market index. Similar techniques can be used to estimate the appropriate project cost of debt and then to estimate the appropriate overall cost of capital.

pure play approach estimating betas and the risk associated with an investment and the optimal financing by estimating the WACC of firms in an industry associated with the project

Several practical difficulties are associated with estimating RADRs. For example, it may be difficult to find an appropriate company to use in the pure play approach, and the regression of project ROA on an index ROA may lead to an inaccurate beta measure. In addition, intuitive adjustments made by managers are subjective in nature and prone to error—though they may be no more so than other techniques. However, despite the associated difficulties, estimating RADRs is preferable to blindly applying one constant discount rate to all projects, regardless of their individual risk characteristics.

CONCEPT REVIEW QUESTIONS

1. What complications arise when firms are rationed in terms of their available capital budget?

2. Explain how firms should decide which projects to accept and which to reject when capital rationing exists.

3. How and why do we adjust the discount rate for multi-divisional firms?

4. What mistakes can occur if firms do not make the appropriate adjustments?

13.5 INTERNATIONAL CONSIDERATIONS

Figure 13-6 depicts foreign direct investment (FDI), which represents investment in real assets and companies by firms. All types of investments across national boundaries are increasing as the world becomes one giant marketplace. Figure 13-6 shows that both outbound FDI by Canadian firms and inbound FDI from foreign countries has increased through time. Figure 13-6 also shows that both outbound and inbound FDI move in similar fashion, which implies they are affected by the same factors. In fact, their correlation over the 1983 to 2011 period was 0.75. Firms make these foreign investments for many reasons: they may want to take advantage of cheaper resources, whether labour or materials; they may want to enter new markets; or they may want to have access to new technology. To exploit such opportunities, many firms establish foreign subsidiaries or enter into joint ventures with firms that are in foreign countries.

Learning Objective 13.5
Explain the importance of international foreign direct investment both inside and outside Canada.

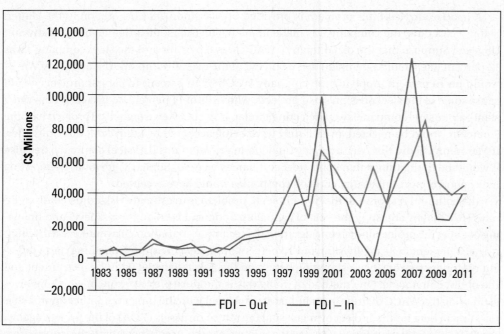

FIGURE 13-6 *Foreign Direct Investment In and Out of Canada (1983–2011)*

Source: Data from Statistics Canada website, www.statcan.gc.ca/pub/61-232-x/2011001/tablesectlist-listetableauxsect-eng.htm.

Regardless of the motives, foreign investment is a capex decision, and firms have to apply the same criteria as they do for domestic projects. However, some practical difficulties arise when attempting to apply the NPV evaluation process to foreign investments:

- How do we account for the political risk of expropriation or insurrection or the imposition of foreign exchange controls that prevent the firm's getting its investment back?[16]

- How do we account for other potential legal and regulatory issues where local competitors may have privileged access to cronies in the government?

- How do we adjust for foreign exchange risk because cash flows are denominated in a foreign currency?

- How do we adjust for the taxes paid in a foreign currency and the possibility that when they are paid back to Canada, they may be taxed again?

- How do we finance a foreign project if the local markets are poorly developed?

Many large Canadian firms are dealing more frequently with these important questions, which are covered in a multinational business finance course. The Export Development Corporation of Canada (EDC) also helps Canadian firms export and make FDI decisions. EDC is a branch of the Canadian government and offers extensive insurance programs to mitigate some of the risks of FDI. For example, EDC offers political risk insurance (PRI) against

- breach of contract risk

- conversion risk

- expropriation risk (including gradual or creeping expropriation)

- risk of non-payment by a sovereign obligor

- political violence risk

---

[16]A survey of companies found that for foreign capital budgeting decisions in which there is substantial political risk, companies tend to use a method such as the payback period. In contrast, in cases in which there is little political risk, companies tend to use the net present value method. Source: Holmen, Martin, and Bengt Pramborg, "Capital Budgeting and Political Risk: Empirical Evidence." *Journal of International Financial Management and Accounting* 20, no. 2 (Summer 2009), pp. 105–34.

- repossession risk
- transfer risk

The terms of the PRI vary from one country to another depending on the risk, but in evaluating FDI, the PRI can, in part, be removed by charging the project with a 1-percent PRI fee based on the capital committed, which is the normal fee for comprehensive political risk insurance for a typical developing country.

The techniques developed in chapters 11 and 12 to manage financial risk are often used to manage foreign exchange risk. Canadian firms routinely use forwards to sell future foreign cash flows forward into Canadian dollars and may also issue foreign currency debt to hedge their investment. Therefore, FDI project analysis involves all the standard domestic problems, plus a variety of complex institutional problems that make it considerably more difficult than domestic project analysis.

CONCEPT REVIEW QUESTIONS

1. What is so different about evaluating FDI compared with domestic projects?
2. Name some unique risks that can arise when evaluating FDI.

APPENDIX **13A**

THE MODIFIED INTERNAL RATE OF RETURN (MIRR)

The assumption, built into the internal rate of return mathematics, that all cash inflows are reinvested at the internal rate of return may be too aggressive a supposition to make. We can modify this assumption by calculating the return on the project with a more realistic view of the reinvestment of cash inflows. The result is the **modified internal rate of return (MIRR)**. The accept/reject criteria for the MIRR is similar to that of the IRR: if a project has an MIRR greater than its cost of capital, it is acceptable; if a project's MIRR is less than its cost of capital, it is not acceptable.

Let's start with a project X that has a project cost of capital of 10 percent and the following cash flows:

Year	End-of-Year Cash Flow
0	–$10,000
1	4,200
2	4,200
3	4,200

Learning Objective 13.6
Understand how the modified internal rate of return (MIRR) is calculated and why this represents a conceptual improvement over the way the IRR is calculated.

modified internal rate of return (MIRR) a variation of the IRR that allows adjustments for the reinvestment rates on cash flows that are generated during the life of the project

The IRR of project X is 12.51 percent, and the NPV is $444.78. The IRR of 12.51 percent assumes all cash flows are reinvested and earn a return of 12.51 percent, which is well above the firm's cost of capital. To illustrate the role of reinvestment, let's assume that the company has no other projects in which to reinvest any of these cash flows. We calculate the return on project X in this situation by comparing the investment of $10,000 with what is available at the end of the project. If each cash flow that comes in is deposited in an account that earns no interest, the company will have $12,600 at the end of three years.

Therefore,

PV = $10,000

FV = $12,600

N = 3

Solve for I/Y → I/Y = 8.01%

Given no other use of the cash, the company has a return, which is the MIRR, of 8.01 percent.

Under these circumstances, project X is not acceptable.

Now let's assume that the company has other investment opportunities available that earn 5 percent. We can represent this in a diagram, indicating the cash flows and how they "grow" when reinvested at 5 percent:

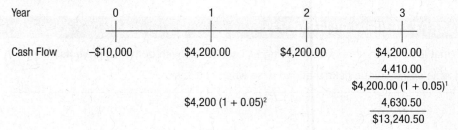

In table form, we have:

Year	End-of-year cash flow	Future value of reinvested cash flows, end of period 3
0	−$10,000.00	
1	$4,200.00	$4,630.50
2	$4,200.00	$4,410.00
3	$4,200.00	$4,200.00
Total		$13,240.50

The future value of the reinvested cash flows, FV, is $13,240.50, and therefore the MIRR is 9.81 percent:

PV = $10,000
FV = $13,240.50
N = 3
Solve for I/Y → I/Y = 9.81%

Again, the project is not acceptable because the return on the project is less than the project's cost of capital.

A common assumption for reinvestment opportunities uses the company's cost of capital, which is the return on the typical or average project of the company. The reasoning is simple: if the company has cash flows from a project, they are most likely reinvested in a typical project for the company. Using the company's cost of capital of 10 percent, the MIRR becomes 11.61 percent.[17] In this case, the project is acceptable because the MIRR of 11.61 percent exceeds the project's cost of capital of 10 percent.

The MIRR is sensitive to the reinvestment assumption, as we show in Figure 13A-1, where we graph the MIRR against the reinvestment rate for project X; the better the reinvestment opportunities, the better the return on the project, as measured by MIRR.[18] In general, the

---

[17]If you are checking this calculation, the future value of the cash flows, considering reinvestment at 10 percent, is $13,902

[18]Using Microsoft's Excel Solver function, we can solve for the reinvestment rate at which the MIRR is equal to the project's cost of capital. We do this by setting the goal of the MIRR equal to 10 percent, and then solve for the reinvestment rate that is applied against the project's cash inflows. For project X, the project is acceptable as long as the return on reinvested cash flows is equal to or greater than 5.5329 percent.

"normal" assumption used in calculating MIRR is that funds will be reinvested at the firm's cost of capital so if you see a reported MIRR and there is no explicit mention of the reinvestment rate used, it is reasonable to assume they used the firm's cost of capital.

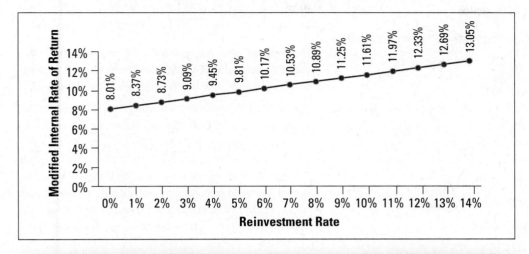

FIGURE 13A-1 *Modified Internal Rate of Return for Project X*

CONCEPT REVIEW QUESTIONS

1. What improvement does MIRR represent over traditional IRR?
2. When will a calculated MIRR be greater than a calculated IRR?

SUMMARY

In this chapter, we discuss the capital budgeting process for companies. We focus most of our discussion on the criteria (NPV, IRR, profitability index, payback period, and discounted payback period) that are commonly used to evaluate capital expenditure decisions. We show why NPV is the preferred measure, although the other criteria also provide useful information. Finally, we consider three specific complexities: those caused by capital rationing, those caused by risk differences within multi-divisional firms, and those caused by FDI. In Chapter 14, we will show exactly how to calculate the cash flows and will work through more detailed examples. We will also delve further into the complex issue of deciding what "incremental" means in practice.

SUMMARY OF LEARNING OBJECTIVES

13.1 Describe the capital budgeting process and explain its importance to corporate strategy.

Capital budgeting refers to the process through which a firm makes capital expenditure decisions by (1) identifying investment alternatives, (2) evaluating these alternatives, (3) implementing the chosen investment decisions, and (4) monitoring and evaluating the implemented decisions.

13.2 Identify and apply the main tools used to evaluate investments.

The main tools used to evaluate investments include net present value (NPV) analysis, internal rate of return (IRR),

payback period, discounted payback period, and profitability index. The most commonly used method is NPV, and the second most commonly used method is IRR.

13.3 Analyze independent projects and explain how they differ from interdependent projects.

Independent projects are analyzed standing alone. As long as there are no capital spending restrictions, the decision rule is to accept projects that generate a positive NPV and reject those that do not. Interdependent projects are related to other projects. In this case, we need to consider the relationships among projects. Contingent projects are projects for which the acceptance of one requires the acceptance of another, either beforehand or simultaneously. For mutually exclusive projects, the firm must decide which project is best.

13.4 Explain what capital rationing is and how it affects firms' investment criteria.

Capital rationing occurs when the total amount of investment capital available is restricted and must be allocated among available investment projects. Projects are ranked on an investment opportunity schedule using NPV and are selected based on positive NPV, from the highest to the lowest, until the maximum capital input is reached.

13.5 Explain the importance of international foreign direct investment both inside and outside Canada.

All types of investments across national boundaries are increasing as the world becomes one giant marketplace. Outbound foreign direct investment (FDI) by Canadian firms has increased in 15 years from 14 percent of gross domestic product to more than 30 percent, while inbound FDI has increased from less than 20 percent to about 26 percent.

13.6 Understand how the modified internal rate of return (MIRR) is calculated and why this represents a conceptual improvement over the way the IRR is calculated.

We calculate the MIRR by adjusting the reinvestment rate applied to interim cash flows received to determine an ending future value (FV). The MIRR is the rate that equates the initial investment outlay (i.e., the PV) with this ending FV. This method represents a more realistic way of adjusting for the reinvestment rate assumed on projects, since we do not blindly assume that all funds are reinvested at the project's IRR, which may be above or below average.

KEY TERMS

bottom-up analysis, p. 497
capital budgeting, p. 495
capital expenditures, p. 494
capital rationing, p. 516
chain replication approach, p. 512
contingent projects, p. 512
crossover rate, p. 507
discounted cash flow (DCF) methodologies, p. 498

discounted payback period, p. 509
equivalent annual NPV (EANPV) approach, p. 513
five forces, p. 496
incremental, p. 500
independent projects, p. 511
interdependent projects, p. 512
internal rate of return (IRR), p. 503
investment opportunity schedule (IOS), p. 516

modified internal rate of return (MIRR) p. 521
mutually exclusive projects, p. 506
net present value (NPV), p. 499
payback period, p. 508
profitability index (PI), p. 510
pure play approach, p. 519
risk-adjusted discount rate (RADR), p. 500
top-down analysis, p. 497

EQUATIONS

Equation	Formula	Page
[13-1] Net Present Value	$NPV = \dfrac{CF_1}{(1+k)^1} + \dfrac{CF_2}{(1+k)^2} + \dfrac{CF_3}{(1+k)^3} + \ldots - CF_0 = \sum_{t=1}^{n} \dfrac{CF_t}{(1+k)^t} - CF_0$	p. 499
[13-2] Internal Rate of Return	$\dfrac{CF_1}{(1+IRR)^1} + \dfrac{CF_2}{(1+IRR)^2} + \dfrac{CF_3}{(1+IRR)^3} + \ldots = CF_0 \text{ or } \sum_{t=1}^{n} \dfrac{CF_t}{(1+IRR)^t} = CF_0$	p. 503
[13-3] Profitability Index	$PI = \dfrac{PV \text{ (cash inflows)}}{PV \text{ (cash outflows)}}$	p. 510
[13-4] Equivalent Annual NPV	$EANPV = \dfrac{Project\ NPV}{\left[\dfrac{1 - \dfrac{1}{(1+k)^n}}{k}\right]}$	p. 514

QUESTIONS AND PRACTICE PROBLEMS

Multiple Choice Questions

1. What will probably happen if a firm does not invest effectively?
   a. The firm could still maintain its competitive advantage.
   b. The cost of capital of the firm will be unchanged.
   c. The long-term survival of the firm will be affected.
   d. The short-term performance will be unaffected.

2. Which of the following is *not* a critical factor that Porter identified in determining industry attractiveness?
   a. bargaining power of suppliers
   b. entry barriers
   c. rivalry among competitors
   d. bargaining power of government

3. What is the NPV for a project with an after-tax initial investment of $17,000 and five equal cash flows of $8,000 at the start of each year, beginning with the third year? The appropriate discount rate is 20 percent. Should it be accepted?
   a. $2,937.41; accept
   b. $6,924.90; accept
   c. –$385.49; reject
   d. $1,998.35; accept

4. When will NPV and IRR have different rankings when we evaluate two mutually exclusive projects? $IRR_A < IRR_B$.
   a. discount rate (k) < crossover rate
   b. discount rate (k) < IRR_A
   c. discount rate (k) > crossover rate
   d. discount rate (k) > IRR_B

5. Which project(s) should a firm choose when the projects are independent? When they are mutually exclusive? Suppose both are within the capital budget and k is 15 percent for both projects.

   Project A: $CF_0 = \$2,000$; $CF_1 = \$1,000$; $CF_2 = \$2,000$; $CF_3 = \$1,500$
   Project B: $CF_0 = \$2,000$; $CF_1 = \$1,000$; $CF_2 = \$1,000$; $CF_3 = \$4,500$

   a. both projects; project A
   b. both projects; project B
   c. project B; project B
   d. neither project; neither project

6. What is the IRR of the following project? After-tax initial investment = $6,000; $CF_1 = \$2,500$; $CF_2 = \$4,000$; $CF_3 = \$5,000$. If $k = 20\%$, should you accept the project?
   a. 15%; no
   b. 35.87%; yes
   c. 25.65%; yes
   d. 35.87%; no

7. We should *reject* a project if:
   a. NPV > 0.
   b. IRR > required rate of return.
   c. discounted payback period < required period.
   d. PI < 1.

8.   Which of the following statements about IRR and NPV is *incorrect*?
     a.   NPV and IRR yield the same ranking when evaluating projects.
     b.   NPV assumes that cash flows are reinvested at the cost of capital of the firm.
     c.   A project may have multiple IRRs when the sign of the cash flow changes more than once.
     d.   IRR is the discount rate that makes the NPV equal zero.

9.   Which of the following would *not* happen if a firm uses WACC for all projects, regardless of the individual risks of the projects?
     a.   Accept a high-risk project with negative NPV
     b.   Reject a low-risk project with positive NPV
     c.   Accept an average-risk project with positive NPV
     d.   Reject a high-risk project with positive NPV

10. To estimate risk-adjusted discount rates, a firm could do all of the following, *except:*
     a.   use the cost of capital ± risk premium method.
     b.   regress the ROA of the project on the ROA of the whole firm.
     c.   regress the ROA of the project on the ROA of the market index.
     d.   use the pure play approach.

11. What is true about evaluating FDI compared with domestic projects?
     a.   We cannot use the NPV rule to evaluate FDI.
     b.   We cannot use IRR to evaluate FDI.
     c.   FDI has some unique risks.
     d.   FDI always has negative NPV.

12. Which is not the unique risk of FDI compared with domestic projects?
     a.   Interest rate risk
     b.   Political risk of expropriation or insurrection or the imposition of foreign exchange controls that prevent the firm's getting its investment back
     c.   Potential legal and regulatory issues where local competitors may have privileged access to cronies in the government
     d.   Foreign exchange risk because cash flows are denominated in a foreign currency

13. What improvement does MIRR represent over traditional IRR?
     a.   It calculates the NPV of a project.
     b.   It relaxes the assumption that cash flows are reinvested at IRR.
     c.   It always gives the same accept/reject decision as IRR.
     d.   It always gives the same accept/reject decision as NPV.

14. In which of the following situations is MIRR likely to be greater than a calculated IRR?
     a.   Reinvestment rate is the same as the cost of capital.
     b.   Reinvestment rate is less than the cost of capital.
     c.   Reinvestment rate is greater than IRR.
     d.   A firm deposits cash flows in a zero-interest account.

Practice Problems

15. Bert has just been hired by your company as a summer co-op student and has been assigned to assist you. Bert is puzzled about why your company is calculating IRR and payback periods for investment projects. According to Bert's finance textbook, NPV gives the best measure of the impact of a project on shareholder wealth.
     a.   Explain to Bert the advantages and disadvantages of payback and IRR.
     b.   Which evaluation techniques are the most popular with companies (i.e., your company's clients)?

c. Given the disadvantages and limitations of payback and IRR, why do you think so many CFOs continue to use them as criteria for evaluating projects?

16. For the following decisions, indicate whether they are examples of a bottom-up analysis or a top-down analysis:
    a. Replacing the printing press at a newspaper
    b. A newspaper's decision to sell all its print services and move into on-line data services
    c. A pharmaceutical company's research investment in developing a cholesterol drug
    d. A car company's research investment in developing a cholesterol drug
    e. Your decision to take an English literature elective rather than a sociology elective this semester
    f. Your decision to do a degree in business rather than medicine

17. State the drawbacks of the payback period and discounted payback period.

Use the following information to answer practice problems 18 to 26.

You have been hired as consultants for BigCo Manufacturing Company. BigCo is considering several projects and has provided the forecasted annual after-tax cash flows in Table 1.

Table 1
Annual cash flows (all amounts in $millions)

	Project A	Project B	Project C	Project D	Project E	Project F	Project G
Year 0	−1,000	−2,000	−8,000	−5,000	−5,000	−10,000	−3,000
Year 1	500	1,500	2,000	4,800	2,000	3,000	1,500
Year 2	1,000	1,000	2,000	1,000	3,000	2,000	1,200
Year 3	1,200	300	8,000	6,000	5,000	1,000	300
Year 4	2,500	500	2,000	−3,000	1,000	1,000	
Year 5	3,000	200	2,500	−4,000	3,000	3,000	

18. Assume that BigCo's cost of capital for all the projects is 7 percent. Calculate the NPV, IRR, payback period, discounted payback, and profitability index for each project in Table 1. The firm requires a payback period of 2 years and a discounted payback period of 2.5 years.

	Project A	Project B	Project C	Project D	Project E	Project F	Project G
NPV							
IRR							
Payback							
Discounted payback							
Profitability index							

19. a. If the firm is not capital constrained and the projects in Table 1 are independent, which projects should the firm undertake using the following criteria?
      i. NPV
      ii. IRR
      iii. Payback period
      iv. Discounted payback period
    b. Are any of your recommendations, based on the above criteria, contradictory? Explain how that would be possible.

20. a. If the firm is not capital constrained and the projects in Table 1 are mutually exclusive, which project should the firm undertake using the following criteria?
    i.   NPV
    ii. IRR
    iii. Payback period
    iv. Discounted payback period
    v.   Profitability index
   b. Are any of your recommendations, based on the above criteria, contradictory? Explain how that would be possible.

21. BigCo Manufacturing Company is also debating whether to invest in Project H (a three-year project) or Project D. Project H has cash flow of –$3,000, $1,500, $1,200, and $750 in years 0, 1, 2, and 3. Determine which project is preferred (assuming that the appropriate cost of capital is 7 percent) using the.
   a. chain replication approach
   b. equivalent annual NPV approach

22. Using projects A to F in Table 1, construct BigCo's investment opportunity schedule. If BigCo has $8,000 available for investment, which projects should it undertake (assume all projects are independent)? Justify your recommendations to the CEO of BigCo.

23. The CFO of BigCo is concerned about the sensitivity of his decisions to the choice of discount rate. For projects A, C, and E, plot the NPV profiles on the same graph. Does the NPV ranking of the three projects remain the same for every possible discount rate? Explain your observations.

24. Calculate the crossover rate for projects B and C from Table 1.

25. You have conducted an analysis of BigCo and have found that the firm is made up of two different divisions: SatellitesRUs (a satellite launching service) and a bank. Projects A to G are all related to satellite launching technology. You have also examined the industry of each division and have found the following:

Firm	Industry	Cost of capital
Crash'n Burn	Satellite launching	27%
Liddy's Launchers	Satellite launching	20%
Reliable Bankers	Banking	5%
Reliance Bank	Banking	4%
VBigCo	Satellite launching and banking	10%

   a. What is the appropriate discount rate for projects A to G? Describe your assumptions.
   b. What will be the impact on the shareholder value of BigCo if the firm used 7 percent, the overall WACC, in the valuation of the satellite launching projects (A to G)?

26. The CEO of BigCo has just bought a fancy financial calculator and calculated the IRR and NPV of Project D from Table 1 and is utterly confused. His calculator is telling him that the IRR is 26 percent, but when he uses a cost of capital of 1 percent, the NPV is negative. The CEO expects that if the IRR is greater than the cost of capital then the NPV should be positive. How are the CEO's observations possible? Hint: See the NPV profile of Project D.

27. Cutler Compacts will generate cash flows of $30,000 in year 1, and $65,000 in year 2. However, if it makes an immediate investment of $20,000, it can instead expect to have cash streams of $55,000 in total in year 1 and $63,000 in year 2. The appropriate discount rate is 9 percent.
   a. Calculate the NPV of the proposed project.
   b. Why would IRR be a poor choice in this situation?

28. Elaine is evaluating two investments—investment 1 has a profitability index (PI) of 2.4 while investment 2 has a PI of 1.2. As these investments are mutually exclusive, Elaine is recommending investment 1. The Chair of the board of BigCo has asked for your comments on Elaine's recommendation.

29. Daria is evaluating two investments—investment 1 will produce cash flows for the next 5 years and has an NPV of $1,000. Investment 2 will produce cash flows for the next 15 years and has an NPV of $700. Based on this analysis, Daria recommends investment 1. Discuss whether this conclusion is appropriate.

30. Given the following: Project A: $CF_0 = -\$23,000$; $CF_1 = \$6,000$; $CF_2 = \$9,000$; $CF_3 = \$15,600$
    Project B: $CF_0 = -\$20,000$; $CF_1 = \$4,000$; $CF_2 = \$8,000$; $CF_3 = \$15,000$
    What is the crossover rate (r)?

31. If the NPV of a project is $5,090 and its after-tax initial investment is $10,050, what is its PI? Should the firm accept the project? Does the PI yield the same decision as the NPV? (Assume all the cash flows except for the initial investment are inflows.)

32. SK Inc. has two projects as follows:

Project	Initial CF	CF_1	CF_2	CF_3	CF_4
A	−2,500	800	1,200	900	2,000
B	−3,000	750	1,500	1,000	4,000

If SK set 2.6 years as a cut-off period for screening projects, which projects will be selected, using the payback period method?

33. Which project(s) will be selected if the company uses the discounted payback period method in Practice Problem 32 and the discount rate is 12 percent?

34. State the decision rules for NPV, IRR, PI, and the discounted payback period. List two possible consequences of using IRR.

✿ 35. Malcolm, a very junior reporter, has asked for your help with his first article for a major national newspaper. He has provided you with the following excerpt from his article and would like your comments:

The BathGate Group, one of the few all-equity firms left in Canada, has recently built a widget manufacturing plant in Whitby. The firm has invested $1 million and, according to our sources, the promised return on the investment (IRR) is over 27 percent! The shareholders of the firm must be ecstatic—they are currently only receiving a return of 10 percent. Just think—in 10 years the value of the plant is expected to be close to $11 million.

   a. What is Malcolm assuming about the reinvestment rate? Does it make sense?
   b. What is Malcolm assuming about the riskiness of the project? Are the shareholders necessarily happy with this decision?

✿ 36. Longlife Company is considering an investment in Ponce Leon Mineral Baths. The investment has the same risk characteristics as the firm. It is assumed that all cash flows are perpetuities and that there are no taxes. Currently the firm has cash flows of $1,000 a year with required debt payments of $300 per year. The current market value of the firm (debt plus equity) is $13,000. The firm is considering an investment of $5,000 in a project that will generate $610 a year forever. Assume that the firm can continue to borrow at 5 percent.
   a. Should the firm undertake the investment?
   b. Demonstrate that the investment will increase/decrease shareholder value (show the impact on cash flows to debt holders and equity holders).

37. The analysis of a two-division company (DV2) has indicated that the beta of the entire company is 1.35. The company is 100-percent equity funded. The company has two divisions: Major League TV (MLTV) and Minor League Shipping (MLS), which have very different risk characteristics. The beta of a pure-play company comparable to MLTV is 1.85 while for MLS the beta of a comparable pure-play company is only 0.75. The risk-free rate is 3 percent and the market risk premium is 5 percent. Assume all cash flows are perpetuities and the tax rate is zero.
    a. Calculate the cost of capital of the entire company.
    b. The company is evaluating a project that has the same type of risk as MLTV. The project requires an initial investment of $10,000 and pays $1,000 per year forever. Should the company undertake this project? Why or why not?

38. Westlake Corp. has a capital structure that has 60 percent debt at a cost of 12 percent and 40 percent equity. Westlake's stock has a beta of 1.2, market risk premium of 8 percent, and a risk-free rate of 5 percent. The firm has a potential project on hand, which requires an initial investment of $120,000 and generates an annual year-end cash flow of $37,500 for five years. Calculate the IRR of this project. Decide if the project should be accepted or not, assuming the project is less risky for the firm. $T_c = 40\%$.

39. A project has an NPV of $50,000. Calculate the cost of capital of this project if it generates the following cash flows for six years after an initial investment of $200,000:

Year 1: $50,000	Year 2: $50,000
Year 3: $30,000	Year 4: $80,000
Year 5: $60,000	Year 6: $70,000

40. Based on the cash flows given below, calculate the PI of a project that has a required rate of return of 15 percent. Also, indicate whether the project should be accepted.

Year 0: –$90,000	Year 1: $20,000
Year 2: $40,000	Year 3: –$15,000
Year 4: $100,000	

41. GiS Inc. has the following four projects on hand:

Project	Initial CF	Accum. CF$_1$	Accum. CF$_2$	Accum. CF$_3$	Accum. CF$_4$
1	–15,067	3,385	8,965	14,078	21,495
2	–14,543	2,578	6,865	12,095	19,067
3	–8,565	3,097	5,674	9,883	15,688
4	–6,500	2,955	4,985	4,985	12,000

    Note the cash flow in the table is accumulative. Assume that $R_F = 5\%$, $ER_M = 12\%$, firm-beta = 1.2, after-tax cost of debt = 6.5%. The firm is financed by 40-percent debt and 60-percent equity. Projects 1, 2, and 3 have the same capital structure as the firm, while project 4 has a 1-percent risk premium. Calculate the cost of capital for the four projects using the following methods:

    a. The payback period for projects 1, 2, and 3: If the cut-off period for screening projects 1 and 2 is 3.5 years and for project 3 is 2.25 years, which project(s) should be rejected?
    b. The discounted payback period method for project 4: If the cut-off period for screening project 4 is 3.25 years, should it be accepted?

42. SK Inc. has a project that requires a $50,000 after-tax initial investment and produces these after-tax cash flows at each year-end: $18,000; $20,000; –$5,000; $40,050; $58,000; and $20,000. The appropriate domestic discount rate is 19.4 percent. The project is in another developing country, where extra risk is assumed to be 4.6 percent. Calculate the project's NPV. Should SK Inc. accept or reject the project?

43. Calculate the NPV and IRR of the following project and check whether they produce the same decision. After-tax initial investment is $66,777; after-tax cash flows at each of the following six year ends are $20,000. The year-end cash flow at year 7 is $40,000. Assume k is 18 percent.

44. You are considering buying a machine that will cost you $12,000. There will be a maintenance cost of $1,000 at the beginning of each year, and the machine will generate cash flows of $5,000 over the next five years. After the five years, the machine will have no salvage value. What is the NPV of this machine if the cost of capital is 12 percent?

45. Your truck has a market value of $60,000. You can sell it to your brother who agreed to buy it now and pay $75,000 three years from now, or you can sell it to your cousin who agreed to pay you $65,000 at the end of the year. To whom should you sell the truck if your cost of capital is 8 percent?

46. You are interested in an investment where the initial investment is $150,000 and your required cost of capital is 11 percent. Cash inflows from this project are expected to be $10,000 at the end of the first year and are expected to grow at 5 percent a year thereafter. Compute the NPV.

47. An investment has the following cash inflows: $2,500 at the end of the first year, $2,000 at the end of the second year, and $1,500 at the end of the third year. What is the discounted payback period if the discount rate is zero percent and the initial cash outflow is $5,000?

48. Name one condition under which the discounted payback period will be equal to the payback period.

49. You have two mutually exclusive projects:

Year	Cash Flow (A)	Cash Flow (B)
0	−150,000	−100,000
1	30,000	60,000
2	30,000	40,000
3	60,000	20,000
4	90,000	20,000

Irrespective of the project, the discount rate is 8 percent. Calculate the payback and discounted payback periods for the projects. Which one will you consider?

50. Using initial cost of I_0, and annual cash inflows of R over N period, express R in terms of I_0 and N such that the payback period is equal to its life.

51. Using NPV, should you invest in a project where the initial cash outflow is $25,000 and the cash inflow in the first year is $2,000 and "grows" at a rate of 2 percent thereafter? Assume cost of capital is 10 percent.

52. A bond is currently trading at par, which is $1,000. If the bond pays an annual coupon rate of 10 percent, calculate the IRR of this bond.

53. What are independent projects? What are mutually exclusive projects?

54. For each pair of investment opportunities, indicate if they are more likely to be mutually exclusive or independent projects. Explain your choices.
    a. Cruise line:
        i. Build a cruise ship to carry 10,000 passengers
        ii. Build two ships each carrying 5,000 passengers

    b. Mining company in northern Alberta:
       i. Use old open pit mine for waste disposal
       ii. Use old open pit mine for fishing and hunting lodge
    c. University:
       i. Use classroom for tutorials
       ii. Use classroom for faculty meetings
    d. You:
       i. Latte
       ii. Cappuccino
    e. You:
       i. Salad
       ii. Steak

55. MedCo, a large manufacturing company, currently uses a large printing press in its operations and is considering two replacements: the PDX341 and PDW581. The PDX costs $500,000 and has annual maintenance costs of $10,000 for the first 5 years and $15,000 for the next 10 years. After 15 years, the PDX will be scrapped (salvage value is zero). In contrast, the PDW can be acquired for $50,000 and requires maintenance of $30,000 a year for its 10-year life. The salvage value of the PDW is expected to be zero in 10 years. Assuming that MedCo must replace its current printing press (it has stopped functioning), it has a 10-percent cost of capital, and all cash flows are after tax, which replacement press is the most appropriate?

56. GiS Inc. now has the following two projects available:

Project	Initial CF	After-tax CF$_1$	After-tax CF$_2$	After-tax CF$_3$
1	−12,095	5,500	6,000	9,500
2	−3,080	3,450	3,000	

Assume that $R_F = 5\%$, risk premium = 10%, and beta = 1.2. Use the chain replication approach to determine which project(s) GiS Inc. should choose if they are mutually exclusive.

57. Solve Practice Problem 56 using EANPV and assuming the market risk premium is 10 percent.

58. A firm is considering two mutually exclusive projects, as follows. Determine which project should be accepted if the discount rate is 15 percent. Use the chain replication approach. Assume both projects can be replicated.

Project	Initial CF	After-tax CF$_1$	After-tax CF$_2$	After-tax CF$_3$
1	−5,000	2,500	4,050	0
2	−3,000	750	1,750	2,000

59. Redo Practice Problem 58 using the EANPV approach.

60. Assume that SK Inc. has a capital budget of $200,000. In addition, it has the following projects for evaluation. Determine which project(s) should be chosen, assuming k is 13 percent.

Project	Initial CF	CF$_1$	CF$_2$	CF$_3$
1	−100,000	80,000	80,000	0
2	−75,000	50,000	60,000	70,000
3	−120,000	55,000	100,000	80,000

61. Briefly explain the pure-play method for estimating beta.

62. LargeCo has a capital budget of $100 million to invest in projects. It has evaluated six independent projects and the results of the analysis are summarized in the following table.

Project	Initial investment	NPV	Salvage value
A	$10 million	$5 million	$3 million
B	$90 million	$15 million	$5 million
C	$25 million	$8 million	$2 million
D	$40 million	$7 million	$1 million
E	$25 million	$3 million	$5 million
F	$15 million	$2 million	$8 million

a. If the company was not capital constrained, which projects should it undertake?

b. Given its capital constraint, which projects do you recommend that it undertake?

c. How can the firm increase its capital budget?

63. What are the practical difficulties when attempting to apply the NPV evaluation process to foreign investments?

64. Project X has a cost of capital of 8 percent and the following cash flows: investment of $10,000 in year 0, cash inflows of $5,000, $ 3,000, and $4,000 in years 1, 2, and 3.

a. What is the IRR? What is the assumption of IRR on reinvesting cash?

b. Suppose the cash is deposited in an account with a 2% annual interest rate. What is the MIRR?

c. Suppose the cash is deposited in an account with a 8% annual interest rate. What is the MIRR?

d. Suppose the cash is deposited in an account with a 10.179% annual interest rate. What is the MIRR?

14 | Cash Flow Estimation and Capital Budgeting Decisions

LEARNING OBJECTIVES

14.1 Outline the basic framework for capital expenditure analysis.

14.2 Estimate the future cash flows associated with potential investments.

14.3 Conduct a sensitivity analysis to see how the value changes as key inputs vary, and determine what is a real option.

14.4 Explain how to make replacement decisions, and explain what is special about them.

14.5 Explain how mistakes can easily be made when dealing with inflation.

Alcoa Inc. released the following press release on January 5, 2012:

> NEW YORK—Alcoa (NYSE: AA) announced today that it intends to close or curtail approximately 531,000 metric tons, or 12 percent of its global smelting capacity, to lower the Company's position on the global aluminum cost curve and improve Alcoa's competitiveness.
>
> The Company will permanently close its smelter in Alcoa, Tennessee, which was curtailed in 2009, along with two of the six idled potlines at its Rockdale, Texas smelter. Together, these closures will reduce Alcoa's global smelting capacity of 4.5 million metric tons per year by 291,000 metric tons, or about 7 percent.
>
> "These are difficult but necessary steps to improve Alcoa's competitiveness, preserve and grow shareholder value and protect jobs in the rest of the Alcoa system," said Alcoa Chairman and CEO Klaus Kleinfeld.
>
> Aluminum prices have fallen more than 27 percent from their peak in 2011. In addition to the curtailments, the Company will accelerate actions to reduce the escalating cost of raw materials.

Alcoa's actions were taken in response to a reduction in the future cash flow estimates associated with these investments, which have become less (un)attractive due to projected lower selling prices and higher production costs.

Source: Alcoa Inc. press release, January 5, 2012. Available at http://www.alcoa.com/global/en/news.

CHAPTER 14 **PREVIEW**

hapter 13 illustrated the capital budgeting process and discussed the most important approaches used to evaluate investment opportunities. However, the inputs to the analysis were largely specified for you. As the Chapter 14 opening vignette illustrates, these inputs, such as the size of estimated future cash flows are critical. This chapter is hands-on, and you'll have many opportunities to practise your skills and estimate inputs yourself.

14.1 GENERAL GUIDELINES FOR CAPITAL EXPENDITURE ANALYSIS

Learning Objective 14.1
Outline the basic framework for capital expenditure analysis.

In Chapter 13, we discussed several capital budgeting evaluation criteria (i.e., NPV, IRR, profitability index, payback period, and discounted payback period). All of these methods require an estimate of the present cash outlay, as well as estimates of the future cash flows associated with the investment opportunity. In this chapter, we discuss how to estimate these important inputs into those evaluation procedures. We will need to draw on our discussions in chapters 3 and 4 regarding the firm's financial statements, as well as our knowledge of the capital cost allowance (CCA) system in Canada.

We begin by providing some general guidelines for estimating the cash flows associated with capital expenditure decisions:

1. Estimate all cash flows on an *after-tax* basis, because taxes can play an important role in any investment decision and because we use an after-tax cost of capital to discount these cash flows. As we will show, there are many ways to approach capital budgeting, but one of the most important principles is to compare like with like, which is why we use after-tax cash flows with an after-tax discount rate.

marginal or **incremental cash flows**
the additional cash flows that result from capital budgeting decisions, generated by new projects

2. Use the appropriate cash flow estimates that represent the **marginal** or **incremental cash flows** arising from capital budgeting decisions, including the changes in existing flows that result from the firm's decisions. For example, suppose a firm is considering introducing a new product line that will generate $100,000 per year in additional after-tax cash flows. However, the introduction of this new product line will "cost" the firm $40,000 in after-tax cash flows as a result of lost sales for an existing product. This is called "cannibalization," and the marginal cash flows that should be used in evaluating the new product line are $60,000 per year (i.e., $100,000 – $40,000).

3. Do *not* include associated interest and dividend payments in estimated project cash flows; they should already be accounted for in the discount rate (i.e., the appropriate cost of capital). This is why we discount with the weighted average cost of capital (WACC), which captures all the financing costs in the discount rate. The WACC is discussed in detail in Chapter 20.

4. Adjust cash flows (particularly the initial cash outlay and the terminal cash flow at the end of the estimated project life) to reflect any additional working capital requirements that are associated with the project. For example, consider a firm that is evaluating a new production process. The process requires the firm to hold additional inventory on hand, which would tie up more funds and would be reflected in the firm's level of working capital (as defined in Chapter 3). This represents a drain of cash that should be considered in the capital budgeting decision, because any funds that are tied up have an associated cost. Of course, a firm could also be considering a process that requires it to hold lower amounts of inventory on hand, which would represent a source of funds for the firm. This should also be considered when evaluating the implementation of that process.

5. Treat **sunk costs** as irrelevant; we are concerned with future cash flows. Suppose a firm has spent $50,000 to get a project up and running. If something happens to make the project undesirable, the firm should not proceed any further; otherwise, it will simply be "throwing good money after bad." In other words, it should accept the $50,000 loss, which makes more sense than losing another $100,000 on the project. Obviously, this is easier said than done.

> **sunk costs** costs that have already been incurred, cannot be recovered, and should not influence current capital budgeting decisions

6. Although sunk costs are irrelevant, **opportunity costs** should be factored into cash flow estimates. Opportunity costs represent cash flows that must be forgone as the result of an investment decision. The following example shows the difference between sunk costs and opportunity costs. Consider a firm that purchased a piece of land several years ago for $150,000. Today, the firm is considering whether or not to use the land as the location for a new storage facility. In this situation, the original outlay of $150,000 is a sunk cost and should be ignored. However, the land cannot be considered "free," because the firm always has the option of using it for another purpose or selling it. Assuming the firm could sell this land today at a market price of $200,000, this would represent the opportunity cost of using the land for the storage facility; as such, it should be included in the cost of the project.

> **opportunity costs** cash flows that must be forgone as the result of an investment decision

7. Determine the appropriate time horizon for the project. We need to know how long a project is likely to continue before it is economical to finish or replace it. In this sense, "abandonment decisions" have to be considered, because projects are finished when it is economical to do so, not when the engineer says the assets are no longer functioning.

8. Ignore intangible considerations that cannot be measured in the financial analysis, unless their impact on cash flows can be estimated. Often, intangible benefits are used to justify poor projects. If there are spinoffs, they should be analyzed and incorporated into the analysis, however difficult it is to do so.

9. Ignore **externalities** in the calculations. Externalities are the consequences that often result from an investment that may benefit or harm unrelated third parties. As with intangible factors, although we do not account for these effects in the financial analysis, they could have a huge impact on the final investment decision.[1] An example is a project that generates employment in a depressed region: it is the government's job to assess the value of these externalities, not the firm's.

> **externalities** the consequences that result from an investment that may benefit or harm unrelated third parties

10. Consider the effect of all project interdependencies on cash flow estimates. This issue was discussed in Chapter 13 in connection with mutually exclusive projects and contingent projects. Undertaking a project now could mean a negative NPV in the short term but might give the firm the option to do other things in the future that may generate value.

11. Treat inflation consistently. This harks back to comparing like with like: discount nominal cash flows with nominal discount rates, and real cash flows with real discount rates.

12. Undertake all social investments required by law. This may be obvious, but many social and infrastructure projects must be undertaken even though they have negative rates of return or no definable impact on the value of the firm.

CONCEPT REVIEW QUESTIONS

1. How should we treat taxes and inflation when determining the present value of future cash flows?

2. What do we mean by incremental cash flows?

3. What are externalities and opportunity costs?

4. Why do we not deduct interest costs from the cash flows to be discounted?

---

[1] This is important to recognize, as we are not suggesting these be ignored. In many cases they could be the deciding factor. We are merely saying that we ignore them for "financial" analysis, which will be one part of the overall investment decision.

14.2 ESTIMATING AND DISCOUNTING CASH FLOWS

Learning Objective 14.2
Estimate the future cash flows associated with potential investments.

Sometimes it is convenient to distinguish among three different categories of cash flows—initial after-tax cash flow, expected annual after-tax cash flow, and ending (or terminal) after-tax cash flow—and estimate each type separately. Each category of cash flow is discussed below.

The Initial After-Tax Cash Flow (CF_0)

initial after-tax cash flow (CF_0) the total cash outlay required to initiate an investment project, including the change in net working capital and associated opportunity costs

capital cost (C_0) all costs incurred to make an investment operational, such as machinery installation expenses, land-clearing costs, and so on; these can be depreciated for tax purposes

The **initial after-tax cash flow (CF_0)** refers to the total cash outlay that is required to initiate an investment project.[2] It includes additional cash flows, such as the change in net working capital (NWC) and associated opportunity costs, both of which were discussed in the previous section. These items may affect the firm's cash flow, but they cannot be expensed for tax purposes. CF_0 differs from the **capital cost (C_0)** of an investment, which includes all costs incurred to make an investment operational, such as machinery installation expenses, land-clearing costs, and so on. These can be depreciated for tax purposes. The CF_0 can generally be estimated using Equation 14-1.

[14-1]
$$CF_0 = C_0 + \Delta NWC_0 + OC$$

where C_0 = the initial capital cost of the asset
ΔNWC_0 = the change in net working capital requirements (as discussed in the previous section)
OC = the opportunity costs associated with the project (as discussed in the previous section)

Example 14-1 illustrates how to estimate the CF_0.

EXAMPLE 14-1 | Calculating CF_0

Brennan Co. is evaluating the proposed acquisition of a new milling machine. The machine's base price is $625,000, and it would cost another $25,000 to modify it for special use by the firm. To use the machine, the firm will need to maintain additional raw materials inventory of $100,000. Estimate the firm's associated after-tax cash outlay.

Solution

Capital cost = C_0 = $625,000 + $25,000 = $650,000

Initial cash outlay = CF_0 = $C_0 + \Delta NWC_0 + OC$ = $650,000 + $100,000 + $0 = $750,000

Note that, in Example 14-1, the cost of the capital asset is not just the $625,000 purchase price but also all other cash outlays that are needed to get the equipment operational. In this case, the $25,000 in modifications have to be capitalized and then depreciated over the life of the machine because, just like the equipment itself, they generate benefits over the life of the equipment. Generally, in any analysis, costs have to be divided into capitalized costs and expenses. The Canada Revenue Agency (CRA) requires anything that generates future benefits to be capitalized; the value is then expensed through depreciation over future periods. In contrast, costs that generate no future benefits can be expensed immediately and are immediately tax deductible.

---

[2] In fact, this could involve a cash *inflow* rather than an outlay for some projects. For example, if a firm is considering selling a division, it will get the cash today (so CF_0 will be negative) and will forgo the future cash flows (CF_t) associated with that division, which will be recognized as *negative* cash flows for capital budgeting decision-making purposes. This is the type of analysis Alcoa would have undertaken before it decided to sell off some existing assets and/or cancel future investments it had planned.

Expected Annual After-Tax Cash Flows (CF$_t$)

The **expected annual after-tax cash flows (CF$_t$)** are those that are estimated to occur as a result of the investment decision. These cash flows comprise the associated expected incremental increase in after-tax operating income (i.e., the operating CFs), as well as any incremental tax savings (or additional taxes paid) that result from the initial investment outlay. The tax savings are associated with the additional depreciation expenses that may be charged for tax purposes as a result of the initial investment. Recall from our discussion in Chapter 3 that the amount of depreciation charged for tax purposes is called the capital cost allowance (CCA) and is prescribed by CRA according to the asset class associated with the cash outlay. Some of the more common asset classes are listed in Table 14-1.

expected annual after-tax cash flows (CF$_t$) the cash flows that are estimated to occur as a result of the investment decision, comprising the associated expected incremental increase in after-tax operating income and any incremental tax savings (or additional taxes paid) that result from the initial investment outlay

TABLE 14-1 Common Asset Classes Established by Canada Revenue Agency

Asset Class	Type of Assets	CCA Rate
Class 1	Buildings	4%
Class 8	Office equipment	20%
Class 30	Automobiles, system software, etc.	30%
Class 43	Manufacturing equipment	30%
Class 45	Computers	45%

Because CCA is a non-cash expense, and we are trying to estimate cash flows, we have two ways to deal with it. The first approach is to deduct CCA from operating income, then deduct the associated taxes payable, and finally add the amount of the CCA expense back (because it is a non-cash expense). The second approach is to recognize that CCA creates tax savings for the firm in the amount of the CCA expense multiplied by the company's effective tax rate (T), which is then added to the after-tax operating income, determined by deducting the taxes associated with the firm's before-tax operating income (before depreciation). These two approaches are shown in Table 14-2 and illustrated in Example 14-2.

TABLE 14-2 Two Ways to Determine Cash Flows after Capital Cost Allowance

(1) Before-tax operating income (before depreciation)	(2) Before-tax operating income (before depreciation)
− CCA	− Taxes payable on operating income
= Taxable income	= After-tax operating income
− Taxes payable	+ CCA tax savings
= After-tax income	= Net cash flow
+ CCA (non-cash expense)	
= Net cash flow	

EXAMPLE 14-2 Calculating Future Annual CF$_t$

With respect to the milling machine purchase that Brennan Co. was considering in Example 14-1, the firm's production department anticipates the machine will generate an additional $450,000 per year in annual operating revenue, while the associated annual operating expenses are projected to be $325,000 per year. The economic life of the machine is expected to be five years. This milling machine is in asset class 9, which has a CCA rate of 30 percent (declining balance method). Estimate the amount of the annual after-tax cash flow for each year, using both approaches described above.

Solution

For all five years, operating income = operating revenue − operating expense = $450,000 − $325,000 = $125,000

continued

EXAMPLE 14 -2   *Calculating Future Annual CF$_t$ continued*

Recall from Chapter 3 that the half-year rule applies in the first year an asset is acquired, which means that only half of the CCA rate is applied in year 1. Therefore, we can estimate CCA in year 1 as:

CCA (year 1) = (C$_0$) × (CCA rate) × (1/2) = ($650,000) × (0.3) × (1/2) = $97,500

Because the full CCA rate is applied to the undepreciated capital cost (UCC) of the asset in all years subsequent to the first year, we can estimate the CCA expense in years 2 through 5 as follows:

UCC (beginning of year 2) = UCC (beginning of year 1) − CCA (year 1) = $650,000 − $97,500 = $552,500

CCA (year 2) = (UCC) × (CCA rate) = ($552,500) × (0.3) = $165,750

UCC (beginning of year 3) = UCC (beginning of year 2) − CCA (year 2) = $552,500 − $165,750 = $386,750

CCA (year 3) = (UCC) × (CCA rate) = ($386,750) × (0.3) = $116,025

UCC (beginning of year 4) = UCC (beginning of year 3) − CCA (year 3) = $386,750 − $116,025 = $270,725

CCA (year 4) = (UCC) × (CCA rate) = ($270,725) × (0.3) = $81,218

UCC (beginning of year 5) = UCC (beginning of year 4) − CCA (year 4) = $270,725 − $81,218 = $189,507

CCA (year 5) = (UCC) × (CCA rate) = ($189,507) × (0.3) = $56,852

UCC (end of year 5) = $189,507 − $56,852 = $132,655

Combining these estimates with the firm's tax rate of 45 percent, we can estimate CF$_t$s as follows:

Approach 1

	Year 1	Year 2	Year 3	Year 4	Year 5
Operating income	$ 125,000	$ 125,000	$ 125,000	$ 125,000	$ 125,000
− CCA expense	−97,500	−165,750	−116,025	−81,218	−56,852
Taxable income	27,500	(40,750)	8,975	43,782	68,148
− Taxes payable (@45%)	−12,375	+18,338*	−4,039	−19,702	−30,667
After-tax income	15,125	(22,412)	4,936	24,080	37,481
+ CCA expense	+97,500	+165,750	+116,025	+81,218	+56,852
Net cash flow	$ 112,625	$ 143,338	$ 120,961	$ 105,298	$ 94,333

Approach 2

	Year 1	Year 2	Year 3	Year 4	Year 5
Operating income	$ 125,000	$ 125,000	$ 125,000	$ 125,000	$ 125,000
− Taxes payable on operating income (@45%)	−56,250	−56,250	−56,250	−56,250	−56,250
After-tax operating income	68,750	68,750	68,750	68,750	68,750
+ CCA tax savings (CCA × T)	+43,875	+74,588	+52,211	+36,548	+25,583
Net cash flow	$ 112,625	$143,338	$ 120,961	$ 105,298	$ 94,333

* In year 2, we assume that the firm can refile the previous year's tax return and get a tax refund, so CRA sends the firm a cheque for $18,338. Alternatively, the assumption is that the firm has other taxable income that it can then shield from tax.

Notice the following points from Example 14-2:

1. Both approaches give the same result. Because it is relatively easy to calculate the amount of the associated CCA tax savings, we will use approach 2. This decision is important be-

cause the use of declining-balance CCA means that the tax deductions last forever and the asset is never fully depreciated. This makes it difficult to put all the cash flows into a spreadsheet unless we make some assumptions about the end of the project's life. As a result, we can estimate the annual operating cash flows by using Equation 14-2.

$$CF_t = CFBT_t(1 - T) + CCA_t(T)$$ [14-2]

where $CFBT_t$ = cash flow before taxes (i.e., incremental pre-tax operating income)

CCA_t = the CCA expense for year t

T = the firm's marginal (or effective) tax rate

2. CCA expense is lower in year 1 because of the half-year rule, is highest in year 2, declines in year 3, and declines every year thereafter as the UCC continually declines.

3. After-tax operating income is the same for each of the five years in Example 14-2, and we could view these cash flows as an annuity. This becomes particularly important because there is a formula that determines the present value of the CCA tax shield associated with capital investments, which we will introduce shortly.

EXAMPLE 14-3   Estimating the PV of Future CF_t

Determine the present value of the cash flows from years 1 to 5, assuming the firm's cost of capital is 12 percent.

Solution[3]

$$PV \text{ (Future } CF_t) = \frac{\$112,625}{(1.12)^1} + \frac{\$143,338}{(1.12)^2} + \frac{\$120,961}{(1.12)^3} + \frac{\$105,298}{(1.12)^4} + \frac{\$94,333}{(1.12)^5}$$

$$= \$100,558 + \$114,268 + \$86,098 + \$66,919 + \$53,527 = \$421,370$$

Examples 14-2 and 14-3 deal with future cash flows in which the CCA tax savings cash flows are determined without considering what happens to the machine at the end of its useful economic life. As discussed in Chapter 3, if this asset is sold at that time, its price may affect the CCA expense (and cash flow) in the terminal year of the project. Before proceeding to this issue, however, we will first deal with the issue of the ending (or terminal) cash flow.

Ending (or Terminal) After-Tax Cash Flow (ECF_n)

The **ending (or terminal) after-tax cash flow (ECF_n)** is the total cash flow that is expected to be generated in the terminal year of a project, aside from that year's expected after-tax cash flow, as determined above. It comprises the estimated selling or **salvage value (SV_n)** of the asset.

As discussed in Chapter 3, this selling price can have tax consequences. First, if the selling price is greater than the original capital cost, a capital gain arises, which is taxable. The converse is not true: depreciable capital assets do not generate tax-deductible capital losses when they are sold below their original purchase price, because this lower price is expected (i.e., because they are depreciable assets, they are expected to depreciate in value below their original cost).

Aside from capital gains, additional tax consequences can arise. In particular, CCA recapture or terminal losses may be generated by the sale of an asset (or assets) if the CCA asset class

ending (or terminal) after-tax cash flow (ECF$_n$) the total cash flow that is expected to be generated in the terminal year of a project, aside from that year's expected after-tax cash flow; the estimated salvage value of the asset

salvage value (SV$_n$) the estimated sale price of an asset at the end of its useful life

---

[3] Note that the CCA tax savings are as risky as the firm's pre-tax income. Without any pre-tax income, the CCA tax shields are worthless, and CRA places restrictions on the transfer of CCA tax shields within different types of firms. For this reason, they are discounted at the firm's WACC. In the United States, where it is easier to file consolidated tax returns and transfer depreciation tax shields between firms, the tax shields are often discounted at the firm's borrowing cost. In practice, this adjustment usually makes little difference in the final DCF analysis.

is terminated by selling the asset. This would occur only if no other assets were included in that asset class for the firm. Under this scenario, the firm would have to pay additional taxes on "excess" CCA charged against the asset (or assets) if the salvage value is greater than the ending UCC for the asset (or asset class). The amount by which the salvage value exceeds the UCC is referred to as "CCA recapture" and is fully taxable.[4] However, if the salvage value is less than the ending UCC, the amount by which the UCC exceeds the salvage value is called a terminal loss and is fully tax deductible.[5] Finally, CCA recapture may occur even if an asset class is not closed, if an asset (or assets) is sold for a price that exceeds the remaining UCC for that asset class.

In addition to the salvage value and all the associated tax implications, the working capital that was associated with the project will be recaptured at the end of the project, which represents a cash inflow. This means that the people to whom you have extended credit will pay off the debts once the project is finished, and all inventory on hand will be sold, so that the net amount after the firm has paid its suppliers is available to finance other projects.

We can estimate the ending cash flow with tax implications by using Equation 14-3. The second-last term of the equation is included only if a capital gain arises, and the last term is included only if a terminal loss or CCA recapture occurs.[6]

[14-3]
$$ECF \text{ (with tax implications)}_n = SV_n + \Delta NWC_n - [(SV_n - C_0) \times T] - [(SV_n - UCC_n) \times T]$$

where ECF(with tax implications)$_n$ = ending cash flow in year n (i.e., at the end of the project life)

SV$_n$ = the estimated salvage value in year n for the asset purchased

ΔNWC_n = the net working capital "released" upon termination of the project

C$_0$ = the original capital cost of the asset

UCC$_n$ = the asset (or asset class) ending UCC balance

T = the firm's effective tax rate

Generally, capital gains are rare for depreciable capital assets since the market price of machinery, equipment, etc., tends to go down and not up due to normal wear and tear, as well as obsolescence. CCA recapture is also rare because most large firms will have several assets in a given CCA pool, and the pool will remain open after the asset is sold. As a result, the asset cost and UCC will usually be greater than the salvage value of any particular asset, so capital gains, terminal losses, and CCA recapture will not happen. In such situations, we can estimate the ending cash flow using Equation 14-4, which eliminates the last two terms of Equation 14-3.

[14-4]
$$ECF_n = SV_n + \Delta NWC_n$$

EXAMPLE 14-4   Calculating ECF$_n$

Regarding the project being considered by Brennan Co. in examples 14-1, 14-2, and 14-3, the production department estimated that the $100,000 in additional net working capital requirements will be released at the end of the economic life of the machine. Management estimates that at the end of five years, the milling machine can be sold for $132,655. Assume the asset class remains open after the milling machine is sold. Determine the ending cash flow and the present value of this ending cash flow.

continued

---

[4] In other words, it is viewed as if the firm charged too much CCA (depreciation), because the asset is sold for more than its depreciated book value for tax purposes (UCC). Therefore, the firm must pay back the amount of tax it saved by charging too much CCA.
[5] In other words, the firm did not charge enough CCA, because the asset was sold below its book value for tax purposes (UCC). Therefore, it is permitted to depreciate the asset to its selling price and deduct this charge for tax purposes.
[6] Notice that the last term "self-adjusts" for terminal losses or CCA recapture, because it will be negative if CCA recapture occurs (i.e., because SV$_n$ is greater than UCC$_n$) and it will be positive if a terminal loss occurs (i.e., because SV$_n$ is less than UCC$_n$).

EXAMPLE 14-4   Calculating ECF$_n$ continued

Solution

Notice in this example that no capital gains arise because SV$_n$ is less than C$_0$. Because the asset class is left open, a terminal loss is not possible. Because SV$_n$ equals UCC$_n$, there is no CCA recapture—we do not need to check against the UCC for the entire class. Therefore, we can use Equation 14-4, as follows:

$$ECF_n = SV_n + \Delta NWC_n = \$132{,}655 + \$100{,}000 = \$232{,}655$$

$$PV(ECF_n) = \frac{\$232{,}655}{(1.12)^5} = \$132{,}015$$

Putting It All Together

Recall from Chapter 13 that the NPV of an investment equals the present value of the future cash flows minus the initial cash outlay. This was expressed in Equation 13-1, which is replicated below:

$$NPV = \sum_{t=1}^{n} \frac{CF_t}{(1+k)_t} - CF_0 = PV(\text{Future CFs}) - CF_0$$

If we decompose the future CF$_t$ in the equation above into annual CFs and the ending cash flow, as discussed above, we obtain Equation 14-5.

$$NPV = PV(\text{Annual CFs}) + PV(ECF_n) - CF_0 \qquad [14\text{-}5]$$

Referring to examples 14-1 through 14-4, we can use Equation 14-5 along with the values we calculated to find the NPV of this project for Brennan Co. We do this in Example 14-5.

EXAMPLE 14-5   Estimating the NPV

Determine the NPV of the project being considered by Brennan Co., using the information in the solutions to examples 14-1 through 14-4. Should Brennan Co. accept or reject this project?

Solution

$$NPV = PV(\text{Operating CFs}) + PV(ECF_n) - CF_0$$

$$= \$421{,}370 + \$132{,}015 - \$750{,}000 = -\$196{,}615$$

Therefore, Brennan Co. should reject the project.

Valuation by Components

Evaluating the project that was considered in examples 14-1 through 14-5 was relatively straightforward. However, it would take much longer to find the NPV if it were a 20-year project, because we would have to calculate cash flows for each year and then discount them back individually. Obviously, the use of a spreadsheet program, such as Excel, is one way to make the calculations. However, if using Excel is not an option, we can use formulas to simplify the calculations by separating the problem into its different components.

Whenever operating cash flows are assumed to be the same every year, as in Example 14-5, we can view these cash flows as an annuity and find their present value using the present value of an annuity formula, which was introduced in Chapter 5. This assumption is reasonable for most replacement decisions in which the cash savings are assumed to be the same each year. The example is depicted in Equation 14-6.

[14-6]
$$PV(\text{Operating Cash Flows}) = CFBT(1-T) \times \left[\frac{1 - \frac{1}{(1+k)^n}}{k} \right]$$

In addition to the annuity formula for the operating cash flows, we can also separately determine the present value of the tax shield created by the CCA expenses for the investment. The first equation can be used in most circumstances, because it applies when there is no CCA recapture or terminal loss. This situation occurs whenever an asset class is left open or when the salvage value is less than the UCC for an entire class, which is generally what happens for long-term capital expenditures.

[14-7]
$$PV(\text{CCA Tax Shield}) = \frac{(C_0)(d)(T)}{d+k} \times \frac{(1+0.5k)}{(1+k)} - \frac{(SV_n)(d)(T)}{(d+k)} \times \frac{1}{(1+k)^n}$$

where d = the applicable CCA rate

The first part of the first term of Equation 14-7 $\left[\frac{(C_0)(d)(T)}{d+k} \right]$ is a variation of the dividend discount model (DDM), which was introduced in Chapter 7 as a method of finding the present value of a growing perpetuity (of dividends). However, in this situation, the starting cash flow in the numerator is the tax savings generated by the CCA expense, $[(C_0)(d)(T)]$, instead of D_1 as it is in the DDM. The denominator, $(d+k)$, is a variation of $k - g$ in the DDM, where d is positive to reflect the fact that the amount of CCA charged actually declines (or displays negative growth) every year.[7] The second part of the first term in the equation reflects the impact of the half-year rule on the CCA tax savings in the first year. This first term, therefore, estimates the present value of CCA tax savings if the asset were held indefinitely. The second term in Equation 14-7 reflects the fact that the CCA tax savings do not, in fact, go on perpetually, because the asset is assumed to be sold at some estimated salvage value at the end of the project's estimated useful life. Therefore, we subtract the present value of this part of the CCA tax savings that the firm will not realize, because this portion would be generated only if the asset were held indefinitely.

Equation 14-7 applies when there are no terminal losses or CCA recapture. Whenever an asset class is terminated, the possibility exists that one of these items will arise. In those cases, we need to use Equation 14-8 to estimate the present value of CCA tax savings. Equation 14-8 would also apply if an asset class were left open and CCA recapture occurred, except that we would replace the UCC for the asset in question with the UCC for the entire asset class.

[14-8]
$$PV(\text{CCA Tax Shield}) = \frac{(C_0)(d)(T)}{d+k} \times \frac{(1+0.5k)}{(1+k)} - \frac{(UCC_n)(d)(T)}{(d+k)} \times \frac{1}{(1+k)^n} - \frac{(SV_n - UCC_n)(T)}{(1+k)^n}$$

The last term in this equation reflects the present value of the cash flow impact of any terminal loss or CCA recapture that arises. Notice that it will be negative when CCA recapture occurs (i.e., when SV_n is greater than UCC_n), and it will be positive if a terminal loss occurs (i.e., when SV_n is less than UCC_n).

Finally, whenever capital gains occur, we must also estimate the present value of the cash flow implications arising from the taxable capital gain. We can do so by using Equation 14-9, which estimates the present value of the capital gain multiplied by the firm's tax rate and is based on the assumption that the firm pays taxes at the full marginal rate on its taxable gains, which may or may not always be the case.[8]

---

[7] In other words, it is the same as $k - g$, except that g is negative.

[8] If the firm faces a different tax rate for capital gains (T_{CG}), we can simply substitute this rate for T in the equation.

$$PV\,(Capital\ Gains\ Taxes\ Paid\,) = \frac{(SV_n - C_0)(T)}{(1+k)^n}$$ [14-9]

We have already accounted for the tax implications at the end of the project, so we must therefore estimate the present value of the ending cash flow by using ECF_n, as defined in Equation 14-4. Combining all this information, we can express the NPV equation as follows:

$$NPV = PV(Operating\ CFs) + PV(CCA\ Tax\ Shield) + PV(ECF_n) - PV\,(Capital\ Gains\ Taxes\ Paid) - CF_0$$ [14-10]

In this equation, the PV(Operating CFs) term can be estimated using Equation 14-6 if the operating cash flows are expected to be the same every year. The PV(CCA tax shield) can be estimated using equation 14-7 or 14-8, depending on whether or not terminal losses or CCA recapture arise, while the PV(Capital Gains Taxes Paid) term applies only if a capital gain arises. It can be estimated using Equation 14-9.

EXAMPLE 14-6	Finding the NPV Using the Valuation by Components Approach I

Use equations 14-6 through 14-10 (as applicable) to estimate the NPV of the Brennan Co. project that was solved using the longer approach in examples 14-1 through 14-5.

Solution

$CF_0 = \$750,000$

$$PV\,(Operating\ Cash\ Flows) = CFBT\,(1-T) \times \left[\frac{1 - \dfrac{1}{(1+k)^n}}{k}\right]$$

$$= [\,\$125,000(1 - 0.45)\,] \times \left[\frac{1 - \dfrac{1}{(1.12)^5}}{0.12}\right]$$

$$= (\$68,750) \times (3.604776) = \$247,828$$

Because there is no terminal loss or CCA recapture associated with the termination of this project, we use Equation 14-7 to estimate the present value of the CCA tax shield:

$$PV\,(CCA\ Tax\ Shield\,) = \frac{(C_0)(d)(T)}{d+k} \times \frac{(1+0.5k)}{(1+k)} - \frac{(SV_n)(d)(T)}{(d+k)} \times \frac{1}{(1+k)^n}$$

$$= \frac{(\$650,000)(0.30)(0.45)}{0.30+0.12} \times \frac{(1+0.5 \times 0.12)}{1+0.12} - \frac{(\$132,655)(0.30)(0.45)}{0.30+0.12} \times \frac{1}{(1.12)^5}$$

$$= \$197,736 - \$24,195 = \$173,541$$

$$PV\,(ECF) = \frac{\$232,655}{(1.12)^5} = \$132,015 \text{ (as calculated in Example 14-4)}$$

There are no capital gains, so this term is zero.
Now we can put these items together to determine the NPV of the project.

$$NPV = PV\,(Operating\ CFs) + PV\,(CCA\ Tax\ Shield) + PV\,(ECF_n) - PV\,(Capital\ Gains\ Taxes\ Paid) - CF_0$$

$$= \$247,828 + \$173,541 + \$132,015 - \$0 - \$750,000 = -\$196,616$$

This is the same answer we obtained when we solved the problem in examples 14-1 through 14-5. (The $1 difference is due to rounding.)

EXAMPLE 14-7	Finding the NPV Using the Valuation by Components Approach II

Redo Example 14-6, assuming that the asset class is now closed upon termination of the project and that the salvage value is

a. $100,000

b. $200,000

Solution

Notice that changing the salvage value affects only the PV(CCA tax savings) and the PV (ECF_n) terms; therefore, we do not need to re-estimate the other terms.

$CF_0 = \$750,000$

PV(Operating Cash Flows) = $247,828

Because there are no capital gains, that term is still zero.

In this example, because the asset class is closed at the termination of the project, we must use Equation 14-8, which accounts for a terminal loss or CCA recapture, to estimate the present value of the CCA tax shield.

a. $ECF_n = \$100,000 + \$100,000 = \$200,00$

$$PV\text{ (CCA Tax Shield)} = \frac{(C_0)(d)(T)}{d+k} \times \frac{(1+0.5k)}{(1+k)} - \frac{(UCC_n)(d)(T)}{(d+k)} \times \frac{1}{(1+k)^n} - \frac{(SV_n - UCC_n)(T)}{(1+k)^n}$$

$$= \frac{(\$650,000)(0.30)(0.45)}{0.30+0.12} \times \frac{(1.06)}{(1.12)} - \frac{(\$132,655)(0.30)(0.45)}{0.30+0.12} \times \frac{1}{(1.12)^5} - \frac{(\$100,000 - \$132,655)(0.45)}{(1.12)^5}$$

$$= \$197,736 - \$24,195 + \$8,338 = \$181,879$$

$$PV\text{ } (ECF_n) = \frac{\$200,000}{(1.12)^5} = \$113,485$$

So,

NPV = PV (Operating CFs) + PV (CCA Tax Shield) + PV (ECF_n) – PV (Capital Gains Taxes Paid) – CF_0

$$= \$247,828 + \$181,879 + \$113,485 - \$0 - \$750,000 = -\$206,808$$

The project is even less attractive because of the lower salvage value, despite the increase in the CCA tax shield through the terminal loss of $32,655 (i.e., $132,655 UCC – $100,000 salvage value).

b. $ECF_n = \$200,000 + \$100,000 = \$300,000$

$$PV\text{ (CCA Tax Shield)} = \frac{(C_0)(d)(T)}{d+k} \times \frac{(1+0.5k)}{(1+k)} - \frac{(UCC_n)(d)(T)}{(d+k)} \times \frac{1}{(1+k)^n} - \frac{(SV_n - UCC_n)(T)}{(1+k)^n}$$

continued

EXAMPLE 14-7 Finding the NPV Using the Valuation by Compnents Approach II *continued*

$$= \frac{(\$650,000)(0.30)(0.45)}{0.30 + 0.12} \times \frac{(1.06)}{(1.12)} - \frac{(\$132,655)(0.30)(0.45)}{0.30 + 0.12} \times \frac{1}{(1.12)^5} - \frac{(\$200,000 - \$132,655)(0.45)}{(1.12)^5}$$

$$= \$197,736 - \$24,195 - \$17,196 = \$156,345$$

$$PV\ (ECF_n) = \frac{\$300,000}{(1.12)^5} = \$170,228$$

So,

NPV = PV (Operating CFs) + PV (CCA Tax Shield) + PV (ECF$_n$) − PV (Capital Gains Taxes Paid) − CF$_0$

$$= \$247,828 + \$156,345 + \$170,228 - \$0 - \$750,000 = -\$175,559$$

The project will still be rejected—although it is more attractive because of the higher salvage value—despite the decrease in the CCA tax shield because of the taxable CCA recapture of \$67,345 (i.e., \$132,655 UCC − \$200,000 SV).

EXAMPLE 14-8 Finding the NPV When *k* Changes

Redo Example 14-6 by assuming, once again, that the asset class is left open, the salvage value is \$132,655, and all else is as in the original example, except that the discount rate is 10 percent instead of 12 percent.

Solution

All of the terms, except for the initial cash outlay, will be affected by the change in the discount rate.

$$CF_0 = \$750,000$$

$$PV\ (\text{Operating Cash Flows}) = CFBT\ (1 - T) \times \left[\frac{1 - \dfrac{1}{(1 + k)^n}}{k} \right]$$

$$= [\ \$125,000(1 - 0.45)\ ] \times \left[\frac{1 - \dfrac{1}{(1.10)^5}}{0.10} \right]$$

$$= (\$68,750) \times (3.79079) = \$260,617$$

Because no terminal loss or CCA recapture is associated with the termination of this project, we use Equation 14-7 to estimate the present value of the CCA tax shield:

$$PV\ (\text{CCA Tax Shield}) = \frac{(C_0)(d)(T)}{d + k} \times \frac{(1 + 0.5k)}{1 + k} - \frac{(SV_n)(d)(T)}{d + k} \times \frac{1}{(1 + k)^n}$$

$$= \frac{(\$650,000)(0.30)(0.45)}{0.30 + 0.10} \times \frac{(1 + (0.5 \times 0.10))}{1 + 1.10} - \frac{(\$132,655)(0.30)(0.45)}{0.30 + 0.10} \times \frac{1}{(1.10)^5}$$

$$= \$209,403 - \$27,799 = \$181,604$$

$$PV\ (ECF_n) = \frac{\$232,655}{(1.10)^5} = \$144,460$$

continued

EXAMPLE 14-8   Finding the NPV When *k* Changes *continued*

So,

NPV = PV (Operating CFs) + PV (CCA Tax Shield) + PV (ECF$_n$) − PV (Capital Gains Taxes Paid) − CF$_0$

= \$260,617 + \$181,604 + \$144,460 − \$0 − \$750,000 = −\$163,319

The project would still be rejected, although the NPV is higher (less negative) because of the use of a lower discount rate, which increases the present value of the future cash flows.

EXAMPLE 14-9   Finding the NPV When Operating Cash Flows Are Higher

Redo Example 14-8 (again assuming *k* = 10 percent), but now assume that all of the annual operating cash flows are 10 percent higher than the original estimates.

Solution

The only term that is affected by this assumption is the present value of the operating cash flows.

CF$_0$ = \$750,000

$$\text{PV (Operating Cash Flows)} = \text{CFBT} (1 - T) \times \left[\frac{1 - \dfrac{1}{(1 + k)^n}}{k} \right]$$

$$= [\, \$137,500 (1 - 0.45)\,] \times \left[\frac{1 - \dfrac{1}{(1.10)^5}}{0.10} \right]$$

$$= (\$75,625) \times (3.79079) = \$286,678$$

PV (CCA Tax Shield) = \$181,604 (as in Example 14-8)

PV (ECF$_n$) = \$144,460 (as in Example 14-8)

So,

NPV = PV (Operating CFs) + PV (CCA Tax Shield) + PV (ECF$_n$) − PV (Capital Gains Taxes Paid) − CF$_0$

= \$286,678 + \$181,604 + \$144,460 − \$0 − \$750,000 = −\$137,258

The project would still be rejected, although the NPV is higher (less negative) because of the increase in estimated operating cash flows.

CONCEPT REVIEW QUESTIONS

1. Why does the initial cash outlay often exceed the purchase price of an asset?

2. How do taxes affect the annual cash flows and terminal cash flows of an investment project?

3. Explain why the valuation by components approach can save computational time and still lead to the correct answer.

Learning Objective 14.3
Conduct a sensitivity analysis to see how the value changes as key inputs vary, and determine what is a real option.

14.3 SENSITIVITY TO INPUTS

Examples 14-7 through 14-9 examine the impact of changing one or more of the inputs into the "base-case" (most likely) project estimates. We used them to illustrate the impact of various estimates on the resulting NPV, as well as to implement various forms of the equations introduced in the previous section. In practice, companies are dealing with estimates of future cash flows, discount rates, and so on. Because any estimate of the future is subject to error, it is often useful to examine the impact on the attractiveness of a project if one or more of the estimates is incorrect. In other words, firms may want to estimate the NPV (or IRR, profitability index, or payback period) of projects using a range of estimates in order to examine the "risks" in their estimates.

In this section, we briefly discuss some commonly used methods for analyzing risks, which are all included in the survey results in Figure 14-1. There isn't much to say about the number one answer (judgement, used by 76.9 percent of firms), as all investment decisions are critical management decisions, which obviously involve some judgement. We discuss the others below in turn.

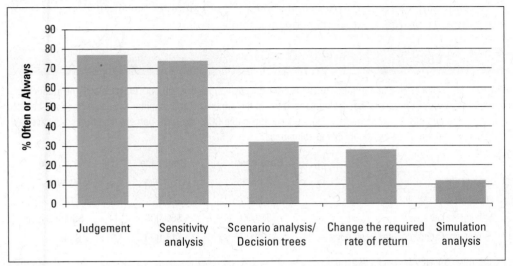

FIGURE 14-1 *Survey Results of Risk Analysis Techniques Used by Canadian Firms When Deciding the Projects or Acquisitions to Pursue*

Source: Baker, Kent H., Shantanu Dutta, and Samir Saadi, "Corporate Finance Practices in Canada: Where Do We Stand?" *Multinational Finance Journal* 15, no. 3/4 (September/December 2011), Table 4, p. 174.

Sensitivity Analysis

The number two response in Figure 14-1 (at 73.5 percent) is **sensitivity analysis**, which examines how an investment's NPV changes as we change the value of one input at a time, just as we did in examples 14-7 through 14-9. For instance, in Example 14-7, we varied the estimated salvage value and recalculated the NPV, which demonstrated how a change in this estimate could affect the attractiveness of a project. Similarly, in examples 14-8 and 14-9, we changed the value of the discount rate (i.e., the number four answer in Figure 14-1) and then the operating cash flow estimates to isolate how sensitive the NPV is to these inputs. This type of analysis allows firms to determine which of their estimates are the most critical in the final decision. Obviously, the most critical estimates require the greatest amount of scrutiny from the firm.

sensitivity analysis an examination of how an investment's NPV changes as the value of different inputs are changed, one input at a time

The number three response in Figure 14-1, **scenario analysis**, examines how an investment's NPV changes in response to differing scenarios with respect to the values of one or more estimates, such as sales or costs. It is also informative to vary the discount rate used in the NPV calculations, because this variable is hard to estimate precisely and can change substantially through time as market, industry, and company conditions change. It often makes sense to vary more than one input variable at a time, because it allows us to account for interactions among the variables and for the fact that many of them can be related to external variables, such as the overall health of the economy or the company's industry. For example, if interest rates decline, it is reasonable to assume that a firm's discount rate may decline, and if the product it sells is sensitive to interest rates, it is also reasonable to assume that the operating cash flows associated with a particular capital expenditure could increase under this favourable scenario. Similarly, if the price of oil declines, this may reduce the expected operating cash flows

scenario analysis an examination of how an investment's NPV changes in response to varying scenarios in terms of one or more estimates, such as sales or costs

from an investment for an oil producer. The decline in oil prices could also cause the market price of the oil producer's common shares to decline, which could increase its cost of capital.

It makes sense to view the impact of certain scenarios that might arise on all variables. Scenario analysis can provide important information, because we know that estimates will rarely be completely accurate and can often be well off the mark.

Scenario analysis is often conducted in the form of a "what if" analysis. For example, a company would typically estimate a base-case scenario. It would then make more optimistic and more pessimistic assumptions to produce, at minimum, an optimistic (or best case) scenario and a pessimistic (or worst case) scenario. In practice, it is common to produce a wide variety of what-if scenarios, which can easily be handled through the use of a spreadsheet program, such as Excel. As Figure 14-1 suggests, some companies will use "simulation analysis" to generate various scenarios using a mathematical or computerized simulation generation procedure. We provide a simple scenario in Example 14-10.

EXAMPLE 14-10 Scenario Analysis

A company has a project that requires an initial after-tax cash outlay of $100,000, which is also the amount for the capital cost of the assets that are purchased to get the project up and running. The asset class will be left open at the end of the project's useful life, and the applicable CCA rate is 20 percent. The firm's effective tax rate is 40 percent. It makes the following estimates:

	Base case	Best case	Worst case
Project life	12 years	15 years	9 years
Discount rate (k)	12%	10%	14%
Salvage value	$50,000	$60,000	$30,000
Annual operating after-tax cash flows	$12,000	$15,000	$9,000

Determine the NPV for each scenario.

Solution

$CF_0 = \$100,000$

Base case:

$$PV \text{ (Operating Cash Flows)} = [\$12,000] \times \left[\frac{1 - \frac{1}{(1.12)^{12}}}{0.12} \right]$$
$$= (\$12,000) \times (6.194374) = \$74,332$$

Because no terminal loss or CCA recapture is associated with the termination of this project, we use Equation 14-7 to estimate the present value of the CCA tax shield. There are no capital gains, so this term is zero.

$$PV \text{ (CCA Tax Shield)} = \frac{(C_0)(d)(T)}{d+k} \times \frac{(1+0.5k)}{1+k} - \frac{(SV_n)(d)(T)}{d+k} \times \frac{1}{(1+k)^n}$$
$$= \frac{(\$100,000)(0.20)(0.40)}{0.20 + 0.12} \times \frac{(1 + (0.5 \times 0.12))}{(1 + 0.12)} - \frac{(\$50,000)(0.20)(0.40)}{0.20 + 0.12} \times \frac{1}{(1.12)^{12}}$$
$$= \$23,661 - \$3,208 = \$20,453$$

$$PV \text{ (ECF}_n) = \frac{\$50,000}{(1.12)^{12}} = \$12,834$$

NPV = PV (Operating CFs) + PV (CCA Tax Shield) + PV (ECF$_n$) − (CF$_0$)
= $74,332 + $20,453 + $12,834 − $0 − $100,000 = +$7,619

The base-case NPV suggests that the project should be accepted because it generates a positive NPV.

continued

EXAMPLE 14-10 Scenario Analysis *continued*

Best case:

$$PV \text{ (Operating Cash Flows)} = [\$15,000] \times \left[\frac{1 - \frac{1}{(1.10)^{15}}}{0.10} \right]$$

$$= (\$15,000) \times (7.60608) = \$114,091$$

$$PV \text{ (CCA Tax Shield)} = \frac{(\$100,000)(0.20)(0.40)}{0.20 + 0.10} \times \frac{(1 + 0.5 \times 0.10)}{1 + 0.10} - \frac{(\$60,000)(0.20)(0.40)}{0.20 + 0.10} \times \frac{1}{(1.10)^{15}}$$

$$= \$25,455 - \$3,830 = \$21,625$$

$$PV \text{ (ECF}_n) = \frac{\$60,000}{(1.10)^{15}} = \$14,364$$

$$NPV = PV \text{ (Operating CFs)} + PV \text{ (CCA Tax Shield)} + PV \text{ (ECF}_n) - CF_0$$

$$= \$114,091 + \$21,625 + \$14,364 - \$0 - \$100,000 = +\$50,080$$

The best-case NPV suggests that the project is extremely attractive and should be accepted.

Worst case:

$$PV \text{ (Operating Cash Flows)} = [\$9,000] \times \left[\frac{1 - \frac{1}{(1.14)^{9}}}{0.14} \right]$$

$$= (\$9,000) \times (4.94637) = \$44,517$$

$$PV \text{ (CCA Tax Shield)} = \frac{(\$100,000)(0.20)(0.40)}{0.20 + 0.14} \times \frac{(1 + 0.5 \times 0.14)}{1 + 0.14} - \frac{(\$30,000)(0.20)(0.40)}{0.20 + 0.14} \times \frac{1}{(1.14)^{9}}$$

$$= \$22,085 - \$2,171 = \$19,914$$

$$PV \text{ (ECF}_n) = \frac{\$30,000}{(1.14)^{9}} = \$9,225$$

$$NPV = PV \text{ (Operating CFs)} + PV \text{ (CCA Tax Shield)} + PV \text{ (ECF}_n) - CF_0$$

$$= \$44,517 + \$19,914 + \$9,225 - \$0 - \$100,000 = -\$26,344$$

The worst-case NPV suggests that the project is extremely unattractive and should be rejected.

Examining these three scenarios tells the company that although the project seems attractive and has significant upside, it could also turn out to be a losing proposition and is not without risk.

Once we conduct scenario analysis, a final step is to consider a what-if scenario analysis. In Example 14-10, we assumed that a variable changed, yet the firm did not change anything in response. In the extreme, we said that the project was extremely unattractive if the worst case materialized and the operating cash flows were only $9,000 a year for nine years, although the risk of the project increased and the salvage value dropped to $30,000. But a firm would not stand by and watch a project deteriorate without doing anything. In practice, firms respond to changing circumstances. For example, *Finance in the News 14-1* discusses just such a situation involving Talisman Energy Inc.'s January 2012 announcement that it would be cutting its capital spending and considering some asset sales because, according to CEO John Manzoni, they "expect gas prices to remain depressed through this year." **Real option valuation (ROV)**, discussed in the next subsection, recognizes that firms respond to different circumstances and change their operating characteristics.

real option valuation (ROV) an assessment that recognizes that firms respond to different circumstances and change their operating characteristics

finance INTHENEWS 14-1   Talisman Trims Capital Spending

SEEING NO RECOVERY in natural gas prices on the horizon, Talisman Energy Inc. plans to spend less this year than it did in 2011 and is eyeing up to $2 billion in asset sales.

"I believe we can expect gas prices to remain depressed through this year—at least that's the basis on which we've set our capital plans," chief executive officer John Manzoni told a conference call with analysts Tuesday.

The Calgary-based company has set a 2012 capital budget of just over $4 billion, a decrease of $500 million or 11 percent from 2011. Capital spending in North America is expected to be approximately $1.8 billion in 2012, which is about $400 million lower than last year.

Talisman plans to spend less on dry natural gas and focus more on areas rich in natural gas liquids, which have been much more robust lately. The company aims to increase liquids production from 25,000 barrels of oil equivalent per day this year to 60,000 barrels by 2015.

The company is looking to pare down its portfolio by $1 billion to $2 billion this year, eyeing opportunities to divest assets in the North Sea, North America and in early-stage international exploration areas.

Mr. Manzoni said that over time, Talisman plans to reduce its footprint in the "mature and relatively volatile" North Sea. Taxes, pipeline outages, and other issues have caused headaches in that region lately.

"I'm not in a position today to describe exactly how we'll achieve that, although we are investigating several options: a combination of some sales, some farm outs and some dilutions will over time result in the North Sea becoming a smaller part of the portfolio."

Talisman will continue to focus on North America, but "some assets are non-core to Talisman and should be sold," Manzoni said.

"In other areas, we'll seek to use other expertise or resources to accelerate activity and optimize value in areas where we would not otherwise direct capital."

John Manzoni, president and CEO of Talisman Energy, speaks to reporters following the company's annual meeting in Calgary, May 4, 2011. (Jeff McIntosh/The Canadian Press)

The oil and gas producer may look to exit some of its international assets—in the Iraqi region of Kurdistan and South America, for example— "as part of the natural evolution of that portfolio."

Lanny Pendill, an analyst with the Edward Jones brokerage in St. Louis, Mo., said he was glad to see Talisman set conservative targets for itself.

"It's always better to set the bar low and exceed targets than it is to try to get aggressive on a target and come underneath, and that's always been Talisman's problem."

Talisman said production averaged about 425,000 barrels of oil equivalent in 2011, an increase of nine percent. Production growth of up to five percent is expected this year.

Source: Krugel, Lauren, "Talisman trims capital spending, eyes assets sales." The Canadian Press, printed in *The Globe and Mail Report on Business*, January 11, 2012, B3.

Real Option Valuation (ROV)

Real option valuation (ROV) was listed as a capital budgeting approach in Figure 13-3, with 10 percent of CFOs saying they used it often or always. ROV places great weight on the flexibility involved in a firm's operations. The classic example of ROV is in mining. Suppose it costs $150 to put into operation a mine that lasts for one year and can produce 100 units of production at a fixed cost of $200 and a variable cost of $6. If the price of the ore is expected to be $10 and the discount rate is 12 percent, then the NPV is:

$$\text{NPV} = -\$150 + \frac{(\$10 - \$6) \times 100 - \$200}{1.12} = \$28.57$$

Clearly the mine is a go because it has a positive NPV. However, suppose the analyst then conducted a sensitivity analysis with respect to the most important factor, which is the ore price, to see what happens when there is an equal probability of the ore price being either $12 and $8, or $14 and $6, or $16 and $4. We might suppose that the mine becomes less valuable as the ore price volatility increases, yet this is not the case. Table 14-3 shows the cash flow estimates under the three ore-price scenarios.

The expected cash flows are highest in scenario 3, in which the ore price variability is highest and the ore price is either $16 or $4. The reason is that the cash flow for the bad price scenario remains at – $200, which is the same as in scenario 2 because there is an explicit option available to the firm: to shut down. According to basic economics, a firm will operate only when the contribution margin is positive or, in other words, when the price exceeds the variable cost. In the case of the mine, when the ore price is at or below its $6 variable cost, the firm can't lose more than its fixed $200 costs or it will shut down. As a result, in the $16 ore price case, it earns $800, while in the $4 case it loses only $200, so the expected cash flow is a 50-percent chance of $800 and a 50-percent chance of –$200 or $300. Therefore, the value of the mine goes up as the volatility of its ore price increases.

We illustrate this with a **decision tree** in Figure 14-2, in which we map out two possibilities for scenario 3.

decision tree a schematic way to represent alternative decisions and the possible outcomes

TABLE 14-3 Real Options Example

	Scenario 1: Ore Price $12 or $8	Scenario 2: Ore Price $14 or $6	Scenario 3: Ore Price $16 or $4
Good price ($p = 0.5$)	$12	$14	$16
Cash flow	$400	$600	$800
Bad price ($p = 0.5$)	$8	$6	$4
Cash flow	$0	–$200	–$200
Expected cash flow	$200	$200	$300

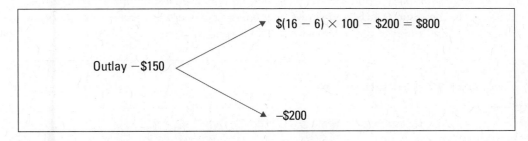

FIGURE 14-2 *Decision Tree on Two Possible Outcomes*

For simplicity, we have assumed no taxes or CCA.

The firm loses the $200 fixed costs regardless of the ore price, because these costs are defined as fixed. However, its contribution depends on the ore price. When the ore price is above $6, there is a positive contribution; when it is below $6, the contribution is zero as the firm shuts down. Although we call this the shutdown option, it is, in fact, a 100-unit call option on the ore. If the ore price is above $6, the firm executes its option to go into business and produce ore; if the ore price is below $6, it throws the option away and does not open the mine.

We can use the binomial option pricing model discussed in Appendix 12A to value this option as long as we have the futures price for the ore. In fact, option pricing is used to value mines producing copper, gold, zinc, and other commodities when they are traded commodities and the cost structure of the mine is clearly defined, as it usually is.

ROV has been applied to other cases in which the firm has the option to defer or delay a project, abandon a project, or switch the use of an asset from producing one product to another. For example, we started out by saying capex decisions could possibly change the risk of the firm and were very important if they involved irrevocable unique assets. However, if the assets involved generic modern production equipment that could be used to do other things, then the flexibility available to close down an unprofitable project and use the assets elsewhere considerably reduced the project's risk. In such a case, scenario analysis combined with these event-changing parameters gives a more accurate NPV than assuming that nothing changes as critical values faced by the project change. As a result, ROV and decision-tree analysis have dramatically increased our understanding of corporate decision-making and the value of flexibility and of the strategic considerations raised by senior management.

ROV is much more difficult to apply than conventional capital budgeting, and you can only use the binomial or Black-Scholes option pricing models in highly restrictive circumstances. However, the following options almost always exist in a capital expenditure decision:

1. When do you undertake the investment, now or at some point in the future?

2. Will the acceptance of this project generate other projects—that is, are investment projects linked or interdependent?

3. Can you put the resources to alternative uses if things don't pan out?

4. Can you terminate the project if cash flows do not materialize?

5. Can you learn, from undertaking the project, how to lower expected cash costs?

Finance in the News 14-2 discusses Magna International's intended purchase of a 20-percent stake in GM Europe (Opel), which, along with the planned 35-percent stake of its partner Sberbank, would have given it control of GM's European operations. The deal fell through after the U.S. and Canadian governments bailed out GM and gave it the resources to keep Opel. However, the story reveals Magna's history of building cars under contract for other brand-name producers in Europe and shows how the purchase of Opel would have given it an integrated car company and the option to produce electric cars, possibly for export back to the United States, in competition with GM, even though the agreement restricted this. Options 2 and 5 certainly applied to Magna's initial involvement in car production for others, as it generated the company's ability to try to buy GM Europe. Even though the deal fell through, it illustrates the value of ROV and shows how building cars under contract for others gave Magna the opportunity to generate positive NPV elsewhere

finance INTHENEWS 14-2 Magna's Opel Dilemma

THE DEAL TO BUILD a Magna International Inc. factory that would assemble vehicles for Chrysler was all but done. The choice had come down to a site in Sarnia, Ont., or a location in Georgia.

Then Chrysler pulled the plug, and plans for a Magna assembly plant vanished. That was three years ago, when the global automotive meltdown was not on the radar screens of a single auto industry executive.

Now Magna's plans are back on the drawing board. Magna founder and chairman Frank Stronach has renewed his longstanding desire to build vehicles in Canada and, more recently, has expressed a dream to create the first major Canadian-owned auto maker in almost a century.

But Mr. Stronach has a dilemma. He has helped save GM from the embarrassment and cost of having its European operations placed in bankruptcy protection. But General Motors has insisted as part of the deal that Opel vehicles not be sold in the U.S. market. Nonetheless, Mr. Stronach wants to build some Opel cars in Canada for sale in North America.

"I would like to see that the first electric car facilities are here in Canada," he told reporters in Ottawa yesterday. "If we would get a loan, we know we could speed it up; we could make sure it's going to be in Canada."

Mr. Stronach expanded on that theme by demonstrating and driving the battery-powered Ford Focus that Magna helped develop.

Mr. Stronach said he is looking for government loans worth half the $300 million he needs to invest—or $150 million—to build electric cars in Canada. He also said that U.S. states and European countries are starting to line up to offer incentives to locate the plants there.

Magna International Inc. Chairman Frank Stronach. (Darren Calabrese/The Canadian Press)

His vehicle for the risky endeavour of establishing a Canadian-owned car maker is Adam Opel GmbH. Opel is the key European division of General Motors Corp., which has signed an agreement that will involve a Magna-led group taking over a controlling stake in the troubled unit.

"But keep in mind [GM] still owns 35 percent," he said.

"I'm a great believer that if you come forward with a good program that makes a lot of common sense, that you can always change a few things. If it makes economic sense, you might change some people to change some contracts."

Assembling cars for the Canadian market alone makes little economic sense, one senior industry executive said yesterday.

continued

Finance in the News 14-2: Magna's Opel Dilemma *(continued)*

Other high-ranking industry sources said Magna could use Opel technology and manufacturing processes as a base for an assembly plant in Canada that could replicate what the Canadian auto parts giant's Magna Steyr division does in Europe.

"That makes a lot of sense," said one industry executive who knows Magna's operations well. "It's almost obvious that Magna Steyr [should] do a North American assembly plant."

Magna Steyr assembles vehicles on contract for several European auto makers, including BMW AG and Mercedes-Benz.

GM and Chrysler LLC have slashed their production capacity so drastically that contract assembly could become an attractive alternative for them if the North American market rebounds strongly during the next decade, the executive said.

Several sources said a Magna Steyr plant in Canada could also assemble vehicles under contract with Saturn, a GM division that is being shed in the auto maker's restructuring.

There are 16 entities examining Saturn, GM's chief financial officer Ray Young said on a conference call yesterday.

Magna is not among that group, Mr. Stronach has said.

Mr. Young said there are issues regarding Opel that still need to be worked out between the Magna-led group and GM.

"There's going to be a management team which, again, Magna [and] ourselves decide how that is going to be structured, whether it's going to be a European organization, or a pan-European Opel organization," he said.

Under the deal, Magna will hold 20 percent of Opel. Sberbank of Russia will own 35 percent, as will GM. Opel employees will hold 10 percent.

Some of Magna's other customers are unhappy about Magna building cars that would compete with their models that carry hundreds, sometimes thousands, of dollars worth of Magna parts.

Volkswagen AG, which competes directly with Opel in most European markets, is particularly unhappy, industry sources said yesterday.

"Competing with your customers is never a good idea," one source said.

Mr. Stronach said other customers should not worry.

"We will create different structures whereby it is absolutely clear that we will create a wall between car manufacturing and parts manufacturing," he said. "I think we can demonstrate to our customers that there is no intermixing."

NPV Break-Even Analysis

Because the annual operating after-tax cash flows are so critical to the success or failure of many investment projects, firms may pay particular attention to how variations in these cash flows affect the viability of a project. Sometimes they will want to know what level of annual operating cash flow is required for a project to "break even" in the sense of producing an NPV of zero. We will denote this as the operating cash flow **NPV break-even point** of a project.[9] The break-even discount rate is the IRR of the project. In Example 14-11, we calculate the operating cash flow NPV break-even point for the project discussed in Example 14-10.

NPV break-even point the level of annual operating cash flow required for a project to produce an NPV of zero

EXAMPLE 14-11 Scenario Analysis

Use the base-case estimates for all inputs other than operating after-tax cash flows for the project examined in Example 14-10. Determine the break-even amount for the annual operating after-tax cash flow.

Solution

$CF_0 = \$100,000$

$PV \text{ (CCA Tax Shield)} = \$20,453$

$PV (ECF_n) = \$12,834$

We can set the NPV equal to 0 and solve for the required value of the PV of the operating CFs, as follows:

$NPV = PV \text{ (Operating CFs)} + PV \text{ (CCA Tax Shield)} + PV (ECF_n) - CF_0$

$\$0 = PV \text{ (Operating CFs)} + \$20,453 + \$12,834 - \$100,000$

$PV \text{ (Operating CFs)} = \$66,713$

continued

[9] Firms pay attention to many other break-even points, such as the accounting break-even point, which occurs when the accounting profit equals zero and is typically measured in units of sales.

EXAMPLE 14-11 Scenario Analysis *continued*

Now we can solve for the annual after-tax CF that satisfies this equation, as follows:

$$PV \text{ (Operating CFs)} = [\text{Break-Even Operating CF}] \times \left[\frac{1 - \dfrac{1}{(1.12)^{12}}}{0.12} \right]$$

$66,713 = (\text{Break-Even Operating CF}) \times (6.194374)$

Break-Even Operating CF = $10,770

Notice that this annual cash flow is less than the $12,000 estimate in the base case, which had produced a positive NPV.

CONCEPT REVIEW QUESTIONS

1. What insights can be gained by using sensitivity analysis, scenario analysis, and NPV break-even analysis?

2. What limitations of scenario analysis does the real option valuation approach address?

14.4 REPLACEMENT DECISIONS

Learning Objective 14.4
Explain how to make replacement decisions, and explain what is special about them.

expansion projects projects that add something extra to the firm in terms of sales or cost savings; their new cash flows are incremental cash flows

replacement projects projects that involve the replacement of an existing asset (or assets) with a new one

Earlier in this chapter, we introduced 12 guidelines for estimating cash flows. Guideline 2 stated that we should focus on *marginal* or *incremental* cash flows that arise as a result of a capital budgeting decision. This refers to the additional cash flows that will be generated for the firm. So far, this has been relatively easy to deal with, because we have been considering **expansion projects**—that is, projects that would add something extra to the firm in terms of extra sales or cost savings. For these types of projects, the new cash flows that arise from the investment decision represent incremental cash flows.

Replacement projects, as their name suggests, involve the replacement of an existing asset (or assets) with a new one. We deal with these types of decisions in the same manner as we deal with expansion problems, except that we must focus more on incremental cash flows. We demonstrate this point in Example 14-12.

EXAMPLE 14-12 Evaluating Replacement Decisions

A firm is considering the purchase of a new machine priced at $350,000 to replace an existing machine. The present market value of the existing machine is $50,000, and it is expected to have a salvage value of $15,000 at the end of eight years. Management estimates that the company will benefit from the new machine by reducing annual operating expenses by $50,000 over the life of the project, which is expected to be eight years. This new machine is expected to have a salvage value of $100,000 at the end of eight years. The firm's marginal tax rate is 40 percent, and its marginal cost of capital is 15 percent. Both machines belong to class 10, which has a CCA rate of 30 percent, and the asset class will remain open. Estimate the NPV of replacement and decide whether or not replacement should occur.

Solution

We must first estimate the incremental capital cost (ΔC_0), which is the difference between the purchase price of the new machine and the salvage price of the old machine. This will be the addition to the asset class and will determine the additional CCA tax savings generated by the new investment. The incremental capital cost also represents a component of the firm's incremental initial after-tax cash outlay (CF_0).

$$\Delta C_0 = C_0^{\text{New}} - C_0^{\text{Old}} = \$350,000 - \$50,000 = \$300,000$$

continued

EXAMPLE 14-12   Evaluating Replacement Decisions *continued*

In this example, there is no mention of opportunity costs arising or of additional working capital being tied up, so we can estimate the initial cash outlay as follows:

$$\Delta CF_0 = \Delta C_0 + \Delta NWC_0 + OC = \$300{,}000 + \$0 + \$0 = \$300{,}000$$

Now we need to estimate the present value of the annual incremental operating cash flows (ΔOperating CFs).

$\Delta CFBT = \$50{,}000$ per year in additional cost savings

$$PV(\Delta Operating\ CFs) = (\Delta CFBT)(1-T)\left[\dfrac{1-\dfrac{1}{(1+k)^n}}{k}\right]$$

$$= (\$50{,}000)(1-0.40)\left[\dfrac{1-\dfrac{1}{(1.15)^8}}{0.15}\right] = (\$50{,}000)(0.60)(4.487322)$$

$$= \$134{,}620$$

Now we estimate the present value of the incremental CCA tax savings generated by the replacement decision. Because the asset class is left open and there is no CCA recapture or terminal loss, we can use Equation 14-7, making sure to use the incremental capital cost (ΔC_0) as estimated above, and also using the incremental salvage value (ΔSV_n), which is estimated below:

$$\Delta SV_n = SV_{New} - SV_{Old} = \$100{,}000 - \$15{,}000 = \$85{,}000$$

$$PV(\Delta CCA\ Tax\ Shield) = \dfrac{(\Delta C_0)(d)(T)}{d+k} \times \dfrac{(1+0.5k)}{(1+k)} - \dfrac{(\Delta SV_n)(d)(T)}{d+k} \times \dfrac{1}{(1+k)^n}$$

$$PV(\Delta CCA\ Tax\ Shield) = \left[\dfrac{(\$300{,}000)(0.30)(0.40)}{0.30+0.15} \times \dfrac{(1+0.5(0.15))}{1+0.15}\right] -$$

$$\left[\dfrac{(\$85{,}000)(0.30)(0.40)}{0.30+0.15} \times \dfrac{1}{(1.15)^8}\right]$$

$$= \$67{,}373$$

Next, we need to estimate the present value of the incremental ending cash flow (ΔECF_n) associated with the replacement decision as follows:

$$\Delta ECF_n = \Delta SV_n + \Delta NWC_n = \$85{,}000 + \$0 = \$85{,}000$$

$$PV(\Delta ECF_n) = \dfrac{\Delta ECF_n}{(1+k)^n} = \dfrac{\$85{,}000}{(1.15)^8} = \$27{,}787$$

We can combine the results above to determine the NPV of the replacement decision, as follows:

$$NPV = PV(\Delta Operating\ CFs) + PV(\Delta CCA\ Tax\ Shield) + PV(\Delta ECF_n) - \Delta CF_0$$

$$= \$134{,}620 + \$67{,}373 + \$27{,}787 - \$300{,}000 = -\$70{,}220$$

Therefore, the firm should not go ahead with this replacement project.

CONCEPT REVIEW QUESTION

1. Discuss any differences in the evaluation of a replacement decision versus the evaluation of an expansion decision.

14.5 INFLATION AND CAPITAL BUDGETING DECISIONS

Learning Objective 14.5
Explain how mistakes can easily be made when dealing with inflation.

Because capital expenditures typically involve the estimation of cash flows several years in the future, inflation can play an important role in determining these estimates, because it will affect future levels of sales and expenses. For example, *Finance in the News 14-3* discusses the significant impact of "sharply" rising industry costs on the estimated price tag for the Kearl oil sands mine. In addition, inflation affects the level of interest rates and therefore affects the cost of capital, which Imperial Oil Ltd. expected to use in discounting these future cash flows when it developed the Kearl mine.

---

finance INTHENEWS 14-3   New Price Tag for Imperial's Kearl Mine Reflects Rising Oil Sands Costs

IMPERIAL OIL LTD. jacked up its spending budget for the massive Kearl oil sands mine, sparking concern the industry's costs are rising sharply as companies plow ahead with multibillion-dollar projects.

The Calgary oil giant, majority-owned by Exxon Mobil Corp. expects to spend about $30 billion developing the Kearl mine, a 25-percent increase over its previous estimate. Imperial provided the revised forecast on Wednesday as it announced plans to build Kearl's $8.9-billion expansion phase.

Oil sands mining projects are notoriously expensive, and the industry wants to avoid repeating the mistakes energy companies made during Fort McMurray's last boom, which culminated around 2008. Companies blew through their budgets before the global economic crisis clobbered the price of oil and forced them to shelve a slew of projects.

Industry officials today are cognizant of creeping costs and are trying not to stoke costs for labour and materials. But as executives, loathe to be left without growth prospects, again earmark large amounts of capital to long-life projects, worries about costs are growing.

"Imperial's [announcement] is yet another data point that costs in the oil sands, and the potential for rampant cost inflation, is a very real threat for producers—at least those in the Fort McMurray region," Justin Bouchard, an analyst at Raymond James in Calgary, said in a note. "Oil sands mining companies are [at today's costs] effectively getting a mine-only operation for the cost of a mine plus an upgrader a few years ago."

Imperial, however, said its new budget is not about competition for labour or steel. Instead, it said, the new budget reflects two key expenses that were not previously included in the calculations: improvements to its tailings-pond system, and pipelines that will connect the Kearl project to other major lines.

Pius Rolheiser, an Imperial spokesman, said many of the changes were made so Kearl could comply with Alberta's new tailings-pond

regulations, known as directive 74. "That includes changes to the mine design, the tailings area design, and also technology changes that will alter the characteristics of the tailings before we deposit [them]," Mr. Rolheiser said. "All of these are geared toward enabling better and faster reclamation." Kearl is not expected to meet directive 74's targets on time, but will meet its objectives over the entire lifetime of the mine.

Kearl was originally designed to be constructed in three phases. Last May, however, Imperial amended the plan and said it would build an initial development, an expansion phase, and then go through a "debottlenecking" period, which would make the whole operation more efficient.

Imperial estimates the capital costs to develop the 4.6 billion-barrel resource at Kearl will be about $6.20 per barrel, up 24 percent from its previous estimate of $5 per barrel. "We have a high degree of confidence on the $6.20 on the initial development and the expansion," Mr. Rolheiser said.

There is still a significant amount of engineering and planning work to finish before the price tag on the debottlenecking phase can be pinpointed, but Imperial expects it to be about $6.20 per barrel as well, he said.

When the company unveiled the new blueprints in May, it increased the cost of the first phase to $10.9 billion from $8 billion, in part reflecting revisions to its tailings-pond system. That revision still expected capital costs to ring in at $5 per barrel.

At completion, Kearl will have the capacity to produce 345,000 barrels of oil per day. Imperial hopes to have wrapped up its capital investments in the project by 2020.

Canadian Natural Resources Ltd., Suncor Energy Inc., and Syncrude Canada Ltd. each have major mining expansion projects teed up, Mr. Bouchard noted. Earlier this month, France's Total SA received regulatory approval to build its Joslyn North project, Canada's fifth oil sands mine.

Source: Tait, Carrie, and Shawn McCarthy, "New price tag for Imperial's Kearl mine reflects rising oil sands costs." *The Globe and Mail*, December 22, 2011. Available at www.theglobeandmail.com. © The Globe and Mail Inc. All rights reserved. Reprinted by permission.

Earlier in this chapter, we introduced guideline 11 for estimating cash flows, which said that we need to treat inflation *consistently*. So far, we have been estimating future cash flows on a nominal basis (i.e., estimating the actual cash flow that will result in year 2, etc., without making adjustments for inflation). As a result, we have been discounting these cash flows using nominal (or actual) discount rates. This approach treats inflation consistently. An alternative is to estimate future *real*, or inflation-adjusted, cash flows and discount these real cash flows using *real* discount rates, which have also been adjusted for inflation. One difficulty with this approach is that the CCA tax-savings estimates represent the actual amount of CCA that can be charged in a given year. Therefore, the easiest way to proceed is usually to estimate the nominal cash flows and discount them using nominal discount rates.

It is important for firms to consider the impact that inflation will have on both sales and expenses, as well as on the discount rate. Although it is often reasonable to assume that both items will be equally affected by inflation, this will not be the case for all firms or all situations. Much depends on the industry firms are in and on the products they sell. For example, sometimes inflation will have a greater impact on selling prices than it will on expenses, and sometimes it will be the opposite. Example 14-13 demonstrates the impact that such variations in the growth of sales and expenses can have on the NPV of a project.

EXAMPLE 14-13 The Impact of Inflation

A firm is considering a project with the following forecasts:

- The initial after-tax cash outflow will be $1,000,000; the entire outflow represents a capital cost of $1,000,000; and the appropriate CCA class is asset class 8 (CCA rate is 20 percent, declining balance method).

- There is no terminal loss or CCA recapture associated with the project.

- Revenues will be $350,000 in the first year and will grow at 5 percent per year after that.

- Costs will be $75,000 in the first year and will grow at 5 percent per year after that.

- The project will last 10 years, and the equipment has an estimated salvage value of $100,000 at that time.

- The firm's required return is 18 percent.

- The firm pays taxes at a marginal rate of 40 percent.

a.   Calculate the NPV of this project.

b.   Redo part a. by assuming the first year's revenue is $350,000; however, there is no growth in revenue beyond that. In addition, costs turn out to be $100,000 the first year and grow at 7 percent per year thereafter.

c.   Redo part a. by assuming the first year's revenue turns out as expected, but revenue grows at a rate of 7 percent per year thereafter until year 10, while costs are $75,000 in the first year and rise at 3 percent per year thereafter until year 10.

Solution

This problem can be solved much more efficiently using a spreadsheet program, such as Excel, but we will proceed using formulas.

The present value of CCA tax savings and the present value of the ending cash flow will be the same for parts a., b., and c., so we solve for these items first.

$$C_0 = \$1,000,000$$

$$CF_0 = C_0 + \Delta NWC_0 + OC = \$1,000,000 + \$0 + \$0 = \$1,000,000$$

$$PV\ (\text{CCA Tax Shield}) = \left[\frac{(\$1,000,000)(0.20)(0.40)}{0.20 + 0.18} \times \frac{1 + 0.5\,(0.18)}{1 + 0.18}\right] - \left[\frac{(\$100,000)(0.20)(0.40)}{0.20 + 0.18} \times \frac{1}{(1.18)^{10}}\right]$$

$$= \$194,469 - \$4,022 = \$190,447$$

$$ECF_n = SV_n + \Delta NWC_n = \$100,000 + \$0 = \$100,000$$

$$PV\ (ECF_n) = \frac{ECF_n}{(1 + k)^n} = \frac{\$100,000}{(1.18)^{10}} = \$19,106$$

continued

EXAMPLE 14-13 The Impact of Inflation *continued*

a. The operating cash flows are expected to grow at a rate of 5 percent per year, because both revenue and expenses are expected to grow at 5 percent per year for 10 years. We *could* estimate all 10 operating cash flows separately and discount each of them. In fact, this would be the appropriate strategy if we were using a spreadsheet. However, when solving this with a calculator, a computationally more efficient method is to use a variation of the constant growth version of the DDM, which gives the present value of a "growing perpetuity." The cash flows in this example do not grow at 5 percent forever, but only for 10 years. We can adjust for this fact by subtracting the present value of the growing perpetuity of operating cash flows from years 11 to infinity from the present value of the perpetuity from time 0 to infinity. This leaves us with the PV of the 10-year annuity. In other words:

$$\text{PV (Operating CFs)} = \frac{\text{CFBT}_1(1-T)}{k-g} - \frac{\text{CFBT}_{11}(1-T)}{k-g} \times \frac{1}{(1+k)^{10}}$$

$$= \frac{(\$350{,}000 - \$75{,}000)(1-0.40)}{0.18-0.05} - \frac{(\$350{,}000-\$75{,}000)(1-0.40)(1.05)^{10}}{0.18-0.05} \times \frac{1}{(1+0.18)^{10}}$$

$$= \frac{\$165{,}000}{0.13} - \frac{(\$165{,}000)(1.628895)}{0.13} \times (0.1910645)$$

$$= \$1{,}269{,}231 - \$395{,}015 = \$874{,}216$$

Combining the above results, we can find the NPV as follows:

$$\text{NPV} = \text{PV (Operating CFs)} + \text{PV (CCA Tax Shield)} + \text{PV (ECF}_n) - \text{CF}_0$$

$$= \$874{,}216 + \$190{,}447 + \$19{,}106 - \$1{,}000{,}000 = \$83{,}769$$

Strictly speaking, the firm should go ahead with the project (however, the NPV is not that high, relative to the $1-million required outlay).

b. Revenues display no growth and remain at $350,000 per year for 10 years. Expenses start at $100,000 (not $75,000) and grow at 7 percent per year thereafter.

The beginning cash flow, tax shield, and ending cash flow calculations are not affected; only the operating cash flows are, so we redo those here. Notice that revenues and expenses now grow at different rates, so we must consider each separately.

$$\text{PV (Operating Revenues)} = \frac{\text{Rev}_1(1-T)}{k-g} - \frac{\text{Rev}_{11}(1-T)}{k-g} \times \frac{1}{(1+k)^{10}}$$

$$= \frac{(\$350{,}000)(1-0.40)}{0.18-0.07} - \frac{(\$350{,}000)(1-0.40)(1.07)^{10}}{0.18-0} \times \frac{1}{(1+0.18)^{10}}$$

$$= \frac{\$210{,}000}{0.18} - \frac{(\$210{,}000)(1.0)}{0.18} \times (0.1910645)$$

$$= \$1{,}166{,}667 - \$222{,}909 = \$943{,}758$$

$$\text{PV (Operating Costs)} = \frac{\text{Cost}_1(1-T)}{k-g} - \frac{\text{Cost}_{11}(1-T)}{k-g} \times \frac{1}{(1+k)^{10}}$$

$$= \frac{(\$100{,}000)(1-0.40)}{0.18-0.07} - \frac{(\$100{,}000)(1-0.40)(1.07)^{10}}{0.18-0.07} \times \frac{1}{(1+0.18)^{10}}$$

$$= \frac{\$60{,}000}{0.11} - \frac{(\$60{,}000)(1.967151)}{0.11} \times (0.1910645)$$

$$= \$545{,}455 - \$205{,}011 = \$340{,}444$$

continued

EXAMPLE 14-13 The Impact of Inflation *continued*

The PV(Operating CFs) = $943,758 − $340,444 = $603,314, which is well below the value of $874,216 calculated in part a. under the previous assumptions.

The NPV can now be calculated as

NPV = PV (Operating CFs) + PV (CCA Tax Shield) + PV (ECF_n) − CF_0

$$= \$603,314 + \$190,447 + \$19,106 - \$1,000,000 = -\$187,133$$

Under this scenario, the project produces a negative NPV and would be unattractive.

c. Revenues grow at 7 percent instead of 5 percent for 10 years. Expenses start at $75,000 and grow at 3 percent per year thereafter. Once again, the beginning cash flow, the CCA tax shield, and the ending cash flow calculations are not affected. Notice that revenues and expenses again grow at different rates, so we must consider each separately.

$$PV \text{ (Operating Revenues)} = \frac{Rev_1(1-T)}{k-g} - \frac{Rev_{11}(1-T)}{k-g} \times \frac{1}{(1+k)^{10}}$$

$$= \frac{(\$350,000)(1-0.40)}{0.18-0.07} - \frac{(\$350,000)(1-0.40)(1.07)^{10}}{0.18-0.07} \times \frac{1}{(1+0.18)^{10}}$$

$$= \frac{\$210,000}{0.11} - \frac{(\$210,000)(1.967151)}{0.11} \times (0.1910645)$$

$$= \$1,909,091 - \$717,537 = \$1,191,554$$

$$PV \text{ (Operating Costs)} = \frac{Cost_1(1-T)}{k-g} - \frac{Cost_{11}(1-T)}{k-g} \times \frac{1}{(1+k)^{10}}$$

$$= \frac{(\$75,000)(1-0.40)}{0.18-0.03} - \frac{(\$75,000)(1-0.40)(1.03)^{10}}{0.18-0.03} \times \frac{1}{(1+0.18)^{10}}$$

$$= \frac{\$45,000}{0.15} - \frac{(\$45,000)(1.343916)}{0.15} \times (0.1910645)$$

$$= \$300,000 - \$77,032 = \$222,968$$

The PV (Operating CFs) = $1,191,554 − $222,968 = $968,586, which is well above the $874,216 that was calculated under the assumptions in part a.

NPV = PV (Operating CFs) + PV (CCA Tax Shield) + PV (ECF_n) − CF_0

$$= \$968,586 + \$190,447 + \$19,106 - \$1,000,000 = \$178,139$$

Under this scenario, the project would produce a much larger positive NPV and would be more attractive.

LESSONS TO BE LEARNED   **In this section**, we discussed how to adjust for inflation when making capital expenditure decisions. Generally speaking, the Bank of Canada's adherence to a target range of 1 to 3 percent (with a 2 percent goal) since 1991 has made this much easier for companies and investors attempting to forecast future inflation rates. On the other hand, the depth of the financial crisis in the United States has been so great that it has prompted the largest increase in the money supply and the largest increase in U.S. government spending since the end of World War II. In finance, we talk about "the law of unintended consequences." In responding to the worst downturn in 70 years, the United States has injected so much stimulus into the economy that concerns abound that if it is not careful in removing the stimulus as the economy recovers, it may overshoot into an inflationary environment. The lesson to be learned is that the government, in solving one problem, may sometimes create another.

CONCEPT REVIEW QUESTIONS

1. Why is it usually more precise to use nominal cash flows and nominal discount rates when evaluating projects?

2. Why might inflation affect cash inflows differently from the way it affects cash outflows?

SUMMARY

In this chapter, we demonstrate several approaches and guidelines for estimating the future cash flows associated with an investment. The chapter involves a lot of number crunching, because in capex evaluation, there are alternative ways of solving many of the problems. We also introduce several equations that can be used to estimate the present value of future cash flows and differentiate between expansion and replacement decisions. We proceed to discuss how sensitivity analysis, scenario analysis, what-if decision-tree analysis, and NPV break-even analysis can be used to determine how variations in estimates might affect the attractiveness of project evaluations. We conclude by illustrating the impact that inflation can have on capital budgeting decisions.

SUMMARY OF LEARNING OBJECTIVES

14.1 Outline the basic framework for capital expenditure analysis.

(1) Estimate all cash flows on an *after-tax* basis. (2) Use the appropriate cash flow estimates that represent the marginal or incremental cash flows arising from capital budgeting decisions. (3) Do *not* include associated interest and dividend payments in estimated project cash flows; they should already be accounted for in the discount rate (i.e., the appropriate cost of capital). (4) Adjust cash flows (particularly the initial cash outlay and the terminal cash flow at the end of the estimated project life) to reflect any additional working capital requirements that are associated with the project. (5) Treat sunk costs as irrelevant; what is of concern are *future* cash flows. (6) Although sunk costs are irrelevant, opportunity costs should be factored into cash flow estimates. (7) Determine the appropriate time horizon for the project. (8) Ignore intangible considerations. (9) Ignore externalities in the calculations. (10) Consider the effect of all project interdependencies on cash flow estimates. (11) Treat inflation consistently. This harks back to comparing like with like: discount nominal cash flows with nominal discount rates, and real cash flows with real discount rates. (12) Undertake all social investments required by law.

14.2 Estimate the future cash flows associated with potential investments.

The cash flows include three categories: initial cash flow, the expected annual after-tax cash flows and the ending cash flow.

- Initial cash flow = initial investment + change in net working capital + opportunity cost

- Expected annual after-tax cash flows = (sales − cost) $\times (1 - t) + t \times CCA$

- Ending cash flow = Salvage value + Change in net working capital. It could get more complicated if a capital gain, capital recapture, or terminal loss is incurred.

14.3 Conduct a sensitivity analysis to see how the value changes as key inputs vary and determine what is a real option.

Sensitivity analysis examines how an investment's net present value (NPV) changes as the value of one input is changed at a time. Scenario analysis examines how an investment's NPV changes in response to differing scenarios with respect to the values of one or more estimates. The real option valuation (ROV) approach places great weight on the flexibility involved in a firm's operations. Using a decision tree, the ROV approach considers alternative decisions and the possible outcomes.

14.4 Explain how to make replacement decisions, and explain what is special about them.

Replacement projects, as their name suggests, involve the replacement of an existing asset (or assets) with a new one. What is special is that one must focus more on incremental cash flows.

14.5 Explain how mistakes can easily be made when dealing with inflation.

Inflation must be treated consistently. More specifically, nominal cash flow needs to be discounted by the nominal discount rate, and real cash flow by the real discount rate. Mistakes can easily be made if the consistency rule is not followed.

KEY TERMS

capital cost (C_0), p. 538

decision tree, p. 553

ending (or terminal) after-tax cash flow (ECF_n), p. 541

expansion projects, p. 556

expected annual after-tax cash flows (CF_t), p. 539

externalities, p. 537

initial after-tax cash flow (CF_0), p. 538

marginal or incremental cash flows, p. 536

NPV break-even point, p. 555

opportunity costs, p. 537

real option valuation (ROV), p. 551

replacement projects, p. 556

salvage value (SV_n), p. 541

scenario analysis, p. 549

sensitivity analysis, p. 549

sunk costs, p. 537

EQUATIONS

Equation	Formula	Page
[14-1] Initial Cash Outlay	$CF_0 = C_0 + \Delta NWC_0 + OC$	p. 538
[14-2] Annual After-Tax Cash Flows	$CF_t = CFBT_t(1 - T) + CCA_t(T)$	p. 541
[14-3] Ending Cash Flow (with tax implications)	$ECF \ (with \ Tax \ Implications)_n = SV_n + \Delta NWC_n - [(SV_n - C_0) \times T]$ $- [(SV_n - UCC_n) \times T]$	p. 542
[14-4] Ending Cash Flow (ignoring tax implications)	$ECF_n = SV_n + \Delta NWC_n$	p. 542
[14-5] Net Present Value	$NPV = PV(Annual \ CFs) + PV(ECF_n) - CF_0$	p. 543
[14-6] Present Value of Operating Cash Flows	$PV(Operating \ Cash \ Flows) = CFBT(1 - T) \times \left[\dfrac{1 - \dfrac{1}{(1 + k)^n}}{k} \right]$	p. 544
[14-7] Present Value of CCA Tax Shield (ignoring CCA Recapture and Terminal Loss)	$PV(CCA \ Tax \ Shield) = \dfrac{(C_0)(d)(T)}{d + k} \times \dfrac{(1 + 0.5k)}{(1 + k)} - \dfrac{(SV_n)(d)(T)}{(d + k)} \times \dfrac{1}{(1 + k)^n}$	p. 544
[14-8] Present Value of CCA Tax Shield (accounting for CCA Recapture or Terminal Loss)	$PV(CCA \ Tax \ Shield) = \dfrac{(C_0)(d)(T)}{d + k} \times \dfrac{(1 + 0.5k)}{(1 + k)} - \dfrac{(UCC_n)(d)(T)}{(d + k)} \times \dfrac{1}{(1 + k)^n}$ $- \dfrac{(SV_n - UCC_n)(T)}{(1 + k)^n}$	p. 544
[14-9] Present Value of Capital Gains Taxes Paid	$PV(Capital \ Gains \ Taxes \ Paid) = \dfrac{(SV_n - C_0)(T)}{(1 + k)^n}$	p. 545
[14-10] Net Present Value (Components)	$NPV = PV(Operating \ CFs) + PV(CCA \ Tax \ Shield) + PV(ECF_n)$ $- PV(Capital \ Gains \ Taxes \ Paid) - CF_0$	p. 545

QUESTIONS AND PRACTICE PROBLEMS

Multiple Choice Questions

1. When making capital expenditure decisions, firms should not consider which of the following?
   a. after-tax incremental cash flows
   b. additional working capital requirements
   c. sunk costs
   d. salvage value

2. Which of the following will yield the same capital expenditure decisions?
   a. Using nominal cash flows and a real discount rate versus using nominal cash flows and a nominal discount rate
   b. Using nominal cash flows and a nominal discount rate versus using real cash flows and a real discount rate

    c. Using real cash flows and a real discount rate versus using real cash flows and a nominal discount rate

    d. Using nominal cash flows and a nominal discount rate versus using real cash flows and a nominal discount rate

3. When making capital expenditure decisions, firms should consider which of the following?

    a. after-tax incremental cash flows

    b. sunk cost

    c. associated interest and dividend payments

    d. externalities

4. When making capital expenditure decisions, firms should not consider which of the following?

    a. change of working capital

    b. opportunity cost

    c. all project interdependencies

    d. intangible considerations whose impact on cash flows cannot be estimated

5. What is the initial after-tax cash flow (CF_0) of a project given the following information: initial cost = \$400,050; R&D costs associated with the project = \$10,000; associated opportunity costs = \$90,000; decrease in inventory = \$15,000; installation costs = \$5,000.

    a. \$480,050

    b. \$510,050

    c. \$490,050

    d. \$530,050

6. Which of the following items is not included in the calculation of the ending (or terminal) cash flow (ECF_n)?

    a. salvage value

    b. change in inventory levels

    c. change in accounts receivable levels

    d. operating cash flows

7. A firm has a project that is expected to generate annual revenue of \$50,000, while incurring an annual cost of \$18,000. The CCA is \$45,000 and the tax rate is 40%. What is the after-tax cash flow?

    a. \$20,000

    b. \$19,200

    c. \$37,200

    d. \$68,000

8. A firm's discount rate is 20%. Suppose annual revenue starts at \$50,000; annual expenses start at \$18,000; and both will grow at a rate of 6 percent from year 2 to year 15. What is the present value of operating cash flows for all 15 years?

    a. \$120,090

    b. \$115,810

    c. \$132,000

    d. \$109,088

9. Which of the following will not decrease the present value of the CCA tax shield associated with an investment project?

    a. an increase in the discount rate

    b. a decrease in the corporate tax rate

    c. a decrease in the CCA rate

    d. a decrease in the discount rate

10. Which of the following statements is false?

    a. CCA recapture occurs when the salvage value is greater than the ending UCC for the asset or asset class.

b. Capital gains occur when the salvage value is greater than the original cost of the asset.

c. CCA recapture is taxable.

d. A terminal loss occurs when the salvage value is greater than the ending UCC for the asset or asset class.

11. What is the terminal cash flow (ECF_n) based on the following information? The release of additional inventory tied up = $2,000; salvage value = $10,000; UCC = $20,000; initial cost ($C_0$) = $35,000; T = 40%. Assume the asset class will remain open.

   a. $12,000
   b. $16,000
   c. $8,000
   d. $14,000

12. Which of the following statements is true about sensitivity analysis and scenario analysis?

   a. Sensitivity analysis examines the impact of the change of one input at a time.
   b. Scenario analysis examines the impact of the change of one input at a time.
   c. Sensitivity analysis examines PV changes in response to differing scenarios.
   d. Sensitivity analysis usually includes a base-case scenario, a best-case scenario, and a worst-case scenario.

13. Oak Inc. is planning to purchase new, faster printers to replace its existing printers. The capital cost of the new printers = $300,000. The current market price of the old printers = $50,000. The applicable CCA rate (d) = 20%; the tax rate = 40%; and k = 20%. It is estimated that the new printers could last for 15 years. What is the second-year incremental CCA expense?

   a. $45,000
   b. $54,000
   c. $25,000
   d. $65,000

14. Which of the following statements is true about replacement decisions?

   a. Incremental cash flow is used.
   b. Only the cash flow generated from the new machine is considered.
   c. The cash flow that would be generated from the old machine is irrelevant.
   d. The salvage value of the new machine is irrelevant.

15. Suppose the nominal cash flow is $1,000 in year 1, the nominal discount rate is 5 percent, and the inflation rate is 2 percent. What is the PV of the cash flow?

   a. $952.38
   b. $970.87
   c. $1,000
   d. $950

Practice Problems

16. Your boss is very puzzled by the finance courses in his MBA program. He has learned that "cash flow is king," but notices that the capital budgeting problems spend a lot of time and effort dealing with depreciation and CCA but not with interest expenses. He knows that depreciation and CCA are non-cash expenses, and he knows that interest is definitely a cash expense. He would like an explanation of why he needs to bother with depreciation and CCA and not with interest expense.

17. Firms A and B are competing for a project. The potential client has provided the following information on a hypothetical project: initial cost is $500,000; building renovation is $600,000; and the building cannot be rented due to the project (currently the building is vacant). Firm B has made the following statement to the board of directors:

   We have conducted an extensive analysis of the project and have concluded that your decision should consider the initial cost of $500,000 only. The $600,000 spent on renovation does not *affect future cash flow; therefore we can ignore it. The potential rental revenue should be ignored also, as the building is currently empty and therefore is not a cost of this project.*

The board of directors has asked for your comments on firm B's statement.

18. An investor has observed that BathGate Company, a shareholder wealth-maximizing company, has just made an investment that appears to have a negative NPV. The investor is very puzzled about why a company would undertake a negative NPV project. Assume that the NPV of the cash flows is in fact negative, and the project is actually shareholder wealth maximizing. What aspect of the project is the investor not considering?

19. Summarize all the cash flows that cannot be used in the capital budgeting process and explain the reasons.

20. Jensen's Juice Bar is considering purchasing a new blender. Indicate which of the following statements is a relevant consideration in the new-blender decision.
    a. Last year, Jensen's spent $500 on a new blender.
    b. Customers would prefer to have their juice made in the new blender and won't buy juice produced in the old one.
    c. The manager of the juice bar just got a raise.
    d. The juice bar's tax rate is 29 percent.
    e. The juice bar's monthly rent is $500.
    f. If Jensen's buys a blender, there will be no space for a coffee maker.
    g. The new blender is blue, and blue is your favourite colour.
    h. Jensen's Juice Bar spent $10,000 in renovations last year.

21. Complete the following table assuming that this project is in its fifth year.

	Tax rate	Annual cash flow before taxes	Discount rate	CCA rate	PV of operating cash flows CBIT (1 − T)
A	24%	$5,000	5%	35%	
B	43%	$3,000	10%	24%	
C	36%	$8,000	8%	19%	
D	50%	$15,000	15%	30%	
E	15%	$9,000	36%	36%	
F	30%	$20,000	12%	20%	

22. Prepare a schedule of the annual capital cost allowance for a major project. The initial investment is $50,000, the tax rate is 27 percent, and the CCA rate is 35 percent. Determine the amount of CCA allowed each year. Assume that the item will continue in use for more than four years.

Year	Opening UCC balance	CCA	Closing UCC balance
1			
2			
3			
4			

23. Complete the following table. Assume that the asset class is left open, and/or the salvage value is less than the UCC for the entire class.

	CCA rate	Tax rate	Discount rate	Initial investment	Salvage value	Project Life (n)	PV (CCA tax shields)
A	15%	35%	10%	$1,000	$0	5	
B	20%	40%	14%	$1,200	$500	4	
C	25%	35%	5%	$5,000	$1,000	8	
D	40%	45%	12%	$3,000	$200	10	
E	30%	50%	8%	$4,000	$300	14	
F	20%	35%	15%	$1,000	$500	7	
G	10%	27%	6%	$9,000	$0	9	

24. Which of the following items, relating to working capital, would be considered a cash inflow or outflow when evaluating a project (and why)?
   a. Increase in inventory
   b. Increase in accounts payable
   c. Increase in accounts receivable
   d. Decrease in inventory

25. KRZ Company's tax rate is 40 percent and the appropriate discount rate is 10 percent. It is considering a project. Each asset class is large and continues after the project terminates. KRZ is not capital constrained. There is no change in net working capital at the beginning or at the termination of the project. The initial investment is $4,000; annual pre-tax operating cash flow is $2,000; salvage value is 0; the CCA rate is 30 percent; and the length of the project is three years. Should KRZ take this project?

26. KRZ Company's tax rate is 40 percent and the appropriate discount rate is 10 percent. It is considering a project. Each asset class is large and continues after the project terminates. KRZ is not capital constrained. There is no change in net working capital at the beginning or at the termination of the project. The initial investment is $12,000; annual pre-tax operating cash flow is $1,600; salvage value is $750; the CCA rate is 20 percent; and the length of the project is 10 years. Should KRZ take this project?

27. Java Cafe's tax rate is 45 percent and the appropriate discount rate is 8 percent. It is considering a project. Each asset class consists only of the project asset and will be terminated at the end of the project. Java Cafe is not capital constrained. The initial investment is $40,000; annual pre-tax operating cash flow is $15,000; salvage value is $30,000; the CCA rate is 10 percent; and the length of the project is three years. Should Java Cafe take this project?

28. Java Cafe's tax rate is 45 percent and the appropriate discount rate is 8 percent. It is considering another project. Each asset class consists only of the project asset and will be terminated at the end of the project. Java Cafe is not capital constrained. The initial investment is $90,000; annual pre-tax operating cash flow is $20,000; salvage value is $50,000; the CCA rate is 30 percent; and the length of the project is five years. Should Java Cafe take this project?

29. Java Cafe's tax rate is 45 percent and the appropriate discount rate is 8 percent. It is considering another project. Each asset class consists only of the project asset and will be terminated at the end of the project. Java Cafe is not capital constrained. The initial investment is $85,000; annual pre-tax operating cash flow is $32,500; salvage value is $65,000; the CCA rate is 30 percent; and the length of the project is six years. Should Java Cafe take this project?

30. KRZ Company has hired you to help evaluate several projects. The firm's tax rate is 40 percent and the appropriate discount rate is 10 percent. Each asset class is small and will be terminated at the end of each project. KRZ is not capital constrained. The initial investment is $4,000; annual pre-tax operating cash flow is $2,000; salvage value is $500; the CCA rate is 30 percent; and the length of the project is three years. Should KRZ take this project?

31. KRZ Company has hired you to help evaluate several projects. The firm's tax rate is 40 percent and the appropriate discount rate is 10 percent. Each asset class is small and will be terminated at the end of each project. KRZ is not capital constrained. The initial investment is $5,700; annual pre-tax operating cash flow is $2,000; salvage value is $500; the CCA rate is 30 percent; and the length of the project is three years. Should KRZ take this project?

32. You are trying to decide whether or not to go to graduate school. If you get a job right after you get your bachelor's degree, you expect to earn $40,000 a year, and you expect your salary to increase by 5 percent a year for the next 40 years. If you go to graduate school, you will spend four more years at school. The tuition and books are expected to cost $8,000 a year.

    Assume living expenses are $15,000 a year. After graduate school, you expect to start at a higher salary that will increase by 7 percent a year. However, you will only be able to work for 36 years. Your savings earn 4 percent a year.

    What is the minimum post-graduate school starting salary you will require to make going to graduate school a positive NPV project? (Note: do not consider the non-monetary benefits of a higher education.) Use Excel "solver" function.

⚙ 33. You are trying to decide whether to continue renting an apartment or to buy a house. In 20 years, you plan on leaving Canada and moving to a warm tropical island and would like to have as much money as possible. You have just won $25,000 in the lottery and will be able to use that money for a down payment. At the moment, your rent is $700 a month and you expect it to increase by 1 percent a year. The long-term forecast for housing in your area is that house prices are expected to rise at a rate of 5 percent a year for the next 20 years. With $25,000 down, you are able to obtain a 5-year, $250,000 mortgage at 7 percent, compounded monthly and amortized over 20 years (the value of the house you are considering is $275,000). Every five years you will have to renegotiate the mortgage, and you expect interest rates to increase by 50 basis points (½ a percentage point) each time. Assume zero taxes.
    a. If you expect to earn 10 percent on your investments, should you buy a house or continue to rent? (Suggestion: use a spreadsheet to solve this problem.)
    b. Would your answer change if you only expected to earn 4 percent on your investments?

34. Calculate the initial cash flows (CF_0) for the following projects. Which project has a larger CF_0?
    a. Project A: equipment purchase price = $200,000; installation cost = $5,000; extra working capital requirement = $50,500
    b. Project B: machine purchase price = $120,500; shipping cost = $10,000; decrease in working capital = $20,000; opportunity cost = $80,500

35. Describe how CCA recapture and CCA terminal losses occur and their tax treatment.

36. You are given the following information: C_0 = $300,000; CCA rate (d) = 0.3; T = 0.4; RF = 4.5%; project beta = 1.2; market risk premium = 10%; SV_n = $35,000; UCC_n = $55,000. This project has a 5-year life.
    a. Calculate the discount rate.
    b. Assuming that the asset class is terminated, calculate the present value of the CCA tax shield.
    c. Calculate the PV (CCA tax shield) if the asset class remains open.

37. You are given the following information: CFBT = $195,000; T = 40%; this project will last for six years. The project has a 1.5-percent extra risk premium compared with the firm's cost of capital. The firm has 30 percent debt at a cost of 6 percent, 50 percent common equity at a cost of 12 percent, and the remainder is preferred shares at 8 percent.
    a. What is the WACC?
    b. What is this firm's cost of capital?
    c. Calculate the present value of operating cash flows.

38. Brigid Co. has the following potential project:

Machine price = $1,600,000; additional inventory requirement = $50,000. Cash flows will be generated at year end. Rev_1 = $250,000 and grows at 5 percent each year for five years, while $Cost_1$ = $100,000 and grows at 4 percent. At the end of the five-year project, the assets can be sold for $20,000, while the additional inventory that was tied up will be released. The applicable CCA rate land purchase and machine is 30 percent. The tax rate = 45%, and RF = 4.5%; project beta = 1.5; ER_M = 9.5%. The ending UCC = $124,500.

Calculate the NPV of the project if the asset class remains open upon termination of the project. Decide whether or not Brigid Co. should accept the project.

39. Calculate the NPV in Practice Problem 38 assuming a best case of the following: project life = 20 years; project beta = 0.8; SVn = $100,000; $Rev1$ = $500,000.

✱ 40. You have been hired as consultants to XrayGlasses Corporation (XGC). XGC is in the process of deciding whether to invest in a new production facility. The new facility will enable it to produce and sell X-ray machines to airports. The manufacturing and marketing process is not very different from their current line of business. The management of XGC has produced certain estimates about the new facility. Review the estimates to:
   a. Calculate beginning UCC, CCA, and ending UCC each year.
   b. Calculate investment, opportunity cost, and changes in net working capital each year. Note that these items are not subject to tax.
   c. Calculate revenue and cost of X-ray machines project each year and the lost revenue and saved cost of X-ray glasses each year.
   d. Calculate after-tax cash flows each year.
   e. Determine the appropriate discount rate for the X-ray machines project.
   f. Determine the NPV of this project to XrayGlasses Corporation. Make a recommendation, with supporting arguments, to the management of XrayGlasses about the project.
   - Cost of the machinery: $45,000; installation costs: $15,000

   - Life of the project: five years; the expected salvage value of the machine is $2,000

   - An environmental assessment of the building site that is already paid: $200,000

   - Charles LeCrook has offered XrayGlasses $150,000 for the building. XrayGlasses paid $45,000 for the building 10 years ago and spent $50,000 last month on renovations.

   - The CCA rate on the machinery is 25 percent, and there are other assets in the pool. At the end the project, the pool is not expected to be closed. The firm's tax rate is 35 percent.

   - Currently work-in-progress inventory is $65,000. This is expected to increase by $2,000 immediately and to remain at that level for the life of the project. This inventory will be sold at the end of the project.

   - Currently accounts receivable are $15,000. This is expected to increase by $3,000 by the end of year 1. The higher level of accounts receivable is expected to continue until the end of the project, at which time the accounts will be paid in full.

   - Currently accounts payable are $25,000. This is expected to increase by $2,000 by the end of year 1. The higher level of accounts payable is expected to continue until the end of the project, at which time the accounts will be paid in full.

   - XGC expects to sell 25 machines in year 1, 30 in year 2, and 40 machines per year for years 3 to 5.

   - Variable costs are expected to be $5,000 per machine; the expected sales price is $50,000.

   - Annual fixed costs for the firm are currently $900,000 per year and will rise to $930,000 during the project.

- Currently the firm sells 400 pairs of x-ray glasses to airport security guards each year. These sales are expected to disappear when the x-ray machines enter service. The price of a pair of glasses is $550 and the cost of production is $50.

- The company will have to borrow to finance the start-up of the project. The expected interest expense is $5,000 per year. Each year the firm will have to repay $3,000 of the principal of the loan. Overall, the firm expects to remain at its optimal capital structure.

- Currently the firm pays $25,000 in dividends. This is expected to increase to $28,000 during the life of the project.

- The yield to maturity of the firm's debt is 5 percent, the cost of equity is 14 percent, and the WACC is 10 percent.

Use the following information to answer practice problems 41 to 45.

41. GG Inc. has a project that requires purchases of capital assets costing $40,000 and additional raw material inventory of $2,000. Shipping and installation costs are $1,500. GG Inc. estimated that the project would generate an annual operating after-tax cash flow of $5,600 for six years at each year end. At the end of the project, the assets can be sold for $4,000, while the additional inventory that was tied up will be released. The assets are in asset class 9, which has a CCA rate of 30 percent. The tax rate = 40%, and k = 15%. The ending UCC = $8,469. Calculate PV of CCA tax shield by formula. Calculate the NPV of the project if the asset class is closed on termination of the project. Decide whether or not GG Inc. should accept the project.

42. Repeat Practice Problem 41 assuming that the project would generate annual revenue of $70,000 and annual costs of $40,000 for six years. Also, assume the asset class will remain open.

43. Repeat Practice Problem 41 assuming that the project would generate annual revenue of $70,000 and annual costs of $40,000 for six years. Also, the asset class will be closed at the end of six years.

44. Calculate the NPV of the project described in Practice Problem 41, but assume that the project would generate annual revenue of $70,000 and annual costs of $40,000 for six years. Assume the discount rate has changed based on the following information: RF = 3.4%; project beta = 1.2; the market risk premium = 5.5%; and the firm is financed entirely by equity. Assume the asset class will remain open. What is the percentage change in the NPV because of the change in the discount rate? Decide whether or not the project should be accepted.

45. Calculate the operating cash flow NPV break-even point for the project described in Practice Problem 41 by using a 15-percent discount rate. Also, the asset class will be closed at the end of six years.

46. Calculate the present value of the operating cash flows if the revenue of a project grows at 5 percent, while expense grows at 4 percent, given that Revenue$_1$ = $15,000 and Expense$_1$ = $7,000. Assume the firm is all-equity financed; RF = 8%; project beta = 0.8; the market risk premium = 5.5%; and T = 40%. The project is expected to last for eight years.

47. a. Describe how CCA expenses change through the life of a project.

   b. Given C0 = $250,000; CCA rate = 0.2%; tax rate = 40%; and year 2 operating income = $150,000, calculate the cash flow in year 2.

48. What is the difference between sensitivity analysis and scenario analysis?

49. You are evaluating a project for a small manufacturing firm. The firm has provided the following data: the initial cost of the project is $2,500; the CCA rate is 10 percent; tax rate is 25 percent; and the cash flow in the first year is $700. Cash flows are expected to increase at 5 percent a year for four years. At the end of the fourth year, the project will end and the machinery acquired to start the project will be scrapped (zero salvage). The asset class is large and will continue. The appropriate discount rate is 7 percent.

a. Calculate beginning UCC, CCA, ending CCA, and after-tax cash flow in each year. Calculate the NPV of this project.

b. You have also obtained the following information about the best- and worst-case scenarios. In the best case, the cash flow in the first year will be $900 and will grow at 8 percent a year. In the worst case, the cash flow in the first year will be $300 and will grow at 2 percent a year. The base case was presented above. The probability of the worst case is 30 percent, best case is 15 percent, and base case is 55 percent. Calculate the expected NPV of the project.

c. You are not very confident about the growth rate assumption and the initial cash flow estimate. Do a sensitivity analysis to assess the impact of possible errors in those estimates. Assume that growth rates could be 3 percent, 5 percent, or 7 percent and the initial cash flow could be $400, $700, or $1,000.

d. Using the base case estimates, determine the NPV break-even initial cash flow.

50. Explain how real option valuation (ROV) is applied.

51. AK Radio has hired a consultant to help in the assessment of a project to launch a satellite to deliver a 24/7 infomercial radio station to the world. The satellite costs $500 million and has a CCA rate of 35 percent. The satellite is expected to last 10 years and then burn up in the earth's atmosphere. AK does not expect to replace the satellite, and the asset class will terminate in 10 years. The launch is expected to take place in two years and will cost $5 million. Satellite launches are risky undertakings, and there is a 40 percent chance that the rocket taking the satellite into space will explode on take-off. If the launch fails, AK will close the business, as it will have only $50 million of cash left and will be unable to acquire another satellite.

A terrestrial (land-based) infomercial radio station is expected to generate annual pre-tax operating cash flows of $50 million per year, while a satellite-based system is expected to generate operating cash flows of –$25 million for the first three years after the satellite goes up, and $150 million per year for the next seven years. Due to licensing restrictions, AK must decide now whether it will be a satellite-based or land-based infomercial station. Radio stations can operate only in one area—terrestrial or space.

The tax rate for AK is 35 percent. The appropriate discount rate for AK is 20 percent.

a. Calculate the NPV of a terrestrial project. Assume it lasts 12 years.

b. If the satellite launch project is successful, calculate beginning UCC, CCA, ending UCC, after-tax cash flow every year. Calculate the present value of CCA terminal loss. Calculate the NPV of the satellite launch project if it is successful.

c. If the satellite launch project fails, calculate beginning UCC, CCA, ending UCC, after-tax cash flow every year. Calculate the present value of CCA terminal loss. Calculate the NPV of the satellite launch project if it fails.

d. Calculate the NPV of the satellite launch project. Do you recommend that AK invest in the satellite launch project?

e. Describe how your analysis would change if the licensing restriction allowed AK to decide on terrestrial or space in two years.

52. The CFO of CanGold Company is considering investing in a gold mine in Mongolia. The mine will cost $200 million to get into production and will last for one year. At the end of one year, it is expected to produce 1 million ounces of gold. The price of gold is expected to be $500 an ounce in one year (the forward price). The current price of gold is $300 an ounce. Fixed costs of production are $50 million and variable costs are $250 per ounce. Assume no taxes or CCA. The appropriate discount rate for the mine is 15 percent. Risk-free borrowing and lending is available at a rate of 3 percent per year.

a. Based on NPV, should CanGold invest in the Mongolian gold mine?

b. If in one year, we know that the price of gold will be either $200 per ounce or $850 per ounce:

i. Describe how having the choice of closing the mine can change the value of the asset.

    ii.   Describe how the volatility of the price of gold could increase the value of the mine.

    iii.   Draw the decision tree for this project.

    iv.   Value the mine as a call option on gold. (Hint: use the arbitrage arguments behind the binomial option pricing model. Think of the mine as a financial security).

53. A consultant has presented the following statement to the board of directors of BigCo:

When comparing two mutually exclusive projects, we only need to consider the NPV. When the two projects have different lives, we recommend comparing the NPV/life (i.e., NPV divided by the number of years) ratios of the projects and choosing the project with the highest ratio. The NPV/life ratio reflects the average annual increase in shareholder value expected from the project.

The Chair of the Board is not convinced and has asked FinCorp Inc. to review this statement. Explain to the Chair why the consultant's approach to dealing with projects of different lives is incorrect. Provide a numerical demonstration to support your arguments.

54. Consider the following scenario and calculate beginning UCC, CCA, ending UCC, after-tax incremental cash flow, and CCA tax shield every year. Annual incremental cash flow includes the lost revenue of the old machine (cash outflow), the saving of maintenance of the old machine (cash inflow), and the maintenance of the new machine (cash outflow). Then decide whether a newspaper, *Weekday*, should replace its current printing press with a new one.

Currently *Weekday* has a printing press in its plant that costs $5,000 a year in maintenance. The maintenance costs are expected to increase by $1,000 a year for the next five years. At the end of the five years, the machine will be scrapped and the salvage value will be zero. The press was fully depreciated eight years ago. The current press has a unique capability to print very large certificates in addition to the regular printing. The revenue from the certificate business is expected to be $1,500 per year for the next five years.

A replacement machine is available at a cost of $25,000 with a life expectancy of five years. At the end of the five years, the salvage value is expected to be $5,000. The CCA rate for the machine is 20 percent. Annual maintenance costs of the new machine are $500 per year.

The company is expected to be very profitable in the future. The real risk-free rate is 2-percent, inflation is expected to remain at 3 percent for the next five years, and the appropriate real discount rate for risky cash flows is 7 percent. The tax rate is 34 percent.

55. GG Inc. is now considering replacing some old equipment. The market price of the old equipment is $50,000 and the salvage value at the end of five years is $15,000. The new equipment will cost $100,000 and could be sold at the end of five years for $35,000. An additional $4,000 in working capital is required and will be released at the end of five years. The new equipment is estimated to generate $10,000 in before-tax operating income, compared with $6,000 for the old one. Assume that $T = 40\%$ and $k = 15\%$. Both the new and old equipment belong to class 10, which has a CCA rate of 30 percent, and the asset class will remain open at the end of five years. Calculate PV of CCA tax shield by formula. Estimate the NPV of the replacement decision and decide whether or not replacement should occur.

56. BathGate Group has just completed its analysis of a project. The CFO has presented the following information to the board of directors:

The initial cost of the project is $15,000. Sales are expected to be 10,000 units in year 1 and are expected to grow by 5 percent per year forever. In year 1, we expect to sell units for $3 each and foresee no real change in unit price. Variable and fixed costs are zero.

The firm's required rate of return is 8 percent. The corporate tax rate is 30 percent. Assume the CCA rate is zero.

   a.   Calculate the NPV of this project if there is zero inflation forecasted.

   b.   Calculate the NPV of this project if inflation is forecasted to be 2 percent per year. Assume the required rate of return is nominal.

   c.   Calculate the NPV of this project if inflation is forecasted to be 2 percent per year, and the firm requires a real rate of return of 8 percent.

15 | Mergers and Acquisitions

LEARNING OBJECTIVES

15.1   Describe the different types of takeovers.

15.2   Explain securities legislation as it applies to takeovers.

15.3   Differentiate between friendly and hostile acquisitions and describe the process of a typical friendly acquisition.

15.4   Explain the various motivations underlying mergers and acquisitions.

15.5   Identify the valuation issues involved in assessing mergers and acquisitions.

15.6   Identify the issues involved in accounting for mergers and acquisitions.

M&A [mergers and acquisitions] activity in Canada kicked off with 120 transactions worth US$34.7b in Q1 2012, an 84.2 percent increase in value compared to Q4 2011 (116 deals worth US$18.8b) and a 118.3 percent increase compared to Q1 2011 (105 deals worth US$15.9b). Aggregate M&A value was at its highest level in Q1 2012 since Q3 2008, which had 133 transactions worth US$36.8b.

Energy, Mining & Utilities was the most active sector in the top deals table, representing six transactions. The consolidated sector represented 46.7 percent of Canada deals by value, with 37 deals worth US$16.2b. The energy sector alone made up 28 deals worth an aggregate US$14.3b.

The largest deal in Q1 2012, which fell into the agriculture sector, was announced at the end of the quarter when Canada-based Viterra Inc. agreed to be acquired by the Switzerland-based commodity provider Glencore. The pending deal, expected to close during the second quarter of 2012, is valued at US$7.3b.

Source: The Mergermarket Group, "Mergermarket's Canadian M&A Round-up for Q1 2012." Mergermarket press release, April 17, 2012. Available at www.mergermarket.com.

CHAPTER 15 **PREVIEW**

In chapters 13 and 14, we discussed the issues surrounding the typical capital expenditure decisions of firms. We focused on typical investments that would help the existing firm grow from within—this is often referred to as "organic growth." However, firms can also grow by acquiring other firms or by acquiring selected assets from other firms. Sometimes an entirely new entity is formed; at other times the acquiring firm simply becomes larger and the "target" firm ceases to exist. In this chapter, we illustrate how financial decisions about mergers and acquisitions can be evaluated using standard discounted cash flow valuation techniques.

15.1 TYPES OF TAKEOVERS

Learning Objective 15.1
Describe the different types of takeovers.

takeover the transfer of control from one ownership group to another

acquisition the purchase of one firm by another

merger the combination of two firms into a new legal entity

Few topics generate more interest from the financial media than the subject of corporate **takeovers**, which refers to the transfer of control from one ownership group to another. The chapter-opening vignette touches upon the level of takeover activity (referred to generically as merger and acquisition or M&A activity) during the first quarter of 2012. In fact, these takeovers can occur in several manners, which are described below.

The terms "mergers," "acquisitions," and "takeovers" are often used in different ways. An **acquisition** occurs when one firm (the acquiring firm or bidder) completely absorbs another firm (the target firm). Under this arrangement, the acquiring firm retains its identity, while the acquired firm ceases to exist. An example is provided by the acquisition of Foster's, an Australian brewer, by SAB Miller of the United States. for AUS$9.9 billion (US$10.2 billion) in December of 2011.[1] Immediately following approval of the acquisition by not only shareholders, but also the Supreme Court in the state of Victoria, Foster's ceased trading. This illustrates the key idea that, in an acquisition, the purchased company disappears as all senior management functions reside with the acquirer.

In contrast, a **merger** is usually the combination of two firms into a new legal entity. Such a situation notionally occurred in 2008, when the TSX Group Inc. and the Montreal Exchange Inc. combined to form the TMX Group Inc., which exists in this form today.

Some "mergers" run into issues over the intent to merge equals. Consider, for example, the proposed 2011 merger between the TMX Group Inc. and the London Stock Exchange (LSE) in the U.K., which failed to materialize due to a lack of investor support. One of the key issues was that the deal called for a "merger of equals," yet LSE shareholders would receive 55 percent of the shares in the new entity, versus 45 percent for TMX shareholders. In addition, the board of directors would consist of eight LSE-appointed directors versus seven TMX-appointed ones.

In some cases, issues arise because after companies have announced their intention to merge as equals, events occur that take them down a different path. For example, on May 2, 1998, Daimler-Benz and Chrysler announced that they were combining as a "merger of equals" worth almost US$40 billion. The combination of the third-largest U.S. car company with the prestigious maker of Mercedes-Benz cars was obviously big news, and the fact that the new company's name was a hybrid of the merging firms' names suggested that it was an integration of the two companies, with neither dominant. For a time, it appeared as if nothing had changed, but in 2003 the *Detroit News* announced that the merger was in fact a takeover or acquisition of Chrysler by Daimler. This sparked multiple lawsuits, since it was clear that Chrysler was becoming a division of Daimler, and effective control and decision-making would take place in Germany.

These examples indicate the elasticity of the terms "merger," "acquisition," and "takeover." The proposed Miller takeover of Foster was clearly an acquisition right from the start, with Foster ceasing to exist, while the TMX Group Inc. was formed out of a merger of the TSX and

---

[1] At the time of writing, the transaction was subject to approval by the Australian government, which put conditions on the acquisition, especially for domestic production of domestically consumed beverages.

the Montreal Exchange. The furor over Daimler's acquisition of Chrysler arose from the fact that it was announced as a merger, with the implication that the two companies would be integrated in the new entity, with shared responsibilities and management, when in reality it was an acquisition that left Daimler in charge. Shortly after, most of the senior Chrysler management left.

Financing Takeovers

One key consideration in classifying acquisitions and mergers is the means by which the deal is financed. Most acquisitions, such as the one discussed in *Finance in the News 15-1*, are made through a **cash transaction**, with the shareholders in the target company receiving cash for their shares. In section 15.2, we will briefly discuss securities legislation as it applies to takeovers, but generally, when one company acquires another, the approval of the target company's shareholders is required, since they have to agree to sell their shares. The shareholders of the *acquiring* company do not normally have to give their approval. Buying another company is regarded as similar to buying a new piece of equipment or any other purchase. Only if there is some specific provision in the company's charter do the shareholders of the acquiring firm get to vote on whether or not the company should make the acquisition.

    The alternative to a cash transaction is a **share transaction**, where the acquiring company

cash transaction the receipt of cash for shares by shareholders in a target company

---

finance IN THE NEWS 15-1 URS to Buy Flint Energy

URS CORP., the San Francisco-based construction company, agreed to buy Flint Energy Services Ltd. for C$1.25 billion in cash to add projects servicing oil and natural gas producers in Western Canada.

Flint shareholders will get C$25 per share, URS said in a statement, about 67 percent more than Flint's C$14.90 closing price in Toronto trading on Feb. 17. URS also plans to assume C$225 million of Calgary-based Flint's debt.

Buying Flint adds 10,000 employees serving companies in the oil and gas producing areas of Western Canada and the Southwest, Appalachian and Rocky Mountain regions of the U.S. to URS's 47,000 staff. The deal will raise URS's 2012 earnings by 20 cents to 30 cents a share and boost its sales from the oil and gas industry to about 22 percent of total revenue, according to the statement.

"Expanding our presence in the oil and gas sector has been a longstanding strategic priority for URS," URS Chief Executive Officer Martin Koffel said in the statement.

The deal values Flint at 14.3 times earnings before interest, tax, depreciation, and amortization, compared with the average of 9.2 times EBITDA for nine comparable deals, according to data compiled by Bloomberg.

Flint, which has dropped 23 percent in the past year, last traded at C$14.90 before markets in the U.S. and Canada were closed. The decline compares with the 7.1 percent decline in the Morgan Stanley Capital International World Energy Small Cap index in the past 12 months.

Flint's operations in Canada accounted for about 80 percent of sales in the 12 months ended in September. The deal is expected to be completed in the second quarter of 2012, the companies said.

Financing in Place

URS, which has financing in place to complete the transaction, plans to use an existing credit facility and new debt for permanent financing, according to the statement. Flint Chief Executive Officer Bill Lingard will continue to manage the company's operations as a new division of URS.

"Flint offers a diversified, full cycle of services, has limited exposure to fixed price contracts, and derives its earnings entirely from operations in the stable North American region," said H. Thomas Hicks, URS's chief financial officer.

The acquisition will generate cost savings of $10 million to $15 million this year, assuming the deal closes in the second quarter, and additional future cost reductions, Hicks said.

Source: Donville, Christopher, and Mider, Zachary, R., "URS to buy Flint Energy for $1.26 billion to boost North American presence." Bloomberg News, February 20, 2012. Available at www.bloomberg.com. Reprinted by permission.

---

offers shares or some combination of cash and shares to the target company's shareholders. For example, the 2012 all-share takeover bid by Glencore International PLC for Xstrata PLC provided 2.8 shares to Xstrata shareholders for each of their Xstrata shares, valuing the deal at $30-billion.[2] In contrast to a cash transaction, a share transaction often does require the approval of the acquiring firm's shareholders, depending on whether the firm has a limit on

share transaction the offer by an acquiring company of shares or a combination of cash and shares to the target company's shareholders

---

[2] Xstrata CEO Poised to Get $46-Million Retention Package." *The Globe and Mail*, May 31, 2012. Retrieved from http://www.theglobeandmail.com/report-on-business/international-business/european-business/xstrata-ceo-poised-to-get-46-million-retention-package/article4219796/.

its authorized share capital. If the firm's authorized share capital is limited to, say, 3 million shares, and it wants to offer shares in excess of this limit, then shareholder approval is needed. To get around this, in recent years, most companies have sought and received shareholder approval to issue an unlimited number of shares. However, this does point to the most basic distinction between a merger and an acquisition.

Amalgamations

amalgamation a genuine merger in which both sets of shareholders must approve the transaction

In a merger, a new company is created, so both sets of shareholders have to agree to exchange their existing shares for shares in the new company. This means that, in a genuine merger, both sets of shareholders are required to approve the transaction. In Canada, this process is called an **amalgamation**. For example, the TSX–Montreal Exchange combination discussed above was referred to as an amalgamation, and the announcement began by stating that 99.6 percent approval had been obtained from the Montreal Exchange shareholders. The two companies approve an amalgamation agreement, and a special meeting of the shareholders is called to vote on the agreement. Under the *Canada Business Corporations Act* (CBCA), 21 days' notice is given for this special meeting, and since the shareholders have to vote, all the normal rules for proxy statements and other information are invoked. The basic rule is that two-thirds of the shareholders of both amalgamating firms have to approve the special resolution to amalgamate.[3] This can sometimes result in tense battles as dissident shareholders refuse to support an agreement crafted by the two sets of managers. An amalgamation also takes place when the acquirer has purchased all the shares in the target, but in this case, since the acquirer owns all the shares, the process is a formality.

going private transaction or **issuer bid** a special form of acquisition where the purchaser already owns a majority stake in the target company

An amalgamation can also become a tense situation after a firm has partially completed a takeover. Sometimes the acquirer can end up with a majority of the shares, say 70 percent, so that it knows it can get the two-thirds majority to approve an amalgamation, yet there are still 30 percent of the shares outstanding and held by dissident shareholders who have not agreed to sell their shares. This is a special form of acquisition called a **going private transaction** or **issuer bid**.

These sorts of transactions have been common in Canada, because there were many Canadian companies with a majority of shares owned by another company and only a minority owned by Canadian shareholders. For example, Imperial Oil's majority owner is Exxon. Similarly, U.S. parent companies have owned the majority of shares for companies like DuPont Canada, Shell Oil Canada, Sears Canada, Goodyear Canada, Ford Canada, and so on. In such cases, the minority of shares traded in the Canadian market were not the result of failed takeover bids but of U.S. companies' desire to keep a public "float" of the shares in the hands of Canadian shareholders. This motivation became less important after Canada signed the Free Trade Agreement (FTA) with the United States and the economies were more closely integrated. A side effect of the FTA was that U.S. multinationals wanted to integrate their companies in the two countries, and buying out the Canadian minority shareholders removed an obstacle to this.[4]

fairness opinion an opinion provided by an independent expert regarding the true value of a firm's shares, based on an external valuation

Regardless of how a public minority of shareholders is created, the issues and principles are the same. When a controlling shareholder seeks approval for an amalgamation, special rules kick in. The presumption is that the controlling shareholder has a much more accurate knowledge of the true value of the shares and will abuse this position unless safeguards are in place. The critical safeguards are that a majority of the minority shareholders approve the special resolution to amalgamate the two companies and that there be a **fairness opinion**. A fairness opinion is an independent expert's opinion about the value of a firm's shares, based on an external valuation. These valuations are particularly difficult given that, with a controlling shareholder, there is little possibility of any other party buying the shares.

---

[3] Note that this is two-thirds of all the shareholders, including groups that do not normally have the right to vote. Moreover, sometimes they have the right to vote as a class, so a small group can defeat an amalgamation proposal.

[4] Under the CBCA, directors of a Canadian company have to act in the best interests of the company as a whole, and not just the majority shareholder. This restricted the ability of the U.S. parents to integrate their Canadian subsidiaries into their North American operations.

A good example of this principle comes from Sears, Roebuck and Co., which on December 5, 2005, announced that it would make a bid for the 46 percent of Sears Canada that it did not own, paying $16.86 a share. Sears' initial aim was to buy enough shares that it would own 90 percent; under Ontario securities law, when minority shareholders hold less than 10 percent of a company's shares, they must accept the offer that has been accepted by the other shareholders. This rule prevents a "holdup" problem that might occur if the last shareholder asks for a ridiculously high price. However, since the offer was an insider bid, Sears Canada set up a committee of six independent members of the board of directors to evaluate the bid. They hired Genuity Capital Markets to do a fairness opinion, which came in at a range of $19 to $22.25 a share—well above the offer from Sears, Roebuck. On this basis, the independent directors unanimously rejected the offer from their own company's parent and also announced that they would not stand for re-election at the May 2006 annual general meeting. (Given the directors' decision, they probably would not have been nominated for re-election.)

In March 2006, Sears, Roebuck announced that it had received only 9.5 percent of the 46 percent of the Sears Canada shares it did not hold. It also announced that instead of trying to buy the shares directly, it would seek a statutory amalgamation at a special meeting of shareholders. In this case, all it needed to amalgamate Sears Canada with Sears, Roebuck was the two-thirds necessary for an amalgamation plus a majority of the minority shareholders. It also sweetened the price marginally to $18. However, a new valuation by Genuity Capital reiterated its valuation and judgements on both sides.

This situation deteriorated when it was discovered that Sears' Canadian financial advisors had entered into a "lock-up agreement" to sell shares they controlled to Sears, Roebuck without disclosing this. The Ontario Securities Commission (OSC) was asked to rule on this and decided that these shares could not be counted as part of the majority of the minority rule, a decision that was upheld by the Ontario Divisional Court.

CONCEPT REVIEW QUESTIONS

1. What is the difference between an acquisition and a merger?
2. What is an amalgamation?
3. What is the majority of the minority rule?

15.2 SECURITIES LEGISLATION

The previous discussion on takeovers highlights the role of securities legislation in determining what can be done and when. In fact, many takeovers are nullified by regulators, such as the proposed merger of the NYSE Euronext and the Deutsche Bourse, which was shot down by European regulators. Authorities can reject takeovers for a variety of reasons, including the following:

Learning Objective 15.2
Explain securities legislation as it applies to takeovers.

- concerns related to national security
- concerns about "sensitive" industries that are seen as critical to the nation (this is why there are foreign ownership restrictions for Canadian banks)
- anti-trust concerns in situations where an amalgamation of two or more businesses would create an entity that would too narrowly restrict competition

In Canada, regulators review foreign takeovers over $1 billion (previously $299 million) and subject them to the so-called net benefit rule. Questions about how, precisely, this rule is implemented have been the cause of much concern in Canada, especially in light of the 2010 rejection of the Australian giant BHP Billiton's proposed takeover of Potash Corporation of Saskatchewan Inc. These issues are discussed in *Finance in the News 15-2*.

finance INTHENEWS 15-2 BHP Billiton Walks Away from PotashCorp

BHP BILLITON has withdrawn its $40-billion hostile-takeover bid of Potash Corporation of Saskatchewan, the Australian company said Sunday.

The company's announcement comes about 10 days after the Canadian government ruled the acquisition would not provide a net benefit to the country.

In a statement, BHP Billiton suggested the government's opinion was incorrect.

"BHP Billiton continues to believe its offer would have resulted in a significant net benefit to Canada …. As a package, the proposed undertakings offered by BHP Billiton … were unparalleled in substance, scope and duration, reflecting the importance of potash to Canada and Saskatchewan," the statement said.

"The company has offered to commit to legally binding undertakings that would have, among other things, increased employment, guaranteed investment and established the company's global potash headquarters in Saskatoon."

Federal Industry Minister Tony Clement publicly declared the government's decision to quash the takeover on Nov. 3 but gave BHP Billiton 30 days to make additional representations so he could make a "final decision."

The *Investment Canada Act* allows Ottawa to block any deal worth $299 million or more if the government finds it doesn't provide "net benefits" to Canadians.

Sunday's development renders the need for a further decision from Clement moot.

Clement Responds

In the wake of Sunday's announcement, Clement issued a statement thanking BHP Billiton for its "good faith and integrity" while Industry Canada evaluated its bid.

Clement hinted he's open to hearing suggestions for how the government could improve the bid-review process for major investments in Canada.

"Our policy has always been clear: we welcome foreign investment for all the benefits it brings, including new ideas, sources of capital, and job creation," he said. "Simply put, foreign investment is in the best interests of Canada and an open global economy."

Federal Minister of Industry Tony Clement holds a press conference after issuing a statement about BHP Billiton and PotashCorp in Toronto on Sunday November 14, 2010. (Chris Young/The Canadian Press)

The Saskatchewan government also opposed the sale of PotashCorp, citing a study that pointed out losses in provincial revenues over the next decade and because potash is a strategic resource in how it's used in food production.

The province produces 30 percent of the world's potash, a crop nutrient.

BHP had offered to offset provincial revenue losses by contributing to an infrastructure fund, a proposal Saskatchewan officials have called inadequate.

Despite the failed bid for PotashCorp, BHP Billiton CEO Marius Kloppers restated his commitment Sunday to the Jansen Lake mine in Saskatchewan.

Kloppers said Sept. 20 that BHP has already invested $400 million in the Jansen project and hopes to start producing potash from the mine by 2015.

Once at full production, Jansen is expected to produce about eight million tonnes per year.

Source: "BHP Billiton Walks Away from PotashCorp." CBC News website, November 14, 2010. Available at www.cbc.ca. Reprinted by permission.

In addition to takeovers that cause anti-trust and/or foreign ownership concerns, securities legislation is relevant for all potential takeovers because it governs the exchange of shares by the target company's shareholders and protects their right to receive full value for their shares. We will examine other aspects of securities law later, when discussing new issues of securities, but the main thing to remember is that this is a provincial responsibility, and there are slight differences between provinces. However, the *Ontario Securities Act*, administered by the OSC, contains many features that are common to all jurisdictions, and we will use it to illustrate some of the usual characteristics of securities legislation.

There are several critical shareholder percentages that investors have to be aware of:

1. 10 percent: early warning

2. 20 percent: takeover bid

3. 50.1 percent: control

4. 66.7 percent: amalgamation

5. 90 percent: minority squeeze-out

The 10-percent early warning threshold (which is set at 5 percent in the United States) refers to the level of shareholding by any one owner that requires a report to be sent to the OSC. This lets the company know who owns its shares and whether a significant block has been bought by a potential acquirer. Once a shareholder holds 20 percent of shares, he or she cannot buy any more shares in the open market without making a takeover bid (we will discuss this in more detail later). The 50.1 percent ownership level gives a company control so that it can call a special meeting of the shareholders (5 percent ownership is required to attend the meeting) and change the membership of the board of directors (BOD). In Canada, but not in the United States, members of the BOD can be removed without cause, so the majority shareholder can change management and take control of the firm's affairs.[5]

As described above, a firm can seek to hold a special meeting of shareholders to vote on an amalgamation, which needs support from owners of 66.7 percent of the shares, but the amalgamation can be disputed by a majority of the minority shareholders. Finally, following a takeover bid, if the firm owns 90 percent of the shares, it can force the minority of the shareholders to sell their shares at the takeover price. This prevents a small minority from frustrating a bid that has been accepted by the majority of shareholders. Otherwise, a few dissidents could wreak havoc by refusing to sell a small number of shares.

These share percentage milestones explain a lot of takeover behaviour. Initially, most firms will acquire less than the 10 percent of shares that trigger the early warning and then purchase up to the 20 percent level of the target's shares in the open market. This is referred to as "obtaining a toehold." Firms do this to acquire the shares at the market price without paying a premium. After acquiring 20 percent, buying any more shares requires a takeover bid, which is an offer to purchase outstanding voting shares that, together with the offeror's shares, equal 50 percent or more of the target's shares.

This definition of a takeover bid applies to individuals alone or "working in concert with others." Otherwise, a company could buy 20 percent itself and then get friendly parties or another subsidiary to buy two more blocks of 20 percent and thereby effect a takeover without making a takeover bid.

Unless the purchase is exempt from the *Ontario Securities Act*, any further takeover bid must then follow strict rules. A takeover circular (similar to a prospectus) describing the bid, financing, and all relevant information must be sent to all shareholders for review. The target then has 15 days to circulate a letter indicating acceptance or rejection, and the bid has to be open for 35 days from its announcement in the newspaper or the mailing of documents to shareholders. Shareholders then **tender** to the offer by signing the authorizations sent to them; in the event that another firm makes a competing offer, they can withdraw their acceptance. A competing bid automatically increases the takeover window by 10 days.

tender to sign an authorization accepting a takeover bid made to target company shareholders

The takeover bid does not have to be for 100 percent of the shares. If the bid is for, say, 60 percent, and more shares are tendered, the acquirer pro-rates the shares tendered so everyone receives an equal proportion. That is, if 80 percent are tendered and 60 percent are bought, then everyone who has tendered gets to sell 75 percent (60 ÷ 80) of the shares tendered. While the tender offer is outstanding, the acquirer can buy another 5 percent of shares

---

[5] In the United States, directors have a fixed term and cannot be forcibly removed simply because of a change in ownership. By having directors serve non-concurrent terms, a firm can prevent a majority owner from immediately changing the board and senior management. As a result, it may take several years for a majority owner to change directors and senior managers.

through the facilities of the stock exchange as long as it announces that it intends to do so. Finally, the tender offer price cannot be for less than the average price of shares that the acquirer has bought in the previous 90 days. This is to prevent a coercive takeover bid, where the acquirer offers one price for the shares needed to get control and then a lower price once it has control. (This kind of bid is called a two-part tender offer and is illegal in Canada because it produces a rush to sell into the higher price at the first stage and "coerces" shareholders.[6])

The basic objective of these rules is to make sure that an acquirer treats all the shareholders fairly and everyone gets the same price. Otherwise there is an economic incentive to lock up shares early at a high price, so that an acquirer has control and can then offer a lower price, knowing that no one else can mount a competing bid. In this way, different classes of shareholders are treated differently, and the shares are sold below their true value. As the Sears, Roebuck example highlights, once you have control, no one else can bid and there is a temptation to try to buy the remaining shares cheaply.

As mentioned earlier, all takeovers have to abide by these rules unless they are exempt from the *Ontario Securities Act* for one of the following reasons:

- Where there is limited involvement by shareholders in Ontario—say a takeover of a Manitoba company in which there are very few Ontario shareholders—securities legislation in another province (in this case, Manitoba) will apply.

- Securities legislation is concerned with the involvement of the public, so takeovers of private firms are exempt.

- An acquirer can also buy shares from fewer than five shareholders as long as the premium over the market price is not more than 15 percent. This is to allow the sale of blocks of shares.

- Finally, and most importantly, a normal tender offer can be made through a stock exchange as long as no more than 5 percent of the shares are purchased through the exchange over a one-year period. This 5-percent rule allows for **creeping takeovers**, where a company acquires a target over a long period of time by slowly accumulating shares.

creeping takeover the acquisition of a target company over time by the gradual accumulation of its shares

There are many other regulations that relate to takeovers. In fact, a "solvency" clause that was inserted by BCE Inc.'s lawyers to protect them against bondholder litigation proved to be a "dagger" that ended the proposed $52-billion takeover of BCE Inc. by the Ontario Teachers' Pension Plan and a group of investors, as KPMG refused to sign off on the deal in November 2008.

CONCEPT REVIEW QUESTIONS

1. What is a tender?
2. What is a takeover circular?
3. What is a creeping takeover?

LESSONS TO BE LEARNED

The termination of the proposed BCE Inc. takeover that was led by the Ontario Teachers' Pension Plan, discussed above, was attributed to an accounting "technicality"; however, this termination followed months of speculation about how Teachers' could possibly carry through with the deal despite insisting that it would. The doubts arose because the credit and private equity markets completely dried up during the period after the deal was originally announced, and people wondered where, or at what cost, Teachers' could possibly obtain the necessary financing. And, of course, stock market prices had plummeted during the fall of 2008, so the agreed-upon purchase price of BCE Inc. seemed extremely high in comparison to prevailing stock prices at the time. Most experts would quietly agree that this accounting technicality saved Teachers' a lot of hardship. In fact, after the deal fell through, Teachers' eventually sold its remaining 4 percent stake in BCE for approximately $23, well below the $42.75 per share offer.[7]

continued

---

[6] Coercive two-part tender offers are allowed in the United States.
[7] BCE Inc. closed trading at $41.78 on June 13, 2012.

15.3 FRIENDLY VERSUS HOSTILE TAKEOVERS

Friendly Takeovers

Learning Objective 15.3
Differentiate between friendly and hostile acquisitions and describe the process of a typical friendly acquisition.

With a knowledge of securities legislation, we can now consider whether an acquisition should be hostile or friendly and discuss how a deal is hammered out. To understand this, think first about the difficulty of valuing a company when an external party has access only to public sources of information. How do you value a small biotech company, for example, when you have no direct information on whether recent lab tests were positive or negative? Similarly, for an oil and gas company or mining firm, it may not be obvious how much potential is left in an oil and gas field or mineral reserve. The obvious thing to do, when faced with this uncertainty, is to go to the target company and ask whether it is interested in being acquired. In this situation, the acquirer hopes for a **friendly acquisition**. The URS–Flint deal discussed in *Finance in the News 15-1* was a friendly deal that resulted in a 70 percent premium offer, while *Finance in the News 15-4* discusses another friendly deal that resulted in a 10.5 percent premium offer—so it is hard to make generalizations about the premiums offered based on the nature of the deal.

friendly acquisition the acquisition of a target company that is willing to be taken over

Friendly acquisitions also start out when the target voluntarily puts itself into play. This can occur for many reasons, but it often happens when the founder is no longer playing a part in the business, and it is time for the firm to leave the controlling owner and be sold to other interests. Such an incident occurred on July 12, 2006, when a deal was reached to sell CHUM Limited to Bell Globemedia for $1.7 billion. In this case, the estate of Allan Waters, the founder of CHUM Limited, agreed to sell its controlling 88.6 percent of the voting shares to Bell Globemedia. If a firm decides to sell itself, it normally consults an investment bank to put together an **offering memorandum** that describes the most important features of the company to potential buyers. This offering memorandum is much like an abbreviated prospectus, which will be discussed in detail with respect to securities issues in Chapter 17. Regardless of whether it is the company that decides to sell itself, or an acquirer that approaches it, the company that is willing to be sold has to provide more information so that its fair value can be estimated.

offering memorandum a document describing a target company's important features to potential buyers

data room a place where a target company keeps confidential information about itself for serious potential buyers to consult

The target firm can disclose more information by setting up a **data room**, where it keeps confidential information. When serious acquirers express interest, they can access the data room by signing a **confidentiality agreement**. Not all acquirers will want to sign a confidentiality agreement, since normally this restricts the acquirer's freedom of action. Typically, the acquirer is prohibited from using the information to damage the target—by hiring away key employees, for example, or approaching key customers. There is also usually a time limit for these restrictions. The objective of the confidentiality agreement is to restrict access to important information to serious potential acquirers. This process of evaluating the target is called **due diligence** and is an important part of the acquisition process.

confidentiality agreement a document signed by a potential buyer to guarantee the buyer will keep confidential any information about a target company that is available in the data room and will not use the data to harm the target company

due diligence the process of evaluating a target company by a potential buyer

Once the confidential data have been evaluated, if the acquirer goes forward, it normally signs a **letter of intent**. This sets out the terms of an agreement and allows the acquirer to do

letter of intent a letter signed by an acquiring company that sets out the terms of agreement of its acquisition, including legal terms

the third stage of the due diligence process,[8] in which its legal team checks the title for property, terms of contracts, and so on, to make sure that all the claims in the data room documents are actually correct, and the firm owns the assets that it says it owns. The letter of intent also usually contains a **no-shop clause**, where the target agrees not to try to find another buyer. In this way, the target shows that it is committed to making the transaction work. There is also usually a termination or **break fee** of approximately 2.5 percent of the value of the transaction. In the case of the URS–Flint deal discussed in *Finance in the News 15-1*, the break fee was $42 million (or 3.4 percent of the deal value), while for the Teacher's–BCE deal the break fee was $800 million (or 1.55 percent of the $51.7-billion deal value).

Break fees have become very controversial. The justification for the break fee is that once companies get into the final round of due diligence, the expectation is that a deal will be completed. However, despite a no-shop clause, sometimes a competing bid does come in. Faced with two alternative offers, a company's BOD has a fiduciary duty to act in the best interests of the shareholders and seek the best possible price. It may then be that the firm that started the process and has committed significant resources to negotiating an agreement finds itself the loser. The break fee is designed to compensate the original acquirer for these costs and to reward it for generating a competing bid and getting the target shareholders a better price.

Once the final due diligence phase has been completed and everything has worked out to the satisfaction of the acquirer, the final sale agreement is reached and ratified, or agreed to, by both parties. If it is a private company, that is the end of the story, but for a firm with public shareholders, the deal then goes to the shareholders for approval.

This typical process is illustrated in Figure 15-1.

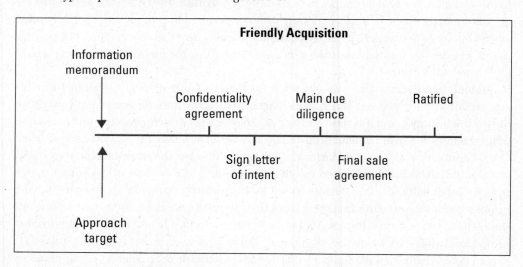

FIGURE 15-1 *Friendly Acquisition*

no-shop clause a clause in a letter of intent stating that the target agrees not to find another buyer, demonstrating its commitment to close the transaction

break fee a fee paid to an acquirer or target should the other party terminate the acquisition, often 2.5 percent of the value of the transaction

With a friendly transaction, there is considerable scope for structuring the acquisition to the mutual benefit of both parties. The key areas usually involve careful tax planning, legal structuring to avoid certain liabilities, providing milestones for incentive agreements, and the possibility of "cherry picking" for certain more valuable assets. We will discuss each of these in turn.

Careful tax planning is important in any transaction. When an acquirer uses cash to purchase a company, that cash is always taxable in the hands of the target company shareholders. If the share price has run up significantly, this could mean the shareholders must pay capital gains tax on the appreciation in the value of their shares. On the other hand, a share swap is usually non-taxable. This is why, in many smaller acquisitions, the target company's shares are swapped for preferred shares in the acquiring company. The target's shareholders, usually the founders, get a steady income from the preferred shares and are relieved of day-to-day

---

[8] The first phase is the examination of public information that is usually included in the offering memorandum; the second phase is the provision of confidential documents in the data room; the final phase is the serious verification process.

concerns about their company. The acquiring firm can then integrate the target into its existing operations.

Tax concerns are also the reason a target company's assets, rather than its shares, are sold to the acquirer. In an **asset purchase**, the target firm receives the proceeds from the sale and uses these proceeds to pay off its debts. The target firm then has the option of either "reinventing itself" or liquidating itself and paying out the proceeds to the firm's shareholders. This approach may be attractive to the acquiring firm, since it can depreciate the assets at the value that it has paid for them; there are usually tax advantages from having a higher CCA value. In contrast, the target may be able to shield any potential tax payments with other losses.

Also, sometimes the target firm has contingent liabilities that the acquirer does not wish to assume. For example, there may be potential warranty claims, which create a huge uncertainty surrounding the firm. Sometimes this warranty can be sidestepped by buying the assets. However, this potential is severely limited in some cases. For example, environmental claims generally follow the assets, so you can't dodge an environmental lawsuit from a polluting factory by selling the factory to someone else. In this case, the contingent liability stays with the asset, not the shareholders. Otherwise, legitimate claims could be avoided simply by reorganizing the firm.[9]

Deals often fall through because of fundamental disagreements concerning the target's value. Often the target's managers or founders are optimistic about the future prospects of the firm and value it based on a scenario in which everything goes right. In contrast, the acquirer may have experience with acquisitions that didn't go so well and approaches this one with a more cautious attitude. To bridge the valuation gap when the acquisition is small, "earn outs" are often used: the acquirer pays an upfront price and then makes future payments conditional on the performance of the target after it has been acquired. These future payments are usually based on divisional sales or other reasonably objective data that both parties agree on.

Of course, not all friendly acquisitions follow this process. Some legal experts tell their clients not to sign a letter of intent, because this is essentially a preliminary sale agreement and the acquirer could be held liable if it backs out of the deal.

Hostile Takeovers

In practice, many deals, far from being friendly, are **hostile takeovers**. In a hostile deal, the target has no desire to be acquired, actively rebuffs the acquirer, and refuses to provide any confidential information. Usually, in such cases, the acquirer has already taken a toehold and has 20 percent of the shares, so the target knows it is in for a fight.

In hostile bids there is usually a **tender offer**, in which the acquiring firm makes a public offer to purchase shares of the target firm from its existing shareholders. Typically, the bidder includes the provision that the offer is only good subject to the bidder being able to obtain a certain minimum percentage of the outstanding voting shares. The advantage of this approach to the bidder is that a formal vote by the target shareholders is not required, since they merely decide on their own whether or not they want to sell their shares to the acquiring firm.

When a hostile tender offer is launched, external parties always look for certain clues. The most obvious is the behaviour of the market price relative to the offer price. If the market price immediately jumps above the offer price, the market is saying that a competing offer is likely or that the bid is too low, and the bidder will have to increase the offer price. Alternatively, if the market price stays close to the offer price, it indicates that the price is fair and the deal is likely to go through.

Professionals then look for the amount of trading in the target's shares. Very little trading is usually a bad sign for the acquirer because it means shareholders are sitting on the shares and are reluctant to sell. On the other hand, a large amount of trading indicates that shares

asset purchase a purchase of the firm's assets rather than the firm itself

hostile takeover a takeover in which the target has no desire to be acquired, actively rebuffs the acquirer, and refuses to provide any confidential information

tender offer a public offer in which the acquiring firm offers to purchase shares of the target firm from its existing shareholders

---

[9] Deliberately selling assets to evade legitimate claims on the firm could also open up both sets of shareholders to lawsuits based on fraudulent conveyance.

are cycling from regular investors into the hands of specialists: people who specialize in predicting what happens in takeovers. These specialists are called **arbs**.[10] This is good for the acquirer, since arbs are only interested in selling as long as the price is right. However, the arbs buy the shares after the announcement, so they pay a premium and then expect to get a bigger premium when they sell. Their motivation is to extract the highest possible price.

arbs (short for **arbitrageurs**), specialists who predict what will happen in takeovers and buy and sell shares in target companies, with the possibility of earning a premium

The attempted takeover of Sears Canada, described in section 15.1, was rejected because the $18 offer price was below what the arbs wanted. They had bought the shares after the Sears, Roebuck announcement, hoping for an increase in the price, and then didn't see it happen. As a result, they pressured Sears, Roebuck to increase the offer price. At that time, 14.1 percent of Sears Canada's shares were owned by three New York hedge funds. These are professionally managed funds with managers who are experts in securities law and tactics designed to get the highest price for their shares. Most of the regular investors in Sears Canada sold out to these professional takeover speculators, so it became a battle of wits among experts in the area.

In the Sears Canada example, there is no question that the arbs would sell their shares—it was only a matter of when and at what price. In contrast, in hostile bids, the target doesn't want to be taken over at any price and resists the bid, often entering into anti-takeover tactics. What the target can do is restricted by securities laws, since the securities commissions in Ontario and elsewhere will take a dim view of any action on the part of the target firm that interferes with the fundamental right of shareholders to dispose of their shares at full market value. As a result, takeover defences that work in the United States, for example, do not work in Canada.

defensive tactic a strategy used by a target company to stave off a takeover or to try to get the best deal for its shareholders

One **defensive tactic** used by some BODs is to implement a **shareholder rights plan**, also known as a **poison pill**. Under such a plan, in the event of a takeover, the non-acquiring company shareholders have the right to buy 50 percent more shares at a discounted price. This increase in the number of shares makes the acquisition much more expensive and, if everything else is constant, forces the acquirer to negotiate with the target company and make a friendly offer, since the BOD can then remove the poison pill through a vote.

shareholder rights plan or **poison pill** a plan by a target company that allows its shareholders to buy 50 percent more shares at a discounted price in the event of a takeover, which makes the target company less attractive

Poison pills are also allowed in the United States. Moore Corporation, a large Canadian company, attempted a hostile takeover of Wallace Computer Services, which had a poison pill. Moore Corporation asked for and got a special meeting of shareholders, 78 percent of whom passed a resolution to nullify Wallace's poison pill. However, the Wallace BOD ignored the resolution and refused to nullify the poison pill, thereby making it prohibitively expensive for Moore to proceed. This decision was supported when Moore took Wallace to court; the U.S. court decided that it was up to the business judgement of the BOD.

In contrast, Canadian securities commissions take a completely different view. The acquirer will go to the securities commission directly to get the poison pill nullified. The securities commission then looks to three basic criteria:

- Is there a likelihood of another offer?

- Can the offer be withdrawn?

- Are the shareholders lobbying for the removal of the poison pill?

In Alberta, Saskatchewan,[11] and Ontario, poison pills have been struck down when shareholders lobbied for their removal because they produced very little chance of a counter bid and a good chance that the existing bid would be withdrawn. In contrast, when MDC Corporation attempted to take over Regal Greetings and Gifts Inc. in September 1994, the OSC allowed the poison pill to remain for three weeks, since the target was actively seeking another

---

[10] "Arbs" is short for "arbitrageurs," but technically these specialists are taking significant risks and their positions are not arbitrage (riskless) positions, which involve buying and selling the same security at different prices.

[11] In 1991, the Saskatchewan Court of Appeals struck down a poison pill used by Producers Pipeline to frustrate a takeover by 347883 Alberta Ltd., saying that it was being used by directors who only wanted to retain control of the company and were not necessarily looking out for the best interests of the shareholders.

bidder. The upshot is that, in Canada, poison pills can be used only as a delaying tactic; they cannot be used to frustrate a bid the way they are in the United States.

Other tactics involve making the target unattractive to the acquirer. There are many ways to do this. One tactic, called **selling the crown jewels**, involves selling the asset the acquirer is really interested in. For example, in 1979, Edper Equities made a hostile bid for Brascan Ltd. Brascan's major asset was $500 million in cash that it had just received from selling a Brazilian power plant, so Edper made a partial bid for Brascan. It was a partial bid because Edper only needed 50.1 percent to control 100 percent of the cash. Regardless, the day after Edper approached Brascan, Brascan responded by making a hostile bid for F.W. Woolworth Co., knowing that Edper wanted the cash, not Woolworth.

The other major defence is to try to find a **white knight** to rescue the company and make a counter bid. In fact, as Figure 15-2 shows, 32 percent of hostile takeover attempts in Canada over the 1994–2011 period resulted in the company being acquired by a white knight. In another 4 percent of the attempts, the entrance of a white knight resulted in a revised higher bid from the initial bidder being successful. Figure 15-2 also shows that hostile bidders are successful less than half of the time.

selling the crown jewels the sale of a target company's key assets, which the acquiring company is most interested in, to make the target company less attractive for takeover

white knight an entity that rescues a target company from a hostile takeover by making a counter bid

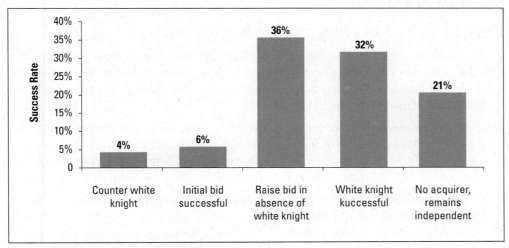

Data source: Data from RBC Capital Markets, April 2012.

FIGURE 15-2 *Hostile Bidder Success Rates, 1994–2011*

An interesting example of a hostile bid that met with many forms of resistance occurred in December 2000, when Indigo Books and Music Inc. made a hostile $13-a-share offer for Chapters Inc., its main bookselling rival, in an attempt to consolidate the Canadian bookselling industry in the face of potential U.S. competition. Chapters fiercely resisted the hostile offer and first tried selling the crown jewels, offering to buy back the minority interest in its Chapters Online Internet bookstore for $3.40 a share (shares in the Internet bookstore had closed trading the previous day at $2.00). This got rid of cash and increased Chapters' ownership in something Indigo did not want. As Gerry Schwartz, who was bankrolling the Indigo bid, said, "Chapters has become virtually the only company in North America to offer cash to bail out the shareholders of a failing e-tailer."[12] When this tactic failed, Chapters paid Future Shop a break fee in order to get it to offer $16.80 a share as a white knight. This forced Indigo to raise its offer to $17.00, which was eventually successful.

Indigo was successful in its hostile bid for Chapters for several reasons. First, the business was straightforward and known to the acquirer, so little due diligence was needed; that is, there was no great uncertainty about the value of Chapters to Indigo. Second, there was no other strategic buyer that could generate similar value by acquiring Chapters. In this respect, a combination of a bookstore (Chapters) and an electronics seller (Future Shop) offered little

---

[12] "Chapters Plots to Fend off Indigo Takeover." CBC News website, December 8, 2000. Retrieved from http://www.cbc.ca/news/business/story/2000/12/08/chapters001208.html.

retail logic—it was simply a mechanism to get Indigo to bid more. Finally, Indigo could afford a long, drawn-out takeover battle, since the value of Chapters was unaffected by the struggle. In contrast, sometimes the value of a target is dissipated as a result of lost contracts or key people leaving the company.

CONCEPT REVIEW QUESTIONS

1. What goes into a confidentiality agreement and why do people sign them?
2. What is due diligence?
3. What is a shareholder rights plan?
4. What are some standard takeover defences?
5. When is it best to mount a hostile bid?

15.4 MOTIVATIONS FOR MERGERS AND ACQUISITIONS

Classifications of Mergers and Acquisitions

Learning Objective 15.4
Explain the various motivations underlying mergers and acquisitions.

Acquisitions are made because the acquirer thinks that the target company will enhance the firm's long-run value. The source of this value depends on the type of acquisition and the structural changes occurring in the economy at various times. There are three broad classifications of mergers and acquisitions:

horizontal merger a merger in which two firms in the same industry combine

1. **Horizontal merger**: This occurs when two firms in the same industry combine. For example, in March 2012, BCE Inc. launched a $3-billion takeover of Astral Media Inc., which is in the same business as BCE but has a very strong presence in the Quebec market, where BCE is lacking. Removing a competitor is often a motive for an acquisition.

vertical merger a merger in which one firm acquires a supplier or another firm that is closer to its existing customers

2. **Vertical merger**: A firm can expand by acquiring a company that is closer to its existing customers ("going forward") or by acquiring a supplier that provides inputs into its production process ("going backward"). Bell Globemedia's acquisition of CHUM Limited is an example of going forward to create an integrated media company, adding CHUM's radio stations to Bell Globemedia's stable of television, print, and other media outlets. AOL's acquisition of Time-Warner—probably the most-storied failed merger in history—was an attempt by AOL to go backward by accessing both media content and a cable distribution system to create an integrated media company. *Finance in the News 15-3* describes Glencore International's $6.1-billion bid for Canadian firm Viterra Inc., one of the world's largest grain companies, which was subsequently approved by 99.8 percent of Viterra's shareholders in May 2012. Glencore is a large Swiss commodities trading company, so this is an example of buying a key supplier, which is critical for most companies, especially a trading company. Notice the following quote in *Finance in the News 15-3* from Curt Vossen, president of Winnipeg-based Richardson International, who noted, "Your greatest fear would be in this global demand environment, can I continue to source the raw materials that I trade?"

conglomerate merger a merger in which two firms in unrelated businesses combine

3. **Conglomerate merger**: This occurs when two firms in unrelated businesses combine. The motivation to create a conglomerate is that the different businesses face different risks, which tend to cancel each other out, lowering the overall risk of the combined company. One classic example comes from November 1981, when the United States Steel Corp. bought control of Marathon Oil Corp. In this case, U.S. Steel was the white knight, bidding in response to a hostile bid for Marathon from Mobil Corp. However, the result was an oil company and a steel company with few economic reasons for the combination. A classic Canadian example of a failed expansion into unrelated business

lines was the 1995 acquisition of Universal Studios by Seagram's, a longstanding Canadian producer of whiskey. This represented an ill-founded desire to branch out into the entertainment business. The business combination faced numerous challenges, and the company ceased to exist after its entertainment and beverage divisions were sold off separately in 2000, ending a legacy that went back to 1857.

Acquisitions can also be classified as domestic or **cross-border (international) M&As**. Many Canadian companies have been involved, as both acquiring firms and as target firms, in high-profile cross-border mergers throughout the years. *Finance in the News 15-3* discusses a situation in which a Canadian company (Viterra) was the target, while *Finance in the News 15-4* discusses an acquisition by a Canadian company looking to expand into new markets. Figure 15-3 shows cross-border M&A activity in Canada from 2004 to the first quarter of 2012. An examination of the reasons underlying this activity leads us to a discussion of some of the common motivations for M&As.

cross-border (international) M&A

a merger or acquisition involving a Canadian and a foreign firm as either the acquiring or target company

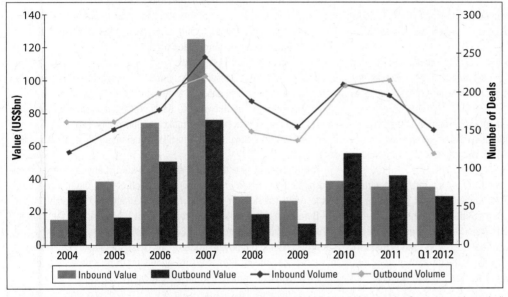

Source: The Mergermarket Group, "Mergermarket's Canadian M&A Round-up for Q1 2012." Mergermarket Group press release, April 17, 2012, p. 3. Available at www.mergermarket.com.

FIGURE 15-3 *Canadian Cross-Border M&A Activity, 2004–12*

finance INTHENEWS 15-3 Glencore's Viterra Deal Spurs Grain Sector Shakeup

GLENCORE INTERNATIONAL PLC has struck a $6.1-billion agreement to buy Viterra Inc., in a deal that would carve up a historic Prairie company and reshape the country's agriculture business.

The transaction, which had been heavily rumoured for days, was also a classic display of Glencore CEO Ivan Glasenberg's style: fast, opportunistic, and politically and strategically clever.

The result is that Glencore, already a global commodities trading giant in everything from oil to sugar, will become the biggest trader of wheat, barley, and canola. "Viterra is a great acquisition for our agriculture business, especially as we had very little exposure to North America," Mr. Glasenberg said in a phone interview Tuesday.

The acquisition came in at $16.25 a share in cash, a hefty 48 percent premium to Viterra's share price on the day before the Canadian company revealed it was in play. But Glencore will recoup $2.6 billion of the

A Viterra grain storage facility in Saskatoon, March 20, 2012. (Liam Richards/The Canadian Press)

continued

Finance in the News 15-3: Glencore's Viterra Deal Spurs Grain Sector Shakeup (continued)

purchase price from two Canadian partners that will take a significant number of Viterra's domestic assets.

The bid was, in a sense, inevitable because of the Conservative government's decision to use legislation to strip the Canadian Wheat Board of its monopoly on export sales of wheat and barley grown in Western Canada.

Glencore and other big names in the agriculture trading business, among them Archer-Daniels-Midland, Bunge and Noble Group, knew that the end of the monopoly in August would open up vast opportunities once Canadian farmers gained the right to sell their own grain.

The pitch to farmers is that Glencore will be able to pay the top price for grain, because it has the best network of end customers abroad who need wheat. The company has offices in 40 countries around the world, seeking buyers for commodities.

For some farmers, the message sounds good, especially if Glencore uses Viterra—Western Canada's largest grain handler—as a base to get even bigger in North America.

"If that gives us more access to the U.S. and other markets, that could be a good thing," said Arlynn Kurtz, a farmer near Stockholm, Sask., and vice-president of the Agricultural Producers Association of Saskatchewan.

Glencore's deal means the likely end of a company that was started in the 1920s as a farmer-owned co-operative that eventually would become known as Saskatchewan Wheat Pool. Viterra, as it was renamed in 2007, will be split into three.

Agrium Inc. of Calgary is buying most of Viterra's retail agricultural products business, which includes a 34 percent interest in an Alberta fertilizer plant, for $1.8 billion. Winnipeg's Richardson International is buying 23 percent of Viterra's Canadian grain-handling business, food-processing plants such as five oat and wheat flour mills, and some farm supply stores for $800 million. Glencore will get the infrastructure prizes, including 63 grain elevators and seven port terminals in Canada, and eight port terminals in Australia.

The major concern for some farmers might be Agrium's purchase of the retail stores, which will give that company a dominant position in that business.

Mr. Glasenberg, the South African former accountant who has been Glencore's CEO since 2002, has been a whirlwind of activity in an industry—commodities—that has been all but moribund since the financial crisis of 2008 and the recession that followed. A year ago, he floated Glencore on the London Stock Exchange, where it immediately became a member of the FTSE-100.

Last month, Glencore offered to buy the 65.6 percent of Xstrata, the mining heavyweight that owns Canada's Falconbridge, that it did not already own in a $90-billion (U.S.) "merger of equals." The new company, to be called Glencore Xstrata, would be one of the world's top five mining companies.

Viterra was next. It was an open secret for at least two weeks that Glencore coveted Viterra, Canada's biggest grain handler and the owner of a significant spread of grain infrastructure, including ports, in South Australia. In truth, Glencore has been sizing up the deal for at least six months.

Glencore did not approach Viterra first. It devised a strategy to increase greatly the odds that the deal would not be scrutinized, and potentially killed, by anti-trust regulators and Investment Canada. The company's executives were well aware that takeovers in Canada have become political; in late 2010, the Harper government blocked BHP Billiton's takeover attempt of Potash Corp. of Saskatchewan, the world's biggest potash producer.

Glencore approached Agrium and Richardson International in the autumn. The Swiss company had a threefold strategy: to "Canadianize" the bid; to find buyers for many of the assets that Glencore did not want in Canada (it is keeping almost all of the Australian assets); and to get a top price for them and avoid competition problems.

"It was basically a general conversation that evolved into this specific discussion," said Curt Vossen, president of Winnipeg-based Richardson, which has sold grain and oilseeds to Glencore for years.

An adviser who did not want to be quoted by name said: "Glencore lined up its ducks well before it spoke to Viterra. For example, it knew it wanted to find a buyer for the fertilizer business before it bid for the company."

The end result is a dramatic shift in western Canada's agricultural landscape. Richardson and Glencore will each control roughly one-third of the grain trade, with the rest handled largely by U.S. giant Cargill Inc. Before this deal, Viterra controlled about 45 percent of the market, Richardson about 25 percent and Cargill 13 percent.

"This is not about buying traders," Mr. Glasenberg said. "This is about infrastructure. Adding infrastructure allows us to put more products on the water and export more in a growing industry."

For a company like Glencore, the key is ensuring a supply of the materials it trades. That means cutting out middlemen and dealing directly with farmers. Owning grain elevators enables Glencore to do just that.

"Your greatest fear would be in this global demand environment, can I continue to source the raw materials that I trade?" Mr. Vossen said. He added that this type of consolidation has been going on for the past two years, with giant traders buying up grain-handling companies.

With Viterra, Glencore has filled a big hole in its agriculture portfolio—North America. Canada offers vast potential for Glencore because it is responsible for 13 percent of the world's wheat exports, 6 percent of barley and an extraordinary 69 percent of canola. Viterra will boost Glencore's agricultural commodities revenues by 50 percent or more.

finance IN THE NEWS 15-4   Fortis Makes $1-Billion Offer for N.Y. Utility

CANADA'S LARGEST investor-owned utility, Fortis Inc., has launched an ambitious U.S. growth strategy with a proposed $1-billion (U.S.) acquisition of CH Energy Group Inc., an electric and gas utility in New York's Central Hudson Valley.

Like other Canadian utilities, St. John's-based Fortis is looking south of the border for expansion due to the paucity of takeover targets among regulated utilities in this country.

"There is just not anything left for us in Canada," Fortis chief financial officer Barry Perry said in an interview from Poughkeepsie, where CH Energy is based.

"This will not be the end of our acquisition plan," Mr. Perry said. "By the end of the decade, we expect to have as many assets in the U.S. as we have in Canada today. We're aiming for a 50/50 mix."

Mr. Perry said the CH Energy deal, which must be approved by regulators, represents a solid first step into the U.S. market, with a well-run, moderate-sized utility that has its own growth plan intact.

Fortis has been scouting for opportunities in the United States for five years. It failed in its first attempt to break into that utility market when Montreal-based Gaz Métro last year outbid it in a hostile takeover for Central Vermont Public Service, whose board had previously agreed to a Fortis acquisition.

Fortis is offering CH Energy shareholders $65 (U.S.) a share, a 10.5-percent premium above the most recent closing price for the stock, which was just below its 52-week high. Fortis said the takeover will benefit CH Energy customers by allowing the company to invest more in service improvements.

Fortis said it will keep CH Energy's management team headquartered in Poughkeepsie, consistent with its practice of maintaining autonomous management structures in each jurisdiction.

Mr. Perry said CH Energy will benefit from Fortis's technological knowhow and low cost of capital to help finance its $100-million-a-year investment plan.

Fortis faces a year-long regulatory review by the New York Public Service Commission and will spell out customer benefits in more detail in the course of that hearing, CH Energy's spokeswoman Denise VanBuren said in a telephone interview.

"We see it as a win for our customers as well as our shareholders and our employees," Ms. VanBuren said.

She added that CH Energy management had not been looking for a buyer, but was approached by Fortis several months ago about a deal.

With $13-billion (Canadian) in assets, Fortis has been on a strong growth track over the past 10 years since acquiring electric and natural gas utilities in booming Alberta and in British Columbia. It is prepared to make acquisitions of up to $5-billion (U.S.) south of the border, with its focus mainly on the northeastern United States.

The company currently serves more than two million gas and electricity customers. Its regulated holdings include electric distribution utilities in five provinces and two Caribbean countries and a natural gas utility in British Columbia.

CH Energy has 300,000 electricity customers and 75,000 gas customers, and its acquisition would increase Fortis's asset base by 16 percent.

In a presentation last month, Mr. Perry assured investors that Fortis would be disciplined in its growth strategy: chasing only acquisitions of regulated utilities that would quickly add to earnings per share, that maintain its growth track, and that do not jeopardize its credit rating.

The CH Energy deal meets those criteria, he said Tuesday.

CH Energy shares jumped more than 7 percent to $66.22 (U.S.) on the New York Stock Exchange on Tuesday, suggesting that some investors expect a competing bid to top Fortis's $65 offer.

M&A Activity

Figure 15-4 shows Canadian M&A activity over the period from 2004 to the first quarter of 2012 and demonstrates a sharp decline in the formerly hot M&A market after 2007. Much of the decline in activity was driven by limited availability of capital and a rapid deterioration in earnings. However, things appeared to be improving during the first quarter of 2012 (as mentioned in the chapter-opening vignette). And prior to 2008, M&A activity soared in the Canadian energy and commodity sectors, fuelled by high energy prices, high commodity prices, a strong currency, and a healthy economy.

That a wave of M&A activity ended during 2008 is nothing new. Dating to the turn of the nineteenth century, M&A activity has tended to occur in periodic waves of robust activity, as depicted in Table 15-1.

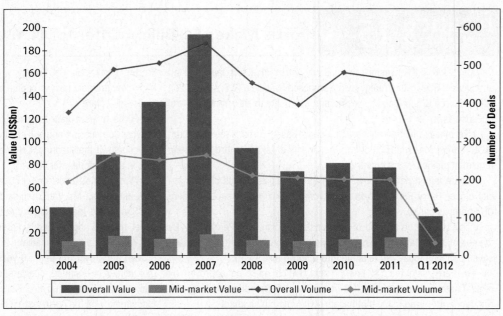

FIGURE 15-4 *Canadian M&A Activity, 2004–12*

Source: The Mergermarket Group, "Mergermarket's Canadian M&A Round-up for Q1 2012." Mergermarket Group press release, April 17, 2012, p. 3. Available at www.mergermarket.com.

TABLE 15-1 M&A Activity in Canada

Period	Major Characteristics of M&A Activity
1895–1904	• Driven by economic expansion, U.S. transcontinental railroad, and the development of national U.S. capital markets • Characterized by horizontal M&As
1922–1929	• 60 percent occurred in fragmented markets (chemical, food processing, mining) • Driven by growth in transportation and merchandising, as well as by communications developments
1940–1947	• Characterized by vertical integration • Driven by evasion of price and quota controls
1960s	• Characterized by conglomerate M&As • Driven by aerospace industry • Some firms merged to play the earnings-per-share "growth game" (discussed in section 15.5 under "The Effect of an Acquisition on Earnings per Share")
1980s	• Characterized by leveraged buyouts and hostile takeovers
1990s	• Many international M&As (e.g., Chrysler and Daimler-Benz, Seagram and Martell) • Strategic motives were advanced (although the jury is still out on whether this was truly achieved)
1999–2001	• High technology/Internet M&As • Many stock-financed takeovers, fuelled by inflated stock prices • Many were unsuccessful and/or fell through as the Internet "bubble" burst
2005–2008	• Resource-based/international M&A activity • Fuelled by strong industry fundamentals, low financing costs, strong economic conditions

Source: Adapted in part from J. Fred Weston, Kwang S. Chung, and Susan E. Hoag. *Mergers, Restructuring, and Corporate Control.* Toronto: Prentice-Hall Canada, Inc., 1990.

Theoretically, the primary motive for a merger or acquisition should be the creation of **synergy**, which causes the value of the combined firm to exceed the sum value of the two individual firms. Synergy is created due to economies of integration that are expected to occur for one reason or another. If V_A is the pre-merger value of the acquiring firm, V_T is the pre-merger value of the target firm, and V_{A-T} is the value of the post-merger firm, we can say that synergy occurs whenever $V_{A-T} > V_A + V_T$. Synergy is the additional value created (ΔV), as expressed in Equation 15-1:

$$\Delta V = V_{A-T} - (V_A + V_T) \qquad [15\text{-}1]$$

synergy value created from economies of integrating a target and acquiring company; the amount by which the value of the combined firm exceeds the sum value of the two individual firms

If the target and acquirer have initial values of $50 million ($V_T$) and $100 million ($V_A$), respectively, and the combined firm is worth $200 million ($V_{A-T}$), then there are synergy values of $50 million. Of course, in this case, the key questions are where do these synergies come from and who gets them? If the acquirer pays $100 million for the target, then all the synergy value flows through to the target shareholders and none to the acquirer. On the other hand, at any value less than $100 million, the synergy gains are split between the acquiring and target firm shareholders. In this case, the acquisition has created value of $50 million.

Value Creation Motivations for M&As

Most M&A announcements go to great lengths to describe the synergies, or total positive gains, associated with the proposed transaction. For example the proposed takeover of Flint Energy by URS, discussed in *Finance in the News 15-1*, indicated cost savings of $10 million to $15 million in year 1, with continued annual savings going forward. Sometimes these gains materialize and sometimes they don't. In this section, we list a variety of "value creation" motives that are often used to justify a merger or acquisition decision. Some of these justifications hold greater merit than others, as we discuss below.

Operating Synergies

1. ECONOMIES OF SCALE

Economies of scale arise whenever bigger is indeed better. Some potential benefits may arise from the following economies:

- Reducing capacity. It may be, for example, that an industry has grown too big and there are too many firms operating in it. A merger or acquisition in this situation is often called an **over-capacity M&A**. For example, in 2003, Alcan, the major Canadian aluminum producer, purchased the French producer Pechiney, while the U.S. bank JPMorgan purchased another American bank, Chase.

over-capacity M&A a merger or acquisition that occurs when an industry has too many firms operating in it

- Spreading fixed costs. Often, significant costs in a business are fixed, independent of scale. By increasing the company's size, these costs are spread over greater volumes, and the firm is more efficient. This was the ostensible motivation for the proposed Royal Bank–Bank of Montreal merger, which was stopped by the Government of Canada in 1998. The banks argued that the costs of information technology could be reduced through a merger since both banks were developing similar technology. The same arguments apply to spreading research and development costs.

- Geographic synergies. Often an industry is fragmented and ripe for consolidation. A **geographic roll-up** occurs when a national firm is created out of a series of regional firms. The original Standard Oil in the United States was created when John D. Rockefeller consolidated the U.S. oil industry, which allowed common marketing and managerial overhead. Retailing has similarly been consolidated, with the creation of national

geographic roll-up the creation of a national firm from a series of regional ones

chains from regional ones to gain economies in purchasing and an improvement in the distribution channel.

2. ECONOMIES OF SCOPE

An economy of scope occurs when the combination of two activities reduces costs. Such economies typically result when two products share similarities in their production process, which can be exploited. A classic example is a distribution system that can be used to sell two lines of product instead of one. On this basis, Seagram (think whisky) purchased Martell (think fine cognac) in 1988. Seagram's rationale was that it could sell Martell's cognac through its U.S. distribution system as easily as its own whisky, and thereby generate expanded sales at little extra cost.

Another example occurred in the early 1980s. Until then, commercial banking (i.e., making corporate loans) was separated from investment banking (i.e., selling corporate securities). The Ontario Securities Commission held a series of hearings to determine whether the investment dealers—firms like Dominion Securities and Wood Gundy—should be allowed to convert from being partnerships to corporations, and whether they should be permitted to be acquired by the banks. The OSC approved the changes largely on the basis that there were efficiencies to be gained if investment banking and commercial banking were carried on by the same institution. However, regulators have so far resisted arguments that banks be allowed to use their distribution systems to sell insurance.

Two of the many other examples of economies of scope achieved by acquisitions are Coca-Cola's purchase of Gatorade to gain entry into the sport drinks market, and Quaker Oats buying Snapple Beverage Corporation.

3. COMPLEMENTARY STRENGTHS

Complementary strengths occur if one firm is more efficient in one or more areas of operations than another. For example, a marketing-oriented firm may acquire a production-oriented firm if it feels the product line is not being sold efficiently. A classic example of this is Remington, the razor company. It was acquired by Victor Kiam, who immediately cut engineering and product development and marketed a smaller range of razors. He did this to great effect by advertising himself, saying, "I liked the razor so much I bought the company."

Another example can be seen in the 2008 acquisition of the American Stock Exchange (Amex) by NYSE Euronext. While Amex was a national stock exchange, it was very small in comparison to the NYSE. However, Amex traded a wider array of exchange-traded funds (ETFs) and options than the NYSE. Hence, it possessed some strengths that complemented those of NYSE Euronext. Of course, the acquisition also presented opportunities to cut costs associated with duplicated efforts, and the Amex trading floor was officially shut down during the summer of 2008.

extension M&A a merger or acquisition that extends a firm's expertise

Another example of complementary strengths is the **extension M&A**. Certain organizational cultures are good at doing certain things. The research part of research and development, for example, usually requires a creative organizational culture that encourages risk taking. The development part, on the other hand, often requires extensive managerial and production skills. As a result, big pharmaceutical companies, like Merck & Co., Inc., and Pfizer Inc., often buy small drug companies after they come up with a potential new drug, since often only the big companies can take the drug through the clinical trials it must pass before it is certified for use by consumers.

Similarly, many mineral finds have been made by small firms, often consisting of a few geologists. After a deposit is found, however, they sell the company to the major international companies that have the skills and resources to develop it. An example in Canada was the Voisey's Bay nickel deposits in Labrador, found by Diamond Fields Resources Inc. in 1994. This was the most significant mineral discovery in Canada in 40 years and sparked a furious bidding war for the rights to develop the deposits, which was eventually won by Inco Ltd.

In this case, the M&A occurred because the exploration and development functions, as opposed to the R&D functions, were best carried out by separate entities.

Efficiency Increases

Efficiency gains materialize whenever one or both of the firms involved have excess capacity—that is, they possess factors that are currently being underused. This is a common motivation for mergers, and, unfortunately for employees, some of the synergy that arises involves the elimination of jobs. Of course, efficiency gains do not always have to result in job losses; the excess capacity could exist in one or more of many factors, such as shipping, storage, and information technology. Another important source of increased efficiency could be improved company management—that is, the acquiring firm believes that its management team will operate more efficiently than the target firm's management team. It is in this sense that people often refer to the "market for corporate control" as a viable corporate governance mechanism, since inefficient management will pay the ultimate price.

Financing Synergy

Financing synergies may arise for a number of reasons. The main ones discussed below are all variations on the theme that larger is better in accessing capital markets.

- **Reduced cash flow variability**. Cash flow volatility tends to be lower for larger entities, especially if the cash flows from the two underlying businesses are not highly correlated. This may enable the company to reduce its need for external financing, since future financing needs can be forecast with greater certainty.

- **Increase in debt capacity**. Debt capacity may rise due to the increase in size and/or reduction in cash flow volatility of the new company. Smaller, riskier firms generally cannot carry as much debt as larger firms, and the use of additional debt provides the firm with greater tax savings, as we will discuss in more detail in chapters 20 and 21.

- **Reduction in average issuing costs**. Since most security issues occur in large increments, the average cost of floating new debt or equity will decrease as the firm issues larger amounts. Additionally, larger firms can access more sources of capital than smaller ones, resulting in cost savings.

- **Fewer information problems**. Larger firms usually attract more external security analysts and have greater exposure in the media. The result is that they attract big institutional investors, which may lower their financing costs.

Tax Benefits

Tax benefits occur when one firm has substantial operating loss credits that it cannot take advantage of because it is not operating profitably. These losses are valuable since they can be carried forward and used against future profits to reduce taxes. However, if the firm is unlikely to become profitable in the near term, these losses may expire worthless. On the other hand, if the firm combines with a profitable one in the same basic line of business, these losses can be used to offset the other firm's profits to reduce taxes. This was the case in the Kmart–Sears merger of 2004. At the time of the merger, Kmart had $509 million in tax-loss carryovers that were due to expire in the 2021–23 tax years. Kmart had little chance of using these losses unless it combined with a profitable company.[13] By combining with a profitable company, the net operating loss carryover could then be used as offsets against future taxable income, hence reducing taxes of the combined company.[14]

---

[13] Information from Kmart Holding Corporation 2004 fiscal year 10-K filing with the Securities and Exchange Commission, p. 49.
[14] Sears Holdings, the parent company after the acquisition, announced store closures at the end of 2011 because of poor holiday earnings, a sign that the company continued to struggle. If Sears Holdings does not generate taxable earnings to apply against those net operating losses, the losses may still expire worthless.

Tax benefits may also arise due to the depreciation of capital assets (i.e., current cost accounting tax shields) that can be claimed by the combined entity, and the increased use of debt financing with more interest tax shields, as discussed above.

Strategic Realignments

The acquisition of new managerial skills and new product/service line growth opportunities, resulting from an M&A, may allow the new entity to pursue strategies that were previously not feasible.

Managerial Motivations for M&A

Creating value for shareholders may be the basic motivation for running a business, but, as we discussed previously, it is the managers that control the company. Therefore, we sometimes get managerial motives for M&A that are distinct from the shareholder motivation. Two of the more common motivations are described below.

1. **Increased firm size**. This may or may not be a good thing, depending on whether any economic synergies are created. Unfortunately, in the past, some M&As have been advocated by managers who were equally concerned with the additional personal compensation and power they would realize as a result of the transaction. The classic example here is the 1998 attempted merger between Glaxo Wellcome and Smith Klein, two big British pharmaceutical companies. In February 1998, the proposed merger was called off because the two CEOs couldn't decide on the management team of the new company. With the announcement of the cancellation of the merger, £13 billion (about C$30 billion) was wiped out from the combined companies' market value. In this case, the personal egos of the senior managers destroyed value; normally value is destroyed by making bad acquisitions rather than cancelling potentially good ones.[15]

2. **Reduced firm risk through diversification.** M&As may also be used to diversify a firm—geographically, across industries, or in its product mix—through conglomerate mergers, as discussed earlier. Unfortunately, the evidence suggests that diversification is generally a poor motive for a merger, often resulting in additional managerial complications and a lack of focus by managers running disparate businesses. The markets recognize this and are not willing to pay a premium for diversification, since it is easy to diversify a portfolio across the same industries and geographic borders. In fact, the evidence suggests quite the opposite: investors tend to pay a premium for "pure play" companies that are focused on one strategic plan.

Gains Resulting from Mergers: Empirical Evidence

So what does the evidence on M&As tell us about the gains? There are numerous empirical studies that examine the gains from mergers. The evidence suggests that the target firm shareholders gain the most, with premiums over the prior stock market price in the 15 to 20 percent range for stock-financed takeovers, and from 25 to 30 percent for cash-financed takeovers. These gains consist of a one-third run-up in the stock price prior to the announcement, plus about a two-thirds gain after the announcement.

There is considerable disagreement about the source of the run-up prior to the announcement. On one hand, some people believe that information about an impending merger is leaked, resulting in insider trading, which is, of course, illegal. On the other hand, many believe that informed industry specialists can make reasonable predictions about takeover activity based on transactions elsewhere. For example, on February 12, 2007, *The Times* of London reported that BHP and Rio Tinto, two huge British-Australian mining

---

[15] The deal did eventually go through, as even managerial egos could not stand in the way of C$30 billion.

companies, had drawn up plans for a $40-billion bid for New York-based aluminum producer Alcoa. In response, rival Alcan's stock price jumped $4 on speculation that if it didn't buy Alcoa, someone might buy Alcan.

Regardless of the source, it always pays for the shareholders of the target firm to be taken over. Short-term gains of 20 to 40 percent are the reasons why the arbs, the M&A specialists discussed earlier, refused to let Sears, Roebuck buy Sears Canada cheaply. In their lexicon, Sears, Roebuck was not playing fair by refusing to let the arbs make a profit.

These takeover gains to the target can be even higher, especially if bidding wars develop, and they tend to be higher still when the deals are 100-percent cash, since the target shareholders usually have to pay capital gains tax. In contrast, the acquiring firm's shareholders, on average, see no change in their stock price. In fact, the stock price usually dips marginally on news of the bid. This implies that acquiring firms pay too much for target firms, acquire them for the wrong reasons, and/or overestimate the benefits resulting from the merger. Numerous studies concerning post-merger value indicate there is little or no increase in value; there are no synergistic gains to the acquirer, which are the supposed rationale for mergers.

A good popular analysis of M&A deals was published by the U.S. periodical *Business Week* on October 12, 2002. The magazine hired the Boston Consulting Group's (BCG) M&A team to do the work. They analyzed 302 deals worth more than US$500 million, done between 1995 and 2001. On average, the acquirer bought a company 47 percent its size, so these were big deals. Of these deals, 61 percent lost value over the next year. BCG estimated this by looking at the subsequent stock market performance relative to the companies' peers. The losers lost about 25 percent of relative value, and overall the average loss was 6.3 percent. The next year didn't get any better. The biggest losers were those deals that were financed with shares, which lost an average 8 percent, whereas those financed with cash lost only 0.3 percent. It seems that acquirers are freer with their shares than they are with their cash, and there is good reason for this.

In a 2010 study of mergers and acquisitions globally, researchers examining over 13,000 mergers in 89 different countries indicated that the gains to acquirers and targets were different in very competitive markets (e.g., the United States and United Kingdom), compared to other markets around the world.[16] They also found that acquirers in these competitive markets tended to underperform relative to acquirers in less competitive markets. The researchers observed that in acquisitions involving cash as a medium of exchange, the acquisition resulted in a shift of wealth from the acquiring shareholders to the target shareholders; in other words, value was not created, merely shifted. In the case of the exchange of shares, the researchers observed synergistic gains only in non-competitive markets.

Consider a $2-billion company that wants to take over a company with a $1-billion value because it thinks there are $0.5 billion in synergies. If it gets into a bidding war and pays $1.5 billion in cash for the company and then finds that there are no synergies, it has lost the $0.5-billion premium it paid. In this case, it has 25 percent of its market value at risk in the acquisition ($0.5 ÷ 2). In contrast, if the acquiring company does a share swap at $1.5 billion, the original shareholders own only 57.14 percent of the new company ($2 ÷ $3.5) and will lose only this fraction of the lost $0.5 billion, or $286 million. The rest has been lost by the shareholders of the target, who accepted shares in the new company only to see them to go down in value.[17]

This analysis is called "shareholder value at risk," or SVAR, in M&As. It illustrates the basic point that, when using cash, the acquirer bears all the risk, whereas when using share swaps, the risk is borne by the shareholders in both companies. For example, Nortel was a major Canadian technology company during the Internet bubble, and it made a large number of acquisitions, almost all of them using its own shares. Nortel used its high share price as an acquisition currency, and unless the target shareholders sold their shares immediately, they lost

[16] Alexandridis, G., D. Petmezas, and Nicholas G. Travlos, "Gains from Merger and Acquisitions Around the World: New Evidence." *Financial Management* (Winter 2010), pp. 1671–95.

[17] Rappaport, A., and M. Sirower, "Stock or Cash." *Harvard Business Review* (November/December 1999), pp. 147-58

as much when the market crashed as did Nortel's original shareholders. Using share swaps for its acquisitions also meant that Nortel survived the crash, whereas if it had borrowed the money to make cash purchases, it could never have supported the debt load after the crash.

SVAR supports the argument that when firms make deals using cash, they are a lot more careful about the acquisition price than when they use their shares. One reason for this is that the managers have less interest in the financing of the deal than in getting it done in the first place.

CONCEPT REVIEW QUESTIONS

1. What is the difference between vertical and horizontal mergers?
2. What is an extension M&A, an over-capacity M&A, and a geographic roll-up M&A?
3. What financial synergies are possible in an M&A transaction?
4. What tax benefits can occur in an M&A?
5. What is the empirical record on the success of M&As in the 1990s?
6. What is SVAR and why do managers prefer to finance with shares rather than cash?

15.5 VALUATION ISSUES

Learning Objective 15.5
Identify the valuation issues involved in assessing mergers and acquisitions.

So far we have discussed how to do an acquisition, different types of acquisitions, and the securities law surrounding acquisitions—almost everything about acquisitions except the critical question of how to value them. Since companies are always buying something, they have to know the basics of valuation, especially in a merger, where they must determine the share exchange ratio. In principle, this involves the same issues as valuing a project (discussed in earlier chapters) and valuing securities like bonds and shares. However, it is considerably more complex for a variety of reasons that we discuss below.

James Needham of Arthur Young and Company summed up some of the issues this way: "In pricing an acquisition, we can always agree on the numbers. What the value is tends to be more in the realm of poets than financial people."[18] In other words, value generically means a willingness to sell or to buy—that is, we are talking about supply and demand curves. The price, on the other hand, is the value at which a deal is consummated. When we look at most commodities that are bought and sold, there are many people in the market buying and selling, so the price is clearly derived. In this sense, it is an equilibrium price. For companies, on the other hand, while the shares may trade between many buyers and sellers, there is a limited market for the company as a whole, so we are dealing with only a few points on the demand and supply curves. This naturally leads to a wide range of possible deal prices.

We illustrate this point in Figure 15-5. Normally, in a basic economics course, we draw a supply and demand curve assuming multiple buyers and sellers so that the equilibrium price is P*. This may be the case if there are many steel companies, for example, and many potential buyers, but in reality what happens is that one company may be "put in play" at any point in time, and the seller may want a price of S1, which is its valuation of the company. There may be only one potential buyer, who places the value at B1. So rather than all the points on the demand and supply curve, we simply have two points. If these two parties can come to an agreement, the transaction price can be anywhere between these two prices. This is the crux of Needham's comment: we may have an idea of what P* should be, but if there are only two parties, their own valuations can be all over the place.

---

[18] Needham, James, "The Leading Edge in Mergers and Acquisitions." *Mergers & Acquisitions* (November/December 1986).

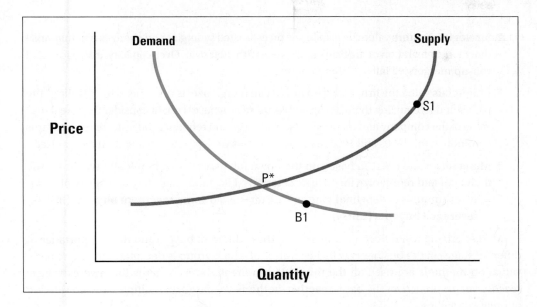

FIGURE 15-5 *Demand and Supply of Company Shares*

This concept underlies the definition of **fair market value (FMV)**, which is described as the highest price obtainable in an open and unrestricted market between knowledgeable, informed, and prudent parties acting at arm's length, with neither party being under any compulsion to transact. We often need to know the value of something for tax and other legal purposes, and FMV reflects this specific valuation, which is not necessarily a transaction price.

If we look at the definition of FMV, there are certain key words and phrases we must understand:

- **Open and unrestricted market:** there are no barriers and anyone can buy or sell.

- **Knowledgeable, informed, and prudent parties:** all the information is in the market, and the value is determined by people who know what they are doing.

- **Arm's length:** the value is determined by parties who do not know each other.

- **Neither party under any compulsion to transact:** it is not a panic sale, causing distressed valuations.

The Canada Revenue Agency (CRA) adopts FMV as the standard definition of selling price, since otherwise a party wishing to avoid capital gains tax could sell an asset to a related party at a "knockdown" price. This is why the definition includes the "arm's length" provision. Indeed, if you look carefully at these four components, you will realize that this is a description of an ideal or perfect market, where everyone is reasonable and arrives at values in an objective, rational way. It is also why the courts have frequently thrown out actual transaction values when these conditions were not met.

The relevance of FMV is that it comes up all the time in valuing transactions, but the requirements for it highlight why transaction values frequently depart from FMV. In a hostile takeover, for example, the acquirer does not have access to a data room or confidential information and often *overbids* for a firm. Similarly, managers selling a single division of a firm or putting the whole firm up for sale on the death of the founder are frequently under a compulsion to act and are dealing in a restricted market.

To put the above comments in perspective, we can think of purchasers as belonging to four different groups:

1. **Passive investors** value the firm based on estimated cash flows as they are at present, with only minor adjustments. Passive investors are mutual funds and any small investor that cannot change what the firm is doing.

fair market value (FMV) the highest price obtainable in an open and unrestricted market between knowledgeable, informed, and prudent parties acting at arm's length, with neither party being under any compulsion to transact

2. **Strategic investors** value the firm based on estimated synergies and changes that may arise due to the integration of the firm's operations with their own. Over-capacity, extension, and roll-up mergers all fall into this category.

3. **Financials** value the firm based on how it can reorganize its operations by "juggling" the pieces and refinancing them. For example, these purchasers might consider the "break-up" value of the company and then sell off some pieces and refinance the rest. This strategy was common in the 1970s and 1980s as conglomerates were purchased and then reorganized.

4. **Managers** value the firm based on their own job potential and their ability to motivate their staff and reorganize the firm's operations. Like financials, they usually involve significant amounts of debt financing and are referred to as **management buyouts (MBOs)** or **leveraged buyouts (LBOs)**.

> **management buyouts (MBOs)** or **leveraged buyouts (LBOs)** buyouts in which the purchasers are a firm's managers; these buyouts usually involve high levels of debt financing

Market pricing will reflect the influence of these different buyers and their importance at different stages of the business cycle. Regardless of which group is dominant, the same basic valuation methods are used all the time. We can break these methods into two extremes: *reactive* versus *proactive*. The basic **reactive methods** are based on multiples and liquidation or break-up values.

> **reactive methods** a valuation method based on general rules of thumb and examining the present pricing of similar securities

1. **Multiples or relative valuation.** This approach involves the use of ratios such as price-earnings (P/E), market-to-book (M/B), price-to-sales (P/S), and price-to-cash flow (P/CF). They are called "multiples" because we are arriving at a market value by using some multiple of an item in the firm's forecast financial statements. The relative valuation comes in because we arrive at these multiples by looking at comparable firms, known as "comps," and deciding what a reasonable multiple is. (We discussed these multiples in Chapter 7.) This approach is used extensively and can also be used as a first step in a proactive analysis. The justifiable multiples are often estimated based on historical trading values, "rules of thumb," "comparables" (such as industry averages or comparable companies), and/or precedent transactions (which refers to the multiples observed in previous takeovers of similar companies). This method provides a starting point for the valuation process by establishing the value in relation to historical values, rules of thumb, and similar companies. The basic multiples valuation approach is illustrated in Figure 15-6 and in Examples 15.1 to 15.3.

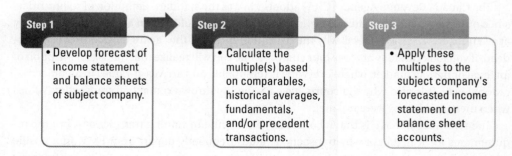

Step 1
- Develop forecast of income statement and balance sheets of subject company.

Step 2
- Calculate the multiple(s) based on comparables, historical averages, fundamentals, and/or precedent transactions.

Step 3
- Apply these multiples to the subject company's forecasted income statement or balance sheet accounts.

FIGURE 15-6 *Multiples Valuation*

2. **Liquidation values.** This approach involves estimating the liquidation value of the company's assets at present market prices. For example, we know that cash is worth 100 percent, and we can estimate accounts receivable at 85 percent; inventory at 75 percent; and property, plant, and equipment at 50 percent of their book values. This can be an especially important consideration if the acquiring firm plans on selling some of the target firm's assets to help pay off the debt financing associated with the purchase.

> **proactive methods** a valuation method to determine what a target firm's liquidation value should be based on future values of cash flow and earnings

In contrast to reactive methods, which are reacting to general rules of thumb and the pricing of other securities, **proactive methods** work out what the value *should be,* based on future values of cash flow and earnings. The most common proactive method is the discounted cash flow (DCF) model.

> **Discounted cash flow (DCF) model.** This approach involves estimating the future cash flows associated with the new combined entity and discounting them back to the present to determine the fair market value. Sound familiar? This is exactly how we evaluated the traditional investment decisions in chapters 13 and 14 and individual securities in chapters 6 and 7. This simply reflects the fact that DCF valuation is the workhorse of finance.

Multiples Valuation

The following three examples illustrate how multiples may be used to evaluate a company and highlight the difficulties that may arise from using this approach.

EXAMPLE 15-1 | Valuation Using Multiples

Let's go back to the example we used in Chapter 7, where we have the following information about a target company (T1) that an acquiring firm (A) is considering buying.

Sales and Income Statement Items

Sales		$10 million
	Volume 1 million	
	Price per unit $10	
		($ million)
Costs		9.0
	Variable costs	5.0
	Fixed cash costs	1.7
	Depreciation	0.8
	Interest	0.5
	Income tax	1.0
Net income		1.0
Dividends		0.5

Capital

Number of common shares outstanding 0.5 million

Invested capital (book values)

Equity	$5 million
Debt	$5 million
Market value of equity	$15 million

Valuation Ratios	T1	T1 5-Yr. Avg.	Industry Avg.
Price-earnings (P/E) (trailing)	15	14.5	16.5
Value/EBIT	8	5.5	7.5
Value/EBITDA	6.06	4.8	6.0
Price/Sales (P/S)	1.50	1.35	1.6
Price/Book value (P/B) (equity)	3	3	3.2
Price per unit of output	$15	$14.5	$16.0
Return on equity (ROE)	20%	16.5%	17.5%

EXAMPLE 15-1 *Valuation Using Multiples continued*

Remember in these ratios that EBIT (earnings before interest and taxes) and EBITDA (earnings before interest, taxes, depreciation, and amortization) belong to all the security holders, not just the shareholders, so these multiples are based on the total market value of the firm—that is, the value of the equity plus the debt. In this case, to get the equity value, we then have to subtract the market value of the debt.[19]

Of course, the actual value ratios for T1 listed above are based on the current market price of T1's common shares, and we cannot use them to value T1 since they just give us back the current value. In order to use the multiples approach to estimate the true value of T1, we would need to estimate "justifiable" P/E ratios drawn from comparables or a bottom-up analysis, as discussed in Chapter 7.

Estimate the value of T1's equity

a.   using the industry averages for the first five valuation ratios presented above.

b.   using the five-year averages for T1 for the first five valuation ratios presented above.

c.   using the forward P/E ratio that is calculated based on the assumptions that
    i.   9 percent is a reasonable cost of equity for T1,
    ii. T1 maintains its present dividend payout ratio, and
    iii. T1's dividends and earnings grow at an annual rate of 6 percent indefinitely.

Solution

a.   Using P/E ratio: Value P/E × Net income = 16.5 × \$1m = \$16.5m

    Using V/EBIT ratio: Value = V/EBIT × EBIT − Debt = 7.5 × \$2.5m − \$5m = \$18.75m − \$5m = \$13.75m

    Using V/EBITDA ratio: Value = V/EBITDA × EBITDA − Debt = 6.0 × \$3.3m − \$5m = \$19.8m − \$5.0m = \$14.8m

    Using P/S ratio: Value = P/S × Sales = 1.6 × \$10m = \$16m

    Using P/B ratio: Value = P/B × BV = 3.2 × \$5m = \$16m

    The industry average multiples indicate that T1's equity may be currently under-valued at \$15 million, and it should be valued somewhere around \$16 million, depending on which multiple is used.

b.   Using P/E ratio: Value = P/E × Net income = 14.5 × \$1m = \$14.5m

    Using V/EBIT ratio: Value = V/EBIT × EBIT − Debt = 5.5 × \$2.5m = \$13.75m − \$5.0m = \$8.75m

    Using V/EBITDA ratio: Value = V/EBITDA × EBITDA − Debt = 4.8 × \$3.3m = \$15.84m − \$5.0m = \$10.84m

    Using P/S ratio: Value = P/S × Sales = 1.35 × \$10m = \$13.5m

    Using P/B ratio: Value = P/B × BV = 3.0 × \$5m = \$15m

    The company's historical (five-year) average multiples indicate that T1's equity should be valued somewhere between \$8.75 million and \$15 million, depending on which multiple is used.

c.   The justifiable forward P/E ratio for T1 based on these assumptions can be calculated as follows:

    P/E (forward) = Payout ÷ $(k - g)$ = (0.5m ÷ 1.0m) ÷ (0.09 − 0.06) = 0.5 ÷ 0.03 = 16.67

    Next year's earnings based on a 6-percent growth rate = (\$1m)(1.06) = \$1.06m

    Value of T1's equity = (P/E)(E$_1$) = (16.67)(\$1.06m) = \$17.67m

---

Example 15-1 demonstrates that various valuation models may be used to estimate justifiable multiples, which can then be used to evaluate a target firm. However, in practice, we cannot just passively use these ratios for several reasons. For one thing, the use of different accounting methods can affect many of the items used in the multiples approach. We illustrate how these differences can affect the ratios and the valuation process in Example 15-2.

---

[19] Often the price-to-sales ratio used may be the total firm market value-to-sales ratio.

EXAMPLE 15-2 Accounting Differences

Consider two companies, A and B, that are identical in sales and profitability. Both have 1 million common shares outstanding. However, their income statements differ significantly as a result of the accounting methods they choose. In particular, their accounting choices differ in the following ways:

a.   Firm A uses LIFO to account for inventory, while firm B uses FIFO.[20]

b.   Firm A uses an accelerated depreciation method, while firm B uses straight-line depreciation.

c.   Firm A fully funds pension costs, while B reports an unfunded pension liability.

d.   Firm B sells surplus property for a gain to beef up earnings, while A has similar unrealized gains available to it.

The differences in the income statements of A and B are illustrated below:

	A($)	B($)
Sales	10,000,000	10,000,000
Cost of goods sold	6,000,000	6,000,000
Selling and general	1,500,000	1,500,000
LIFO difference	400,000	0
Depreciation	400,000	300,000
Pension costs	200,000	50,000
Gain on property sale		150,000
Earnings before tax	1,500,000	2,300,000
Income tax expense @ 40%	600,000	920,000
Net income	900,000	1,380,000
Earnings per share	0.90	1.38

Estimate the price of A's and B's shares using a P/E ratio of 15.

Solution

	A	B
Price using P/E ratio of 15x	$13.50	$20.70
Total Equity Value	$13.5m	$20.7m

Notice that the "only" differences in the companies are their accounting choices, yet we get very different valuations if we blindly use a P/E multiple of 15. This implies the importance of taking such factors into consideration in the valuation process.

Example 15-2 illustrates how different accounting choices can affect income statement items. Of course, a firm's capital structure decisions will also affect valuation ratios, as illustrated in Example 15-3.

EXAMPLE 15-3 Differing Capital Structures

Consider two companies, C and D, that are identical in sales and operating profitability (as measured by EBIT), but have different capital structures, as shown in the following. Calculate the P/E ratio for both companies.

continued

---

[20] Canadian firms tend to use FIFO; U.S. firms tend to use FIFO or LIFO.

EXAMPLE 15-3	*Differing Capital Structures continued*	
	C($)	**D($)**
EBIT	2,000,000	2,000,000
Interest	500,000	0
EBT	1,500,000	2,000,000
Income taxes (40%)	600,000	800,000
Net income	900,000	1,200,000
Debt (Book value)	10,000,000	0
Equity (Book value)	10,000,000	20,000,000
Equity (Market value)	12,000,000	20,000,000

Solution

	C	**D**
P/E ratio	(12,000,000 ÷ 900,000)	(20,000,000 ÷ 1,200,000)
	13.333x	16.667x

Notice the significant difference in P/E ratios that is caused by the fact that C uses $10 million in debt financing while D is all equity financed. Obviously, capital structure decisions can have a big impact on valuation multiples, as we discuss in Chapter 21 when we consider the question of an optimal capital structure.

In order to avoid the problems associated with the multiples approach, we can make adjustments to the financial statements and/or to the multiples we use for valuation purposes. Alternatively, we can use a different valuation framework that avoids some of the problems associated with using multiples. But note that if we have to use a multiple, most corporate valuations focus on the EBITDA and EBIT multiples, since they remove the problem with capital structure and focus higher up the income statement, avoiding some of the accounting problems that result from firms focusing on the bottom line (i.e., net income).

Liquidation Valuation

This approach can be implemented following a process such as the one below:

1. Estimate the liquidation value of current assets based on their "realizable value." For example, if a company's accounts receivable are with firms of good credit quality, and most of them are current, it might be reasonable to value them at 80 percent of their book value. This percentage could be lower for firms whose customers are of lower average credit quality, or if they have a large percentage of overdue receivables. Similarly, inventory could be valued according to its marketability, etc.

2. Estimate the present market value of tangible assets such as machinery, buildings, and land.

3. Subtract the value of the firm's liabilities from the total estimated liquidation value of all the firm's assets. This represents the liquidation value of the firm.

The liquidation value approach is useful, but it can involve several estimates that may be imprecise at best, especially when a company has a lot of assets. More importantly, it values companies based on existing assets and is not forward looking. Therefore, we will devote most of our attention to the discounted cash flow valuation approach, which is discussed below. This approach must also overcome several challenges, as we shall see.

Discounted Cash Flow Analysis

The discounted cash flow (DCF) approach was applied to specific securities in chapters 7 and 8. Now we apply it to the valuation of a company. The first step in this process is to estimate the future after-tax cash flows associated with a company. This step is fraught with difficulties, as alluded to in Professor Finagle's three laws of information, quoted below:[21]

1. The information we have is not what we want.

2. The information we want is not what we need.

3. The information we need is not available.

Let's examine these three "laws" one at a time, modifying the last statement so that we have a viable way of approaching the issue.

1. *The information we have is not what we want.*

   What we *have* (i.e., what we can find from the company's financial statements) is accounting earnings, which represents the bottom line, is affected by accounting choices, and can be manipulated by accounting "trickery."

   What we *want* is cash flow. The typical solution is to add back non-cash items such as depreciation, amortization, and deferred taxes, which leaves us with the traditional cash flow.

2. *The information we want is not what we need.*

   What we *want*, or what analysts typically try to estimate, is cash flow from operations (CFO). Recall from Chapter 3 that CFO may be estimated as traditional cash flow minus the increase in accounts receivable and/or inventory, plus the increase in accounts payable and/or other accruals.

   Using CFO helps eliminate the issues involved with accounting differences, such as the use of LIFO/FIFO and different revenue recognition policies. However, CFO does not truly reflect what we need, which is discussed below.

3. *The information we need, we can have, if only we look.*

   What we really need is an estimate of the cash that can be withdrawn from a business after the firm has made all required investments to sustain its future growth. This is best described as the free cash flow of a firm, which was defined in Chapter 3, and can be estimated using the following formula:

   Free cash flow = CFO – "Normal" capital expenditure (capex) requirements

   This cash flow estimate not only adjusts for the accounting problems discussed in items 1 and 2 above, but also ensures the firm grows in the long term and does not "run down" its assets to sustain profitability in the short term.

To summarize, the cash flows we will use in the DCF valuation approach will be the company's free cash flows. These free cash flows, which are defined in Equation 15-2 below, are the free cash flows to equity holders, since they represent the cash flows left over after all obligations, including interest payments, have been paid.[22]

---

[21] Hunt, Pearson, "Funds Position: Keystone in Financial Planning." *Harvard Business Review* (May/June 1975).

[22] This also assumes the firm does not issue any new debt, which would be added to the free cash flow amount. We ignore this component of free cash flow to equity for valuing takeover targets, since the new financing would presumably come from the acquiring firm going forward. The free cash flow to the firm (both equity and debt holders) would simply be the free cash flow to equity plus the after-tax amount of the interest payments (less any new debt issued that was added to determine free cash flow to equity).

[15-2]   *Free cash flow to equity = Net income +/– Non-cash items*
          (amortization, deferred taxes, etc.) +/– Changes in net working capital
          (not including cash and marketable securities) – Net capital expenditures

The next step in DCF valuation is to discount all of the future cash flow estimates back to the present, as depicted in Equation 15-3. Notice that this is identical to Equation 7-5 from Chapter 7, which depicted the generalized version of the dividend discount model (DDM); the only difference is that we use cash flows in the numerator instead of dividends. Since we are using free cash flow to equity, the appropriate discount rate (k) will be the risk-adjusted cost of equity for the target firm.[23]

[15-3]
$$V_0 = \frac{CF_1}{(1+k)^1} + \frac{CF_2}{(1+k)^2} + \ldots + \frac{CF_\infty}{(1+k)^\infty} = \sum_{t=1}^{\infty} \frac{CF_t}{(1+k)^t}$$

Like the constant-growth version of the DDM, this equation can be simplified, as shown in Equation 15-4, if we assume that these cash flows grow at some constant annual rate (g) to infinity.

[15-4]
$$V_0 = \frac{CF_1}{k-g}$$

In practice, it is common to refine this process so that we can focus on estimating cash flows that will arise in the short to medium term and then make some simplifying assumption about cash flows beyond some terminal date (T). This process is depicted in Figure 15-7.

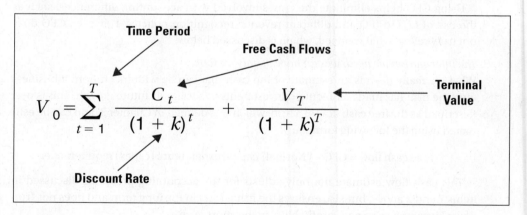

FIGURE 15-7 *The DCF Valuation Framework*

The final term in the equation in Figure 15-7 is the terminal value (V_T). This value is the present value of all future cash flows from time T to infinity, and it is usually estimated assuming some reasonable sustainable annual growth rate in cash flows from some time T forward. Notice that this is the same approach we used when we applied the multiple-stage growth DDM in Chapter 7. For future reference, we number and present the following equation from Figure 15-7.

[15-5]
$$V_0 = \sum_{t=1}^{T} \frac{CF_t}{(1+k)^t} + \frac{V_T}{(1+k)^T}$$

---

[23] If we instead had decided to use free cash flow to the firm, we would need to use the target firm's weighted average cost of capital as the appropriate discount rate. Our discussion in Chapter 20 shows that this discount rate reflects all financing costs, and therefore we should not include interest payments in our cash flow estimates. By using free cash flow to the firm, we have already made this adjustment, since we added back the after-tax interest amount to the free cash flow to equity estimates.

We now illustrate this valuation approach using some simple examples.

EXAMPLE 15-4   DCF Valuation I

We are given the following information about a potential takeover candidate firm (T2) for next year, based on what it is expected to contribute after it is acquired (i.e., with any arising synergies included): expected EBIT = $2 million; expected interest payments = $200,000; expected depreciation and amortization expense = $100,000; expected deferred taxes = $50,000; tax rate = 42 percent; expected increase in net working capital = $200,000; and expected net capital expenditures = $150,000.

a. Estimate T2's free cash flow to equity next year.

b. Estimate the value of T2's equity in total and on a per-share basis, assuming that next year's free cash flow increases annually at a 5-percent rate indefinitely. The firm has 500,000 shares outstanding. The appropriate beta is 1.2, the expected return on the market is 10 percent, and the risk-free rate is 4 percent.

Solution

a. Net income = (2,000,000 − 200,000) × (1 − 0.42) = $1,044,000
    Free cash flow to equity = Net income + Non-cash expenses − Increase in net working capital − Net capital expenditures = 1,044,000 + 100,000 + 50,000 − 200,000 − 150,000 = $844,000

b. Since we are assuming constant growth in the cash flows to infinity, we can use Equation 15-4.

$k = 4 + (10 − 4) (1.2) = 11.2\%$

$CF_1 = \$844,000; g = 5\%$

$$V_0 = \frac{CF_1}{k - g} = \frac{844,000}{0.112 - 0.05} = \$13,612,903$$

Therefore, the per-share value = $13,612,903 ÷ 500,000 = $27.23

EXAMPLE 15-5   DCF Valuation II

We are given the following information about a potential takeover candidate firm (T3) for the next three years.

$	Year 0	Year 1	Year 2	Year 3
Net income	1,450	1,500	1,550	1,600
Depreciation	100	100	100	100
Deferred taxes	50	50	50	55
Accounts receivable	200	230	250	260
Inventory	150	160	180	190
Accounts payable	210	230	240	250
Capital expenditures	80	70	80	90
Dividends	150	150	160	160

After three years, free cash flow is expected to grow at 6 percent per year indefinitely. Estimate the value of T3's equity using DCF analysis, assuming the appropriate discount rate is 12 percent.

Solution

$	Year 1	Year 2	Year 3
Net income	1,500	1,550	1,600
+Depreciation	+100	+100	+100
+Deferred taxes	+50	+50	+55

continued

EXAMPLE 15-5 *DCF Valuation II continued*

$	Year 1	Year 2	Year 3
−Increase in accounts receivable	−30	−20	−10
−Increase in inventory	−10	−20	−10
+Increase in accounts payable	+20	+10	+10
−Capital expenditures	−70	−80	−90
Free cash flow to equity	1,560	1,590	1,655

$$k = 12\%; \ CF_1 = \$1,560; \ CF_2 = \$1,590; \ CF_3 = \$1,655$$

Since we are assuming constant growth after three years, we can use Equation 15-5.

$$V_0 = \sum_{t=1}^{T} \frac{CF_t}{(1+k)^t} + \frac{V_T}{(1+k)^T}$$

We can estimate the terminal value after three years using the constant growth version of the DCF formula, since $g = 6\%$ per year from year 3 to infinity.

$$V_T = \frac{CF_{T+1}}{k-g} = \frac{(1,655)(1.06)}{0.12 - 0.06} = \$29,238.33$$

Now we can estimate the value of T3 today:

$$V_0 = \frac{1,560}{(1.12)} + \frac{1,590}{(1.12)^2} + \frac{1,655}{(1.12)^3} + \frac{29,238.33}{(1.12)^3}$$

$$= 1,392.86 + 1,267.54 + 1,178.00 + 20,811.27 = \$24,649.67$$

The Acquisition Decision

In the section above, we discussed different methods of determining the value of a takeover candidate. This is a critical part of the takeover decision process, since an acquisition will make sense only if the target firm can be acquired for a price that is less than its value to the acquiring firm. For example, the acquiring firm in Example 15-5 should acquire firm T3 only if it can acquire T3 at a cost less than or equal to $24,650. Example 15-6 demonstrates that the cost of acquiring T3 depends on how the target firm is purchased, by cash or shares.

EXAMPLE 15-6 The Cost of an Acquisition

Firm A estimates that it can purchase firm T3 from Example 15-5 in one of two ways:
(1) by paying $24 per share in cash; or (2) by giving T3's shareholders two shares in the new combined firm A-T3 for each share of T3.

Prior to the merger, T3 had 1,000 shares outstanding, which are trading at $20 per share, and A had 3,000 shares outstanding, trading at $12 per share.

Assuming that A is properly priced prior to the acquisition, should A acquire T3? If so, which method should it use to acquire T3?

continued

EXAMPLE 15-6 *The Cost of an Acquisition continued*

Solution

We estimate the cost under each method:

a. **Cash:** The cost is $24 \times 1,000 = \$24,000$, which means that purchasing T3 by cash would generate an NPV of $\$24,650 - \$24,000 = +\$650$.

b. **Stock:** Since A is giving T3's shareholders two of its shares (worth $12 each) for every share of T3, and since T3 has 1,000 shares outstanding, the cost appears to be 2,000 shares $\times \$12 = \$24,000$; however, this is not correct since what A is really giving to T3's shareholders is 2,000 shares in the new company, A-T3, which is created from the merger.

To estimate the cost, we must therefore estimate the value of A-T3 after the merger:

Post-merger value of A-T3 = Value of A + Value of T3 to A = $(3,000)(\$12) + \$24,650 = \$60,650$

Since there will be $3,000 + 2,000$ (new shares issued) = 5,000 shares outstanding in the new firm, each share will be worth $\$60,650 \div 5,000 = \$12.13$.

So, the actual cost of giving T3's shareholders 2,000 shares equals:

Cost = (2,000 shares)($12.13 per share) = $24,260

Thus, the NPV under this scenario would be $\$24,650 - \$24,260 = +\$390$.

Example 15-6 highlights the SVAR analysis. Using cash lets the original shareholders keep the expected NPV, whereas using a share swap lets the target firm shareholders share in the NPV. Clearly, if the firm is very confident in the NPV, it should use cash, but if the NPV is highly uncertain, then a share swap reduces the risk to the original shareholders.

The Effect of an Acquisition on Earnings per Share

Table 15-1 referred to the earnings per share (EPS) "growth game" as a motive for several M&As during the 1960s. An acquiring firm can increase its EPS if it acquires a firm that has a P/E ratio lower than its own, even if no synergies arise from the merger. This is illustrated in Example 15-7.

EXAMPLE 15-7 **The EPS Effect**

Firm A2 acquires firm T4 for cash at T4's present market value, and no synergies arise. The following pre-merger information is provided. What is the EPS of the new firm (A2-T4)?

	A2	T4
Total earnings	$10,000	$3,000
Number of common shares outstanding	4,000	2,000
EPS	$2.50	$1.50
Market price per share (P_0)	$20	$9
P/E ratio	8 times	6 times
Total market value of equity	$80,000	$18,000

continued

EXAMPLE 15-7 *The EPS Effect continued*

Solution

New firm A2-T4:

Total earnings = $10,000 + $3,000 = $13,000

Total shares outstanding = 4,000 (i.e., the number of shares A2 had outstanding)

Post-merger EPS = $13,000 ÷ 4,000 = $3.25 (well above A2's pre-merger EPS of $2.50)

Notice that if the market were inefficient and the P/E ratio for A2 remained at 8, the value of A2-T4 would equal EPS × P/E ratio = $3.25 × 8 = $26.

Therefore, the market value of A2-T4 would equal $26 × 4,000 = $104,000.

    This is well above what it should be in an efficient market, since we know the combined market value should equal the market value of A2 plus the market value of T4, assuming no synergies were created. In other words, the combined market value of A2-T4 should equal 80,000 + 18,000 = $98,000. Total market value of A2 (after paying cash for T4) is $80,000. This implies that the P/E ratio should be $98,000 ÷ $13,000 = 7.54, and the share price for A2-T4 should be $3.25 × 7.54 = $24.50, not $26.

    In an efficient market, the market value of the combined firm in Example 15-7 should be $98,000 and not $104,000. Given full disclosure, analysts are aware of the earnings multiplier game and see through such accounting gimmicks. This would mean that the accounting motivation for M&A is not significant. However, many firms do not seem to disclose the full extent of their acquisitions. For example, Tyco, the large U.S. conglomerate, was the target of much criticism for its disclosure of its M&A activity, with some suspicion that its earnings were in part from accounting and not organic growth. As a practical matter, many analysts and companies entering into M&As prefer those that are "accretive" to (i.e., increase) EPS.

CONCEPT REVIEW QUESTIONS

1. What is the difference between value and price?
2. What is fair market value?
3. What key multiples are used in valuing companies?
4. Why do differing capital structures cause problems with using P/E multiples?
5. What is free cash flow?
6. When does EPS increase when using a share swap?

15.6 ACCOUNTING FOR ACQUISITIONS

Learning Objective 15.6
Identify the issues involved in accounting for mergers and acquisitions.

purchase method a method of accounting for business combinations in which one firm assumes the fair market value of all the assets and liabilities of the other (target) firm and all operating results from the date of acquisition going forward

Historically, Canadian companies could use one of two methods to account for business combinations: the **purchase method** or the pooling-of-interests method. However, the Canadian Institute of Chartered Accountants (CICA) worked closely with the Financial Accounting Standards Board (FASB) of the United States to eliminate the pooling-of-interests method as of June 30, 2001. This caused fewer difficulties in Canada than in the United States, since the pooling method was permitted only in the rarest of circumstances in Canada. It had been used more frequently in the United States. The International Accounting Standards Board (IASB) also no longer permits the use of the pooling method. Given the conversion of Canadian GAAP to the IFRS standards in 2011, this means Canadian firms still have no choice and cannot use the pooling method. Since this method is no longer used, we will not elaborate on its application.

    Under the purchase method, one firm basically assumes all of the assets and liabilities of the other (target) firm and all operating results from the date of acquisition going forward.

No restatement of prior periods' results is necessary. At the time of the acquisition, all the assets and liabilities of the target firm are restated to reflect its FMV as of the acquisition date. Since we know that equity is defined as assets minus liabilities, this implies the difference between the FMV of the target firm's assets and liabilities is the FMV of its equity. If the purchase price exceeds the FMV of the target firm's equity, the excess amount is referred to as **goodwill**, which is reported on the asset side of the balance sheet for the new entity. Example 15-8 illustrates the purchase method of accounting for an acquisition.

goodwill the amount of a target firm's purchase price that exceeds the fair market value of its equity

---

EXAMPLE 15-8   The Purchase Method

Assume company A1 acquires company T5 for $1,250 in cash on June 30, 2014. The table below provides the balance sheets for A1 and T5 on that date, as well as the estimated market values for T5's assets and liabilities. Construct A1's balance sheet after the acquisition, using the purchase method.

$	A1	T5 (Book Value)	T5 (FMV)
Current assets	10,000	1,200	1,300
Long-term assets	6,000	800	900
Goodwill			
Total	16,000	2,000	2,200
Current liabilities	8,000	800	800
Long-term debt	2,000	200	250
Common stock	2,000	400	1,250
Retained earnings	4,000	600	
Total	16,000	2,000	2,300

Solution

$	A1 (Pre-Merger)	T5 (Book Value)	T5 (FMV)	A1 (Post-Merger)
Current assets	10,000	1,200	1,300	11,300[1]
Long-term assets	6,000	800	900	6,900[2]
Goodwill				100[3]
Total	16,000	2,000	2,200	18,300
Current liabilities	8,000	800	800	8,800
Long-term debt	2,000	200	250	2,250
Common stock	2,000	400	1,250	3,250
Retained earnings	4,000	600		4,000
Total	16,000	2,000	2,300	18,300

[1] 10,000 + 1,300 = 11,300
[2] 6,000 + 900 = 6,900
[3] Goodwill = 1,250 (Price paid) − MV (T5's Equity) = 1,250 − [2,200 MV(T5's assets) − 1,050 MV (T5's liabilities)] = 1,250 − 1,150 = 100

In addition to the accounting rule changes with respect to purchase versus pooling accounting, rules have also been implemented about the valuation of goodwill and intangibles. One of the most important rule changes is that the goodwill resulting from an acquisition may not be amortized. Prior to the rule change, amortization was mandatory. Instead, the market value of goodwill must be assessed annually, and it is written down and charged directly to earnings per share if the value is deemed to have been permanently "impaired." As a result of this treatment of goodwill, its fair value is subject to an annual impairment test. As discussed above, the value of goodwill on the balance sheet is what is left over after properly valuing everything else. This means companies are required to employ common valuation techniques, such as detailed discounted cash flow analysis, in order to determine fair value.

CONCEPT REVIEW QUESTIONS

1. Explain how the purchase method gives rise to goodwill.
2. How is goodwill treated for accounting purposes in Canada and the United States?

SUMMARY

In this chapter, we discuss the various forms of business combinations, paying particular attention to mergers and acquisitions. We examine some of the most common motives that exist for takeovers, as well as some desirable characteristics of potential takeover "targets." We then demonstrate how to evaluate a potential takeover candidate using the multiples approach and using discounted cash flow analysis. We conclude with a discussion of how acquisitions should be accounted for in the financial statements, and we show the impact that acquisitions can have on earnings per share.

SUMMARY OF LEARNING OBJECTIVES

15.1 Describe the different types of takeovers.

Takeover: the transfer of control from one ownership group to another

Acquisition: the purchase of one firm by another

Merger: the combination of two firms into a new legal entity

Amalgamation: a genuine merger in which both sets of shareholders must approve the transaction

Going private transaction (issuer bid): a special form of acquisition in which the purchaser already owns a majority stake in the target company

15.2 Explain securities legislation as it applies to takeovers.

Securities legislation governs the exchange of shares by the target firm's shareholders and protects the shareholders' right to receive full value for their shares. Securities legislation falls under provincial jurisdiction; therefore, there are differences between the provinces. The *Ontario Securities Act*, administered by the Ontario Securities Commission, contains many features that are common to all jurisdictions. Critical shareholder percentages are:

- 10 percent: early warning
- 20 percent: takeover bid
- 50.1 percent: control

- 66.7 percent: amalgamation
- 90 percent: minority squeeze-out

15.3 Differentiate between friendly and hostile acquisitions and describe the process of a typical friendly acquisition.

In a friendly acquisition, the management of the target company agrees to the takeover. In a hostile acquisition, the management of the target company resists the acquirer, so the acquirer makes a tender offer directly to the shareholders of the target.

The steps in a typical friendly acquisition process are:

1. The target issues an information memorandum.
2. The potential acquirers conduct due diligence.
3. The most interested acquirers sign letters of intent.
4. The winning acquirer makes a final agreement with the board of the target.
5. The offer is approved by the shareholders of the target company.

15.4 Explain the various motivations underlying mergers and acquisitions.

Mergers and acquisitions are most commonly motivated by the following benefits:

- Economies of scale: increased size produces benefits, such as reducing over-capacity in the industry

- Economies of scope: combined activities reduce costs

- Complementary strengths: one firm's strength benefits the other

- Efficiency increases: e.g., eliminating excess capacity increases efficiency

- Financing synergies: larger is better for accessing capital markets

- Tax benefits: e.g., one firm's losses can be used to offset the other firm's profits to reduce taxes

- Strategic realignments: e.g., the acquisition of new managerial skill and new product/service line growth opportunities

15.5 Identify the valuation issues involved in assessing mergers and acquisitions.

1. *Multiples or relative valuation* involves the use of ratios, such as price-earnings (P/E), market-to-book (M/B), price-to-sales (P/S), and price-to-cash flow (P/CF).

2. *Liquidation valuation* involves estimating the liquidation value of the firm's assets at present market prices.

3. *Discounted cash flow (DCF) analysis* involves estimating the future cash flows associated with the new combined entity and discounting them back to the present to determine the fair market value.

15.6 Identify the issues involved in accounting for mergers and acquisitions.

Under the purchase method, the assets of the target are restated to reflect their fair market value (FMV). The FMV of the assets is added to the assets of the acquiring firm. If the purchase price exceeds the FMV of the assets, then the difference is recorded as goodwill on the acquiring firm's balance sheet.

KEY TERMS

acquisition, p. 574
amalgamation, p. 576
arbs, p. 584
asset purchase, p. 583
break fee, p. 582
cash transaction, p. 575
confidentiality agreement, p. 581
conglomerate merger, p. 586
creeping takeover, p. 580
cross-border (international) M&A, p. 587
data room, p. 581
defensive tactic, p. 584
due diligence, p. 581
extension M&A, p. 592
fair market value (FMV), p. 597

fairness opinion, p. 576
friendly acquisition, p. 581
geographic roll-up, p. 591
going private transaction/issuer bid, p. 576
goodwill, p. 609
horizontal merger, p. 586
hostile takeover, p. 583
letter of intent, p. 581
management buyouts (MBOs)/leveraged buyouts (LBOs), p. 598
merger, p. 574
no-shop clause, p. 582
offering memorandum, p. 581
over-capacity M&A, p. 591

proactive methods, p. 598
purchase method, p. 608
reactive methods, p. 598
selling the crown jewels, p. 585
share transaction, p. 575
shareholder rights plan/poison pill, p. 584
synergy, p. 591
takeovers, p. 574
tender, p. 579
tender offer, p. 583
vertical merger, p. 586
white knight, p. 585

EQUATIONS

Equation	Formula	Page
[15-1] Synergy	$\Delta V = V_{A-T} - (V_A + V_T)$	p. 591
[15-2] Free Cash Flow to Equity	*Free cash flow to equity = Net income +/– Non-cash items (amortization, deferred taxes, etc.) +/– Changes in net working capital (not including cash and marketable securities) – Net capital expenditures*	p. 604
[15-3] Firm Value (long version)	$V_0 = \dfrac{CF_1}{(1+k)^1} + \dfrac{CF_2}{(1+k)^2} + \ldots + \dfrac{CF_\infty}{(1+k)^\infty} = \sum_{t=1}^{\infty} \dfrac{CF_t}{(1+k)^t}$	p. 604

EQUATIONS *continued*

Equation	Formula	Page
[15-4] Firm Value (constant growth version)	$V_0 = \dfrac{CF_1}{k - g}$	p. 604
[15-5] Firm Value (multi-stage growth version)	$V_0 = \sum\limits_{t=1}^{T} \dfrac{CF_t}{(1 + k)^t} + \dfrac{V_T}{(1 + k)^T}$	p. 604

QUESTIONS AND PRACTICE PROBLEMS

Multiple Choice Questions

1. Which of the following statements about takeovers is *false*?
   a. Mergers create a new firm, while acquisitions do not.
   b. Both mergers and acquisitions require two-thirds votes from both firms.
   c. In the tender offer, the acquiring firm makes a public offer to purchase shares of the target firm.
   d. Acquisition of assets is one of the types of takeover.

2. Which of the following firm structures is least likely to be the target for a bidder?
   a. Common shares are widely held.
   b. The stock is undervalued.
   c. It has a simple corporate structure.
   d. There are many legal problems.

3. Which of the following critical shareholder percentages is *false*?
   a. 10%: early warning
   b. 20%: takeover bid
   c. 50.1%: control
   d. 100%: minority squeeze-out

4. Which of the following statements about hostile takeovers is *false*?
   a. In hostile takeover bids, there is usually a tender offer.
   b. A formal vote by the target shareholders is required.
   c. The target has no desire to be acquired.
   d. The target actively rebuffs the acquiring firm and refuses to provide any confidential information.

5. Which of the following statements is *false* when the market price immediately jumps above the tender offer price in a hostile bid?
   a. A competing offer is likely.
   b. The bid is too low.
   c. The bidder will have to increase the offer price.
   d. The bid is too high.

6. Which of the following statements is *false* regarding a tender offer during hostile takeovers?
   a. If there is little trading, this is usually a bad sign for the acquiring firm, since shareholders are sitting on the shares and are reluctant to sell.
   b. A large amount of trading indicates that shares are cycling from regular investors into specialist hands.

    c. Arbitrageurs are only interested in selling as long as the price is right.

    d. The motivation of arbitrageurs is to take control of the target.

7. Which of the following is *not* a defensive tactic in a hostile takeover?

    a. A shareholder rights plan (a poison pill)

    b. Selling the crown jewels

    c. Finding a white knight

    d. Cooperating with the acquirer

8. Which of the following is *not* one of the three types of merger?

    a. Vertical M&A

    b. Horizontal M&A

    c. Proxy contest

    d. Conglomerate

9. Which of the following M&As is valid?

    a. $V_{A-T} = \$400,000$; $V_A = \$200,000$; $V_T = \$205,000$

    b. $V_{A-T} = \$390,000$; $V_A = \$200,000$; $V_T = \$190,000$

    c. $V_{A-T} = \$410,000$; $V_A = \$200,000$; $V_T = \$190,000$

    d. $V_{A-T} = \$600,000$; $V_A = \$400,000$; $V_T = \$210,000$

10. Which of the following is a poor motive for M&As as suggested by evidence?

    a. Diversification

    b. Economies of scale

    c. Economies of scope

    d. Complementary strengths

11. Which of the following is *not* a reason for financial synergies?

    a. Fewer information problems

    b. Reduced average issuing costs

    c. Reduced cash flow volatility

    d. Increased need of external financing

12. What is the market value of the equity of a firm that has a trailing P/E ratio of 4.5 and expected earnings (E_1) of \$550,000? The firm is expected to grow at 5 percent.

    a. \$2,475,000

    b. \$2,357,143

    c. \$1,850,000

    d. \$2,050,099

13. Which of the following cash flow measures should be used in the DCF valuation approach?

    a. Cash flow from operations (CFO)

    b. Free cash flow

    c. Cash flow from investing (CFI)

    d. Cash flow from financing

14. Which of the following statements about liquidation valuation is *false*?

    a. Current accounts receivable with good credit firms should be realized at a relatively high percentage of book value.

    b. Liquidation value equals book value of current assets plus market value of tangible assets minus the value of the firm's liabilities from the total estimated liquidation value of all the firm's assets.

    c. Overdue accounts receivable with bad credit firms should be realized at a relatively low percentage of book value.

    d. The liquidation valuation approach is not forward-looking.

Practice Problems

15. List and briefly describe the two types of takeovers.

16. Marcel owns 12 percent of Steam Forge Company (SFC). SFC trades on the Toronto Stock Exchange and has been the subject of a takeover attempt by Iron Forge Company (IFC). Assuming that Marcel is the only minority shareholder who will not co-operate with IFC, determine the minimum level of ownership IFC needs in order to do the following. (Round your answer to one decimal.)
    a. Call a special meeting of the shareholders.
    b. Replace the board of directors.
    c. Replace the firm's management.
    d. Force Marcel to sell at the takeover price.
    e. Win a vote on amalgamation.
    f. Make a takeover bid.

17. Julius is a shareholder in a public corporation, which has recently acquired another company, and the consequences for the bidding firm have been catastrophic. Julius is suing the bidder's board of directors for breach of duty as he believes that they failed in their duties to the shareholders. The board of directors, in their response to the suit, said: "A board member is from British Columbia, and he knew about a timber company that was for sale and we could get it cheap. We saw that the profits of lumber companies had increased over the past two years, so we bought it. We did not waste time and money looking at other possible candidates because we had found a good deal. We knew the deal was good because the CEO of the target was the cousin of the board member from B.C." The bidding company, prior to the acquisition, was in the business of making sewing machines. The board of directors of the bidding firm has 12 members, 8 of whom are either current or former executives with the firm.

    Discuss at least four serious problems with the board's approach toward this acquisition.

18. The Bynum Private Equity group has just made a tender offer for, at most, 60 percent of Vendall Company. Vendall has 1,000 shares outstanding. Mr. VanDuun is a shareholder of Vendall and has tendered his shares. For each situation below, indicate the number of shares accepted by Bynum and how many of Mr. VanDuun's shares will be accepted by Bynum.

	Total shares tendered by Vendall shareholders	Mr. VanDuun's tendered shares	Total number of shares accepted by Bynum	Number of Mr. VanDuun's shares accepted by Bynum
A	1,000	400		
B	1,000	300		
C	500	400		
D	500	300		
E	500	100		
F	500	200		

19. Describe the process of a friendly acquisition.

20. Briefly describe three common defensive tactics against a takeover and the difference between U.S. and Canadian practice on poison pills.

21. Describe the possible market price change after a tender offer and the possible reasons.

22. You are a risk arbitrageur and you observe the following information about a deal: the current price of the target is $20 per share and the current price of the bidder is $15 per share. The bidder is offering two bidder shares per target share, and you expect the deal to be completed in one year. Neither company is expected to pay dividends over the next year. Assume you can freely short sell and there are no margin requirements. You do not use any leverage.
    a. i.   Calculate the offer premium.
       ii. Describe the transaction you will undertake to capture the premium.
       iii. Show how your transaction will make money.
    b. Is it possible that your actual return will be less than the expected return? Describe two situations that can cause the risk in risk arbitrage.

23. Describe horizontal M&A, vertical M&A, and conglomerate.

24. Describe the economies of scale of M&A.

25. Describe the financing synergies of M&A.

26. Describe the empirical evidence on the actual gains or losses resulting from mergers.

27. Carla is the CEO of The Superior Sausage Company (a Canadian firm, listed on the Toronto Stock Exchange) and believes that the best way for the company to grow is through acquisitions. She has identified a likely target, Bunns & Bagels (B&B), which is also listed on the Toronto Stock Exchange.
    a. Describe two different possible types of motives for this acquisition.
    b. Carla is very uncertain about the value of B&B. Describe how she can structure the deal to reduce the risk to Superior Sausage.
    c. Carla has just publicly announced that she feels that the senior management of B&B is not only incompetent, but likely to have been committing fraud.
       i.   Is a takeover by Superior Sausage more likely to be friendly or hostile? Why?
       ii. Is Superior more likely to use a tender offer or a merger offer? Why?
       iii. Describe three ways B&B could try to defend itself from Superior.
    d. Before the market opened on Monday, B&B announced that it had received a merger offer from Franks' Fine Franks. By the end of trading on Monday, B&B has earned a return of – 2 percent (negative 2 percent). The return on the market that day was 4 percent and the daily risk-free rate was close to zero. The beta for B&B is 2, with a standard deviation of the regression of 2 percent.
       i.   What is the expected return for B&B on Monday based on CAPM?
       ii. What is the abnormal return for B&B on Monday?
       iii. Given the empirical evidence on mergers and acquisitions, is the market's reaction unusual? Why or why not?

        Use the following information to answer practice problems 28 to 32.

Sales	$1,550,000
Cost of goods sold	350,000
Depreciation	400,000
Interest	150,000
Income tax	260,000
Dividends	300,000
Common shares outstanding	500,000
P/EBITDA	10x

28. Calculate the market price of the company's common shares using a relative valuation approach. (Round your answer to one decimal.)

29. Calculate the trailing and forward P/E ratios using the price calculated in Practice Problem 28. Assume a 6 percent earnings growth. (Round your answer to one decimal.)

30. Calculate the trailing and forward P/E ratios using the following assumptions: RF = 5 percent; β = 0.65; market risk premium = 5 percent; dividends and earnings grow at 6 percent indefinitely; and the firm maintains its current dividend payout ratio. (Round your answer to one decimal.)

31. Calculate the market value of the *firm* given the following additional information: cost of equity is 8.25 percent, free cash flow to equity grows at 6 percent indefinitely; total debt outstanding = $1,000,000; increase in current assets = $400,000; increase in current liabilities = $300,000; and capital expenditures = $100,000. (Round your answer to the nearest dollar.)

32. In Practice Problem 31, if the free cash flow to equity grows at 8 percent for the first two years and then grows at 5 percent indefinitely, what is the market value of the firm now? (Round your answer to the nearest dollar.)

33. ABC Inc. is planning to purchase DEF Inc. in one of two ways: (1) by paying $22 per share in cash; or (2) by giving DEF's shareholders two shares in the new combined firm ABC-DEF for each share of DEF. Prior to the merger, DEF had 500,000 shares outstanding, trading at $20 per share. ABC had 600,000 shares outstanding, trading at $18 per share. Assume that ABC is properly priced prior to the acquisition. DEF is valued at $15,875,000 to ABC. Should ABC acquire DEF? If so, which method should it use to acquire DEF?

34. Calculate the post-merger EPS and market value of equity, assuming no synergies arise in the following acquisition settled *in cash*. Analyze the difference, if there is any. Further, calculate the *new* P/E ratio and share price for post-merger B-T. Additional information is given as follows:

	Bidder	Target
Total earnings	$25,000	$7,000
Number of common shares outstanding	8,000	3,500
EPS	$3.13	$2.00
Market price per share (P_0)	$29.50	$12.00
P/E ratio	9 times	6 times
Total market value of equity	$236,000	$42,000

35. A bidder paid $1,250 for a target. The target's market asset is $2,000 and market liability is $1,050. What is the goodwill created during the acquisition?

36. Describe the purchase method in accounting for acquisitions.

37. The balance sheets of a bidder and target companies are as follows:

Balance Sheet (Bidder) as of 31/12/1x

Tangible assets	$50,000			
Accumulated depreciation	$32,000		Total debt	$15,000
Net tangible assets		$18,000		
Goodwill		3,000	Equity	6,000
Total assets		$21,000	Total claims	$21,000

CHAPTER 15 | Questions and Practice Problems   617

Balance Sheet (Target) as of 31/12/1x

Tangible assets	$31,000				
Accumulated depreciation	$10,000		Total debt	$19,000	
Net tangible assets		$21,000			
Goodwill		0	Equity	2,000	
Total assets		$21,000	Total claims	$21,000	

The tax rate for both companies is 25 percent. The acquisition will be accounted for using the purchase method. Prior to the acquisition, the bidding firm had 10,000 shares outstanding, with a share price of $20. The target had 5,000 shares outstanding, with a market price of $10. The bidder acquired the target by offering 0.80 bidder shares per target share.

After analyzing the target, the bidder has decided that the market value of the target's assets is $65,000, and the market value of the bidder's assets are $45,000.

a. How many shares will be outstanding for the combined firm, B-T?
b. What fraction of the combined company will be owned by the original bidder shareholders?
c. How much goodwill was created by this transaction?
d. How much is the net tangible assets for the combined firm?
e. Show the consolidated balance sheet for B-T (use the template provided).

Combined Firm Balance Sheet as of 31/12/1x

Net tangible assets		Total debt	
Goodwill		Equity	
Total assets		Total claims	

38. Complete the following balance sheet for the post-merger firm B-T. The bidder acquired the target for $2,000 in cash.

$	Bidder	Target (book value)	Target (FMV)	B-T (post-merger)
Current assets	25,000	3,500	2,900	
Long-term assets	10,000	1,000	1,300	
Goodwill				
Total assets	35,000	4,500	4,200	
Current liabilities	11,000	1,500	1,500	
Long-term debt	5,000	800	1,000	
Common stock	15,000	1,800	2,000	
Retained earnings	4,000	400		
Total	35,000	4,500	4,500	

16 | Leasing

LEARNING OBJECTIVES

16.1 Identify the basic characteristics of leases and differentiate between operating and financial (or capital) leases.

16.2 Describe the accounting treatment of both operating and financial leases.

16.3 Evaluate the lease decision using discounted cash flow valuation methods.

16.4 Explain the various motives for leasing.

More than 200 members of the Canadian Finance & Leasing Association (CFLA) are active in the asset-based financing, equipment, and vehicle leasing industry in Canada. Members range from large multinationals to national and regional domestic companies, crossing the financial services spectrum from manufacturers' finance companies and independent leasing companies, to banks, insurance companies, and suppliers to the industry.

The asset-based financing and leasing industry is the largest provider of debt financing to business customers and consumers in Canada after the traditional lenders (banks and credit unions).

In 1998, the federal (MacKay) Task Force on the Future of the Canadian Financial Services Sector reported that the assets of the asset-based financing and leasing industry in 1997 totalled $50 billion. By 2007, the value of assets financed had risen to $105.4 billion. But, with the worldwide economic crisis of 2008–2009, total assets financed in Canada declined to $79.7 billion in 2010.

Source: Canadian Finance and Leasing Association (CFLA), *2010/2011 Annual Report*, p. 8. Available at www.cfla-acfl.ca.

CHAPTER 16 **PREVIEW**

This chapter discusses leasing arrangements, which may represent attractive alternatives for companies looking to finance both short- and long-term investments. This chapter deals with basic financial issues faced by Canadian individuals as well as firms. Think of this chapter the next time you decide to buy or lease a new car.

16.1 LEASING ARRANGEMENTS

Learning Objective 16.1
Identify the basic characteristics of leases and differentiate between operating and financial (or capital) leases.

asset-based lending financing that is tied directly to a particular asset

secured financing financing based on an underlying asset that serves as collateral in the event of a default

In earlier chapters, we considered the purchase of a piece of equipment separate from its financing, which will be discussed in later chapters. In **asset-based lending**, these two decisions are combined into one decision, with the financing tied directly to the particular asset being purchased. This is an example of **secured financing**, in which the financing is based on an underlying asset that serves as collateral in the event of a default. Examples of asset-based lending are secured loans, conditional sales contracts, and leases. We will talk about the differences between these types of asset-based financing in this chapter, but the main focus is on leases. While most textbooks discuss leasing as either a financing or investment decision, we have chosen to discuss it as a capital budgeting decision because it provides a further chance to develop basic valuation skills in discounting cash flows. Also, a firm may choose to lease rather than purchase one of the long-term assets considered in capital budgeting. Figure 16-1 shows the level of leasing activity in Canada, which closely follows the pattern of business investment.

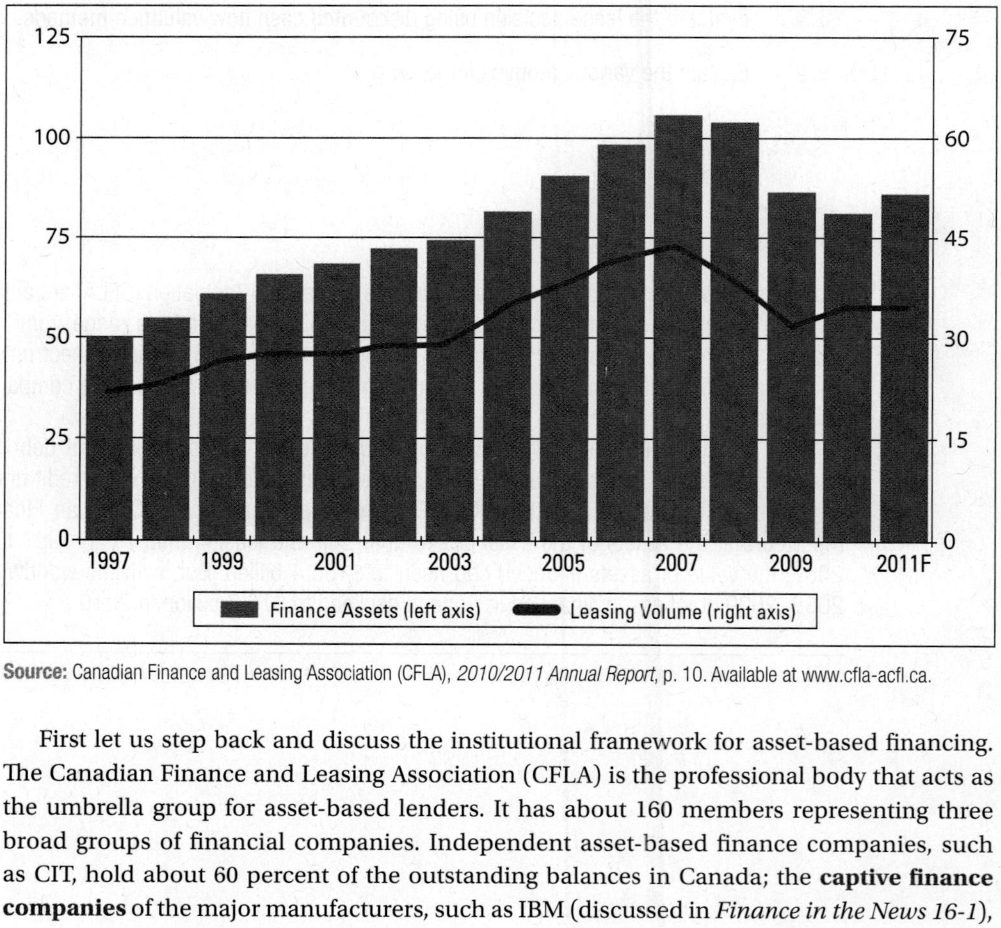

FIGURE 16-1 *Equipment and Vehicle Leasing Market in Canada ($billions)*

Source: Canadian Finance and Leasing Association (CFLA), *2010/2011 Annual Report*, p. 10. Available at www.cfla-acfl.ca.

captive finance companies finance companies that are divisions of major manufacturers and provide loans to purchase or lease their products

First let us step back and discuss the institutional framework for asset-based financing. The Canadian Finance and Leasing Association (CFLA) is the professional body that acts as the umbrella group for asset-based lenders. It has about 160 members representing three broad groups of financial companies. Independent asset-based finance companies, such as CIT, hold about 60 percent of the outstanding balances in Canada; the **captive finance companies** of the major manufacturers, such as IBM (discussed in *Finance in the News 16-1*), hold about 29 percent of the outstanding balances; and the remainder is with the chartered banks. There are restrictions in the *Bank Act* that prevent the chartered banks from leasing consumer household property, vehicles (except for commercial transportation equipment), and real property (land and buildings). As a result, this is one major segment of the capital market where the banks are not as important as they are elsewhere.[1]

finance INTHENEWS 16-1 | IBM to Offer Special Finance Packages

IBM IS OFFERING special finance packages through the remainder of 2009 for its System x family of servers that bundle the newly released VMware vSphere 4 virtualization platform. Qualified customers are eligible for financing on purchases as small as $5,000.

IBM's System x lineup includes BladeCenter servers, System x rack and tower models, and the System x3950 M2 enterprise server, the single-system "reference platform" for the development of VMware vSphere 4 scalability.

The new financing plan is offered by IBM Global Financing in response to customer demands for the packaging and financing of total solutions—

hardware, software, and service. All of IBM's System x and BladeCenter servers are currently eligible for the special finance plan, with financing for IBM's iDataPlex servers planned to be available later this year.

IBM Global Financing offerings are provided through IBM Credit LLC in the United States and other IBM subsidiaries and divisions worldwide to qualified commercial and government clients. Rates are based on a client's credit rating, financing terms, offering type, equipment type, and options and can vary by country.

Source: "IBM Global Financing to Offer Bundled Server Financing Program for '09." *World Leasing News*, July 1, 2009. Available at http://worldleasingnews.com. Reprinted by permission.

Asset-based financing is always tied directly to some underlying asset. Table 16-1 shows the split among three major categories (commercial equipment, commercial vehicles, and retail vehicles) in 2009 and 2010. The major assets financed in this way are broadly distributed between the different types of financial companies. The independents are mainly involved in machinery and equipment financing; approximately 20 to 25 percent of all machinery and equipment is leased, with 60 percent of their customers being **small and medium-sized enterprises (SMEs)**. Approximately 40 percent of the assets financed are either transportation equipment, such as buses, trucks, and trailers, or office equipment. As we will discuss, this financing tends to be extremely flexible, is often tailored to meet the needs of the original manufacturers, and ranges across the whole spectrum of asset-based financing. Often an SME will approach a manufacturer for a piece of equipment and will be offered on-the-spot financing as a pre-arranged package with the asset-based financier.

small and medium-sized enterprises (SMEs) businesses that generally have fewer than 50 employees

TABLE 16-1 Asset-Based Financing Market in Canada

	2010	2009	2009–2010 % change
New Business Total ($billions)	33.8	30.4	11
Commercial equipment	13.0	10.8	20
Commercial vehicles	3.1	2.7	14
Retail vehicles	17.8	16.9	5
Assets ($billions)	79.7	87.1	−9
Commercial equipment	31.8	32.2	−1
Commercial vehicles	7.0	8.5	−17
Retail vehicles	40.9	46.5	−12

Source: Canadian Finance and Leasing Association (CFLA), *2010/2011 Annual Report*, p. 8. Available at www.cfla-acfl.ca.

---

[1] Banks are continually lobbying for greater access to this market. Currently, chartered bank leasing has to be done through separate subsidiaries, where 80 percent of the assets are leases and the balance are bridge financing to leases.

lessor the owner of the asset; the party in a lease agreement who conveys the right to use the asset in return for payment

lessee the party in a lease agreement who pays to obtain the right to use the asset

operating lease a lease in which some of the benefits of ownership do not transfer to the lessee but remain with the lessor

financial lease a lease in which essentially all the benefits of ownership transfer to the lessee; also known as a capital or full payout lease

In contrast, the captive finance companies are subsidiaries of the major manufacturing companies and finance the purchase of the equipment they sell. This sector is dominated by the big vehicle manufacturers like GM, Ford, and Toyota. It is estimated that about a third of all new vehicles are leased, a third paid for with cash, and a third paid for through borrowing. The final group of financial companies, the chartered banks, are much more restricted since they primarily finance through capital leases, a direct alternative to a secured loan.

So what is a lease and how is it distinct from other asset-based forms of financing? The CFLA provides the following definition: "A lease contract is an agreement where the owner conveys to the user the right to use an asset in return for a number of specified payments over an agreed period of time. The owner of the asset is referred to as the **lessor**, the user the **lessee**."[2]

Thus, what leasing does is give lessees an alternative to purchasing an asset that they need.

As indicated above, there are different types of asset-based financing, and, unfortunately, the definitions differ from one accountant, lawyer, and tax authority to another. As a result, some forms of asset-based financing are specifically structured to meet one interpretation for accounting and a different one for tax purposes. However, broadly speaking, we can differentiate between **operating leases** and **financial leases**, which are also commonly referred to as full payout or capital leases.

Types of Asset-Based Financing

In 1983, the Canada Revenue Agency (CRA) released an interpretation bulletin (IT-233R) spelling out when a lease should be considered a lease for tax purposes. In 2001, CRA repealed IT-233R, stating that "it is our view that the determination of whether a contract is a lease or sale is based on the legal relationship created by the terms of the agreement."[3] Although the bulletin was repealed, it is useful to take a look at its text to see how CRA formerly viewed a lease. IT-233R implied that CRA viewed a lease as a sale of equipment through a *conditional sales agreement* if one of the following occurred:

- The lessee automatically acquired ownership at some point.

- The lessee was required to buy the asset at some point or guarantee that the lessor got a certain value for it.

- The lessee had the right to buy the asset at some point for substantially less than the likely fair market value.

- The lessee had the right to buy the asset at a price that would cause a reasonable person to conclude that he or she would buy it.

The CRA concern was that if any of the above conditions were satisfied, a reasonable person would conclude that the expectation was that ownership of the asset was being transferred to the user of the asset, even though that party had to make a series of future payments that "looked like" a loan or lease payment. CRA was interested in this because the owner of the asset had the right to claim capital cost allowance (CCA) for tax purposes. So if any of the above conditions had been satisfied, CRA would have regarded the user—and not the party receiving the payments—as the party with the right to claim CCA.

---

[2] "The Asset Based Financing, Equipment and Vehicle Leasing Industry." Canadian Finance and Leasing Association (CFLA), backgrounder for the House of Commons Finance Committee, September 4, 1998.

[3] For information about the cancellation of IT-233R, see Canada Revenue Agency, *Income Tax Technical News*. No. 21, June 14, 2001, available at http://www.cra-arc.gc.ca/E/pub/tp/itnews-21/itnews-21-e.pdf.

The accounting profession's view of a financial lease is that all the benefits of ownership transfer to the lessee. In this interpretation, the payments to the lessor are compensation for the initial purchase of the equipment and provide the lessor with a financial return. In this case, the lease usually

- requires the lessee to carry out maintenance and insure the asset,
- provides the lessee with a fixed-purchase option,
- covers at least 75 percent of the economic life of the asset,
- is structured so that the present value of lease payments exceeds 90 percent of the cost, and
- involves fixed rental payments.

The lessee is assumed to own the asset and thus claims depreciation on the firm's income statement and records the value of the asset as an asset and the financing obligation as a liability on its balance sheet.

In contrast, the critical feature of an operating lease is that some of the benefits of ownership do not transfer to the lessee but remain with the lessor. As a result, the conditions are the opposite to those for a financial lease. For example, operating leases are usually, though not always, *full-service* leases in which the lessor is responsible for maintaining the asset, providing any insurance, and paying property taxes on the asset (if the asset is land or a building).

When we compare financial leases with operating leases, we can see that the criteria for operating leases are all different ways of saying that the lessor maintains significant residual exposure to the value of the asset. In fact, under the *Bank Act*, chartered banks cannot write a lease if they have significant exposure to the residual value of the asset.

Another type of leasing arrangement is a **sale and leaseback (SLB) agreement**. In an SLB, the owner of an asset sells it (usually to an insurance company or pension fund) and then signs an agreement to lease the asset back. Thus, the lessee retains the use of the asset and receives a large, one-time cash inflow at the time of the sale. At one time, this type of arrangement was particularly popular for organizations in very low tax brackets. Universities, for example, pay no tax. They are therefore unable to claim any tax deductions for depreciation on the assets that they own. A university could sell an asset to someone who did pay taxes and could use the depreciation deduction. When the university leased the asset back, part of the tax savings that the new owner was enjoying could be passed back to the university in the form of lower lease payments.

> **sale and leaseback (SLB) agreement** an agreement in which the owner of an asset sells it to another party and then leases the asset back

The 1989 federal budget changed the tax rules concerning SLB agreements so that the lessor could deduct depreciation on leased assets only from the income derived from leasing, which has made them less attractive from a tax minimization point of view. As a result of this legislation, the number of SLBs for non-profit organizations, such as universities and hospitals, has declined substantially.[4]

A **leveraged lease**, which is depicted in Figure 16-2, is a popular financing vehicle in the United States. It is a three-way agreement between the lessee, the lessor, and one or more external lenders. As with other lease arrangements, the lessee uses the asset and makes regular lease payments, while the lessor purchases (or owns) the asset, delivers it to the lessee,

> **leveraged lease** a three-way agreement between the lessee, lessor, and third-party lender(s) in which the lessor buys the asset with only a small down payment, and the lender supplies the remaining financing

---

[4] One prominent Canadian university sold its library and then leased it back. At the time, some observers could understand why the institution sold the library, but not why it leased it back.

and receives lease payments. However, the lessor puts up only a small portion (usually in the 20 to 50 percent range) of the purchase price of the asset, and lenders supply the remaining financing, in return for interest payments from the lessor. The lenders are protected against default because they have a first lien on the leased asset and because the lease payments go directly to the lenders in the event of a loan default by the lessor.

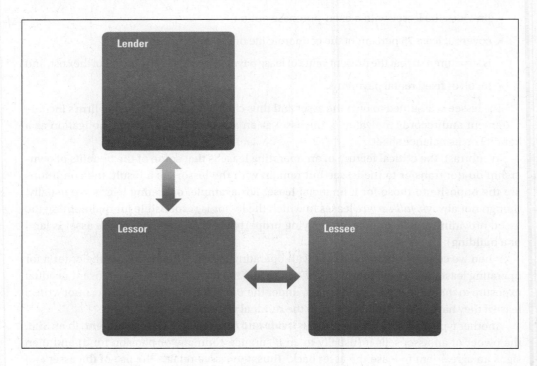

FIGURE 16-2 *A Leveraged Lease*

The attractiveness of leveraged leases in the United States is that the lessor puts up only a portion of the asset purchase price but receives all of the tax benefits of ownership and has lease payments available to service the loan payments. Leveraged leases are not popular in Canada, because CRA restricts the use of CCA deductions to the party at risk, and the deductions cannot be carried over into other income. In the United States, however, they can be, and the lessee can realize a benefit in the form of lower lease payments whenever the lessor's costs are reduced.

CONCEPT REVIEW QUESTIONS

1. What is the difference between an operating and a financial lease?
2. What type of leases do chartered banks normally make?
3. What is a sale and leaseback agreement (SLB)?

16.2 ACCOUNTING FOR LEASES

Learning Objective 16.2
Describe the accounting treatment of both operating and financial leases.

While analysts tend to use the broad definitions of operating and financial leases discussed above, accountants use a more stringent definition of financial leases. This is important because financial leases are included on the balance sheet of the lessee, while operating leases are not—the lessor retains the leased asset on its balance sheet. Operating leases are an example of **off-balance-sheet financing** (for the lessee) and are included only in the notes to the financial statements. For a financial lease, the present value of all lease payments is entered as a liability along with debt on the right side of the lessee's balance sheet. The same amount is entered on the left side of the balance sheet as the value of the asset that is leased.

As discussed in Chapter 3, Canada adopted International Financial Reporting Standards (IFRS) as of January 2011. We mentioned in the chapter that IFRS seek to limit off-balance-sheet financing, which means that IFRS propose to have operating leases listed on the balance sheet and capitalized; however, the exact manner in which this will be done is still not known. In addition, U.S. (GAAP) are supposed to be adopting the new IFRS rules regarding the treatment of leases at the same time as IFRS. In fact, this is one of the joint projects undertaken by the U.S. Financial Accounting Standards Board and the International Accounting Standards Board as part of the overall convergence between the two sets of standards. This issue is discussed in *Finance in the News 16-2*.[5]

> **off-balance-sheet financing** a financing arrangement that does not appear in a company's balance sheet but only in the notes to the financial statements

---

finance INTHENEWS 16-2 Proposed Lease Accounting Changes: Impact on Asset Finance Deals

IN AUGUST 2010, the International Accounting Standards Board (IASB) issued a proposal which, if adopted, will overhaul lease accounting for all companies reporting under IFRS.

Executive Summary

In Canada, publicly accountable enterprises (PAE), with few exceptions, will be required to apply International Financial Reporting Standards (IFRS) for financial periods beginning after January 1, 2011. PAEs, in particular public issuers, face a substantial challenge in preparing for the transition and reporting their first quarter for 2011 in accordance with IFRS ...

Another equally significant change proposed to IFRS relates to the accounting for leases. The proposal for leases will end the financial reporting practice of off-balance-sheet financing. Once implemented, lessees who previously entered or will enter into a lease arrangement that satisfies the current Canadian GAAP definition of an operating lease will be required to record an asset for the right to use the leased asset and a corresponding liability on their balance sheets. Such leases will be treated as capital leases, referred to as finance leases under IFRS ...

As a result, lessees must anticipate the impact of these accounting changes. For instance, lessees may have other financing arrangements which are subject to financial covenants that include ratios tied to "balance

sheet" position. The proposed changes will have a direct impact on the calculation of these ratios. There will also be an impact on profitability as accounting for finance leases will require the recording of both amortization of the right-of-use asset and imputed interest expense based on the estimated term of the lease ...

Current Canadian GAAP Rules

A capital lease (referred to as a finance lease under IFRS) is distinguished from an operating lease as a transaction that transfers substantially all the risks and rewards incidental to ownership of an asset from a lessor to a lessee. Canadian GAAP sets quantitative thresholds with respect to transfer of ownership, lease term and present value of lease payments which must be attained before a lease is accounted as a capital lease.

Current IFRS Rules That Apply to Leases

Like Canadian GAAP, a transfer of substantially all the risks and rewards means a lease transaction must be accounted as a finance lease. However, quantitative thresholds to help classify leases do not apply. IFRS requires an approach that considers the substance of a transaction rather than the form of the contract.

Source: Garellek, Michael, "Proposed Lease Accounting Changes: Impact on Asset Finance Deals." Article from Gowling Lafleur Henderson LLP, December 2010. Available at www.gowlings.com. Reprinted by permission.

In addition to the balance sheet differences noted above, the income statement is affected by the classification of a lease as operating or financial. For operating leases, the full amount of the lease payments is classified as a rental expense for the lessee and as rental income for the lessor. Since the lessor retains the asset on its balance sheet, it charges depreciation expense against the asset.

For financial leases, the lease payments will be broken down into interest expense and principal repayment. The latter is not an expense but is reflected in the declining value of the liability reported on the balance sheet. As a result, for financial leases, the lessee's associated

---

[5] At the time of writing, this issue had not yet been finalized in Canada nor was the co-ordination with U.S. GAAP complete. Hence, we believe it is still important to distinguish between operating and financial leases and their impact on financial statements and financial ratios.

expenses will be in two forms: interest associated with the financing arrangement and depreciation expense associated with the asset. The lessor reports income in the form of a gain (or loss) on the asset at the time the lease arrangement (i.e., the sale) is initiated, and then it reports periodic interest income based on the interest portion of the lease payments it receives. These accounting differences are summarized in Table 16-2.

TABLE 16-2 Operating versus Financial Leases

	Operating		Financial	
	Lessee	**Lessor**	**Lessee**	**Lessor**
Asset	Not on balance sheet (B/S); disclose in notes to financial statements	Report on B/S	Report on B/S	Not on B/S
Lease payments	Expense the full amount as rental expense	Claim as rental income	Decompose into interest and principal repayment, and expense the interest portion	Claim the interest portion of payments received as interest income
Depreciation expense (associated with leased asset)	Cannot claim	Claim	Claim	Cannot claim

Obviously, there are some potential benefits for firms when leases are classified as operating leases rather than financial leases. We will elaborate on these in the next section. However, there are certain guidelines that must be followed. For accounting purposes, leases are classified as financial leases if at least one of the following criteria is met:

- The lease transfers ownership of the property to the lessee by the end of the lease term.
- The lessee has a bargain purchase option—that is, it can purchase the asset at a price below fair market value when the lease expires.
- The lease term is 75 percent or more of the estimated economic life of the asset.
- The present value of lease payments is 90 percent or more of the asset's fair market value at the inception of the lease.

Financial Statement Effects of Lease Classification

Given our discussion above, it is not surprising that classification of a lease as operating or financial can have a significant impact on a firm's financial statements. As a result, many of the ratios that analysts use to examine company performance (discussed in Chapter 4) can be affected, as can the firm's cash flow statements. The examples in this section illustrate some of the major differences that can arise.

EXAMPLE 16-1   Income Statement and Cash Flow Statement Effects

Assume a company leases an asset with a present fair market value of $317,000. The lease arrangement requires four annual payments of $100,000. The appropriate interest rate is 10 percent. Assume the asset has a zero salvage value at the end of its useful life of four years, and that it can be depreciated using straight-line depreciation. Contrast the income statement and cash flow statement impacts of classifying the lease as financial versus operating.

continued

EXAMPLE 16-1 *Income Statement and Cash Flow Statement Effects continued*

Assume the following are the firm's expected income and cash flow statements for the next four years, ignoring the effect of this lease arrangement:

	Year 1	Year 2	Year 3	Year 4
Revenue	$10 million	$10 million	$10 million	$10 million
Net income (excluding lease)	$500,000	$500,000	$500,000	$500,000
Cash flow from operations (CFO)	$600,000	$600,000	$600,000	$600,000
Cash flow from financing (CFF)	$100,000	$100,000	$100,000	$100,000
Cash flow from investing (CFI)	−$300,000	−$300,000	−$300,000	−$300,000
Net cash flows	$400,000	$400,000	$400,000	$400,000

Solution

Operating Lease

The annual charge to the income statement = Rental expense = $100,000

The annual effect on CFO = $100,000

The annual effect on total cash flow = $100,000

Net effects

	Year 1	Year 2	Year 3	Year 4
Net income	$400,000	$400,000	$400,000	$400,000
CFO	$500,000	$500,000	$500,000	$500,000
CFF	$100,000	$100,000	$100,000	$100,000
CFI	−$300,000	−$300,000	−$300,000	−$300,000
Net cash flows	$300,000	$300,000	$300,000	$300,000

Financial Lease

Effect on Income Statement

Annual depreciation expense = (317,000 − 0) ÷ 4 = $79,250

Interest expense (year 1) = $317,000 × 0.1 = $31,700

Principal repayment (year 1) = $100,000 − $31,700 = $68,300

Principal outstanding (end of year 1) = $317,000 − $68,300 = $248,700

Interest expense (year 2) = $248,700 × 0.1 = $24,870

Principal repayment (year 2) = $100,000 − $24,870 = $75,130

Principal outstanding (end of year 2) = $248,700 − $75,130 = $173,570

Interest expense (year 3) = $173,570 × 0.1 = $17,357

Principal repayment (year 3) = $100,000 − $17,357 = $82,643

Principal outstanding (end of year 3) = $173,570 − $82,643 = $90,927

Interest expense (year 4) = $90,927 × 0.1 = $9,093

Principal repayment (year 4) = $90,927 (i.e., the total principal outstanding at the beginning of the year, which must be fully paid)

continued

EXAMPLE 16-1 *Income Statement and Cash Flow Statement Effects continued*

Associated Expenses

	Year 1	Year 2	Year 3	Year 4
Depreciation expense	− $79,250	− $79,250	− $79,250	− $79,250
Interest expense (@10%)	− $31,700	− $24,870	− $17,357	− $9,093
Charges on net income	− $110,950	− $104,120	− $96,607	− $88,343

Effect on Cash Flow Statement

	Year 1	Year 2	Year 3	Year 4
CFO				
Interest expense	− $31,700	− $24,870	− $17,357	− $9,093
CFF				
Principal repayment	− $68,300	− $75,130	− $82,643	− $90,927
Net effect on total cash flow	− $100,000	− $100,000	− $100,000	− $100,020*

*The extra $20 is required to fully amortize the purchase price.

	Year 1	Year 2	Year 3	Year 4
Net income	$389,050	$395,880	$403,393	$411,657
CFO	$568,300	$575,130	$582,643	$590,907
CFF	$31,700	$24,870	$17,357	$9,073
CFI	− $300,000	− $300,000	− $300,000	− $300,000
Net cash flows	$300,000	$300,000	$300,000	$299,980*

*As explained above, the $20 difference is required to fully amortize the purchase price.

Example 16-1 makes two things obvious:

1. Net income will generally be higher for operating leases in the early years, and it will generally be lower in the later years. This is because the interest expense charged for financial leases declines as the liability (lease obligation) is amortized by the lease payments. This means that the expense associated with a financial lease will decrease over time, since the depreciation expense usually is constant, whereas the lease expense for an operating lease remains constant through the years (i.e., it equals the amount of the lease payments).

2. The cash flow from operations (CFO) will be lower when a lease is classified as operating, since the full lease payment will be subtracted from CFO. For financial leases, only the interest portion of these payments is subtracted. On the other hand, the cash flow from financing (CFF) will be higher for operating leases because, unlike financial leases, they have no principal repayment component. Even more important to note is that the overall effect on total cash flow will be the same as for financial leases. It is merely the classification of the cash flows that is affected.

Example 16-2 demonstrates that the firm will appear larger and will have more debt if a lease is classified as financial, as opposed to operating.

Example 16-3 shows the impact of the lease classification on some commonly used ratios that were discussed in Chapter 4.

EXAMPLE 16-2   Balance Sheet Effects

Assume the company from Example 16-1 decides to lease the asset worth $317,000 considered in that example. The company's balance sheet, excluding the lease, is given below. Depict the firm's balance sheet after the lease arrangement has been entered into, assuming the lease is classified as (1) an operating lease and (2) a financial lease.

Current assets	$2,000,000	Current liabilities	$1,000,000
Long-term assets	8,000,000	Long-term debt	6,000,000
		Equity	3,000,000
Total assets	$10,000,000	Total liabilities and equity	$10,000,000

Solution

Operating Lease

The balance sheet remains unchanged—it is exactly the same as the one given above. The only difference is that the firm would have to disclose the lease in the footnotes to the financial statements.

Financial Lease

The new balance sheet would reflect the $317,000 on both sides.

The $317,000 on the liability side would be broken down into the current portion of the obligation (i.e., the first year's required principal repayment component of the lease payment) and the remaining part of the lease, which would be classified as long-term debt.

Addition to current liabilities = $68,300 (principal repayment as calculated in Example 16-1)

Long-term debt = $317,000 − $68,300 = $248,700

Current assets	$2,000,000	Current liabilities	$1,068,300
Long-term assets	8,317,000	Long-term debt	6,248,700
		Equity	3,000,000
Total assets	$10,317,000	Total liabilities and equity	$10,317,000

EXAMPLE 16-3   Financial Ratio Effects

Calculate the following ratios for the company in examples 16-1 and 16-2 for year 1: current, debt, leverage, net income (NI) margin, asset turnover, return on assets (ROA), return on equity (ROE), price-earnings (P/E).

Use the balance sheet items from Example 16-2 and the income statement information from Example 16-1, assuming the lease in question is classified as an operating lease or as a financial lease. Assume the firm has 1 million common shares outstanding and that its share price is $10 per share regardless of the method of accounting for the lease. Comment on any differences in the ratios.

continued

EXAMPLE 16-3 *Financial Ratio Effects continued*

Solution

Ratio	Operating	Financial
Current (CA/CL)	2,000,000 ÷ 1,000,000 = 2.0	2,000,000 ÷ 1,068,300 = 1.87
Debt (TL/TA)	7,000,000 ÷ 10,000,000 = 0.70	7,317,000 ÷ 10,317,000 = 0.71
Leverage (TA/E)	10,000,000 ÷ 3,000,000 = 3.33	10,317,000 ÷ 3,000,000 = 3.44
NI margin (NI/S)	400,000 ÷ 10,000,000 = 4.00%	389,050 ÷ 10,000,000 = 3.89%
Asset turnover (S/TA)	10,000,000 ÷ 10,000,000 = 1.00	10,000,000 ÷ 10,317,000 = 0.97
ROA (NI/TA)	400,000 ÷ 10,000,000 = 4.00%	389,050 ÷ 10,317,000 = 3.77%
ROE (NI/E)	400,000 ÷ 3,000,000 = 13.33%	389,050 ÷ 3,000,000 = 12.97%
P/E (P_0/EPS)	10 ÷ 0.40 = 25.00	10 ÷ 0.38905 = 25.70

It is obvious from these calculations that when leases are classified as financial instead of operating, the firm will report lower current ratios, higher debt and leverage ratios, lower asset turnover ratios, and lower profitability ratios (at least in the early years). Since the classification of a lease has no impact on a firm's total cash flows, its price should be unaffected; therefore, the P/E ratios should be higher to reflect the lower earnings per share (EPS). However, note that if the P/E ratio remained at 25, the share price would be lower, reflecting the lower EPS. This is obviously inappropriate and should not happen in efficient markets.

Example 16-3 shows that there will be a significant impact on a company's financial ratios depending on whether a lease is classified as operating or financial. We can see that managers have an incentive, from a financial-ratio point of view, to have leases classified as operating rather than financial. Therefore, one would suspect that managers might try to make sure their leases are categorized as operating leases in an attempt to "fool" the readers of their company's financial statements. However, while operating leases are not included on the balance sheet, companies are required to disclose information about such leases in the notes to the financial statements. Hence, the information is publicly available and, if markets are efficient, any attempt to fool readers should be a waste of time, since most analysts would see through this type of manipulation.

LESSONS TO BE LEARNED   While analysts and investors should recognize the liabilities associated with operating leases and other off-balance-sheet items, in practice they often neglect or underestimate the associated risks. Such was the case with Enron, whose demise was caused to a large extent by the massive amount of off-balance-sheet liabilities it accrued through special purpose entities (SPEs). While this information was publicly available, it was ignored to a large extent by analysts and investors in aggregate. Indeed, many analysts had "buy" recommendations on Enron stock in the weeks preceding its collapse.

The lesson to be learned is that proper analysis requires looking beyond the surface numbers; otherwise, significant risks can be overlooked or underestimated.

CONCEPT REVIEW QUESTIONS

1. What are the cash flow from operations and the free cash flow implications of an operating lease versus a financial lease?

2. Which type of lease, operating or financial, gives a higher asset turnover ratio?

16.3 EVALUATING THE LEASE DECISION

Learning Objective 16.3
Evaluate the lease decision using discounted cash flow valuation methods.

Leasing provides an alternative to buying an asset. This is a decision most of us face when we are deciding whether to lease or buy a car, and the same principles apply to companies considering leasing any asset. *Finance in the News 16-3* offers some perspectives on the automobile buy-versus-lease decision.

finance IN THE NEWS 16-3   Leasing a Car Is the Worst Financial Option for Most

CANADA'S AUTO GURU Dennis DesRosiers has a quick response to the question of whether it's best to lease or finance a new car: pay cash.

That's what he does, for the simple reason that it's the least expensive option.

But he realizes most Canadians can't just lay down tens of thousands of dollars at one go, or don't want to, so when asked about the remaining options, his response is more nuanced.

"It depends," he says, on what you expect out of your driving experience and whether you are more sensitive to the size of monthly payments or the end-of-use total cost of the purchase. And it depends whether owning a vehicle is important to you.

"The general rule of thumb is that if you are a consumer that changes vehicles every two, three, or four years, leasing is a highly attractive option in most cases, though not all. The longer you keep your vehicle the more attractive loans become."

First, if you are the type of person who is addicted to the new-car smell, lease if you can afford it, he says.

But if you are looking for the least costly option and don't mind hanging on to your car longer—the average length of first ownership on a new vehicle is 9.2 years—then leasing is likely the worst thing you can do, Mr. DesRosiers adds.

The funny thing is that it may not appear that way when negotiating a financing arrangement at the local car dealer.

Invariably, the monthly payments on a lease are lower than on loans even though the posted interest rate is almost always higher. And leasing appears so worry-free. Take a new car, drive it for three years, then return it and get another new car. Repeat the process.

"It's the voodoo of leasing," Mr. DesRosiers says. "Leasing is absolutely the highest cost of borrowing in the market place. Hands down, no exceptions, but it doesn't look that way."

Why is that? Monthly payments are comprised of two components—interest on the principal or cost of the vehicle, and paying down the principal. On a loan, the paying down the principal portion can be quite steep because the buyer is paying off the entire cost of the vehicle during the financing term. On a lease, depending on the end residual value, the consumer may be only paying down half the cost of the vehicle.

That's why monthly payments are usually lower, but at the end of the lease, the consumer doesn't own the vehicle and will have paid more in interest than on a loan.

"The embedded interest in a lease is typically about $100 a month higher than the interest on a loan," Mr. DesRosiers says.

As well, there are additional costs that could accrue on a lease, and they can be substantial. Leasing companies insist a vehicle be returned in good working order and with "normal wear and tear."

What that means is open to interpretation—with the consumer having little input—but it usually requires replacing tires, possibly a brake job, and body work for bumps and scrapes that may have occurred. The end-of-lease surprise can add up to hundreds and even thousands of dollars.

(Londoneye/iStock)

As well, Mr. DesRosiers says many consumers wind up paying hefty penalties if they put on more than 25,000 kilometres a year, not that unusual since the average driver in Toronto clocks in at over 30,000 annually.

"So leasing is a consumer beware item," he says.

That doesn't mean it's the worst choice, however. Silvana Aceto of the Canadian Automobile Association says her organization advises members to do the math, but also to consider their personal circumstances.

"Some people like the flexibility of a lease, they like to have a new car every two or three years, and they don't have to worry about maintenance because when the car is new, usually that's when repairs are the fewest," she says.

You may not own the car at the end of the lease term, but then you don't have the worries older cars can bring, including breakdowns and repair costs.

Ms. Aceto says the CAA does not pick sides, but advises members to "do the math" and consider carefully their preferences.

Mr. DesRosiers agrees. If he has one hard-and-fast rule, it's never get into an open-ended lease where the customer is responsible for assuming the residual value—what's left owing on the car at the end of the lease period.

"Residuals are extremely volatile and nearly impossible to predict. Billions have been lost in residual value [usually by auto companies] over the years," he says.

By Mr. DesRosiers' calculations, about 18 per cent of Canadians leased their vehicle last year, while the vast majority financed. That's about right, he says.

"For 15 to 20 per cent of customers, leasing is a viable option, but for the rest they would be better off financially with a loan," he says.

"The issue is not whether you would like a new vehicle every three years, it's whether you can afford a new vehicle every three years, and most consumers can't."

As suggested in *Finance in the News 16-3*, if a company needs an asset and has the opportunity to either lease or buy it, the company must compare the cash flows from leasing with the cash flows from buying in order to determine which is better. There are four main differences in the cash flows for a company that leases an asset instead of buying it:

1. It does not have to pay for the asset up front.

2. If it is an operating lease or if title is not transferred through a financial lease, the company does not get to sell the asset when it is finished with it.[6]

3. It makes regular lease payments. If the lease is an operating lease, the full amount of the lease payments is tax deductible; if it is classified as a financial lease, then only the interest portion of the payments is deductible.

4. It does not get to depreciate the asset for tax purposes if it is an operating lease. If it is a financial lease, it does get to charge depreciation.

Example 16-4 provides a discounted cash flow (DCF) framework for evaluating the attractiveness of leasing.

EXAMPLE 16-4   Leasing versus Buying

A firm wishes to obtain a limousine for its executives. The limousine would cost $1 million to buy (it is very luxurious and also bulletproof). It would be depreciated at a rate of $100,000 per year for tax purposes. Assume the limousine could be sold in five years for $500,000. The firm could also sign a five-year operating lease for the limousine, with lease payments of $140,000 per year. Each payment would be due at the beginning of the year.[7] The firm's effective tax rate is 40 percent. Determine whether or not the firm should lease the limousine, assuming its before-tax cost of borrowing is 7 percent.

Solution
The following cash flows need to be considered:

- The firm saves $1 million in today's dollars by not buying the asset.

- If the firm buys the limousine, it will get $100,000 per year in depreciation. Each year, this will result in a tax savings of (0.4 × $100,000) = $40,000, which can be assumed as an inflow at the end of the year (i.e., when the firm pays its taxes). If the firm leases, it forgoes this tax benefit.

- The firm must make regular tax-deductible lease payments at the beginning of each of four years.[8] Using an effective tax rate of 40 percent, these payments translate into after-tax payments of $140,000 (1 − 0.4) = $84,000 per year.[9]

The table below presents the cash flows associated with leasing rather than buying (in $000s).

Year	0	1	2	3	4	5
Initial cost	1,000					
After-tax lease payment	−84	−84	−84	−84	−84	
Forgone tax shield	0	−40	−40	−40	−40	−40
Forgone salvage value						−500
Total	916	−124	−124	−124	−124	−540

continued

---

[6] Note that in many cases the salvage value would be discounted at a higher rate, reflecting the risk attached to the future value. For simplicity we abstract from this, but it is often an important component of the analysis.

[7] Most lease payments are made monthly, not annually; however, we assume annual payments for simplicity.

[8] Notice that since it is an operating lease, the lessee can deduct the full amount of the lease payments.

[9] Technically, it is not correct to adjust for the tax savings from the "beginning"-of-year lease payments, since the tax savings will arise at year end. We do this for simplicity and demonstrate that it does not make a substantial difference in the answer.

EXAMPLE 16-4   *Leasing versus Buying continued*

Now that we have estimated the incremental cash flows that result from leasing instead of buying, the question is how to evaluate these cash flows. It is usually appropriate to consider leasing as a form of debt financing, since it represents a legal obligation to make periodic payments to another party (i.e., the lessor). Viewing the lease arrangement in this manner, we can say it is like a $1-million loan, and we can estimate the interest rate that the firm is paying on this "loan-like arrangement," which we can then compare to the firm's after-tax borrowing cost. To solve for this rate, we simply treat it like the following internal rate of return (IRR) problem, with k denoting the IRR:

$$0 = 916 - \frac{124}{1+k} - \frac{124}{(1+k)^2} - \frac{124}{(1+k)^3} - \frac{124}{(1+k)^4} - \frac{540}{(1+k)^5}$$

$$k = 3.32\%$$

Recall from Chapter 13 that we can solve for the IRR by longhand or, more simply, by using a financial calculator, as shown in the following.[10]

EXAMPLE 16-4   **Solution Using a Financial Calculator**

 (TI BA II PLUS)

CF	2ND	CLRWORK		−124	ENTER	↓	↓
+916	ENTER	↓		−124	ENTER	↓	↓
−124	ENTER	↓	↓	−540	ENTER	↓	
−124	ENTER	↓	↓	IRR	CPT	gives 3.32%	

EXAMPLE 16-4   **Solution Using Excel**

 XLS

For this example, if we "guessed" an IRR of 10 percent, and we had the year 0, 1, 2, 3, 4, and 5 cash flows in cells B2 through B7, respectively, we could express the required Excel function as follows:

= IRR (B2:B7, 0.1). This would also give us an answer of 3.32 percent.

EXAMPLE 16-4   *Leasing versus Buying continued*

Thus, leasing instead of buying involves receiving financing at an effective rate of 3.32 percent. This rate should be compared with the *after-tax* rate at which the firm can normally borrow.

For this example, we have been told that the before-tax cost of borrowing is 7 percent, so the after-tax cost of borrowing will be:

$$7\% \times (1 - 0.4) = 4.2\%\ [11]$$

Therefore, since 3.32% is less than 4.2%, the firm should lease the limousine, because leasing provides cheaper financing than normal borrowing does.

An easier way to evaluate the lease is to simply use the after-tax borrowing rate as a discount rate and calculate the net present value (NPV) of leasing versus buying.

continued

---

[10] See Example 13-3 of Chapter 13 for the "longhand" version.

[11] This approach to estimating the after-tax cost of borrowing is correct if the borrowing is in the form of traditional bonds, because they pay interest only, and the interest payments are completely tax deductible. It would not be strictly correct if the before-tax borrowing cost were applied to a loan with blended payments of principal and interest, since only the interest portion of these payments is tax deductible. However, for practical purposes, this estimate is close enough.

EXAMPLE 16-4 *Leasing versus Buying continued*

For this example, we can estimate the NPV of leasing versus buying as follows (numbers in thousands):

$$NPV \text{ (leasing)} = 916 - \frac{124}{1.042} - \frac{124}{(1.042)^2} - \frac{124}{(1.042)^3} - \frac{124}{(1.042)^4} - \frac{540}{(1.042)^5}$$

$$= +28.41 \text{ (in \$000s)}$$

EXAMPLE 16-4   Solution Using a Financial Calculator

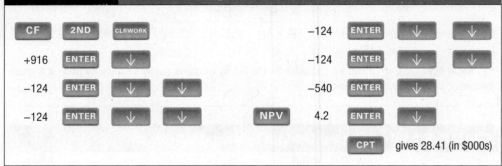

EXAMPLE 16-4   Solution Using Excel

The following function may be used to determine the present value (PV) of the "future" cash flows (CFs) (not including CF_0):

= NPV(rate, value 1:value 5)

If we had the discount rate of .042 in our Excel spreadsheet cell B2 and had the years 1 through 5 cash flows in cells B3 through B7, respectively, we could express the Excel function above as follows:

= NPV(B2, B3:B7), which would give the PV of future CFs as −887.59, which, when added to +916, gives an NPV of +28.41 (in \$000s).

EXAMPLE 16-4 *Leasing versus Buying continued*

We could also estimate the NPV of leasing by finding the present value of the various kinds of cash flows, which can be expressed as follows:

NPV(leasing) = CF_0 (purchase price savings) − PV(forgone depreciation tax savings) − PV(forgone salvage value) − PV(after-tax lease payments) CF_0 = \$1,000,000

Depreciation tax savings = $0.4 \times \$100,000 = \$40,000$ per year end

$$PV \text{ (Depreciation tax savings)} = 40,000 \times \left[\frac{1 - \frac{1}{(1.042)^5}}{0.042} \right] = \$177,077$$

$$PV \text{ (Salvage value)} = 500,000 \times \left[\frac{1}{(1.042)^5} \right] = \$407,035$$

$$PV \text{ (After-tax lease payments)} = 84,000 \times \left[\frac{1 - \frac{1}{(1.042)^5}}{0.042} \right] \times (1.042) = \$387,479$$

Now, we can put all of these factors together to estimate the NPV of leasing:

NPV(leasing) = CF_0 − PV(forgone depreciation tax savings) − PV(forgone salvage value) − PV(after-tax lease payments)

$$= 1,000,000 - 177,077 - 407,035 - 387,479 = +28,409 \text{ (difference due to rounding)}$$

So the NPV = \$28,409, which is positive, so it is better to lease the limousine than buy it.

Note that in the example above, the positive NPV of leasing tells you that leasing is better than buying, but not whether you should acquire the asset in the first place. This question should be answered based on the total NPV of the project, as discussed in chapters 13 and 14. To incorporate lease financing into an overall NPV problem, simply calculate the NPV of the project, assuming that you buy the asset, then add on the NPV of leasing. This gives the NPV of the project, including the advantage of financing the asset through leasing.

As mentioned previously, leases normally involve monthly, rather than annual, payments, with each payment due at the beginning of the month. In addition, the tax savings associated with these payments will be realized at year end, when the firm pays its taxes. We removed these complications in Example 16-4 to make things simpler, but Example 16-5 addresses these issues, demonstrating that the end result is not greatly affected by the simplifying assumptions employed in the previous example.

EXAMPLE 16-5 Leasing versus Buying with Monthly Payments

Find the NPV of leasing the limousine described in Example 16-4, assuming that everything is the same except that lease payments of $11,667 (i.e., $140,000 ÷ 12) are made monthly, and that we treat the tax benefits of these payments appropriately (i.e., assuming they occur at the end of each year).

Solution

We can estimate the NPV of leasing using the following expression, in which we have replaced the final term from the formula solution to Example 16-4—PV(after-tax lease payments)—with the following two terms:

+ PV(tax savings from lease payments) − PV(before-tax lease payments).

$$NPV(leasing) = CF_0 - PV(forgone\ depreciation\ tax\ savings) - PV(forgone\ salvage\ value) + PV(tax\ savings\ from\ lease\ payments) - PV(before-tax\ lease\ payments)$$

We begin by stating the PV of the cash flows from Example 16-4 that remain unchanged:

$CF_0 = \$1,000,000$

PV(depreciation tax savings) = $177,077

PV(salvage value) = $407,035

Next, we estimate the PV of the tax savings associated with the lease payments.

Annual lease payments = $11,667 × 12 = $140,000

Annual tax savings due to lease payments = $140,000 × 0.4 = $56,000 per year

Assuming these tax savings are realized at year end, we get

$$PV\ (Tax\ savings\ from\ lease\ payments) = 56{,}000 \times \left[\frac{1 - \frac{1}{(1.042)^5}}{0.042}\right] = \$247{,}908$$

Number of monthly lease payments: $n = 5\ years \times 12\ months = 60$

Monthly discount rate = $(1.042)^{1/12} - 1 = 0.3434379\%$

Before-tax payments = $11,667

continued

EXAMPLE 16-5 *Leasing versus Buying with Monthly Payments continued*

So, assuming beginning-of-month lease payments, we have:

PV(Before-tax lease payments)

$$\text{PV (Before-tax lease payments)} = 11{,}667 \times \left[\frac{1 - \dfrac{1}{(1.003434379)^{60}}}{0.003434379} \right] \times (1.003434379) = \$633{,}798$$

Now we can put all these factors together to estimate the NPV of leasing:

NPV(leasing) = CF_0 − PV(forgone depreciation tax savings) − PV(forgone salvage value) + PV(tax savings from lease payments) − PV(before-tax lease payments)

= 1,000,000 − 177,077 − 407,035 + 247,908 − 633,798 = +$29,998

This number is slightly larger (by $1,589) than the NPV of $28,409 that we calculated using the simplifying assumptions that lease payments were made annually at the beginning of the year and that tax savings were realized at the same time. The reason the NPV is larger is because the last two terms in the expression above [i.e., + PV(tax savings from lease payments) − PV(before-tax lease payments)] equalled $385,890, while the last term in the simplified version in Example 16-4 that they replace [i.e., − PV(after-tax lease payments)] equalled − $387,479. This is due to the assumption of beginning-of-year payments versus beginning-of-month payments, which translates into a higher PV of the outlay, despite the fact that the tax savings are appropriately valued at year end.

In most cases, it is reasonable to make the assumptions we did in Example 16-4, since the end result was quite close. However, in situations where precision is critical, it will be worthwhile to use the more accurate (and somewhat lengthier) approach that was used in Example 16-5.

We made one other simplification in Example 16-4: we assumed depreciation for tax purposes was a constant amount per year. In practice, we have learned that depreciation that may be charged for tax purposes—the capital cost allowance (CCA)—is calculated using the declining balance method. Example 16-6 adjusts for this fact.

EXAMPLE 16-6 **Leasing and CCA Tax Shields**

A firm is considering whether to purchase or lease a machine that costs $100,000 and is subject to a 20 percent CCA rate, calculated using the declining balance method. The required lease payments are $25,000 per year for four years (with beginning-of-year payments as usual). The lessor has agreed to provide maintenance as part of the lease contract, and the firm has estimated $10,000 per year in maintenance expenses would be incurred if it decided to purchase the machine. It estimates the asset could be sold for $46,080 after four years. The firm's before-tax borrowing rate is 10 percent, and its effective tax rate is 40 percent. Should it purchase or lease the machine, assuming the acquisition of the machine has a positive NPV and that the lease would qualify as an operating lease?

Solution

First, we estimate the cash flows.

After-tax annual lease payments = $25,000 × (1 − 0.4) = $15,000

After-tax borrowing cost = 0.1 × (1 − 0.4) = 6%

After-tax annual maintenance savings = $10,000 × (1 − 0.4) = $6,000

continued

EXAMPLE 16-6 *Leasing and CCA Tax Shields continued*

CCA Tax Shield (CCA × 0.4)

UCC (beginning year 1)	100,000	
CCA (year 1)	(10,000)	$4,000
UCC (beginning year 2)	90,000	
CCA (year 2)	(18,000)	$7,200
UCC (beginning year 3)	72,000	
CCA (year 3)	(14,400)	$5,760
UCC (beginning year 4)	57,600	
CCA (year 4)	(11,520)	$4,608
UCC (end year 4)	46,080	

(Cash flows in $000s)

Year	0	1	2	3	4	5
Initial cost	100					
After-tax lease payment	−15	−15	−15	−15		
After-tax maintenance savings		+6	+6	+6	+6	
Forgone tax shield	0	−4	−7.2	−5.76	−4.608	
Forgone salvage value					−46.08	
Total	85	−13	−16.2	−14.76	−44.688	

We can estimate the NPV of leasing as follows:

$$NPV \text{ (Leasing)} = 85,000 - \frac{13,000}{1.06} - \frac{16,200}{(1.06)^2} - \frac{14,760}{(1.06)^3} - \frac{44,688}{(1.06)^4}$$

$$= 85,000 - 12,264 - 14,418 - 12,393 - 35,397$$

$$= +\$10,528$$

EXAMPLE 16-6 **Solution Using a Financial Calculator**

(TI BA II PLUS)

CF	2ND	CLRWORK		−14,760	ENTER	↓	↓
85,000	ENTER	↓		−44,688	ENTER	↓	↓
−13,000	ENTER	↓	↓	NPV 6	CPT	gives +10,528	
−16,200	ENTER	↓	↓				

EXAMPLE 16-6 **Solution Using Excel**

XLS

The following function may be used to determine the PV of the "future" CFs (not including CF₀):

= NPV(rate, value 1:value 4)

If we had the discount rate of .06 in our Excel spreadsheet cell B2, and had the years 1 through 4 cash flows in cells B3 through B6, respectively, we could express the Excel function above as follows:

= NPV(B2, B3:B6), which would give the present value of the years 1 to 4 cash flows as −74,472. Adding 85,000 to this amount gives the NPV of +10,528

EXAMPLE 16-6 *Leasing and CCA Tax Shields continued*

As in our solution for Example 16-4, we could also estimate the NPV of leasing by finding the present value of the various kinds of cash flows, which can be expressed as follows:

NPV(leasing) = CF$_0$ (purchase price savings) + PV(maintenance savings) – PV(forgone depreciation tax savings) – PV(forgone salvage value) – PV(after-tax lease payments)

CF$_0$ = $100,000

$$PV \text{ (Maintenance savings)} = 6,000 \times \left[\frac{1 - \frac{1}{(1.06)^4}}{0.06}\right] = \$20,791$$

We can estimate the PV of the CCA tax shield using Equation 14-7 from Chapter 14, which applies when there is no terminal loss or CCA recapture. This equation is appropriate here because we assume the salvage value is the ending UCC at the end of four years.

$$PV \text{ (CCA tax shield)} = \frac{(C_0)(d)(T)}{d+k} \times \frac{(1+0.5k)}{(1+k)} - \frac{(SV_n)(d)(T)}{(d+k)} \times \frac{1}{(1+k)^n}$$

$$= \frac{(100,000)(0.20)(0.40)}{0.20 + 0.06} \times \frac{(1 + 0.5 \times 0.06)}{(1 + 0.06)} - \frac{(46,080)(0.20)(0.40)}{0.20 + 0.06} \times \frac{1}{(1.06)^4}$$

$$= 29,898 - 11,231 = \$18,667$$

$$PV \text{ (Salvage value)} = 46,080 \times \left[\frac{1}{(1.06)^4}\right] = \$36,500$$

$$PV \text{ (After-tax lease payments)} = 15,000 \times \left[\frac{1 - \frac{1}{(1.06)^4}}{0.06}\right] \times (1.06) = \$55,095$$

Now we can put all of these factors together to estimate the NPV of leasing:

NPV(leasing) = CF$_0$ + PV(maintenance savings) – PV(forgone depreciation tax savings) – PV(forgone salvage value) – PV(after-tax lease payments)

$$= 100,000 + 20,791 - 18,667 - 36,500 - 55,095 = \$10,529 \text{ (difference due to rounding)}$$

So the NPV = +$10,528, which is positive, so it is better to lease than to buy.

In Example 16-7, we consider how to evaluate a financial lease. Two key differences to note are that the firm will likely get to claim the depreciation tax savings, and it may also take owner-ship of the asset at the end of the lease term, so it will be able to sell the asset for the estimated sal-vage value if it chooses, which means this cash flow is not forgone. In addition, the entire amount of the lease payment is not tax deductible, as is the case for operating leases. Rather, only the interest portion may be expensed. However, this is exactly the same as it would be for a loan—that is, only the interest portion of the loan payment is tax deductible. Therefore, the only real differ-ence between a standard financial lease and a loan is that the lease payments are made at the beginning of the period, while the loan payments are made at the end of the period.[12]

EXAMPLE 16-7   Entering into a Financial Lease versus Borrowing

A company is given the option of entering into a five-year, $10,000 financial lease arrangement that calls for monthly payments based on a 6-percent lease rate, or borrowing $10,000 through a five-year loan that calls for monthly payments based on a 6.12-percent lending rate. Which option should the firm choose?

continued

---

[12] In reality, loans require some form of down payment, whereas leases may provide 100-percent financing.

EXAMPLE 16-7 *Entering into a Financial Lease versus Borrowing continued*

Solution

Notice that we cannot blindly select the lease option just because 6 percent is less than 6.12 percent, because the lease involves beginning-of-month payments, while the loan involves end-of-month payments.

First, we calculate the monthly payments for each option.

Lease

Monthly lease rate = 6% ÷ 12 = 0.5%

Number of monthly payments = 5 years × 12 months = 60

$$\text{Monthly lease payments} = \frac{10{,}000}{\left[\dfrac{1 - \dfrac{1}{(1.005)^{60}}}{0.005}\right](1.005)} = \$192.37$$

Loan

Monthly loan rate = 6.12% ÷ 12 = 0.51%

$$\text{Monthly loan payments} = \frac{10{,}000}{\left[\dfrac{1 - \dfrac{1}{(1.0051)^{60}}}{0.0051}\right]} = \$193.89$$

Now we need to find the PV of the payments under each option, but which discount rate should we use? It turns out it does not matter, but it makes the most sense to use the loan rate, since we are evaluating the lease option.

Trivially, the PV of the loan payments using the monthly loan rate = $10,000 (since that is the amount we used to determine the required payments).

Now we need to estimate the PV of the beginning-of-month lease payments using the loan rate.

$$\text{PV (Lease payments)} = 192.37 \times \left[\dfrac{1 - \dfrac{1}{(1.0051)^{60}}}{0.0051}\right](1.0051) = \$9{,}972.39$$

This implies that the firm should enter into the lease arrangement, since the effective cost of the asset would be less than $10,000, which is the cost under the loan arrangement.[13] Notice that we could have come to the same conclusion if we had used the monthly lease rate to evaluate both options. We would have found that the PV of the lease payments was $10,000, while the PV of the loan payments was $10,029.07.

The solution to Example 16-7 may appear somewhat lengthy, but it is a useful framework because it accommodates other variations in the loan versus lease decision, such as differences in required down payments, any services provided through leasing arrangements, and any bargain purchase options.

CONCEPT REVIEW QUESTIONS

1. Explain how to calculate comparisons in the lease-versus-buy decision when the lease in question is an operating lease.

2. How does the analysis change when the lease is a financial lease?

---

[13] In fact, we could say the NPV of leasing versus borrowing = 10,000 − 9,972.39 = +$27.61.

16.4 MOTIVATION FOR LEASING

In the previous section, we showed how leases could, under some circumstances, provide "cheaper" financing than typical loan arrangements. The attraction of leases in such cases is obvious; however, leases provide other benefits to lessees. Below, we provide a description of some of the most common reasons why firms enter into lease arrangements; some are better reasons than others.

1. **Cheaper financing.** This can be the case for operating leases because the entire lease payment is tax deductible. In addition, the lessee may end up receiving attractive leasing rates if the lessor is better able to take advantage of the CCA tax savings associated with ownership of the underlying asset, and if market conditions induce the lessor to pass these benefits on to the lessee.

2. **Reduce the risks of asset ownership.** Leasing allows companies to acquire needed equipment without assuming the risk of having to resell the asset or of having it become obsolete. This is particularly important for assets whose technological capabilities are constantly changing, which is one reason many companies lease computers rather than purchasing them. Essentially, this means that the equipment manufacturer or other lessor, rather than the user, bears the risk of the salvage value of the asset at the end of the lease.

3. **Implicit interest rates.** Leasing usually offers firms fixed-rate financing over the life of the lease, whereas small firms, in particular, are often forced to use variable-rate, prime-based lending when borrowing from banks.

4. **Maintenance.** Under a full-service lease arrangement, the lessor will provide maintenance. Often, the lessor will be a specialist in this type of equipment and is therefore better able to provide maintenance than the lessee.

5. **Convenience.** It is often more convenient to lease an asset than to purchase it, especially if it is only needed for a relatively short period of time and/or if it is a very specialized or illiquid asset that may be hard to sell in the future.

6. **Flexibility.** Leases often offer more flexibility. For example, they often include the option to cancel the lease, which may be important when obsolescence is a possibility. The CFLA also offers the example of a ski-lift operator that financed its lifts with a lease in which payments were seasonal, coinciding with the winter months, for obvious reasons.

7. **Capital budget restrictions.** Since leasing requires a very limited initial capital outlay (just the first lease payment plus any arrangement fees), managers may be able to circumvent capital budget constraints by leasing assets, rather than buying them. This is a dubious reason for leasing, since it allows division managers to circumvent broader-based company policies.

8. **Financial statement effects.** As demonstrated in examples 16-1 through 16-3, the use of operating leases versus debt or financial leases enhances the appearance of the firm's financial statements since they provide off-balance-sheet financing. The use of operating leases can also lead firms to report higher net income, lower debt ratios, and higher liquidity ratios. However, this should not affect the firm's value in efficient markets, because it does not affect the level of its cash flows or the nature of the financial risks it faces. It merely changes the way these items are reported in the financial statements. Therefore, this is not a good reason for leasing. In addition, operating leases will be shown on the balance sheet under new IFRS-based accounting standards in the near future, and discussions are under way to have them show up on the balance sheet under U.S. GAAP.

Case Example

The CFLA offers the following example of how a lease is useful for an SME.

The usual leasing transaction of interest to a business would likely target a particular core asset that will directly contribute to revenue production. For an SME, typically, it would be a "small-ticket" transaction for specific equipment or vehicles between $15,000 and $100,000. The acquisition of new equipment or of new vehicles is an important way for SMEs to grow their businesses and enhance productivity. These acquisitions are building blocks or discrete investment projects that allow for relatively simple business planning: matching projected incremental revenue to the business generated by the investment to incremental expenses and to incremental productivity—on a step-by-step basis.

By way of illustration, consider the possible example of a $50,000 photocopier for a street-corner photocopy business. Often, an entrepreneur will know the particular equipment needed by the business. The manufacturer or a dealer/distributor is contacted. Normally the equipment sales representative of the manufacturer or dealer/distributor meets the customer on the customer's premises or at the dealer/distributor's offices. With the long hours put in by entrepreneurs, "house calls" can be very helpful.

The sales representative will likely have been trained by either the manufacturer's finance company or by the independent financing institution associated with the manufacturer to understand how to structure the financing. The sales representative usually has an in-depth knowledge of the equipment in question and the business of the customer. This knowledge base is very helpful in structuring practical financing for SMEs.

A business customer will usually be offered a financing/leasing package that will include not only the cost of the equipment but also the cost of delivery, installation, servicing, and insurance. The credit decision is usually part of a highly automated process that can be concluded very rapidly, often at the point-of-sale.

The single question of greatest interest to most lessees is the amount of the monthly payment. The lease payment schedule can be tailored to the customer's anticipated revenue stream (example—a lower monthly lease payment in year 1 of the lease with a sliding scale increasing the amount of the monthly payment over the lease term). The lease payment schedule is fixed at the start of the lease such that the lessee will know the amounts and due dates throughout the lease term.

If, during the term of the lease, the customer decides that a new model of the copier would be to the advantage of the business, the lessor will generally negotiate the replacement of the old technology with the new one, rolling the costs into a new lease with a new payment schedule.

Under Canadian Generally Accepted Accounting Principles (GAAP), an operating lease is not capitalized on the financial statements of the lessee. Lease payments are considered an expense for the lessee. In contrast, typical bank financing or finance leases are capitalized and recorded as a debt liability on the borrower's financial statement, thereby affecting the debt/equity ratios impacting the business. This "off-balance-sheet" feature—acquiring needed plant, equipment, and vehicles by way of an operating lease—can be a real advantage, particularly to SMEs.

Also for non-production assets, that is, equipment and vehicles not considered as part of the core production of a business—for example, photocopiers in an office (rather than in a photocopy shop) or trucks—if acquired by way of a loan, the total of the GST and PST must be paid upfront by the customer (although the GST will be refunded eventually). The total sales tax plus the down payment can be a significant upfront amount. On the acquisition of non-production assets by way of lease, the sales taxes are levied generally on each monthly lease payment over the full term of the lease rather than as a single lump sum, upfront payment.[14]

The CFLA example highlights the fact that, in practice, the leasing decision is not a simple investment versus financing decision, but is an integration of both. In this example, the lease is an operating lease that allows the SME to transfer many of the business risks of ownership to a party—the manufacturer—better equipped to manage those risks.

CONCEPT REVIEW QUESTIONS

1. Why are leases often more flexible than a borrow-purchase option?
2. Why do you think the major market for leasing is often SMEs, rather than large corporations?
3. If you were opening a copy centre, do you think you would lease or borrow to buy the equipment and why?

SUMMARY

In this chapter, we discuss leasing as a financing source. In a lease arrangement, the lessor retains ownership rights to an asset but makes the asset available for use by the lessee, who in turn agrees to make periodic lease payments to the lessor. We discuss the general differences between operating and financial (or capital) leases and how they are treated by the CRA for tax purposes and by companies for accounting purposes. We demonstrate that, as a result of these differences, with all else being equal, classifying a lease as operating rather than financial will result in a company reporting higher net income, lower debt ratios, and higher liquidity ratios. We proceed to show how firms can evaluate a potential lease decision using the discounted cash flow (DCF) analysis framework. We conclude by discussing various motivations that firms might have for entering into leasing arrangements, and we focus on the flexibility of lease contracts and the close relationship that exists between manufacturers and equipment-leasing firms.

SUMMARY OF LEARNING OBJECTIVES

16.1 Identify the basic characteristics of leases and differentiate between operating and financial (or capital) leases.

A lease is an agreement where the owner conveys to the user the right to use an asset in exchange for a set of payments over a specified time period. Leasing an asset is an alternative to borrowing money and buying the asset. An operating lease is one in which some of the benefits of ownership do not transfer to the lessee but remain with

the lessor—e.g., a short-term lease is an operating lease. A financial lease is a lease in which essentially all of the benefits of ownership transfer to the lessee.

16.2 Describe the accounting treatment of both operating and financial leases.

With an operating lease, the leased asset does not appear on the lessee's balance sheet—it remains on the lessor's balance sheet. With a financial lease, the asset appears

---

[14] "The Asset-Based Financing, Equipment & Vehicle Leasing Industry." Canadian Finance & Leasing Association (CFLA), backgrounder for the House of Commons Finance Committee, September 4, 1998.

on the lessee's balance sheet. The present value of the lease payments appear as an asset and as a liability. With a financial lease, the lessee depreciates the asset for tax purposes; with an operating lease, the lessor depreciates the asset. With an operating lease, the lessee can expense the lease payments. With a financial lease, the lessee expenses the interest component of the lease payments and gets the depreciation tax shield associated with the asset.

16.3 Evaluate the lease decision using discounted cash flow valuation methods.

A lease is an optimal form of financing (compared to borrowing and buying) if the present value of the incremental benefits exceeds the present value of the in-cremental costs. The main benefit of a lease is the fact that the asset does not have to be purchased. Another benefit of an operating lease is the after-tax maintenance expense savings. The cost of an operating lease includes the after-tax lease payments, the foregone depreciation tax shield and the foregone salvage value of the asset.

16.4 Explain the various motives for leasing.

- Leases can be a cheaper source of financing—especially operating leases because the whole lease payment is tax deductible.
- Leases reduce the risk of ownership, because the asset can be returned at the end of the lease term.
- Leases provide a form of fixed-interest-rate financing (as opposed to variable rate).
- For operating leases, the lessor usually provides maintenance of the asset.
- Leasing can be more convenient than buying, especially for items that are needed for a relatively short period, are very specialized, and may be hard to sell in future.
- Leases often provide flexibility through a cancellation option.
- Managers may be able to circumvent capital budget con-straints by leasing assets, rather than buying them.
- Leases enhance the appearance of the firm's financial statements since they provide off-balance-sheet financing.

KEY TERMS

asset-based lending, p. 620
captive finance companies, p. 620
financial lease, p. 622
lessee, p. 622
lessor, p. 622
leveraged lease, p. 623

off-balance-sheet financing, p. 625
operating lease, p. 622
sale and leaseback (SLB) agreement, p. 623
secured financing, p. 620
small and medium-sized enterprises (SMEs), p. 621

QUESTIONS AND PRACTICE PROBLEMS

Multiple Choice Questions

1. Which of the following statements about an operating lease is *false*?
   a. The lessor is responsible for maintaining the asset.
   b. The lessee is responsible for maintaining the asset.
   c. An operating lease is usually a full-service lease.
   d. Payments of one operating lease term are usually not enough to fully cover the asset cost.

2. Financial leases are:
   a. leases for which the lessees are responsible for maintenance of the assets.
   b. short-term leases.
   c. leases for which the lessors are responsible for maintenance of the assets.
   d. leases that cover less than 75 percent of the economic life of the asset.

3. Which of the following statements about leveraged leases is *false*?
   a. The lease involves an external lender, lessor, and lessee.
   b. The lender receives interest payments from the lessee.
   c. The lessee can bargain for lower lease payments if the market is competitive.
   d. The lender has the first lien on the leased asset.

4. Which of the following organizations is *most likely* to enter into a sale and leaseback agreement?
   a. factory
   b. university
   c. investment firm
   d. real estate firm

5. Which of the following leases is classified as a financial lease?
   a. The lessee could purchase the asset at $90,000, while the market value of the asset is $81,000 when the lease expires.
   b. The lease term is 7.5 years and the economic life of the asset is 9 years.
   c. The lease does not transfer the ownership of the asset to the lessee when the lease expires.
   d. In the lease inception, the fair market value of the assets is $70,000, while the present value of the lease payments is $58,000.

6. Given the following operating lease information, what is the asset/liability recognized on the lessee's balance sheet at the beginning of the lease? Minimum annual lease payment at the beginning of each year = $15,000; lease term = 7 years; appropriate discount rate = 5 percent; salvage value = $0.
   a. $72,293.62
   b. $78,765.45
   c. $0
   d. $88,517.01

7. Given the following information, what is the asset/liability recognized on the lessee's balance sheet at the beginning of the lease? Salvage value = $0; minimum annual lease payment at the beginning of each year = $15,000; lease term = 5 years; appropriate discount rate = 5 percent.
   a. $68,189.26
   b. $64,942.15
   c. $58,764.46
   d. $75,000.00

8. Which of the following is *higher* under operating leases?
   a. NI and CFO
   b. NI in the early years and CFF
   c. Depreciation and NI
   d. Total cash flow and CFO

9. Under financial leases, the following ratio is *higher* compared with that for an operating lease:
   a. current ratio
   b. leverage ratio
   c. NI margin
   d. ROE

10. Which of the following financial figures is *unchanged* regardless of the type of lease?
    a. leverage ratio
    b. P/E ratio
    c. total cash flow
    d. asset turnover

Practice Problems

11. Financial statements for Canadian public corporations are available from corporate websites or from the System for Electronic Document Analysis and Retrieval (SEDAR) at www.sedar.com.
    a. Review a copy of Air Canada's annual report for fiscal year end December 31, 2011 and determine the portion of Air Canada's long-term debt and financial leases that was made up of financial leases. (Hint: see page 100, note 9.)

b. Obtain the same ratio for TELUS. (Hint: see page 154, note 20.)

12. Briefly describe three motivations for leasing.

13. White River Manufacturing Company has just signed several leases and has hired FinCorp Inc. to do the initial classification of the leases as operating or financial for accounting purposes. White River could have bought each asset for $1 million instead of leasing. The appropriate discount rate is 10 percent per year; all lease payments are paid annually at the end of the year. Classify each of the following leases as operating or financial and explain your reasoning.

	Expected economic life of the asset	Annual lease payments	Length of lease	Purchase price at end of lease
A	10 years	$175,000	8 years	$10,000
B	5 years	$115,000	2 years	$900,000
C	10 years	$30,000	5 years	$500,000
D	9 years	$180,000	8 years	$1,000
E	25 years	$110,000	22 years	$8,000
F	10 years	$195,000	5 years	$800,000

14. Igor, the intern at FinCorp Inc., has just presented your boss, Mr. Cabinet, with his valuation of Kitchen Gadget Company (KGC). Igor has identified two other companies, Kitchen Widgets and Kitchen Thingies, in exactly the same line of business as KGC and carried out his valuation using multiples. All three companies use 100-percent equity. Igor presents the following analysis:

	Kitchen Widgets	Kitchen Thingies	Average P/E
P/E ratio	18	25	$21.50

As KGC has an EPS of $1, Igor has valued it at $21.50 per share. Mr. Cabinet looks at Igor's work, tells him to do it again, and mumbles something about "notes to the statements." Igor is utterly confused and has come to you for help. You have quickly reviewed Igor's work and noticed that KGC has a policy of buying all its assets; in contrast, Kitchen Widgets uses operating leases while Kitchen Thingies uses financial or capital leases.

a. Explain to Igor what the "notes to the statements" are.
b. Explain how he should have done the valuation.
c. Is this likely to affect his valuation of KGC?

✿ 15. A firm decides to enter into a lease agreement. The lease term is four years, while the economic life of the asset is five years. The annual lease payment is $10,000 at the beginning of each year, and the appropriate discount rate is 8 percent. There is no salvage value at the end of the lease. The lessee uses the straight-line depreciation method. Estimate the NPV of the lease payments). Estimate the change in NI, CFO, and CFF at the end of the first year.

✿ 16. Estimate the change in NI, CFO, and CFF if the economic life of the lease described in Practice Problem 15 is six years instead of five years.

✿ 17. What are the changes in current assets, long-term assets, current liabilities, and long-term liabilities at the end of the first year in Practice Problem 15?

18. What are the changes in current assets, long-term assets, current liabilities, and long-term liabilities at the end of the first year if the economic life of the lease described in Practice Problem 15 is six years instead of five years?

19. Expedic Utility Corp. needs to increase its electricity production capacity. It is interested in a slightly used reactor located in Ontario. It has been offered two alternatives: buy the reactor for $16 billion (and hold onto it for 20 years) or lease it for 10 years at $2.5 billion per year. At the end of 10 years, Expedic would have the option of either buying the reactor for $3.5 billion or renewing the lease at annual payments of $3 billion. Expedic has a cost of capital of 7 percent. Assume the economic life of the reactor is 20 years, the CCA rate is $800 million per year, and the tax rate is 40 percent. At the end of 20 years, the reactor will have a salvage value of zero. Assume all lease payments are made at the beginning of the lease; all leases are operating leases; maintenance costs of $12 million per year will be covered by the lessor; and all CCA is taken at the end of the year (do not apply the half-year rule).

    a. Draw the decision tree for Expedic. What choices does it have to make and when?

    b. Ignoring the real options value, evaluate the NPV of the three alternatives: 1. Buy asset; 2. Lease and renew lease in year 10; and 3. Lease and then buy asset in year 10. What is your recommended course of action to the CEO of Expedic?

20. Sharon McKee has been appointed finance minister and is convinced that the leasing business is just a way to avoid paying taxes. She has hired FinCorp Inc. to evaluate the cash flow effects for both the lessee and the lessor in financial leases. McKee wants to determine if there is any loss of tax revenue to the government. Use the information given below to answer the following questions.

    - The cost of the asset is $1.5 million. The lessor will have to buy the asset in order to lease it to lessee.

    - The cost of capital for both firms is 10 percent.

    - The annual cash flow (before tax) generated by the asset is $800,000 regardless of who uses the asset.

    - To acquire the asset, the firm will make annual interest payments at the end of each year and repay the principal of $1.5 million at the end of the fifth year (just like a bond).

    - Maintenance and insurance costs are $0.

    - The economic life of the asset, and the term of the lease, is five years.

    - A CCA of $300,000 is claimed at the end of each year (for convenience, we are assuming the firm uses the straight-line depreciation method).

    - Annual lease payments of $500,000 are made at the end of the year.

    - The tax rate of both the lessee and lessor is 40 percent.

    - Assume that both firms make sufficient income to claim any tax benefits.

    a. Complete the following table assuming the firm buys the asset (lease payments equal 0).

	Firm buys asset					
	Year 1	Year 2	Year 3	Year 4	Year 5	Principal repayment
Cash flow from asset						
Interest payments						
Lease payments						
CCA on asset						
Tax payment						
After-tax cash flows						

    b. Complete the following table assuming the firm uses a financial lease (interest payments equal 0). For simplicity, assume that the entire lease payment is treated as a financing charge (like interest).

	Firm uses financial lease					
	Year 1	Year 2	Year 3	Year 4	Year 5	Principal repayment
Cash flow from asset						
Interest payments						
Lease payments						
CCA on asset						
Tax payment						
After-tax cash flows						

c. Complete the following table for the lessor in the financial lease. For simplicity, assume that the entire lease payment is treated as a financing charge (like interest). The lessor borrows money to acquire the asset. The lessor will make annual interest payments at the end of each year and repay the principal of $1.5 million at the end of the fifth year (just like a bond).

	Lessor in financial lease					
	Year 1	Year 2	Year 3	Year 4	Year 5	Principal repayment
Cash flow from asset						
Interest payments						
Lease payments						
CCA on asset						
Tax payment						
After-tax cash flows						

d. Are Ms. McKee's suspicions about loss of tax revenue correct?

e. How could the firms (the sum of lessee and lessor) gain from leasing activities? In other words, why would a lessor lease the asset to the operating firm rather than use the asset itself?

21. A firm plans to either lease a piece of equipment or purchase it. The upfront purchase price is $800,000, and it is depreciated at $80,000 per year for tax purposes. The equipment could be sold in nine years for $80,000. If the firm leases the equipment under an operating lease, it pays annual lease payments of $40,000 at the beginning of each of nine years. The firm's effective tax rate is 40 percent. Determine whether or not the firm should lease the equipment, assuming the before-tax cost of borrowing is 8 percent.

22. A firm plans to either purchase or lease a machine that costs $250,000 and is subject to a 20-percent CCA rate, using the declining balance method. The required lease payments are $30,000 at the beginning of each of four years. The lessor has agreed to provide maintenance as part of the lease contract, and the firm has estimated it would incur $20,000 per year in maintenance expense if it decided to purchase the machine. It estimates the asset could be sold for $115,200 after four years (the ending UCC at the end of year 4). The firm's before-tax borrowing rate is 8 percent, and its effective tax rate is 40 percent. Should it purchase or lease the machine, assuming the acquisition of the machine has a positive NPV and that the lease would qualify as an operating lease?

23. Suppose you are going to enter into a six-year, $22,000 financial lease that requires monthly payments based on an 8-percent lease rate. Alternatively, you could borrow $22,000 via a six-year loan that requires monthly payments based on a 7-percent lending rate. Which option should you choose?

24. Paolo, the CEO of Paola Bros Inc., wants to have a Ferrari as a company car. The Ferrari costs S1.5 million. For tax purposes, assume that the car will depreciate at a rate of $180,000 per

year. In five years, the Ferrari could be sold for $800,000. The Ferrari could be leased on a five-year operating lease for $200,000 per year. The lease payment would be made at the beginning of the year. If the effective tax rate of Paolo Bros Inc. is 35 percent, and its before-tax cost of borrowing is 8 percent, should Paolo lease the Ferrari or buy it?

25. In Practice Problem 24, what would the lease payment have to be for Paolo to be indifferent about whether the company buys or leases the Ferrari?

26. Nash Business School is considering whether to lease or buy a shuttle bus for students travelling between its two campuses. The bus costs $1.8 million, with a CCA rate of 25 percent. The lease payments are $400,000 per year for the next five years, with payments made at the beginning of each year. There is no maintenance cost, and the expected market value of the bus after five years is zero. Assuming the lease qualifies as an operating lease and the cost of borrowing is 5 percent, should Nash Business School lease the bus or buy it? Note that universities do not pay tax.

27. In Practice Problem 26, assuming that Nash Business School has an effective tax rate of 40 percent, should the shuttle bus be bought or leased?

28. A firm has the option of borrowing $2.5 million through a 10-year loan with monthly payments based on a 7-percent lending rate, or entering into a 10-year, $2.5-million financial lease arrangement with monthly payments based on a 7-percent lease rate. Which option is more advantageous to the firm?

29. A used car that currently costs $25,000 will have a market value of $5,000 in four years. As a student, you cannot afford to pay $25,000, but you want to have a car while you are going to university for the next four years. Your father agrees to lend you $25,000 on the condition that you pay him $300 at the end of every month for the next four years and $25,000 at the end of the four years. The car dealer provides financing facilities, and you are qualified to get a lease for which you will have to make monthly, end-of-month payments of $650 for 48 months. Which option will leave you better off, assuming your cost of capital is 6 percent?

30. Charles Zhang, the owner of a small moving company, has decided that economic conditions are perfect for him to expand his business. Such an expansion will require him to buy five new moving trucks at a total cost of $250,000. Mr. Zhang's company has $8,000 in cash and a $45,000 line of credit at the bank. It is a small company, so it does not have the option of issuing public debt, and Mr. Zhang is not comfortable mortgaging his family home to buy the trucks. Describe two ways Mr. Zhang can acquire the trucks. Discuss the advantages and disadvantages of each.

Part 7

LONG-TERM FINANCING

Having considered the left-hand side of the balance sheet in Part 6, we now consider the right-hand side and examine how a firm finances its operations. This involves securities law, because obtaining funds from the public is heavily regulated due to the possibility of fraud. We discuss the role of provincial securities commissions and how securities are issued to the public. We then discuss the different types of securities that firms issue, how equities differ from debt securities, and the range of securities in between these two extremes, commonly referred to as hybrids. We conclude by examining how to estimate a firm's cost of capital based on its use of the various financing alternatives.

17 | Investment Banking and Securities Law

LEARNING OBJECTIVES

17.1 Explain what is meant by "information asymmetries" and how these affect the raising of capital.

17.2 Explain the purpose of securities laws and regulations in the financial markets.

17.3 Explain what a prospectus is, what it contains, and why it is critical for initial public offerings (IPOs).

17.4 Outline the basic stages in taking a firm public through an initial public offering (IPO) of securities.

17.5 Explain why continuous disclosure requirements are important for investors and how they affect secondary offerings.

In the most notorious stock-market fraud in Canadian history, Bre-X claimed it had discovered a massive gold strike in Indonesia. The scheme unravelled in 1997 when it was revealed the company had been salting the core samples from the deposit. Former Bre-X chief geologist John Felderhof was the only person ever charged. In 2007, he was found not guilty on charges of illegal insider trading and acquitted of issuing false press releases.

Source: Waldie, Paul and McFarland, Janet. "The end of the trail." *The Globe and Mail*, August 3, 2007.

CHAPTER 17 **PREVIEW**

In chapters 17, 18, and 19, we develop an overview of corporate financing and an understanding of the cost of capital as the overall cost of the funds invested in a firm. To understand how this cost of capital is determined, we need to understand why certain types of securities exist and the basic reasons firms issue debt securities rather than equity securities and vice versa. In chapters 6 and 7, we discussed the basics of bonds and equities and how to value them. However, we did not discuss why these securities exist or, just as important, the difference between private and public markets for securities—that is, why some securities are traded while others aren't.

To understand these issues, we will discuss some major financial scandals in which investors (both equity and debt investors) lost millions and sometimes billions of dollars. The underlying reasons for these losses are fraud and criminal activity. It is an unfortunate truth that financial markets, by their very nature, are subject to potential abuse because it is difficult for investors to separate frauds from legitimate investments. And as our opening vignette shows, proving a case of fraud is extremely difficult. In this chapter, we discuss the basic problem of raising external capital and separating good from bad investments. The problem arises because of asymmetric information: fraudsters know that they are fraudsters, whereas investors do not. Differences in information have a huge impact on the design of financial securities and the practice of corporate financing. (In chapters 18 and 19, we discuss how these differences in information cause firms to issue different types of securities.).

After considering this basic problem and illustrating it with recent and classic frauds, we discuss securities regulation and the reasons all those legal requirements exist. We then discuss the process of taking a firm public and explain how to raise capital through both initial public offerings (IPOs) and seasoned equity offerings (SEOs). We show how this process applies to both debt and equity securities.

17.1 CONFLICTS BETWEEN ISSUERS AND INVESTORS

The Basic Problem of Asymmetric Information

Learning Objective 17.1
Explain what is meant by "information asymmetries" and how these affect the raising of capital.

asymmetric information information that one party in a deal has and the other doesn't; an extreme example is someone knowingly selling worthless securities that the investor doesn't know are worthless

We begin by considering the most basic case of investors investing in what, unknown to them, is a deliberate fraud. This is an example of **asymmetric information**, or information that one side has and the other doesn't. This is an extreme case in which one side knows that the securities being offered are worthless—that is, they are completely fraudulent—while the investors think they are being offered a legitimate business opportunity. In Chapter 1, we introduced Bernard Madoff, who committed arguably the biggest fraud in history. However, as the stock market crashed in 2008, more and more frauds came to light as investors tried to cash in their investments and retreat from the market, only to find that they had invested in a Ponzi scheme and their money had disappeared. This has reinforced the importance of securities legislation and what we referred to as due diligence, which is, simply, not accepting things at face value but doing basic background checks.

In chapters 6 and 7, we discussed the valuation of common stocks (equities) and bonds and developed discounted cash flow valuation formulas. In all cases, there is an initial outflow to buy the security and then a series of expected future cash inflows. These future inflows are discounted back to the present to estimate the present value of a security. However, think about an initial issue of securities from the issuer's perspective. The issuer receives an immediate cash inflow based on the assumption that it will, in turn, pay a series of expected future cash flows. If both the investor and issuer agree on the expected stream of future cash flows, the situation is *symmetric*: what the investor expects to receive is what the issuer expects to pay, so the investor's expected rate of return is equal to the issuer's cost of raising capital.

This is the basic approach of corporate finance: we look to the capital markets to get an indication of the cost of certain types of financing, which is the reason, in this textbook, we discussed the essentials of capital markets before discussing corporate financing. If the current interest rate on long-term debt is 6 percent, we say that the cost of long-term debt financing to the firm is 6 percent; if we estimate the capital asset pricing model (CAPM) required rate of return on equity is 12 percent, we say the cost of common equity financing is 12 percent. We will deal with some of the nuances later, but the principal assumption is that the investor and the issuer agree on the value of the expected stream of cash flows and come up with the same estimate. The problem, however, is that capital markets exhibit information asymmetries, which is a fancy way of saying that people frequently have different information about the same future stream of cash flows, and thus they value the securities differently. In fact, they can disagree so much that a market may not exist, and a firm that cannot find anyone to buy its securities experiences a "financing gap."[1]

The classic example of market failure in the presence of information asymmetries was demonstrated by Professor George Akerlof, who formalized the notion of a market for lemons. Consider the most familiar "lemons market," which is that for used cars. Suppose that for a given make and year of used car, there are two types: good cars, which were driven by responsible drivers who regularly maintained them, and lemons, which were driven by people who drove them excessively and never properly maintained them. However, let's assume the lemon looks as good as the good-quality car because the owner has turned the odometer back and put heavier oil in the transmission. Suppose the true value of the good car is $15,000, and that of the lemon is $10,000. If there are equal numbers of both types of car in the market, the average price for the car will be $12,500 or, more likely, less than this amount, taking into account the risk of buying a lemon. So let's say it is $11,000.

At a market price of $11,000, the owners of good cars will not offer them for sale. Instead, these owners will sell their cars privately to someone who trusts them, like a relative or close friend. After all, the owners know the true mileage and know they have completed the scheduled maintenance. As a result, they will not offer a $15,000 car for sale to the general public for $11,000, so the supply of good cars will go down. For the lemon, the situation is the opposite. Because their owners know they own a lemon and know the going market price exceeds its true value, they will put their cars up for sale. The result is that there will be an unequal supply of good cars and lemons; the market supply will consist entirely of lemons plus a few good cars sold by people with no friends or relatives to sell to. As a result, the overall market for cars fails.

This market for lemons is an example of "Gresham's law." Sir Thomas Gresham, who coined the phrase "bad money drives out good," observed that in 16th-century England, gold and silver coins circulated at their par value; for example, a one-shilling coin was valued at one shilling. However, the metallic value of the coins, based on their gold and silver content, would vary as some coins were "clipped." This was a practice in which people deliberately clipped or shaved off some of the coin and used the gold and silver for other purposes. The result was that, if someone had two coins in hand—a new, fully valued silver coin and a clipped one—the owner would spend the clipped one and save (or clip) the fully valued coin. Hence, the bad money drives good money out of circulation. Gresham's law applies to any situation in which there is a single market price, yet the value of the commodity traded differs. Inevitably, it is the inferior-valued commodity that is passed on, as is the case in Akerlof's car example, in which the car market becomes dominated by lemons.[2]

---

[1] Governments are constantly worried about financing gaps and the fact that good companies cannot get financing on reasonable terms. Of course, people disagree profoundly on what constitutes reasonable terms.

[2] Gresham's law also explains why coins have traditionally been "milled" with a defined edge, so that everyone knows the coin has not been tampered with. This practice has continued, even though most coins now have little monetary value.

Of course, there are mechanisms to adjust for this market failure. In Gresham's time, people would weigh the coins and refuse to accept badly clipped ones at face value. Similarly, in Akerlof's example, one solution is to get a mechanic's report. However, a buyer may not have any faith in the seller's choice of mechanic, requiring that the buyer also get a mechanic's report, adding two layers of cost. Another solution is to buy from the dealer who originally sold and serviced the car, thus relying on the car dealer's reputation. In this case, the lemons would be sold at auction, where only the pros (mechanics and used-car dealers) buy. Failing that, a last solution is to buy a used car from someone who clearly has no friends or relatives! The point is that we get a richer set of markets with alternative market mechanisms. This is what happens in financial markets: much of the richness of financial markets is derived from arrangements developed to deal with these information asymmetries.

Let's return to our discussion of an investor who wants to buy a new issue of securities but doesn't realize the issue is fraudulent. From the issuer's perspective, this is a fantastic deal: for the initial cash received from selling the securities, the criminal promises to make a series of future payments. All he or she has to do for this cash is provide some "legal" documentation and a few certificates, essentially some paper. If the criminal can raise, say, $200 million from a group of investors, he or she only needs to make a few payments before jumping on a plane to a jurisdiction that won't extradite him or her back to Canada. The criminal enjoys a $200-million inflow in return for printing up a few certificates.

Real-World Examples of Fraudulent Activities

Historically, financial markets have been rife with fraud and abuse. A little more than 100 years ago, many of the securities sold to the general public were frauds. However, frauds occur at all levels and not just with the general public. The U.S. Securities and Exchange Commission's (SEC) website shows that frauds are still happening. For example, William E. Lyons is accused of trying to sell US$220 million in fraudulently issued zero coupon bonds to Bear Stearns Companies, Inc. (Bear Stearns), a major U.S. investment bank that subsequently figured prominently in the financial crisis and that collapsed in March 2008. In the SEC complaint, section 16 alleges that

> Lyons' efforts to market the bank guarantee offering to Bear Stearns were designed to persuade representatives of Bear Stearns to tender the $200 million payment for the purchase of a purported $220 million bank guarantee. Such a payment by Bear Stearns would have generated a total of approximately $1 million in compensation to SV Group and Lyons.

Lyons was a former broker at Bear Stearns, and the SEC complaint in section 13 further alleges that,

> had Lyons conducted an independent inquiry, he would have discovered that the purported bank guarantees that he was offering and their associated funding and issuing transactions had the hallmarks of a fraudulent prime bank securities scheme.

Bear Stearns rejected Lyons' proposal in December 2002, indicated that the transaction was probably fraudulent, and suggested he check the SEC website. However, Lyons then apparently tried to sell the securities to Merrill Lynch & Co., Inc. (Merrill Lynch), Goldman Sachs Group, Inc., and Chase Manhattan Bank, three other prominent U.S. financial institutions. This is when the SEC intervened.

Lyons' alleged actions illustrate that if a criminal wants to steal, he or she goes where the money is: the major financial institutions. If Lyons had tried to sell these securities to the general public, it would have taken a lot more effort over a much longer period of time, with a lot more publicity, to raise US$200 million. It is interesting that he tried to sell zero coupon bonds: if he had sold regular interest-bearing bonds, the fraudsters who originally issued the bonds would have had to pay interest, and the lack of interest payments would have caused the purchasers to contact the SEC or police soon after the missed interest payment. In contrast, zero coupon bonds offer no payments until maturity, so there is no tipoff that they are fraudulent until they are redeemed.

Bearer bonds are unregistered bonds; the owner is the person who has the bonds at a particular time. Bearer bonds are popular in Europe, where they are allegedly often used for tax evasion. However, in North America, almost all bonds are registered and maintained as (computer) book entries, and there are just a tiny number of bearer bonds. In contrast to bearer bonds, the interest payments and repayments of principal for registered bonds go to the individual who is the registered owner. This produces a paper trail for the cash that all can see, including Canada Revenue Agency.[3]

> **bearer bonds** unregistered bonds that are payable to whomever holds them

One of the biggest frauds in England involved a fraudulent issue of 10-year zero coupon bonds, sold into a small regional market, away from the major market in London where it would have quickly been noticed. The fraud became known only after the bonds were sold and the bearer bonds were warehoused. A lowly clerk happened to notice that the new bonds didn't seem to be as stiff as other bonds that he had previously catalogued and put away. On checking, he discovered they all had the same serial number! It turned out the bonds had been copied on reasonably sophisticated photocopiers, but the paper was different. *Zero Coupon* (1993), a popular novel by Paul Erdman, was loosely based on this real-life fraud.

In advising investors, the SEC points to five major warning signs of fraud:

- Excessive guaranteed returns: 20 to 200 percent
- Fictitious financial instruments
- Extreme secrecy
- Exclusive opportunity
- Inordinate complexity

As we pointed out in Chapter 8, common equities average returns of only 10 to 11 percent, so to be offered a guaranteed—that is, risk-free—return in excess of 20 percent is a sure sign that something is wrong. If this opportunity is then dressed up as a complicated financial instrument that is only available to a small number of investors by "invitation" in a transaction that has to be "secret" and for which you have to sign a non-disclosure agreement, the best thing is to say you'll get back to them, and then contact the OSC and SEC. However, frauds don't have to be that complicated.

For example, zero coupon bonds aren't really needed for fraud; all that is needed is some mechanism for keeping investors happy while the fraudster tries to defraud more people. The classic way of doing this is to sell enough new fraudulent securities so that the cash inflow from their sale can make the interest payments on the earliest fraudulent bonds. This type of fraud is called a **Ponzi scheme**, after Carlo Ponzi, an Italian born in 1882, who emigrated to the United States. When dealing with a customer in Spain, Ponzi noticed that he received an international postal reply coupon that could be exchanged for U.S. stamps. What he also noticed was that he could buy these coupons in Spain and exchange them for U.S. stamps worth six times as much. In financial terms, we say that he recognized an *arbitrage* opportunity—he could buy something in one market (i.e., Spain and other countries) and resell it for more in another market (i.e., the United States). Technically, arbitrage implies the ability to earn a profit without assuming any risk. In any event, Ponzi subsequently discovered that the cost of the round-trip transaction involved so many administrative details that he could not make a profit. However, his idea was easily understood, and friends and relatives had wanted in on

> **Ponzi scheme** a fraud that involves selling enough new fake securities so the cash inflow can be used to make the interest payments on the earliest fake securities

---

[3] In Canada, the Canadian Depository for Securities (CDS) is owned by the major banks and handles 413 million transactions a year, with $4 trillion on deposit. Purchases and sales are made through computer entries at CDS and are regulated by the Quebec Securities Commission and Bank of Canada.

his investment before it occurred to him that it was not profitable. He took their money and issued them notes promising a 50 percent return in six months, ostensibly so he could buy more postal coupons. He then paid off the notes as they came due with the money from new investors as word of his genius spread. The more he bragged about his financial acumen, and the more satisfied customers he had, the more the money rolled in.

Several groups warned investors that something was wrong, but as long as Ponzi paid off the 50-percent interest-bearing notes, he had an army of satisfied investors who were vociferous in their support of his enterprise. His status was enhanced after he paid off a horde of investors who panicked and demanded their money back. It seemed that Ponzi could do no wrong. However, auditors looking at his books eventually declared that he was bankrupt, and the U.S. federal authorities arrested him on August 13, 1920. It turned out that in order to fulfill his scheme, he needed to buy 180 million postal certificates, and he had bought only two. He was sentenced to five years in jail by the U.S. government, and seven to nine in Massachusetts, but he skipped bail and was later found selling "underwater" building lots in Florida for $10, promising investors they could be resold for $5.3 million within two years.

Bernard Madoff's fraud was similar to Ponzi's, although much more sophisticated. One major difference is that Madoff was a prominent financier who at one time was chair of the board of directors of the National Association of Securities Dealers (NASD) in the United States. He owed this position to his company's role as a market maker, trading shares in small companies at very low spreads and undercutting the major companies. It is now known that this activity was increasingly a front or loss leader for his illegal activity, which was managing money for other institutional accounts. Madoff was very cunning; he did not sell any securities directly to the public and did not advertise, so he avoided the eyes of the watchdogs. Instead, feeder funds brought him money as he "earned" higher and higher rates of return, and his fame spread by word of mouth. However, like Ponzi, he did not really earn these rates of return; they were simply an illusion created as new money came in from new investors. When the stock market crashed in 2008 and investors wanted some of their money back, his whole scheme came crumbling down. On June 29, 2009, Madoff was sentenced to 150 years in prison. The actual size of his scam is difficult to determine—the high estimate of US$65 billion includes the impact of his promised high rates of return—but even allowing for no income on the invested funds, it still appears to be at least a US$10-billion fraud.

The examples of Lyons and Madoff, and the classic case of Ponzi, illustrate the problems of information asymmetry in issuing securities. In all three cases, the issuers knew that what they were selling was not worth what investors were paying. These are extreme cases of information asymmetry, but in the face of any such fraudulent activity, financial markets cannot survive. As an example, take two possible issuers: one a fraudster, like Ponzi, and the other a legitimate company. If the investor cannot distinguish between them, then he or she has to bear this fraud risk, keeping in mind that every dollar invested in the fraudulent scheme will be lost. Increasing the interest rate to compensate for the risk of fraud might solve this problem, but such a solution is self-defeating.

Consider a simple case in which the market interest rate is 10 percent for non-fraudulent bonds. If one in five bonds in a given market is fraudulent, then introducing a "fraud premium" would put the interest rate at 37.5 percent, based on a one-year investment horizon and assuming the market does not require a risk premium. This rate may be calculated as follows:

$$4 \times (1 + k) = 5 \times (\$1.10)$$

$$k = 0.375$$

In other words, the investor wants 10 percent or $1.10 (principal plus interest) on each $5 invested but will only get $(1 + k)$ on the $4 invested in the legitimate businesses and will get $0 from the fraudster. As the amount of fraudulent activity in the market increases, so too does the market interest rate applied to all borrowers.

However, there is a problem with increasing the market interest rate, just as there was a problem with the market rate in Akerlof's market for lemons. We know that Ponzi was willing to pay 37.5 percent—after all, he actually paid 50 percent on six-month notes—but fraudsters usually have no intention of paying all the money back. As a result, they will *promise* to pay any market interest rate, because they don't expect to pay it at all. Conversely, legitimate businesses can't normally generate the profits required to pay 37.5 percent and will balk at paying such a high rate when they have no intention of committing fraud. Consequently, they will not issue securities to the general public, just as the owner of a good car doesn't sell to the public. Instead, legitimate businesses will rely on private financing, and the public markets will be left to the fraudsters and will inevitably dry up. In this case, an issuer's willingness to pay an exorbitant interest rate should be a tipoff to any sensible person not to lend them money.

This insight drives almost all securities law. Quite simply, if investors cannot distinguish good investments from lemons offered by fraudsters, they will not invest in the public markets. As the OSC points out, "The OSC mandate is set by statute: To provide protection to investors from unfair, improper, or fraudulent practices and to foster fair and efficient capital markets and confidence in capital markets."[4] The fact is investors have to be confident that they are being treated fairly in the capital market; otherwise they will invest offshore, where they are treated fairly, or they will invest in real assets, such as houses and gold. There is then a social loss from the collapse of financial markets. This explains why there is a direct (positive) correlation between the existence of public capital markets and respect for the "rule of law." In countries where there is no confidence in the enforcement of laws against fraud, or where there is a belief that markets are rigged, financial transactions are done mostly through private placements in which the borrower and lender know each other. In these cases, there are also usually social enforcement costs to mitigate fraud. These generally involve either social costs, such as being excluded from the best "clubs,"[5] or draconian punishment for criminals.[6]

Finance in the News 17-1 discusses an OSC case with two broad conclusions. The first is that the wheels of justice often grind along quite slowly, since the accused have legal rights as well. In the interim, it is well to remember the words of the "victim": "Maybe I should have educated myself. Sometimes you have to take responsibility for your actions. I really dropped the ball on this." So what can regulators and individuals do?

---

finance INTHENEWS 17-1   Ponzi Scheme Duped GTA Dentists

DR. JOSEPH RADICE had every reason to believe his money was in good hands.

The Woodbridge dentist had invested $617,000 of hard earned savings with a dental colleague he believed was a financial whiz who had made a killing on the New York and Toronto stock exchanges.

Today, Radice alleges he is one of at least 50 investors—many of them prominent dentists—looking for $50 million in lost funds. In allegations filed in court Radice accuses former colleague Peter Sbaraglia and wife Mandy, both dentists, of being key cogs in a sophisticated Ponzi scheme.

What Radice and investors did not know was that the Ontario Securities Commission (OSC) was actively investigating the scheme, even as they were being reassured that their money was safe and earning vast returns.

"If they are a protective government agency then, they (the OSC) should have stepped up," Radice said in an interview. "What safeguards are in place to protect investors from unscrupulous people?"

For Radice, it all started around the dentist chair at his Woodbridge practice in 2005.

When the veteran family dentist needed a dental anesthesiologist to help treat a patient, Radice called for Sbaraglia. Radice grew to trust him.

Over time, according to Radice, Sbaraglia boasted that he and his wife had great "prowess" in trading private and public securities in Toronto and New York. So much prowess, Radice recalled in a court action he started against his old dental colleague, that Sbaraglia was planning to leave his own practice and become a full-time investor.

continued

---

[4] Ontario Securities Commission, "About the OSC." On the OSC website, http://www.osc.gov.on.ca/en/About_about_index.htm.

[5] Traditionally, in Canada, as in many other countries, the perpetrators of fraud were disciplined by being designated social outcasts and having their families excluded from the best schools, clubs, and so on. The loosening of social bonds has weakened the effectiveness of these types of constraints in Canada but not in more socially cohesive cultures.

[6] In Russia, the capitalists who bought formerly state-owned enterprises at reduced prices have not fared very well. Mikhail Khordovsky is in jail for 10 years for fraud and tax evasion, while Yukos, the oil and gas company he owned and operated, faces a $27.5-billion tax bill and a forced merger with Gazprom, the state-owned oil company.

Finance in the News 17-1: Ponzi Scheme Duped GTA Dentists (continued)

According to the OSC, Sbaraglia was, by 2006, hooked up with Robert Mander, the mastermind of a Ponzi scheme that would take at least $40 million from investors. A Ponzi scheme is a financial operation that pays returns to investors from money that new investors contribute.

Radice said he had no idea that Mander and Sbaraglia were working together.

The OSC, in a release last week, alleges both men participated in a "fraudulent scheme" through their company, C.O. Capital Growth. Radice would have liked to have known that years ago.

"When someone is under investigation you know what they should have done. They should have frozen the assets and stopped the whole process from tumbling and falling down," said Radice.

"Maybe I should have educated myself. Sometimes you have to take responsibility for your actions. I really dropped the ball on this," Radice said. He estimates 50 investors lost $50 million in the scheme, though the regulator has pegged the amount at $40 million.

Between November 2006 and August 2008, Radice said he invested $617,000 in six different contributions to Sbaraglia, who promised a 25 percent return on the dentist's investments. Radice acknowledges he made a mistake in trusting his former colleague who, he said, promised his money would continue to grow as long as he resisted the urge to withdraw it.

Other investors continued to invest in 2009, according to the receiver's report on the case.

Radice, in a statement of claim filed in court in 2010, said he often dropped by Sbaraglia's office to get a report on the investments. Radice said Sbaraglia typically told him they were doing well and "there was no possibility of him losing his money."

According to the OSC, Sbaraglia and wife Mandy were on a spending spree by this time, racking up whopping credit card bills while dining at fine restaurants and using some of the investor money to support a dental hygiene business owned by Mandy, a periodontist.

Last December, an Ontario judge put the Sbaraglia's assets into receivership, including their $2.9 million heritage home in Oakville. It was listed for sale recently.

Source: Mathieu, Emily and Popplewell, Brett. "Ponzi Scheme Duped GTA Dentists." *Toronto Star*, March 1, 2011. Available at www.thestar.com. Reprinted by permission.

As in the used-car market, alternative market mechanisms have evolved in the financial markets so that individuals can invest with some assurance that they are not buying lemons. The main mechanisms are basic research, securities legislation, and corporate law, which keep known criminals out of the markets and require that those interacting with the public are registered and that any securities offered to the public are checked to ensure they are legitimate. This overall process of checking securities offered to the public and providing basic information is called **due diligence**, and it can be very expensive and time consuming. It is as a result of fraud that so much checking and legal documentation is required. We will discuss some more Canadian cases of fraudulent activity in the next section.

due diligence the process of checking securities offered to the public to ensure they are legitimate

Some Canadian Examples of Fraudulent Activities

In 1908, Carlo Ponzi served 20 months in jail for a similar pyramid scam in Canada. If U.S. securities laws had been as tough in 1920 as they are now, he would never have been allowed to sell securities to the public, because his criminal background would have disqualified him from registration as a securities broker-dealer. Likewise, one of the charges the SEC levied against William Lyons was that he was not registered to sell financial securities. Keeping known criminals out of the business, and making sure that those in it understand the basics of the business and abide by professional standards, is a necessary, if insufficient, condition for minimizing fraud in the markets.

In her book *Contrepreneurs* (1988), Diane Francis details how Toronto used to be the "bucket shop" capital of the world. "Bucket shops" were basically basements in large buildings with banks of dedicated telephones, where salespeople would call wealthy doctors and dentists in the United States, touting junior resource stocks on the Vancouver Stock Exchange (VSE).[7] The broker-dealers selling these "penny stocks" would often trade among themselves in "wash sales," in which the sum of the external sales activity was zero. By selling among themselves at ever higher prices, they generated the appearance of momentum, which attracted investors

---

[7] The Vancouver Stock Exchange no longer exists and has been replaced by the TSX Venture Exchange. To avoid alerting Canadian authorities to the scam, the salespeople in the bucket shops took pains not to sell to Canadians.

looking at the statistics in the newspaper. These securities were highlighted as emerging "growth" stocks, with great potential to attract investors looking for a quick profit. However, once the price had been artificially inflated to attract enough external investors, the insiders sold out, and the external investors discovered that there was no one else to sell to. This example of "pumping and dumping" illustrates the basic proposition that although it is easy to buy securities, they are often difficult to sell. These types of activities have now been shut down by securities regulators, but as *Finance in the News 17-2* shows, they are impossible to stop entirely.

---

finance INTHENEWS 17-2 | Stock Selling Scheme

TWO MEN who ran a high-pressure operation to sell shares of Shallow Oil and Gas Inc. have each been sentenced to 27 months in prison for fraud and trading violations.

The boiler room operation was started in the Toronto-area city of Markham in the fall of 2007 and was shut down by Ontario authorities in January 2008.

At the time of the raid, the accused were soliciting investors across Canada.

Abel Da Silva and Eric O'Brien were each sentenced to 18 months for running a "boiler room" and nine months consecutively for breaching cease trade orders.

A third man, Abraham Grossman, was sentenced in June to three years in prison for his part in the Shallow Oil and Gas scheme.

The Ontario Securities Commission alleged that Shallow Oil didn't carry on any legitimate business and none of the defendants was registered with the province.

Source: The Canadian Press, "Two Men Who Ran High-Pressure Stock Selling Scheme Jailed for 27 Months Apiece." *Canadian Business*, November 16, 2011. Copyright © 2011 The Canadian Press. Reprinted by permission.

If buying securities directly from a company or through a broker-dealer, is considered risky, why not buy them through an asset manager selling mutual funds? Buying a mutual fund holding many securities is less risky—right? Not necessarily. In Quebec, Norbourg Asset Management Inc. (Norbourg) was closed down and its founder, Vincent Lacroix, was charged by Quebec's main regulator, the Autorité des marchés financiers (AMF), with misappropriating investor funds. The AMF claimed Lacroix stole $84 million from Norbourg and Evolution mutual funds, and it is claiming $10 million in punitive damages. The AMF froze Norbourg's assets in August 2005, and a later audit revealed that $130 million was missing. Luckily for the 9,200 investors in this case, they got almost all their money back as a result of legal claims against the regulators and others who should have been aware of what was going on.[8]

Regulators and police try hard to stop criminal activity, but they can never shut it down completely. It's like trying to stop people from speeding—the laws are there, as is the enforcement, but the police can't be everywhere. Investors need to remember the old adage that "if it sounds too good to be true, it probably is."

This warning may be obvious, but it is remarkable how gullible people can be. Moreover, the statistical evidence is that gullible investors tend to be of above-average intelligence and are workaholics who consider themselves to be financially literate. This is why doctors and dentists are prime candidates for fraudsters: they have lots of money and are eager to get more, while they are also clever enough to think they understand what's going on and don't need expert advice. It appears that the easiest person to defraud is someone who has a high opinion of himself or herself, as *Finance in the News 17-1* indicates.

CONCEPT REVIEW QUESTIONS

1. How does the existence of asymmetric information lead to market inefficiencies?

2. Why can increases in interest rates not be used to solve the "lemons problem" in markets?

3. Why are securities legislation and corporate laws essential for markets to perform properly?

---

[8] See Marotte, Bernard, "Norbourg Investors Declare a Victory for Us." *The Globe and Mail*, January 31, 2011.

17.2 A PRIMER ON SECURITIES LEGISLATION IN CANADA

Securities Legislation—Basic Responsibilities

Learning Objective 17.2
Explain the purpose of securities laws and regulations in the financial markets.

Canada has no federal securities regulator because financial markets are a provincial and territorial responsibility. There has been a great deal of debate over this format, with many parties pushing for the establishment of a federal securities regulator. *Finance in the News 17-3* discusses this topic and the Supreme Court of Canada's decision that the federal government's proposal for a national securities regulator was illegal because securities regulation is a shared responsibility with the provinces.

---

finance INTHENEWS 17-3　Why Is a National Securities Watchdog So Controversial?

THE SUPREME COURT ruled on December 22 that the federal government's attempt to create a single Canadian securities regulator is "not valid" under the Constitution.

What is the issue?
Canada is one of the few G8 countries that doesn't have an umbrella agency that governs companies that want to sell stocks or issue bonds or other financial products to the public.

Since he took office in 2006, Finance Minister Jim Flaherty has advocated for a national securities watchdog. He argues that such an agency would be more "comprehensive" and effective than the disparate collection of provincial regulators in stopping Earl Jones-style Ponzi schemes and other financial frauds that have arisen in Canada in the past few years.

Why is this controversial?
Regulating the stock and commodities markets is currently the jurisdiction of the 10 provinces and three territories.

A number of provinces and territories, including Ontario, are on board with Flaherty's proposal. There are several holdouts, however, which is why the finance minister has sought agreement from the Supreme Court.

What the Supreme Court delivered on December 22 was an "advisory opinion" on the legality of establishing a national securities regulator without the approval of all provinces and territories.

Who's in favour of a national securities regulator?
Among the provinces, Ontario is the main proponent, while others have voiced varying degrees of support. The idea also has the backing of much of the Canadian business community, including the Canadian Bankers Association, as well as international bodies like the Organization for Economic Co-operation and Development (OECD) and the International Monetary Fund (IMF).

Supporters say a national securities regulator will help discourage white-collar crime by making enforcement much more effective.

Who's opposed?
Alberta and Quebec are the main holdouts, saying they don't want to lose control of their local economies to a federal agency. Lower courts in both of those provinces have already ruled that Ottawa is overstepping its bounds in trying to set up the national body.

What did the Supreme Court say?
In its opinion on Flaherty's proposal, the court ruled that the Proposed Canadian Securities Act "is not valid" under the Constitution.

"In submitting this proposal, the Canadian government invoked its general trade and commerce power under section 91(2) of the Constitution." The court ruled, however, that this power "cannot be used in a way that denies the provincial legislatures the power to regulate local matters and industries within their boundaries."

The court's opinion really comes down to one thing—namely, that the federal and provincial governments have a shared desire to protect investors, promote fairness and competition, and ensure stability in the markets. As a result, the court sees no need for "a wholesale takeover of the regulation of the securities industry which is the ultimate consequence of the proposed federal legislation."

Source: CBC News Online, "Why Is a National Securities Watchdog So Controversial?" December 22, 2011. Available at www.cbc.ca. Reprinted by permission.

Securities and Exchange Commission (SEC) a U.S. agency that is, in effect, a national securities regulator

As it stands today, the main regulators in Canada are the Ontario, British Columbia, and Quebec provincial securities commissions. However, when securities are sold in other provinces and territories, the issue must be cleared with their authorities as well. Similarly, securities regulation in the United States is a state responsibility, but so many issues in the United States are national in scope and cross state lines that the U.S. **Securities and Exchange Commission (SEC)** is, in effect, a national securities regulator. However, issues can be sold within a state if no out-of-state investors are involved. This raises the basic point that securities regulation is designed to protect investors in a specific jurisdiction, so the provincial and territorial authorities exert authority whenever its citizens are involved. This is the reason that scam artists in Toronto sold into the United States and not within Canada: it meant the Ontario Securities Commission (OSC) was not directly involved. For the same reason, a majority of Internet fraud now seems to come from Russia, where regulation is lax.

A security, according to the *Ontario Securities Act (OSA)*, includes "any document, investment, or writing commonly known as a security,"[9] such as bonds and common equities. The critical fact is that the list is not exhaustive. In practice, the OSC and other provincial and territorial securities commissions aim to protect investors not just from fraud but also from "the imposition of unsubstantial schemes"—that is, misleading and bad investments.

In determining whether a security exists, the OSC looks at several factors, including the following:

- whether the promoter raises money and leads the investor to expect a profit
- whether the investor has any control on how the money is spent
- whether there is risk involved

Other factors are also important, but these are the major ones, and taking a broad interpretation of these criteria implies that almost any document can be construed as a security. For example, securities have been found to exist when a half interest in a pair of royal chinchillas was sold, when warehouse receipts were sold to indicate ownership of casks of whiskey, and when leases were sold that gave drilling rights. The critical point seems to be the protection of the public interest, and courts have taken a broad view of what this interest is.

A classic case involved Pacific Coast Coin Exchange of Canada (PCCE), which sold silver on a 35 percent margin (that is, purchasers put up only 35 percent of the money for the silver). Purchasers could then sell the silver back to PCCE; pay interest on the loan, storage, and handling charges; and receive the difference (positive or negative) in the price of silver. PCCE promoted its business, emphasizing silver as a store of value during a highly inflationary period.[10] The OSC shut down PCCE's operations because it was in violation of the OSA, a decision that the Supreme Court of Canada confirmed. Although PCCE's operations did not technically meet the definition of a security as it then existed, the Supreme Court stated that the important point was the policy behind the legislation, and that "substance not form" dictated whether or not something was a security. All that is necessary for the OSC to claim jurisdiction is that a transaction has an effect on Ontario residents sufficient to prejudice the public interest.

This broad interpretation of what constitutes a security and where securities laws can be applied means that the OSC is involved in five major areas in which securities are transferred or traded:

- *primary market offerings* (where money is raised directly from investors by the company)
- *secondary market trading* (where existing securities are traded between investors)
- *activities of investment professionals* (where professionals are trading or advising on these securities and thereby affecting market prices)
- *insider trading* (where people who have privileged information about a company, not available to the general public, are buying or selling shares at prices that do not reflect their true value)
- *takeover bids* (where shareholders are being asked to sell their shares to a purchaser)

---

[9] See the OSC's current investigations and rules at its website, www.osc.gov.on.ca. This section is heavily based on MacIntosh, Jeffrey, and Christopher Nicholls, *Securities Law*. Toronto: Irwin Law, 2002; and Nicholls, Christopher, *Corporate Finance and Canadian Law*. Toronto: Carswell, 2000.

[10] The case was settled in 1978, and the 1970s saw inflation at double-digit levels.

The broad definition of a trade is a *sale* of a security for valuable consideration. It also includes the activities of traders on an organized exchange, registrants who take orders to buy and sell securities, and any "act, advert, solicitation, conduct or negotiation to directly or indirectly further a trade." Traders and individuals registered to buy and sell securities (i.e., registrants) are regulated; however, given the broad scope of what constitutes a security, many individuals are traders and do not realize it. For example, lottery tickets sold at the corner store could be regarded as securities, with the storekeeper required to register with the OSC. However, the fact that lotteries are well known, with no public interest issues involved, means that, in practice, they are not treated as securities.[11]

Security Offerings

The other main implication of the definition of a trade is the promotion aspect. Anyone who phones someone to generate a sale is involved in trading, as is any website that promotes particular securities. Moreover, the OSC has broad powers to restrict such activity before a trade is effected, meaning that documents used to generate sales of securities are highly regulated. The most significant area involves **initial public offerings (IPOs)** of securities, because the assumption is that information asymmetry is greatest with IPOs. IPO trades are "primary offerings"—that is, they are a first-time distribution of securities. Most provinces in Canada, including Ontario, have a closed system for the distribution of securities. What this means is that any distribution of securities has to be accompanied by a **prospectus**, a formal summary of the security that describes the costs, investment objectives, and risks involved. It is illegal to distribute securities without delivering a prospectus to the purchaser. The system is "closed" because there are a limited number of *exemptions* from the prospectus requirement.

There are two types of prospectuses: long form and short form. For IPOs, a firm has to have a **long-form prospectus** that consists of many pages of dense discussion about the firm.[12] The overriding requirement is that the prospectus supply "full, true and plain disclosure of all material facts relating to the securities proposed to be distributed." This definition has important components. The "full, true and plain" means that it has to be understandable (not in "legalese") and it must correctly portray the situation of the firm. Further, every "material fact" has to be disclosed. A material fact is something that can reasonably be expected to affect the price of the securities being distributed. This also means that half-truths, even if they are technically correct, and omissions do not represent full, true, and plain disclosure. The prospectus has to be signed by both the chief executive officer (CEO) and the chief financial officer (CFO) on behalf of the issuing firm's board of directors (BOD) and the investment dealer helping to sell the securities. This makes all signatories liable for damages in the event of misrepresentation.[13]

The possibility of a lawsuit is what ensures that the investment dealer and the issuing firm do a comprehensive job of explaining the firm's position. This involves performing their due diligence, defined earlier, and doing a reasonable investigation of the facts to ensure that there has been no material misrepresentation. The standard applied is "that required of a prudent person in the circumstances of the particular case." The investment dealers and the lawyers preparing the prospectus have to check and recheck the statements made by the issuing firm to assure themselves that the prospectus fairly represents the firm's position.[14]

---

[11] The fact that only about 35 percent of the gross proceeds from lotteries are returned as payouts should be a concern. In Ponzi's scheme, the eventual liquidation of his "business" resulted in about a 35 percent payout as well.

[12] All legal documents in Canada can be retrieved from the OSC's System for Electronic Document Analysis and Retrieval (SEDAR) website at www.sedar.com. Investors can search for both long-form and short-form prospectuses.

[13] Before *Sarbanes-Oxley (SOX)*, discussed in Chapter 3, the standard advice was not to trust the annual report but, instead, look to the last prospectus, because an investor could sue for misrepresentation in the prospectus but not in the annual report. This is still true for Canadian companies that are not subject to SOX.

[14] This does not mean that the prospectus includes "full, true and plain disclosure of all material facts." If the firm deliberately wants to commit fraud, then even diligent work by the investment dealer and its lawyers may not uncover it.

The British Columbia Securities Commission (BCSC) has a 66-page document dictating what has to be included in a prospectus.[15] Broadly speaking, this document says that a prospectus must contain the following information:

- a description of the securities being issued and who can buy them

- the price of the securities, the fees to the investment dealer involved with the distribution, and the net proceeds

- the market for the securities—that is, whether they will be traded

- the business of the issuer and its subsidiaries, with a discussion of the past three-year history

- risk factors involved with buying the securities

- summary financial information

- management's discussion and analysis

Under each of these general groupings are extensive lists of what needs to be discussed, as well as specific requirements for different types of distributions, such as those by mining firms or mutual funds. It is easy to understand, from reviewing the BCSC document, why the cost of preparing a prospectus is at least $500,000 for a $20-million offering. Despite the cost, a prospectus is required for all distributions.

The OSC has determined that there are three types of distributions. The first is a distribution by an issuer. The assumption here is that the issuer is raising money in the primary market from investors and, by definition, knows more about the true value of the securities than the investors do. Hence, the prospectus is designed to remedy this information asymmetry. Imagine, for example, if Carlo Ponzi had had to describe his business with a "full, true, and plain" disclosure, and an investment bank and legal firm had to sign off on his prospectus.

The second type of distribution is one being sold from a control block.[16] The assumption here is that someone owning a control block also has privileged access to the firm; as a result, there is an information asymmetry that the prospectus is designed to remedy. In this case, a prospectus has to be prepared even if the firm is raising no money; this is an example of a secondary market transaction rather than a primary market transaction. Again, the fact the firm has to bear this cost is not a factor. What is important is that investors buying the securities are protected.

The third type of distribution is one in which restricted shares are being sold to the public for the first time.

As indicated above, a prospectus is required for most distributions of securities. In the process, the securities are registered, which means that trades in the securities can be effected by a securities firm that is registered with the appropriate securities commission. In this way, the Canadian Depository for Securities (CDS) is normally the registered owner of the securities, and trades in the securities are effected by means of computer (book) entries. What this means is that the prospectus requirement goes hand in hand with the registration of the securities, which allows them to be subsequently bought and sold in the public markets. Without a prospectus, the securities are not registered and cannot be publicly traded. The market for non-registered securities is called the **exempt market**.

If a firm wants to raise a small amount of money, preparing a $500,000 prospectus and engaging an investment dealer to distribute the securities does not make much sense. As a result, there are exemptions from the prospectus requirement based on smaller issues, the sophistication of the potential investors, and the low-risk nature of the securities. To prevent

exempt market the unregulated market for non-registered securities that raise money from private investors

---

[15] BC Securities Commission, *BC Form 41-601F: Information Required in a Prospectus*. This form is on the commission's website at www.bcsc.bc.ca.

[16] Control blocks are not defined in law. Clearly, 50.1 percent effects legal control, but a prospectus may also be required to distribute smaller blocks, even down to 5 percent, if there are grounds for believing that there is inside information.

securities that are sold in the exempt market from slipping into the public markets—what is called "backdoor underwriting"—the exempt purchasers can sell only to other exempt purchasers. Under certain circumstances, they can sell the securities in the public market after holding them for a certain time,[17] if the issuer has effectively met the prospectus requirements by becoming a "reporting issuer," which will be discussed later.

offering memorandum a document with the same objectives as a prospectus but that provides significantly less information, which lowers the cost of preparing it

For the exempt market, the issuer normally prepares an **offering memorandum**, rather than a prospectus. Although both of these documents have the same objective and have to be correct, the amount of information in an offering memorandum is significantly less, which lowers the cost of preparing it.[18]

The sophisticated purchasers of the exempt market are essentially individuals and institutions that can be expected to hire their own experts to conduct the necessary due diligence. For example, securities can be sold without a prospectus to accredited investors, such as banks, governments, wealthy investors (net assets of more than $1 million and $300,000 a year in family income), investment dealers, and individuals owning control blocks.

Similarly, government debt issues are exempt, as are the debt issues of many financial institutions. Finally, securities issued as part of a takeover or corporate reorganization are exempt because they are covered by corporate law requirements to provide proxy circulars and similar documents.

The only other major exemption is for private firms, now called "closely held issuers." As long as no promotion is done and less than $3 million is raised, securities can be sold to no more than 35 individuals with the approval of the BOD. In this case, the issue has to be accompanied by an information statement containing basic information about the issuer.

Although securities regulations are comprehensive, they cannot prevent all possible abuses. One major area of concern involves situations where companies change their strategy and their operations. Although such changes are revealed through mandatory disclosures, it is possible, through a takeover of a firm that has reduced its operations, to bypass the IPO process and thereby avoid a long-form prospectus. Such a reverse takeover also means that a private firm can buy a publicly traded firm and thereby acquire a listing on the Toronto Stock Exchange (TSX). This is also often called a "backdoor" listing, where, after the takeover, the name of the listed firm is usually changed and it enters a completely different line of business. This became a major issue when a Chinese firm, Sino-Forest, acquired a TSX listing through a reverse takeover. The price of shares in Sino-Forest increased dramatically as the company was thought to control vast acreages of land in China. However, as *Finance in the News 17-4* discusses, an analyst report questioned the extent of the holdings of Sino-Forest and drew attention to its governance.

finance INTHENEWS 17-4   Questions Linger As Panel Winds Up Sino-Forest Probe

A FINAL REPORT into fraud allegations at Sino-Forest Corp left many questions unanswered, with scant new detail on the value of its timber holdings or its opaque ties with suppliers.

The report by an internal committee, released late on Tuesday, is unlikely to pacify investors, who have been clamoring for answers since June, when short-seller Carson Block and his Muddy Waters firm likened the Canadian-listed Sino-Forest to a "Ponzi scheme" and accused it of inflating the size of its Chinese forestry assets.

Regulators and law enforcement officials are investigating the company, which denies the allegations. Sino-Forest said in November that preliminary evidence from its internal probe had found no evidence of fraud.

In its final report, the committee admitted it has failed to answer all the questions on the company's business practices in China, including ones about related-party transactions and the valuation of its forestry holdings.

"I don't think the report addresses most of the issues highlighted in

continued

---

[17] Normal hold periods are four months to two years, after which the securities are regarded as seasoned.

[18] In some cases, the OSA requires an offering memorandum, which is delivered to the OSC but is not publicly available. In other cases, the issuer decides, or the investment dealer insists, on the preparation of an offering memorandum to help market the issue.

Finance in the News 17-4: Questions Linger As Panel Winds Up Sino-Forest Probe*(continued)*

the last one and restores investors' confidence; it looks like it's just trying to meet the deadline," said Annisa Lee, Asia credit analyst at Nomura in Hong Kong.

"The valuation of the assets has not been done, which is one of the key things because this is crucial to determine the valuation of the company."

Sino-Forest shares fell more than 70 percent in the two days after the Muddy Waters report, and trade in the stock was halted in August. Canada's top securities regulator recently extended the cease trade order to April 16.

In a highly technical 13-page report, the panel of lawyers and auditors said it had not been able to assess whether Sino-Forest had a proper "arm's length" relationship with the owners of land on which it had contractual rights over the timber and businesses to whom it sold its wood.

"There remain issues which have not been fully answered," the report said. The probe was "at the point of diminishing returns, because much of the information which it is seeking lies with non-compellable third parties, may not exist or is apparently not retrievable from the records of the company."

Nomura's Lee said the report had not addressed the very close relationship between the company and its suppliers and customers, a key allegation from Muddy Waters.

"Without doing this, I don't think investors will have the confidence to conclude that there were no related-party transactions," he said.

Reverse Takeover

Sino-Forest was founded in the 1990s by Hong Kong entrepreneur Allen Chan and listed in Toronto through a reverse takeover of a dormant Canadian firm, a practice since criticized as a way to circumvent the more rigorous regulatory standards of a new share offering.

It is the most prominent of the Chinese companies listed in North America whose shares were suspended or delisted last year amid suspicions about their business practices and Chinese regulatory safeguards.

The firm had agreed with its debt holders it would make its final report by January 31.

Sino-Forest's bondholders have greater influence over the company since earlier this month, when they agreed not to force it into default following a covenant breach related to its failure to release third-quarter results.

Sino-Forest also said it intended to vigorously defend a class action lawsuit brought against it in the United States.

The class action, filed in New York state on Friday, was brought on behalf of investors who bought Sino-Forest shares on the over-the-counter market and non-Canadian buyers of Sino-Forest debt securities. It targets current and former management, along with auditor Ernst & Young and underwriters Bank of America and Credit Suisse.

The company is already facing a possible class action lawsuit in Canada.

The panel looked at two of Sino-Forest's Chinese forestry concessions in a sampling exercise and found the company's statements of its assets to be accurate to within 6 percent. But it said it could not extrapolate those findings to Sino-Forest's broader forestry assets.

The two parcels represent less than 150 hectares of the more than 800,000 hectares of timber Sino-Forest has said it controls.

Sino-Forest said it has engaged Singapore-based consultancy Stewart Murray to assist it in verifying and valuing its entire forestry assets.

Source: Prasad, Sakthi, and Rachel Armstrong, "Questions Linger as Panel Winds up Sino-Forest Probe." CNBC.com, February 1, 2012.

Sino-Forest was, at the time, the most prominent Chinese firm listed on a North American stock exchange, but after the report its stock price crashed by 70 percent, triggering a round of lawsuits against all the parties involved, including its auditors Ernst & Young and the investment banks that helped sell its shares, including Bank of America and Credit Suisse.

Securities legislation has come a long way since the days of Carlo Ponzi. The definition of a security is now so broad as to cover any attempt to sell an interest in something to someone with an expectation of making a profit. All such distributions must be accompanied by a prospectus, unless they are sold into the exempt market by means of what is referred to as a "private placement." The prospectus is designed to minimize problems of information asymmetry so that Ponzi schemes and other frauds are rare and so that investors will have confidence in the public markets. This confidence is encouraged by the breadth and depth of the information required in a prospectus and the fact that almost everyone involved in its production can be sued if there are material misrepresentations. The restrictions on "hyping" securities while they are being issued and the requirement that professionals involved in their subsequent trading be registered are both designed to enhance the confidence in secondary as well as primary markets.

However, the legal system is constantly having to react to the dynamic nature of financial markets. One particular change is that investors are increasingly diversifying internationally, and stock markets are also globalizing as they compete for listings and trading. It is only a little over 10 years ago that we had four "largish" stock exchanges in Canada, whereas now we have only one and that one was almost taken over by the London Stock Exchange in 2011.[19] In response to this competition among exchanges, the Toronto Stock Exchange has tried to position itself as a resource-based exchange and has actively sought out non-Canadian firms to list. The Sino-Forest situation has alerted securities regulators to the problems arising from the fact that making these firms accessible to Canadian investors means they have to abide by the same disclosure and governance rules of Canadian firms. This can be difficult and expensive given that their operations are often thousands of miles away.

Finance in the News 17-5 discusses a review by the OSC, which stated that firms from emerging markets have to abide by Canadian securities laws if they are to list in Canada and sell shares to the Canadian public. The overriding objective of Canadian securities regulators is to protect Canadians and ensure that they have faith in any securities offered to them, whether they are from Canadian or non-Canadian firms. This means non-Canadian companies can't use reverse takeovers to bypass securities regulations and the due diligence process designed to protect Canadians. In the sections below, we will discuss the IPO process, where this due diligence is at its highest level; why firms choose to go public rather than sell securities through a private placement or the exempt market; and how ongoing supervision of firms is carried out after they have filed their initial long-form prospectus.

---

finance INTHENEWS 17-5 | OSC Aims to Improve Compliance for Emerging Market Issuers

THE ONTARIO SECURITIES COMMISSION (OSC) is proposing a series of recommendations for issuers, underwriters, and auditors aimed at improving compliance for companies that are largely based overseas, but are listed on Canadian markets.

The review, which the OSC launched in July 2011 following the revelation of apparent disclosure problems at China-based forestry firm, Sino-Forest Corp., examines a sample of 24 issuers listed on Canadian exchanges that have significant business operations in emerging markets. The regulator focused on the adequacy of issuer disclosure and corporate governance practices, as well as the roles played by auditors, underwriters and exchanges in bringing these issuers to market.

No specific policy actions are recommended as a result of the review. Instead, it identifies a variety of areas of regulatory concern, including issues related to the quality of emerging market issuer governance and disclosure, the adequacy of the audit function, the adequacy of the due diligence conducted by underwriters in these sorts of offerings, and the nature of the exchange listing approval process.

"One of our central concerns was the apparent 'form over substance' approach to compliance with applicable standards for disclosure, issuer governance, board oversight, audit practices and due diligence practices," the report says. "In our view, the level of rigor and independent-mindedness applied by boards, auditors and underwriters in doing their important jobs—management oversight, audit, due diligence on offerings—should have been more thorough."

One of the basic reasons that auditor and underwriter due diligence appears to be lacking is the fact that the core operations and assets of many of the issuers are located in emerging markets, and the firms have very little presence in Canada, it notes. A lack of understanding of local business practices, language barriers, and translation issues, also contributed to these problems, it says.

The review found several areas of potential concern for auditors including a lack of professional skepticism, a lack of knowledge about local cultural and business practices, too much delegation to foreign auditors, difficulty in obtaining domestic auditor working papers, and language barriers.

Similarly, for underwriters, the review found wide variation in due diligence practices and documentation, and a lack of professional skepticism and rigor, among other things. "We noted several instances where 'red flags' should have prompted further probing or questions. Our review indicated little or no follow-up in these instances to either understand or analyze the concerns, or disclose them," it says.

In terms of exchanges, the review says that no particular form of listing, whether by IPO, reverse takeover, or direct listing, was specifically problematic. It did have concerns though, including whether additional listing requirements for emerging market issuers are necessary, a lack of transparency when exchanges waive certain listing requirements, and a heavy reliance on third parties in conducting due diligence.

The report says that the OSC will follow up with issuers, auditors, and underwriters in areas that it has identified for improvement, and that some issues uncovered in the review have been referred to enforcement. It also says that it will continue to work with the Canadian Public Accountability Board to address audit related concerns, with staff at the exchanges to address concerns related to the listing process, and with the Investment Industry Regulatory Organization of Canada on underwriting practices.

continued

---

[19] The "merger" between the TSX and LSE was killed on June 29, 2011, when it failed to get enough shareholder approval in the face of a rival bid from a consortium of Canadian financial institutions.

Finance in the News 17-5: OSC Aims to Improve Compliance for Emerging Market Issuers (continued)

The report proposes a list of recommendations, which it says do not necessarily require the creation of new policies or rules, but instead involve the development of guidance, best practices or enhanced vigilance to improve compliance with current requirements.

For issuers, this includes guidance to improve corporate governance practices, clarifying the regulatory expectations of CEOs and CFOs in conducting reasonable due diligence, better disclosure of complex corporate structures, better risk disclosure, ensuring the maintenance of appropriate books and records in Canada, the possibility of imposing a minimum language competency component for board members in the firm's local language, and possible minimum Canadian director residency requirements.

For auditors, it calls for improved access to audit working papers; examining whether securities rules need to be enhanced to allow more information sharing for the oversight of audit firms, whether suitability standards for auditors should be developed, and whether auditors should be required to publicly disclose and explain their resignation from a file. It also calls for greater cooperation among securities regulators and audit oversight bodies.

For underwriters, the report recommends: establishing a consistent and transparent set of requirements for the conduct of due diligence, developing best practices for documenting due diligence, and best practices for due diligence calls and site visits.

Finally, it says that the exchanges will need to assess whether additional listing requirements are needed, provide greater transparency regarding waivers of any listing requirements, assess the extent of reliance on third parties in conducting due diligence and whether additional due diligence steps are warranted, and review the role of sponsors in bringing issuers to market, "to ensure that there is adequate accountability placed on the sponsor and if there is an appropriate level of transparency regarding the sponsor's due diligence work."

"The OSC expects issuers and gatekeepers to act in a manner that promotes investor protection and supports confidence in our capital markets," said Howard Wetston, chair and CEO of the OSC.

Source: Langton, James, "OSC aims to improve compliance for emerging market issuers." *Investment Executive*, March 20, 2012. Available at www.investmentexecutive.com. Reprinted by permission.

CONCEPT REVIEW QUESTIONS

1. What are some of the more important issues arising from the fact that securities regulation is a provincial and territorial, not a federal, responsibility in Canada?

2. Why are prospectuses so important for public market issues?

3. Explain how offering memorandums differ from prospectuses and how exempt markets differ from public markets.

4. What is a reverse takeover and a backdoor listing?

17.3 IPOS AND INVESTMENT BANKING

The Motivation for IPOs

The principles that we have discussed apply to all public offerings of securities, whether they are debt or common equity securities and whether or not this is the first time such securities have been offered. In this section, we discuss a particularly important public offering of securities: namely, offering common shares to the public for the first time (i.e., an IPO). Although it is not strictly necessary, such public offerings are almost always listed on an organized exchange, such as the Toronto Stock Exchange (TSX) or TSX Venture Exchange, which allows these shares to be easily traded.

Most firms that "go public" have had this as a long-term goal for many years before they actually become a publicly traded company. The response to a Conference Board of Canada survey indicates that firms have several reasons for going public.[20] One of the most frequently cited reasons is the desire on the part of some investors to "cash out." Sometimes this is a way

Learning Objective 17.4
Outline the basic stages in taking a firm public through an initial public offering (IPO) of securities.

---

[20] For some case histories see Andrews, Michael, *Initial Public Offerings: The Experience of Eight Canadian Growth Companies.* Ottawa: Conference Board of Canada, 1995.

to pay off private equity investors and other venture capitalists who financed the firm in its earlier stages of development. At other times, the founders of the company might want to cash out if they are no longer actively involved in managing the company. As we discussed in Chapter 2, an *agency relationship* exists when people hire someone else to execute their wishes. In this respect, managers are agents for the owners of the firm. As a firm grows, it makes the switch from being an owner-managed firm to one that has a *separation* of ownership from control (which is what normally happens when a firm goes public). The managers then face the choice of either selling the company to someone else privately or going public and combining a sale of shares by the company with the sale of the founders' shares. In this situation, an important part of going public is the fact that a market price exists and shareholders can evaluate and liquidate their investment more easily.

Other firms go public because they want access to a more diversified set of financing options. In particular, two often-expressed motives are to escape dependence on bank lending and to increase the use of common equity as an acquisition currency. We discussed the closed system of securities regulation in the previous section, but if a firm wants to buy another firm through an exchange of shares, the purchasing firm's ability to exchange shares is restricted, unless it is publicly traded, because the shares are not registered and can only be sold to exempt purchasers and not to the general public. This lack of liquidity in the stock makes the firm's shares unattractive as a means of financing takeovers. As discussed in Chapter 15, any firm making extensive acquisitions will find it advantageous to have publicly traded shares.

It is also important to recognize that many private firms are extremely dependent on their bank for financing. Even if they have a good relationship with their bank, there is a perception that this relationship improves after they go public. This may be due to the belief that being a "listed company" has significant value. The listing of a firm's shares on a major exchange, coupled with the prospectus requirement, dramatically increases the flow of information about the firm, which the bank may find comforting. Several respondents to the Conference Board of Canada study reported that the relationships with suppliers and customers did improve as a result of a public listing, which provides a kind of "seal of approval" that the firm has arrived.

The reasons given by the participants in the Conference Board's eight case studies are broadly consistent with the ideas advanced by Stewart Myers.[21] Myers also emphasizes the use of the stock price as an incentive mechanism to enhance managerial efficiency.

Suppose, for example, we divide a new firm's development into five stages:

1. technological experimentation

2. pilot studies and sales

3. improvement in production and scaling up manufacturing

4. full-scale marketing and production

5. expansion into other lines

These five stages roughly correspond to the product life cycle discussed in strategy classes. What Myers added is the need to provide incentive for the founders and reward them for their industry and innovation, which will vary across the product life cycle.

In Myers' view, the entrepreneur is essential at stages 1 and 2, valuable at stage 3, useful but replaceable at stage 4, and not needed at all at stage 5. So suppose at stages 1 and 2 the entrepreneur is willing to commit "sweat equity" and all his or her savings to the enterprise but needs some external finance. The company can't raise external equity at this stage, because the informational problems are too large. Instead, the firm raises **private equity** or **venture capital** from a partner. In this way, the funds are provided from the exempt market.

private equity or **venture capital**
money raised from private investors in the exempt market

---

[21] Myers, Stewart, "Financial Architecture." *European Financial Management* 5, no. 2 (1999), pp. 133–41.

The entrepreneur, as well as the partner, then needs a commitment to go public at either stage 3 or certainly by stage 4, as the proportion of intellectual or human capital versus real capital in the value of the firm goes down. Essentially, if the venture is successful after stage 2, then the entrepreneur's value has been validated by an increase in the value of the firm. Yet at this stage, significant external funds are needed to formalize the firm's business plan and buy real assets. This is the ideal point to take the firm public so the investment by the entrepreneur or founder and backers can be monetized. Otherwise, the value will be diluted by the new funds raised to take the firm to the next stage. Also at this stage, the entrepreneur is no longer as important to the firm as it moves into a classic production mode with a formal managerial culture, with less need to provide incentive on the creative side of the business.

Myers was writing at the time of the Internet bubble and was clearly influenced by the large number of hi-tech firms going public at that time. The basic idea is consistent with **agency theory**—the study of relationships between shareholders and a company's managers and the costs of resolving conflicts between them and aligning their interests—and with the observation that private firms involve a higher proportion of "intellectual" capital. Such firms go public when the proportion of intellectual capital is less important and when they face increased financing needs. The corollary is that firms with little need to provide incentives for management have less need to go public. It is hardly surprising, for example, that utility firms, like the local water company, are run under private (normally municipal) management; they have less need to motivate management to be efficient and create value. (There may be other reasons, however, such as external monitoring.)

Agency theory also explains why divisions are sometimes spun off from larger firms. Entrepreneurial activity cannot be properly rewarded within a large firm when there is little correspondence between the effort expended by entrepreneurial managers and the value they create. In contrast, entrepreneurial activity is often stimulated in a wave of innovation as a division is spun off from a bureaucratic parent company, and the managers start focusing on creating enough value to take the firm public.

Going public can thus be seen as a longer-term objective of many firms to monetize the value created by the founders when their value to the firm starts to wane, and the firm moves to stage 3 or 4. Even before this point, the firm will have been in constant contact with its investment dealer as it sought different sources of financing.

agency theory the study of relationships between shareholders and a company's managers and the costs of resolving conflicts between them and aligning their interests

The Stages of the IPO Process

A typical IPO involves four basic stages and normally involves an investment dealer (or investment bank in the United States) that specializes in raising capital for firms and being their "eyes and ears" on the capital market. The first stage involves the initial discussion with the investment dealer, which then triggers the formal IPO process. The second stage consists of drafting an initial prospectus. The third stage, commonly called the waiting period, involves finalizing the prospectus and obtaining clearance from the securities commission. The final stage involves pricing and distributing the issue and providing after-market stabilization. The process is illustrated in Figure 17-1.

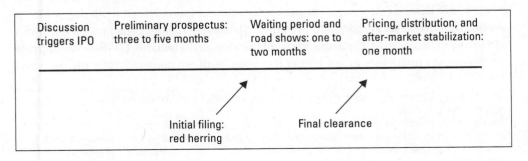

FIGURE 17-1 *The Stages of an IPO*

The First Stage: Discussion

The Conference Board of Canada survey referred to earlier indicates that, in this first phase of going public, the firm will use its existing investment dealer but will frequently add other dealers to broaden the distribution of its shares and increase the number of analysts who will subsequently follow, and make recommendations on, the firm. At this early stage, the firm will also "clean up" its legal structure by removing different classes of shares, changing its bylaws and its board of directors, and generally making itself more marketable.

The Second Stage: Preliminary Prospectus

The second phase involves preparing the **preliminary prospectus**,[22] a document produced for prospective investors by an underwriter, with the understanding that it may be modified significantly before the final prospectus is published. This usually takes from three to five months to complete. It is this stage that illustrates a Catch-22. The investment dealer would like to do some pre-marketing to gauge the amount of interest in the company. However, promoting and discussing the sale of shares is regarded as trading, and this cannot happen until a prospectus has been delivered. Consequently, the firm will normally sign a "letter of intent" with its investment dealer, indicating that the firm will cover all out-of-pocket costs as the dealer helps it prepare a preliminary prospectus. During this period, the firm, its lawyers, and the investment dealer are not allowed to hype or promote the stock, and communications with the public have to remain unchanged. Further, the investment dealer has to restrict the flow of information.

It is at this stage that the firm and the investment dealer decide on the broad type and terms of the public offering. They can choose from four different types of public offerings: a **best efforts offering**, a **firm commitment offering**, a **bought deal**, and a **standby** or **rights offering**. The last two can only be used with seasoned offerings, and most IPOs are firm commitment offerings. In a best efforts offering, the investment dealer signs an agency agreement to do its best to sell the shares, with no guarantee of success. The investment dealer is rewarded on the basis of the shares that it sells—that is, it is paid a certain amount for each share it sells. Such offerings are rare, because firms do not like the uncertainty attached to the process. If this is the only option that is available to the firm after it contacts several investment dealers, it may be a warning sign that the firm should not go public. Occasionally, a firm commitment offering will be converted into a best efforts offering after the investment dealer discovers there is limited investor interest.

In a firm commitment offering, the investment dealer buys the new securities from the issuer and guarantees the sale of a certain number, while in a bought deal, the underwriter buys all the shares of a seasoned issue to resell later, even before the drafting of the preliminary prospectus. In a standby or rights offering, common shares are offered at a discount to investors who already own shares.

The standard IPO contract is a firm commitment arrangement in which the investment dealer buys the shares for a fixed price and resells them to the public at a slightly higher price, thus earning profits on this **spread** (i.e., the difference between the purchase and reselling price). In this case, the investment dealer **underwrites** or guarantees the offering, which is why investment dealers are commonly referred to as *underwriters*.[23] Larger issues will have a **lead investment dealer** that manages the whole process, and a **banking (or dealer) syndicate** that is formed temporarily to sell part of the issue. Both groups underwrite the issue and

---

preliminary prospectus a document produced for prospective investors by an underwriter, with the understanding that it may be modified significantly before the final prospectus is published

best efforts offering an offering in which an investment dealer signs an agency agreement to do its best to sell shares, but with no guarantee of success; investment dealers are paid a certain amount for each share they sell

firm commitment offering an offering in which the investment dealer buys the new securities from the issuer and guarantees the sale of a certain number

bought deal an offering in which the underwriter buys all the shares of a seasoned issue to resell later, even before the drafting of the preliminary prospectus

standby or **rights offering** an offering of common shares at a discount to investors who already own shares; can only be used with seasoned offerings

spread the difference between the price at which an investment dealer buys shares and the slightly higher price at which they are resold to the public

underwrite to assume risk by guaranteeing an offering

lead investment dealer a securities firm that manages the process of selling larger issues

banking (or dealer) syndicate a group formed temporarily to jointly underwrite and sell a new security offering

---

[22] The preliminary prospectus is often called a "red herring" because of the notice in red type, required by law on the first page, indicating its status.

[23] Canadian investment banks are often called investment dealers, as discussed in Chapter 2, because the use of the term "bank" was restricted under the *Bank Act* in Canada. Because most of the dealers are now owned by the chartered banks, the use of the American term "investment bank" is becoming more common, although we still use "investment dealer" throughout most of our discussion.

guarantee the proceeds to the firm. However, sometimes an investment dealer joins as part of the **selling group** on a best efforts basis, and any shares it cannot sell are returned to the banking syndicate.

The compensation to the investment dealer comes from the standard 4 percent underwriting fee, based on the gross proceeds of the issue,[24] and the difference between the price the dealer pays the issuer for the shares and the price at which the dealer sells them to the public. The **Investment Industry Regulatory Organization of Canada (IIROC)**, the national self-regulatory organization of the Canadian securities industry, enforces rule 29.2 on business conduct, which expressly prohibits selling securities at a price higher than that provided in the prospectus during the course of the distribution.

The underwriting agreement includes standard clauses that provide the issuer with the authority to issue the securities, require it to prepare a prospectus, prevent it from issuing any other securities while the underwriting is underway, and obligate it to pay the underwriter. The contract also stipulates when the securities will be transferred to the underwriter and when the underwriter will pay the issuer. This payment is normally conditional on a **market or disaster "out" clause**.[25] If the state of the financial markets deteriorates so much that the underwriter cannot market the issue profitably, then the issue can be cancelled. This is clearly a huge safety net for the underwriter, but "deterioration" in the state of the market has not been clearly defined. The B.C. Supreme Court stated that the market out clause referred to the state of the issuing company's shares and not the market generally. Like many legal interpretations, this one has yet to be tested in other cases, but if this holds, it lessens the value of a firm commitment offering and brings it closer to a best efforts offering.

Another standard underwriting clause is an **overallotment or "green-shoe" option** that gives the underwriter the option of buying more shares from the issuer (usually 15 percent more) if investor demand is strong. Finally, many agreements also contain a **lock-up period** that prevents the founders of the company from selling their shares for a given time. Because cashing out the founding entrepreneur's or some other private equity investors' shares is a common motive for going public, as discussed above, the last thing the investment dealer wants is a large number of shares being sold just as it is marketing the issue. For this reason, the investment dealer almost always negotiates a lock-up period so that these shares cannot be sold for six months. The actual lock-up period depends on the investment dealer's assessment of how many of the existing common shares are likely to flood the market. If the number of shares is large, the dealer might impose a *phased* period in which only a certain percentage of the shares can be sold over certain intervals.

The Third Stage: The Waiting Period

Once the preliminary prospectus has been drafted, it is sent to the securities commission to be examined for any deficiencies. This third phase is generally called the **waiting period**, as the investment dealer and the issuer wait for final clearance to sell the securities. This period usually lasts at least three weeks. It is longer for IPOs because there is less information already available for them than there is for seasoned offerings.[26] During the waiting period, the underwriter can market the issue and collect "expressions of interest." However, the final price has not been set, so the underwriter indicates a range of possible prices, usually $2 apart, because it is illegal to sell the securities until the prospectus is final.

The marketing of the issue will involve "road shows" (or "dog and pony shows") to describe the issuer and the issue itself in the major financial cities where the issue will be marketed.[27]

selling group everyone who works to sell an issue

Investment Industry Regulatory Organization of Canada (IIROC) the national self-regulatory organization of the Canadian securities industry

market or disaster "out" clause a clause that gives the underwriter the right to cancel an issue if financial markets deteriorate so much that the underwriter cannot market the issue profitably

overallotment or "green-shoe" option a clause that gives the underwriter the option of buying more shares from the issuer if investor demand is strong

lock-up period a time during which the founders of the company are prohibited from selling their shares

waiting period the time after the preliminary prospectus has been drafted and sent to the securities commission to be examined for deficiencies, during which the investment dealer and the issuer wait for final clearance to sell the securities

---

[24] In the United States, the fee is 7 percent, as there is less competition among the investment banks.

[25] The difference between the two is the extent of deterioration in the markets and the amount of margin that the investment dealer is allowed to post. All investment dealers finance their inventory of securities with borrowings, mainly from the chartered banks.

[26] It is no longer the practice of the OSC, as it has been in the past, to examine every prospectus in detail.

[27] The prospectus needs to be cleared in each province and territory in which the securities will be sold.

Typically, exempt purchasers (i.e., the major financial institutions) will be contacted by different members of the selling group and invited to these presentations by senior management and the lead underwriter. Because it is important to the underwriter to sell the issue as quickly as possible, the focus is on institutional clients that can buy large blocks of shares. Significant retail investors may also be invited to attend, although this is less common now than in the past.

It is important to note that at this stage the "expressions of interest" are not firm orders. In the case of major institutions, the expressions of interest are usually in the form of **limit orders**, in which they indicate that they are willing to buy so many shares at a certain price. For retail investors, expressions of interest generally take the form of **market orders**, which means they are for fixed amounts of shares at whatever the final price is. This interaction between the investment dealer and the market is useful for setting the final terms of the issue and confirming that the issue can be sold.

If the securities commission finds any deficiencies in the prospectus, the issuer has a minimum of 10 days to rectify them—although it may take longer if the deficiencies are significant. Once the revised prospectus has been accepted by the commission, it becomes a final prospectus. The securities regulator will then issue a receipt, and the prospectus will be sent for printing. It is at this stage that the issuer and the investment dealer finalize their underwriting contract and meet to set the final price and quantity of shares being issued. Normally, the price is set after the market closes early in the week so that the issue can be sold quickly. As a guideline, the underwriter sets the price assuming that the issue will be at least twice oversubscribed, based on the earlier expressions of interest. In this way, the underwriter hopes that the price will rise above the issue price on the first day of trading. The fact that the price is expected to rise and generate short-run profits to the purchasers is partly why IPOs tend to be oversubscribed. The practice of short-term trading by buying IPOs is referred to as "stagging" the new issue and can be very profitable when many attractive issues come to the market.

The Fourth Stage: Distribution Period

Once the issue is cleared for sale by the securities regulator, the underwriters go into high gear to convert the expressions of interest into firm sales. This is the beginning of the fourth phase and is formally called the **distribution period**. Its length depends on the nature of the issue. Normally, the underwriter has to write a cheque to the issuer within three days or so of the issue as the issuer delivers the shares to the underwriter. The underwriter is under great pressure to sell the shares as quickly as possible. The issuer is under a continuing obligation to amend the prospectus if a material change occurs during the distribution. This obligation continues after the issuer is paid by the underwriter and only finishes when the underwriter has informed the issuer that the shares have been sold. This distribution period usually lasts about a month. During that time, the underwriter is under special restrictions.

The first restriction is that this is the "quiet" period. Essentially, all the relevant information should have been included in the prospectus, so the underwriter and issuer are both prohibited from hyping the stock to help sell it. The investment dealer, in particular, cannot issue an analyst report recommending the shares. Also during this period, the underwriters as a group are normally restricted from reducing the price—otherwise, one member of the group could dump its shares if market conditions deteriorate. Finally, the lead underwriter has the right to trade in the shares to maintain an orderly market and help make the issue successful.[28]

The basic way in which an underwriter supports the share price during the distribution period is through the overallotment option. First, the underwriter will try to sell more shares than are issued and will be short the stock if it is successful. In this case, the underwriter exercises its option and gets more shares from the company. However, under Canadian laws (and the laws of most other countries), investors have a two-day "cooling off" period and can

limit orders expressions of interest that are not firm orders but indications from major institutions of how much they are willing to buy at a certain price

market orders orders from retail investors for fixed amounts at whatever the final price is

distribution period the period after the issue has been cleared for sale by the securities commission, when the underwriters convert the expressions of interest into firm sales

---

[28] This is also the reason that the other members can't sell below the stated price; otherwise, they would be selling to the lead underwriter.

renege on an offer to purchase the shares. Alternatively, if the issue appears to be having trouble, many of the expressions of interest may disappear, and even those investors that honour their commitments may dump the shares if they learn that the issue is in trouble or if they want to take short-term profits.

The underwriter will quickly realize if an issue is in trouble as it makes a market in the stock and sees the selling pressure. Because the underwriter is short the stock, it can buy it back in the open market. This constant buying by the underwriter is what supports the price during the distribution period if the issue is "cold" or if shares are being dumped for short-term profits. If this price support is ineffective, then, after supporting the price, the underwriter will give up and the price will drift (sometimes quickly) lower. The underwriter will then take a loss or try to exercise its *market out* clause at the cost of its reputation.

Remember that all the investment dealer has before it begins selling the shares are expressions of interest. Given the common knowledge that there is a first-day run-up in the share price for IPOs, many investors order more shares than they want to hold for the long term. As a result, the investment dealer faces the risk that these expressions of interest either do not materialize as actual purchases or are quickly sold into the market. To counter this risk, the investment dealer tries to place as much of the issue as possible in the friendly hands of investors that have demonstrated they will honour their commitments and not cut and run. A corollary is that for cold issues, when large-scale institutional purchases dry up, the banking group is forced to turn to the retail or ordinary investor to try to sell the issue. When an investor gets a call from a retail broker selling an IPO, it is often a signal that the issue is cold and institutions have already turned it down.

IPO Underpricing

One controversial issue in the IPO process is the size of the first-day return earned by investors. If the investment dealer had a fiduciary duty to the issuer to get the best possible price for the issue, then nothing would happen on the issue day. However, the first-day return tends to be very high, meaning that the issuer could have sold at a higher price but, instead, "left money on the table." In other words, the IPO is priced at less than its market value, and the price on the first day of trading is much higher. This is referred to as **underpricing**. Jay Ritter has surveyed the literature on first-day underpricing in North America versus other countries and reports the first-day returns, shown in Table 17-1.

underpricing pricing an IPO at less than its market value; it is the difference between the initial offering price and the price on the first day of trading

These countries were chosen because their capital markets are very similar, based on external capital and English common law. What is of interest is that Canada's first-day return is by far the lowest, at 6.3 percent, and is about one-third of first-day returns in the United States. The first-day return of 6.3 percent is the lowest of any of the 38 countries sampled by Ritter except Denmark, where the sample was very limited.

When investment dealers are asked why underpricing is so low in Canada, they respond that there is too much competition for business in Canada, and Canadian firms do not need to tolerate high underpricing because they want the best price for their shares. In contrast, a number of reasons have been given for the underpricing in the United States, none of them entirely convincing. The most obvious is that it lowers the risk that the underwriter will lose money on the issue. However, this implies that the U.S. investment banks are more powerful than their equivalents in Canada, and although there is anecdotal evidence of this, it is difficult to prove.

Another reason that has been advanced for the high level of underpricing in the United States is the litigious nature of the U.S. economy. If the share price falls, then the risk is high that someone will mount a class action suit against the underwriter for misleading the purchasers. In support of this is the observation that some U.S. law firms specialize in suing underwriters, and they do this routinely if the share price falls by 20 percent shortly after the IPO, which seems to be the magic number.

TABLE 17-1 Evidence of IPO Underpricing

Country	Sample	Period	Return (%)
Canada	500	1971–99	6.3
United Kingdom	3,122	1959–2001	17.4
United States	14,840	1960–2001	18.4
Australia	381	1976–95	12.1
New Zealand	201	1981–99	19.1

Source: Ritter, Jay, "Differences between European and American IPO Markets." *European Financial Management* 9, no. 4 (2002), pp. 421–34.

It has also been suggested that a well-received public offering paves the way for subsequent offerings by the firm and builds momentum into the share price. However, the relative rarity of equity issues makes this rationale dubious.

Finally, **spinning** has been offered as a reason for high underpricing. In this process, the underwriter allocates IPOs to favoured clients, knowing that they will make a large profit on the first day, making some people very wealthy. Spinning was popular among investment dealers during the Internet bubble, when first-day returns on hot Internet stocks were often more than 100 percent. Allocating IPOs to favourite clients was then essentially a way of bribing them with millions of dollars to get future investment banking business. The bribe was paid at the expense of the issuing firm, which did not receive full value for its securities.

Spinning is obviously unethical. It was severely criticized after the stock market crashed in 2001 and investors became aware of the corruption in the marketing of Internet stocks in the United States in the 1990s. In April 2003, Eliot Spitzer, then the attorney general for New York, reached a global settlement with most of the major U.S. investment banks in which they agreed to pay US$1.4 billion in restitution. Most of the settlement was related to the biased nature of security analyst reports, which were used to pump up Internet and technology stock prices. However, part of the settlement was related to spinning, which became illegal and was banned. In May 2003, Spitzer reached a settlement with Philip Anschutz, former chair of Qwest Communications International, Inc. (Qwest), a major U.S. telecom company. As part of the settlement, Anschutz "disgorged" US$4.4 million in profits on IPO shares he received from Salomon Smith Barney, a major U.S. investment bank. According to Spitzer, the IPO allocations were awarded to Anschutz as a reward for investment banking business from Qwest and were never disclosed.

spinning a process by which the underwriter allocates IPOs to favoured clients, knowing that they will make a large profit on the first day

CONCEPT REVIEW QUESTIONS

1. Briefly discuss the possible motivation for firms to enter into IPOs, and relate these motivations to the five stages of firm development discussed by Myers (1999).

2. List and briefly describe the four basic stages of the IPO process.

3. List and briefly describe some possible reasons for the existence of IPO underpricing.

17.4 POST-IPO REGULATION AND SEASONED OFFERINGS

The Post-IPO Market

Learning Objective 17.5
Explain why continuous disclosure requirements are important for investors and how they affect secondary offerings.

After the quiet period has ended, the investment dealer's research analyst can initiate coverage on the company because it is assumed that by this time the prospectus no longer contains all relevant information, and the analyst may add value. In fact, promising analyst coverage of the firm's shares is a key part of the pitch that an investment dealer makes to win investment banking business. The analyst coverage, plus the investment dealer's agreement to make a market in the firm's shares, offers the firm the possibility of enhancing liquidity in its shares and increasing its recognition within the investment community.

Unfortunately, these practices were also taken to excess in the United States during the Internet bubble. In the settlement that Eliot Spitzer extracted from the major U.S. investment banks, he not only stopped the practice of spinning, but also revealed the depth to which research analysts were compromised in their pursuit of investment banking business. It was routine to reward analysts with a share of the investment banking business they brought in, in effect turning research analysts into promoters of the company's stock rather than providers of objective research.

In the settlement reached with Eliot Spitzer, two analysts, Jack Grubman of Salomon Brothers and Henry Blodget of Merrill Lynch, were charged with issuing fraudulent research reports and agreed to pay penalties of US$15 million and US$4 million, respectively. They were both also banned from the securities business for life. The SEC charged Credit Suisse First Boston (CSFB) with issuing fraudulent research on two stocks and producing misleading research on three others. Allegations were made that investment banks paid other investment banks to provide analyst research coverage to avoid the appearance that the "buy" recommendations were coming from within.

The excesses evident in the United States were not evident in Canada, and regulatory changes in the United States have made research analysts independent of investment banking. However, it is obviously difficult to win investment banking business from a company if a research analyst is trashing the stock. Hence, even when a formal separation exists between research and investment banking, it is sensible to discount recommendations from the company's investment dealer, which leaves investors reliant on analysis from the investment dealers who want to win the firm's business in the future.

The other holdover from the IPO is that the lock-up period usually lasts around six months. During the Internet boom, share prices tended to dip, sometimes as much as 20 percent, after six months, when the lock-ups expired and insiders sold some of their shares. This was particularly evident for technology and Internet stocks, because insiders usually continued to hold more than 80 percent of the shares—that is, the IPOs were so sought-after at the time that only 20 percent of the shares were sold on the IPO date. Consequently, insiders were under tremendous pressure to diversify their own portfolios by selling shares. To counter this tendency for prices to drop as the lock-ups expired, research coverage was often initiated with buy recommendations at about the six-month mark.

Continuous Disclosure Requirements

IPOs are not as hot as they were in the late 1990s, so the fraction held by insiders is usually much less than 80 percent. However, common advice is to be wary of IPOs when the founders are left with a high percentage of the shares, because the market will likely have to absorb some of this supply in the future. After the IPO, people who buy the shares in the secondary market do not get a copy of the prospectus. After all, the information in the prospectus rapidly becomes outdated, so it is of little value to secondary market investors. To remedy this, almost all issuers are required to become **reporting issuers** and provide **continuous disclosure**. The main components of continuous disclosure are the filing of quarterly and annual financial statements, annual information forms (AIFs), and proxy and information circulars.

Although firms normally include financial statements in their annual report, in Ontario there is no requirement to include all the material normally contained in the annual report, much of which is promotional. Since 1982, the OSC has required larger firms (i.e., those with a market value greater than $75 million or sales of more than $10 million) to file an AIF complete with a comprehensive management discussion and analysis (MD&A) of its operations. The

reporting issuers issuers that are required to provide continuous information disclosure

continuous disclosure the filing of quarterly and annual financial statements, annual information forms, and proxy and information circulars

AIF and MD&A provide prospectus-type disclosure for all larger firms with securities traded in Ontario. Under corporate law, an annual proxy statement has to be filed for the annual general meeting in order to change the company's bylaws and elect members of the BOD, so this is regarded as part of continuous disclosure as well.[29]

Firms are also required to disclose any "material changes" in the affairs of a reporting issuer. Note that material *facts* are also required to be disclosed, but a material *change* is broader and encompasses more than a material fact. A material change can occur even when all the facts are already known. However, the exact definition of a material change is elusive; the interpretation seems to be that "investors should know it when they see it."

The OSC requires that firms issue a press release and file a material change report in its System for Electronic Document Analysis and Retrieval (SEDAR), on the OSC's website, as soon as is practical and within 10 days of a material change. It is important that firms cannot selectively disclose facts, not even to industry professionals, such as security analysts. This first became important in the United States, where regulation FD, which stands for **fair disclosure**, mandated that information given to security analysts, such as earnings guidance, had to be made available to all. The result has been a surge in webcasts where analysts ask questions of the company—for example, about its quarterly earnings results. Ordinary investors can now listen to these webcasts and get the same information as the professionals. Checking the section of a company's website for investor relations usually reveals information about upcoming webcasts.

In Canada, selective disclosure became a hot issue in October 2000 after the CFO of Air Canada instructed staff to leave telephone messages on the answering machines at major investment dealers. The messages indicated that Air Canada's upcoming results would be worse than expected. The next day, it released most of this information in a press release, but by then the share price had already dropped. Air Canada paid both the Ontario and Quebec Securities Commissions $500,000 plus costs in restitution. In October 2001, the recommendations of the Crawford Committee on analyst standards led to the formal adoption of FD in Canada.

Seasoned Offerings and Short-Form Prospectuses

The upshot of these requirements for continuous disclosure is that the preparation of a long-form prospectus for a seasoned equity issue by a reporting issuer is redundant, because the information should be available already. The result has been the development of the **short-form prospectus**. Essentially, any reporting issuer with an existing AIF can issue securities under a short-form prospectus, which indicates the nature and pricing of the securities, omits all corporate information, and incorporates existing documents by reference. As long as the securities are not "novel," they can be cleared by the OSC in a matter of days, so that issues can be brought to market very quickly.[30]

The short-form prospectus has changed the basic way firms raise both debt and equity capital, and it has led directly to the growth of the bought deal, in which the underwriting contract is signed even before the drafting of the preliminary prospectus. The OSC allows this because it knows that the prospectus now includes only details of the offering, rather than of the issuer, and that the prospectus will follow within two days. This allows the investment dealer to market the issue to major institutions and close the transaction usually within two to three days after the initial discussions with the issuer. Often the investment dealer directly approaches the issuer and tells the issuer that, based on its knowledge of the market, it can raise a certain amount of money. As a result, it is often the investment dealer that initiates the transaction and not the issuer.

fair disclosure the requirement that all information given to security analysts, such as earnings guidance, be made available to everyone

short-form prospectus a document that indicates the nature and pricing of the securities, omits all corporate information, and incorporates existing documents by reference

---

[29] These requirements also explain why investing in small-cap stocks is so risky. The fact is that these companies do not provide the same level of disclosure as reporting issuers, and information asymmetry can be more acute.

[30] Examples of short-form prospectuses are available at www.sedar.com, but long-form prospectuses are now quite rare.

To show how dynamic seasoned equity offerings have become, we consider the $180 million in common equity raised by BC Gas in October 2001. BC Gas (now FortisBC) is primarily a local gas distribution company in the lower B.C. mainland. As a largely regulated utility, there is little unknown about its operations. In late 2001, it bought the gas distribution assets of another utility company on Vancouver Island from Westcoast Energy Inc. To pay for this acquisition, on the closing of the deal, BC Gas invited bids from a series of investment dealers and then awarded the underwriting contract to RBC Dominion Securities Inc. (RBCDS) and Scotia Capital Inc. Apart from the standard 4 percent underwriting fee, the underwriters agreed to pay BC Gas $36.15 a share. The only snag was that the closing price for the BC Gas shares was $36.10.

The BC Gas financing deal shows how competitive the investment dealer business has become now that the prospectus requirements have been reduced in favour of continuous disclosure. It downplays the importance of the other skills provided by the investment dealer in favour of its raw trading and marketing power. In the BC Gas case, the market was so short of deals that both RBCDS and Scotia Capital were willing to incur a trading loss (because they knew the closing price) and eat into their 4 percent commission, simply to generate activity for their investment dealer teams. The example illustrates how seasoned offerings have developed in Canada to enable larger firms to rapidly access markets to raise capital.

The Size of the Investment Banking Market

The **Investment Industry Association of Canada (IIAC)** is the organization that represents the securities industry in Canada. IIAC members raise the financing needed for new and existing businesses and police the trading practices of its members so that investors can "trade with confidence in open and fair capital markets." IIAC also collects important information that helps investors understand the capital markets and freely distributes this information from its website at www.iiac.ca. Table 17-2 lists the total value of new equity issues in Canada for 2007 and 2011.

Investment Industry Association of Canada (IIAC) a member-based, professional association that advances the growth and development of the Canadian investment industry

For example, in 2007 there was $40 billion raised in new common shares, of which $5.73 billion was through initial public offerings. That had increased marginally by 2010, but in 2011 was only $5,308 billion—still less than the 2007 high.. In the next few chapters, we will discuss why firms issue these different types of securities, but it is clear that the common share issue is the most important type of new equity issue in terms of both volume and value. In contrast, while there are relatively few preferred share issues, they raise about 20 percent of the value of common share issues. This indicates that they tend to be very large issues, and in fact most of them were issued on behalf of Canadian financial firms, for regulatory purposes, to raise capital during the 2008–9 financial crisis.

TABLE 17-2 Total New Equity Issues in Canada, 2007 and 2011

$Billions	2007	2011
Equity IPOs	5,734	5,308
Non IPO Equities	34,307	35,936
Preferred shares	5,157	4,269

Source: Data from IIAC *New Issues Annual*, April 20, 2012. Available at www.iiac.ca/welcome-to-iiac/resources/publications/.

These data put some flesh on the discussion of the investment banking process. What we can conclude is that the IPO market is very sensitive to the state of the equity markets, while the seasoned equity offerings (SEO) market is a little more stable. So who does all this activity? It is hardly surprising that the bulk of it is done by the investment banks, which are part of the Big Five chartered banks. In 2010, the dealers of the big integrated firms that are national in scope (i.e., mainly the Canadian banks) earned 65 percent of the total investment banking income of $4.8 billion. The rest was scattered among the other 195 members of the IIAC.

CONCEPT REVIEW QUESTIONS

1. Explain why the lock-up period is an important consideration for investors, especially for issues that are still largely held by insiders.

2. How do continuous disclosure requirements protect investors?

3. Briefly explain why short-form prospectuses are permitted by regulators for a large percentage of seasoned issues, and explain why they have led to the growth in popularity of bought deals.

LESSONS TO BE LEARNED

During 2008 and 2009, we have relearned some old lessons about the securities markets. One of the most fundamental is that, despite extensive securities regulations that intrude into almost all the operations of raising money and trading securities, there are still crooks in the capital market. The Madoff Ponzi scheme came as a shock to many, and even the size of it was a shock to the U.S. Securities and Exchange Commission, which had actually investigated the firm on several occasions. The fact is that Madoff was part of the establishment and operated by word of mouth and personal recommendations. This very secrecy enhanced his reputation, especially when he did not solicit money himself but obtained it through feeder funds, which many people invested in, unaware that the funds were actually going to Madoff.

It is often said that a "rising tide lifts all boats," to which Warren Buffett replied, "You only find out who is swimming naked when the tide goes out." When the tide went out in 2008 as the stock market collapsed, more scams came to light than ever before, simply because those monthly statements from the securities firms telling you how much money you have are easy to produce; actually sending you a cheque if you want to sell has turned out to be more difficult than some ever imagined.

SUMMARY

A prerequisite for understanding corporate financing is understanding the basics of securities laws. Investment bankers (dealers) who assist firms in raising capital must abide by these laws, which severely restrict what they can and cannot do.

In this chapter, we discuss how one of the core problems in raising capital is the existence of information asymmetry—some people have access to privileged information and have a clearer idea of the value of the securities being offered than others do. In the extreme case of fraud, there is a clear asymmetry of information. In fact, it was the existence of fraud in the financial markets that led to the creation of securities commissions and the tight regulation of the offering process. We show how broad the legal definition of a security is, what constitutes a prospectus, and why it takes so much time and effort to raise money through an IPO. In contrast, once the information is available in the capital markets, the requirement for continuous disclosure for larger firms means that secondary offerings (SEOs) and private placements can be accomplished incredibly quickly in today's markets, at very low cost.

SUMMARY OF LEARNING OBJECTIVES

17.1 Explain what is meant by "information asymmetries" and how these affect the raising of capital.

The term "information asymmetry" is applied to transactions where the counterparties have differing private information about the asset/good/service being exchanged. Information asymmetry is a significant problem in new issues, since the issuer has much more information about the value of the security than the prospective investor. Information asymmetry can lead to outright fraud, such as when issuers sell worthless securities to investors.

17.2 Explain the purpose of securities laws and regulations in the financial markets.

Securities laws are designed to protect investors from being defrauded due to their informational disadvantage. Securities laws require firms to make full, true, and plain disclosure of all material facts—both at the IPO through the prospectus and through continuous disclosure. Securities laws also restrict corporate insiders from trading on the basis of undisclosed material information. These insider trading rules protect investors against information asymmetry.

17.3 Explain what a prospectus is, what it contains, and why it is critical for initial public offerings (IPOs).

A prospectus is a formal summary of a security that describes the costs, investment objectives, risks, and performance. There are two types: long form and short form. All material facts about the company must be included in the prospectus. For example, a description of the security being issued, the price of the security, underwriter fees, where the security will be traded, business history, historical financial statements, risk factors, and MD&A (management discussion and analysis). A long-form prospectus is required in all initial public offerings. The extra detail is required since there are no securities analysts writing reports on the company, and the information asymmetry is greatest at this point.

17.4 Outline the basic stages in taking a firm public through an initial public offering (IPO) of securities.

There are four basic steps in an IPO:

1. discussion
2. preparation of the preliminary prospectus (red herring)
3. waiting period and road show
4. pricing and distribution

Negotiation of deal type occurs during the preparation stage or during the waiting period.

17.5 Explain why continuous disclosure requirements are important for investors and how they affect secondary offerings.

The prospectus protects investors from asymmetric information during the IPO; however, the information becomes stale and does not help investors during subsequent secondary market trading. Continuous disclosure requires firms to file quarterly financial statements and information circulars. Thus, firms must continue to disclose all material information in a full, true, and plain manner. Reporting issuers (who make continuous disclosure) can issue new securities using a short-form prospectus instead of a regular prospectus—this makes the new issue process quicker and cheaper.

KEY TERMS

QUESTIONS AND PRACTICE PROBLEMS

Multiple Choice Questions

1. Which of the following statements about due diligence is *false*?
   a. It is designed to ensure the legitimacy of securities offered to the public.
   b. It is designed to ensure that there is no misleading information when companies issue shares.
   c. It is expensive to implement.
   d. There is no cost to implement it.

2. Which of the following statements about asymmetric information is *false*?
   a. There is asymmetric information between managers and investors.
   b. There is no asymmetric information in the used car market.
   c. A prospectus is designed to reduce information asymmetry in the capital market.
   d. Information asymmetry varies across corporations.

3. Which of the following statements about Ponzi schemes is *false*?
   a. Such schemes are named after Carlo Ponzi, an Italian born in 1882 who immigrated to the United States.
   b. Ponzi schemes are legal in Canada.
   c. There were cases of Ponzi schemes in the United States.
   d. There were cases of Ponzi schemes in Canada.

4. Which of these pieces of information is not required in an IPO prospectus by the British Columbia Securities Commission?
   a. A description of the securities being issued and who can buy them
   b. The price of the securities, the fees to the investment dealer involved with the distribution, and the net proceeds
   c. The market for the securities—that is, whether they will be traded
   d. The CEO's resume

5. Which of the following regulators does not exist in Canadian securities markets?
   a. Ontario Securities Commission
   b. British Columbia Securities Commission
   c. Federal Securities Commission
   d. Quebec Securities Commission

6. Which of the following statements is *false*?
   a. An IPO is assumed to have the least information asymmetry.
   b. An IPO is the distribution of securities from the corporation to the investors.
   c. An IPO is the first-time distribution of securities.
   d. "Full, true, and plain" means every material fact has to be disclosed.

7. The market for non-registered securities is called the:
   a. non-registered market.
   b. secondary market.
   c. primary market.
   d. exempt market.

8. Which of the following statements about the exempt market is *false*?
   a. "Backdoor underwriting" refers to the practice of slipping securities from the exempt market into the public market.
   b. In the exempt market, the issuer prepares a prospectus too.
   c. Only if the issuer becomes a reporting issuer can the issuer sell securities in the public market.

   d. The exemption from prospectus requirement is based on smaller issues, the sophistication of the potential investors, and the risk of the securities.

9. Which of the following issuers is not exempt?
   a. government debt issuers
   b. financial institution debt issuers
   c. securities issued as part of takeovers
   d. private firms issuing large amounts of stocks

10. Which of the following statements about public offerings is *false*?
   a. There are four types of offerings: a best efforts offering, a firm commitment offering, a bought deal, and a standby or rights offering.
   b. Bought deal offerings and standby offerings are used only for seasoned offerings.
   c. Most IPOs are best efforts offerings.
   d. A lead investment dealer and a banking syndicate are involved in larger issues.

11. Which of the following is not a main component of continuous disclosure?
   a. filing of quarterly financial statements
   b. filing of annual financial statements
   c. filing of proxy and information circulars
   d. filing of monthly financial statements

12. Which of the following statements about seasoned offerings is *false*?
   a. A seasoned offering's prospectus has the same content as the prospectus for an IPO.
   b. A seasoned offering has less information asymmetry than an IPO.
   c. A seasoned offering allows the use of a short-form prospectus.
   d. A seasoned offering is the offering after the firm goes public.

Practice Problems

13. In late 2006, Canada Post began issuing "permanent" stamps. Purchased at the current first-class letter rate ($0.51 at the time), these stamps may be used indefinitely even if the price of stamps increases. Arthur Ponzarelli (known to his friends as "Ponzi") is always looking to make a quick buck, and he thinks these stamps present a lucrative opportunity. Expecting the price of postage to increase by $0.01 very soon, he decides to "invest" in 100,000 stamps.
   a. If Canada Post raises the postal rate to $0.52 two weeks later, and Arthur resells his securities (the stamps) at the new price, how much profit will he make?
   b. To avoid running afoul of securities laws, Arthur decides to sell his stamps to someone in another province and will have to pay $249 for shipping and insurance. Unfortunately, his reputation for shady deals has preceded him, so the purchaser is only willing to pay $0.5125 per stamp. Will Arthur still make a "quick buck"?
   c. To avoid running afoul of securities laws, Arthur decides to sell his stamps to someone in another province and will have to pay $249 for shipping and insurance. He successfully sells the stamps at $0.52 each. How much money will he make?

14. If the interest rate for non-fraudulent bonds is 12 percent, and chances are that one out of five bonds is fraudulent, what is the interest rate based on a one-year investment and assuming the market does not require a risk premium?

15. State the five major areas in which the Ontario Securities Commission (OSC) is involved.

16. State three types of distributions of securities determined by the OSC.

17. Describe three major categories of exempt purchasers.

18. Describe the basic stages of IPOs.

19.   Describe limit orders and market orders.

20.   What is the "quiet period"?

21.   Describe four different types of public offerings.

22.   Describe the market or disaster "out" clause.

23.   Describe the overallotment or "green-shoe" option.

24.   What is the lock-up period?

25.   What is the waiting period?

26.   What is a "road show"?

27.   Why is IPO underpricing less severe in Canada than it is in the United States? What causes underpricing?

28.   Back in their college days, David and Douglas Finn started renting refrigerators to other students for use in their dormitory rooms. Over the years, Finns' Fridges has grown and financed its operations by retaining most of the profits it made. Now, however, the brothers would like to "cash out" by taking the company public through an IPO. Together, the brothers own one million shares and will sell half of their holdings. In addition, the company will issue 250,000 new shares as part of the IPO to provide additional growth financing. What percentage of the firm's shares will the Finns own after the IPO?

29.   If the IPO for Finns' Fridges (see Practice Problem 28) goes well, the contract with the investment bankers has a "green-shoe" clause that permits them to sell 15 percent more shares than originally planned. These additional shares would all be issued by the company, not sold by the Finn brothers themselves. How much of the firm will the brothers own if this overallotment option is taken up?

30.   Niagara Vineyards and Winery needs to raise $2 million in new equity.
      a.   If the costs of the share issue are estimated to be 7 percent of gross proceeds, how large does the offering need to be? How much will Niagara pay in flotation costs?
      b.   If the underwriters give a discount and only charge 5 percent of gross proceeds, how large does the offering need to be? How much will Niagara save on flotation costs?

31.   Winnipeg Water & Gas Co. recently issued a series of bonds; the gross proceeds were $25 million. The underwriting fees were 1.8 percent, and additional issuance costs were $100,000. How much did the company actually receive from the sale? As a percentage of the gross proceeds, what were the total costs of the bond issue?

32.   Lansdowne Ltd. needs to raise $10 million and intends to sell additional shares. The company's existing shares are trading on the Toronto Stock Exchange for $28. However, the investment dealer hired by Lansdowne has cited investors' concerns about information asymmetry to justify an offering price of $25 per share. Underwriting costs charged by the investment dealer are 5 percent of the issue price. How many shares must the firm sell to net $10 million? Why does the investment dealer suggest an offering price less than the trading price?

33.   The little company you and your friend started in your parents' garage has grown so much that you are now ready to take the firm public. In your discussions with one of the top investment dealers, you have been given a choice between two alternatives:

      Plan I: The investment dealer will underwrite the issue of one million shares at $14 per share. There will be an underwriting fee of 6.5 percent of the gross proceeds.

Plan II: The investment dealer will accept the 1 million shares on a "best efforts" basis. The price will be $15 per share, and it is believed that 95 percent of the shares will be sold. The investment dealer's fee will be $950,000.

What will the net proceeds be under each plan? What will the investment dealer charge under each plan? Which plan should you accept?

34. Pills4u.com and Drugs-R-Us Co. both sell prescription medications over the Internet. Each company has recently announced an IPO at $15 per share. At this price, one of the companies is undervalued by $1.50, while the other is overvalued by $1.00. Unfortunately, you have no way of knowing which is which, as you have no particular expertise in pharmaceuticals or Internet sales. Nonetheless, you plan to buy 1,000 shares of each company's stock at the offer price.

   a. If you are allocated the full 1,000 shares of each new issue, how much profit will you make when the shares adjust to their true value?

   b. If an issue is undervalued, it will be rationed, and you will only get half your order. What profit do you expect in this situation?

   c. If an issue is undervalued, it will be rationed, and you will only get one-fifth of your order. What profit do you expect in this situation?

35. Sous-Chef Inc. is an employment agency that specializes in the restaurant industry. The company intends to sell 800,000 shares in its IPO and the investment dealers working on the issue have been seeking expressions of interest in the shares from various investors (pension plans, mutual funds, and so on). As the dealers sit down with the company's management to price the issue, the "book" looks like this:

Investor	Number of shares	Limit price
A	200,000	$21.00
B	150,000	$20.50
C	300,000	$20.00
D	200,000	$19.25
E	250,000	$19.00
F	350,000	$18.75
G	250,000	$18.50
H	100,000	$18.00
I	150,000	$17.50
J	200,000	$17.00

   a. What is the highest issue price that the shares can command if all the investors live up to their intentions as shown in the table?

   b. Suppose the investment dealers want to set the price so that the issue is two-times oversubscribed. That is, all the shares will sell even if the investors only purchase half the number of shares indicated in the table. At what price should the shares be issued?

   c. Assume the IPO was priced at $18.50 and will trade on the Toronto Stock Exchange. If the amount of underpricing is the same as the historical average for Canadian stocks, what do you expect the price of the stock to be at the end of its first day of trading? What would its price be if the first-day return is the same as what is typically seen in the United States?

36. What are continuous disclosure requirements?

18 | Debt Instruments

LEARNING OBJECTIVES

18.1   Define "debt" and identify the basic features that distinguish debt from equity financing.

18.2   Identify and describe the different types of short-term debt issued in the money market.

18.3   Describe the types of debt financing provided by banks.

18.4   Identify the requirements that must typically be satisfied for public debt issues.

18.5   Explain how debt ratings are determined, what they mean, and how useful they are in predicting default and recovery rates associated with public debt issues.

Manulife Financial Corp.'s debt rating has been dropped by DBRS [Dominion Bond Rating Service] one level to AA (low) from AA, with DBRS saying in its analysis that the company may be forced to go back to the market to get more cash.

Manulife's big loss dropped its key capital ratio enough that "another negative quarter will force the company to raise additional capital."

That is not what equity investors want to hear, after enduring two big share sales in 2008.

DBRS said that Manulife's financial flexibility is "increasingly constrained, as the most readily available sources of capital have already been tapped"—pointing to the two share issues in 2008 equity raises totalling $5 billion, a halving of the company's dividend, and close to $1.5 billion in debt and preferred share financings.

The result was an increase in "financial leverage ratios to the point where DBRS was no longer comfortable with the company's pre-existing ratings."

DBRS said that at the new rating level, Manulife could issue more debt, rather than having to go to the equity markets, and still keep the ratings intact.

CHAPTER 18 **PREVIEW**

I n Chapter 17, we described the steps involved in raising capital and the role of securities regulation in protecting the public through mandatory disclosure. However, no matter how much information is disclosed, investors will disagree on the interpretation of that information and view the firm's prospects differently. Consequently, they will invest in different types of securities. In this chapter, we discuss the implications for debt securities, one of the two classic types of securities. In Chapter 19, we will discuss the implications for equity securities, the second classic type of security, and so-called hybrids, which are part debt and part equity.

18.1 WHAT IS DEBT?

Learning Objective 18.1
Define "debt" and identify the basic features that distinguish debt from equity financing.

Debt is a contract between a lender and a borrower that stipulates the terms of repayment of the loan. As a contract, these terms are limited only by the imagination of the contracting parties. However, a critical component is that the interest on debt securities is fully deductible for tax purposes by the borrower (payer or issuer) and fully taxable for the lender (recipient or investor). As a result, one of the major factors determining whether or not a security is debt is its treatment by the Canada Revenue Agency (CRA). In this sense, debt is what the CRA accepts as debt for tax purposes. We will see that many factors determine whether a firm issues debt or equity securities or some form of hybrid, but tax consequences are always a factor.

It might seem obvious what debt is. After all, many of us have borrowed money from friends, relatives, or financial institutions. For example, you might borrow $1,000 at 10 percent interest and agree to pay the loan back in one year's time. In this case, you have to pay back $1,100 at the end of the year; 10 percent interest is the cost of "renting" the $1,000 in principal for the year. In this way, the 10 percent interest rate is the cost of borrowing money.

fixed contractual commitments
contractual terms that commit the parties involved to adhere to specific requirements

All of this is straightforward, but it is important to point out that the interest cost and principal repayment are **fixed contractual commitments**, and failing to honour them has serious implications that we discuss later. The fact that the principal and interest payments are fixed contractual commitments is the essential difference between debt and equity. With equity, an investor is an owner, shares in the profits of the business, and has no "contractual" rights because equity is not a contract in the way that debt is. Instead, a shareholder owns a share in the business and, as an owner, has the rights allocated in the company's articles of incorporation and bylaws (discussed in Chapter 2) as well as in the general provisions of corporate and securities laws. However, shareholders do not have a specific contract that details the cash flows they can expect to receive from the investment. An owner is a "residual claimant," which means that he or she gets what is left after all the firm's contractual commitments have been met.

The fact that payments on debt are a fixed contractual commitment puts them in the same category as the firm's rental payments on property, its wage bill to its workforce, and its other business expenses. They are legitimate costs of doing business and are tax deductible. In contrast, equity costs are not a cost of doing business in the same sense. Instead, they represent returns to the *owners* of the business after the company has paid all its legitimate expenses. As such, equity securities are treated differently for tax purposes. By investigating this difference, we can understand why and how debt and equity securities differ.

Suppose, for example, that a firm has $10 million in assets and expects to generate 10 percent of this amount (or $1 million) in earnings before interest and tax (EBIT). If the corporate tax rate is 30 percent, then the firm will pay $300,000 in tax, assuming it makes no interest payments. However, if the firm borrows $5 million at 7 percent, it will have a $350,000 interest expense deduction, reducing its taxable income to $650,000 and its tax bill to $195,000. The firm's tax bill drops by $105,000 because of its decision to finance part of its operations with debt instead of equity. The calculations are shown below.

TABLE 18-1 Common Asset Classes Established by Canada Revenue Agency

	No Debt ($)	**$5 Million in Debt ($)**
EBIT	1,000,000	1,000,000
Interest	0	350,000
Taxable income	1,000,000	650,000
Tax (30%)	300,000	195,000
Net income	700,000	455,000

Of the $350,000 in interest expense paid by the firm, only 70 percent, or $245,000, is actually paid by the owners of the firm; the other 30 percent, or $105,000, is paid through a reduction in income taxes remitted to the government. We can see this in the fact that net income has dropped by only $245,000 despite the increased interest payments of $350,000.

This simple example highlights a very important point: the firm's net cost for using debt is the after-tax cost. In our example, this was the 7 percent interest rate multiplied by one minus the tax rate $(1 - 0.3)$ or 70 percent. This gives the debt cost as 4.9 percent. Generally, we can use Equation 18-1 to determine this **after-tax cost of debt (K)**.

after-tax cost of debt (K) the net cost to the firm for using debt, calculated as the before-tax interest cost of the firm's debt multiplied by one minus the corporate tax rate

$$K = K_d (1 - T)$$ [18-1]

In Equation 18-1, K_d is the before-tax interest cost of the firm's debt, and T is the corporate tax rate.

We will generically use K as the yield, or required return, on a security and indicate what type of security it is by using subscripts; in this case, the subscript is d, indicating debt.

This discussion illustrates a basic rule: if a business is taxable, it makes sense to correctly identify all legitimate costs of doing business, because these reduce the taxable income and thus the tax bill. For corporations, it means they legitimately try to ensure that their financing costs are tax deductible, because it reduces their income taxes. Conversely, the CRA has to make sure that the *Income Tax Act* is enforced and that firms take only legitimate deductions for genuine debt securities.

The CRA uses three basic tests to make sure that the interest on debt is tax deductible:

1. Interest is compensation for the use or retention of money owed to another.

2. Interest must be referable to a principal sum.

3. Interest accrues from day to day.

These criteria make sense. Using the example of a $1,000 loan again, the $1,000 is the principal sum, and the interest of 10 percent is referable back to that principal to get the $100 in interest. If the loan is paid off late, the borrower would expect to pay more than $100 in interest, because he or she has rented the principal for a longer time. This is the way in which the interest accrues as the loan is outstanding: the longer the loan is outstanding, the more interest is paid. However, as simple as this appears to be, a huge amount of litigation has been involved in deciding whether these three factors actually hold for a particular security.

For example, Richardson shows that the second requirement (i.e., that interest is referable to a principal sum) dates to a Supreme Court of Canada decision concerning the *Saskatchewan Farm Security Act* of 1944.[1] At that time, the Province of Saskatchewan wanted to reduce the debt burden faced by its farming community. It could not waive interest payments because

---

[1] Richardson, Stephen, "New Financial Instruments: A Canadian Tax Perspective." In *New Financial Management*. Toronto: Canadian Tax Foundation, 1993.

they are a federal responsibility and are stipulated in the federal *Income Tax Act*. Therefore, the province passed a law reducing the principal value associated with the required interest payments but stipulated that the interest payments would not be reduced, even though the principal value was. Effectively, the reduction in principal payments was set so that it would offset the interest paid, thereby removing the burden of the interest payments and helping Saskatchewan farmers. However, the Supreme Court of Canada ruled that the interest payments could no longer be regarded as interest, because the principal sum was being reduced and the interest had to be tied back to this principal.

This is a typical pattern in finance. "Innovative" financing vehicles are created to exploit the wording in the *Income Tax Act* in an attempt to make things appear to be debt, and tax deductible, when they really are not. As the Saskatchewan example highlights, this isn't just a corporate or personal activity; governments do it as well.[2] It may take years for the CRA to dissect an income statement and challenge a deduction, but when it does respond, the matter often ends up in tax court. The courts rule on whether these securities comply with the definitions of interest and the intent of the *Income Tax Act*. If the deduction is disallowed, the loophole is then closed until clever financiers find another way to do the same thing. However, before we talk about some of the "grey area" securities between debt and equity, we will consider "plain vanilla" debt securities. First, we will discuss short-term debt.

CONCEPT REVIEW QUESTIONS

1. Distinguish debt from equity.

2. Explain how to estimate the after-tax cost of debt.

3. What three characteristics does the CRA look for to determine whether interest payments are tax deductible?

18.2 SHORT-TERM DEBT AND THE MONEY MARKET

Learning Objective 18.2
Identify and describe the different types of short-term debt issued in the money market.

We will discuss different types of debt in this chapter, but two key features are the maturity of the debt—that is, how long until the debt has to be repaid—and whether the debt is marketable and can be traded in a secondary market. We start with the most debt-like of all debt securities, which is short-term debt, since the probability of being repaid in full without any loss in value is generally highest for this type of debt.

Government Treasury Bills

The simplest sort of debt contract is one that most of us have made by lending friends a few dollars and telling them to pay us back next week. This is obviously a loan, but it is not backed by anything other than the friend's promise to repay in a week's time. If this promise is documented in a written contract that says, "I promise to pay $X to YYY on April 30," the contract is a security called a **promissory note**. The next time a friend borrows money from you, get him or her to sign such a note; you will have created the most basic type of financial security and will be on your way to becoming a financier!

promissory note a written promise to pay back a loan

Governments issue such short-term promissory notes, which are generically called **treasury bills (T-bills)** because the promise is issued by the treasury department of the government. Generally, any debt instrument with a maturity of less than a year is called a

treasury bills (T-bills) a promissory note issued by a government treasury department

---

[2] Another example of provincial activity was the sale and leaseback of Ontario's GO Transit rolling stock. The provincial government, as a non-taxable entity, cannot use any tax shields. However, by selling the rolling stock to a private enterprise that can use the tax shields, and then leasing the equipment back at a favourable rate, the province gained at the expense of the federal government.

"bill" or "paper"; if it matures in one to seven years it is called a "note," and if it has a maturity of more than seven years it is a "bond." All the bills and short-term paper outstanding are generically referred to as the money market.

At the end of 2010, the Government of Canada had $174 billion in T-bills outstanding. The standard reference point in the money market is the 91-day federal government T-bill. The implicit interest rate for this is commonly referred to as "the" T-bill yield. However, the Government of Canada sells T-bills of varying maturities up to one year, depending on its financing needs. It does this by auctioning off a stock of bills and requiring government securities dealers to place minimum bids on these securities.

The Bank of Canada acts as the Government of Canada's fiscal agent in selling these securities and maintaining an orderly auction market. It does this by requiring that all orders for T-bills be submitted through government securities distributors (GSDs) and by dividing orders into "competitive" and "non-competitive" bids. Competitive bids are orders to buy securities at a particular price at the auction, whereas non-competitive bids are orders to buy them at the average price determined in the auction. A special group of GSDs, the largest and most active dealers, are called "primary dealers" and are given preferential treatment because of their importance to the implementation of monetary policy.[3] These primary dealers then have to bid for a certain amount of T-bills at each auction. The Bank of Canada sets special limits on how much of the auction each dealer can buy to avoid market manipulation.[4]

As of 2011, the primary dealers in the treasury bill market were the Bank of Montreal, Canadian Imperial Bank of Commerce, Deutsche Bank Securities Limited, HSBC Bank Canada, Laurentian Bank Securities Inc., Merrill Lynch Canada Inc., National Bank Financial Inc., RBC Dominion Securities Inc., Scotia Capital Inc., and the Toronto-Dominion Bank. As is to be expected, this group is dominated by the Big Six integrated Canadian banks.[5]

As discussed in Chapter 6, T-bills, like most money market instruments, are normally sold on a discount basis. This means that the Bank of Canada might auction off $500 million in T-bills, but the bills do not pay a specific interest rate. Instead, they are sold at a discount to their par value, and the "interest" is earned by the investor being paid the full par value at the maturity date. For example, suppose that, in an auction, the winning bid for a $1,000 par value, 91-day T-bill is $990.099. The interest is the difference between the market price of $990.099 and the $1,000 paid back by the government in 91 days, or $9.901. This means the 91-day interest rate is 1 percent, which we can calculate as

$$990.099 = \frac{1,000}{(1 + K)}$$

We do not deal with T-bill yields and pricing in great detail here because we did so in Chapter 6; however, we can see that if we solve for K, it is 1 percent, because $1,000/(1.01) = $990.099. In order to establish interest rates, this 1 percent is converted to an annual rate by multiplying by the number of 91-day periods in a year, which means the rate would be quoted as 4.011 percent (i.e., 1% × 365/91).[6] Most money market issues are traded on a discount basis, but some commercial paper is issued in interest-bearing form.[7]

---

[3] The Bank of Canada controls interest rates by buying and selling treasury bills and moving government deposits around, and the dealers are important for these processes.

[4] These new procedures were introduced when the number of dealers declined in response to reduced government financing requirements. In particular, three major U.S. dealers withdrew from the Canadian auction in 2001 as there simply wasn't enough government borrowing.

[5] The Bank of Canada's website, www.bankofcanada.ca, is the critical source of information on government debt markets.

[6] There are many quoting conventions. One of the most common in the United States is to treat each month as if it had 30 days. Thus, when the U.S. government issues 90-day treasury bills, not 91-day as in Canada, the annual rate is exactly four times the quarterly rate.

[7] For tax purposes, the CRA regards the increase from the purchase price to the par value as interest and not capital gains, because the "gain" is locked in at the time of purchase.

Although the federal government's T-bill auction plays a pivotal role in the money market, there are other T-bills outstanding. The larger provinces, particularly Ontario and Quebec, sell T-bills through the major investment dealers, as do some of the larger municipalities. As of the end of 2010, there was $42.58 billion in outstanding T-bills issued by the provinces and major municipalities.

Commercial Paper

commercial paper (CP) short-term debt instruments, usually unsecured, issued by companies

For corporate financing, companies can issue **commercial paper (CP)**, an instrument that is similar to T-bills. Unlike T-bills, however, CP is normally issued with maturities of 30 and 60 days, rather than 91 days. One major problem with CP is that corporations have credit risk: they may default on their obligation to pay investors back in 30 or 60 days. This is a major problem for all corporate debt obligations, but it is particularly acute for CP because it is almost always unsecured, which means the investor has no underlying assets to seize in the event of a default. Further, the dollar amounts involved are frequently very large, for reasons we will come to shortly.

To understand the importance of credit risk, consider a 30-day, interest-bearing CP issue (instead of a discount issue) of $100 million with the same interest rate as the T-bill yield of 6 percent (or approximately 0.5 percent per 30 days). However, now there is a 1 percent chance of the CP issuer defaulting. If it does, the investor gets nothing. We represent this in Figure 18-1.

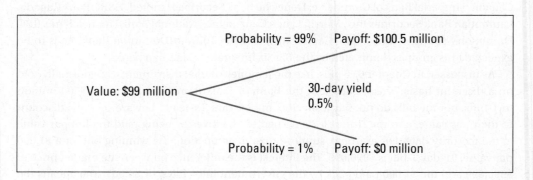

FIGURE 18-1 *Commercial Paper Payoffs*

Because money market instruments are quoted on an approximate interest rate basis, the 6 percent annual rate translates to 0.5 percent per month (i.e., 6%/12). On a $100-million investment, if the issuer does not default, the investor gets $100.5 million after one month; if the issuer defaults, the investor gets nothing. The investor has a 99 percent chance of getting $100.5 million and a 1 percent chance of getting $0; the average of these two, or the expected payoff, is $99.495 million (i.e., 0.99 × $100.5 + 0.01 × $0). If this expected payoff is discounted back for one month at 0.5 percent, the $100-million CP is worth only $99 million (i.e., $99.495 million/1.005).

promised yields the quoted interest rates received if the issuer does not default and the investor is paid off on time, as promised

This example illustrates an important point: the quoted interest rates are called **promised yields**. They are the rates investors would get if the issuer does not default and they are paid off on time, as promised. For Canadian government issues, where there is virtually no default or credit risk, these promised yields are also expected rates of return. However, for corporate issues, which have default risk, the expected rate of return is always *lower* than the promised yield because the promised yield is the maximum rate the investor can hope to earn by holding the security to maturity.

In our example, the company could not issue $100 million of CP at the T-bill yield of 6 percent, because if it did, the CP would be worth only $99 million. Instead, to raise the $100 million par value, the company would have to increase the promised yield higher than the default-free T-bill yield. The value of the 30-day CP issue can be found using Equation 18-2.

$$V = \frac{PAR(1 + R)P + RECOVER(1 - P)}{(1 + K)} \qquad \text{[18-2]}$$

In this equation, par value (PAR) is \$1,000, R is the promised yield, P is the probability of not defaulting, $(1 - P)$ is the probability of defaulting, RECOVER is the recovery rate if the company defaults, and K is the investor's required return.

In our example, we simplified this equation by setting RECOVER equal to zero and the investor's required rate of return equal to the T-bill yield. If we continue with these assumptions, we can find the promised yield necessary for the CP to be issued at PAR, that is, PAR = V:

$$R = \frac{(1 + K_{TB})}{P} - 1 \qquad \text{[18-3]}$$

where K_{TB} is the required return for investing in T-bills. In the absence of default risk (P = 1), the promised yield on CP would be the same as that on T-bills. However, with the 1 percent chance of default, the promised yield has to be 1.515 percent per month (i.e., 1.005/0.99 − 1) or 18.2 percent per year (i.e., 1.515% × 12).

The difference between the promised yield on CP and the yield on the equivalent-maturity T-bill is called the **default or credit yield spread**. In this case, given a 1 percent chance of default, the yield spread is 12.2 percent (i.e., 18.2% to 6%). The 12.2 percent yield spread is compensation for the fact that if the CP defaults, the investor gets nothing. Obviously, as the probability of default goes up, P goes down and the yield spread increases. The important point to note from this example is the huge impact that default risk has on promised yields. Even if the risk of default drops from 1 percent to 0.1 percent, the monthly promised yield for CP is still 0.6 percent (versus 0.5 percent) for a yield spread of 1.2 percent on an annual basis.

default or credit yield spread the difference between the yield on a default-risky debt instrument and the yield on an equivalent-maturity Government of Canada instrument

For reference purposes, on March 14, 2012, the yields on three-month T-bills and "prime" CP were 0.9 percent and 1.16 percent, respectively, resulting in a yield spread of 0.26 percent. This indicates the extremely low default risk attached to prime CP in Canada.[8] This yield spread had a volatile ride during the financial crisis of 2008–9, for reasons we will discuss shortly. However, it indicates that the actual risk of investing in CP is extremely low, so only the best companies can access the CP market. This is because assessing default risk requires time as well as analytic skills. This outlay may be worthwhile when investing for a long period, but few investors are inclined to do this analysis for an investment with a three-month maturity or less. In this sense, investors in the paper market are not so much investing as simply "parking" money for a short period of time. However, as we noted, default risk does have a huge impact on yields. To solve this problem, the market has developed alternative risk-assessment measures. Credit rating agencies have developed the most basic measure, which provides default or credit ratings to investors, thereby relieving investors of the need to do individual analyses.

The most important credit rating agency in Canada is the Dominion Bond Rating Service (DBRS). Two U.S. rating agencies, Moody's and Standard & Poor's (S&P), also provide ratings on Canadian firms, although they mainly provide ratings on longer-term issues, particularly those issued in the U.S. market, rather than money market instruments. However, S&P, in particular, has evolved into a major competitor to DBRS since it took over the Canadian Bond Rating Service (CBRS) in 2001.

DBRS rates CP, longer-term bonds, and preferred shares and has separate rating categories for each. Generally, the ratings are very similar, but sometimes the short-term risk of investing in CP is less than the longer-term risk of investing in the same company's long-term bonds, so the ratings may differ slightly.

---

[8] Or it indicates the extremely high recovery rates in the event of default.

For CP, DBRS has three basic rating categories:

R-1 Prime credit quality
R-2 Adequate credit quality
R-3 Speculative

Within these categories, DBRS adds sub-ratings of high, mid, and low, so R-1 (high) is the highest rating, while R-3 (low) is the lowest. In practice, these rating categories are moot to some extent, because as of December 2010, the percentage distribution of CP by rating category was as follows:

TABLE 18-2 Distribution of CP by DBRS Rating Category

Type	Companies (%)	Securitizations (%)	Total (%)
R-1 (high)	20.8	48.4	69.2
R-1 (mid)	6.8	0.1	6.9
R-1 (low)	23.9	0.0	23.9
Below R-1 (low)	0.0	0.0	0.0

The two rating groups are for CP issued by companies and CP issued as securitizations. We will discuss these latter issues later in this chapter and again when we talk about working capital management in Chapter 24. However, the important point is that in 2010, no CP was issued in the Canadian market with other than a prime R-1 rating. This is important since even R-2 is rated adequate quality or "investment" grade.

The distribution of DBRS CP ratings confirms the fact that the CP market is only accessible to firms with the best credit ratings. However, even for these firms, investors are wary of investing in CP unless the companies have **liquidity support**, ensuring that money will be available to pay off the CP if the firms cannot roll it over by selling to new investors. Liquidity support is usually a dedicated backup line of credit from a bank. The firm can draw on the credit line to pay off the CP if needed when it comes due. The commitment fee to establish a bank line of credit for liquidity support is about 0.125 percent per year, but varies with credit market conditions, which adds to the overall cost for a company issuing CP. We will discuss these facilities shortly when we discuss bank financing.

CP is sold directly from the dealing rooms by the major investment banks. The trading or dealing room is a huge room with areas or desks allocated for selling different securities; each desk is flanked by a series of computer screens. The "money market desk" is an area in which traders sell CP. The traders call major institutional investors and sell them the CP that the bank has arranged to sell on behalf of its clients. Usually the bank charges 0.125 percent as a selling commission, but this is often bid down, depending on market conditions. CP is usually sold on the basis of its credit rating, and an investor will ask, "What do you have R-1 (low)?" This is why the credit ratings are so important because, to a large extent, all the R-1 (low) issues are interchangeable.

Bankers' Acceptances (BAs)

If an issuer does not have a good enough credit rating to access the CP market, it is forced to rely more heavily on its bank for financing. One way of doing this is to have its bank guarantee or "accept" its commercial paper by selling the CP to the bank, which then stamps "accepted" on it and sells it from its own money market desk. These accepted CP issues are called **bankers' acceptances (BAs)**. If the issuer defaults, the bank will pay off the CP at maturity, thereby converting the instrument's credit status into that of the major bank that guarantees it.

In many countries, including the United States, BAs are created as a result of international trade. Typically, an exporter will receive a "bill of exchange" in return for the export of its goods. This bill of exchange is essentially a promissory note issued by the foreign importer, usually guaranteed by its local bank. The exporter will then have this note accepted by its own

liquidity support money available to pay off a debt, often in the form of a dedicated backup line of credit from a bank, which ensures that companies have money to pay off the CP if the firms cannot roll it over by selling to new investors

bankers' acceptances (BAs) short-term paper sold by an issuer to a bank, which guarantees or accepts it, obligating the bank to pay off the debt instrument at maturity if the issuer defaults

bank so that note can be sold for cash. This is how BAs are created in the United States and many other countries, but BAs in Canada have nothing to do with trade. They are a method by which lower-rated companies can issue short-term paper into the money market.

BAs trade as bank CP. Because most Canadian banks are rated R-1 (mid), BA yields are usually marginally lower than prime commercial paper, which is generally a mixture of R-1 (low) and R-1 (mid). However, this is not currently the case. As of March 14, 2012, yields on T-bills, BAs, and CP were as shown in Table 18-3.

TABLE 18-3 Yields on T-Bills, BAs, and CP, March 14, 2012

Type	1 Month (%)	3 Month (%)
T-bills	0.82	0.93
BAs	1.13	1.18
CP	1.07	1.16

As we can see, the yields on CP and BAs were close, with prime commercial paper slightly lower than the yield on BAs.

In terms of the cost to a firm, issuing CP involves the actual interest cost plus the bank fees. These fees typically include the issuing or dealing fee of 0.125 percent and the cost of a line of credit of 0.125 percent, so the total cost of issuing three-month CP as of March 14, 2012, would be about 1.16 percent plus typically 0.25 percent and any other incidental fees. These incidental fees consist of the costs of computer screens and data services, part of the time the firm devotes to managing the issue, and the costs of actually printing the CP notes and selling and redeeming them. In total, the cost of a CP issue is usually the CP yield + 0.375 percent. In contrast, a firm's cost for issuing BAs is the yield on the BA plus the bank's stamping or acceptance fee. This fee is usually 0.5 to 0.75 percent, depending on the credit risk involved. So taking these fees as typical, on March 14, 2012, the total cost to the firm of financing by using BAs was 1.68 percent to 1.93 percent. CP tends to be significantly cheaper only for the largest creditworthy companies that do not need 100 percent backup from a line of credit and that raise significant amounts of money.

Overall, as of December 2010, the Canadian money market consisted of the amounts outstanding shown in Table 18-4.

TABLE 18-4 Canadian Money Market (December 2010)

	$ Million
Corporate commercial paper	26,616
Securitizations	25,099
BAs	45,817
Provincial T-bills	42,455
Canada T-bills	174,532
Total	314,519

With $314 billion of securities, most with a maturity of one to three months, there is a huge amount of money turning over every day as most of the debt is simply renewed by issuing new securities. The money market is therefore a huge liquid market of short-term securities that are regarded as virtually default free and very safe. However, if that promise to repay becomes doubtful, the market evaporates in a hurry, which is what happened starting in July 2007. Figure 18-2 shows the default yield spreads for both BAs and CP starting in January 2006, before the financial crisis developed. These spreads were at the normal level of 10 to 11 basis points in August 2007, when the Canadian money market was rocked by the revelation that some commercial paper was backed by securities linked to U.S. sub-prime mortgages.

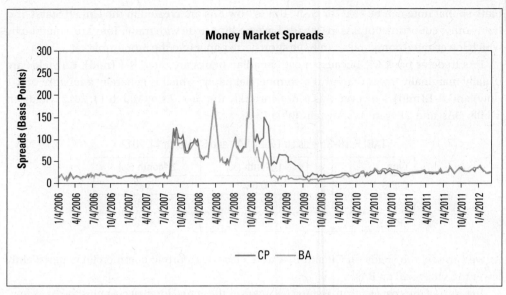

FIGURE 18-2 *Money Market Spreads in Basis Points (1/100 of a Percent)*

Source: Data from Bank of Canada, www.bankofcanada.ca/rates/interest-rates; CANSIM V121812, V121778, and V121775.

The financial crisis first became apparent in July 2007, when a prominent U.S. investment bank, Bear Stearns, revealed that two of its hedge funds were almost worthless because their underlying assets, tied to U.S. sub-prime mortgages, had lost significant value. These two failures initiated a hunt for U.S. sub-prime exposure, and on August 13, 2007, Coventree, a major manager of asset-backed commercial paper (ABCP), was unable to refinance its maturing paper. In short order, the ABCP market in Canada "froze up."

ABCP is an example of the "securitizations" that we mentioned above. We will discuss how these are used in Chapter 24, but, in essence, ABCP consists of commercial paper issued not by a specific company but by a special-purpose vehicle (SPV), with the CP paid from the proceeds of the underlying assets in the SPV. Typically, the underlying assets are things like car loans, mortgages, or other short-term debts owed to companies. These loans are sold to the SPV, which finances the purchase by issuing CP. The advantage is that investors in the CP are not at risk from other corporate activities; they are simply at risk of the loans not being paid off. This risk is usually reduced by various credit enhancement techniques, so ABCP is given a high credit rating by DBRS and can easily be sold.

This changed on August 13, 2007, when Coventree indicated that a small percentage of the underlying assets of the ABCP it managed was backed by debt obligations linked to U.S. sub-prime mortgages. As indicated earlier, a mere hint of default is enough to cause promised yields on debt to increase dramatically. In this case, as the ABCP came due, investors demanded their money back and refused to finance new issues of ABCP. This meant Coventree and others were forced to pay off the ABCP, with no cash coming in from new issues of ABCP. In this liquidity crisis, Coventree called on its banks to honour their liquidity agreements, but they refused, for reasons we will discuss shortly. The result was a freeze in the ABCP market, and $32 billion of ABCP instantly went from being liquid commercial paper to totally illiquid securities of questionable value as investors shied away from anything that could be linked to U.S. sub-prime debt.

Default spreads on CP and BAs remained high after August 2007 as, first, Bear Stearns was bailed out by the U.S. government in March 2008 when it verged on bankruptcy, and then Lehman Brothers was allowed to fail on September 14, 2008, when the U.S. government decided it could not bail out yet another investment bank. The failures of two major U.S. investment banks caused investors around the world to wonder who was next and to retreat from any form of risk. This forced drastic actions on the part of the U.S. government to calm the markets, and gradually money market spreads returned to normal, where they have been for the past three years. However, it points out that the money market is usually a very boring market punctuated by periods of extreme panic.

CONCEPT REVIEW QUESTIONS

1. Explain how interest is received on most money market instruments.

2. Contrast treasury bills, commercial paper, and BAs in terms of who issues them, their basic structure and default risk, and the yields they provide.

3. Define yield spreads and explain how they arise.

18.3 BANK FINANCING

In short-term financing, the chartered banks are important. For example, when issuing CP, most firms are required to have a backup line of credit to ensure that, in the event of a disruption in the money market, funds are available to pay off the CP.[9] However, the line of credit is not available if the credit condition of the company or security deteriorates, and the credit condition is reviewed continually by the bank. This is why the banks refused to honour their liquidity support when Coventree called on them after announcing that its ABCP was backed in part by assets linked to U.S. sub-prime debt. In the banks' view, Coventree's problem was not caused by external factors but by a deterioration in the credit quality of Coventree's ABCP.

Whether the banks were right in not honouring their liquidity support hinges on whether investor refusal to buy new issues of ABCP was due to a deterioration in credit quality or a general flight to quality that affected all of the CP market. This question will doubtless be the cause of significant litigation, since hundreds of millions of dollars were lost. However, the Coventree example reinforces the critical role of the banks in the money market. We have already seen that if a CP issuer wants an unconditional guarantee from a bank, the issuer can have the CP guaranteed so it becomes a BA. This costs 50 to 75 basis points, because the bank is then exposed to credit risk. The Office of the Superintendent of Financial Institutions (OSFI) requires that banks provide the right amount of capital when making such guarantees, since they are not costless.

However, the CP and BA markets are useful only for companies that have reasonably large and continuous financing needs because CP and BAs are sold in large amounts, usually at least $1 million. For smaller, irregular-sized financing requirements, firms rely more on traditional bank financing. These consist of term loans and lines of credit.

Lines of Credit (LCs)

We have already mentioned **lines of credit (LC)** in our discussion of CP. The different types of LCs are a basic financing tool provided by banks. The standard type is an **operating or demand LC**. These are lending facilities that are made available by the bank for the firm's operating purposes—they generally cannot be used to back up a CP program. Technically, operating LCs are demand loans that can be cancelled at any time. However, in practice, banks are reluctant to do anything that might trigger financial problems for a firm, because this might leave them legally liable for damages. In structure, an LC is a loan for a maximum dollar amount that the firm can draw down by electronically transferring funds from the operating line to its chequing (or current) account.

The standard cost of the operating line is the **prime lending rate**. Prime is an example of a **floating interest rate** because it changes regularly, so the cost of a firm's demand loan

Learning Objective 18.3
Describe the types of debt financing provided by banks.

lines of credit (LCs) a basic financing tool provided by banks that establishes a loan with a specified limit to a firm based on its creditworthiness

operating or demand LCs lending facilities that are made available by the bank for the firm's operating purposes and that generally cannot be used to back up a CP program; these demand loans can be cancelled at any time

prime lending rate the interest rate banks use to calculate their other interest rates; it is also the standard cost of an operating line of credit

floating interest rate an interest rate that changes regularly

---

[9] Sometimes, external factors, such as an unexpected major default, cause investors to stop buying CP, even though the credit status of an issuer is unchanged.

will float with the bank's prime lending rate. As prime changes, the bank will inform the firm of the change in the cost of its loan for the upcoming month. Whereas CP costs between 1.68 and 1.93 percent, on March 14, 2012, prime was 3 percent, generally making it cheaper to "escape the bank." The bank will make loans available to its most creditworthy customers at rates below prime, particularly if they are large enough to access the money market, since otherwise this is what they will do, taking their business away from the bank. However, most firms are "prime plus" borrowers, so borrowing rates are quoted as prime plus 0.5 percent, prime plus 1 percent, and so on.

term or revolving LC a line of credit extended by a bank to a firm for a specific amount that automatically adjusts as payments are made or received

The second type of bank line of credit adds more stability to the firm. This is the **term or revolving LC**. The term is usually at least 364 days and can be as long as five years, renewable every six months. Often a five-year "revolver" is renewed at the end of each year, making it an "evergreen" five-year line of credit. Because the revolver is a commitment of credit, the bank has to provide capital against these commitments to ensure the liquidity of the bank. These LCs are commonly for 364 days because more capital is required against a one-year or 365-day LC.

Revolving LCs are flexible financing tools for both the bank and the firm. In addition to being used to provide straight borrowings, they are also used to back up CP programs or other commitments, such as forward foreign currency contracts. However, banks have tightened up on the potential uses for these bank LCs, observing the general principle that lines of credit are for "liquidity" and not "credit enhancement" purposes. This means that the bank will withdraw or adjust the line of credit if a "material adverse change" occurs—that is, if the credit quality of the firm deteriorates. The LC provides the firm with liquidity that it can draw down only if its credit quality is constant. The OSFI, which regulates the banks, monitors lines of credit to make sure that they are used for liquidity purposes. What the OSFI is worried about is the possibility that a deterioration in credit quality could cause large numbers of firms with poor credit to suddenly draw down their lines of credit, thus endangering the stability of the banking system.

Firms have to meet a variety of restrictions to maintain access to the funds in an LC. Typically, the maximum value of the LC is determined by using a standard formula—for example, that it cannot exceed 75 percent of a company's receivables plus 50 percent of its inventory. Normally, the firm must provide periodic abbreviated financial statements, sometimes monthly. The firm may then have to meet certain credit restrictions, or **covenants**, such as maintaining the following:

covenants promises or restrictions in a contract

- a minimum current ratio of 1.4 or net working capital of $100 million
- net worth (shareholders' equity) in excess of $250 million
- a minimum interest coverage ratio (times interest earned) of 1.75
- an asset coverage ratio in excess of 2 and a debt ratio less than 0.75

The covenants in the revolving loan allow the bank to pull the loan (i.e., demand repayment) and/or prevent the firm from drawing the loan down beyond a certain amount as its credit quality deteriorates. However, the restrictions are only of limited effectiveness; firms usually have more than one bank account, and they know before the bank does whether they are going to violate the conditions. In that case, they can simply draw down the line of credit before informing the bank of the violations and transfer the funds to another bank where they have full use of the money. Of course, this will damage their reputation, which could impede their ability to borrow in the future.

In addition to the interest costs, the banks normally charge a commitment fee of around 0.5 percent for setting up the LC, which is also charged on the unused balance. As with the operating line, most revolvers are based on prime, with less creditworthy firms paying higher spreads above prime. However, larger customers, who may be able to access the money market directly, are increasingly being offered lines that can be drawn down in either Canadian or

U.S. dollars. The Canadian dollar funds are then based on BA plus 0.5 percent to 0.75 percent, while the U.S. rate is based on LIBOR. This is consistent with our discussion in Chapter 11, where we saw that the base borrowing rates for banks are the BA rate in Canadian dollars and LIBOR for U.S. dollars.

Term Loans

The idea behind LCs is that the funds are used for working capital: financing receivables, inventory, and ongoing corporate activity, such as hedging by using swaps and forwards. In fact, some more traditional banks still require "cleanup" periods, in which the firm has a zero balance on its line of credit, to make sure that the bank is not providing "permanent" financing, which should be financed with longer-term funds. **Term loans** differ from lines of credit because they have a fixed maturity, require repayment to be made on a fixed schedule, and are meant to finance longer-term requirements such as equipment purchases.

term loans loans to finance longer-term requirements, such as equipment purchases; they have a fixed maturity and require repayment to be made on a fixed schedule

These loans are structured in a variety of ways. They are usually for a term of at least three years and may go out to 10 years or longer. Some involve "bullet" or "balloon" payments: only interest is paid until maturity, at which time the entire principal is due and payable. Such loans generally provide permanent financing of the firm's operations, rather than financing a particular asset. In contrast, amortizing loans are similar to conventional loans made to individuals, in which a monthly payment consists of both interest and principal payments. These are similar to a car loan or mortgage, which are valued as annuities, as discussed in Chapter 5.

Similar to other forms of bank financing, term loans may be based on the prime lending rate and thus float with the general level of interest rates. However, term loans are often offered with a fixed interest rate over the term of the loan. In addition, term loans are also offered by insurance companies and specialized business finance companies, often for longer periods than those offered by the chartered banks.

The big advantage of term loans to a borrowing company is that they are easy to arrange. All firms have banking relationships because they need chequing accounts to gain access to the payments system, and they also need banks for short-term financing and to arrange hedging contracts, such as swaps and forwards. Consequently, the firm's bank already has inside knowledge of its activities and can readily arrange a term loan if it judges the firm to be creditworthy. Further, the term loan can often be structured to fit with a firm's operating and revolving LCs. For example, sometimes a revolver is structured to switch into a term loan at the end of its five-year life.

CONCEPT REVIEW QUESTIONS

1. Briefly describe operating LCs, revolving LCs, and term loans.
2. Why do banks typically impose debt covenants on their borrowing customers?
3. Why is it reasonable to assume that most firms will have a banking relationship?

18.4 LONG-TERM DEBT AND THE MONEY MARKET

Long-term financing generally refers to any debt issued with a term longer than one year. It is often called "funded" debt. This is because short-term debt is not regarded as permanent capital; therefore, when a firm accumulates "too much" short-term debt, it funds this debt by issuing long-term debt. As discussed above, banks provide medium-term financing through term loans, which are also provided by insurance companies and other specialized financial companies. These are examples of private financing, because the debt is not offered to the general public. For bank financing, the firm generally does not have to provide any extra

Learning Objective 18.4
Identify the requirements that must typically be satisfied for public debt issues.

information, because it already provides information in support of its existing bank relationship. For term loans from other entities, the firm will have to provide an offering memorandum. As described in Chapter 17, this document contains much the same type of information as a prospectus does, but in less detail.

The remaining forms of financing involve public financing, and here it is important to realize that securities legislation, with the requirement that a prospectus be filed, applies to debt as well as equity offerings. As discussed in Chapter 17, most financing in the capital markets is done by reporting issuers, who can raise capital, both debt and equity, through the issue of a short-form prospectus. These documents are filed with the provincial or territorial securities commissions and are publicly available. (For example, the documents filed with the Ontario Securities Commission are available on www.sedar.com.)

On November 21, 2001, BC Gas (now FortisBC) filed a short-form prospectus to raise $500 million in medium-term note debentures (MTNs).[10] (The word "debenture" formerly meant "unsecured bonds" but now generically refers to any bond, so we refer to secured and unsecured debentures.) The prospectus indicated that the MTNs would be in either interest-bearing or discount form and would be registered for sale either in Canada or as global debentures. The interest rates were to be determined by the company, after consultation with its dealers, for an amount of up to $500 million for 25 months from the date of the prospectus, bringing the total MTN borrowing up to $1,400 million.

The short-form prospectus simply gave notice that BC Gas intended to raise $500 million in some form or another over the next two years. The exact terms of any issue would then be documented in a pricing supplement or "term sheet" negotiated between the company and its investment dealers, who would be canvassing major institutional purchasers to work out the most attractive issue at any point in time. As we discussed in Chapter 11, BC Gas could always use the swap market to convert the terms of a particular issue into something more attractive to it.

Apart from the information included in the prospectus, the following was included "by reference":

- annual information form

- audited financial statements

- unaudited six-month statements

- any other information filed with the securities commission after the date of the prospectus but before the termination of the offering

Essentially, all the regular documents filed by BC Gas as a reporting issuer were part of the prospectus. The BC Gas short-form prospectus is an example of the new "continuous disclosure" practices that allow larger firms to access the capital markets on an almost continuous basis.

When firms issue securities to the general public, some basic mechanical problems have to be solved. For example, who keeps track of who owns the securities, makes sure they get their interest or dividends, and ensures that the company meets its obligations? Securities offered to the general public are normally held by the Canadian Depository for Securities (CDS). CDS physically holds the securities and maintains book entries regarding security ownership, but as we pointed out in Chapter 17, this is usually a major institution rather than the ultimate owner. A **transfer agent** looks after the day-to-day administration of the securities. For the BC Gas MTNs, CIBC Mellon Trust Company (CIBC Mellon) was the transfer agent and registrar. It maintained a record of the individuals who owned the MTNs and who therefore expected to receive interest and principal payments. Payment of interest, for example, could be made by electronic funds transfer or by cheque (dated on the interest date) to the owner in CIBC Mellon's records.

transfer agent a company that handles the day-to-day administration of securities and maintains records, including purchases, sales, and account balances

---

[10] The following discussion paraphrases the information in the prospectus.

The transfer agent also makes sure that the legal documentation is satisfied. For example, the BC Gas MTNs were issued under a 1977 indenture between CIBC Mellon and a predecessor company (Inland Gas and Oil, Ltd.). This indenture had been updated many times since, but it stipulated the rights of the MTN holders. For example, it stipulated that BC Gas could issue an unlimited amount of MTNs, but the bonds would rank equally with all other unsecured and unsubordinated debt of the company. What does this mean?

First, it means that the MTNs ranked behind any secured debt outstanding in the event of default—that is, the secured debt holders had first claim on the particular underlying assets in the event of default. In the case of BC Gas, two different types of secured bonds technically ranked ahead of the MTNs. The first were BC Gas's "first mortgage bonds." Mortgage bonds are similar to residential mortgage arrangements, in which the lender has registered a claim on the underlying real property that is financed. For BC Gas, this real property largely consisted of small-diameter pipelines used for distributing natural gas to customers in British Columbia. These were "first" mortgage bonds because they had first claim on the underlying assets, whereas "second" bonds would rank behind them.

BC Gas also had $275 million in **purchase-money mortgages** outstanding. These are mortgages that constitute all or part of the compensation received for the sale of property and are used when the seller is also the lender. These were issued for the purchase of the gas-distribution assets of another B.C. company.

purchase-money mortgages mortgages that constitute all or part of the compensation received for the sale of property; used when the seller is also the lender

For BC Gas, the impact of these secured bonds was moot because none of the first mortgage bonds were still outstanding, while the purchase-money mortgages were specialized financing tools. Generally, mortgage bonds have been declining in popularity because, as with a regular mortgage, the claim of the lender has to be registered, which involves significant legal costs, particularly for companies with assets across Canada. Furthermore, what is a creditor going to do if it has to seize kilometres and kilometres of underground gas mains?[11] The problem is that many underlying assets are specific to the firm; if it does go bankrupt, forcing the lender to seize the assets, they have little value. So, de facto, there were few claims above BC Gas's MTNs.

The term **unsubordinated debt** means that no other unsecured debt ranked ahead of these MTNs. BC Gas did not have any subordinated debt outstanding at the time, but if it did, it would simply mean that this class of unsecured debt ranked behind the MTNs. If BC Gas had "junior" subordinated debt, it would mean that this debt ranked even farther behind. This ranking has the same interpretation as the terms "first" and "second" when used in reference to mortgage bonds.

unsubordinated debt unsecured debt that ranks first with the company; no other unsecured debt ranks ahead of it

The BC Gas trust indenture also indicated the actions of the company that could trigger default:

1. nonpayment of principal when due

2. nonpayment of interest after 30 days

3. an order for the winding up or liquidation of the firm

4. issuance of a general assignment of debts or declaration of bankruptcy

5. any execution enforced against the property of the company that was not paid after 45 days to the extent that it had not been challenged

6. default on its first mortgage bonds or purchase-money mortgages

7. violation of a covenant provision and failing to make good on such a violation in 60 days

The first two clauses are clear: failing to make a contractual payment of principal or interest causes default. Clause 6 indicates that default on its other long-term obligations also

---

[11] The alternative uses for small-diameter natural gas pipes are rather limited.

cross-default clause a clause that indicates that default on one obligation also constitutes default on another

constitutes default on the MTNs; this is referred to as a **cross-default clause**. Under clause 5, if someone goes to court and is allowed to claim any of the assets of BC Gas, and this claim has not been settled in 30 to 45 days (depending on the type of asset), this also causes default. This clause is similar to the cross-default clause in that it indicates an inability to pay a court order. Clauses 3 and 4 indicate that even if the company has not defaulted on any of its obligations, if it initiates procedures to wind down its business or go into bankruptcy, this constitutes default.

All these actions constitute "default," so how does this happen? It is the job of the trustee, CIBC Mellon, to monitor BC Gas's situation and, at its discretion or on the direction of the holders of 25 percent of the outstanding value of the MTN bonds, inform BC Gas that all of the outstanding MTN debt and accrued interest are due immediately. If BC Gas fails to pay on demand the full principal and interest owed, CIBC Mellon, at its discretion or again at the request of holders of 25 percent of the value of the outstanding MTNs, proceeds to get a court order to enforce payment. It is this movement to enforce payment that usually triggers the defaulting firm to go into bankruptcy protection.

Clause 7 refers to violations of the covenant provisions in the BC Gas MTN indenture, which restrict what BC Gas can do. These particular MTNs were relatively "clean" in that they had few restrictions. The major covenants were as follows:

1. BC Gas will not "mortgage, pledge, charge, or otherwise encumber" any of its assets unless the MTNs are given the same security. The only exception is the existing first mortgage bonds and purchase-money mortgages.

2. BC Gas will not guarantee any debt that is not necessary for carrying on its existing business.

3. The company will not issue any additional debt unless its earnings in 12 of the past 23 months satisfy a 2.0 times interest coverage ratio after the new debt has been issued and other debt retired.

4. The company will maintain its facilities for the supply of gas to enable it to carry on its business and will not sell shares that cause certain designated subsidiaries to cease to be subsidiaries.

negative pledge a clause that stipulates that a borrower may not create higher-priority debt without giving the other debt holders the same security

The first covenant is a standard **negative pledge** clause. It means that BC Gas cannot create higher-priority debt that ranks above the MTNs without giving the MTN holders the same security. All BC Gas can do is issue more debt under its two existing secured debt indentures. The idea behind the negative pledge is simply to prevent the company from issuing large amounts of senior debt that ranks above the MTNs, thereby making them riskier. The second covenant prevents BC Gas from issuing guarantees. The reason for this restriction is that BC Gas is part of a holding company, and the bondholders are worried that its parent might make the company guarantee other assets of the company. If the guarantee were then called, it would endanger the credit of the company, making the MTNs riskier. The fourth covenant ensures that BC Gas remains a utility that distributes natural gas.

The most interesting covenant provision is the third one, which is standard to most gas-distribution utilities. This is the interest coverage restriction (ICR). Although the company could issue an unlimited amount of MTNs under the indenture, the ICR restricts such issues to make sure they do not make the existing MTNs riskier. As we discussed in Chapter 4, the interest coverage ratio is determined by taking the earnings before interest and tax (EBIT) and dividing this figure by the interest payments. The ICR ensures the firm does not issue so much debt that this ratio drops below 2.0. In doing this, it allows the company to "smooth" its earnings a bit by taking the best 12 out of 23 months. The interest on the new debt is then added to the existing interest costs, and the interest on any retired debt is subtracted. The focus on the ICR is common for utilities because their earnings are stable. For other firms, the restriction is more often in terms of the debt ratio.

An ICR of 2.0 would be very low for a typical firm, but utilities have low business risk because they are regulated and provide an essential service. The result is that utility debt is also low risk. A critical element in the prospectus for the MTNs was the fact that BC Gas debt was rated A by DBRS and, in the opinion of BC Gas's legal counsel, was an eligible investment under most of the legislation governing prudent investments for major financial institutions.[12] These rules are often referred to as "legal for life" rules and mean that the BC Gas MTNs could be sold to the widest possible group of investors.

This discussion of an actual bond issue by a major Canadian company is important because it emphasizes that bonds are a contractual obligation. The bond contract is exactly that—a contract—and the company cannot violate its terms without the trustee taking them to court or at least forcing them to negotiate. *Finance in the News 18-1* is a press release from Sino-Forest, which continues the discussion of the company started in Chapter 17. Following a securities analyst's devastating critique of the company in June 2011 and the collapse in its share price, Sino-Forest was investigated and forced to suspend the release of its 2011 Q3 financial results, which contravened securities laws and a covenant in its bond contract. This meant that the bondholders could seek court action to protect their interest. Instead, they pressured Sino-Forest to make major changes to address the serious concerns raised by the securities analyst. In the interim, the Ontario Securities Commission suspended trading in Sino-Forest's common shares because there was so much uncertainty about the true state of the company.

finance INTHENEWS 18-1 — Sino-Forest Corporation's Noteholders Waive Default under Senior Notes on Agreed Terms

SINO-FOREST CORPORATION ("Sino-Forest" or the "Company") today announced that holders of a majority in principal amount of its Senior Notes due 2014 and its Senior Notes due 2017 have agreed to waive the default arising from the Company's failure to release its 2011 third quarter financial results (the "Q3 Results") on a timely basis. The Company also announced the terms under which its noteholders agreed to waive the default.

As disclosed in the Company's December 18, 2011, press release, Sino-Forest received written notices of default dated December 16, 2011, in respect of its two series of Senior Notes. The notices referenced the Company's previously disclosed failure to release the Q3 results on a timely basis. The Company's breach of the Senior Note indentures relating to the Q3 results could be waived for a series of Senior Notes by the holders of at least a majority in principal amount of that series.

Following extensive discussions with an ad hoc committee of noteholders (the "Ad Hoc Noteholders"), holders of a majority in principal amount of the Company's two series of Senior Notes agreed to waive the default. The material terms of the waiver agreements are described below.

The Company will file the waiver agreements on SEDAR www.sedar.com and on the Company's website www.sinoforest.com.

Payment of Interest on Notes, Waiver Fee, and Advisor Costs

Pursuant to the waiver agreements, the Company has agreed to make the US$9.775 million interest payment on its 2016 Convertible Notes that was due on December 15, 2011. The Company also has agreed to continue to pay when due interest on the Convertible Notes due 2013 and 2016 and on the Senior Notes due 2014 and 2017.

The Company has agreed to pay a waiver fee of 1% of the principal amount to all holders of the Senior Notes due 2014 and 2017. The aggregate waiver fee to be paid is US$9,991,870. In addition, the Company has agreed to pay the fees of the advisors to the Ad Hoc Noteholders (the "Ad Hoc Committee Advisors"). Goodmans LLP and Hogan Lovells LLP are acting as legal advisors to the Ad Hoc Noteholders.

Release of Q3 Financial Results

Sino-Forest has agreed to use its reasonable best efforts to address outstanding issues noted in its press release dated December 12, 2011, in order to file its Q3 Results.

Ontario Securities Commission Cease Trade Order

On August 26, 2011, the Ontario Securities Commission issued a temporary cease trade order against the Company and others. On September 8, 2011, the Company consented to an extension of the cease trade order against the Company to January 25, 2012. The Company has agreed to a further extension of the cease trade order, and there are ongoing discussions between the Company and staff of the Ontario Securities Commission with respect to the term of any extension. In the waiver agreements, the Company has agreed to file an application to lift the cease trade order as soon as practicable.

Maintenance of Cash Balances

The Company has agreed that it and its subsidiaries will maintain in aggregate a minimum cash balance inside the People's Republic of China (excluding Hong Kong) of US$165 million and a minimum cash balance outside of the People's Republic of China (including Hong Kong)

continued

---

[12] These regulations include, for example, the *Insurance Companies Act*, the *Trust and Loan Companies Act*, and the *Pension Benefits Standards Act (Canada)*.

Finance in the News 18-1: Sino-Forest Corporation's Noteholders Waive Default under Senior Notes on Agreed Terms (continued)

of US$140 million. The Company also has agreed to take steps to manage liquidity and to monetize assets for the repayment of the Company's indebtedness.

Strategic Plan

The Company has agreed to provide a strategic plan to the Ad Hoc Committee Advisors on or before March 31, 2012, and to keep them informed of the progress of this effort. The strategic plan will include an indicative timeline for any sale process, capital or equity process and will address to the extent practicable such other steps that are necessary to maximize value in respect of the Company's assets.

Governance

The Company also has agreed that the constitution and size of, and governance matters related to, the Board of Directors of the Company and any committees, including the Strategic Restructuring Committee of the Board of Directors, will be satisfactory to the Ad Hoc Committee Advisors, on behalf of the Ad Hoc Noteholders, by no later than March 31, 2012. Thereafter, any governance changes must be satisfactory to the Ad Hoc Committee Advisors on behalf of the Ad Hoc Noteholders. Sino-Forest has agreed that there shall be no appointment of any new members to the Board of Directors, senior officers, or any chief restructuring officer unless such appointment is on terms satisfactory to the Ad Hoc Committee Advisors on behalf of the Ad Hoc Noteholders.

Access to Information

To the extent permitted by law and the terms of any contractual confidentiality obligations, the Company has agreed to provide the Ad Hoc Committee Advisors with access to the Company's premises, assets, accounts, books and records, and to make advisors to the Company and appropriate officers of the Company with relevant information available for discussions with these advisors. The Ad Hoc Committee Advisors have executed confidentiality agreements with the Company. The waiver agreements contemplate that the Ad Hoc Noteholders also may receive confidential information upon execution of confidentiality agreements in a form acceptable to the Company.

The Company has also agreed to keep the Ad Hoc Committee Advisors reasonably informed regarding any material discussions with any party with respect to any material transactions concerning the Company. Where deemed appropriate by the Company, the Company also will provide the Ad Hoc Noteholders or the Ad Hoc Committee Advisors with an opportunity to participate in such discussions.

Restrictions on Material Transactions and Shareholder Distributions

The waiver agreements also contain restrictions on the Company's ability to enter into material transactions, sell all or substantially all of its assets, and to enter into transactions outside of the ordinary course of business.

The Company has agreed not to make or pay any dividend, charge, fee, or other distribution to its shareholders or subsidiaries. The Company has agreed to restrictions on the additional indebtedness it may incur.

Final Report of the Independent Committee

The Company has agreed that the Independent Committee of the Board of Directors will deliver its final report and that such report will be made public by January 31, 2012. Thereafter, any residual matters or issues identified in the final report or earlier reports of the Independent Committee shall be addressed by the Company and its advisors in consultation with the Ad Hoc Committee Advisors.

The Company believes that any residual matters or issues identified by the Independent Committee are best and more efficiently addressed by the Audit Committee or the Special Restructuring Committee, working in consultation with the Ad Hoc Committee Advisors.

Conditions to and Termination of Waiver

The waiver will terminate on the earlier of April 30, 2012, and any earlier termination of the waiver agreements in accordance with their terms, unless extended by the parties. The waiver agreements contain covenants (many of which have to be satisfied by March 31, 2012), the breach of which would entitle the Ad Hoc Noteholders to terminate the waiver upon 30 days' notice to the Company. In addition, the waivers will immediately terminate upon the Company or any of its subsidiaries becoming subject to certain insolvency, receivership, or bankruptcy proceeding without the prior written consent of holders of a majority of the principal amount of the series of notes to which the waiver relates.

Source: Sino-Forest press release, January 12, 2012. Retrieved from http://www.sinoforest.com/companyreleases.asp.

CONCEPT REVIEW QUESTIONS

1. Define mortgage bonds, secured debentures, unsecured debentures, and subordinated debt.

2. Discuss the rationale for including debt covenants in a public issue.

3. Briefly describe negative pledge and cross-default clauses.

18.5 BOND RATINGS

Interpreting Debt Ratings

We have already seen that DBRS rates commercial paper and that a rating is essential to access the CP market. When investments have such a short maturity, it makes credit analysis expensive. For longer-term debt issues, most purchasers, like the major institutions mentioned above, do their own credit analysis. However, bond ratings are still important. In Chapter 6, we listed Standard & Poor's (S&P) debt-rating categories; in Table 18-5 we show DBRS's rating structure for long-term debt.

Learning Objective 18.5
Explain how debt ratings are determined, what they mean, and how useful they are in predicting default and recovery rates associated with public debt issues.

TABLE 18-5 DBRS's Rating Structure for Long-Term Debt

AAA	Highest credit quality
AA	Superior credit quality
A	Satisfactory credit quality
BBB	Adequate credit quality
BB	Speculative
B	Highly speculative
CCC/CC/C	Very highly speculative

In addition, each rating may be modified with a high or low rating. The lowest **investment-grade** bond rating is BBB (low); below this the bonds are commonly referred to as **junk bonds**, although they are more politely referred to as "high-yield bonds."

The long-term bond ratings are similar in meaning to the CP ratings we discussed earlier. In fact, normally there is a direct correspondence, with R-1 (high) being equivalent to AAA, R-1 (mid) to AA, and R-1 (low) to A.

We previously noted that there is currently no R-2-rated CP outstanding in the Canadian money market, where R-2 is equivalent to a BBB long-term bond rating and is still regarded as investment-grade debt. Similarly, until recently there was little BBB-rated original issue long-term debt in Canada. The relatively few issues outstanding were either from smaller regulated utilities or from issuers that started out as some form of A and were subsequently downgraded—the so-called fallen angels. The rule of thumb is that non-investment-grade issuers, below BBB (low), generally raise debt in the U.S. high-yield market and then swap back into the Canadian market, because there are more investors willing to invest in original issue high-yield debt in the United States.

The most common DBRS rating is A, which DBRS defined in the following way:

> Long-term debt rated "A" is of satisfactory credit quality. Protection of interest and principal is still substantial, but the degree of strength is less than that of AA-rated entities. While "A" is a respectable rating, entities in this category are considered to be more susceptible to adverse economic conditions and have greater cyclical tendencies than higher-rated securities.[13]

investment grade a bond rating that means the issuer is likely to meet payment obligations

junk bonds speculative bonds with ratings below investment grade; often called "high-yield bonds"

Determining Bond Ratings

DBRS determines a bond rating after extensive consultation with the company—which includes a site visit in which the company can state its view of its business and future prospects—and after examining at least five years of financial statements. The rating agency also usually has prior knowledge of the company from its extensive industry surveys. DBRS will issue a draft report to the company so it can check for any analytic or data errors before the agency issues a final rating. In determining its rating, DBRS is guided by two basic principles: the stable rating philosophy and the hierarchy principle.

---

[13] Dominion Bond Rating Service, "Bonds, Long Term Debt and Preferred Share Ratings." DBRS press release, January 2000.

stable rating philosophy the idea that ratings are based on structural and not cyclical factors; changes in ratings are not made in response to temporary changes in the economy but only when there are clear structural changes in a company's credit

credit watch a status applied to a firm by a rating agency when it is monitoring the firm

hierarchy principle a principle based on the fact that rating agencies rate debt issues and not companies; rating agencies rate each class of debt lower than the previous class, unless there is little of the higher-ranked debt outstanding

The **stable rating philosophy** is founded on the idea that the rating is based on structural and not cyclical factors. The fortunes of most companies will fluctuate with the business cycle: when the economy is hot, most companies will make money; conversely, when it is in recession, most companies will struggle. Holders of 20- or 30-year debt can expect the company to operate through many ups and downs of the business cycle. DBRS aims to see through these predictable effects and change ratings only when a clear structural change occurs in the company's credit. This sounds easier than it is because, in practice, it can be difficult to maintain ratings when the economy is in deep recession, even though the company is responding to that recession in a predictable manner. This is the stage when many rating agencies put companies on **credit watch**, rather than cutting the rating.

The **hierarchy principle** is based on the fact that DBRS rates debt issues and not companies. Although we think of a rating as applied to a particular company, this is not the case: DBRS generally takes off a level for each class of debt. So the first mortgage bonds of a company might be rated as A (high), unsecured MTNs as A, and junior subordinated bonds as A (low). DBRS departs from this rule when there is little of the higher-ranked debt outstanding, in which case the next class of debt assumes the rating of the more senior debt. For this reason, it is inappropriate to compare the rating of one company's first mortgage bonds with another firm's junior subordinated debentures.

In determining its rating, DBRS looks at six basic factors:

1. *Core profitability:* This is an assessment based on standard profit measures, such as the return on equity, return on assets, the "quality" of a firm's earnings, its cost structure (i.e., whether it is a low-cost producer, etc.), its growth opportunities, and its pricing structure.

2. *Asset quality:* Assets are made up of many different types, so DBRS looks at the importance of intangibles (for example, how valuable is the goodwill on the firm's balance sheet), the market value of the firm's assets, and its use of derivatives and risk management to see whether it is managing its operational and market risks effectively.

3. *Strategy and management strength:* Ultimately, a firm comprises assets and management, so the capabilities of the senior management group are vitally important to an assessment of a firm's credit risk. This is particularly important if the firm is actively involved in mergers and acquisitions, where a clear strategic approach and skills at integrating acquired companies are valuable.

4. *Balance sheet strength:* If the lenders have to initiate bankruptcy proceedings, it is important that they know where they stand in the overall liabilities of the firm, so awareness of standard debt ratios, coverage tests, and the amount of financial flexibility available to the firm is important. The latter includes an assessment of the firm's reliance on short-term debt, its commitment to a capital expenditure program that cannot be easily stopped, and the support potentially available from other parties, such as affiliated companies. Size is important because larger firms are usually less risky and have more market power.

5. *Business strength:* This category looks at standard factors, including market share; key intangibles, such as the quality of the work force; industry issues, such as the degree of unionization and competition; growth prospects for the industry; and issues specific to the company, such as its implementation of a defensible base of diversified operations and up-to-date management information systems.

6. *Miscellaneous issues:* This is a "catch-all" category, including such issues as the quality of the firm's financial statements and whether there have been frequent restatements, the structure of the bond indenture, and the importance of the firm and industry to the province or territory or to Canada.

Overall, the DBRS approach combines standard financial analysis, based on the ratios discussed in Chapter 4, with a broader firm and industry analysis. The result is a mixture of quantitative and qualitative factors. In 2011–12, for example, the Canadian economy was relatively stable, with few downgrades. This was not the case in Europe, where the sovereign debt problems of the eurozone countries created problems for institutions in those markets. *Finance in the News 18-2* discusses S&P's downgrades of 34 Italian banks following on its downgrade of Italy's debt to BBB+.

---

finance INTHENEWS 18-2 S&P Downgrades 34 Italian Banks after Reducing Nation's Rating

UniCredit SpA (UCG), Intesa Sanpaolo SpA and Banca Monte dei Paschi di Siena SpA (BMPS) were among 34 Italian financial firms downgraded by Standard & Poor's, after the credit-ratings company reduced the nation's grade last month.

UniCredit, Italy's biggest bank, and No. 2 Intesa had their long-term ratings lowered to BBB+ from A, S&P said yesterday in a statement. Monte dei Paschi, the No. 3 bank, was reduced to BBB from BBB+. All three have a negative outlook, S&P said.

Italy's credit rating was cut two levels to BBB+ from A on Jan. 13 as S&P said European leaders' struggle to contain the region's debt crisis would complicate the country's efforts to finance borrowings. S&P yesterday revised its banking industry country risk assessment, known as Bicra, for Italy to group 4 from group 3, citing mounting risks.

"Italy's vulnerability to external financing risks has increased, given its high external public debt, resulting in Italian banks' significantly diminished ability to roll over their wholesale debt," S&P said in a separate statement on the country's financial industry. "We anticipate persistently weak profitability for Italian banks in the next few years."

European nations are grappling with a debt crisis now in its third year as they seek to restore budget order and shore up the region's financial

UniCredit headquarters in Rome, Italy. (Alessia Pierdomenico/Bloomberg via Getty Images)

industry. Spreads on some Italian banks are trading as if they were rated at the cusp of investment grade.

Source: Clark, Patrick, "S&P downgrades 34 Italian banks after reducing nation's rating." *Bloomberg News*, February 10, 2012. Copyright ©2013 Bloomberg. Reprinted by permission.

Empirical Evidence Regarding Debt Ratings

We can assess the quality of the DBRS ratings by looking at how accurately they correlate with future default rates. In April 2005, DBRS assessed the default experience in Canada by using what is termed a static pool analysis.[14] What this amounts to is looking at the ratings for all the firms, then tracking the default rates for these classes in the future, ignoring any subsequent changes in rating. The basic results, based on averages in the number of companies (and not on the dollar amounts outstanding) after 5, 10, and 20 years, are shown in Table 18-6.

---

[13] Dominion Bond Rating Service, *DBRS Corporate Default Study*. Toronto: DBRS, April 2005.

TABLE 18-6 Average Default Rates (%) in Canada

DBRS Rating	Number of Years Examined		
	5	10	20
AAA	0.00	0.00	0.00
AA	0.56	0.63	0.63
A	0.95	1.60	2.33
BBB	2.34	3.82	5.03
BB	6.37	8.99	10.11
B	28.33	28.33	28.33
CCC	33.33	33.33	33.33

The DBRS analysis makes several important points. First, the default rates clearly increase as the DBRS rating goes down, so the ratings provide a good indicator of credit risk. Second, for the investment-grade bond ratings, we can see why BBB is the cutoff point between the investment and non-investment-grade ratings. For the AAA, AA, and A ratings, the default rates are low, with no AAA-rated issuers actually defaulting, and only 0.63 percent of the AAs defaulting. However, there is an exponential increase as credit quality deteriorates, with 2.33 percent of the As defaulting after 20 years, 5.03 percent of the BBBs, 10.11 percent of the BBs, and 28.33 percent of the Bs. From this, we can understand why many major institutional investors restrict their bond portfolio holdings to debt with a minimum rating of A, or utilities with BBB. Finally, for the really risky low-rated debt—B and CCC—default either happens quite early or doesn't happen at all, because the default rates are essentially stable beyond five years.

Of course, DBRS does not leave its ratings unchanged when structural changes affect the underlying credit risk. As a result, ratings migrate as the credit quality of a firm deteriorates. DBRS gives the example of Trizec Properties Inc., formerly a major Canadian property developer. Three years before bankruptcy, it was rated AA (low); two years before bankruptcy, it was rated BBB (low); one year before bankruptcy, it was B rated; and three months before bankruptcy, it was CCC.

The DBRS study is rather limited simply because defaults generally occur during recessions, when firms experience cash flow problems, so just because there are no defaults does not mean there is no risk. There are also relatively few firms in each industry in Canada with which to assess industry default levels. In the United States, S&P has a larger sample of default rates because the U.S. economy is approximately 11 times bigger than Canada's. In Figure 18-3, a graph from S&P shows the weighted average default rates, with the defaults weighted by the issuer base of debt outstanding at the start of the year. There are clear differences in default rates across different industries. The lowest default rates are generally in regulated industries, with gas and electric utilities the lowest risk. The highest default rates occur in more competitive industries that are more sensitive to the business cycle, with leisure time and media at the top of the list.

Of course, defaulting is only part of the story, because investors want to know how much they are likely to get in the event of a default. Information on recovery rates is difficult to gather because it depends on the industry the firm is in and the nature of the underlying assets.

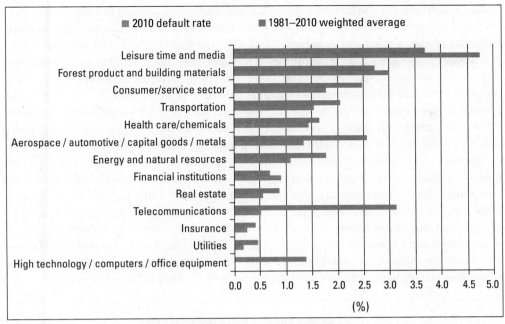

FIGURE 18-3 *Global Corporate Default Rates by Industry, 2010 versus Long-Term Average*

Source: Standard & Poor's Global Fixed Income Research and Standard & Poor's CreditPro®. Retrieved from www.standardandpoors. com/ratings/articles/en/us/?assetID=1245302234237. © Standard & Poor's 2011.

TABLE 18-7 Default Recovery Rates

Type	Market Value/Par Value (%)
Senior secured	54.6
Senior unsecured	40.6
Senior subordinated	31.3
Subordinated	30.1
Junior subordinated	23.0
All bonds	34.2

However, in 1995, Stuart Gilson reported on a Salomon study that gave the market values for different types of debt after a firm defaulted.[15] Table 18-7 shows these market values, which reflect the recovery rates.

The Salomon data indicate that after going into default, the average ratio of market price to face value was only 34.2 percent. However, this rate clearly declines with the ranking of the debt, because senior secured debt traded for 54.6 percent of face value, while junior subordinated debt traded for only 23 percent of face value.

The data on default and recovery rates indicate what we would expect: high-risk bonds have both a higher probability of defaulting and a lower recovery rate. Figure 18-4 shows the yield spreads between different bond ratings. In each case, the bond yield is from an index of long-term bonds maintained by Scotia Capital Markets; the spread is the difference between the yield on this index and the yield on an index of long Canada bonds. The spreads are weekly values from January 1980 until January 2012, but in the earlier period, only monthly values are available. For the overall period, the average AA spread over long Canada bonds was 0.82 percent, the A spread was 1.07 percent, and the BBB spread was 1.79 percent.

---

[15] Gilson, Stuart, "Investing in Distressed Situations: A Market Survey." *Financial Analysts Journal* 51, no. 6 (November–December 1995), pp. 8–27.

Unfortunately, there are no longer enough AAA-rated bonds outstanding to make up an index. However, averages are deceptive. What also matters is the variability. In this case, the standard deviation of the spreads is 0.5 percent (AA), 0.47 percent (A), and 0.82 percent (BBB), indicating that the spreads are not only higher with the lower-rated debt but also much more variable. We can see this during the slowdown experienced in the Canadian economy during the early 1990s and again after the stock market peaked in October 2000. Each time, the BBB spreads reached over 3 percent, whereas the spreads on A and AA bonds were much more stable. In contrast, during the crisis of 2008–9, it was not just the BBB spreads, but also the A and AA spreads that dramatically increased, with the latter reaching record highs.

The spread experience indicates that during economic slowdowns there is a "flight to quality"; investors are reluctant to invest in riskier securities and invest more heavily in low-risk investments, like Canada treasury bills and, to a lesser extent, other Canada bonds. During these recessionary or slowdown periods, some firms experience financing problems and discover that they cannot access long-term funds on reasonable terms. In fact, these spreads are on **seasoned bond issues** (or actively traded bond issues), and they do not indicate whether new funds are available on those terms. For this reason, during these periods, lower-rated companies usually have to finance with shorter-term debt or rely on bank borrowings.

seasoned bond issues actively traded bond issues that have been outstanding for some time

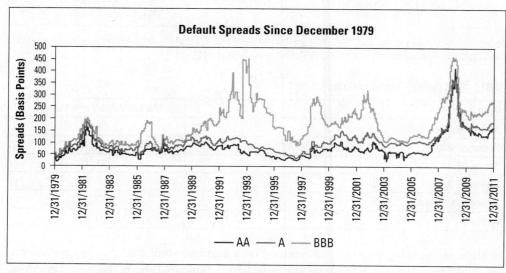

FIGURE 18-4 *Canada Bond Yield Spreads in Basis Points (1/100 of a Percent)*

Source: Data from Datastream series SCM3BLG, SCM1ALG, SCM2ALG, SCMCLNG.

CONCEPT REVIEW QUESTIONS

1. Differentiate investment-grade debt from junk debt.

2. Briefly describe the main factors DBRS considers in determining its debt ratings.

3. Briefly summarize the evidence regarding how well debt ratings work.

SUMMARY

In this chapter, we discuss the basic features of debt financing. Debt is a fixed contractual commitment. In order to be tax deductible, debt payments have to represent compensation for money owed, be referable back to a principal sum, and accrue from day to day. We then distinguish between short-term funds in the money market and long-term funds in the capital market. Money market securities are normally traded on a discount basis and are referred to as paper or bills. The biggest component of the money market is the treasury bill market, but commercial paper and bankers' acceptances are also important. Firms also use bank borrowings in the form of lines of credit and term loans.

Longer-term debt must be issued under a prospectus when sold to the general public. Most large companies in Canada are now reporting issuers and so can issue using a short-form prospectus. The information in the prospectus includes the type of debt and the major covenant provisions that restrict what the firm can do. The critical clauses are usually cross-default clauses, negative pledge clauses, and interest coverage restrictions. The bonds will then need a bond rating in order to be sold to major institutional purchasers. DBRS is the major bond-rating agency in Canada for both CP and long-term issues. Bond ratings run from AAA down to C, but, in practice, most Canadian bonds are rated A or higher, just as there is currently no CP rated lower than R-1 (low) outstanding. These ratings are highly correlated with actual default rates and the recovery rates that investors can expect in case of default.

SUMMARY OF LEARNING OBJECTIVES

18.1 Define "debt" and identify the basic features that distinguish debt from equity financing.

Debt is a contract between a lender and a borrower that stipulates the terms of repayment of the loan. Three basic features distinguish debt from equity financing:

- With debt, interest cost and principal repayment are fixed contractual commitments; with equity, an investor is an owner, shares in the profits of the business, and has no contractual rights, because equity is not a contract in the way that debt is.

- Debt costs are legitimate costs of doing business and are tax deductible. In contrast, equity costs are not a cost of doing business in the same sense.

- Interest on debt is paid before corporate tax, but dividends on stocks are paid after tax.

18.2 Identify and describe the different types of short-term debt issued in the money market.

The short-term debt issued in the money market include government treasury bills, commercial paper (CP), and bankers' acceptances (BAs). Treasury bills are promissory notes issued by a government treasury department. CP are short-term debt instruments, usually unsecured, that are issued by companies. BAs are short-term paper sold by an issuer to a bank, which guarantees or accepts it, obligating the bank to pay off the debt instrument at maturity if the issuer defaults.

18.3 Describe the types of debt financing provided by banks.

Banks provide a backup line of credit in CP and provide support in the BA market. However, the CP and BA markets are useful only for companies that have reasonably large and continuous financing needs because CP and BAs are sold in large amounts, usually at least $1 million. For smaller, irregular-sized financing requirements, firms rely more on traditional bank financing. This consists of term loans and lines of credit.

18.4 Identify the requirements that must typically be satisfied for public debt issues.

The company must offer a prospectus. The following items are incorporated in the prospectus by reference: annual information form, audited financial statements, unaudited six-month statements, and any other information filed with the securities commission after the date of the prospectus but before the termination of the offering.

18.5 Explain how debt ratings are determined, what they mean, and how useful they are in predicting default and recovery rates associated with public debt issues.

In determining its rating, the Dominion Bond Rating Service looks at six basic factors: core profitability, asset quality, strategy and management strength, balance sheet strength, business strength, and miscellaneous issues. The ratings are AAA for highest credit quality, AA for superior credit quality, A for satisfactory credit quality, BBB for adequate credit quality, BB for speculative, B for highly speculative, and CCC/CC/C for very highly speculative. Bond rating is very important for investors making investment decisions. It indicates the credit quality of a bond (i.e., the likelihood that it will default).

KEY TERMS

after-tax cost of debt (K), p. 687

bankers' acceptances (BAs), p. 692

commercial paper (CP), p. 690

covenants, p. 696

credit watch, p. 704

cross-default clause, p. 700

default or credit yield spread, p. 691

fixed contractual commitments, p. 686

floating interest rate, p. 695

hierarchy principle, p. 704

investment grade, p. 703

junk bonds, p. 703

lines of credit (LCs), p. 695

liquidity support, p. 692

negative pledge, p. 700

operating or demand LC, p. 695

prime lending rate, p. 695

promised yields, p. 690

promissory note, p. 688

purchase-money mortgages, p. 699

seasoned bond issues, p. 708

stable rating philosophy, p. 704

term loans, p. 697

term or revolving LC, p. 696

transfer agent, p. 698

treasury bills (T-bills), p. 688

unsubordinated debt, p. 699

EQUATIONS

Equation	Formula	Page
[18-1] After-Tax Cost of Debt	$K = K_d (1 - T)$	p. 687
[18-2] Commercial Paper Issue	$V = \dfrac{PAR(1 + R)P + RECOVER(1 - P)}{(1 + K)}$	p. 691
[18-3] Promised Yield to Issue at PAR	$R = \dfrac{(1 + K_{TB})}{P} - 1$	p. 691

QUESTIONS AND PRACTICE PROBLEMS

Multiple Choice Questions

1. Which of the following statements about debt is *incorrect?*
   a. Interest payments and principal payments are fixed commitments.
   b. Interest payments are not tax deductible.
   c. Bond holders are paid a series of fixed periodic amounts before the maturity date.
   d. Debt indenture is a legal document, specifying payment requirements.

2. What is the after-tax cost of debt, assuming T = 30%; before-tax cost of debt = 8%.
   a. 3.2%
   b. 7.5%
   c. 5.6%
   d. 6.0%

3. What is the promised yield to issue at PAR, assuming RECOVER = 0, P = 90%, and $K = K_{TB} = $ 2%?
   a. 12%
   b. 13.33%
   c. 11%
   d. 10%

4. What is the yield spread, if the promised yield on 30-day CP is 6 percent, the yield on the 91-day T-bill is 3 percent, and the yield on the 30-day T-bill is 1 percent?
   a. 2%
   b. 3%
   c. 4%
   d. 5%

5. Which of the following money market instruments could a firm without a very sound credit rating use when seeking financing?
   a. commercial paper
   b. bankers' acceptance
   c. bill of exchange
   d. both A and B

6. Which of the following investments is considered to be the safest?
   a. commercial paper
   b. corporate bonds
   c. treasury bills
   d. treasury bonds

7. Which of the following sources of financing is likely to provide the most favourable rates for large, highly rated firms seeking short-term financing?
   a. Selling commercial paper
   b. Selling secured long-term debt
   c. Getting an unsecured line of credit from a bank
   d. Selling bankers' acceptances

8. Parts of the indenture that limits certain actions a company takes during the term of the loan to protect the lender's interests are called
   a. debentures.
   b. negative pledge clauses.
   c. bond ratings.
   d. covenants.

9. Which of the following reflects the negative pledge clause?
   a. The issuing firm must make its interest payments.
   b. The issuing firm must fulfill its supplies to promised customers.
   c. The issuing firm has to maintain a current ratio of more than 2.5.
   d. The issuing firm must not issue any new debt with existing assets as collateral.

10. Which of the following statements about lines of credit is *false?*
    a. An operating or demand line of credit is the standard type.
    b. A revolver has less stability than an operating line of credit.
    c. Prime is the cost base of an operating line of credit and is a floating rate.
    d. A revolver is usually at least 364 days.

11. Which of the following ratings is the highest?
    a. BB
    b. CCC
    c. A
    d. AA

Practice Problems

12. State the three basic tests the CRA uses to ensure interest payments are tax deductible.

13. Determine the selling price of a Government of Canada treasury bill that has a quoted annual interest rate of 2.1 percent and will mature in 180 days. Assume a par value of $1,000.

14. On a one-year loan of $5,000, a bank charges interest at 10 percent. The bank also charges an application fee of $50 to cover processing expenses. What is the effective interest cost (annual rate) being paid by the borrower?

15. Collingwood Corp.'s 60-day commercial paper has a promised yield of 9 percent per year, but the expected yield is just 1 percent due to the risk of default. If the current 60-day T-bill yield is 1 percent, what is the yield spread on this commercial paper?

16. As the newly appointed treasurer for Collingwood Corp., you have to decide how to raise $50 million in short-term financing. You believe you could issue commercial paper with a promised yield of 9 percent. However, your bank will charge a commitment fee of 0.125 percent on the line of credit to back up this paper, as well as 0.125 percent as a selling commission. As an alternative, the bank suggests using bankers' acceptances that would have a lower yield of 8.75 percent. The bank's "stamping" fee for these BAs is 0.325 percent. Which financing alternative should you choose?

17. Calculate the price of a 91-day T-bill if the face value is $1 million and the quoted interest rate is 4.8 percent. Round to nearest dollar.

18. Calculate the value of the one-month CP given the following: PAR = $500,000; r (promised yield) = 5%; probability of not defaulting = 95%; RECOVER = 0; k = 15%. Round to nearest dollar.

19. Discuss the important characteristics of money market debt instruments. How are these characteristics important to money market participants?

20. Jackie would like to borrow $150,000 to expand her small business, but needs to understand the impact of the 8-percent interest payments. Last year, her company did not pay any interest and had total earnings before tax of $123,500. The tax rate was 25 percent. Determine the company's net income for the year. Assuming that EBIT and the rate of taxation will not change, calculate how much the net income figure will change if Jackie proceeds with the loan. Explain to Jackie why her company's net income does not fall by the full amount of the interest payments.

21. The cost (interest rate) of the loan Jackie needs for her business is 8 percent per year. Given that the company's net income will fall by less than the amount of interest paid (see Practice Problem 20), is Jackie correct to think that the after-tax cost of the loan is lower than 8 percent? With a tax rate of 25 percent, what is the after-tax cost of this loan?

⚙ 22. Michael M. specializes in buying high-risk commercial paper; his required return on these investments is 12 percent per year. He is considering buying some 60-day paper from Collingwood Corp. with a promised yield of 9 percent per year. However, Michael believes there is a 1-percent chance that Collingwood will default on this debt, in which case he would only recover 80 percent of the face value. How much will Michael be willing to pay for each $1,000 par value of this paper?

⚙ 23. Collingwood Corp. is able to issue its 60-day commercial paper at par with a promised yield of 9 percent per year. The current T-bill yield is 6 percent per year (or 1 percent for the 60-day period), which is also the expected return on the commercial paper, as there is some risk of default. If Collingwood were to default, investors would recover 80 percent of the face value of the debt. Based on this information, what is the probability that Collingwood will default on its commercial paper? Round to two decimals.

⚙ 24. When Collingwood Corp. issued its 60-day commercial paper the promised yield was 9 percent, whereas the 60-day T-bill yield was 6 percent. There is a 2-percent chance that Collingwood will default on this debt. If investors were willing to pay the full par-value amount ($1,000) to purchase the paper, how much do they expect to recover in the event of a default?

25. In your job as treasurer of Collingwood Corp., you have to arrange a line of credit for the firm. The following is taken from the company's balance sheet.

Current assets	
Cash	$ 1,271,987
Accounts receivable	18,536,000
Inventory	74,196,000
	94,003,987
Property and equipment (net)	126,323,000
Goodwill	46,888,000
Total assets	$267,214,987

The bank will provide credit up to the sum of 75 percent of the value of receivables, and 50 percent of the inventory value. What is the maximum credit limit that Collingwood can obtain?

26. Collingwood Corp. has a revolving line of credit on which it owes $50 million. One of the restrictions imposed with this financing arrangement is that the company must maintain a minimum interest coverage ratio of 2. If this is the only borrowing, and the annual interest rate is 9.75 percent, how much does the company have to earn to live up to the covenant?

27. Why do corporations issue long-term bonds, knowing that interest rate risk is higher for longer-term bonds?

28. Collingwood Corp.'s bank is willing to provide it with a 10-year term loan for $50 million. The annual payments on this loan will be $5.25 million, and there is a "bullet" payment of $50 million at maturity. What is the interest rate being charged by the bank? Does it make sense that this loan would have a higher cost than the alternatives presented in Practice Problem 16?

29. List and briefly describe the six basic factors used to determine a DBRS rating.

⚙ 30. Rather than take a term loan from the bank, Collingwood Corp. has decided to issue $50 million of 10-year bonds. DBRS has assigned a rating of "BB" to this bond issue.
   a. Determine the probability that no default occurs during the life of these bonds, based on historical average default rates provided in Table 18-6.
   b. Valuing long-term bonds with default risk is quite difficult. For simplicity, assume that the bonds mature in one year and can be valued in the same manner as commercial paper (Equation 18-2). Collingwood Corp. will pay coupon interest (the promised yield) of 10 percent, whereas the current yield on treasury bonds is 6 percent. Use the estimated default rate from part (a) to determine the value of the bonds. You may assume that the bonds are worthless in the event of a default.

⚙ 31. Sometimes, bonds are completely worthless when a company defaults on payments. However, in practice, bonds typically have some market value (recovery rate) even after a default. Collingwood's bonds are unsecured, but are senior to any other debt. Use the information in Table 18-7 and the information in Practice Problem 30 to determine the value of the bonds.

⚙ 32. Assume two bonds in the market—bond A and bond B—have the same rating and the same YTM. Discuss three reasons that might make one bond preferable to the other.

19 | Equity and Hybrid Instruments

LEARNING OBJECTIVES

19.1   Explain the basic rights associated with share ownership.

19.2   Identify and describe the various classes of shares and the shareholders' rights associated with each.

19.3   Explain how preferred shares differ from common shares and outline the various features associated with preferred shares.

19.4   Explain how combining warrants with debt issues or issuing convertible bonds or debentures can provide firms with attractive financing options.

19.5   Identify and describe the various hybrid financing options available to firms, and explain how they are constructed.

Warrants are an example of the hybrid instruments discussed in Chapter 19. They are similar to options but have a longer time horizon (two to five years). They provide excellent leverage for the longer-term investor seeking exposure to a particular security or industry—they trade like the underlying security to which they are attached, but they cost less. Unlike regular options, they are exercised against the company so it receives new financing. As a result, and unlike regular options, the expiration date of the warrant is often extended, because the company's intention is to raise financing. On March 23, 2012, AgriMarine Holdings issued the following press release:

AgriMarine Holdings Inc. (the "Company" or "AgriMarine"), the leader in floating closed containment technology and production for sustainable aquaculture, announces that it has applied to the TSX Venture Exchange (the "Exchange") for approval to extend the expiry dates of certain common share purchase warrants issued as part of a non-brokered private placement, which closed in tranches in April and June 2010.

Each warrant expiry date shall be extended for an additional twelve (12) months, as follows:

1. 9,393,010 warrants shall be amended to expire April 19, 2013;
2. 677,500 warrants shall be amended to expire April 29, 2013; and
3. 1,250,000 warrants shall be amended to expire June 18, 2013.

All other terms and conditions of the warrants, including the exercise price of $0.30, remain unchanged. For information pertaining to the warrants please see the Company's news release dated April 1, 2010. The proposed extension remains subject to Exchange approval.

Source: AgriMarine press release, March 23, 2012. Available at http://agrimarine.com/news/agrimarine-announces-proposed-warrant-extension.

CHAPTER 19 **PREVIEW**

In Chapter 18, we discussed debt and how one of the major factors determining whether or not a security is debt is its treatment by the Canada Revenue Agency (CRA) for tax purposes. In this chapter, we consider non-debt securities, beginning with equity, both common shares and preferred shares, which are part of shareholders' equity. We show that the basic rights provided to common shareholders can be distributed among different classes of common shares. As a result, all common shares are not equal. In particular, some of them have voting rights, others don't, and some of them have larger dividends than others do.

Preferred shares in Canada come in a wide variety of forms because of the way dividends are taxed. This means some preferred shares are similar to commercial paper (CP), mid-term notes, or long-term financing, with the major difference being that preferred shares pay dividends rather than interest.

We then show how conversion features in warrants and convertibles make convertible bonds part common equity and part debt, depending on the structure of the conversion feature. We also look at the non-tax features of different securities and how they are treated by the major rating agencies.

A good understanding of the material in this chapter is necessary to comprehend the range of corporate financing activities undertaken by firms and the ways firms can mix them in an attempt to lower their overall financing cost, which will be discussed in Chapter 20.

19.1 SHAREHOLDERS' EQUITY

Learning Objective 19.1
Explain the basic rights associated with share ownership.

In Chapter 7, we defined "equity securities" as ownership interests in an underlying business, usually a corporation. We defined "common shares" as certificates of ownership interest in a corporation, which means that common shareholders represent the true "owners" of the corporation. Finally, we defined "preferred shares" as shares that provide the owners with a claim to a fixed amount of equity that is established when the shares are first issued. However, MacIntosh and Nicholls point out that the terms "common share" and "preferred share" have no statutory definition in Canada; they are used only to describe classes of shares.[1] Our discussion in this chapter distinguishes between the two forms of equity and examines the implications for investors and for the underlying business.

Shareholder Rights

In Chapter 18, we saw that the basic definition of debt flows from what the CRA determines to be tax-deductible interest. Equity can be regarded as a security for which the payments are not tax deductible. In addition, the *Canada Business Corporations Act (CBCA)* 24(3) provides that:

> Where a corporation has only one class of shares, the rights of the holders thereof are equal in all respects and include the rights
> a) to vote at any meeting of shareholders of the corporation;
> b) to receive any dividend declared by the corporation; and
> c) to receive the remaining property of the corporation on dissolution.

Provincially incorporated companies operate under provincial laws with similar provisions. These three provisions define the basic rights of common shareholders.

The most basic right of common shareholders is the right to vote. Because they own a "share" of the business, shareholders have the right to make important decisions at the annual

---

[1] MacIntosh, Jeffrey, and Christopher Nicholls, *Securities Law*. Toronto: Irwin Law, 2002.

general meeting. These include the right to elect the members of the board of directors (BOD), appoint the auditors of the firm, make changes in the articles of incorporation and bylaws of the company, and vote on major changes in the firm's operations. What constitutes a major or fundamental change in the firm's operations is difficult to define, but it normally includes the acquisition of another firm through an exchange of shares or the disposition of major assets.

However, even these rights can be severely circumscribed. At one time, most equity holders also had a **pre-emptive right**, which was the right to maintain proportional ownership in a company when new shares were issued. If the firm were to issue, say, 50 percent more shares in a seasoned offering, all shareholders had the right to buy 50 percent more shares to maintain their proportional interest. If there is no pre-emptive right, it means that the company can sell shares to "new" shareholders and dilute or reduce the ownership interest of existing shareholders. The pre-emptive right meant that, historically, most new issues of shares were made by means of a "rights offering" to existing shareholders. Table 19-1 lists the largest rights issues in the world as of November 24, 2009, compiled by Reuters.

pre-emptive right the right of shareholders to maintain proportional ownership in a company when new shares are issued

TABLE 19-1 Top 10 Rights Issues as of November 2009

Issuer	Date	USBillions at Current Foreign Exchange	Billions in Local Currency	USBillions at Historic Foreign Exchange
1. Lloyds Banking Group	Nov 09	22.3	£13.5	22.1
2. HSBC	Apr 09	21.8	£13.2	19.4
3. RBS	Jun 08	20.4	£12.3	24.4
4. Fortis	Oct 07	20.3	€13.6	19.3
5. UBS	May 08	15.8	16.0 Swiss francs	15.4
6. Rio Tinto	Jul 09	12.4	£7.5	12.3
7. Enel	Jun 09	11.9	€8.0	11.1
8. Santander	Nov 08	10.7	€7.2	9.3
9. Sberbank Rossii	Feb 07	10.0	€6.7	8.8
10. Imperial Tobacco	Jun 08	8.3	£5.0	9.9

What is striking about the companies in Table 19-1 is not who is there, but who is not. For example, we might expect to see no Canadian companies, but it is surprising that there are no American companies. The list is dominated by European, principally British, companies and by banks, which reflects the enormous fundraising efforts they had to make in the aftermath of the financial crisis.

Starting in the early 1950s, Canadian companies changed their corporate structure, removing the pre-emptive right so they could sell shares more quickly and cheaply to new, principally institutional, investors. We saw in Chapter 17, for example, that bought deals can be accomplished very quickly by having an investment bank buy shares directly from a company and then resell them very quickly into the market. This is only possible if the shares can be sold to major institutions like pension funds, mutual funds, and insurance companies. In the process, the ordinary retail investor is largely cut out and forced to buy the shares once they enter the market. As a result, very few rights offerings are now made in Canada, and shareholders cannot prevent their ownership share from being diluted by the sale of new shares to other investors.[2]

The loss of the pre-emptive right has been exacerbated by the fact that most companies now have authorized an unlimited number of common shares or have increased the authorized

---

[2] In fact, a standard takeover defence is to sell shares to a friendly investor, thereby reducing the stake of a potentially hostile acquirer. *Poison pills*, discussed in Chapter 15, are another example of the lack of pre-emptive rights and its impact on shareholder dilution.

capital so that they no longer need shareholder approval to issue more common shares. Again, for reporting issuers, this means that firms can sell new shares very quickly by means of a bought deal. However, while a firm can raise capital more cheaply, it also means it no longer needs shareholder approval for the new share issue or, most of the time, what it intends to do with the financing. The result has been a significant reduction in oversight of corporate activities by a firm's owners, the shareholders, and increased power for its senior management. The shareholders' two remaining rights—to receive a dividend and to receive any remaining property on the dissolution of the corporation—reflect the equity shareholders' rights as the **residual owners**. For example, the equity holders have no right to a dividend until it is declared by the company's BOD. Legally, the shareholders cannot force a company to pay a dividend—this decision is the prerogative of the BOD. Furthermore, there are extensive legal restrictions on when the company can declare a dividend; the major one is that the firm has to have the resources to pay the dividend without impairing its ability to meet its fixed contractual commitments. Otherwise, a company going bankrupt could simply strip out all its cash through a dividend prior to declaring bankruptcy. In this sense, payment of a dividend reflects the fact that the equity holders are last in line after all other claims on the firm's earnings stream have been met. In the same way, if the firm is liquidated, all other claimants on the firm's assets have to be paid before the equity holders receive any payment.

A right not explicit in the CBCA description, although fundamental to the CBCA itself, is the right to limited liability, which was discussed in Chapter 2. The equity holders commit initial equity to the firm, but they are legally protected from being forced to put more money into the firm. As a result, if the firm cannot meet its fixed commitments to pay interest and so on, the equity holders do not have to inject more money into the firm so it can meet these commitments. If the creditors then force the firm into bankruptcy, and there is not enough money to pay off all the claims on the firm, the equity holders are still not required to invest more money in the firm. Limited liability ensures that the shareholders can only lose their initial investment. This means their *downside* risk is limited, while they have unlimited *upside* potential. In this sense, common shares have some of the characteristics of call options, discussed in Chapter 12. We will use this insight when discussing financial strategy.

Different Classes of Shares

The CBCA definition qualifies the three rights of the common shareholders by stating these rights apply "where a corporation has only one class of shares." When a company has more than one class of shares, it must indicate in its articles of incorporation how these rights are allocated among the various classes of shares. The only legal requirement is that each of these three rights has to be attached to a class of shares.

For example, the following share structure could be set up:

A Shares

- no voting rights as long as dividend payments are made
- a $0.05 dividend in addition to any dividend paid to class B shares, but only if class C dividends are not in arrears
- an equal share with class B shares in any residual receipts on the winding up of the company

B Shares

- full voting rights
- no dividends if dividends on class C shares are in arrears

---

residual owners equity owners who receive any remaining cash flows or property (on the dissolution of the corporation) after all other commitments have been satisfied

Learning Objective 19.2
Identify and describe the various classes of shares and the shareholders' rights associated with each.

- an equal share with class A shares in any residual receipts on the winding up of the company

C Shares

- no voting rights unless dividends are in arrears for two years, after which each share gets one vote

- a dividend of $0.30 per share every quarter when declared by the BOD; no dividends on class A and B shares can be paid if these dividends are in arrears

- payment of $25 par value before any payments to class A and B shares on the winding up of the company

This is a loose description of a relatively simple share structure that meets the CBCA requirements. The voting rights rest with the class B shares, and all shares have clearly specified rights in the event of a dividend payment or the winding up of the company. In this case, the class B shares would be regarded as common shares. The class A shares have no voting rights but have a slight preferential dividend and would commonly be referred to as **non-voting** or **restricted shares**. The class C shares are preferred shares because they have a preferred dividend over both the A and B shares.

There are no limitations on the share structure a company can set up, but this example of two classes of common shares and one class of preferred shares is common for Canadian firms. However, it raises the problem of allocating voting rights.

Voting rights give shareholders control and the ability to choose the BOD and, through it, senior management and the strategic direction of the company. In the event of a takeover, voting shares are more valuable than non-voting shares because of this control value. A company wishing to take over another can do so only by buying the voting shares. A good example of the importance of voting shares is provided by Bell Globemedia Inc.'s takeover offer for CHUM Ltd. on July 12, 2006.

CHUM had a dual-class share structure, which means that it had A and B shares similar to those described above. In CHUM's case, 90 percent of the class A shares were held by the Waters family, descendants of CHUM's founder, Allan Waters. These shares had normal voting rights. The family also owned 10 percent of the class B non-voting shares, which were otherwise widely held. Bell Globemedia (now called CTVglobemedia Inc.) offered $52.50 for the class A shares and $47.50 for the class B shares. In both cases, the offer price was about a 60 percent premium over the average price for CHUM's shares. However, the fact that the A shares received a $5 per share premium rankled many big institutional shareholders. If the same offer had been made to both classes of shares, the price would have been $48.50. As a portfolio manager at AIC said, "The overall price is not the issue. It's the difference and discrimination, if you will, that's fairly large."[3] The offer price difference in the CHUM bid was relatively mild compared with previous cases. For example, in 1988, holders of the voting shares in Canadian Tire Corporation, Limited, received a takeover premium and the non-voting shares did not. To prevent this from happening again, the Toronto Stock Exchange (TSX) changed its rules after the Canadian Tire case, creating "coattail" provisions so that both classes of shares have to be purchased; the non-voting shares ride the coattails of the voting shares, which the acquirer needs to get control. However, the rules apply only to new listings, and CHUM, like many companies, was grandfathered because its shares were already outstanding.

The decision to establish or maintain classes of shares with different voting rights is common to many family-run businesses in which the founder needs external capital but wants to maintain control. A classic example was Four Seasons Hotels Inc., a chain founded by Isadore

non-voting or **restricted shares**
common shares that have no voting rights but a slight preferential dividend

---

[3] Sethi, Chanakya, "CHUM Investors Criticize Dual-Class Discount." *The Globe and Mail*, July 13, 2006, p. B4.

Sharpe, whose family controlled 67 percent of the votes through multiple voting shares.[4] In September 1996, Four Seasons proposed to reorganize its two main classes of shares. The subordinated voting shares were to be renamed limited voting shares, and the multiple voting shares owned by Sharpe family members, who already had 12 votes each, were to be renamed variable voting shares. The plan was to increase the voting power of these shares to keep the Sharpe family at 67 percent of the votes as more limited voting shares were issued. In essence, without putting up any more money, the Sharpe family would always control the company through these variable voting shares. Many institutional investors refuse to invest in limited or non-voting shares, but on the day the Four Seasons plan was announced, the stock price went up 55 cents and reached a 52-week high.

What both the CHUM and the Four Seasons examples highlight is the role of the *founder* of the company. When the voting rights are concentrated in the hands of a visionary leader who has built the company, investors are often only too happy to see control concentrated in his or her hands because the company is the senior management. For this reason, many institutional investors were relatively indifferent to the Four Seasons' plan. The problems arise when the bloodline "thins out," and the second and third generations of the family do not have the managerial skills evident in the original founder, or when the firm is sold. This was the case with CHUM: when control passed out of the hands of the founder, there was no clear strategic direction for the company. CHUM became a takeover target, and investors were upset by the price differential between the voting and non-voting shares.

The value of these voting rights depends on who has control of the company and whether it is good or bad for shareholder value creation. Empirical studies estimating the value of these voting rights have produced mixed results, as have studies of the stock market's reaction when firms recapitalize their share structure to create or remove voting differentials. The problem is that differential voting rights may not affect value when the founder runs the company, but they do when that founder ceases to be involved. Regardless, the limited or non-voting shares usually offer a slight premium in the form of the right to a dividend to offset the lost value of control.

Another well-known example of a method for maintaining the founding family's control is provided by Ford Motor Company, in which 71 million B shares, with 40 percent of the voting rights, are in a **family trust**. Trusts solve the problem of what happens after the founder ceases to be involved and the wealth gradually disperses over succeeding generations. Trusts are a standard way of separating ownership from control. For example, when an inheritance goes to an heir under the age of majority, the wealth is typically put into a trust. The minor receives the income from the inheritance but cannot control it until he or she reaches a given age, normally 25. In similar fashion, the shares in the Ford family trust ensure that income flows through to the hundreds of individuals descended from Henry Ford, but all the votes are held by the trustees.

Family members installed Clay Ford, great-grandson of Henry Ford, as president and CEO of Ford in 2001. In the next decade, Ford's stock price fell from just over $20 in 2001 to less than $2 in November 2008, and things became so desperate that Ford hired investment bankers to see how the company could be reorganized or broken up. One extreme option considered was to sell off Ford's assets except its truck division, which continues to make record profits. Luckily for Ford's external shareholders, Clay Ford had the good sense to pull back, becoming Ford's executive chairman, and to install Alan Mullaly in his place as CEO. Mullaly pledged Ford's assets and raised a significant amount of money before the stock market collapse and recession. If he had not taken this route, Ford could easily have followed General Motors and Chrysler into bankruptcy. Ford's share price has recovered to the $12 range, and shareholder resolutions to change Ford's share structure have been defeated each of the past several years, but each year the number of votes in favour of a change has increased.

family trust a trust that ensures income flows to the people descended from the company founder, while all the votes are held by the trustees

---

[4] Shecter, Barbara, "Four Seasons Plan Assailed." *Financial Post*, September 27, 1996.

This discussion of shareholder rights indicates that not all shares are created equal, as discussed in *Finance in the News 19-1*. Although the differences between shares are not as great as the contractual differences between different classes of bonds, it is still important to be aware of the class of shares. It is also interesting to see that as the Canadian economy has matured, the importance of founders and different classes of shares has decreased. Figure 19-1, taken from research by professors at Wilfrid Laurier University and the University of Lethbridge, shows the persistent decline in the importance of dual-class shares on the TSX.

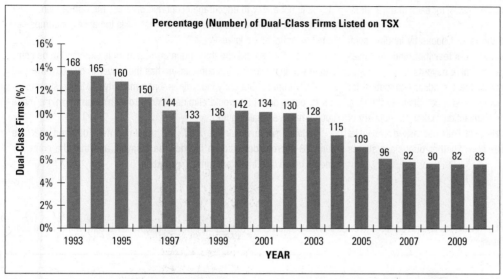

FIGURE 19-1 *Decline of Dual-Class Shares on the TSX*

Source: Amoako-Adu, Ben, Brian F. Smith, and Vishaal Baulkaran, "Assessing the Cost of Parting with Stronach and Dual-Class Shares." *Canadian Investment Review*, January 18, 2012. Retrieved from www.investmentreview.com/analysis-research/magna-the-true-cost-of-share-unification-5694. Reprinted with the permission of *Canadian Investment Review*.

finance INTHENEWS 19-1 | Not All Shares Are Created Equal

IT IS NOT JUST Magna Int'l. $860-million sendoff to controlling shareholder Frank Stronach that will be on trial when the Ontario Securities Commission opens its hearing on Wednesday.

Nor is the conduct of Magna's directors—who are getting heat for not making a recommendation either way on the matter—the sole sore point. The real point of contention in the OSC hearing, arguably, is a long-standing skeleton in the closet of corporate Canada: dual-class shares.

The concept of giving some shareholders more power than others dates back to a time in Canadian business when the country was dominated by family-owned companies, whose founders wanted to raise cash to build their businesses without ceding control. The solution was dual-class stock structures, which allowed families to keep control by owning multiple-voting shares, while single-vote or non-voting shares were sold to Joe Mainstreet.

According to a federal study in 2005, public companies with dual-class shares accounted for more than 20 percent of all companies listed on the Toronto Stock Exchange, compared with just 2 percent of listed companies in the United States.

Owners of supercharged stock sometimes enjoy the right to pocket enormous premiums over what other shareholders are paid during takeovers and other transactions that trigger changes of control. That is the

case at Magna. Mr. Stronach's $860-million farewell package of cash and stock amounts to a premium of nearly 1,800 percent over the value of Magna's regular shares the day before the deal was announced. Although Mr. Stronach owns less than 1 percent of the company's equity, his holding of Magna stock with multiple-voting privileges gives him substantial leverage to demand special treatment.

The TSX tried in 1987 to push Canada into the modern era by requiring all newly listed companies to effectively attach protections, known as "coattail provisions," to multiple-voting shares. These provisions ensured that all classes of shareholders would receive equal terms and compensation when control of public companies changed hands.

There was, however, a footnote to the TSX's blueprint: all companies with dual-class shares in 1987 were exempted from the obligation to protect shareholders with coattail provisions. In other words, investors in dozens of companies continued to face the risk that they would be treated as second-class citizens when controlling shareholders were bought out.

More than two decades and several takeovers and corporate bankruptcies later, about a dozen grandfathered companies remain on the TSX, experts say. The group includes Power Corp., Rogers Communications Inc., Astral Media Inc., and Shaw Communications Inc. (A spokeswoman for

continued

Finance in the News 19-1: Not All Shares Are Created Equal *(continued)*

the TSX said the exchange does not keep track of how many grandfathered companies remain.)

In recent years, shareholders have balked at a number of special deals for owners of multiple-voting stock. In 2006, the Waters family faced shareholder complaints after it demanded a richer premium for its voting stake in CHUM Ltd. The deal, which was approved despite the complaints, saw acquirer Bell Globemedia pay a 12-percent premium for each of the Waters' family's voting shares.

Now that Mr. Stronach has entered the record books by landing such a huge premium for his stake in Magna, investors fear that other multiple-voting share owners will be tempted to seek similar payouts.

Ermanno Pascutto, executive director of the Canadian Foundation for Advancement of Investor Rights (FAIR), which filed a complaint to the OSC about the proposed Magna deal, said the transaction makes "a mockery of corporate governance in this country." He said FAIR has asked provincial securities regulators across Canada to review whether dual-class shares should be allowed to continue.

"If dual-class shares are going to be used to abuse public shareholders, then we have to revisit whether we permit these shares any longer," Mr. Pascutto said.

Foreign investors tend to steer away from Canadian companies with dual-class shares, a legacy that John Coffee, of Columbia University's law school in New York, warns could handicap Canada's capital markets.

"It is not a way to encourage economic growth," Mr. Coffee said. "Over the long run, dual-class capitalization at least chills the ability of companies to raise capital at the lowest cost."

The OSC's hearing into the Magna arrangement is expected to be completed within two days. The commission has the power to overturn the deal with Mr. Stronach. But early indications that a majority of Magna shareholders favour a deal that would eliminate Mr. Stronach's control might make such a reversal challenging.

Instead, some observers said, the regulator may demand that the June 28 shareholder vote on the deal be delayed, and that the company and its board give investors more information.

Some Basic Ratios

We now return to our previous example of Tim Hortons, Inc. Its shareholders' equity figures for the fiscal year ends of January 2, 2011 and January 1, 2012, are presented in Table 19-2.

TABLE 19-2 Tim Hortons Shareholders' Equity (in millions of dollars)

	2011	2012
Preferred stock	0	0
Capital stock	474.5	443.8
Retained earnings	962.3	708.8
Total shareholders' equity	1,442.4	1,154.4
Total liabilities and equity	2,481.5	2,204.0
Shares outstanding year end (million)	170.6	157.8
Book value per share ($)	8.46	7.31
Diluted earnings per common share ($)	3.58	2.35
Common dividend per share ($)	0.52	0.68

Notice that Tim Hortons had no preferred shares outstanding, just common shares. Its 2012 common equity figure consisted of $443.8 million contributed by shareholders through public offerings and adjustments to the capital stock and $708.8 million contributed through retaining earnings within the firm rather than paying them out as dividends. Tim Hortons was owned by the U.S. company Wendy's International, Inc., until a portion of its shares were sold to the public in 2006. Residual shares were "spun off" (that is, given as a dividend) to the shareholders of Wendy's soon after. In Tim Hortons' annual report, the company's shares have a par value of US$0.001. However, since 1975, it has not been permissible for firms incorporating under the

CBCA to issue common shares with a par value in Canada. As we saw earlier in the chapter, there is no reason to have a par value for common shares.[5]

As of its January 1, 2012 year end, Tim Hortons had 157.8 million shares outstanding, so each common share had a book value per share (BVPS) of $7.32, calculated as

$$BVPS = \frac{Common\ Equity}{Number\ of\ shares} = \frac{1,154.4}{157.8} = \$7.32$$

Tim Hortons' BVPS indicates the amount of money that Tim Hortons shareholders have invested in the firm. As we discussed in Chapter 4, Tim Hortons is currently very profitable, and its market price reflects the current and future expected profits. As a result, the market price (P) of its shares at year end was $49.17, compared with a BVPS of only $7.32, which translates into a market-to-book ratio (M/B) of 6.72, calculated as

$$\frac{M}{B} = \frac{Price}{BVPS} = \frac{49.17}{7.32} = 6.72$$

Tim Hortons is a moderate growth company. In 2011, it paid a dividend of $0.68, so its dividend yield at the end of 2012 was this dividend per share divided by its market price of $49.17 or 1.38 percent, calculated as

$$Dividend\ yield = \frac{Dividend\ per\ share}{Stock\ price} = \frac{\$0.68}{\$49.17} = 1.38\%$$

However, its latest quarterly dividend per share has increased to $0.21, so its expected dividend per share for 2012 will probably be at least $0.84, for a forecast dividend yield of 1.71 percent. We will discuss dividend policy in detail in Chapter 22, but note that while Tim Hortons paid out $110.2 million in dividends to common shareholders in 2011, it also paid out $572.5 million to repurchase its own common shares, which is why the year-end number of shares dropped from 170.6 million in 2011 to 157.8 million as of January 1, 2012.

A dividend yield of 1.38 percent on its own would be relatively low for a stable company. Figure 19-2 plots the dividend yield on the S&P/TSX Composite Index since January 1956, which is the longest period available. The dividend yield has averaged 3.07 percent over this period, but there has been considerable volatility because the dividend yield decreases as market prices increase as well as when the dividend per share is reduced. We can clearly see the significant increase in the dividend yield on the S&P/TSX index during the 1970s, when high levels of inflation hurt the stock market. We can also see the impact of the financial crisis starting in the fall of 2008 as the stock market crashed. At year-end 2011, the yield on the S&P/TSX index was 2.85 percent, which exceeded the 2.46 percent yield on the long Canada bond. Since common share dividends normally increase with growth in the economy, as we saw in Chapter 7 when discussing the dividend discount model, this is a highly unusual situation. In 2012, however, it is not so much that the dividend yield on the TSX is high as that the yield on the long Canada bond is too low. In August 2011, the U.S. Federal Reserve Board announced a new bond-buying program known as Operation Twist. The specific objective of this program was to "twist" the yield curve and lower U.S. long-term interest rates, but this has had the unintended effects of lowering long-term rates around the world.

Dividends are very attractive for corporations and individuals in Canada for tax reasons. As we discussed in Chapter 3, dividends received by one Canadian corporation from another Canadian corporation are not taxed. This is in order to avoid double taxation of income at the

---

[5] Note: Tim Hortons' accounts are in Canadian dollars but the company uses U.S. GAAP, which reflects its prior ownership by Wendy's. Only 6.5 percent of the company's revenues come from the United States; the rest are earned in Canada.

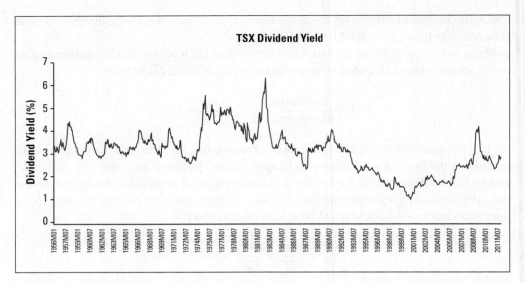

FIGURE 19-2 *TSX Dividend Yield*

corporate level.[6] In contrast, interest income paid by one corporation to another is taxable because, as we discussed before, interest expense is tax deductible.

Dividend income is attractive for individuals because of the dividend tax credit system in Canada. Traditionally, this system was structured so that the effective tax rate paid by owners of small private corporations was the same whether they withdrew their compensation as dividends or as salary. However, in the May 2006 budget, the federal government reformed the tax rates to reduce the overall tax rate on dividend income from public corporations. Since then, most of the provinces have also reformed their taxation of dividend income.

For tax purposes, Canadian-sourced dividend income is "grossed up" by 45 percent for federal income tax purposes. This means that for every dollar of dividends, you have to include $1.45 in your taxable income. The federal government then allows a dividend tax credit applied against the federal tax. Further, each province allows a provincial dividend tax credit to offset against provincial taxes, which results in a dividend tax credit of about 31 percent against the grossed-up dividend. The result is that the combined tax rate on dividend income for an Ontario resident in the top tax bracket is 29.54 percent, compared with 46.41 percent for interest income and 23.2 percent for capital gains income. The dividend tax rate has been increasing in Ontario as the provincial corporate tax rate has declined to keep the overall tax rate roughly the same as for other income. All these tax rates may change in the future as all levels of government deal with the budget deficits they now face as a result of the debt overhang they incurred during the recession. However, it is unlikely that the relative tax preference for dividend income will change, since it reflects the fact that, unlike interest income, dividends are paid out of after-tax income and have already borne the effect of corporate income taxes. The result is that every investor in Canada has a tax preference to receive dividend rather than interest income.[7]

CONCEPT REVIEW QUESTIONS

1. What are the basic rights associated with equity securities? How do these differ across different categories or classes of equities?

2. Why do voting rights affect the prices of some common shares and not others?

3. Why is dividend income preferred by both corporations and individual investors?

---

[6] Of course, the income is eventually taxed twice in total because individual investors pay taxes on any dividends received. However, eliminating the tax on dividends paid to other corporations avoids having the same dollar of income taxed three times—twice at the corporate level and once again when received by individual investors.

[7] See the current tax calculators provided by Ernst & Young on its website, http://www.ey com/CA/en/Services/Tax/Tax-Calculators-2012-Personal-Tax.

19.2 PREFERRED SHARE CHARACTERISTICS

The fact that interest and dividend income are taxed differently is well known in the capital market. BMO Capital Markets, the investment dealer arm of the Bank of Montreal, produces a monthly preferred share statistics report that tracks the performance of the preferred share market. The February 2012 issue of *Preferred Share Statistics* provided the yields on various instruments, as shown in Table 19-3.

Table 19-3 reports the yields on three different types of preferred shares, which we discuss below. Because of the favourable tax treatment accorded dividends in Canada, a variety of different types of preferred shares exist in the capital market. Many of these issues are designed to mimic different types of bonds and appeal to bond investors who want the more favourable tax treatment. This is why BMO reports the after-tax yields to both corporate investors and ordinary or retail investors: some of these preferreds are specifically designed for corporate investors, while others are for the traditional retail market. Remember that although preferred shares are a type of equity and the dividends are not legally an obligation until they are declared, for low-risk companies their payment is virtually assured.

TABLE 19-3 Preferred Share Yields, February 2012

Straight Preferreds	(%)
Dividend yield	4.83
Long Canada yield	2.60
After-tax spread (corp.)	3.01
After-tax spread (indiv.)	2.01
Retractable Preferreds	**(%)**
Dividend yield	1.12
Mid Canada yield	1.44
After-tax spread (corp.)	0.12
After-tax spread (indiv.)	0.02
Floating Rate Preferreds	**(%)**
Dividend yield	3.02
BA (3-month)	1.18
After-tax spread (corp.)	2.19
After-tax spread (indiv.)	1.50

Source: Data from BMO, *Preferred Share Statistics*, February 2012.

The first type of preferred share reported in Table 19-3 is the traditional **straight preferred share**. These are preferreds that have no maturity date and pay a fixed dividend at regular intervals (usually quarterly). As discussed in Chapter 7, these can be viewed as perpetuities and are valued accordingly. These were the most common type of preferreds in the Canadian market until the 1970s. In Table 19-3, the straight preferred yields are 4.83 percent, compared with a yield of 2.6 percent for long Canada bonds, implying a positive yield spread of 2.23 percent.

There are several reasons for this spread. The most obvious is that bonds issued by the Government of Canada are clearly a lower risk than preferred shares issued by a firm that may default. In addition, straight preferred shares that have no maturity date have a longer life than even the longest-term government bonds, so they will have greater maturity risk, as discussed in Chapter 6. These risks, particularly the default risk, are reflected in this yield spread, even before we take taxes into account.

The 2.23 percent spread is based on before-tax yields, so it does not take into account the **tax value of money**: the fact that dividends are taxed more favourably than interest income

Learning Objective 19.3
Explain how preferred shares differ from common shares and outline the various features associated with preferred shares.

straight preferred share a preferred share that has no maturity date and pays a fixed dividend at regular intervals, usually quarterly

tax value of money the fact that some sources of income, like dividends, are taxed at preferential rates and are thus more valuable than other sources of income, like interest income

and so are more valuable than interest income. To account for the tax differences, BMO Capital Markets also estimates the after-tax spreads, which are based on the dividends being in the hands of a corporate investor in the 30 percent tax bracket, for whom the dividend income is non-taxable, and in the hands of a private investor in the highest tax bracket. In this case, the after-tax spread would increase to 3.01 percent for a corporate investor, and 2.01 percent for a personal investor.

retractable preferred share a share that gives the investor the right to sell it back to the issuer, thus creating an early maturity date

The second type of preferred share presented in Table 19-3 is the **retractable preferred share**. Retraction means that the investor has the right to sell the shares back to the issuer at a date prior to maturity. Retractable preferreds permit early retirement, with the typical retraction date being set at five years. Therefore, even though the preferred shares may end up being outstanding for longer periods, they are valued as if the maturity is five years. For this reason, BMO Capital Markets compares the yields on retractable preferreds with those on mid-term bonds. In February 2012, the retractable preferreds yielded 1.12 percent, while the mid-term Canada bonds yielded 1.44 percent, producing a negative spread (–0.32 percent) between the yields on the riskier preferred shares and on the less risky bonds. Of course, the reason for this is the different tax treatment of dividends and interest. Indeed, when we look at the after-tax spread, we see that it is 0.12 percent for the corporate investor and 0.02 percent for the individual investor, which means the traditional risk-return relationship prevails on an after-tax basis.

floating rate preferred share a share that has a long maturity date but that has its dividend reset by an auction mechanism every three or six months so that the dividend yield is in line with market interest rates

The final type of preferred share reported in Table 19-3 is the **floating rate preferred share**. These shares generally have a long maturity date, but every three or six months, their dividend is reset by an auction mechanism so that the dividend yield will be in line with current market interest rates. Alternatively, many of the floating rate preferred shares issued by the major banks have their dividend rate float with 75 percent of the prime rate, usually to some maximum rate. The result is that they always sell close to their par value because their dividend rate is always close to the current market rate. In Table 19-3, the yield on these "floaters" is compared with the yield on three-month bankers' acceptances (BAs), which represent an alternative short-term fixed-income investment. The yield on the floaters was 3.02 percent compared to the 1.18 percent yield on the BAs, producing a pre-tax spread of 1.84 percent. The after-tax spread was 2.19 percent for corporate investors and 1.5 percent for individual investors.

Three important points about the yield data emerge. First, although the time and risk value of money are important, so too is the tax value of money. Second, the capital market is creative in its ability to design securities that meet investor demand: preferred shares have been designed to match similar fixed-income debt securities, but with the tax advantage of dividends.[8] Finally, the comparisons are never perfect because preferred shares are unambiguously riskier. Generally, the after-tax spreads are smallest for the shorter-term securities, where the risk differences are the lowest, and largest for the infinite-lived straight preferred shares, when compared with long-term Canada bonds. However, the current impact of monetary policy and Operation Twist in the United States has affected all these spread comparisons.

The basic risk attached to investing in preferred shares is that they have "equity risk" in addition to the investment risks attached to fixed-income securities. As mentioned above, equity securities do not provide a contractual right to anything except the residuals after all other claimants have been paid off. If, in any quarter, the BOD decides *not* to pay a dividend, the holders of preferred shares cannot seek legal action to force payment. This rule gives a firm some flexibility if it runs into serious financial trouble, because it can conserve cash by suspending the dividend payments.

cumulative provision a stipulation that no dividends can be paid on common shares until preferred share dividends, both current and arrears, are paid in full

However, because they don't carry a right to receive a dividend, most preferred shares do have a **cumulative provision**, which states that no dividends can be paid on common shares until preferred share dividends, both current and arrears, are paid in full. This ensures that the

---

[8] At one point in the 1980s, there was an attempt to issue 30-day preferred shares to directly mimic BAs. The CRA closed this down.

common shareholders, who have voting rights, don't suspend payment on the preferred share dividends while continuing to pay dividends on the common shares. Some preferred shares gain limited voting rights as the arrears accumulate, which allows the preferred shareholders to exercise some control over the company. However, these rights depend on the structure of the preferred shares.[9]

Commonly, firms experiencing financial trouble will suspend dividend payments on all classes of shares, including preferred shares, to conserve cash. If the firm then recovers, it must make significant cash payments to clear off the preferred dividend arrears. In practice, what often happens in these situations is that the arrears are paid through the issue of common shares or some combination of cash and shares. This allows the firm to clean up its balance sheet and start fresh.

An example of a traditional straight preferred issue is the series F preferred shares issued by Great-West Lifeco Inc. Great-West Lifeco has several series of preferred shares outstanding, each with slightly different features. As with other classes of shares, Great-West Lifeco's authorized capital allows it to issue more of these shares if it wants, or it can start another series. As of March 22, 2012, there was $193,544,750 of the F series outstanding, each with a par value of $25. Unlike common shares, preferred shares have a par value so their value is known in the event of bankruptcy. In addition, as is the case for bonds, the amount of the dividend payments is sometimes expressed as a percentage of par. In the case of these particular preferred shares, the dividend is $1.48 per year and they are traded on the TSX under the symbol "GWO. PR.F," similar to common shares. An interesting feature of Great-West Lifeco's preferred shares is that the series F through P do not have dividends that cumulate, and it has now redeemed its preferred share series A through E, which did have cumulative dividends.

Preferred shares are a popular financing vehicle for Great West Lifeco because it is a regulated life insurance company and relatively low risk. For similar reasons, preferreds are also issued by regulated utilities and banks. *Finance in the News 19-2* discusses a recent over–subscription to an issue of preferreds by Canadian Utilities.

---

finance INTHENEWS 19-2 | Canadian Utilities Boosts Preferred Share Offering after Strong Investor Demand

CANADIAN UTILITIES LIMITED says strong investor demand has led the Calgary company to boost a planned preferred share offering to $275 million from $200 million.

The pipeline and energy services unit of Atco Ltd. (TSX:ACO.X) said Tuesday it will now issue 11 million second preferred shares at $25 each, up from earlier plans to issue eight million shares.

The money will be used for capital spending, to pay down debt, and for other corporate purposes.

The preferred share financing is slated to close September 21.

Canadian Utilities has more than 6,000 employees and assets of $11 billion. The company operates in pipelines, natural gas and electricity transmission and distribution, power generation, gas and liquids processing, and other businesses.

Source: The Canadian Press, "Canadian Utilities Boosts Preferred Share Offering after Strong Investor Demand," September 13, 2011. © The Canadian Press, 2011. Reprinted by permission.

Like many preferred share issues, this series is "callable" by Great-West Lifeco. They were callable at $26 in September 2008 and at $25.75 in September 2009, declining by $0.25 each year until they are callable at par. This means that at Great-West Lifeco's option, it can call the preferred shares away from their owners by paying the fixed call price. As of March 22, 2012, the Great West Life preferreds were selling at $25.40, and the fact that they were callable at $25 meant that their price was unlikely to increase even if the market interest rate fell.

---

[9] Note that many of the short-term preferred shares, particularly those issued by the banks, do not have this cumulative feature, because the risk of non-payment is very low.

From this description of Great-West Lifeco's preferred shares, we can see that they have many of the characteristics of bonds. Like bonds, they have different features that require that each series of preferred shares be evaluated separately. We have discussed retraction features and call features, but some preferred shares (convertibles) can be converted into other securities, usually common shares, which we will discuss shortly. Other preferred shares have "purchase funds," which act like sinking funds for debt securities (discussed in Chapter 6). Like sinking funds, purchase funds require the company to buy back a certain number of shares each year, creating a "two-edged" sword: in the short run, this increases the number of purchasers and ensures a ready market for the shares; in the long run, however, as the number of shares goes down, it has the opposite effect.

Just like bonds and commercial paper, preferred shares are rated by the rating agencies, such as Dominion Bond Rating Service (DBRS). However, because preferred shares are riskier than either bonds or CP, the rating structure is more limited. Pfd-1 is equivalent to both AAA- and AA-rated bonds, Pfd-2 to A-rated bonds, Pfd-3 to more highly rated BBB bonds, Pfd-4 to lower-rated BBB and BB-rated bonds, and Pfd-5 to B- or lower-rated bonds. The Great West Lifeco preferreds are all rated Pfd-1 (low) by DBRS.

We have discussed preferred shares in the context of shareholders' equity because, legally, they are equity securities. However, as the discussion above demonstrates, they share many characteristics with debt and are commonly regarded as a **hybrid security**, part debt and part equity. In fact, there is a continuum of financial securities that run the full range from common shares to what people typically think of as debt. Some of the hybrids can be very important for corporate financing, and we will discuss them in the following sections.

> **hybrid security** a security that is part debt and part equity

CONCEPT REVIEW QUESTIONS

1. Briefly describe the following types of preferred shares: straight, retractable, and floating rate.

2. Briefly describe the following features that may be associated with preferred shares: cumulative provision, callable feature, and purchase funds.

3. Why are preferred shares sometimes called hybrid securities?

4. Why would you want a cumulative feature when purchasing preferred shares?

19.3 WARRANTS AND CONVERTIBLE SECURITIES

> **Learning Objective 19.4**
> Explain how combining warrants with debt issues or issuing convertible bonds or debentures can provide firms with attractive financing options.

We now consider the last major class of securities issued by companies, which includes warrants, convertible bonds, and convertible preferred shares.

Warrants

> **warrants** the corporate finance equivalent of call options: they are issued by firms to raise capital; when they are exercised, more shares are created; they usually have long maturities, which makes them more valuable

Warrants are the corporate finance equivalent of call options, so they are affected by the same factors as those that affect call options, as discussed in Chapter 12. However, there are two major differences.

- First, call options are transactions between two external investors; what one investor gains, the other loses, but there is no impact on the firm. Warrants are issued by firms to raise capital; when they are exercised, more shares are created.

- Second, call options are usually issued with very short maturities because they are standardized. Warrants almost always have longer maturities, which makes them more valuable.

The data in Table 19-4 come from the *Financial Post* and list the first four warrants outstanding on the Canadian exchanges in March 2012 as well as a long-dated warrant for Franco-Nevada Corp.

TABLE 19-4 Warrant Listings, March 22, 2012

Company	Stock Close	Stock Exchange	Exercise Price	Recent Close	Bid/ Ask	Intrinsic Value	Time Value	Years Left	Expiry Date
Aberdeen Intl. Inc.	0.50	TSX	1.00	0.500		0	0.05	0.3	June 6, 2012
Ainsworth Lumber Co. Ltd.	1.56	TSX	2.500	12.00	Bid	0	0.150	1.40	July 22, 2013
Air Canada	0.97	TSX	2.20	0.04	Bid	0	0.70	0.70	October 28, 2012
Andina Minerals Inc.	0.80	TSX	2.250	0.01	Bid	0	0.01	0.30	June 2, 2012
Franco-Nevada Corp.	43.72	TSX	75.0	6.02		0	6.02	5.3	June 16, 2017

Source: Data from *Financial Post*, http://www.financialpost.com/markets/data/group-warrants.html. Retrieved March 22, 2012.

Note that almost all of these warrants are for mining firms or other resource companies. In fact, most warrants are issued by junior firms looking for equity financing. The company receives initial financing by issuing the warrants; then, if events turn out well (for example, if a drilling operation is successful), the stock price rises and the firm sees a further infusion of equity as the warrants are exercised. In contrast to the situation with calls, when the warrants are exercised, the warrant holder pays the exercise price to the company in return for shares. Warrants thus provide *primary* financing because the issuing company raises capital from their sale. Note that the maturities of these warrants run from a few months for the Aberdeen International warrants to 5.3 years for the warrants of Franco-Nevada, another gold company.

The fact that the number of shares outstanding increases when warrants are exercised means that warrants can be valued by using a variant of the standard option pricing model. We denote the existing number of shares as n and the number of shares issued on exercise of the warrants, at an exercise price of X, as m. If the value of the firm, without taking into account the warrants, is V, then the payoff if the warrants are exercised can be expressed as shown in Equation 19-1:

$$\text{Payoff to warrant holders} = \frac{m}{n+m}(V+mX) - mX \qquad [19\text{-}1]$$

Equation 19-1 indicates that after the warrants are exercised, the value of the firm must be the value without the warrants (V) plus the proceeds to the firm from the exercise of the warrants (mX), for a total value of $V + mX$. Of this total value, the percentage owned by the warrant holders is $m/(n+m)$, whereas the cost to them is the exercise value of mX. As a result, the payoff to the warrant holders is the difference between these two values. If we multiply the exercise value mX by $(n+m)/(n+m)$ and simplify, the payoff reduces to Equation 19-2:

$$\text{Payoff to warrant holders} = \frac{m}{n+m}(V-nX) \qquad [19\text{-}2]$$

In Equation 19-2, $V - nX$ can be viewed as the standard payoff to n secondary market calls with the same strike price of X—in other words, if we divide both of these terms by n, the first

dilution factor the amount by which ownership is reduced when additional shares are issued

term is the share price (i.e., V/n), and the second term is the exercise price (X). The first term, $m/(n + m)$, is the **dilution factor**, which results from the additional shares that are created as the warrants are exercised. Consequently, however the value of a secondary market call is determined, the value of the warrant is this amount multiplied by the dilution factor, whether we use the Black-Scholes or the binomial option pricing models discussed in Chapter 12 and Appendix 12A, respectively.

EXAMPLE 19-1   Estimating Payoffs to Warrants

A company has 10 million shares outstanding that are trading at $20 per share. The company has 1 million warrants outstanding that have an exercise price of $18 each. What is the payoff to the warrant holders of exercising them?

Solution

$m = 1$ million

$n = 10$ million

$V = \$20 \times 10$ million $= \$200$ million

$X = \$18$

By using Equation 19-2, we can estimate the payoff as

$$\text{Payoff} = \frac{m}{n + m}(V - nX) = 1/(10 + 1) \times (200 - (10)(18)) = (1/11) \times (20) = \$1.818 \text{ million}$$

As long-term options, warrants are often extremely valuable, as they often trade at significant premiums over their intrinsic value—that is, they possess a significant time value. For example, the Franco-Nevada warrants have an exercise price of $75, while the current share price is only $43.72, so they have no intrinsic value but have a time value of $6.02 because their value is heavily dependent on the future price of gold, which has been reaching record highs.

Because they are valuable, warrants are frequently used as "sweeteners" to make issues more attractive and thereby access financing that would not otherwise be available. For example, junior mines often have significant capital expenditures and limited cash flow to meet interest payments on financing. If they approach a venture capitalist for debt financing, they may be asked to pay a very high interest rate, given the risks involved. This compounds the problem of a lack of cash flow to make the interest payments. In these circumstances, the combination of a low-cost loan and warrants may allow the firms to raise debt. The low interest rate helps alleviate a firm's cash flow problems, while the warrants make new equity financing available if the firm is successful. Investors may be willing to buy these warrants, which might provide a significant payoff if the firm does well and its share price increases.

Furthermore, the very risk that makes debt financing expensive also makes the warrants valuable. Recall from our discussion in Chapter 12 that call options are more valuable when the underlying asset price is volatile. This is also true for warrants, which are simply corporate-issued call options. As a general rule, we often see warrants and convertibles (which are discussed below) being issued by firms that face significant uncertainty and possess correspondingly low bond ratings. They have difficulty raising debt capital without resorting to the use of some form of sweetener. For these firms, using warrants or adding convertible features reduces the cash outlay for interest payments, thus lowering the risk of financial distress.[10]

For similar reasons, warrants are often part of staged financing by a company. If the company is successful, the stock price will go up, so by issuing warrants that include the right to buy further warrants, a company can generate an automatic sequence of financing. The warrants in this kind of financing strategy are often referred to as "bunny warrants", for obvious reasons. The document in *Finance in the News 19-3* is a press release for $48 million in warrant financing that includes the possibility of a second round of warrant financing.

---

[10] A basic problem of debt financing is that increasing the interest rate for risky borrowers makes the borrowers even riskier.

finance INTHENEWS 19-3 — Intertainment Receives Commitments for $48 Million Special Warrant Financing

INTERTAINMENT MEDIA INC. ("Intertainment" or the "Company") is pleased to announce that it has received commitments to complete a non-brokered private placement of up to 40 million special warrants (each a "Special Warrant") at a price of $1.20 per Special Warrant for gross proceeds of up to approximately $48,000,000 (the "Offering"). Each Special Warrant will be exchangeable, for no additional consideration, for one common share in the capital of Intertainment (each a "Common Share") and one-half of one common share purchase warrant (each a "Warrant").

The Company will consider the financing commitment in 2 tranches; the first tranche of up to $28 million, and will consider the second tranche of up to $20 million based on assessment of corporate opportunities and expansion. The Company may elect, at its sole discretion, to take less than the amount offered.

The offering group consists of institutional investment firms including Toronto-based AlphaNorth Asset Management Inc., a prominent U.S.-based investment fund, accredited investors, and Intertainment board and management.

Proceeds will be used to accelerate the Company's core new media offering, including Ortsbo, Ad Taffy, and itiBiti; potential acquisition opportunities, and for working capital purposes.

The Special Warrants will expire on the earlier of (i) the date of issuance of a receipt being issued in respect of a final prospectus filed in certain Canadian jurisdictions (the "Prospectus") qualifying the securities issuable upon exchange of the Special Warrants; and (ii) four months following the closing date of the Offering. Each Special Warrant will be subject to statutory resale restrictions and, absent the clearing of the Prospectus in Canada, neither the Special Warrants nor the underlying securities may be traded in Canada during the period of four months following closing of the Offering, except in accordance with applicable securities legislation and TSX Venture Exchange policies.

Each whole Warrant will entitle its holder to purchase one additional Common Share for $2.00 and will expire 24 months after the date of the closing of the Offering. In the event that the Common Shares trade at a closing price on the TSX Venture Exchange of $4.00 or higher for a period of 15 consecutive trading days at any time after four months and one day after the closing of the Offering, the Company may accelerate the expiry date of the Warrants by giving notice to holders thereof and in such case the Warrants will expire on the 30th day after the date on which such notice is given by the Company.

The Company may pay finder's fees of up to 7% cash and 7% broker warrants in accordance with the TSX Venture Exchange policies. The completion of the Offering is subject to TSX Venture Exchange acceptance, standard conditions, and other regulatory approval.

Source: Press release from Ortsbo/Intertainment Media Inc., May 2, 2011. Retrieved from www.ortsbo.com/about/press-releases.

If the warrants are "detachable," the institution providing the debt may sell the warrants to other investors. If they are not detachable, issuing bonds plus warrants is similar to issuing convertible bonds.

Convertible Securities

Convertible bonds, as described in Chapter 6, are bonds (preferred shares) that can be converted into a specified number of common shares at the option of the bondholder. In many ways, they are similar to bonds (preferred shares) with warrants. The key difference is that when convertibles are converted, the bonds are exchanged for common shares and are no longer outstanding, whereas for debt with warrants attached, the debt remains outstanding and the exercise price is paid in cash. This means that the firm does not get any new financing when convertibles are converted; all that happens is that the debt is converted into common shares. In contrast, with warrants, the firm gets new financing from the sale of new shares at the exercise price.

On March 22, 2012, the *Financial Post* reported the data shown in Table 19-5 for the first five convertible bonds outstanding in Canada.

Like companies offering warrants, companies that issue convertible bonds tend to be high risk. The first company listed in Table 19-5 is Advantage Energy, whose outstanding convertible bond has a 5 percent coupon and is selling for $97.26. These bonds have just under three years to maturity, a yield to maturity of 6.06 percent, and a reported **conversion ratio (CR)** of 11.63. This means that each bond could be converted into approximately 11.63 Advantage Energy common shares. Remember that bonds have a $1,000 par value but are always quoted

conversion ratio (CR) the number of shares for which a convertible security can be exchanged

TABLE 19-5 Convertible Bond Listings, March 22, 2012

Issuer	Coupon	Maturity	Last Price	Parity	Yield to Maturity	Premium	Conversion Ratio	Conversion Price	Share Price, March 22, 2012
Advantage Energy	5.00%	30-Jun-2015	97.26	43.26	6.06%	124.85%	11.63	8.60	3.72
AECON Group	7.00%	30-Sept-2014	105.75	70.84	4.55%	49.16%	5.26	19.0	13.47
AG Growth	7.00%	31-Dec-2014	108.00	90.91	3.91%	18.20%	2.22	44.98	41.10
Alacer Gold	4.75%	30 Mar 2012	105.22	103.25	−437.29%	1.66%	12.50	8.00	8.28
Algoma Central	6.00%	31-Mar-2018	106.00	74.84	4.84%	40.72%	0.65	154.00	116.00

Source: Data from *Financial Post*, http://www.financialpost.com/markets/data/bonds-debentures.html.

conversion price (CP) the price at which a convertible security can be converted into common shares based on its conversion ratio

as $100, so if we divide the 11.63 into $100, we can say that the **conversion price (CP)** is $8.60 (i.e., $100/11.63), as reported in the listing. Advantage Energy is effectively selling common shares for $8.60 if the bonds are converted. We depict this relationship in Equation 19-3.

[19-3]
$$CP = \frac{Par}{CR}$$

conversion value (CV) the value of a convertible security if it is immediately converted into common shares

At the time, however, the market price (P) of Advantage Energy's common shares was only $3.72, so the **conversion value (CV)** for these convertibles, denoted as "Parity" in the listing, was 11.63 times this current share price or $43.26. The conversion value is the value of the bonds if they are immediately converted into common shares, as expressed in Equation 19-4.

[19-4]
$$CV = CR \times P$$

Because the bonds were selling for $97.26 at the time, and their value if immediately converted into common shares was only $43.26, the bonds were selling for a premium over their conversion value of 124.85 percent (i.e., (97.26–43.26)/43.26). Equation 19-5 estimates this conversion premium.

[19-5]
$$Conversion\ premium = \frac{(Market\ value - CV)}{CV}$$

We can view this 124.85 percent premium as the percentage by which the Advantage Energy share price would have to increase before it began to make sense to convert the bonds into common shares. Recall from Chapter 12 that when the stock price is less than the exercise price for call options, we say the option is "out of the money" and has an intrinsic value of zero; no one would exercise the call. Similarly, with the Advantage Energy convertible, when the conversion value is less than the bond's market value, no one will voluntarily convert the bonds into common shares.

The Advantage Energy bonds are an example of an out-of-the-money call option since the conversion value or parity is such a small proportion of the bond's current market value. The reason for this is not that Advantage Energy is a poor company. In fact, quite the opposite—it is an innovative oil and gas company and one of the major players in finding new reserves of "shale gas" in northeastern British Columbia and Alberta. The problem is simply that companies like Advantage Energy have been so successful at finding new reserves of natural gas that the market is flooded with natural gas and prices are depressed. This, in turn, has affected the stock price of all predominantly natural gas companies in Canada. Because it is out of the money, it is highly unlikely that the Advantage Energy convertible will be converted to common shares in the time left before the bond matures in January 2015. In this case, the convertible is largely selling on its **straight bond value (SBV)**. The SBV can be determined by using the standard bond pricing equation that was introduced in Chapter 6, using the yield on similar non-callable bonds as the market rate (k_b). Using Equation 6-1, we can calculate SBV.

straight bond value (SBV) the price that a convertible bond would sell for if it could not be converted into common stock

$$SBV = I \times \left[\frac{1 - \frac{1}{(1+k_b)^n}}{k_b} \right] + F \times \frac{1}{(1+k_b)^n} \qquad [19\text{-}6]$$

In Equation 19-6,

SBV = the straight bond value

I = interest (or coupon) payments

k_b = the yield on similar non-callable bonds

n = the term to maturity

F = the face (par) value of the bond

For Advantage Energy, there are no non-convertible bonds outstanding, as its other debt is all short-term bank loans. It records its bank debt as costing 5.5 percent. In Table 19-5, the *Financial Post* simply reversed the bond-pricing Equation 19-6, using the current market price of $97.26 to calculate the yield to maturity on the convertible bond of 6.06 percent. A default spread of 4.64 percent (6.06 percent to 1.42 percent) is consistent with the pricing of the short-term debt of a risky junior oil and gas company that is otherwise bank financed at 5.5 percent, leaving relatively little time value left in the option to convert.

Every convertible bond has a **floor value (FV)**, because it will always sell *for no less than* the larger of its straight bond value or its conversion value. This is logical because even if the company's shares are trading at a price well below the conversion price, so that the value of the conversion feature is negligible, the bond would still be held by investors and valued as a straight bond, as seems to be the case for the Advantage Energy bond. Therefore, it will never trade below the SBV. Similarly, a convertible bond would never sell below its conversion value because if it did, arbitrageurs would buy the bond, convert it into common stock, and sell the shares, thus earning riskless profits. If we look at Alacer Gold's convertible bond, included in the Financial Post table, its conversion value (parity) is $103.25 and it only has eight days left before maturity. In its case, the recorded yield is −437.29 percent, since it would soon mature for $100. The premium of the convertible over its conversion value is due to the value of this very short-term option, which was implicitly tied to the value of gold. As we can see, the convertible for Advantage Energy is selling only slightly above its straight bond value, while that for Alacer is selling slightly above its conversion value. This confirms that we can estimate the FV of a convertible using Equation 19-7.

floor value (FV) the lowest price a convertible bond will sell for, which is equal to the larger of its straight bond value or its conversion value

$$FV = Max(SBV, CV) \qquad [19\text{-}7]$$

Of course, in practice, convertibles usually sell at prices higher than their minimum value because of the time value of the conversion option, in the same way that warrants and calls sell above their intrinsic value. However, for Advantage Energy, the option is deep out of the money, while for Alacer Gold it is deep in the money.

EXAMPLE 19-2   Convertible Bond Values

A 10 percent coupon bond has 10 years to maturity when market rates on similar non-convertible bonds are 8 percent. It is convertible into 50 common shares and has a $1,000 par value. Estimate the following for this convertible:

a.   conversion price

b.   straight bond value (SBV), assuming it pays annual coupons

c.   conversion value (CV), if the shares are trading at $25 per share

d.   floor value (FV)

e.   conversion premium, if it was trading at $1,350

Solution

a.   CP = Par/CR = $1,000/50 = $20

b.   Par = $1,000; I = coupon rate $\times F$ = 0.1 $\times$ $1,000 = $100; n = 10; k_b = 0.08.

   With this information, we can use Equation 19-6 to find the price, or we can solve it by using a financial calculator or Excel.

$$SBV = 100 \times \left[\frac{1 - \frac{1}{(1.08)^{10}}}{0.08} \right] + 1,000 \times \frac{1}{(1+0.08)^{10}} = \$1,134.20$$

EXAMPLE 19-2   Solution Using a Financial Calculator

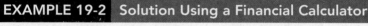

PMT → −100;   N → 10;   FV → −1,000;   I/Y → 8%   CPT   PV = $1,134.20

EXAMPLE 19-2   Solution Using Excel

= PRICE(date(2012,11,06), date(2022,11,06), .10, .08, 100, 1, 0) produces $1,134.20.

EXAMPLE 19-2   Convertible Bond Values *continued*

Solution

   c. CV = CR $\times$ P = 50 shares/bond $\times$ $25/share = $1,250

   d. Floor value (FV) = Max(SBV, CV) = Max(1,134.20, 1,250) = $1,250

The convertible *cannot* trade below this.

   e. Conversion premium = (1,350 − 1,250)/1,250 = 8%

(TI BA II PLUS)

Conceptually, we can view a convertible bond as a straight bond plus the option to convert the bonds into common shares. The convertibles are thus a hybrid. This hybrid characteristic can be illustrated by thinking about what happens at maturity, when the purchasers can surrender them for their par value. Essentially, there are two alternatives: either the share price goes higher than the conversion price or it does not. If the price goes higher, then investors will convert the bonds into the common shares, because the conversion value will exceed the bond value of the convertible. To make sure that conversion occurs, most convertible bonds are also callable by the issuer. Therefore, if the conversion value exceeds the par value, the company can state its intention to buy them back at par, thereby forcing conversion by the investors because they will get a higher price by converting than by selling them back at par.

   If the company did not have the right to buy the bonds at $100 plus accrued interest, investors would continue to hold the bonds and would not convert them into common shares because there would still be time value attached to the option to convert. If, on the other hand,

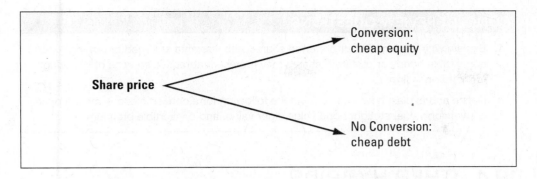

FIGURE 19-3 *Convertible Scenarios*

the share price is less than the conversion value at the maturity date, the holders will simply demand their par value of $100 for the bond, and the conversion privilege will expire worthless, just like an out-of-the-money call option. These two scenarios are illustrated in Figure 19-3.

Note that if the convertibles are converted, the company ends up with "cheap" equity, which is the case for Alacer Gold. This is because convertibles are normally issued with a conversion premium of about 25 percent, which means that the share price is less than the conversion price and the company has effectively sold equity with a time lag for a higher price. However, suppose the share price is now $20. In this case, an even better strategy, in retrospect, would have been to finance with straight debt and then issue shares for $20 years later. The after-the-fact best financing choices would have been, in order, debt, convertibles, and common shares. However, firms (or investors) do not have the luxury of perfect foresight.

Now consider what happens if the bonds aren't converted, as will likely be the case for Advantage Energy. In this situation, the company will be forced to redeem the bonds at par value, but it will have had the benefit of five-year debt that paid only 6 percent, when similar straight debt would have cost much more (remember that the company is paying 5.5 percent on its short-term bank debt). As a result, Advantage Energy will have ended up with cheap debt financing. However, the stock price only had to increase about 25 percent over a five-year period to get the holders of the convertible bonds to convert them into common shares, which is less than the cost of equity capital for these small risky companies, so the original expectation was that the convertibles would be converted. The fact that they will probably not be means that the shareholders have received an inadequate rate of return. The best scenario would then have been for Advantage Energy to have sold common shares rather than convertibles, because the shares will almost certainly be worth less on the maturity date than was originally expected. After-the-fact best financing choices for Advantage Energy would have been common shares, convertibles, and debt.

This what-if scenario analysis indicates that convertibles are rarely the "right" decision, but they are never the "wrong" decision, because the firm gets either cheap debt or cheap equity financing. It is this compromise that makes convertibles popular for many high-risk junior companies that have trouble accessing debt markets because of the high interest rate. Convertibles are also popular when a company's management is reluctant to issue more common shares because it believes its share price is undervalued.

This discussion has emphasized that convertibles are hybrids: they are part equity and part debt. When Advantage Energy and Alacer Gold issued their convertibles, straight debt financing would have been expensive. However, issuing convertibles did not mean that they got cheap debt, since on the issue date they were both partly debt and partly equity. How much they were of each depends on the terms of the convertible, but the fact they were hybrids means we cannot consider them to be either debt or equity in isolation.

As we look at the other convertibles, we note that what the *Financial Post* lists as the "premium" is the market price minus the conversion value, divided by the conversion value. This will always be positive because the convertibles will always sell for more than the higher of their conversion value or bond value due to their option value.

CONCEPT REVIEW QUESTIONS

1. Explain why issuing debt or preferred shares with warrants attached or issuing convertible bonds or preferred shares may represent attractive sources of financing for higher-risk firms.

2. Define and explain how to determine the following for a convertible: conversion price, conversion value, straight bond value, floor value, and convertible premium.

19.4 OTHER HYBRIDS

Categorizing Hybrids

Learning Objective 19.5
Identify and describe the various hybrid financing options available to firms, and explain how they are constructed.

Warrants, convertible bonds, and convertible preferred shares are the most obvious types of hybrids. However, there has been enormous innovation in corporate financing aimed at creating hybrids that satisfy multiple objectives. Our focus on hybrids so far has been on the CRA's definition of interest for tax purposes. However, there is also the question of how these securities are categorized on the firm's financial statements—are they treated as debt or equity?—and by the rating agencies. The financial criteria for viewing hybrids as debt, equity, or some mix of the two are different from the CRA's criteria. DBRS, for example, looks at four factors to determine whether a security is debt or equity: the permanence factor, the subordination factor, the legal factor, and the subjective factor.

permanence factor the length of time for which the security will be outstanding; a major factor in determining whether a security is debt or equity

The **permanence factor** relates to whether or not the security will be outstanding for a long period. Common shares are the gold standard because they have no maturity date and no requirement to redeem them at any point. BAs, conversely, are the ultimate debt instrument because they have a very limited life, 30 or 60 days, and then have to be redeemed. The **subordination factor** refers to the priority of the claim on the firm's assets and income stream. Again, common shares are the gold standard and BAs are obvious debt because they have an absolute claim to be paid off in 30 or 60 days. The **legal factor** refers to the legal rights of the investors—that is, do they have a contractual right to receive income or is it in some way discretionary, such as the declaration of a dividend by the BOD? Finally, the **subjective factor** is the intention of the company when it issues the securities.

subordination factor the priority of the claim on the firm's assets and income stream; a major factor in determining whether a security is debt or equity

legal factor the rights, contractual or discretionary, of the investors to receive income; a major factor in determining whether a security is debt or equity

Standard & Poor's (S&P), one of the two major U.S. bond-rating agencies, has gone into the issue of hybrids in more detail because there are more outstanding in the U.S. market. S&P has four criteria that are similar to those of DBRS.[11]

1. Does it have ongoing payments that could lead to default?

2. Does it have a maturity or repayment requirement?

3. Does it provide a "cushion" for creditors in case of distress?

4. Is it expected to remain in the capital structure?

subjective factor the intention of the company when it issues securities; a major factor in determining whether a security is debt or equity

Clearly, S&P criterion 1 is the same as DBRS factor 3, which is the contractual commitment to pay interest, where failure leads to default. S&P 2 is the same as DBRS 1, which is the question of permanence versus a maturity date. S&P 3 is similar to DBRS 2, where the deeper the subordination, the more "cushion" is provided to senior bondholders. Finally, S&P 4 is similar to DBRS 4, where the question is the intention of the company and whether the security is expected to remain part of the firm's long-term financing or its capital structure.

An example illustrating the DBRS and S&P criteria might help. In our discussion of preferred shares, we noted that there are different types of preferred shares that mimic debt but attract the tax treatment of dividends. One class of these preferred shares was retractable pre-

---

[11] Corporate Equity Criteria—Equity Credit, S&P 28, October 2004.

ferred shares, which BMO Capital Markets compared with five-year Government of Canada bonds. What we didn't discuss was what these preferred shares were retractable into—that is, when the holders ask for their money back, what do they get?

A **hard retraction** requires that the preferred shares be paid off in cash. In effect, this makes them very bond-like, because apart from getting dividends for five years instead of interest at the end of five years, the investor gets cash back. A **soft retraction** allows the preferred shares to be paid off with common shares or other preferred shares. In this case, the firm has no commitment to pay cash; it simply issues more shares with no cash outlay.

In terms of the S&P/DBRS criteria, preferred shares with a hard retraction are very debt-like, because they are not permanent, have a fixed contractual commitment to pay off at maturity with cash, and are not a permanent part of the firm's capital structure. The soft retractables have no fixed contractual commitments, have no maturity because they are simply replaced with other types of equity, and are more likely to be a permanent part of the firm's capital structure. Hence, they are more like equity. DBRS and S&P would give them greater equity weight because they do not strain the firm's cash flow.

> **hard retraction** the requirement that preferred shares be paid off in cash
>
> **soft retraction** the allowance for preferred shares to be paid off with common shares or other preferred shares

Creative Hybrids: Some Examples

Another security that looks like debt but is closer to equity is an **income bond**. These bonds are generally issued after a reorganization, so the "interest" is tied to some cash flow level for the firm. **Cash flow bonds** are now sold in the United States with the same objective. In both cases, the maturity dates have been quite long, usually at least 30 years, and the fact that the "interest" payments are conditional on the firm meeting certain thresholds reduces the contractual commitment to pay interest. As a result, income bonds are given significant equity weight. In fact, in Canada, the payments are not tax deductible and are classified as dividends. This reduces their attractiveness as far as the company is concerned, which is why they have mainly been a "desperation play" after a major reorganization (when the company has lots of tax-loss carry forwards and little use for tax shields).

> **income bonds** bonds issued after a reorganization, with interest tied to some cash flow level for the firm and with long maturity dates
>
> **cash flow bonds** bonds sold in the United States that have the same objectives as income bonds in Canada

Some firms achieve the same type of objective with the **commodity bond**. Suppose a gold producer has fixed mine costs to produce gold but faces uncertain revenues because they are tied to the price of gold. One way to manage this gold-price risk is through the use of derivatives that are tied to the price of gold, such as those discussed in Chapter 11, or through long-term fixed-price contracting. However, an alternative is to tie the bond payments to the price of gold. This can be done in two ways: either the interest payment or the principal is tied to the price of gold. If the principal is tied to the price of gold, then as the gold price increases, so too does the principal; because interest is expressed as a percentage of the principal, the investor receives more interest. If the bond payments are structured carefully, CRA criteria are met and the interest is tax deductible, but the bonds are less risky to the firm because the interest payments are tied to its major risk, which is the price of gold.

> **commodity bond** a bond whose interest or principal is tied to the price of an underlying commodity, such as gold

Commodity bonds, in which the principal is tied to some external index, are an example of indexed bonds. The most common of these are the "real return bonds" issued by the Government of Canada (discussed in Chapter 6). In this case, the principal is tied to the consumer price index (CPI). As the CPI increases, the principal increases, and the interest is expressed as a percentage of this increasing principal. In this way, the investor's income increases with inflation, thereby preserving a real rate of return. As of March 22, 2012, the yield on the real return bond, equivalent to the regular 30-year fixed-rate Canada bond, was a paltry 0.57 percent. In this instance, the investor could choose between the real return bond, yielding 0.57 percent, and the regular long-term Canada bond, yielding 2.77 percent. The difference is that with the regular bond, the investor runs the risk that inflation will erode the real purchasing power of both the income and the maturity value of the bond. The difference between these two yields (2.2 percent) is slightly above the middle of the Bank of Canada's target inflation band of 1 percent to 3 percent. However, on a simple comparison basis, if investors are worried about inflation or think the rate of inflation will be greater than this break-even rate of 2.2 percent, they should buy the real return bond.

The problem with the real return bond is that the increase in the value of the principal is regarded by the CRA as income and is taxed as such. As a result, ordinary investors holding these bonds are taxed on this income, even if they do not receive any cash. This makes the bonds unattractive for many investors unless they can hold them in tax-preferred savings plans, like Registered Retirement Savings Plans (RRSPs). For the same reason, these bonds are popular with institutional investors that do not pay tax, such as pension plans.

Real return bonds are not issued by corporations, but they do have one attractive property: the immediate interest payments are much lower than those from regular fixed-income bonds. Note, for example, that the yield on the real return bond was 0.57 percent versus 2.77 percent for the regular bond. The offset is that, at maturity, the firm has to pay a much larger principal back to the investor, as the nominal $100 has increased with the CPI. For firms that are short of immediate cash but have good long-run prospects, this is an attractive proposition because it minimizes immediate cash payments, deferring them to a period when, it is hoped, the firm will be more valuable. Corporations achieve this same result by issuing **original issue discount bonds (OIDs)** or **low-yield notes** that similarly sell at a discount.

original issue discount bonds (OIDs) or **low-yield notes** bonds that sell at a discount from par value when issued by firms

Table 19-6 shows the time path of the cash payments on two bonds: a 10-year regular interest bond with a 10 percent annual yield versus an OID with a 10 percent yield but a zero coupon. The principal for both bonds is set at $42.40 (for reasons we will come to in a minute). The regular bond has annual cash outflows of $4.24 and, in year 10, a bullet payment of the principal of $42.40. The OID has no annual interest payments; instead, the 10 percent yield is earned by paying $42.40 today and receiving $100 at maturity in 10 years. As a result, the principal increases each year from $42.40 in year 1, to $46.65 in year 2, and so on, until it reaches $100 at the end of year 10.

TABLE 19-6 OID versus Regular Bond Payments

Year	Regular Bond	OID Bond	
		Principal	"Interest"
2	$4.24	$46.65	$4.24
3	4.24	51.32	4.67
4	4.24	56.45	5.13
5	4.24	62.09	5.64
6	4.24	68.30	6.21
7	4.24	75.13	6.83
8	4.24	82.64	7.51
9	4.24	90.91	8.26
10	46.65	100.00	9.09

From the company's point of view, the discount bond involves no annual payments but a much larger payment at maturity. This time pattern of cash flows is useful for many cash-poor, opportunity-rich companies. However, from a tax point of view, the CRA regards the discount bond as locking in interest in the same way an issue of treasury bills on a discount basis does. The CRA has several ways of determining interest, but the correct way is to compound the $42.40 forward to the $100 maturity value. This provides the series of "interest" payments in the fourth column, which the CRA allows the company to deduct. Although this cash is not paid, investors have to pay tax on this imputed interest just as they do with the interest from the real return bond.

The zero-coupon bond is an example of an "off-market" interest rate that causes the market value to deviate from par. Another variant is a low-yield note, in which the coupon is not zero but is less than the going market interest rate. This means that the cash flow pattern falls between the two extremes documented above. In some cases, these low-yield notes are combined with a convertible feature, in which case they are called **liquid yield option notes (LYONs)**. LYONs are accretive convertibles, because the principal accretes or increases over time. Rogers Communications Inc. issued LYONs when it needed to conserve cash while building its cable network.

Another way to address the problem of tying interest payments to cash flow is to make the interest payments conditional on prior dividend payments. **Adjustable rate convertible subordinated securities (ARCS)** do just this. They have fixed principal and maturity, and the interest normally comprises two parts: a fixed interest rate, and some function of the dividend paid in the prior six months. These securities are almost all convertible into common shares, so the dividend is expressed as a percentage of the conversion price. If the conversion price is $50 and the dividend per share is $1, it would be expressed as 2 percent. The ARCS would then pay 5 percent plus twice this 2 percent dividend rate, or 9 percent in total. The ARCS are then subordinated to the firm's senior debt.

ARCS combine debt and equity features. Because the interest is represented as a percentage, is tied to the principal value, and legally accrues, it is tax deductible. However, as a deeply subordinated debt issue in which the interest could drop to 5 percent if the dividend is not declared in the prior six-month period, it has some equity-like features.

Another debt-versus-equity variant is **preferred securities**. Note that these are not preferred shares, because the payments are tax deductible. Texaco Inc. was the first to issue tax-deductible preferred securities in 1991. They have grown in popularity since then. Texaco set up a 100-percent-owned subsidiary in the Turks and Caicos Islands (a tax haven) to issue preferred securities. The proceeds were then loaned to the parent, for whom the interest paid was tax deductible. The interest flowed to the subsidiary, where it was not taxed, and all of it was used to make the dividend payments. The key provision was that Texaco would not let a 100-percent-owned subsidiary be forced into bankruptcy if it failed to make the interest payments. In turn, the preferred securities were sold with a five-year deferral of dividend payments, a 30-year life, and deep subordination.

Subsequently, trusts have been used to sell preferred securities; these are commonly called "trust preferred securities" and have been very popular with Canadian companies. Typically, they are rated BBB or lower and have been sold into the U.S. market as there is little appetite in the Canadian market for any type of high-yield debt.

Finally, there are **Canadian optional interest notes (COINs)**, often referred to as **prepaid bonds**. With COINs, a firm issues 99-year bonds with a par value of $100 and an interest rate of, say, 10 percent, which sell at par. After the bonds are issued, the firm immediately prepays the interest from years 11 to 99 ($38.546), leaving it with a net inflow of $61.454. This is why COINs are also called prepaid bonds. The firm has met all the legal requirements to continue deducting annual interest payments on $100, even though it has only effectively borrowed $61.454, not $100. Remember that this $100 represents the present value of each interest payment, as well as the $100 par value in 99 years. However, the discounting process means that the current value of the $100 par value in 99 years at 10 percent is only $0.008—that is,

$$\$0.007982 = \frac{\$100}{1.10^{99}}$$

By the same process, the present value of the interest payments from years 11 to 99 is $38.546, and that for years 1 to 10 is $61.446. The market value of $100 is the sum of these three components.

Some European companies using COINs reportedly wrote off the prepaid interest of $38.546 immediately, but the CRA has now limited the deduction of interest on these prepaid bonds to the imputed interest—that is, 10 percent of the actual amount raised, or $61.454. The speedy reaction of the CRA represents the dynamic interplay between innovative financing instruments and the tax authorities.

liquid yield option notes (LYONs) low-yield notes that are combined with a convertible feature and are accretive convertibles because the principal accretes or increases over time

adjustable rate convertible subordinated securities (ARCS) securities that have fixed principal and maturity, and interest that normally comprises a fixed interest rate and some function of the dividend paid in the previous six months; typically convertible into common shares

preferred securities securities generated by a company by creating a 100-percent-owned subsidiary that issues the shares and then loans the proceeds to the parent company, for whom the interest is tax deductible; interest flows to the subsidiary, where it is not taxed, and is used to make dividend payments

Canadian optional interest notes (COINs) or **prepaid bonds** 99-year bonds that are sold at their par values of $100; the firm immediately prepays the interest from years 11 to 99, leaving the firm with a net inflow and allowing it to continue to deduct annual interest payments of $100, even though it has effectively borrowed less

A Financing Hierarchy

S&P has ranked many types of hybrids according to their debt-equity mix, and Table 19-7 shows a synopsis of the main securities that we have discussed.[12] They range from common shares, which are rated at 100 percent, to commercial paper or BAs, which are rated at –100 percent, because they are the most debt-like form of security.

TABLE 19-7 S&P Financing Rankings

	Equity Share (%)
Common shares	100
Mandatory convertible preferred shares*	90
Straight preferred shares	50
Trust preferred shares	40
Convertible preferred shares	20
Re-marketed preferred shares†	–10
Normal convertible debt	–50
Accreting convertible bonds (LYONs)	–60
Very long-term bonds	–70
Medium-term bonds	–80
Auction preferred shares	–60
Commercial paper	–100

*Preferred shares for which conversion into common shares is structured to be automatic.
†Preferred shares that are repriced and resold after five to seven years.

As the S&P equity weighting scheme indicates, the risk of these instruments differs according to how much equity weight they have. At one extreme, common shares, as the riskiest security, are the most expensive, because investors require the highest rate of return to compensate them for the risk. At the other extreme, CP has the least equity weight and is the most like debt, with the lowest risk and lowest required rate of return. The costs of the various securities fall between these extremes. A typical hierarchy of financing cost is shown in Figure 19-4.

In practice, the actual rates depend on the level of interest rates and the state of the economy, but common equity is the most expensive, and the cost decreases as the equity share falls.

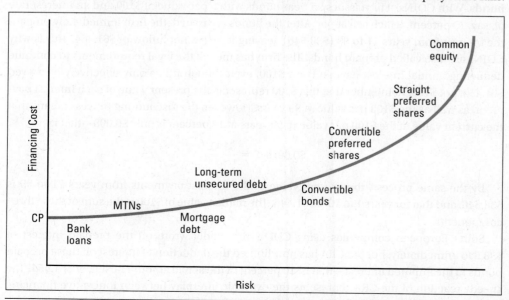

FIGURE 19-4 *Financing Hierarchy Costs*

[12] Table 19-7 is our interpretation of the S&P rankings based on Canadian issues.

CONCEPT REVIEW QUESTIONS

1. Name and discuss the four criteria used by DBRS to classify a security as debt versus equity.

2. Define the following types of hybrids: income bonds, commodity bonds, real return bonds, original issue discount bonds, LYONs, ARCS, preferred securities, and COINs.

3. Relate the costs of various financing options to their equity-like characteristics.

19-1 ETHICS AND CORPORATE GOVERNANCE
Ontario Teachers Pension Plan Halts Lending of Shares to Short Sellers

The Ontario Teachers Pension Plan has taken the rare step of halting the lending of shares to short sellers and plans to set up a new internal lending operation, arguing it wants to maintain tighter control over its voting rights as an investor.

Teachers senior vice-president Brian Gibson said the pension plan halted its lending late last year after two companies in which it held stakes called for shareholder voting on closely contested matters, but Teachers couldn't vote shares that had been borrowed by short sellers.

Mr. Gibson said Teachers had standard arrangements with its securities custodian to allow it to recall shares when necessary, but found the system didn't work well, and the shares could not be retrieved in time for votes.

When shares are lent by an investor for short selling, the voting rights transfer to the borrower. The situation has led some major U.S. companies to criticize the power of hedge funds to sway corporate votes using shares they have only borrowed and do not actually own.

It's not clear that any Canadian votes have been decided by hedge funds using borrowed shares. Mr. Gibson wouldn't identify the cases Teachers encountered, but said that in the end, the missing votes were not needed to clinch a vote. Teachers' move comes as corporate governance experts are increasingly urging institutional investors to get more closely involved in voting their shares and make more in-house decisions about how to vote on key issues.

David Beatty, managing director of the Canadian Coalition for Good Governance, which represents institutional investors, said institutional investors have a fiduciary responsibility to their beneficiaries to ensure the priority is to manage their voting.

In the United States, proposals have been floated to toughen rules on voting borrowed shares, or to require companies to announce the issues that will be up for a vote at a future shareholder meeting when they set the record date for voting. That would allow institutions to see if there are important issues on the ballot and recall their shares before the record date passes.

There has been little public debate of the issue in Canada, where activity has been confined to the internal steps taken by institutional shareholders to control their votes.

Peter Chapman, executive director of the Vancouver-based Shareholder Association for Research and Education, says some investors try to control lending during voting periods. "Some institutions don't track it, so they lose their votes. The better practice would be not to lend during the windows when you lose your voting rights."

Doug Pearce, chief executive officer of the B.C. Investment Management Corp., which manages investments for the B.C. government and public sector pension plans, said his fund rarely needs to recall shares for voting. "It is an issue, but we make sure that we secure our vote first, and lending will be secondary to that."

An official at the Ontario Municipal Employees Retirement System said OMERS hasn't had any occasion to recall shares in recent years for voting purposes and has made no changes to its lending practices.

But Mr. Gibson said Teachers has found the system not only works imperfectly, but has not been economically worthwhile. He said Teachers was earning little income from its lending because most of the proceeds went to the custodian who administered the program.

"Losing votes costs us a lot more economically than the little bit we were making on lending."

He said Teachers has decided to develop an in-house lending program so it can maintain close control over the process.

The extra cost of managing its own lending will be offset by the additional income Teachers will receive by not sharing the revenue with a custodian, Mr. Gibson said.:

Source: McFarland, Janet, "Why Teachers Halted Stock Loans to Short Sellers; Seeks to Maintain Tighter Control over its Voting Rights as Shareholder." *The Globe and Mail*, April 3, 2007, p. B11. © The Globe and Mail Inc. All rights reserved. Reprinted by permission.

DISCUSSION QUESTIONS

1. One share equals one vote, so when shares are lent to someone to sell, the new holder gets to vote. Who do you think should get to vote the shares: the underlying owner, such as Teachers, or the institution to whom it has lent the shares? Why?

2. Large institutions like Teachers have a lot of influence with their large shareholdings and actively intervene to improve corporate governance. Is Teachers giving up its fiduciary duty to its pensioners by lending its shares and giving up the right to vote?

SUMMARY

This chapter discusses equity and hybrid securities. Securities are financial contracts, and their level of risk depends on the design of the contract—specifically, how they are treated for tax purposes, and how much equity weight they have, which determines the risk they impose on the firm. Common shares impose the least risk because, according to S&P's criteria, they are a permanent part of the firm's capital structure, impose no commitments that might cause the firm to default, provide a cushion to senior debt that the firm can issue, and have no maturity date. CP and BAs are the opposite in that they have fixed payments, short maturities, a higher priority charge, and a lack of permanency. However, the interest on CP and BAs is tax deductible, whereas the dividends on common shares are not.

Between these two extremes are all the securities that firms issue. Conventional fixed-rate preferred shares, retractable preferred shares, and floating rate preferred shares take advantage of the fact that dividends in Canada attract the dividend tax credit and are non-taxable between corporations. Convertible securities and warrants are the most equity-like securities, particularly if they are structured so that conversion is mandatory. They also have the advantage of deferred equity financing or cheap debt financing, depending on what happens to the firm's share price.

This chapter describes the menu of corporate financing opportunities available. How firms choose between them is the topic of chapters 20 and 22.

SUMMARY OF LEARNING OBJECTIVES

19.1 Explain the basic rights associated with share ownership.

- (Some) equity holders can vote at shareholder meetings.
- Equity holders are entitled to dividends as declared by the corporation.
- Equity holders are residual claimants to the company's assets on dissolution.

19.2 Identify and describe the various classes of shares and the shareholders' rights associated with each.

The differentiating features across classes are voting rights, rights in the event of a dividend payment, and rights in the event of terminating the company. An example of a share structure:

- Class A shares: referred to as non-voting shares or restricted shares and have no voting rights, as long as dividends are paid; in the event of the winding up of the company, these shares are equal to class B shares.
- Class B shares: regarded as common shares and have full voting rights; there are no dividends paid if class C shares are in arrears, and these shares are equal with class A shares on the winding up of the company.
- Class C shares: have no voting rights unless dividends are in arrears for two years; no dividends can be paid on class A and B shares if class C shares are in arrears; for class C shares, there is a payment of $25 par value before any payments to class A and B shares on the winding up of the company.

19.3 Explain how preferred shares differ from common shares and outline the various features associated with preferred shares.

Dividends for preferred shares can be skipped (unlike those for bond coupons) because, unlike interest, there is no contractual right to receive a dividend, as it has to be declared by the board of directors. To protect the preferred shareholders, most preferred shares have a cumulative feature that requires skipped dividends to be made up at some future date before the common shareholders may receive a dividend. Preferred shareholders have a more senior claim to the company's assets than common shareholders in the event of dissolution, but the claim is limited to their par value (and to dividends in arrears). Straight preferred shares have no maturity date. Retractable preferred shares give the holder the right to redeem the share for the par value.

Some preferred shares pay a variable dividend rather than a fixed dividend. The dividend varies with a benchmark interest rate.

19.4 Explain how combining warrants with debt issues or issuing convertible bonds or debentures can provide firms with attractive financing options.

Risky companies with low bond ratings (e.g., young or start-up companies) can have difficulty borrowing money through the issue of debt. Warrants or convertibles can act as sweeteners to help raise capital. The option portion of the security (warrant or convertible) gives the holder some advantage if, as a result of the company's success, the stock price increases. In this case, if the company is successful, it automatically gets some equity financing. Since this option is valuable, the company can issue debt at a lower interest rate, so if it is not successful it ends up with "cheap" debt. In this way, the convertible feature reduces the cash outlay for interest and lowers the risk of financial distress.

19.5 Identify and describe the various hybrid financing options available to firms, and explain how they are constructed.

- Warrants are call options issued by the firm. When the options are exercised, the company acts as the writer and sells new shares in the company. The number of shares outstanding rises after warrant exercise, and the company raises new equity financing.

- Convertible bonds combine a coupon bond with a warrant. If the company is successful and the share price increases, the holder surrenders the bond in exchange for shares in the company. In this way, the firm's common equity increases and its debt decreases, opening up the ability to raise more debt.

- Convertible preferred shares combine a preferred share with a warrant and have the same impact as convertible debt.

KEY TERMS

adjustable rate convertible subordinated securities (ARCS), p. 739
Canadian optional interest notes (COINs), p. 739
cash flow bonds, p. 737
commodity bond, p. 737
conversion price (CP), p. 732
conversion ratio (CR), p. 731
conversion value (CV), p. 732
cumulative provision, p. 726
dilution factor, p. 730
family trust, p. 720
floating rate preferred share, p. 726

floor value (FV), p. 733
hard retraction, p. 737
hybrid security, p. 728
income bonds, p. 737
legal factor, p. 736
liquid yield option notes (LYONs), p. 739
low-yield notes, p. 738
non-voting or restricted shares, p. 719
original issue discount bonds (OIDs), p. 738
permanence factor, p. 736
pre-emptive right, p. 717
preferred securities, p. 739

prepaid bonds, p. 739
residual owners, p. 718
retractable preferred share, p. 726
soft retraction, p. 737
straight bond value (SBV), p. 733
straight preferred share, p. 725
subjective factor, p. 736
subordination factor, p. 736
tax value of money, p. 725
warrants, p. 728

EQUATIONS

Equation	Formula	Page
[19-1] Payment to Warrant Holders	$\text{Payoff to warrant holders} = \dfrac{m}{n+m}(V+mX)-mX$	p. 729
[19-2] Payment to Warrant Holders	$\text{Payoff to warrant holders} = \dfrac{m}{n+m}(V-nX)$	p. 729
[19-3] Conversion Price	$CP = \dfrac{Par}{CR}$	p. 732
[19-4] Conversion Value	$CV = CR \times P$	p. 732
[19-5] Conversion Premium	$\text{Conversion premium} = \dfrac{(Market\ value - CV)}{CV}$	p. 732
[19-6] Straight Bond Value	$SBV = I \times \left[\dfrac{1 - \dfrac{1}{(1+k_b)^n}}{k_b} \right] + F \times \dfrac{1}{(1+k_b)^n}$	p. 733
[19-7] Floor Value	$FV = Max(SBV, CV)$	p. 733

QUESTIONS AND PRACTICE PROBLEMS

Multiple Choice Questions

1. Which of the following does not appear in the share structure of a firm?
   a. Preferred shares
   b. Common shares
   c. Restricted shares
   d. None of the above

2. Which of the following statements about preferred shares is false?
   a. Retractable preferred shares allow the shareholders to bring forward the maturity date.
   b. The most common preferred shares in Canada are straight preferred shares.
   c. Preferred shareholders can force bankruptcy if the firm defaults on the dividend payment.
   d. Floating rate preferred share dividends are reset periodically.

3. A(n)_____is a bond that may be exchanged for the common stock of the same corporation.
   a. exchangeable bond
   b. retractable bond
   c. convertible bond
   d. warrant

4. Which of the following statements is true?
   a. Bonds are exchanged for common shares when convertibles are converted.
   b. The current market price is paid in cash when warrants are exercised.
   c. Debt is exchanged for common shares when its attached warrant is exercised.
   d. A conversion ratio is not specified in convertibles.

5. Which of the following is a correct ranking of after-the-fact best financing choices, assuming that the share price increases beyond the conversion price?
   a. Debt, convertibles, common shares, and preferred shares
   b. Preferred shares, common shares, debt, and convertibles
   c. Preferred shares, common shares, convertibles, and debt
   d. Debt, convertibles, preferred shares, and common shares

6. Assume a warrant carries a right to buy two shares of common stock at $20 per share. If the market price of a share is $30, what is the theoretical value of the warrant?
   a. $20
   b. $10
   c. $5
   d. $0

7. A convertible bond selling for $1,000 can be converted to 20 shares of common stock that is currently selling for $55 per share. What is most likely to happen?
   a. The bondholder will choose not to convert because the bond is worth more than the common shares.
   b. The bondholder will choose to convert.
   c. The stock price will go down to $50.
   d. It is impossible to predict using only the information provided.

8. A company has just issued convertible bonds with a face value of $1,000 and a conversion ratio of 50. Which of the following is most likely to be the current price per share of the company's common stock?
   a. Under $20
   b. $20

    c. Between $20 and $40

    d. Above $40

9. Which of the following is not one of the factors used to judge whether a security is debt or equity?

    a. Subordination

    b. Legal

    c. Subjective

    d. Coupon payment

10. Which of the following statements is false?

    a. A hard retractable means preferred shares must be paid off in cash.

    b. Commodity bonds help commodity producers to control the commodity price risks.

    c. Real return bonds are tied to the CPI.

    d. Preferred securities are another name for preferred shares.

11. What is the correct ranking of cost from the highest to the lowest?

    a. Common shares, convertible preferred shares, straight preferred shares

    b. Convertible preferred shares, convertible bonds, straight preferred shares

    c. Medium-term note debentures, bank loans, mortgage debt

    d. Common shares, long-term unsecured debt, mortgage debt

Practice Problems

12. State the three basic rights of common shareholders.

13. Discuss three reasons why firms issue preferred shares.

14. A firm has just filed for bankruptcy and is likely to be liquidated. The creditors, such as equipment suppliers and employees, are owed $1.5 million.

    a. How much will the equity holders receive if, when liquidated, the firm's assets are worth

        i. $1.7 million?

        ii. $1.2 million?

    b. Suppose that equity holders did not have limited liability. How much would they receive for each asset value above?

15. With the savings from your summer job you were able to buy 500 shares of a hot new Internet company last year. A few months after your purchase, the company was low on cash and needed to raise more equity capital. The company's charter provided a pre-emptive right to shareholders, so you were offered the chance to buy one additional share for each five owned.

    a. What percentage of the firm's equity will you own after your initial purchase if there are 500,000 shares outstanding?

    b. What percentage of the firm's equity will you own if you buy the extra shares offered?

    c. If you decline to buy the additional shares (but they are sold to other investors), how much of the firm's equity will you own?

16. When a firm needed to raise capital to expand, the founder was concerned about losing control of the firm if he sold too many shares. The solution devised by his investment banker was to create two different classes of shares. The founding member would retain 250,000 class A shares, which are entitled to two votes apiece; 750,000 common shares with one vote would be sold to the IPO investors. What percentage of the company's equity will the founder own? How much control (percentage of the votes) will the founder maintain?

17. A firm has 50 million common shares outstanding, on which it pays a quarterly dividend of $0.20 per share. The firm's capital structure also includes two million cumulative preferred

shares with a $25 par value that yield 8 percent per year (or 2 percent per quarter). After making some bad loans in the sub-prime mortgage market, the firm suffered a big loss, and suspended its dividend payments on all forms of equity. Six months later, the company is once again in the black having earned $6 million (after tax), which it intends to pay as dividends. How much will the common shareholders receive per share?

18. Collingwood Corp. has decided to invest some of its excess cash in straight preferred shares issued by other companies. It will earn a yield of 6.5 percent on the $10-million investment. How much net income will Collingwood earn if its corporate tax rate is 25 percent?

19. A firm has just issued convertible preferred shares with a $50 par value. The conversion price for these shares is $12.50 (per common share). What is the conversion ratio?

20. A firm has just issued convertible preferred shares (See Practice Problem 19). These shares have a call feature that permits the firm to repurchase the shares at par value (or, in effect, force the conversion into common shares). Usually, the common stock will be trading at least 20 percent above the conversion price before the call feature is invoked. At what price of its common stock will the firm consider calling the preferred shares?

21. The common shares of a firm are currently trading at $10.00, while its preferred shares trade at par (see Practice Problem 19). Calculate the convertible premium on the preferred shares. What does this premium mean?

22. What are the differences between call options and warrants?

23. Calculate the conversion price and conversion value of the convertible bonds given the following: selling price $95; each bond is convertible into four common shares; current common share price $40. Will the convertible bonds be converted?

24. In December 2009, Collingwood Corp. decided to issue 100,000 convertible bonds, maturing in December 2017. The bonds have a face value of $1,000 and promise an annual coupon payment of 5.75 percent. Conversion ratio of these bonds is 25.32, and it is known that Collingwood Corp.'s common shares were trading at $32.50 in December 2009. These bonds are rated A-, and straight bonds from similar companies with similar maturity yield 9 percent. Current market price of these bonds is $1,051. Calculate the conversion price, conversion value, SBV, floor value, and the conversion premium for these bonds.

25. Calculate the payoff of fully exercising warrants given the following: 900,000 existing shares are outstanding (n); 100,000 warrants (m) are outstanding and are exercisable at $10 (X). The firm is valued at $10 million (V) before the warrants are exercised. Calculate the payoff to warrant holders and the dilution factor.

26. Orion's Belt Mining Co. has 12 million common shares outstanding, which are currently trading for $4.75 apiece. In addition, the company has issued three million share purchase warrants with a strike price of $4.00 that are just about to expire.
    a. Determine the equity value of the firm before the warrants are exercised.
    b. What is the total cost to the warrant holders to purchase the new shares?
    c. Calculate the value of the shares that the holders of the warrants will own after they are exercised.
    d. What is the payoff to warrant holders? How much would you be willing to pay for each warrant?

27. A firm's common shares currently trade at $20 per share. The firm has warrants outstanding that entitle the holder to purchase two shares at an exercise price of $18 per share. The expiry date is two years from today.

a. Calculate the minimum value (floor value) for the warrants.

b. Show that the warrants cannot trade at a price that is below this floor value.

c. Show the percentage change in the floor value of the warrants given a 10 percent change in the market price of the shares.

28. Straight preferred shares issued by a firm have a discount rate of 8 percent per year, whereas these shares are yielding 6 percent on the $50 par value. The conversion value of these shares is calculated to be $40. Determine the straight preferred value (SPV) and the floor value for the convertible preferred shares. Assume the shares have no maturity and can therefore be valued as a perpetuity.

29. Jack and Jill Inc. very nearly tumbled into bankruptcy last year. To refinance the firm, the firm issued $25 million worth of 30-year income bonds. These bonds have an 8-percent coupon that is payable only if the firm achieves earnings before interest and tax (EBIT) of $3 million. Suppose the firm exactly achieves its target and pays out the full coupon interest amount. Determine the company's net income if the tax rate is 25 percent.

20 | Cost of Capital

LEARNING OBJECTIVES

20.1 Explain how the three major problem areas in finance—valuation, cost of capital, and determining cash flows—are related.

20.2 Calculate the weighted average cost of capital (WACC) and explain its significance.

20.3 Estimate the cost of capital and its non-equity components.

20.4 Explain how operating leverage and financial leverage affect a firm's risk.

20.5 Apply the discounted cash flow model to estimate the equity cost and describe this model's advantages and disadvantages.

20.6 Estimate the cost of equity using risk-based models and describe the advantages and limitations of these models.

20.7 Explain how WACC interacts with the investment decision framework introduced in chapters 13 to 17.

"We earn a premium on our cost of capital" is one of the four pillars of our strategy. To create value and survive in the long term, a company's earnings must exceed the costs of stockholders' equity and debt capital. To secure BASF's sustainable success, we encourage all employees to think and act entrepreneurially within the framework of our value-based management concept. Our goal: to create awareness about how every employee can find value-oriented solutions and implement these in an efficient and effective manner in day-to-day business.

Source: BASF. "We earn a premium on our cost of capital." BASF website, January 17, 2013. Available at www.basf.com/group/corporate/en/investor-relations/strategy/cost-of-capital/index.

CHAPTER 20 **PREVIEW**

In chapters 17 to 19, we discussed securities legislation; the differences between debt, equity, and hybrid securities; and how securities are issued. We finished by describing a risk hierarchy that essentially corresponds to a particular security's resemblance to debt or equity. As we move from types of security that are 100 percent debt, such as commercial paper, to those that are 100 percent equity, they become riskier. This risk hierarchy corresponds to a cost hierarchy for a firm because investors require compensation for additional risk, which translates into higher costs for the firm. In this chapter, we discuss how firms synthesize this information as they determine their overall cost of funds, called "the cost of capital."

The cost of capital is the most basic piece of information a firm needs, since it determines how the firm is valued and is often the appropriate "hurdle rate" to be used for making corporate investment decisions.[1] In this chapter, you will learn what the cost of capital means, how to calculate it, and how to avoid some basic yet common mistakes in corporate financing. During the process, we will discuss some of the problems that result when using the discounted cash flow models described in Chapter 7 (for valuing equities) and the capital asset pricing model (CAPM) described in Chapter 9. These two models are the "workhorses" of corporate finance for estimating the cost of capital.

After you master the material on the cost of capital, you will learn, in Chapter 21, how firms determine their financing decisions.

20.1 FINANCING SOURCES

Capital Structure

Learning Objective 20.1
Explain how the three major problem areas in finance—valuation, cost of capital, and determining cash flows—are related.

We begin by returning to the balance sheet to review the major accounts, as depicted in Table 20-1.

TABLE 20-1 Main Balance Sheet Accounts

Cash and marketable securities	Accruals
Accounts receivable	Accounts payable
Inventory	Short-term debt
Prepaid expenses	Current liabilities
Current assets	Long-term debt
Net fixed assets	Shareholders' equity
Total assets	Total liabilities and shareholders' equity

On the asset side, we have current (short-term) assets consisting of cash and marketable securities, accounts receivable, inventory, and, usually, some accounting items, such as prepaid expenses. When the current assets are added to the net fixed assets (i.e., gross fixed assets less accumulated depreciation), we have total assets. We call the method of financing total assets the "financial structure decision," which reflects all of the firm's liabilities, including invested capital.

For our purposes, it is useful to distinguish between debt and other types of liabilities that do not represent debt contracts in the strictest sense. In particular, many accruals are strictly accounting items required to prepare the statements according to International Financial Reporting Standards (IFRS) as well as generally accepted accounting principles (GAAP). As

---

[1] As noted in Chapter 13, the firm's cost of capital is the appropriate discount rate for evaluating projects that possess "average" risk for the company.

such, they do not represent a decision on the part of an investor or creditor to finance the firm. For example, both the authors are paid by their universities with a two-week to one-month lag, which would show up as wages payable on their universities' balance sheets. However, neither of us would consider this delay in getting paid as a financial investment in the university on our part. Instead, because the university does not pay us on a daily cash basis, the accountant accrues a liability. Similarly, as long as a firm's credit is good, accounts payable arise as the result of a telephone or computerized order, where the invoice arrives with the order. Again, in most cases the supplier is not explicitly thinking of the value of its shipment as an investment in the company.[2] It is simply the way business is done between companies. In this sense, the only current liability items that do reflect a creditor investing in the company are bank debt, other short-term debt, and the current portion of any long-term debt that is due within a year.

When it comes to long-term liabilities, the basic distinction is again between accounting items and money that has been invested in the firm. On the simple balance sheet presented in Table 20-1, all the liabilities are invested capital because we do not have any headings that are strictly accounting items. However, firms often report the value of benefits owing to workers as a liability since they customarily pay health benefits after retirement, even when they are made on a "pay-as-you-go" basis. There are also often deferred income taxes, as discussed in Chapter 3, as well as other accounting items that do not reflect invested capital. In almost all cases, these "non-debt" accounting items are ignored when it comes to estimating firm capital. Apart from explicit debt and the shareholders' equity accounts, the only other item that is included as capital is minority interest, since this reflects the amount of shareholders' equity in a subsidiary that is not owned by the shareholders of the parent firm.[3] Decisions about the **capital structure** of the firm involve questions of how this invested capital is financed, including what proportion will be financed through debt and what proportion through equity. How the firm arrives at these decisions is the focus of Chapter 21.

capital structure how a firm finances its invested capital

The simplified balance sheet in Table 20-2 gives an example of one firm's capital structure.

TABLE 20-2 A Simplified Balance Sheet

Cash and marketable securities	50	Accruals	100
Accounts receivable	200	Accounts payable	200
Inventory	250	Short-term debt	50
Prepaid expenses	0	Current liabilities	350
Current assets	500	Long-term debt	650
Net fixed assets	1,500	Shareholders' equity	1,000
Total assets	2,000	Total liabilities and shareholders' equity	2,000

The financial structure is $2,000, while the capital structure components total $1,700, consisting of $1,000 in shareholders' equity and total interest-bearing debt of $700 (i.e., $50 + $650), producing a **debt-to-equity ratio** of 0.7 (i.e., $700 ÷ $1,000). This hypothetical capital structure is typical of Canadian firms. Figure 20-1 is from the January 2012 monetary policy report of the Bank of Canada, which shows that the average debt-to-equity ratio for Canadian firms was about 1.2 in the early 1990s but has been declining since then and was at 0.9 in 2011.

debt-to-equity ratio the ratio of interest-bearing debt to shareholders' equity plus minority interest

---

[2] Note that this is not always the case. For firms in serious financial trouble, a shipment may be seen as an investment with an explicit interest charge.

[3] Minority interest arises when a firm reports consolidated financial statements. GAAP requires consolidated statements when a subsidiary is not 100 percent owned, but is controlled. (This usually means more than 50 percent ownership). As a result, all of the subsidiary's debt and assets are included on the consolidated statements, and the portion of the subsidiary's equity that is not owned is shown as minority interest.

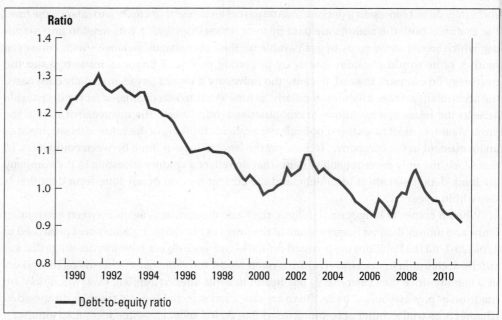

FIGURE 20-1 *Debt-to-Equity Ratio (Quarterly Data)*

Source: Bank of Canada, *Monetary Policy Report*, January 2012, Chart 28, p. 27. Data from Statistics Canada. Retrieved from www.bankofcanada.ca/wp-content/uploads/2012/01/mpr-january2012.pdf.

The numbers in Table 20-2 come from the firm's financial statements and represent historical book values. For our purposes, we can convert them to market values. We can assume that the book and market values of the firm's debt are very close; this is often the case now, since interest rates have been relatively stable in Canada for the past nine years.[4] However, suppose that the firm's equity is selling for 2.5 times its book value, so that its **market-to-book (M/B) ratio**, defined in Chapter 4, is 2.5. For the example in Table 20-2 then, the total market value of the equity would be $2,500 (i.e., $1,000 × 2.5), and the total market value of the firm would be $3,200 (i.e., $700 + $2,500). Therefore, the firm's "market valued" debt-to-equity ratio is 0.28 (i.e., $700 ÷ $2,500), which again is fairly typical of Canadian non-financial firms. The two key issues in corporate financing are to attempt to increase this market value by changing the mix of debt and equity, and to determine the minimum rate of return necessary to maintain this market value.

market-to-book (M/B) ratio the market price per share divided by the book value per share

Three Ways of Using the Valuation Equation

Before addressing these key issues, let's review the most basic implication of the simple perpetuity valuation problem, discussed in Chapter 5. Recall that the present value of a perpetuity is found by dividing the amount of the regular payment by the appropriate discount rate. For our purposes, let's assume the perpetuity is future estimated earnings, which are expected to remain at the same level indefinitely, thus experiencing no growth. We can discount these earnings using the investors' required rate of return to find the present value of those future earnings, as shown in Equation 20-1.

[20-1]
$$S = \frac{X}{K_e}$$

where X is the forecast earnings, S is the value of the perpetuity, and K is the investors' required rate of return, subscripted *e* for equity.

---

[4] Recall that long-term debt will usually be issued at coupon rates, approximately equal to prevailing market rates, so that they are sold at close to their face value. If the interest rates do not change very much, the market value of such debt will remain close to the book value.

If a firm's common shares are expected to earn and pay out $1 in perpetuity, and investors require a 10 percent rate of return, the value of this perpetuity (which in this example is the value of the firm's common equity) is simply $10—that is:

$$S = \frac{X}{K_e} = \frac{1}{0.1} = \$10$$

We often use perpetuities in finance because they are easy to value, and the results almost always hold with more complicated patterns of earnings. However, note that this is one equation, and we can easily rearrange it to solve for any of the three values. We just happened to have focused on the valuation problem, which tells us what the perpetuity is worth. When we valued securities in chapters 5 to 7, we focused on estimating the values of different securities, such as common shares and bonds. In order to do this, we took the investors' required rate of return as given.

However, if we rearrange Equation 20-1 to solve for K_e we get Equation 20-2.

$$K_e = \frac{X}{S} \qquad\qquad [20\text{-}2]$$

Given a $10 market price and forecast perpetual earnings of $1 per year, we can estimate the investors' required rate of return as:

$$K_e = \frac{X}{S} = \frac{1}{10} = 10\%$$

This estimate of the investors' required rate of return or the cost of equity capital to the firm, is called the **earnings yield** because it is the forecast earnings divided by the market price, similar to the dividend yield.[5] In practice, the earnings yield is rarely used as an estimate of K_e; most firms have some expectation for growth, so the stock price reflects these growth opportunities as well as the current earnings. However, the earnings yield was commonly used in the 1950s when inflation and growth expectations were minimal. On the other hand, the basic approach of estimating the discount rate that sets the forecast stream of earnings or cash equal to the current price is used for all discounted cash flow (DCF) methods of estimating the cost of equity capital. We will discuss DCF estimation techniques in more detail later in the chapter. For now, recognize that this way of rearranging the valuation equation addresses the need to estimate what return investors require. In this example, we estimate that investors require a 10 percent return for holding this perpetuity.

earnings yield the estimate of the investors' required rate of return, which is also the cost of equity capital to the firm

Finally, we can rearrange the same equation and solve for the forecast earnings, as shown in Equation 20-3.

$$X = K_e \times S \qquad\qquad [20\text{-}3]$$

If the security is worth $10, and the investor requires a 10 percent rate of return, the firm must generate forecast earnings of $1, as shown below:

$$X = K_e \times S = 0.1 \times 10 = \$1$$

This explicitly tells the firm's managers what their earnings targets must be to support the current valuation. That information is crucial for regulated industries, like utilities, which can only earn a set amount of profit. The regulator determines what prices utility companies can charge to realize this return, and in setting these prices, regulators use this last version of the valuation equation. In other words, Equation 20-3 is used to regulate utilities as well as in basic corporate finance applications. (Note that the concepts and processes described in this chapter have been used to set your telephone, water, gas, and electric bills.)

---

[5] Notice that it is also the reciprocal of the firm's forward price-earnings (P/E) ratio, which was discussed at length in chapters 4 and 7.

The same equation can therefore be used in three different ways. To illustrate the concept of the cost of capital, we will use this third approach. For the time being, let's assume that our example firm's earnings are perpetual, the required rates of return are known, the yield on the firm's debt is 6 percent, and equity holders require a rate of return of 12 percent. We already know that the debt is worth $700 and the equity is worth $2,500, so with these data we can estimate the following:

$$\text{Interest for the bond holders} = K_d \times D = 0.06 \times \$700 = \$42$$

$$\text{Return to the shareholders} = K_e \times S = 0.12 \times \$2,500 = \$300$$

What this tells us is that with a $700 market value for the debt (D) and a 6 percent yield or required return on debt (K_d), the firm has to earn $42 to pay the bondholders. Similarly with the firm's common shares worth $2,500 ($S$), and the shareholders requiring a 12 percent return (K_e), the firm has to earn $300 to meet these expectations. So in total, with this mix of debt and equity and a $3,200 current market value, the firm has to earn $342.

Deriving the *Required* Income Statement

Once we have this information, we can work up the firm's income statement. Suppose, for example, that the firm has a 25 percent corporate income tax rate, and its operating costs are $558, composed of $300 of variable costs and $258 of fixed costs. The forecast income statement in this case is presented in Table 20-3.

TABLE 20-3 A Forecasted Income Statement

Sales	$1,000
Variable costs	300
Fixed costs	258
EBIT	442
Interest	42
Tax (25%)	100
Net Income	300

If the firm has 1,000 shares outstanding, its earnings per share (EPS) are $0.30 (i.e., $300 ÷ 1,000).

Note that rather than starting with sales and working down the income statement, we have done the opposite. This is exactly what regulators do in setting prices. They first start with a fair return to the common shareholders and then add in these other forecast costs to establish the firm's revenue or sales requirement, from which they set individual prices. This approach is common in all "rate of return regulated" industries, with the exception that they use book values for invested capital instead of market values.[6] Since regulated industries are capital intensive, and individual firms tend to have relatively high amounts of debt, these financial costs are an important part of their cost structure.

We now have a lot of information about the firm. Given its total market value and investor return requirements, the firm has to have sales of $1,000. We also note that the firm's total assets are $2,000, so its **asset turnover ratio**, defined in Chapter 4 as sales divided by total assets, has to be 0.5 (i.e., $1,000 ÷ $2,000), and its **return on assets (ROA)**, defined in Chapter 4 as net income divided by total assets, is 15 percent (i.e., $300 ÷ $2,000). The book value of its invested capital is $1,700, and its EBIT is $442, so its **return on invested capital (ROIC)**, defined as EBIT divided by the book value of invested capital (IC), is 26 percent. ROIC, often referred to simply as ROI, can also be expressed on an after-tax basis by multiplying the ROI by

asset turnover ratio sales divided by total assets

return on assets (ROA) net income divided by total assets

return on invested capital (ROIC) earnings before interest and taxes divided by the book value of invested capital

---

[6] Regulators use book values based on the rationale that investors require a fair return on the money they have invested in the utility.

$(1 - T)$, which in our case is 0.75, producing an after-tax ROI of 19.5 percent. The firm's **return on equity (ROE)**, defined as net income divided by the book value of equity, is $300 divided by $1,000, or 30 percent, which is very high.

return on equity (ROE) net income divided by the book value of equity

The very high ROE explains the firm's M/B ratio. Remember that the earnings per share equals the ROE times the book value per share (BVPS), as shown below:

$$EPS = \frac{NI}{Number\ of\ shares} = \frac{NI}{Equity} \times \frac{Equity}{Number\ of\ shares} = ROE \times BVPS$$

For our example, the BVPS is $1 ($1,000 shareholders' equity divided by 1,000 shares), and the EPS equals this $1 times the 30 percent ROE, or $0.30.

Since we are dealing with a perpetuity, the price per share can be expressed as shown in Equation 20-4.

$$P = \frac{EPS}{K_e} = \frac{ROE \times BVPS}{K_e} \qquad [20\text{-}4]$$

Using the numbers given, the share price is just the $0.30 EPS discounted in perpetuity at 12 percent, the investors' required rate of return or cost of equity capital.

$$P = \frac{EPS}{K_e} = \frac{ROE \times BVPS}{K_e} = \frac{0.30 \times \$1}{0.12} = \$2.50$$

If we divide both sides of Equation 20-4 by the BVPS, we get the basic relationship that drives the M/B ratio:

$$\frac{P}{BVPS} = \frac{ROE}{K_e} \qquad [20\text{-}5]$$

For the numbers in this example, we get

$$\frac{P}{BVPS} = \frac{ROE}{K_e} = \frac{0.30}{0.12} = 2.50$$

Equation 20-5 simply says that if what the firm earns (ROE) exceeds what investors require (K_e), then the price goes above the book value of the investment. This is a basic relationship in finance: if you exceed investor expectations, prices go up!

Remember that in Chapter 6 we discussed the pricing of bonds and how, when interest rates increase, the price of bonds goes down, and vice versa. Further, we indicated that if the current interest rate exceeds the coupon rate on a bond, that bond sells at a discount from par value. However, if the interest rate is less than the coupon rate, the bond sells at a premium. The current interest rate is analogous to the investors' required return for investing in bonds. As a result, saying that bonds sell at a discount (or a premium) when required returns exceed (or are less than) the coupon rate is another way of saying their M/B ratio is less than (or greater than) 1.0. Similarly, in our example, the equity M/B ratio exceeds 1.0 because the ROE of 30 percent significantly exceeds the investors' required rate of return on equity of 12 percent.

Now that we have drawn the link between book values and market values, we will discuss the concept of the cost of capital.

CONCEPT REVIEW QUESTIONS

1. Why is the earnings yield not usually an adequate measure of the investors' required return on equity?

2. How are the ROE and K_e related to a firm's growth opportunities and its M/B ratio?

20.2 THE COST OF CAPITAL

Determining the Weighted Average Cost of Capital (WACC)

Learning Objective 20.2
Calculate the weighted average cost of capital (WACC) and explain its significance.

So far we have considered only the equity market value, but now let's look at the overall market value of the firm—that is, the value of the debt plus the value of the equity $(D + S)$, which for our example is $3,200. We also know that the firm's after-tax ROI on its $1,700 book value is 19.5 percent, based on EBIT$(1 – T)$ of $331.50 or $442(1 – 0.25)$. This is an important number because EBIT$(1 – T)$ indicates the net income of the firm if it is financed 100 percent with equity—that is, if there is no deduction for interest payments on the firm's debt. It is also equal to a firm's net operating income if there are no items such as income from investments or capital gains and losses.

We now have two of the three numbers needed in a valuation equation. We know the overall firm value is $3,200 and the EBIT$(1 – T)$ is $331.50, so we can find the discount rate that sets them equal. First we rewrite EBIT minus taxes as ROI × IC and re-express the valuation equation, as shown in Equation 20-6.

[20-6]
$$V = \frac{ROI \times IC}{K_a}$$

Here we are still using the perpetuity equation, but have simply replaced S (the value of the firm's equity) with V, which stands for the total value of the firm, and have denoted the required return as K_a, indicating it is the average, or overall, required rate of return. For the numbers in this example, ROI × IC = $0.195 \times \$1,700 = \$331.50$, so we get

$$V = \frac{ROI \times IC}{K_a} = \frac{331.5}{K_a} = \$3,200$$

Just as we did with the earnings yield previously, we can rearrange to find the overall required rate of return, which is given below:

[20-7]
$$K_a = \frac{ROI \times IC}{V}$$

For the numbers in this example, we get

$$K_a = \frac{ROI \times IC}{V} = \frac{331.5}{3,200} = 10.36\%$$

So if we discount the EBIT minus taxes figure using this average required rate of return, we get the overall market value of the firm.

This is obviously a very important number. To understand where it comes from, remember that the total amount needed for the equity holders is $300, or $K_e \times S$, whereas the total amount needed for the bondholders is $42, or $K_d \times D$. This exceeds the amount the firm has to earn ($331.50) by $10.50. This $10.50 is the reduction in the firm's corporate income taxes due to the fact that interest is tax deductible. The exact amount needed to pay the bondholders is $K_d(1 – T) \times D$ or $0.06 \times 0.75 \times 700 = \$31.50$. It is this $31.50 that gives us the EBIT minus taxes of $331.50 when we add it to the required earnings for the equity holders. If we substitute these definitions into the equation for the average required return, we get Equation 20-8.

[20-8]
$$K_a = \frac{ROI \times IC}{V} = \frac{K_e S + K_d(1-T)D}{V} = K_e \frac{S}{V} + K_d(1-T)\frac{D}{V}$$

weighted average cost of capital (WACC) or **cost of capital** an estimate of a firm's average cost for $1 of financing

In this equation, the average required rate of return is a **weighted average cost of capital (WACC)**, commonly referred to as the **cost of capital**. In this context, the cost of capital reflects the average rate of return required by all the investors who have contributed invested capital to the firm.

Estimating the cost of capital is a way of calculating the overall required rate of return needed to meet investor expectations. There are three steps involved in estimating the WACC:

1. Estimate market values for the firm's sources of capital.

2. Estimate the current required rates of return for these various sources of capital invested in the firm.

3. Weight the costs of all sources of capital on the same corporate tax basis, recognizing that interest on debt is tax deductible, whereas the return to the equity holders is not.

For our example firm, we have a market-valued debt ratio of 21.875 percent ($700 ÷ $3,200) and a market-valued equity ratio of 78.125 percent (i.e., $2,500 ÷ S3,200). We assumed a required return on equity of 12 percent and on debt of 6 percent. Finally, the interest cost is tax deductible, so on an after-tax basis, with a corporate income tax rate of 25 percent, it is 4.5 percent (or 6% × [1 − 0.25]). Putting this all together we get

$$K_a = K_e \frac{S}{V} + K_d(1-T)\frac{D}{V} = 0.12 \times 0.78125 + 0.06 \times (1 - 0.25) \times 0.21875 = 0.1036 = 10.36\%$$

The key result is that the cost of capital is just a *weighted average* of the after-tax costs of the different sources of capital, where the weights are the proportion of each in the total market value of the firm.

Before we proceed, we should note that Equation 20-8 is incomplete when a firm uses preferred share financing. In this case, we also replace the term $K_d(1 - T)$ with K_i to denote the after-tax cost of debt, as shown in Equation 20-9.

$$WACC = K_e\frac{S}{V} + K_p\frac{P}{V} + K_i\frac{D}{V} \qquad [20\text{-}9]$$

P is the market value of the firm's preferred shares, K_p is the cost of preferred shares, and the value of the firm, V, now equals $S + P + D$. Notice that we do not need to adjust K_p for taxes, since preferred shares pay dividends out of after-tax income, just like common shares.

Estimating Market Values

Estimating the market value of a firm's common equity (S) is straightforward whenever a firm has shares that are traded publicly. We simply multiply the firm's market price per common share (P_o) by the number of shares outstanding (n), as shown in Equation 20-10.[7]

$$S = P_o \times n \qquad [20\text{-}10]$$

Estimating the market value of a firm's preferred shares is also straightforward if it has preferred shares outstanding that are publicly traded, in which case we can simply use Equation 20-10, replacing the common share information with the market price of the preferred shares (P_p), multiplied by the number of preferred shares outstanding. In the event that the firm's preferred shares are not actively traded, we can estimate the market value of each of its preferred shares using Equation 20-11, which was first introduced in Chapter 7 for valuing straight perpetual preferred shares.

$$P_p = \frac{D_p}{K_p} \qquad [20\text{-}11]$$

Estimating the market value of a firm's debt can be somewhat more complicated, as it also is for non-traditional preferred shares. As mentioned earlier, if interest rates have not changed

---

[7] Notice that in deriving the market value of the equity we could have also multiplied the firm's book value of common equity figure by its M/B ratio.

much since the debt was first issued by the firm, then the book value of the firm's long-term debt is close to its market value, so we can use the book value. When a firm has bonds outstanding, we can be more precise and use the following bond valuation equation, introduced in Chapter 6 to estimate the market value of bonds.

[20-12]

$$B = I \times \left[\frac{1 - \frac{1}{(1+K_b)^n}}{K_b} \right] + F \times \frac{1}{(1+K_b)^n}$$

where
B = the bond price
I = interest (or coupon) payments
K_b = the bond discount rate (or market rate)
n = the term-to-maturity
F = the face (par) value of the bond

If the firm has more than one series of bonds or other types of long-term debt issues outstanding, we can repeat this process and add up all the calculated market values to determine the total market value of the firm's outstanding debt.

EXAMPLE 20-1 Estimating Market Values

Suppose firm ABC has the following balance sheet figures:

	Book Value
Debt (D): 8% coupon rate, annual coupons 10 years to maturity	$1.0 million
Preferred shares (P): 10% dividend rate	$1.0 million
Common equity (CE):	
Common shares (C/S) – 100,000 shares (originally issued at $15/share)	$1.5 million
Retained earnings (RE)	$0.5 million
Total	$4.0 million

Assume the marginal tax rate (T) is 40 percent.

The present market conditions are the following:
  Debt: The present market rate on similar risk 10-year bonds is 6 percent.
  Preferred shares: Similar risk preferred shares are providing yields of 8 percent.
  Common equity: Common share price is currently $25.

Find the market value proportions of these components, assuming the firm wants to raise new funds in order to maintain its present capital structure based on these market value proportions.

Solution
Long-term debt (D):

$$D = \$80,000 \times \left[\frac{1 - \frac{1}{(1+0.06)^{10}}}{0.06} \right] + \$1m \times \left[\frac{1}{(1+0.06)^{10}} \right] = \$1,147,202$$

Preferred shares:

$$P = \frac{D_p}{K_p} = \frac{(\$1m)(.10)}{0.08} = \frac{\$100,000}{0.08} = \$1,250,000$$

continued

Example 20-1 illustrates how to combine these concepts.

EXAMPLE 20-1   *Estimating Market Values continued*

Common equity:

$S = P_0 \times n = (\$25)(100,000 \text{ shares}) = \$2.5\text{m}$

So, according to the "market" value of the firm's balance sheet, we obtain the solution:

$V = D + P + SE = 1,147,202 + 1,250,000 + 2,500,000 = \$4,897,202$

$$\text{and } \frac{D}{V} = 0.234, \frac{P}{V} = 0.255, \text{ and } \frac{CE}{V} = 0.511$$

CONCEPT REVIEW QUESTIONS

1. Why is the weighted average cost of capital (WACC) so important?

2. What are the steps involved in estimating a firm's WACC?

3. How can we estimate the market value of common equity, preferred equity, and long-term debt?

20.3 ESTIMATING THE NON-EQUITY COMPONENT COSTS

Flotation Costs and the Marginal Cost of Capital (MCC)

To derive the cost of capital in the previous section, we were given the cost of equity, as well as the before-tax cost of debt. In this section, we show how we can calculate the cost of debt and preferred equity if we do not have this information. In following sections, we discuss estimating the cost of common equity.

One complication that arises with respect to all sources of capital, except for internally generated funds, is that the firm incurs **issuing** or **flotation costs** when it issues new securities. These include any fees paid to the investment dealer and/or any discounts provided to investors to entice them to purchase the securities. As a result, the cost of issuing new securities will be *higher* than the return required by investors, since the net proceeds to the firm from any security issue will be lower than that security's market price.

It is especially important to be aware of this fact when we consider the cost of common equity to the firm. In particular, remember that there are two sources of common equity financing: reinvested earnings, which show up on the firm's balance sheet in the retained earnings figure, and new common share issues. When the common equity portion of financing comes entirely from reinvested earnings, the firm's cost of equity will equal the return required by its shareholders, as discussed previously. However, when the firm is forced into issuing new common shares, it must pay flotation costs for issuing these shares, so the cost to the firm is higher than the cost of using internally generated funds.

At this point, it is useful to introduce the concept of the **marginal cost of capital (MCC)**, which may be defined as the weighted average cost of the "next dollar" of financing to be raised. Sometimes the terms WACC and MCC are used interchangeably, although they are not really the same, since the WACC represents the weighted average cost of each dollar raised in total. The two tend to be the same for most levels of financing. However, they will differ when, at some financing level, the firm's cost of raising new money increases, causing the MCC to exceed the WACC. Given the discussion in the paragraph above, it's clear the most common

Learning Objective 20.3
Estimate the cost of capital and its non-equity components.

issuing or **flotation costs** costs incurred by a firm when it issues new securities

marginal cost of capital (MCC) the weighted average cost of the next dollar of financing to be raised

cause of this increase in the MCC occurs when the firm cannot supply all of its required common equity financing from reinvested earnings (i.e., internal funds). Therefore, it must issue new common shares and bear the brunt of issuing costs, in addition to providing common shareholders with their required rate of return. This causes the cost of common equity to increase, meaning the MCC increases. The reason MCC and WACC are often identical is that many firms restrict their investment outlays so that all of the common equity finance portion can be provided by internal funds. (Recall from Chapter 13 that this procedure is referred to as capital rationing.)

In short, the MCC often exceeds the WACC due to the costs of raising additional funds. Changes in securities regulation have led to a drop in these issuing costs, so for large firms, like Tim Hortons, they are relatively minor. However, for small firms these issue costs can be significant, causing the MCC to jump dramatically.

Currently, issuing costs are approximately as shown in Table 20-4.

TABLE 20-4 Average Issuing Costs

Commercial paper	0.125%
Medium-term notes	1%
Long-term debt	2%
Equity (large)	5%
Equity (small)	5% to 10%
Equity (private)	10% and up

What this means is that there is a "financing wedge" between what the investor pays and what the firm receives, the difference being the money that is lost to these issue costs.

Debt

We can determine the cost of debt to the firm by using a variation of Equation 20-12, in which we replace the bond price with the net proceeds (NP) the firm receives when it issues new bonds after paying its flotation costs. We would note here that flotation costs are tax deductible immediately. (On the other hand, when debt securities are issued at a discount from their face value, this cost will be amortized over the life of the debt.) We must make one more adjustment to Equation 20-12 to reflect the fact that the interest payments are tax deductible, whereas the principal repayment (i.e., the face value) is not. After making these substitutions, we merely solve for the firm's after-tax cost of debt (K_i) in the same manner by which we solved for the yield to maturity (YTM) in Chapter 6. This equation is given below.

[20-13]
$$NP = I \times (1-T) \times \left[\frac{1 - \frac{1}{(1+K_i)^n}}{K_i} \right] + F \times \frac{1}{(1+K_i)^n}$$

EXAMPLE 20-2   Determining the Cost of Debt

Suppose firm ABC from Example 20-1 can issue new 10-year bonds at par value. The bonds pay 6 percent annual coupons. The before-tax issuing costs are 2.5 percent of par. Estimate the firm's before- and after-tax cost of debt.

Solution

Using $100 par value, we get the following values that can be substituted into Equation 20-13:

$$NP = 100 - 100 \, (0.025) \, (1 - 0.4) = 100 - 1.50 = \$98.50$$
$$I = (0.06) \, (\$100) = \$6$$

continued

EXAMPLE 20-2 *Determining the Cost of Debt continued*

So we have:

$$98.50 = 6 \times (1 - 0.4) \left[\frac{1 - \frac{1}{(1+K_i)^{10}}}{K_i} \right] + 100 \times \frac{1}{(1+K_i)^{10}}$$

Solving for K_i using a financial calculator,[8] as shown in Chapter 6, we get the solution below.

EXAMPLE 20-2 **Solution Using a Financial Calculator**

Then **CPT** **I/Y** will give 3.78 percent.

So the firm's after-tax cost of debt is 3.78 percent. This is slightly higher than the 3.6 percent that we get from the 6 percent yield and 40 percent tax rate, since we have taken into account the fact that the firm is not receiving all of the $1,000 market value of the bonds. Instead, there is $15 of after-tax issuing costs.

Preferred Shares

The cost of preferred shares can also be determined by accounting for flotation costs. In Equation 20-11, replace P_p with NP and then solve the equation for K_p, as shown in Equation 20-14.

$$K_p = \frac{D_p}{NP} \tag{20-14}$$

EXAMPLE 20-3 **Determining the Cost of Preferred Equity**

Suppose firm ABC from Example 20-1 can issue new preferred shares at par value of $100, which pay annual dividends at an 8 percent rate. The net after-tax flotation costs are 2 percent of par. Estimate the firm's after-tax cost of preferred equity.

Solution
Based on their $100 par value, we get the following values, which can be substituted into Equation 20-14:

$$NP = \$100 \, (1 - 0.02) = \$98.00; \; D_p = (0.08) \, (\$100) = \$8$$

So we have:

$$K_p = \frac{D_p}{NP} = \frac{\$8}{\$98} = 8.16\%$$

Now that we have discussed how to estimate the cost of debt and preferred equity, let's see how we can apply them to Tim Hortons. First, Tim Hortons does not have any preferred equity, so it is simply a question of estimating its debt costs. Note 14 to Tim Hortons' annual report discusses its financing. As of January 1, 2012, Tim Hortons had no public debt outstanding. Instead, of its $354.2 million debt, $52.3 million was for a capital lease for some restaurants owned by Tim Hortons, and $301.9 million was for a private placement of notes with a remaining term to maturity of 5½ years—that is, they mature on June 1, 2017. Tim Hortons also has a revolving line of credit with a syndicate of seven Canadian and U.S. banks for $250 million, but as of January 1, 2012, it had a zero balance.

The features of the private placement of Tim Hortons' senior notes loans were quite "clean," without extensive covenant restrictions, similar to those described in Chapter 18. The notes ranked equally, that is "pari passu," with other notes issued under the trust indenture and with the bank line of credit and were rated A(Low) by Dominion Bond Rating Service.

---

[8] Students who have not yet mastered the financial calculator can solve using the trial-and-error method illustrated in Chapter 6.

There are no extensive restrictions on the notes because they involve a call option—that is, if there is a change in control and the notes are downgraded below investment grade, Tim Hortons has to repurchase them at 101 percent of their par value plus accrued interest to the redemption date. This protects the note holders from possible losses if Tim Hortons is taken over by another party.

To some extent, Tim Hortons' notes "piggyback" on top of the restrictions in the bank line of credit, since they rank equally. This revolver bears a floating interest rate at either the yield on LIBOR for U.S. dollars or the yield on bankers acceptance for Canadian dollars, plus a spread of about 1 percent. The company had to maintain certain covenants; the most important ones relate to a minimum fixed charge coverage ratio and a maximum debt coverage ratio similar to those discussed in Chapter 4.

While Tim Hortons reported an effective interest cost of 6 percent on its debt financing as of January 1, 2012, interest rates had fallen considerably since its notes were issued. As a result, Tim Hortons reported the fair market value of its debt at $427.4 million or a premium of $73.2 million over the values reported in its financial statements. At the end of 2012, the yield on three- to five-year Canada bonds was 1.18 percent, and the spread of an A issuer over the Government of Canada was about 1.2 percent, so Tim Hortons' debt had a market yield of about 2.38 percent. Corporate tax rates in Canada have been falling over the five years since 2006, and Tim Hortons reported that its statutory tax rate, reflecting both the United States and Canada, was 36.8 percent in 2009 but had dropped to 29 percent during 2011. If scheduled tax cuts are implemented, it will fall further in 2012. However, we will use the 2011 tax rate of 29 percent, so the after-tax cost of Tim Hortons' debt at year-end 2011 is 2.38 percent $\times (1 - 0.29)$ or 1.69 percent.

Estimating the cost of common equity is more complicated, and we elaborate on various approaches in the following sections.

CONCEPT REVIEW QUESTIONS

1. How do flotation costs affect the cost of capital sources for a firm?
2. Explain how to estimate the cost of debt and preferred equity for a firm.

20.4 THE EFFECTS OF OPERATING AND FINANCIAL LEVERAGE

Sales Changes and Leverage

Learning Objective 20.4
Explain how operating leverage and financial leverage affect a firm's risk.

Before we formally consider how to estimate a firm's cost of common equity, we return to the firm from Table 20-3, which had to generate sales of $1,000 to cover its operating and financing costs. Suppose that the firm issued a report stating that sales potential had increased and it now expected to sell 20 percent more widgets; as a result, sales revenues were expected to be $1,200, all else remaining constant (Table 20-5).

TABLE 20-5 Forecasted Income Statement after a 20% Sales Increase

Sales	$1,200
Variable costs	360
Fixed costs	258
EBIT	582
Interest	42
Tax (25%)	135
Net income	405

In this example, the firm's variable costs increase by the same 20 percent that sales increase, rising to $360, but EBIT increases by 31.7 percent, to $582. This is because some of the firm's operating costs are fixed and do not increase with sales, a circumstance referred to as **operating leverage**. In addition to the fixed operating costs, the firm's interest costs of $42 are also fixed. As a result, the firm's net income increases by 35 percent, from $300 to $405. If this $405 is viewed as a perpetuity, as before, and is discounted back at the 12 percent cost of equity, the market value of the equity also increases by 35 percent, to $3,375 from $2,500.

operating leverage the increased volatility in operating income caused by fixed operating costs

We might also ask what happens to the market value of the firm's debt. One way to determine this is to go back and look at the times interest earned (TIE) or coverage ratio, which was defined in Chapter 4 as EBIT divided by interest expense. At sales of $1,000, if we divided the EBIT of $442 by the interest expense of $42, the TIE ratio was 10.52, which is very high. This means that there was $10.52 of EBIT available for every dollar of interest payments, so the firm's EBIT could drop precipitously and still be able to cover the interest payments. At the new sales and EBIT levels, the coverage ratio increases to 13.86 (i.e., $582 ÷ $42), which means the debt is even safer.

This might mean that the debt is marginally less risky, but as we discussed earlier, debt is normally issued under a trust indenture that indicates how much the firm can issue. For example, under the FortisBC indenture discussed in Chapter 18, FortisBC could issue as much debt as it wanted, provided it satisfied a specified interest coverage ratio test. As a result, with a higher coverage ratio, the bondholders would expect the firm to issue more debt so that the required return on the debt would stay the same and all the increased value would "drop through" to the common shareholders.[9] So with a constant market value for the example firm's debt, the overall firm value increases from $3,200 to $4,075.

Now let's consider what happens if sales drop by 20 percent, to $800. Table 20-6 illustrates how the income statement would appear in this case.

TABLE 20-6 Forecasted Income Statement after a 20% Sales Decrease

Sales	$800
Variable costs	240
Fixed costs	258
EBIT	302
Interest	42
Tax (25%)	65
Net income	195

Now the effect of fixed operating and financial costs works in reverse. With fixed operating costs of $258, the firm's EBIT drops by 31.7 percent, to $302; with fixed interest costs, the net income drops by 35 percent, to $195. If this net income is expected to continue in perpetuity, then discounting it at 12 percent gives an equity market value of $1,625, which is also a drop of 35 percent.

With the lower sales level, the TIE ratio drops from 10.52 to 7.19. This is still very high, so the sales drop would not unduly concern the firm's bondholders, and the market value of the debt might stay the same. The result is that the overall firm value drops from $3,200 to $2,325 and is again fully borne by the shareholders.

This example illustrates the basic proposition that risk "drops down" through the income statement. The first claim on the firm's sales is the variable costs. Remember from microeconomics that the firm will not produce anything unless it covers its variable costs; otherwise, it is increasing its losses as it produces more. The next claim is the fixed operating costs, such

---

[9] Note that some of the increased value drops through to the government, because with a proportional corporate income tax, the government is a compulsory shareholder in all private-sector activity.

as space rentals or leases on cars and equipment. These costs are not tied to the level of sales and are incurred regardless of the level of sales. Once the EBIT is determined, the first financial claim is that of the debt holders, since it is a fixed contractual commitment. The last and residual claim is that of the equity holders. When times are good and sales increase, net income increases proportionately more than sales, depending on the size of the firm's fixed operational and financial commitments. This sensitivity was referred to in Chapter 4 as the degree of total leverage (DTL), which was defined as the contribution margin divided by the earnings before tax. In our example, the contribution margin at a sales level of $1,000 is $700 (sales minus variable costs), so the degree of total leverage is this divided by the earnings before tax of $400, which gives us 1.75. This indicates that for every 1 percent variation in sales, net income varied by 1.75 percent (i.e., a 20 percent change in sales produces a 35 percent change in net income).

The example also indicates the residual nature of the common shareholders and the fact that they are last in line. As the firm's sales drop, everyone has a higher priority claim than the common shareholders do, so they see much greater volatility in their return than either the debt holders or others with a stake in the firm's operations. It also explains why the stock market is so sensitive to sales and earnings announcements, given the great difficulty in forecasting future profit levels.

CONCEPT REVIEW QUESTIONS

1. Distinguish between operating and financial leverage.
2. Why do we say that equity holders bear the brunt of the effects of leverage?

20.5 GROWTH MODELS AND THE COST OF COMMON EQUITY

The Importance of Adjusting for Growth

Learning Objective 20.5
Apply the discounted cash flow model to estimate the equity cost and describe this model's advantages and disadvantages.

When we talk of adjusting for growth, we are referring to forecasting a firm's future earnings and dividends. One way to assess a firm's growth prospects is to look at the stock market's time horizon, estimate the value of the firm's current dividend when viewed as a perpetuity, and then compare this value with the stock price. If the values are significantly different, it means that the stock market is valuing something other than the firm's current earnings and dividends. Table 20-7 breaks down the stock price for a number of stocks into this no-growth perpetuity value and the remaining percentage of the stock price, which is attributed to future growth opportunities.

TABLE 20-7 Stock Prices and Growth Prospects

Company	Price ($)	DPS ($)	Dividend Yield (%)	Perpetuity ($)	Growth Value (%)
			Stock Market Time Horizon		
AGF	25.75	0.283	1.1	5.66	78
BC Gas	30.60	1.13	3.7	22.60	26
CAE	11.50	0.161	1.4	3.22	72
Dennings	3.50	0.102	2.9	2.04	42
EL Financial	285	0.570	0.2	11.40	96
GSW(A)	26.75	0.428	1.6	8.56	68

continued

TABLE 20-7 Stock Prices and Growth Prospects *(Continued)*

Company	Price ($)	DPS ($)	Dividend Yield (%)	Perpetuity ($)	Growth Value (%)
Hammersen	14.05	0.197	1.4	3.94	72
Intrawest	6.95	0.292	4.2	5.84	16
Jannock	29.60	0.148	0.5	2.96	90
Average			1.89		62.22

Source: Booth, Laurence. Table 1 from "What Drives Shareholder Value." *Financial Intelligence* IV-6, Spring 1999.

The firms in Table 20-7 were chosen randomly as the first firm in each alphabetical group that paid a dividend, according to the stock market pages of the *Financial Post*. The first column gives the share price, the second the dividend per share (DPS), and the third the dividend yield. The fourth column gives the perpetuity value of the dividend using the yield on conventional preferred shares (which was 5 percent at the time) to value each firm's dividend. This is the value of the shares if nothing changes and the firm pays this dividend forever. The final column gives the proportion of the share price not explained by the dividend, which by definition is the value attributed to the firm's growth prospects. Overall, an average of 62.22 percent of the market value of this sample of firms could be attributed to growth opportunities, with the remaining 37.78 percent attributed to the present value of the current dividend. However, there is huge variation, from a low of only 16 percent attributed to growth for Intrawest to a high for EL Financial, with 96 percent of the share price attributed to growth. The important point of the data in the table is that the simple perpetuity model only works for firms with no growth prospects, and the data show that this is a valid assumption for only a limited number of firms, if any.[10]

In Chapter 7, we discussed how to value common shares when the earnings were not expected to be constant in perpetuity. The general principle was that the value of a common share was equal to the present value of its dividends. In order to make this equation practical, we had to impose some assumptions; otherwise, we would be forced to discount dividends to infinity, since common shares have no maturity date. One of the most important models we discussed in that chapter was the constant growth version of the dividend discount model (DDM), as expressed in Equation 7-7, which determines the present value of a growing perpetuity. We discuss this model in the next subsection.

The Constant Growth Model

The constant growth DDM is commonly referred to as the Gordon model after the late Professor Myron Gordon of the University of Toronto. The basic valuation equation was introduced in Chapter 7 and is reproduced below as Equation 20-15.

$$P_0 = \frac{D_1}{K_e - g} \qquad [20\text{-}15]$$

where the price of a share (P_0) equals the expected dividend (D_1) divided by the required return by common share investors (K_e), minus the forecast long-run growth rate (g) in dividends and earnings.

As discussed in Chapter 7, we can rearrange this equation to estimate the common equity investors' discount rate or required rate of return. This process is called the discounted cash flow (DCF) method for estimating the investors' required rate of return. Equation 20-16 is used for the DCF method.

---

[10] Note that the data also show why the stock market reacts so quickly to news about a firm's future prospects. With so much of the value of most firms' share price coming from future growth, small changes in these future prospects have a huge impact on the share price. The data also indicate how "far-sighted" the stock market is.

[20-16]
$$K_e = \frac{D_1}{P_0} + g$$

In this equation, the required rate of return is composed of the expected dividend yield ($D_1 \div P_0$) plus the expected long-run growth rate (g). The long-run growth rate is then the estimate of the increase in the share price and the investors' capital gain. As discussed previously, this is the appropriate cost of equity capital for the firm when the firm can raise the required funds internally (i.e., when it uses reinvested profits). Example 20-4 illustrates how to use this equation.

EXAMPLE 20-4   **Determining the Cost of Common Equity—Internal Funds**

Let's revisit firm ABC from Examples 20-1 through 20-3, and assume the firm paid a dividend per share last year of $1, which is expected to grow at 5 percent per year indefinitely. Recall that its share price is $25. Estimate the cost of common equity using internal funds.

Solution
First, we need to find D_1:

$$D_1 = D_0 (1 + g) = \$1 (1.05) = \$1.05$$

Now we can use Equation 20-16 to estimate K_e:

$$K_e = \frac{D_1}{P_0} + g = \frac{1.05}{25} + 0.05 = 0.042 + 0.05 = 0.0920 = 9.20\%$$

Example 20-4 shows how we can estimate the cost of common equity for a firm if it does not need to issue new common equity, since it is simply the return required by common equity investors. However, what if a company needs to raise new common equity financing through a share issue? In this case, we need to account for the share issuance costs, as discussed previously. Equation 20-17 shows that the necessary adjustment to Equation 20-16 is straightforward. We simply replace the share price (P_0) with the net proceeds (NP) received by the firm. This accounts for the fact that the firm does not receive the full share price that investors are willing to pay, since a portion of these funds goes to pay for issuing costs. We provide Equation 20-17 below, denoting the cost of issuing new common equity as K_{ne}.

[20-17]
$$K_{ne} = \frac{D_1}{NP} + g$$

EXAMPLE 20-5   **Determining the Cost of Common Equity—New Issues**

We revisit firm ABC from Example 20-4 and assume the firm can issue new shares with net after-tax flotation costs of 5 percent of the share price. Estimate the cost of new common equity to the firm.

Solution
First, we need to find NP:

$$NP = P_0 (1 - 0.05) = \$25 (0.95) = \$23.75$$

Now we can use Equation 20-17 to estimate K_{ne}:

$$K_{ne} = \frac{D_1}{NP} + g = \frac{1.05}{23.75} + 0.05 = 0.0442 + 0.05 = 0.0942 = 9.42\%$$

We can see that the firm's cost of equity is 0.22 percent higher for new share issues than when it uses internal funds.

Before we proceed further, it is important to note that equations 20-15 and 20-16 are the same; therefore, if Equation 20-15 does not hold, then neither does Equation 20-16 nor Equation 20-17. We mention this because Equations 20-16 and 20-17 are commonly used to estimate the cost of equity capital, but the assumptions used to derive them are often forgotten. As a result, it is easy to misuse them.

Consider the case of a firm that pays no dividends and is growing at 20 percent per year, a growth rate that is expected to continue for the foreseeable future. A simple application of Equation 20-16 would suggest the cost of equity capital (internal funds) is 20 percent. Yet if we go back to Equation 20-15 and plug in 20 percent as a growth rate for a firm paying no dividends, we get results that make no sense. The reason for this is that 20 percent *cannot* be a long-run growth rate; in deriving Equation 20-15, we assume that the growth rate is constant forever and that the dividends start from a positive amount. If nominal GDP is growing at 5 to 6 percent a year, a firm that is growing at 20 percent will be capturing an ever bigger share of GDP. In fact, it is easy to show that such a firm would eventually be bigger than the whole economy. In this case, the assumption of constant growth used to derive Equation 20-15 is implausible, so using Equation 20-16 or 20-17 to estimate the cost of equity capital is *wrong*.

Unfortunately, people often try to squeeze the data used in equations 20-16 and 20-17 in an attempt to make them work; for example, they assume a small dividend and then reduce the short-run growth forecast to bring it more in line with what is possible in the long run. However, you cannot torture a model that doesn't fit the assumptions of a particular firm. Instead, you need to use a model that better fits the firm, such as the multi-stage growth models that were discussed in Chapter 7. Before discussing how to use these models, let's explore the constant growth model a bit more.

Growth and ROE

In Chapter 7, we pointed out that one way to estimate growth was the sustainable growth method, in which the growth rate is the product of the firm's retention rate (b), defined as one minus the firm's payout ratio, multiplied by its forecast ROE, as shown in Equation 20-18.

$$g = b \times ROE \tag{20-18}$$

This equation makes it obvious that even if the firm retains all of its profits and reinvests them in the firm, it is not plausible that it could earn a 20 percent ROE on this investment forever. Such an assumption would imply that no other firm can enter the industry and compete with the firm for these high ROEs. If other firms can enter the market, which will normally be the case, these high ROEs will be reduced to normal levels due to competitive pressures.

We have to remember that Professor Myron Gordon developed the constant growth model for use in public utility regulation, where the allowed ROEs should be reasonable and where the problem of rapid growth rates does not exist. Further, a result of regulation is that all common equity earns virtually the same regulated ROE. In this case, the average and marginal ROE are exactly the same, and every dollar the firm retains earns the same ROE. In contrast, many extremely profitable firms cannot reinvest at the same ROE because they cannot find opportunities as good as their existing ones. In determining the growth rate, the ROE is the return on incremental investment, which may be greater or smaller than what the firm is currently earning.

However, for the time being let's return to the constant growth DDM with the assumption of a constant ROE. Substituting the sustainable growth rate, as expressed in Equation 20-18 (i.e., $b \times ROE$), into the constant growth DDM in place of g, we get Equation 20-19.

$$P_0 = \frac{D_1}{K_e - b \times ROE} \tag{20-19}$$

Further, we then recognize that the expected dividend per share (D_1) is the expected earnings per share (X_1) times the dividend payout rate (i.e., one minus the retention rate), since a dollar can either be paid out or retained and reinvested in the firm. Making this substitution for D_1, we get Equation 20-20.

[20-20]
$$P_0 = \frac{X_1(1-b)}{K_e - b \times ROE}$$

This equation shows that the price per share is determined by the firm's forecast earnings per share (X_1), its dividend payout $(1 - b)$, its ROE, and the return required by common equity shareholders (K_e).

One important use of Equation 20-20 is to see how growth and the firm's ROE affect its share price. Suppose, for example, that the firm's retention rate is 50 percent, its cost of equity capital is 12 percent, and its forecast earnings per share figure is $2. If the firm's ROE is 12 percent, then the forecast growth rate is 6 percent (i.e., 12% × 0.5), and the forecast dividend per share is $1, using the 50 percent payout ratio. In this case, the shares are worth $16.67—that is, $1 divided by 6 percent (i.e., $K_e - g = 12\% - 6\%$). Now suppose instead of a 12 percent ROE, the firm is expected to earn 10 percent or 14 percent. At a 10 percent ROE, the firm's forecast growth rate drops to 5 percent and its share price is only $14.29, whereas at a 14 percent ROE, the firm's growth rate is 7 percent and its shares are worth $20.

What this example illustrates is that the higher the growth rate, the higher the share price, since investors will forecast larger future dividends and earnings. If we rearrange Equation 20-20, we get the following variation of the constant growth DDM:

[20-21]
$$K_e = \frac{D_1}{P_0} + g = \frac{X_1(1-b)}{P_0} + b \times ROE$$

In this equation, the first term is the forecast dividend yield, and the second is the sustainable growth rate. However, note what happens when we use this equation to estimate the cost of equity capital (internal) for our three growth scenarios, as depicted in Table 20-8.

TABLE 20-8 Growth and K_e

ROE	P_0	Expected Dividend Yield	Sustainable Growth Rate	K_e
10%	14.29	7%	5%	12%
12%	16.67	6%	6%	12%
14%	20.00	5%	7%	12%

Since the shares were valued using a constant 12 percent discount rate, when we "reverse engineer" from the share price, we get the same 12 percent back as the estimate of the cost of equity capital. In this case, the higher forecast growth rate leads to a higher market price and a lower dividend yield. Generally, firms with high dividend yields have lower forecast growth rates and vice versa. The only exception to this general rule is when a firm is under a lot of stress and is about to cut its dividend. However, there is no reason for the cost of equity capital to be the same, since the composition of the return between dividends and growth changes. This is a question of the firm's dividend policy, which will be discussed in detail in Chapter 22.

However, note that the firm's retention rate, and thus its dividend payout ratio, is reflected in the constant growth DDM as "b." Table 20-9 gives the share price if this retention rate changes under the three scenarios in which the firm's ROE is 10, 12, or 14 percent.

TABLE 20-9 Retention Rates, ROE, and Share Prices

b	ROE		
	0.14	0.12	0.10
0.40	18.75	16.67	15.00
0.41	18.85	16.67	14.94
0.42	18.95	16.67	14.87
0.43	19.06	16.67	14.81
0.44	19.18	16.67	14.74
0.45	19.30	16.67	14.67
0.46	19.42	16.67	14.59
0.47	19.56	16.67	14.52
0.48	19.70	16.67	14.44
0.49	19.84	16.67	14.37
0.50	20.00	16.67	14.29
0.51	20.16	16.67	14.20
0.52	20.34	16.67	14.12
0.53	20.52	16.67	14.03
0.54	20.72	16.67	13.94
0.55	20.93	16.67	13.85
0.56	21.15	16.67	13.75
0.57	21.39	16.67	13.65
0.58	21.65	16.67	13.55
0.59	21.93	16.67	13.44
0.60	22.22	16.67	13.33

Let's look first at the last column in the table, where the ROE is 10 percent. We already saw that at a 50 percent retention rate, the firm's share price was $14.29, but now we see that its share price *decreases* as the firm retains more money and reinvests it in the firm. In contrast, when the ROE is 14 percent, the share price increases as the firm retains more, while for the 12 percent ROE, the share price is independent of the retention rate.

The reason for these results is that when the firm's ROE is 10 percent, it is less than the investors' required rate of return of 12 percent. So as the firm invests more by increasing its retention rate, the shareholders are unhappy. Why would they invest in a firm where they require a 12 percent rate of return and be happy with the firm investing at 10 percent? In this case, the share valuation model is telling the firm's management to reduce investment and return the funds saved as a larger dividend. The shareholders can then take these funds and invest them elsewhere to earn their 12 percent required rate of return. Conversely, when the firm is expected to earn 14 percent, the shareholders are saying the opposite: "Don't give us a dividend. We can only earn 12 percent elsewhere, so please reinvest more and earn 14 percent." As a result, the share price increases as the firm invests more. Finally, for the 12 percent ROE case, the shareholders are saying: "We don't care what you do, since you are not doing anything for us if you invest or give us a dividend." As a result, there is no impact on the share price.

The example in Table 20-9 is very important in finance. For a long time it was felt that this result was due to the firm's dividend policy because the firm's retention rate and dividend payout were changing. However, this is not the case. What is really changing is the amount of investment the firm is making, and the stock market is valuing whether the firm is creating or destroying value. When ROE is more than K_e, the firm is creating value when it reinvests;

hurdle rate the return on an
investment required to create value;
below this rate, an investment would
destroy value

when ROE is less than K_e, it is destroying value. This result is independent of how much the firm decides to pay out as a dividend, since it can always raise money to pay a dividend. This points to another aspect of the cost of capital: not only is it important to value the firm's shares, but it is also a **hurdle rate** for making investment decisions. This is the meaning of the phrase "required return": unless an investment jumps this hurdle, it destroys value and should not be undertaken. We will discuss this more at the end of the chapter.

The example with the different ROEs and different retention rates also emphasizes another key point in finance: there is a big difference between a *growing* firm and a *growth* firm. When ROE equals K_e, the share price is independent of how much the firm reinvested. If the firm pays out all its earnings and does not grow at all ($b = 0$), the share price is \$16.67, whereas if it reinvests all its earnings ($b = 1$) and grows at 12 percent per year, the share price is still \$16.67. (This ignores taxes, which were discussed in Chapter 18.) This is an example of a growing firm that, because it simply reinvests at its cost of capital, is "not doing anything" for the shareholders; as a result, they don't care whether it is growing or not. Note also that the earnings yield for this growing firm at a 50 percent retention rate is 12 percent, which equals its forecast earnings per share divided by its stock price (i.e., \$2 ÷ \$16.67). So for growing firms, the earnings yield is a good estimate of their cost of equity capital.

On the other hand, when ROE is greater than K_e, the firm is doing something that the shareholders cannot do, which is reinvest at 14 percent. We call these firms "growth firms" and say they have "growth opportunities." In this case, note that the earnings yield is \$2 divided by \$20, or 10 percent, which underestimates the required return by common shareholders.

Finally, there are some firms that destroy shareholder value by investing where ROE is less than K_e. For these firms, the earnings yield is \$2 divided by \$14.29, or 14 percent, which overestimates their cost of internal equity. These results confirm that the earnings yield is not a good estimate of a firm's cost of internal equity capital. Dividends or earnings may be growing, but the crucial piece of information is whether the firm is investing at rates of return greater or less than its cost of equity capital—that is, whether growth opportunities exist. We can consider these cases by looking again at multi-stage growth models.

Multi-Stage Growth Models

multi-stage growth DDM a
version of the DDM that accounts for
different levels of growth in earnings
and dividends

Another version of the DCF model to consider is the **multi-stage growth DDM,** which was also discussed in Chapter 7. In practice, there is no limit to the extent of the growth stages, but let's consider a very simple case in which the firm has some investment today, which we assume equals the firm's book value per share (BVPS), which is earning a return (ROE$_1$) in perpetuity. The firm is expected to invest a similar amount next year (Inv), which will again earn a return (ROE$_2$) in perpetuity. This particular version of the multi-stage model is expressed in Equation 20-22.

[20-22]
$$P_o = \frac{ROE_1 \times BVPS}{K_e} + \frac{Inv}{(1+K_e)}\left[\frac{(ROE_2 - K_e)}{K_e}\right]$$

The first term in this equation equals the perpetuity value of the current earnings, as discussed previously, where the firm is expected to earn an ROE equal to ROE$_1$. The second term represents further investment (Inv), which we assume is invested at ROE$_2$ and is discounted back one period, since it is one period further off in the future. However, it adds a perpetual amount, represented by the difference between the firm's ROE on this investment of ROE$_2$ minus K_e. As before, if ROE$_2$ equals K_e, this future investment adds nothing to the value of the firm, since it does not create value, and the second term will equal zero. However, if ROE$_2$ is greater than K_e, this future investment adds value, with the amount of value depending on the amount of investment (Inv) that can be invested at this rate, and by how much ROE$_2$ exceeds K_e. Equation 20-22 is a simple approach to valuation that breaks out the value of shares into the **present value of existing opportunities (PVEO)**, the first term, and the **present value of growth opportunities (PVGO)**, as a result of investment in the future, the second term. Note that although we conventionally refer to the second term as PVGO, it is actually the *net* present value (NPV), since we have to subtract the future cost of the investments.

We apply this equation by setting the investment amount arbitrarily at $20 for both the current book value and the next period's investment, and use a discount rate of 12 percent to value this stock. We now consider four scenarios:

A. In this scenario, PVEO is high, with ROE_1 of 20 percent and BVPS of $20, so PVEO is $33.33. The ROE for the next period is expected to remain high, at 20 percent, so PVGO is $11.90. Thus, the share price would be $45.23. Note in this case that the PVGO of $11.90 is less than the PVEO of $33.33, since it is actually the NPV of these future growth opportunities.

B. In this scenario, ROE_2 is less than or equal to 12 percent, so the firm has no PVGO and does not make any future investments, but we assume it has the same high ROE for current earnings of 20 percent, so its share price would be $33.33.

C. In this scenario, the firm has very poor current earnings, with ROE_1 of 2 percent, but it has the same great future prospects as it does in scenario A. Thus, its PVEO equals $3.33, and its PVGO would be $11.90, translating into a share price of $15.23.

D. In the final scenario, the firm has the same poor current prospects as in scenario C, so its PVEO would be $3.33. On top of that, it is destroying value by reinvesting in the future at an ROE_2 of 10 percent, so PVGO is –$2.98, and its share price would be a trivial $0.35 (i.e., $3.33 – $2.98)!

If we classify these four cases as types of firms, we have the following:

A. High PVEO and high PVGO

B. High PVEO and low (zero) PVGO

C. Low PVEO and high PVGO

D. Low PVEO and low PVGO

We can put them into a two-by-two matrix and classify them according to a conventional corporate description pioneered by the Boston Consulting Group, as shown in Figure 20-2.

present value of existing opportunities (PVEO) the value of the firm's current operations, assuming no new investment

present value of growth opportunities (PVGO) the net present value (NPV) today of the firm's future investments

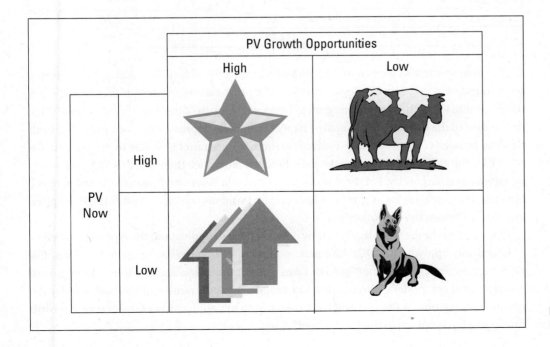

FIGURE 20-2 *Growth Opportunities and Firm Type*

star a firm with high PVEO and high PVGO

cash cow a firm with high PVEO but low PVGO

turnaround a firm with low PVEO and high PVGO

dog a firm with low PVEO and low PVGO

Firm A would be classified as a **star** in Figure 20-2, having everything going for it—both very good PVEO and excellent PVGO. Firm B would be the **cash cow**, generating significant cash flows from its current opportunities and thus possessing a high PVEO, but with no good investment opportunities, so its PVGO is zero. Firm C is the **turnaround** candidate; its current operations are a drag on performance so PVEO is low, but everything is about the future, so its PVGO is high. Finally, Firm D is the **dog**, with poor current operations so its PVEO is low. On top of that, it has been investing in projects that provide returns lower than its cost of internal equity, so it possesses a negative PVGO.

We developed these four stylistic views of firm valuation to show that for every firm, there is a "story" that has to match its valuation. If you can understand this, then estimating each firm's cost of equity capital becomes easier as you know the biases in using DCF estimates. For example, A has the highest market price because both PVEO and PVGO are high. This could be a large capitalization stock (large cap) such as Apple, where everything is going right. The cash cow would be a utility like TransCanada Pipelines Ltd., with an excellent profitable core business but limited growth prospects. The cash cow might also be called a value stock, depending on its price. The turnaround company could be a pure growth stock, with very limited current value but great growth potential. Classic examples of turnarounds or growth stocks would be the Internet and tech stocks of the late 1990s, or companies like Google Inc. today, where investors are paying a huge premium for the PVGO. Finally, dogs *should* be scarce, since they are candidates for hostile takeovers. Regardless of the poor quality of their current operations (low PVEO), their value could be increased just by stopping them from throwing good money after bad by investing at less than their equity cost.

Note that we valued these four firms using the same 12 percent discount rate, so the cost of equity capital is exactly the same. However, the market-to-book ratio and earnings yield are different for each, as shown in Table 20-10.

TABLE 20-10 The Impact of Growth Opportunities on Share Prices

	Earnings Yield (%)	Market-to-Book
Star	8.84	2.26
Cash cow	12.00	1.67
Turnaround	2.63	0.76
Dog	114.29	0.02

The actual numbers are not that important, but the critical feature is that the star and the turnaround have very low earnings yields (or high price-earnings ratios). Both of these types of companies would be regarded as growth firms, since much of the value comes from PVGO. In the case of the turnaround company, its PVEO actually depresses its stock price. For both of these types of companies, DCF estimation methods are unreliable due to the importance of PVGO. The cash cow gives back the true discount rate, since there is no PVGO, and it may be viewed as a perpetuity. For the dog, the earnings yield is very high, exceeding 100 percent, because it is forecast to lose value from its future investments, which depresses the share price and thus increases the earnings yield.

The point of these examples is to show that you have to understand the type of firm before mechanically applying the DCF formulas; otherwise, it is very easy to make mistakes. The DCF models work best for non-growth firms and for the market as a whole, where growth opportunities are moderate and easiest to estimate. A good example of the latter use for the economy as a whole is the U.S. Federal Reserve System's application of the constant growth model in what is known as the "Fed model," discussed next.

The Fed Model[11]

The Fed model was used to estimate whether the stock market was over- or undervalued and whether the U.S. Fed should "talk down" market values that might be excessive and cause problems if they collapsed. The exact equation used was:

$$\frac{V_{actual}}{V_{Fed}} = \frac{V_{actual}}{Exp\,(EPS)/(K_{TBond}-1.0\%)} \qquad [20\text{-}23]$$

In this equation, V_{actual} was the actual value for the U.S. stock market, and V_{Fed} was the estimate from the Fed's model, which was the expected earnings per share on the Standard & Poor's 500 Index (Exp(EPS)), as reported by security market analysts, divided by the yield on the long-term U.S. treasury bond (K_{TBond}) minus 1 percent. That is,

$$V_{Fed} = \frac{Exp\,(EPS)}{K_{TBond}-1.0\%} \qquad [20\text{-}24]$$

Valuation is easier when you aggregate across all securities, since you remove the "non-systematic risk" attached to individual securities. (This was discussed in chapters 8 and 9.) In the case of the market as a whole, after-tax earnings should grow at approximately the long-run real growth rate of GDP plus inflation, while the cost of equity for the market as a whole should be the treasury bond yield plus a market risk premium. So the Fed model implies that for fair valuation, the market risk premium is 1 percent less than the growth rate in nominal GDP.

The actual "performance" of the Fed model is illustrated in Figure 20-3. We can see that the model tracked the U.S. equity market quite well for much of the period until the late 1990s, when actual market values deviated significantly from the values implied by the Fed model. The stock market actually peaked in August 2000 and then went into a freefall that lasted almost three years. This suggests that investors who used the signals provided by the Fed model and decided to get out of the stock market in 2000, when it indicated significant overvaluation, would have saved themselves from large losses.

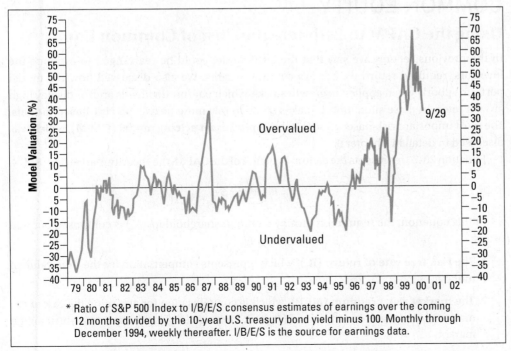

* Ratio of S&P 500 Index to I/B/E/S consensus estimates of earnings over the coming 12 months divided by the 10-year U.S. treasury bond yield minus 100. Monthly through December 1994, weekly thereafter. I/B/E/S is the source for earnings data.

FIGURE 20-3 *The U.S. Fed's Stock Valuation Model**

Source: Yardeni, Edward. "US Stock Valuation Models." Deutsche Bank, October 4, 2000, www.yardeni.com.

[11] This discussion follows that in Yardeni, Edward. "US Stock Valuation Models." Deutsche Bank, October 4, 2000.

Denoting Exp(EPS) as X, we can see that if the Fed model is rearranged, it also indicates that the market is fairly valued when the following condition exists:

[20-25]

$$\frac{X}{P_{S\&P500}} - 1.0\% = K_{TBond} - 1.0\%$$

This equation says that the earnings yield on the S&P 500 is equal to the long-term treasury bond yield minus 1 percent. As discussed previously, the earnings yield is the appropriate discount rate for the no-growth case (i.e., for perpetuities), whereas we would expect the market as a whole to grow at the nominal GDP growth rate. So if this nominal GDP growth rate is 5 percent, another way of interpreting the Fed model is to say that the required return on the equity market as a whole averages the long-term treasury bond yield plus a 4 percent risk premium (i.e., the 5% nominal GDP growth rate – 1%). With U.S. treasury bonds yielding about 3 percent on March 22, 2012, this would indicate an overall cost of equity for the U.S. market of 7 percent, which seems reasonable given the very low expected inflation rate consistent with the slow growth experienced by the United States as it works to escape the recession.

CONCEPT REVIEW QUESTIONS

1. Explain how we can use the constant growth DDM to estimate the cost of firms' internal common equity, as well as the cost of new common share issues.

2. Explain the relationship between ROE, retention rates, and firm growth.

3. How can we relate the existence of multiple growth stages to four commonly used firm classifications?

4. Describe the Fed model and how it may be used to estimate the required rate of return of the market as a whole.

20.6 RISK-BASED MODELS AND THE COST OF COMMON EQUITY

Using the CAPM to Estimate the Cost of Common Equity

Learning Objective 20.6
Estimate the cost of equity using risk-based models and describe the advantages and limitations of these models.

risk-based models models that estimate costs based on the associated risks

capital asset pricing model (CAPM) a pricing model that uses one factor, beta, to relate expected returns to risk

risk-free rate of return compensation for the time value of money

market risk premium (MRP) compensation for assuming the risk of the market portfolio

beta coefficient a measure of a firm's systematic or market risk

In the previous section, we saw that the DCF model could be rearranged to estimate the investors' required return on a firm's common shares. We also discussed how the model performs poorly when applied to growth stocks, which pay low dividends and/or display high growth rates. In these situations, it makes sense to rely more heavily on **risk-based models**. The most important risk-based model is the **capital asset pricing model (CAPM)**, which was discussed in detail in Chapter 9.

Equation 20-26 represents the central equation of the CAPM, the security market line (SML).

[20-26]

$$K_e = R_F + MRP \times \beta_e$$

In this equation, the required return by common shareholders (K_e) is composed of three terms:

1. The **risk-free rate of return (R_F)**, which represents compensation for the time value of money

2. The **market risk premium (MRP)**, which is compensation for assuming the risk of the market portfolio and is defined as $E(R_M) - R_F$, where $E(R_M)$ is the expected return on the market

3. The **beta coefficient** (β_e) for the firm's common shares, which measures the firm's systematic or market risk and represents the contribution that this security makes to the risk of a well-diversified portfolio

The CAPM is derived as a single-period model, but just what is meant by a single period is an unresolved issue, since investment horizons differ from investor to investor. In testing the CAPM, it is common to use a 30-day time horizon, yet such a short time horizon is rarely useful in making corporate finance decisions. In fact, when we talked about the characteristics of common equity in Chapter 19, one of the most important was the absence of a maturity date. While individual investors may invest for 30 days, at that time, they will sell the shares to other investors, so the security is still outstanding. In addition, as we will see when we discuss corporate investment decisions, the cost of capital or WACC is used to evaluate long-term investment decisions made by the firm. For this reason, the risk-free rate used in *corporate* applications of the CAPM is usually the yield on the longest-maturity Government of Canada bond, which is currently the 30-year bond.

In order to estimate the MRP, we generally use long-run averages supplemented by knowledge of the prevailing economic scenario. The basic idea is that over long periods of time, what people expect to happen should on average occur—that is, they are biased in forming their expectations if they consistently over or under predict returns. In contrast, over short periods of time, expectations are unlikely to be realized. It's like tossing a die: you may get three consecutive 1s, but if you throw it enough times, eventually you will get 1s one-sixth of the time, 2s one-sixth of the time, and so on. Let's keep this in mind as we consider the performance of the S&P/TSX Composite Index over the 2006 to 2011 period, as reported in Table 20-11.

TABLE 20-11 Returns on the S&P/TSX Composite Index

	Returns (%)
2006	17.26
2007	9.83
2008	−33.0
2009	35.05
2010	17.61
2011	−8.71

Clearly, it is difficult to argue that in any one particular year the performance of the S&P/TSX Composite Index was what was expected at the time. For example, nobody would have held shares in 2008 if they expected the stock market to crash the way it did! Similarly, the performance in 2009 was exceptional; indeed, if you consistently earned returns of more than 20 percent, you would become very rich very quickly. In both cases, it is like observing three consecutive 1s when throwing a die; it can happen but is not what was expected.

Table 20-12 (formerly Table 8-2 in Chapter 8) shows estimates of average investment returns over the period 1938 to 2011.

TABLE 20-12 Average Investment Returns and Standard Deviations, 1938 to 2011

	Annual Arithmetic Mean (%)	Annual Geometric Mean (%)[12]	Standard Deviation of Annual Returns (%)
Government of Canada treasury bills	4.96	4.88	4.24
Government of Canada bonds	6.44	6.08	8.99
Canadian stocks	11.35	10.03	16.82
U.S. stocks	12.16	10.77	17.53

Source: Data are from the Canadian Institute of Actuaries and from Datastream.

---

[12] This was referred to as the "Annual Compound Return" in Table 5-1 of Chapter 5. This is because the geometric mean is the mean used in compounding, as discussed below.

Over this long period of time, the difference between the average return on bonds and the average return on common equities in Canada was just under 5 percent (i.e., 11.35% – 6.44%), which would represent one estimate of our long-term MRP.[13] This MRP has fallen over the past few years due to the collapse in long-term government bond yields, which has generated great bond market returns and weak equity markets. It is only representative of the expected MRP if events of the past 74 years are expected to repeat themselves in the future. This would accord with the expectations of market professionals, like security analysts and company executives. Most people believe that the Canadian MRP over the long-term bond yield is between 5 and 6 percent. Therefore, with the 2.7 percent long Canada bond yield that prevailed at the time of writing, the Canadian stock market could be expected to earn between 7.7 and 8.7 percent going forward over a very long period. The overall estimate of the stock market's expected return is important, because it is broadly consistent with the result of the Fed model for the United States. However, both would be regarded as "low," since current long-term interest rates are so low as a result of central bank monetary policy, particularly given the Bank of Canada's 2 percent inflation target.

In 2011, TD Economics came up with forward-looking estimates, presented in Table 20-13. The Dex Universe Bond Index mentioned in the table is a portfolio of long-term bonds maintained by Scotiabank. It is riskier than the long Canada bond, since some of the portfolio's contents are corporate bonds with default risk, so the TD Economics estimate of the MRP is at least 4.1 percent over the long Canada bond yield of 2.7 percent. However, remember the discussion in Chapter 8 of arithmetic mean (AM) versus geometric mean (GM) returns, where we suggested that arithmetic mean returns (or simple averages) are always higher than geometric mean (or compound) returns, and that this difference increases with the variability in the arithmetic returns. In fact, the approximate relationship is expressed in this equation:

$$AM = GM + \frac{\sigma^2}{2}$$

TABLE 20-13 Long-Run Financial Projections

Financial Forecasts	Average Annual Percent Return
Cash: 3-Month T-bills	3.4
Income: Dex Universe Bond Index	4.0
Canadian Equities: S&P/TSX Composite Index	7.5
U.S. Equities: S&P 500 Index	7.5
International Non-U.S. Equities: MSCI EAFE Index	7.5

Source: TD Economics, "An Economics, Perspective on Long-Term Financial Returns." March 17, 2011.

With annual stock market returns having a standard deviation of about 16 percent, as indicated in Table 20-12, half of their variance is 1.3 percent, so the long-run MRP estimated by TD Economics is consistent with an arithmetic MRP of 5.4 percent (i.e., 4.1% + 1.3%). This figure is higher than that obtained using the long-run average MRP of 5 percent since 1938 due to the current low long Canada bond yield.

Estimating Betas

The beta coefficient is the final piece of information needed in order to use the SML to estimate required returns. The beta coefficient adjusts the risk of the market to the risk of an individual security, so it is an absolute number like 0.5 for a low-risk security and 1.5 for a high-risk security. It measures the degree to which securities move in relation to market movements: the more they move together, the fewer diversification gains there are and the riskier the

---

[13] Notice that this figure differs from the market risk premium for treasury bills, alluded to in Chapter 9.

security. Betas are normally estimated using the prior five years' monthly return data, but it is important to realize that if nothing happened during this period, this will be reflected in the estimate. Conversely, if something special happened during this period, the beta will reflect that. (In other words, beta estimates, particularly those for individual stocks, tend to be sensitive to the chosen estimation period.) For this reason, we tend to go back over long periods of time and again analyze what happened during the estimation period.

Figure 20-4 gives the beta coefficients estimated for the major subindexes of the S&P/TSX Composite Index, using the prior five years of monthly data. Since it is difficult to read the betas of all the major subindexes from the graph, we also report them in Table 20-14.

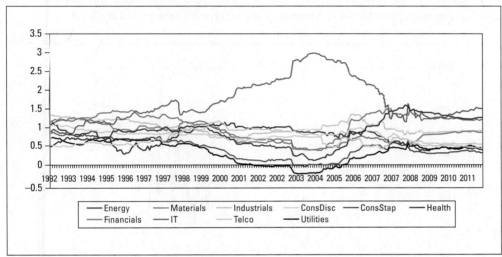

Source: Data from the Canadian Financial Markets Research Centre (CFMRC) stock return data

FIGURE 20-4 *Estimated Betas for Major Subindexes of the S&P/TSX Composite Index*

TABLE 20-14 S&P/TSX Subindex Beta Estimates

	Energy	Materials	Industrials	ConsDisc	ConsStap	Health	Fin	IT	Telco	Utilities
1995	0.93	1.41	1.19	0.82	0.68	0.36	0.92	1.25	0.53	0.67
1996	0.93	1.28	1.10	0.83	0.66	0.39	1.02	1.36	0.61	0.65
1997	0.98	1.33	0.97	0.82	0.62	0.60	0.93	1.56	0.62	0.53
1998	0.85	1.12	0.94	0.80	0.60	1.02	1.11	1.40	0.92	0.55
1999	0.91	1.04	0.78	0.73	0.43	1.00	1.00	1.55	1.11	0.30
2000	0.67	0.74	0.73	0.69	0.23	1.10	0.79	1.78	0.92	0.14
2001	0.50	0.60	0.82	0.68	0.10	0.98	0.67	2.12	0.94	+/−0.03
2002	0.43	0.57	0.86	0.73	0.11	0.99	0.67	2.27	0.92	−0.06
2003	0.27	0.42	0.91	0.74	−0.04	0.85	0.39	2.75	0.82	−0.26
2004	0.17	0.42	1.04	0.81	−0.02	0.84	0.41	2.89	0.55	−0.14
2005	0.48	0.78	1.12	0.84	0.14	0.74	0.58	2.71	0.71	−0.01
2006	1.01	1.34	1.05	0.87	0.48	0.88	0.70	2.14	0.49	0.24
2007	1.41	1.47	0.95	0.74	0.54	0.56	0.55	1.22	0.59	0.44
2008	1.42	1.36	0.79	0.52	0.32	0.64	0.58	1.49	0.53	0.43
2009	1.35	1.24	0.83	0.56	0.28	0.42	0.79	1.23	0.48	0.42
2010	1.24	1.21	0.87	0.55	0.33	0.42	0.84	1.37	0.47	0.42
2011	1.25	1.19	0.89	0.53	0.31	0.39	0.85	1.49	0.45	0.44

Source: The Canadian Financial Markets Research Centre (CFMRC) stock return data

What is striking about the estimates and the graph is that one subindex (the IT subindex) shows rapidly increasing and then decreasing beta coefficients from 1999 until 2007, whereas most of the other beta coefficients show a constant or decreasing trend. In fact, consumer staples and utilities actually had *negative* beta estimates, indicating that they moved in the opposite direction to the stock market as a whole and reduced the risk of a diversified portfolio.

As discussed in Chapter 9, if we sum up all the beta coefficients, their value-weighted average has to equal 1, which is the beta of the market as a whole. What these estimates indicate is that the IT subindex was very important during this period, and as it increased, by definition, the other betas *had* to decrease on average. In fact, the more recent beta estimates are somewhat anomalous, since they reflect the Internet bubble of the late 1990s and its subsequent burst in the early 2000s. Figure 20-5 summarizes this phenomenon, showing the stock price of Nortel Networks Corporation until the end of 2005.

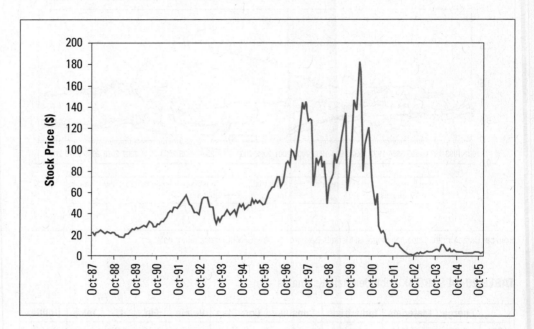

FIGURE 20-5 *Nortel Stock Price (1987–2005)*

Nortel was originally a telecommunications manufacturer controlled by BCE Inc. However, during the Internet mania of the late 1990s, investor interest shifted to companies making the equipment for the backbone of the Internet. Two Canadian companies, Nortel and JDS Uniphase, attracted a huge amount of interest. As can be seen from Figure 20-5, Nortel's stock price jumped from the $20 to $40 range to peak at over $170 before collapsing to the penny stock range.[14] The prices of JDS and other IT companies followed similar patterns over this time. At one point, Nortel and JDS combined to make up more than one-third of the market value of the S&P/TSX Composite Index; they pushed the value up along with them when they soared and dragged it back down again when they crashed. This is why the IT subindex beta increased so dramatically: it was essentially dictating the major market movements and *was* the market.

What this means is, if a repeat of the IT-driven stock market boom and bust is expected, these beta estimates are good estimates. If such a boom and bust is not expected, these estimates are of little value. Also note that the energy subsector had betas around 1 until 2000; it then dropped to well below 1 until 2006 and for the past several years it has been well over 1. Does this make sense? The answer again is to understand what has generated these estimates. For the past several years, the stock market has been driven by commodity prices, in particular

---

[14] At the time of writing, Nortel's stock price was $0.015 and the company had almost finished selling off its assets under bankruptcy protection. To all intents and purposes, Nortel is now dead.

the price of oil. The Canadian market is rich in energy and resource stocks, so for the past several years the betas of these stocks have increased as they have been driving the overall market return. The message is never to take a statistic at face value; instead, try to understand what has happened in the economy to generate it.

To estimate the risk of an individual company, we can take the industry grouping as a major input, along with the individual beta estimate. If we take Tim Hortons as an example, we have a slight problem, because it has only been a publicly traded company since March 2006, so there are barely five and a half years of data available. In Chapter 9 we indicated that Tim Hortons' beta over the past five years has been 0.68. As Tim Hortons is a consumer products company, we would expect it to have a low beta because consumer spending is not as volatile as spending on industrial products. It is interesting to note that the most recent consumer discretionary subindex beta is 0.53, while the beta of the consumer staples subindex is lower, at 0.31. Tim Hortons is classified as consumer discretionary, along with companies like Sears Canada, Canadian Tire, Corus Entertainment, and Magna International, but may have more in common with consumer staples companies like Shoppers Drug Mart and Loblaws. For the authors, coffee *is* a staple!

As a result, it may be reasonable to use a range of beta estimates, running from a lower beta estimate of 0.53, reflecting the consumer discretionary subindex beta, to Tim Hortons' own beta of 0.68. Using the long-term Canada bond yield of 2.7 percent, the consumer discretionary beta of 0.531, and the lower estimate for the MRP of 5 percent, we estimate Tim Hortons' cost of (internal) equity capital using the CAPM as:

$$K_e = 2.7 + (0.53) \times 5 = 5.35\%$$

This is very low, even though, as we estimated earlier, Tim Hortons' after-tax debt cost is barely 1.7 percent. If we use the higher beta estimate of 0.68 and the upper estimate of the MRP of 6 percent, we get:

$$K_e = 2.7 + (0.68) \times 6 = 6.78\%$$

This range of 5.35 to 6.78 percent is based on both the low and high ends of the market risk premium and beta ranges. In this way, we acknowledge that estimating the cost of equity financing involves less precision than estimating the cost of debt. However, as we mentioned in Chapter 9, risk premiums tend to vary over time with capital market conditions, in which case we talk of the *conditional* risk premium—that is, the risk premium conditional on current capital market conditions. One clear indication of what the market expects is the yield spread between the borrowing cost for Canadian corporations and that for the Government of Canada. In Chapter 18 we saw that from January 1980 to January 2012 the spread between A-rated corporate debt yields and those of the Government of Canada averaged 1.07 percent. However, at the time of writing, this spread was almost 1.8 percent, which indicates that investors view corporate debt as less valuable than normal. Researchers at the Bank of Canada attributed about 37 percent of this larger-than-normal spread to the increased risk of default on the part of typical A-rated issuers; the balance was due to decreased liquidity.[15] This suggests that the MRP was at least 0.25 percent higher than normal (0.37×0.71) at the time of writing, but we would place it slightly higher, at 0.4 percent. Overall, we consider a reasonable cost of equity for Tim Hortons to be below 7 percent and use the estimate we derived in Chapter 9 of 6.84 percent.

If 6.84 percent is the cost of equity for Tim Hortons, and the 1.69 percent mentioned previously is its after-tax cost of debt, all we now need are the equity and debt weights. We already know that the market value of Tim Hortons' debt was $427.4 million at year-end, and from Chapter 19 we know there were also 157.8 million shares outstanding, at a year-end stock price of $49.17, so the equity market capitalization for Tim Hortons was $7.759 billion. What this means is that the equity weight in Tim Hortons' capital structure was 95 percent and the

---

[15] Garcia, A., and J. Yang, "Understanding Corporate Bond Spreads Using Credit Default Swaps." *Bank of Canada Review*, Autumn 2009.

debt weight only 5 percent. Combining these cost estimates and capital structure weights, we get the following estimate of the company's weighted average cost of capital.

$$WACC = (0.95)(6.84) + (0.05)(1.69) = 6.58\%$$

Notice two things about Tim Hortons' WACC: first, the company uses little debt, so with an equity market value of almost $8 billion, the $427.4 million in debt is a very minor 5 percent of Tim Hortons' financing. The corollary of this is that the WACC is driven by Tim Hortons' equity cost. Second, the overall cost is quite low, at 6.58 percent, but perhaps not that low when we consider that inflation was only slightly over 2 percent, and we also recognize how low risk Tim Hortons is. Figure 20-6 tracks Tim Hortons' stock price relative to the S&P/TSX Composite Index from its initial listing in 2006 to March 23, 2012.

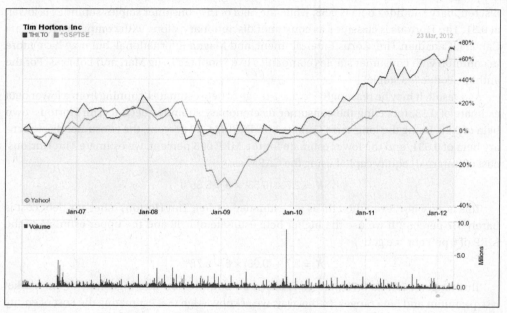

FIGURE 20-6 *Tim Hortons' Stock Price versus the S&P/TSX Composite Index*

Source: Note: THI is Tim Hortons' stock ticker, and Yahoo uses .TO to indicate Canada (Toronto). Reprinted with permission from Yahoo! Inc. © 2013 Yahoo! Inc. YAHOO! and the YAHOO! logo are trademarks of Yahoo! Inc.

What is striking is that while the TSX at its worst lost over 40 percent of its market value from its previous high, Tim Hortons' stock price showed no great trend. The price at the market low on March 9, 2009, was down from its previous year's high but did not drop with the horrendous bear market of September 2008–March 2009. By March 2012, the TSX was about back to where it had been almost six years earlier, while Tim Hortons was up almost 80 percent. Most investors would have loved to have had all their money invested in Tim Hortons, rather than the TSX, for 2008–9!

However, remember that when we make estimates we are looking forward, not backward; just because Tim Hortons has been low risk does not mean it will continue to be low risk. Starbucks Corporation is a good example of a competitor that was similarly regarded as low risk until the recession hit. Then its premium coffee strategy turned into a millstone as low-end competitors like McDonald's Corporation started offering premium coffee at much lower prices. This is one of the reasons firms generally push up their cost of capital estimates by at least 1 percent: they are attempting to take into account uncertainties that have not played out in the capital market and, as a result, have not yet affected their beta estimate.

We conclude this section by revisiting firm ABC from Examples 20-1 through 20-5 and determining its cost of internal and external common equity, as well as its WACC.

EXAMPLE 20-6 Determining the Cost of Internal Common Equity Using CAPM

Assume the beta for firm ABC from Examples 20-1 through 20-5 is 1.15 and that the risk-free rate is 4.5 percent, while the MRP is 4.5 percent. Estimate the firm's cost of equity for internal funds using CAPM.

Solution

$$K_e = 4.5 + (4.5) \times (1.15) = 9.68\%$$

Notice that with the CAPM approach, the equity share price is not explicitly considered, which adds a complication if we want to estimate the cost of new common equity to the firm. There are two common ways to deal with this issue. The first is to take the premium over the cost of internal funds that was estimated using the constant growth DDM approach, which does include the price. For this company, the premium was 0.22 percent, since the cost of internal equity was estimated at 9.2 percent, while the cost of new common equity was estimated to be 9.42 percent. However, this will not work when we are unable to use the DDM, which is exactly when we will want to use a risk-based approach such as the CAPM, as discussed previously. In this case, we can merely "scale" our estimate of K_e by the following factor, which relates the share price to the net proceeds after flotation costs: $P_0 \div NP$. This adjustment leads to the following estimate of the cost of new common equity (K_{ne}):

$$K_{ne} = K_e \times \frac{P_0}{NP}$$ [20-27]

Example 20-7 applies both approaches.

EXAMPLE 20-7 Determining the Cost of External Common Equity Using CAPM

Use the estimate of internal common equity for firm ABC, obtained in Example 20-6, to estimate the firm's cost of external equity.

Solution

Approach #1

Use the premium determined using the DDM approach, which equals:

$$K_{ne} - K_e = 9.42 - 9.2 = 0.22\%$$

Adding this premium to the estimated K_e of 9.68 percent, we get

$$K_{ne} = K_e + 0.22 = 9.68 + 0.22 = 9.9\%$$

Approach #2

Adjust K_e:

$$K_{ne} = K_e \times \frac{P_0}{NP} = 9.68 \left(\frac{25}{23.75} \right) = 10.19\%$$

Using this approach we get a much larger premium of 0.29 percent.

EXAMPLE 20-8 Determining the WACC

Use the estimates for firm ABC determined in Examples 20-1 through 20-7. Assume that, based on your analysis, you decide to use the common equity costs as determined using the constant growth DDM.

a. Estimate ABC's WACC and MCC, assuming it has more than sufficient internal funds to provide the required common equity financing.

b. Estimate ABC's MCC if it needs to issue new common shares to provide the required amount of financing.

continued

EXAMPLE 20-8   *Determining the WACC continued*

Solution

a.   Since the firm raises all its common equity internally, we can assume that its WACC equals its MCC.

$$WACC = MCC = K_e\frac{S}{V} + K_p\frac{P}{V} + K_i\frac{D}{V} = (9.2)(0.511) + (8.16)(0.255) + (3.78)(0.234) = 7.67\%$$

b.   If the firm has to raise new common equity financing, its cost of common equity will rise, as will its MCC.

$$MCC = (9.42)(0.511) + (8.16)(0.255) + (3.78)(0.234) = 7.78\%$$

CONCEPT REVIEW QUESTIONS

1.   Explain how we can use the CAPM to estimate the cost of common equity.

2.   Explain why beta estimates are "period specific," and outline the potential problems that may arise. Allude to problems with recent beta estimates.

20.7 THE COST OF CAPITAL AND INVESTMENT

Learning Objective 20.7
Explain how WACC interacts with the investment decision framework introduced in chapters 13 to 17.

If investors in Tim Hortons want an overall cost of capital of 6.57 percent, as calculated in the previous section, Tim Hortons should not reinvest funds in its operations, which earn a rate of return less than this hurdle rate. This suggests that the WACC is not just a valuation tool—it is also used going forward as a tool to evaluate investments. A stylized version of this investment decision is shown in Figure 20-7.

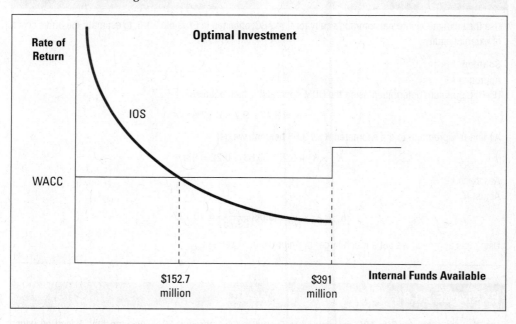

FIGURE 20-7 *Tim Hortons' Investment Opportunities Schedule (2011)*

investment opportunities schedule (IOS) the ranking of a firm's investments from highest to lowest profitability according to the rate of return they are expected to earn

We discussed how to evaluate firm investment decisions in chapters 13 and 14. Recall that the firm can look at its investments and rank them from highest to lowest profitability according to the rate of return they are expected to earn. This provides us with the downward sloping line in Figure 20-7, indicating the firm's **investment opportunities schedule (IOS)**. This curve represents the firm's demand curve for funds. Corresponding to this is the firm's supply curve for funds, which is initially represented assuming all common equity is supplied by internal funds.

Remember from Chapter 3 that traditional cash flow is net income plus amortization and deferred taxes (i.e., net income plus the non-cash items in the firm's income stream). For Tim Hortons, we indicated in Chapter 3 that cash flow from operations (CFO), less the change in working capital during 2011, was $391 million. This is the amount of money that Tim Hortons had to invest at its WACC of 6.57 percent. It is indicated by the horizontal line in Figure 20-7. In 2011, Tim Hortons actually had $152.7 million in capital expenditures and expenditures on acquisitions. This is depicted by the spot where Tim Hortons' IOS intersects its WACC for the optimal investment.[16] In 2011, Tim Hortons' total investment was significantly below the amount of internal cash flow it generated, which is why Tim Hortons was a cash cow: it could not profitably invest all the funds from its operations, even after including money spent on acquisitions. This is consistent with the funds forecast we made for Tim Hortons in Chapter 4, where we predicted excess cash being generated.

If Tim Hortons' IOS shifted to the right (very far to the right!), so that its internal demand for funds outstripped its supply of funds, then eventually it would have to raise additional capital. In this case, its MCC would increase above its WACC. This is indicated by the vertical jump in its supply of funds schedule. As discussed, in this scenario, the MCC would be above the WACC, simply due to the cost of raising additional funds.

So how does this discussion of what firms should do accord with what they actually do? In the spring of 2006, Kent Baker, Shantanu Dutta, and Samir Saadi surveyed Canadian firms to determine the answer to that question.[17] In particular, they asked firms what discount rate they used when evaluating a new project. The answers are in Table 20-15.

TABLE 20-15 Survey Results on Estimating the Discount Rate

Discount Rate	Percentage of Answers Saying "Often" or "Always"
1. The company's WACC	63.6
2. A rate based on management experience	43.5
3. The cost of specific funds of the project	38.2
4. A risk-matched discount rate for the project	36.6
5. A different discount rate for each cash flow	14.1
6. A divisional discount rate	11.3

Overwhelmingly, the most popular discount rate was the WACC, followed by experience—but then, you would hope that all companies take into account the experience of their senior executives. What is more important are the final four answers. In deriving our WACC, we explicitly looked at what investors required for investing in the firm's shares and debt, so the WACC is an overall cost of capital for the firm. However, what if the firm itself is composed of many different lines of business? TransCanada Corporation, for example, owns the Mainline natural gas pipeline that runs from western Canada east to central Canada; this has traditionally been the core of the company. However, it also has an interest in nuclear power generation in Ontario, an oil pipeline that will take heavy Canadian crude down to the Gulf of Mexico, and U.S. and Canadian power operations. TransCanada Corporation's WACC reflects the average risk of all these businesses and is probably not reflective of any particular one of them.

To solve the problem of evaluating a company with multiple lines of business, the WACC should be adjusted to reflect a risk-based WACC appropriate for each individual business. This is what the last four answers essentially do. A divisional discount rate (answer 6) simply indicates that TransCanada should adjust its overall WACC up or down, depending on whether it is applied to its nuclear power operations or the Mainline. This divisional discount

---

[16] The WACC estimates are not provided by Tim Hortons; only the cash flow and investment numbers are provided.

[17] Baker, H. Kent, Shantanu Dutta, and Samir Saadi, "Corporate Financial Practices in Canada: Where Do We Stand?" *Multinational Finance Journal* 15–3 (2011): 157–92.

rate should reflect the different risks involved in the different divisions (answer 5), and the different financing of each (answer 3). From this perspective, answers 3, 5, and 6 are simply more sophisticated applications of the WACC to multi-divisional firms.

Answer 4 is the most sophisticated, since in any project there are, in fact, different cash flows. We discussed this in Chapter 14, where we described it as valuation by components. For example, as soon as a project is undertaken, the investment gives rise to future capital cost allowances and tax shields, which are largely independent of the other project cash flows. Technically, these different components of the future cash flow stream should be discounted at different discount rates. Table 20-15 indicates that some firms actually use this more sophisticated approach to capital budgeting, which affects their choice of the discount rate. In the future, this more sophisticated approach may generate more interest on the part of Canadian companies.

LESSONS TO BE LEARNED   **There are silver linings** in all thunderstorms. There is no question that the financial crisis has caused all sorts of financing problems for many aggressive firms that financed heavily with debt. However, to refloat the economy and prevent excessive damage, the Bank of Canada and the Federal Reserve in the United States have dramatically dropped interest rates. As a result, prime at 3 percent is the lowest it has been for decades. When we consider that the interest is tax deductible at just over 1.5 percent, we see that the cost is less than the Bank of Canada's target inflation rate of 2 percent.

Who are the beneficiaries of this? Clearly, the firms that would otherwise have gone bankrupt benefit, but conservative firms like Tim Hortons could also, if they wanted, take advantage of these very low interest rates to increase their capital expenditures or make acquisitions. Rather than simply surviving, they could expand, since they have the financial flexibility to take on more debt. This is the wish of the Government of Canada, which is keeping interest rates artificially low in order to stimulate investment and get Canada working so that the unemployment rate comes down.

CONCEPT REVIEW QUESTIONS

1. Explain the importance of using the WACC as a hurdle rate for making investment decisions.

2. Why does the MCC suddenly jump up and become expensive?

SUMMARY

In this chapter, we synthesize information on the types of securities a firm may issue to finance its operations. In Chapter 19, we pointed out that these different types of securities differ in their degree of "equityness," so they all have different required rates of return. However, the firm as a whole has to earn enough money to pay the investors their required rate of return. Taking into account these different securities and their associated required rates of return and market values, we can determine how much the firm has to earn to meet these commitments. This is the basis for the weighted average cost of capital (WACC), which is the overall cost of the capital invested in the firm.

The WACC is a market-value-weighted average of the after-tax costs of all these securities. If the firm earns its WACC, then its present market values are supported, but if it is expected to earn less (more) than its WACC, its market value will fall (increase). In most cases, this change in market value drops through to the common shareholders, who are the residual claimants; as a result, they hold the riskiest of all the securities issued by the firm. In this sense, risk increases as we drop down the income statement.

We then show that the most difficult estimate in the WACC is determining the cost of common equity capital. In estimating this, we discuss the discounted cash flow (DCF) model, which "reverse engineers" the valuation equation to use the current market price in order to estimate the discount rate used by the investor. In doing so, we emphasize that since there are many different types of DCF models, there are also many different ways to estimate the cost of common equity. While the constant growth DDM is by far the most popular model, it also leads to serious errors for high-growth companies. To illustrate which model to use in different situations, we discuss a simple characterization of types of firms based on the present value of existing and growth opportunities.

Alternatively, rather than using DCF models, the capital asset pricing model (CAPM) can be used to minimize estimation errors. We know that the market risk premium has averaged between 4 and 5.5 percent historically, so the discount rate on the stock market as a whole is currently in the 6.5 to 8 percent range, with long-term Canada bond yields of around 2.5 percent. In adjusting for the risk of individual securities, we show how beta estimates are critically dependent on the time period over which they are estimated. We show that if we don't make appropriate adjustments for what has happened in the stock market over the past 10 years, recent beta estimates are seriously misleading. As with the DCF model, use of the CAPM requires judgement, common sense, and an understanding of recent financial history.

SUMMARY OF LEARNING OBJECTIVES

20.1 Explain how the three major problem areas in finance—valuation, cost of capital, and determining cash flows—are related.

Valuation of any securities is the sum of the discounted future cash flow. To do valuation, estimated cash flow and cost of capital (discount rate) are necessary inputs.

20.2 Calculate the weighted average cost of capital (WACC) and explain its significance.

The weighted average cost of capital (WACC) formula is given in Equation 20-8, in which WACC is the weighted average cost of equity and the after-tax cost of debt. It is significant because it is used in the valuation of projects.

20.3 Estimate the cost of capital and its non-equity components.

Cost of capital is the weighted average cost of equity and the after-tax cost of debt. Its non-equity component is the after-tax cost of debt.

20.4 Explain how operating leverage and financial leverage affect a firm's risk.

Operating leverage is generated by fixed costs. Companies with a greater proportion of fixed costs have a higher break-even sales level than firms with a lower proportion of fixed costs. As a result, they are riskier (because there is a higher variability in operating income). Financial leverage is generated by borrowing. Firms with debt have a higher variability of earnings per share but also have higher average return on equity than equivalent unlevered firms.

20.5 Apply the discounted cash flow model to estimate the equity cost and describe this model's advantages and disadvantages.

Equations 20-16 and 20-17 show how to apply the discounted cash flow model to estimate the equity cost. The method is easy to use. However, it depends on assumptions, which may lead to misuse. For example, it assumes that dividends grow at a constant rate.

20.6 Estimate the cost of equity using risk-based models and describe the advantages and limitations of these models.

Equation 20-26 shows that cost of equity equals the risk-free rate plus market risk premium multiplied by beta. It is derived from the capital asset pricing model and is easy to understand. However, empirically, it is difficult to estimate market risk premium and beta, and even the proxy of the risk-free rate is highly debatable.

20.7 Explain how WACC interacts with the investment decision framework introduced in chapters 13 to 17.

Chapters 13 and 14 are about investment decisions and focus on the method and estimation of cash flow. Cash flow and the cost of capital are the two most important factors in capital expenditure. Thus, Chapter 20 completes the discussion on capital investment. Chapters 15 and 16 cover two specific examples of investment: mergers and acquisitions, and leasing, respectively. Chapter 17 covers how to raise cash flows for investment purposes and discusses securities law. They are important parts of capital investment as well.

KEY TERMS

asset turnover ratio, p. 754

beta coefficient, p. 774

capital asset pricing model (CAPM), p. 774

capital structure, p. 751

cash cow, p. 772

cost of capital, p. 756

debt-to-equity ratio, p. 751

dog, p. 772

earnings yield, p. 753

hurdle rate, p. 770

investment opportunities schedule (IOS), p. 782

issuing or flotation costs, p. 759

marginal cost of capital (MCC), p. 759

market-to-book (M/B) ratio, p. 752

market risk premium (MRP), p. 774

multi-stage growth DDM, p. 770

operating leverage, p. 763

present value of existing opportunities (PVEO), p. 771

present value of growth opportunities (PVGO), p. 771

return on assets (ROA), p. 754

return on equity (ROE), p. 755

return on invested capital (ROIC), p. 754

risk-based models, p. 774

risk-free rate of return (R_F), p. 774

star, p. 772

turnaround, p. 772

weighted average cost of capital (WACC), p. 756

EQUATIONS

Equation	Formula	Page
[20-1] Perpetuity Valuation Formula	$S = \dfrac{X}{K_e}$	p. 752
[20-2] Earnings Yield	$K_e = \dfrac{X}{S}$	p. 753
[20-3] Required Earnings	$X = K_e \times S$	p. 753
[20-4] N/A	$P = \dfrac{EPS}{K_e} = \dfrac{ROE \times BVPS}{K_e}$	p. 755
[20-5] Price to Book for Perpetuity	$\dfrac{P}{BVPS} = \dfrac{ROE}{K_e}$	p. 755
[20-6] Total Enterprise Value (TEV)	$V = \dfrac{ROI \times IC}{K_a}$	p. 756
[20-7] TEV Discount Rate	$K_a = \dfrac{ROI \times IC}{V}$	p. 756
[20-8] Weighted Average Cost of Capital (WACC)	$K_a = \dfrac{ROI \times IC}{V} = \dfrac{K_e S + K_d(1-T)D}{V} = K_e\dfrac{S}{V} + K_d(1-T)\dfrac{D}{V}$	p. 756
[20-9] WACC with Preferred Shares	$WACC = K_e\dfrac{S}{V} + K_p\dfrac{P}{V} + K_i\dfrac{D}{V}$	p. 757
[20-10] Equity Market Value	$S = P_o \times n$	p. 757
[20-11] Perpetuity Preferred Share Value	$P_P = \dfrac{D_p}{K_p}$	p. 757
[20-12] Bond Valuation Formula	$B = I \times \left[\dfrac{1 - \dfrac{1}{(1+K_b)^n}}{K_b}\right] + F \times \dfrac{1}{(1+K_b)^n}$	p. 758

continued

Equation	Formula	Page
[20-13] Net Bond Proceeds	$NP = I \times (1-T) \times \left[\dfrac{1 - \dfrac{1}{(1+K_i)^n}}{K_i} \right] + F \times \dfrac{1}{(1+K_i)^n}$	p. 760
[20-14] Cost Of Perpetuity Preferreds	$K_p = \dfrac{D_p}{NP}$	p. 761
[20-15] Constant Growth Model (CGM)	$P_0 = \dfrac{D_1}{K_e - g}$	p. 765
[20-16] Equity Cost from the CGM	$K_e = \dfrac{D_1}{P_0} + g$	p. 766
[20-17] Cost of New Equity (after Issue Costs)	$K_{ne} = \dfrac{D_1}{NP} + g$	p. 766
[20-18] Sustainable Growth Rate	$g = b \times ROE$	p. 767
[20-19] CGM with Sustainable Growth	$P_0 = \dfrac{D_1}{K_e - b \times ROE}$	p. 767
[20-20] N/A	$P_0 = \dfrac{X_1(1-b)}{K_e - b \times ROE}$	p. 768
[20-21] N/A	$K_e = \dfrac{D_1}{P_0} + g = \dfrac{X_1(1-b)}{P_0} + b \times ROE$	p. 768
[20-22] Two ROE Model	$P_0 = \dfrac{ROE_1 \times BVPS}{K_e} + \dfrac{Inv}{(1+K_e)} \left[\dfrac{(ROE_2 - K_e)}{K_e} \right]$	p. 770
[20-23] Fed Model	$\dfrac{V_{actual}}{V_{Fed}} = \dfrac{V_{actual}}{Exp\,(EPS)/(K_{TBond} - 1.0\%)}$	p. 773
[20-24] Fed's CGM	$V_{Fed} = \dfrac{Exp\,(EPS)}{K_{TBond} - 1.0\%}$	p. 773
[20-25] N/A	$\dfrac{X}{P_{S\&P500} - 1.0\%} = K_{TBond} - 1.0\%$	p. 774
[20-26] CAPM	$K_e = R_F + MRP \times \beta_e$	p. 774
[20-27] N/A	$K_{ne} = K_e \times \dfrac{P_0}{NP}$	p. 781

QUESTIONS AND PRACTICE PROBLEMS

Multiple Choice Questions

1. Which of the following statements is false?
    a. Financing total assets is called the financial structure decision.
    b. Capital structure is how invested capital is financed.
    c. The financial structure is $34,000 if the total assets are $34,000.
    d. The invested capital is $50,000 if the total assets are $50,000.

2. If an all-equity firm is expected to earn and pay out a $2.50 dividend forever (in perpetuity), what is the value of the firm's stock given a cost of equity of 10 percent?
   a. $25.00
   b. $25.50
   c. $12.50
   d. $22.50

3. What is the earnings yield given a $75,000 earnings figure, a $20 market price per share, and 10,000 shares outstanding?
   a. 0.625
   b. 0.375
   c. 0.400
   d. 0.275

4. What does a firm have to earn given the following? MV of debt = $60,000; MV of equity = $140,000; $K_e = 10\%$; $K_d = 5\%$
   a. $17,000
   b. $3,000
   c. $14,000
   d. $13,000

5. Which of the following statements is true?
   a. When ROE < K_e, management is adding value to the firm.
   b. When ROE > K_e, management is decreasing the firm's value.
   c. When ROE > K_e, the market price goes above the book value of the investment.
   d. When ROE = K_e, the market price goes above the book value of the investment.

6. Which of the following is not an input in the calculation of WACC?
   a. Book values of equity and debt
   b. Market values of equity and debt
   c. Cost of equity
   d. Corporate tax rate

7. To increase the stock price of a firm that is assumed to grow at a constant rate g,
   a. increase the cost of equity.
   b. increase the constant growth rate.
   c. decrease the dividend payout ratio.
   d. increase the retention ratio.

8. Northern Star Inc. just paid a $3 dividend, which is expected to grow at a constant rate. Recent EPS is $6 and net income is $250,000. Total equity is $1.25 million and the cost of equity is 12 percent. What is the share market price?
   a. $165
   b. $150
   c. $50
   d. $300

9. Which of the following firms is a growth firm?
   a. ROE > K_e
   b. ROE < K_e
   c. ROE = K_e
   d. Net income = K_e

10. Which of the following statements is false?
    a. Star firms have both high PVGO and PVEO.
    b. Google and Yahoo are examples of turnarounds.
    c. Cash cows could be called growth stocks as well.
    d. Utility firms are examples of cash cows.

Practice Problems

Use the information below to answer practice problems 11 to 13.

BALANCE SHEET			
Cash	$140,000	Accounts payable	200,000
Marketable securities	200,000	Wages payable	100,000
Accounts receivable	40,000	Short-term debt	250,000
Inventory	1,000,000	Long-term debt	690,000
		Total liabilities	**$1,240,000**
Fixed assets	900,000	Common stock	950,000
		Retained earnings	90,000
Total assets	**$2,280,000**	**Total equity and liabilities**	**$2,280,000**

INCOME STATEMENT	
Sales	$2,000,000
CGS	$400,000
Amortization	$90,000
Interest	$56,400
EBT	$1,453,600
Taxes	$435,000
NI	$1,018,600
Shares outstanding	500,000

11. What is the cost of equity (K_e) given R_F = 2%, beta (β) = 1.5, expected market return (ER_M) = 12%?

12. What is the market price and market-to-book ratio, assuming the firm's stock is a perpetuity and all earnings are paid out as cash dividends (i.e., the retention ratio is zero)?

13. Calculate invested capital and before-tax ROI.

14. Provide two reasons why the cost of a security to a company differs from its required return in capital markets.

15. A firm's market values of equity and debt are $750,000 and $250,000, respectively. The before-tax cost of debt = 6%; R_F = 4%; beta (β) = 0.8; the market risk premium = 10%; and the tax rate = 20%. Calculate the WACC (weighted average cost of capital).

16. What is V_{Fed} given the expected earnings per share on the S&P 500 is $23.50 and the long-term U.S. bond rate is 4.75 percent?

17. Rocky Mountain Depot just announced its EPS of $4.50. Retention ratio (b) = 0.6. The earnings are expected to grow at 10 percent for one year and then at 5 percent indefinitely. Given that K_e = 17%, what is the market price?

18. Calculate the cost of issuing new equity for a firm, assuming issue costs are 3 percent of the share price after taxes; market price per share = $40; current dividend = $2.75; and the constant growth rate in dividends is 5 percent.

19. A firm has common shares outstanding with a discount rate of 12 percent. The current market price is $22.75, and dividend payments for this year are expected to be $0.60. What is the per-share implied growth rate?

20. A firm's earnings and dividends are expected to grow at a constant rate indefinitely, and it is expected to pay a dividend of $8.75 per share next year. Expected EPS and BVPS next year are $12 and $48, respectively. The cost of equity is 10 percent and there are 10,000 shares outstanding. Calculate the firm's value, assuming that the retention ratio stays the same and the market value of debt is $500,000.

21. Calculate the cost of equity using the constant growth DDM given the following: current dividend = $3; payout ratio = 0.5 (assume it is not changing); ROE = 12%; and the current market price of the stock = $24. Is the current management adding to or reducing the shareholders' value?

22. Calculate PVGO and PVEO given the following information: $ROE_1 = 20\%$; $ROE_2 = 25\%$; further investment (Inv) = $100; BVPS = $10; and $K_e = 10\%$. Is this firm a star? If not, what is it according to Boston Consulting Group?

23. A firm is going to finance a new project 100 percent with debt, through a new bond issue. Since the firm is using only debt to finance the project, the NPV of the project should be calculated using the cost of debt as the discount rate. Is this statement true, false, or uncertain? Explain.

24. Montreal Brokers, a small brokerage firm and PEItronics, a software development company, are both separately considering developing and marketing a new software package. Neither party is aware that the other is considering this project and it is not at any point going to become a joint venture. These new software packages will organize mutual fund data into a new type of database and then run a series of complicated algorithms on that new database. The beta of the brokerage firm is 0.9 and the beta of the software firm is 2.3. The risk-free rate is 2 percent and the market risk premium is 10 percent. The NPV of the project, using an 11 percent discount rate, is +$1 million. However, using a 19 percent discount rate, the project has a $500,000 NPV. Should either or both parties go ahead with the project?

25. Suppose a firm uses a constant WACC to calculate the NPV of all of its capital budgeting projects, rather than adjusting for the risk of the individual projects. What errors will the firm make in its capital budgeting decisions?

26. A firm has the following capital structure based on market values: equity 65 percent and debt 35 percent.

The current yield on government T-bills is 2 percent, the expected return on the market portfolio is 10 percent, and the firm's beta is approximated at 2.1. The firm's common shares are trading at $25, and the current dividend level of $3 per share is expected to grow at an annual rate of 4 percent. The firm can issue debt at a 3 percent premium over the current risk-free rate. The firm's tax rate is 40 percent, and the firm is considering a project to be funded out of internally generated funds that will not alter the firm's overall risk. This project requires an initial investment of $12 million and promises to generate net annual after-tax cash flows of $2 million perpetually. Should this project be undertaken?

27. A firm has the following balance sheet items:

Common stock: 300,000 shares at $8 each	$2,400,000
Retained earnings	1,200,000
Debt: 10% coupon, 15 years to maturity	1,800,000
Preferred shares: 6% dividend	1,200,000

The before-tax interest cost on new 15-year debt would be 7.5 percent, and each $1,000 bond would net the firm $975 after issuing costs. Common shares could be sold to net the firm $8 per share, a 12 percent discount from the current market price. Current shareholders expect a 15 percent return on their investment. Preferred shares could be sold at par to provide a yield of 5 percent, with after-tax issuing and underwriting expenses amounting to 5 percent of par value. The firm's tax rate is 45 percent, and internally generated funds are insufficient to finance anticipated new capital projects. Compute the firm's marginal cost of capital.

28. A company can issue new 20-year bonds at par that pay 5 percent annual coupons. The net proceeds to the firm (after taxes) will be 98 percent of par value. They estimate that new preferred shares providing a $2 annual dividend could be issued to investors at $25 per share to "net" the firm $22 per share issued (after taxes). The company has a beta of 1.10, and present market conditions are such that the risk-free rate is 1 percent, while the expected return on the market index is 10 percent. The firm's common shares trade for $30, and they estimate the net proceeds from a new common share issue would be $28.50 per share (after tax considerations). The firm's tax rate is 20 percent.
   a. Determine the firm's cost of long-term debt, preferred shares, and common equity financing (internal and external sources) under the conditions above.
   b. What is the firm's weighted average cost of capital, assuming that it has a "target" capital structure consisting of 30 percent debt, 10 percent preferred equity, and 60 percent common equity? Assume that it has $3 million in internal funds available for reinvestment and requires $3 million in total financing.
   c. Suppose everything remains as above, except that the company decides it needs $5 million in total financing. Calculate the firm's marginal cost of capital.

29. a. Kitchener Consumer Products plans to issue 25-year bonds with an 11.5 percent coupon rate, with coupons paid semi-annually and a par value of $1,000. After-tax flotation costs (issuing and underwriting costs) amount to 0.35 percent of par value. The firm's tax rate is 50 percent. Determine the firm's effective annual after-tax cost of debt.
   b. Kitchener Consumer Products plans to issue $50 par preferred shares (P/S) with annual dividends of $3 (i.e., a 6-percent dividend yield). It estimates flotation costs to be $1 per share after taxes. Find the firm's cost of P/S.
   c. Kitchener Consumer Products wishes to make a new issue of common shares (C/S). The current market price (P_o) is $25, D_1 = $1.75 (expected dividend at the end of this year), while g = 6 percent per year indefinitely. Flotation costs and discounts amount to $1 per share after taxes. Find the firm's cost of issuing new common shares

      i. using the dividend valuation approach.

      ii. using CAPM, given that the risk-free rate is 11 percent, the expected return on the market is 12 percent, and the beta for Kitchener Consumer Products is 0.95.

   d. Find the cost of internally generated common equity
      i. using the dividend model approach.
      ii. using the CAPM approach.

30. A firm wishes to raise funds in the following proportions: 20 percent debt, 20 percent P/S, and 60 percent CE (common equity). Assume the cost of internally generated funds is 15 percent. Annual after-tax cost of debt is 5.86%. Cost of preferred equity is 6.12%. It believes all of the CE component can be raised using internally generated funds.
   a. Find the WACC.
   b. Now suppose the firm wants to raise $10 million for investment purposes, and it has only $4 million of internally generated funds available. Determine the "break point" of the CE component. Break point is the maximum investment in which all targeted equity can be financed internally.
   c. Determine the marginal cost of capital (MCC) if the firm must raise funds beyond the break point. Assume the cost of new common equity issues is 20 percent.

Part 8

FINANCIAL POLICIES

Having discussed the range of financial securities available to the firm in the previous section, we now consider the critical aspects of financial policy: how the firm combines its outstanding securities to find an optimal financing policy and how it decides its dividend policy. These are two of the most contentious areas of corporate finance and lead to Franco Modigliani and Merton Miller, Nobel Prize winners in economics, who surprisingly showed that there is no optimal financial policy.

21 | Capital Structure Decisions

LEARNING OBJECTIVES

21.1 Explain how business and financial risk affect a firm's ROE and EPS, and identify the financial break-even points.

21.2 Identify the factors that influence capital structure.

21.3 Explain how Modigliani and Miller (M&M) "proved" their irrelevance conclusion that the use of debt does not change the value of the firm.

21.4 Explain how the introduction of corporate taxes affects M&M's irrelevance result.

21.5 Describe how financial distress and bankruptcy costs lead to the static trade-off theory of capital structure.

21.6 Explain how information asymmetries and agency problems lead firms to follow a pecking-order approach to financing.

21.7 Describe other factors that can affect a firm's capital structure in practice.

21.8 Explain how the introduction of personal taxes on investment income affects the corporate tax advantage to using debt.

TELUS is a major Canadian telecommunications company. In its 2008 annual report, TELUS states that its objectives when managing capital are "(i) to maintain a flexible capital structure that optimizes the cost of capital at acceptable risk; and (ii) to manage capital in a manner that balances the interests of equity and debt holders." How does it do this? TELUS manages the capital structure "in light of changes in economic conditions and the risk characteristics of the underlying assets. In order to maintain or adjust the capital structure, the company may adjust the amount of dividends paid to shareholders, purchase shares for cancellation pursuant to normal course issuer bids, issue new shares, issue new debt, issue new debt to replace existing debt with different characteristics, and/or increase or decrease the amount of sales of trade receivables to an arm's-length securitization trust." It was this quest for a lower cost of capital that led TELUS to consider its conversion to an income trust structure before the federal minister of finance withdrew that option in 2006. TELUS highlights the importance of an optimal capital structure as a financial objective for firms, since reducing the cost of capital enhances shareholder value as much as reducing operating costs. In this chapter, you will learn the basic techniques firms use to manage their capital structure.

Source: TELUS 2008 annual report available at http://about.telus.com/community/english/investor_relations/financial_documents.

CHAPTER 21 **PREVIEW**

In Chapter 20, we discussed how a firm can estimate the cost of each source of funds and average them to estimate its overall cost of capital, which we refer to as the weighted average cost of capital (WACC). In this chapter, we discuss how the firm may attempt to minimize its WACC through its financing choices. Just as a firm can increase its value by lowering its production costs, it can also increase its value by lowering its capital costs as measured by its WACC. This is much more difficult than lowering production costs, involving sophisticated concepts that have been hotly debated for almost 50 years and that, to some extent, remain unsettled.

In discussing these issues, you will learn how firms may use OPM—other people's money—and its impact on the common shareholder. You will also learn how to assess the limits placed on a firm's ability to issue debt as creditors and bond-rating agencies calculate the risk attached to corporate debt issues. You will then learn how this qualitative assessment conflicts with the celebrated Modigliani and Miller (M&M) proposition that, given some simplifying assumptions, the capital structure decision does not affect firm value.

The chapter finishes by showing how issuing debt may create value when we relax the two critical assumptions of M&M: there are no taxes and there are no bankruptcy or financial distress costs. You will learn that there are tax advantages to issuing debt and, therefore, the firm could do so up to the point where the associated risks of financial distress and bankruptcy outweigh these gains. The result is the static trade-off model, which indicates the general determinants of a firm's target or optimal debt ratio. Firms may then depart from this target by using a pecking order, issuing equity only when they are forced to do so or when the markets are particularly receptive.

21.1 FINANCIAL LEVERAGE

Risk and Leverage

Learning Objective 21.1
Explain how business and financial risk affect a firm's ROE and EPS, and identify the financial break-even points.

invested capital (IC) a firm's capital structure, consisting of shareholders' equity and short- and long-term debt

We begin by returning to the example we used in Chapter 20, where the firm had a capital structure of $1,700, composed of $1,000 of shareholders' equity and $700 of short- and long-term debt. This capital structure represented the firm's **invested capital (IC)**. We used this example to illustrate a discussion of the cost of capital, but we also worked out the required income statement, which is shown in Table 21-1.

TABLE 21-1 Example Income Statement

Sales	$1,000
Variable costs	300
Fixed costs	258
EBIT	442
Interest	42
Taxable income	400
Tax (25%)	100
Net income	300

return on invested capital (ROI) the return on all the capital provided by investors; EBIT minus taxes, divided by invested capital

return on equity (ROE) the return earned by equity holders on their investment in the company; net income divided by shareholders' equity

Based on these data, we indicated that the firm's **return on invested capital (ROI)** equalled its EBIT-minus-taxes figure of $331.50, where we ignore the interest charge, divided by the invested capital of $1,700, or 19.5 percent. Its **return on equity (ROE)** equalled its net income of $300 divided by shareholders' equity of $1,000, or 30 percent. The manner in which this ROE varies with changes in ROI is due to the firm's **financial leverage**.

financial leverage the effect of using debt as a source of capital

To understand how financial leverage works, consider the equation for ROE:

$$ROE = \frac{(EBIT - R_D B)(1 - T)}{SE} \qquad [21\text{-}1]$$

This simply says we work down the income statement from EBIT. First we subtract the interest expense, which is the interest cost of the firm's debt (R_D) times the book value of the firm's debt. As before, we use R to indicate actual costs, and now, since we are looking at book values, we use B to represent the book value of the firm's debt (bonds or B).[1] We then pay taxes, so $(1 - T)$ [2] flows through to the common shareholders, where we represent the book value of equity using SE for shareholders' equity.

We now use the definition of ROI from Chapter 20, which is shown in Equation 21-2.

$$ROI = \frac{EBIT(1 - T)}{SE + B} \qquad [21\text{-}2]$$

If we re-express Equation 21-2 in terms of EBIT $(1 - T)$ and substitute into Equation 21-1, we get Equation 21-3, the financial leverage equation.

$$ROE = ROI + (ROI - R_D(1 - T))\frac{B}{SE} \qquad [21\text{-}3]$$

The importance of the financial leverage equation is that ROI measures the return the firm earns from its operations and does not explicitly consider how the firm is financed, because it uses EBIT minus taxes in the numerator and the *total* invested capital in the denominator. This is why we think of the firm's ROI as a reflection of its **business risk**, which was discussed in Chapter 20, while the ROE reflects business risk as well as **financial risk**. The financial leverage equation shows how these two risk factors in combination affect the ROE—that is, they show how much of the risk is due to the firm's operations and how much is due to the way the firm is financed.

business risk the variability of a firm's operating income (EBIT) caused by its operations

financial risk the variability of a firm's net income caused by the use of financial leverage

Consider again our example, in which we found that ROI = 19.5 percent. In this case, the interest cost was 6 percent, which is 4.5 percent after tax (i.e., $6 \times (1 - 0.25)$), and the book debt-equity (D/E) ratio was $700 \div 1,000$ or 0.7. Substituting these numbers into Equation 21-3, we get:

$$ROE = 19.5 + (19.5 - 4.5) \times 0.7 = 30\%$$

This is exactly what we calculated directly from the firm's net income and the shareholders' equity (i.e., $300 \div 1,000$). If we get the same answer, you might ask why we went to the trouble of calculating the ROE through this roundabout method. The answer is that doing so allows us to examine the impact of how the firm is financed.

Remember that each dollar invested in the firm earns the same ROI—that is, for investment purposes, a dollar is a dollar. There is no such thing as an equity dollar or a debt dollar. It is the corporate financing or capital structure decision that allocates the ROI to different claimants and causes differences in the returns to equity and debt holders. In our example, the debt holders want a fixed 6 percent return; because this cost is tax deductible, it costs the

---

[1] Notice the difference from Chapter 20, where we used D to denote the market value of the firm's debt and S for the market value of its equity.

[2] In the chapter, "T" represents the corporate tax rate since we are dealing with only one tax rate. In Appendix 21-A where we also have personal tax rates, we will subscript it "c" to avoid confusion.

firm's shareholders only 4.5 percent after taxes. So each dollar borrowed from the debt holders earns the firm an ROI of 19.5 percent at a cost of 4.5 percent, and the spread of 15 percent drops through to the common shareholders. The only question is how many dollars of debt are carried by each dollar of equity, and this is answered by the debt-equity ratio of 0.7.

What is happening is that each dollar of equity earns 19.5 percent directly, but in addition, each dollar of equity also supports $0.70 of debt, which earns the spread of 15 percent, which also goes to the common shareholders. So, indirectly, the shareholders earn another 10.5 percent, which is the spread of 15 percent times 0.7. The ROE of 30 percent is the direct return from investing at the ROI of 19.5 percent, plus the indirect return of 10.5 percent by "trading on the equity" and borrowing money at an after-tax cost of 4.5 percent while investing it at 19.5 percent. Previously, we used the term "OPM" to refer to the option pricing model. However, historically, OPM referred to this process of using "other people's money," or financial leverage.

In our example, financial leverage is extremely favourable for the firm because it adds another 10.5 percent to the common shareholders' ROE. However, remember that the cost of the debt is a fixed contractual commitment of 6 percent before tax, whereas the ROI reflects the business risk of the firm and can vary. If we rearrange Equation 21-3 to group the terms involving the ROI, we get:

[21-4]

$$ROE = ROI\left(1 + \frac{B}{SE}\right) - R_D(1 - T)\frac{B}{SE}$$

We express the financial leverage equation in this way to show that the second term in Equation 21-4 is fixed, whereas the first term depends on the firm's uncertain ROI. This means we can graph the ROE against the firm's ROI as a straight line. This is what we do in Figure 21-1, with ROE plotted along the y-axis, and ROI plotted along the x-axis.

Figure 21-1 maps out the ROE that results from different levels of ROI for two financing strategies. The first strategy, labelled ROI, is to simply finance using 100 percent equity and not use any debt. In this case, the financial leverage equation suggests that ROI = ROE. The second strategy is the one employed by our example firm, where the firm's debt-equity ratio is 70 percent, which we will refer to as the 70-percent strategy in our further discussion.

The Rules of Financial Leverage

To understand Figure 21-1, you must work through several important points. Since the graph is a straight line, there are two break-even points. The first is where each financial strategy cuts the horizontal axis. For the 100 percent equity financing strategy, which we label "ROI," this point occurs where the ROI and ROE are zero, because if the firm's ROI is zero, so too is its ROE. However, in the case of the 70 percent strategy, which we label as ROE, when the ROI is zero, the ROE is –3.15 percent. This 3.15 percent is the product of the 0.7 debt-equity ratio multiplied by the 4.5 percent after-tax debt cost. The reason for this is that even if the ROI is zero, the firm still has to pay the debt holders their 6 percent interest rate, so with a 70 percent debt-equity ratio, each dollar of equity loses 4.2 percent. Assuming that the firm can use this loss to recapture previous income taxes paid, the after-tax cost is 3.15 percent.[3] If the firm cannot go back and reclaim previous taxes paid, the loss will be 4.2 percent. These break-even points are often called the **financial break-even points**.

The second break-even point is where the two financing strategies give the same ROE. This point is also often called the **indifference point**, because at this point the ROE is the same re-

financial break-even points points at which a firm's ROE is zero

indifference point point at which two financing strategies produce the same ROE

---

[3] Remember from our discussion of corporate income tax in Chapter 3 that the firm can carry back losses from the current year to recapture previous income taxes paid. If it has not paid taxes in the past few years, it can carry this loss forward and hope to offset future profits.

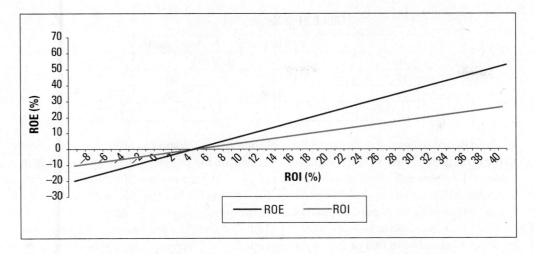

FIGURE 21-1 *Financial Leverage*

gardless of how the firm is financed. We can calculate this point by setting the two ROEs to be the same using Equation 21-3. For the 100 percent equity strategy, this point is where the ROI equals the after-tax debt cost of 4.5 percent, since at this point the ROE must equal 4.5 percent regardless of how the firm finances its operations.[4]

We can see from this analysis that with a 70 percent debt-equity ratio, the firm has to earn an ROI of 3.15 percent to break even so that it will have a zero ROE. At any ROI greater than 4.5 percent, it will have a higher ROE with the 70 percent strategy than with 100 percent equity financing. Given that the firm's ROI is 19.5 percent, the use of debt financing increases the firm's ROE from 19.5 percent to 30 percent and is very favourable. In this case, using other people's money generated extra profits to the firm's shareholders.

This result shows that using OPM tends to increase the ROE because the firm only has to earn more than the after-tax cost of debt. This should be easy for any firm! Remember from our discussion of the cost of capital that the firm should only make investments where it expects to earn more than its WACC, which is the weighted average of this after-tax debt cost and the cost of equity. Given that equity is almost always the most expensive form of capital, it follows that the WACC *is always* higher than the after-tax cost of debt. So the first "rule" of financial leverage is: ***for value-maximizing firms, the use of debt increases the expected ROE, so shareholders expect to be better off by using debt financing, rather than equity financing***. In this situation, the firm expects to be to the right of the indifference point; the farther to the right the firm expects to be, the greater the value of using debt financing.

This is an important result, but it can also be misleading because it implies that the firm should always finance with debt, as the WACC is always higher than the after-tax cost of debt. We must consider what we are ignoring, since we have a result that says we must always make the same decision, when, in practice, firms make multiple decisions. This leads us to consider the second principle of finance, which is the **risk value of money**.

Remember that the behaviour of the ROI reflects the business risk of the firm. The expected ROI can be represented by a point estimate, such as 19.5 percent in our example. However, we have to take into account the business risk of the firm, which is the variability in the ROI. Suppose, for example, the forecast ROI was expected to be between 10 and 30 percent. Would this affect the judgment that debt financing increases the ROE? We can examine this by looking at the ROE for the two strategies on the graph in Figure 21-1 at the 10 percent and 30 percent ROI levels. These values are calculated in Table 21-2.

risk value of money the principle that future cash flows (money) involving different amounts of risk have different present values

---

[4] Generally, the indifference point is close to the after-tax cost of debt. It will differ depending on the firm's historical financing rates (i.e., the costs of debt).

TABLE 21-2 Varying ROI Values

	70% D/E Ratio	100% Equity
ROI (%)	**ROE (%)**	
10	13.85	10
30	47.85	30
Range	34	20

At an ROI of 10 percent or 30 percent, the 100 percent equity strategy produces ROEs equal to the ROIs, generating a range of 20 percent. In contrast, the 70 percent strategy leads to ROE values of 13.85 percent and 47.85 percent, for a range of 34 percent. Thus, the range or variability of the ROE increases with debt financing. This reflects the fact that the financial leverage line is steeper with the 70 percent strategy, since the debt-equity ratio is higher.

Would this increase in risk affect the firm's shareholders? In this example, the answer is no, since the minimum ROI of 10 percent exceeds the indifference point of 4.50 percent. As a result, at all forecast levels of ROI, the firm's ROE is higher with the use of debt financing. However, the important point is that the variability of the ROE increases as the firm finances with more debt. This is because there are fixed financial charges—that is, the fixed interest costs—that the firm has to pay, which are independent of the firm's ROI. If we increase the range of ROI possibilities from –10 to 40 percent, we get the ROE values shown in Table 21-3.

TABLE 21-3 Varying ROI Values

	70% D/E Ratio	100% Equity
ROI (%)	**ROE (%)**	
–10	–20.15	–10
40	64.85	40
Range	85	50

With this wider range in ROI values, the ROE for the 70 percent strategy is –20.15 percent on the low end, which is much lower than the ROE for the strategy with no debt. As before, the range of ROE values is much higher for the leveraged position.

This leads to the second rule of financial leverage: ***financing with debt increases the variability of the firm's ROE, which usually increases the risk to the common shareholders.***

As the above examples illustrate, the range of ROE values always increases with debt financing, but, depending on the numbers, this does not necessarily mean that risk increases. Sometimes, as in the first example, the firm is better off at all ROI levels with debt financing regardless of the greater variability in the ROE. In this case, it simply says that the firm is not using enough debt, as it could raise more debt and unambiguously increase the ROE to the common shareholders. This means that variability does not always mean risk.[5]

Since the range of ROE values increases with debt financing, the firm has to find the cash to cover the fixed interest payments. In the worst-case scenario above, where the firm has an ROI of –10 percent, it still has to cover the 4.5 percent after-tax and 6 percent before-tax interest payments. If the firm's underlying health remains sound, it will be able to borrow from the bank (as long as the bank continues to lend to the firm) or use up some of its cash reserves to make these payments. However, sometimes a series of poor operating results can cause serious financial problems for a highly indebted firm. This situation can compound, as the firm's owners might change their operating procedures if there is a significant risk of financial distress or bankruptcy. We will discuss such a situation in more detail later in the chapter, but at this point we simply note the third rule of financial leverage: ***financing with debt increases the likelihood of the firm running into financial distress and possibly even bankruptcy.*** Figure 21-2 illustrates this proposition.

---

[5] In more advanced finance courses, you will learn that this is a case of stochastic dominance.

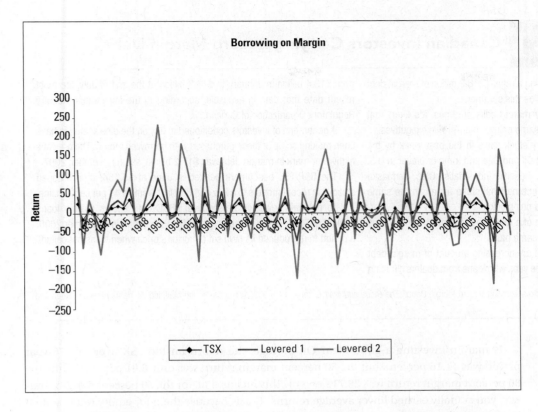

Borrowing on Margin

FIGURE 21-2 *Investing Using Leverage*

Figure 21-2 graphs the annual returns from investing in the S&P/TSX Composite Index using three different financing strategies. The first (denoted TSX) is simply the annual return generated from investing in the S&P/TSX Composite Index. The second (denoted Levered 1) assumes that investors borrow 50 percent on margin[6] —that is, they put up $1 for every $2 borrowed. The third (Levered 2) assumes they borrow 80 percent on margin, putting up $1 for every $4 borrowed. For these two leverage strategies, we assume the investors pay the treasury bill rate plus 2 percent per year. For convenience, we will ignore taxes. The graphs are generated simply by plugging the actual TSX returns and the actual treasury bill yields each year since 1936 into Equation 21-4.

You should notice two things about the graph. The first is the increased variability in the return from the two leverage strategies, which is predicted by the second rule of financial leverage. As before, we can see this by simply looking at the range of the outcomes, which always increases with leverage. The second is that on some occasions the return from the highly leveraged strategy drops below –100 percent. For example, in 2008 the S&P/TSX Composite Index dropped over 33 percent, but the return for investors using the 50 percent debt financing strategy was –76 percent; for the 80 percent leverage strategy it was –185 percent. These "leveraged" investors would have been pretty much wiped out during that brutal bear market. In fact, long before that happened, they would have received a margin call from their brokers, insisting they put up more capital. If they didn't, they would have been sold out before losing everything. This is because margin debt is essentially a demand loan, callable at the whim of the bank. However, the graph illustrates the fact that margin investors in 2008 lost a lot of money, as they do on a regular basis when the stock market crashes. *Finance in the News 21-1* indicates that margin debt was at an all-time record high prior to the stock market crash and that this is exactly what happened to some very wealthy and astute investors.

---

[6] Margin loans are debt provided by a broker to finance the purchase of securities. The amount of margin or debt that the broker will provide varies with the price of the security and its risk; 80 percent is an extreme case to illustrate the impact of leverage. In practice, this is so risky you cannot borrow this amount.

finance IN THE NEWS 21-1   Canadian Investors Carrying Record Margin Debt

CANADIAN INVESTORS WERE carrying a record $16.3 billion of margin debt when the stock market began to slide this summer.

As the first evidence of nasty margin calls emerges, it's likely that individual investors are facing the same pain as high-profile executives.

Margin calls forced involuntary stock sales in the past week by the CEOs of Calgary-based Connacher Oil and Gas and a major player in U.S. natural gas, Chesapeake Energy. Russian industrialist Oleg Deripaska liquidated his $1.5-billion Magna International stake for much the same reason: banks called loans made to buy stocks.

Unless Tuesday's rally is a sign of a real turn in the market, numerous individual investors are feeling the same pain.

Canadian investors shouldered an increasing amount of margin debt through the first seven months of the year, with loans from dealers climbing from $13.4 billion in January to $16.3 billion at the end of July, the most recent date that data is available, according to the Investment Industry Regulatory Organization of Canada.

A generation of investors conditioned to buy on the dips seems to have been making some of those purchases with borrowed money. The previous highwater mark in margin debt was $15.2 billion, set in November, 2007.

The S&P/TSE benchmark peaked in June at 15,154, then dropped steadily in recent months to a low of 8,850 last week, a 41 per cent decline.

To put debt levels in perspective, IIROC data shows margin loans peaked at $11.3 billion at the height of the tech boom, in November 2000, a period that produced its own set of horror stories when loans got called.

Source: Willis, Andrew, "Canadian Investors Carrying Record Margin Debt." *The Globe and Mail*, October 14, 2008. ©The Globe and Mail, Inc. All rights reserved. Reprinted by permission.

Is margin investing a good idea? On average, the return on the TSX over this 76-year period was 11.16 percent, but the 50 percent margin return was only 8.81 percent, while the 80 percent margin return was 28.71 percent. This means that, for the 50 percent margin strategy, you actually earned lower average returns. This is because the poor equity returns often occurred in years when treasury bill yields were high, and when we add an extra 2 percent, this really hurts the levered investment strategy.[7] For the 80 percent margin strategy, on average, financial leverage is worthwhile. However, statisticians joke that you can drown in a river with an average depth of one metre,[8] and it is the same with stock market returns: on average you make money using financial leverage, but you can also get financially killed in the process.

Figure 21-2 shows that the effects of financial leverage are not confined to corporations. In fact, they apply to any economic entity, whether a firm, an individual, or a government. Financial leverage tends to increase returns, but it also increases the risk of variability and financial distress. Consequently, the amount of debt a firm or individual can carry very much depends on the underlying business risk of the asset being financed. As we saw in Figure 21-2, financing an investment in the stock market with a 50 or 80 percent debt strategy is very risky. In contrast, Canadians are happy to finance their house purchase with 80 percent debt. Indeed, with high-ratio mortgages, the amount of debt financing is frequently as high as 95 percent. In this case, the asset being financed is perceived to be lower risk than the stock market, so people are comfortable financing it with more debt. However, even here there have been times when 80 percent mortgage financing has been risky.[9]

Indifference Analysis

Before leaving our discussion of financial leverage, we will examine one more set of financial leverage charts, which relate to the firm's earnings per share (EPS). We noted in Chapter 20 that the example firm has 1,000 shares outstanding, so the EPS in relation to the firm's EBIT can be defined using Equation 21-5.

---

[7] Without the extra 2 percent, the 50 percent margin strategy gives an average return of 12.81 percent, but only the government can borrow at this rate.

[8] This is because rivers don't have the same depth throughout their run or at all times during the year.

[9] Below 80 percent financing, a mortgage is a prime mortgage; above 80 percent it is sub-prime. When U.S. house prices dropped in some areas by over 40 percent from 2007 to 2009, even prime mortgages became risky, which was the basic cause of the U.S. financial crisis.

$$EPS = \frac{(EBIT - R_D B)(1 - T)}{\#} \qquad [21\text{-}5]$$

This is identical to the ROE-ROI relationship, except that instead of the book value of equity in the denominator, we now have the number of shares (#). As a result, we can rearrange the equation and show how EPS varies with the EBIT.

$$EPS = \frac{-R_D B(1 - T)}{\#} + \frac{EBIT(1 - T)}{\#} \qquad [21\text{-}6]$$

Note that this is also a simple linear relationship; we plot the impact of EBIT (horizontal line) on EPS (vertical line) in Figure 21-3. If the firm has no debt, the first term is zero and the EPS is simply the EBIT minus taxes divided by the number of shares, which is the EPS for a firm financed 100 percent by equity, denoted as EPS(0%). If the firm finances with debt, it incurs the after-tax fixed-interest expense per share and then has fewer shares outstanding. The result is that the EPS-EBIT line pivots and gets steeper as more debt is used—denoted as EPS(70%). In this case, the same increase in the EBIT causes a bigger impact on the EPS. This is illustrated in Figure 21-3, where the firm is assumed to have 1,280 shares outstanding in the no-debt situation.

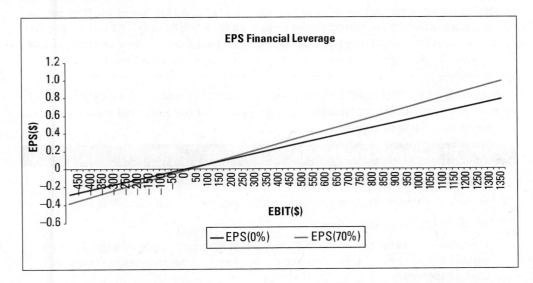

FIGURE 21-3 EPS-EBIT Charts

Note that, as in the ROE-ROI chart, the 0 percent D/E line has a lower intercept (because there are no after-tax fixed-interest payments to make) and is not as steep as the other line. In the EPS-EBIT chart, the 70 percent debt-equity line (EPS70%) is steeper since there are fewer shares outstanding, whereas in the ROE-ROI chart it was steeper because of the larger debt-equity ratio. Either way, the result is the same: as the firm finances with more debt, its EPS and ROE are more sensitive to its operating results—that is, to its EBIT and ROI. All firms look at the impact of financing on their ROE and EPS, and the charts they create for this analysis are often called **profit planning charts**.

Like the ROE indifference point, discussed in connection with Figure 21-1, the **EPS indifference point** is the point in Figure 21-3 where the two lines intersect. We can solve for this indifference point in terms of EBIT by setting the EPS, as expressed in Equation 21-5, equal for two alternative financing plans under consideration. Then we merely solve for the EBIT level at which the two financing alternatives generate the same EPS, which we denote as EBIT*. This will give the firm some useful direction when it comes to choose between financing alternatives, because firms generally want to maximize their bottom line, as measured by EPS, and they usually have an estimate of their expected EBIT. Example 21-1 illustrates this process.

profit planning charts charts showing ROE-ROI and EPS-EBIT that allow firms to analyze the impact of financing on their profits

EPS indifference point the EBIT level at which two financing alternatives generate the same EPS

EXAMPLE 21-1   EPS Indifference Analysis

Calculate the EPS indifference point, EBIT*, for the firm discussed above, assuming it maintains its present 70 percent D/E ratio, and then assuming it uses all equity financing. Its pre-tax cost of debt is 6 percent under the present structure, and there are 1,000 common shares outstanding. Further, assume that under the all-equity plan, the firm has 1,280 shares outstanding.[10] Which plan is preferable at the current level of sales and EBIT?

Solution

$$EPS(70\%) = \frac{(EBIT - 0.06 \times 700)(1 - 0.25)}{1,000} = \frac{0.75EBIT - 31.5}{1,000}$$

$$EPS(0\%) = \frac{0.75 \times EBIT}{1,280}$$

Setting the two EPS equations together and solving for EBIT* will give us the indifference EBIT, as shown below:

So, $750EBIT^* = 960EBIT^* - 40,320$

And $210EBIT^* = 40,320$

So $EBIT^* = \$192$

Notice that this is the point where the two lines intersect in Figure 21-3. Beyond this EBIT level, the 70 percent debt-equity option is preferred because it produces a higher EPS; below this EBIT level, the all-equity option is preferred. Therefore, at the current EBIT level of $442, which is well above $192, the more leveraged financing option (i.e., the 70 percent debt-equity option) gives a significantly higher EPS and generally would be preferred.

Conducting EPS-EBIT indifference analysis is a useful beginning point for firms trying to evaluate potential financing plans. We will discuss some of the additional issues, which are considerable, in the sections below.

CONCEPT REVIEW QUESTIONS

1. Define business risk and financial risk.
2. How does financial leverage affect the relationship between ROI and ROE?
3. What are the three rules of leverage?
4. Describe how we determine the ROE and EPS indifference points for a firm based on various financing alternatives, and explain why this analysis provides the firm with useful information.

21.2 DETERMINING CAPITAL STRUCTURE

Learning Objective 21.2
Identify the factors that influence capital structure.

In 1990, the Conference Board surveyed 119 U.S. companies to determine how they set their capital structures. The results of the survey are presented in Table 21-4.

TABLE 21-4 Determinants of Capital Structure

1. Analysis of cash flows	23.0%
2. Consultations	18.3%
3. Risk considerations	16.5%
4. Impact on profits	14.0%
5. Industry comparisons	12.0%
6. Other	3.4%

Source: Conference Board, 1990.

[10] We "guesstimate" this figure by assuming the firm can retire the $700 worth of debt by issuing 280 shares at $2.50 (i.e., $700 ÷ $2.50 = 280), using the market share price for this firm that was provided in Chapter 20.

We will present some more recent survey results later in the chapter, but the Conference Board survey is useful because it reflects a professional focus. For example, it is clear that firms will consult with their advisors (#2) and look at other firms in their industry (#5) to check on what is reasonable. However, neither of these are primary methods of deciding on capital structure because they do not indicate how their advisors or other firms determine their capital structure. The three primary determinants are impact on profits (#4), risk (#3), and analysis of cash flows (#1). The profit planning charts discussed in the previous section are the basic way to assess the impact on profits. By varying EBIT and ROI, they can also be used to assess the impact of risk. What is left to discuss is cash flow.

However, let's first consider some standard, commonly used financial ratios. We can think of these as stock or flow ratios. *Stock* ratios are measures like the debt-equity and debt ratios. They measure the stock of outstanding debt relative to the total capital structure of the firm or the amount of equity. In contrast, *flow* variables measure the flow of income over a period, such as EBIT, and the flow of payments the firm is required to make, such as interest. Stock ratios are clearly useful: bond-rating agencies and others use them to do a quick check on the firm's financing, and they are also often used to limit the amount of debt the firm can raise through its trust indenture, as we discussed in Chapter 18. However, we must consider just how useful these ratios really are.

In Chapter 18, we discussed some of the features of different types of debt. For example, we noted that bankers' acceptances had a maturity of 30 days, whereas long-term bond issues typically had a life of 20 or 30 years. It obviously matters a great deal to a firm if its debt has a 30-day versus a 30-year maturity. For one thing, if the firm has to "roll over" its debt every 30 days, it must be confident that it has the cash to pay off this debt if the lenders refuse to renew it. Similarly, if the debt has sinking fund payments, where the firm is contractually obliged to pay off a certain amount of debt each year, this increases the firm's commitments to the debt holders and requires that it have the cash ready to fulfill this commitment. In both cases, it is not the stock of debt outstanding that matters so much as the maturity of the debt. That is why this information must be provided in the notes to the firm's financial statements. Further, it suggests that the stock ratios are not completely adequate, since they ignore some of the cash flow commitments attached to debt.

In the same way, consider the great emphasis we placed on the interest coverage ratio in Chapter 18, defined as EBIT divided by interest expense. This is a flow variable, since it is the ratio of the flow of EBIT to the flow of interest payments. Remember that there is often a clause in the trust indenture that states the firm cannot issue any more debt unless it has an interest coverage ratio of 2.0 or more. However, this also does not include all of the firm's commitments. The most basic limitation is that interest payments are made from cash and not from accounting earnings. Further, similar to the problems with the stock ratios, the interest coverage ratio does not show the impact of any sinking fund payments or other commitments, such as dividends to the preferred shareholders.

fixed burden coverage ratio an expanded interest coverage ratio that looks at a broader measure of both income and the expenditures associated with debt; EBITDA divided by a firm's fixed financing payment requirements

We can get around some of these problems by modifying the interest coverage ratio to include these other commitments. One way is to estimate the **fixed burden coverage ratio**, which is defined in Equation 21-7.

$$Fixed\ burden\ coverage = \frac{EBITDA}{I + (Pref.\ Div. + SF)/(1-T)} \qquad [21\text{-}7]$$

In the numerator, instead of EBIT, we have EBITDA, which is EBIT before subtracting the non-cash deductions for depreciation and amortization. As such, it is a "better" estimate of the firm's cash flow.[11] In the denominator, along with interest, we have added the firm's

---

[11] Some analysts simply add depreciation to net income.

commitment to make sinking fund payments (SF) on its debt and its preferred share dividends (Pref. Div.). Since both dividends and sinking fund payments are paid out of after-tax income, we "gross them up" by dividing by one minus the corporate tax rate $(1 - T)$ to determine their pre-tax equivalent, which is then comparable to the interest payments. We ignore the common share dividends since these can be cut more easily than the dividends to the preferred shareholders.

Another way to modify the flow and stock variables is to combine them. One key ratio that does this is the **cash flow-to-debt ratio (CFTD)**, which directly measures the cash flow available over a period to cover the firm's stock of outstanding debt. This ratio may be calculated using Equation 21-8.

cash flow-to-debt ratio (CFTD)
a direct measure of the cash flow available over a period to cover a firm's stock of outstanding debt

[21-8]
$$CFTD = \frac{EBITDA}{Debt}$$

Again, as with many ratios, cash flow is measured either as net income plus non-cash charges like depreciation, or simply as EBITDA.

These last two ratios are very important. In Chapter 19, we discussed Tim Hortons' financing. The company had to meet certain covenant provisions for its term loan and its revolver, and the two most important ones were a fixed burden coverage ratio, similar to Equation 21-7, and a debt-to-cash flow ratio, which is the inverse of Equation 21-8. In both cases, the actual ratios and the method of calculating them were spelled out in some detail so Tim Hortons could not make accounting changes to alter the values.

As the financial ratios depart more and more from standard definitions, they become more analyst specific, but the general point is simply that there are serious drawbacks to using either stock or flow variables based on the firm's financial statements to measure how much debt a firm can handle. The best procedure is for the firm to generate its own forecast of expected cash flows over a short- to medium-term horizon, and then calculate internally what level of fixed commitments the firm can handle without exposing it to serious harm. This "scenario-based" approach to determining capital structure was pioneered by Gordon Donaldson.[12] However, the key question is whether lenders will lend to the firm based on its internal scenario-based assessment of how much debt it can carry. This requires that sensitive information be divulged to lenders and that the lenders believe the data. Consequently, there is still heavy reliance on standard ratios.

Financial Ratios and Credit Ratings

Moody's periodically provides data on the most commonly used credit ratios and how they correlate to Moody's credit ratings. (See the data provided in Table 21-5.) Moody's defines these ratios in its own way, but they broadly conform to the ratios described above. The simple average of investment-grade (IG) companies—firms with at least a BBB bond rating—has higher coverage, less debt (leverage), a larger cash flow-to-debt ratio, less liquidity (cash plus marketable securities as a percentage of total assets), higher profit margins, and a higher return on assets (ROA) than the simple average of firms with non-investment-grade (non-IG) bond ratings. IG firms also tend to have more stable sales and are growing faster than non-IG firms with greater capital expenditures to depreciation (asset growth).

---

[12] Donaldson, Gordon, "New Framework for Corporate Debt Policy." *Harvard Business Review* (September/October 1978), pp. 149–64.

TABLE 21-5 Moody's Average Credit Ratios

	IG	Non-IG
Coverage	11.4	1.7
Leverage (%)	36.1	76.0
Cash flow-to-debt (%)	63.0	11.8
Profit margin (%)	16.9	7.1
Return on assets (%)	15.1	6.4
Sales stability	15.1	17.2
Asset growth	1.3	1.0
Altman Z score*	2.17	1.62

*From Mocdy's Investor Services, "The Distribution of Common Financial Ratios by Rating and Industry for North American Non-Financial Corporations," December 2004.

Source: Calculated using *Moody's Financial Metrics: Key Ratios by Rating and Industry for North American Non-Financial Corporations*, 2008. January 2009.

All of these ratios make sense. Firms with better credit ratings tend to be larger and more profitable, generate more cash, and have more stable sales, meaning lower business risk. They also tend to have better investment opportunities so are reinvesting at a higher rate than firms with inferior credit ratings. Moody's looks at other ratios in addition to these and also adjusts these ratios across industries to reflect differences in business risk. As a result, the final credit rating is based on both quantitative as well as qualitative assessments.

The final value in Moody's set of ratios is the Altman Z score. This is a weighted average of several key ratios that Professor Ed Altman found were useful for predicting a firm's probability of bankruptcy.[13] Equation 21-9 is his prediction equation.

$$Z = 1.2X_1 + 1.4X_2 + 3.3X_3 + 0.6X_4 + 0.999X_5 \qquad\qquad [21\text{-}9]$$

Where

X_1 = working capital divided by total assets

X_2 = retained earnings divided by total assets

X_3 = EBIT divided by total assets

X_4 = market value of total equity divided by non-equity book liabilities

X_5 = sales divided by total assets

Note that most of the variables are scaled by total assets to standardize them, so we will refer to them by the numerator. However, they all have simple intuitive meanings.

High working capital generally means more receivables and inventory, which are usually more liquid than fixed assets. The existence of retained earnings generally means that the firm has earned money in the past, and therefore it proxies for age and past profitability, among other things. EBIT is a measure of operating profitability. The market value of equity divided by non-equity book liabilities is another way to calculate a market-valued debt ratio. Finally, sales divided by assets is the turnover ratio, so it measures how productively the firm is using its assets.

---

[13] Altman, E., "Financial Ratios, Discriminant Analysis and the Prediction of Corporate Bankruptcy." *Journal of Finance* 23, no. 4 (September 1968), pp. 589–609.

The Altman Z score was the first of many such measures that attempt to summarize a large number of financial ratios into a simple score. In the case of the Z score, the larger the better. Altman estimated it using a sample of 66 U.S. manufacturing firms, equally divided between firms that did and did not go bankrupt. His bankrupt firms had an average Z score of about 1.5. What is interesting is that even though Altman estimated this function more than 40 years ago, Moody's (and many other debt analysis reports) still report Altman's Z score, and it is still working in the sense that the IG firms have higher Z scores than the non-IG firms.

In terms of capital structure, we know that firms pay a lot of attention to the impact that issuing debt will have on their future profit levels and risk, so assessing their underlying business risk is very important. As firms issue more debt, most of their key ratios covered by Moody's deteriorate. As a result, their credit rating weakens, they pay higher interest charges, and they have to submit to more trust indenture provisions to lessen the risk involved. Consequently, it is vital that we understand how issuing debt affects the firm's credit rating.

However, a key question is not raised by the results of the Conference Board survey: does issuing debt increase or decrease the firm's market value? So far, our discussion has simply addressed the question of whether a firm can issue debt or not, and on what terms. It involves important factors like taxes and financial flexibility, but it does not answer the question of whether the firm should issue debt. This question is addressed in one of the most famous papers in finance, which is discussed in the next section. Surprisingly, the authors initially answered the question by saying that capital structure is irrelevant!

CONCEPT REVIEW QUESTIONS

1. What are the main determinants of capital structure?

2. Explain how ratios may be used to assess a company's ability to assume more debt.

3. What is Altman's Z score and what does it measure?

21.3 THE MODIGLIANI AND MILLER (M&M) IRRELEVANCE THEOREM

M&M and Firm Value

Learning Objective 21.3
Explain how Modigliani and Miller (M&M) "proved" their irrelevance conclusion that the use of debt does not change the value of the firm.

Franco Modigliani and **Merton Miller (M&M)** economists who devised a proposition stating that, under some simplifying assumptions, the capital structure decision does not affect firm value

In this section, we will discuss a theorem—a proposition based on a series of assumptions about how financial markets should work. It is, in fact, a very powerful theorem for which (in part) the authors, **Franco Modigliani** and **Merton Miller** (also known as M&M), won the Nobel Prize in economics.[14] Unfortunately, the "M&M results" are only as good as their assumptions, and most of them have been shown to reflect the "real" world poorly. However, their research pointed the way for many of the significant developments in corporate finance theory and practice over the past 50 years, as later researchers examined how M&M's assumptions affected their result.

The following are M&M's key assumptions:

• There exist two firms in the same "risk class" with different levels of debt.

• The earnings of both firms are perpetuities.

• Markets are perfect in the sense that there are no transaction costs or asymmetric information problems.

• There are no taxes.

• There is no risk of costly bankruptcy or associated financial distress.

---

[14] Modigliani, Franco, and Merton Miller, "The Cost of Capital, Corporation Finance and the Theory of Investment." *American Economic Review* 48, no. 3 (June 1958), pp. 261–97.

Of these five assumptions, two are modelling assumptions and three are assumptions about the real world. In 1958, relatively little was known about the pricing of risk. M&M finessed this by assuming two firms with the same business risk. We could get M&M's result now by using the capital asset pricing model (CAPM) or some other risk-adjustment model to adjust for risk, so this is a simple modelling assumption. Similarly, we have already seen that assuming perpetuities makes valuation easy, since we just divide the expected cash flows by the required rate of return. Again, we can get the M&M results if we assume some growth in the underlying earnings, but this introduces needless complexity. The critical assumptions are the last three: markets are perfect, with no transaction costs and perfect information availability; there are no taxes; and there is no costly bankruptcy or financial distress risk. Later in the chapter we will discuss what it means to relax these assumptions, but right now we will discuss the basic M&M model.

M&M proved their proposition by means of an "arbitrage argument." As we discussed, with respect to the option pricing model, arbitrage arguments are the strongest in finance since they rely on two assumptions: there is no such thing as "free money," and investors prefer more money to less. Let's think about what this means to two firms with the same business risk but different levels of debt. We assume the first firm, which we will refer to as the unlevered firm (U), has no debt; the second firm, the levered firm (L), does have debt because it uses financial leverage. If we buy some arbitrary percentage (α) of the unlevered firm, we simply get this percentage of the firm's earnings, which is paid out as a dividend. Since there is no interest paid by an unlevered firm, and since M&M assumed there were no taxes, the firm's EBIT is also its net income. Therefore, our share of the firm's earnings and dividends equals αEBIT, which we have assumed will be paid out as a perpetuity.

If we buy the same share of the equity of the levered firm, we have to subtract the interest payments, so we receive a smaller amount as a dividend. In this case, our share is $\alpha EBIT - K_D D$, where the interest cost is the market value of the debt multiplied by the required return on debt. The values for the "payoff" from buying the equity of either firm are identical except for the interest charges, since we assumed that the two firms were in the same risk class. In other words, it would be like buying shares in two very similar steel companies or two drug companies.

M&M then asked the following question: if the levered firm sold at a discount to the unlevered firm (i.e., if investors did not like the effects of financial leverage), what could an investor do? To answer this question, they drew up the M&M arbitrage table depicted in Table 21-6.

TABLE 21-6 M&M Arbitrage Table I

Portfolios (Actions)	Cost	Payoff
Portfolio A: Buy α of unlevered firm	αV_U	αEBIT
Portfolio B: Buy α of levered firm's equity	αS_L	$\alpha(\text{EBIT} - K_D D)$
Buy α of levered firm's debt	αD	$\alpha K_D D$
Total portfolio B	$\alpha(S_L + D)$	αEBIT

The first row, Portfolio A, is the cost of, and payoff from, investing in the unlevered firm. The next two rows are the cost of, and payoff from, buying the same proportion of the equity and debt of the levered firm, where the levered firm's equity is subscripted "L" for levered (αS_L). The final row is the cost of, and payoff from, this Portfolio B, which is composed of buying the same percentage of the levered firm's debt and equity. Note that what the levered firm pays as interest goes to the investors, because they have bought the levered firm's debt. Therefore, a portfolio of debt and equity in the levered firm ends up with the same amount of EBIT (i.e., αEBIT) as if we had invested in the unlevered firm. Notice that the share of the levered and unlevered firm that you buy makes no difference, as α can be any number.

This is a powerful result. If you don't like the negative effects of financial leverage (e.g., the increased variability of returns), you can remove them by effectively "unlevering" the levered firm's equity by buying some of the firm's debt. This is where the arbitrage comes in: if the payoff is exactly the same, these two sets of cash flows must sell for exactly the same value, so their cost must be the same. That is:

[21-10]
$$V_U = S_L + D = V_L$$

This equation says that the value of the levered firm (V_L) is the value of its debt plus the value of its equity ($S_L + D$), and this must equal the value of the unlevered firm (V_U). What this proof says is that, under M&M's assumptions, adding debt cannot destroy value, since the investor can undo the negative effects.[15]

If debt cannot destroy value, the next logical question is whether it can create value. Suppose the levered equity sells at a premium because of the favourable effects of financial leverage—what can the investor do then? M&M's answer to this was that an investor can create the effects of corporate leverage through the use of personal leverage. Remember that the effects of leverage are the same whether it is a firm, an individual, or a government borrowing money. In each case, it is simply the effect of using other people's money. So M&M came up with the arbitrage table shown in Table 21-7.

TABLE 21-7 M&M Arbitrage Table II

Portfolios (Actions)	Cost	Payoff
Portfolio C: Buy α of levered firm's equity	αS_L	$\alpha(EBIT - K_D D)$
Portfolio D: Buy α of unlevered firm	αV_U	$\alpha EBIT$
Borrow α of levered firm's debt	αD	$-\alpha K_D D$
Total portfolio D	$\alpha(V_U - D)$	$\alpha(EBIT - K_D D)$

The strategy for Portfolio C is to buy the levered firm's equity at a cost of αS_L, with a payoff of $\alpha(EBIT - K_D D)$. In Portfolio D, the individual replicates this payoff to see whether it can be bought more cheaply. First, the payoff from the unlevered firm at a cost of αV_U is $\alpha EBIT$. As before, the only difference is the absence of interest payments, and this is one thing everyone knows how to create: all you have to do is borrow money. So the individual borrows enough to pay the same interest payments of $-\alpha K_D D$ (the negative sign indicates that these are an outflow—i.e., a payment). This is where the perfect market assumption comes in, since M&M assume that the individual pays the same interest rate when borrowing against the unlevered firm's assets as the levered firm pays. In this case, the cost of generating these interest payments is the same as the cost of money borrowed by the levered firm (i.e., $-D$).

The cost to the portfolio that replicates the payoff from the levered firm's equity is therefore $V_U - D$, which has to equal the levered firm's equity value, S_L. Rearranging Equation 21-10, we get the same result as before: the levered firm's total value, equity plus debt, equals that of the unlevered firm. Therefore, the capital structure decision has no value. So now we have M&M's second proof. If you like the effects of financial leverage, you don't have to pay for them, because you can create the same effect through personal leverage. This is often referred to as M&M's **homemade leverage** result.

In proving this result, M&M made use of our recognition that the effects of financial leverage are the same whether the debt is issued by a company, an individual, or a government. In fact, M&M took this a step further: with their assumptions, the effects are not only the same but are identical! This means homemade leverage and corporate leverage are perfect substitutes.

homemade leverage creating the effect of a firm's financial leverage through the use of personal leverage

---

[15] This result underpins the income trust market, where the trust owns both the equity and the debt of the operating company. If you are both the creditor and the debtor, the amount of debt clearly does not matter.

M&M's two results suggest that you can undo the effects of financial leverage if you don't like them, and you can create them if you do like these effects. These results rely heavily on the assumption that capital markets are perfect. They assume that individuals can buy both the debt and the equity of the levered firm to undo the effects, and that they can borrow on margin to create homemade leverage. Further, they assume that the interest rate investors pay for the debt is the same as that paid by the firm. However, nowhere is the investor defined or described. It could be a large financial institution or a hedge fund facing the same type of transaction costs faced by the firm. For this reason, most of the focus of the academic literature has been on the key assumptions of no taxes, no costly bankruptcy or financial distress costs, and no asymmetric information or agency costs. Before considering these assumptions, we should first work through what the initial M&M irrelevancy result means for the cost of capital.

M&M and the Cost of Capital

The M&M results assume that the firm's earnings represent a perpetuity, so we can value the firm's equity as the present value of these earnings, as shown in Equation 21-11.

$$S_L = \frac{(EBIT - K_DD)}{K_e} \qquad [21\text{-}11]$$

In this case, the cost of equity capital is the earnings yield, as we discussed in Chapter 20. As a result, we can estimate the equity cost using Equation 21-12, which divides the perpetual earnings (dividends) by the market value of the common shares (S_L).

$$K_e = \frac{(EBIT - K_DD)}{S_L} \qquad [21\text{-}12]$$

Since M&M proved that the value of the firm is unchanged by leverage, we can define the unlevered value (V_U) by discounting the firm's expected EBIT by its unlevered equity cost (K_U), as shown in Equation 21-13.

$$V_U = \frac{EBIT}{K_U} = S_L + D = V_L \qquad [21\text{-}13]$$

EXAMPLE 21-2   M&M's First Model and Firm Value

a. An unlevered firm (U) has an EBIT of $2 million, which is expected to remain constant indefinitely. Its cost of capital is 10 percent. What is the market value of this firm?

b. An identical risk-levered firm (L) has $5 million in debt outstanding. What is the value of this firm, and what is the value of its equity?

Solution

a. $V_U = \dfrac{EBIT}{K_U} = \dfrac{2}{0.1} = \$20$ million

b. $V_L = V_U = \$20$ million

   $S_L = V_L - D = \$20 - \$5$ million $= \$15$ million

Returning to Equation 21-13, we can solve for EBIT, substitute it for the EBIT in the leveraged equity cost equation (Equation 21-12), and rearrange to determine how the equity cost varies with the debt-equity ratio.[16] This is shown in Equation 21-14.

---

[16] Using Equation 21-13, we can find EBIT = $K_U(S_L + D)$, which we substitute into Equation 21-12 to get: $K_e = [K_U(S_L + D) - K_DD)]/ S_L = K_U + (K_U - K_D) D/S_L$.

$$[21\text{-}14] \qquad K_e = K_U + (K_U - K_D)\frac{D}{S_L}$$

M&M equity cost equation an equation used to determine how the equity cost varies with the debt-equity ratio

financial leverage risk premium the difference between the unlevered equity cost and the cost of debt, multiplied by the D/E ratio

This is referred to as the **M&M equity cost equation**. It states that if the firm has no debt in its capital structure, the investor requires a cost of equity of K_U, which is referred to as the cost of unlevered equity. This cost reflects the business risk of the firm and will depend on the risk class of the firm. As the firm uses debt, the equity cost increases due to the **financial leverage risk premium**, which is the difference between the unlevered equity cost and the cost of debt, multiplied by the D/E ratio.

Note that M&M's equity cost equation is not the same as the financial leverage equation (Equation 21-3). The financial leverage equation is based on book values, and in every case the sum of the debt plus equity equals the invested capital. However, the M&M equation holds because, according to their assumptions, the sum of the market value of debt plus equity equals the unlevered firm value. As we will see later, this is not the case when we relax M&M's assumptions. What this means is that M&M's equity cost equation (Equation 21-14) is a corollary of their constant value result (Equation 21-10).

A final implication of the M&M result applies to the cost of capital. If value is independent of financial leverage, we can ignore it and simply discount the EBIT cash flows with the unlevered equity cost. The problem is how to estimate this discount rate, because if the firm uses debt, all we observe is the levered equity cost (K_e). The solution is to go back to Equation 21-14 and rearrange it to solve for K_U.[17] If we do this, we get:

$$[21\text{-}15] \qquad K_U = K_e\frac{S}{V} + K_D\frac{D}{V}$$

This is, of course, the weighted average cost of capital (WACC), as discussed in Chapter 20. However, there is one difference from the equation we provided there: in Equation 21-15, we have not adjusted K_D for taxes, since in this ideal M&M world there are no taxes.

EXAMPLE 21-3   M&M's First Model and the Cost of Capital

Estimate the cost of equity and the WACC for the levered firm in Example 21-2, assuming that its cost of debt is 6 percent.

Solution

$$K_e = K_U + (K_U - K_D)\frac{D}{S_L} = 10 + (10 - 6)\frac{5}{15} = 11.33\%$$

$$\text{WACC} = \frac{15}{20}(11.33) + \frac{5}{20}(6) = 10\%$$

So M&M's results are really quite simple. The value of the firm is unaffected by the use of debt. This means that as the firm uses debt, the equity cost increases—by enough to exactly offset the advantage of using "cheap" debt. The result is that the firm's WACC is constant. This is illustrated in Figure 21-4.

---

[17] Dropping the "L" subscripts and rearranging Equation 21-14 to group the unlevered equity cost terms, we get $K_U + K_U$ (D/S) = $K_e + K_D$ (D/S), or K_U (1 + D/S) = $K_e + K_D$(D/S). Substituting S/S into the left-hand side for 1, we have K_U [(S + D)/S] on the left, which can also be expressed as K_U (V/S), since V = S + D. This leaves us with K_U (V/S) = $K_e + K_D$ (D/S). Multiplying both sides by S/V leaves $K_U = K_e$ (S/V) + K_D (D/V).

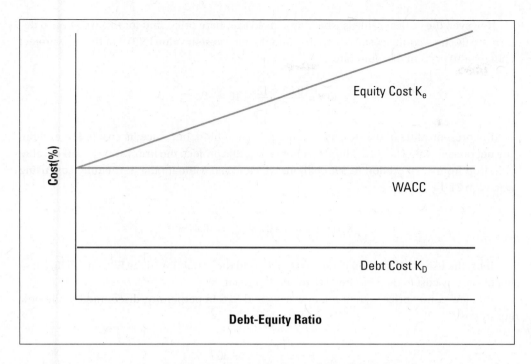

FIGURE 21-4 *M&M and the Cost of Capital*

This is a very important figure. M&M were the first to logically analyze the capital structure decision and derive the relationship between the WACC and the firm's financing decision. Previously, people had speculated about it without imposing any logical structure. Even now, when first confronted with the M&M argument, people say that the firm's WACC must fall if the unlevered equity cost is, say, 10 percent and debt only costs 6 percent. Obviously 6 percent is less than 10 percent, so the WACC must fall! The error in this logic is that these people over-look the fact that the equity becomes riskier due to the financial leverage risk premium. With the M&M argument, the equity cost rises by exactly enough to offset the cheap debt, leaving the WACC unchanged.

Other people go back to the financial leverage equation and say that the EPS must increase as long as the ROI exceeds the cost of debt, so that is the correct cut-off rate for evaluating investments, not the firm's WACC. This argument is also faulty, because the use of debt financing will increase the equity cost, which means the value of the shares may fall, even if the expected EPS goes up. Further, it is the firm's objective to maximize market values, not EPS.

Consider an unlevered firm with an expected EBIT of $10 million and an unlevered equity cost (K_U) of 10 percent. This means that its value is $100 million (i.e., $10 million ÷ 0.1). If it has 10 million shares outstanding, the share price is $10. Now suppose the firm finds a $10-million project with an ROI of 8 percent. Clearly, with a 10 percent equity cost, this project should not be accepted. However, suppose someone says, "We can borrow debt at a cost of 6 percent, so let's accept it, since the expected EPS will go up." This statement is partly true; we can work out the new higher expected EPS using the following equation:

$$\text{EPS} = \frac{10 + 0.08 \times 10 - 0.06 \times 10}{10} = \$1.02$$

This is higher than the original EPS of $1.00 (i.e., $10 million ÷ 10 million shares). The new EPS reflects the existing $10-million EBIT plus the EBIT from the new project of $0.8 million (8 percent × $10 million) minus the new interest charges of $0.6 million (6 percent × $10 million).

However, the critical value is what happens to the share price, and for this we need to determine the new equity cost. We can first find the net present value (NPV) of the new project using the 10 percent discount rate.

$$\text{NPV} = \frac{0.08 \times 10}{0.1} - 10 = -\$2$$

The present value of the project's earnings is $8 million, but since its cost is $10 million, the net present value is –$2 million. So after taking this project, the firm's equity market value will drop from $100 million to $98 million. We can then estimate the new equity cost using Equation 21-14.

$$K_e = 0.1 + (0.1 - 0.06)\frac{10}{98} = 10.41\%$$

Thus, the use of $10 million in debt has increased the variability in the EPS and ROE, causing the equity cost to increase from 10 to 10.41 percent.

The new equity price is then the new expected EPS in perpetuity, discounted at the new equity cost.

$$P = \frac{1.02}{0.1041} = \$9.80$$

Just as the value of the equity drops by $2 million, so the share price drops by $0.20, despite the increase in the expected EPS.

Remember that financial leverage has three effects: increased expected ROE, increased ROE variability, and increased risk of financial distress and bankruptcy. M&M's assumptions rule out the third effect, so we are left with one favourable and one unfavourable effect. In this example, the favourable increase in expected EPS is outweighed by the unfavourable effect of increased financial leverage. As a result, financing an 8 percent project with 6 percent debt increases the expected EPS, but when the WACC is 10 percent, the stock price still falls due to the higher financial leverage. *Only if the expected ROI of a project exceeds the WACC will the share price go up.*

CONCEPT REVIEW QUESTIONS

1. State the assumptions underlying the M&M irrelevance theory.
2. Explain the importance of this theory.
3. What is the basic argument that M&M use to arrive at the irrelevancy result?
4. In this ideal M&M world, what will affect firm value?

21.4 THE IMPACT OF TAXES

Introducing Corporate Taxes

Learning Objective 21.4
Explain how the introduction of corporate taxes affects M&M's irrelevance result.

Even back in 1958 there were taxes, and the impact of government on corporate investment and financing decisions still existed. Unfortunately, tax is amazingly complex, and a full discussion is beyond the scope of this text. However, one key feature we emphasized in Chapter 18 is that the interest on debt is tax deductible. This has a profound impact on the M&M results, since debt is favoured for tax reasons in Canada.[18] We will incorporate taxes into our

---

[18] Debt is not as much favoured in Canada as it is in the United States, as we shall see when we discuss the dividend tax credit system in Chapter 22.

discussion simply by making all the payments to the equity holders after corporate income taxes in the M&M arbitrage table. What this means is that we multiply all values by $(1 - T)$ as shown below.

The first thing to note is that the value of any firm will be reduced as taxes are introduced, since this reduces the earnings available to the shareholders. For example, the value of the unlevered firm, assuming perpetual EBIT, reduces to:

$$V_U = \frac{EBIT\,(1 - T)}{K_U}$$

[21-16]

Notice that for the same level of EBIT, the firm value (as reflected in the numerator of this equation) is reduced as taxes are introduced. Further, the higher the tax rate, the lower the firm value, all else being equal.

We now focus on the value of the levered equity, since this is what decreases in value for the levered firm when we consider corporate income taxes.

In Table 21-8, everything is as in Table 21-7 except now buying the levered equity results in an after-tax net income and dividend of $\alpha(EBIT - K_DD)(1 - T)$; similarly the payoff to the unlevered equity is $\alpha EBIT(1 - T)$. Under this scenario, getting the same payoff for the homemade leverage portfolio formed by borrowing to invest in the unlevered equity requires interest payments of $\alpha K_DD(1 - T)$. If these interest payments are discounted at the cost of debt, then the investor has to borrow $-\alpha D(1 - T)$ in order to generate these interest payments.[19] As a result, to avoid arbitrage, the value of the firm must equal $V_U - D(1 - T) = S_L$. Noting that $V_L = S_L + D$, we can rearrange the equation above to get the following:

$$V_L = V_U + DT$$

[21-17]

TABLE 21-8 M&M with Taxes

Portfolios (Actions)	Cost	Payoff
Portfolio E: Buy α of levered firm's equity	αS_L	$\alpha(EBIT - K_DD)(1 - T)$
Buy α of unlevered firm	αV_U	$\alpha EBIT(1 - T)$
Borrow α of levered firm's debt	$\alpha D(1 - T)$	$-\alpha K_DD(1 - T)$
Total portfolio D	$\alpha\,[V_U - D(1 - T)]$	$\alpha(EBIT - K_DD)(1 - T)$

Equation 21-17 is M&M's valuation equation (Equation 21-10) extended to recognize that interest payments are tax deductible by the corporation. It is sometimes referred to as M&M's second model. The value of the firm *with* leverage is the value without leverage plus the **corporate debt tax shield** from debt financing.

Remember that interest is tax deductible, so in our cost-of-capital example, where the interest rate was 6 percent and the corporate tax rate 25 percent, the after-tax cost to the firm was only 4.5 percent. This means that 25 percent of the cost of the interest was paid for by a reduction in the firm's tax bill. If the firm is a perpetuity, this debt is outstanding forever; discounting this reduction in the interest cost to perpetuity gives the tax shield value DT. This is the implication of the M&M arbitrage argument.

Another way of thinking about this is to remember that the value of the firm is the value of the equity and the value of the debt. If the firm has no debt outstanding, the value is split between the government in tax revenues and the equity market value, since the taxes are proportional to the firm's taxable income. If the corporate income tax rate is 25 percent, then the government is getting 25 percent of the overall value, and the shareholders are getting 75 per-

corporate debt tax shield the value added when a firm uses debt that is attributable to the associated tax benefits

___

[19] In this example we ignore personal taxes and whether the individual borrowing the money gets a tax deduction.

cent. However, if the firm raises debt, the government share of the pie falls as its tax revenue falls. Consequently, the value of the debt plus the equity goes up. This is illustrated in Figure 21-5. Also note that if there are no taxes, it makes no difference how you slice up the pie between debt and equity holders.

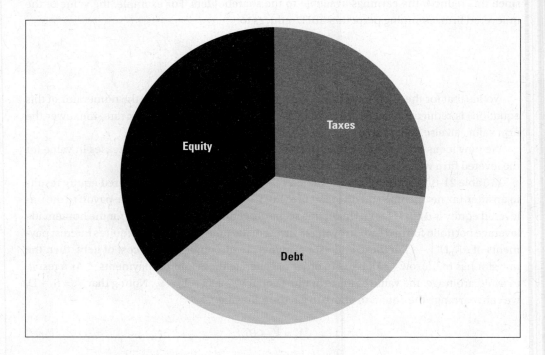

FIGURE 21-5 *Firm Value with Corporate Taxes*

The tax subsidy for using debt explains why so many of the corporate financing vehicles described in Chapter 18 are designed with the intention of making the associated payments tax deductible as interest.

If the use of debt makes the value of the firm go up, the WACC must go down as the firm generates a bigger tax shield value and reduces the government share of the value of private enterprise. To see how this works, we can substitute the M&M tax value (Equation 21-17) into the earnings yield and get the new tax-corrected value of Equation 21-14. This is shown in Equation 21-18 below.

[21-18]
$$K_e = K_U + (K_U - K_D)(1-T)\frac{D}{S_L}$$

In this case, the financial leverage premium is reduced by $(1 - T)$. If the government pays for 25 percent of the debt through a reduction in taxes, then the effective debt-equity ratio is only $(1 - T)D/S_L$. As a result, the equity cost does not increase by the same amount it would if there were no taxes paid. This is illustrated in Figure 21-6.

The key differences between Figure 21-6 and Figure 21-4 are that the interest cost and the financial leverage risk premium on the equity cost are both reduced by $(1 - T)$. As a result, as more debt is used, the cost of equity does not increase enough to offset the use of the cheaper debt. Therefore, the WACC declines continuously with the use of debt financing. Notice also that the equation to determine the WACC must be adjusted to reflect taxes and would now be the same as the WACC equation introduced in Chapter 20 (ignoring preferred shares). This is shown in Equation 21-19.

[21-19]
$$WACC = \frac{S}{V}K_e + \frac{D}{V}K_D(1-T)$$

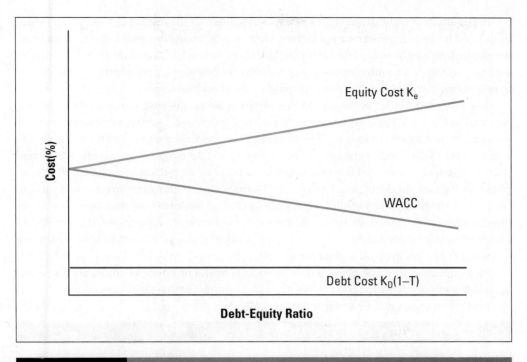

FIGURE 21-6 *M&M with Corporate Taxes*

EXAMPLE 21-4   M&M with Corporate Taxes

Let's revisit the firms in Example 21-2 and assume that they both face a corporate tax rate of 30 percent, and they still generate an expected EBIT of $2 million perpetually.

a.   Find the value of the unlevered firm (U), assuming its cost of capital is 10 percent.

b.   Find the value of the identical risk-levered firm (L), which has $5 million in debt outstanding.

c.   Find the cost of L's equity and its WACC.

Solution

a. $V_U = \dfrac{EBIT(1-T)}{K_U} = \dfrac{2(1-.30)}{0.1} = \$14$ million

Notice the decline of $6 million in U's market value. This is the present value of the future tax payments made to the government.

b. $V_L = V_U + DT = 14$ million $+ (0.3)(5) = \$15.5$ million
$S_L = V_L - D = 15.5$ million $- 5 = \$10.5$ million
Notice that L is worth $1.5 million more than U due to the tax shield value of debt (DT).

c. $K_e = K_U + (K_U - K_D)(1 - T)D/S_L = 10 + (10 - 6)(1 - 0.3)(5/10.5) = 11.33\%$
$WACC_L = (10.5/15.5)(11.33) + (5/15.5)(6)(1 - 0.3) = 9.03\%$
This explains why $V_L > V_U$, since L's WACC of 9.03 percent is below U's WACC of 10 percent (which equals its cost of equity because it is all equity financed).

Historically, the tax-extended M&M equity cost equation was often used in corporate finance because it captures one of the key features of corporate financing: the tax deductibility of interest payments. However, the M&M equity cost equations are rarely used anymore because there are now models—in particular the capital asset pricing model (CAPM)—that can adjust for risk. Assuming that the CAPM holds, the "beta" version of Equation 21-18 is

$$K_e = R_F + MRP \times \beta_U\left(1+(1-T)\ \frac{D}{S_L}\right)$$ [21-20]

The equity cost without any debt is the risk-free rate plus the market risk premium (MRP) multiplied by the unlevered beta coefficient. With debt financing but ignoring corporate taxes, we get the financial leverage effect, and the unlevered beta is multiplied by one plus the debt-equity ratio. However, with corporate income taxes, as before, we multiply the debt by $(1 - T)$ to reflect that not all of the debt costs are paid by the shareholders.

Given the importance of the CAPM in estimating the equity cost, Equation 21-20 is used more often than the M&M equations from which it is derived.[20] Given the simplicity of the adjustment, it is relatively easy to unlever betas to get the unleveraged equity cost, and then relever them to account for changes in the firm's financial leverage. Although this is common practice, it contains a crucial flaw: the adjustment is based on the M&M equation, which implies that 100 percent debt financing is optimal—since there is always more tax shield value to using more debt, why stop? While it seems obvious on an intuitive level that firms should not finance with 100 percent debt, we can address the question more formally by relaxing M&M's assumptions that there are no costs related to the risk of financial distress or bankruptcy. We discuss these issues in detail in the next section.

The conclusion that 100 percent debt is optimal in the presence of corporate taxes also ignores the impact of personal taxes. We discuss the impact of personal taxes on M&M's conclusions regarding capital structure in Appendix 21-A.

CONCEPT REVIEW QUESTIONS

1. How do taxes affect the M&M argument?
2. What are the practical difficulties associated with the implications of M&M's corporate tax model?

21.5 FINANCIAL DISTRESS, BANKRUPTCY, AND AGENCY COSTS

Learning Objective 21.5
Describe how financial distress and bankruptcy costs lead to the static trade-off theory of capital structure.

The problem with M&M's corporate tax model is that it recognizes the benefits of using debt (i.e., the tax shield DT), but disregards the associated risks, which include the increased risk of financial distress or bankruptcy. The important thing about financial distress and bankruptcy costs is that they produce a flow of value away from both the debt holders and the equity holders. In the simple M&M world, anyone can buy both the firm's debt and equity, and what the equity holder loses, the debt holder gains. This is an example of a "zero-sum game." All that is happening is value is being rearranged but none is being destroyed. The key feature of bankruptcy and financial distress is that value is destroyed. So while the use of debt creates value by reducing the government's share of taxes, it also destroys value by causing increased risk of financial distress and bankruptcy. Before we go on, we must first explain what we mean by distress and bankruptcy.

bankruptcy a state of insolvency that occurs when a firm commits an act of bankruptcy, such as the non-payment of interest, and creditors enforce their legal rights to recoup money, or when a firm voluntarily declares bankruptcy in an effort to gain protection while it reorganizes so it can become solvent again

Bankruptcy is a legal state. It can occur in two ways: (1) when the firm commits an act of bankruptcy, such as the non-payment of interest, and creditors enforce their legal rights as a result; or (2) when the firm voluntarily declares bankruptcy. Under either scenario, in Canada, the firm is reorganized under the *Companies' Creditors Arrangements Act* (CCAA) or the *Bankruptcy and Insolvency Act* (BIA).

The CCAA is primarily for larger, more complicated firms (the debt must exceed $5 million) and is exceedingly flexible. Essentially, the court appoints a monitor, normally a trustee in bankruptcy working for one of the larger accounting firms, who then reports back to the court. The monitor has considerable flexibility to prevent creditors from exercising their

---

[20] Hamada, R., "The Effect of the Firm's Capital Structure on the Systematic Risk of Common Stocks." *Journal of Finance* 27, no. 2 (May 1972), pp. 435–52.

claims against the firm, to restructure contracts, and to allow the management of the firm to develop a plan to reorganize in the hope of continuing operations. During this period, the firm is allowed to raise new financing, called debtor-in-possession (DIP) financing, with a higher priority over existing unsecured claims. It is this financing that gives the firm some breathing space to reorganize and present a plan to all creditors, which the court can impose, providing enough of the creditors agree. *Finance in the News 21-2* is a press release on the establishment of a $1-billion DIP fund during the aftermath of the financial crisis to help Canadian firms reorganize.

---

finance INTHENEWS 21-2 Brookfield Establishes C$1 Billion DIP Financing

BROOKFIELD ASSET MANAGEMENT and Export Development Canada [EDC] today announced that Brookfield has established a C$1 billion fund (the "Fund") with the backing of EDC to provide debtor-in-possession ("DIP") loans and other specialty finance solutions to Canadian companies undergoing a restructuring or reorganization.

Brookfield has committed to provide 10 per cent of the Fund's capital and will manage the Fund, identifying and evaluating investment opportunities. EDC played a lead role in structuring the Fund, and is the largest investor with an initial participation of C$450 million that could grow to C$1 billion.

"Brookfield's history of specialty bridge lending and expertise in corporate restructuring positions us well to provide tailored solutions to support companies through the restructuring process. We believe that providing financing for companies undertaking a restructuring will help viable enterprises emerge from the current recession in a strong competitive position," said Joe Freedman, the Senior Managing Partner responsible for the Fund at Brookfield.

DIP financing provides companies seeking protection from creditors with capital to continue to operate their business while they complete a plan of reorganization. The Fund will target mid-market and larger scale opportunities where at least C$20 million of financing is required.

"This Fund will help Canadian companies gain access to credit during restructuring, when it's most needed," said Eric Siegel, President and CEO of EDC. "This new partnership with Brookfield enables us to further assist even more Canadian companies during the current downturn."

Fund investors also include Canadian Imperial Bank of Commerce ("CIBC") and Sun Life Financial Inc.

"CIBC is pleased to be a part of this initiative, which will help support Canadian companies in these uncertain economic times," said Laura Dottori-Attanasio, Global Head of Corporate Credit Products at CIBC.

Source: Brookfield Asset Management, "Brookfield Establishes C$1 Billion DIP Financing," press release, August 19, 2009. Retrieved from http://brookfield.com

---

The BIA is much more rigid. There is very limited scope for preventing creditors from seizing assets; the firm cannot raise DIP financing, and there is no provision for imposing a settlement on all creditors, even if a significant majority agree to it. If a restructuring plan is rejected, creditors can seize the assets and the firm is liquidated. Anything left after the secured creditors are paid is proportionally allocated to the unsecured creditors. The BIA is much simpler and more predictable than the CCAA and is used mainly by smaller companies, where the major creditor is a commercial bank. As a result, it is a lot easier to negotiate a settlement. In contrast, the CCAA is mainly used for large companies with many creditors, where a "stay" or breathing space is needed to sort things out.

Either way, a reorganization is expensive, particularly under the CCAA, where there are much more significant legal, accounting, and court fees. All of these fees represent an outflow of value that goes to neither the debt holders nor the equity holders. If the firm is actually wound up and liquidated, there are even more costs, as the major asset of a failing firm is usually a history of tax losses. These losses can be carried forward and used against future profits and are thus valuable to the firm. However, if the firm is wound up, these losses disappear and the major beneficiary is the government. In addition, the process of winding up a firm usually results in sales of assets to third parties at "bargain" prices that are less than their value in place, so again there is a value loss to the firm.

direct costs of bankruptcy costs incurred as a direct result of bankruptcy including liquidation of assets, the loss of tax losses, and legal and accounting fees

indirect costs of bankruptcy or **financial distress costs** losses to a firm before it declares bankruptcy

financial distress a state of business failing where bankruptcy seems imminent if dramatic action is not taken

agency costs the costs associated with agency problems, as discussed in Chapter 2

Firms try hard to reorganize prior to a formal bankruptcy and liquidation because of these deadweight losses to liquidation from reduced asset prices in distress sales, the loss of tax losses, and the costs of legal and accounting fees associated with a liquidation. These costs are often referred to as the **direct costs of bankruptcy**.

While the direct costs can be substantial, even greater losses in value may occur before the firm deteriorates into a bankruptcy situation. These latter losses are often referred to as the **indirect costs of bankruptcy** or, more simply, **financial distress costs**. Financial distress is a situation in which the firm has yet to commit the act of bankruptcy, although it knows that unless something dramatic happens, it will likely go bankrupt. Suppose, for example, the firm still has $10 million in cash, but its business is failing, it is worth only $20 million, and it has a $50-million loan coming due in a year. Clearly, if the firm doesn't do anything, in a year's time its creditors will insist on payment, and the $20-million business and the $10 million in cash will belong to the creditors. Ignoring any fees and other associated costs, the creditors will get $0.60 on the dollar for their debt, and the shareholders will lose everything. This is a situation of financial distress.

During periods of financial distress, there is an increase in the **agency costs** due to the growing divergence of the interests of equity holders and debt holders. In the example discussed in the previous paragraph, the debt holders have a chance to get back $0.60 on the dollar, while the equity holders' stake in the firm is zero. Therefore, the equity holders (who get to vote) may try to implement measures in an attempt to get something for themselves, at the expense of the debt holders. For example, the shareholders might vote to pay out the $10 million in cash as a dividend. This will give them some cash now, and in a year's time the creditors will get only $20 million instead of $30 million when they seize the firm's assets. However, this is illegal as well as being unethical.

The responsibility of the board of directors (BOD) is to act in the best interests of the company. For a solvent company, this means pursuing the best interests of the shareholders. However, for an insolvent company, the responsibility of the BOD shifts to all the stakeholders in the firm, including the creditors. In particular, once the firm is reorganized under the CCCA or BIA, all the dividend decisions of the previous year, and sometimes of the previous three years, are reviewed to see whether they were prudent and reasonable at the time. A sudden cash dividend of $10 million shortly before a firm goes bankrupt would immediately make the board members at the time the dividend was declared personally liable, and would cause the court to order the payments reversed.[21]

However, just because something is illegal doesn't mean there is no way to achieve the same result. Funny things happen in failing firms: assets are sometimes sold to related companies owned by the shareholders at "knock down" prices, or the firm pays for joint venture activities that seem, on the surface, to offer little benefit. In all cases, these are simply more sophisticated ways to try to strip cash out of the company before it goes bankrupt, since these assets will belong to the creditors and not the shareholders when it does go bankrupt. Part of the expense of reorganizing or liquidating a company is simply working out what has happened in the previous few years and determining whether any assets have been fraudulently stripped out of the company.

A more subtle issue than outright fraud is the recognition that the shareholders essentially have a one-year call option on the underlying firm; the exercise price is the value of the debt. In one year's time, the value of the firm described above will either exceed $50 million or it won't. If it exceeds $50 million, the firm can refinance and pay off its creditors, and the shareholders will have some residual value. On the other hand, if the value of the firm is less than $50 million, the shareholders are protected by limited liability and can simply walk away and hand the firm over to the creditors. The existence of limited liability, and the fact that

---

[21] Note that this is also why directors usually resign as the firm gets into serious financial trouble. There have been times when all the directors have tried to resign, but the *Canada Business Corporations Act* requires at least one director.

shareholders are only exposed up to the value of their investment, create this call option. The shareholders' value is depicted in Figure 21-7.

If there is no limited liability, the shareholders have to pay off the $50 million in debt regardless, so they gain (lose) if the underlying firm value (the unlevered value) is greater (less) than the face value of the debt. However, with limited liability, they can't be forced to make up the losses if the value of the firm is less than the face value of the debt that is due. As a result, the value of the equity behaves like a call option, with the minimum value represented by the heavy intrinsic value line in Figure 21-7. The important thing to understand about the change in the characteristics of the shares in a firm in financial distress is that options react differently than ordinary common shares. For example, two major factors increasing the value of a call option are time and risk—both of which increase the option value. So with $10 million in cash, the shareholders can possibly increase the risk of the firm and extend the time until they go bankrupt.

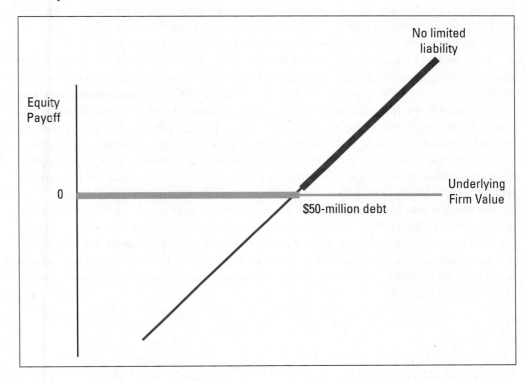

FIGURE 21-7 *The Firm as a Call Option for Shareholders*

Whether or not they can extend the time period will depend on the type of debt that they have outstanding. In this example, all $50 million is due the next year. But if, instead, it were long-term debt with only the interest payments due in a year, the firm could continue to make the interest payments until all $10 million in cash was used up. During this period, the firm could devote all its time and energy to survival. It would skip normal maintenance, not replace machines, stop advertising and R&D, and generally allow the operations to run down. In this case, the shareholders would be hoping that something might happen to give value to the firm, while the worst that could happen is a delayed bankruptcy. For the creditors, this is a nightmare scenario because they are seeing the value of the operations, as well as the $10 million in cash, go down period by period until, by the time they can finally force bankruptcy, they don't get $30 million—they get much less.

The second major problem is that there is an incentive for the shareholders to gamble, since they are gambling with the debt holders' wealth. They might make risky investments that they would not otherwise make, because if the investments pay off, they could get the firm out of bankruptcy. If they don't pay off, it doesn't matter to the shareholders because they are essentially bankrupt anyway. This attitude often shows up in the form of poorly researched new product introductions, where the product hasn't been properly tested and the proper research and development has not been carried out. Unfortunately, the opposite scenario also occurs: if the firm is going bankrupt, the equity holders have no incentive to put in new money for minor projects, even if they are very profitable, since all this does is create more value for the creditors, not the shareholders.

All these examples illustrate the fact that the incentives for shareholders and the firm change once there is significant bankruptcy risk. Instead of making positive NPV decisions, where the equity holders bear the risk, they face a situation where it is the creditors who bear the risk. This is because the firm really belongs to the creditors, yet they cannot alter what the firm is doing until it commits the act of bankruptcy by non-payment of interest or principal.

During this period of financial distress, the underlying operations of the firm are often poorly managed due to this change in incentive structure. What this means in terms of the M&M argument is that if the firm raises too much debt, the underlying EBIT of the levered firm will change as poor projects are accepted, good ones ignored, operations neglected, and cash stripped out of the company. Again, as with direct bankruptcy costs, there is a value loss that is not being fully captured by either the debt holders or the equity holders.

Creditors are well aware that distressed firms may take these types of actions, which is why they take offsetting measures. One standard approach is not to make long-term loans to risky firms. Instead, debt is short term or includes sinking fund payments that create a continuous cash payment to the creditors, thereby reducing the maturity of the call option. This also explains all the stipulations in the BC Gas trust indenture we discussed in Chapter 18, in which the firm agrees to insure its assets, maintain them in good order, not sell them unless it meets certain tests, not exceed a particular debt ratio, and maintain certain levels of working capital. In all cases, the lender is simply trying to reduce the value of this call option and gain greater control over the affairs of the firm.

The result is that there are significant costs attached to raising too much debt, since too much debt increases the risks of financial distress and bankruptcy, and the associated value outflows to third parties. This leads to a theory referred to as the **static trade-off**, which says a firm will use debt to maximize its tax advantages up to the point where these benefits are outweighed by the associated estimated costs of financial distress and bankruptcy. The model is illustrated in Figure 21-8.

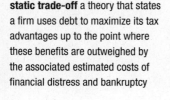

static trade-off a theory that states a firm uses debt to maximize its tax advantages up to the point where these benefits are outweighed by the associated estimated costs of financial distress and bankruptcy

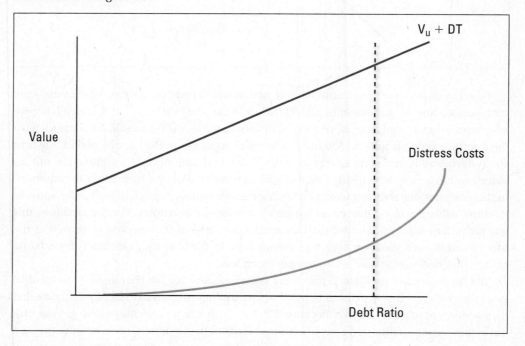

FIGURE 21-8 *Firm Value and Financial Distress Costs*

The straight line in Figure 21-8 is the M&M value of the levered firm, taking into account the existence of corporate taxes. In other words, it is the value of the unlevered firm plus the tax shield value, where the slope of the line is determined by the tax rate, T, since value increases with debt by the corporate tax rate. The curved line is the expected value loss from financial distress and bankruptcy. Notice that the slope of this line increases with the debt ratio. This is because there is little risk of distress or bankruptcy at low levels of debt, but this risk and its consequences increase with the debt level. The optimal level of debt occurs where the slope of the financial distress curve is the same as that of the tax-corrected value line, because at this point the marginal tax shield benefit equals the marginal cost of financial distress and bankruptcy. In this way, the tax advantages of debt are traded off against the distress and bankruptcy disadvantages.

The conclusions of the static trade-off model are depicted in Figure 21-9. The top diagram shows that the cost of equity increases throughout as more debt is added, as expected. Initially, the effect of this increase on the WACC is more than offset by the use of the cheaper debt. As a result, the WACC initially declines as more debt is added. However, beyond a certain point, depicted as D/E*, the WACC begins to increase, reflecting the higher costs of both debt and equity in response to the increased risk of financial distress and bankruptcy. So the WACC is minimized at D/E*. As a result, as can be seen in the bottom diagram in Figure 21-9, the value of the firm is maximized at this same point. This point, D/E*, represents the optimal capital structure according to the static trade-off model.

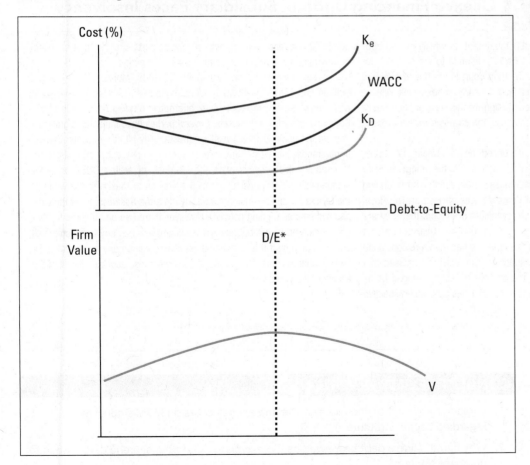

FIGURE 21-9 *The Static Trade-Off Model*

How significant are these financial distress and bankruptcy costs? As we discussed earlier, a firm with too much debt and no financial flexibility cannot react to changing market conditions. A classic example of this is Oilexco, which was (note the tense) a Calgary-based oil and gas exploration company whose major activities were in the North Sea, through its British subsidiary. It had excellent technical know-how in extracting oil from fields that were felt to be dry, but at a relatively high cost. It became a darling of the stock market: as the price of crude oil hit $147 a barrel, its stock price went to $19.50, giving the company a value of $4.5 billion. However, it financed this activity through two series of bank loans syndicated through the Royal Bank of Scotland (RBS). When the financial crisis hit, RBS lost 28 billion pounds sterling (about $50 billion) and pulled the plug on all manner of risky loans. Remember that most bank loans are demand loans. *Finance in the News 21-3* reprints the Oilexco news release that explains what happened when the price of oil dropped below $50 a barrel.

Eventually, Oilexco's UK subsidiary was sold for less than the value of its debt of about $600 million. Unfortunately, Oilexco had guaranteed its subsidiary's debt. On July 16, 2009, Oilexco was forced to liquidate its remaining assets to make good on the guarantee. The result was that Oilexco went from a $4.5-billion market value to zero in the space of a year because it had no financial flexibility and could not access capital. Prior to the financial crisis of 2008, Oilexco could have raised financing with oil prices at $50, but in the middle of the crisis no one was willing to extend any credit. In recessions, "cash is king," and those without it run the risk of going bankrupt, like Oilexco.

finance INTHENEWS 21-3 Oilexco Financing Update: Subsidiary Faces Insolvency

OILEXCO INCORPORATED ANNOUNCED today that its wholly owned subsidiary, Oilexco North Sea Limited ("ONSL"), intends to file petitions for administration ("Administration") in the High Court in the United Kingdom as soon as reasonably practicable but likely as early as next week. Oilexco Incorporated is considering its options in light of this development but at this time remains solvent and committed to the strategic review process that was previously announced.

As the Company previously announced on December 17, 2008, incremental funding was necessary in addition to the bridge funding announced that day, although no assurances were given that such funding would become available. Today, the Company was advised by The Royal Bank of Scotland plc on behalf of the syndicate of lenders that they are not prepared to advance any further funding to ONSL. Oilexco does not have any other source of funding at this time and has therefore concluded that an Administration must be pursued. Oilexco has been advised that funding for an Administration is in the process of being arranged by its senior secured lenders, subject to settlement of terms with the prospective administrators and counsel. Accordingly, all parties expect that safe and orderly operations will continue throughout this period.

As also announced on December 17, 2008, Morgan Stanley & Co. Limited and Merrill Lynch International have been retained by Oilexco in a strategic review process to seek alternative funding or the sale of the Company or some of its assets. Several parties have indicated significant interest in acquiring ONSL or all or substantially all of its assets. Oilexco understands that it is the intention of the proposed administrators to continue this process, with the intention of selling ONSL or all or substantially all of its assets in such a way as to maximize the value of the assets for all stakeholders, and maintain the business, its employees and systems as a going concern. However, there can be no certainty that any binding offers will be received or accepted or that any transaction will be completed or, if it is completed, that there will be any equity value for Oilexco shareholders. The shares of ONSL comprise substantially all of the assets of the Company.

Source: Oilexco, "Oilexco Financing Update: Subsidiary Faces Insolvency," press release, December 31, 2008. Retrieved from www.oilexco.com.

CONCEPT REVIEW QUESTIONS

1. Explain the impact of financial distress and agency costs on M&M's conclusions regarding capital structure.

2. Why can the firm's debt be viewed as the exercise price to the shareholders' option to purchase the firm?

3. Explain the static trade-off theory.

21.6 OTHER FACTORS AFFECTING CAPITAL STRUCTURE

How well does the static trade-off model explain capital structures? It certainly captures the main effects. However, it ignores two important issues:

1. **Information asymmetry problems:** the effect of informational differences among shareholders, creditors, and management

2. **Agency problems:** the fact that managers make decisions on behalf of the shareholders but have their own interests at stake as well

First let's consider the impact of information differences. Suppose a firm has a market value of $20 million and, after careful consideration, decides to undertake a new project that costs $5 million and has a $5-million NPV. The firm has 1 million shares outstanding, so the share price prior to undertaking the new project is $20. What should it do and how should it finance this project? Theoretically, the CEO should call a news conference and announce this great new investment, the media and security analysts in attendance should clap their hands, the market value of the firm should go up by $5 million to $25 million, and the stock price should rise to $25. The firm should then issue 200,000 shares at $25 each to finance the project, spending the $5 million so the total value increases to $30 million and the stock price remains at $25 (i.e., $30m ÷ 1.2m).

However, the real world does not react like this. Investors will yawn, bombard the CEO with questions, and generally be extremely critical, since they have heard this story before and cannot distinguish between good firms telling the truth and poor firms spinning a story to boost the stock price. What is more likely to happen, therefore, is the stock price will stay at $20, forcing the firm to issue 250,000 shares at $20 to finance the project. Then, when the truth is revealed and the project does add value, the firm's value will increase to $30 million. So the firm value still gets to $30 million, but with 1.25 million shares outstanding and a stock price that only reaches $24.

The situation may be even worse than this, since stock prices often drop when firms announce a new share issue. This is because investors suspect that management thinks the stock price is overvalued and are therefore trying to issue common shares while they are trading at inflated prices. Suppose, for example, that the stock price drops to $18 on the announcement of the share issue. In that case, the firm will have to issue 277,778 shares to raise the $5 million, and even if the market value ultimately rises to $30 million, the stock price will only rise to $23.48. In both of these cases, the ownership of this positive NPV project is being shared by the existing shareholders and the new shareholders who are buying in at below "true" market price.

How can the firm handle this problem of information asymmetry? The obvious answer is to raise $5 million in debt. In this case, when the value of the firm rises to $30 million after the profits flow from the new investment, the equity will be worth $25 million and the debt $5 million, but there will still be only 1 million shares outstanding, and the stock price will rise to $25.

This suggests that firms should only issue equity as a last resort. Instead, they should finance using internal cash flow, then debt, and, finally, common equity, in what Stewart Myers refers to as a **pecking order**.[22]

Myers' argument that firms follow a pecking order is based on divulging information. If the firms use internal cash flow, they do not need anyone's permission. Even the shareholders can't force the firm to pay a dividend. Similarly, the firm can talk to a bank and divulge privileged information to secure a loan. However, when it issues new common shares, as we have

Learning Objective 21.6
Explain how information asymmetries and agency problems lead firms to follow a pecking-order approach to financing.

pecking order the order in which firms prefer to raise financing, starting with internal cash flow, then debt, and finally common equity

---

[22] Myers, S. "The Capital Structure Puzzle." *Journal of Finance* 39, no. 3 (July 1984), pp. 574–92.

seen, the firm has to file a prospectus and reveal all material facts that affect the share price. In the process, the firm has to be careful not to reveal facts to a competitor that may give it a jump-start and allow it to compete away the NPV benefits of the project.

The pecking order was discussed in a different context by Gordon Donaldson, who justified the pecking order through what we would now call "agency arguments."[23] He showed that managers' commitment to the firm is a result of their human capital, in contrast to the "short-term" financial commitment of shareholders. As a result, managers are more concerned about the long-term survival of the firm and less inclined to take risks. For these agency reasons, he argued that managers had a preference for financing by using internal cash flow (retained earnings), then debt, and finally by issuing new common equity. In an agency model, this financing hierarchy imposes the least risk on the firm and requires the least justification by managers.

Regardless of whether it is for agency reasons, information problems, or some combination of the two, we do see firms using the pecking order. Profitable firms tend to have the least debt simply because they don't need it and have more than enough internal funds. Leveraged recapitalizations involve issuing debt and using the funds to buy back shares. These tend to address the lack of debt over time, but only with a significant lag. The real puzzle is that there are some firms that simply don't use much debt, even though they could. Microsoft, for example, is relatively low risk, hugely profitable, and has no significant debt. It could undoubtedly lower its tax bill by using debt financing and buying back shares, yet it hasn't done so.

CONCEPT REVIEW QUESTION

1. Explain how the existence of information asymmetries and agency problems may lead firms to follow a pecking order to financing.

21.7 CAPITAL STRUCTURE IN PRACTICE

Learning Objective 21.7
Describe other factors that can affect a firm's capital structure in practice.

So what do we make of all these factors? First we can say that the static trade-off theory suggests you should take advantage of the tax shields from debt, so the first question is: *Is the firm profitable?*

If the firm has no profits, it can't use the tax shields from debt. In this case, it might as well finance with equity. More to the point, it has no ability to make interest payments.

The second question deals with whether or not the firm can issue debt. As we saw, lenders make credit evaluations and won't lend if they fear financial distress. In particular, if firms have hard tangible assets that can be sold elsewhere, lenders may lend to them even if they are worried about the survival prospects of the firm. This is because they can always seize the assets, sell them, and recover most of their principal. This leads to the second question: *What type of assets does the firm have?* If they are tangible assets that can be used elsewhere, they can be used as collateral for a secured loan.

If the firm's assets are not good collateral, the lender has to look to the firm's cash flow rather than its assets for security. In this case, the lender will be concerned about the firm's business risk and the variability of its operations. This leads to the third question: *How risky is the firm's underlying business?*

It is a basic law of finance, illustrated by our discussion of financial leverage, that you do not layer significant financial risk on top of significant business risk.

---

[23] Donaldson, G. "Financial Goals: Management versus Stockholders." *Harvard Business Review*, May/June 1963.

Generally, financial markets are size constrained. This means that, because preparing a prospectus and other necessary documents is time-consuming and costly, only larger firms access the public markets. Further, larger firms tend to have more diversified operations and more market power. This is not an absolute, but larger firms tend to be less risky than smaller firms, so the fourth question is: ***How big is the firm?***

Finally, there is the basic question of whether the firm needs the money, which is very much a function of its profitability and growth rate. Growing firms need cash, whereas profitable firms generally spin off cash, so we ask: ***What is the firm's growth rate, and how profitable is it?***

These five questions go a long way to determining how much debt a firm can carry and what its optimal debt ratio will be. Of course, firms deviate from their target capital structure when they are offered a good deal. Like everyone else, we may do something we didn't intend to if someone offers us a good deal. In terms of financing, this means that if the firm can obtain attractive interest rates, it might lean more heavily on debt financing. This pattern is discussed in *Finance in the News 21-4*, which alludes to investors and firms taking advantage of so-called cheap money as a result of U.S. government monetary policy keeping interest rates extremely low.

---

finance INTHENEWS 21-4 | Thought of No More Cheap Money Scaring Investors

ANOTHER QUARTER of a million U.S. jobs created in February—excellent news that markets are hardly celebrating. Oil fell on the news. The S&P 500 stock index is at a post-recession high, but is far from flying—up only 4 percent since Feb. 1. Jobs may be good for investors, but money for almost nothing from central banks is better. And economic strength means that money may not be coming so freely.

Markets are addicted to cheap money and withdrawal may be painful. When Ben Bernanke, chairman of the U.S. Federal Reserve, failed even to hint at QE3—a third round of quantitative easing—in a speech on Feb. 29 the spot gold price suffered its biggest one-day fall in three years.

No wonder. The speculation has been that QE3 would be similar in size to the $600 billion (U.S.) of QE2. These huge sums dwarf Greek GDP, not just the current €130-billion bailout. If the cash doesn't come, fans of the yellow metal would not be the only ones to suffer. No QE3 would be a challenge. Safe haven bonds, equities, and oil have all recently scaled peaks.

Nor is QE3 the only stimulant that risks going missing. There's also LTRO 3. The European Central Bank's two long-term refinancing operations put a trillion euros of fresh cash into European banks. But Jens Weidmann, president of the German Bundesbank, has not been shy about expressing his discomfort with exceptional monetary support. LTRO 3 is unlikely unless markets get really ugly.

Globally, markets continue to face high uncertainty. The United States, Japan, and Germany are all showing signs of improving, though not high, growth. Emerging markets are growing more slowly than before, but still quite fast. Euro trouble will keep brewing. The big change and the biggest threat is that better economic news makes the liquidity tap gush less freely.

Yet trouble for markets might not be all bad. The inflated oil price threatens the recovery. If it were to fall it would help growth. What is bad for inflated markets could be good for growth and jobs. That's something the central banks need to ponder.

If a firm's share price is very high and increasing, and the firm believes the stock is overvalued, it may decide to take advantage of this window of opportunity to issue common shares. This is why we observe more equity financing in a strong equity market than a weak one. (In fact, firms often issue equity when they think it is overvalued. This opportunistic financing causes significant departures from their long-run target debt ratios.) Therefore, one other question we might ask is: ***How high is the stock price, how much has it appreciated over the last year, and how cheap is it to borrow?***

These are the basic questions that are asked in determining a firm's financing decisions. Let's finish with a survey carried out by Deutsche Bank. Figure 21-10 presents results from the survey, in which companies were asked to rate the importance of the factors listed in determining an appropriate level of debt—from "not important" (0) to "very important" (5).

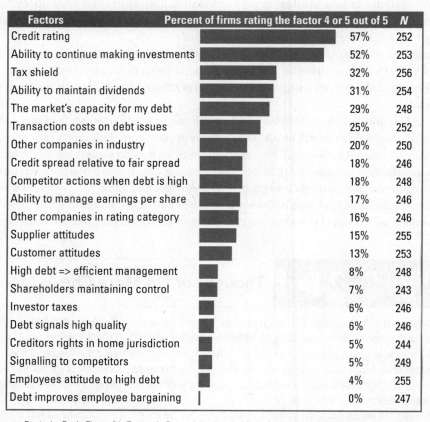

Factors	Percent of firms rating the factor 4 or 5 out of 5	N
Credit rating	57%	252
Ability to continue making investments	52%	253
Tax shield	32%	256
Ability to maintain dividends	31%	254
The market's capacity for my debt	29%	248
Transaction costs on debt issues	25%	252
Other companies in industry	20%	250
Credit spread relative to fair spread	18%	246
Competitor actions when debt is high	18%	248
Ability to manage earnings per share	17%	246
Other companies in rating category	16%	246
Supplier attitudes	15%	255
Customer attitudes	13%	253
High debt => efficient management	8%	248
Shareholders maintaining control	7%	243
Investor taxes	6%	246
Debt signals high quality	6%	246
Creditors rights in home jurisdiction	5%	244
Signalling to competitors	5%	249
Employees attitude to high debt	4%	255
Debt improves employee bargaining	0%	247

FIGURE 21-10 *Factors in Determining Level of Debt*

Source: Deutsche Bank, Figure 21: Factors in Determining Level of Debt. In *Corporate Capital Structure*. January 2006.

There were many more factors presented here than in the survey conducted by the Conference Board, which we discussed earlier in the chapter, but the implications are similar. The number one factor mentioned is credit rating: firms often take drastic measures simply to maintain their A or BBB rating. Other factors consistent with our discussion are number 3, the tax shield value of debt, which reflects the tax deductibility of interest; and numbers 2 and 4, which reflect risk, since firms do not want to be put in a position where they have to restrict investments or cut their dividends. After that, the factors tend to be technical, such as who is willing to buy the debt (capacity), what costs are involved in issuing it, and the old standby: what do other companies do?

Figure 21-11 presents results from the same Deutsche Bank survey. Firms were asked whether they have a target or optimal capital structure. If M&M are correct, the answer should be "No, we don't care." However, 90 percent of companies domiciled in Latin America and 85 percent in North America, have a target capital structure. The number is slightly less in Germany and the rest of Western Europe, but it turns out their tax systems do not give the same level of subsidy to interest payments as the systems in North America. Overall, the survey data provided by Deutsche Bank confirm the idea that we have been discussing: firms have an optimal capital structure, and it tends to be a trade-off between tax advantages and the loss of financial flexibility.

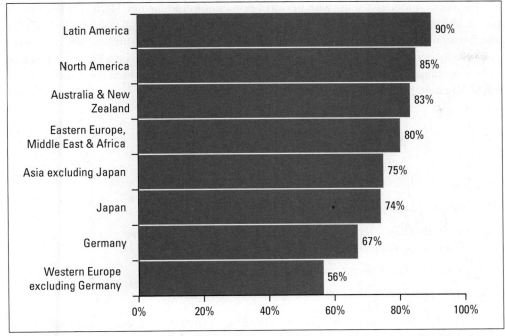

Source: Deutsche Bank, Figure 18: Proportion of Firms with a Target Capital Structure by Region. In *Corporate Capital Structure.* January 2006.

FIGURE 21-11 *Proportion of Firms with a Target Capital Structure by Region*

LESSONS TO BE LEARNED **The Modigliani and Miller theorems** are the core of corporate finance, but they rest on critical assumptions of perfect markets and investor rationality. In particular, they assume that good projects, like good firms, can always get financing, yet during the financial crisis, this was not the case. The problem was that the key people at the centre of the financial system—the banks—were under enormous pressure due to loan losses from the U.S. sub-prime market and had to attend to their first priority, which was their survival. Despite the U.S. government's huge injection of capital into the banks during the six months from September 2008 to March 2009, the financial system was not working and funds were not available. During this time, cash was king and financing was only available for very low-risk institutions like utilities.

The crisis has reaffirmed the perils of excessive debt and the cost of financial distress. To some extent, we are seeing a response similar to that of the 1930s, when all types of debt were shunned. This is happening at all levels, from the household sector to corporations to government.

CONCEPT REVIEW QUESTION

1. Explain four of the most important factors influencing capital structure decisions as indicated in the survey results and how they relate to the conceptual discussion of an optimal capital structure.

APPENDIX **21A**

PERSONAL TAXES AND CAPITAL STRUCTURE

Recall from our discussion of taxation in Chapter 3 that dividend income and interest income are taxed differently at the personal level, with dividends receiving preferential tax treatment. Since investors will base their valuations of securities on the after-tax cash flows they expect to receive from them, it is reasonable to assume that individual taxes may affect firm value and thus capital structure decisions.

Learning Objective 21.8
Explain how the introduction of personal taxes on investment income affects the corporate tax advantage to using debt.

One popular model dealing with personal taxes was introduced by Merton Miller (one of the Ms of M&M).[24] He argued that a firm should strive to minimize all taxes, both corporate and personal, paid on corporate income. By doing so, the firm maximizes total cash flows available to security holders after corporate and personal taxes. Based on a number of technical assumptions, Miller arrived at the following valuation equation, which is a variation of the M&M valuation model that also accounts for personal tax rates:

[21A-1]
$$V_L = V_U + D\left[1 - \frac{(1-T_C)(1-T_D)}{(1-T_P)}\right]$$

where

T_C = the corporate tax rate

T_P = the individual's personal tax rate on ordinary income
    (which also applies to interest income)

T_D = the individual's tax rate on dividend income

Technically, we can note several things from this equation.

1. If $(1 - T_P) = (1 - T_C)(1 - T_D)$, then $V_L = V_U$, and we get the M&M irrelevancy proposition. This is referred to as an integrated tax system and has historically been the tax system in use in western Europe, where individuals get a tax credit for the corporate taxes paid on their behalf. Obviously, in this case there are no tax advantages to using debt.

2. If $(1 - T_P) < (1 - T_C)(1 - T_D)$, then $V_L < V_U$, which suggests the firm loses value by issuing debt. In this case, there is an incentive for individuals to borrow money, rather than the firm, since they generate larger tax shields.

3. If $(1 - T_P) > (1 - T_C)(1 - T_D)$, then $V_L > V_U$, which suggests the firm enhances value by issuing debt, since there are more debt tax shields at the corporate than the personal level. This is the system we have in Canada and is referred to as a partially integrated tax system.

4. If the personal tax rate on dividends (T_D) equals the tax rate on interest income (T_P), then we have what is referred to as a classic tax system, in which all personal income is taxed at the same rate. This is historically the system in place in the United States. The ratio $(1 - T_D)/(1 - T_P)$ equals one, and the M&M corporate tax shield holds even with personal taxes—that is, $V_L = V_U + T_C D$.

Generally, the third case tends to hold—that is $(1 - T_P) > (1 - T_C)(1 - T_D)$, so that $V_L > V_U$. It is the case in Canada that $T_D < T_P$, so the amount by which V_L exceeds V_U is less than the "$T_C D$" term included in M&M's corporate tax model. In other words, there are usually gains to firm value associated with the use of debt, but the gains are not as great as that predicted by M&M's corporate tax valuation model.

For example, based on 2012 federal and provincial tax rate estimates, the combined federal and provincial corporate tax rate for a company operating in Ontario that does not qualify for the small business tax deduction is 26 percent. This is a full 10 percent drop over the past eight years as Canada has attempted to reduce corporate tax rates to attract new investment. Further, assume an Ontario individual in the highest federal and provincial tax brackets has a personal tax rate of 46.41 percent on personal income and 29.54 percent on dividend income.[25]

---

[24] Miller, M., "Debt and Taxes." *Journal of Finance* 32, no. 2 (May 1977), pp. 261–75.

[25] A good site for determining current tax rates is the tax calculator provided on the Ernst & Young website at www.ey.com/CA/en/Services/Tax/Tax-Calculators.

Using these rates, we have the following:

$$(1 - T_P) > (1 - T_C)(1 - T_D)$$

$$(1 - 0.4641) > (1 - 0.26)(1 - 0.2954)$$

$$0.5359 > 0.5214$$

Notice that these numbers imply the following gains to using debt:

$$V_L = V_U + D\,[1 - (0.5214/0.5359)] \text{ or } V_L = V_U + 0.027D$$

Notice that the last term (0.027D) in this expression is much lower than that suggested by M&M's second model, which would be 0.26D based only on the corporate tax rate. Further, at these rates the combined tax on income earned through a large corporation is almost the same as that earned directly on interest income, implying a very low value for corporate leverage. This has been a major change in Canada due to the progressive reduction in the corporate tax rate.

While these results might appear useful at first glance, the model itself is based on several assumptions and is subject to several difficulties. First, as we have discussed several times throughout the text, the financial markets, and hence securities prices, are heavily influenced by the investing behaviour of institutional investors such as pension funds, insurance companies, and mutual funds, and most of these are not subject to tax. Second, individual investors face a variety of different marginal tax rates on both ordinary income and dividend income. As a result, the estimates of the tax advantages of using debt are a lower bound (a lower limit on the value). In fact, the dividend tax credit system was originally set up to fully integrate the tax system for small businesses based on their lower tax rate. This is because they have considerable discretion in paying out funds either as dividends or interest or salary, and the government wanted to remove any incentive for them to do one thing rather than another. However, if the system is neutral for a small business, it can't also be neutral for a larger business facing a higher corporate tax rate.

What we can say is that the Canadian tax system marginally favours corporate debt financing, and firms get a corporate tax shield from using debt. When we consider personal taxes, the advantage is not as large as that predicted from the corporate tax shield alone, since the government has set personal tax rates to reduce the double taxation of equity income in Canada. As a result, the tax advantages to using debt are between the value implied using personal taxes of 2.7 percent and that assuming no differential taxes at the individual level of 26 percent.

SUMMARY

In this chapter, we discuss some of the most important issues in finance. Long before OPM stood for the option pricing model, it stood for "other people's money" and was at the heart of financing activities. We show the three effects of financial leverage: expected ROE tends to increase, the variability of the ROE increases, and the risk of financial distress increases. These principles apply to the use of OPM regardless of who the borrower is: they are simply the effects of financial leverage. However, this text is concerned with corporate decisions, and the Conference Board shows that the major determinants of a firm's capital structure decision are that structure's impact on profits, risk, and cash flows. These impacts can be assessed by profit planning charts or financial break-even (indifference) analysis, as well as by the use of standard ratios calculated by the major rating agencies. However, these tools do not indicate how the use of debt creates value.

The classic M&M arguments assess whether the capital structure decision creates value. Their startling conclusion was that under some simplifying assumptions, issuing debt does not create value. This is because the firm is not doing anything that others can't do just as well—that is, borrow money. In essence, the M&M argument is that firms should stick to doing things where they have a comparative advantage, and it is difficult to see how borrowing money is such an activity, since we can all do it. However, what this means is that the WACC is independent of the debt ratio, and simple statements like "debt is cheaper than equity" and "using debt lowers the WACC" are fundamentally wrong.

However, once we introduce the fact that interest on debt is tax deductible, whereas dividends to the common shareholders are not, we see that there is a tax shield value to raising debt. At a 40-percent tax rate, the fact that interest is tax deductible as a cost of doing business means that, for a profitable firm, 40 percent of the value of the debt is effectively being paid by the government in reduced taxes. Hence, there is a transfer of wealth to the private sector from the government as the firm finances with debt. This tax incentive to using debt is offset by the resulting financial distress and bankruptcy costs, as discussed in the static trade-off model.

As its name implies, the static trade-off model does not take into account dynamic effects. The pecking order theory, on the other hand, does account for these dynamic effects, as firms tend to use internal cash flow first and then debt, and will only raise new common equity as a last resort. The result is that firms depart from the static trade-off optimal debt ratio over time, and then refinance to bring their debt ratio back in line with their target ratio. Therefore, actual capital structures are constantly changing as firms take advantage of market conditions.

SUMMARY OF LEARNING OBJECTIVES

21.1 Explain how business and financial risk affect a firm's ROE and EPS, and identify the financial break-even points.

Business risk is the variability in operating income caused by operational risk. Business risk can be thought of as the factors that cause variation in EBIT (e.g., operating leverage). Financial risk is the variability in net income (EPS) caused by leverage. The expected EPS and ROE rise as more debt is added as long as the firm earns more than the interest cost, but they also become more volatile. At low levels of EBIT, ROE/EPS is lower for a leveraged firm than for an all-equity firm, and the firm can run into financial difficulty because of the interest payments. At high levels of EBIT, ROE/EPS is higher for a leveraged firm than for an all-equity firm.

21.2 Identify the factors that influence capital structure.

A firm's use of debt is a trade-off between the tax advantages of debt (since the interest payments are tax deductible) and the loss in financial flexibility (since in a recession the firm may not have the ability to make the interest payments). In the case of a recession, the firm may end up bankrupt or in severe distress, or at the very least may find itself making sub-optimal decisions just to survive. In the latter case, the firm may have to defer capital expenditures, curtail dividends, and devote all corporate resources to paying off

creditors at a time when better-financed competitors can take advantage of its situation. Firms also take advantage of market opportunities and deviate from their optimal financing mix. For example, firms may not use their full debt capacity if the equity markets are buoyant, and they feel that it is cheaper to issue equity. Conversely, they will use as much debt as possible if they feel their equity is undervalued.

21.3 Explain how Modigliani and Miller (M&M) "proved" their irrelevance conclusion that the use of debt does not change the value of the firm.

The key assumptions underlying M&M's irrelevance argument are: perfect markets (no transaction costs and no asymmetric information), no taxes, no costs associated with financial distress, all earnings paid out as dividends, and individuals borrowing and lending at the same rate as companies. M&M showed that under these conditions, without taxes, firm value and WACC are completely unaffected by leverage. The irrelevance argument makes an analogy between firm value and a pie—how the pie is sliced does not affect the size of the pie. Similarly, how the firm structures the right-hand side of its balance sheet does not affect overall firm value. The irrelevance argument shows that investors can use leverage in their own account (homemade leverage) to offset corporate leverage.

21.4 Explain how the introduction of corporate taxes affects M&M's irrelevance result.

Corporate taxes change the M&M irrelevance conclusion. With taxes, a firm's value increases (and WACC decreases) with increased leverage due to the tax deductibility of interest. However, whether this remains true once we consider personal taxes is controversial, since individuals can also deduct the interest payments when they borrow money to buy shares.

21.5 Describe how financial distress and bankruptcy costs lead to the static trade-off theory of capital structure.

M&M assume costless bankruptcy and financial distress. However, bankruptcy includes costs, such as administrative, legal, and accounting costs as well as the loss of value due to distress sales. Financial distress includes costs too, such as customers buying elsewhere for fear that warranties will not be honoured, suppliers demanding cash payments for inputs fearing they may not be paid otherwise, and agency costs. The present value of these expected costs reduces slightly the benefits of the interest tax shield. Under the static trade-off theory, companies use debt to maximize their tax advantages up to the point where these benefits are outweighed by the associated costs of financial distress and bankruptcy.

21.6 Explain how information asymmetries and agency problems lead firms to follow a pecking-order approach to financing.

Information asymmetry is a significant problem for new equity issues, since the issuer has much more information about the value of the security than the prospective investor. The asymmetry leaves investors vulnerable to buying overpriced securities. To compensate for this risk, most new issues are underpriced, which makes issuing new equity unattractive for companies. Companies prefer internal equity first, debt second, and new equity last. Agency costs refer to costs incurred when managers do not act in the best interest of shareholders. If managers are self-interested, they prefer little oversight so they can use company resources for their own purposes. The desire to avoid scrutiny leads to a preference for internal cash over debt or equity, since capital markets and lenders place restrictions on management's actions.

21.7 Describe other factors that can affect a firm's capital structure in practice.

In practice, firms are restricted in the amount of debt they can issue since they are the "supply" side, but there is also a "demand" side to the debt markets. During the financial crisis of 2008, we saw many well-run businesses shut out of the debt markets and unable to raise money; some even went bankrupt. Consequently, many firms follow a policy of maintaining an investment-grade bond rating or spare debt capacity. This is why the rating agencies are so important. By downgrading a firm's rating to junk or less than BBB, they restrict the firm's financing flexibility. In response, firms only use as much debt as they can issue and stay within the covenant provisions of their bond contract so they will maintain a BBB or higher rating.

21.8 Explain how the introduction of personal taxes on investment income affects the corporate tax advantage to using debt.

The Government of Canada has recognized that equity income is double taxed by being taxed at both the corporate and personal level. This is why there is the dividend tax credit system, where the credit is designed to offset the corporate income tax so that the overall taxation of interest and dividend income is very similar. If the firm recognizes this, the tax advantage to using debt in Canada is much reduced. Whether it is reduced is complicated by the fact that much of the equity is owned either directly or indirectly by institutions or tax-preferred retirement vehicles so that in practice it remains an open question whether personal taxes affect capital structures for widely owned corporations.

KEY TERMS

agency costs, p. 820
bankruptcy, p. 818
business risk, p. 797
cash flow-to-debt ratio (CFTD), p. 806
corporate debt tax shield, p. 815
direct costs of bankruptcy, p. 820
EPS indifference point, p. 803
financial break-even points, p. 798
financial distress, p. 820

financial leverage, p. 797
financial leverage risk premium, p. 812
financial risk, p. 797
fixed burden coverage ratio, p. 805
homemade leverage, p. 810
indifference point, p. 798
indirect costs of bankruptcy or financial distress costs, p. 820
invested capital (IC), p. 796

M&M equity cost equation, p. 812
Modigliani and Miller (M&M), p. 808
pecking order, p. 825
profit planning charts, p. 803
return on equity (ROE), p. 796
return on invested capital (ROI), p. 796
risk value of money, p. 799
static trade-off, p. 822

EQUATIONS

Equation	Formula	Page
[21-1] Return on Equity	$ROE = \dfrac{(EBIT - R_D B)(1 - T)}{SE}$	p. 797
[21-2] Return on Investment	$ROI = \dfrac{EBIT(1 - T)}{SE + B}$	p. 797
[21-3] Return on Equity	$ROE = ROI + (ROI - R_D(1 - T))\dfrac{B}{SE}$	p. 797
[21-4] Return on Equity	$ROE = ROI\left(1 + \dfrac{B}{SE}\right) - R_D(1 - T)\dfrac{B}{SE}$	p. 798
[21-5] Earnings per Share	$EPS = \dfrac{(EBIT - R_D B)(1 - T)}{\#}$	p. 803
[21-6] Earnings per Share	$EPS = \dfrac{-R_D B(1 - T)}{\#} + \dfrac{EBIT(1 - T)}{\#}$	p. 803
[21-7] Fixed Burden Coverage Ratio	$Fixed\ burden\ coverage = \dfrac{EBITDA}{1 + (Pref.\ Div. + SF)/(1-T)}$	p. 805
[21-8] Cash Flow-to-Debt Ratio	$CFTD = \dfrac{EBITDA}{Debt}$	p. 806
[21-9] Altman Z Score	$Z = 1.2X_1 + 1.4X_2 + 3.3X_3 + 0.6X_4 + 0.999X_5$	p. 807
[21-10] Value of Unlevered Firm	$V_U = S_L + D = V_L$	p. 810
[21-11] Equity Value of Levered Firm	$S_L = \dfrac{(EBIT - K_D D)}{K_e}$	p. 811
[21-12] Cost of Equity	$K_e = \dfrac{(EBIT - K_D D)}{S_L}$	p. 811
[21-13] Unlevered Value	$V_U = \dfrac{EBIT}{K_U} = S_L + D = V_L$	p. 811
[21-14] M&M Equity Cost Equation	$K_e = K_U + (K_U - K_D)\dfrac{D}{S_L}$	p. 812
[21-15] Cost of Unlevered Equity	$K_U = K_e\dfrac{S}{V} + K_D\dfrac{D}{V}$	p. 812
[21-16] Value of Unlevered Firm, Assuming Perpetual EBIT	$V_U = \dfrac{EBIT(1 - T)}{K_U}$	p. 815
[21-17] Value of Firm with Leverage	$V_L = V_U + DT$	p. 815
[21-18] M&M Equity Cost	$K_e = K_U + (K_U - K_D)(1 - T)\dfrac{D}{S_L}$	p. 816
[21-19] Weighted Average Cost of Capital	$WACC = \dfrac{S}{V}K_e + \dfrac{D}{V}K_D(1 - T)$	p. 816
[21-20] CAPM Version of the Equity Cost Equation	$K_e = R_F + MRP \times \beta_U\left(1 + (1 - T)\dfrac{D}{S_L}\right)$	p. 817
[21A-1] Value of the Firm with Debt and Both Corporate and Personal Income Taxes	$V_L = V_U + D\left[1 - \dfrac{(1 - T_C)(1 - T_D)}{(1 - T_P)}\right]$	p. 830

QUESTIONS AND PRACTICE PROBLEMS

Multiple Choice Questions

1. What is the invested capital given the following? Accounts receivable = $50,000; current assets = $200,000; total assets = $700,000; shareholders' equity = $440,000; accounts payable = $10,000; short-term debt = $100,000; and long-term debt = $150,000.
   a. $700,000
   b. $740,000
   c. $690,000
   d. $590,000

2. Which of the following statements is true?
   a. Equity dollars are different from debt dollars.
   b. ROI is not affected by business risk.
   c. Each new dollar invested in a firm earns an incremental and different ROI.
   d. ROE is affected by financial risk.

3. Which of the following statements is false?
   a. The slope of the financial leverage line is (1 + debt-equity ratio).
   b. ROE = ROI if a firm is 100 percent financed by debt.
   c. The intercept of the financial leverage line is the debt-equity ratio times the after-tax cost of debt.
   d. One of the break-even points is when two financial strategies have the same ROE.

4. Which of the following statements of rules of financial leverage is false?
   a. The use of debt normally decreases the expected ROE.
   b. The higher the debt-equity ratio, the steeper the financial leverage line.
   c. Debt financing increases the risk to common shareholders.
   d. Debt financing increases the chances of financial distress.

5. The EPS-EBIT line
   a. is steeper if there are more shares outstanding.
   b. has a slope equal to $EBIT(1 - T)/\#$.
   c. has an intercept equal to $R_D B(1 - T)/\#$.
   d. indicates that if EBIT = 0, $EPS = -R_D B(1 - T)/\#$.

6. Which of the following is not an assumption of M&M's irrelevance theorem?
   a. Two firms exist with different levels of debt.
   b. There is no tax.
   c. Transaction costs are minimal.
   d. There is no risk of costly bankruptcy.

7. Which of the following will result in a decrease in the weighted average cost of capital (WACC)?
   a. A decrease in T_C
   b. An increase in the cost of debt
   c. An increase in the cost of equity
   d. A decrease in the weight of equity

8. In the M&M irrelevance world, which of the following is false?
   a. The cost of equity increases as the debt-equity ratio increases.
   b. If the expected ROI of a project is greater than the WACC, the share price will go up.
   c. The firm's objective is to increase the market value of the share price, not EPS.
   d. The WACC always increases as the debt-equity ratio increases.

9. What is the cost of equity for a levered firm given the following? $K_U = 10\%$; $K_D = 5\%$; $T = 20\%$; and $D/S_L = 0.6$.
    a. 13%
    b. 10.6%
    c. 12.4%
    d. 14.8%

10. Which of the firms below is the most likely to raise debt in the capital market?
    a. A profitable firm that has a risky underlying business
    b. A large and profitable firm with stable earnings and cash from operations
    c. A less profitable firm that has a non-risky business and cyclical cash flows
    d. A small firm that has seen its share price decrease in the past

Practice Problems

11. State the two rules of financial leverage.

12. Calculate ROE and ROI given the following.

Sales	$250,000	Taxes	$ 50,750
Cost of goods sold	$ 40,000	R_D	8%
Depreciation	$ 25,000	SE	$500,000
Selling, general, and administrative expenses	$ 16,000	Book value of debt (B)	$300,000

13. Calculate ROE if ROI = 12%, R_D = 10%, B = $200,000, SE = $300,000, and T = 0.35. Identify the business risk and financial risk.

14. What is the intercept and slope of the financial leverage (ROE-ROI) line in Practice Problem 13? Explain the meaning of the slope. What is the pecking order according to Myers' argument?

15. What is the ROE indifference point of the two strategies of Arctic Inc. as follows? $T_C = 30\%$, Strategy 1: debt-equity ratio = 0.7. Strategy 2: debt-equity ratio = 1.0. Arctic Inc.'s after-tax cost of debt is 10 percent.

16. Use two different methods to calculate ROI given the following information for Brandon Corp. Sales = $500,000; Cost of goods sold = $100,000; Interest cost $22,500; $T_C = 40\%$. The firm's debt (B = $300,000) accounts for 25 percent of the invested capital. After-tax cost of debt is 4.5 percent.

17. Calculate the fixed burden coverage and cash-flow-to-debt ratio given the following: EBIT = $700,000; depreciation and amortization = $60,000; preferred dividend $50,000; sinking fund payments = $10,000; tax rate = 20%; debt = $200,000. Why do analysts use EBITDA more often than EBIT?

18. Calculate Altman's Z score for Home Depot in fiscal year 2011 (as of January 29, 2012) and then compare it with Moody's rating chart. Is this company an IG or non-IG? All numbers are in millions.

Current assets	CA	$14,520	Retained earnings	RE	$2,251
Current liabilities	CL	$9,376	EBIT	EBIT	$6,661
Non-equity book liability	BL	$22,620	Market value of equity	MVE	$67,618
Total assets	TA	$40,518	Sales	S	$70,395

19. Explain the elements of Altman's Z score as used in Practice Problem 18.

20. Calculate the EPS indifference EBIT* level given the following information. The corporate tax rate is 20 percent. Under a 75-percent D/E ratio, the number of common shares outstanding

is 30,000; pre-tax cost of debt is 10 percent; and outstanding debt is $675,000. Under a 30-percent D/E ratio, the number of common shares outstanding is 65,000; pre-tax cost of debt is 6 percent; and outstanding debt is $420,000. Discuss the implication of the indifference EBIT* and indicate which option is better given an EBIT of $125,000.

21. In order for the M&M irrelevance theorem to hold, what key assumptions must be met?

22. In the M&M no-tax world, calculate the value of the levered firm (V_L). Cost of unlevered equity (K_U) = 15%; cost of debt (K_D) = 7%; debt (D) = $400,000; and NI = $520,000. What is the cost of levered equity?

23. With reference to the M&M irrelevance theorem, calculate the market value of an unlevered firm (U) and an identical risk-levered firm (L). The expected EBIT of the unlevered firm (U) = $1.5 million, which will remain constant indefinitely. The cost of capital is 12 percent. If the levered firm (L) has $6 million debt outstanding, what is the market value of the equity?

✸ 24. In the M&M no-tax world, an unlevered firm has a cost of equity of 10 percent and expected EBIT of $375,000. The firm decided to issue $2 million of debt at a cost of 6 percent to finance a project, which has an ROI of 15 percent. It has 100,000 shares outstanding.
   a. Calculate the value of the firm and price per share before issuing the debt.
   b. Calculate the firm's new earnings per share after issuing the debt.
   c. Calculate the value of the firm and the value of equity after the firm issues the debt.
   d. Calculate the cost of equity after the firm issues the debt.
   e. Calculate the new share price of the firm after it issues the debt.

25. In the M&M tax world, what is the value of levered firm (V_L) in Practice Problem 22 if the tax rate is 30 percent? What is the cost of levered equity? What is the market risk premium (MRP) given $\beta_U = 1.2$ and $R_F = 2\%$?

26. In the M&M tax world, calculate the value of the unlevered firm (U) and the identical risk-levered firm (L). Corporate tax rate = 20%; perpetual EBIT for U and L = $2 million; cost of capital of U = 16%; L's outstanding debt = $4 million; pre-tax cost of debt = 5%. What is the WACC of L?

✸ 27. Susan and Celia are twins but have very different attitudes toward debt. Susan believes that firms should have a D/E ratio of 0.2 while Celia believes that the D/E ratio should be 1.1. Both sisters have agreed that Okanagan Produce Inc. (OPI) is an excellent investment. However, the D/E of 0.5 is not quite right. OPI has an EBIT of $750,000 per year and pays interest of $100,000 per year. The cost of debt is 10 percent, and the twins can also borrow and lend at that rate. All cash flows are permanent and there are zero taxes.
   a. Determine what the cash flows from OPI would be if the firm had the desired D/E ratio in the table below:

		Desired by Susan	Desired by Celia
	OPI with D/E = 0.5	OPI with D/E = 0.2	OPI with D/E = 1.1
Value of firm	$3,000,000		
Value of debt	$1,000,000		
Value of equity	$2,000,000		
EBIT	$750,000		
Interest	$100,000		
Cash flows to equity	$650,000		

   b. Show the sisters how they can invest in OPI and still obtain their desired cash flows through borrowing and lending.

28. The Saskatchewan Botanicals Company expects a free cash flow of $1.2 million every year forever. Saskatchewan Botanicals currently has no debt, and its cost of equity is 20 percent. The corporate tax rate is 20 percent. The firm can borrow at 10 percent. All cash flows are perpetual. Saskatchewan Botanicals has 1 million shares outstanding.
    a. What is the value of Saskatchewan Botanicals with zero debt?
    b. If Saskatchewan Botanicals issues $3 million of debt and uses the proceeds to repurchase stock, determine the number of shares outstanding and the price per share after the repurchase.
    c. What is Saskatchewan Botanicals' cost of equity after the debt issue?
    d. Value Saskatchewan Botanicals' equity using the cost of equity. What is the cash flow to equity?

29. Athabascan Drilling is currently unlevered and is valued at $10 million. The company is considering including debt in its capital structure and would like to know the likely impact on its value and cost of capital. The current cost of equity is 22 percent. The firm is considering offering $2 million of new debt with an interest rate of 14 percent. Athabascan Drilling will use the proceeds of the debt issue to repurchase stock. There are currently 1 million shares outstanding and the marginal tax rate is 34 percent.
    a. What is the new value of Athabascan Drilling?
    b. What is the new WACC for Athabascan Drilling?

30. Straightforward Theatre Company has an EBIT of $1 million per year. The WACC of the firm is 10 percent and the before-tax cost of debt is 4 percent. The debt is risk free and all cash flows are perpetual. The current D/E ratio is 2/3. The corporate tax rate is 20 percent. The new CEO of Straightforward believes that the D/E ratio is too high and would like to reduce it to 1/3. She will issue stock to repay the debt.
    a. What is the impact on the EPS of Straightforward Theatre with this change in the D/E ratio?
    b. What is the impact on the cost of equity for Straightforward Theatre?

31. Explain how the static trade-off model can be used to find an optimal capital structure.

32. What important issues does the static trade-off model ignore?

33. Describe the factors that can affect a firm's capital structure in practice.

34. State the two possible ways bankruptcy can occur. What is the role of a monitor appointed by the court under the Companies' Creditors Arrangement Act (CCAA)? Compare the difference of recognizing firm bankruptcy under CCAA and the Business Insolvency Act.

35. Describe the relationship between the debt ratio and firm value when we consider the existence of bankruptcy costs. How do you view the agency costs when bankruptcy occurs?

36. What is the pecking order according to Myers' argument?

37. Summarize the main factors you need to consider if the CFO of your firm asks you to evaluate your firm's capital structure.

38. Gus Fitzgerald, a local shipping tycoon, is very confused. He has issued stock to finance a positive NPV investment. He expected the stock price to rise, as positive NPV projects are supposed to increase shareholder value. However, the stock price fell! Explain how this is possible in an efficient market.

39. Your cousin has just started his MBA and is confused. He understands that without taxes, capital structure is irrelevant. He also understands that with taxes, firms should use 100 percent debt. However, his professor is saying that with taxes, there are times that the investor will prefer an unlevered firm. How is this possible? Assume that there is no bankruptcy cost, information asymmetry, or agency problems. Assume that there is personal tax.

22 | Dividend Policy

LEARNING OBJECTIVES

22.1   Explain what a cash dividend payment is, how dividend payments are made, and why dividend payments are different from interest payments.

22.2   Describe typical dividend payouts and explain the importance of dividends.

22.3   Explain how Modigliani and Miller proved that dividend payments are irrelevant, due to the existence of homemade dividends, and therefore have no impact on market value.

22.4   Explain why dividend payments generally reflect the business risk of the firm, and explain what the "bird in the hand" argument is.

22.5   Explain why firms are reluctant to cut their dividends and why they smooth their dividends.

22.6   Explain why dividends are not a residual, as implied by M&M.

22.7   Describe what a share repurchase program is and explain how it can substitute for dividend payments.

MARKHAM, Ontario—Apple today announced plans to initiate a dividend and share repurchase program commencing later this year.

Subject to declaration by the Board of Directors, the Company plans to initiate a quarterly dividend of $2.65 per share sometime in the fourth quarter of its fiscal 2012, which begins on July 1, 2012.

Additionally, the Company's Board of Directors has authorized a $10 billion share repurchase program commencing in the Company's fiscal 2013, which begins on September 30, 2012. The repurchase program is expected to be executed over three years, with the primary objective of neutralizing the impact of dilution from future employee equity grants and employee stock purchase programs.

"We have used some of our cash to make great investments in our business through increased research and development, acquisitions, new retail store openings, strategic prepayments and capital expenditures in our supply chain, and building out our infrastructure. You'll see more of all of these in the future," said Tim Cook, Apple's CEO. "Even with these investments, we can maintain a war chest for strategic opportunities and have plenty of cash to run our business. So we are going to initiate a dividend and share repurchase program."

"Combining dividends, share repurchases, and cash used to net-share-settle vesting RSUs, we anticipate utilizing approximately $45 billion of domestic cash in the first three years of our programs," said Peter Oppenheimer, Apple's CFO. "We are extremely confident in our future and see tremendous opportunities ahead."

Source: Apple Inc. press release, March 19, 2012. Available at www.apple.com/ca/pr.

CHAPTER 22 **PREVIEW**

I In Chapter 21, we discussed how a firm decides on its capital structure—that is, the mix between debt and equity securities. The second major topic in corporate financing is how to decide on a payout policy: how much of a firm's earnings to pay out to common shareholders and how to do this. Payout policy is more commonly referred to as dividend policy, but as we saw in the opening vignette, there are several ways to pay out cash to the shareholders apart from paying a cash dividend; one way is to repurchase shares. We have previously discussed how to value common shares by discounting the expected future dividends, so it might seem obvious that dividends matter. Yet it turns out this may not necessarily be true. Having challenged conventional wisdom in terms of capital structure, Modigliani and Miller (M&M) went on to challenge the notion that dividends matter and derived their second irrelevance theorem: given certain assumptions, how much a firm pays out in dividends is completely irrelevant.

In this chapter, you will learn why dividends may be irrelevant and what critical assumptions are needed to reach this conclusion. In the process, you will understand what "realities" M&M assumed away and how they can affect dividend policy. We will show how dividends are paid out, what types of dividends there are, and why a share repurchase is sometimes seen as a substitute for a regular cash dividend.

22.1 DIVIDEND PAYMENTS

The Mechanics of Cash Dividend Payments

Learning Objective 22.1
Explain what a cash dividend payment is, how dividend payments are made, and why dividend payments are different from interest payments.

As we discussed in connection with common shares, there is no legal obligation for firms to pay common shareholders a dividend. A dividend has to be declared by the board of directors (BOD), after which it is announced and then becomes a contractual commitment. However, shareholders cannot force the members of the BOD to declare a dividend. Further, there are legal restrictions on whether or not the firm can declare a dividend. As we discussed in connection with bankruptcy in Chapter 21, the BOD cannot declare a dividend if by doing so it causes financial distress and makes the firm unable to fulfill its contractual commitments. If the BOD declares a dividend anyway, the members of the BOD can be held personally liable for damages. The *Canada Business Corporations Act* (CBCA) also expressly states that after the dividend payment, the value of the firm's assets has to exceed the total of its liabilities plus stated share capital. This is another way of saying that the dividend cannot be used to strip cash out of a firm in a period of financial distress.

declaration date the date on which the board of directors decides that the firm will pay a dividend

holder of record person who officially owns a share or shares on a given date

On February 14, 2012, TransCanada Corporation issued a press release announcing that "the Board of Directors of TransCanada declared a quarterly dividend of $0.44 per common share for the quarter ending March 31, 2012 on the Company's outstanding common shares, a five per cent increase over the $0.42 per share paid in each of the previous four quarters. The common share dividend is payable on April 30, 2012 to shareholders of record at the close of business on March 30, 2012." In this case, February 14, 2012, is the **declaration date**; after this declaration, TransCanada is legally obliged to pay a dividend of $0.44 per share. At this point, the amount of the dividend is transferred from retained earnings to an accrued liability in the firm's financial statements. The press release also indicates the **holder of record** date, which is March 30, 2012. This means whoever is the owner of record of TransCanada's shares on March 30, 2012, will be entitled to receive the dividend. The dividend will then be paid on April 30, 2012, to all those owners.

One obvious question is "When can I buy the shares and get the dividend?" Or alternatively, "When can I sell the shares and not receive the dividend?" The answer is that on most exchanges, common share transactions are settled three business days after the trade. For this reason, most exchanges, as well as most investment dealers for the over-the-counter market, establish an **ex-dividend date** two business days prior to the holder of record date. From this date on, the shares trade without the right to receive the dividend (i.e., ex-dividend). So for TransCanada, the ex-dividend date would be March 28: if you sold the shares on March 27, you would not receive the dividend, since the shares would be registered to the new owner by March 30. However, if you sold them on March 28, you would receive the dividend, since you would still be the holder of record on March 30.

We chose to look at TransCanada in this example because as a major Canadian pipeline utility, it pays a regular cash dividend and has a long history of doing so. Figure 22-1 shows TransCanada's quarterly dividend per share history since 2000. We can see that in 2000, TransCanada paid a quarterly dividend per share of $0.20, this was increased to $0.23 in 2001, and then by a few cents every year until March 2012, when it reached $0.44. We can also see that the BOD sets the dividend at the end of TransCanada's fiscal year, and this quarterly dividend is maintained each quarter until the BOD reviews the annual results the next year. This also is typical of major corporations; the dividend per share is typically set once a year unless something dramatic happens.

ex-dividend date date after which shares trade without the right of the purchaser to receive a dividend

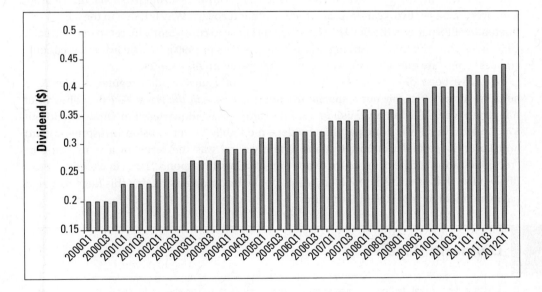

FIGURE 22-1 *TransCanada Dividend per Share (DPS) History*

The dividend per share information for TransCanada comes directly from the company's website.[1] TransCanada also paid dividends prior to 2000, and Figure 22-2 plots the annual dividend and earnings per share since 1998. During the mid-1990s, TransCanada made a disastrous foray into non-regulated businesses, and its EPS dropped to $0.77 in 1998, significantly below the $1.18 dividend set at the start of the year. Although its operations improved during 1999 to $0.97, this was still below the established dividend, so the BOD cut the dividend in both 1999 and 2000 to establish a new starting level of $0.20 a quarter. This raises three important questions: when and why does a BOD cut the dividend and what is the stock market's reaction to both a cut in a dividend and its restoration?

---

[1] The URL for the TransCanada website is www.transcanada.com.

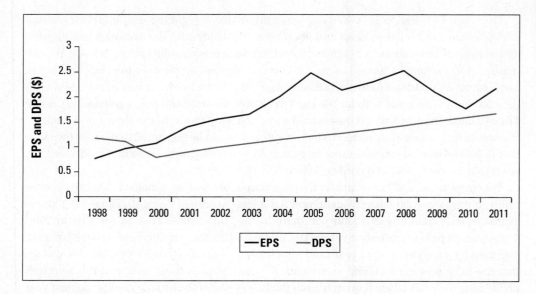

FIGURE 22-2 *TransCanada Annual Dividend and Earnings per Share*

One final observation on the TransCanada DPS history is that the annual DPS shows a nice pattern of pretty much constant growth since 2000. However, the EPS pattern is nowhere near as pretty! There is a quite dramatic EPS increase from 1998 through to 2005, then a drop, a recovery, a bigger two-year drop, and then another recovery. Why is it that in the face of this fluctuating EPS pattern, the BOD of TransCanada chose to consistently increase the DPS each year, even while the EPS was falling, when it cut the DPS in 1999 and 2000 in similar circumstances? These are questions we will be addressing later in this chapter.

We have been discussing the dividend history of TransCanada's regular dividend. In addition, firms often pay out a **special dividend**. *Finance in the News 22-1* describes what happened when Telesat, a Canadian satellite company headquartered in Ottawa, paid out $705 million to its two principal shareholders, the Public Sector Pension Investment Board and Loral Space and Communications. The dividend was the result of a refinancing or "recapitalization" of the company, so was a one-off affair. In response, Loral declared a special dividend so that its own shareholders would not be led into thinking that this huge dividend payment might be repeated in the future.

special dividend a dividend over and above a firm's normal dividend that the BOD indicates is not likely to be repeated

finance INTHENEWS 22-1 Dividend Payable

LORAL SPACE & COMMUNICATIONS INC. today announced that its Board of Directors has declared a special dividend of $13.60 per share for an aggregate dividend of up to $421 million. The dividend is payable on April 20, 2012, to holders of record of Loral voting and non-voting common stock as of April 10, 2012. As of March 27, 2012, there were outstanding 21,117,311 shares of Loral voting common stock and 9,505,673 shares of Loral non-voting stock.

Loral's declaration of this special dividend is a direct result of Telesat's completion today of a refinancing and recapitalization transaction which resulted in a dividend from Telesat to Loral. As part of the transaction, Telesat entered into a new credit agreement that replaced its existing credit agreement and increased its indebtedness by approximately $490 million. Commenting on Telesat's refinancing, Michael B. Targoff, Chief Executive Officer of Loral, said: "I am particularly gratified that Telesat was able to raise approximately $2.5 billion of bank financing with an average annual

interest rate of approximately 4.4%, another testament to the strength of the Telesat business."

In addition, the Board of Directors and shareholders of Telesat approved payments to Telesat's option holders and distributions to Telesat's shareholders of C$705 million in the aggregate, of which a total of C$420 million will be paid to Loral. The distributions by Telesat to its shareholders were authorized to be paid in two tranches; the first tranche was paid by Telesat on March 28, 2012, the closing date of the transaction, with Loral receiving C$375 million, and the second tranche is planned for payment in the third quarter of 2012 with Loral to receive C$45 million. The dividend to be paid to Loral's shareholders approximates the full amount of both dividend tranches to be received by Loral from Telesat. Pending receipt of the second tranche from Telesat, Loral will use its available cash balance to fund the difference between the Loral dividend being paid and the proceeds received from Telesat.

continued

Finance in the News 22-1: Dividend Payable *(continued)*

Regarding the dividend, Mr. Targoff said: "Our investment in Telesat has provided Loral with handsome book returns and growth since our acquisition. Receipt of this significant dividend from Telesat is a partial realization of this investment, and we are pleased to be able to share that with Loral's shareholders."

Source: "Loral Declares Dividend of $13.60 Per Share." Loral press release, April 20, 1012. Available at http://investor.loral.com.

Dividend Reinvestment Plans (DRIPs), Stock Dividends, and Stock Splits

If the investor does not want to receive a dividend, many Canadian firms offer the option of using the cash dividend proceeds to buy new shares by way of a **dividend reinvestment plan (DRIP)**. These shares are then issued by the company without any brokerage fees or transactions costs. Generally, DRIPs will buy as many shares as the cash dividend allows, with the residual deposited as cash. At one time, firms allowed the shares to be purchased at a 5 percent discount to the closing market price as an incentive for investors to reinvest, but many companies, such as BCE Inc., have now phased out the discount.

> **dividend reinvestment plan (DRIP)** a plan that allows investors to use dividends to buy new shares

DRIPs are popular with both investors and companies. For companies, it means that shares are issued continuously at no cost, while they are also seen to be paying a regular dividend. DRIPs foster a more ongoing relationship with investors, who often end up holding **odd lots** of shares, so that their total share holdings are in odd numbers, like 123 shares, instead of a round lot of some multiple of 100. This has become less important in recent years as trading has become more efficient and is no longer done in round lots of 100 shares each. For long-term investors who are not reliant on income from their portfolios, the automatic reinvestment averages their investment, since they are buying shares at a range of prices. It also removes the problem of accumulating funds to reinvest. However, even though less cash is received by the investor, the full cash dividend is still taxable, which represents an obvious disadvantage.

> **odd lots** groups of shares that are purchased in odd-numbered lots instead of in multiples of 100

A cash dividend along with a DRIP is similar to a **stock dividend**. In this case, rather than giving the investor cash and then taking it back for shares, the company simply gives more shares. A stock dividend is defined as any share distribution in which the number of shares issued is less than 25 percent of the outstanding shares. So a company may give a 10 percent stock dividend in which each investor gets 10 percent more shares. In terms of accounting, it is treated like a regular cash dividend, so the value of the shares issued is transferred from retained earnings into the capital stock account. As a result, stock dividends are limited by the amount of retained earnings available.

> **stock dividend** a dividend paid in additional shares rather than cash

However, there is one significant difference between a cash dividend plus DRIP and a stock dividend. With the cash dividend plus DRIP, the cash is distributed first, and it is up to the investors to decide whether they want to buy more shares. Regardless of the investors' decisions, the firm has to have the cash to make the distribution. With the stock dividend, on the other hand, firms often do not have the cash and simply issue a stock dividend to give the investor "something." Whether the investors pay attention when they get more pieces of paper is another question, since all that is happening is the value of the common shares is being divided among more shares, which will cause the stock price to fall. In addition, the amount of the stock dividend is fully taxable, despite the fact that no cash is received. Finally, the fact that retained earnings have decreased reduces the firm's ability to pay subsequent cash dividends, which also have to be paid out of retained earnings.

An extreme version of a stock dividend is a **stock split**. In this case, there is a greater-than-25-percent increase in the number of shares outstanding. For example, a 50-percent increase

> **stock split** a greater-than-25-percent increase in the number of shares outstanding

in the shares outstanding would be referred to as a "three for two" stock split rather than a 50 percent stock dividend. This simply means that investors get three shares for every two they already hold, or 50 percent more. There are some accounting advantages to this because the retained earnings account is not altered, but the number of shares outstanding is simply increased (in this example, by 50 percent). In addition, in contrast to the case with stock dividends, investors face no tax implications arising from a stock split, except that the average purchase price for shares will be adjusted downward to reflect the split.

Both stock dividends and stock splits simply divide the value of the common shares among more shares and, all else remaining constant, reduce the price per share. Why firms do this is something of a mystery, since there is no underlying change in the firm. One reason often advanced is that by increasing the number of shares, the price per share falls, which may be useful if there is an optimal trading range for the share price. This allows the shares to be traded in round lots at a reasonable value. For example, 100 shares at a price of $30 each means a $3,000 trade, but if the share price is $300, it means a $30,000 trade, which may be too big for small investors.

This argument had some validity when there were significant costs attached to trading shares and round lots of 100 shares meant something. However, trading costs are now deregulated, and odd lots of, say, 50 shares can be traded without excessive transactions costs. Further, if the share price gets too high, what constitutes a round lot changes. For example, shares of Berkshire Hathaway (whose largest shareholder and CEO is Warren Buffett, the second-richest man in the world) traded down $1,119.97 a share on March 29, 2012. That sounds like a lot but was actually only a 0.91 percent drop in price to $121,655.03 a share. These shares trade in round lots of one share and have no trouble attracting investors. On the other hand, foreign securities are often repackaged into bundles of shares known as American Depository Receipts (ADRs) to get their U.S. dollar price in New York into a "proper" trading range. UK stocks are repackaged for the U.S. market, for example, because they trade in the United Kingdom in pence and would be regarded as "penny" stocks in New York if they weren't bundled. Barclays, one of the largest banks in the world, with a market capitalization of $50 billion, trades as BCS in New York and was priced at $15.66 on March 28, 2012, while it traded in London as barc.l at 234 pence or about $4.

It is difficult to know whether these strategies have any economic significance, but exchanges do have rules for shares trading under $2 that are different from the rules for shares trading above $2. These rules affect the requirements for listing status as well as brokerage commission rates. Also, securities regulations in North America often make it difficult to sell, or get margin to buy, short stocks when they are priced under $5. In practice, Canadian and U.S. firms with large market capitalizations like to have their stock price trade well above $5. This became a problem for Nortel Networks Corporation when its stock price collapsed from US$122 down to the $2 range. Nortel's stock price bounced around the $2 level for over two years, and it was an embarrassment for Canada's premier technology company to be regarded as a penny stock. In response, at the company's annual shareholder meeting on June 29, 2006, the shares were consolidated in a "1-for-10" reverse split. Nortel explained that "the transaction was implemented to increase investors' visibility into the Company's profitability on a per share basis, reduce share transaction fees for investors and certain administrative costs for Nortel, and broaden interest to institutional investors and investment funds."[2]

If investors hadn't been paying attention, they might have thought the Nortel stock price boom of the 1990s had happened all over again; once the consolidation took place on December 1, 2006, Nortel's stock price was miraculously above $30 for the first time in six years. However, all that had happened was the number of Nortel shares they owned had been cut by 90 percent.

---

[2] The information is available in Nortel's filings with the Ontario Securities Commission at www.sedar.com; this quote was taken from the Nortel website at www.nortel.com/corporate/investor/faq.html, but has since been removed.

To emphasize: with stock splits and stock dividends, the firm's value is being divided by a greater number of shares, which means the share price should fall. With a reverse split, the price should rise. If there is an optimal trading range, it might be that the share price does not decrease proportionally with the greater number of shares. This is easy to test. In a pioneering study, Fama et al. examined 940 stock splits in the United States from 1927 to 1959 and found no significant wealth change in the month of each split.[3] However, there were two important results. First, the researchers found that firms that split their stock did so after exceptionally good stock market performance. Consistent with the optimal trading range idea, they split their stock in order to bring the stock price back to a "normal" range. Second, they found that two-thirds of the firms in their sample increased their aggregate dividend payments; for those firms, the shares performed better in the next year. In contrast, for the one-third of the sample that kept their aggregate dividend constant, the share price underperformed the market.

The Fama study has been repeated several times since, and the basic message is the same. North American firms like to keep their share prices in a "normal" trading range and use stock dividends and stock splits to accomplish this. If the price run-up that causes the split results in higher dividends, the stock price continues to outperform the market; if there is no change, the share price slips back. This leads to the conclusion that it is not the stock split or dividend itself that is causing the price behaviour but expectations about the firm's future performance, and investors take the stock split as a signal that management agrees with this assessment. We will discuss this "signalling role" for dividends in more detail after we consider some data on dividends. However, whereas the stock split is a positive signal when firms maintain their dividend per share, a reverse stock split is rarely a good signal because such firms hardly ever pay a dividend in the face of a falling stock price. For example, the reverse stock split did nothing for Nortel, and its stock price continued to deteriorate because cutting the number of shares outstanding did nothing for its underlying business operations. Nortel then entered bankruptcy protection and is now in the final stages of selling its remaining assets.

CONCEPT REVIEW QUESTIONS

1. Define four important dates that arise with respect to dividend payments.
2. Explain the similarities and differences of DRIPs, stock dividends, and stock splits.

22.2 CASH DIVIDEND PAYMENTS

We can look at dividends from both macro- and micro-level perspectives. At the macro level, dividends are income, and data about them are collected on tax returns. These data end up in the National Income Accounts and are included as part of the gross domestic product (GDP). Figure 22-3 shows the after-tax profit and dividends paid by corporate Canada divided by GDP, since 1961. We divide by GDP simply to standardize the dollar numbers and because, as income, the figures are also part of gross national income.

The graph shows that after-tax profits generally run at about 6 percent of GDP but are highly variable because they reflect all the uncertainty in the business cycle. During recessions, when GDP weakens, firms lose money because, while their sales decline, their fixed operating and financing costs do not drop proportionally. We can see the impact of the recessions in the early 1980s and early 1990s, when after-tax profits dropped to just below 3 percent and then barely 1 percent of GDP. We can also see the dramatic drop in 2009 as weaker commodity prices hit Canada very hard. The recession in the early 1990s was particularly painful due to the adjustment to the Free Trade Agreement (FTA) with the United States, when corporate

Learning Objective 22.2
Describe typical dividend payouts and explain the importance of dividends.

---

[3] Fama, E., L. Fisher, M. Jensen, and R. Roll, "The Adjustment of Stock Prices to New Information." *International Economic Review* 10, no. 1 (February 1969), pp. 1–21.

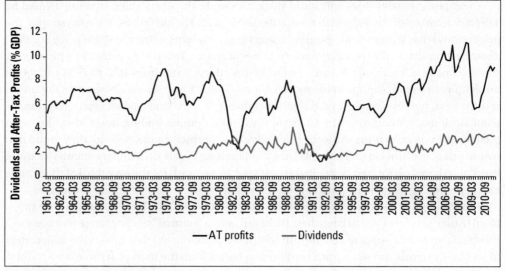

FIGURE 22-3 *Aggregate Dividends and After-Tax Profits as a Percentage of GDP*

Source: Data from Statistics Canada.

Canada had to learn how to compete against larger, more competitive U.S. firms. Finally, we can see the surge in profits earned by corporate Canada in the early to mid-2000s as natural resource prices hit record levels. In recent years, after-tax profits have been at an all-time high, in the 10 percent range.

In contrast to the volatility in after-tax profits, dividends have remained relatively stable. Note that while dividends roughly tracked after-tax profits from 1961 to 1980, they were not cut during the recession of 1981–82 or during the deeper recession of 1991–93. Further, since 2000 we have seen a large increase in after-tax profits, which has not been matched by an equivalent increase in dividends, although dividends in 2011 were running at 3.4 percent of GDP, which is higher than the average since 1961 of 2.45 percent. We can see these effects more clearly when we look at the aggregate dividend payout, which is aggregate dividends divided by aggregate after-tax profits. Figure 22-4 indicates that the median or typical payout is just less than 40 percent of after-tax profits, but it increased to over 100 percent during the two recessions when profits dropped dramatically but dividends remained relatively stable. Further, we have seen the payout rate trending downwards since 2000, to an all-time low of 26 percent of after-tax profits in the second quarter of 2008, as a result of recent record-high profits.

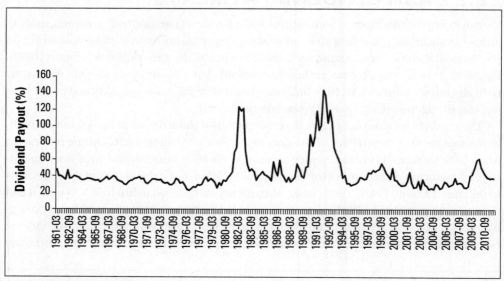

FIGURE 22-4 *Payout Based on Aggregate Profits and Dividends (Median Payout 37%)*

Source: Data from Statistics Canada.

Looking at the aggregate dividend and profits data confirms the results of looking at the same data for TransCanada and naturally raises the first of two important questions:

1. *Why are dividends smoothed and not matched to profits?*

Another way of asking this is: why don't firms just pay a constant proportion of profits out as dividends and cut them when their profits and cash flows drop, as they usually do during recessions? We saw, for example, that TransCanada Corporation did not cut its dividend per share in 2009 and 2010, even as its earnings per share fell. We can see the same phenomenon in Figure 22-3 when we aggregate across all Canadian firms.

It is also interesting to look at the micro level—that is, the dividends paid by individual companies. Table 22-1 contains the dividend per share and **dividend yield** (defined in chapters 4 and 7 as the annual dividend per share divided by the share price) for the firms in the S&P/TSX 60 Index as of March 28, 2012.

dividend yield annual dividend per share divided by the share price

Looking at the dividend yields, we see that they range from a low of zero for several firms, including Research In Motion (RIM), to a high of almost 10 percent for Enerplus, which used to be an income trust before it converted back to being a regular corporation. Even discounting Enerplus, we still see the Canadian banks with dividend yields of about 4 percent in 2012. This raises the other important question:

2. *Why is there such a substantial difference in dividend yields (and payouts) across major Canadian companies? Why do some firms have very high dividends and some very low or non-existent dividends?*

To answer this question, we consider the second major contribution of Modigliani and Miller and consider what value is created by paying a dividend.

TABLE 22-1 S&P/TSX 60 Index Dividend Yields, as of March 2012

Company	DPS	Div. Yld.
Agnico-Eagle Mines Ltd.	0.2	2.4
Agrium Inc.	0.25	0.58
ARC Resources Ltd.	0.1	5.21
Bank of Montreal	0.7	4.73
Bank of Nova Scotia	0.55	3.89
Barrick Gold Corporation	–	–
BCE Inc.	0.54	5.43
Bombardier Inc.	0.25	2.44
Brookfield Asset Management Inc.	0.14	1.77
Cameco Corporation	0.1	1.86
Canadian Imperial Bank of Commerce	0.9	4.71
Canadian National Railway Company	0.38	1.9
Canadian Natural Resources Limited	0.11	1.29
Canadian Oil Sands Limited	0.3	5.6
Canadian Pacific Railway Limited	0.3	1.57
Canadian Tire Corporation, Limited	0.3	1.85
Cenovus Energy Inc.	0.22	2.46
Eldorado Gold Corporation	0.09	1.35
Enbridge Inc.	0.29	2.91
Encana Corporation	0.2	4
Enerplus Corporation	0.18	9.65
First Quantum Minerals Ltd.	0.13	0.95

continued

TABLE 22-1 S&P/TSX 60 Index Dividend Yields, as of March 2012 *continued*

Company	DPS	Div. Yld.
Fortis Inc.	0.3	3.72
George Weston Limited	0.36	2.29
Gildan Activewear Inc.	0.08	0.11
Goldcorp Inc.	0.05	1.22
Husky Energy Inc.	0.3	4.76
Iamgold Corporation	0.13	3.84
Imperial Oil Limited	0.12	1.07
Inmet Mining Corporation	0.10	0.36
Kinross Gold Corporation	0.08	1.64
Loblaw Companies Limited	0.21	2.47
Magna International Inc.	0.28	2.34
Manulife Financial Corporation	0.13	3.86
Metro Inc.	0.22	1.63
National Bank of Canada	0.75	3.77
Nexen Inc.	0.05	1.11
Penn West Petroleum Ltd.	0.27	5.55
Potash Corporation of Saskatchewan Inc.	0.14	1.2
Power Corporation of Canada	0.29	4.37
Research In Motion Limited	–	–
Rogers Communications Inc.	0.395	4.07
Royal Bank of Canada	0.57	3.93
Saputo Inc.	0.19	1.76
Shaw Communications Inc.	0.08	4.6
Shoppers Drug Mart Corporation	0.27	2.42
Silver Wheaton Corp.	0.09	1.11
SNC-Lavalin Group Inc.	0.22	2.21
Sun Life Financial Inc.	0.36	6.11
Suncor Energy Inc.	0.11	1.36
Talisman Energy Inc.	0.14	2.13
Teck Resources Limited	0.4	2.31
TELUS Corporation	0.61	4.19
Thomson Reuters Corporation	0.32	4.36
Tim Hortons Inc.	0.21	1.55
Toronto-Dominion Bank	0.72	3.41
TransAlta Corporation	0.29	6.26
TransCanada Corporation	0.44	4.09
Valeant Pharmaceuticals International, Inc.	–	–
Yamana Gold Inc.	0.55	1.42

CONCEPT REVIEW QUESTIONS

1. What obvious question arises when we examine historical patterns in aggregate dividend payouts?

2. What obvious question arises when we examine cross-sectional patterns in the dividend payouts of individual companies?

22.3 MODIGLIANI AND MILLER'S DIVIDEND IRRELEVANCE THEOREM

M&M, Dividends, and Firm Value

After "proving" in 1958 that, under certain circumstances, a firm's capital structure did not matter, Franco Modigliani and Merton Miller (M&M) went on in 1961 to "prove" that dividend policy did not matter either,[4] thereby showing that two of the major activities of corporate finance were irrelevant. Needless to say, this position was highly controversial then and remains so today. However, the importance of the M&M argument is not that it is actually correct, but that it points the way to finding where value can be created with dividend policy and why.

It might seem obvious that dividends matter; after all, one of the most basic equations used to value common shares is Equation 22-1.

$$P_0 = \frac{D_1 + P_1}{(1 + K_e)} \qquad [22\text{-}1]$$

The price of a share today (P_0) is the present (discounted) value of next period's expected dividend per share (D_1) and price per share (P_1). The dividend per share is part of the valuation equation, so dividends must be important. However, M&M showed that all is not what it seems.

To understand the M&M proof, first multiply the price per share by the current number of shares outstanding (m). This simply converts the price-per-share equation into an equation that values the total amount of common equity, or the **equity market capitalization** (V_0).

$$mP_0 = V_0 = \frac{m(D_1 + P_1)}{(1 + K_e)} \qquad [22\text{-}2]$$

As they did for their capital structure argument, M&M then made some very important assumptions:

1. There are no taxes.

2. Markets are perfect.

3. All firms maximize value.

4. There is no debt.

The last assumption is there simply because they proved in 1958 that debt is irrelevant so that in this paper, they could concentrate on dividend policy; it also helps simplify their use of the sources and uses of funds constraint. Remember from accounting that the cash flow statement, like all financial statements, always balances. Therefore, without any debt, the sources and uses of funds identity (i.e., sources = uses) can be expressed as:

$$X_1 + nP_1 = I_1 + mD_1 \qquad [22\text{-}3]$$

Here, X represents cash flow from operations and I represents investment, so $X - I$ is what we termed **free cash flow** in Chapter 3. This free cash flow can either be paid out as a dividend to the current shareholders (mD_1), or new funds can be raised by selling new shares (n) to investors next period at the price P_1.

Learning Objective 22.3
Explain how Modigliani and Miller proved that dividend payments are irrelevant, due to the existence of homemade dividends, and therefore have no impact on market value.

equity market capitalization (V_0)
total common equity market value

free cash flow the result of subtracting the capital expenditures from the cash flow from operations

---

[4] Miller, M., and F. Modigliani, "Dividend Policy, Growth, and the Valuation of Shares." *Journal of Business* 34, no. 4 (October 1961), pp. 411–33.

It is important to realize that Equation 22-3 is not an assumption; it is just a constraint indicating that the sources and uses of funds have to balance given the absence of debt financing. Consequently, we can solve for the dividends paid out (mD_1) to get:

$$mD_1 = X_1 + nP_1 - I_1$$

Notice that this relationship implies that if the firm pays out dividends that exceed its free cash (X – I), it must issue new common shares to pay for these dividends. When we substitute this term into the valuation Equation 22-2 for mD_1, we get the following:

[22-4]
$$V_0 = \frac{X_1 - I_1 + [(m + n)P_1 = V_1]}{(1 + K)}$$

So the value of the firm is simply the value of next period's free cash flow ($X_1 - I_1$) plus next period's equity market value (V_1, which equals $(m + n)\,P_1$). By repeatedly substituting this to find the value of the firm at all future points in time, we get the fundamental equity valuation formula, Equation 22-5. This is the basic equation we use to determine the total market value of the firm's equity as opposed to the price per share. It says that firm value is determined as the present value of the free cash flows to the equity holders.

[22-5]
$$V_0 = \sum_{t=1}^{\infty} \frac{X_t - I_t}{(1 + K)^t}$$

It is important to realize that Equation 22-1 says that, in order to value a share of common stock, we simply discount all the future expected dividends, since this is the cash received by the investor. Yet Equation 22-5 says that to value the aggregate of all the shares (i.e., the total market value of equity), we value the free cash flows to all the equity holders. Obviously these two approaches must give exactly the same value, which implies that the dividend is equal to the free cash flow each period. In this view, the dividend is the residual that remains after the firm has taken care of all its investment requirements, so we call this the **residual theory of dividends**.

So what does all this mean? To answer, let's return to the investment opportunity schedule (IOS) for Tim Hortons for 2011, previously depicted in Figure 20-7 of Chapter 20 and reproduced in Figure 22-5.

residual theory of dividends the theory that the dividends paid out should be the residual cash flow that remains after the firm has taken care of all its investment requirements

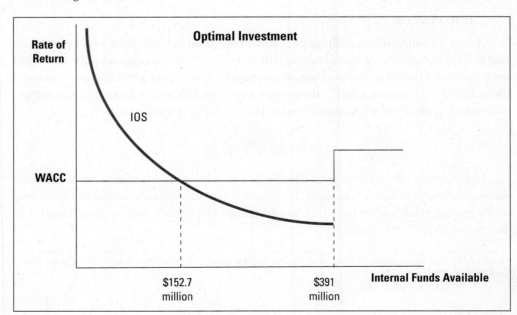

FIGURE 22-5 *Tim Hortons' Internal Funds, Investment, and Dividends*

In this figure, we see Tim Hortons' 2011 cash flow from operations of $391 million and investment of $152.7 million. In the case of Tim Hortons,

$$X - I = \$238.3 \text{ million}$$

So we can say that Tim Hortons would normally be regarded as a **cash cow**. Or we could say that the residual theory of dividends suggests that Tim Hortons should pay a high dividend, but it does not. In Chapter 19, we showed that Tim Hortons' dividend yield at the 2011 year end was 1.38 percent; on March 28, 2012, it was 1.55 percent. The dividend yield fluctuates with market prices and so is constantly changing, but Tim Hortons' dividend yield is not very high. So where does the rest of Tim Hortons' money go? In 2011, the company spent a whopping $572.5 million repurchasing common shares. Moreover, this was not unusual, as Tim Hortons spent $242.6 million and $113.4 million repurchasing shares in the two prior years, and the company recently announced a $200-million share repurchase program for 2012.

As M&M's theory showed, paying cash dividends or repurchasing common shares accomplishes the same purpose. Both actions return cash to the shareholders, confirming that Tim Hortons is a cash cow. If these numbers were reversed, and Tim Hortons had cash flow from operations of only $152.7 million and investment of $391 million, it would be classified as a growth stock. In this case, the residual theory of dividends would indicate that it should not pay out a dividend since it would have to raise equity through new share issues to finance its investment. In fact, Tim Hortons has the best of both worlds: its major mode of expansion is through franchised restaurants, which do not tap its cash as much as owner stores, so it has the luxury of being a cash cow with growth potential, and a relatively low-risk one at that. It is a star! This is why its market price is so high.

The key insight from the M&M argument is that the firm always accepts the optimal amount of investment, so investment is independent of the firm's dividend policy. The main assumptions that generate this conclusion are that firms maximize value and markets are perfect. This means firms can always raise the necessary capital to undertake all positive net present value (NPV) projects, so they are not financially constrained. If firms are financially constrained, the idea that dividend policy is irrelevant falls apart, as we will show shortly.

With investment fixed and cash flow from operations determined by the firm's real operations, it is clear from the sources and uses of funds constraint, Equation 22-3, that new share issues and dividend payments are the opposite of each other. If all else is constant, an increase in cash dividends paid means the firm has to raise more cash by selling new shares.

cash cow a firm with a high present value of existing opportunities but a low present value of growth opportunities

---

EXAMPLE 22-1   Dividends and Free Cash Flow

A firm has cash flow from operations of $100 million and needs $90 million for investment purposes, leaving $10 million of free cash flow. Assume the firm has 10 million shares outstanding and its shares are presently trading at $20 per share. How many new shares must be issued if it plans to pay out a dividend per share of $2?

Solution

$$nP_1 = mD_1 - (X_1 - I_1) = (10)(2) - (100 - 90) = \$10 \text{ million}$$

New proceeds required = $10 million

Since its share price is $20, with 10 million shares outstanding, we can say that the value of the firm's equity is $20 × 10 million = $200 million.

When it issues new shares, this $200 million must be divided among the new shareholders (n) as well as the existing shareholders (m), so the new share price at time 1 will be:

$$P_1 = \frac{V}{m+n} = \frac{\$200}{10+n}$$

This reduces to:

$$10P_1 + nP_1 = \$200$$

continued

EXAMPLE 22-1   Dividends and Free Cash Flow *continued*

Since we know that $nP_1 = \$10$ million, we know that

$$10P_1 = \$200 - \$10 = \$190$$

So the new $P_1 = \$190 \div 10 = \$19$

This implies the firm will need to issue the following number (n) of new shares:

$$n = 10 \text{ million} \div \$19 = 526{,}316 \text{ shares}$$

Notice that the firm value remains the same, at $200 million, in M&M's world, since it is simply the present value of the firm's future free cash flows to infinity. There are simply more shares outstanding (10,526,316), which are each worth $19.

EXAMPLE 22-2   Residual Dividend Policy

Consider the firm from Example 22-1.

a.   How much would it pay out in dividends per share if it was all equity financed and the firm followed a strict residual dividend policy?

b.   Redo part (a), but assume the firm plans to finance its future investments, including this year's total investment outlay of $90 million, using 30 percent debt financing.

Solution

a.   Dividends per share = Free cash flow per share = \$10 million/10 million shares = \$1

b.   In this case, only $63 million of the required investment is from operations (i.e., 70 percent of the $90 million in total investments), since the other $27 million (i.e., 30 percent of $90 million) will be financed using debt. Therefore:

Dividends per share = Free cash flow per share = (100 million − 63 million) ÷ 10 million = \$3.70

M&M's Homemade Dividend Argument

homemade dividends dividends created or eliminated by investors through their own behaviour

M&M's argument is often illustrated using the concept of **homemade dividends**. This refers to the ability of individuals to create (or eliminate) dividends through their own behaviour in a perfect M&M world, with no taxes, transactions costs, or other market imperfections. In essence, according to M&M's assumptions, investors will buy shares regardless of the firm's underlying dividend policy, since they can create any dividend policy they want, as illustrated by Example 22-3.

EXAMPLE 22-3   Homemade Dividends in an M&M World

Consider a no-growth company (NG) whose shares are presently trading at $10 per share. The company has just announced that it plans to pay out all of its free cash flow of $1 per share in the form of a $1 dividend per share at the end of the year, and these dividends will be maintained indefinitely.

a.   Estimate the expected value of the company's shares after one year (P_1), assuming investors require a 10 percent return on these shares.

b.   Investor A holds 1,000 NG shares and does not want to receive any dividends next year, but then wishes to sell all her shares and collect all her investment income from NG. Explain what she can do and show how much she will receive after two years.

continued

EXAMPLE 22-3   Homemade Dividends in an M&M World *continued*

c. Investor B also holds 1,000 NG shares but wishes to receive $6,000 in income from his shares at the end of this year and collect his remaining investment income at the end of the second year, at which time he wishes to sell all his shares. Explain what he can do and show how much he will receive after two years.

d. Explain why the amount of income received by the two investors differs.

Solution

a. $P_1 = \$1 \div 0.1 = \$10$ per share

b. Investor A can take the $1,000 in dividends she receives (i.e., $1 × 1,000 shares) and buy new shares in NG at the end of the year. Assuming the shares are trading at $10 per share, as calculated in part (a), the investor can purchase an additional 100 shares (i.e., $1,000 ÷ $10 per share) with the $1,000 in dividends she receives. At the end of two years, assuming the $1 free cash flow per share and the 10 percent discount rate remain constant, the shares will still be trading at $10 per share. Therefore, she will receive $11,000 for selling her 1,100 shares at $10 a piece, plus $1,100 in dividends, for a total of $12,100.

c. Investor B can take the $1,000 in dividends he receives and sell an additional 500 shares at $10 each to generate an additional $5,000 in investment income, for a total of $6,000. At the end of two years, assuming the $1 free cash flow per share and the 10 percent discount rate remain constant, the shares will still be trading at $10 per share. Therefore, he will receive $5,000 for selling his remaining 500 shares, plus $500 in dividends (i.e., 500 shares × $1 per share), for a total of $5,500.

d. Investor A receives a total of $12,100 at the end of year two. Notice that investor B receives $6,000 at the end of year one and $5,500 at the end of year two, for a total of only $11,500. The difference of $600 represents the forgone return of 10 percent on the $6,000 that investor B withdraws at the end of year 1, which investor A leaves invested in firm NG. Recall that our share price calculations are based on the assumption that the firm's shares provide investors with a 10 percent return.

Example 22-3 shows how investors can buy or sell shares in an underlying company to create their own cash flow patterns or simulated dividend streams. In fact, when you answered part (b) in the example, you were simply using a homemade dividend reinvestment plan or DRIP, which we discussed earlier. Investors who don't like dividends can sign up for a DRIP and undo the effects of a firm's dividend policy. Conversely, in answering part (c), you saw an investor creating a cash flow from the firm simply by selling some or all of his shares.

What the example illustrates is that, given the M&M assumptions, the investor is indifferent to a firm's dividend policy. However, in the real world there are several practicalities to consider, such as transactions costs, risk, taxes, and other market imperfections. We will elaborate on these matters in the following sections.

CONCEPT REVIEW QUESTIONS

1. Explain how, and under what assumptions, M&M show that dividends are irrelevant.

2. Explain the relationship between M&M's argument and the use of a residual dividend policy.

3. Briefly describe the notion of homemade dividends as it relates to M&M's irrelevancy argument.

22.4 THE "BIRD IN THE HAND" ARGUMENT

M&M's dividend irrelevance proposition was as controversial in 1961 as it remains today, since it seems to conflict with the intuition that firms paying cash dividends are less risky than ones where the investors' return comes by way of a capital gain. It would seem to follow that firms that do not pay a cash dividend are riskier because this causes the cost of equity capital to increase and the stock price to fall. This idea is called the **"bird in the hand" argument** on the basis that a "bird in the hand" (cash dividend) is worth more than "two in the bush" (twice as much in capital gains).

In thinking through this argument, remember that in Chapter 20, we used the version of the two-stage growth model that is expressed in Equation 22-6.

$$[22\text{-}6] \qquad P = \frac{ROE_1 \times BVPS}{K_e} + \frac{Inv}{(1 + K_e)}\left(\frac{ROE_2 - K_e}{K_e}\right)$$

This model drove a discussion about the value of a firm being split between the present value of existing opportunities (PVEO), as measured by the first term in Equation 22-6, and the present value of growth opportunities (PVGO), as measured by the second term. We then used this to discuss four stereotypes of firms: the cash cow, the star, the dog, and the turnaround. These different stereotypes are usually perceived to have varying risk, since PVEO is generally regarded as less risky than PVGO.

Think for a moment about where PVGO comes from: it requires that the firm earn a return on equity (ROE) that exceeds its cost of equity capital (K_e), so in the second term of Equation 22-6 we are adding the present value of all these future net present values. However, from basic economics we know that there will be new entrants to a market when firms earn more than a normal level of profits, where "normal" is defined as a fair rate of return on the funds invested or the cost of equity capital. As a result, if PVGO is high, we can expect other firms to try to enter the market and compete for these excess profits. This makes the PVGO part of the firm's market value extremely vulnerable, as future competition could see it diminish, if not disappear completely.

Of course, PVEO can also be vulnerable to market entry and competition if it, too, is partly derived from excess profits. However, for PVEO there is more information about potential entry and new competition for existing operations than there is for PVGO, which may stretch far into the future. Further, there is more information about the stability of PVEO, since the firm has an earnings history and has actually generated the PVEO. For these basic reasons, capital gains, or expected increases in the share price, are generally regarded as riskier than current dividends. This is the basic idea that the "bird in the hand" argument captures: that investors value current dividends more highly than future capital gains. The implication is that investors perceive non-dividend-paying firms to be riskier, and they apply a higher discount rate to value them, causing share prices to fall. The "answer" then seems to be for these firms to pay a dividend.

The "dividends-are-better" theory is normally associated with Myron Gordon, developer of the Gordon growth model.[5] It captures the notion that dividends are more stable than capital gains and, as a result, are more highly valued. It is commonly accepted that cash cows such as utilities and banks are less risky than high-tech firms such as RIM. Further, if you look at the dividend yields listed in Table 22-1 and ignore the income trusts, you will see that low-risk utilities and banks do indeed have high dividend yields, while cyclical resource stocks and high-risk tech firms rarely pay a dividend—and when they do, it tends to be very low. So, intuitively, the dividends-are-better argument seems to make sense. In addition, in practice, the share prices of high-dividend-paying stocks have tended to perform as well as, or better than,

[5] Gordon, M., "Optimal Investment and Financing Policy." *Journal of Finance* 18, no. 2 (May 1963), pp. 264–72.

stocks with low dividend payouts, which indicates that investors need not sacrifice growth for income.

Finance in the News 22-2 elaborates on this point and discusses the results of applying the "dogs of the Dow" strategy to Canada. This is a strategy of buying the 10 U.S. stocks in the Dow-Jones 30 index with the highest dividend yield at the end of the year. They are called "dogs" because the high dividend yield is in part caused by the low stock price. As the analyst explains, such a strategy beat the S&P/TSX Composite by 6 percent annualized over the past 20 years. The news story suggests that if investors choose the "right" high-dividend-paying stocks, they can "have it all"—both yield and capital gains.

---

finance INTHENEWS 22-2 Dogs of the Dow

INVESTORS WHO FOLLOW the Dogs of the Dow strategy buy the top-yielding stocks on the Dow Jones industrial average once per year. (A high yield can be a sign that a stock is unloved and must offer a larger payout to woo investors.) Historically, this strategy has outperformed the Dow, although that hasn't been the case in recent years.

Morningstar CPMS helped us adapt the strategy for Canada.

CPMS is an equity research and portfolio analysis firm owned by Morningstar Canada. It maintains a database of about 680 of the largest and more liquid Canadian stocks, plus another 2,100 U.S. stocks, and spends a lot of time adjusting for unusual accounting items in each company's quarterly results to make sure screens can perform correctly.

Jamie Hynes, CPMS senior consultant, first decided to look for stocks in the S&P/TSX Composite Index that have higher quality or safer dividends, as well as high yields. He screened for high-yield stocks that have increased dividends over the last year or that have a low payout ratio (expected dividends per share as a percentage of expected earnings per share).

Payout must be less than 41 percent or dividends must have grown in the last year. Regardless, payout must be less than 100 percent.

Mr. Hynes created a portfolio of 20 stocks that is annually reselected every year on March 31. He also allowed no more than five stocks per sector and he excluded trusts.

Mr. Hynes found out that the strategy beat the S&P/TSX composite total return benchmark index by 6 percent annualized over the past 20 years. In other words, the portfolio returned 15.7 percent annually, versus 9.7 percent for the benchmark.

In recent years, it hasn't kept up with the benchmark because of its low exposure to commodities, but it still has outperformed over the long term.

"It beats the TSX in all four years the TSX was down, but can have a hard time keeping up when the TSX is up [it beat the TSX in nine of 16 years when the TSX is up]," Mr. Hynes said.

CPMS Portfolio of High-Yielding Canadian Stocks					
	Company	Symbol	Price $ (April 21)	Market Cap ($ mil.)	Dividend Yield %
1	BCE Inc.	BCE-T	35.58	26773.6	5.5
2	AGF Management Ltd.	AGF.B-T	19.29	1840.6	5.4
3	Mullen Group Ltd.	MTL-T	20.3	1603.9	4.9
4	Shaw Communications	SJR.B-T	19.6	8517.6	4.7
5	Reitman's (Cda.) Ltd.	RET.A-T	17.39	1153.3	4.6
6	Emera Inc.	EMA-T	30.95	3746	4.2
7	TransCanada Corp.	TRP-T	40.08	28035.5	4.2
8	Telus Corp.	T-T	50.24	23587.1	4.2
9	Rogers Communications	RCI.B-T	34.4	19021.6	4.1
10	TMX Group Inc.	X-T	40.07	2980	4
11	Genworth MI Canada	MIC-T	26.05	2729.9	4
12	CI Financial Corp.	CIX-T	23.13	6669.5	3.9
13	Corus Entertainment	CJR.B-T	19.98	1566.8	3.8
14	Fortis Inc.	FTS-T	31.83	5563.7	3.6

Data source: Morningstar Canada

Disclosure: The article's author owns shares of Fortis Inc.

Figure 22-6 illustrates the difference between the M&M and Gordon arguments. The M&M argument is that dividends and capital gains are perfect substitutes. If investors want a 10 percent rate of return, they can get this as a 10 percent dividend yield (D_1/P_0), or they can cut the dividend and reinvest more, which they receive as a capital gain ($(P_1 - P_0)/P_0$). The slope of the line as they cut the dividend is then -1, indicating that the investors' required rate of return or discount rate is constant. Gordon, on the other hand, argues that if investors want a 10 percent return from a 10 percent dividend yield, they will want an ever higher required

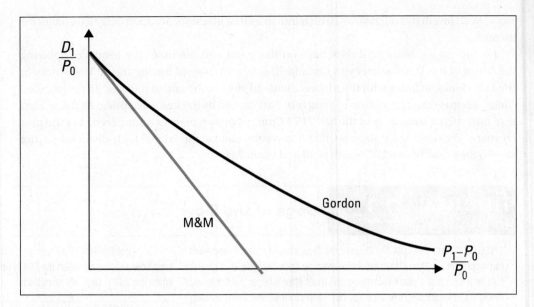

FIGURE 22-6 *M&M versus Gordon's "Bird in the Hand" Argument*

rate of return as the dividend payout is cut, due to the increase in risk. As a result, they might want a 15 percent required return if there is no dividend, because all of the return is coming from risky capital gains.

So how do we balance the obvious intuition of the "bird in the hand" argument against the formal "proof" offered by M&M? The easiest way is to work through an example. Suppose that a firm has a market value of $50 million and has $5 million in cash flow that equals its required investment level. Using Equation 22-4, we can see that this firm has zero residual cash and generally should not pay a cash dividend according to the residual theory of dividends. Further, if the discount rate is 10 percent, the market value of its equity is $45.45 million, as shown below.

$$\$45.45 = \frac{\$50 + \$5 - \$5}{(1.1)}$$

If we further assume there are one million shares currently outstanding (m), the price per share is $45.45. In this case, the investor expects to get a zero dividend and a 10 percent capital gain ($4.55 ÷ $45.45).

Now suppose the firm pays out the $5 million in a $5 per share cash dividend. In this case, M&M assume that the firm still has to find $5 million to pay for the required level of investment, since value creation requires that all positive NPV projects are undertaken.

As a result, the firm will have to issue more shares next period at the then-market price (P_1). We can designate these new shares as n, so the price per share is

$$P_0 = \frac{5m + \dfrac{50m}{1 + n}}{(1.1)}$$

The price today is the dividend of $5 per share that will be paid to the existing owners. They will also have the new share price, which is the $50 million in market value divided by the current shares outstanding of 1 million, plus the new shares that will have to be issued (n). Note that the assumption of value creation means that all positive NPV projects are undertaken and the total market value next period of $50 million is the same regardless of the firm's dividend policy.

To find the number of shares that have to be issued, we can solve the following equation.

$$n\left[P_1 = \frac{50}{1+n}\right] = \$5 \text{ million}$$

This means that the number of shares (n) issued, multiplied by the price next period (P_1), is equal to the proceeds of the share issue, which is $5 million. Solving, we find that the firm has to issue 111,111 shares at $45 a share. The price per share is then

$$P_0 = \frac{5 + 50/1.1111}{1.1} = \$45.45$$

Notice that this is the same as in the no-cash-dividend case.

In this case, the shareholders will get an expected dividend yield of 11 percent ($5 ÷ $45.45), but due to the extra shares being issued, their ownership in the firm will be diluted and they will actually suffer a capital loss of 1 percent as the share price declines from $45.45 to $45. Therefore, they obtain a 10 percent return. By varying the cash dividend amount, we can come up with different numbers for the expected dividend yield and capital gain (loss), but under the M&M assumptions, the investors' return stays the same.

Now that we see that the M&M argument "works," we can also see how to reconcile it with Gordon's argument. First, note that the capital gain in our M&M example is not far off in the future as it is with risky high-tech stocks—it is immediate, when the dividend is paid. As soon as the $5 million in cash is paid out as a dividend, the firm has to issue 111,111 shares at $45 per share to fund its investment. As a result, the capital gain—or in this case, loss—is like a stock split. Second, with the M&M assumptions, the underlying operations of the firm are unaffected by the dividend—this is the significance of the constant value of $50 million next period. What it means is that by changing from a firm with a zero percent dividend yield to a firm with an 11 percent dividend yield, as in our example, the firm is not changing itself from a RIM into a Royal Bank. The firm stays exactly the same. What is important to recognize is that *RIM is riskier than Royal Bank due to its business risk, not because of its lack of a dividend.* In other words, the dividend policy of the firm should follow the business risk of the firm, and changing that dividend policy cannot change the risk of the firm.

Gordon is right in arguing that the dividend yield does indicate the risk of the firm, and firms that pay large amounts of dividends are less risky than non-dividend-paying firms. However, M&M are also right, because changing the dividend cannot change the underlying risk of the firm; this comes from its underlying operations. In this sense, the dividend should reflect the firm's operations through the residual value of dividends, and the firm should not be able to change these underlying operational characteristics by merely changing the dividend. This reconciliation also leads to some implications as to why the stock market reacts to changes in a firm's dividend policy.

CONCEPT REVIEW QUESTIONS

1. Explain the "bird in the hand" argument about dividends.
2. Reconcile the predictions of M&M with Gordon's arguments about dividend policy.

22.5 DIVIDEND POLICY IN PRACTICE

Learning Objective 22.5
Explain why firms are reluctant to cut their dividends and why they smooth their dividends.

Accepting the M&M argument as a valid description of the real world leads to some problems. One is that if dividend policy doesn't matter, why is it we see such stability in dividend policy? The M&M proof indicates that the firm is valued based on the residual or free cash flows, so paying a dividend just means more share issues and lower capital gains. If this is true, the firm can cut the dividend if it is short of cash and increase it when it has surplus cash. In this way, the dividend is a residual and as volatile as the firm's free cash flow. However, we saw in Figure 22-1 that aggregate dividends are much more stable than earnings (and cash flow), so firms smooth their dividends. But there is nothing in M&M's proof that indicates there is any value to dividend smoothing. Further, M&M's concern was with dividend policy in general, and they indicate no difference between a regular and a special dividend, or a cash dividend versus a share repurchase. So why is it that firms declare both regular and special dividends or, like Tim Hortons, buy back shares as well as pay a dividend?

The standard explanation for this observed dividend behaviour is to suggest that firms smooth their dividends over time as they move toward a new target level of dividends. The original work in this area was done by John Lintner, who suggested using the partial adjustment model specified in Equation 22-7.[6]

$$[22\text{-}7] \qquad \Delta D_t = \beta(D_t^* - D_{t\text{-}1})$$

This equation simply says that the change in the dividend at time t (ΔD_t) is equal to an adjustment factor (β) times the difference between the target dividend for the period (D_t^*) and the dividend for the prior period ($D_t - 1$). If the firm adjusts immediately to the target dividend, then the adjustment coefficient (β) is equal to 1, and the cash dividend is always optimal. If it doesn't adjust at all, then the dividend is constant and β is equal to zero.

Lintner took the target dividend (D_t^*) to be a function of the firm's optimal payout rate of the firm's underlying earnings (E_t), which leads to the model in Equation 22-8.

$$[22.8] \qquad D_t = a + (1-b)D_{t\text{-}1} + cE_1$$

This equation suggests that dividends are a function of the previous period's dividends and current earnings. Lintner estimated the coefficient on lagged dividends to be 0.7, indicating an adjustment speed (b) coefficient of 0.3. He also estimated the coefficient on current earnings (c) of 0.15. When the adjustment to the target dividend is complete, Lintner's estimates imply an optimal payout ratio for U.S. companies of 50 percent (b/c). This is consistent with the aggregate evidence that U.S. companies do pay out about 50 percent of their earnings as dividends, which is slightly higher than the median payout in Canada of just less than 40 percent. Lintner's results have been replicated many times, and their importance is twofold. First, the speed of adjustment is only 30 percent, which means that, during each period, the average firm moves only 30 percent of the way toward its target dividend. Alternatively, this means firms are reluctant to fully adjust, so their dividends are "sticky." Second, the coefficient on earnings is only 15 percent, so firms do not follow a policy of paying out a constant proportion of earnings as dividends.

The fact that actual dividend policy does not accord with the irrelevance theorem of M&M means, obviously (and not surprisingly), that some of their assumptions are not realistic. The

---

[6] Lintner, J., "Distribution of Incomes of Corporations among Dividends, Retained Earnings and Taxes." *American Economic Review* 46, no. 2 (1956), pp. 97–113.

critical suspect assumptions are that markets are perfect and there are no taxes. *Finance in the News 22-3* describes the Bank of Montreal's very long history (180 years) of paying a dividend and its current CEO's decision to pay a dividend during the financial crisis to indicate the bank's "core earning power," a clear indication of BMO's dividend policy. In the next section, we will discuss why the bank would do this.

---

finance INTHENEWS 22-3 Canadian Bank's Long History of Steady Dividends

SOME OF THE LARGEST banks in the world had collapsed and central bankers were still in the midst of a costly bail out of financial institutions.

The directors of the Bank of Montreal were carefully balancing the pressure to pay out a dividend to shareholders and the need to contain the effects of an international financial crisis.

The year was 1829, and as stock markets recovered from the failure of six English banks caught out by bad bets on Latin American credit markets, bank directors decided to proceed with a dividend payment to shareholders.

The move established a tradition that has endured for 180 years and was reaffirmed on Tuesday as Canada's oldest bank maintained its dividend at 70 cents.

There was no sign that BMO's management had given any serious consideration to cutting the dividend ahead of Tuesday's annual general meeting.

But Bill Downe, chief executive, took time out to reassure shareholders, saying dividends were of perennial importance to retail investors.

"Shareholders of Canadian banks place a high value on consistency," he said, noting BMO had "extended its unmatched record of continuous dividend payment".

The executive acknowledged the payout ratio had climbed to a relatively high level above 50% of net income when the bank was accumulating excess capital three years ago, and that since then the credit crisis had crimped income.

But he indicated the bank plans to stay the course, in keeping with its "core earnings power".

The executive hinted that the most likely scenario for the bank to reduce its dividend would be further down the road in the context of a big acquisition.

Stephen Foerster, professor at the Richard Ivey School of Business, said Canadian banks had a long history of sustaining dividends during downturns.

"I think Canadian banks will at least maintain their dividends," said the professor, who conducted an extraordinary study of BMO's dividend policy over 175 years.

BMO Financial Group president and CEO William Downe addresses the audience at the bank's 2009 annual shareholder meeting. (Clement Allard/The Canadian Press)

The professor's detailed financial research explored the trends and factors that contributed to the bank's dividend ratios in each year and found BMO had a long history of generous pay outs.

The study showed bank management had consistently sought to balance the need to reinvest for growth and preserve capital with "the traditional role of dividends" as a source of succour to "the proverbial widows and orphans".

The professor said demand for dividends had only increased as the population aged and more Canadians sought to fund their retirement.

Banks, he said, would remain a favourite for investors who want "some equity exposure but like the stability of a steady dividend".

Source: Callan, Eoin, "Canada banks' long history of steady dividends." *Financial Post*, March 3, 2009. Available at www.financialpost.com. Reproduced by permission.

CONCEPT REVIEW QUESTIONS

1. What does real-world evidence imply about how firms manage their dividend payments?

22.6 RELAXING THE M&M ASSUMPTIONS: WELCOME TO THE REAL WORLD!

Learning Objective 22.6
Explain why dividends are not a residual, as implied by M&M.

The perfect markets assumption contains a number of unrealistic aspects, the most important of which are the absence of transactions costs and the belief that all information is freely available and understood.

Transactions Costs

Transactions costs are important because it is assumed, in the M&M model, that the firm can pay a dividend and then issue shares to raise the money needed to make the required level of investment.[7] Let's take an extreme situation in which transactions costs are very high and the firm cannot raise new capital. In this case, the payment of the cash dividend reduces the amount of money available to invest and causes the firm to forgo positive NPV projects. The value of the firm would go down, since it is not creating value by accepting positive NPV projects.

Faced with significant costs attached to raising new money, cash-poor growth firms have little incentive to pay a dividend, since all they are doing is compounding their financing problems. Similarly, firms with volatile earnings, whose cash flow fluctuates significantly from year to year, will attempt to "store" cash from one period to another. As a result, they will conservatively maintain their dividend payments at a level that minimizes the need to constantly access the capital markets.

How important are these concerns? It turns out they are very important. In Chapter 21, Figure 21-10 listed the most important concerns for firms when making their capital structure decision: the first two factors were their credit rating and their ability to continue to make investments, while the fourth was their ability to continue to make dividend payments. Overall, we regard this as "financial flexibility." To illustrate this concept, we saw in Chapter 12 that Oilexco went from being a $4-billion market capitalization firm to bankrupt in eight months when what should have been routine financing became unavailable during the financial crisis. The result is that firms are reluctant to "stretch" and put themselves at the mercy of capital markets by paying out "surplus" cash as a dividend. Similarly, they are reluctant to issue new shares to finance a dividend payment; instead, they would rather cut or defer investments. In Baker et al.'s survey of Canadian firms, fully 40 percent of the time the respondents considered themselves constrained in terms of capital.[8] The upshot is that dividends are not a residual, consistent with Lintner's empirical work.

This brings us to a second unrealistic aspect of the perfect markets assumption, which is that everyone has the same amount of information.

Dividends and Signalling

The M&M model assumes perfect markets in which all participants have access to the same information. In practice, however, capital markets are rife with information asymmetries, with some parties knowing more than others. Even though the main focus of securities regulation is to ensure all material facts are public information, agents in the capital market often have widely different views about a firm's future prospects and value—that is, they interpret the same information differently.

---

[7] Alternatively, it is assumed that investors can create homemade dividends by buying or selling shares without cost to generate any desired cash flows, which makes the firm's dividend decision irrelevant.

[8] Baker, H. Kent, Shantanu Dutta, and Samir Saadi, "Corporate Finance Practices in Canada: Where Do We Stand?" *Multinational Finance Journal* 15, no. 3/4 (2011), pp. 157–92.

For example, management usually knows more than external investors, so the firm has to have some way of signalling to investors that their press releases can be believed. As we discussed in Chapter 21, investors tend to view such information with a great deal of scepticism, so one way to signal a firm's credibility is to increase the dividend only when the firm believes it will not have to reduce future payouts. The fact that paying the cash dividend reduces the funds available to the firm and its financial flexibility means the firm will make the payment only when it thinks its internal funds are increasing and are enough to support the dividend payment.[9] Otherwise, as we just discussed, paying a dividend will impose more transactions costs on the firm when it has to raise more funds in the future. This "signalling model" explains why share prices tend to increase when dividends are initiated or increased unexpectedly. In both cases, the dividend increase indicates good news because it suggests that management believes it can support the dividend out of future earnings.

Another explanation for the favourable stock market reaction associated with dividend increases is provided by **agency theory**. Many investors are wary of senior management because managers tend to view the firm as their firm and not as something belonging to the shareholders. Investors fear that senior management may waste corporate resources over-investing in poor (negative NPV) projects, since it is not "their" money but the money of the shareholders that they are using. This view is supported by the argument put forward by Gordon Donaldson (discussed in detail in Chapter 2 and again in Chapter 21): for agency reasons, senior management follows a pecking order when raising capital. This means, for example, that managers prefer to finance projects using internal cash flow (retained earnings), then debt, and finally by issuing new common equity. Shareholders, on the other hand, would prefer that cash be disgorged as a dividend, with management then explaining why it needs the money back by filing a prospectus and issuing new common shares.[10] From an agency perspective, paying a large dividend and forcing the firm to justify future expenditures creates value by controlling management. However, while an agency perspective justifies the stock market's reaction to dividends, it cannot explain the phenomenon of dividend smoothing.

agency theory the recognition of conflicts of interest whereby managerial decision-making may not be in the best interests of shareholders

Figure 22-7 helps explain the signalling model.

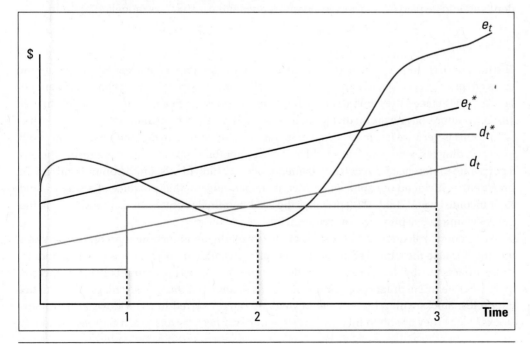

FIGURE 22-7 *The Signalling Model*

---

[9] This also means that it is expensive for poor-quality firms to mimic this cash dividend payment.

[10] In fact, this argument has been cited as one factor contributing to the popularity of income trusts, which pay out virtually all of their earnings, forcing them to access capital markets for future financing needs.

The starred values in Figure 22-7 represent management's view of the underlying or permanent earnings (e_t^*) and dividends (d_t^*) per share, whereas the unstarred values are the actual values. Note that the underlying earnings and dividends are increasing through time, so the firm has some long-run target payout. However, actual earnings vary with "predictable" factors such as the state of the economy or the inflation rate. So when the actual earnings increase in line with underlying earnings, the firm increases the dividend per share as at time 1. However, when there are poor earnings at time 2, the firm does not cut its dividend, since to do so would signal to the market that these poor earnings are not temporary, but permanent. At this point in time, the firm cannot cover its dividend from its earnings, but it signals to investors that this earnings drop is expected to be temporary by maintaining the dividend.

Figure 22-3 shows that this is what many Canadian companies did during the recessions in the early 1980s and 1990s. During both these recessions, dividends in aggregate were maintained even in the face of cyclically low earnings as managers signalled that this was cyclical and not fundamental. Similarly, in Figure 22-2, we saw that TransCanada maintained and even increased its dividend in 2009 and 2010, even as its EPS fell. Again, it was signalling that nothing fundamental had changed. In contrast, in 1998 and 1999, TransCanada's EPS dropped, but not because of normal cyclical reasons (in fact, the stock market and economy were both strong). Instead, TransCanada cut its dividend because it went through an extensive corporate reorganization and wrote off hundreds of millions of dollars in bad investments: it was telling the market that it had suffered a serious loss in earnings power that was fundamental and not cyclical.

At time 3, the firm increases its dividend again to signal that the earnings increase this time is in line with the firm's underlying earnings increase.

This signalling model indicates that dividend changes have "information content," which provides an important role for dividend policy. The signalling model, when combined with the residual theory of dividends, provides the major theories that explain actual dividend policy. The residual theory of dividends explains generally which types of firms should pay a dividend and the general level of their payout. The signalling model explains how these dividends should be paid out as a slowly adapting dividend per share, as modelled by Lintner.

Taxes

The final imperfection that affects all financial policy is the impact of taxes. Working out how taxes affect financial policy is difficult because different classes of investors have different tax brackets. With taxes, the general rule is that "one size does not fit all." As discussed in Chapter 19, corporations pay no tax on dividend income if it is received from another Canadian corporation. This is because it is taxed when paid out to an individual; to do otherwise would result in a cascading tax, where the rate could end up greater than 100 percent.[11] As a result, there is a corporate preference for receiving dividend income. Individuals, on the other hand, might prefer either dividend or capital gains income depending on their province of residence and their income level.[12] Table 22-2 provides the 2011 marginal tax rates for dividend and capital gains income in five provinces, as reported by Ernst & Young.[13]

As a general rule, marginal tax rates are lower on dividend income than on capital gains income because the capital gains tax rate is half the marginal tax rate, whereas dividend income attracts the dividend tax rate. This differential narrows as the amount of taxable income increases due to the progressive nature of our tax system, but the system still gives rise to **tax clienteles**. Stocks with a high dividend yield are often referred to as "widows and orphans stocks," since they are often held by investors in lower tax brackets (often retirees), who rely

tax clienteles a phenomenon reflecting the fact that investors in different tax brackets face different marginal tax rates on dividends versus capital gains income and thus have different preferences for receiving dividend income

---

[11] This is because tax would be paid every time a dividend passed between different companies.

[12] It is, therefore, obvious that M&M's homemade dividend argument is negated by the existence of differential tax rates as well as by the existence of transactions costs.

[13] The rates were calculated using the tax calculator at www.ey.com/CA/en/Services/Tax/Tax-Calculators-2012-Personal-Tax.

on the dividends for income. In contrast, stocks with a low dividend yield tend to be held by younger investors, who have longer-term horizons and are intent on holding for a long time to defer taxes. So although the payment of a dividend may not have an impact on the general level of share prices, it will have a major influence on the type of investors a firm attracts. The general advice that flows from this is not to drastically change dividend policy, because that upsets the existing ownership base.

TABLE 22-2 Individual Tax Rates (%) on Dividends and Capital Gains for 2012

	Income Level	$25,000	$50,000	$75,000	$100,000
British Columbia	Dividends	0.0	9.6	10.7	18.6
	Capital gains	11.6	14.9	16.3	19.2
Alberta	Dividends	0.0	9.6	9.6	15.2
	Capital gains	13.0	16.0	16.0	18.0
Ontario	Dividends	0.0	13.4	14.2	25.4
	Capital gains	10.5	17.4	16.5	21.7
Quebec	Dividends	5.7	19.2	19.2	29.4
	Capital gains	14.3	19.2	19.2	22.9
Nova Scotia	Dividends	0.0	18.1	20.4	27.1
	Capital gains	11.9	18.5	19.3	21.8

Repackaging Dividend-Paying Securities

The tax clienteles identified above are interested in different parts of the return generated by the firm. The problem is that the return comes packaged in one security, so each group gets part of what it wants and part of what it doesn't want. This has led to some interesting security repackaging products and **income stripping**.

income stripping the process of repackaging securities to provide different types of income based on different parts of the return

Stripping is common in finance and is entirely respectable. It refers to the process of repackaging securities to provide different types of income based on different parts of the return. Take BCE Inc., for example, whose major asset is Bell Canada, which has a history of being a reasonably stable firm paying a high dividend. However, the telecommunications revolution of the past 20 years has provided BCE with growth prospects. As a result, it attracts both growth investors and dividend yield investors, but they both have to buy the same package of returns from BCE. McLeod Young Weir (MYW), a company that is now owned by the Bank of Nova Scotia, found a way around this problem in 1986.

MYW bought $454 million in BCE common shares and repackaged them. The shares were placed in a trust company named "B" Corporation, which raised the $454 million by issuing two classes of securities backed by the BCE shares. One class of securities was special preferred shares. Investors buying these securities had the right to receive all the dividends on these shares for six years. At the end of six years, they got either the minimum of $30 or the BCE share price minus $1. MYW sold these preferred shares for $330 million. The second class of securities was referred to as "instalment receipts" (IR) and provided investors with the right to purchase the BCE shares at the end of six years by paying the minimum of $30 or the BCE share price minus $1. MYW sold these securities for $143 million.

The pattern of the securities is illustrated in Figure 22-8, but the upshot is that $454 million of BCE shares were repackaged and sold for $473 million, and MYW pocketed $19 million in fees to cover expenses.

The top box in Figure 22-8 is the valuation of the BCE shares at $454 million. This is the present value of six years of dividends plus the share price at the end of the six years. The bottom two boxes are the values of the preferred shares and IRs. Note that if you add the payoffs from the two securities together, they equal the payoff from the BCE shares. So MYW is just stripping the BCE shares into two new securities.

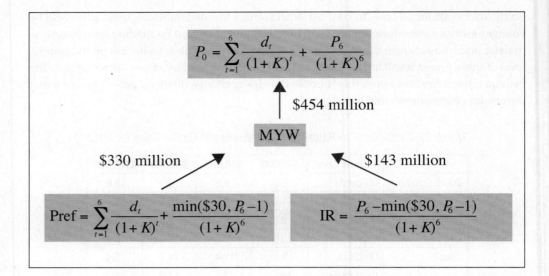

FIGURE 22-8 *MYW's "B" Corporation Shares*

One interesting feature of these shares is the instalment receipts. Whenever you see minimums or maximums, you should think options, as in Chapter 12. In this case, the IR holders will pay only $30 to buy the BCE shares if the share price is above $30, so this is a straight call option. If the BCE share price is less than $30, they will pay $1 less than the shares are worth. Either way, the IR holders end up owning the shares at the end of six years, and the preferred shareholders simply receive the dividends on all the shares for the previous five years and either $30 or the BCE share price minus $1. Effectively, the IRs are long-term "in the money" call options on BCE common shares.

So instead of holding BCE shares and getting a package of dividends and capital gains, investors can buy the preferred shares and get more dividends than they can buy directly for $330 million, or they can buy the IRs and get all capital gains through a long-term call option. The fact that MYW made $19 million in fees indicates that the parts were worth more than the whole and that investors would prefer to own a pure dividend or pure capital gains stream of cash flows. In turn, this implies that tax clienteles do exist.

"B" Corporation was the first dividend strip of common shares in Canada. Since then there have been many examples of what are now termed **split shares**. The Bank of Nova Scotia now has the largest split share mutual fund, where instead of stripping the income on one company, such as BCE, they split it on a pool of companies. Allbanc Split Corporation II has a market value of $300 million and splits the dividends and capital gains from a portfolio of bank shares, which, like BCE, have high dividends. The investor can either buy the preferred shares, which have a fixed dividend (ALB.PR.B), or buy the capital shares, which receive any increase in dividends plus the capital appreciation (ALB). The shares are issued in the ratio of two capital shares for one preferred share as a unit, but they trade separately.

In its 2006 annual report, Allbanc described its two classes of shares as follows:

> The Capital Shares provide their holders with a leveraged investment, the value of which is linked to changes in the market price of the Portfolio Shares. It is the policy of the Board of Directors to declare and pay quarterly dividends in an amount equal to the dividends received by the Company on the Portfolio Shares minus the distributions payable on the Preferred Shares and all administrative and operating expenses. The Preferred Shares provide their holders with quarterly fixed cumulative preferential distributions equal to $0.26563 per Preferred Share.

The popularity of split shares has two major implications. First, there are investor dividend clienteles, and dividends do matter to some investors. This emphasizes that companies need

split shares shares sold as the dividends and capital gains parts of a security

to consider dramatic dividend changes as a serious event, not to be taken lightly. Second, the capital shares are marketed as a leveraged investment and can be considered an application of the homemade leverage theorem advanced by M&M. In this case, given investor preference for leverage and dislike of dividends, they can buy, for example, the Allbanc capital shares. The result is that the financial policies of the six banks in the Allbanc portfolio are being changed to the benefit of the capital shareholders in exactly the way suggested by M&M.

There are now almost 40 families of split shares traded on the TSX, with a market value of $4.2 billion. These firms strip the dividends from the capital gains for a wide class of common shares ranging from bank and utility stocks to global telecom stocks. The existence of these families of split shares is an example of the M&M theorems in action, as well as an example of the efficiency with which financial markets adapt to "imperfections" that provide an opportunity to create value.

CONCEPT REVIEW QUESTIONS

1. Explain why dividend policy will be relevant in the presence of transactions costs, informational asymmetry and agency problems, and taxes.

2. Describe split shares and explain what their popularity implies about investor preferences for dividends in the real world.

22.7 SHARE REPURCHASES

The final aspect of dividend policy we will consider is share repurchases. These are important because, as we noticed with Tim Hortons, some firms regularly make significant cash payments to repurchase some of their outstanding shares. Note that in the sources and uses of funds constraint expressed in Equation 22-3, we can always set the dividend as equal to zero. This means that if the free cash flow is negative, the firm issues shares; if it is positive, the firm, instead of paying a cash dividend, repurchases shares.

Let's return to our example of the firm with a $50-million value in the next period and one million shares outstanding. Further assume that it has an expected free cash flow of $5 million in the next period. So its value, with a $5 per share cash dividend, is now $50, as below:

$$P_0 = \frac{5m + 50m}{(1 + 0.10)} /1{,}000{,}000 = \$50$$

However, if the firm used the $5 million in free cash flow generated during the year to buy back 90,909 shares at $55 each at the end of the year, in the next period the market value of the shares would be:

$$P_1 = \frac{50m}{909{,}090} = \$55$$

Therefore, the present value of $55 today, using the 10 percent discount rate, is once again $50.

This example shows that the firm can use the $5 million in cash to either pay a cash dividend or repurchase shares. Either way, with perfect capital markets, the shares are worth $50 today. The example also illustrates how share repurchase is simply another form of payout policy. It is an alternative to a cash dividend, where the objective is to increase the price per share rather than paying a dividend and forcing the shareholders to immediately pay tax on the dividend.

Of course, in this example the firm has to buy back the shares at $55, which is the ongoing value of the firm ($50) plus the $5 million in cash on hand, divided by the current one million

Learning Objective 22.7
Describe what a share repurchase program is and explain how it can substitute for dividend payments.

shares outstanding. If it offers to buy the shares at $60, all the shareholders should tender their shares, as they are only worth $55. Similarly, if it offers $50 a share, no one should tender them. The advantage for the shareholders is that they can either hold their shares and receive a larger capital gain in the future or sell out now. Such a persistent policy of share repurchase is technically illegal, since there are rules against the improper accumulation of funds within the firm.[14] Consequently, firms sometimes adopt a policy of large, infrequent, share repurchase programs. At these points, insiders often hold on to their shares so that they defer any capital gains and associated taxes.

This example illustrates how a share repurchase program can act like a cash dividend by providing a payout of funds to the shareholders. However, unlike a dividend, share repurchases can be motivated by several other factors, so it is easy to think that it is part of a payout policy when in fact it is not. Some of the other factors motivating share repurchases are listed below:

- *Offset the exercise of executive stock options (ESOs).* ESOs are call options granted to senior executives. When exercised, they result in more shares outstanding. Firms frequently repurchase shares to meet these exercise requirements, thereby leaving the number of shares outstanding constant.

- *Carry out a leveraged recapitalization.* Often debt is raised and the proceeds used to repurchase shares to move the firm back to its optimal capital structure.

- *Send a signal.* Management often repurchases shares to signal to the market that it thinks the stock is undervalued.

- *Repurchase dissident shares.* If there is substantial disagreement among shareholders about the future of the firm, a share repurchase program gives the dissidents an opportunity to sell their shares without depressing the market price, thereby removing an "overhang" of shares.

- *Remove cash without generating expectations for future distributions.* A large share repurchase can return cash to the shareholders without generating expectations about receiving such distributions in the future, similar to a special dividend payout.

- *Take the firm private.* A share repurchase to buy all the firm's outstanding shares takes the firm out of the public markets.

LESSONS TO BE LEARNED

Earlier in the chapter, we indicated that BMO decided to maintain its long string of dividend payments because Canadians valued consistency, and the dividends reflected BMO's earnings power. This was a clear statement of the dividend signalling model discussed earlier. However, as we have noted several times, the financial crisis was much more severe in the United States than it was in Canada. Moreover, almost all the major U.S. financial services companies faced the same problems of bad loans and a deteriorating economy. As a result, the signals they sent by cutting their dividends did not entail the same cost. In fact, the market responded positively as investors preferred to see their dividends cut rather than have the banks selling shares at seriously depressed prices. *Finance in the News 22-4* reports on one of the biggest "shocks" of all—GE cutting its dividend for the first time since the Great Depression—and explains the reasons why this happened.

The lesson to be learned is that dividends signal firm-specific information, not macroeconomic information. By cutting its dividend, GE did not signal that anything specific to itself had changed. Quite the opposite: it signalled the company was serious about supporting the value of the GE share price and wanted to avoid selling shares at deeply depressed prices. In doing so, it was following in the footsteps of most of the big U.S. financial institutions.

---

[14] Until the late 1940s, the U.S. Treasury, for example, investigated for improper accumulation of funds any firm that did not pay out 70 percent of its earnings as dividends. The onus was on the firm to justify a reinvestment rate above 30 percent of earnings.

1. Why can share repurchases be viewed as an alternative to paying a cash dividend?

2. What factors may influence a firm's decision to enter into share repurchases?

22-1 ETHICS AND CORPORATE GOVERNANCE
CompuCredit's Surprise Dividend Is Target of Suit

Nearly two dozen investment funds, including a handful managed by Whitebox Advisors of Minneapolis, filed a federal lawsuit this week accusing a Georgia-based sub-prime lender of fraudulently transferring millions of dollars in assets to company insiders and shareholders at the expense of its debt holders as the company nears insolvency.

The lawsuit, filed Monday in U.S. District Court in Minneapolis, cited CompuCredit Holdings Corp.'s recent regulatory filings as evidence it is "hemorrhaging cash" and facing a liquidity crisis that raise doubts about its ability to make debt payments barring an "extreme, unexpected and immediate improvement" in operations. Yet, according to the lawsuit, CompuCredit recently announced it was departing from its policy of not paying stock dividends by declaring a dividend of 50 cents a share payable early next year.

"The announced dividend flies in the face of the company's staggering ongoing losses, its acknowledgement of the dire credit environment in which it is operating, and its stated goal of preserving capital to shore up its operations," the suit says. It says the dividend "will result in the stripping of almost $25 million of the company's rapidly dwindling assets, with over half of that amount going to corporate insiders."

The investment funds say CompuCredit is trying to force its debt holders to convert the outstanding debts at a discount by demonstrating the company has no intent to pay them. To drive home the message, they

say, CompuCredit announced recently that it's considering a tax-free spin-off of its U.S. and U.K. micro-loan businesses into a publicly traded company called Purpose Financial Holdings Inc. The lawsuit says the company's proposal would excise the only segment of CompuCredit's business that had been producing cash.

Source: Browning, Dan, "CompuCredit's surprise dividend is target of suit." [Minneapolis] *Star Tribune*, December 22, 2009. Available at www.startribune.com/business/.

DISCUSSION QUESTIONS

1. CompuCredit is planning to spin off its profitable micro-loan business into a separate company and also initiate a cash dividend—all while it is hemorrhaging cash. Why is this seen as an attempt to force bondholders to convert their debt into equity at a discount?

2. Shareholder value creation assumes that no other stakeholders lose as a result of a corporate decision. In this case, discuss the reaction of shareholders and bondholders, and whether the proposed dividend and spin-off is ethical.

3. The board of directors has to agree to this plan. What legal protection do bondholders have in the face of such a plan, and what should they have done to protect against such actions?

SUMMARY

In this chapter, we look at different types of dividends, including regular and special cash dividends, stock dividends, and stock splits, as well as share repurchases. As in our discussion of capital structure theory, we present the major argument of M&M, which suggests that in a perfect market, the payment of a cash dividend should not affect the value of the firm. According to the M&M assumptions, this is because the value of the firm is determined by real factors such as the firm's free cash flow. Therefore, all a dividend does is create a greater financing need that has to be met by selling more common shares. This leads us to look at the role of M&M's assumptions.

One common argument that justifies the importance of dividends is that they create value because they are safer than capital gains. However, we see that while dividend-paying firms are generally lower risk than capital-gains-oriented ones, this tends to reflect the risk of their basic operations, as well as the residual theory of dividends. A more substantial critique is that transactions costs make it difficult for firms to follow the residual dividend policy implicit in the M&M argument, since it is expensive to raise capital.

The existence of transactions costs also leads firms to increase or initiate dividend payments to signal a higher level of earnings. As a result, dividends have information content, and the unexpected payment of a dividend generally causes stock prices to increase. Agency theory predicts the same results but cannot explain the most salient feature of actual dividend policy, which is that firms tend to smooth their dividends.

We recognize the existence of tax clienteles, since investors' preference for dividends versus capital gains depends on their tax bracket and level of income. This provides a tax motivation for firms to use share repurchases as a means of payout policy, because a repurchase leads to an increase in share prices and capital gains rather than dividends. However, we see that there are many other reasons why firms might want to repurchase their shares.

SUMMARY OF LEARNING OBJECTIVES

22.1 Explain what a cash dividend payment is, how dividend payments are made, and why dividend payments are different from interest payments.

A cash dividend is the cash payment that shareholders receive periodically. A dividend has to be declared by the board of directors (BOD), after which it is announced and becomes a contractual commitment. However, shareholders cannot force the members of the BOD to declare a dividend. An interest payment is different in that it is a legal obligation.

22.2 Describe typical dividend payouts and explain the importance of dividends.

Typical dividend payouts are around 40 percent, but increase to over 100 percent during recessions. They trend downwards in booms. Dividends are an important source of holding period return.

22.3 Explain how Modigliani and Miller proved that dividend payments are irrelevant, due to the existence of homemade dividends, and therefore have no impact on market value.

Modigliani and Miller argue that dividend policy is irrelevant under certain assumptions: there are no taxes and there is a perfect market. Investors can create homemade dividends by selling off a small part of the stock that has appreciated in value, or they can also undo dividends by reinvesting the dividend cash. M&M show that a dividend with offsetting new issue is irrelevant—the same as doing nothing.

22.4 Explain why dividend payments generally reflect the business risk of the firm, and explain what the "bird in the hand" argument is.

Firms that do not pay dividends are typically growth firms that need to retain cash to finance new projects.

Growth firms have little residual cash flow to pay out. Low-growth firms have no new projects or investments and so have high residual cash flow—low-growth firms can pay high dividends. The "bird in the hand" argument stems from the belief that firms that do not pay a cash dividend are riskier because this causes the cost of equity capital to increase and the stock price to fall; therefore, a cash dividend ("bird in the hand") is worth more (twice as much—"two in the bush") than capital gains. The fallacy is that firms that pay dividends are perceived to be safer—to have a lower cost of equity and a higher stock price. Conversely, firms that do not pay dividends are perceived to be riskier and to have a higher cost of equity and a lower stock price.

22.5 Explain why firms are reluctant to cut their dividends and why they smooth their dividends.

Firms are reluctant to cut their dividends because it signals that the value of a firm's asset in place has decreased and causes the share price to drop. Firms smooth dividends for the following reasons: first, the transactions costs of raising new equity is so high that changing dividends will compound financing problems. Second, thanks to the signalling function of dividends, smoothing dividends creates a reputation that the firm's performance is stable and less risky. Third, drastically changing dividend policy upsets the existing ownership base, so smoothing dividends appeals to a firm's tax clientele.

22.6 Explain why dividends are not a residual, as implied by M&M.

M&M's perfect markets assumption contains a number of unrealistic aspects, the most important of which are the absence of transactions costs and the belief that all information is freely available and understood. (1) Transactions costs: faced with significant costs attached to raising new money, cash-poor growth firms have little incentive to pay a dividend, since all they are doing is compounding their financing problems. Similarly, firms with volatile earnings, whose cash flow fluctuates significantly from year to year, will attempt to "store" cash from one period to another. (2) Dividends and signalling: the fact that paying the cash dividend reduces the funds available to the firm means the firm will only make the payment when it thinks its internal funds are increasing and are enough to support the dividend payment. (3) Taxes: the general advice that flows from tax clienteles is not to drastically change dividend policy because that upsets the existing ownership base.

22.7 Describe what a share repurchase program is and explain how it can substitute for dividend payments.

In a share repurchase, a company buys back its own shares on the open market. A share repurchase reduces shares outstanding but it also reduces corporate resources. If a company repurchases its shares at a fair price, then its stock price is unchanged by the repurchase. If a company repurchases shares, then shareholders can sell the same proportion of shares as are repurchased and so receive some cash without changing their proportionate control of the company. In this way, repurchases are an alternative means of distributing cash to shareholders.

KEY TERMS

EQUATIONS

Equation	Formula	Page
[22-1] Single Period Valuation Model	$P_0 = \dfrac{D_1 + P_1}{(1 + K_e)}$	p. 849
[22-2] Required New Share Issue	$mP_0 = V_0 = \dfrac{m(D_1 + P_1)}{(1 + K_e)}$	p. 849
[22-3] Cash Flow Constraint	$X_1 + nP_1 = I_1 + mD_1$	p. 849
[22-4] Single Period Free Cash Flow	$V_0 = \dfrac{X_1 - I_1 + [(m + n)P_1 = V_1]}{(1 + K)}$	p. 850
[22-5] Free Cash Flow Valuation	$V_0 = \sum\limits_{t=1}^{\infty} \dfrac{X_t - I_t}{(1 + K)^t}$	p. 850
[22-6] Existing and Growth Opportunities Valuation	$P = \dfrac{ROE_1 \times BVPS}{K_e} + \dfrac{Inv}{(1 + K_e)}\left(\dfrac{ROE_2 - K_e}{K_e}\right)$	p. 854
[22-7] Adaptive Dividend Model	$\Delta D_t = \beta(\dot{D}_t - D_{t-1})$	p. 858
[22-8] Lintner Equation	$D_t = a + (1-b)D_{t-1} + cE_1$	p. 858

QUESTIONS AND PRACTICE PROBLEMS

Multiple Choice Questions

1. Dividend-payout ratio is defined as:
    a. the dividend yield plus the capital gains yield.
    b. dividends per share divided by earnings per share.
    c. dividends per share divided by income per share.
    d. dividends per share divided by current price per share.

2. Which of the following statements about stock splits is incorrect?
    a. Market price per share is reduced after the split.
    b. The number of outstanding shares is increased.
    c. Retained earnings are changed.
    d. Proportional ownership is unchanged.

3. When is the ex-dividend date if the holder of record date is April 13, 2012?
    a. April 15
    b. April 14
    c. April 11
    d. April 12

4. On January 7, a firm declared a $0.25-per-share quarterly dividend payable March 3 to share-holders of record on Friday, February 8. What is the latest date by which you could purchase the stock and still receive the recently declared dividend?
    a. March 1
    b. February 5
    c. February 6
    d. February 7

5. Which of following has a negative impact on the share price?
    a. Unexpected dividend increase
    b. Unexpected dividend initiation
    c. Unexpected dividend decrease
    d. None of the above

6. Which of the following is an M&M assumption?
    a. There are personal taxes.
    b. Not all firms maximize value.
    c. There is no debt.
    d. Markets are imperfect.

7. What is the market value of equity if next-period cash flow from operations is $400,000 and investment is $200,000, respectively, and $k = 15\%$?
    a. $173,913
    b. $347,826
    c. $175,000
    d. $359,499

8. A Firm's target dividend is $4.50 and the prior-period dividend is $3. What is the change in dividends if the firm adjusts dividends immediately?
    a. 0
    b. −$1.50
    c. $0.75
    d. $1.50

9. Suppose that the pre-tax holding period returns on two stocks are the same. Stock A has a low dividend payout policy and stock B has a high dividend payout policy. If you are an individual in a high marginal tax bracket and do not intend to sell the stocks during the holding period, which stock should you purchase?
    a. A because it will have a higher after-tax return than stock B
    b. B because it will have a higher after-tax return than stock A
    c. A or B (indifferent) because the after-tax returns on stocks A and B will be the same
    d. It is impossible to determine which stock to purchase given the information available.

10. Which of the following arguments supports the relevance of dividends?
    a. Informational release
    b. Reduction of uncertainty
    c. Some investors' preference for current income
    d. All of the above

11. Which of the following statements regarding motivation for a stock repurchase is incorrect?
    a. Firms could be privatized using stock repurchases.
    b. Investors consider a firm's stock overvalued when a stock repurchase occurs.
    c. Firms use stock repurchases to move capital structure back to some optimum level.
    d. Stock repurchases are sometimes used to satisfy dissident shareholders.

12. If a firm repurchased 50 percent of its outstanding common stock, the result would be
    a. a decline in *EPS*.
    b. an increase in retained earnings.
    c. a decrease in total assets.
    d. a decrease in the number of shareholders by 50 percent.

Practice Problems

13. Describe the difference between a stock dividend and a cash dividend plus a DRIP.

14. A firm has a dividend yield of 3.14 percent and a payout ratio of 35.84 percent. If its earnings are $25 million and there are 7 million shares outstanding, what is the price per share?

15. CGC Company is considering its dividend policy. Currently CGC pays no dividends, has cash flows from operations of $10 million per year (perpetual), and needs $8 million for capital expenditures. The firm has no debt and there is no tax. The firm has 2 million shares outstanding, which are currently trading at $50 per share. George, the majority owner of CGC (he owns 60 percent), would like to take $20 million out of the company to fund his various charities. You have been hired by CGC to consider different alternatives.
    a. George could sell stock to the market to raise the $20 million he requires. What are the advantages and disadvantages of this strategy (i.e., the impact on the value of CGC and George's control)?
    b. CGC could pay a dividend so that George receives the $20 million.
        i. Describe how the company can issue stock to create the dividend.
        ii. What is the effect on the value of CGC and on George's control of the firm?

16. Explain the implications of M&M's homemade dividend argument.

17. What is the market price per share if the next period's dividend is $2, $P_1 = \$25$, and $K = 20\%$?

18. According to equity market capitalization, what is the cost of capital for the stock of the following firm? Current market value of the equity is $1.2 million with 100,000 shares outstanding. The stock price is expected grow 5 percent in a year, and the firm is expected to pay out a $1.50 dividend per share at the end of the first year.

19. Currently a firm has an operating cash flow of $350 million and there is a promising project available, which costs $200 million. There are 100 million shares outstanding with a current price of $40 per share. The firm is expected to pay out a dividend of $2.50 per share to existing shareholders. It will raise the money needed through issuing new shares.
    a. What amount of new proceeds is required?
    b. What is the new share price? Hint: the firm's equity market value is not changed.
    c. How many new shares does the firm have to issue?

20. A firm has one million shares outstanding. After-tax earnings have been constant at $10 per share. The firm pays out all earnings in dividends at the end of each year. The shareholders' required rate of return is 15 percent.
    a. Calculate the current share price.
    b. The firm considers a one-time retaining of all earnings for the current year. It will revert to a zero retention policy from next year. Assume the new investment promises a return of 10 percent, 15 percent, or 16 percent in perpetuity. Calculate the new share price in each separate case.
    c. Is it reasonable for the firm to claim that it would always find enough positive *NPV* opportunities yielding at least 16 percent, and therefore, it will never pay dividends?

21. Assume that the shareholders of a firm pay a net tax of 30 percent on cash dividends received. After-tax earnings have been constant at $10 per share. The firm pays out all earnings in dividends at the end of each year. The market requires a 15 percent rate of return, which implies that shareholders require an after-tax return of $(1 - 0.3) \times 0.15 = 10.5\%$.
    a. Calculate the share price if the firm pays out all earnings as dividends.
    b. Calculate the share price if the firm retains the current year earnings and reinvests it at 15 percent. Starting next year, the firm reverts to a zero retention policy. What is the capital gain? Do shareholders prefer dividends or capital gains?

22. A firm's next-period market value of equity is $2.5 million and there are 100,000 shares outstanding, with $K = 15\%$.
    a. What is the current stock price if the firm pays $500,000 in cash dividends?
    b. What is the number of shares outstanding if a firm spends its extra $500,000 to buy back shares at $30 per share instead of paying $500,000 in cash dividends?
    c. What is the current stock price if a firm spends its extra $500,000 to buy back shares at $30 per share instead of paying $500,000 in cash dividends?

23. MCC Corporation currently has cash flow from operations of $10 million, capital expenditures of $8 million, and pays a dividend of $2 million (all are perpetuities). The firm has no growth prospects or debt, and shareholders expect an annual return of 5 percent. The total number of shares outstanding is 1,000. For the following investors, describe how they can achieve their desired cash flow patterns and the value of their strategy (future value) at the end of the second year. Each investor owns 10 percent of the firm and there are no taxes or transactions costs.
    a. Marie lives in a very high-cost city and would like to receive a dividend of $400,000 at the end of year 1. She needs this money to finance her lifestyle.
    b. Charlie has found another investment opportunity that will cost $400,000 at the end of year 1, pay him 15 percent, and pay back his initial investment of $400,000 at the end of year 2.
    c. Radha is very frugal and would rather not receive dividends at the end of year 1.

24. A dividend-paying company has a current dividend yield of 8 percent and a stock price of $100. The company has paid the same dividend for the past 15 years and it is not expected to change. Alice believes that the company is an excellent investment opportunity for her clients and has been contacting them. Here are some of the responses she has received:

    Client A: I need income, I don't trust capital gains—they aren't real, just paper. I'm not interested in this stock; I'd rather just have a bond and get a nice fixed income.

Client B: Who cares about dividends? I pay more taxes on the dividends so I want capital gains where I can control the timing of the tax bill. The dividend is too high, and I will pay too much tax so I'm not interested in the stock.

    a. Which statement is consistent with the "bird in the hand" argument about dividends?

    b. Describe how income stripping would allow Alice to satisfy the needs of both clients.

25. Discuss the "bird in the hand" argument in support of dividend payments.

26. According to John Lintner, what is the adjustment factor β? Interpret the calculated adjustment factor.

27. A firm follows a strict residual dividend policy. This firm will have profits of $500,000 this year. After screening all available investment projects, the firm has decided to take three out of the 10 projects and those three will cost $410,000. The current equity market value of this firm is $5,000,500 and the current market price of its shares is $45.60. Estimate the current year dividend per share. What is the shortcoming of this policy?

28. Explain why firms do not simply pay out dividends as a fixed portion of their profits. What do most firms do in terms of dividend policy?

29. How do personal taxes affect preference for high versus low dividend yields?

30. Describe the implication of releasing the assumptions of no transactions costs.

⚙ 31. The current stock price of Abacus is $50. For the past 20 years, the firm has paid an annual dividend of $5. On July 26, it announced a dividend of $6 payable on September 10 to shareholders of record at the close of business on September 1.

    a. What do you expect to happen to the price of Abacus stock on July 26?

    b. If the shareholders of Abacus pay no taxes on dividends, what do you expect to happen to the price of Abacus on the ex-dividend date?

    c. If the shareholders of Abacus pay taxes on dividends, do you expect the stock price reaction on the ex-dividend date to be greater, the same, or less than in (b)?

32. Investor A's personal tax rate is 25 percent while Investor B's is 29 percent. Investor A owns 100 shares of SNS Company and receives an annual dividend of $1.60 per share. Investor B owns 100 shares of CGC Company and receives an annual dividend of $1.36 per share. Which investor receives the larger after-tax dividend amount?

⚙ 33. Kumar expected his firm to earn $1,000 per year forever, with no growth. Given a cost of capital of 10 percent, the value of the firm is $10,000. Kumar identified a new project, which costs $1,000 but would earn 11 percent per year forever. To invest in this project, Kumar cancelled this year's dividend. Given that he is investing in a positive NPV project, he expected his stock to rise. However, it fell dramatically. Explain what happened. Does this mean that investors do not like positive NPV projects?

34. Describe possible reactions from the market of the following dividend payout changes: dividend initiation, dividend increase, and dividend decrease.

    a. Dividend initiation

    b. Dividend increase

    c. Dividend decrease

35. A company has announced an increase in its quarterly dividend from $0.25 to $0.33 per share. If an investor who owns 700 shares is in the 20 percent tax bracket, calculate the amount by which the investor's tax would increase annually due to the dividend.

36. List the main reasons why firms repurchase shares.

Part 9

WORKING CAPITAL MANAGEMENT

Last, but certainly not least, is the issue of managing working capital. This topic may appear at the end of the textbook, but it is critically important for two reasons. First, most new financial recruits in non-financial companies start their careers managing working capital. These new finance professionals will need to learn whether to extend credit to a trade customer, whether to invest surplus cash balances in marketable securities, and how to decide how much inventory a firm really needs. Second, if a firm is having financial problems, they will show up in the firm's short-term cash flow. The ultimate test of a firm's financial health is whether or not it has enough cash or cash equivalents to cover cash expenditures. These decisions involve interacting with that most important institution, the Canadian chartered bank, which frequently lends against working capital assets and actively monitors the financial health of the firm to make sure that its loans are sound.

23

Working Capital Management: General Issues

LEARNING OBJECTIVES

23.1 Explain why the management of net working capital is critical for the survival of a firm.

23.2 Explain how managing receivables, inventory, and payables is related in an integrated approach to net working capital management.

23.3 Explain how financing and current asset investment decisions interact to determine a company's overall working capital position.

23.4 List and describe some common ways to analyze a firm's management of its net working capital.

Liquidity is adequate, but we expect cash to continue to decline due to normal seasonal working capital patterns, ongoing losses (we expect a fourth-quarter 2011 loss to push the full-year deficit well over $1 billion), and debt maturities. Fourth-quarter debt maturities are a substantial $1.1 billion, though much of that is already refinanced using proceeds from the $726 million 2011-2A enhanced equipment trust certificates that American sold in October. We forecast year-end cash in the $3.5 billion-$4 billion range (in the mid-teens as a percent of revenues), but above our $3 billion potential downgrade trigger. In reviewing any possible downgrade, we would also consider expected future cash generation, financing activities, and cash uses (including $1.8 billion of 2012 debt maturities).

Source: Standard & Poor's Rating Service on American Airlines as reported in the *Dallas Morning News*, October 20, 2011. Available at http://aviationblog.dallasnews.com/2011/10/analysts-offer-opinions-on-amr.html. Reprinted with permission of *The Dallas Morning News*.

CHAPTER 23 **PREVIEW**

net working capital (NWC) the difference between a firm's current assets and its current liabilities

working capital management the way in which a firm manages both its current assets (i.e., cash and marketable securities, accounts receivable, and inventories) and its current liabilities (i.e., accounts payable, notes payable, and short-term borrowing arrangements)

Learning Objective 23.1
Explain why the management of net working capital is critical for the survival of a firm.

illiquidity the inability of an entity to raise funds on reasonable terms, unrelated to its creditworthiness

insolvency the inability of an entity to meet its financial obligations as they come due, leading to a default

I n this chapter, we introduce the concept of working capital management and discuss various methods firms can use to make decisions about managing working capital.

In Chapter 4, we defined working capital as the sum of the firm's current assets. In Chapter 3, we talked about **net working capital (NWC)** as the difference between a firm's current assets and its current liabilities. **Working capital management** refers to the way in which a firm manages both its current assets (i.e., cash and marketable securities, accounts receivable, and inventories) and its current liabilities (i.e., accounts payable, notes payable, and short-term borrowing arrangements).

23.1 THE IMPORTANCE OF WORKING CAPITAL MANAGEMENT

Managing working capital (W/C) effectively is critical to both the short-term and the long-term viability of any firm. In fact, W/C *mismanagement* often causes liquidity problems, which, in extreme cases, can force a firm into bankruptcy. The opening vignette alludes to the critical nature of liquidity issues, as it describes how American Airlines was struggling to raise funds as its liquidity deteriorated. In this case, the efforts appeared to be unsuccessful, as American Airlines went into voluntary bankruptcy protection. However, all is not as it appears, which highlights the difference between illiquidity and insolvency.

Illiquidity is the inability of an entity to raise funds on reasonable terms, unrelated to its creditworthiness. **Insolvency**, on the other hand, is the inability of an entity to meet its financial obligations as they come due, leading to a default.[1] Clearly the two concepts are closely related. However, financing relies on both the supply of securities (that is, the demand for cash) and the demand to purchase those securities (the supply of cash), so illiquidity can come about simply because the lender decides not to buy the securities. Consequently, the firm can be "short of cash" or illiquid even if its creditworthiness has not changed. If the firm can find no other source of cash, this illiquidity may lead the firm to default on its obligations and become insolvent. Conversely, a firm may be liquid but still default or seek bankruptcy protection, which is what happened to American Airlines. On the day that this happened, an analyst at JPMorgan was reported as saying, "We were wrong." Previously, JPMorgan had described a voluntary bankruptcy filing as highly unlikely. "The company has approximately $4.1 billion in unrestricted cash and short-term investments...[which] is anticipated to be more than sufficient to assure that its vendors, suppliers and other business partners will be paid timely and in full... So, this WASN'T about liquidity (liquidity is about 18 percent of LTM revenue)." In JPMorgan's view, the filing by American Airlines was all about reducing costs and achieving a more viable competitive position in the long run for the airline, rather than signalling an inability to meet its commitments.[2]

The distinction between illiquidity and insolvency is highlighted in *Finance in the News 23-1*, which discusses liquidity problems faced by Italy. Although this textbook is about corporate finance, it was government financial problems that dominated the headlines in 2011 and 2012, particularly those facing the United States and countries in the eurozone. Countries often need to finance their expenditures, just as corporations do, and they similarly have to rely on the willingness of others to buy their securities. If this willingness disappears, a country, like Italy, or a corporation can face a liquidity crisis, which simply confirms the critical importance of managing working capital.

---

[1] Technically, a company is insolvent if the value of its liabilities exceeds the value of its assets.
[2] Grocer, Stephen, "Analysts React American's Bankruptcy Filing: 'This WASN'T about Liquidity.'" (blog), *Wall Street Journal, Deal Journal*, November 29, 2011, http://blogs.wsj.com.

finance INTHENEWS 23-1 | Why Italy's Days in the Eurozone May Be Numbered

WITH INTEREST RATES on its sovereign debt surging well above seven percent, there is a rising risk that Italy may soon lose market access. Given that it is too-big-to-fail but also too-big-to-save, this could lead to a forced restructuring of its public debt of €1,900bn. That would partially address its "stock" problem of large and unsustainable debt but it would not resolve its "flow" problem, a large current account deficit, lack of external competitiveness, and a worsening plunge in gross domestic product and economic activity.

To resolve the latter, Italy may, like other periphery countries, need to exit the monetary union and go back to a national currency, thus triggering an effective break-up of the eurozone.

Until recently the argument was being made that Italy and Spain, unlike the clearly insolvent Greece, were illiquid but solvent given austerity and reforms. But once a country that is illiquid loses its market credibility, it takes time—usually a year or so—to restore such credibility with appropriate policy actions. Therefore unless there is a lender of last resort that can buy the sovereign debt while credibility is not yet restored, an illiquid but solvent sovereign may turn out insolvent. In this scenario, sceptical investors will push the sovereign spreads to a level where it either loses access to the markets or where the debt dynamic becomes unsustainable.

So Italy and other illiquid, but solvent, sovereigns need a "big bazooka" to prevent the self-fulfilling bad equilibrium of a run on the public debt. The trouble is, however, that there is no credible lender of last resort in the eurozone.

Source: Excerpted from Roubini, Nouriel, "Why Italy's Days in the Eurozone May Be Numbered," *Financial Times*, November 10, 2011.

LESSONS TO BE LEARNED

The importance of maintaining adequate liquidity has been highlighted over the past five years, as we have witnessed numerous dramatic corporate bankruptcies and an ongoing euro crisis resulting from a lack of liquidity. This lesson was also learned by many individuals. The number of individuals declaring bankruptcy, particularly in the United States, has soared as consumers also borrowed too much and were not prepared to weather the economic storms we have recently endured. The lesson is that it is important to maintain adequate liquidity or financial reserves and not to leverage yourself with too much debt, particularly short-term debt that forces you to rely on someone else to continue to finance you. When times are tough it is difficult to distinguish between illiquidity and insolvency, and financing may be withdrawn even if you believe that you are solvent.

Many entry-level jobs for finance graduates are in the field of working capital management. This is because every firm has to manage its working capital day to day, whereas decisions regarding capital structure, dividend policy, and capital budgeting are made infrequently. Consequently, this chapter covers "bread-and-butter" topics that anyone working in a finance capacity in a non-financial company must be familiar with.

What constitutes good W/C management? The answer is complicated; however, we can say that good W/C management is characterized by

1. the maintenance of optimal cash balances;

2. the investment of any excess liquid funds in marketable securities that provide the best return possible, considering any liquidity or default-risk constraints;

3. the proper management of accounts receivable;

4. an efficient inventory management system; and

5. the maintenance of an appropriate level of short-term financing in the least expensive and most flexible manner possible.

We deal with these points in Chapter 24. In this chapter, we address the concept of W/C management in general. However, before we discuss this concept, read the excerpt from *Business Week* of April 28, 1956, in *Finance in the News 23-2*. This topic is as important now as it was then.

finance INTHENEWS 23-2   How to Go Broke...While Making a Profit

AS THE YEAR STARTED, Mr. Jones of the ABC Co. was in fine shape. His company made widgets—just what the customer wanted. He made them for 75¢ each, sold them for $1. He kept a 30-day supply in inventory, paid his bills promptly, and billed his customers 30 days net. Sales were right on target, with the sales manager predicting a steady increase. It felt like his lucky year, and it began this way:

Jan. 1 Cash $1,000 Inventory $750 Receivables $1,000

In January, he sold 1,000 widgets; shipped them at a cost of $750; collected his receivables—winding up with a tidy $250 profit.

Feb. 1 Cash $1,250 Inventory $750 Receivables $1,000

This month sales jumped, as predicted, to $1,500. With a corresponding step-up in production to maintain his 30-day inventory, he made 2,000 units at a cost of $1,500. All receivables from January sales were collected. Profit so far: $625

Mar. 1 Cash $750 Inventory $1,125 Receivables $1,500

March sales were even better: 2,000 units. Collections: On time. Production to adhere to his inventory policy: 2,500 units. Operating result for the month: $500 profit. Profit to date: $1,125

Apr. 1 Cash $375 Inventory $1,500 Receivables $2,000

In April, sales jumped another 500 units to 2,500—and Jones patted his sales manager on the back. His customers were paying right on time. Production was pushed to 3,000 units, and the month's business netted him $625 for a profit to date of $1,750. He took off for Florida before he saw the accountant's report.

May 1 Cash $125 Inventory $1,875 Receivables $2,500

May saw Jones' company really hitting a stride—sales of 3,000 widgets, production of 3,500, and a five-month profit of $2,500. But suddenly he got a phone call from his treasurer: "Come home! We need money!" His books had caught up with him.

June 1 Cash $000 Inventory $2,250 Receivables $3,000

He came home—and hollered for his banker.

23.2 AN INTEGRATED APPROACH TO NET WORKING CAPITAL (NWC) MANAGEMENT

A Classic Working Capital Problem

Learning Objective 23.2
Explain how managing receivables, inventory, and payables is related in an integrated approach to net working capital management.

The *Business Week* article in *Finance in the News 23-2* is a classic because it highlights a basic problem: profits are not cash, and a firm can only pay its bills with cash. In this example, Mr. Jones' "books caught up with him" and he had to come home from his Florida vacation after getting a phone call from his accountant/treasurer. ABC's rapid growth was causing cash flow problems even though it was very profitable. Let's analyze what went wrong—or more accurately, what was going right and what the treasurer should have done to head off an entirely predictable problem.

First, look at the cash flow statement as of June 1, shown in Table 23-1, to find out what happened. Recall from Chapter 3 that firms produce three statements: the income statement, the balance sheet, and the cash flow statement. Of the three, financial analysts tend to look at the cash flow statement the most, because the other two frequently have accounting adjustments that make it difficult to find the firm's problems. The ABC example helps us contrast the usefulness of the income statement with that of the cash flow statement.

TABLE 23-1 ABC Company: Sources and Uses of Funds

Cash Flow Statement	January–June 1
Sales	$10,000
Cost of goods sold	7,500
Profit	2,500
Operating cash flow	2,500
(No depreciation)	
Increase in accounts receivable	2,000
Inventory	1,500
Change in working capital	3,500
Change in cash	−1,000

We know that Mr. Jones was running a profitable company. When we add up the sales from January to May, we see that he sold $1,000 worth of widgets in January and $500 more each month, so by the end of May, he had cumulative sales of $10,000. These widgets had a $0.75 cost, so he had $7,500 in cost of goods sold. The operating profit was $2,500. We have not included any depreciation charge for wear and tear on his machines, and even if we had, we would just add it back to get operating cash flow, because depreciation is a non-cash charge. So if ABC had cash flow of $2,500, why the telephone call telling Mr. Jones to hurry back?

The problem was the change in ABC's working capital. Mr. Jones sold his widgets on credit; his customers paid him with a 30-day lag. This is typical of **trade credit**, in which a customer orders ABC's widgets and the firm ships them out, along with an invoice indicating the terms of payment, which in this case is 30 days. By June 1, ABC's accounts receivable had risen from $1,000 to $3,000, an increased investment in receivables of $2,000. The reason for the increase was the increased sales level, from $1,000 in January to $3,000 in May, which meant that more credit was being granted to ABC's customers, even though ABC's credit policy had not changed.

Similarly, ABC had an inventory policy of keeping a 30-day supply on hand, so when customers placed an order, it could be boxed and sent out immediately. In January, Mr. Jones had $750 worth of widgets on hand; by June 1, this had increased to $2,250 worth of widgets as ABC's sales level rose. Again, the reason for the increased inventory was the increase in sales level from $1,000 to $3,000. ABC required a similar increase in inventory of $2,000 worth of widgets, because the firm's policy was to keep one month's sales on hand. However, the widgets were carried in inventory at the "lower of cost and market," so the inventory investment was the $0.75 cost rather than the $1 selling price. ABC had an increased inventory investment of $1,500.

ABC paid its bills immediately, so there were no accounts payable. The change in net working capital was the change in receivables plus inventory minus the change in payables: −$3,500. When the change in NWC was added to the operating cash flow, ABC had cash flow from operations of −$1,000. ABC started with $1,000 cash in the bank, but by the end of May the cash had been depleted and ABC had no cash to finance its operations. At that point, ABC's cheques would bounce.

Finance in the News 23-3 alludes to the critical nature of this issue, stating "Cash is the lifeblood of business," and later, "The essence of effective working capital management is proper cash flow forecasting."

trade credit a form of credit in which a customer orders a product or service and the firm delivers it, along with an invoice indicating the terms of payment

finance INTHENEWS 23-3   How to Improve Working Capital Management

"CASH IS THE LIFEBLOOD OF BUSINESS" is an oft-repeated maxim amongst financial managers. Working capital management refers to the management of current or short-term assets and short-term liabilities. Components of short-term assets include inventories, loans and advances, debtors, investments and cash and bank balances. Short-term liabilities include creditors, trade advances, borrowings and provisions. The major emphasis is, however, on short-term assets, since short-term liabilities arise in the context of short-term assets. It is important that companies minimize risk by prudent working capital management.

What Affects Working Capital Management

- Organizations are generally focused on cash, accounts payable and supply chain issues. On the other hand, external issues like the legal and business environment, or internal mechanisms like organization structure, information systems, can significantly impact working capital.

- Owing to market pressures, companies are led to pay a lot of attention to producing good quarterly results quarter after quarter. Undue focus on this may sometimes produce a flattering but inaccurate snapshot of working capital performance. This also happens in companies that have a marked seasonality of operations, with working capital requirements varying widely from quarter to quarter.

Measures to Improve Working Capital Management

- The essence of effective working capital management is proper cash flow forecasting. This should take into account the impact of unforeseen events, market cycles, loss of a prime customer and actions by competitors. The effect of unforeseen demands on working capital should be factored in.

- It pays to have contingency plans to tide over unexpected events. While market-leaders can manage uncertainty better, even other companies must have risk-management procedures. These must be based on an objective and realistic view of the role of working capital.

- Addressing the issue of working capital on a corporate-wide basis has certain advantages. Cash generated at one location can well be utilized at another. For this to happen, information access, efficient banking channels, good linkages between production and billing, internal systems to move cash and good treasury practices should be in place.

- An innovative approach, combining operational and financial skills and an all-encompassing view of the company's operations will help in identifying and implementing strategies that generate short-term cash. This can be achieved by having the right set of executives who are responsible for setting targets and performance levels. They are then held accountable for delivering, encouraged to be enterprising and to act as change agents.

- Effective dispute management procedures in relation to customers will go a long way in freeing up cash otherwise locked in due to disputes. It will also improve customer service and free up time for legitimate activities like sales, order entry and cash collection. Overall, efficiency will increase due to reduced operating costs.

- Collaborating with your customers instead of being focused only on your own operations will also yield good results. If feasible, helping them to plan their inventory requirements efficiently to match your production with their consumption will help reduce inventory levels. This can be done with suppliers also.

Working capital management is an important yardstick to measure a company's operational and financial efficiency. This aspect must form part of the company's strategic and operational thinking. Efforts should constantly be made to improve the working capital position. This will yield greater efficiencies and improve customer satisfaction.

Source: Gordon, Alexander, "How to Improve Working Capital Management." EzineArticles.com, http://ezinearticles.com/?How-to-Improve-Working-Capital-Management&id = 397977.

It is important to note that cash flow from operations is the correct measure of the cash-generating ability of the firm. All finance instructors emphasize that depreciation and amortization are non-cash charges and need to be added to net income to get cash flow, but this is only part of the story; other cash items need to be considered in determining cash flow. If ABC had a cash-only sales policy and did not extend credit, the firm would receive $10,000 in cash with the same level of sales. However, the fact that sales were on credit with a 30-day payment period meant that ABC did not get any cash from the $3,000 of sales in May. The receivables did not increase by $3,000, because the firm got the $1,000 from receivables that were outstanding in January. When firms sell on credit, they have to make sure that they are actually collecting the cash from those sales. Similarly, the income statement includes only the cost of producing items that are sold. If production is unsold, it goes into inventory, but the firm has still paid to produce it, so there is still a cash outflow. The increase in receivables and inventory, net of payables, are the most important net working capital items.

The Cash Budget

If Mr. Jones had estimated ABC's cash flow statement for May, he would have realized that he had a cash flow problem. However, he would need to do a cash flow statement for every month to know exactly *when* this problem would become acute. Firms do project a **cash budget**, which is essentially a cash flow statement for each month.

So let's think through ABC's problem. The sales level was $1,000, and Mr. Jones was forecasting a $500 increase every month. We can start the sales at $1,000 for month 1 and then increase by $500 for every future month. Mr. Jones could forecast the cash inflow from these sales, which for ABC, with a 30-day credit policy, meant that each month the firm would receive as an inflow the previous month's credit sales. (In practice, things are slightly more complicated, as we will discuss later.)

Remember that the only source of cash from operations was from sales; all the other items were uses of cash. ABC spent $0.75 producing every widget. Two types of widgets were produced: those that were sold and those that were held in inventory. For each month, ABC had a cash outflow for the cost of the widgets produced and sold, which for month 1 was $750, for month 2 was $1,000, and so on. However, in month 2, in addition to production for sales, there was an additional $375 outflow for the 500 widgets produced for inventory, because sales had increased by 500 units and ABC had an inventory policy of keeping a one-month supply on hand. In reality, for month 2, at a sales level of $1,500, ABC was receiving only the $1,000 from the previous month's sales, while it was paying $1,125 to produce for the current month's sales and an additional $375 to increase inventory, translating into a net cash outflow of $500.

The cash inflows and outflows record the change in the cash budget each month. ABC started with $1,000 in cash, which increased to $1,250 after month 1 and then decreased to $750 after month 2. If Mr. Jones had decided that ABC needed 20 percent of sales in cash "just in case," then the excess cash in month 1 would have been $1,050.[3] This excess cash could have been invested for a month. However, by month 2 the drop in cash flow from operations meant that the excess cash had dropped precipitously, to $450. By month 3, the cash budget would have indicated to Mr. Jones that ABC had no excess cash and was now below its desired holding of cash. This was two months *before* ABC actually ran out of cash, which would have given Mr. Jones plenty of time to talk to the bank about arranging some short-term credit. Table 23-2 provides ABC's cash budget for six months.

The important thing about the cash budget is that it forecasts cash inflows and outflows over a forecast horizon and their cumulative impact on the firm's cash balances. All the problems we discuss in this chapter and Chapter 24 revolve around the cash budget. Typically, firms prepare a cash budget for at least the upcoming year on a monthly (and sometimes even a weekly or daily) basis. These cash budgets are important planning tools for the firm. For example, they indicate when and for how long a firm can expect to have excess cash balances that can be invested in marketable securities. For ABC, this was the first two months of the year. Cash budgets also show when and for how long a firm may need to arrange some short-term borrowing to cover any cash shortfalls.

cash budget a cash flow statement for each month

TABLE 23-2 ABC's Six-Month Cash Budget

$	1	2	3	4	5	6
Sales	1,000	1,500	2,000	2,500	3,000	3,500
Cash inflow	1,000	1,000	1,500	2,000	2,500	3,000
Cash outflow						

continued

---

[3] Note that the JP Morgan analyst quoted earlier in the chapter indicated that American Airlines' liquidity was 18 percent of revenues.

TABLE 23-2 ABC's Six-Month Cash Budget *(continued)*

$	1	2	3	4	5	6
Current sales	750	1,125	1,500	1,875	2,250	2,625
Inventory	0	375	375	375	375	375
Operating cash	250	−500	−375	−250	−125	0
Start cash	1,000	1,250	750	375	125	0
End cash	1,250	750	375	125	0	0
Required cash	200	300	400	500	600	700
Surplus/deficit	1,050	450	(25)	(375)	(600)	(700)

Banks often require a cash budget as part of the documentation for a loan application, because they need to see whether the loan is necessary for a short period or is, in fact, permanent financing. The cash budget will indicate this and help the bank structure an operating line of credit or longer-term financing. A careful look at Table 23-2 indicates that the operating cash flow shortfall is declining: it peaks at $500 and declines to $0 by month 6. If Mr. Jones had presented this cash flow forecast to the bank at the beginning of the year, the lending officer would have requested he complete it for the whole year instead of just the first six months. This 12-month budget is presented in Table 23-3.

TABLE 23-3 ABC's 12-Month Cash Budget

$	1	2	3	4	5	6	7	8	9	10	11	12
Sales	1,000	1,500	2,000	2,500	3,000	3,500	4,000	4,500	5,000	5,500	6,000	6,500
Cash inflow	1,000	1,000	1,500	2,000	2,500	3,000	3,500	4,000	4,500	5,000	5,500	6,000
Cash outflow												
Current sales	750	1,125	1,500	1,875	2,250	2,625	3,000	3,375	3,750	4,125	4,500	4,875
Inventory	0	375	375	375	375	375	375	375	375	375	375	375
Operating cash	250	−500	−375	−250	−125	0	125	250	375	500	625	750
Start cash	1,000	1,250	750	375	125	0	0	125	375	750	1,250	1,875
End cash	1,250	750	375	125	0	0	125	375	750	1,250	1,875	2,625
Required cash	200	300	400	500	600	700	800	900	1,000	1,100	1,200	1,300
Surplus/deficit	1,050	450	(25)	(375)	(600)	(700)	(675)	(525)	(250)	150	675	1,325

By completing the cash budget for the whole year, it becomes apparent that with the $500 increase in sales each month, ABC's cash flow problems peak in months 5 and 6 (May/June) and then correct themselves. By month 7 (July), operating cash flow is positive, at $125, and from then on the operating cash flow increases every month. By month 10, ABC has surplus funds again and can start to invest the excess in marketable securities.

Mr. Jones would not have enhanced his reputation with the people at the bank if he went to see them in May, saying, "Please help me. I am out of cash." At the least, it would have indicated poor cash management, and the lending officer would have paid close attention to any loans made to ABC. If Mr. Jones had, instead, completed the cash budget at the beginning of the year and explained that he needed to set up a facility whereby he could invest surplus funds at the start and end of the year, and that he needed some short-term borrowing in the middle months, the bank could have designed a borrowing and lending facility for ABC. Establishing a good reputation with the bank lending officer is critical, especially for small firms, and the tool for doing this is the cash budget, because it enhances an understanding of the cash inflows and outflows through the firm.

The key components of a cash budget are sales forecasts, estimated production schedules, and estimates of the size and timing of any other major inflows (e.g., from the sale of an asset) or outflows (e.g., capital expenditures, dividend payments) that the firm expects. Example 23-1 provides a simplified exercise in constructing a cash budget.

EXAMPLE 23-1   Cash Budget

A firm has estimated its sales, purchases from suppliers, and wages and miscellaneous operating cash outlays for the first four months of next year as follows:

Month	Sales	Purchases	Wages and Miscellaneous
January	$10,000	$6,000	$3,000
February	$12,000	$7,500	$3,500
March	$15,000	$5,500	$4,000
April	$11,000	$5,000	$3,000

The firm estimates that 50 percent of its sales will be for cash and that 80 percent of its credit sales will be collected one month after the sale, with the remainder being collected in the following month. It also estimates that 50 percent of its purchases will be paid 30 days from the purchase date, while the remaining 50 percent will be paid in 60 days. Assume that sales and purchases were the same in November and December as they are estimated to be in January. Finally, the firm plans to pay dividends of $3,000 in March and expects to receive $1,500 in January from the sale of a used truck. The beginning cash balance is $1,000, which is the minimum cash balance the firm wants to maintain. Estimate the firm's cash budget for the first four months of next year.

Solution

	January	February	March	April
Cash inflows ($)				
Sales				
Current month's sales	5,000	6,000	7,500	5,500
Previous month's sales	4,000	4,000	4,800	6,000
Sales from two months ago	1,000	1,000	1,000	1,200
Total sales receipts	10,000	11,000	13,300	12,700
Other cash inflows	1,500*			
Total cash inflows	11,500	11,000	13,300	12,700
Cash outflows ($)				
Purchases				
Previous month	3,000	3,000	3,750	2,750
Two months ago	3,000	3,000	3,000	3,750
Total purchase outflows	6,000	6,000	6,750	6,500
Wages and miscellaneous	3,000	3,500	4,000	3,000
Other cash outflows			3,000†	
Total cash outflows	9,000	9,500	13,750	9,500
Net cash flow	2,500	1,500	(450)	3,200
Beginning cash	1,000	3,500	5,000	4,550
Ending cash	3,500	5,000	4,550	7,750

* From sale of truck

† Dividend payment

The firm's cash balance is expected to climb to $3,500 in January and not go below that figure any time before April. In fact, cash is expected to increase to $7,750 by the end of April. This implies that the firm could invest as much as $2,500 for at least three months in marketable securities and still maintain the $1,000 minimum amount in cash. In fact, if the surplus cash position was expected to last longer, the excess funds could be invested in other assets. We could just as easily have constructed an example in which a firm forecast a deficit cash position in a future month or months. In that case, the amount of the expected deficit would provide the firm with a starting estimate of how much short-term borrowing it needed to arrange—in practice, the firm would probably arrange to borrow an amount that exceeded the projected cash deficit, just to be cautious.

CONCEPT REVIEW QUESTIONS

1. What is the difference between profit and cash flow from operations?
2. Why should all firms prepare a cash budget?

23.3 ANALYZING CASH INFLOWS AND OUTFLOWS

Cash Changes and Sales Growth

Learning Objective 23.3
Explain how financing and current asset investment decisions interact to determine a company's overall working capital position.

The cash budget is the basic tool for forecasting the cash inflows and outflows through a firm. Unfortunately, although it helps to identify key items, it does not explain the exact cause of the problem. Let's look at the problem faced by ABC in more detail. ABC's sales in the previous month can be represented as S_{t-1}, because it receives its cash with a one-month lag due to its collection policy. In this example, ABC is selling 500 units for $1 each. ABC's cash outflows are then $0.75 for production for current sales and $0.75 for inventory to support the increased sales. Algebraically, we can represent the change in cash (ΔCash) as

$$\Delta \text{Cash} = S_{t-1} - bS_t - b(S_t - S_{t-1})$$

The change in cash equals last month's sales minus the cost of production for this month (bS_t) and the cost of producing goods for inventory ($b[S_t - S_{t-1}]$), where b is the $0.75 cash production cost or, conversely, $1 - 0.75$ (i.e., $0.25) is the contribution margin. If we define g as the monthly sales growth rate, so that $S_t = S_{t-1} \times (1 + g)$, we get Equation 23-1.

[23-1]
$$\Delta \text{Cash} = S_{t-1}[1 - b(1 + 2g)]$$

Finance professors love equations like Equation 23-1 because the change in cash is linear in the growth rate in sales—that is, if we graph the change in cash against the monthly sales growth rate, we get a straight line. We will do this shortly with a more general problem, but note that with ABC's problem, $b = 0.75$, so if we divide both sides by last period's sales, the equation reduces to

$$\frac{\Delta \text{Cash}}{S_{t-1}} = 0.25 - 1.5g$$

We have divided by last period's sales to standardize the problem and focus on the critical issues. Think about the equation. If the sales growth rate is zero, then last period's sales are the same as this period's sales, so with a 30-day credit policy, ABC's cash inflow is the same as this month's sales. Further, there is no production for inventory, so the cash outflow is the $0.75

production cost. As a result, with $g = 0$, ABC makes $0.25 on every dollar of sales, and its cash inflow is the 25 percent contribution margin for each sale (i.e., $\Delta Cash = \$0.25 \ S_{t-1}$). So what about the g coefficient?

Given ABC's credit policy, this month's sales increase has no impact on cash inflows, because these were fixed last month; all that a sales increase does is increase cash outflows. For ABC, there is increased cash outflow for production for the incremental sales and incremental inventory. With a "current monthly sales in inventory policy," this means that for every unit increase in sales, there is a cash outflow to produce two units: one for sales and one for inventory. As a result, the coefficient on the sales growth rate is twice the cost of production. Clearly, ABC's credit and inventory policies mean that the cash flow from operations is very sensitive to the sales growth rate. In fact, we can set the left side equal to zero and find the **break-even sales growth rate** at which the monthly cash flow from operations is zero. For ABC, this is 1/6 or 16.67 percent (i.e., $0.25 - 1.5g = 0$; so $g = 0.25/1.5 = 1/6$). This means that as long as ABC's monthly sales growth rate is less than 16.67 percent, it generates cash; above that rate, it needs cash.

Returning to the annual cash budget for ABC, we can see why ABC changes from needing cash to generating cash. The key is that Mr. Jones assumed a $500 increase in sales each month. For month 1, there was no increase, so ABC generated 0.25 times the $1,000 sales level or $250. For month 2, the sales increase was 50 percent, well above the 16.67 percent break-even rate, so ABC needed cash. In fact, using the above equation, we can see that the cash changed by $0.25 - (1.5 \times 0.5)$, or –50 percent of the previous month's sales of $1,000 (i.e., –$500), which is exactly what happened. This need for cash changed in month 6, when sales increased by $500 from the $3,000 level of the previous month, or by exactly 16.67 percent, so the change in cash was zero. After that, the constant $500 sales increase on ever-larger previous month's sales figures caused the growth rate to drop below the 16.67 percent break-even rate, so ABC generated cash.

The importance of the growth rate on cash flow from operations—specifically, whether that cash flow is positive or negative—is equivalent to our discussion in Chapter 4 on the importance of the sustainable growth rate. In both cases, a higher sales growth rate creates an external financing need. In Chapter 4, we were concerned with the overall financing needs of the firm over a long period and how it should raise long-term capital. In this chapter, the concern is for the firm's financing needs over a shorter horizon, and we are mainly concerned with NWC management. However, the fundamentals are the same: for most firms, the structure of their financial and operating policies means that higher growth rates generate a need for financing. Now we can see how NWC management policies interact in a more general way.

break-even sales growth rate the sales growth rate that makes the monthly cash flow from operations zero

Credit, Inventory, and Payables

We can define the firm's credit policy with α as the percentage of sales collected this month and the balance $(1 - \alpha)$ collected with a one-month lag. In practice, sales can be collected after two or more months, but the important thing is that by varying α, we are changing the firm's credit policy to see how this affects its cash flow from operations. β is the proportion of this month's production costs that are paid this month, and $(1 - \beta)$ is the proportion paid next month. In this way, we can have the firm pay for some of its current production costs with a one-month lag, reflecting credit provided to it by suppliers and the firm's workforce.[4] Finally, γ is the percentage of the firm's monthly sales tied up in inventory, so $1/\gamma$ is the monthly inventory turnover ratio.

With these assumptions and the same notation as before, the change in cash each month is as shown in Equation 23-2.

---

[4] Workers generally are paid at the end of the week or month, so implicitly they finance some of the firm's operations, as discussed in Chapter 20.

[23-2]

$$\Delta Cash = \alpha S_t + (1 - \alpha)S_{t-1} - b\beta S_t - b(1-\beta)S_{t-1} - b\gamma(S_t - S_{t-1})$$

Equation 23-2 looks cumbersome, but all that has changed is that cash inflows come from this month's and last month's sales; cash outflows for current sales also occur this month and the following month; and production for inventory depends on the inventory policy (γ). In ABC's case, $\alpha = 0$, because it collects all this month's sales the following month; $\beta = 1$, because it pays all this month's expenses this month; $b = \$0.75$; and $\gamma = 1$, because it tries to maintain the next month's projected sales in inventory. So for ABC, the equation reduces to the equation shown previously:

$$\Delta Cash = 0 + (1)S_{t-1} - (\$0.75)(1)\ S_t - \$0.75(0)S_{t-1} - (\$0.75)(1)(S_t - S_{t-1})$$

$$= S_{t-1} - \$0.75S_t - \$0.75(S_t - S_{t-1})$$

If we again remove the different sales levels by including the sales growth rate, $S_t = (1 + g) S_{t-1}$, in Equation 23-2, and simplify, we get Equation 23-3:

[23-3]

$$\frac{\Delta Cash}{S_{t-1}} = (1 - b) + [\alpha - b(\beta + \gamma)]g$$

As before, with no sales growth, we get the contribution margin of $(1 - b)$, and the firm generates cash. However, this time the coefficient on the growth rate is more complex, as we are allowing the firm's policies regarding receivables, payables, and inventory to change. For example, previously we assumed cash inflows were from the previous month's sales, so $\alpha = 0$. Similarly, we assumed that all bills were paid immediately, so $\beta = 1$, and the firm kept 100 percent of monthly sales in inventory, so $\gamma = 1$. The coefficient on the sales growth rate was 1.5. Now we allow this coefficient to change with the firm's working capital policy.

First, however, in Figure 23-1, we graph the change in cash against the sales growth rate.

We can now see several things. First, as before, growth normally causes cash flow problems as the investment in NWC soaks up cash more quickly than the incremental sales generate

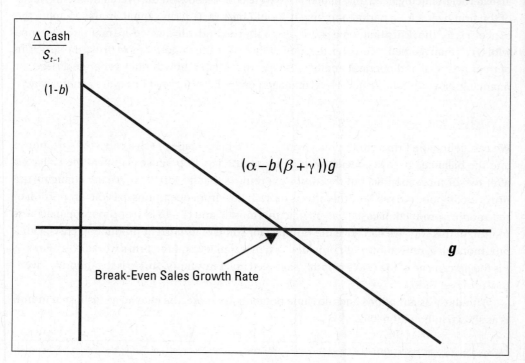

FIGURE 23-1 *Change in Cash and Sales Growth*

cash: this is generally referred to as the firm's **burn rate**. (This is also the reason why slow-growing profitable firms are referred to as "cash cows.") Fast-growing firms need to have more liquidity or external financing to offset this higher burn rate. Second, we can see what affects this burn rate. What the firm would like to do is flatten the slope of the line so that it reduces the amount of cash needed to finance the firm's growth—that is, it would like to lower its burn rate.

> **burn rate** the rate at which a firm uses up its cash reserves; it is synonymous with monthly cash flow deficits

In the example for ABC Company, its burn rate was rapidly decreasing as its growth rate was declining, so if it held on long enough, its problem would reverse. However, this is not the case for companies suffering financial distress. Companies in financial distress worry about their *cash burn rate*. *Cash burn rate* refers to a company's cash on hand and the rate that cash is used in operations due to negative operating cash flows. The *burn rate* then indicates how long a company can operate before it has to raise funds, either by issuing stock or borrowing. For example, Ford burned through $4.7 billion of cash in the first six months of 2009, but was able to slow that burn with a significant positive cash flow in the fourth quarter of 2009, burning just $300 million for the entire year of 2009. The fate of Ford depended on its ability to slow the cash burn, which it did.

Many companies suffer from cash burn leading up to bankruptcy, including United Airlines in 2002 and Consolidated Freightways in 2002. Consider Borders Group, a U.S. retail bookstore chain that filed for bankruptcy in 2011. Borders burned through cash as it approached bankruptcy (Figure 23-2).

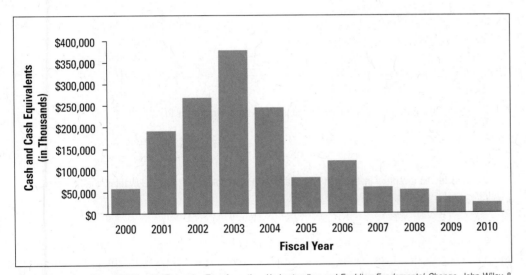

FIGURE 23-2 *Borders Group's Cash Burn*

Source: Data from Rouse, William B., *Enterprise Transformation: Understanding and Enabling Fundamental Change*, John Wiley & Sons, 2006; Borders Group 10-K filings, various years.

One way to lower the burn rate is to increase α and hope that it changes the slope of the line from negative to positive. Increasing α essentially means collecting receivables more quickly. This changes the firm's **credit policy**. Alternatively, we can reduce β and γ; b has to remain positive as it is the firm's production cost. Reducing β means delaying paying the bills; the greater β is, the higher the percentage of bills paid in the current month. This changes the firm's **payment policy**. Finally, reducing γ means having less inventory, which in turn means increasing the turnover ratio and changing the firm's **inventory policy**. For a given sales growth rate, the firm's main levers for growing faster are to collect its invoices more quickly, delay paying its bills, and reduce its stock of inventory. These policy changes may slow the growth rate, as we will see in Chapter 24. If the firm can't change these policies, another alternative is to increase its prices and slow its growth rate that way, which has the added advantage of increasing its contribution margin and lowering b.

> **credit policy** decisions on how a firm grants, monitors, and collects payment for outstanding accounts receivable

> **payment policy** decisions on how quickly the firm pays its bills

> **inventory policy** decisions on the levels of inventory the firm holds

As before, we can work out the monthly sales growth rate the firm can grow at without needing or generating cash. Equation 23-4 shows the extended example case.

[23-4]
$$g = \frac{(1-b)}{[b(\beta + \gamma) - \alpha]}$$

As can be seen from Equation 23-4, the firm can grow faster if it has a higher gross margin $(1-b)$, has lower production costs (b), collects its receivables more quickly (higher α), pays its bills more slowly (lower β), and has less inventory (lower γ).

EXAMPLE 23-2   Break-Even Sales Growth Rates

A firm collects 10 percent of its monthly sales immediately and the rest a month later. Its production costs are 80 percent of sales. It holds two months' worth of sales in inventory, and it pays half its bills immediately and half after 30 days.

a.   What is its break-even sales growth rate?

b.   What happens to this rate if the firm reduces its inventory to one month's sales and speeds up its collection of receivables to 50 percent immediately and 50 percent after 30 days?

Solution

a. $\alpha = 0.1$; $b = 0.8$; $\beta = 0.5$; and $\gamma = 2$

Plugging these values into Equation 23-4, we get

$$g = \frac{(1-b)}{[b(\beta + \gamma) - \alpha]} = \frac{(1-0.8)}{[0.8(0.5+2) - 0.1]} = 0.1053 = 10.53\%$$

b.   With the new policy, $\gamma = 1$ and $\alpha = 0.5$, so the growth rate increases to

$$g = \frac{(1-0.8)}{[0.8(0.5+1) - 0.5]} = 0.2857 = 28.57\%$$

By reducing its inventory investment and speeding up the collection of its receivables, the firm can grow faster.

Another way of looking at the information in Figure 23-1 is to consider something called the "cash conversion cycle," which is a measure of how many days of financing are required. This topic is addressed in the next section.

CONCEPT REVIEW QUESTIONS

1.   What is the relationship between the break-even sales growth rate and a firm's collection policy, payables policy, and inventory policy?

2.   Why does cash flow from operations increase if the firm speeds up the collection of receivables, delays paying its bills, or increases its inventory turnover ratio?

Learning Objective 23.4
List and describe some common ways to analyze a firm's management of its net working capital.

23.4 WORKING CAPITAL MANAGEMENT

We have discussed what characterizes good working capital management and how such decisions can be integrated. We now discuss some common ways to assess or summarize a firm's W/C management.

Working Capital Ratios

We defined two common measures of firm liquidity in Chapter 4: the current ratio and the quick (or acid test) ratio. We repeat those definitions below:

$$\text{Current ratio} = \frac{\text{Current assets (CA)}}{\text{Current liabilities (CL)}} \qquad [23\text{-}5]$$

$$\text{Quick ratio} = \frac{\text{Cash (C) + Marketable securities (MS) + Accounts receivable (AR)}}{\text{CL}} \qquad [23\text{-}6]$$

Recall that the current ratio measures a firm's ability to repay current obligations from current assets. The quick ratio is a more conservative estimate of liquidity that reflects the fact that inventory is generally not as liquid as other current assets, while prepaid expenses are virtually worthless in the event of firm liquidation. There are no general rules setting out what are "good" values for these ratios, and optimal ratios vary by industry. For both of these ratios, higher values indicate that a firm has more liquidity. However, this does not necessarily mean that the firm is practising effective W/C management. In fact, it could indicate quite the opposite—that is, perhaps the firm is being too conservative and maintaining *excessive* liquidity, or perhaps it has high ratios because its credit policy is too lenient, which has left it with high levels of receivables outstanding.[5]

Although the current and quick ratios are useful summary statistics, they do not tell the whole story of working capital management. To gain better insight into a company's strengths and weaknesses, we need to look at how it arrived at these levels of CA and CL. We can again turn to Chapter 4, in which we introduced several efficiency ratios that are specifically related to working capital items. We begin by looking at two ratios that are related to accounts receivables:

$$\text{Receivables turnover (RT)} = \frac{\text{Rev}}{\text{AR}} \qquad [23\text{-}7]$$

$$\text{Average collection period (ACP)} = \frac{\text{AR}}{\text{Average daily revenue (ADR)}} = \frac{365}{\text{RT}} \qquad [23\text{-}8]$$

The receivables turnover (RT) ratio measures the revenues (Rev) that are generated for each dollar that is tied up in receivables, while the average collection period (ACP) measures how long it takes the average customer to pay his or her account. The ACP is 365 divided by the receivables turnover—that is, if accounts receivable turn over 10 times per year, the ACP is 36.5 days (365/10). Technically, both of these ratios should be calculated by using credit revenues and not total revenues; however, because most companies do not break out revenues into cash and credit revenues, it is common to use the total revenues figures.

In Chapter 4, we also introduced some efficiency ratios that are related to inventory. One of these, the inventory turnover (IT) ratio, is defined in Equation 23-9.

$$\text{Inventory turnover (IT)} = \frac{\text{Cost of goods sold (CGS)}}{\text{Inventory}} \qquad [23\text{-}9]$$

The numerator of this ratio will be the CGS, because when inventory is sold, it is expensed through this account. However, in practice, because of accounting differences, the CGS figure is not always reliable nor always comparable across firms. As a result, CGS is often replaced by revenues in the IT ratio, which is then defined as shown in Equation 23-10.

---

[5] The same could be said with respect to the current ratio if the firm maintains excess inventory. This would obviously not affect the quick ratio.

$$[23\text{-}10] \qquad \text{Inventory turnover (IT)} = \frac{\text{Rev}}{\text{Inventory}}$$

We will use this definition of IT for the remaining discussion.

Similar to our derivation of the ACP in Equation 23-8, we can divide 365 days by the IT ratio to find the average days of revenues in inventory (ADRI), which is given in Equation 23-11.

$$[23\text{-}11] \qquad \text{Average days revenues in inventory (ADRI)} = \frac{\text{Inventory}}{\text{ADR}} = \frac{365}{\text{IT}}$$

Notice that higher receivables turnover and higher inventory turnover are generally indicative of more efficient management of these current assets. However, they would cause a firm's current ratio (and its quick ratio, in the case of receivables turnover) to decline, all else being equal. This in itself demonstrates why current and quick ratios, when viewed in isolation, are insufficient measures of working capital management.

Finally, we focus on the current liability side of the W/C management issue by introducing the following two ratios that are related to a firm's management of its accounts payable:

$$[23\text{-}12] \qquad \text{Payables turnover (PT)} = \frac{\text{Rev}}{\text{Accounts payable}}$$

$$[23\text{-}13] \qquad \text{Average days of revenues in payables (ADRP)} = \frac{\text{Accounts payable}}{\text{ADR}} = \frac{365}{\text{PT}}$$

The payables turnover (PT) ratio shows how many times a year a firm pays off its suppliers, on average. The average days of revenues in payables (ADRP) ratio represents how long a firm defers payments to its suppliers, on average.[6]

Operating and Cash Conversion Cycles

Two additional summary measures of W/C management deal specifically with the amount of time a firm must wait for cash to be generated from its sales and how much financing it will require. The **operating cycle (OC)** represents the average time required for a firm to acquire inventory, sell it, and collect the sale proceeds. As such, the OC can be estimated as the sum of the average days of revenues in inventory (ADRI) and the average collection period (ACP), as expressed in Equation 23-14.

operating cycle (OC) the average time required for a firm to acquire inventory, sell it, and collect the proceeds

$$[23\text{-}14] \qquad \text{Operating cycle (OC)} = \text{ADRI} + \text{ACP}$$

The OC measures the average number of days a firm holds items in inventory before they are sold, plus the average time it takes to collect on sales. Large OC figures indicate that a firm has a long operating cycle that requires large average investments in receivables or inventory. However, to estimate the amount of financing a firm requires, we must also consider how long it is able to delay making payments to suppliers. This can be measured by using the firm's average days of revenues in payables (ADRP) ratio, which measures how long it defers paying payables on average.

cash conversion cycle (CCC) an estimate of the average time between when a firm pays cash for its inventory purchases and when it receives cash for its sales; the average number of days of revenues that a firm must finance outside the use of trade credit

The **cash conversion cycle (CCC)** takes the payable deferral period into account and provides an estimate of the average time between when a firm pays cash for its inventory purchases and when it receives cash for its sales. In essence, the CCC represents the average

---

[6] Technically, we should use the CGS instead of revenues in each of these ratios, because these payments represent costs that would be included in the CGS. However, for the same reasons we cited with respect to the use of revenues to calculate inventory turnover, it is common to use revenues.

number of days of revenues that a firm must finance outside the use of trade credit. As such, it is an important ratio that firms and their creditors consider when arranging financing. It can be broken into two components: the OC and the ADRP, as shown in Equation 23-15.

$$\text{Cash conversion cycle (CCC)} = \text{OC} - \text{ADRP} \text{ or } \text{CCC} = (\text{ADRI} + \text{ACP}) - \text{ADRP} \qquad [23\text{-}15]$$

We now return to our discussion of Mr. Jones' ABC Company. ABC had a policy of keeping one month's revenues in inventory, allowing 30 days of credit, and paying bills immediately. Therefore, ABC's ADRI was 30 days, as was its ACP, while its ADRP was zero. This translates into an OC of 60 days and a CCC of 60 days. If ABC immediately pays its bills for its widgets, it then has to finance them for 30 days while they sit in inventory and for another 30 days before the firm receives payment for them after they are sold. In other words, ABC has to finance 60 days' worth of revenues.

The CCC is clearly related to Figure 23-1. If the firm speeds up its collection policy, it gets its cash earlier and the number of days in receivables goes down. Similarly, if it increases its inventory turnover ratio, it needs less inventory and the number of days of revenues that are tied up in inventory goes down. Finally, if it delays paying its bills, it has larger accounts payable. As a result of undertaking any of these actions, the firm can grow at a faster rate without needing cash, and the cash conversion cycle gets shorter.

EXAMPLE 23-3   Cash Conversion Cycle

Use the data provided for the company in Example 23-2 to calculate its cash conversion cycle under the policies outlined in parts (a) and (b) of that example.

Solution

a. The average days in receivables is 27, because 10 percent are collected immediately and 90 percent after 30 days; that is, days $= \alpha \times 0 + (1 - \alpha) \times 30$. The days in inventory is 60, because the inventory is $\gamma \times 30$, while the days in payables is 15, which is $\beta \times 0 + (1 - \beta) \times 30$. So the cash conversion cycle is 72 days (i.e., $27 + 60 - 15$). The company has to finance its widgets while they sit in inventory for 60 days and then for another 27 days until the company gets paid, which is partially offset by the 15-day trade credit the company gets by paying its bills with a lag.

b. With the higher inventory turnover rate, as γ is reduced from 2 to 1, the days in inventory goes down to 30 days, while the quicker collection of receivables, as β increases to 0.5, reduces the collection period to 15 days. Overall, the cash conversion cycle drops from 72 to 30 days (i.e., $15 + 30 - 15$). With a shorter cash conversion cycle, the firm's break-even growth rate goes up.

Industry "Norms"

Dun and Bradstreet (D&B) is a major data provider that operates in over 100 countries worldwide, with a global database of information on over 140 million companies, including more than a million in Canada. One part of its service is to provide a database of financial ratios for different industries so that firms can benchmark themselves against industry norms. These industries are sorted by their standard industry classifications (SIC). For our purposes, we will look at the median ratios for the eating and drinking places classification (SIC 58) for firms with over $1 million in assets. D&B reports 14 key business ratios for a sample of 13 firms that meet this classification, but we will report only the ratios for 2008 and 2009 , shown in Table 23-4.

TABLE 23-4 D&B Key Business Ratios

	2008	2009
Quick ratio	0.9	0.5
Current ratio	1.1	1.1
Collection period	0.0	7.2
Inventory turnover	44.6	49.2
Payables to sales	1.6%	1.3%

These are the median values, or those for the "middle" firm, so they are not distorted by very high or low numbers. These are for the five standard working capital ratios, except that D&B reports the payables ratio as a percentage of sales, rather than as the average days in sales as it is normally calculated. This simply means that D&B divided by sales instead of dividing sales by 365. If we used the average days of revenues in payables ratio (ADRP) presented in the previous section, we would get 5.8 days for 2008 and 4.75 for 2009.

An Illustrative Example

We now return to the financial statements for Tim Hortons Inc., which were analyzed in chapters 3 and 4, to demonstrate how to calculate and interpret the ratios discussed above. Tim Hortons' balance sheets and income statements for 2010 and 2011 were presented in figures 3-4 and 3-5 of Chapter 3.

We calculate the 2011 ratios for Tim Hortons for illustrative purposes, beginning with the current and quick ratios.

$$\text{Current ratio} = \frac{CA}{CL} = \frac{621.0}{476.7} = 1.30$$

$$\text{Quick ratio} = \frac{C + MS + AR}{CL} = \frac{126.5 + 0 + 173.7}{476.7} = 0.63$$

The current ratio of 1.30 indicates that Tim Hortons has $1.30 in CA for every dollar in CL, while its quick ratio is slightly less than half its current ratio.

Now we move on to calculate the various efficiency ratios, beginning with those related to receivables.

$$\text{Receivables turnover} = \frac{Rev}{AR} = \frac{2{,}853}{173.7} = 16.4$$

$$ACP = \frac{365}{\text{Receivables turnover}} = \frac{365}{16.4} = 22.3 \text{ days}$$

The receivables turnover ratio indicates that for every dollar invested in receivables, Tim Hortons generated $16.40 in revenues. The ACP indicates that if Tim Hortons' revenues were all on credit, its customers were paying, on average, 22.3 days after purchase.

Next, we examine the company's ratios related to inventory management. We use revenues instead of cost of goods sold in our calculations, for the reasons discussed above.

$$\text{Inventory turnover} = \frac{Rev}{Inv} = \frac{2{,}853}{137} = 20.8$$

$$ACP = \frac{365}{\text{Inventory turnover}} = \frac{365}{20.8} = 17.5 \text{ days}$$

The high inventory turnover (or low ADRI) reflects the nature of Tim Hortons' product, which must be sold quickly while it's fresh.

So Tim Hortons has only 17.5 days of revenues tied up in inventory and only 22.3 in receivables. This translates into an operating cycle of 39.8 days:

$$OC = ADRI + ACP = 17.5 + 22.3 = 39.8 \text{ days}$$

We know that Tim Hortons does not have to finance all 39.8 days of revenues because it can lean on its suppliers to a certain extent. We can measure its payables policy during 2011 by using the following two ratios:

$$\text{Payables turnover (PT)} = \frac{\text{Rev}}{\text{Accounts payable}} = \frac{2{,}853}{177.9} = 16$$

$$\text{Average days of revenues in payables (ADRP)} = \frac{365}{PT} = \frac{365}{16} = 22.8 \text{ days}$$

We can use this information to estimate Tim Hortons' cash conversion cycle:

$$CCC = OC - ADRP = 39.8 - 22.8 = 17 \text{ days}$$

On average, Tim Hortons has to finance 17 days of revenues or

$$\text{Required financing} = 17 \text{ days} \times \frac{2{,}853 \text{ million}}{365} = \$132.9 \text{ million}$$

This is a small number relative to its sales, and if we look at the balance sheet, we see that it does not have any short-term loans outstanding. This indicates that Tim Hortons essentially finances its CCC (which is minimal) using long-term financing.

23-1 ETHICS AND CORPORATE GOVERNANCE

Bristol-Myers Squibb Company

The Securities and Exchange Commission today announced that it filed an enforcement action against Bristol-Myers Squibb Company, a New York-based company whose largest division, the U.S. Medicines Group, is based in New Jersey. The Commission's complaint, filed today in the United States District Court for the District of New Jersey, alleges that Bristol-Myers perpetrated a fraudulent earnings management scheme by, among other things, selling excessive amounts of pharmaceutical products to its wholesalers ahead of demand, improperly recognizing revenue from $1.5 billion of such sales to its two largest wholesalers and using "cookie jar" reserves to meet its internal sales and earnings targets and analysts' earnings estimates.

In settling the Commission's action, Bristol-Myers agreed to an order requiring it to pay $150 million and perform numerous remedial undertakings, including the appointment of an independent adviser to review and monitor its accounting practices, financial reporting and internal controls.

Stephen M. Cutler, Director of the SEC's Division of Enforcement, said, "Bristol-Myers' earnings management scheme distorted the true performance of the company and its medicines business on a massive scale and caused significant harm to the company's shareholders. The company's conduct warrants a stiff civil sanction. As our investigation continues, we will be focusing on, among other things, those individuals responsible for the company's failures."

Timothy L. Warren, Associate Regional Director of the SEC's Midwest Regional Office, added, "For two years Bristol-Myers deceived the market into believing that it was meeting its financial projections and market expectations, when, in fact, the company was making its numbers primarily through channel-stuffing and manipulative accounting devices. Severe sanctions are necessary to hold Bristol-Myers accountable for its violative conduct, and deter Bristol-Myers and other public companies from engaging in similar schemes."

continued

ETHICS AND CORPORATE GOVERNANCE: Bristol-Myers Squibb Company *(continued)*

Specifically, the Commission's complaint alleges, among other things, that:

> From the first quarter of 2000 through the fourth quarter of 2001, Bristol-Myers engaged in a fraudulent scheme to inflate its sales and earnings in order to create the false appearance that the company had met or exceeded its internal sales and earnings targets and Wall Street analysts' earnings estimates.

> Bristol-Myers inflated its results primarily by (1) stuffing its distribution channels with excess inventory near the end of every quarter in amounts sufficient to meet its targets by making pharmaceutical sales to its wholesalers ahead of demand; and (2) improperly recognizing $1.5 billion in revenue from such pharmaceutical sales to its two biggest wholesalers. In connection with the $1.5 billion in revenue, Bristol-Myers covered these wholesalers' carrying costs and guaranteed them a return on investment until they sold the products. When Bristol-Myers recognized the $1.5 billion in revenue upon shipment, it did so contrary to generally accepted accounting principles.

> When Bristol-Myers' results still fell short of the Street's earnings estimates, the company tapped improperly created divestiture reserves and reversed portions of those reserves into income to further inflate its earnings.

> At no time during 2000 or 2001 did Bristol-Myers disclose that (1) it was artificially inflating its results through channel-stuffing and improper accounting; (2) channel-stuffing was contributing to a build-up in excess wholesaler inventory levels; or (3) excess wholesaler inventory posed a material risk to the company's future sales and earnings.

> In addition, as a result of its channel-stuffing, Bristol-Myers materially understated its accruals for rebates due to Medicaid and certain of its prime vendors, customers of its wholesalers that purchased large quantities of pharmaceutical products from those wholesalers.

Bristol-Myers has agreed, without admitting or denying the allegations in the Commission's complaint, to the following relief:

- a permanent injunction against future violations of certain antifraud, reporting, books and records and internal controls provisions of the federal securities laws;

- disgorgement of $1;

- a civil penalty of $100 million;

- an additional $50 million payment into a fund for the benefit of shareholders;

- various remedial undertakings, including the appointment of an independent adviser to review, assess and monitor Bristol-Myers' accounting practices, financial reporting and disclosure processes and internal control systems.

Source: Securities and Exchange Commission press release, "Bristol-Myers Squibb Company Agrees to Pay $150 Million to Settle Fraud Charges," August 4, 2004. Available at www.sec.gov/news/press.

DISCUSSION QUESTIONS

1. Bristol-Myers Squibb (BMS) was accused of channel-stuffing. What is channel-stuffing?

2. When does GAAP recognize a sale as occurring, and did a sale occur if BMS covered its distributors' costs and guaranteed them a return on their purchase of BMS products?

3. How did BMS's channel-stuffing affect its sales and cash flow? How could an analyst have picked up on BMS's channel-stuffing?

CONCEPT REVIEW QUESTIONS

1. What are the limitations of the current ratio and the quick ratio as measures of working capital management?

2. What are the operating cycle and the cash conversion cycle, and how are they related to working capital policy?

SUMMARY

In this chapter, we discuss the importance of effective net working capital management and demonstrate the classic problem faced by growing firms. We present an integrative approach to working capital management that focuses on the importance of the sales growth rate and demonstrates the usefulness of cash budgets, which allow firms to forecast their cash requirements. We conclude by showing how to use some common ratios to assess a firm's overall approach to working capital management.

SUMMARY OF LEARNING OBJECTIVES

23.1 Explain why the management of net working capital is critical for the survival of a firm.

Sales growth may create a cash shortage, as increased inventory and accounts receivable consume cash. While sales growth also increases payables, the increase usually does not offset inventory and receivables. This cash shortage can lead to insolvency—for a growing firm! Even in a firm without growth, cash is used in production before it is collected from sales. This gap can lead to cash shortages, which can lead to a firm's insolvency if they are not planned for and accommodated through short-term financing.

23.2 Explain how managing receivables, inventory, and payables is related in an integrated approach to net working capital management.

Net working capital is the difference between current assets and current liabilities. Current assets usually include cash, receivables, and inventory. Current liabilities include payables. Thus, net working capital = cash + receivables + inventory – payables. This is why receivables, inventory, and payables must be managed as part of the integrated approach to net working capital management.

23.3 Explain how financing and current asset investment decisions interact to determine a company's overall working capital position.

For most firms, the structure of their financial and operating policies means that higher growth rates generate a need for short-term financing. If current assets are less than current liabilities, net working capital becomes negative, which generates a need for outside financing. A company's overall working capital can also be affected by its policies concerning collection of receivables, payment of bills, and inventory management.

23.4 List and describe some common ways to analyze a firm's management of its net working capital.

Current ratio: restates working capital as a ratio of current assets over current liabilities

Operating cycle: the amount of time between the time when inputs are purchased and the time when cash is collected from the sale of a finished product; the sum of days in inventory and the average collection period

Cash conversion cycle: the amount of time between when inputs are paid for and when cash is collected from the sale of a finished product; equal to the operating cycle less days in payables

KEY TERMS

break-even sales growth rate, p. 887
burn rate, p. 889
cash budget, p. 883
cash conversion cycle (CCC), p. 892
credit policy, p. 889

illiquidity, p. 878
insolvency, p. 878
inventory policy, p. 889
net working capital (NWC), p. 878
operating cycle (OC), p. 892

payment policy, p. 889
trade credit, p. 881
working capital management, p. 878

EQUATIONS

Equation	Formula	Page
[23-1] Change in Cash	$\Delta\text{Cash} = S_{t-1}[1 - b(1 + 2g)]$	p.886
[23-2] Change in Cash (general working capital)	$\Delta\text{Cash} = \alpha S_t + (1 - \alpha)S_{t-1} - b\beta S_t - b(1 - \beta)S_{t-1} - b\gamma(S_t - S_{t-1})$	p. 888
[23-3] Change in Cash Percentage of Sales	$\dfrac{\Delta\text{Cash}}{S_{t-1}} = (1 - b) + [\alpha - b(\beta + \gamma)]g$	p. 888

continued

EQUATIONS *(continued)*

Equation	Formula	Page
[23-4] Break-even Sales Growth Rate	$g = \dfrac{(1 - b)}{[b(\beta + \gamma) - \alpha]}$	p. 890
[23-5] Current Ratio	$\text{Current ratio} = \dfrac{\text{Current assets (CA)}}{\text{Current liabilities (CL)}}$	p. 891
[23-6] Quick Ratio	$\text{Quick ratio} = \dfrac{\text{Cash (C) + Marketable securities (MS) + Accounts receivable (AR)}}{\text{CL}}$	p. 891
[23-7] Receivables Turnover (RT)	$\text{Receivables turnover (RT)} = \dfrac{\text{Rev}}{\text{AR}}$	p. 891
[23-8] Average Collection Period (ACP)	$\text{Average collection period (ACP)} = \dfrac{\text{AR}}{\text{Average daily revenue (ADR)}} = \dfrac{365}{\text{RT}}$	p. 891
[23-9] Inventory Turnover (IT)	$\text{Inventory turnover (IT)} = \dfrac{\text{Cost of goods sold (CGS)}}{\text{Inventory}}$	p. 891
[23-10] Inventory Turnover (IT)	$\text{Inventory turnover (IT)} = \dfrac{\text{Rev}}{\text{Inventory}}$	p. 892
[23-11] Average Days of Revenues in Inventory	$\text{Average days revenues in inventory (ADRI)} = \dfrac{\text{Inventory}}{\text{ADR}} = \dfrac{365}{\text{IT}}$	p. 892
[23-12] Payables Turnover (PT)	$\text{Payables turnover (PT)} = \dfrac{\text{Rev}}{\text{Accounts payable}}$	p. 892
[23-13] Average Days of Revenues in Payables (ADRP)	$\text{Average days of revenues in payables (ADRP)} = \dfrac{\text{Accounts payable}}{\text{ADR}} = \dfrac{365}{\text{PT}}$	p. 892
[23-14] Operating Cycle (OC)	$\text{Operating cycle (OC)} = \text{ADRI} + \text{ACP}$	p. 892
[23-15] Cash Conversion Cycle (CCC)	$\text{Cash conversion cycle (CCC)} = \text{OC} - \text{ADRP}$ or $\text{CCC} = (\text{ADRI} + \text{ACP}) - \text{ADRP}$	p. 893

QUESTIONS AND PRACTICE PROBLEMS

Multiple Choice Questions

1. Which of the following is not a warning sign of potential liquidity problems?
   a. Declines in working capital and daily cash flows
   b. Increases in accounts receivable and longer collection periods
   c. Decreases in debt and debt ratios
   d. A buildup of inventory and declining inventory turnover

2. Which of the following is true?
   a. Cash budgets should not be prepared with uncertain numbers.
   b. Cash budgeting is a one-time process.
   c. It is helpful to prepare separate cash budgets for alternative forecasts of key variables.
   d. Cash budgets should not be used to evaluate the impact of different scenarios.

3. Which of the following usually does not increase as sales increase?
    a. cash
    b. accounts receivable
    c. trade credit
    d. short-term debt

Use the following information to answer questions 4 to 6 and practice problem 31.

Cash	$ 500,000
Marketable securities	800,500
Accounts receivable	700,000
Inventory	1,203,000
Short-term loans	100,000
Accounts payable	800,000
Sales	1,287,555
Cost of goods sold	550,000

4. What are the current ratio and quick ratio?
    a. 4.57; 2.86
    b. 3.56; 2.86
    c. 3.56; 2.22
    d. 2.22; 3.56

5. What is the average collection period (ACP)?
    a. 227 days
    a. 142 days
    a. 150 days
    a. 198 days

6. Calculate the operating cycle (OC) using COGS to calculate the inventory turnover ratio.
    a. 1,025 days
    b. 539 days
    c. 996 days
    d. 940 days

7. What is the period of time between the outflow of cash from buying raw materials and the collection of cash from selling finished goods?
    a. collection period
    b. inventory period
    c. net financing period
    d. operating cycle

8. The period of time between the purchase of raw materials and the sale of the finished goods produced from the raw materials is called the:
    a. collection period.
    b. inventory period.
    c. cash conversion cycle.
    d. operating cycle.

9. The period of time between the sale of finished goods on credit and the collection of the cash is called the:
    a. collection period.
    b. inventory period.

    c. net financing period.

    d. operating cycle.

10. What changes will occur if an inventory policy change causes a firm to hold less inventory?

    a. The current ratio and the quick ratio will both decrease.

    b. The current ratio will decrease but the quick ratio will be unchanged.

    c. The inventory turnover ratio will decrease.

    d. The average days' revenues in inventory (ADRI) will increase.

11. What changes will occur if a payment policy change causes a firm to pay its suppliers faster?

    a. The current ratio and the quick ratio will both decrease.

    b. The current ratio will increase, but the quick ratio will be unchanged.

    c. The payables turnover ratio will decrease.

    d. The average days of sales in payables (ADSP) will decrease.

12. What changes will occur if a credit policy change causes a firm to allow its customers more time to pay their invoices?

    a. The current ratio and the quick ratio will not change as accounts receivable changes to cash.

    b. The current ratio will increase but the quick ratio will be unchanged.

    c. The receivables turnover ratio will increase.

    d. The average collection period (ACP) will decrease.

Practice Problems

13. Explain how trade credit allows firms to use their suppliers as sources of short-term funds.

14. State the characteristics of sound net working capital management.

15. How is net working capital calculated?

16. Why is the efficient utilization of net working capital important?

17. Describe the types of cash inflows and outflows in a cash budget.

18. What is the connection between cash budgets and pro forma financial statements?

19. For 2012, Ontario Manufacturing Company provided the following accounting information:

Net operating income	$60,000
Depreciation on equipment and building	10,000
Sale of land	25,000
Purchase of equipment	15,000
Retirement of long-term debt	30,000
Dividends declared	15,000
Long-term investments	10,000

    a. Which of the above are sources of funds?

    b. Which of the above are uses of funds?

    c. What is the overall increase or decrease in cash?

20. Christmas Inc. is a wholesaler of Christmas decorations and wrapping paper. It is a seasonal business and, due to the timing of cash inflows and outflows, it frequently experiences a cash shortfall in the fourth quarter of the year, before it can liquidate its current assets. Christmas Inc. has a cash balance as of October 1 of $40,000. Cash receipts for October, November, and

December are expected to be $20,000, $30,000, and $70,000, respectively. Fixed-cash operating expenses are $40,000 per month, and variable-cash operating expenses are generally 30 percent of the cash receipts for that month. If the line of credit is paid off the month after it is used, there is no interest charged. Prepare a cash budget for Christmas Inc., and determine whether Christmas Inc. will need to make use of its $10,000 credit line.

21. A firm has estimated its sales, purchases from suppliers, and wages and miscellaneous operating cash outlays for the first four months of next year as follows:

Month	Sales	Purchases	Wages & Misc.
January	$100,000	$60,000	$20,000
February	$102,000	$70,000	$30,000
March	$105,000	$55,000	$35,000
April	$110,000	$50,000	$25,000

It estimates that 50 percent of its sales will be for cash, and that it will receive the remaining portion in two equal amounts at the end of the subsequent two months. It plans to pay for all of its purchases two months after the purchase date.

The firm is scheduled to pay dividends of $40,000 in January, and to pay $20,000 for new equipment in March. Its beginning cash balance is $30,000, and the firm wishes to maintain a minimum balance of $10,000. Wages & misc. must be paid monthly without delay. Estimate the firm's cash budget for the first four months of next year. Assume that the sales and purchases were the same in November and December as they are estimated to be in January.

22. Calculate the ending cash balance of the current month for the following:

Beginning cash	$ 20,000
Prior month sales	50,000
Current month sales	100,000
Current purchases	35,000
Prior month purchases	20,000
Sale of old equipment	70,000
Dividend payment	80,000
Wages and others	35,000

23. A firm collects 60 percent of its monthly sales immediately and the rest a month later; its production costs are 80 percent of sales, and it holds two months of sales in inventory. It pays 40 percent of its bills immediately and the remainder after 30 days.
   a. What is its break-even sales growth rate?
   b. What happens to this rate if it increases its inventory to three months' sales and offers more lenient credit terms that result in only 40 percent of its sales being for cash, with the remainder being collected after 30 days?

24. Atlantic Transport collects 75 percent of its monthly sales immediately and the rest at the end of the month; has production costs that are 50 percent of sales; pays 50 percent of its bills immediately and the rest at the end of the month; and has four months of sales in inventory.
   a. Calculate the break-even sales growth rate.
   b. Suppose that Atlantic Transport adopts a more efficient inventory policy that reduces the size of its inventory to three months of sales. Atlantic Transport also reduces its production costs to 40 percent of sales. What is the new break-even sales growth rate?

25. Would each of the following changes increase or decrease the break-even sales growth rate?
   a. An increase in the amount of inventory held

    b. An increase in the proportion of invoices that are paid immediately

    c. A decrease in the amount of inventory held

    d. A decrease in the proportion of invoices that are paid immediately

    e. An increase in the proportion of sales for cash

    f. An increase in the proportion of sales collected at the end of one month

26. a. What can you conclude if a firm's planned sales growth exceeds its break-even sales growth rate?

    b. What can you conclude if a firm's planned sales growth is less than its break-even sales growth rate?

27. Explain the difference between the receivables turnover ratio and the average collection period (ACP).

28. Discuss measures businesses can implement to improve working capital management.

29. Explain the difference between the operating cycle (OC) and the cash conversion cycle (CCC).

30. Explain the difference between the quick ratio and the current ratio.

31. Calculate the cash conversion cycle (CCC) for the company examined in questions 2 to 4.

32. Great Northern Manufacturing presently has net working capital of $100,000 and sales of $150,000. It is considering entering into a new project that would increase next year's sales by $7,500. The project would result in a decrease in the average collection period of receivables (or days receivables) by two days (from 32 days to 30 days), but would have no impact on the other working capital items. Estimate the accounts receivable before and after the firm undertakes the project. Estimate the change in net working capital that will result for this firm if it undertakes the project.

33. Manitoba Services is considering undertaking a new order that would cause its average days of revenues in payables (ADRP) to decrease from 58 days to 45 days, while its average collection period (ACP) will remain at 90 days and its average days revenues in inventory (ADRI) will fall from 98 days to 80 days. What will be the effect on its operating cycle and cash cycle if these estimates are correct?

34. Determine the operating cycle and cash conversion cycle for a company with inventory turnover of 6.25 times per year, receivables turnover of 10 times per year, and an average days of revenues in payables (ADRP) of 40 days.

⚙ 35. MB Corporation has a receivables turnover of 10, an inventory turnover of 15, and a payables turnover of 5. Calculate its cash conversion cycle. What does a negative cash conversion cycle tell you about MB Corporation's business?

24 Working Capital Management: Current Assets and Current Liabilities

LEARNING OBJECTIVES

24.1 Explain the motivation for holding cash, and describe how to implement effective cash management techniques.

24.2 Describe how accounts receivable are managed.

24.3 Describe how inventory is managed.

24.4 List and describe the major sources of short-term financing.

Cash is something companies love to have. But can they have too much? What about a company's cash position? If excess debt is a bad thing, does it follow that a lot of cash is a good thing? At first glance, it makes sense for investors to seek out companies with plenty of cash on the balance sheet. After all, cash offers protection against tough times, and it also gives companies more options for future growth. Unfortunately, nothing is quite that simple. For investors digging into company fundamentals, a big pile of cash can signal many things—good and bad. How investors interpret cash reserves depends on how the cash got there, the kind of business the company is, and what managers plan to do with the cash. To play it safe, investors should look at cash position through the sieve of financial theory and work out an appropriate cash level. By taking into account the firm's future cash flows, business cycles, capital expenditure plans, emerging liability payments, and other cash needs, investors can calculate how much cash a company really needs.

Source: Excerpted from McClure, Ben, "Cash: Can A Company Have Too Much?" Investopedia. Available at www.investopedia.com. Reprinted with permission from Investopedia.com © 2013 Investopedia US. Reprinted with permission from Investopedia.com © 2013 Investopedia US.

CHAPTER 24 **PREVIEW**

I n Chapter 23, we discussed the importance of net working capital management to the firm, as well as ways to assess a firm's working capital position. In this chapter, we deal with the management of the individual working capital components. We begin by considering the decisions firms make with respect to their investments in current assets, and then we discuss the short-term financing decisions made by firms.

24.1 CASH AND MARKETABLE SECURITIES

Reasons for Holding Cash

Learning Objective 24.1
Explain the motivation for holding cash, and describe how to implement effective cash management techniques.

transactions motive one of the reasons firms hold cash: to pay for normal operations, such as paying bills

precautionary motive one of the reasons firms hold cash: to take care of unanticipated required outlays of cash, such as unexpected repairs on equipment

finance motive one of the reasons firms hold cash: in anticipation of major outlays, such as lump-sum loan repayments and dividend payments

speculative motive one of the reasons firms hold cash: to take advantage of "bargains," such as the opportunity to purchase raw materials very cheaply

Why do firms hold cash? Basically, they hold cash for the same reasons we do: to handle day-to-day spending requirements; to take care of emergencies; to finance any major outlays, such as tax instalments; and sometimes to buy a bargain that requires cash. Following this logic, we can break down the firm's motives for holding cash into the following categories.

1. **Transactions motive**: This refers to the cash that is required for a firm's normal operations. For some companies, such as manufacturing firms, the actual "cash" portion required will be minimal, but they will require money in their chequing account (which is called a "current account" for companies) to handle bill payments, and so on. Other firms, such as retail stores or restaurants, will need to have actual cash on hand, as well as money in their current account to cover cheques.

2. **Precautionary motive**: This refers to the cash that firms keep on hand to take care of unanticipated required outlays of cash, such as unexpected repairs on equipment.

3. **Finance motive**: This refers to the cash that firms will accumulate in anticipation of any major outlays, such as lump-sum loan repayments, dividend payments, and so on.

4. **Speculative motive**: Firms may keep extra cash available to take advantage of unexpected "bargains," such as the opportunity to purchase raw materials very cheaply.

This review of the motives for holding cash highlights the fact that when we speak of "cash," we really mean "cash on hand," money in the firm's current account and money in short-term marketable securities. This is because when we refer to "cash" in the definitions above, what we are really talking about is the need to have funds available almost instantaneously. Such items as investments in short-term marketable securities are often referred to as "near-cash" or "cash equivalents" and include all items that can be quickly and inexpensively converted into cash. These items are typically short-term marketable securities such as treasury bills, bankers' acceptances, commercial paper, and so on. These money market instruments were discussed in detail in Chapter 18, so we will not elaborate on them here.

How much a firm holds in cash and cash equivalents is also partly determined by its ability to borrow on an operating line of credit or to run an overdraft. In fact, most firms will hold more liquidity in borrowing facilities than they will in cash and equivalents because the cost of standby lending facilities is relatively cheap compared with the opportunity cost of raising capital from the firm's shareholders to invest in marketable securities. In particular, motives 2 through 4 can all be satisfied by using near-cash items, such as investments in marketable securities, and by maintaining additional short-term borrowing capacity.

As individuals, we are certainly familiar with the concept of the importance of near-cash as a substitute for cash in our pockets. We can purchase almost anything using debit or credit cards, which have greatly reduced the need to carry actual cash. In addition, writing cheques is becoming outdated, as most of us pay our bills via automatic debit from our accounts or by using the Internet or automated banking machines (ABMs). From now on, for exposition purposes, when we refer to cash, we are talking about both cash and near-cash, unless we make the distinction clear.

Determining the Optimal Cash Balance

Finance in the News 24-1 suggests that "the faster a business expands, the more cash it will need for working capital and investment," which we also demonstrated in Chapter 23. *Finance in the News 24-1* goes on to discuss the working capital cycle and the importance of dealing with the various components, which are discussed in this chapter, before concluding with an important message: "More businesses fail for lack of cash than for want of profit." On that note, we turn to the question of how to determine the optimal amount of cash to maintain on hand. Like most decisions in finance, it comes down to a classic trade-off between risk and expected return. In general, cash and near-cash provide very low returns relative to investments in other assets; however, by definition, they provide the ultimate in liquidity and usually have minimal additional risks (i.e., usually cash and near-cash items are virtually default free). So it is appropriate to assume that cash is low risk, low expected return.

---

finance INTHENEWS 24-1 | Working Capital Cycle

CASH FLOWS in a cycle into, around and out of a business. It is the business's life blood and every manager's primary task is to help keep it flowing and to use the cash flow to generate profits. If a business is operating profitably, then it should, in theory, generate cash surpluses. If it doesn't generate surpluses, the business will eventually run out of cash and expire.

The faster a business expands, the more cash it will need for working capital and investment. The cheapest and best sources of cash exist as working capital right within business. Good management of working capital will generate cash, will help improve profits and reduce risks. Bear in mind that the cost of providing credit to customers and holding stocks can represent a substantial proportion of a firm's total profits.

There are two elements in the business cycle that absorb cash—*inventory* (stocks and work-in-progress) and *receivables* (debtors owing you money). The main sources of cash are payables (your creditors) and *equity* and *loans*.

Each component of working capital (namely inventory, receivables and payables) has two dimensions: time and money. When it comes to managing working capital—time is money. If you can get money to move faster around the cycle (e.g., collect monies due from debtors more quickly) or reduce the amount of money tied up (e.g., reduce inventory levels relative to sales), the business will generate more cash or it will need to borrow less money to fund working capital. As a consequence, you could reduce the cost of bank interest or you'll have additional *free* money available to support additional sales growth or investment. Similarly, if you can negotiate improved terms with suppliers, (e.g., get longer credit or an increased credit limit,) you effectively create *free* finance to help fund future sales.

If you	Then . . . .
Collect receivables (debtors) faster	You release cash from the cycle
Collect receivables (debtors) slower	Your receivables soak up cash
Get better credit (in terms of duration or amount) from suppliers	You increase your cash resources
Shift inventory (stocks) faster	You free up cash
Move inventory (stocks) slower	You consume more cash

It can be tempting to pay cash, if available, for fixed assets (e.g., computers, plant, vehicles). If you do pay cash, remember that this is no longer available for working capital. Therefore, if cash is tight, consider other ways of financing capital investment—loans, equity, leasing etc. Similarly, if you pay dividends or increase drawings, these are cash outflows and, like water flowing down a plug hole, they remove liquidity from the business.

More businesses fail for lack of cash than for want of profit.

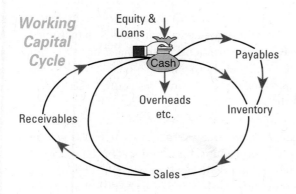

Source: Planware, "Working Capital Management." Retrieved January 3, 2012 from the PlanWare website at www.planware.org/workingcapital.htm. Reprinted by permission.

A firm can always take a conservative approach and choose to maintain a large amount of its assets in cash and near-cash. This will minimize the risk of the firm being unable to satisfy its liquidity requirements. Unfortunately, this approach sacrifices potential returns, which may not be optimal. (In addition, it may make the firm an attractive takeover candidate, because the acquiring firm can use some of this cash to pay down its takeover financing.) Another firm may choose to take an aggressive approach to cash management and maintain minimal balances. This approach might produce higher returns; however, it also increases the risk of the firm becoming illiquid and having to generate liquidity in a hurry. Creating liquidity quickly is often very expensive, because the firm may have to negotiate short-term loans with higher borrowing rates. In more extreme situations, the firm may be forced to sell less-liquid assets, such as inventory or even fixed assets, at discounted prices.

optimal cash balance the amount of cash that balances the risks of illiquidity against the sacrifice of expected returns that is associated with maintaining cash

Given our discussion above, it is reasonable to conclude that the **optimal cash balance** is one that balances the risks of illiquidity against the sacrifice of expected returns that is associated with maintaining cash. Therefore, the optimal cash balance as a percentage of total assets, for example, will differ substantially across firms; some firms have lower and more predictable cash requirements than others—these firms will require proportionately lower amounts of cash. Other firms with higher cash requirements for transaction purposes, or with less predictable cash flows (and therefore a greater need for precautionary liquidity), will hold higher levels of cash.

Near-cash items provide a method for alleviating the problem of the low returns associated with holding cash without sacrificing too much in the way of liquidity. For example, a firm can create excess borrowing capacity in the form of an operating line of credit. However, borrowers usually have to pay fees on the unused portion of these credit lines, which may offset the firm's advantage from holding less in cash. In addition, firms often maintain a large portion of their liquidity requirements in money market instruments, which provide a higher return than cash held in a traditional bank account. The level of investment in marketable securities is dictated to a large extent by the firm's liquidity urgency and by how accurately it is able to forecast its future cash requirements. The latter will be a function partly of the volatility of the firm's cash flows and partly of the firm's ability to design an efficient cash budgeting system. Firms that have well-developed cash management systems and more predictable cash flows will be able to maintain a higher portion of their liquidity in marketable securities and less in cash.

Cash Management Techniques

The general approach to good cash management is to speed up inflows *as much as possible* and delay outflows *as much as possible*. We discussed this in Chapter 23 in terms of increasing α in the cash budget and decreasing β. The qualifier "as much as possible" is important because firms always face constraints that will delay inflows and prevent them from delaying outflows too much. For example, a firm can always speed up its inflows from sales by refusing to give credit to customers, but this will likely have a large impact on its sales, so it may not be a viable strategy. Similarly, a firm may delay making payments to suppliers; however, if the firm is perpetually late in making payments, it will develop a poor relationship with the suppliers. In extreme cases, suppliers may end up selling to the firm on a "cash only" basis, which would, in fact, speed up cash outflows rather than delaying them.

float the time that elapses between the time the paying firm initiates payment and the time the funds are available for use by the receiving firm

An important part of speeding up inflows is the establishment of an efficient credit policy, which specifies the policies for collecting receivables from customers. We will discuss this later in this chapter. Once the payment procedures for customers have been specified, it is important that firms process the payments as efficiently as possible. One objective at this stage should be to minimize **float** time, which can be defined as the time that elapses between the date the paying firm initiates payment—for example, mails the cheque—and the date the funds are available for use by the receiving firm. During this float period, the receiving firm does not have the funds available for use.

There are three major sources of float:

1. the time it takes the cheque to reach the firm after it is mailed by the customer

2. the time it takes the receiving firm to process the cheque and deposit it in an account

3. the time it takes the cheque to clear through the banking system so that the funds are available to the firm

Historically, the first source of float time has been the longest. Of course, firms can always obtain postdated cheques or stipulate that they require payment by a certain date, both of which minimize the float associated with mail and processing times. However, over the past decade in particular, firms have made great strides in eliminating float time by providing payment options that eliminate the need to mail cheques and making them available to (or mandatory for) customers. Today, most retailers accept debit cards, which automatically debit the customer's accounts. This eliminates the problems associated with accepting cheques (i.e., checking for identification, risking the account not having sufficient funds, taking the time to process and deposit the cheque). Many firms also make use of preauthorized payments, which automatically debit customer accounts on the payment date. Other companies use more advanced electronic collection systems, such as electronic funds transfer (EFT) and electronic data interchange (EDI) systems.

Although many advances have occurred, many firms still do things the "old-fashioned way": they bill their customers, and their customers pay by cheque. However, even these firms can take steps to speed up the process and reduce float time. Many firms establish centralized or "concentrated" banking arrangements. Under these arrangements, local offices receive customer payments and deposit them into a local bank account, which is combined with similar local accounts into one central account. This minimizes mail float. A similar strategy, which can be used concurrently with the concentrated bank account option, is to establish "lock box" banking arrangements. This involves setting up local post office boxes, to which customers mail their payments, and authorizing the local bank to empty these boxes and deposit the cheques into the company's account.

Although float works to a firm's disadvantage with respect to collections, it works to the firm's benefit with respect to disbursements. However, it is reasonable to assume that many of the firm's suppliers will employ the same strategies to minimize *their* float, which implies there is little benefit in trying to maximize disbursement float. In addition, as discussed above, trying to delay payments may cause poor relations with suppliers. Even so, firms can still take steps to improve the efficiency of their cash outflows and minimize the cash they need to maintain on hand for required disbursements. Just as it makes sense for firms to have a centralized system to monitor collections, it makes sense to have a similar centralization for payments. This will ensure that payments are made on time, but not early (or late), to the greatest extent possible. In addition, most firms establish "zero-balance accounts," which are centralized accounts that combine the cash balances of many individual accounts into one central account. Under this system, funds are transferred from the central account to cover cheques written against the individual accounts as required. This system reduces the need for cash at the aggregate firm level, because it effectively transfers funds from individual accounts that have excess cash to those that need it. In addition, firms usually tie their operating loans to this central account, reducing the total amount of borrowing required by the firm.

Firms can use these methods to speed up cash inflows and slow down outflows to the greatest extent possible. However, another critical component in any cash management system is the actual tracking of cash requirements through time. This can be especially important for planning and for assessing short-term financing requirements. As demonstrated in Chapter 23, firms use the cash budget to forecast cash balances and borrowing requirements. This important planning tool will let firms know when, and for how long, they can expect to have excess cash balances that can be invested in marketable securities. It also shows firms how much they may require in excess borrowing capacity to cover any shortfalls, and the firms can arrange their short-term lending facilities accordingly. In fact, banks often require a cash budget as part of any loan application package.

The Cash Balance "Puzzle"

The previous discussion of cash management techniques shows how firms have become more efficient at reducing their cash holdings. This discussion is primarily related to the transactions motive for holding cash. However, *Finance in the News 24-2* indicates that actual cash holdings have increased dramatically and that U.S. companies are now sitting on a cash hoard of over $1.24 trillion. These increased cash holdings represent a "puzzle" to many observers. Why, after all, should any entity simultaneously both borrow and lend? Borrowing rates are always higher than lending rates, so this simply costs firms this spread.

The answer is that these cash holdings are being driven by the precautionary and speculative demands for cash. Firms are aware that the U.S. economy is underperforming, and they remember the 2008–9 credit crunch when many of them were cut off from bank credit due to the financial crisis. Moody's notes that this cash hoard also coincides with $498 billion of new bond issues, which has reduced the corporate debt-to-cash ratio to its lowest since 2006. As a result, U.S. firms are currently borrowing long-term through bond issues while simultaneously building up their cash hoard in anticipation of both a recovery of the global economy and an uptick in mergers and acquisitions activity and capital expenditures. Only time will tell whether this increased precautionary and speculative demand for cash was the right decision.

---

finance INTHENEWS 24-2   Corporate Cash Holdings Surpass US$1 Trillion: Moody's

U.S. COMPANIES are sitting on a cash hoard of US$1.24 trillion, which should lead to more capital spending, shareholder distributions, and mergers and acquisitions (M&A).

According to a new report from Moody's Investors Service, U.S. non-financial corporate cash holdings rose 11.2 percent from the end of 2009 to the end of 2010. The growth in cash holdings came even as companies spent far more on capital expenditures, shareholder distributions, and M&A in 2010 than they did in 2009, Moody's said. The rating agency believes the pace of corporate spending on most of these non-operating purposes will increase.

Still, Moody's notes that this sort of corporate spending remains below peak levels "as companies await sustainable economic improvement in the United States and Europe and clarity over the European debt crisis. Additionally, management teams remember the rapid shutdown of the financial markets in 2008 and prefer to hold large cash balances even though the money is earning a low return," says the report.

The top cash-heavy U.S. industries continue to be technology, pharmaceuticals, energy, and consumer products, representing around half of the corporate cash total. Technology held around US$264 billion in cash, pharmaceuticals around US$141 billion, and energy and consumer products each held more than US$100 billion.

Moody's survey of the top cash-rich companies also found that almost half of that cash, approximately US$600 billion, is being held overseas. "We believe companies will keep this cash outside the U.S. as they pursue international acquisitions, invest in their own overseas operations or await tax breaks on overseas earnings they bring back to the U.S.," says Steve Oman, a Moody's senior vice president and author of the report.

Even with near-record-low interest rates and high levels of corporate debt issuance, companies are adding little debt on a net basis, Moody's also noted. Despite US$483 billion of new bond issuance in 2010, the corporate debt-cash ratio is at its lowest since 2006 as companies use new proceeds to retire old debt.

Source: Langton, James, "Corporate cash holdings surpass US$1 trillion." *The Investment Executive*, July 27, 2011. Available at www.investmentexecutive.com.

CONCEPT REVIEW QUESTIONS

1. Why do firms hold cash?

2. What is float and why is it important to the firm?

24.2 ACCOUNTS RECEIVABLE

As soon as a firm decides to extend credit to its customers, it has consciously made a decision to allow some of its funds to be tied up in accounts receivable. This decision should be based on a cost-benefit analysis, just as the decision to have funds tied up in cash—or in any other asset, for that matter—should be. The expected benefits of extending credit are expanded sales and perhaps even improved relationships with customers. The costs may include losses, due to an increase in non-payment by customers, as well as the cost of financing the receivables, which is associated with the time the firm has to do without the cash payment for goods that have already been sold and whose production costs have already been paid (or at least partially paid, depending on the firm's ability to delay paying its suppliers and employees).

Although it is technically true that all firms face the decision of whether or not to provide credit for their customers, as a practical matter many firms really do not have much choice. For example, it is hard to imagine a furniture retailer or car dealer that could remain competitive within its industry if it did not provide customers with financing options. However, these types of companies typically provide financing for their customers through a finance subsidiary of the parent company or through arrangements made with one or more banks or financial institutions. Many companies extend credit to their customers by providing them with additional time to make payment on purchases. For these companies, the first decision they need to make is whether to extend credit at all. The second decision is to decide which customers will be granted credit. Next, the firms must determine the credit terms to be offered to customers (which may vary from customer to customer). Finally, they must decide on the details of the collection process.

Learning Objective 24.2
Describe how accounts receivable are managed.

The Credit Decision

For most companies, the decision of whether or not to extend credit—the "trade credit decision"—will be largely determined by the nature of the product they sell, the industry they are in, and the prevailing policy of competitors. Assuming the firm decides to extend credit, it must then determine which of its customers will qualify for it. This decision is often based on a formal **credit analysis** process, which is designed to assess the risk of non-payment by potential customers. The process involves collecting information about their credit history; their ability to make payments, as reflected in their expected cash flows (which is closely related to income); and their overall financial stability (as reflected in their net worth and their level of existing debt obligations).

Before considering how firms make these decisions, it is important to note that a firm's decision to extend trade credit is subtly different from a bank's decision to make a loan. Suppose, for example, a firm is considering a $10,000 order for widgets. The customer promises to pay in 60 days. If the cost of trade credit is 12 percent per year, the firm might sell the widgets for $10,200, due in 60 days. We will talk about trade credit terms later, but this is similar to a bank lending the customer $10,000 to buy the widgets for cash, then charging 2 percent interest on the loan so that the customer pays $10,200 in 60 days. In both cases, the purchaser owes $10,200, either to the company or to the bank. The bank's profit from the loan is limited to the interest rate,[1] and if the customer defaults, the bank could be out the full $10,000 loan. However, the firm is in a slightly different position.

First, the firm's cost is not the $10,000 it charges for the widgets, because it has to factor a profit margin into the calculation. If the firm's profit margin is 10 percent, and if it can't sell the widgets to other customers, then its decision involves a potential loss of $9,000 if the customer does not pay, rather than the $10,000 the bank would lose. Further, if the customer does pay, it may become an established customer that makes further purchases, generating

credit analysis a process designed to assess the risk of non-payment by potential customers, which involves collecting information about their credit history, their ability to make payments (as reflected in their expected cash flows), and their overall financial stability

---

[1] More likely, in this situation, the bank would let the company advance the trade credit to the customer and then buy the receivable for $9,803.92. The bank would make its 2 percent interest when the customer paid off the $10,000 debt. This is called factoring.

further profit margins for the firm. The fact that the firm thinks in terms of future profit margins from developing a good customer and loses only its production cost in the case of default means that trade credit is granted to customers who could not secure credit from a bank on the same terms.

This discussion also explains why some firms grant credit, whereas others do not. For example, we have already seen that eating-and-drinking establishments generally have very low collection periods; that is, they generally do not give credit. This is because they tend to be low-margin, high-volume businesses, for whom an additional sale is not very valuable and may not generate many future sales. Instead, purchases are made on bank credit cards rather than store cards, and they tend to use loyalty cards or gift cards to generate repeat business. In contrast, high-margin low-volume businesses, such as automobile and equipment manufacturers, do have in-house credit facilities to finance sales of their products. It is for these higher margin businesses that the corporate credit decision is more important.

In making these decisions, firms can use a number of sources of information to assess the creditworthiness of a particular customer. Usually, firms begin by turning to professional credit agencies, such as Dun & Bradstreet (D&B) Canada Limited, which provide credit ratings and comprehensive credit reports on companies. Unlike the major bond rating agencies, such as Dominion Bond Rating Service, Moody's, and Standard & Poor's, D&B rates private companies that do not access the public markets. These reports are based on available financial data, the firm's competitive position, and the company's credit history. In many cases, this report will provide sufficient information to make a credit decision; however, for larger accounts or for arrangements that are expected to last for a long time, the firm may decide to do some additional investigation. An important source of information can be the company's financial statements. Firms may also ask the company to provide a letter from its main banker. Finally, firms can always look for information regarding a company's past credit relationships from a variety of sources, such as trade associations, other firms that have had prior dealings with the company, and so on.

The evaluation of the credit information that has been gathered can vary significantly from one company to the next. Some companies will have very detailed and mechanical evaluation systems, while others will rely more on judgement. In either case, the key issue potential creditors are assessing is the likelihood of the customer paying the bills as they come due. There are two sides to this coin.

capacity the customer's ability to pay

The first side is the potential customer's *ability* to pay. This is often referred to as the firm's **capacity**. As discussed in chapters 3 and 4, two of the most important factors affecting a firm's ability to meet future obligations are the amount of cash flow it expects to generate, and the number of other obligations it has to satisfy. Thus, it is important to examine a firm's expected future profitability, as well as its level of debt and the amount of debt payments it has accumulated. In addition, because most, if not all, trade credit is of a short-term nature, potential creditors are particularly interested in a potential customer's liquidity. As a last resort, creditors can always turn to the assets pledged as security for a loan. In this way, a firm's ability to offer collateral enhances its ability to secure credit. In many cases, items are sold on an **open account** basis, which means that the collateral is simply the assets sold to the customer. In such situations, the creditor must be wary because some assets do not hold their value. In addition, creditors may have difficulty getting the assets from the customer if it defaults on its obligation.

open account credit in which the collateral is the assets sold to the customer

character the customer's willingness to pay, its reliability, and trustworthiness

This leads us to the other side of the coin referred to above—how *willing* the firm is to pay. This is often referred to as the **character** of the firm. In other words, how reliable and trustworthy is the firm? This is an important question, because even if a firm is *able* to make the required payments, this makes little difference if it chooses not to. Creditors look for clues as to the character of the customer's management team by examining, among other things, its payment history and details of the customer's past dealings.

These two sides to the credit decision are often referred to as the "two C's of credit," with collateral representing the third C. In addition, both capacity and character can be affected by the state of the economy. In a recession, the firm's capacity to pay is tested as cash flow dries up and finances are under pressure. So economic **conditions** affect the credit decision, and analysts include it as the fourth C of credit: capacity, character, collateral, and conditions. All four are interrelated.

conditions the state of the economy

Because the process of checking creditworthiness can be lengthy and costly, firms tend to prioritize the amount of time and effort devoted to the analysis. For example, all else being equal, larger orders require more scrutiny than do smaller ones.

Credit Policies

Once a firm has decided to grant credit, it then chooses what **terms of credit** to offer its customers, such as the due date and the discount date and discount amount, where applicable. In practice, the terms a firm offers can vary from one customer to the next, based on credit analysis and on the importance of the account. In other words, key accounts with an impeccable credit rating will likely demand, and receive, better credit terms than smaller accounts or those with weaker credit ratings. For ease of exposition in our discussion, we will assume that most customers receive the same credit terms.

terms of credit the due date and the discount date and discount amount, where applicable, offered to customers

Credit terms of "2/20 net 45" offer customers a 2 percent discount if they pay the full amount due by day 20, with the full amount being due by day 45. Terms of "net 30" require full payment by day 30 and provide no discount options. We use these credit terms to work out how much taking trade credit costs. For example, 2/10 net 45 means that the customer pays either 98 percent after 10 days or 100 percent after 45 days. The cost is 2/98 for getting an extra 35 days to pay, so the effective annual interest rate for not paying on time is

$$k = \left(1 + \frac{2}{98}\right)^{\frac{365}{35}} - 1 = 23.45\%$$

We express the 2 percent discount in terms of a simple interest rate (2/98 or 2.05 percent) and then express it on an annual basis by working out how many 35-day periods are in a year.

In this example, the real cost is 98 percent of the quoted price if the customer pays immediately on receipt of the widgets, during the 10-day grace period. After that, the invoice has to be paid by 45 days, and the cost of getting this extra 35 days' credit is 23.45 percent. Most firms can borrow from their banks more cheaply than this, so, as a basic rule, firms should always take those discounts. If a customer doesn't take the discount, the full 100 percent comes due. It is best to pay by 45 days and avoid the payment reminder telephone calls. Paying on time lowers the effective cost to a more reasonable level.

Generally, when firms decide to extend more lenient credit terms, they expect revenues to increase because they will increase the number of units sold and, possibly, because they will charge higher prices. The costs include the increase in financing costs and the increased risk of non-payment by customers. Conversely, when firms adopt a more restrictive policy, it results in collections being accelerated, at the possible expense of sales. Firms can evaluate such decisions by using the now-familiar net present value (NPV) framework, as given in Equation 24-1.

$$NPV = PV(\text{Future CFs}) - CF_0 \qquad [24\text{-}1]$$

The future cash flows (CFs) will generally be positive when firms loosen their credit terms and will be negative when they tighten them. CF_0 will represent an outlay when the credit terms are loosened, because that requires an additional investment in receivables; it will represent an inflow when the terms are tightened, because that will reduce the level of receivables. The after-tax cost of short-term debt is usually the appropriate discount rate to use, because receivables are low risk and are generally financed by using short-term debt (and the operating line of credit, in particular). Example 24-1 demonstrates how this framework can be used.

EXAMPLE 24-1   The NPV of Extending Additional Credit

Suppose a firm that currently does not grant credit is considering adopting a credit policy that permits its customers to pay the full price for purchases (with no penalties) within 40 days of the purchase (i.e., the credit terms are net 40). The firm estimates that it can increase the price of the product by $1 per unit as a result of the new policy, which results in a new price per unit of $111. The firm expects that unit sales will increase by 1,000 units per year (to 11,000 units) and that variable costs will remain at $99 per unit. It also estimates that bad debt losses will amount to $6,000 per year. The firm will finance the additional investment in receivables by using its line of credit, which charges 6 percent interest. The firm's tax rate is 40 percent. Should the firm begin extending credit under the terms described?

Solution

Because the firm did not previously have any receivables, the initial investment (CF_0) can be viewed as the amount of additional funds that will be tied up in receivables, which equals the number of days that sales must be financed, multiplied by the estimated sales per day:

$$40 \text{ days} \times \text{sales per day} = 40 \times [(\$111 \times 11,000 \text{ units})/365 \text{ days}]$$

$$= 40 \text{ days} \times \$3,345.21/\text{day} = \$133,808$$

Now we need to estimate the PV(Future CFs), which equals the present value of the incremental after-tax cash flows generated by extending credit.

$$\text{Incremental before-tax annual CFs} = (1,000 \text{ extra units sold}) \times [(\$111 - \$99) \text{ profit per unit}] +$$
$$(10,000 \text{ units sold}) \times (\$1 \text{ increase in price per unit sold}) - (\$6,000 \text{ in bad debt losses}) =$$
$$(1,000)(\$12) + (10,000)(\$1) - \$6,000 = \$12,000 + \$10,000 - \$6,000 = \$16,000$$

The appropriate after-tax discount rate is

$$6\% \times (1 - 0.4) = 3.6\%$$

If we assume the firm reaps the benefits of this change in policy indefinitely, we can find the present value of the future benefits by viewing the incremental after-tax annual CFs as a perpetuity:

$$\text{PV(Future CFs)} = \text{Annual after-tax incremental CFs}/k$$

$$= [\$16,000 \times (1 - 0.4)]/0.036 = \$266,667$$

$$\text{NPV} = \text{PV(Future CFs)} - CF_0 = \$266,667 - \$133,808 = \$132,859$$

Thus, the firm should begin extending credit under the terms described above.

In Example 24-1, we considered a firm that decided to extend credit, thus adopting a more lenient credit policy. Of course, firms can always choose to adopt a more stringent credit policy. In this case, the firm will free up cash by reducing the amount of receivables it has outstanding, and the cost will be the forgone additional future cash flows that may result if the firm loses sales or has to reduce its selling price, as Example 24-2 demonstrates.

EXAMPLE 24-2   Adopting a More Stringent Credit Policy

Suppose the firm from Example 24-1 adopts the net 40 credit policy, but one year later, it considers changing the terms to net 30. The firm estimates that it can maintain the same price for the product (i.e., $111 per unit) but that unit sales will decline by 500 units per year (to 10,500 units). Variable costs will remain at $99 per unit. The firm estimates that bad debt losses will be reduced by $2,000 per year (to $4,000) as a result of the new policy. As in Example 24-1, the appropriate after-tax discount rate is 3.6 percent and the tax rate is 40 percent. Should the firm switch to the new policy?

continued

EXAMPLE 24-2 *Adopting a More Stringent Credit Policy continued*

Solution

The initial investment (CF_0) in this case can be viewed as the reduction in the amount of accounts receivable (AR) that need to be financed:

$$AR(new) - AR(old) = \{30 \text{ days} \times [(\$111 \times 10{,}500 \text{ units})/365 \text{ days}]\} - \{40 \text{ days} \times$$
$$[(\$111 \times 11{,}000 \text{ units})/365 \text{ days}]\} = [30 \text{ days} \times \$3{,}193.15/\text{day}] - [40 \text{ days} \times$$
$$\$3{,}345.21/\text{day}] = \$95{,}795 - \$133{,}808 = -\$38{,}013$$

Now we need to estimate the PV(Future CFs), which equals the present value of the incremental after-tax cash flows generated by changing the credit policy. In this case, it will be negative because the firm *loses* future cash flows as a result of tightening its credit policy.

$$\text{Incremental before-tax annual CFs} = (500 \text{ less units sold}) \times (\$111 - \$99 \text{ profit per unit})$$
$$+ (\$2{,}000 \text{ reduction in bad debt losses}) = (-500)(\$12) + \$2{,}000 = -\$4{,}000$$

If we assume the firm reaps the benefits of this change in policy indefinitely, we can find the present value of the future CFs (forgone CFs, in this case), by viewing the incremental after-tax annual CFs as a perpetuity:

$$\text{PV(Future CFs)} = \text{Annual after-tax incremental CFs}/k$$

$$= [-\$4{,}000 \times (1 - 0.4)]/0.036 = -\$66{,}667$$

$$\text{NPV} = \text{PV(Future CFs)} - CF_0 = -\$66{,}667 + \$38{,}013 = -\$28{,}654$$

Thus, the firm should not switch from its existing credit policy to the new one.

When firms offer discounts to customers, two things happen: (1) they lose profits when customers take advantage of the discounts; and (2) they receive payment sooner, so less money is tied up in receivables. The decision to offer discounts (or eliminate them) can be evaluated by using the NPV framework, as Example 24-3 demonstrates.

EXAMPLE 24-3 **Offering a Discount**

Suppose the firm from Examples 24-1 and 24-2 is maintaining the net 40 credit policy evaluated in Example 24-1 but is now considering adopting a new policy that would involve a discount. In particular, it is considering adopting a 2/10 net 40 policy. The firm estimates that 60 percent of customers will take advantage of the discount, while the remaining 40 percent will pay on day 40. The firm expects that it can maintain the same price for the product (i.e., $111 per unit); unit sales will remain at 11,000 per year; variable costs will remain at $99 per unit; and that bad debt losses will not be affected. As in Example 24-1, the after-tax discount rate is 3.6 percent and the tax rate is 40 percent. Should the firm switch to the new policy?

Solution

The initial investment (CF_0), in this case, can be viewed as the reduction in the amount of accounts receivable (A/R) that need to be financed.

The average collection period (ACP) under the new policy will be reduced to $[0.6 \times 10 \text{ days} + 0.4 \times 40 \text{ days}] = 22$ days. The old ACP was assumed to be the net date (i.e., 40 days). The change (reduction) in receivables is

$$(22 - 40) \times [(\$111 \times 11{,}000 \text{ units})/365 \text{ days}] = (-18 \text{ days}) \times (\$3{,}345.21/\text{day})$$
$$= -\$60{,}214$$

Now we need to estimate the PV(Future CFs), which equals the present value of the incremental after-tax cash flows generated by changing the credit terms. In this case, it will be negative because the firm loses future cash flows as a result of customers taking advantage of the discount.

$$\text{Incremental after-tax annual CFs} = (\text{number of units sold at a discount}) \times (\text{discount amount per unit}) \times$$
$$(1 - \text{tax rate}) = (60 \text{ percent of customers taking discount} \times 11{,}000 \text{ annual sales in units}) \times$$
$$(0.02 \text{ discount amount} \times \$111 \text{ per unit}) \times (1 - 0.4) = (6{,}600 \text{ units}) \times (\$2.22) \times (0.6) = \$8{,}791.20$$

continued

| EXAMPLE 24-3 | *Offering a Discount continued* |

PV(Future CFs) = Annual after-tax incremental CFs/k

$$= [-\$8,791.20]/0.036 = -\$244,200$$

NPV = PV(Future CFs) − CF_0 = −$244,200 + $60,214 = −$183,986

Thus, the firm should not offer the discount.

The Collection Process

Firms have many options when deciding how their customers will pay for their purchases. As discussed, several electronic methods are available, such as automatic debit of customers' bank accounts or the use of EFT or EDI systems. These approaches not only reduce payment processing time but also reduce (or eliminate) the risk of late payment and obviously represent attractive collection systems for many firms. However, some firms still invoice their customers at the time of sale and then collect and deposit cheques as they are received.

When firms are forced to wait for payments from customers, several issues arise. First, they must closely monitor their collections and receivables to avoid having many late payments or, worse yet, non-payments. Second, they must determine what to do when late payments occur. Usually, firms establish a systematic process to deal with such accounts. As a start, most firms will charge interest on overdue accounts as a deterrent. After a predetermined interval, companies will usually notify the customer that the account is in arrears and ask the customer to "settle up." This notification can be done by mail, e-mail, or phone. If payment is still not received, firms will generally issue a follow-up reminder (or two). Eventually, if they still have not received payment from the customer, firms must decide what to do next. One of the first things they will do, if they have not already done so, is not allow that customer to make any more purchases on credit. They must then decide whether to hand the bill over to a collection agency or take legal action against the customer. Both of these options can be costly, so in many cases, firms will just write off the debt and inform the credit agency. This decision will be influenced by the amount that is due, among other things.

Sometimes firms avoid the collection process by entering into **factoring arrangements**, whereby they sell their receivables at a discount to a financial company called a "factor," which specializes in collections. Alternatively, many factors do not actually purchase the receivables but agree to handle the collections, for a fee of course.

It can be difficult to assess how well a firm manages its accounts receivable. In Chapter 4, we identified some common ratios that do provide useful insight into this issue: the average collection period (ACP) and the receivables turnover ratio. All else being equal, it is preferable to have a lower ACP and higher receivables turnover. However, firms can always make improvements in these ratios by sacrificing sales growth and/or profit margins, so it is not as simple as merely examining these ratios. In addition, these ratios do not tell us a great deal about the *quality* of a firm's receivables.

One tool that is useful for this purpose is the aged accounts receivable report, which categorizes the balances in receivables according to how long they have been outstanding. For example, a firm might provide a list that shows how much of its receivables are outstanding before the due date, after the due date, a month after the due date, and so on. Generally, receivables that have not been outstanding very long are regarded as higher quality than those that have been outstanding well beyond their due date. In fact, banks often require that borrowing firms provide them with this list each month to support any financing the banks provide in support of receivables. However, this report also has its limitations. For example, it would be preferable to have many receivables due from high-quality customers (such as government agencies) that are 30 days late than it would be to have many 10-day-old receivables

factoring arrangements the sale of a firm's receivables, at a discount, to a financial company called a "factor," which specializes in collections; the outsourcing of the collections to a factor

from customers with low-quality credit. In fact, to accurately assess the quality of a company's receivables, it would help to have a list of the customers underlying the receivables and perhaps even a credit analysis of these customers, at least for the larger accounts.

Despite these limitations, aging of receivables is a very valuable tool. In fact, it applies to all debts and payments. As we have discussed throughout this text, the U.S. economy is very weak and still suffering from the "debt hangover" resulting from the financial crisis. One aspect of this is the continuing weakness in the U.S. housing market. In early 2012, 28 percent of all mortgages in the United States were at least 60 days delinquent—that is, the last two months of mortgage payments had not been made—with 9 percent of prime mortgages and 18 percent of non-prime mortgages actually in default.[2]

While "old" receivables clearly indicate that the debt is of less than sterling quality, current receivables are not necessarily that much better: paying on time is sometimes an indication that the purchaser does not want to be examined too closely and is actually a crook. General Motors Acceptance Corporation (GMAC), at the time the financing arm of GM, found this out the hard way. In the 1980s and 1990s, John McNamara, a Buick-Pontiac dealer in the United States, operated a Ponzi scheme and defrauded GMAC of US$1 billion through fraudulent loans for thousands of vans that were never actually purchased. He claimed to be buying the vans for conversion and export and faked invoices for GMAC to finance. By paying GMAC invoices on time, he developed a reputation as a very good customer and was actively courted by GMAC and given more favourable terms than other purchasers, when in actuality he was simply paying off his old loans with new ones. His fraud only came to light when internal auditors at GMAC could not find evidence for the matching purchases.[3]

CONCEPT REVIEW QUESTIONS

1. Why is trade credit different from bank credit?

2. What are the four C's of credit?

3. What does 2/10 net 30 mean, and what is the implicit interest cost?

4. What is an aged accounts receivable report?

24.3 INVENTORY

A firm's decision about the level of inventory it will hold is based on a trade-off between benefits and costs, similar to the decisions about investments in cash, marketable securities, and accounts receivable. One reason firms hold large amounts of inventory is that they may have received discounts on large-volume purchases. However, the more important benefits of holding inventory are that having sufficient levels of raw materials minimizes disruptions in the production process, while maintaining adequate levels of finished goods on hand helps minimize lost sales (and lost customer goodwill) because of shortages.

The benefits of holding inventory do not come without significant costs. Aside from the obvious cost of financing the funds tied up in inventory, a number of other costs are important, including storage, handling, insurance, spoilage, and the risk of obsolescence. Thus, inventory decisions are critical to a firm's performance. In fact, the field of operations management devotes a great deal of attention to modelling efficient inventory control systems. We provide a brief discussion of some of the more common approaches to inventory management, but we do not elaborate on the technical details.

Learning Objective 24.3
Describe how inventory is managed.

---

[2] These statistics are from RBC Wealth Management, "U.S. Housing: Stability Sooner, Recovery Later." *Global Insight/2012 Outlook*, December 2011, http://dir.rbcinvestments.com/scroller_view.asp?content_id=53589.
[3] McQuiston, Johh, T., "Car dealer admits fraud of billions." *The New York Times*, September 10, 1992.

Inventory Management Approaches

Most inventory control systems used by large companies employ highly automated computerized systems that can easily track all kinds of inventory items as they flow into and out of the company. These systems control inventory levels by relating them to the production process, which in turn is related to the firm's projected sales levels.

Any approach to inventory management must balance the benefits of holding inventory and the costs, as discussed above. We will briefly describe four of these approaches.

1. The **ABC approach**: This approach divides inventory into several categories based on the value of the inventory items, their overall level of importance to the firm's operations, and their profitability. The higher the priority of the inventory item, the more time and effort will be devoted to its management.

2. The **economic order quantity (EOQ) model**: The EOQ model defines (and determines) the optimal inventory level as the one that minimizes the total of "shortage costs" and "carrying costs." As such, it determines the inventory level that balances out the benefits (i.e., reduced shortage costs) against the carrying costs (i.e., financing, storage, insurance, spoilage, obsolescence). The model shows that, under certain assumptions, the minimum total cost occurs at the point at which carrying costs equal shortage costs. One of the key assumptions of the EOQ model is that items are sold relatively evenly throughout the year, so it works well for inventories that follow this pattern and not as well when they don't.

3. **Materials requirement planning (MRP)**: MRP is a detailed computerized system that orders inventory in conjunction with production schedules. The central idea is to determine the exact level of raw materials and work-in-process that must be on hand to meet finished-goods demand. With this capability and good sales forecasts, a company can run on extremely low levels of inventory.

4. **Just-in-time (JIT) inventory systems**: JIT systems fine-tune the receipt of raw materials so they arrive exactly when they are required in the production process. The objective is to reduce inventory to its lowest possible level. JIT systems require close relationships with suppliers in order to work properly.

Evaluating Inventory Management

Although effective inventory management is critical to the success of most firms, it is, like accounts receivable management, difficult to evaluate. In Chapter 4, we introduced two ratios—the inventory turnover ratio and the days in inventory ratio—that outsiders commonly use to evaluate inventory management. Generally, high inventory turnover is recognized as a good sign, while lower or declining turnover is a warning sign. In particular, a declining inventory turnover ratio indicates that sales are declining, inventory levels are accumulating, or both. The greater the inventory buildup, the greater the financing, storage, spoilage, and insurance costs, and the greater the risk of obsolescence.

Although the inventory turnover ratio is a useful indicator, it is far from comprehensive. For example, it does not measure shortage costs or explicitly measure financing costs. As discussed above, these are critical considerations in the implementation (and evaluation) of any inventory management system. In addition, turnover ratios cannot be compared across companies that use different methods of accounting for inventory (i.e., FIFO, average cost), because the reported inventory levels will differ substantially. Finally, inventory turnover says nothing about the breakdown of inventory in terms of raw materials, work-in-process inventory, and finished goods, which can make a big difference in establishing the market value of inventory.

CONCEPT REVIEW QUESTIONS

1. Identify the costs and benefits of holding inventory.

2. What are the drawbacks to using the turnover ratio to measure inventory policy?

24.4 SHORT-TERM FINANCING CONSIDERATIONS

A common trait of investments in current assets, such as cash, accounts receivable, and inventory, is that they all tend to increase automatically as sales increase. The same cannot be said for short-term financing, with the exception of trade credit. Therefore, it is critical that firms forecast their short-term financing requirements as accurately as possible and ensure they have adequate financing in place.

Because there are many potential sources of short-term financing, firms need to assess the cost effectiveness of alternative financing mechanisms. We use the following variation of Equation 5-9, which was introduced in Chapter 5, to estimate the annual effective rate of return or cost (k) associated with any financing alternative:

$$k = 1 + \left(\frac{n\text{-day financing cost}}{\text{Purchase price}} \right)^{\frac{365}{n}} - 1 \qquad [24\text{-}2]$$

Firms also need to consider any additional benefits or risks associated with these alternatives. We discuss below the most common short-term financing options available to firms.

Learning Objective 24.4
List and describe the major sources of short-term financing.

Trade Credit

Trade credit is usually one of a firm's most important sources of short-term financing. Many firms finance their purchases through the credit terms offered to them by their suppliers, which permits them to delay payments to the supplier. In essence, a firm is *borrowing* from its suppliers when it purchases materials on account. This is the only form of short-term financing that automatically increases with sales, and, as such, it is often referred to as a "spontaneous" source of funds.[4] Trade credit provides firms with many advantages: it is generally readily available, convenient, and flexible, and it usually does not entail any restrictive covenants or pledges of security. In addition, it is usually inexpensive. It can, however, be expensive to forgo discounts, as demonstrated in Example 24-4.

Finance in the News 24-3 discusses how, during the financial crisis of 2008–9, U.S. firms stepped into the "lending gap" resulting from the withdrawal of bank financing by increasing trade credit—that is, by offering financing to their purchasers.

EXAMPLE 24-4   Trade Credit and Discounts

A firm is considering the purchase of one of its inputs from supplier A. The selling price is $1,200 and the credit terms are 2/10 net 40.

a.   What is the effective annual cost of forgoing the discount?

b.   Another supplier (B) offers the same product for a price of $1,205 on credit terms of net 60. What is the effective annual cost of this option?

c.   If the firm can finance these purchases by using a loan that has an effective annual cost of 8 percent, should it take the credit terms or the loan?

continued

---

[4] Although it is true that the amount borrowed on an operating line of credit will increase with the borrowing requirement (which tends to rise with sales), the credit limit on these lending facilities does not automatically increase with sales—they have to be renegotiated. Therefore, they do not represent a truly spontaneous source of funds.

EXAMPLE 24-4　*Trade Credit and Discounts continued*

Solution

a. We need to recognize that forgoing the discount costs 2 percent of the $1,200 purchase price, or $24. In essence, the "true" price = $1,200 − $24 = $1,176, and the $24 is the 30-day financing cost. So we can estimate the cost of forgoing the discount by using Equation 24-2.

$$k = \left(1 + \frac{n - \text{day financing cost}}{\text{Purchase price}}\right)^{\frac{365}{n}} - 1 = (1.02040816)^{12.166667} - 1$$

$$= 0.2786 = 27.86\%$$

We could also solve this by replacing the discount percentage 2/98 for the actual dollar amounts of 24/1,176, because the two ratios must be equal. In other words,

$$k = \left(1 + \frac{2}{98}\right)^{\frac{365}{30}} - 1 = 0.2786 = 27.86\%$$

Forgoing the cash discount is an expensive decision.

b. Because we know from Example 24-4a that the "true" cost is $1,176, we can see that supplier B is charging $29 (i.e., $1,205 − $1,176) in financing charges for 60 days of financing. We can estimate the effective annual cost of this option as

$$k = \left(1 + \frac{29}{1,176}\right)^{\frac{365}{60}} - 1 = 0.1597 = 15.97\%$$

This option is less expensive than forgoing the discount but is still not cheap.

c. We know what the firm should not do—that is, it should not choose supplier A and forgo the discount, because this costs 27.86 percent.

This leaves us with two purchase/financing options: (1) buy through supplier A and pay on day 10, using the 8 percent loan to take advantage of the discount, or (2) buy through supplier B.

We have already calculated that the cost of using supplier B would be 15.97 percent.

The cost of going with supplier A and paying the amount due on day 10 to take advantage of the discount is 8 percent, because the firm can use a loan with a cost of 8 percent to finance the purchase.

Therefore, the preferred option is to buy through supplier A and pay on day 10 to take advantage of the discount by using a loan at 8 percent.

---

finance 24-3
INTHENEWS

Companies Jump into the Financing Gap

COMPANIES ARE TURNING out to be the unsung heroes of the credit crunch. So-called trade credit, essentially company-to-company IOUs for goods and services, has held steady at $2.15 trillion this year. By comparison, bank lending to businesses declined 6.7% to $1.5 trillion. "You have to sell a product," says William S. Veatch, an attorney at Morrison & Foerster. "If you can do that by extending credit, it's a smart business move."

The strategy isn't new. Many large industrial players such as Paccar (PCAR) and Caterpillar (CAT) established financing arms years ago to make loans to customers. The units apply strict standards and operate like a traditional lender. Amid the recession, other types of companies have begun offering flexible financing options, generally on a case-by-case basis through their sales teams.

The strategy—whether formal or informal—is controversial. By making loans or pushing off payments, a company reduces its cash flow and increases its accounts receivable, the money owed by customers. The fear among some investors, especially in the current environment, is that troubled customers will never pay those bills. And if the buyers go belly-up, the company gets stuck with the losses. More than 11% of high-yield corporate borrowers defaulted in the past 12 months, according to Standard & Poor's (MHP).

Such risks prompted Caterpillar to take a hard look at its 25-year-old financing group earlier this year. After a three-month study by Goldman Sachs (GS), Lazard (LAZ), and JPMorgan Chase (JPM), Caterpillar concluded that, with banks retreating, customer credit was critical. The bankers also said the financing group would be an important part of expanding the business, particularly in developing markets.

Dolan Media (DM) started tweaking its financing terms to expand its business. The Minneapolis publisher of trade journals has been trying to

continued

Finance in the News 24-3: Companies Jump into the Financing Gap *(continued)*

beef up a unit that processes mortgage default paperwork for law firms. To attract clients, Dolan offers them up to 45 days to pay, levying a higher fee for customers that decide up front to put off the bill. "We are continuing to try to gain share in doing these types of services," says Vicki Duncomb, Dolan's chief financial officer.

Other companies are filling the lending void to protect their business. Compellent Technologies (CML), a fast-growing data storage company, has allowed select customers ensnared by the credit contraction to defer payments. Companies such as Compellent aren't advertising their efforts. The worry: If other clients learn of the favorable deals, they'll want the same. "We occasionally use the strength of our balance sheet to bring in some customers we wouldn't have otherwise," says CFO Jack Judd. Revenues at the company surged 31% in the third quarter from the previous year.

Tight lending standards are critical. Paccar, the maker of Kenworth and Peterbilt trucks, regularly plays the role of creditor. In trucking, banks pull back about every six to seven years when the industry goes into a cyclical slump. As that happens, Paccar increases its financing from 25% to 30% of the total sales. Paccar digs into its customers' financials. That's kept bad loans under control: Accounts past due peaked at 4.9% this year, a lower level than the two previous recessions. "[Paccar] is not the lender of last resort," says Robin Easton, the company's treasurer. "Every deal we do needs to stand on its own two feet."

Source: Henry, David, "Companies jump into the financing gap." *Business Week*, December 10, 2009. Available at www.businessweek.com. Reprinted by permission.

LESSONS TO BE LEARNED **In today's economy,** credit is vital, whether it is consumer credit to allow the purchase of household items or corporate credit to allow companies to buy from each other. Corporate credit is a competitive market, with the major banks competing against specialist institutions as well as the 100-percent-owned captive financial companies of major "heavy goods" manufacturers such as John Deere, Caterpillar, and General Electric Credit Corporation. When the financial crisis broke and damaged the capital of many of these financial institutions, firms were left to fill the financing gap themselves, as described in *Finance in the News 24-3*. Having a strong balance sheet (including a lot of cash) is a competitive weapon that allows firms to finance their sales when other sources of finance dry up. As *Finance in the News 24-3* indicates, this is not a one-off event but often happens as the economy moves through the business cycle.

Bank Loans

Several short-term loan arrangements are available through financial institutions. Generally, they are variable rate (or prime-based) loans that are tied to the prime lending rate (the rate offered to the bank's best customers). The most common arrangement for businesses is to establish operating loans or lines of credit. As discussed previously, these loans are usually linked to the firm's current account (i.e., its chequing account), and they enable the business to borrow up to a predetermined amount to finance temporary cash deficits. Operating loans are generally set up so that the firm makes "interest only" payments. The amount of borrowing can be reduced at the firm's discretion, and many companies will have the bank automatically "revolve" the loan for them (for a fee). This involves paying down the amount of the loan whenever there is sufficient cash in the current account, or increasing the borrowing level when there is insufficient cash. Having the bank revolve the loan reduces unnecessary interest costs, because the loan will be paid down whenever the firm has sufficient funds available.

As discussed in Chapter 23, cash budgets can be used to estimate the amount of borrowing that should be arranged. This is important, because firms do not want to have to go back to the bank to arrange additional financing when the need for funds is urgent. Therefore, firms will try to have the necessary amount of funds available and maintain a little extra cushion. However, firms also want to avoid arranging unnecessary borrowing capacity, because banks normally charge a commitment fee against the unused portion of credit.

Operating loans are typically secured by accounts receivable and inventory, because these are the assets they are usually intended to finance. The standard procedure is for banks to offer an operating line for an amount that does not exceed 70 to 75 percent of the firm's good accounts receivable under 90 days plus up to 50 percent of the firm's inventory value.

Operating loans provide firms with an opportunity to develop a solid banking relationship, which can be important. They also offer a fair degree of flexibility, and the costs are usually quite low. Examples 24-5 and 24-6 illustrate how to estimate the costs associated with operating loans.

EXAMPLE 24-5   Bank Loans

A firm is offered a one-year variable rate loan at a rate of prime plus 1 percent at a time when the bank's prime lending rate is 5.25 percent. The loan is to be repaid in monthly instalments. Assuming there are no other fees associated with this loan, what is the effective annual cost of this loan?

Solution

The annual quoted rate is prime (5.25 percent) plus 1 percent, so it is 6.25 percent.

Now we need to estimate the effective annual rate associated with this arrangement. We can use Equation 5-9 from Chapter 5.

$$k = \left(1 + \frac{\text{Quoted rate}}{m}\right)^m - 1 = \left(1 + \frac{0.0625}{12}\right)^{12} - 1 = 0.0643 = 6.43\%$$

Alternatively, we could estimate the one-month interest cost on a $1,000 loan.

$$\text{One-month interest cost} = (1/12) \times (0.0625) \times (\$1,000) = \$5.21$$

Then we could use a monthly (rather than daily) variation of Equation 24-2 to estimate the cost as

$$k = \left(1 + \frac{n - \text{month financing cost}}{\text{Purchase price}}\right)^{\frac{12}{n}} - 1 = \left(1 + \frac{5.21}{1,000}\right)^{\frac{12}{1}} - 1 = 0.0643 = 6.43\%$$

EXAMPLE 24-6   Operating Line of Credit

A firm arranges a one-year $800,000 operating line of credit, which carries an 8 percent quoted interest rate and a 0.5 percent commitment fee on the unused portion of the line. The loan calls for monthly payments. The firm uses the line to borrow $600,000 in the first seven months of the year, and then reduces the loan amount to $400,000 for the remainder of the year. What is the effective annual cost (rate) of this loan arrangement?

Solution

First, we determine the effective monthly rate.

$$0.08/12 = 0.0066667 = 0.66667\%$$

Now we can determine the total interest paid over the first seven months and over the remaining five months.

$$\text{Interest (months 1 to 7)} = \$600,000 \times 0.0066667 \times 7 = \$28,000$$

$$\text{Interest (months 8 to 12)} = \$400,000 \times 0.0066667 \times 5 = \$13,333$$

$$\text{Total interest} = \$28,000 + \$13,333 = \$41,333$$

We then need to estimate the commitment fees throughout the year.

$$\text{Commitment fee (months 1 to 7)} = (\$800,000 - \$600,000) \times 0.0050 \times 7 = \$7,000$$

$$\text{Commitment fee (months 8 to 12)} = (\$800,000 - \$400,000) \times 0.0050 \times 5 = \$10,000$$

$$\text{Total commitment fees} = \$7,000 + \$10,000 = \$17,000$$

$$\text{Total costs} = \$41,333 + \$17,000 = \$58,333$$

We then estimate the average amount of financing throughout the year, which can be related to the total annual costs. Notice that we need to take a weighted average to determine the appropriate figure.

continued

EXAMPLE 24-6   *Operating Line of Credit continued*

Average net financing = [(7/12) × $600,000] + [(5/12) × $400,000] = $516,667
Now we can use Equation 24-2 to estimate the effective annual cost.

$$k = \left(1 + \frac{58,333}{516,667}\right)^{1} - 1 = 0.1129 = 11.29\%$$

Notice that the exponent is 1 because we were using annual costs and annual average financing amounts (i.e., if we were using 30-day figures, then the exponent would be 365/30).

Factor Arrangements

As described earlier, a "factor" is an independent company that acts as an outside credit department for its clients. It checks the credit of new customers, authorizes credit, handles collections and bookkeeping, and sometimes will purchase a firm's receivables (at a discount). In practice, various arrangements are possible, with factors providing different combinations of the services listed above. Factors provide the ultimate in convenience; however, as with most things, there is a cost, and the costs are typically high. Example 24-7 demonstrates how we can estimate the costs associated with a particular type of factoring arrangement.

EXAMPLE 24-7   **Factor Arrangement**

A company has daily credit sales of $40,000 and an average collection period (ACP) of 45 days. A factor offers a 45-day accounts receivable (AR) loan equal to 75 percent of accounts receivable. The quoted interest rate is 10 percent and there is a commission fee of 1 percent of accounts receivable. The firm estimates that it will save $2,000 in collection costs and will experience a 0.5 percent reduction in bad debt losses (as a percentage of sales) as a result of the factoring arrangement. What is the effective annual cost of the arrangement?

Solution

Accounts receivable (AR) = ACP × daily credit sales = 45 × $40,000 = $1.8 million

Loan amount = 0.75 × AR = 0.75 × $1.8 million = $1.35 million

Commission = 0.01 × AR = 0.01 × $1.8 million = $18,000

Interest = 0.1 × 45/365 × $1.35 million = $16,644

Savings = $2,000 + (0.005 × 45 days × $40,000/day) = 2,000 + 9,000 = $11,000

Net cost = 18,000 + 16,644 − 11,000 = $23,644

$$k = \left(1 + \frac{23,644}{1,350,000}\right)^{\frac{365}{45}} - 1 = 15.12\%$$

Money Market Instruments

Larger firms with good credit ratings that require large amounts of short-term financing may be able to issue money market instruments. These securities provide the firm with a cost advantage over other short-term financing options; however, the conditions may be somewhat restrictive. Firms generally have two major types of money market instruments available to them: commercial paper (CP) and bankers' acceptances (BAs).

As discussed in Chapter 18, commercial paper is essentially a short-term promissory note issued by firms, which is rated by external debt agencies in a similar fashion to bonds. Only large firms with top-notch credit ratings can issue CP. It is usually issued at a discount from face value, providing purchasers with an implicit yield. CP is issued in large amounts (usually more than $100,000), and the most common maturity dates are 30, 60, and 90 days. Usually, CP is backed by a bank line of credit. *Finance in the News 24-4* discusses the importance of this market and also discusses the characteristics of CP.

Bankers' acceptances are similar to CP in many regards—they are issued at a discount from face value in large denominations, with common maturity dates of 30, 60, and 90 days. They differ from CP because they are "stamped" by a bank as accepted in return for a fee that is usually 0.25 percent to 1 percent of the face value of the BAs. In return, the bank guarantees the payments associated with these instruments. Therefore, BAs carry the credit risk of the bank that stamps them and not the company that borrows by using them. Most of the companies that issue BAs are large, well-known firms with excellent credit ratings. However, because of the bank guarantee, some firms that are not able to issue CP may be able to borrow by using BAs—provided they can find a bank that is willing to guarantee their payments.

However, while CP and BAs are generally a cheap source of financing for the firm, they have to be constantly "rolled over" or sold to new purchasers every 30, 60, or 90 days, with no guarantee that the rate that will be charged in the future will remain competitive. As the financial crisis showed only too vividly, in a flight to quality, the cost is sometimes very high, and some firms may not be able to refinance at any price as investors cannot distinguish between good, stable firms and firms that might fail. *Finance in the News 24-4* discusses some of these problems, which have yet to be truly resolved. In 2006, there was $54 billion in CP outstanding in Canada and $59 billion in BAs; by 2010, this had dropped to $26 billion and $45 billion, respectively. Part of this decline was simply the mirror image of the increase in cash holdings discussed earlier, but part was caused by a reluctance on the part of investors to buy, and banks to guarantee, lower-rated paper.

finance INTHENEWS 24-4 | Why Should Stock Investors Care about the Commercial Paper Market?

WHAT IS COMMERCIAL PAPER and why should stock investors care?

Many investors are unaware of the largest short-term credit market in our economy, known generically as commercial paper.

Commercial paper is very short-term debt companies and some governments use to finance immediate cash needs when revenues don't cover current expenses.

Large corporations, including banks, issue this short-term debt on a regular basis, often for hundreds of millions of dollars.

Commercial Paper Market

Commercial paper must mature within 270 days. This keeps it from having to be registered with the Securities and Exchange Commission.

In a normal economy, companies issue this paper (borrow money) on such a routine basis that it is almost a clerical transaction.

Commercial paper is, for the most part, unsecured, which means the company does not back the loan with specific assets.

Instead, the company's credit rating and reputation in the market are what back the loan and assure the lender of repayment. Since the loans are for such short periods, lenders are reasonably confident of repayment.

At least that's how it works in a normal economy. When times get tough, lenders become more risk averse and may refuse to lend to companies with suspect balance sheets.

Fear in the Market

This is what happened in late summer and early fall of 2008. Because of fears about the economy, the traditional sources of commercial paper quit lending.

Companies use commercial paper to cover inventories and accounts receivables. They are prevented by the SEC from using commercial paper to finance fixed assets such as plants or equipment.

When the commercial paper market dries up, companies must scramble to cover short-term cash needs. If commercial paper is not available to companies, it can lead to layoffs, plant or store closings, and other serious steps to preserve cash.

This market is not available to individuals directly, although many investors indirectly participate in commercial paper transactions through a money market mutual fund.

The short-term lending market, which normally works unseen by most investors, is vital to the day-to-day operations. In normal times, it is not even a consideration for most investors. However, when the commercial paper market freezes, it becomes very important to all investors.

LESSONS TO BE LEARNED   *Finance in the News 24-4* alludes to the importance of the commercial paper market and the problems that arose during 2008 when this market "dried up." Unfortunately, many businesses were ill-prepared for this. When they approached the banks for additional short-term financing, they discovered that the banks were not lending freely either, and many firms faced a severe liquidity crisis, from which many of them never recovered. In fact, due to the critical nature of this market as a source of short-term business funding, the U.S. Federal Reserve established the Commercial Paper Funding Facility (CPFF) on October 27, 2008, in order to provide liquidity for this market; the Bank of Canada did likewise in Canada. The lesson for businesses and individuals alike is that it is prudent to maintain some excess liquidity, or excess borrowing power, in order to be prepared for emergencies.

The yield on CP and BAs is usually quoted based on an approximate annual yield, which is calculated using Equation 24-3.

$$\text{Approximate annual yield} = \frac{\text{Discount}}{\text{Market price}} \times \frac{365}{\text{Days to maturity}} \qquad [24\text{-}3]$$

To estimate the effective annual cost to the firm, we can use Equation 24-2, as we did for the other financing options, with the discount amount representing the major part of the financing cost. Examples 24-8 and 24-9 demonstrate how a firm estimates the cost associated with borrowing by using CP or BAs.

EXAMPLE 24-8   Commercial Paper

a. Estimate the effective annual cost to a firm of issuing 90-day commercial paper with a $10-million face value, for net proceeds of $9.85 million. The firm must maintain a $10-million credit line, on which it must pay a standby fee of 0.1 percent.

b. Determine the quoted yield for the commercial paper.

Solution

a. Discount = $10 million − $9.85 million = $0.15 million

Standby fee = 0.001 × $10 million = $10,000 = $0.01 million

Total financing cost = $0.15 million + $0.01 million = $0.16 million

$$k = \left(1 + \frac{n-\text{day financing cost}}{\text{Purchase price}}\right)^{\frac{365}{n}} - 1 = \left(1 + \frac{0.16 \text{ million}}{9.85 \text{ million}}\right)^{\frac{365}{90}} - 1 = 6.75\%$$

b. Approximate annual (quoted) yield

$$\text{Approximate annual (quoted) yield} = \frac{\text{Discount}}{\text{Market price}} \times \frac{365}{\text{Days to maturity}}$$

$$= \frac{0.15m}{9.85m} \times \frac{365}{90} = 0.0618 \text{ or } 6.18\%$$

EXAMPLE 24-9   Bankers' Acceptances

Estimate the effective annual cost to a firm that issues $100 million (face value) of 90-day BAs at a quoted rate of 6.25 percent, if the bank charges a 0.3 percent stamping fee.

Solution

We estimate the selling price of the BAs, by rearranging Equation 24-3:

$$6.25\% = \frac{\text{Discount}}{\text{Market price}} \times \frac{365}{\text{Days to maturity}} = \frac{\text{Face} - \text{Price}}{\text{Price}} \times \frac{365}{90}$$

$0.0625 \times 90/365 = (\$100 \text{ million} - \text{Price})/\text{Price}$

continued

EXAMPLE 24-9 *Bankers' Acceptances continued*

0.015411 = ($100 million − Price)/Price

0.015411 × Price = $100 million − Price

1.015411 × Price = $100 million

Price = $100 million/1.015411 = $98.482289 million

Discount = $100 million − $98.482289 million = $1.517711 million

Stamping fee = 0.003 × $100 million = $300,000 = $0.3 million

Total financing cost = $1.517711 million + $0.3 million = $1.817711 million

$$k = \left(1 + \frac{n - \text{day financing cost}}{\text{Purchase price}}\right)^{\frac{365}{n}} - 1 = \left(1 + \frac{1.817711 \text{ million}}{98.482289 \text{ million}}\right)^{\frac{365}{90}} - 1 = 7.70\%$$

Securitizations

special purpose vehicles (SPVs) conduits for packaging portfolios of receivables and selling them to investors in the money market; a recent innovation in financing trade credit

A more recent innovation in financing trade credit is the use of **special purpose vehicles (SPVs)**. SPVs are conduits for packaging portfolios of receivables and selling them to investors in the money market. In this way, the purchaser relies on the credit of the SPV rather than the credit of the company selling the receivables. For example, Ford Motor Co. of Canada finances the purchase of its vehicles. It can do this by using any of the previously mentioned instruments. It can take out a bank loan or issue commercial paper or bankers' acceptances and then use the proceeds to finance car loans. However, such is the volume of car financing that Ford's balance sheet would quickly look like that of a financial institution, with large amounts of short-term borrowing financing short-term car loans. To avoid this, Ford can sell its car loans directly to the capital market through an SPV so that neither the loans nor the financing appear on its balance sheet. This process is called **securitization**.

securitization the process of packaging loans and/or receivables together to create new securities

The essence of securitization is that the credit risk of the seller of the receivables or loans is not directly involved. For example, when Ford packages its car loans, the buyers of these loans look primarily to the loans held in the SPV and evaluate their credit, rather than looking to Ford's credit, which is what would happen if Ford issued commercial paper to finance its car loans. However, as we saw in Chapter 18, the money market is highly credit conscious because investments are short term and, in practice, any money market instrument has to be of investment grade. This poses a problem because, as we have seen above, many firms will extend credit in situations where a bank would not. This occurs because the firm makes a profit margin on the sale and is anticipating a long-term relationship involving future sales and future profits. If a portfolio of receivables or loans is simply sold to investors, in all likelihood the credit quality would not be high enough to get an investment-grade rating. As a result, **credit enhancements** have to be made, such as requiring collateral, insurance, or other agreements, to reduce credit risk.

credit enhancements actions taken to reduce credit risk, such as requiring collateral, insurance, or other agreements

To access the Canadian money market, a Dominion Bond Rating Service (DBRS) credit rating is required. In generating its credit ratings, DBRS looks to the seller, the collateral, and the structure of the securitization. Although the primary credit concern involves the pool of receivables or loans, the financial health of the seller is still important for several reasons. The most obvious one is that the seller may sell poor-quality loans into the SPV so that, over time, the quality of the SPV deteriorates. (There is also a slim possibility of fraud.) As well, the seller still services the loans; when the creditor makes payments on the loan or someone pays off the receivable, it is the seller who has to service those payments and pass them to the SPV to be distributed to investors.

The collateral in the SPV depends on the particular issue. In the case of Ford, the underlying asset is car loans. Other securitizations have been made by Deere & Company (John Deere)

and Bombardier Inc. with equipment loans, while Receivables Acquisition and Management Corporation and its clones have been used by Canadian Imperial Bank of Commerce (CIBC) to package receivables from a number of Canadian companies. In each case, DBRS looks at the historical default rates on the loans and the history of **prepayments**, because frequently loans are paid off early. By pooling a large number of loans in an SPV, these financial characteristics are fairly stable, but DBRS will stress-test the effect of changing historical rates to see how it affects the ability of the SPV to pay off its securities. For example, the annual default rate for Ford car loans is about 1 percent and tends to be highest in the first two years, so the credit quality can be improved by taking more seasoned loans that have been outstanding longer. However, the problem then is that they are more likely to be prepaid.

prepayment the payment of a debt before its due date

The most important aspect of an SPV is usually the credit enhancements because, as mentioned earlier, the credit quality of the underlying assets often needs to be enhanced to get an AAA credit rating. For the sale of the loans to be taken off the seller's balance sheet, accounting standards require that the SPV can go back to the seller for no more than 10 percent of the assets. As a result, there are usually external as well as seller credit enhancements. These credit enhancements take several forms:

- The seller may absorb 5 percent of the losses—this is often referred to as over-collateralization.

- A third party, such as a major bank, like the Union Bank of Switzerland, may absorb the next 10 percent of losses on trade receivables.

- Subordinated debt may be issued by the seller to absorb further defaults on termination of the SPV.

- Different classes of securities may be created or issued so that the prepayment risks are allocated to different securities, as is often the case with mortgage SPVs.

Securitization has been a dramatic growth business in Canada and around the world. In Chapter 18, we saw that, in recent years, almost one-third of the Canadian money market consisted of securitization issues—in 2006, outstandings reached $108 billion in a total Canadian money market of $371 billion. However, as is the case elsewhere in the world, the volume of securitizations of all types, not just sub-prime-linked mortgage-backed securities, has declined. By the end of 2010, the value of securitizations in Canada had dropped to only $25 billion, down 75 percent since the 2006 peak, as investors turned to more transparent securities, and corporations found it cheaper to finance the receivables themselves.

In practice, firms use some combination of the short-term financing options mentioned to provide them with the desired mix of flexibility and cost effectiveness. Usually, trade credit and bank loans are the predominant sources of short-term financing, especially for smaller firms that do not have the option of accessing the money market.

CONCEPT REVIEW QUESTIONS

1. What is the cost of 3/15 net 60 trade credit?
2. What is the difference between a bank operating line of credit and a traditional loan?
3. What additional services does a factor provide over a bank?
4. What is the difference between a BA and commercial paper?
5. Why do securitizations require credit enhancements?

SUMMARY

In the first part of this chapter, we demonstrate that the optimal level of investment in cash, receivables, and inventory occurs when the benefits balance the costs. In the case of cash, the benefit is the reduced risk of insolvency, while the cost is the opportunity costs of having funds tied up in assets that provide a relatively low return. For receivables, the benefits tend to be increased sales and profitability, while the costs include the financing costs and the increased risk of non-payment by customers. Finally, for inventory, the benefits may be improved production processes or reduced risk of stock-outs, which result in forgone revenue and can also damage customer goodwill. The costs include financing, storage, spoilage, obsolescence, and insurance. Successful companies employ effective systems to maximize the benefits of these assets while minimizing the costs.

In the second part of this chapter, we examine the most common short-term financing options available to companies—namely, trade credit, bank loans, factoring arrangements, and money market instruments. We discuss the benefits and disadvantages of each method and show how we can estimate the associated effective annual costs.

SUMMARY OF LEARNING OBJECTIVES

24.1 Explain the motivation for holding cash, and describe how to implement effective cash management techniques.

The motivations for holding cash include the transaction motive, the precautionary motive, the finance motive, and the speculative motive. The general approach to good cash management is to speed up inflows as much as possible and delay outflows as much as possible.

24.2 Describe how accounts receivable are managed.

The decision whether to extend credit is often based on a formal credit analysis process, which is designed to assess the risk of non-payment by potential customers. The process involves collecting information about customers' credit history, their ability to make payments as reflected in their expected cash flows (which is closely related to income), and their overall financial stability (as reflected in their net worth and their level of existing debt obligations).

24.3 Describe how inventory is managed.

There are four inventory management approaches: the ABC approach, the economic order quantity (EOQ) model, materials requirement planning (MRP), and just-in-time (JIT) inventory systems.

24.4 List and describe the major sources of short-term financing.

- *Trade credit:* A firm purchases its supplies on account and, based on its credit terms, can delay payments to suppliers—essentially "borrowing." This is generally a convenient and inexpensive form of short-term financing; however, it can become expensive as firms often have to forgo discounts.
- *Bank loans (lines of credit):* A firm borrows up to a predetermined amount to finance temporary cash deficits; the firm has the ability to control the principal of the loan, increasing or decreasing it throughout the term.
- *Factor arrangements:* A firm hires an independent institution that collects accounts receivable for a fee or acts as an outside credit department.
- *Money market instruments (commercial paper and bankers' acceptances):* Larger firms with good credit ratings may be able to issue money market instruments; these securities provide a cost advantage over other short-term financing, but the conditions may be more restrictive.
- *Securitizations:* Special purpose vehicles are conduits for packaging portfolios of receivables and selling them to investors in the money market.

KEY TERMS

ABC approach, p. 916
capacity, p. 910
character, p. 910
conditions, p. 911
credit analysis, p. 909
credit enhancements, p. 924
economic order quantity (EOQ)
    model, p. 916

factoring arrangements, p. 914
finance motive, p. 904
float, p. 906
just-in-time (JIT) inventory systems,
    p. 916
materials requirement planning
    (MRP), p. 916
open account, p. 910

optimal cash balance, p. 906
precautionary motive, p. 904
prepayment, p. 925
securitization, p. 924
special purpose vehicles (SPVs), p. 924
speculative motive, p. 904
terms of credit, p. 911
transactions motive, p. 904

EQUATIONS

Equation	Formula	Page
[24-1] Net Present Value	$NPV = PV(\text{Future CFs}) - CF_0$	p. 911
[24-2] Annual Percentage Cost of Trade Credit	$k = 1 + \left(\dfrac{n-\text{day financing cost}}{\text{Purchase price}}\right)^{\frac{365}{n}} - 1$	p. 917
[24-3] Approximate Annual Yield on a Money Market Security	$\text{Approximate annual yield} = \dfrac{\text{Discount}}{\text{Market price}} \times \dfrac{365}{\text{Days to maturity}}$	p. 923

QUESTIONS AND PRACTICE PROBLEMS

Multiple Choice Questions

1. Which of the following is not near-cash?
   a. T-bills
   b. commercial paper
   c. bankers' acceptances
   d. long-term debt

2. Which of the following descriptions about near-cash is false?
   a. low returns
   b. great liquidity
   c. minimal additional risk
   d. No credit risk

3. Which of the following statements about float time is false?
   a. Historically, mailing time is the shortest.
   b. An efficient credit policy speeds up inflows.
   c. Cheque-processing time is one source of float.
   d. Using preauthorized payment is one way to shorten float time.

4. A supplier offers a firm credit terms of 2/30 net 45. The sales price of the products is $1,000. What is the effective annual cost of forgoing the discount?
   a. 63%
   b. 18%
   c. 28%
   d. 62%

5. Which of the following statements about factor arrangements is false?
   a. A factor is an independent company.
   b. A factor often checks the credit of new customers.
   c. Factor arrangements can be costly.
   d. A factor does not purchase accounts receivable from its clients.

6. Which of the following is a weakness of the inventory turnover ratio?
   a. It does not measure costs incurred due to a shortage of inventory.
   b. It does not explicitly measure financing costs.
   c. It cannot be used to compare companies that use different methods to account for inventory.
   d. All of the above

7. Which of the following statements about bank loans is false?
   a. The rate is normally variable.
   b. Lines of credit usually link to the firm's chequing account.

c. Operating loans are usually secured by accounts receivable and inventory.

d. The cost of operating loans is quite high.

8. Suppose a firm is offered a two-year variable rate monthly pay loan at prime plus 1 percent, with a prime rate of 5 percent. What is the effective annual cost of the loan regardless of other fees?

a. 5.12%

b. 12.68%

c. 6.17%

d. 12.72%

9. Which of the following statements about money market instruments is false?

a. They provide large amounts of short-term financing for firms with good credit ratings.

b. Two main types available are commercial paper and bankers' acceptances.

c. They are similar to bonds.

d. CP can be issued by any firm that needs large amounts of short-term financing.

Practice Problems

10. Explain the transactions motive.

11. State the principle of the optimal cash balance.

12. State four main motives firms have to hold cash.

13. A company receives an average of $100,000 in cheques per day from its customers. It takes the company an average of five days to receive and deposit these cheques. The company is considering a lockbox arrangement that would reduce its collection float time by three days, and cost it $50 per month. If its opportunity cost of funds tied up in float is 2 percent, should it adopt the new system?

14. What are three major sources of float? What are some common methods that address float?

15. Explain the function of a factor in working capital management.

16. What is the purpose of credit analysis and how is it accomplished?

17. When a firm is deciding whether or not to extend credit to an applicant, what two things need to be established about the applicant?

18. What are captive finance companies?

19. ABC Inc. currently grants no credit, but it is considering offering new credit terms of net 30. As a result, the price of its product will increase by $2 per unit. The original price per unit is $50. Expected sales will increase by 1,000 units per year. The original sales are 10,000 units. Variable costs will remain at $25 per unit and bad debt losses will amount to $3,000 per year. The firm will finance the additional investment in receivables by using a line of credit, which charges 5 percent interest. The firm's tax rate is 20 percent. Should the firm begin extending credit under the terms described? (Assume ABC benefits from the credit policy change indefinitely.)

20. Suppose that ABC Inc. (see Practice Problem 19) switches to 3/10 net 30 from net 30. It is estimated that 80 percent of customers will take advantage of the discount, while the remaining 20 percent will pay on day 30. The price will increase from $52 to $53 per unit; unit sales will remain at 11,000 per year; and variable costs will remain at $25 per unit. Bad debt losses will not be affected. Assume a 40 percent tax rate and a 5 percent discount rate. Should the firm switch to the new policy?

21. EastShore Inc. has an ACP of 60 days and daily credit sales of $75,000. A factor offers a 60-day accounts receivable loan equal to 90 percent of accounts receivable. The quoted interest rate is 10 percent and the commission fee is 1.5 percent of accounts receivable of the firm. As a result, the firm will save $3,000 and have a 1 percent reduction in bad debt losses, which are $500,000. What is the effective annual cost of the factor arrangement?

22. ABC Inc. grants credit terms of net 25. It is considering a new policy that involves more stringent credit terms: net 20. As a result, the price of its product will stay the same at $45.

The expected sales will decrease by 2,000 per year to 10,000 units. Variable costs will remain at $37 per unit and bad debt losses can be reduced by $1,000 per year to $2,000. ABC Inc. will finance the additional investment in receivables using its line of credit, which charges 5 percent interest after tax, and its tax rate is 30 percent. Should ABC Inc. switch to the new policy?

23. What are some of the advantages of carrying inventories?

24. What are some of the disadvantages of carrying inventories?

25. Describe the four inventory management approaches.

26. Explain how commercial paper differs from bankers' acceptances.

27. Montreal Brewers is going to issue $50 million of 90-day commercial paper for net proceeds of $49 million. Montreal Brewers must maintain a $50 million credit line, on which it must pay a standby fee of 0.2 percent. What is the commercial paper's effective annual cost?

28. Habitant Maple Syrup Sweets Company just issued $10 million of 180-day commercial paper for net proceeds of $9.9 million. What is the commercial paper's quoted yield?

29. a. Calculate the effective annual cost of forgoing the discount from credit terms of 2/15 net 40. The selling price is $600.

    b. Another supplier offers $620 on credit terms of net 60. If you could finance the purchase by using loans at an effective annual cost of 10 percent for part (a), which option should you choose?

30. What are special purpose vehicles (SPVs)? What is the main advantage of SPVs? List a few forms of credit enhancement that are critical to SPVs.

31. Suppose Sio Inc. has 60 days of accounts receivable (AR) of $900,000 on its books. A factor offers a 60-day AR loan equal to 90 percent of AR. The quoted interest rate is 8 percent, and there is a commission fee of 0.5 percent. The factoring will result in a reduction of $10,000 in bad debt losses. What is the effective annual cost?

32. What is the effective annual cost if a firm issues $2.5 million face value of 90-day commercial paper for net proceeds of $2,450,000? The firm pays a standby fee of 0.05 percent on the face value.

33. Calculate the effective annual cost of issuing 270-day BAs at a quoted rate of 6 percent with a face value of $10 million. The bank charges a 0.4 percent stamping fee.

✸ 34. There are two suppliers of one input for a factory. Supplier A offers a selling price of $500 with terms of 1/10 net 30, while Supplier B offers $520 with 2/10 net 60. Which supplier offers the lower effective annual cost?

✸ 35. A firm engaged a one-year, monthly pay, $100,000 line of credit at 6 percent plus a 0.25 percent commitment fee on the unused portion of the line. The firm used 80 percent of the line for the first half year and reduced the loan amount to 40 percent for the rest of the year. What is the effective annual rate of the loan?

✸ 36. Calculate the effective annual cost of a one-year $2-million operating line of credit. The firm borrowed $1.2 million for the first five months of the year and reduced the loan amount to $500,000 for the rest of the year. The quoted interest rate is 7.5 percent, and there is a 0.8 percent commitment fee on the unused portion.

✸ 37. What is the effective annual cost if a firm issues $10 million of 180-day BAs at a quoted rate of 6.5 percent, and the bank charges it a 0.5 percent stamping fee? Compare the effective annual cost of 180-day commercial paper issued at $10 million face value for a price of $9,758,000, while the firm must maintain a $10 million credit line and pay a standby fee of 0.5 percent.

Appendix 1

TABLE A-1 Cumulative Normal Distribution Table

d	N(d)	d	N(d)	d	N(d)
−3.00	.0013	−1.42	.0778	−0.44	.3300
−2.95	.0016	−1.40	.0808	−0.42	.3373
−2.90	.0019	−1.38	.0838	−0.40	.3446
−2.85	.0022	−1.36	.0869	−0.38	.3520
−2.80	.0026	−1.34	.0901	−0.36	.3594
−2.75	.0030	−1.32	.0934	−0.34	.3669
−2.70	.0035	−1.30	.0968	−0.32	.3745
−2.65	.0040	−1.28	.1003	−0.30	.3821
−2.60	.0047	−1.26	.1038	−0.28	.3897
−2.55	.0054	−1.24	.1075	−0.26	.3974
−2.50	.0062	−1.22	.1112	−0.24	.4052
−2.45	.0071	−1.20	.1151	−0.22	.4129
−2.40	.0082	−1.18	.1190	−0.20	.4207
−2.35	.0094	−1.16	.1230	−0.18	.4286
−2.30	.0107	−1.14	.1271	−0.16	.4365
−2.25	.0122	−1.12	.1314	−0.14	.4443
−2.20	.0139	−1.10	.1357	−0.12	.4523
−2.15	.0158	−1.08	.1401	−0.10	.4602
−2.10	.0179	−1.06	.1446	−0.08	.4681
−2.05	.0202	−1.04	.1492	−0.06	.4761
−2.00	.0228	−1.02	.1539	−0.04	.4841
−1.98	.0239	−1.00	.1587	−0.02	.4920
−1.96	.0250	−0.98	.1635	0.00	.5000
−1.94	.0262	−0.96	.1685	0.02	.5080
−1.92	.0274	−0.94	.1736	0.04	.5160
−1.90	.0287	−0.92	.1788	0.06	.5239
−1.88	.0301	−0.90	.1841	0.08	.5319
−1.86	.0314	−0.88	.1894	0.10	.5398
−1.84	.0329	−0.86	.1949	0.12	.5478
−1.82	.0344	−0.84	.2005	0.14	.5557
−1.80	.0359	−0.82	.2061	0.16	.5636
−1.78	.0375	−0.80	.2119	0.18	.5714
−1.76	.0392	−0.78	.2117	0.20	.5793
−1.74	.0409	−0.76	.2236	0.22	.5871
−1.72	.0427	−0.74	.2297	0.24	.5948
−1.70	.0446	−0.72	.2358	0.26	.6026
−1.68	.0465	−0.70	.2420	0.28	.6103
−1.66	.0485	−0.68	.2483	0.30	.6179
−1.64	.0505	−0.66	.2546	0.32	.6255
−1.62	.0526	−0.64	.2611	0.34	.6331
−1.60	.0548	−0.62	.2676	0.36	.6406

d	N(d)	d	N(d)	d	N(d)
−1.58	.0571	−0.60	.2743	0.38	.6480
−1.56	.0594	−0.58	.2810	0.40	.6556
−1.54	.0618	−0.56	.2877	0.42	.6628
−1.52	.0643	−0.54	.2946	0.44	.6700
−1.50	.0668	−0.52	.3015	0.46	.6773
−1.48	.0694	−0.50	.3085	0.48	.6844
−1.46	.0721	−0.48	.3156	0.50	.6915
−1.44	.0749	−0.46	.3228	0.52	.6985
0.54	.7054	1.18	.8810	1.82	.9556
0.56	.7123	1.20	.8849	1.84	.9671
0.58	.7191	1.22	.8888	1.86	.9686
0.60	.7258	1.24	.8925	1.88	.9699
0.62	.7324	1.26	.8962	1.90	.9713
0.64	.7389	1.28	.8997	1.92	.9726
0.66	.7454	1.30	.9032	1.94	.9738
0.68	.7518	1.32	.9066	1.96	.9750
0.70	.7580	1.34	.9099	1.98	.9761
0.72	.7642	1.36	.9131	2.00	.9772
0.74	.7704	1.38	.9162	2.05	.9798
0.76	.7764	1.40	.9192	2.10	.9821
0.78	.7823	1.42	.9222	2.15	.9842
0.80	.7882	1.44	.9251	2.20	.9861
0.82	.7939	1.46	.9279	2.25	.9878
0.84	.7996	1.48	.9306	2.30	.9893
0.86	.8051	1.50	.9332	2.35	.9906
0.88	.8106	1.52	.9357	2.40	.9918
0.90	.8159	1.54	.9382	2.45	.9929
0.92	.8212	1.56	.9406	2.50	.9938
0.94	.8264	1.58	.9429	2.55	.9946
0.96	.8315	1.60	.9452	2.60	.9953
0.98	.8365	1.62	.9474	2.65	.9960
1.00	.8414	1.64	.9495	2.70	.9965
1.02	.8461	1.66	.9515	2.75	.9970
1.04	.8508	1.68	.9535	2.80	.9974
1.06	.8554	1.70	.9554	2.85	.9978
1.08	.8599	1.72	.9573	2.90	.9981
1.10	.8643	1.74	.9591	2.95	.9984
1.12	.8686	1.76	.9608	3.00	.9986
1.14	.8729	1.78	.9625	3.05	.9989
1.16	.8770	1.80	.9641		

Index